REGULATION OF DERIVATIVE FINANCIAL INSTRUMENTS

(SWAPS, OPTIONS AND FUTURES)

CASES AND MATERIALS

■ ■ ■

by

Ronald H. Filler

*Professor of Law, Director of the Financial Services Law Institute
and Program Director of the LL.M. in Financial Services Law,
New York Law School, New York, New York*

Jerry W. Markham

*Professor of Law, Florida International University
College of Law at Miami*

AMERICAN CASEBOOK SERIES®

Mat #41510731

American Casebook Series is a trademark registered in the U.S. Patent and Trademark Office.

© 2014 LEG, Inc. d/b/a West Academic
    444 Cedar Street, Suite 700
    St. Paul, MN 55101
    1-877-888-1330

West, West Academic Publishing, and West Academic are trademarks of West Publishing Corporation, used under license.

Printed in the United States of America

ISBN: 978-0-314-28970-4

PREFACE

Derivatives trading was once an esoteric field of finance that was concerned only with transactions in agricultural commodities. Such instruments were of little interest to Wall Street until the 1970s, when the commodity exchanges began trading futures and options on financial instruments. Trading in those financial derivatives exploded over the next few decades and today comprises the vast majority of derivative transactions.

This casebook will provide you with an understanding of the derivative instruments that are found in the financial and commodity markets. It will trace the history of the regulation of these instruments and the role they played in various financial crises over the years, including the Stock Market Crash of 1987 and the Financial Crisis in 2008.

This casebook will explore the regulation of derivatives under both the federal securities laws and the Commodity Exchange Act of 1936 (CEA). However, its principal focus is on the latter. This is because most derivative trading occurs under the auspices of the CEA. Moreover, much of the regulation created by the federal securities laws is the subject of other courses, such as Business Organizations, Securities Regulation and Corporate Finance. Nevertheless, this casebook will show how the jurisdiction over financial derivative instruments is divided between the Commodity Futures Trading Commission (CFTC) and the Securities and Exchange Commission (SEC). It will address differences in the regulatory approaches of these two agencies.

This casebook will also describe the market participants that are regulated by the CFTC and SEC, including "contract markets," "clearinghouses," "broker-dealers," "futures commission merchants," "commodity pool operators," "commodity trading advisors," "investment advisers," "swap execution facilities," "swap dealers," "major swap participants," "swap data repositories," and the various industry self-regulatory organizations, such as the Financial Industry Regulatory Authority (FINRA) and the National Futures Association (NFA).

The following pages will also identify market abuses that have come to be associated with the trading of derivative instruments, including price manipulations and fraudulent trading and sales practices. Finally, this casebook will conduct a comparative analysis of derivative trading abroad.

RONALD H. FILLER

JERRY W. MARKHAM

February 15, 2014

ACKNOWLEDGMENTS

The authors would like to thank Elizabeth Peiffer for her research and editing assistance.

"Special thanks to my wife, Paula Filler, and my entire family for being true and loyal supporters throughout my career and to the University of Illinois for laying the foundation that led to this book. I bleed orange and blue." Ronald Filler

We are also indebted to the following sources for their generosity in giving us permission to reprint excerpts from original copyrighted materials:

Norman Menachem Feder, "Deconstructing Over-the-Counter Derivatives," 2002 Colum. Bus. L. Rev. 677 (2002). Reprinted with permission.

Ronald H. Filler, "Ask the Professor: What is the Impact on MF Global From The Recent UK Supreme Court Decision Involving Lehman Brothers International (Europe)?", 32 Fut. & Deriv. L. Rep. 1 (April 2012). Reprinted with permission.

Ronald H. Filler, "Ask the Professor: How Will The Seventh Circuit Rule In Sentinel II?", 33 Fut. & Deriv. L. Rep. 21 (November 2013). Reprinted with permission.

Ronald H. Filler, "Are Customer Segregated/Secured Amount Funds Properly Protected After Lehman?", 29 Fut. & Deriv. L. Rep. 1 (November 2008). Reprinted with permission.

Ronald H. Filler, "Ask the Professor: What is Margin and How Is It (Or Should Be) Determined?", 29 Fut. & Deriv. L. Rep. 15 (March 2009). Reprinted with permission.

Ronald H. Filler, "Ask the Professor: Portfolio Margining—How Will Dodd-Frank Impacts Its Utilization?", 30 Fut. & Deriv. L. Rep. 8 (November 2010). Reprinted with permission.

Ronald H. Filler and Elizabeth Ritter: "Ask the Professors: Did the European Court of Justice Properly Rule By Dismissing the U.K.'s Attempt to Annul ESMA's Regulation Banning Short Selling?", 34 Fut. & Deriv. L. Rep (March 2014). Reprinted with permission.

Futures Industry Association, for the FIA International Uniform Execution (Give-Up) Agreement (see Appendix C). Reprinted with pemission.

Roberta S. Karmel, "IOSCO's Response to the Financial Crisis,"37 J. Corp. L. 849 (2012). Reprinted with permission.

Jake Keaveny, "In Defense of Market Self-Regulation," 70 Brook. L. Rev. 1419 (2005). Reprinted with permission.

Jerry W. Markham, "Prohibited Floor Trading Activities Under the Commodity Exchange Act," 58 Fordham L. Rev. 1 (1989). Reprinted with permission.

Jerry W. Markham & David J. Gilberg, "Stock and Commodity Options- Two Regulatory Approaches and Their Conflicts," 47 Alb. L. Rev. 741 (1983). Reprinted with permission.

Jerry W. Markham, "There's Trouble In the Futures Trading Pits," Legal Times 26 (June 3, 1991). Reprinted with permission.

Jerry W. Markham, "Merging the SEC and CFTC—A Clash of Cultures," 78 U. Cin. L. Rev. 537. Reprinted with permission.

Jerry W. Markham & Rita M. Stephanz, "The Stock Market Crash of 1987—The United States Looks at New Recommendations," 76 Geo. L. J. 1993 (1987). Reprinted with permission of the publisher, Georgetown Law Journal © 1987.

Jerry W. Markham, "The Commodity Exchange Monopoly—Reform Is Needed," 48 Wash. & Lee L. Rev. 977 (1991). Reprinted with permission.

Jerry W. Markham "The Financial Stability Oversight Council—Risk Manager or Debating Society," 33 Capco Instit. J. of Fin. Trans. 35 (2011). Reprinted with permission.

Jerry W. Markham, "Confederate Bonds, General Custer, and the Regulation of Derivative Financial Instruments," 25 Seton Hall L. Rev. 1 (1994). Reprinted with permission.

Jerry W. Markham, "The Seventh Amendment and CFTC Reparations Proceedings," 68 Iowa L. Rev. 87 (1982). Reprinted with permission.

Jerry W. Markham & Daniel Harty, "For Whom the Bell Tolls: The Demise of Exchange Trading Floors and the Growth of ECNs," 33 J. Corp. L. 865 (2008). Reprinted with permission.

Jerry W. Markham, "Fiduciary Duties Under the Commodity Exchange Act," 68 Notre Dame L. Rev. 199 (1992). Reprinted with permission. © *Notre Dame Law Review*, University of Notre Dame (the publisher bears any responsibility for any errors which have occurred in reprinting or editing).

Jerry W. Markham, "Super Regulator: A Comparative Analysis of Securities and Derivatives Regulation in the United States, the United Kingdom and Japan," 28 Brook. J. Int'l L. 319 (2003). Reprinted with permission.

Jerry W. Markham, *Law Enforcement and the History of Financial Market Manipulation* (2013). Reprinted with permission from M.E. Sharpe.

Jerry W. Markham & Thomas Hazen, *Broker-Dealer Operations Under Securities and Commodities Law* (2011). Reprinted with permission from West Publishing.

Jerry W. Markham, "Regulation of Hybrid Instruments Under the Commodity Exchange Act: A Call for Alternatives," 1990 Colum. Bus. L. Rev. (1990). Reprinted with permission.

SUMMARY OF CONTENTS

TABLE OF CONTENTS

TABLE OF CASES

The principal cases are in bold type.

———

REGULATION OF DERIVATIVE FINANCIAL INSTRUMENTS

(SWAPS, OPTIONS AND FUTURES)

CASES AND MATERIALS

CHAPTER 1

INTRODUCTION TO DERIVATIVES

■ ■ ■

1. A PRIMER ON DERIVATIVES

A derivative contract has been defined as one "whose value depends (or 'derives' from) the value of an underlying asset, reference rate, or index." Group of Thirty, Derivatives: Practices and Principles 2 (July 1993).

The most popular derivative contracts are futures, options and swaps. The following is a primer explaining the elements of those instruments and their relationship to the underlying commodity through which they derive their value.

(A) THE CASH AND FORWARD MARKETS

A key to understanding derivative contracts is an analysis of their essential building blocks. We begin with their base, i.e., the commodities that underlie derivative contracts. Each derivative instrument has an underlying "cash" commodity, which may be an agricultural product, such as wheat, or a financial instrument, such as the value of a stock index. The derivative contract derives its price and value from that underlying cash commodity.

Transactions in the underlying commodities are conducted in what is variously called the "spot," "cash," "physical" or "actual" market. A transaction in that market involves the actual purchase and immediate or near-immediate delivery of the physical commodity.

An example of a cash market transaction is the buying of groceries at your local supermarket. In buying those groceries, you are engaging in a spot market transaction because delivery is immediate. Payment need not be immediate; the cash market purchase could be made on credit, but delivery is nearly always immediate or nearly immediate.

The next building block in understanding derivative contracts is the "forward" contract (a.k.a., "deferred delivery contract"). In a forward contract, the commodity is actually being purchased and delivered. However, the forward contract differs from the spot contract because delivery of the commodity is deferred until some agreed-upon time in the future.

For example, you are a producer of oil that will be extracted from your wells in the future, but you might agree today to sell that oil to a refiner for delivery months later after it is pumped from the ground. Actual delivery is then made at the agreed upon future date.

Payment terms may vary under forward contracts. The oil in the above example could be paid for in advance of delivery, or payment could be deferred until the oil is delivered, or at some other time as agreed to by the parties. See, Dunn v. CFTC, 519 U.S. 465, 472 (1997) (describing: " 'forward contracts' (agreements that anticipate the actual delivery of a commodity on a specified future date) and 'spot transactions' (agreements for purchase and sale of commodities that anticipate near-term delivery)").

Spot market transactions and forward contracts are not regulated by the Commodity Exchange Act of 1936 (CEA) [7 U.S.C. § 1 et seq.]; they are, however subject to its anti-manipulation prohibitions. In order for a cash or forward contract to be exempt from regulation under the CEA, actual delivery must occur. An exchange of monies representing a net price differential in the value of the underlying commodity does not meet the "forward contract" or "cash" market test.

It is now time to turn to a popular form of a derivative contract, one that is traded on exchanges regulated by the Commodity Futures Trading Commission (CFTC)—the "commodity futures" contract. Those contracts evolved from cash and forward contracts.

Historically, commodity futures contracts were traded primarily on agricultural products, but, today, most commodity futures contracts involve some type of financial instrument.

(B) FUTURES CONTRACTS

A futures contract is a contractual obligation on the part of the purchaser (the "long") to buy a stated amount of a commodity from the seller of a commodity (the "short"). That transaction must be conducted through a commodity exchange regulated by the CFTC as a "designated contract market." (DCM) [7 U.S.C. § 6].

The long trader agrees to take delivery under a futures contract at a future date and at a location specified by the rules of the commodity exchange on which the futures contract is traded. Historically, the buyer, or long, was obligated to take delivery of the cash commodity. When delivery occurred, a negotiable instrument, such as a warehouse receipt or a vault receipt, was transferred between the parties to evidence ownership and delivery of the commodity.

The seller in this arrangement incurs a reciprocal obligation to deliver the commodity at the specified date and agreed upon price. In fact, the seller initiates all deliveries that occur on a futures exchange.

Commodity futures contracts are available in a number of standardized delivery months set by the exchange for the commodity being traded. The parties could, for example, enter into a futures contract for December (DEC) 2014 delivery rather than for March (MAR) 2015 delivery.

A December 2014 futures contract means that delivery will take place sometime during that month, with the last permissible delivery date for that month established by exchange rules. Typically, the last delivery or trading date is around the 21st or 22nd calendar day of the respective month.

Once this last trading day occurs, that contract may no longer be traded, and the next "spot" futures contract becomes the next delivery month, for example, the March (MAR) 2015 futures contract. Financial futures contracts typically have delivery months for the four calendar quarters—March, June, September and December—whereas the delivery months for agricultural futures typically reflect seasonal months when planting and harvesting occur.

Futures contracts are otherwise standardized in the specifications for the quantity and quality of the commodity. The contract specifications are established by the respective exchange and are set forth in the exchange's rules. The only term that is not standardized is the price of the commodity, which is negotiated through a DCM, such as the Chicago Mercantile Exchange (CME).

Standardizing the terms of exchange-traded futures make them interchangeable, and thereby allows a secondary market for their trading. This secondary market allows the holders of futures contracts to liquidate their long or short positions simply by entering into an offsetting contract, i.e., an opposite, short or long position of the same futures contract traded on the exchange. For example, if a customer initially buys a December 2014 Treasury Bond futures contract, then she could close the transaction by selling a December 2014 Treasury Bond futures contract on the same exchange. This constitutes an offsetting or liquidating transaction.

The result of the offsetting trades is that the parties will keep just the profits or pay the losses determined by the difference between the price set by the initial contract and the price set by the liquidating contract.

This offset mechanism thus allows a trader to exit the market and take a profit or loss from price changes without incurring the expense of making or taking delivery of the underlying commodity.

Because of the efficiency of this liquidation process, delivery occurs in only a very small percentage of futures and options contracts. Some financial futures contracts allow only for cash settlement of the price differences (e.g., the S & P 500 Stock Index futures contract traded on the CME). No actual delivery of the underlying "physical" commodity ever occurs with a cash settled contract, just an exchange of cash.

To illustrate how a commodity futures contract is traded: assume that a speculator in Texas believes that the price of oil will increase over the next several months and wants to profit from that expected advance. He could buy the actual oil but has no place to store it and does not want to incur the expenses of such a purchase, which can include the entire price of oil being purchased plus storage, borrowing and insurance costs. Instead, he goes long in a crude oil futures contract on a futures exchange for say DEC 2014 delivery, assume it is now May 2014.

As described in Chapter 3, the traders involved in a futures contract will have to post "margin" to secure their trades. This margin is only a small portion of the purchase price of the oil, but it serves as a security deposit to assure that the parties will meet their contract obligations. This "initial margin" feature of a futures contract thus represents a performance bond concept, that is, the futures customer agrees to perform by maintaining the initial margin amount in her futures account at all times as long as the futures contract remains open in her account. In contrast, "margin" in a securities account involves an actual loan between the broker-dealer and its customer, which is used to purchase the underlying stock. Securities margin thus constitutes stock lending.

Another person in the above oil futures example has an opposite view of the long trader, i.e., she thinks oil prices will decline over the same period and would like to speculate on that possibility by taking a short position.

The buy and sell orders given by the long and short futures traders in the forgoing example are matched on a DCM. Assume that these orders were matched with each other (or with orders of other traders) at say $100 per barrel.

After execution of the initial transaction, the oil futures contract is held on the books of the respective futures commission merchants (FCM), i.e., the brokerage firms that executes and clears the orders of the parties on the DCM, with the margin forwarded from their respective FCMs to the exchange's "clearinghouse."

The clearinghouse plays a critical role in this transaction because it is interceded between each of the long and short traders. The clearinghouse thus becomes the buyer to every seller of futures contracts and the seller to every buyer of those contracts.

As a result of that intercession, the parties need not liquidate their contracts with each other. They can liquidate at any time with other traders.

The intercession of the clearinghouse also means that the traders are not at risk if the other party defaults. Thus, the clearinghouse acts as a financial guarantor of the trades, relieving the parties of the concern that the counterparty with whom they executed their order will default on their obligations.

Returning to the example of an oil futures contract: Sometime before December 2014 assume that each party will liquidate his or her positions through an offsetting position on the exchange. This will result in each party making a profit or incurring a loss on that trade.

In the above example assume that the price of oil rose to $110 per barrel and the long trader liquidates his position in July 2014 and receives a profit of $10 per barrel. If the buyer offsets his trade, that means that he entered into a short or opposite position of the same oil futures contract, e.g., the DEC 2014 contract. The buyer of that new contract, which occurred in July 2014, then becomes the long or buyer to the original contract entered in May 2014. There must always be an equal number of futures contracts reflecting long and short contracts.

Further assume that the short trader, who acquired the short position in May 2014, stays in the market for a longer period and oil prices continue to rise to $120 per barrel, when the short liquidates her short position in say September 2014. The short will have sustained a loss of $20 per barrel because she agreed to sell something she did not own and must now buy the commodity at the now higher price for resale at the lower agreed price.

In other words, the short must make a theoretical purchase of oil for $120 per barrel and receive only a theoretical $100 per barrel as agreed in the original futures contract entered into in May 2014, resulting in the $20 per barrel loss.

In this example, the initial buyer made a profit of $10 per barrel, and the second buyer liquidating the initial buyer's contract also made a profit of $10 per barrel (if he liquidated at the same time), or a total of $20 per barrel for the long portion of this trade. The short lost $20 per barrel. This is called a "zero sum" game, whereby the profits and losses of each futures contract traded must equal the same amount. $10 + $10 = $20.

(C) OPTION CONTRACTS

Another form of derivative contract is the "option." A "call" option contract gives the purchaser the contractual right, but not the obligation, to buy something at a specified price for a specified period of time. This is referred to as a "call" option because it gives you the right to "call" (buy) the commodity away from the seller of the option.

In contrast, a "put" option allows the purchaser to "put" (sell) the commodity to the seller of the option at an agreed upon price for a specified period of time. This means that, if the price of the underlying commodity declines, the seller of the put option must pay the buyer the higher price agreed to in the put option contract (the "strike price").

The purchaser of a put or call option, who is also called the "holder" or "buyer," will pay a "premium" to the seller of the option, who is also called the "grantor" or "writer" of the option.

That premium payment is paid to the seller of the option for accepting the contractual obligation to deliver the stock in the event that the purchaser calls for the stock or pays for the securities if the purchaser puts the actual "cash" commodity underlying the option.

The premium will be valued on the basis of the expected risks from the option that is based on the perceived price volatility of the option and the remaining time of the option's life, i.e., the time value. This means that the premium on a long term option on a volatile underlying commodity will normally be greater than the premium for a shorter term option on a less volatile commodity.

In an "American" option, the long may exercise the option at any time before the expiration date of the option. In contrast, "Bermuda" and "European" options restrict the dates on which the option may be exercised, such as limiting exercise to the expiration date. European options contemplate a cash settlement.

Like futures contracts, the terms of commodity options traded on an exchange are standardized. As is also the case for futures contracts, exchange traded option contracts are generally liquidated by offset, rather than through the exercise of the option and the delivery of the underlying commodity.

Like futures contracts, there is usually no delivery of the underlying commodity when an exchange-traded option is exercised. Rather, the parties will have their price differences cash settled by offsetting transactions on the exchange. However, if the transaction involves an option on a futures contract and that option is exercised, the "commodity" delivered to the buyer of the option is the underlying futures contract. The buyer of a call option thus receives a "long" futures contract in the underlying commodity whereas the buyer of a put option receives a "short" futures contract. Most exchange rules automatically offset the futures contract if the buyer exercises the option, especially if the underlying futures contract is "in the money," i.e., it is profitable.

To illustrate how an exchange treated option contract works: Assume that Party A enters into an American call option contract with Party B covering 1,000 barrels of crude oil. The option gives Party A the right to purchase that oil from Party B at any time during the next three months at a price of $100 per barrel. Party A pays a premium of say $1,000 to the grantor of the option. The option will expire on the date set by the exchange for that option (the expiration date).

Assume further that, after thirty days, the price of oil rises to $110 per barrel. Party A then "exercises" the option on the exchange and the prior trade is thereby offset at the clearinghouse for the exchange. This leaves the buyer of the option (Party A) with a gross profit of $10,000. However, that profit must be offset in the amount of the $1,000 premium paid to the seller of the option, resulting in a net gain of $9,000 before payment of commissions paid to the FCM that executed the trade.

The seller in this transaction would have an offsetting loss in the same amount. This is because the seller agreed to sell the oil at $100 per barrel of oil, but must now make a theoretical purchase of that oil at $110 per barrel to cover that obligation. That results in a gross loss of $10,000, which is reduced by the $1,000 premium paid to the seller by the buyer, exclusive of commissions.

Note there are critical differences between futures and options. For example, the purchaser of a futures contact pays no premium. The initial margin acts as a performance bond, and both parties to the futures contract deposit the initial margin with their respective FCM. That initial margin is returned to the parties, net of any loss that might have impaired the margin deposit, after liquidation of the futures contract.

Further, as described in the above example of a futures contract, the long trader will incur the entire loss or gain of the price movement. In contrast, the options buyer's loss is limited to the amount of the premium paid. In both examples, however, the short seller of the options or futures has unlimited liability (down to zero in the case of a put option) for any price changes in the underlying commodity. The loss to the seller of an option will be reduced by the amount of the premium. There is no such reduction for the seller of a futures contract.

(D) SWAP CONTRACTS

Still another form of derivative contract is the "swap." A swap contract involves an exchange of cash flows or values between the parties to the contract, commonly referred to as the "counterparty" or the "dealer."

For example, in a "plain vanilla" interest rate swap, one party might exchange a floating interest rate on a notional amount of a loan for a fixed interest rate on that same notional amount with the counterparty to the swap.

The parties to this plain vanilla interest rate swap would periodically compute the differences between the fixed interest rate set by the swap agreement and the current market interest rate that is set by some market based index, such as Libor (the London Inter-Bank Offered Rate).

To illustrate: Assume that Party A is a property developer that has an outstanding loan from a bank that is to mature in five years in the amount of $10 million at a fixed interest rate of 5 percent per annum. Party A believes that interest rates are likely to decline slowly over the next five years.

Party A would like a floating rate mortgage, instead of the fixed rate mortgage, so that the interest payments on the $10 million loan will gradually be lowered as market rates fall. In the absence of a swap, Party A could refinance the loan and convert it to a floating rate mortgage. However, that would be expensive and time consuming.

Party B is a financial institution that has an outstanding floating rate loan from a bank in the amount of $10 million. The loan has a twenty-year term but only five years remain on that tenor. Unlike Party A, Party B believes that interest rates will gradually increase over the next five years. If that occurs, and in the absence of a swap, Party B would have to make higher interest rate payments over the next five years than it would have to make under a fixed rate loan.

Both parties can resolve their respective concerns through a swap in which Party A pays Party B a floating interest rate (as determined by Libor) starting at an annual rate of 5 percent on a notional loan amount of $10 million. Conversely, Party B will pay Party A a fixed 5 percent annual interest rate on that notional amount. Payments will be exchanged on a net basis each month.

To illustrate: Assume that during the first month of the year Libor rates fall by 1 percent. Party A will have to pay Party B a floating rate amount $33,333 ($10,000,000 × .04 percent = $400,000 ÷ 12 (to reflect this is a payment for only one month's interest on the annual rate) = $33,333).

Conversely, Party B will have to pay Party A a fixed amount payment of $41,666 ($10,000,000 × .05 percent = $500,000 ÷ 12 = $41,666).

The parties net their payments so that Party B writes Party A a check for $8,333 ($41,666 less $33,333). Party A can use that money to reduce the amount he pays on his fixed monthly loan, thereby effectively converting Party A's fixed interest rate loan into a floating rate loan. These payments will flow back and forth each month as interest rates increase or decrease.

More complex swaps may swap the value of an asset in exchange for a flow of cash payments. For example, as will be shown in Chapter 6, credit default swaps involve periodic payments in exchange for credit protection in the event of a loan default.

There are also many other exotic combinations that are used as a part of a swap agreement. For example, a "swaption" is a combination of a swap and an option.

JERRY W. MARKHAM
"CONFEDERATE BONDS," "GENERAL CUSTER," AND THE
REGULATION OF DERIVATIVE FINANCIAL INSTRUMENTS
25 Seton Hall Law Review 1 (1994)

Historians have traced transactions in derivative instruments to 2000 B.C. Yet, in the United States, futures style contracts were slow to develop. The State of Massachusetts Bay did issue some derivative instruments that appear to contain a crude form of cost of living index. One such instrument was a two year note for three hundred seventy pounds at six percent to be paid in currency "in a greater or less Sum, according as Five Bushels of CORN for, Sixty-eight Pounds and four-seventh Parts of a Pound of BEEF, Ten Pounds of SHEEPS WOOL, and Sixteen Pounds of SOLE LEATHER shall then cost, more or less than One Hundred and Thirty Pounds current Money, at the then current Prices of said Articles." Nevertheless, it was not until the middle of the nineteenth century that a fully functioning futures market was established in Chicago.

Modern futures trading stems from the grain marketing problems that occurred in the mid-west during the early 1800s. Prior to the development of futures trading, the Chicago markets were flooded with grain at harvest time, and prices would drop to levels below production costs. This devastated the farmers, and grain was left to rot in the streets. Later, prices would skyrocket as surpluses were consumed.

To even out this boom and bust cycle, so-called "forward" contracts were developed in which grain was sold for delivery at a future date. These were quite similar to the "to arrive" contracts that had been previously used in England, and which involved goods that were being shipped. The goods could be sold even while they were afloat through the use of negotiable bills of lading. Title was passed, but the goods arrived at a later date.

The forward contract allowed farmers and middlemen to develop storage facilities because the grain no longer needed to be brought to market at harvest time. By the close of the Civil War, forward contracts had evolved into what we now know as futures contracts. This occurred when the terms of the contracts were standardized, with the grade of the commodity and delivery date becoming uniform. The only item negotiated was price. With contract uniformity, traders could offset positions and could more easily speculate in the prices of commodities. This allowed the development of our modern grain distribution system, which permits producers and users of commodities to hedge against price changes. Futures contracts also perform a price discovery function.

The bulk of the trading in futures contracts occurred initially on the Board of Trade of the City of Chicago. The futures contract traded on the Chicago Board of Trade was a true derivative product. The futures contract's price and function was based upon the value of another item—usually an agricultural commodity. * * *

Trading in "privileges," "puts and calls," and "price differences" also accompanied the speculation aroused by the Civil War. Traders in Chicago, for example, used privileges in their grain trading. For a fee, the purchaser was given the "privilege" or option to buy or sell grain at a specified price. In 1865, the Board of Trade prohibited such transactions because they were viewed to be gambling contracts. That bar was ineffective in stopping such trading, as were later efforts by the exchange, including one investigation that involved a round up of members and the use of private detectives. It was reported that the investigation had implicated half the members of the Board of Trade. * * * *

2. SPECULATION VERSUS GAMBLING

JUSTH V. HOLLIDAY
2 Mackey 346 (D.C. Sup. 1883)

MR. JUSTICE HAGNER delivered the opinion of the court.

This is an action brought by the plaintiff against the defendant, upon a promissory note, of which the following is a copy:

$8,500 NEW YORK, Feb. 10, 1876.

"Six months after date I promise to pay to the order of myself, with interest at 7 per cent, eighty-five hundred dollars, at the office of Justh & Co., 19 Broad street, value received.

"G. A. CUSTER.

"Endorsed:

"G. A. CUSTER.

"BEN. HOLLIDAY.

"Received, New York, March 21, 1878, nine hundred and twenty-six dollars ($926.00).

"JUSTH & CO.

A. F., JR."

Besides the pleas of non assumpsit and not indebted, the defendant interposed the following:

"And for further plea, the said defendant says that the note in the declaration mentioned was executed by the said Custer, and endorsed by this defendant for the amount of an alleged account which the said plaintiffs claimed to have against the said Custer, growing out of certain alleged purchases and sales of stock by the said plaintiffs for and on account of the said Custer. And the defendant avers that there were no *bona fide* sales of stocks by the plaintiffs, to or for said Custer, but the alleged amount for which said note was given was for the difference between the price of said stocks at the time of the pretended sale of them by the said plaintiffs to said Custer, or the pretended purchasing thereof by them for him, and the prices thereof at the time of the pretended sale thereof by said plaintiffs for said Custer, and that said Custer did not deal in said stocks, or buy them of or sell them to the said plaintiffs, or buy or sell them through the agency of the said plaintiffs, or otherwise, and no stocks were ever delivered to said Custer by or through the plaintiffs, or intended so to be, but that the transactions between them, in consideration of which said note was made and endorsed, were wagers upon the prices of said stocks, and that no other or different consideration passed between the said plaintiffs and Custer, or defendant, for the giving or endorsement of said note, and the defendant did not know, at the time he endorsed the same, what the consideration thereof was."

Issue was joined upon these pleas, and the case was tried before a jury, which rendered a verdict for the plaintiff for the amount of the note and interest, after crediting the $926, which the plaintiff stated he had received on account from the estate of Custer.

At the trial, the plaintiff proved the execution and endorsement of the note and its due protest, and there rested.

The defendant thereupon read in evidence the testimony taken under a commission issued on the order of the plaintiff, who was the only witness examined.

He testified in chief, in his own behalf, and was cross-examined by the defendant. There were produced by the plaintiff, and returned with the commission, three communications addressed by General Custer to the plaintiff, and several accounts, which he stated represented the transactions between him and General Custer, so far as he was able to furnish the same. And this being all the evidence in the case, the defendant prayed the court to grant the following instruction:

"If the jury believe from the evidence that the note in the declaration mentioned was given by the said Custer and endorsed by defendant for a balance of accounts, alleged to be due from said Custer to the plaintiff, and that such alleged balance arose upon alleged purchases and sales of stocks by Justh & Co., in the name of said Custer, or to or for him, and that no stocks so alleged to be purchased by Justh & Co., in the name of said Custer, or alleged to be sold to or for him, were ever delivered to him, and that it was the intention of the said parties that such stocks should not be delivered to said Custer, but that he should receive only the profits on the alleged purchases and sales of said stocks, if any should be made, or be liable for the losses, if any should occur, then such transactions were illegal, and the plaintiff cannot recover."

The case comes here upon exceptions to the refusal of the court to give this instruction to the jury:

1st. The general principle is well settled as to the conditions which will invalidate contracts of the description referred to in the prayer.

In the excellent work of Mr. Dos Passos, of the New York bar, on the Law of Stock Brokers, it is thus stated: "Where a contract is made for the delivery or acceptance of securities at a future day, at a price named, and neither party, at the time of making the contract, intends to deliver or accept the shares, but merely to pay differences, according to the rise or fall of the market, the contract is void, either by virtue of statute or as contrary to public policy." P. 477.

All observers agree that the inevitable effect of such dealings is to encourage wild speculations; to derange prices to the detriment of the community; to discourage the disposition to engage in steady business or labor, where the gains, though sure, are too slow to satisfy the thirst for gaming when once aroused; and to fill the cities with the bankrupt victims of such disasters as any "Black Friday" may develop. As was well expressed in 55 Pa. State, 298, Bruce's Appeal, "Anything which induces men to risk their money or property without any other hope of return than to get for nothing any given amount from another, is gambling, and demoralizes the community, no matter by what name it may be called."

The extent of this form of speculation now rife in our country is unprecedented, unless perhaps by the almost universal gambling transactions that distinguished the era of the famous South Sea Bubble.

Mr. Dos Passos states in his work that according to financial authorities the sales of stocks alone, at the New York Stock Exchange, in the year 1881, reached the enormous total of 128,162,466 shares, representing in cash at $100 each share, the prodigious sum of twelve billion eight hundred and sixteen millions two hundred and forty-six thousand dollars. No one doubts that much the larger part of these transactions were illicit as gaming contracts. And when it is remembered that this fierce greed for gain without labor has to so great an extent subjected to the same wild speculation the commodities necessary to sustain life, that the humblest housekeeper is frequently the innocent sufferer by mere wagering transactions, the far-reaching extent of this pernicious traffic may, in some degree, be realized. The plainest principles of propriety and public policy, therefore, should warn the courts to adhere tenaciously to such protection against the further spread of the evil, as they have been able to interpose to the recovery upon contracts originating in stock gambling.

2nd. That the endorser of a note given on account of such dealings as are recognized as gaming transactions can rely upon their illegality as a defense to an action on the note, was settled as far back as 1794, in the case of Steers *vs.* Laskley, 6 T. R., 61. There the defendant was engaged in stock-jobbing transactions through a broker, and the plaintiff had acted as one of the referees to determine the amount due to the broker on the dealings. The broker drew upon the defendant to pay part of the adjudged sum. The bill was accepted by the defendant and endorsed by the broker to the plaintiff, who sued the defendant to recover the amount of the bill. Lord Kenyon non-suited the plaintiff, being of the opinion that as the bill grew out of a stock-jobbing transaction, which was known to the plaintiff, he could not recover upon it.

In overruling the motion for a new trial his lordship said: "The bill on which the action is brought was given for these very differences, and Wilson (the broker) could not have enforced payment of it. Then the security was endorsed over to the plaintiff, he knowing of the illegality of the contract between Wilson and the defendant, for he was the arbitrator to settle their accounts; and under such circumstances he cannot be permitted to recover on the bill in a court of law."

And so the law remains to this time. Dos Passos, 478. * * *

We have failed, however, to find in the record, any evidence to show that the plaintiff did purchase any stocks for Custer from other brokers or any other persons.

The real question for determination was as to the *bona fides* of the alleged purchases and sales; whether, in effecting such alleged purchases, any stock was actually obtained from the possession of any other person and transferred or communicated either to Custer personally or to his agent; and further, whether it was the intention of the plaintiff and Custer that the stock was to be obtained from the possession of any person and transferred to that of Custer or his agent, so that Custer would take title to what some one else parted with, or whether, on the other hand, it was their intention that there should be no such surrender of stock by any third person and no equivalent gain of such stock by Custer. And, with the view of presenting this idea of reception of title or interest by the alleged buyer, the expression "*delivered* to Custer" was used, and in no other. A purchaser in London this morning, who *bona fide* has bought stocks by telegraph through a broker in New York, may correctly be said to have had them *delivered to him* today, as a mode of expressing the *bona fides* and completeness of the transaction, while the word would not be applicable to a stock-jobbing bargain concocted between two parties in New York, though sitting side by side in the Stock Exchange. In view of the pleadings and evidence in the case, it is inconceivable that the defendant's counsel could have thought of placing his case upon the point whether it was the intention of the parties that the stocks should be delivered to *Custer* rather than *to his broker*. The expression, "and that it was the intention of the said parties that such stocks should not be *delivered to the said Custer*," was the equivalent of saying, "and that it was the intention of said parties that such stocks should not *pass to or become the property of* Custer." * * * *

During the six months of the speculation the profits credited to Custer amount to $552, and the broker's commissions to $1,840, and Custer's net losses are stated at $8,578. The aggregate of the stock transactions during this period appears to have been $389,983.

It appears that Custer was unable to pay the balance due in December, 1875, and the dividend paid from his estate in 1878 on the claim, would indicate that it could not pay more than ten cents on the dollar.

The disparity between the pecuniary ability of Custer and this immense amount of purchases and sales within half a year's time, would certainly be regarded by business men as a circumstance in contradiction of the idea that he intended to make actual contracts so much beyond his means of payment. In *In re* Green, 7 Bissell, 344, the court, speaking of a transaction insignificant in comparison with this, says: "It is self-evident from the testimony and the condition of the parties that these sales were not *bona fide*. The bankrupt was not a dealer in grain, he was a country merchant of little or no means, and had no money to invest in wheat, which fact both Green, his brother, and Norris knew. The idea that they bought for him several thousand bushels of wheat with the expectation that he was to pay for it was preposterous."

It would be infinitely more preposterous to suppose that this broker bought more than a quarter of a million of dollars worth of stock for this soldier within these few months with the expectation that he was to pay for it. * * * *

In the case at bar, we cannot resist the conclusion that there was abundant evidence legally sufficient to go to the jury, in support of the supposal of the defendant's prayer; and believing that the instruction correctly stated the law, we think it was error to refuse it.

Judgment reversed and new trial awarded.

Notes

1. General Custer lost an even bigger gamble at the Little Bighorn, but the opinion in this case represented a widely held view that speculative trading in stocks or commodities fell within the purview of state gambling statutes. Under those statutes, such wagers were null and unenforceable. However, the Supreme Court, in the same year that Justh v. Holliday was decided, rejected a claim that exchange traded futures contracts were prohibited gambling because delivery usually did not occur:

> Evidence was given that a very large proportion of all the contracts made for the sale of produce at the board of trade of Chicago, were settled by payment of differences, and that nothing else was expected by the parties to them, and the number of these in proportion to the number of bona fide contracts, in which delivery was expected and desired, is said to be so large as to justify the inference that it was so in these cases.

> But since the plaintiff testifies that he had no such understanding, since nothing is proved of the intention of the other parties, and since the contracts were always in writing, we do not think the evidence of what other people intended by other contracts of a similar character, however numerous, is sufficient of itself to prove that the parties to these contracts intended to violate the law, or to justify a jury in making such a presumption.

Roundtree v. Smith, 108 U.S. 269, 276 (1883). In Irwin v. Williar, 110 U.S. 499, 508 (1884), the Supreme Court further ruled that an intent to deliver would be presumed, if the contracts called for delivery, even if delivery was not made and the contract was settled by offset. *See also,* Bibb v. Allen, 149 U.S. 481 (1893); Hansen v. Boyd, 161 U.S. 397 (1896) (making similar rulings).

2. Concerns that futures trading was immoral gambling were also raised on the federal level in the nineteenth century. As one author has noted:

> By 1892 thousands of petitions to Congress called for the prohibition of "speculative gambling in grain." And, attacks from state legislatures were seemingly unrelenting.... Two nineteenth century challenges to futures trading are particularly noteworthy. The first was the so-called Anti-Option movement ... [which] was fueled by agrarians and their sympathizers in Congress who wanted to end what they perceived as wanton speculative abuses in futures trading. Although options were (are) not futures contracts, and were nonetheless already outlawed on most exchanges by the 1890s, the legislation did not distinguish between the two instruments and effectively sought to outlaw both. In 1890 the Butterworth Anti-Option Bill was introduced in Congress but never came to a vote. However, in 1892 the Hatch (and Washburn) Anti-Option bills passed both houses of Congress, and failed only on technicalities

during reconciliation between the two houses. Had either bill become law, it would have effectively ended options and futures trading in the United States.

Joseph Santos, A History of Futures Trading in the United States, http://eh.net/encyclopedia/article/Santos.futures (citations omitted) (accessed September 5, 2011). See generally, John V. Rainbolt II, Symposium on Commodity Futures Regulation: Regulating the Grain Gambler and His Successors, 6 Hofstra L.J. 1 (1977) (describing how concerns over speculation drove Congress to regulate the futures markets).

3. Germany banned futures trading as gambling in 1896. The result of that legislation was that "the market became highly susceptible to unfavorable developments and rumors; and, in the absence of all steadying influence, any adverse factors were accompanied by fluctuations such as had rarely been witnessed in former times. . . . German capital was diverted to the financial centers of other countries." G. Plochman, The German Bourse Law, 187 North American Rev..742, 743, 746–747 (MAY 1908). Nearly one century later, however, Germany repealed that law, legalized derivatives, and Eurex, a German exchange, soon competed with the U.S. futures exchanges for volume.

4. The CEA now specifically preempts state gambling laws and certain other state statutes with respect to trading on regulated exchanges. However, the Dodd-Frank Wall Street Reform and Consumer Protection Act of 2010 (Dodd-Frank Act) amended the preemption provisions in the CEA and eliminated some state statutes from the list of preempted laws. Nevertheless, the preemption of state gaming and anti-bucketing laws for regulated transactions was continued [7 U.S.C. § 16(e)(2)]. In addition, state common law claims involving a futures commission merchant and its customers are not preempted by federal law unless they create a conflict with CFTC jurisdiction. 13A Jerry W. Markham, Commodities Regulation: Fraud, Manipulation & Other Claims §§ 21:5 et seq. (2013).

5. As described in Chapter 6, unregulated trading in off-exchange price "difference" contracts, such as those engaged in by General Custer, was occurring in recent years, but such trades are now regulated by the CFTC.

3. HEDGING AND SPECULATION

Linked to price difference trading, like that in General Custer's case and other such speculation, were the so-called "bucket shops." These operations did not actually execute customer orders on an organized exchange. Instead, they simply took the customer's funds as a bet on future price changes. If the customer was wrong in his prediction of the direction of the price of the commodity that was subject to the bet, the bucket shop operator would keep the customer's funds. If the customer

won the bet, the bucket shop operator often simply disappeared, moving their operations to a new locale.[1]

The Chicago Board of Trade (CBOT) found that the bucket shops were hurting its credibility, as well as providing unwanted competition. The CBOT reacted strongly to that threat by embarking on an anti-bucket shop crusade that sought to stop those operations. The CBOT did so by cutting off their use of the CBOT's price quotations, which the bucket shop operators needed to fuel their business.

BOARD OF TRADE OF THE CITY OF CHICAGO v. CHRISTIE GRAIN AND STOCK COMPANY

198 U.S. 236 (1905)

MR. JUSTICE HOLMES delivered the opinion of the court.

These are two bills in equity brought by the Chicago Board of Trade to enjoin the principal defendants from using and distributing the continuous quotations of prices on sales of grain and provisions for future delivery, which are collected by the plaintiff and which cannot be obtained by the defendants except through a known breach of the confidential terms on which the plaintiff communicates them. It is sufficient for the purposes of decision to state the facts without reciting the pleadings in detail. Special charter of the State of Illinois incorporated the plaintiff on February 18, 1859. The charter incorporated an existing board of trade, and there seems to be no reason to doubt, as indeed is alleged by the Christie Grain and Stock Company, that it then managed its Chamber of Commerce substantially as it has since. The main feature of its management is that it maintains an exchange hall for the exclusive use of its members, which now has become one of the great grain and provision markets of the world. Three separate portions of this hall are known respectively as the Wheat Pit, the Corn Pit, and the Provision Pit. In these pits the members make sale and purchases exclusively for future delivery, the members dealing always as principals between themselves, and being bound practically, at least, as principals to those who employ them when they are not acting on their own behalf.

---

[1] The term bucket shop:

was first used in the late [18]70s, but it is very evident that it was coined in London as many as fifty years ago, when it had absolutely no reference to any species of speculation or gambling. It appears that beer swillers from the East Side (London) went from street to street with a bucket, draining every keg they came across and picking up cast-off cigar butts. Arriving at a den, they gathered for social amusement around a table and passed the bucket as a loving cup, each taking a "pull" as it came his way. In the interval there were smoking and rough jokes. The den soon came to be called a bucketshop. Later on the term was applied, both in England and the United States, as a by-word of reproach, to small places where grain and stock deals were counterfeited.

John Hill, Gold Bricks of Speculation 39 (1904).

The quotation of the prices continuously offered and accepted in these pits during business hours are collected at the plaintiff's expense and handed to the telegraph companies, which have their instruments close at hand, and by the latter are sent to a great number of offices. The telegraph companies all receive the quotations under a contract not to furnish them to any bucket shop or place where they are used as a basis for bets or illegal contracts. To that end they agree to submit applications to the Board of Trade for investigation, and to require the applicant, if satisfactory, to make a contract with the telegraph company and the Board of Trade, which, if observed, confines the information within a circle of persons all contracting with the Board of Trade. The principal defendants get and publish these quotations in some way not disclosed. It is said not to be proved that they get them wrongfully, even if the plaintiff has the rights, which it claims. But as the defendants do not get them from the telegraph companies authorized to distribute them, have declined to sign the above-mentioned contracts, and deny the plaintiff's rights altogether, it is a reasonable conclusion that they get, and intend to get, their knowledge in a way which is wrongful unless their contention is maintained.

It is alleged in the bills that the principal defendants keep bucket shops, and the plaintiff's proof on that point fails, except so far as their refusal to sign the usual contracts may lead to an inference, but if the plaintiff has the rights which it alleges the failure is immaterial. The main defense is this. It is said that the plaintiff itself keeps the greatest of bucket shops, in the sense of an Illinois statute of June 6, 1887, that is, places wherein is permitted the pretended buying and selling of grain, etc., without any intention of receiving and paying for the property so bought, or of delivering the property so sold. On this ground it is contended that if under other circumstances there could be property in the quotations, which hardly is admitted, the subject matter is so infected with the plaintiff's own illegal conduct that it is *caput lupine*, and may be carried off by any one at will.

It appears that in not less than three-quarters of the transactions in the grain pit there is no physical handing over of any grain, but that there is a settlement, either by the direct method, so called, or by what is known as ringing up. The direct method consists simply in setting off contracts to buy wheat of a certain amount at a certain time, against contracts to sell a like amount at the same time, and paying the difference of price in cash, at the end of the business day. The ring settlement is reached by a comparison of books among the clerks of the members buying and selling in the pit, and picking out a series of transactions which begins and ends with dealings which can be set against each other by eliminating those between—as, if A has sold to B five thousand bushels of May wheat, and B has sold the same amount to

C, and C to D and D to A. Substituting D for B by novation, A's sale can be set against his purchase, on simply paying the difference in price. The Circuit Court of Appeals for the Eighth Circuit took the defendant's view of these facts and ordered the bill to be dismissed. 125 Fed. Rep. 161. The Circuit Court of Appeals for the Seventh Circuit declined to follow this decision and granted an injunction as prayed. 130 Fed. Rep. 507. Thereupon this Court granted writs of certiorari and both cases are here.

As has appeared, the plaintiff's chamber of commerce is, in the first place, a great market, where, through its eighteen hundred members, is transacted a large part of the grain and provision business of the world. Of course, in a modern market contracts are not confined to sales for immediate delivery. People will endeavor to forecast the future and to make agreements according to their prophecy. Speculation of this kind by competent men is the self-adjustment of society to the probable. Its value is well known as a means of avoiding or mitigating catastrophes, equalizing prices and providing for periods of want. It is true that the success of the strong induces imitation by the weak, and that incompetent persons bring themselves to ruin by undertaking to speculate in their turn. But legislatures and courts generally have recognized that the natural evolutions of a complex society are to be touched only with a very cautious hand, and that such coarse attempts at a remedy for the waste incident to every social function as a simple prohibition and laws to stop its being are harmful and vain. This court has upheld sales of stock for future delivery and the substitution of parties provided for by the rules of the Chicago Stock Exchange. *Clews* v. *Jamieson*, 182 U.S. 461.

When the Chicago Board of Trade was incorporated we cannot doubt that it was expected to afford a market for future as well as present sales, with the necessary incidents of such a market, and while the State of Illinois allows that charter to stand, we cannot believe that the pits, merely as places where future sales are made, are forbidden by the law. But again, the contracts made in the pits are contracts between the members. We must suppose that from the beginning as now, if a member had a contract with another member to buy a certain amount of wheat at a certain time and another to sell the same amount at the same time, it would be deemed unnecessary to exchange warehouse receipts. We must suppose that then as now, a settlement would be made by the payment of differences, after the analogy of a clearinghouse. This naturally would take place no less that the contracts were made in good faith for actual delivery, since the result of actual delivery would be to leave the parties just where they were before. Set-off has all the effects of delivery. The ring settlement is simply a more complex case of the same kind. These settlements would be frequent, as the number of persons buying and selling was comparatively small.

The fact that contracts are satisfied in this way by set-off and the payment of differences detracts in no degree from the good faith of the parties, and if the parties know when they make such contracts that they are very likely to have a chance to satisfy them in that way and intend to make use of it, that fact is perfectly consistent with a serious business purpose and an intent that the contract shall mean what it says. There is no doubt, from the rules of the Board of Trade or the evidence, that the contracts made between the members are intended and supposed to be binding in manner and form as they are made. There is no doubt that a large part of those contracts is made for serious business purposes. Hedging, for instance, as it is called, is a means by which collectors and exporters of grain or other products, and manufacturers who make contracts in advance for the sale of their goods, secure themselves against the fluctuations of the market by counter contracts for the purchase or sale, as the case may be, of an equal quantity of the product, or of the material of manufacture. It is none the less a serious business contract for a legitimate and useful purpose that it may be offset before the time of delivery in case delivery should not be needed or desired.

Purchases made with the understanding that the contract will be settled by paying the difference between the contract and the market price at a certain time, *Ember* v. *Jemison*, 131 U.S. 336, *Wearer Commission Co.* v. *People*, 209 Illinois, 528, stand on different ground from purchases made merely with the expectation that they will be satisfied by set-off. If the latter might fall within the statute of Illinois, we would not be the first to decide that they did when the object was self-protection in business and not merely a speculation entered into for its own sake. It seems to us an extraordinary and unlikely proposition that the dealings which give its character to the great market for future sales in this country are to be regarded as mere wagers or as "pretended" buying or selling, without any intention of receiving and paying for the property bought, or of delivering the property sold, within the meaning of the Illinois act. Such a view seems to us hardly consistent with the admitted fact that the quotations of prices from the market are of the utmost importance to the business world, and not least to the farmers; so important indeed, that it is argued here and has been held in Illinois that the quotations are clothed with a public use. It seems to us hardly consistent with the obvious purposes of the plaintiff's charter, or indeed with the words of the statute invoked. The sales in the pits are not pretended, but, as we have said, are meant and supposed to be binding. A set-off is in legal effect a delivery. We speak only of the contracts made in the pits, because in them the members are principals. The subsidiary rights of their employers where the members buy as brokers we think it unnecessary to discuss.

In the view which we take, the proportion of the dealings in the pit which are settled in this way throws no light on the question of the proportion of serious dealings for legitimate business purposes to those which fairly can be classed as wagers or pretended contracts. No more does the fact that the contracts thus disposed of call for many times the total receipts of grain in Chicago. The fact that they can be and are set-off sufficiently explains the possibility, which is no more wonderful than the enormous disproportion between the currency of the country and contracts for the payment of money, many of which in like manner are set off in clearing houses without any one dreaming that they are not paid, and for the rest of which the same money suffices in succession, the less being needed the more rapid the circulation is.

But suppose that the Board of Trade does keep a place where pretended and unlawful buying and selling are permitted, which as yet the Supreme Court of Illinois, we believe, has been careful not to intimate, it does not follow that it should not be protected in this suit. * * *

Decree in No. 224 reversed. Decree in No. 280 affirmed.

MR. JUSTICE HARLAN, MR. JUSTICE BREWER and MR. JUSTICE DAY Dissent.

* * * *

Despite the Supreme Court's deference to the role of the speculator and widespread recognition that speculators provide valuable liquidity and price discovery benefits, the speculator has long been reviled in history. Speculators are viewed by many to be gamblers that distort prices and thereby injure producers and consumers.

JERRY W. MARKHAM
FROM THE PHARAOHS TO PAUL VOLCKER—A SHORT HISTORY OF THE WAR AGAINST SPECULATION

Address before the American Bar Association Derivatives and Futures Committee,
Naples, Fl., Feb. 25, 2013

* * * To illustrate the view of many towards speculators, I quote from a recent biography on Paul Volcker [the former Federal Reserve Board chairman]:

> Speculators look like normal people, except they smoke big fat Cuban cigars. They try to buy something (anything) in anticipation of selling at a profit after the price goes up. Or they sell first and try to buy later at a lower price. Some speculators focus on stocks, others on bonds, and still others on Super Bowl Tickets. (Ticket scalpers are speculators by another name).

William L. Silber, *Volcker: The Triumph of Persistence* (2012).

Our disdain for speculators seems to be derived from the "just price" theory traceable to St. Thomas Aquinas. He preached that raising prices in response to increased demand was a form of theft. That concept found its way to colonial America where, among others, Robert Keayne was fined 200£ (later reduced to 80£) in 1639 for selling nails above their "just price."

This just price concept underlies a continuing suspicion and even distaste for speculators (and ticket scalpers) that spurs popular distrust of the commodity and stock traders as gamblers who distort prices.

This concept remains alive today. Yet, history is strewn with unsuccessful efforts to proscribe speculation in order to assure that prices are just. For example, "regrating" and "forestalling" were prohibited by Roman law because such speculative practices were believed to interfere with grain supplies, and a check was "put upon their avarice both by imperial instructions and by enactments. . . . The penalties were banishment from trading or relegation to an island for merchants and forced labor for those of the 'lower orders.' "

England also attacked such practices during medieval times. There, a *forestaller* was a speculator who sought to profit by purchasing goods on their way to a market. . . . A *regrator* was a speculator who bought grain in one market and sold it in another market located within a radius of four miles. An *engrosser* was a speculator who bought up commodities for resale.

These "crimes" of speculation were taken seriously in England and were enforced by the infamous Court of the Star Chamber, which operated in secrecy and from which there was no appeal from its sometimes arbitrary decisions. "Indeed, for a ten-year period in the fourteenth century, forestalling was punishable by death, although it appears that no one was ever actually executed." Herbert Hovenkamp, The Law of Vertical Integration and the Business Firm: 1880–1960, 95 Iowa L. Rev. 863, 878 (2010) (footnote and citation omitted). Efforts by the Star Chamber to order corn to be brought to the market at set prices was found to have actually worsened shortages by increasing the temptation to ship grain where higher prices could be obtained.

These prohibitions proved to be unworkable and unenforceable. As Adam Smith wrote in *The Wealth of Nations* in 1776 fears of engrossing and forestalling may be compared to the "popular terrors and suspicions of witchcraft." Nevertheless, George Washington blamed inflated commodity prices during the Revolution on "monopolizers, forestallers, and engrossers." He viewed such individuals to be "murders of our cause" who should be "hung in gibbets." Washington also complained that "[v]irtue and patriotism are almost extinct. Stock-jobbing, speculating, engrossing seem to be the great business of the multitude."

Our Supreme Court later noted that, because of:

> development of more accurate economic conceptions and the changes in conditions of society, it came to be recognized that the acts prohibited by the engrossing, forestalling, etc., statutes did not have the harmful tendency which they were presumed to have when the legislation concerning them was enacted, and therefore did not justify the presumption which had previously been deduced from them, but, on the contrary, such acts tended to fructify and develop trade."

Standard Oil Company of New Jersey v. United States, 221 U.S. 1, 55 (1910). * * * *

Yet, even today, speculators remain the target of populist politicians when adverse price changes occur. A Senate subcommittee issued a bipartisan staff report in 2006, which claimed that speculators had made "tens and perhaps hundreds of millions of dollars in profits trading in energy commodities." The staff report found "substantial evidence" that these speculators had "significantly increased prices" and that the speculative purchases of oil futures have added as much as $20–$25 per barrel to the current price of crude oil. * * *

Attacks on speculators continued. President Obama stated in 2012 in a speech from the White House's Rose Garden that "we can't afford a situation where speculators artificially manipulate markets by buying up oil, creating the perception of a shortage, and driving prices higher—only to flip the oil for a quick profit."

Bill O'Reilly, the populist Fox News commentator, called oil speculators "crooks" and wanted to increase their margin requirements to fifty percent. Another Fox news commentator John Stossel pointed out to O'Reilly that government efforts to control speculation usually fail. Pulling out an onion he just happened to have in his pocket, Stossel noted that Congress had tried to stop volatility in onion prices by banning futures trading in that commodity in 1958. Onion prices became more volatile after that ban. There is still hope for onion futures, however, after all Japan repealed its 72-year ban on rice futures trading in 2011.

Attacks against oil speculators went global in 2009 when British Prime Minister Gordon Brown and French President Nicolas Sarkozy jointly warned about the dangers of "damaging speculation" and sought government supervision of oil prices. Sarkozy later delivered a speech in which he urged that commodity price speculators be treated in the same fashion as the "mafia."

In 2010, the Greek Prime Minister blamed his country's severe economic problems on speculators, an accusation echoed by his counterpart in Italy. The *Wall Street Journal* opined that their "view seems to be that their fiscal troubles are the result of insidious outside 'manipulation,' not years of wasteful spending and antigrowth policies."
* * * *

JERRY W. MARKHAM
FIDUCIARY DUTIES UNDER THE COMMODITY EXCHANGE ACT
68 Notre Dame L. Rev. 199 (1992)

Commodity futures trading began on the Chicago commodity exchanges in the middle of the nineteenth century. Trading in futures grew steadily over the years, and today, these markets play an important role in the nation's economy. This is due principally to the fact that futures contracts are used to hedge commercial risks. When used for hedging, futures markets effectively operate as insurance contracts against adverse price changes. To illustrate, a large trucking company is concerned that rising fuel costs will impair its profitability because its long-term haulage contracts do not allow price adjustments for fuel price increases. To guard against the risk of fuel price increases, the trucking company could buy petroleum futures contracts on the New York Mercantile Exchange. In the event fuel oil prices increase, the trucking company will experience a profit on the futures contract. The trucking company can then use the profits to offset the increased prices paid for the actual diesel oil. If prices were to instead decrease, the trucking company would experience a loss on the futures contract. That loss, however, would be offset by the decreased cost of the actual diesel fuel. Consequently, whether prices went up or down, the trucking company would assure itself of a stable price for its fuel oil, and its profit margin would be assured.

The same approach could be taken by the airline company that fears another outbreak of violence in the Middle East, which would cause a drastic increase in jet fuel prices. Similarly, large commercial farmers can assure themselves of a specified price before planting crops, and those concerned with interest rate risks can guard against such dangers by using futures contracts on a broad array of interest-bearing instruments. Portfolio managers may also guard against market risks through so-called stock index futures contracts. Indeed, many institutional investors now seek to "index" their portfolios so as to assure that they perform as well as the overall market. This is because modern portfolio theory suggests that it may not be possible to outperform the market. Stock index futures can be used to assist in this indexing or to guard against anticipated market drops. For example, a portfolio manager anticipating a drop in the stock market will not want to sell out a broad-based portfolio because of the transaction costs involved. Moreover, the manager may want to hold the securities on a long-term basis. In that situation, the portfolio manager can simply sell futures contracts on a stock index in an amount equivalent to the value of the portfolio. In the event of a market decline, the profits will offset the diminished value of the portfolio. In the event that the trader erred, and the market does not drop, there will be a loss on the futures contracts that can be offset against the portfolio gain. The cost of the error in judgment, therefore, becomes the relatively low transaction costs associated with the futures contracts plus the giving up of the profits on the portfolio. If, however, the portfolio manager is correct in his judgment, then the profitability of the portfolio will be much enhanced.

Futures contracts also make available a broad array of strategies for traders. These include such things as dynamic hedging, arbitrage transactions, and so-called program trading. Dynamic hedging involves complicated strategies used to adjust hedges to meet changing market conditions. Arbitrage transactions are many and complicated in form, but generally involve an effort to take advantage of price disparities between markets, including the cash markets and related futures or options contracts. Program trading involves computerized programs that signal traders when to buy or sell upon the occurrence of certain market events. * * *

Price discovery is another benefit of the futures markets. It is thought that traders bring information to the market. That information sets prices in the trading pits by competitive auction bids and offers. Those prices are then widely reported through newspapers and on radio and television. Farmers depend on these price reports to determine what crops to plant or when to market their livestock. Futures prices also provide a mechanism for determining the value of precious metals, for pricing oil, and even for pricing the securities markets. This is an important economic contribution, and this pricing function underscores the importance of the futures markets to the national and international economy.

Speculators are necessary to provide liquidity to the marketplace. Speculators offset the risks of hedgers and provide a source of liquidity when hedging risks cannot exactly be offset in the marketplace. That is, commercial firms requiring sales transactions to hedge risks will not exactly offset, either in time or quantity, the hedging needs of other commercial firms with risks that involve the purchase of futures contracts. Speculators fill this gap and provide the cushion and liquidity necessary to assure that hedging transactions can be effected. Speculators also bring information to the marketplace to aid its pricing function. Of course, excessive speculation is not desirable. It may distort prices and prevent the efficient operation of the marketplace. Excessive speculation can cause a market collapse and loss of public confidence. To lessen these concerns, Congress has authorized limits on the amount of speculation that may be engaged in by any one trader or group of traders acting together.

NOTES

1. Since the adoption of the CEA, special treatment has been given to firms that use the U.S. futures markets for bona-fide hedging purposes. This special regulatory treatment for hedgers does not exist in any other country; in other countries, all users of the futures markets are treated in the same manner. In the U.S., bona fide hedgers receive three special regulatory treatments, namely: (i) each U.S. futures exchange establishes a lower initial margin requirement for bona-fide hedgers (the reduced margin savings can be from 25 to 35 percent of the initial margin amount required for speculators), (ii) hedge trades are not subject to the speculative position limits described in Chapter 9, and (iii) in the event of an FCM's bankruptcy, bona-fide hedgers are protected from having their open futures positions being liquidated by the bankruptcy trustee appointed to oversee the FCM's estate.

2. CFTC Rule 1.3(z) [17 C.F.R. 1.3(z)] defines a "bona-fide hedger." Until recently, this definition was left intact and without change for over thirty-five years. Recently, the CFTC has made several changes to this rule, with different tests applicable to different types of transactions. This concept of hedging also impacts the applicability of the "Volcker Rule," which was required by Section 619 of the Dodd-Frank Wall Street Reform and Consumer Protection Act of 2010. The Volcker Rule, which was named after Paul Volcker, the former Federal Reserve Board chairman who championed it, prohibits banks from engaging in speculative "proprietary" trading for their own accounts. Some hedging transactions are exempted from that rule. On December 10, 2013, three federal banking agencies (the Board of Governors of the Federal Reserve System, the Office of the Comptroller of the Currency and the Federal Deposit Insurance Corporation), together with the SEC and the CFTC, all approved a final regulation implementing Section 619. See http://www.federalreserve.gov/aboutthefed/boardmeetings/final-common-rules–20131210.pdf

3. To illustrate how hedging works: assume that Farmer A in North Carolina is trying in March to determine what crop to plant for the coming crop year. He looks to the prices reported on a commodity futures exchange to make that decision. Those prices show that corn for delivery in November (about when the farmer's crop will be fully harvested) are $7 per bushel, soybean prices for that delivery month are $13 per bushel, and cotton is trading at 80 cents per pound.

> Farmer A concludes that he should plant his crop in soybeans because the $13 price would result in a very profitable year for his farm. However, other farmers may have the same idea, resulting in

overproduction that could cause a drastic drop in the price of the soybeans before their harvest. To guard against that possibility, Farmer A sells the soybeans through a futures contract on a DCM in Chicago that calls for November delivery to warehouses approved by the exchange. Consequently, whatever happens to soybean prices thereafter, Farmer A will be assured of a $13 per bushel price.

Farmer A is thus "hedged" against any decline in soybean prices for his crops. If soybean prices decline in the cash market before harvest, Farmer A will still receive $13 from the soybean futures contract. However, if soybean prices unexpectedly increase beyond $13 per bushel at harvest time, Farmer A would still only receive $13 per bushel. He would forgo any further profit above $13 in exchange for the assurance that he will not receive any less than $13 per bushel.

To further illustrate: assume that, based on past production, Farmer A's harvested soybean crop will be at least 75,000 bushels (Farmer A has crop insurance if the crop fails due to adverse weather conditions). He therefore sells fifteen soybean futures contracts on the exchange, each of which calls for the delivery of 5,000 bushels of soybeans for November delivery.

Further assume that soybean prices have dropped to $10 per bushel in the cash market at the time when Farmer A's crop is harvested in late October. The harvest is approximately 75,000 bushels, as expected. Farmer A will receive $10 per bushel for his crop sold to a grain elevator in November. This is deemed a "cash" transaction. However, since he hedged his soybean crop via the futures contract, he will receive a $3 per bushel profit when he offsets his underlying futures contracts, for a total of $13 per bushel.

Alternatively, Farmer A could also deliver his soybeans to a designated grain elevator in Chicago pursuant to the futures contract and receive $13 per bushel from this delivery. However, it is often not convenient to deliver the soybeans to the warehouses designated by the exchange. Instead, Farmer A will probably sell the crop to his local elevator.

In the event that Farmer A had not hedged the crop through futures contracts, $10 is the price he would have received for his soybeans. As it is, however, the hedge means that he will receive $13 per bushel.

The mathematics of this transaction are as follows:

75,000 bushels sold in the cash market at $10 per bushel =	$750,000
Profit of $3 per bushel ($13 less $10) on the DCM for 75,000 bushels =	<u>$225,000</u>
Total	$975,000

Received from futures and cash market = $975,000 ÷ 75,000 bushels = $13 per bushel

Now assume that, instead of declining, soybeans increased in price from $13 to $15. In that case, Farmer A will sell his crop to the local elevator for $15 per bushel. However, he will have to pay the Chicago exchange $2 per bushel for the loss on the futures contract. This is because Farmer A has agreed to sell his soybeans at $13 per bushel but must make a theoretical purchase of the soybeans for theoretical delivery at a price of $15.

The mathematics of this transaction are as follows:

75,000 bushels sold in the cash market at $15 per bushel =	$1,125,000
Loss of $2 per bushel ($15 less $13) on the DCM for 75,000 bushels =	<u>−$150,000</u>
Total	$975,000

Received from cash market less futures loss = $975,000 ÷ 75,000 bushels = $13 per bushel.

In sum, whether prices go up or down, Farmer A will receive $13 per bushel for his soybeans, or a total of $975,000.

4. Hedging can be used wherever there is a commercial risk that is covered by a futures contract. For example, one of an airline's largest costs arises from its purchase of fuel, which is highly susceptible to large price increases. However, the airline can hedge against those price increases by buying futures contracts that will cover its anticipated needs. Similarly, a portfolio manager can hedge against anticipated declines in the stock market that will protect the value of the portfolio. Of course the portfolio manager could sell the stocks in the portfolio and repurchase those same stocks after the market falls to the anticipated level. However, such a sale would be costly and could disrupt the market further.

4. REGULATORY HISTORY

MERRILL LYNCH, PIERCE, FENNER & SMITH INC. V. CURRAN
456 U.S. 353 (1982)

JUSTICE STEVENS delivered the opinion of the Court.

* * * * The Commodity Exchange Act (CEA), 7 U.S.C. 1 et seq. (1976 ed. and Supp. IV) has been aptly characterized as "a comprehensive regulatory structure to oversee the volatile and esoteric futures trading complex." * * * *

Prior to the advent of futures trading, agricultural products generally were sold at central markets. When an entire crop was harvested and marketed within a short time-span, dramatic price fluctuations sometimes created severe hardship for farmers or for processors. Some of these risks were alleviated by the adoption of quality standards, improvements in storage and transportation facilities, and the practice of "forward contracting"—the use of executory contracts fixing the terms of sale in advance of the time of delivery.

When buyers and sellers entered into contracts for the future delivery of an agricultural product, they arrived at an agreed price on the basis of their judgment about expected market conditions at the time of delivery. Because the weather and other imponderables affected supply and demand, normally the market price would fluctuate before the contract was performed. A declining market meant that the executory agreement was more valuable to the seller than the commodity covered by the contract; conversely, in a rising market the executory contract had a special value for the buyer, who not only was assured of delivery of the commodity but also could derive a profit from the price increase.

The opportunity to make a profit as a result of fluctuations in the market price of commodities covered by contracts for future delivery motivated speculators to engage in the practice of buying and selling "futures contracts." A speculator who owned no present interest in a commodity but anticipated a price decline might agree to a future sale at the current market price, intending to purchase the commodity at a reduced price on or before the delivery date. A "short" sale of that kind would result in a loss if the price went up instead of down. On the other hand, a price increase would produce a gain for a "long" speculator who had acquired a contract to purchase the same commodity with no intent to take delivery but merely for the purpose of reselling the futures contract at an enhanced price.

In the 19th century the practice of trading in futures contracts led to the development of recognized exchanges or boards of trade. At such exchanges standardized agreements covering specific quantities of graded agricultural commodities to be delivered during specified months in the future were bought and sold pursuant to rules developed by the traders themselves. Necessarily the commodities subject to such contracts were fungible. For an active market in the contracts to develop, it also was essential that the contracts themselves be fungible. The exchanges therefore developed standard terms describing the quantity and quality of the commodity, the time and place of delivery, and the method of payment; the only variable was price. The purchase or sale of a futures contract on an exchange is therefore motivated by a single factor—the opportunity to make a profit (or to minimize the risk of loss) from a change in the market price.

The advent of speculation in futures markets produced well-recognized benefits for producers and processors of agricultural commodities. A farmer who takes a "short" position in the futures market is protected against a price decline; a processor who takes a "long" position is protected against a price increase. Such "hedging" is facilitated by the availability of speculators willing to assume the market risk that the hedging farmer or processor wants to avoid. The speculators' participation in the market substantially enlarges the number of potential buyers and sellers of executory contracts and therefore makes it easier for farmers and processors to make firm commitments for future delivery at a fixed price. The liquidity of a futures contract, upon which hedging depends, is directly related to the amount of speculation that takes place.

Persons who actually produce or use the commodities that are covered by futures contracts are not the only beneficiaries of futures trading. The speculators, of course, have opportunities to profit from this trading. Moreover, futures trading must be regulated by an organized exchange. In addition to its regulatory responsibilities, the exchange must maintain detailed records and perform a clearing function to discharge the offsetting contracts that the short or long speculators have no desire to perform. 9 The operation of the exchange creates employment opportunities for futures commission merchants, who solicit orders from individual traders, and for floor brokers, who make the actual trades on the floor of the exchange on behalf of futures commission merchants and their customers. The earnings of the persons who operate the futures market—the exchange itself, the clearinghouse, the floor brokers, and the futures commission merchants—are financed by commissions on the purchase and sale of futures contracts made over the exchange.

Thus, in a broad sense, futures trading has a direct financial impact on three classes of persons. Those who actually are interested in selling or buying the commodity are described as "hedgers"; their primary financial interest is in the profit to be earned from the production or processing of the commodity. Those who seek financial gain by taking positions in the futures market generally are called "speculators" or "investors"; without their participation, futures markets "simply would not exist." Finally, there are the futures commission merchants, the floor brokers, and the persons who manage the market; they also are essential participants, and they have an interest in maximizing the activity on the exchange. The petitioners in these cases are members of this third class whereas their adversaries, the respondents, are speculators or investors. * * *

Because Congress has recognized the potential hazards as well as the benefits of futures trading, it has authorized the regulation of commodity futures exchanges for over 60 years. In 1921 it enacted the Future Trading Act, 42 Stat. 187, which imposed a prohibitive tax on grain futures transactions that were not consummated on an exchange designated as a "contract market" by the Secretary of Agriculture. The 1921 statute was held unconstitutional as an improper exercise of the taxing power in *Hill* v. *Wallace*, 259 U.S. 44 (1922), but its regulatory provisions were promptly reenacted in the Grain Futures Act, 42 Stat. 998, and upheld under the commerce power in *Chicago Board of Trade* v. *Olsen*, 262 U.S. 1 (1923). Under the original legislation, the principal function of the Secretary was to require the governors of a privately organized exchange to supervise the operation of the market. Two of the conditions for designation were that the governing board of the contract market prevent its members from disseminating misleading market information and prevent the "manipulation of prices or the cornering of any grain by the dealers or operators upon such board." The requirement that designated contract markets police themselves and the prohibitions against disseminating misleading information and manipulating prices have been part of our law ever since. * * *

In 1936 Congress changed the name of the statute to the Commodity Exchange Act, enlarged its coverage to include other agricultural commodities, and added detailed provisions regulating trading in futures contracts. Commodity Exchange Act, ch. 545, 49 Stat. 1491. Among the significant new provisions was § 4b, prohibiting any member of a contract market from defrauding any person in connection with the making of a futures contract, and § 4a, authorizing a commission composed of the Secretary of Agriculture, the Secretary of Commerce, and the Attorney General to fix limits on the amount of permissible speculative trading in a futures contract. The legislation also required registration of futures commission merchants and floor brokers.

In 1968, the CEA again was amended to enlarge its coverage and to give the Secretary additional enforcement authority. Act of Feb. 19, 1968, 82 Stat. 26. The Secretary was authorized to disapprove exchange rules that were inconsistent with the statute, and the contract markets were required to enforce their rules; the Secretary was authorized to suspend a contract market or to issue a cease-and-desist order upon a showing that the contract market's rules were not being enforced. In addition, the criminal sanctions for price manipulation were increased significantly, and any person engaged in price manipulation was subjected to the Secretary's authority to issue cease-and-desist orders for violations of the CEA and implementing regulations.

In 1974, after extensive hearings and deliberation, Congress enacted the Commodity Futures Trading Commission Act of 1974. 88 Stat. 1389. Like the 1936 and the 1968 legislation, the 1974 enactment was an amendment to the existing statute that broadened its coverage and increased the penalties for violation of its provisions. The Commission was authorized to seek injunctive relief, to alter or supplement a contract market's rules, and to direct a contract market to take whatever action deemed necessary by the Commission in an emergency. The 1974 legislation retained the basic statutory prohibitions against fraudulent practices and price manipulation, as well as the authority to prescribe trading limits. The 1974 amendments, however, did make substantial changes in the statutory scheme; Congress authorized a newly created Commodities Futures Trading Commission to assume the powers previously exercised by the Secretary of Agriculture, as well as certain additional powers. The enactment also added two new remedial provisions for the protection of individual traders. The newly enacted § 5a(11) required every contract market to provide an arbitration procedure for the settlement of traders' claims of no more than $15,000. And the newly enacted § 14 authorized the Commission to grant reparations to any person complaining of any violation of the CEA, or its implementing regulations, committed by any futures commission merchant or any associate thereof, floor broker, commodity trading adviser, or commodity pool operator. This section authorized the Commission to investigate complaints and, "if in its opinion the facts warrant such action," to afford a hearing before an administrative law judge. Reparations orders entered by the Commission are subject to judicial review.

NOTES

1. Derivative contracts were virtually unregulated until the 1920s when legislation was enacted to govern the trading of futures contracts on organized exchanges. Concerns had been expressed for decades over abuses in commodity futures and options trading, particularly large-scale manipulations of agricultural commodity prices. Gold was also a target of speculators during and after the Civil War. In 1864, Congress prohibited short sales of gold. Gold prices immediately rose 30 percent after the enactment of this legislation, and it was repealed only two weeks after its passage.

In 1869, Jay Gould and Jim Fisk engaged in a spectacular effort to corner the gold market, but failed. Fisk and Gould knew that the public supply of gold was limited, and they tried to keep the Treasury Department from selling gold into the market by suborning officials in the administration of President Grant and by arguing that high gold prices meant that farmers' crops were worth more. This corner was broken after President Grant discovered its existence and ordered his Treasury Secretary to sell gold into the market in large quantities. One author described the result as follows:

> Operators old at the game lost their heads and dashed hatless and crazed through the streets, eyes bloodshot and brains afire; the crowd in New Street became a mob. The price of gold plunged downward thirty points. The Gold Exchange Bank could not clear transactions, amounting to over $400 million, and clearances were suspended for a month, and gold dealings for a week.

Edward J. Dies, The Plunger, A Tale of the Wheat Pit 63 (1929).

2. Despite numerous price manipulations in grain on the Chicago Board of Trade, Congress was reluctant to act until after concerns over abuses in the trading of those instruments arose in the wake of World War I. The Federal Trade Commission then conducted a massive study of the grain trade. Congress did not await the end of that study before passing the Future Trading Act of 1921 [42 Stat. 187]. That statute required futures trading in grain products only on boards of trade designated as "contract markets" by the Secretary of Agriculture. However, in Hill v. Wallace, 259 U.S. 44 (1922), the Supreme Court held that the Future Trading Act was an unconstitutional exercise of the taxing power of Congress.

3. One day after the Supreme Court's decision Hill v. Wallace, a blatant manipulation of the wheat futures market occurred. Congress responded to that market disruption by repackaging the Future Trading Act into the Grain Futures Act of 1922 [42 Stat. 999]. In order to pass constitutional muster, the Grain Futures Act was based on the commerce power of Congress under the Constitution. The Supreme Court upheld the Grain Futures Act under that power in Chicago Board of Trade v. Olsen, 262 U.S. 1 (1923).[2]

4. The Grain Futures Act of 1922 proved to be unsuccessful in stopping grain price manipulations. As a result of those problems, derivatives regulation became a part of Franklin D. Roosevelt's "New Deal." In 1936, the Grain Futures Act was replaced by the Commodity Exchange Act (CEA) [7 U.S.C. § 1 *et seq.*]. The CEA extended regulatory jurisdiction over some previously unregulated futures trading on other commodities, *i.e.*, cotton, rice, mill feeds, butter, eggs, and potatoes. Wool tops, fats and oils, cottonseed meal, cottonseed, peanuts, soybeans, and soybean meal were added to that list in 1938. Note that these were all agricultural-based commodities. Futures

---

[2] Ironically, the Supreme Court took the opposite approach in upholding the Patient Protection and Affordable Care Act ("Obamacare"), finding that the individual mandate in that act was supported by Congress' taxing power but not by the Commerce clause. National Federation of Independent Business v. Sebelius, 567 U.S. ___ (2012).

trading on non-agricultural products did not become subject to regulation until the CEA was amended in 1974. Prior to 1974, non-agricultural futures contracts were deemed to be "unregulated" futures contracts and were required to be held in a different account at the customer's FCM. Options trading on "regulated" commodities was prohibited.

5. The CEA was initially administered under the oversight of the Commodity Exchange Commission, which was comprised of the Secretaries of Agriculture and Commerce and the Attorney General. The Secretary of Agriculture was given day-to-day regulatory authority over the commodity futures markets, and he created a small bureau, the Commodity Exchange Authority, to carry out those functions under the CEA.

6. Inflation of commodity prices in the 1970s and concerns over market abuses gave rise to new legislation in 1974. That statute created the U.S. Commodity Futures Trading Commission (CFTC) and expanded its jurisdiction to cover all commodity futures and options trading, including such trading on financial instruments [Commodity Futures Trading Commission Act of 1974, 88 Stat. 1389].

7. Congress subsequently amended the CEA several times to further expand the CFTC's powers. Among other things, the CEA was amended in 1982 to allow the CFTC to regulate the offer and sale of foreign futures contracts in the United States, but it was prohibited from setting the terms of such contracts. Most recently, as described below, Congress, through the Dodd-Frank Wall Street Reform and Consumer Protection Act of 2010 (Dodd-Frank Act), expanded the CFTC's jurisdiction into the OTC swap market.

* * *

CHAPTER 2

CFTC AND SEC JURISDICTION

■ ■ ■

1. THE CFTC

The Commodity Futures Trading Commission (CFTC) is composed of five commissioners appointed by the President, with the advice and consent of the Senate. These commissioners serve staggered five-year terms. No more than three of the commissioners may be from the same political party. One of their number is designated by the President to be the agency's chairman. CFTC Organization, available at http://www.cftc. gov/About/CFTCOrganization/index.htm (visited Feb. 24, 2013).

The CFTC commissioners meet periodically as a body to decide matters that are the subject of Commission orders or other agency action. Many CFTC meetings are public, but enforcement matters are held in closed-door sessions that are not subject to public attendance.

The CFTC's staff carries out many of the day-to-day activities of the agency. The staff is organized into various divisions and offices. The Division of Clearing and Risk (DCR) oversees derivatives clearing organizations (DCOs). The Division of Market Oversight (DMO) oversees the commodity exchanges, i.e., "designated contract markets" (DCMs), and seeks to assure that those exchanges are meeting their core regulatory principles. This division also conducts market surveillance for disruptive trading activity, and it reviews new exchange applications and new products.

The CFTC's Swap Dealers and Intermediary Oversight Division (DSIO) oversees registration and compliance by intermediaries and self-regulatory organizations. It is also responsible for monitoring compliance with regulations addressing business conduct standards, capital adequacy and margin requirements for swap dealers

The CFTC's Division of Enforcement investigates and prosecutes violations of the Commodity Exchange Act of 1936 (CEA) or CFTC rules. It may be authorized by the CFTC to issue subpoenas and compel the production of documents and deposition testimony.

The CFTC also has several "offices," in addition to its divisions. They include the Office of the Chief Economist, which provides economic support and economic advice to the CFTC. The Office of Data and Technology provides technology and data management support for the

CFTC. The Office of the Executive Director is responsible for the allocation of the CFTC's resources and is the overall staff manager for the agency.

The Office of General Counsel (OGC) acts as the CFTC's own lawyer. It represents the agency in appellate, bankruptcy and other litigation, including actions brought against the CFTC. The CFTC's Office of the Inspector General (OIG) acts as the agency's own internal watchdog.

The Office of International Affairs is responsible for providing guidance to the CFTC with respect to international issues. The globalization of the commodity markets has increased the importance of this office. The Office of Legislative Affairs and the Office of Public Affairs also provide support services to the CFTC.

CFTC Organization, available at http://www.cftc.gov/About/CFTC Organization/index.htm (visited Feb. 24, 2013).

2. THE SEC

The Securities and Exchange Commission (SEC) is, like the CFTC, composed of five commissioners appointed by the President with the advice and consent of the Senate. They serve five-year staggered terms, and no more than three commissioners can be members of the same political party.

The federal securities laws that are administered by the SEC seek to prohibit fraud manipulation and other abuses associated with securities transactions. The most prominent of these prohibitions is found in Section 10(b) of the Securities Exchange Act of 1934 (34 Act) [15 U.S.C. § 78j(b)] and Rule 10b–5 promulgated thereunder by the SEC [17 C.F.R. § 240.10b–5]. There are, however, additional anti-fraud provisions in the other so-called federal securities laws, including the Securities Act 1933 (33 Ac) [15 U.S.C. § 77q] and the Investment Advisers Act of 1940 (IAA) [15 U.S.C. § 80b–6].

The SEC staff is structured in a manner similar to that of the CFTC. Most of the work of the SEC is carried out by its staff in Washington, DC, but, like the CFTC, it also has regional offices.

The SEC staff is structured into divisions, which include Enforcement, Trading and Markets, Economic and Risk Analysis, Investment Management and Corporate Finance. Like the CFTC, the SEC also has several offices that carry out a number of duties, such as the Office of General Counsel.

The SEC and its staff are responsible for regulating trading in securities, including stock and bonds and some derivatives such as stock options, single stock futures and security-based swaps. Firms that buy and sell securities to retail customers are required to register with the

SEC as broker-dealers (BDs), which are the counterparts to the futures commission merchant (FCM) in the futures industry.

3. THE ROLE OF SELF-REGULATION AND FINRA

A concept unique to the derivatives and securities markets is the statutorily imposed requirement of self-regulation. This means that industry participants must belong to a government registered and regulated self-regulatory organization (SRO) that will police its members. The role of the SEC and CFTC in this self-regulatory structure is to oversee the respective SROs that fall under their jurisdiction, as well as to act directly where SRO oversight fails.

The SRO concept is based on a belief that, if the industry acts to prevent violations, it will be unnecessary for the government to interfere with the market and will lessen the cost of regulation to taxpayers. Supreme Court Justice William O. Douglas, a former SEC chairman, has described this process as:

> One of letting the exchanges take the leadership with Government playing a residual role. Government would keep the shotgun, so to speak, behind the door, loaded, well oiled, cleaned, ready for use but with the hope it would never have to be used.

William O. Douglas, Democracy and Finance 82 (James Allen ed., 1940).

The U.S. financial regulatory system is comprised of two basic principles. One principle posits that there should be a governmental regulatory agency in place to regulate specific financial firms and products. Under this principle, regulation seeks to protect market participants who may deal with the regulated financial firms and who may trade regulated financial products. These federal regulations consist of a market protection model and a customer protection model.

The second basic principle of financial services regulation requires the financial industry, both the exchanges that offer the financial products and the financial firms that offer these financial products to market participants, to regulate themselves through the concept of self-regulation.

Each futures, swap and securities exchange, being a membership organization with members and member firms, must establish a comprehensive set of regulations that apply to its members and procedures to enforce their regulations. Each such exchange is deemed to be a SRO. As such, each exchange is required to regulate all firms and market participants that do business on the exchange and the products traded on that exchange.

Just like the exchanges, which are permitted to do business pursuant to specific legislation, other industry SROs have also been created by

Congress. There are two principal industry wide SROs. One is Financial Industry Regulatory Authority (FINRA) for the securities industry and the National Futures Association (NFA) for CEA regulated entities.

In 1938, the Maloney Act amended the Securities Exchange Act of 1934 by granting the SEC supervisory authority over the National Association of Securities Dealers, Inc. (NASD). The NASD was a securities industry organization that sought to self-police trading in the over-the-counter securities market, i.e., non-exchange trading.

After the enactment of the Maloney Act, the NASD became the SRO for all registered broker-dealers (BDs), regardless of whether the BD was a member of an exchange or not, and their employees, e.g., securities "registered representatives" (RRs or stock brokers). Thus, BDs that were also exchange member firms were subject to the rules of two SROs, whereas the smaller BDs were only subject to the NASD rules. The creation of FINRA removed that anomaly.

FINRA was created in 2007 as a result of the merger of two industry SROs, the NASD and the regulatory unit of the New York Stock Exchange (NYSE). NYSE's regulatory unit dealt with BDs that were NYSE member firms, and their RRs, who dealt with customers whereas the NASD regulated all registered BDs regardless of whether they were exchange member firms or not.

Following the merger, FINRA commenced a rule harmonization process that adopted many of the existing regulations of both the NASD and the NYSE. FINRA also modified many such regulations to the extent of any inconsistencies.

FINRA only regulates broker-dealers. It does not regulate other SEC registrants such as investment advisers, investment companies or securities-based swap dealers.

4. ROLE OF THE NFA

The NFA was authorized to become an industry wide SRO by the legislation that created the CFTC in 1974. However, membership was not mandatory, rendering such an organization ineffective. That flaw was corrected by legislation enacted in 1978. In 1982, Congress also authorized the NFA to carry out the CFTC's registration functions for industry professionals through Title III of the CEA.

The NFA acts as the SRO for all firms and persons required to be registered with the CFTC and their employees. Historically, these firms included futures commission merchants (FCMs), introducing brokers (IBs), commodity trading advisors (CTAs) and commodity pool operators (CPOs).

As a result of the Dodd-Frank Act, the NFA now has regulatory responsibility over swap dealers (SDs) and major swap participants (MSPs).

The NFA does not regulate "floor brokers" or "floor traders," who are required to be registered with the CFTC [17 C.F.R. § 3.11]. This is because the NFA does not have jurisdiction over exchange-related activities.

All firm registrants must become a NFA member firm under their respective category by filing applications online with the NFA. See Chapter 4 for more information on this registration process. In addition to handling all registration applications, the NFA is responsible for auditing all of its member firms. The NFA's Compliance Department handles all such audits.

The NFA acts as the principal SRO for most registrants in the futures industry. However, all U.S. futures exchanges, such as the CME Group, also act as a SRO for its members and member firms.

Both FINRA and the NFA have responsibility to audit firms that are subject to their jurisdiction. Because of its broader responsibility over all CFTC registrants, the NFA tends to apply a consistent regulatory approach to all such registrants, as all CFTC firm registrants must become members of the NFA. This mandatory NFA membership requirement thus provides an important uniform regulatory model. The NFA also reflects this diversified model by requiring that each of the major registration categories have representation on its Board of Directors.

SROs may form committees to coordinate their audit responsibilities. One example is the Joint Audit Committee (JAC), which consists of all of the SROs in the futures industry. The JAC allocates primary audit responsibilities over FCMs to different SROs.

The NFA is headquartered in Chicago, IL. It has one other office in New York City. FINRA is headquartered in Washington, DC. It has field offices in several U.S. cities, with very large staffs in its offices in New York City, Boston and Chicago.

FINRA and the NFA are financed by the industry or from fees charged to the underlying customers. No U.S. tax dollars are used to support these two SROs.

5. SEC AND CFTC DIVIDE THEIR JURISDICTION

The CFTC and the SEC often clash over the application of their respective jurisdiction over derivatives. In 1978, during the CFTC's first congressional reauthorization hearings, the SEC sought jurisdiction over futures contracts where the underlying commodity was a security. The

Government Accountability Office (GAO) supported the SEC's request. The Treasury Department also sought amendments that would have granted it a regulatory role over futures contracts where the underlying commodity was a government security. Congress rejected both of those requests but did require the CFTC to "maintain communications" with the SEC, the Treasury Department, and the Federal Reserve Board. Jerry W. Markham, Merging the SEC and CFTC—A Clash of Cultures, 78 U. Cinn. L. Rev. 537, 569–570 (2009). This by no means resolved the SEC's concerns over CFTC jurisdiction over derivatives related to underlying financial instruments.

NOTE

Remember, as noted in Chapter 1, the States are preempted by the CEA from affirmatively regulating futures trading. In contrast, each state has its own set of securities laws, known as the Blue Sky Laws, which have been preempted only in part by the federal securities laws.

JERRY W. MARKHAM
SUPER-REGULATOR: A COMPARATIVE ANALYSIS OF SECURITIES AND DERIVATIVES REGULATION IN THE UNITED STATES, GREAT BRITAIN & JAPAN
28 Brooklyn J. Intl. Law 319 (2003)

Though the securities and commodity futures regulatory schemes differed, no one really noticed before the 1970s. The product mix of the two industries was such that, aside from some mobile speculators, there was little overlap between commodity and futures trading. The situation began to change dramatically as inflation heated the economy during the Vietnam War. The resulting price hikes turned investors' attention toward inflation hedges such as gold and silver. The removal of restrictions on trading allowed these metals to be the subject of commodity futures trading. Similarly, President Nixon's removal of the U.S. from the gold standard and out of the International Monetary Fund's fixed rate currency regime led to fluctuating exchange rates that provided a basis for currency trading.

Price volatility also led the commodity exchanges to consider commodity futures trading on interest rates and stock prices. A committee of the Chicago Board of Trade began to explore whether commodity futures trading principles could be applied to stocks. The result was the CBOE. Prior to the creation of the CBOE, stock options were sold only on a limited basis in the over-the-counter market. The CBOE introduced a commodity futures concept of trading standardized options contracts on an exchange floor. This standardization, along with the introduction of a clearinghouse, the Options Clearing Corporation ('OCC'), created a secondary market in options. The CBOE trading floor borrowed from both the securities and commodity exchanges. Instead of a specialist, competing market makers were used to create liquidity in an open outcry system like that on the commodity exchanges.

The SEC asserted regulatory control over the CBOE under the provisions of the Securities Exchange Act of 1934, and also became involved in the regulation of over-the-counter commodity options. * * *

The decision of the CFTC to approve commodity futures trading on Government National Mortgage Association ("GNMA") certificates set off an explosion at the SEC. The SEC contended that such contracts were the equivalent of "when issued" GNMAs that were already regulated by the SEC. This resulted in an exchange of acrimonious correspondence between the two agencies. At the end of the day, the SEC lost the battle and GNMA futures continued to trade. Undaunted, the CFTC also approved a futures contract on treasury bills on the Chicago Mercantile Exchange in 1976.The SEC, however, had a long memory and, as will be seen, would retaliate against the CFTC. * * *

Another threat to the SEC was the decision by the CFTC to approve futures trading on stock indexes. These contracts were almost immediately popular and spread to other commodity exchanges. The SEC retaliated by approving the trading of options on GNMA certificates on the CBOE. The commodity exchanges challenged this action in court and won before the Seventh Circuit. By this point, the SEC realized that it was fighting a losing battle in trying to encroach on the CFTC's jurisdiction; it had learned that it could not win a confrontation in Congress over this matter. The futures industry lobby was simply too strong, and the agricultural committees were captive of those interests. The natural result was to establish an administrative demarche: an agreement was hammered out between the Chairmen of the SEC and CFTC (the "Shad-Johnson Accords"), which allocated jurisdiction between their two agencies. Thereafter, Congress enacted the Shad-Johnson Accords into law. Pub. L. No. 97–303, 96 Stat. 1409 (1982). In brief, the CFTC was given exclusive jurisdiction over all commodity futures trading on any instrument, except that single stock futures were prohibited, joining onions as the only commodity on which futures trading was banned. The SEC was given what amounted to a veto over commodity futures contracts on indexes, and retained jurisdiction over options trading on the stock exchanges, including options on indexes. The SEC and CFTC shared jurisdiction over options trading on foreign currency.

6. THE STOCK MARKET CRASH OF 1987

JERRY W. MARKHAM & RITA M. STEPHANZ
THE STOCK MARKET CRASH OF 1987—THE UNITED STATES
LOOKS AT NEW RECOMMENDATIONS
76 Geo. L. J. 1993 (1988)

Between October 13 and October 19, 1987, the stock market suffered its worst decline since the Great Depression. New York Stock Exchange (NYSE) stocks lost $1 trillion in value and the Dow Jones Industrial Average plunged 508 points in a day that came to be known as Black Monday. In the wake of the crash, trading volume sank as fears of a crash-induced recession spread across the nation. The Chicago Board Options Exchange (CBOE) fired more than 108 employees and plans for a $600 million building to house New York's commodity futures exchanges were dropped. Thousands of brokerage-firm employees were laid off and a few small firms suffered serious problems; some even failed.

Various segments of the financial industry blamed each other for the 1987 market break. The New York Stock Exchange, for example, blamed the futures exchanges for helping precipitate the crash. Its report charged that activities associated with commodity exchanges, such as "program trading" and "portfolio insurance," accelerated the decline. The NYSE reported that on Black Monday three portfolio insurers, pursuant to such trading programs, bought and sold $2 billion of stocks and $2.8 billion in futures. On the other hand, the commodity exchanges claimed that their products prevented even greater losses. The media, for its part, alleged that New York Stock Exchange specialists had abandoned their duty to maintain orderly markets and that a stock-index futures contract had been manipulated. Federal agencies prepared their own reports, which, not surprisingly, defended their respective turfs. Congress, meanwhile, held hearings.

To obtain a less partisan analysis, President Reagan created the Presidential Task Force on Market Mechanisms to investigate the collapse and propose regulatory reforms. The resulting report (the Brady Report) concluded, among other things, that the stock and commodity markets are inextricably linked and require coordinated regulation. * * *

"Portfolio insurance" is a sophisticated type of hedging used primarily by institutional traders; it was the focus of many explanations of the October 1987 crash. For instance, a portfolio manager expecting the stock market to drop would sell an S & P 500 futures contract, which obligates him to deliver in the future a basket of stock at today's prices. If the market declines, he profits because he then can buy the basket for less than the price at which he has agreed to sell it. If the stock market rises, he profits on his stock portfolio although he loses money on the stock-index futures contract. When the market declines, the profit on the index offsets, in whole or in part, the loss on the stocks. The degree of offset increases as the manager's portfolio more closely resembles the S & P index. By giving up a portion of his potential profit in such a manner, a manager is able to *insure* his portfolio against sudden drops in the market, yet avoids the transaction costs and the depressing effect that the outright selling of stocks has on the stock price.

"Program trading," often cited as a cause of the 1987 crash, refers to trading systems, including portfolio insurance, that are directed by computer programs. Changes in market prices prompt these programs to issue orders to buy or sell futures contracts and baskets of stock. For example, in response to a two-point drop in a stock index, programs may order the sale of futures based on a prediction that the market will continue to drop. These programs, although proprietary, confidential, and tailored to specific portfolio strategies, share many characteristics, including a tendency to issue sell orders in response to large drops in prices. Many experts believed that this common characteristic accentuated the October crash. A large market drop prompted virtually all programs to issue sell orders, causing additional massive selling. This additional selling prompted the programs to issue even more sell orders, contributing to an accelerating downward spiral.

The "triple witching hour" refers to the once shared expiration date of certain equity options, stock-index and other commodity futures, and stock index options. Before federal regulators stepped in, the triple witching hour was infamous for the volatile price fluctuations in the stock market and the unusually heavy trading it produced—a reflection of the close link between the market securities and the futures market. The CFTC and the SEC jointly solved this problem by improving order handling and by separating expiration times to avoid the compounding effect of simultaneous expirations.

In "index arbitrage," traders seek to make a profit off minor differences in the prices of certain stock-index futures and the underlying stocks. If the underlying stocks sell for more than the stock-index futures, the arbitrageur buys futures and sells the underlying stocks. Arbitrageurs, during the triple witching hour, used to take advantage of the chaotic trading conditions and the disparate prices created by common expiration times. This increased buying and selling by arbitrageurs escalated market confusion.

Portfolio insurance and index arbitrage, in combination, have the potential to create a self-perpetuating downward spiral known as the "cascade scenario." Portfolio managers forecasting a drop in stock prices sell index futures to offset expected losses. The price of the futures then declines and sells at a discount to the underlying stocks. In an effort to profit from the difference, arbitrageurs buy futures and sell stocks. This may depress stock prices and prompt portfolio managers to begin the cycle anew. * * *

Within days of the crash, President Reagan created the Brady Task Force and gave it sixty days to "determine what happened and why" and to provide guidance on how to avert a recurrence. The following is a summary of the resulting report.

In 1982, all major stock markets began a long period of growth spurred by rising corporate earnings, reduced inflation, and falling interest rates. The Dow Jones Industrial Average rose from 777 in August 1982 to 1,896 in December 1986. In 1987, stock prices continued to climb despite rapidly rising interest rates. In August of that year, the Dow hit 2,722 due, in part, to increased foreign investment in United States equities. The growing popularity of portfolio insurance strategies also contributed to the market's rise. On October 14, 1987, however, the "U.S. equity market began the most severe one-week decline in its history." From the morning of Wednesday, October 14, to the following Tuesday, the Dow plummeted from over 2,500 to barely 1,700, a drop of nearly one third.

Two events contributed to the October 14 "revaluation of stock prices": (1) the announcement that the August merchandise trade deficit was $15.7 billion, $1.5 billion more than anticipated by financial markets; and (2) the House Ways and Means Committee's proposal to eliminate tax benefits associated with the financing of corporate takeovers. In response, arbitrageurs and other investors sold their positions in takeover candidates and the prices of those stocks collapsed. On October 14 alone, the Dow dropped 95 points on a trading volume of 207 million shares. Index-arbitrage sales accounted for seventeen percent of the volume. The twenty largest New York Stock Exchange members sold $689 million of stock while futures investors sold $500 million of futures.

The next day, October 15, traders in the United States awoke to news of continued selling in Tokyo and London. The Dow opened twenty points down from its close on the previous day; during the first half hour of trading, some 2,500 futures contracts and 48 million shares were traded. Although the Dow recovered slightly during the course of the day, it fell fifty-three points in the final half hour of trading, closing fifty-seven points down for the day. Index arbitrageurs sold almost $175 million on the NYSE that day, and sales of "stock baskets" totaled another $100 million. These two strategies accounted for a quarter of the volume during the last half hour of trading.

On Friday, October 16, the Dow dropped another 108 points, its largest single-day drop to that point. In the securities markets, four trading institutions sold over $600 million of stock, indicating heavy, concentrated institutional trading. In the futures markets, portfolio insurers and index arbitrageurs sold the equivalent of $2.1 billion of stock. Index arbitrageurs also accounted for $1.7 billion of sell orders. The following Monday—Black Monday—was "perhaps the worst day in the history of U.S. equity markets."

On Black Monday the Dow plummeted *508* points on a trading volume of 604 million shares. This 23-percent drop is almost twice the percentage drop of 1929's "Black Thursday." S & P 500 futures fell 29 percent on a total volume of 162,000 contracts. This sudden decline had been foreshadowed by precipitous drops in stock markets abroad, which open earlier than U.S. markets. In Tokyo, the Nikkei Index, the Dow equivalent, fell 2.5 percent; by midday, the London market had dropped ten percent. The U.S. markets, including the Major Market Index (MMI) futures and the S & P 500 futures, opened down. Large order imbalances forced many specialists to halt trading in their stocks during the first hour. Nevertheless, two billion shares had traded hands thirty minutes after the opening bell. One mutual fund group accounted for a quarter of that volume.

Index arbitrageurs and portfolio insurers also engaged in heavy trading during the first hour of Black Monday. The discounted openings of stock-index futures resulted in an apparent record discount for futures in relation to stocks. New York Stock Exchange specialists, however, opened trading in their stocks at sharply lower levels. Index arbitrageurs, who had sold stock in anticipation of large futures discounts, rushed to cover their positions by purchasing futures. By 11:00 A.M., rising index-futures prices made stocks more attractive and the stock market rallied.

Between 11:40 A.M. and 2:00 P.M., portfolio insurance sales and rumors that the NYSE might close squelched the rally; the Dow and the futures index fell nine percent and fourteen percent, respectively. During this period, portfolio insurers had sold approximately 10,000 futures contracts, the equivalent of $1.3 billion or forty-one percent of total futures volume, and unloaded $900 million worth of stock on the NYSE. Portfolio insurers in the stock and futures markets provided over $3.7 billion of selling pressure by early afternoon. Selling pressure paused, however, because delays in transmitting orders slowed index-arbitrage activities and because one institution that had already sold $1.3 billion of stock discontinued a sell program. As a result, the Dow rallied to the 2,000 level by 2:45 P.M.

The remainder of the afternoon "was disastrous." In the last hour and a half of trading, one portfolio insurer sold over 6,000 futures contracts, the equivalent of $660 million of stock. Some index arbitragers refused to sell stock through DOT and withdrew from the futures market, causing the futures market to fall to a discount of twenty index points. The DOW closed at 1738, with a near 300-point loss in the last seventy-five minutes of trading.

A small number of institutions, portfolio insurers, and mutual funds were central to Monday's crash. In the stock market, the four largest sellers accounted for $2.85 billion or fourteen percent of the total sales. A few mutual fund groups sold $900 million; one such group accounted for 90 percent of these sales. Three portfolio insurers sold approximately $2 billion or about ten percent of total NYSE sales. Futures-market portfolio insurers, in all, sold the equivalent of $4 billion of stocks. Yet, portfolio insurance sales, although large, comprised a small portion of the total sales dictated by computer model formulas.

After the U.S. markets closed on October 19, the Tokyo and London stock markets fell almost fifteen percent. Nevertheless, U.S. stock and futures markets opened with dramatic increases the next day, partly due to the Federal Reserve's statement that it would provide badly needed liquidity for the financial system. By midmorning, the rally ended and a number of exchanges temporarily halted trading. The Chicago Board Options Exchange suspended trading because New York Stock Exchange trading was not open in at least eighty percent of the stocks constituting the option index. Shortly after noon, the Chicago Mercantile Exchange, reacting to closings on the New York Stock Exchange, suspended trading of the S & P 500. The closing of the markets created a virtual free fall. Typically, the futures market discount would have attracted buyers, but many were afraid of the perceived credit risk. And the buying of stocks was stifled because the huge discount made stocks seem so expensive. Thus, both markets were imbalanced by sell orders. In the afternoon, however, the stock market received reassurance when several major corporations announced stock purchase programs. But the financial markets had "approached breakdown" on Tuesday because of a complete disconnection between the futures and stock markets.

The failure of the stock and futures markets to act as one coordinated financial market led the Brady Commission to recommend strengthening market infrastructures by authorizing one agency to impose intermarket regulations in a few key areas. These regulations would include margin requirements, circuit breaker mechanisms (such as price limits and trading halts), clearing and credit mechanisms, and information systems that monitor intermarket activities.

The Brady Report also explored which government agencies could best perform this task. It concluded that the Department of Treasury is too political and the SEC, although an attractive choice, is too focused on regulating the stock market. It did not even consider the CFTC for this task, presumably because of the agency's even more narrow focus on futures trading. The Brady Commission believed that a merger of the

SEC and the CFTC, although combining the expertise of the two market regulators, would not produce an effective intermarket regulator. The Brady Report recommended that the Federal Reserve assume the role.

NOTES

1. The recommendations in the Brady Report were largely ignored. The only substantive regulation that resulted from the 1987 crash was the introduction of "circuit breakers" that stopped trading when the market dropped a specified amount during the trading day. Trading was halted on exchanges in various products 265 times during a one-year period after such restrictions were imposed. Nathaniel Popper, BATS Flaw, Not So Rare, Data Shows, N. Y. Times, March 29, 2012, at B1.

2. The SEC did adopt new trading restrictions in June 2012 that require "limit-up" and "limit-down" trading halts for individual stocks. Market-wide circuit breakers were also broadened. SEC Approves Proposals to Address Extraordinary Volatility in Individual Stocks and Broader Stock Market, http://www.sec.gov/news/press/2012/2012–107.htm (accessed June 21, 2012). Such trading limits had long been in use on the futures exchanges.

3. As will be seen in the following cases, the rivalry between the SEC and the futures industry continued after the Stock Market Crash of 1987.

7.   MORE JURISDICTIONAL BATTLES

CHICAGO MERCANTILE EXCHANGE V. SECURITIES & EXCHANGE COMMISSION

883 F.2d 537 (7th Cir. 1989), cert. denied sub nom.,
Investment Co. Institute v. SEC, 496 U.S. 936 (1990)

EASTERBROOK, CIRCUIT JUDGE

The Commodity Futures Trading Commission has authority to regulate trading of futures contracts (including futures on securities) and options on futures contracts. The Securities and Exchange Commission has authority to regulate trading of securities and options on securities. If an instrument is both a security and a futures contract, the CFTC is the sole regulator because "the Commission shall have exclusive jurisdiction with respect to . . . transactions involving . . . contracts of sale (and options on such contracts) for future delivery of a group or index of securities (or any interest therein or based upon the value thereof)", 7 U.S.C. § 2a(ii). See also 7 U.S.C. § 2 ("the Commission shall have exclusive jurisdiction, except to the extent otherwise provided in section 2a of this title"); *Chicago Board of Trade v. SEC*, 677 F.2d 1137 (7th Cir.), vacated as moot, 459 U.S. 1026, 74 L. Ed. 2d 594, 103 S. Ct. 434 (1982) (*GNMA Options*). If, however, the instrument is both a futures contract and an option on a security, then the SEC is the sole regulator because "the [CFTC] shall have no jurisdiction to designate a board of trade as a contract market for any transaction whereby any party to such transaction acquires any put, call, or other option on one or more securities . . . including any group or index of such securities, or any interest therein or based on the value thereof." 7 U.S.C. § 2a(i).

The CFTC regulates futures and options on futures; the SEC regulates securities and options on securities; jurisdiction never overlaps. Problem: The statute does not define either "contracts . . . for future delivery" or "option"—although it says that " 'future delivery' . . . shall not include any sale of any cash commodity for deferred shipment or delivery". See Lester G. Telser, *Futures and Actual Markets: How They Are Related*, 59 J. Business S5 (1986). Each of these terms has a paradigm, but newfangled instruments may have aspects of each of the prototypes. Our case is about such an instrument, the index participation (IP). We must decide whether tetrahedrons belong in square or round holes.

Index participations are contracts of indefinite duration based on the value of a basket (index) of securities. The seller of an IP (called the "short" because the writer need not own the securities) promises to pay the buyer the value of the index as measured on a "cash-out day". Any index, such as the Standard & Poor's 500, can be used. The buyer pays for the IP in cash on the date of sale and may borrow part of the price (use margin) on the same terms the Federal Reserve sets for stock—currently 50%. The exchange designates a conversion ratio between the index and the IP, so that (say) each IP unit entitles the holder on cash-out day to the value of the index times 100. Until cash-out the IP may trade on the exchange just like any other instrument. At the end of each quarter the short must pay the buyer (the "long") a sum approximating the value of dividends the stocks in the index have paid during the quarter. From the perspective of the long, then, an IP has properties similar to those of a closed-end mutual fund holding a value-weighted portfolio of the securities in the index: the IPs last indefinitely, pay dividends, and may be traded freely; on cash-out day the IP briefly becomes open-end, and the investor can withdraw cash without making a trade in the market.

Things differ from the short's perspective. Unlike the proprietor of a mutual fund, the short need not own the securities in the index; it will own them (equivalently, a long futures contract based on the same index) only to reduce risk. The short receives the long's cash but must post margin equal to 150% of the value of the IP, similar to the margin required for a short sale of stock. The short sees the IP as a speculative or hedging instrument scarcely distinguishable from a futures contract that terminates on the cash-out day, plus an option held by the long to roll over the contract to the next cash-out date. Cash-out days for an IP generally are the third Friday of March, June, September, and December, the expiration dates of the principal stock-index futures contracts, making the link even more apparent.

Longs and shorts do not deal directly with each other. After the parties agree on the price, the Options Clearing Corporation (OCC) issues the IP to the long, receiving the cash; at the same time the OCC pays the short and "acquires" the short's obligation to pay at cash-out time. OCC guarantees the short's obligations to the long, to secure which it holds the short's 150% margin. As the quarter progresses the short must pony up cash to cover dividend-equivalent obligations. When a long exercises the cash-out privilege, the OCC chooses a short at random to make the payment. Any link between the original buyer and seller of an IP thus does not extend beyond the formation of the instrument; after that instant, each person's rights and obligations run to the OCC exclusively. This arrangement also permits either party to close its position by making an offsetting transaction. If the seller of an IP buys an identical contract in the market, the OCC cancels the two on its books.

The Philadelphia Stock Exchange asked the SEC in February 1988 for permission to trade IPs. The American Stock Exchange and the Chicago Board Options Exchange later filed proposals of their own. Each exchange's IP differs slightly from the others. Philadelphia's IP, called a "Cash Index Participation", allows the long to exercise the cash-out privilege on any business day, at a discount of 0.5% from the value of the index. (The long may cash out on a quarterly date without penalty.) The AMEX's IP, called the "Equity Index Participation", permits the long to cash out quarterly for money or shares of stock in a ratio matching the index. Holders of 500 or more EIP trading units based on the S & P 500 index (each the equivalent of 100 multiples of that index) may exercise the right to receive securities, and they must pay a "delivery charge" to be established by the AMEX. Writers of EIPs may volunteer to deliver stock; if not enough do, a "physical delivery facilitator" at the AMEX will buy stock in the market, using money provided by the shorts whose positions have been liquidated. The CBOE's product, the "Value of Index Participation", has a semi-annual rather than quarterly cash-out date. CBOE's wrinkle is that the short as well as the long may cash out, by tendering the value of the index on the cash-out date. If shorts seeking to close their positions exceed the number of longs who want cash, the OCC will choose additional long positions at random to pay off.

The three stock exchanges and the OCC asked the SEC to allow them to trade these varieties of IP. Each contended that the SEC has exclusive jurisdiction because IPs are securities and not futures contracts. The AMEX added that in its view an IP is an option on securities, activating the savings clause of § 2a(i). The Chicago Board of Trade and the Chicago Mercantile Exchange, supported by the CFTC, asked the SEC to deny the requests. Each futures market, and the CFTC, argued that IPs are futures and not securities, so that the CFTC's jurisdiction is exclusive under 7 U.S.C. §§ 2 and 2a(ii). Complicating the picture, the Investment Company Institute argued that if IPs are securities and not futures, the OCC is an "investment company," offering a product combining features of closed-end and open-end mutual funds, and must register under the Investment Company Act of 1940, 15 U.S.C. §§ 80a–1 to 80a–64.

On April 11, 1989, the SEC granted the exchanges' requests. Release No. 34–26709, 54 Fed.Reg. 15280 (1989). At the same time, its Division of Market Regulation, acting with delegated authority, allowed the OCC to change its rules so that it could issue, settle, and clear IPs. Release No. 34–26713, 54 Fed.Reg. 15575 (1989). The SEC concluded that IPs are "stock" within the meaning of § 3(a)(10) of the Securities Exchange Act of 1934, 15 U.S.C. § 78c (a)(10). IPs are negotiable, pay dividends, may appreciate in value, and may be hypothecated; the only attribute of stock missing from IPs is voting rights, which the SEC thought unimportant. 54 Fed. Reg. at 15285–86. If not stock, the SEC concluded, IPs are "certificates of interest or participation in" stock, another of the instruments defined as "securities" in § 3(a)(10). See 54 Fed. Reg. at 15286. Next the SEC found that IPs are not "futures", *id.* at 15286–89, because they lack two features the SEC thought essential: "futurity" and "bilateral obligation". "Futurity" means that value is set in the future, while as the SEC observed the buyer of an IP pays a price fixed at the time of sale; "bilateral obligation" means that the contract is executory on both sides until expiration or settlement, while the long on an IP performs at the time of purchase, leaving only the short with executory obligations. The SEC went on to say, *id.* at 15289–90, that the OCC need not register under the Investment Company Act because there is no "issuer" within the meaning of § 3(a)(1) of that statute, 15 U.S.C. § 80a–3(a)(1). Concluding that IPs may serve as substitutes for "program trading", provide "an additional layer of liquidity to the market", and afford "an alternative vehicle for retail customers to invest in 'the market'", 54 Fed.Reg. at 15290, the SEC allowed the exchanges to proceed with their plans. We denied the futures markets' request for a stay but accelerated the hearing of the case on the merits. IPs have been trading on the three exchanges since May. * * *

A futures contract, roughly speaking, is a fungible promise to buy or sell a particular commodity at a fixed date in the future. Futures contracts are fungible because they have standard terms and each side's obligations are guaranteed by a clearinghouse. Contracts are entered into without prepayment, although the markets and clearinghouse will set margin to protect their own interests. Trading occurs in "the contract", not in the commodity. Most futures contracts may be performed by delivery of the commodity (wheat, silver, oil, etc.). Some (those based on financial instruments such as T-bills or on the value of an index of stocks) do not allow delivery. Unless the parties cancel their obligations by buying or selling offsetting positions, the long must pay the price stated in the contract (e.g., $1.00 per gallon for 1,000 gallons of orange juice) and the short must deliver; usually, however, they settle in cash, with the payment based on changes in the market. If the market price, say, rose to $1.50 per gallon, the short would pay $500 (50 cents per gallon); if the price fell, the long would pay. The extent to which the settlement price of a commodity futures contract tracks changes in the price of the cash commodity depends on the size and balance of the open positions in "the contract" near the settlement date. When the contract involves financial instruments, though, the price is fixed by mechanical computation from the instruments on which the contracts are based. * * *

A security, roughly speaking, is an undivided interest in a common venture the value of which is subject to uncertainty. Usually this means a claim to the assets and profits of an "issuer". Shares of stock entitle their holders to receive dividends and payments on liquidation (or a change in corporate form), see *Landreth Timber Co. v. Landreth*, 471 U.S. 681, 85 L. Ed. 2d 692, 105 S. Ct. 2297 (1985); bonds and other debt instruments promise interest plus a balloon payment of principal at the end. Unusual interests such as rights in orange groves still may be "securities" if they represent a pro rata share of a variable pool of earnings. *SEC v. W.J. Howey Co.*, 328 U.S. 293, 90 L. Ed. 1244, 66 S. Ct. 1100 (1946). See generally Louis Loss & Joel Seligman, 2 *Securities Regulation* 926–89 (3d ed. 1988).

Securities usually arise out of capital formation and aggregation (entrusting funds to an entrepreneur), while futures are means of hedging, speculation, and price revelation without transfer of capital. So one could think of the distinction between the jurisdiction of the SEC and that of the CFTC as the difference between regulating capital formation and regulating hedging. Congress conceived the role of the CFTC in that way when it created the agency in 1974 to assume functions that had been performed by the Department of Agriculture but which were no longer thought appropriate for that Department as futures markets expanded beyond commodities into financial instruments. See *GNMA Options* for a recap of the history. Unfortunately, the distinction between capital formation and hedging falls apart when it comes time to allocate the regulation of options.

A call option is a promise by the writer to deliver the underlying instrument at a price fixed in advance (the "strike price") if the option is exercised within a set time. The buyer pays a price (the "premium") in advance for the opportunity; the writer may or may not own the instrument he promises to deliver. Call options are written "out of the money"—that is, the exercise price exceeds the market price at the outset. The writer will make money if by the time the option expires the market price is less than the strike price plus the premium (plus the interest earned on the premium in the interim); the buyer of the option hopes that the market price will rise above the strike price by enough to cover the premium, the time value of money, and the transactions costs of executing the option. Options play valuable roles in price-discovery, and they also allow the parties to adjust the net riskiness of their portfolios. Writers of call options reduce the risk they bear if the market falls while limiting gains if the market rises; buyers hope for large proportional gains if the market rises while accepting the likelihood that the options will turn out to be worthless. Options are side deals among investors, which do not augment an entrepreneur's coffers (except to the extent greater liquidity and opportunities to adjust risk increase social marginal propensity to invest). Dwight M. Jaffee, *The Impact of Financial Futures and Options on Capital Formation*, 4 J. Futures Markets 417 (1984). Unlike financial and index futures, options call for delivery of the underlying instrument—be it a share of stock or a futures contract.

The SEC consistently has taken the position that options on securities should be regulated as securities. For some years the CFTC maintained that options on securities should be regulated as futures because options are extrinsic to capital formation and because it is almost always possible to devise an option with the same economic attributes as a futures contract (and the reverse). Matters came to a head in 1980, when both agencies asserted jurisdiction over options on securities based on pools of notes. The Government National Mortgage Association (GNMA) sold pass-through certificates representing proceeds of mortgage notes, and persons started writing options on them to allow hedging against movements in interest rates. The SEC observed that options written on securities are securities under § 3(a)(10) of the '34 Act; indeed the SEC contended that because options are securities it should regulate all options. The CFTC countered that options on financial instruments are futures under § 4c(b) of the CEA, 7 U.S.C. § 6c(b), and added that because its jurisdiction is exclusive, it is the sole lawful regulator. When the SEC allowed stock exchanges to start trading GNMA options, the futures markets sought review in this court and the CFTC howled bloody murder.

While the case was pending, the agencies reached a pact, which the SEC calls the Shad-Johnson Agreement and the CFTC calls the Johnson-Shad Agreement. (John Shad was the SEC's Chairman at the time, and Phillip Johnson the CFTC's.) This Accord (as we shall call it to avoid offending either agency) provided that jurisdiction over options follows jurisdiction over the things on which the options are written. So the SEC received jurisdiction of options on securities, while the CFTC got jurisdiction of options on futures contracts. Things were not quite done, though, because we held in *GNMA Options* that the agencies could not alter their jurisdiction by mutual agreement. 677 F.2d at 1142 n. 8. Starting from the proposition that options on GNMAs are both securities and futures, we held that the CFTC's jurisdiction is exclusive in light of 7 U.S.C. §§ 2 and 2a.

Congress then enacted the Accord almost verbatim, producing the explicit reference to options in § 3(a)(10) of the '34 Act, the SEC savings clause in § 2a(i) of the CEA, and a small change in 7 U.S.C. § 6n to implement an understanding about pools. The legislature thought that this Accord would resolve things and restore a regime in which the SEC supervises capital formation and the CFTC hedging. See S. Rep. No. 97–384, 97th Cong., 2d Sess. 21–24 (1982); H.R. Rep. No. 97–565, 97th Cong., 2d Sess., Part I at 38–40 (1982); H.R. Rep. No. 97–626, 97th Cong., 2d Sess., Part II at 3 (1982); 128 Cong. Rec. 24910 (1982) (Rep. De La Garza); Loss & Seligman, 2 *Securities Regulation* at 1064–80; Jerry W. Markham & David J. Gilberg, *Stock and Commodity Options—Two Regulatory Approaches and Their Conflicts*, 47 Albany L. Rev. 741 (1983).

The legislation implementing the Accord left in place the premise on which *GNMA Options* was founded: if an instrument is *both* a security and a futures contract, then the CFTC's jurisdiction is exclusive. Section 2a(ii) has no other possible meaning. Like many an agreement resolving a spat, the Accord addressed a symptom rather than the problem. Options are only one among many instruments that can have attributes of futures contracts as well as securities. Financial markets work best when they offer every possible combination of risk and return—a condition financial economists call "spanning"—so that investors can construct a portfolio to each need and taste. Exchanges and professional investors therefore continually devise financial products to fill unoccupied niches. See Dennis W. Carlton, *Futures Markets: Their Purpose, Their History, Their Growth, Their Successes and Failures*, 4 J. Futures Markets 237 (1984); William L. Silber, Innovation, Competition and New Contract Design in Futures Markets, 1 J. Futures Markets 123 (1981). These products are valuable to the extent that they do *not* match the attributes of instruments already available. New products, offering a new risk-return mixture, are designed to depart from today's models.

Which means that the dispute of 1980–82 about options will be played out—is being played out—about each new instrument. Today's case repeats the conflict. Other novel instruments are being handled by regulation. For example, on July 17, 1989, the CFTC adopted rules exempting from its regulation certain hybrid instruments combining equity or debt with payments based on the price of commodities. 17 C.F.R. Part 34, 54 Fed.Reg. 30684 (1989). Only merger of the agencies or functional separation in the statute can avoid continual conflict. Functional separation is hard to achieve (new instruments will appear at any border). The SEC favors merger; it has asked Congress repeatedly for jurisdiction over all products (including stock-index and financial futures) based on securities, which would relegate the CFTC to its original role as superintendent of commodities futures. The CFTC has so far defended its position, in part with the argument that multiple regulatory bodies allow greater competition and experimentation—a new product can reach market if either agency approves the variant within its domain.

Unless Congress changes the allocation of jurisdiction between the agencies, the question a court must resolve is the same as in *GNMA Options*: is the instrument a futures contract? If yes, then the CFTC's jurisdiction is exclusive, unless it is also an option on a security, in which case the SEC's jurisdiction is exclusive. So long as an instrument is a futures contract (and not an option), whether it is also a "security" is neither here nor there. Still, if IPs really are "stock" they almost certainly are not "futures contracts", so the inquiries aren't so distinct as the statutes imply.

From the perspective of the long, IPs look like an interest in a portfolio of stock. IPs last indefinitely (except for the chance that a long may be cashed out involuntarily on the CBOE), may be sold like stock or used to secure margin and other loans, change in value with the market, and pay dividends. IPs lack other common attributes of stock: they do not confer voting rights and are not "certificated"; owners of IPs receive dividend-equivalent payments quarterly, not when the firms pay dividends. We need not debate whether these differences come to anything, for they pale beside the larger difficulties in calling IPs "stock". The greatest is that IPs are not stock *in* anything. There isn't an issuer— which the SEC emphasized when concluding that the Investment Company Act is inapplicable, 54 Fed.Reg. at 15289–90. Stock is an equity interest in an issuer, the residual claim to the profits of a venture. *United Housing Foundation, Inc. v. Forman*, 421 U.S. 837, 44 L. Ed. 2d 621, 95 S. Ct. 2051 (1975). *Landreth* rejected the "sale-of-business doctrine" because the owner of 100% of the equity interest in a firm still owns "stock". Purchasers of IPs don't own equity, directly or indirectly; they don't have a claim to the proceeds and liquidating distribution of a business; there isn't an underlying pool of assets; there is only a "short" on the other side. The absence of an issuer—IPs don't carry votes because they don't have anything to do with equity—tells all. There is no common venture, not even the commonality represented by a mutual fund (which reinvests in real stock and creates the risk that the stakeholder will join Robert Vesco with the kitty).

IPs do not fit comfortably into any of the other pigeonholes of § 3(a)(10). A "certificate of interest or participation in . . . any of the foregoing" securities is a security too, but IPs do not represent an "interest or participation" in the stocks in the index; they are based on the value *of* stock without creating a legal interest *in* stock. Perhaps the closest match is the language, part of the Accord in 1982, covering a "privilege on any security . . . or group or index of securities (including any interest therein *or based on the value thereof)*". Then there's the catch-all: "in general, any instrument commonly known as a 'security'". IPs convey privileges based on the value of an index, and what is "commonly known as a security" changes as new instruments come into use. So there is a basis for drawing IPs within § 3(a)(10), even though they do not duplicate a recognized category. See also, e.g., *SEC v. United Benefit Life Insurance Co.*, 387 U.S. 202, 87 S. Ct. 1557, 18 L. Ed. 2d 673 (1967).

Although the SEC found IPs to be securities by looking at the promises made *to* the longs, the CFTC found them to be futures by virtue of the promises made *by* the shorts, a perspective implied by the CEA's references to "contracts . . . for future delivery"—emphasizing the shorts' obligation. Shorts on IPs make the same pledge as shorts on stock-index futures contracts: to pay the value of an index on a prescribed day (the expiration date for the futures contract, the cash-out date for the IP). The short owes this obligation to the clearing house rather than to the long. IPs may be settled by buying or selling an offsetting obligation, after which the clearing house cancels the two on the books, just as with futures contracts. Shorts on IPs must put up more margin than shorts on futures contracts and must make dividend-equivalent payments, but the CFTC did not find these differences any more dispositive than the SEC found the IPs' lack of voting rights. Shorts also face an obligation of indefinite duration on the Philadelphia and AMEX IPs, but the CFTC and the futures markets treat this as no more than a prepaid rollover privilege.

Despite the congruence of futures and IPs on the short side, the SEC and the stock exchanges say that both "futurity" and "bilateralism" are missing. According to the SEC, IPs lack "futurity" because an IP is the "present obligation to pay current value". And IPs are not bilateral because the long performs in full by paying up front, although in a futures contract both sides must perform on settlement or expiration.

With respect to bilateralism, the SEC's point is inescapable. With respect to futurity, the SEC is wrong. IPs are no more a "present obligation to pay current value" than are futures contracts. The holder of either an IP or a stock-index futures contract may go to market and trade it; the price necessarily tracks current value. Neither the long on an IP nor the long on a futures contract can compel the short to *pay* current value, however. Both the futures contract and the IP are settled quarterly (the same dates for both kinds of instrument, except for the CBOE's omission of two of the four dates). The short's obligation is to pay the value of the index *on that date*—which lies in the future to the same extent as the settlement date of any futures contract. Even from the long's point of view, IP and futures contract ultimately look the same. The long pays up front for the IP, but the long on a futures contract *promises* up front to make a defined payment on the settlement date; the difference in the timing of the payment does not affect the fact that valuation comes at the defined future date.

So the IP has futurity but not bilateralism. It looks like a futures contract to the short—except that it is of indefinite duration, carries a dividend-equivalent obligation, and requires higher margin. It looks like a mutual fund to the long—except that it has no voting rights, does not represent any interest in an underlying pool of stock, and may be settled by executing an offsetting transaction. Fact is, it is no less a future than it is a security, and no more. It just doesn't fit. Which is the whole point. It isn't supposed to be just like something else; the IP was designed as a novel instrument so that it could offer attributes previously missing in the market.

The only thing of which we are sure is that an IP is not an option on a security. The AMEX contends that it is a prepaid option, with a premium equal to the full value and an exercise price of zero. The SEC did not accept this contention, writing:

> While IPs contain some characteristics of stock index options (*e.g.*, the issuance and clearance and settlement features of IPs are analogous to those of stock index options), the Commission believes that IPs predominantly have the attributes of a portfolio of common stock.

54 Fed.Reg. at 15286 n. 57. The only "characteristics of stock index options" that either the AMEX or the SEC identified are those introduced by the presence of a clearing house—characteristics that the IP shares with stock-index futures to the last detail. Unless we were to say that all futures are also options (they aren't), these features do not make IPs options. The very features that the SEC emphasizes to show that IPs are securities—indefinite duration, payment up front in cash, dividend equivalency, and so on—show that IPs cannot be options. Options are written out of the money, limited in time, and establish a careful balance among premium, strike price, and duration; the writer retains dividends. IPs possess none of these distinguishing features. As the AMEX defines an "option", someone who buys an automobile for cash and drives it away really has obtained an option with a high premium, zero strike price, perpetual duration, and 100% probability of exercise. Words are useful only to the extent they distinguish some things from others; symbols that comprise everything mean nothing. IPs are not options. * * *

To the extent instrumental arguments influence the coverage of the laws, they do not necessarily cut for the SEC. The futures markets' reply brief invites us to imagine a "Wheat Index Participation" (WIP) having the same characteristics as the IP except that it is based on an index of wheat prices rather than of stock prices. The buyer would pay cash for the WIP and be able to trade it freely; on a date identical to the expiry of the wheat futures contracts, the writer could be required to pay cash measured by the value of the wheat index. According to the SEC, such an instrument would not be a futures contract because it would lack both futurity and bilateralism (and we would agree on the latter point). So the CFTC could not allow it to be traded, no matter how valuable participants in the market might find it. On the other hand, the WIP certainly would not be "stock" and probably would not meet the criteria for being a "security" of any kind. So the SEC could not allow it to be traded on stock exchanges (anyway, the WIP would be a duck out of water on the AMEX!). We could escape from such silliness by reaching the logical conclusion that a WIP would be a futures contract. Yet if the WIP is a futures contract, it is hard to avoid the conclusion that the IP is one, too.

The petition for review in No. 89–1538 is dismissed for want of jurisdiction. The Investment Company Institute's petition, No. 89–2012, presents questions that we need not reach in light of our disposition of the futures markets' claims. On petition Nos. 89–1763 and 89–1786, the SEC's orders approving the applications of the stock exchanges and the OCC are set aside.

BOARD OF TRADE OF THE CITY OF CHICAGO v. SECURITIES & EXCHANGE COMMISSION

187 F.3d 713 (7th Cir. 1999)

EASTERBROOK, CIRCUIT JUDGE.

Although the Dow Jones Industrial Average may be the world's most famous stock market index, the Dow Jones Transportation Average is its most venerable, having been established in 1884. The Dow Jones Utilities Average, which dates from 1929, is another well known indicator. An index uses a few stocks to approximate the performance of a market segment. For example, the 20 stocks in the transportation index are designed to track a portfolio of approximately 145 transportation stocks with a capitalization exceeding $200 billion. The 15 stocks in the utilities index stand in for a utilities segment of 145 firms with a capitalization near $300 billion. When Charles Dow designed these indexes, long before instantaneous worldwide networks, a "computer" was a person who calculated tables of artillery trajectories in longhand on foolscap. In that era a reference to a few stocks as an approximation of many was a valuable time-saving device. Today it is easy to follow the average value-weighted price of a whole market, which an electronic computer can produce at the touch of a button. Each investor can specify and follow the portfolio that seems most interesting or important. Still, indexes have retained their fascination with the media and the public, and they have developed a new use—as the base of futures contracts. Our case presents the question whether futures exchanges may trade contracts based on the Dow Jones Utilities Average and the Dow Jones Transportation Average. For many years Dow Jones was unwilling to license its indexes (rather, the trademarks used to denote them) for use in futures contracts. In 1997 it changed its mind and set in train these proceedings.

"A futures contract, roughly speaking, is a fungible promise to buy or sell a particular commodity at a fixed date in the future. Futures contracts are fungible because they have standard terms and each side's obligations are guaranteed by a clearing house. Contracts are entered into without prepayment, although the markets and clearing house will set margin to protect their own interests. Trading occurs in 'the contract', not in the commodity." The classic futures contract involves a commodity such as wheat, but in principle any measure of value can be used. Financial futures usually take the form of a contract that depends on the value of an index at some future date. Thus, for example, the buyer (the "long") of a futures contract based on the Standard & Poor's 500 Index future might promise to pay 100 times the value of that index on a defined future date, and the seller (the "short") will receive that price. Either side may close the position by buying or selling an offsetting obligation before the expiration date of the contract.

Financial futures contracts are useful for hedging or portfolio adjustment. They facilitate risk management—that is, assignment of the inevitable risks of markets to those best able to bear them. Someone who owns a mutual fund containing all of the Standard & Poor's 500 stocks can cut risk in half by selling a futures contract based on the S & P 500 index, or double the market return (and the risk of loss) for the same financial outlay by buying a S & P 500 futures contract. A futures contract based on a market segment (such as utilities) also may be used for portfolio adjustment. Suppose the investor wants to hold a diversified portfolio of stocks that does not include utilities. This investor might own a broadly representative mutual fund and then sell a futures contract based on a utilities index. Similarly, a person who wants to obtain the returns (and take the risks) of particular market segments that do not have their own mutual fund—for example, a combination of utilities and transportation stocks, but no industrials—could purchase an appropriate combination of futures contracts. Using these contracts for portfolio adjustment is attractive because the transactions costs of trading futures are much smaller (by an order of magnitude) than the costs of trading the underlying stocks in equivalent volumes. A pension fund that wants to move from stocks to the equivalent of a mixed stock-and-bond portfolio, without incurring the costs of trading the stocks, can do so by selling a futures contract on an index.

For many years the traditional futures markets, such as the Chicago Board of Trade, have been at odds with the traditional stock markets, such as the New York Stock Exchange, about where financial futures would be traded—and whether they would be traded at all. The stock exchanges prefer less competition; but, if competition breaks out, they prefer to trade the instruments themselves. The disagreement has spilled over to the regulatory bodies. The Securities and Exchange Commission, which regulates stock markets, has sided with its clients; the Commodities Futures Trading Commission, which regulates boards of trade, has done the same. In 1982 this court held that institutions within the CFTC's domain are authorized to trade financial futures (including options on these futures), and, because of an exclusivity clause in the Commodity Exchange Act, that the stock markets are not. Because the stock exchanges long had traded options, a financial derivative related to futures, a political donnybrook accompanied the regulatory dispute among the markets and agencies. Shortly after our opinion issued, Congress amended the Commodity Exchange Act to reflect a compromise among the CFTC, the SEC, and the exchanges.

Congress allocated securities and options on securities to exchanges regulated by the SEC, futures and options on futures to boards of trade regulated by the CFTC. If an instrument is both a security and a futures contract, then it falls within the CFTC's domain. (This is the basis of Chicago Mercantile Exchange which held that a novel "index participation" is a futures contract that belongs to boards of trade.) Options on single securities are allowed, but futures contracts on single securities are not. This allocation appears to be a political compromise; no one has suggested an economic rationale for the distinction. Having drawn this line, however, Congress had to make it stick. Futures contracts thus must reflect "all publicly traded equity or debt securities or a substantial segment thereof". 7 U.S.C. § 2a (ii)(III). Finally, both agencies participate in the process of reviewing applications to trade new financial futures contracts. Before a new contract may start trading, both the SEC and the CFTC must certify that it meets the statutory criteria. Regulation of the trading process belongs exclusively to the CFTC.

A year after this statute was enacted, the SEC and the CFTC issued a Joint Policy Statement spelling out the kinds of financial futures that the agencies believed suitable for trading. 49 Fed. Reg. 2884 (Jan. 24, 1984). The Joint Policy Statement is not a regulation and lacks legal force, but for many years the markets observed its limits when proposing new contracts. One element of the Joint Policy Statement is that any index used as the basis of a futures contract contain at least 25 domestic equity issuers. The Dow Jones Transportation Average is based on 20 stocks, the Utilities Average on 15. The second element is that, in a price-weighted index, no single security may have a weight exceeding 10% of the entire index, if its price weighting exceeds its capitalization weighting by a factor of three. In April 1997 Dow Jones replaced one firm in its Utilities Average with Columbia Gas, which accounts for 2.93% of the Utilities Average by capitalization weight, but 12.56% by price weight. The Transportation Average does not contain a stock with a similar disparity.

A brief detour into price-weighting may be helpful. All Dow Jones averages are price weighted, the only practical way to construct an index before electronic calculation. Price weighting means that the prices of all stocks in an index are added together, then divided by a number that the maintainer of the index selects to preserve consistency over time as stocks are split, firms enter or leave the index, and so on. If one stock in a price-weighted index undergoes a rapid rise in price, that stock can come to have an influence disproportionate to its capitalization. (Think of a stock of a small company that doubles in price. This will drive up the value of the index more than a 15% increase in the price of a much larger company, even though the bigger company's increase yields a larger improvement in investors' wealth.) Indexes constructed since the advent of electronic computers are value-weighted (that is, each stock affects the level of the index according to the ratio of its total market capitalization to that of all other securities in the index), and value weighting in principle leads an index to be a more accurate reflection of the portfolio. *See* James H. Lorie & Mary T. Hamilton, *The Stock Market: Theories and Evidence* 55–57 (1973). Nonetheless, price-weighted indexes have been highly correlated with value-weighted indexes (and with the market as a whole) through the years. *Id.* at 60–69. Movements in the Dow Jones Industrial Average, a small (30-stock) price weighted index, track very closely movements in the Standard & Poor's 500, a large value-weighted index. The law of large numbers plays a major role, as does the skill of index maintainers in keeping divisors up to date. Thus both price weighted and value-weighted indexes continue to be useful to investors.

When Dow Jones & Co. agreed to license its trademarks for use in financial products based on its market indexes, both stock markets and futures markets sought to trade products based on these indexes. The SEC promptly approved trading (at the stock markets) in options on the Dow Jones Industrial Average, the Dow Jones Transportation Average, and the Dow Jones Utilities Average. But when the futures exchanges sought permission to trade futures contracts based on these indexes, the SEC was less accommodating. It approved a futures contract based on the Dow Jones Industrial Average but blocked trading in the others, which have fewer than 25 stocks in the index. Release No. 34–40216, 1998 SEC LEXIS 1454. The SEC recognized that the Joint Policy Statement of 1984 lacks the force of law. *Id.* at *13. Nonetheless, the SEC concluded, its criteria would be applied as part of the totality of the circumstances that the agency considered. *Id.* at *42. But of course the circumstances an agency considers must implement the statute. One can't have a totality-of-the-circumstances approach in the abstract. * * *

Normally, when a court of appeals concludes that an agency's decision is not adequately supported, it remands so that the agency may enlarge the record or apply correct legal principles to the existing record. *South Prairie Construction Co. v. Operating Engineers*, 425 U.S. 800, 48 L. Ed. 2d 382, 96 S. Ct. 1842 (1976). Section 2a has an unusual proviso that makes the normal approach inappropriate. The SEC has a strict timetable for decision. 2 U.S.C. § 2a(iv)(II). Once the time has elapsed, control passes to the CFTC. This means that if, within the statutory time, the SEC has not given a satisfactory reason for rejecting a proposed futures contract, it does not get a second chance. We have held that the SEC's reasons are not satisfactory. Accordingly, we vacate the SEC's order concluding that the proposed futures contracts do not meet the criteria of § 2a(ii). With the SEC's order vacated, the subject now goes to the CFTC for its decision, just as if the SEC had failed to act within the statutory time.

The order of the Securities and Exchange Commission is vacated.

NOTE

1. Another SEC-CFTC jurisdictional battle was decided by the Seventh Circuit in Grede v. FCStone LLC, Nos. 13–1232, 13–1278 (7th Cir. March 19, 2014) (Sentinel II). The principal issue in Sentinel II involved whether custodial accounts holding assets managed by a firm, registered as both a futures commission merchant (FCM) with the CFTC and as an investment adviser (IA) with the SEC, should be treated as equitable statutory trusts with equal stature in bankruptcy. This treatment would have required remaining customer funds to be distributed on a pro rata basis when a firm files for bankruptcy and a shortfall of the total assets has occurred. See, Ronald H. Filler, Ask the Professor: How Will the Seventh Circuit Rule in Sentinel II? 33 Fut. & Derv. L Rep. 21 (Nov. 2013) and Chapter 4 discussing the issues decided in that case.

8. FUNCTIONAL REGULATION—A FIRST LOOK

JERRY W. MARKHAM
MERGING THE SEC AND CFTC—A CLASH OF CULTURES
78 U. Cinn. L. Rev. 537 (2009)

The massive subprime losses at Citigroup, UBS, Bank of America, Wachovia, Washington Mutual, and other banks [in 2008] astounded the financial world. Equally shocking were the failures of Lehman Brothers, Merrill Lynch, and Bear Stearns. The conversion of Goldman Sachs and

Morgan Stanley into bank holding companies left no large independent investment banks standing. If all that was not enough, Bernard Madoff's incredible $50 billion Ponzi scheme was a new milestone in the nation's financial history. Those failures and Madoff's fraud were unforeseen and undetected by the regulator, the Securities and Exchange Commission (SEC), which was responsible for overseeing the broker-dealers that failed and monitoring the investment advisers such as Madoff. That once-proud agency seemed helpless and hapless in the face of the subprime crisis, during which the investment banks it regulated lost hundreds of billions of dollars, threatening the entire economy. Although those debacles touched the very core of the SEC's regulatory role, it appeared clueless of the risks that the country's largest and most venerable investment banks undertook in subprime-related transactions. The SEC was completely surprised by the failures of Bear Stearns and Lehman Brothers. It was equally surprised by the Madoff fraud, despite several warnings that Madoff's reported profits were unrealistic.

The derivatives counterpart to the SEC, the Commodity Futures Trading Commission (CFTC), was also under fire from the press and Congress in 2008 for its inability to control volatile commodity prices. Those price fluctuations were widely believed, without proof, to be caused by speculators acting with impunity in the commodity markets. Prices exploded to $147.27 a barrel in 2008, pushing gasoline prices to over $4 a gallon in July 2008, before dropping back to about $37 in February 2009. Widespread concerns were also raised about the transparency of the over-the-counter derivatives (OTC derivatives) markets that had been largely deregulated by the Commodity Futures Modernization Act of 2000.

Some of the criticism of the SEC and CFTC is not justified. These two agencies were not responsible for the spike in commodity prices or the residential housing bubble. But the public has lost confidence in their ability to regulate markets because they have proved unable to deter or detect fraud. As the subprime crisis exploded, exposing the shortcomings of these agencies, the Treasury Department was considering its "Blueprint" for regulatory reform. Among the Blueprint's wide-ranging proposals was a recommendation for combining the CFTC and SEC into a single financial services regulator.

Responding to widespread concerns over overlapping and unnecessary regulation in the existing regulatory structure, then-Secretary of the Treasury Henry M. Paulson, Jr. launched an initiative in October 2007 to consider how those concerns might be alleviated. The backdrop for that study was a widely expressed concern that excessive regulation in the United States was undermining the nation's competitive position in the world. Before the subprime crisis reached its peak, even politicians normally in favor of regulation were advocating a roll back of at least some aspects of the Sarbanes-Oxley Corporate Reform Act of 2002 (SOX).

New York Senator Charles Schumer coauthored an op-ed in the Wall Street Journal with New York City Mayor Michael Bloomberg that called for a study to determine if New York was losing its position as the world's leading financial center because of over-regulation and abusive shareholder litigation. The resulting study stated that its findings were:

> Quite clear: First, our regulatory framework is a thicket of complicated rules, rather than a streamlined set of commonly understood principles, as is the case in the United Kingdom and elsewhere. The flawed implementation of the 2002 Sarbanes-Oxley Act (SOX), which produced far heavier costs than expected, has only aggravated the situation, as has the continued requirement that foreign companies conform to U.S. accounting standards rather than the widely accepted—many would say superior—international standards. The time has come not only to re-examine implementation of SOX, but also to undertake broader reforms, using a principles-based approach to eliminate duplication and inefficiencies in our regulatory system. And we must do both while ensuring that we maintain our strong protections for investors and consumers.
>
> Second, the legal environments in other nations, including Great Britain, far more effectively discourage frivolous litigation. While nobody should attempt to discourage suits with merit, the prevalence of meritless securities lawsuits and settlements in the U.S. has driven up the apparent and actual cost of business—and driven away potential investors. In addition, the highly complex and fragmented nature of our legal system has led to a perception that penalties are arbitrary and unfair, a reputation that may be overblown, but nonetheless diminishes our attractiveness to international companies. To address this, we must consider legal reforms that will reduce spurious and meritless litigation and eliminate the perception of arbitrary justice, without eliminating meritorious actions.

Efforts to reform the reforms continued with a 2007 report from the blue ribbon Committee on Capital Markets Regulation (CCMR), which found that excessive regulation was hurting the securities markets and making foreign markets more competitive. The CCMR concluded that the United States' competitive position in financial services was "seriously eroding" and had "deteriorated significantly" in recent years. The CCMR U.S. share of global initial public offerings (IPOs) by foreign companies also significantly declined between 1996 and 2007. In 2007, only about

10% of such foreign based IPOs were listed on a U.S. exchange, in contrast to 44.5% in 1996.

In 1996, eight of the twenty largest global IPOs were listed on a U.S. exchange. In 2006, only one such offering was listed on a U.S. exchange, and foreign firms delisting from U.S. exchanges set a record that year. Statistics also evidenced that foreign firms were turning to unregulated private offerings when they sought to raise funds in the United States. IPOs by U.S. companies abroad also significantly increased. The CCMR recommended that Congress decrease the burden of regulation and litigation in order to make the United States more competitive. The Committee predicted that within ten years, unless its recommended changes were made, the United States would no longer be the financial capital of the world.

The U.S. Chamber of Commerce appointed a bipartisan, independent commission, which issued a report that also raised concerns with unnecessary regulation. That commission found that "in recent years, the U.S. has experienced a steady decline in its share of the global capital markets activity as international financial centers have grown to challenge this historical dominance." Another report by the Financial Services Roundtable noted:

> Effective regulation and the competitiveness of U.S. financial markets and firms are vital to consumers, capital formation, job creation, and sustained economic growth. Consumers of all kinds—small savers, first-time homebuyers, college students, small businesses and medium-sized enterprises, large corporations, issuers, investors, pension funds, and even governments—benefit when markets are safe, stable, and secure as well as when they are vibrant and innovative, and financial services firms actively compete for their business. Today, financial services firms directly account for five percent of total US employment, and eight percent of U.S. gross domestic product (GDP).

The Roundtable's report urged the adoption of principles-based regulation (as opposed to the current rules-based methodology) that would be risk-based, cost-effective, and standard across the same financial markets. The authors of the report included James Dimon, Chief Executive Officer of J.P. Morgan Chase, and Richard Kovacevich, Chairman of Wells Fargo—two banks that would be deeply involved in the subprime crisis as rescuers of failing institutions. * * *

Reform is sorely needed. The United Sates now operates under a "functional" regulatory system. Under this system, different regulators are appointed to regulate particular financial services, even if those services are offered by the same firm. This has resulted in much overlap and regulatory conflict, and created a system that failed to anticipate the subprime crisis. That the functional regulatory system failed should not be a surprise. It is a haphazard system of regulation that is not the result of a design or reasoned blueprint. Rather, it is a set of accumulated responses to a long history of financial crises, scandals, happenstance, personalities, and compromises among a broad and competing array of industry and governmental bodies.

Under functional regulation, financial service firms are regulated by fifty state insurance commissioners acting collectively through the National Association of Insurance Commissioners (NAIC), fifty state securities commissioners (plus the District of Columbia) acting collectively through the North American Securities Administrators Association (NASAA), fifty state attorneys general who operate in wolf packs when attacking financial service firms, and fifty state bank regulators. Union pension funds support that cast by acting as "private attorneys general" in bringing class action lawsuits whenever a company announces bad news.

At the federal level, functional regulators include the Federal Reserve Board (Fed), the Office of the Comptroller of the Currency in the Treasury Department (OCC), the Federal Deposit Insurance Corporation (FDIC), the Office of Thrift Supervision (OTS), the Treasury Department's anti-money laundering group (FinCEN), and the Office of Foreign Asset Control (OFAC), which is also in the Treasury Department and handles financial embargoes imposed on troublesome countries. The Justice Department, together with the FBI and Postal Inspectors, has also become a financial services regulator by criminalizing bad corporate decision making. In addition, the SEC, CFTC, Federal Trade Commission (FTC), Occupational Safety & Health Agency (OSHA) (for SOX whistleblower claims), and self-regulatory bodies such as the Financial Industry Regulatory Authority (FINRA) and National Futures Association (NFA) regulate various aspects of the financial services industry.

In 2006, Treasury Secretary Paulson warned that the country was "creating a thicket of regulation that impedes competitiveness." The Treasury Department sought public comment on regulatory efficiency issues in its study on the flaws in functional regulation. Of particular interest was the Department's request for comment on whether the "increasing convergence of products across the traditional "functional' regulatory lines of banking, insurance, securities, and futures" justifies changes in the regulatory system to ensure that regulatory boundary lines do not unnecessarily inhibit competition. The Department received more than 350 letters in response, indicating the financial community's interest. The Treasury Department published its report in March 2008

(Treasury Blueprint) [Dep't of the Treasury, Blueprint for a Modernized Financial Regulatory Structure (2008)].

The study that led to the Treasury Blueprint was commenced at a time when inefficient regulation was thought to be impairing financial services. Even while the Treasury study was ongoing, however, a sea change was occurring as the subprime crisis arose and intensified. The Wall Street Journal declared in a front-page article on March 24, 2008, that a new era of increased regulation could be expected due to problems in the subprime market. The Treasury Blueprint, which recommended a broad restructuring of the chaotic financial services regulatory structure, was published a few days after the Wall Street Journal article. It sought more centralized and rational regulation because of concern that functional regulation was ineffective and was undermining America's traditional competitive advantage in financial services. The Treasury Blueprint prophetically found that functional regulation:

> exhibited several inadequacies, the most significant being the fact that no single regulator possesses all of the information and authority necessary to monitor systemic risk, or the potential that events associated with financial institutions may trigger broad dislocation or a series of defaults that affect the financial system so significantly that the real economy is adversely affected.

The Blueprint contrasted the functional regulatory approach in America with regulatory mechanisms abroad. England, Germany, Japan, and dozens of other countries use a single consolidated regulator, along with a central bank, to regulate; those countries eschew the "rules-based" approach used by most of the most regulators in the United States. Rather, foreign regulators use a "principles-based" approach that sets broad regulatory goals and permits the industry to decide how to meet those goals. A principles-based approach reduces the need for volumes of regulations that seek to control every aspect of financial services operations—which is the approach taken by the SEC. The SEC has an institutional culture that seeks to dictate every aspect of corporate behavior. In contrast, the CFTC administers a principles-based regulatory structure put in place by the Commodity Futures Modernization Act of 2000. * * *

In seeking to abandon functional regulation, the Treasury Blueprint did not advocate a single regulator system for the United States. The Blueprint rejected a single regulator model for many reasons:

> While the consolidated regulator approach can deliver a number of benefits, several potential problems also arise. First, housing all regulatory functions related to financial and consumer regulation in one entity may lead to varying degrees of focus on

these key functions. Limited synergies in terms of regulation associated with financial and consumer protection may lead the regulator to focus more on one over the other. There may also be difficulties in allocating resources to these functions. Second, a consolidated regulatory approach to financial oversight might also lead to less market discipline as the same regulator would regulate all financial institutions, whether or not they have explicit government guarantees. This would seem to be particularly important in the United States where a number of financial institutions have access to explicit government guarantees of varying degrees. Third, since regulatory reform must consider the role of the central bank, the consolidated regulatory approach must maintain some degree of close coordination with the central bank if the central bank is going to be ultimately responsible for some aspect of market stability. The United Kingdom's recent experience with Northern Rock highlights the importance of this function in the consolidated regulator approach. Finally, the scale of operations necessary to establish a single consolidated regulator in the United States could make the model more difficult to implement in comparison to other jurisdictions.

Instead of a single regulator, the Blueprint recommended that the United States adopt the "twin peaks" approach used in Australia and the Netherlands. This concept is attributed to Michael Taylor, a former official at the Bank of England who wrote a 1995 article entitled "Twin Peaks': A Regulatory Structure for the New Century. The Twin Peaks approach is objectives-based and focuses on specific regulatory goals.

Twin Peaks envisions a central bank that focuses on prudential supervision, and a single business practices regulator that focuses on business conduct and consumer protection. From this the Treasury Blueprint created a "Three Peaks" approach that would have three separate bodies implementing three specific regulatory goals: (1) market stability regulation, (2) prudential financial regulation, and (3) business conduct regulation. This objectives-based approach would require consolidating and reshuffling the existing functional regulators in the United States into essentially three principal regulators. The market stability regulator would be the Federal Reserve Board. A new agency would be created for prudential financial regulation that would regulate financial institutions with a government guarantee, such as banks insured by the FDIC and broker-dealers insured by the Securities Investor Protection Corporation (SIPC). A new agency would also have to be created for the business conduct regulator, which would create and apply principles-based regulation.

The Treasury Blueprint recommended that in the interim, the SEC and CFTC be merged. It also recommended that the SEC adopt a principles-based regulatory approach, like that of the CFTC, to make the merger more workable. The Parts below discuss the many obstacles to such a merger. Prior efforts to merge the two agencies revealed strongly entrenched constituencies willing to battle to keep themselves separate, and a vast gulf in the two agencies' regulatory approaches, creating differing cultures that often clashed.

NOTES

1. The Financial Crisis of 2008 derailed the efforts to streamline the regulatory process and led to the passage of the massive (2,300 page) Dodd-Frank Wall Street Reform and Consumer Protection Act of 2010 (Dodd-Frank Act). The Dodd-Frank Act rejected the Treasury Blueprint's recommendations for a three peak regulatory approach. Instead, that legislation added even more layers to the existing functional regulatory system.

2. Among other things, the Dodd-Frank Act created a new Financial Stability Oversight Council (FSOC), which as described in Chapter 12, acts as a super regulator in dealing with systemic financial risks. A new Bureau of Consumer Financial Protection (BCFP) was also added to the already lengthy list of regulators.

3. Compare our vast financial regulatory model, which consists of both federal and state layers of regulation, to the U.K. regulatory model, which, before 2008, only had one financial regulator, the U.K. Financial Services Authority (FSA). As described in Chapter 12, more recently, two regulatory agencies replaced the FSA, but this is still a far cry from the large number of financial regulators that exist in the U.S.

CHAPTER 3

MARKET REGULATION

■ ■ ■

1. CONTRACT MARKET DESIGNATION AND REGULATION

The Commodity Exchange Act of 1936, as amended (CEA) [7 U.S.C. § 6], requires all futures contracts to be traded on a "contract market" designated as such by the Commodity Futures Trading Commission (CFTC). These "Designated Contract Markets" (DCMs) are also commonly called "boards of trade" or simply "futures exchanges." These exchanges are membership organizations through which their members trade.

Part 38 of the CFTC's regulations [17 C.F.R. Part 38] sets forth the requirements for an exchange to become a registered DCM. Futures contracts cannot be traded on an exchange without such registration.

Appendix A to Part 38 of the CFTC's regulations [17 C.F.R. Part 38] includes a Form DCM, which provides instructions and a list of necessary information and documentation that a DCM must submit to the CFTC to initiate the designation process.

Among other things, as a part of its self-regulatory obligations, exchanges seeking DCM status must have their own set of regulations governing all aspects of the exchange's trading, clearing and membership obligations and must make sure that their members and member firms comply with its regulatory structure. Among the documents required for the DCM application is a set of the exchange's proposed rules that will govern trading.

In addition, with respect to each futures contract to be traded on the DCM, proof must be provided by the applicant showing that that the respective futures contract will be traded in a manner that satisfies the twenty-three core principles added to the CEA by the Commodity Futures Modernization Act of 2000 (CFMA), and which are described below.

See the following link for the list of DCMs now registered with the CFTC.

http://sirt.cftc.gov/SIRT/SIRT.aspx?Topic=TradingOrganizations&implicit=true&type=DCM&CustomColumnDisplay=TTTTTTTT (accessed on November 25, 2013).

Once registered, DCMs may implement new rules or amend existing rules by filing a certification with the CFTC. The exchange must either (a) certify that the rule or rule amendment complies with the CEA and applicable CFTC regulations, or (b) request formal approval from the CFTC for the respective rule or rule amendment. The certification process or the rule approval process applies to all DCM rules, except for certain administrative-related exchange regulations. This includes each new futures contract to be traded on a DCM as well as any amendments to existing futures contracts.

2. PRINCIPLES-BASED VS. PRESCRIPTIVE-BASED REGULATION

Financial regulations typically fall into one of two categories, namely, whether they are "principles-based," meaning that they take a broader, more macro approach, or are "prescriptive-based," meaning that they are quite specific and detailed in nature.

Historically, most federal regulations involving derivatives have been prescriptive-based in nature. The underlying regulations provide specific requirements or guidelines as to how a registrant must comply with the respective regulation.

More recently, financial regulators have utilized the concept of "principles-based" regulation in adopting new rules, to take into consideration the ever-changing financial products that are traded on exchanges. In other words, as Moses did on Mount Sinai, they believe that a Ten Commandments approach, such as "thou shall not commit fraud," may be the preferred regulatory model rather than being specific as to what constitutes fraud.

The best example of this principles-based regulatory model are the twenty-three core principles, which are outlined below, that were adopted by the CFMA in 2000.

In contrast, stock exchanges, which are regulated by the SEC, do not have similar core principles regarding their rules or rule amendments. Therefore, each stock exchange may only adopt a new rule or amend an existing rule through a request for approval by the SEC. This more formal rule approval process has placed stock exchanges at a competitive disadvantage to DCMs when both stock exchanges and DCMs are offering products that compare favorably from an economic equivalent perspective.

Prescriptive-based regulations used by both the SEC and CFTC should be distinguished from the "prudential" regulatory approach of the banking regulators. The SEC and CFTC seek to regulate through high profile court or administrative cases that draw big headlines and involve large fines. In contrast, bank regulators prefer to work quietly with the banks they regulate. Bank regulators use their discretion in discouraging banks from engaging in unsafe and unsound practices that might affect the financial stability of a bank.

It is difficult to judge which regulatory model is preferable, since they both failed in the run up to the Financial Crisis in 2008. It is clear, however, that financial institutions have become milk cows for prescriptive-based regulators. Hardly a day goes by without an announcement in the news of another massive settlement in a regulatory action against a large financial institution by one regulator or another.

3. DCM REVIEWS

The CFTC's Division of Market Oversight's Examination Branch conducts regular reviews of the operations and activities, in particular, of the market surveillance programs, at each DCM. The examination includes, among other things, evaluating the DCM's compliance with the twenty-three core principles, determining whether the DCM is properly enforcing its rules and preventing market manipulation and market abuses, and ensuring that the DCM is properly maintaining its records and trade data. These CFTC reviews are known as "rule enforcement reviews (RERs). These RERs are conducted normally every fifteen to eighteen months.

A RER of the Chicago Mercantile Exchange is set forth in the following link:

http://www.cftc.gov/PressRoom/PressReleases/pr6658–13 (accessed on November 25, 2013).

4. CORE PRINCIPLES

As noted above, the CFMA added twenty-three core principles to the regulation of DCMs and clearinghouses, also known as "designated clearing organizations" (DCOs). They are set forth in detail in Part 38 of the CFTC's regulations [see also, 7 U.S.C. § 7]. To maintain its designation as a DCM, the exchange must comply, on both an initial and ongoing basis, with these core principles. They are:

1. To be a DCM
2. Compliance with Rules
3. Contracts Not Readily Subject to Manipulation
4. Prevention of Market Disruption
5. Position Limitations and Accountability
6. Emergency Authority

7. Availability of General Information

8. Daily Publication of Trading Information

9. Execution of Transactions

10. Trade Information

11. Financial Integrity of Transactions

12. Protection of Markets and Market Participants

13. Disciplinary Procedures

14. Dispute Resolution

15. Governance Fitness Standards

16. Conflicts of Interest

17. Composition of Governing Boards of Contract Markets

18. Recordkeeping

19. Antitrust Considerations

20. System Safeguards

21. Financial Resources

22. Diversity of Boards of Directors

23. SEC swaps reporting and inspection

These core principles provide invaluable flexibility to DCMs. The futures exchange thus merely needs to certify that any new rule or rule amendment satisfies these core principles. Each new product traded on the DCM constitutes a new exchange rule. Therefore, futures exchanges can easily add a new futures contract to be traded on the exchange through this rule certification process, without a prior economic review by the CFTC. Previously, such reviews by the CFTC were required and often led to considerable delay and expense in introducing new products.

Since this "core principles" model does not exist in the securities industry, stock exchanges, such as the Chicago Board of Options Exchange (CBOE), must submit any new rule or rule amendment, including any new product to be traded, to the SEC for review and approval. This review and approval process can take months to complete. As noted above, this puts stock exchanges at a competitive disadvantage to their futures exchanges counterparts.

5. CONTRACT MARKET EMERGENCIES

Pursuant to Core Principle Six, each DCM has the authority to exercise emergency powers to ensure that futures contracts traded on the exchange are not subject to market manipulation or abuse. CFTC Rule

38.350 [17 C.F.R. § 38.350], which incorporates Core Principle Six, gives the DCM the authority to: (i) liquidate or transfer open positions, (ii) suspend or curtail trading in a futures contract, or (iii) require market participants to provide special margin requirements.

The CFTC also maintains oversight over DCMs and may direct the DCMs to take action in the event of a market emergency [12 U.S.C. § 12a(9)]. However, such power has not always been effective when market emergencies actually arise.

The legislation that created the CFTC thus included a provision that allowed the CFTC to declare a market emergency and to direct contract markets to take measures to combat the emergency, and to restore or to maintain "orderly trading." These emergency powers include, but are not limited to, "the setting of temporary emergency margin levels on any futures contract, and the fixing of limits that may apply to a market position acquired in good faith prior to the effective date of the Commission's action." [7 U.S.C. § 12a(9)].

These emergency powers are extraordinary, since they can require the liquidation of contracts at inopportune times, introducing a political risk of such action into an already volatile market. The power to increase margin requirements introduces a similar risk of forced liquidation and reduced liquidity as speculators exit the market to avoid those demands.

An "emergency" that is subject to these extraordinary powers includes, "in addition to threatened or actual market manipulations and corners, any act of the United States or a foreign government affecting a commodity or any other major market disturbance which prevents the market from accurately reflecting the forces of supply and demand for such commodity." [7 U.S.C § 12a(9)].

In 1976, the CFTC faced its first significant market emergency after traders defaulted on the May 1976 Maine potato futures contract traded on the New York Mercantile Exchange (NYMEX). That default occurred in a classic battle between short and long traders in which deliverable supplies of Maine potatoes proved to be unavailable.

The CFTC declared a market emergency and used its new emergency powers prior to the potato default by ordering NYMEX to increase potato futures margins one hundred percent and to trade for liquidation only. See, Jerry W. Markham, Manipulation of Commodity Futures Prices— The Unprosecutable Crime, 8 Yale J. on Reg. 281, 335 (1991) (describing that event). However, that action did not "prevent the largest default in the history of commodities futures trading." Strobl v. NYMEX, 768 F.2d 22, 23 (2d Cir. 1985), cert. denied, 474 U.S. 1006 (1985).

On November 23, 1977, the CFTC declared another emergency. This time for the December 1977 coffee futures contract that was traded on the

New York Coffee and Sugar Exchange. That exchange had declared a market emergency just before the CFTC endorsed that action by declaring its own emergency. That emergency was the result of an unusual frost and other extraordinary conditions that disrupted supplies and caused coffee prices to skyrocket. The CFTC was concerned that governments in leading coffee producing countries were trying to manipulate coffee prices upward. Challenges by traders to that emergency action were rejected. Compania de Salvadorena v. CFTC, 446 F. Supp. 687, 689 (S.D.N.Y. 1978) and Equitable Trust Co. v. CFTC, 669 F.2d 269 (5th Cir. 1982).

Unusual market conditions in the March 1979 wheat futures contract that was traded on the Chicago Board of Trade (CBOT) resulted in another market emergency. Long traders in that contract held dominant positions that far exceeded deliverable supplies. The CFTC requested that the CBOT take emergency action, but the exchange refused that request. The CFTC then declared a market emergency, and suspended trading for one day so that the CBOT could act to prevent a price manipulation. The CBOT once again refused that request, and the CFTC then suspended all trading in the March contract and directed that outstanding contracts be settled at the then prevailing settlement price. The CBOT sought and received a court order enjoining the CFTC's action. That order was later reversed on appeal by the Seventh Circuit, a decision that came too late to affect trading in the March 1979 contract. CBOT v. CFTC, 605 F.2d 1016 (7th Cir. 1979), cert. denied, 446 U.S. 928 (1980).

The decision by the Seventh Circuit in the CBOT case raised concerns in Congress because the court had held that CFTC actions taken under its emergency powers was not subject to meaningful judicial review. The CEA was amended by the Futures Trading Act of 1982 [Pub. L. No. 97–444] to allow some limited judicial review.

Thereafter, the CFTC tended to defer to the exchanges in declaring a market emergency. See, Jerry W. Markham, "Manipulation of Commodity Futures Prices—The Unprosecutable Crime," 8 Yale J. on Reg. 281, 347 (1991) (describing emergency actions taken by exchanges and CFTC deference).

During 1979, there was rapid run up in silver prices as the result of a massive silver speculation by the Hunt family of Texas and several foreign traders. The exchanges on which the Hunts and other speculators traded futures contracts, including the Commodity Exchange Inc. (Comex), were first blamed for allowing silver futures prices to be manipulated upward. The exchanges then were criticized for taking actions that pricked the silver bubble. However, a district court found that the silver futures exchanges had not acted in bad faith. The court noted that:

From August through September 1979 the per-ounce price of silver, which had been stable at the six dollar level from 1974 to 1978, rose from nine to eighteen dollars. By December 1979, silver reached twenty-five dollars per ounce, and in mid-January, the price of silver peaked at about fifty dollars per ounce. During this period, which amounted to a crisis in the view of many market participants, concern was expressed that the silver futures market was becoming congested and that a possible manipulation of silver prices might be in progress.

In response to these unusual events in the silver market, the Comex Board of Governors convened for at least twenty-five special or emergency meetings in addition to its regular monthly board meetings. Among the actions that the Comex Board took were the following: On October 4, 1979, the Board voted unanimously to appoint "disinterested" members of the Board to serve on a Special Silver Committee to "deal with the silver situation" and to "take all action with respect to the silver market that could otherwise be taken by the Board." The Special Silver Committee consisted of Dr. Andrew F. Brimmer, a public member, who chaired the Committee, and three additional members representing each of the three other groups which comprised the Board. The Special Silver Committee held at least nine formal meetings during this period and also conducted depositions, surveys and negotiations with market participants.

Next, the Board, in conjunction with the Special Silver Committee, began to raise periodically the margin requirements for silver futures contracts and engaged in "jawboning" with market participants holding long silver futures positions to attempt to achieve voluntary position reductions. On January 7, 1980, the Board imposed position limits on holders of silver futures contracts. Two members abstained from the vote; all other members present voted in favor of the limits. On January 21, 1980, the Board imposed liquidation-only trading on the silver market: no new contracts could be bought and the only trading permitted was the liquidation of existing contracts. Of the governors present, ten voted in favor of the liquidation-only rule and five abstained.

By the beginning of March 1980, the price of silver had dropped to thirty-five dollars per ounce. By the end of March 1980 silver plummeted further, dropping to as low as ten dollars per ounce.

Minpeco, S.A. v. Hunt, 693 F. Supp. 58 (S.D.N.Y. 1988).

Still another market emergency arose in the July 1989 soybean contract traded on the CBOT. Drought conditions reduced soybean supplies and a large Italian operation, Ferruzzi Finaziaria S.P.A. (Ferruzzi), was found to be holding a dominant position in that contract. The CBOT then declared a market emergency and ordered Ferruzzi to liquidate a substantial portion of its long position, which was supposed to be a hedge, but which was determined actually to be a speculation. See, In re Soybean Futures Litigation, 892 F. Supp. 1025 (N.D. Ill. 1995) (describing these events).

A group of soybean farmers sued the CBOT under the antitrust laws claiming that the exchange acted in bad faith in issuing the liquidation order, which caused soybean prices to drop. The Seventh Circuit held that the CBOT did not have anti-trust immunity because the CFTC had not approved the exchange's emergency order. American Agric. Movement v. CBOT, 977 F.2d 1147, 1167 (7th Cir. 1992). The case was subsequently dismissed, however, because the court could find no evidence to support the charge that the CBOT's emergency action was undertaken in order to protect a politically powerful member of the exchange. Zimmerman v. CBOT, 360 F.3d 612 (7th Cir. 2004).

Ferruzzi also sued the CBOT over its emergency action and the CBOT countersued. That matter was later settled. See, Jerry W. Markham, Law Enforcement and the History of Financial Market Manipulation § 4:13 (2014) (describing those actions).

NOTE

1. Section 8 of the CEA [7 U.S.C. § 12] grants the CFTC broad authority to investigate the operations of the markets it regulates. That provision states that:

> (a) For the efficient execution of the provisions of this Act, and in order to provide information for the use of Congress, the Commission may make such investigations as it deems necessary to ascertain the facts regarding the operations of boards of trade and other persons subject to the provisions of this Act. The Commission may publish from time to time the results of any such investigation and such general statistical information gathered therefrom as it deems of interest to the public: *Provided,* That except as otherwise specifically authorized in this Act, the Commission may not publish data and information that would separately disclose the business transactions or market positions of any person and trade secrets or names of customers; *Provided further,* That the Commission may withhold from public disclosure any data or information concerning or obtained in connection with any pending investigation of any person. . . .

> (c) The Commission may make or issue such reports as it deems necessary, or such opinions or orders as may be required under other provisions of law, relative to the conduct of any board of trade

or to the transactions of any person found guilty of violating the provisions of this Act or the rules, regulations, or orders of the Commission thereunder in proceedings brought under Section 6 of this Act. In any such report or opinion, the Commission may set forth the facts as to any actual transaction or any information referred to in subsection (b) of this section, if such facts or information have previously been disclosed publicly in connection with a congressional proceeding, or in an administrative or judicial proceeding brought under this Act.

6. GOVERNANCE REQUIREMENTS

The CFTC requires each DCM to satisfy certain acceptable practices relating to exchange governance in order for the FCM to be in compliance with Core Principle Sixteen. [7 U.S.C. § 7(d)(16)]. Core Principle Sixteen states:

> "CONFLICTS OF INTEREST—The board of trade shall establish and enforce rules to minimize conflicts of interest in the decision-making process of the contract market and establish a process for resolving such conflicts of interest."

In the Federal Register release adopting exchange governance acceptable practices, the CFTC stated that acceptable practices "address conflicts of interest that exist within DCMs as they operate in an increasingly competitive environment and transform from member-owned, not-for-profit entities into diverse enterprises with a variety of business models and ownership structures." 72 Fed. Reg. 6936, 6937 (Feb. 14, 2007).

In particular, among the acceptable practices now required, each DCM must establish a board of directors, as well as an executive committee, which must contain at least thirty-five percent of the directors as "public directors." A public director is in essence a person who has no material relationship with the DCM that could somehow reasonably affect a director's independent judgment.

In addition, each DCM must establish a Regulatory Oversight Committee (ROC), which must be comprised solely of public directors. The ROC must have complete and independent review and maintain responsibility over the DCM's enforcement responsibilities as an SRO. The purpose of this requirement is to maintain all core regulatory functions separately and apart from the DCM's commercial activities.

KLEIN & CO. FUTURES, INC. V. BOARD OF TRADE OF THE CITY OF NEW YORK

464 F.3d 255 (2d Cir. 2006)

B.D. PARKER, CIRCUIT JUDGE:

Klein & Co. Futures Inc. is a futures commission merchant ("FCM") and a clearing member of New York Clearing Corporation ("NYCC"). Klein appeals the dismissal by the United States District Court for the Southern District of New York (Daniels, J.) for lack of standing to bring claims against Defendant-Appellees the Board of Trade of the City of New York ("NYBOT"), New York Clearing Corporation ("NYCC"), Norman Eisler, and others (collectively "NYBOT Defendants") under Sections 22 (a) and (b) of the Commodity Exchange Act (CEA), 7 U.S.C. § 25. After dismissing Klein's claims under the CEA, the district court declined to exercise jurisdiction over its supplemental state law claims and dismissed them without prejudice. The NYBOT defendants cross-appeal that dismissal. For the reasons set forth below, we affirm. Except as noted, the facts are drawn from the complaint.

As a FCM, Klein facilitated the trading and fulfilled certain obligations of its customers who traded through the NYBOT. Prior to May 2000, Defendant Norman Eisler, whose conduct is the focus of Klein's complaint, was the Chairman of the New York Futures Exchange ("NYFE"). The NYFE is a futures and options exchange designated by the Commodity Futures Trading Commission ("CFTC") as a contract market for the trading of commodities futures and options, including P-Tech Futures and Options ("P-Tech contracts"). Eisler was also a member of the NYFE's Settlement Committee for the Pacific Stock Exchange Technology Index Futures Contract & Options (the "Committee"). The Committee's primary responsibility was to calculate the price of P-Tech contracts for the purposes, among other things, of calculating margin requirements in customers' accounts. Eisler was also a customer of Klein and the principal of First West Trading Inc. ("First West"), another Klein customer. Eisler traded in P-Tech contracts for the account of First West. The trades were unsolicited and were made without input or advice from Klein.

Allegedly, Eisler, in his capacity as a member of the Committee, secretly manipulated the settlement prices of P-Tech contracts. This manipulation benefitted Eisler's P-Tech positions but, at the same time, caused Klein to miscalculate the margin requirements for the First West account. Around March 2000, the NYBOT began receiving complaints regarding the P-Tech settlement prices but failed to make proper inquiries or to place Klein or other members of the industry or public on notice of potential irregularities.

In early May 2000, Klein, based on the incorrect settlement prices, computed the required margin in First West's account at $700,000, but Eisler was unable to post that amount. Klein then contacted the NYBOT and expressed concerns regarding the illiquidity of the P-Tech contracts, Eisler's inability to meet First West's margin call, and his inability to liquidate First West's contracts. Klein reported that the First West margin deficit, if not covered, would impair Klein's net capital and cause Eisler significant losses. Klein requested that the NYFE Board halt trading in P-Tech contracts, but no such action occurred.

At that point, the scheme began to unravel. In mid-May, Eisler's NYBOT membership privileges were suspended and he was dropped from the Committee. Once this occurred, the remaining Committee members recalculated the settlement prices and First West's margin deficit ballooned to $4.5 million, an obligation it could not meet. As a result, Klein was required to take an immediate charge against its net capital, forcing it below the minimum required for clearing members of the NYCC and the New York Mercantile Exchange ("NYMEX"). Its membership privileges were suspended and Klein collapsed.

Klein then sued on various claims. Klein's first claim alleged that NYFE violated § 5b of the CEA by failing to enforce its rules, and sought a declaration that NYFE should be suspended as a contract market. Klein further alleged that the NYBOT Defendants violated the anti-fraud provisions in CEA § 4b and 17 C.F.R §§ 33.9 and 33.10, and the insider provisions of CEA § 9. In addition, the complaint alleged a variety of state law claims.

The NYBOT Defendants moved to dismiss principally on the ground that Klein was not a purchaser or seller of futures contracts or options and, therefore, lacked standing under § 22 of the CEA. They also they moved to dismiss Klein's state law claims with prejudice on the ground that they were preempted by the CEA. The district court agreed and dismissed Klein's claims under the CEA for lack of standing. Specifically, the district court concluded:

> Plaintiff Klein lacks standing under Section 22 to bring this suit. Klein does not allege that it was either a purchaser or a seller of P-Tech Futures and Options. Furthermore, Klein does not claim that it traded for its own account. Rather, it is undisputed that *First West*, not Klein, traded in P-Tech Futures and Options. Indeed, Klein claims that these trades were effected "without input, counsel, advice or any type of recommendation whatsoever from Klein & Co." Klein further alleges that it "had no equity or financial interest in the First West account nor did Klein & Co. exercise control over the trade in said account."

Klein & Co. Futures, Inc. v. Bd. of Trade of N.Y., 2005 U.S. Dist. LEXIS 2720, No. 00–CV–5563–GBD, 2005 WL 427713, at *4 (S.D.N.Y. Feb. 18, 2005 (internal citations omitted)).

The court further reasoned that § 22 precluded an action by a plaintiff that "did not suffer its damages in the course of its trading activities on a contract market." *Id.* Without addressing preemption, the district court declined to exercise supplemental jurisdiction over the state law claims and dismissed them without prejudice. This appeal followed.

We review *de novo* the district court's dismissal of a complaint for lack of standing under Fed. R. Civ. P. 12(b)(1) and 12(b)(6). *See Kaliski v. Bacot (In re Bank of N.Y. Deriv. Litig.)*, 320 F.3d 291, 297 (2d Cir. 2003). We review the court's decision to decline supplemental jurisdiction over state law claims for abuse of discretion. *See Valencia ex rel. Franco v. Lee*, 316 F.3d 299, 304 (2d Cir. 2003).

CEA § 22 enumerates the only circumstances under which a private litigant may assert a private right of action for violations of the CEA. Section 22 includes two types of claims. Section 22(a) relates to claims against persons other than registered entities and registered futures associations. 7 U.S.C. § 25(a). Section 22(b) deals with claims against those entities and their officers directors, governors, committee members and employees. The text of the two subdivisions requires that a putative plaintiff fall within one of the four required relationships set forth in § 22(a)(1)(A–D).

The common thread of these four subdivisions is that they limit claims to those of a plaintiff who actually traded in the commodities market. Specifically, the remedies afforded by CEA § 22(b) are available only to a private litigant "who engaged in . . . transaction[s] on or subject to the rules of" a contract market. *Id.* § 25(b)(1)–(3). The section contains another important limitation. Subsection 22(b)(5) provides that the private rights of action against the exchanges enumerated in § 22(b) "*shall be the exclusive remedy* . . . available to *any person* who sustains a loss as a result of" a violation of the CEA or an exchange rule by a contract market or one of its officers or employees. *Id.* § 25(b)(5) (emphasis added).

Klein does not fall within any of the required subdivisions of § 22(a)(1)(A)–(D). To fit under one of the four, Klein must essentially either have (1) received trading advice from Eisler or First West for a fee; (2) traded through Eisler or First West or deposited money in connection with a trade; (3) purchased from or sold to Eisler or First West or placed an order for the purchase or sale through them; or (4) engaged in certain market manipulation activities in connection with the purchase or sale of a commodity contract.

Here, Klein was a FCM and a clearing member of the NYCC that cleared First West's trades through NYCC. Klein does not contend that it purchased or sold P-Tech contracts. Klein was not a trader of P-Tech contracts; nor did it own the P-Tech contracts at issue. To the contrary, Klein's complaint admits that it had no financial interest in the First West account and that all the trades in question were unsolicited by First West. Klein's losses were not the result of its purchases or sales in the commodities market. Klein functioned merely as a broker or agent that earned commissions for handling its customer's trades. As a clearing member, Klein cleared their trades and was obligated to post margins for them as required. Under NYCC Rules governing clearing members, Klein was liable for its own failure to post the required margin on its customers' positions, whether or not Klein collected that margin from defaulting customers such as First West. In view of the provisions of sections 22(a) and (b) expressly limiting the categories of persons that can seek remedies under the statute we conclude, as did the court below, that a plaintiff such as Klein who falls outside those categories lacks standing. *See Water Transp. Ass'n v. ICC*, 722 F.2d 1025, 1028–29 & n. 2 (2d Cir. 1983); *see also Am. Agric. Movement Inc. v. Chicago Bd. of Trade*, 977 F.2d 1147, 1153 (7th Cir. 1992) (finding that § 22 of the CEA forecloses remedies on behalf of non-traders), *aff'd in part, rev'd in part on other grounds by Sanner v. Chicago Bd. of Trade,* 62 F.3d 918 (7th Cir. 1995). *Cf. Nicholas v. Saul Stone & Co.*, 224 F.3d 179, 187 (3d Cir. 2000).

Klein's main response to this reading of the statute is that the remedies of § 22 are not limited to those who actually traded and that it has standing because, as the legislative history demonstrates, Congress intended to protect those such as itself who were injured in the course of trading on a contract market. According to Klein, the legislative history shows that Congress's main concern in drafting § 22 was to protect "market participants" who suffered actual losses arising from a transaction on the futures market. Klein contends that Congress intended the restrictions on standing to prevent suits on speculative damages to assets subject to price fluctuations on the commodities markets but which are not the subject of transactions. Affording standing to a FCM, such as Klein, is consistent with these purposes because a FCM that has experienced catastrophic losses, that were caused by a customer who had engaged in manipulation, has suffered what Congress had in mind: actual, non-speculative damages resulting directly from transactions on a commodities exchange.

This argument founders on the clear text of the statute. Section 22(b)'s remedies are expressly available only to a private litigant who "engaged in any transaction on or subject to the rules" of contract markets or other registered entities. As noted, Klein was not an owner of P-Tech contracts traded by First West. To the contrary, Klein was required by NYCC Rules to keep the options in a segregated First West account and not to co-mingle assets. Klein did not fall within any of the categories enumerated in § 22(a)(1)(A–D). Because we conclude the statute is clear, we decline Klein's invitation to parse the legislative history. *See* 7 U.S.C. § 25(a); *Lee v. Bankers Trust Co.*, 166 F.3d 540, 544 (2d Cir. 1999) ("It is axiomatic that the plain meaning of a statute controls its interpretation and that judicial review must end at the statute's unambiguous terms." (internal citations omitted)).

In the alternative, Klein contends that it has standing under CEA to challenge the NYBOT Defendants as a "forced" purchaser and seller of securities. Klein contends that the Supreme Court in *Blue Chip Stamps v. Manor Drug Stores*, 421 U.S. 723, 95 S. Ct. 1917, 44 L. Ed. 2d 539 (1975), after confirming that the federal securities laws confer an implied private right of action, granted standing under § 10(b) of the Securities Act of 1934 to securities brokers as "forced" purchasers or sellers, in situations where they, as clearing members, suffered damages arising from obligations to guarantee their customers' trades. Klein argues that as a FCM and clearing member, it was subject to federal statutes as well as the rules and by-laws of NYBOT, NYFE, and NYCC that required Klein to maintain funds guaranteeing its customers' transactions on the contract market. In his brief on appeal, Klein asserts that it assumed "a very real investment risk that the commodity contracts its customers traded would maintain or increase in value, a risk that is identical to that taken by any purchaser or seller of a commodity contract who is granted standing under the CEA." In sum, Klein argues that it has standing because it faced essentially the same risks as a purchaser or seller of commodities contracts. We disagree.

It is undisputed that Klein was not a trader of P-Tech contracts. Moreover, Klein did not own the P-Tech contracts at issue. Rather, First West, not Klein, traded in P-Tech contracts. Indeed, as the district court recognized, Klein stated in its complaint that it had no financial interest in the First West trading activity and had nothing to do with its trading decisions. Consequently, regardless of whether the First West trading position rose or declined in value, Klein had no interest in any of the resulting profits or investments losses. As the district court observed, "Klein suffered damages because of its customer First West's inability to cover its margin call. . . ." *Klein*, 2005 U.S. Dist. LEXIS 2720, 2005 WL 427713, at *4. Thus, Klein's loss was a credit loss, not a trading loss.

Because § 10(b) and Rule 10(b)(5) are implied causes of action, their "boundaries are left to judicial inference." *Grace v. Rosenstock*, 228 F.3d 40, 46 (2d Cir. 2000). The securities laws discussed in *Blue Chip Stamps*—§ 10(b) of the Securities Act of 1934 and Rule 10(b)(5)—contain no corollary to the express limitations on standing expressly imposed by CEA § 22(b). Section 22 was enacted as part of the Futures Trading Act of

1982 in response to *Merrill Lynch, Pierce, Fenner & Smith, Inc. v. Curran*, 456 U.S. 353, 102 S. Ct. 1825, 72 L. Ed. 2d 182 (1982), where the Supreme Court recognized an implied right of action under the CEA. In response, Congress enacted CEA § 22 but enumerated the only circumstances under which a civil litigant could assert a private right of action for a violation of the CEA or CFTA regulations. *See* H.R. Rep. No. 565, Pt. I, 97th Cong., 2d Sess. 57 (1982), reprinted in 1982 U.S.C.C.A.N. 3871, 3906. Congress went on to emphasize that the private right of action in CEA § 22 "shall be the exclusive remedy . . . available to any person who sustains a loss as a result of" a violation of the CEA. 7 U.S.C. § 25(b)(5). Enforcing the statute that Congress wrote, we conclude Klein lacks standing because it was not "engaged in any transaction on or subject to the rules" of a contract market and did not suffer any "actual losses that resulted from such transaction" as required by § 22 of the CEA. * * *

For the reasons discussed, the judgment of the district court is affirmed.

NOTE

1. The Supreme Court granted a writ of certiorari in the Klein case. 550 U.S. 956 (2007). Oral arguments were heard. However, before a decision was rendered, the parties settled the matter, thus leaving the Second Circuit decision intact. 552 U.S. 1085 (2007) (cert. dismissed).

BOSCO V. SERHANT

836 F.2d 271 (7th Cir. 1987), cert. denied sub nom., 486 U.S. 1056 (1988)

POSNER, CIRCUIT JUDGE.

This unwieldy commodities-fraud case, rich in parties and issues, comes to us after a five-week trial that produced a record of several thousand pages. However, the essential facts are simple (and we shall make them even simpler, to the extent this can be done without distorting our analysis), and many of the issues require little or even no discussion.

At the heart of the fraud was Robert Serhant, who between 1980 and 1982 offered investors a "Hedge-Spread Program" that he said would work as follows. For every $100,000 invested, Serhant would use $97,000 to buy a 90-day U.S. Treasury bill having a value at maturity of approximately $100,000 (this was a period of high interest rates) and would invest the remaining $3,000 in Treasury bill futures traded on the Chicago Mercantile Exchange, of which he was a member. He told investors that their risk would essentially be limited to the interest on the Treasury bill, because, at worst, at the end of 90 days they would have $100,000 (more or less)—the $97,000 principal of the Treasury bill plus interest thereon for 90 days. They would have lost only the interest they would have earned if the full $100,000 rather than $97,000, had been invested in Treasury bills. The "Program" was a gimmick, of course; the investors would be no better off than if they gave Serhant just $3,000 each. And it was misleading, as we shall see, to suggest that an investor could lose no more than the amount of the investment used to buy futures.

To do the actual trading of the futures Serhant needed the services of both a clearing member of the Exchange, whose function is to guarantee that each party to a trade will make good on his commitment, and a futures commission merchant, who acts as custodian of the investors' funds. (On the mechanics of commodities trading, and especially the role of the clearing member, see *United States v. Dial*, 757 F.2d 163, 164–66 (7th Cir. 1985); *Bernstein v. Lind-Waldock & Co.*, 738 F.2d 179, 181 (7th Cir. 1984); *Leist v. Simplot*, 638 F.2d 283, 286–88 (2d Cir. 1980), aff'd under the name of *Merrill Lynch, Pierce, Fenner & Smith v. Curran*, 456 U.S. 353, 72 L. Ed. 2d 182, 102 S. Ct. 1825 (1982); Fishman, *Commodities Futures: An Introduction for Lawyers*, 65 Chi. Bar Record 306, 309 (1984); Chicago Board of Trade, Commodity Trading Manual (1982).) For most of the period of the fraud, Serhant used K & S Commodities, Inc. (owned by Messrs. Schiller and Krumhorn) as both his clearing agent and futures commission merchant.

Serhant's scheme was fraudulent in three respects. First, he invested not 3 percent but almost 100 percent of the investors' money in Treasury bill futures, thus making the investments far riskier than the investors had originally supposed they would be. Erroneously predicting trends in short-term interest rates, Serhant lost $21 million of the $51 million invested in the Hedge-Spread Program. He didn't pocket the money; he just lost it in trading.

Second, he tried to conceal the losses from the investors by various dishonest tricks such as "allocating" profits to investors who had suffered losses. Suppose Serhant made a "block" sale (that is, a consolidated sale of futures contracts held in different accounts, see *United States v. Dial, supra*, 757 F.2d at 165, in this case accounts of different customers) of two futures contracts, at a price of $2 a contract. And suppose that he had paid $3 for one of the contracts and $1 for the other and that the first contract had been bought for the account of an investor who had later suffered large losses and the second contract for the account of a new investor, who had suffered no losses; Serhant might switch the accounts so that the account of the first investor would show a profit (of $1) that offset some of that investor's losses. As in a Ponzi scheme, Serhant was using newly invested money to make old investors think they were earning profits rather than losing their shirts.

Third, Serhant exaggerated the degree to which the Hedge-Spread Program, had it been implemented as represented, was secure. In commodities trading you can lose more money than you invest, even if you ignore margin calls. A futures contract is a contract to buy or sell a commodity or a financial instrument at a specified price on a specified date, and should an investor be unsuccessful in unloading the contract as the price shifts against him (he might be unsuccessful because the price changed precipitately or simply because his broker failed to offset the contract), he may end up having to ante up more than he invested.

For these various frauds Serhant is now serving an 11-year prison sentence.

The investors whom he fleeced brought this civil suit (actually suits, but we'll suppress that irrelevant detail to simplify the opinion) against a variety of individuals and institutions. Many of the defendants settled before trial, to the tune of more than $8 million. Some did not settle—Serhant, and companies owned by him which he used as vehicles for the fraudulent scheme; K & S, and one of its co-owners, Krumhorn; the Chicago Mercantile Exchange; and the First Bank of Schaumburg. The district court granted summary judgment for the exchange and for the bank but allowed the case to go to the jury against the other defendants, which is to say against the Serhant and K & S groupings. The jury, asked to assess compensatory damages separately against each defendant, returned a verdict that awarded total damages—after some trebling under RICO, see 18 U.S.C. § 1964(c), which Serhant and his companies were held to have violated—of about $3.3 million. Most of the assessment is against the Serhant group of defendants. Only $120,001 was assessed against K & S and $60,001 against Krumhorn. Schiller, the co-owner of K & S, had settled before trial for $350,000.

The plaintiffs appeal from the judgment in favor of the exchange and the bank, and from the district court's refusal to set aside the damage judgment against the other defendants as being too low. Those defendants cross-appeal, contending that they should have had judgment in their favor. We discuss the liability of the Mercantile Exchange first, then the adequacy of the damages judgment, then the liability of K & S and Krumhorn and the bearing of the settlements generally, and last the liability of the First Bank of Schaumburg. There are a few other issues worthy of some discussion and we'll tuck them in at convenient places.

The plaintiffs seek to rope in the Exchange under either of two sections of the Commodity Exchange Act. Section 5a(8), 7 U.S.C. § 7a(8), as it read in the period relevant to this case, required each exchange to "enforce all by-laws, rules, regulations, and resolutions, made or issued by it . . ., which relate to terms and conditions in contracts of sale . . ., and which have been approved by the [Commodity Futures Trading]

Commission. . . ." Section 13(a), 7 U.S.C. § 13c(a), provided that "any person who . . . willfully aids, abets, counsels, . . . [etc.] a violation of any of the provisions of this [Act] . . . may be held responsible in administrative proceedings under this [Act] for such violation as principal." The Act nowhere expressly authorized private damages suits against violators of either section. The Futures Trading Act of 1982 changed this, see 7 U.S.C. § 25(b)(1)(A); 7 U.S.C. § 13c(a), but the parties agree that the changes are inapplicable to this case. Proceeding under the unamended statute, the district court held that a private right of action is implicit in section 13c(a) (aiding and abetting) but not in section 5a(8) (failure to enforce rules), and so dismissed the section 5a(8) claim. Then he granted summary judgment for the defendants on the aiding and abetting claim, on the ground that there was insufficient evidence to create a triable issue. * * *

In the case of a massive multi-million dollar fraud facilitated by an exchange's failure to enforce rules designed to prevent fraud, it can be argued that the remedies provided by the Act are inadequate and that that is why Congress amended the Act in 1982 to make the right to sue an exchange guilty of such failures explicit. Since we are proceeding under the Act as it stood before 1982, Congress's intentions in 1982 are relevant only insofar as they cast light on the understanding of the earlier Congresses that created the Act in the form in which it existed at that time. They cast this much light: Congress did not believe in 1982 (or at least did not say) that it was changing course and revising an earlier compromise that had ruled out effective remedies for violations of the Act.

. . . The fact that the cases decided before 1974 did not involve any violations of exchange rules designed to prevent fraud as such, but only violations of rules designed to prevent price manipulation, is immaterial, for some of the cases involved violation of the *statutory* prohibition against fraud, and anyway price manipulation is a species of fraud. Although *Curran* jostles uneasily with other, and apparently still authoritative, statements of the principles governing implied rights of actions, see, e.g., *Cort v. Ash*, 422 U.S. 66, 78, 45 L. Ed. 2d 26, 95 S. Ct. 2080 (1975), the Mercantile Exchange concedes that if the plaintiffs can fit themselves within the principles of *Curran* they have an implied right of action.

Even if the district judge erred in dismissing the plaintiffs' section 5a(8) claim at the threshold, however, the error would be harmless if as the Exchange argues there was not enough evidence to create a triable issue with regard to its alleged failure to enforce its rules.

The express private right, created in 1982, to sue an exchange for failing to enforce rules that it is required to enforce is limited to situations where the exchange's failure is in "bad faith." 7 U.S.C.

§ 25(b)(4). In so limiting the right Congress was merely codifying what had become the settled understanding of the scope of the implied right of action recognized in *Curran* and other cases. *Brawer v. Options Clearing Corp.*, 807 F.2d 297, 302 (2d Cir. 1986); *Sam Wong & Son, Inc. v. New York Mercantile Exchange, supra*, 735 F.2d at 676 n. 30. By "bad faith," however, the cases did not mean actual participation in fraud (or other misconduct), for such conduct would make the exchange liable directly under section 4b, 7 U.S.C. § 6b, the anti-fraud section. Yet, read naturally, the words seem to imply that the exchange's failure to enforce must be more than merely negligent. How much more? In ordinary English "bad faith" implies a deliberate wrong rather than just failing to come up to an objective standard of care, which is what negligence is. Therefore, as an original matter (an important qualification, as will appear) we might conclude that the plaintiffs in this case would have to prove that the Mercantile Exchange knew that a rule it was required to enforce was being violated, or—what is in fact a form of knowledge—deliberately closed its eyes so that it would not discover what it strongly suspected was going on. This is the form of reckless disregard that we discussed recently in the context of prison officials' liability for failing to protect prisoners from dangers to their health or safety. See *Duckworth v. Franzen*, 780 F.2d 645, 651–56 (7th Cir. 1985); cf. *United States v. Ramsey*, 785 F.2d 184, 189 (7th Cir. 1986); *United States v. Josefik*, 753 F.2d 585, 589 (7th Cir. 1985).

The Mercantile Exchange's Rule 536 requires that "at the time of execution [of an order], every order received from a customer . . . must be in writing, *with the customer's designation indicated.*" One purpose of the language we have italicized is to prevent what we earlier called "allocation"—an integral part of Serhant's fraud. When a member of the Exchange wants to make a trade, he must transmit his order to the floor. This is usually done by phone to save time. The floor broker writes down the order dictated over the phone, then steps away from the phone booth and, by means of hand signals, transmits the order to the "pit," where it is executed. He then makes a note of the transaction, which is later posted to the customer's account with the futures commission merchant. Often Serhant would be placing a block order on behalf of a number of investors in his Hedge-Spread Program. Each investor had a customer designation (a number), which Serhant could have dictated over the phone to the floor broker; but he refused to do this, on the ground that it was too time-consuming and that recording the customer designations when the memo of the transaction came back from the floor satisfied the rule. An officer of K & S disagreed and complained to the Exchange. At a conference where she and Serhant argued their opposing points of view, the Exchange's representative agreed that it would be too much of a burden on Serhant to require him to dictate the customer designations to the floor broker. Later the Exchange conducted an audit of Serhant's records to make sure that the customer designations appeared on the office copies of the floor brokers' memos of transactions; they did.

So the Exchange knew that Serhant was not dictating customer designations to the floor broker, but the anterior question, on which liability under section 5a(8) depends, is whether in failing to do this Serhant was violating Rule 536. Although read literally the rule requires that the customer designation be on the order at the moment of execution, the Exchange interpreted the rule as requiring merely that the designation appear on it within a reasonable time after execution. Is this a permissible interpretation? There is a danger that if the order is executed before the customer designation is placed on it, the customer's representative (Serhant) will bide his time and not place the designation on the order when it comes back to his office until he knows how each customer is doing and can shuffle designations around as may be necessary to conceal losses. In fact this is what happened. But the issue presented to the Exchange was not whether Serhant was likely to play any such games but whether the customer designation could be affixed to the floor order immediately after rather than immediately before execution. Concerned with the delay that would be created if the designations had to be on the floor order before it was executed, the Exchange decided that Serhant could wait till right after the order was executed. Even if this interpretation of Rule 536 was incorrect or even unreasonable, it would not be in bad faith under the demanding standard suggested. Cf. *Trans World Airlines, Inc. v. Thurston*, 469 U.S. 111, 126– 27, 83 L. Ed. 2d 523, 105 S. Ct. 613 (1985).

Now in fact Serhant often waited much longer than this to put on the customer designations, and therefore he was violating the rule even as interpreted by the Exchange. The Exchange argues that there is no evidence either that it knew this or that it went out of its way to avoid knowing because it was fearful of discovering something it would rather not know. It argues, in short, that it acted in good faith. But this argument works only if "bad faith" in the 1982 amendments, and (what is more germane to this case, which arises under the earlier statute) in the case law that the amendments codified, has the same meaning it bears in ordinary English. The law does not always use the words "bad faith" in their ordinary-language sense, see, e.g., *Harlow v. Fitzgerald*, 457 U.S. 800, 818, 73 L. Ed. 2d 396, 102 S. Ct. 2727 (1982); 1 Anderson on the Uniform Commercial Code § 1–201:86 (3d ed. 1981), and, in the present setting, involving an exchange's failure to enforce its rule in accordance with the exchange's own interpretation, the courts, including our own, have treated the term "bad faith" as if it read "negligence." See *Hochfelder v. Midwest Stock Exchange*, 503 F.2d 364, 368 n. 2 (7th Cir. 1974), a case involving the duty of self-regulation under the Securities Exchange Act rather than the Commodity Exchange Act but not distinguishable on any principled ground; also *Rich v. New York Stock Exchange*, 522 F.2d 153, 155 n. 4 (2d Cir. 1975).

Thus, if an exchange's regulation imposes a duty that the exchange *should* know is being flouted, the exchange is acting wrongfully—in an attenuated sense, perhaps, but one sufficient under the cases we have cited to demonstrate bad faith. The test is different if the exchange injures a trader through the exercise of a discretionary power, such as the power to take emergency actions to prevent substantial losses; then more must be shown to constitute bad faith—either that the exchange acted unreasonably or that it had an improper motivation. See *Sam Wong & Son, Inc. v. New York Mercantile Exchange, supra,* 735 F.2d at 670–78; *Daniel v. Board of Trade of City of Chicago,* 164 F.2d 815, 819 (7th Cir. 1947). Discretion implies latitude for judgment, and commodity exchanges must not be deterred from exercising judgment by the prospect of heavy liability if they make a mistake.

Thus in the present case, if the alleged bad faith were just the Mercantile Exchange's interpreting its rule to allow Serhant to place customer designations on orders shortly after rather than before or at the moment of execution, the higher standard for proving bad faith would be applicable. Interpretation is often, and was here, discretionary, cf. *Homemakers North Shore, Inc. v. Bowen,* 832 F.2d 408, slip op. at 7–8 (7th Cir. 1987); and the Exchange's interpretation, while somewhat free, was not unreasonable, and there is no evidence of improper motivation. But with regard to Serhant's violations of Rule 536 (as interpreted by the Exchange), there was no scope for the exercise of discretion and hence no excuse (under the cases) for the Exchange's carelessness in ignoring evidence that such violations were being committed. Furthermore, despite the audit there is some evidence that the Exchange knew that Serhant was delaying up to six hours in placing customer designations on the order form—a delay too long for the Exchange to deem him in compliance with its regulation, even when the regulation is interpreted to allow reasonable delay.

So the plaintiffs appear to have a strong case under section 5a(8)—though not one on which they can recover any damages from the Mercantile Exchange in this case * * * [Auth. note: damage discussion omitted]

Affirmed In Part And Reversed In Part.

7. CLEARINGHOUSE REGULATION

Each futures contract traded on a DCM must be cleared through a designated clearing organization (DCO), commonly referred to as a clearinghouse or central counterparty (CCP). Each DCO, like a DCM, must be approved by and registered with the CFTC [7 U.S.C. § 7a–1]. A

DCO must meet certain core principles, including governance standards, system safeguards, default procedures, treatment of customer funds, settlement procedures, risk management and financial resources. [7 U.S.C. § 7a–1(c)].

BEFORE THE DEPARTMENT OF THE TREASURY
WASHINGTON, D.C.
Treas–Do–2007–0018 (2007)

The Department of Justice ("Department") is pleased to submit these comments in response to the Department of the Treasury's ("Treasury's") request for comments on the Regulatory Structure Associated with Financial Institutions, 72 F.R. 58939, October 17, 2007.

Based on its extensive experience investigating competitive conditions in various financial markets, including financial futures, options, and equities, the Department believes that certain regulatory policies governing financial futures may have inhibited competition among financial futures exchanges, potentially discouraging innovation and perpetuating high prices for exchange services.

More specifically, the Department believes that the control exercised by futures exchanges over clearing services—including (a) where positions in a futures contract are held ("open interest"), and (b) whether positions may be treated as fungible or offset with positions held in contracts traded on other exchanges ("margin offsets")—has made it difficult for exchanges to enter and compete in the trading of financial futures contracts. If greater head-to-head competition for the exchange of futures contracts could develop, we would expect it to result in greater innovation in exchange systems, lower trading fees, reduced tick size, and tighter spreads, leading to increased trading volume.

In contrast to futures exchanges, equity and options exchanges do not control open interest, fungibility, or margin offsets in the clearing process. This lack of control appears to have facilitated head-to-head competition between exchanges for equities and options, resulting in low execution fees, narrow spreads, and high trading volume. Equities and options execution systems are also very sophisticated and feature-rich, more so than futures contract execution systems.

Although characteristics of the equities and options markets differ from those of financial futures markets, the clearing processes and related regulatory framework in equities and options markets appear to provide useful lessons in the futures arena. In light of the potential competitive benefits that could flow from regulatory changes that would facilitate competition in financial futures exchange markets, the Department recommends that Treasury propose a thorough review of futures clearing and its alternatives. * * *

Under the current clearing framework, competition tends to be limited to that which occurs when a new contract, *i.e.*, one addressing a market risk not addressed or not adequately addressed by existing products, is introduced. The introduction of a new contract by one futures exchange frequently prompts another exchange to offer a similar contract, and a battle to garner all the liquidity in the contract ensues. After one exchange wins most of the liquidity in the contract, the other exchange usually exits. In its investigations, the Department has found that, in each significant financial futures contract traded in the United States, one exchange has virtually all of the liquidity. Using the 10-year Treasury note future as an example, CME has a market share of essentially 100%. The "winner-takes-all" character of futures exchange competition is a function of liquidity: the more liquid the market, the greater the chance of execution at favorable prices. As a result, the market for a particular contract will tend to concentrate on a single exchange. This in turn gives the exchange a marked advantage over smaller firms and new entrants.

While network effects provide a significant impetus toward the concentration of trading in any particular type of futures contract on a single exchange, they are not by themselves an insurmountable barrier to competition. Liquidity network effects of this sort have been successfully overcome in financial markets where regulatory policy facilitates competition among exchanges. In financial futures markets, however, efforts by competitors to overcome an initial liquidity disadvantage are further handicapped by the liquidity advantages of incumbent exchanges that flow from their control of clearing. Specifically, the Department believes that the control of clearing by incumbent futures exchanges prevents buyers and sellers from accessing *existing* liquidity if they trade the same (or highly correlated) contract on another exchange, thereby making it significantly more difficult for entrants to gain sufficient liquidity to provide sustained competition with the incumbent.

Efforts over the last decade by exchanges to enter the U.S. financial futures markets with products that competed head-to-head with existing products, all of which failed, show the effect of exchange-controlled clearing and the potential competitive benefits of successful entry. In a number of instances where entry has been attempted, the prospect of entry forced a substantial, but only temporary, competitive response from the incumbent exchange. These competitive responses benefitted the market, but those benefits proved transitory because, under the existing regime of clearing, the entrant was unable to establish sufficient liquidity to maintain a sustained competitive presence and exited the market.

The Department is aware of three principal arguments in favor of the current regime of exchange controlled clearing in futures markets: (1) that sufficient reward to promote innovation can only be assured if replica contracts are kept off the market and that exchange controlled clearing helps achieve that objective; (2) trading of futures on multiple exchanges could adversely affect traders by fracturing liquidity and diminishing market depth; and (3) the current system minimizes the risk of default

The first contention, that the current structure is necessary to provide exchanges an incentive to innovate new futures contracts, boils down to the contention that competition is inconsistent with incentives to innovate. In fact, however, experience indicates that competition can spur firms to innovate by developing new products or making their existing products more attractive (including though product change as well as reduced prices and improved quality). Thus, any study of regulatory change that would eliminate exchange control of clearing would need to consider the important incentives that may be created by competition.

A second argument offered in favor of preserving the current regime is that a change in regulatory policy that would facilitate the trading of futures contracts on multiple exchanges would adversely impact buyers and sellers by fracturing liquidity, diminishing market depth and price transparency, and by making it more difficult for buyers and sellers to find the best price to execute transactions. The market response to Eurex's and Euronext Liffe's suggests that such concerns are not well founded. In both cases, new entry coincided with substantial *increases* in trading activity in the products traded. Experience with new entrants in the options and equities markets is to the same effect. In each case, market volumes increased and all indicators of market performance—fees, volume, spreads—either improved or did not change. Indeed, experience in options markets suggests that the likely effect of a change would be significantly lower exchange fees, narrower spreads, and greater trading volume.

A third argument is that the current system reduces risk to the market of participant default as transparency of market exposure is enhanced when related market positions of individual customers can be captured in one place. Exchange control of where products are cleared, however, does not appear necessary to achieve this result. Both the options and equities models have successfully protected investors from default.

NOTES

1. In approving a merger of the two largest U.S. futures exchanges in 2007, the Department of Justice also stated that:

> WASHINGTON—June 11, 2007: The Department of Justice's Antitrust Division issued the following statement today after announcing the closing of its investigation into the proposed acquisition of CBOT Holdings Inc. by Chicago Mercantile Exchange Holdings Inc.:

After an extensive investigation of both the Chicago Mercantile Exchange's (CME) proposed acquisition of CBOT and the 2003 agreement under which CME provides clearing services to CBOT, the Antitrust Division determined that the evidence does not indicate that either the transaction or the clearing agreement is likely to reduce competition substantially. More specifically, the Division determined that although the two exchanges account for most financial futures (and in particular, interest rate futures) traded on exchanges in the United States: their products are not close substitutes and seldom compete head to head, but rather provide market participants with the means to mitigate different risk; and they are, absent the merger, unlikely to introduce new products that compete directly with the other's entrenched products, in part due to the difficulty of overcoming an incumbent exchange's liquidity advantage in an established futures contract.

The Division also looked carefully at whether the combination would lead to less innovation and fewer new products. While the evidence suggests that competition between CME and CBOT has, at times, provided some incentive for them to develop and offer new products, it does not indicate that continued innovation depends on competition between the parties. Rather, the evidence indicates that the two principal impetuses for innovation have been, and will continue to be, the prospect of winning business from the over-the-counter market and the potential to offer products that the OTC community can use to hedge the risk associated with its activities.

Finally, the Division investigated whether the combination might foreclose entry by other exchanges into financial futures as a result of the integration of virtually all financial future contracts into a single clearinghouse. The evidence indicates that neither the clearing agreement nor the transaction will foreclose entry by other exchanges. Indeed, the New York Stock Exchange, in connection with its acquisition of Euronext.liffe, recently announced its intention to offer futures products, and the Intercontinental Exchange (ICE), in connection with its bid to purchase control of CBOT, has publicly stated its intent to offer interest rate futures regardless of whether its bid succeeds.

Statement Of The Department Of Justice Antitrust Division On Its Decision To Close Its Investigation Of Chicago Mercantile Exchange Holdings Inc.'s Acquisition Of CBOT Holdings Inc. (June 11, 2007).

2. Stock options, as described in Chapter 5, are traded on multiple stock exchanges but are cleared only through one securities clearinghouse, i.e., the Options Clearing Corporation (OCC). In contrast, DCMs have each established their own clearinghouse to clear futures contracts traded on the respective DCMs. This lack of fungibility, which exists within the stock option industry, has resulted in strict "vertical" clearing models whereby

products traded on a DCM may only be cleared through the affiliated DCO. This model has adversely prevented new futures exchanges from emerging and offering similar futures products. As also described in Chapter 5, a single clearinghouse for stock options fostered competition, resulting in better pricing.

3. Under the Dodd-Frank Act that was enacted in 2010, each facility that will offer swaps to be traded, whether the facility is a DCM or a newly-designated "swap execution facility" (SEF), must give the counterparty the right to choose the DCO to clear the swap. This "horizontal" clearing model is obviously significantly different than the vertical clearing model used for futures.

8. MARGIN REQUIREMENTS

RONALD H. FILLER
ASK THE PROFESSOR—WHAT IS MARGIN AND HOW IS IT (OR SHOULD BE) DETERMINED?
29 Fut. & Derv. L. Rep. 15 (March 2009)

"Margin" for futures contracts is such a strange and complex term. Whoever first called minimum exchange-traded futures deposits "margin" should be shot in my opinion as it has created much confusion over the past many years. The term "margin" for futures, which implies a performance bond or surety bond concept, is entirely different from the term "margin" for securities, which reflects a stock loan arrangement. I will try and explain the concept of margin, and its purpose, in this column.

The Board of Governors of the Federal Reserve System ("FED") has adopted Regulation T ("Reg. T") which states, in essence, that a broker-dealer may not lend its customers more than 50%, nor extend credit in an amount greater than 50%, of the value of the securities acquired in a securities account. Reg. T thus governs the amount of margin that a broker-dealer must collect and maintain in the customer's securities account whenever securities are bought or sold short. It also governs the amount of customer funds that may be withdrawn if that customer has opened a margin account with that broker-dealer.

These so-called margin accounts are also governed by securities SROs, such as the New York Stock Exchange ("NYSE"). NYSE Rule 431 [now superseded by FINRA Rule 4210], in particular, establishes a minimum maintenance margin requirement of 25% for long positions and 30% for short positions held in the underlying margin account.

Accordingly, margin in a securities account, in essence, reflects a loan arrangement between the broker-dealer and the customer, the amount of the loan being the difference between the respective stock purchase amount and the current equity value in the account. This is real debt that is incurred. For example, if Customer A buys 100 shares of XYZ stock @ $50.00 per share, Customer A would need to deposit a minimum of $2,500.00 with the broker-dealer and borrow the balance.

Pursuant to the standard Stock Margin Agreement, if the customer does not maintain the minimum maintenance margin requirements established by that broker-dealer for its margin account, then the broker-dealer may take certain actions against the customer, including the liquidation of some or all of the open securities positions in the margin account which, in effect, transforms the equity in the margin account to cash. The customer is nevertheless liable for any outstanding indebtedness still owed by that customer to the broker-dealer following such liquidation or close-out. So, even though the concept of "margin" is so dramatically different between a futures account and a securities margin account, this concept of permissible actions that may be taken by a broker-dealer or futures commission merchant ("FCM") is a constant, as explained below. In futures, margin takes on a different meaning.

Margin, or "initial margin" ("IM") as it is often called, reflects a performance bond or surety bond, whereby the customer of an FCM agrees, pursuant to the Futures Customer Agreement, to deposit and maintain, at all times, the initial margin required by the FCM for that customer's account. Typically, for most large institutional futures customers, the IM requirement represents the minimum margin requirement set by the respective exchange for that particular futures product but the FCM may, pursuant to the Futures Customer Agreement, reserve the contractual right to require the futures customer to maintain an amount of initial margin greater (but never lower) than the minimum amount set by the exchange. As in a securities margin account, the futures customer must maintain an amount of equity, often called the net liquidating value ("NLV"), in its account that equals or exceeds the initial margin requirements. And if a futures customer does not meet this minimum amount requirement each day, the FCM may exercise its contractual right by claiming that the customer's account has resulted in an Event of Default, as defined in the Futures Customer Agreement, and may thus liquidate any and all of the open futures positions.

With respect to futures, the amount of margin required by an exchange is normally calculated based on an historical price basis, typically a one day, two standard deviation methodology. This mathematical analysis rationalizes that the minimum margin requirement for that particular futures product should cover, historically, approximately 95% of the underlying price changes that occurred over a certain period of time, typically the past 30 to 60 days, depending on the formula used by that clearing house. FCMs may, or even should, evaluate their large futures customers in different light, applying a higher standard, such as a three day or even a five day, two or more standard deviation test, especially if such customers are engaged in a prime brokerage arrangement with that firm, as other products involved in the prime brokerage arrangement apply a different margin payment obligation.

For example, the payment for stock purchases is T+3 whereas the payment for futures is typically T+1. Thus, unlike margin for securities, which, as noted above, involve a loan arrangement, margin in a futures account takes on a more credit risk feature as no loan exists. However, while the end game is the same, that is, the broker-dealer and/or FCM may protect itself by contract by claiming that an Event of Default has occurred, thus initiating the contractual right to take further action (e.g., liquidate some or all of the open positions), the amount of futures margin required to be paid may vary by each firm depending on the creditworthiness of the client and by the product traded. In a securities margin account, for example, FED and Reg. T rules set the requirements for the minimum amount of equity that must be maintained at all times in the margin account. However, in a futures account, exchange rules normally dictate the minimum amount of initial margin that must be maintained but the FCM may impose margin requirements greater than the amount set by the respective exchange.

Certain CFTC rules also impact the margin requirements. Another important concept involving margin is the amount that an FCM or BD must pay their respective clearing houses based on margin amounts due for their customer accounts. Most global clearing houses require the underlying clearing member firm to deposit an amount equal to the margin required for all positions on a "net" clearing basis. Thus, if one customer is long CBOT Treasury Bond futures contracts and another customer of that FCM is short CBOT Treasury Bond futures contracts, the FCM must still collect the required margin from both customers but would not be required to deposit any required margin amounts with the CME Clearing House.

Conversely, if the clearing house requires margin to be paid on a "gross" clearing basis, then the FCM would deposit the full amount of the IM due on all futures contracts, the aggregate amount of both the long and short positions, cleared by that respective clearing house. This concept of "net" vs. "gross" clearing dramatically impacts the obligations due customers of a defaulting clearing member firm. * * *

NOTES

1. Although several efforts had been made to grant the CFTC or other regulators authority to set margin for futures contracts, those efforts were largely defeated over the course of a number of years after the enactment of the CEA. The CFTC was given authority for oversight of margins on stock

index futures contracts after the stock market crash of 1987, but the CFTC delegated that authority back to the exchanges. See, Helen Parry, et al., Futures Trading Law and Regulation: 216 (1993) (describing that legislation). That circular action may seem strange, but the CFTC has the residual authority to act on those margins in the event of abuse or a systemic crisis.

2. The Dodd-Frank Act that was enacted in 2010 granted the CFTC limited authority to require margins that will protect the financial integrity of DCOs. However, the CFTC is prohibited from setting specific margin amounts. [7 U.S.C. § 12a(7)(D)]. Dodd-Frank Section 731 also allows regulators to set margins for uncleared swaps.

3. The concept of "portfolio margining" allows traders to aggregate their portfolio risk assessment in computing their margin requirements. This allows traders to reduce their margin requirements where they have positions that offset the risk in other positions. This process was hampered by requirements that customer funds and securities be held in separate segregated accounts when they fell under SEC control. The Dodd-Frank Act amended the Securities and Exchange of 1934 Act and the CEA to authorize joint broker-dealers/futures commission merchants to hold securities that are part of a portfolio margining program in a futures account. Securities products held in a futures account will be treated as futures contracts for purposes of the U.S. Bankruptcy Code. See, Ronald H. Filler, Ask the Professor: Portfolio Margining—How Will Dodd-Frank Impact Its Utilization?, 30 Fut. & Derv. L. Rep. 8 (Nov. 2010). See also a sample of a Cross Margin Netting Agreement (CMNA), which is used by brokerage firms when they provide margin financing to their clients (Appendix A to this Casebook).

4. As of November 2012, all futures margins received by an FCM must be forwarded to the respective clearinghouse on a "gross" margin basis. This means that the margin requirements for the FCM's customer short and long positions, even in the same futures contract month, cannot be netted against each other. Netting would permit only the net amount to be sent to the clearinghouse. In contrast, the gross margin requirement will require margins for both the long and short positions to be sent to the clearinghouse. See, CFTC, Derivatives Clearing Organization General Provisions and Core Principles, 76 Fed. Reg. 69334, 69439 (Nov. 8, 2011).

5. As discussed in Chapter 4, all futures customer assets, deemed to be "customer property," must be held by the FCM in a protected customer segregated account solely for the benefit of the customers. See Ronald Filler, Consumer Protection: How U.K. Client Money Rules Differ From the U.S. Customer Segregated Rules When a Custodian Firm Fails to Treat Customer Property Properly? 24 J. of Tax & Reg. of Fin. Instit. 25 (2011).

6. See also ADM Investor Services, Inc. v. Collins, 515 F.3d 753, 757–758 (7th Cir 2008), in which Judge Easterbrook stated:

"It should now be apparent that margin requirements in futures markets are not designed to protect investors . . . from adverse price movements. Margin protects counterparties from investors who may be unwilling or unable to keep their promises."

He then stated:

"Another way to see this point is to observe that balky customers are not in the zone of interests protected by margin-posting requirements."

MERRILL LYNCH, PIERCE, FENNER & SMITH, INC. V. BROOKS
548 F.2d 615 (5th Cir. Tex. 1977), cert. denied, 434 U.S. 855 (1977)

PER CURIAM

Essentially this case may be summarized as one where a commodities broker extended credit—over-extended that is—to a sophisticated commodity futures investor who at all times possessed knowledge of his deficient margin account status and who now contends he should not be required to pay back any remaining indebtedness because the extension of credit violated a rule or regulation of the Chicago Board of Trade. To adopt such an argument would permit commodity futures investors knowingly to accept extensions of credit from a broker which violate the Board of Trade's rules or regulations and repudiate losses that ensue or accept profits that follow. The only risk to the investor would be his initial deposit in a margin account, "initial margin", which represents only a fraction of the potential losses or hoped for profits. We do not accept this position and affirm on the basis of the District Court's opinion, *Brooks v. Merrill Lynch, Pierce, Fenner & Smith, Incorporated*, N.D. Tex., 1975, 404 F. Supp. 905.

In 1964, Brooks (Investor) initially opened a commodities margin account with Merrill Lynch, Pierce, Fenner & Smith, Inc. (Merrill Lynch) so he could buy and sell commodity futures contracts for investment purposes. Unlike many, Investor was not a speculator or dilettante. Rather, he has in general great business acumen and possesses in particular extensive knowledge about commodity investing.

During April 1973, Investor utilized his margin account and acquired twenty-four soybean meal futures contracts calling for delivery in July 1973. Unfortunately, his visions of aggrandizement vanished as the price of soybean meal increased which, under Rule 210 and Regulation 1822, P14 of the Chicago Board of Trade, necessitated that Investor increase the balance in his margin account. This increase is called the "maintenance margin".

Merrill Lynch did not notify Investor on April 12, 1973, the day his margin account became insufficient or "under margined", and not until May 1, 1973 did it demand that Investor deposit the contractually required "maintenance margin". Despite this failure to timely demand, Investor knew at all times of the deficiency in his account. In fact Investor went to Merrill Lynch's local office daily to check on his commodities transactions. Faced with this demand to meet the maintenance margin requirement, on May 7, 1973, Investor agreed in writing to be liable to Merrill Lynch for all amounts, including losses, that might be due under the margin contract.

As this letter agreement turned out to be insufficient to the broker's management and no effort was made by Investor to meet the known margin deficiency, Merrill Lynch proceeded on May 9 under its Commodity Account Agreement with Investor to cover Investor's twenty-four contracts and liquidated his margin account at an indebtedness of $198,262. This liquidation occurred later than it could have had the demand for maintenance margin been made on April 12. Rule 209 of the Chicago Board of Trade allows reasonable time to meet such a demand which is interpreted to be one hour in usual circumstances. * * *

When a business person with expertise in commodities trading and with full knowledge of all happenings and their ramifications accepts credit from a broker, as Investor has done, this Court will not relieve this Investor or any investor of an obligation unless singular circumstances exist. That a loss was incurred is not such a circumstance. For the foregoing reasons, the judgment of the District Court is affirmed.

BAKER v. EDWARD D. JONES & CO.

Comm. Fut. L. Rep. (CCH) ¶ 21,167 (C.F.T.C. 1981)

Opinion And Order Of The Commission

In an initial decision Administrative Law Judge Arthur L. Shipe found that a margin call made by respondent Edward D. Jones & Co., a registered futures commission merchant ("Jones & Co."), on complainant Robert L. Baker's commodity futures trading account was invalid because it was calculated in a manner inconsistent with the customer's reasonable expectations. The judge concluded, therefore, that Mr. Baker's refusal to meet the call was not improper and Jones & Co.'s subsequent trades, which liquidated the positions in Mr. Baker's commodity futures account over his objections, were unauthorized and thus violated Section 4b of the Commodity Exchange Act, as amended, 7 U.S.C. § 6b (1976). The judge awarded the complainant damages in the amount of $3,359.22, plus commissions and interest at a rate of 8% from January 1, 1976.

On June 21, 1978, the Commission granted Jones & Co.'s application for review of the initial decision to consider, inter alia, whether the

Administrative Law Judge correctly ruled that respondent's liquidation of complainant's commodity account on December 30, 1976, constituted unauthorized trading in violation of Section 4b of the Act.

In the initial decision, the judge found that Mr. Baker, who had previously traded in securities and commodities, opened an account with respondent on January 22, 1975. The complainant signed a standard Jones & Co. customer agreement and was also given a margin sheet which generally set forth Jones & Co's initial margin and maintenance margin requirements for commodity futures contracts. On December 18, 1975, the complainant held three long May 1976 plywood contracts. The initial margin requirement specified by the Jones & Co. margin sheet was $750 per plywood contract, and the maintenance margin was then $500 per plywood contract. At the end of trading on December 18, Mr. Baker had a credit balance in his trading account of $3,419 and an equity balance of $3,460.

The following day, December 19, Mr. Baker placed an order for an additional long March 1976 plywood contract at $153.50. Later that day he offset that contract at $150.00 resulting in a loss of $272.35 on the trade. The Administrative Law Judge described the subsequent turn of events:

> The market for May 1976 plywood closed at $151.00 on December 19, 1975, resulting in an unrealized loss to complainant of $787.74 on the three contracts that remained outstanding. This amount, plus the $272.35 loss on the day trade, reduced the equity in complainant's account to $2,359.19. A margin call was then issued, and received by complainant on December 24, 1976, for $368.46, computed as follows: $3,000 (initial margin for four contracts), less $2,359.19 (amount of equity remaining in complainant's account at the close of business on December 19, 1975), less $272.35 (the loss on the day trade). Record at 63–65 and Complaint and Answer. (Initial Decision at 5).

Upon receipt of the margin call, Mr. Baker visited respondent's local office and disputed it. Respondent's local agent referred the matter to his home office where the margin call was recomputed and confirmed. The complainant, continuing to dispute the propriety of the call, refused to meet it. On December 30, respondent's local agent informed the complainant that unless the amount due as the result of the December 19 margin call was paid immediately, respondent would liquidate Mr. Baker's account. Mr. Baker again refused to meet the call, and Jones & Co. offset Mr. Baker's three remaining contracts at $145.60. Respondent sent to Mr. Baker $1,118.27, the balance left in his account after liquidation. Mr. Baker claimed that the liquidation of his account under the circumstances was improper and that, since the price of plywood advanced after his positions were liquidated, he was entitled to an award in the amount of profit he would have realized had respondent not acted to liquidate his account.

The Administrative Law Judge agreed with complainant. The judge held that a futures commission merchant does not have absolute and unbridled discretionary power to liquidate a customer account, and that any liquidation must be in good faith and in light of the surrounding facts and circumstances (Initial Decision at 8–9). The judge concluded that the margin calls and the margin computation itself reflected internal policies of respondent that were: unknown to the customer; not contemplated by the customer agreement and margin sheet provided; not in conformity with his reasonable expectations; and, therefore, improper, in light of the surrounding facts and circumstances (Initial Decision at 10–14). On that basis the judge found that respondent had traded Mr. Baker's account without proper authorization and had thereby violated section 4b of the Act.

This case raises questions which are central to the relationship between margin and the financial integrity of all futures commission merchants and of this nation's commodity futures markets. We are asked to consider whether in the absence of any evidence that the firm computed its margin demand in bad faith or that the customer was misled or otherwise defrauded in connection with the firm's margin policy when entering into or maintaining a contractual relationship with Jones & Co., a customer may decline to meet a margin call with which he disagrees and, should his open positions be liquidated as a result, whether that liquidation may properly be held to constitute unauthorized trading in violation of Section 4b of the Act. For reasons which differ somewhat from those advanced by respondent and the amicus curiae who supports respondent, we conclude that Mr. Baker may not properly recover here and we reverse the Administrative Law Judge's decision.

Central to the Administrative Law Judge's disposition here is his conclusion that

> [t]he reasonable expectation of a customer under the considered contractual instruments would be that if his account met initial margin requirements when an order was completed, no additional margin would be required unless the account thereafter fell to a maintenance margin level. There is no indication in any of these instruments that an account will be "called back" to initial margin requirements merely because the market moves adversely after the order is completed. An internal policy of the broker contrary to the reasonable expectation created by the governing instruments cannot be

considered binding on the customer. While it is entirely possible that there may be circumstances where raising margins on existing positions may be warranted, or required, when such circumstances arise, the action can be taken in a straight-forward manner, not in an abstruse, retroactive computation of existing margin requirements. (Initial Decision at 11)." In our view, this statement fails to take sufficient cognizance of the special status accorded margin under the Commodity Exchange Act or under the contractual instruments and the exchange rules in question here. That status derives from the important role played by margin in the necessarily flexible process by which futures commission merchants control financial risk to themselves.

Turning first to the Commodity Exchange Act, we note that Sections 5a(12) and 8a(7) specifically except from the Commission's authority to approve, disapprove or alter contract market rules, those rules relating to the setting of margin levels. It is left to the exchanges to decide the appropriate margin levels necessary to assure that members and the members' customers have the financial wherewithal to effect and maintain market positions. Rule 210 of the Chicago Board of Trade is the basis upon which that exchange sets the margin levels for its members. Further, in terms broader than Rule 210, Rule 209 empowers firms which are members of the exchange, such as Jones & Co., to require from its customers additional deposits beyond the margin levels set by the exchange. Thus, Jones & Co. was clearly authorized by the contract market involved here to demand that its customers deposit funds in excess of the margin required by the contract market itself and in such amounts as respondent might deem necessary. But perhaps most importantly here, Mr. Baker himself agreed in paragraph 8 of the customer agreement he signed that he would "at all times maintain margins for said accounts, as required by [Jones & Co.] from time to time" (Exhibit No. II). This provision is not contrary to the Act, nor is it contrary to contract market rule. Rather, it contemplates, as does Rule 209, that the business judgment of Jones & Co. will govern the amount of margin which must be provided from time to time.

This leads us to a conclusion contrary to that reached by the Administrative Law Judge. Under the circumstances here Jones & Co. had the power to demand of customers such additional deposits as it deemed necessary at any time and for any reason based upon its own good faith business judgment. At least where that power is reserved by the customer agreement to the futures commission merchant, that is what the "reasonable expectation" of any customer must be. And given the agreement found here we cannot agree with the judge that Mr. Baker could have had any understanding other than that Jones & Co. possessed the power to demand the deposit of additional funds for any good faith business reason. While Mr. Baker might have hoped that the funds demanded would be no greater than that reflected on the margin sheet to which the Administrative Law Judge attaches such great significance, in light of the customer agreement we cannot conclude that Mr. Baker was entitled to rely solely upon the margin sheet as setting an absolute upper limit on his margin exposure.

This is not to say that if a futures commission merchant misrepresents its margin policy, thereby inducing transactions, or acts in bad faith in demanding additional deposits the result will be the same as that reached by us here. To the contrary, we will not permit the power to make legitimate business judgments to be perverted in a way which is tantamount to fraud. But under the circumstances of this case we are not persuaded by the evidence adduced by Mr. Baker that respondent either misrepresented its powers vis-à-vis margin or acted in bad faith in making its demand upon Mr. Baker.

In conclusion we want to stress that this decision is both a function of the special status of margin in the Act's regulatory scheme and of our desire that futures commission merchants have adequate means to assure their own financial integrity and thereby contribute to the financial integrity of the entire marketplace. Particularly in those market situations where a prompt response is required, a futures commission merchant is free to exercise its power to demand the deposit of additional funds by its customer and to liquidate an account without hesitation if the demand is not met. The exercise of those powers is available as a matter of business judgment, a judgment not curtailed by fear of subsequent claims of constructive fraud which have no basis.

Accordingly, IT IS HEREBY ORDERED that the initial decision is reversed and the complaint is dismissed.

NOTE

1. A claim that is sometimes made by securities market customers trading on margin is that they were damaged by a broker-dealer's violations of Regulation T, which imposes limits on the amount of money that can be borrowed to purchase stocks. [12 C.F.R. Part 220]. At one time, some courts found that such a private right of action was implied under the margin requirements of the Federal Reserve Board and the Securities Exchange Act of 1934 (Securities Exchange Act). Most courts, however, rejected such claims. Also, in 1970 Congress amended the Securities Exchange Act to make it illegal for any person to purchase securities in violation of Regulation T. This extended the prohibitions of the margin requirements of Regulation T to customers as well as to brokerage firms. This meant that the customer was in violation of margin requirements and could hardly claim greater fault on the part of the broker-dealer. See, 23A Jerry W. Markham and Thomas Lee

Hazen, Broker Dealer Operations Under Securities and Commodities Law: Financial Responsibilities, Credit Regulation, and Customer Protection, § 8:13 (discussing those cases).

9. MEMBERSHIP DENIAL PROCEEDINGS

Each SRO, including both DCMs and the other industry SROs, is a membership organization. As such, it must establish procedures to permit new members and member firms. One such procedure requires the SRO to establish a due process hearing whereby any firm or person, who is denied membership by the SRO's membership committee, has the right to a hearing.

These hearings are held before the SRO's Membership Committee. The Respondent is entitled to present evidence on his/her behalf and be represented by counsel. The Legal Department of the SRO represents the SRO. A transcript of the hearing is maintained. An adverse decision by the Membership Committee may be appealed to the SRO's Board of Directors and from there to the CFTC and then to the judiciary.

10. REVIEW OF SRO ACTIONS BY THE CFTC

The SRO disciplinary process is normally initiated by the issuance of a Complaint or Order filed against the member or member firm.

While each SRO does it slightly different, normally, most SROs have a Probable Cause Committee (PCC), which reviews the evidence provided by the SRO enforcement or market surveillance department and determines whether a Complaint should be issued. The PCC acts in essence like a grand jury, and is comprised of representatives from member firms of that SRO and public representatives.

The Respondent who receives the Complaint may try and settle the matter and not pursue further hearings. Most SROs utilize a different body or group to review the settlement offer discussions and accept or not accept their respective terms. The second group is commonly known as the Business Conduct Committee (BCC), which is also comprised of member firms of the SRO and public representatives. Persons who sit on the PCC and the BCC all come from the same pool.

If a settlement order is agreed to by all of the parties, this results in a final decision. The Respondent may instead elect to pursue a hearing so that the Respondent may be heard on the issues and matters comprising the Complaint. This hearing will also be heard by a different set of individuals who comprise the BCC. Once a final decision is rendered by the BCC, following the hearing, then the matter becomes final.

Either party to the hearing, including both the DCM and the Respondent, may appeal the decision to the DCM's Board of Directors.

The Board will then hold a hearing, and a final decision will be made. Any final Board of Directors decision may then be appealed to the CFTC, which will act as an appellate body. The CFTC's decision is reviewable by the judiciary. See, 13 Jerry W. Markham, Commodities Regulation: Fraud, Manipulation & Other Claims § 26:9 (2013) (describing cases addressing whether such an appeal is to be made to a district court or to a circuit court of appeals).

11. FLOOR BROKERS AND FLOOR TRADERS

There are several important benefits of becoming an exchange member. One benefit involves the generally much lower exchange transaction fees that a member must pay versus non-member customers. Another benefit gives the member the privilege to trade directly on the exchange trading floor. Before the advent of electronic trading as noted in Chapter 11, this exchange trading privilege provided material monetary benefits to exchange members because of the time and place advantage the floor provided over other traders who had to phone in orders off the floor.

Exchange floor members fall within two primary groups. One group is registered with the CFTC as "floor traders" [7 U.S.C. § 6e]. These are exchange members who trade for their own accounts. They are often referred to as "locals." Floor traders may be "scalpers" who are seeking trading profits while trying to minimize their trading losses each day. Few scalpers carry trades on an overnight basis. Instead, they are strictly "day-traders" who shout and scream all day long, five days a week or enter rapid buy and sell orders through a computer in order to pick up quick profits.

The other group trading on exchange floors is the "floor broker," which executes customer orders, acting as their agent. You must be registered as a floor broker with the CFTC in order to handle customer orders on the exchange floor [7 U.S.C. § 6e].

As noted in Chapter 2, floor brokers and floor traders are the only group of registrants that are not subject to the NFA's regulations.

IN THE MATTER OF SOLOMON MAYER, ET AL.
Comm. Fut. L. Rep. (CCH) ¶ 27,259 (C.F.T.C. 1998)

By the Commission (CHAIRPERSON BORN, COMMISSIONERS TULL, HOLUM and SPEARS).

* * *

On April 24, 1992, the Commission issued a 23-count complaint charging Solomon Mayer ("SMayer"), Barry Mayer ("BMayer"), SHB

Commodities, Inc. ("SHB"), Mayer Commodities Corp. ("MCC"), Robert S. Halper ("Halper"), Steven Gelbstein ("Gelbstein"), Edmond Mekertichian ("Mekertichian"), and Isaac Mayer ("IMayer") with multiple violations of the Act and Commission regulations arising out of their trading activities in the heating oil pit of New York Mercantile Exchange ("NYMEX") from April 1987 through June 1989. The complaint alleged violations of the Act's recordkeeping, supervision, registration, and trade practice requirements. * * *

The alleged trade practice violations relate to the accounts allegedly owned and controlled by the Mayers. The complaint alleged that SMayer, BMayer, and Mazel each owned one-third of SHB and were the only members of the board of directors. The complaint alleged that SMayer, president, directed and controlled the activities of SHB. While the trades for the SHB house account were generally executed by BMayer, vice-president, SMayer had authority to trade the account and did in fact do so.

The complaint also alleged that SMayer was president and BMayer vice-president of MCC, that SMayer directed and controlled the firm and its activities, that they both directed and controlled trading of the MCC proprietary account, and that while the trades for the MCC house account were generally executed by SMayer, BMayer had authority to trade the account and did in fact do so. The complaint also alleged that both SMayer and BMayer each directly or indirectly had an ownership interest in MCC. The complaint listed seven accounts that SMayer controlled or directed and in which he had an ownership interest.

The complaint alleged four categories of trade practice violations. Specifically, the complaint alleged that SMayer, BMayer, SHB, and MCC knowingly engaged in a series of noncompetitive trades to achieve wash results by trading the SHB and MCC house accounts opposite each other ("the Schedule A trades"). The Schedule A trades were divided into: (1) Schedule A–1, 73 alleged occasions between April 28, 1987, and June 27, 1989, in which the MCC house account bought and sold heating oil futures contracts from and to the SHB house account in spread transactions; and (2) Schedule A–2, 41 alleged occasions from May 13, 1987 through May 24, 1989, in which the MCC house account bought and sold heating oil futures contracts from and to the SHB house account in outright transactions.

In the second category of trade practice violations, the complaint alleged that on various trading days between February 18, 1987 and December 14, 1987 in simultaneous or nearly simultaneous transactions which were executed opposite one or two floor brokers or traders, SMayer bought futures contracts for one of the seven accounts he controlled while selling an equal number of the same contracts at the same price for another of the controlled accounts. Consequently, the complaint alleged, SMayer, SHB, and MCC knowingly engaged in a series of noncompetitive trades to achieve wash results, and Gelbstein, Halper, and Mekertichian accommodated them by buying and selling the same or a similar quantity of the same contracts at the same or nearly the same price ("the Schedule B trades").

Third, the complaint alleged that between June 29, 1987, and May 4, 1989, SMayer knowingly engaged in a series of noncompetitive trades by bucketing customers' orders or willfully and knowingly, and without the prior consent of such customers, becoming the buyer in respect to selling orders or the seller in respect to buying orders. The complaint further alleged that Gelbstein, Halper, Merkertichian, and other floor traders and brokers accommodated SMayer by buying (or selling) contracts from or to SMayer and then selling (or buying) the same or similar quantity of the same contracts at the same or almost the same price in simultaneous or near simultaneous transactions ("the Schedule C trades").

Fourth, the complaint alleged that from January 19, 1988, through December 19, 1988, SMayer bucketed his customers' orders or willfully and knowingly, and without the consent of his customers, became the buyer in respect to selling orders or became the seller in respect to buying orders. The complaint alleged that SMayer achieved this result by engaging in simultaneous or nearly simultaneous transactions whereby a floor broker employed by SHB sold (or bought) heating oil contracts to Gelbstein for a customer of SHB with SMayer's knowledge and SMayer, trading for the MCC house account, bought (or sold) an equal or nearly equal number of the same contracts from Gelbstein at the same or nearly the same price ("the Schedule D trades").

With respect to the alleged trade practice violations, the complaint charged that certain respondents cheated and defrauded customers in violation of Section 4b(A) of the Act, 7 U.S.C. § 6b(A) (1988); bucketed customer orders or took the opposite side of customers' orders without their prior consent in violation of Section 4b(D) of the Act, 7 U.S.C. § 6b(D) (1988), and Commission Rule 1.38, 17 C.F.R. § 1.38 (1988); entered into wash, fictitious, and accommodation trades in violation of Section 4c(a)(A) of the Act, 7 U.S.C. § 6c(a)(A) (1988); caused non-bona fide prices to be reported in violation of Section 4c(a)(B) of the Act, 7 U.S.C. § 6c(a)(B) (1988); and engaged in noncompetitive trading in violation of Commission Rule 1.38(a), 17 C.F.R. § 1.38(a) (1988). Pursuant to Section 2(a)(1)(A) of the Act, 7 U.S.C. § 4 (1988), and Commission Rule 1.2, 17 C.F.R. § 1.2 (1988), the complaint charged that SHB and MCC were liable for any and all violations of SMayer and BMayer because they acted within the scope of their employment. * * *

"The central characteristic" of fictitious trades is the "use of trading techniques that give the appearance of submitting trades to the open market while negating" risk and price competition. In re Collins, [1986–1987 Transfer Binder] Comm. Fut. L. Rep. (CCH) P 22,982 at 31,902 (CFTC Apr. 4, 1986) clarified, P 23,401 (Nov. 26, 1986), rev'd on other grounds sub nom., Stoller v. CFTC, 834 F.2d 262 (2d Cir. 1987). Wash trades and accommodation trades are forms of fictitious trades. In a wash sale, the trader effectively buys from and sells to himself so that there is no change in financial position. Collins, P 22,982 at 31,902. The price of the orders is of little consequence. Id. The intentional creation of a nullity is not deemed a bona fide transaction "even when the trader's facially independent purchase and sale are executed by open and competitive outcry." In re Bear Stearns & Co., [1990–1992 Transfer Binder] Comm. Fut. L. Rep. (CCH) P 24,994 at 37,663 (CFTC Jan. 25, 1991).

The schedules attached to the complaint depict a pattern of trading between various entities owned and controlled by SMayer and BMayer. The accounts ("Mayer family accounts") include SHB and MCC house accounts, two MCC pension accounts, the personal accounts of SMayer and Sarah Mayer Hammerman, and a joint account of SMayer and BMayer. The distinctions between the financial interests of the Mayer family entities appear to be largely illusory. While he denied being a part owner of MCC, SMayer reported capital gains from MCC in an amount equal to that of his mother, the only avowed owner. Consequently, we conclude that SMayer owned half of MCC. SMayer and BMayer together owned two-thirds of SHB. SMayer admitted that he had a financial interest in both accounts. SMayer controlled the trading at MCC. Both SMayer and BMayer traded the SHB account. SMayer managed and controlled the operations of SHB. Funds were transferred between the two entities without documentation of any underlying obligation, and witnesses were unable to explain the reasons for various transfers. Additionally, all family members had authority to withdraw funds from the accounts at their own discretion.

Because the accounts had a common ownership, a losing trade in one account was offset by a winning trade in the other account. Since the Mayers had a financial stake in both sides of the trades, we conclude that there could not have been a change in the overall financial position of the Mayers. Accordingly, we find that the transactions listed in the Schedules between Mayer accounts were wash trades.

In addition to the wash character of the trades, the trading activity between the Mayer brothers bears additional indicia of fictitious trading. BMayer traded primarily in the platinum/palladium pit. SMayer traded primarily in the heating oil pit. Every so often, during 1987–1989, BMayer walked out of the platinum/palladium pit into the heating oil pit, executed a trade, and went back to the palladium pit. In the years 1987–

1989, 30 percent of the transactions that BMayer executed in the heating oil pit, constituting 64 percent of his heating oil contracts, were with his brother SMayer. Further, while there is no prohibition against two brothers trading with each other, the brothers asked an exchange official to sign the pit card attesting to open outcry. The brothers state that they followed the cross trading procedure and obtained the signature because they "wanted everything to be above board." Since the certification procedure they followed is used only when a broker trades two of his own customer orders and two customer orders were not being traded, the brothers were misusing the procedure. Consequently, we believe that the attestation to open outcry, rather than helping the Mayers' cause, raises further questions as to why they went out of their way to ensure that there was a witness to the open outcry.

SMayer managed both SHB and MCC and reviewed daily the daily trade register listing every transaction in the SHB account which traded opposite the MCC account. SMayer testified that he knew when he traded opposite BMayer that they both could have been trading accounts that belonged to the Mayer family. They carpooled into work together each morning. SMayer was in the heating oil pit daily and tracked the trading in all energy pits. BMayer traded primarily in the platinum and palladium pit and entered the heating oil pit only rarely. Sometimes BMayer was in the heating oil pit only long enough to execute a single trade. The street book shows that, on more than one occasion, BMayer executed two trades in both pits during the same minute. SMayer testified that traders in one energy pit must actively keep abreast of the prices in other energy pits because there is an economic relationship between the prices. Yet BMayer testified that he traded the SHB account "arbitrarily." Under those circumstances and given their joint financial interests in the accounts, it strains credulity to assume that the brothers traded independently. Further, we note the testimony of the accommodators who stated that they executed accommodation trades with the Mayers through open outcry. We conclude that the weight of the evidence demonstrates that SMayer and BMayer prearranged trades using a cooperative strategy.

Prearrangement is one of the more common forms of fictitious sales forbidden by Section 4c(a)(A) and is also a form of anticompetitive trading that violates Commission Rule 1.38. The transaction may appear to be the result of open outcry but negates both the risk and price competition incident to an open outcry market because it is in reality a private transaction arranged outside the trading pit. Collins, P 22,982 at 31,903; In re Gimbel, [1987–1990 Transfer Binder] Comm. Fut. L. Rep. (CCH) P 24,213 at 35,003 (CFTC Apr. 14, 1988). When a prearranged transaction in the pit is structured to produce a wash result, it is both a fictitious sale and a wash sale under Section 4c(a)(A) of the Act. We conclude that

BMayer and SMayer prearranged the 113 trade sequences of wash transactions found in Schedule A in violation of Section 4c(a)(A) of the Act. Accordingly, we find that: (1) BMayer committed 113 violations of Section 4c(a)(A) of the Act and Commission Rule 1.38 by entering into 113 prearranged wash transactions; (2) SMayer committed 113 violations of Section 4c(a)(A) of the Act and Commission Rule 1.38 by entering into 113 prearranged wash transactions; and (3) since BMayer and SMayer were acting within the scope of their employment, SHB and MCC are liable for 113 violations of Section 4c(a)(A) of the Act and Commission Rule 1.38 pursuant to Section 2(a)(1)(A(iii) of the Act and Commission Rule 1.2.

In addition to the wash nature of the trades between the Mayer family accounts, there is both direct and indirect evidence that the trading activity underlying the sequences listed in Schedule B had the character of a wash sale. Schedule B depicts 16 trade sequences in which there is one trade between one of the Mayer family accounts and an account owned or controlled by another individual and then a trade a short time later at the same or similar price with the same individual (in two transactions, there are two individuals involved in between) and one of the Mayer family accounts. SMayer executed these trades with various accommodators.

In appropriate circumstances a pattern marked by characteristics unlikely to occur in an open and competitive market is indicative of noncompetitive trading. In re Rousso, [Current Transfer Binder] Comm. Fut. L. Rep. (CCH) P 27,133 at 45,308 (CFTC July 29, 1997) citing In re Buckwalter, [1990–1992 Transfer Binder] Comm. Fut. L. Rep. (CCH) P 24,995 at 37,682–37,683 (CFTC Jan. 25, 1991), and Bear Stearns, P 24,994 at 37,663. "Moreover, the existence of such a pattern permits the inference that the trades that form the pattern were intentionally achieved by noncompetitive means." In re Rousso, P 27,133 at 45,308 citing Collins, P 22,982 at 31,900 n.16 and Gimbel, P 24,213 at 35,003 n.6. The NYMEX street book indicates that SMayer repeatedly traded, for the Mayer family accounts, the opposite sides of the same or similar quantity of the same commodity at the same price with the same individuals within very short time intervals. This pattern strongly supports the inference that the trades were noncompetitive.

Further, several of the individuals who traded opposite SMayer in these trades testified that they had accommodated SMayer and that the trades had no economic purpose. Helfer specifically described three of the transactions in his testimony. This testimony supports the inference that the pattern set forth in the trade sequences was intentionally achieved by accommodation trading.

Gelbstein participated in three of the Schedule B trade sequences, B–9, B–14, B–15. There is no discernible difference between the transactions executed by Gelbstein and those executed by the witnesses. In all three trade sequences, Gelbstein sold heating oil to SMayer who acted on behalf of one of the Mayer family accounts and, either in the same minute or one minute later, purchased the same quantity at the same price from SMayer acting on behalf of another Mayer family account. We therefore find unpersuasive Gelbstein's assertion that there is no pattern of improper trading and that his trades are consistent with an inference that he was merely scalping or engaging in spread trades.

Consequently, we affirm the ALJ's finding that all 16 of the trade sequences listed in Schedule B show SMayer participating in wash trades with an accommodator. We find that: (1) SMayer committed 16 violations of Section 4c(a)(A) of the Act by entering into 16 wash sale transactions; (2) Gelbstein accommodated SMayer in three wash sale transactions and thereby committed three violations of Section 4c(a)(A); and (3) since SMayer was acting within the scope of his employment, SHB and MCC are liable for 16 violations of Section 4c(a)(A) of the Act pursuant to Section 2(a)(1)(A(iii) of the Act and Commission Rule 1.2.

Schedule C lists trade sequences showing Gelbstein and others trading with SMayer, who was acting as a broker trading a customer account, and within a short time frame thereafter, trading the same commodity at the same or similar price with SMayer who was then trading one of the Mayer family accounts. The Schedule D trade sequences depict Gelbstein as buying and selling the same commodity at the same or similar price within a short time frame between trades executed by either SMayer or another SHB broker (including four by BMayer) on behalf of a customer account and then on behalf of one of the Mayer family accounts.

In the complaint, Schedule C contained 174 alleged bucketed and fictitious trade sequences by SMayer. The Division filed a corrected complaint on March 15, 1994, and reduced the number of alleged illegal trade sequences to 172. With the Division's agreement, the ALJ dropped trades 151 and 170 from the list. Thus, 170 trade sequences were alleged to be bucketed. In his initial decision, the ALJ found that 67 of the listed trades were bucketed by SMayer aided by Gelbstein and that SMayer bucketed 102 listed trades with the aid of brokers and traders not respondents in this proceeding in violation of Section 4b(D) of the Act. The ALJ also found that SMayer knowingly engaged in the 28 trade sequences listed in Schedule D which resulted in the bucketing of SHB customers' orders in violation of Section 4b(D) of the Act. Based on these findings, the ALJ decided that SMayer had cheated and defrauded his customers in violation of Section 4b(A) of the Act.

Respondents and their expert argue that the pattern identified by the Division is consistent with scalping. In their testimony, they gave several examples of legitimate flat trading which can be attributed to scalping or other legitimate purposes. Although these examples explain why a broker or trader may publish a flat trade, they do not explain why another trader would agree to both sides of the flat trade. Generally, when a broker or trader legitimately publishes a flat market, it would be expected that each side of the flat trade would be executed with different traders. Here, in trade after trade, both sides of the flat market were executed with the same trader. Respondents' examples do not explain why these flat trades, with no apparent economic purpose, happened so often with the same individuals.

SMayer denies bucketing customer orders, apparently relying on the argument that if his customers received a competitive market price the orders were not bucketed. The Mayers contend that the ALJ concluded that the customers were harmed because the ALJ mistakenly analyzed the trades as if they were outrights rather than spreads and that, had he examined the trades properly as spreads, he would have found that the customers received good prices. Bucketing consists of a broker's trading opposite his or her own customer's order without open and competitive execution. The price the customer received is irrelevant to a determination of whether SMayer bucketed SHB customer orders. SMayer's attempt to argue that the trades were spreads is unavailing. If SMayer traded against his customer noncompetitively, it does not matter whether the trade was outright or spread. It is still illegal. The evidence clearly indicates that SMayer executed SHB customer orders against Mayer family accounts by using Gelbstein and others to execute wash trades between SHB's customers and Mayer family accounts. Consequently, we find that SMayer bucketed these customer orders in violation of Section 4b(D) of the Act.

Furthermore, SMayer breached his fiduciary duty by not submitting orders to the pit and pursuing the best price possible. "Failure to pursue the best price possible can, without more, constitute fraud regardless of whether the customer is harmed financially." In re Rousso, P 27,133 at 45,310 citing U.S. v. Ashman, 979 F.2d 469, 477–478 (7th Cir. 1992), cert. denied, 510 U.S. 814 (1993) (finding failure to submit customers' orders to the marketplace deprives them of economic opportunity and constitutes fraud). Consequently, we find that SMayer cheated and defrauded his customers in violation of Section 4b(A) of the Act.

As an accommodator, Gelbstein facilitated SMayer's bucketing of trades by executing wash trades between the Mayer family accounts and SHB customers. Gelbstein makes several arguments with respect to the lack of a definitive pattern. (GBr. at 46 nn.36–37, attempting to refute the C and D trades the ALJ discussed in his initial decision). Specifically, Gelbstein states that "75% of the cited trades involving Gelbstein do not fit within [the pattern]," asserting that there are "slight deviations" in the price and/or quantity involved in some of the trade sequences, and that many trades were not executed simultaneously. (GBr. at 30, 47.) However, de minimis differences in price, time, and quantity do not change the substantive nature of the wash trades evident in the schedules.

Gelbstein also contends that the Division did not prove his knowing participation in the illegal trades. To determine whether participation was willful, we look for factors that are relevant to a facilitating respondent's knowledge of wrongdoing at the time he participated in a challenged trade and are independently significant. Bear Stearns, P 24,994 at 37,665. Gelbstein was at the center of the bucketed trades. For each bucketed trade, Gelbstein executed a buy order and a sell order for the same commodity at the same time or shortly thereafter at the same or similar price with brokers who were acting on behalf of an SHB customer for one trade and a Mayer family account for the other. Gelbstein was a longtime friend of SMayer. He stood next to him in the trading pit. Gelbstein could not help but be aware of the pattern of trading that he was facilitating. Gelbstein played a critical role in both stages of the transaction. Given his central role as accommodator, the frequency of the violative trades, and his close relationship with SMayer, we believe there is an adequate basis for concluding that Gelbstein knew of the wrongful nature of the challenged trade at the time of his participation. Id. See also, Gilchrist, P 24,993 at 37,651.

Gelbstein challenges the ALJ's finding that his testimony was not credible:

> Unlike the other witnesses who openly acknowledged that accommodation trades were a regular practice in the pit, SGelbstein testified that he never took SMayer's or anyone else's bid and offers when they did a flat market, he never saw accommodation trading, and he did not know how to define accommodation trading.

Mayer, P 26,736 at 44,052 (emphasis added). Gelbstein argues that this statement demonstrates that the ALJ believed that it would be highly unusual to find a trader acting properly and that a trader who makes such a claim is not credible. However, in light of the number of examples in Schedules C and D of flat trading by Gelbstein that appear to contradict his testimony, we see no reason to deviate from our usual practice of deferring to the credibility determination of the ALJ. Heilman v. First Nat'l Monetary Corp., [1986–1987 Transfer Binder] Comm. Fut. L. Rep. (CCH) P 23,207 at 32,569 (CFTC Aug. 14, 1986). Because Gelbstein repeatedly enabled SMayer to trade against either customer orders or accounts in which he had a financial interest, we find that

Gelbstein knowingly participated with SMayer in his violations of Section 4c(a)(A) of the Act. * * *

Respondents were charged with reporting, and the ALJ found that respondents had reported, non-bona fide prices. The only bona fide prices are those obtained competitively in the pit. In re Murphy, [1984–1986 Transfer Binder] Comm. Fut. L. Rep. (CCH) P 22,798 at 31,352. Because the noncompetitive transactions in which respondents engaged were reported to NYMEX, they resulted in prices being reported, registered, or recorded which were not true and bona fide prices. Bear Stearns, P 24,994 at 37,666 and Buckwalter, P 24,995 at 37,684. Accordingly, SMayer committed 145 violations of Section 4c(a)(B) by causing non-bona fide prices to be reported in connection with 73 spread transactions and 40 outright trades set forth in Schedule A and 30 outright trades and two spread transactions listed in Schedule B. BMayer committed 113 violations of Section 4c(a)(B) by causing non-bona fide prices to be reported in connection with 113 trade sequences listed in Schedule A. Gelbstein committed three violations of Section 4c(a)(B) by causing non-bona fide prices to be reported in connection with three outright trades in Schedule B. SMayer committed 376 violations of Section 4c(a)(B) by causing false reports to be made in connection with 376 trades in Schedules C and D. Gelbstein committed 200 violations of Section 4c(a)(B) by causing false reports to be made in connection with 200 trades (two of the trades were spreads, the rest were outrights) set forth in Schedules C and D. Since SMayer and BMayer were acting within the scope of their employment, SHB and MCC are liable for their 634 violations of Section 4c(a)(B) pursuant to Section 2(a)(1)(A(iii) of the Act and Commission Rule 1.2.

JERRY W. MARKHAM
THERE'S TROUBLE IN THE FUTURES TRADING PITS
Legal Times 26 (June 3, 1991)[1]

[In July of 1989 federal grand juries in Chicago returned indictments against forty-six traders on futures exchanges in that city]. The now famous sting operations on the Chicago Board of Trade and the Chicago Mercantile Exchange raise the specter of wholesale fraud on the commodity exchange floors. Closer inspection of the indictments, however, suggest that the amount of money at stake was not enormous, possibly a few million dollars—petty theft in the world of high finance, particularly compared with the sums involved in Wall Street insider-trading scandals.

---

[1] Reprinted with permission from the June 3, 1991 edition of the Legal Times © 1991, ALM Properties, Inc. All rights reserved. Further duplication without permission is prohibited.

The success of the Chicago prosecutions has been mixed. The first trial, which involved traders in the Swiss Franc pit resulted in only a few convictions and a hung jury on many charges. The second trial, involving traders in the soybean pit, did lead to serious and substantial convictions in January 1991. But, in a third trial in March, the jurors looking at the Japanese yen pit announced that they were hung on many counts, even after a so-called *Allen* charge from the judge ordering them to reach some resolution. That jury also acquitted some defendants.

As a result of these setbacks, the head of one major exchange announced that its members had been, in large measure, exonerated. The industry has also shown a tendency to dismiss the events in Chicago as a mere aberration.

Not so fast. Some thirty of the forty traders indicted as a result of the sting have been convicted, either by guilty plea or by trial. . . . Something is seriously wrong, and it's no aberration.

In theory, commodity futures markets are the essence of competition. Brokers are required to expose all orders to the trading pit, where traders compete with each other to ensure the best price for customers. And at a superficial level, the exchanges do bear the hallmarks of competition. From the galleries, one observes hundreds of frenzied traders screaming for orders.

The federal sting operations in Chicago burrowed below the surface, however, and produced stark evidence that competition on the exchanges has been undermined by surreptitious, non-competitive execution of many small customer orders. Floor traders execute customer orders and floor traders (also called *locals*) trading for their own accounts are not giving the public the benefits of competition. Recent cases brought by the Commodity Futures Trading Commission against locals and floor traders on the New York exchanges suggest that these practices are not limited to Chicago.

In the Chicago cases, floor brokers were willing to execute customer orders with locals at non-competitive prices. Profits from these fraudulent transactions were kicked back to floor brokers. In many instances, the transactions were used to cover floor broker errors, which totaled thousands of dollars. In exchange for noncompetitive executions (which assured the locals a profit), the locals would cover floor broker errors on other trades by taking those trades at artificial prices. This, of course, resulted in losses to the locals—but they were repaid, or prepaid, by kickbacks from profits obtained by cheating other customers of the floor brokers.

Government witnesses have testified in the Chicago prosecutions about such fraudulent trade practices as "edges," leads, "matches," and "trading off an order." An edge is simply a competitive advantage in the form of a preferred or first opportunity to bid on customer orders. This edge is given particular traders because of their willingness to trade in larger volumes with floor brokers executing customer orders. An edge does not guarantee the floor trader a profit, but it does better ensure that result—and it detracts from the competitive equal-access-to-orders concept for all traders on which futures trading is based.

A more malignant trading practice is the "lead" where a floor broker gives an order to a floor trader at a price that is slightly different (e.g. higher in the case of a customer buy order) from that existing at other points in the trading pit. This allows an almost assured profit, and certainly a greater competitive edge for the local. A lead is intentionally designed to permit the execution of customer orders at non-competitive prices.

"Matches" occur when floor brokers pair off customer orders, sometimes using intermediary locals to disguise what is occurring, without executing the orders in the pit. Similarly, "trading off an order" happens when a floor broker uses traders in a way that allows the broker to take the opposite side of his own customer's order.

All of these practices could be prevented—or at least substantially reduced—if there were an automated small order execution system on the commodity futures exchanges, such as those being developed in the stock markets. * * * These systems will allow small orders to be automatically queued, bids and offers matched, and trades executed. These systems will permit trades to be moved to final settlement faster and more efficiently, without broke intermediation; they will also create an audit trail. * * *

To be sure, automation may not be a complete panacea. Automated order systems in the securities industry have proved faulty in such high-volume moments as a stock market crash of 1987 and the mini-crash 1989. Nevertheless, improvements are being made to assure better performance. * * *

NOTES

On January 19, 1989, the Chicago Tribune published an article exposing the above described sting operation by the FBI and the United States Attorney in Chicago. Undercover FBI agents posing as traders purchased seats on the Chicago Board of Trade and the Chicago Mercantile Exchange in order to gain access to the their trading floors. The FBI agents pretended to be floor traders and secretly recorded hundreds of conversations in the trading pits of those two exchanges. The FBI agents also leased expensive apartments and provided elaborate entertainment to exchange members in order to ingratiate themselves into the club-like atmosphere on the exchange floors. See, Jerry W. Markham, Prohibited Floor Trading Activities Under the

Commodity Exchange Act, 58 Fordham L. Rev. 1–2 (1989) (describing that operation).

Chapter 11 describes the growth of electronic trading, which has sidelined most of the floor broker and floor trader communities. However, as that and other readings below will show, electronic trading has brought its own regulatory concerns.

12. TRADING ON FOREIGN EXCHANGES BY U.S. PERSONS

Pursuant to Part 30 of the CFTC rules [17 C.F.R. Part 30] a U.S. person may trade, under specified circumstances, futures traded on a non-U.S. exchange. This process involves two tests, namely whether (i) the products traded on the respective non-U.S. exchange have been approved for sale to U.S. persons by the CFTC, and (ii) whether the foreign brokerage firm may do business directly with the U.S. person.

Under the first test, a U.S. person can, for the most part, purchase futures contracts traded on non-U.S. exchanges if those products do not involve a non-U.S. stock index contract. If the underlying futures contract involves a non-U.S. stock index product, then a different analysis applies, which requires some explanation.

In 1981, the chairs of the CFTC and the SEC established the Shad-Johnson Jurisdictional Accord which divided up jurisdiction between those two agencies over both U.S. and non-U.S. stock indices. This jurisdictional accord was later codified by Congress and was continued in the Dodd-Frank Act when Congress applied this same test to the definitions of "swaps" and "security-based swaps."

If a U.S. person wants to trade a broad-based non-U.S. stock index product traded on a non-U.S. exchange, then that non-U.S. exchange must apply to the CFTC for approval for sale of the underlying stock index product to U.S. persons. The SEC may only oppose the approval of that broad-based index for sale to U.S. persons.

If the non-U.S. stock index involved a "narrow-based" index, then the SEC, and only the SEC, would have jurisdiction over that product and application would have to be made to it in order to trade such an index.

The determination of whether the index is broad-based or narrow-based utilizes two tests:

(1) the number of securities that comprised the index, and

(2) a weighted formula of the underlying securities that comprise the index.

Basically, if the stock index is comprised of less than twenty-five stocks, then the index would be deemed to be "narrow-based."

SEC Rule 15a–6 [17 C.F.R. § 240.15a–6] also deals with the ability of U.S. persons to trade on non-U.S. securities exchanges. Historically, the SEC has applied a more restrictive regulatory approach as it grants permissibility for such trading solely to institutional customers. In contrast, CFTC Part 30 is much more expansive as it permits retail U.S. persons to trade on non-U.S. futures exchanges.

13. PROPRIETARY TRADING

The CEA and applicable CFTC regulations are designed, for the most part, to protect customers who use the futures markets. One element of this customer protection regime is to require FCMs to separate from their customer accounts all "propriety" trading activities done directly for the benefit of the FCM or its affiliates. This includes separation of the funds required to margin such FCM and affiliated futures contracts.

The concept of customer segregation, as noted in more detail in Chapter 4, thus seeks to separate proprietary trading activities from those of customers. That is, no monies, securities or property provided by a customer to an FCM may be commingled with the assets of the FCM, and all amounts held in the segregated account constitute "customer property" and do not belong in any way to the FCM or its creditors until customer claims are resolved. [17 C.F.R. § 1.20].

To assure separation, each FCM establishes two "omnibus" accounts at each DCO where it does business. One of those accounts is held in the name of the FCM but for the benefit of its customers. The customer funds are held collectively in that omnibus account as customer property. This omnibus account is distinguished from a "fully-disclosed" account where the funds would be held in each respective customer's name.

The second omnibus account created by the FCM at the DCO is for holding proprietary funds or assets used for proprietary trading.

Other CFTC regulations, such as its net capital rules [17 C.F.R. 1.17], also impose different capital requirements on FCM that hold both customer funds and proprietary funds.

CHAPTER 4

REGULATION OF FUTURES COMMISSION MERCHANTS & BROKER-DEALERS

■ ■ ■

1. INTRODUCTION

Firms or persons that solicit or sell a financial product to the public must be registered in some capacity with a U.S. financial regulatory agency and become a member of one or more self-regulatory organizations (SROs).

As described in Chapter 2, the U.S. regulatory scheme is primarily driven by the financial product being sold to the customer. If the financial product constitutes a "security," then the firm that sells the security must be registered as a broker-dealer (BD) with the Securities and Exchange Commission (SEC) and be a member firm of the Financial Industry Regulatory Agency (FINRA). The employee of that BD, who sells or solicits the security to the customer, must be registered as a securities registered representative (RR) and be a member of FINRA.

Similarly, if the financial product constitutes a futures contract, then the brokerage firm must register as a futures commission merchant (FCM) with the Commodity Futures Trading Commission (CFTC) and become a FCM Member Firm with the National Futures Association (NFA), the futures industry's equivalent to FINRA within the securities industry. The non-clerical employees of the FCM must be registered as Associated Persons (APs) with the CFTC and become an Associate Member of NFA. As will be discussed below, each individual who registers in any capacity with the SEC or with the CFTC is also required to take certain fitness examinations.

Applicants seeking to become registered as a RR or as an AP must answer questions regarding his or her prior experiences, including whether the applicant has ever been sanctioned by a regulatory agency, whether the person has been convicted of any felony or certain misdemeanors and whether the person has filed for bankruptcy. If the applicant checks the "YES" box next to any of these questions, the applicant must provide background information regarding the reason for those adverse events. The NFA also requires applicants to be fingerprinted, and it conducts a background check on each applicant See, 7 U.S.C. § 12a (authorizing finger printing). Failure to answer the questions properly can lead to actions brought by FINRA or by the NFA against the applicant denying the application or subsequently withdrawing the application if it was originally granted before the NFA learned of the discrepancy.

If the applicant committed a crime that results in a statutory disqualification (e.g., a felony), then the application must be automatically denied. [7 U.S.C. § 12a]. The denied applicant may then appeal to the Membership Committee of the respective SRO. Keep in mind that both FINRA and NFA are membership organizations, and each can thus deny membership to any applicant who meets a statutory disqualification.

2. BROKER-DEALER REGISTRATION

A key component of the SEC's market regulation function is the broker-dealer (BD) licensing provision. That registration requirement allows the SEC to exclude those unfit for the business and provide a regulatory handle so that customer protection provisions can be imposed on those engaging in broker-dealer activities.

The SEC thus views the broker-dealer registration requirement to be the "keystone" for its regulation of broker-dealers. Frank W. Leones, Securities Exchange Act Release No. 23,524 (S.E.C. Aug 11, 1986), noted in Roth v. S.E.C., 22 F.3d 1108, Fed. Sec. L. Rep. (CCH) ¶ 98206 (D.C. Cir. 1994).

The term "broker-dealer" has two components, either of which may require registration as a BD. Simply stated, a "broker" is someone effecting securities for the accounts of others. A "dealer" is someone engaging in market making activities through transactions for its own account.

Section 15 of the Securities Exchange Act of 1934 [15 U.S.C. § 78o] requires registration as a BD where a person is effecting transactions or is inducing or attempting to induce the purchase or sale of any security other than an exempted security or commercial paper, bankers' acceptances, or commercial bills.

Section 3(a)(4) of the Securities Exchange Act [17 U.S.C. § 78c(a)(4)] defines a "broker" as a person, other than a bank with respect to certain defined transactions, "engaged in the business of effecting transactions in securities for the accounts of others."

A "dealer" is defined by Section 3(a)(5) of the Securities Exchange Act [17 U.S.C. § 78c(a)(5)] as one who buys or sells securities for his own account through a broker or otherwise.

The SEC Staff has defined activities that will require broker-dealer registration to include the following:

A person effects transactions if he or she participates in securities transactions "at key points in the chain of distribution." Such participation includes, among other things, selecting the market to which a securities transaction will be sent, assisting an issuer to structure prospective securities transactions, helping an issuer to identify potential purchasers of securities, soliciting securities transactions (including advertising), and participating in the order taking or order-routing process (for example, by taking transaction orders from customers). Factors indicating that a person is "engaged in the business" include, among other things: receiving transaction-related compensation; holding one's self out as a broker, as executing trades, or as assisting others in completing securities transactions; and participating in the securities business with some degree of regularity. In addition to indicating that a person is "effecting transactions," soliciting securities transactions is also evidence of being "engaged in the business."

BD Advantage, Inc., 2000 WL 1742088 (S.E.C. Oct. 11, 2000) (citations and footnotes omitted).

EASTSIDE CHURCH OF CHRIST V. NATIONAL PLAN, INC.
391 F.2d 357 (5th Cir. 1968)

GRIFFIN B. BELL, CIRCUIT JUDGE:

This case presents the not unusual question of which of the innocent parties, appellants on the one hand and appellees on the other, must bear a loss sustained through the defalcation of a third party with respect to church bonds. The appellants, seven churches, are seeking recovery against the two appellees, National Plan, Inc. and its president and principal owner, Robert H. Knox. The churches, asserting that they never received payment for certain bonds which they issued and which were purchased by National, claim that they are entitled to recover the bonds still in National's possession and damages for any which National has transferred to innocent purchasers. National answers that the bonds are valid and subsisting obligations of the churches. The District Court agreed with National. Unfortunately we cannot finally resolve the question in full. We affirm in part; but, because of a basic error of law in the District Court in the area of securities regulation, the case must be reversed in part and remanded for further proceedings. * * *

This brings us to the pertinent facts. National acquired the bonds in the following manner. Paden, a church contractor, agreed to construct buildings for each of the appellant churches. To finance the construction of the buildings, the churches issued bearer bonds to Paden, either selling them to him outright or delivering them to him as agent to sell, or as the church witnesses said, 'to place' the bonds on behalf of the churches. The churches claim that Paden was obligated to remit to them the full face value of the bonds, without commission, either promptly or, in the case of certain bonds, as the money would be needed for construction of the buildings. Paden sold bonds in the face amount of $215,750 to National at a discount. In the case of a few the discount was ten per cent; in the case of most, fifteen per cent. National, as directed by Paden, paid for the bonds either directly to Paden or to a company called World Oil & Gas of Delaware, Paden having told National that World Oil & Gas would absorb the discount and pay Paden the full face value of the bonds as he needed it for the church construction projects. The evidence was that Paden failed to remit to the churches on the National purchases.

The churches entrusted Paden with the bonds. They issued the bonds in negotiable form. They printed on the face of each bond: 'This is a bearer bond and as such may be transferred by delivery'. In addition, each bond bore the certificate that payment had been received for the bond but, of course, with respect to those bonds purchased by National on the representation from Paden that he was acting as agent for the churches in an effort to sell the bonds, National knew that the churches had not been paid.

The churches claim that National purchased the bonds in violation of three provisions of the federal securities laws. First, they assert that National was an unregistered broker-dealer and, accordingly, that National's purchase of the bonds violated § 15(a)(1) of the Act, 15 U.S.C.A. § 78o(a)(1), prohibiting an unregistered broker-dealer from effecting securities transactions. Second, they claim that National violated the antifraud provisions in § 15(c)(1) of the Exchange Act, 15 U.S.C.A. § 78o(c)(1), and Rule 15c1–4 thereunder, 17 CFR § 240.15c1–4, by failing to send written confirmations of the purchases to the churches. Third, they claim that National violated the antifraud provisions in § 15(c)(2) of the Exchange Act, 15 U.S.C.A. § 78o(c)(2), and Rule 15c2–4 thereunder, 17 CFR § 240.15c2–4, in that it neither transmitted its purchase payments directly to the churches nor deposited the money in a separate bank account or in an escrow account for their benefit. * * *

We consider first the failure of National to register and the result which ensues because of § 15(a)(1) of the Act. It was stipulated that National had not registered as either a broker or dealer under the Act, that the mails were used in the transactions in question and that they took place in interstate commerce.

One church securities exemption is from the registration provisions of the Securities Act of 1933, something not here involved. We are concerned with the Securities Exchange Act of 1934. Section 12(g)(2)(D) of that Act, 15 U.S.C.A. § 78l(g)(2)(D), contains an exemption of church bonds, but that exemption, again, relates only to their registration, It does not relate to the antifraud or broker-dealer registration provisions. There is simply no exemption in the Exchange Act from these provisions even when the broker or dealer is handling church bonds.

The District Court did not decide whether National was a broker or a dealer within the meaning of the Exchange Act. This question was not reached due to the erroneous view that church bonds were exempt securities even for the purposes of the broker-dealer registration provisions. Section 3(a)(4) of the Exchange Act, 15 U.S.C.A. § 78c(a)(4), defines a broker as any person engaged in the business of effecting transactions in securities for the account of others. The evidence shows conclusively that National was a broker. Mr. Knox testified that the principal business of National was to 'put on bond issues to build churches'. He stated that National went to churches where they had been requested to put on bond programs, assisted the church in doing all of the legal work concerning the bond program, took care of necessary printing, handled all of the paper work in connection with the bond issue, acted as fiscal agent and trustee of the property, and directed the bond sales program. He testified that the sales were made throughout the country.

Section 3(a)(5) of the Exchange Act, 15 U.S.C.A. § 78c(a)(5), defines a dealer as any person engaged in the business of buying and selling securities for his own account, through a broker or otherwise. The evidence demands a finding that National was so engaged. National purchased many church bonds prior to the ones in question for its own account as a part of its regular business and sold some of them. Thus National was a broker and a dealer within the meaning of the Act. See 2 Loss, securities Regulation, 1295, 1297 (2d ed. 1961). * * *

NOTES

1. The receipt of per trade compensation (e.g., a brokerage commission) for the execution of customer orders has been generally viewed as indicative of "broker" status. See, Jerry W. Markham & Thomas Lee Hazen, 23 Broker Dealer Operations Under Securities and Commodities Law: Financial Responsibilities, Credit Regulation, and Customer Protection, Ch. 3 (2013) (describing broker registration requirements).

2. "Dealer" activities that may require registration include underwriting securities, purchasing or selling securities as principal from or to customers, carrying a dealer inventory, quoting a market in securities or publishing quotations through a quotation system used by dealers, brokers, or institutional investors, or otherwise quoting prices other than on a limited basis through a retail broker-dealer, holding oneself out as a dealer or market-maker or as otherwise willing to buy or sell particular securities on a continuous basis, and extending or arranging for the extension of credit in connection with securities transactions. See, Edward F. Green, et al., U.S.

Regulation of the International Securities and Derivatives Markets § 10.03(b) (2008).

3. Securities Exchange Act Section 3(a)(5)(B) [15 U.S.C. § 78c(a)(5)(B)] creates an exception from the dealer registration requirement. It states that:

> The term "dealer" does not include a person that buys or sells securities . . . for such person's own account, either individually or in a fiduciary capacity, but not as a part of a regular business.

BD registration has not been required for "traders", who are trading for their own accounts, even though their trading is a part of their regular business and even if their trading is a highly active and for speculative purposes. VI Louis Loss, et al., Securities Regulation, Ch. 8 at 514 (4th ed. 2011) (describing the "Dealer-Trader Distinction"). For example, so-called "high frequency traders" are not required to register as BDs even though their algorithmic trading is dominating securities market trading volumes.[1]

4. To become registered as a BD, the firm must file a Form BD with the Central Registration Department (CRD) of FINRA. This registration form requires the applicant to provide important basic information regarding the applicant including, but not limited to:

A.   Organizational structure and ownership

B.   List of all Officers and Board Members

C.   List of the Headquarters and all Branch Offices

D.   Types of securities products to be offered for purchase and sale

E.   Net capital (the BD must submit a recent audited financial statement)

F.   List of person responsible for various activities

G.   Answers to several questions regarding whether the applicant has ever been subject to a laundry list of sanctions

H.   List of States it intends to register with (or can check the box: "ALL").

5. In addition to the Form BD, the applicant must submit, among other documents, the following documents:

A.   Audited Financial Statement, not less than 90 days old

B.   Compliance Policy and Procedures Manual

C.   Anti-Money Laundering (AML) Policy

6. A person seeking to become registered as a RR with the BD must submit a Form U-5 with FINRA's CRD unit. This application requires the applicant to provide information, including but not limited to:

---

[1]   The IRS also distinguishes between "investors," "dealers" and "traders" and "investors" for tax purposes. http://www.irs.gov/taxtopics/tc429.html (accessed on Nov. 5, 2013).

A. Name and Address

B. Employment history

C. Residential history

D. Educational history

E. List of other registrations held by the applicant

F. Whether the person has been subject to a laundry list of sanctions that are asked on the form

G. List of States will the applicant intend to become registered in (or can check the box: "ALL")

7. The RR must also provide the following documents:

A. Proof of completing the Series 7 and Series 63 examinations (which test the competency of the applicant to engage in the securities business) administered by FINRA.

B. Set of fingerprint cards

8. Once a person is registered as RR and has taken the Series 7 and 63 examinations, additional examinations may be required depending on what securities products the RR may sell and/or what role that the person may play at the BD. There are over forty such examinations that may apply. The more popular licenses include:

A. Branch Manager—Series 9/10 examination

B. General Securities Principal—Series 24 examination

C. Financial Operations Principal—Series 27 examination

D. Registered Options Representative—Series 42 examination

E. Registered Options Principal—Series 4 examination

F. Compliance Officer—Series 14 examination

G. Registered Options Principal—Series 4 examination

H. Municipal Securities Representative—Series 52 examination

I. Municipal Securities Principal—Series 53 examination

See FINRA Compliance Page: http://www.finra.org/industry/compliance/registration/qualificationsexams/qualifications/p011051

9. All registrations for BD and RR status are filed with the CRD unit of FINRA. Note that the SEC and not FINRA handles applications for other types of registrants required by the federal securities laws, such as investment companies, investment advisers and security-based swap dealers whereas the NFA handles all firm registrations required by the CEA.

3. FUTURES COMMISSION MERCHANT REGISTRATION

The CEA requires entities acting as an FCM to register and be subject to CFTC oversight. [7 U.S.C. § 6d]. The CEA defines a FCM to include entities that accept orders and funds from customers for CFTC regulated products. [7 U.S.C. § 1a(28)].

A sample of a Futures Customer Agreement is set forth in Appendix B to this Casebook. This Agreement contains the contractual provisions between the FCM and the futures customer.

In futures, there are two primary functions—the execution of the order and the clearing of the order. The Futures Customer Agreement is signed when the futures customer opens an account with the FCM. A customer, however, may bifurcate these two functions, by executing the order through another firm and clearing the trade with the FCM where it has opened the futures account. See a sample of the Uniform Give-Up Agreement that is typically used when one firm executes the order and another firm (e.g., the FCM) clears the order on behalf of the customer (Appendix C to this Casebook).

A FCM receiving customer funds in connection with their orders is required, as described in Section Seven of this Chapter, to maintain those funds in specially segregated accounts. The following case considers whether a firm was subject to that segregation requirement where it was registered as an FCM but did not operate as a FCM because it did not accept customer orders.

CFTC v. SENTINEL MANAGEMENT GROUP

2012 U.S. Dist. LEXIS 109747 (N.D. Ill.)

CHARLES P. KOCORAS, DISTRICT JUDGE:

This matter comes before the Court on the motion of Plaintiff Commodity Futures Trading Commission ("CFTC") for partial reconsideration of our March 30th, 2012 judgment denying the CFTC's motion for summary judgment against Eric A. Bloom ("Bloom") and Charles K. Mosley ("Mosley") (collectively, "Defendants"), and granting Defendants' cross-motion for summary judgment. For the following reasons, Plaintiff's motion is denied in part and granted in part.

On March 30th, 2012, we issued a Memorandum Opinion ("March 30th Opinion") denying the CFTC's motion for summary judgment and granting Defendants' cross-motion for summary judgment. *CFTC v. Sentinel Mgmt. Group, Inc.*, 08 C 2410, 2012 U.S. Dist. LEXIS 46198 (N.D. Ill. Mar. 30, 2012). We held that Defendants, as a matter of law, did not violate Sections 4b(a)(2), 4d(a)(2), 4d(b), 4g(a), and 6(c) of the

Commodity Exchange Act ("CEA"). 7 U.S.C. §§ 6b(a)(2), 6d(a)(2), 6d(b), 6g(a), and 9. The CFTC now requests that we reconsider our ruling with respect to Section 4b(a)(2), 7 U.S.C. § 6b(a)(2), and Section 4d(b), 7 U.S.C. § 6d(b). We briefly recite the facts relevant to the instant motion.

Sentinel Management Group ("Sentinel") was an investment group registered as both an "investment advisor" with the United States Securities and Exchange Commission ("SEC"), and as a "futures commission merchant" ("FCM") with the CFTC. Bloom was Sentinel's president and chief executive officer for nearly twenty years, controlling the company's day-to-day operations. He also served as Sentinel's chief compliance officer from January 2006 through August 2007. Mosley served as Sentinel's vice president, head trader, and portfolio manager for approximately five years.

Sentinel's business strategy relied on recruiting FCMs to invest their excess margin funds with Sentinel. CFTC regulations allow FCMs to deposit their customers' excess margin funds only with banks, clearing houses, or other FCMs. Sentinel sought the CFTC's advice on how to legally accept and invest FCMs' funds. The CFTC recommended that Sentinel register as an FCM pursuant to 17 C.F.R. § 1.49(d)(2), which Sentinel did. Soon after Sentinel's registration, the CFTC issued Sentinel a "No Action Letter," whereby exempting Sentinel from the net capital requirements otherwise applicable to FCMs, provided that Sentinel abstained from trading commodities. Sentinel represented that its registration as an FCM was "solely so that it may [4] hold customer's funds deposited with it by other FCMs for the exclusive purpose of investing such funds."

Sentinel held the assets of its client portfolios in segregated custodial accounts with the Bank of New York Mellon Corporation ("BONY"). It also maintained a House Portfolio with BONY, which Sentinel held for its own proprietary trading. BONY maintained these accounts and provided Sentinel with financing through nightly overnight loans. BONY required Sentinel to maintain enough securities in its clearing accounts on a daily basis to collateralize the loan. Crystal York ("York"), Sentinel's employee primarily responsible for booking the loan each night, testified that she indiscriminately chose which securities to pledge as collateral with no consideration for how Sentinel allocated the BONY loan among the portfolios. York testified that she generally used the highest valued securities, which most often were funds belonging to Sentinel's FCM-clients. In the summer of 2007, Bloom instructed Sentinel employees to collateralize the BONY loan with Sentinel's FCM-clients' excess margin funds only if other securities were insufficient.

In 2004, the CFTC allowed for FCMs to use reverse repurchase agreements ("reverse repos") as a form of leverage. *See* 17 C.F.R. § 1.25.

On Bloom's recommendation, Sentinel began using reverse repos, whereby it would sell securities to a broker at an amount that was below-market value with a commitment to repurchase that security at a pre-determined higher price. Sentinel profited through these arrangements if the securities' value at the time of repurchase exceeded the difference between the sale price and the repurchase price.

Sentinel's troubles began in June 2007, when a broker who held over $1 billion in outstanding reverse repos with Sentinel began to redeem them. The following month, another broker with $600 million in outstanding reverse repos followed suit. At first, Sentinel paid these brokers with money obtained from the nightly BONY loans. By August 13th, 2007, Sentinel lacked the capital to meet its clients' redemption orders. BONY sent Bloom a letter on August 17th notifying him that Sentinel had defaulted on the loan agreement, and that it had the right to sell the securities that Sentinel had pledged as collateral. Sentinel filed for Chapter 11 bankruptcy the same day.

On April 28th, 2008, the CFTC filed a complaint alleging that Bloom, Mosley, and Sentinel violated various sections of the Commodities Exchange Act ("CEA"). On March 30th, 2012, we denied the CFTC's summary judgment motion and granted Defendants' cross-motion for summary judgment in its entirety. The CFTC filed the instant motion on April 26th, requesting that we revisit our ruling.

. . . [T]he CFTC asks us to reconsider our ruling with respect to Section 4d(b) of the CEA. The CFTC asserts that Sentinel violated Section 4d(b) because it allegedly removed securities from its FCM-clients' segregated accounts and placed them in alienable clearing accounts, where they were commingled with Sentinel's proprietary securities and improperly pledged as collateral for the BONY loan for the benefit of the House Portfolio. CFTC contends that our ruling was in error because Section 4d(b) protects FCMs' customer funds from commingling and misappropriation by third parties like Sentinel.

In the March 30th Opinion, we held that Sentinel could not be liable under Section 4d(b) [10] because it did not receive customer funds as described in Section 4d(a)(2). *Sentinel Mgmt.*, 2012 U.S. Dist. LEXIS 46198, at *21–22. But as CFTC now points out, our ruling misinterpreted the scope of Section 4d(b), as made evident by the text and the purpose of the statute.

Section 4d(a)(2) funds, or "customer funds," are money, securities, or property that an FCM receives from its customers in order to margin, guarantee, or secure the trades or contracts of these customers. 7 U.S.C. 6d(a)(2). The CEA imposes strict segregation requirements on these funds. *Id.* A Section 4d(b) violation occurs when a person who receives Section 4d(a)(2) funds treats those funds as if they belonged to anyone other than the FCM's customer. 7 U.S.C. § 6d(b). It is undisputed that Sentinel's FCM-clients held Section 4d(a)(2) funds, that the FCM-clients invested those funds with Sentinel, and that Sentinel held those funds in its own segregated accounts at BONY. In the March 30th Opinion, we ruled that because FCMs' handling of its customers' funds were the target of Section 4d(a)'s regulation, only FCMs could be held liable under Section 4d(b).

The rationale underlying our ruling is belied by a more natural reading of the statute and the purpose behind the statute. The scope of Section 4d(b) plainly encompasses persons beyond FCMs. Section 4d(b) is entitled "Duties of clearing agencies, depositories, and others in handling customer receipts." 7 U.S.C. § 6d(b). Additionally, the statute and corresponding regulations state that liability may extend to "any person." *Id.*; *see* 7 U.S.C. § 1a(38). Furthermore, Sentinel legally held and invested its FCMs' clients' funds with the CFTC's consent. Section 4d(b)'s non-exhaustive list of the types of entities that could legally hold FCMs' customers' funds indicates that Congress intended to hold entities like Sentinel liable in the event they misappropriated or commingled any of the FCMs' customers' funds. Interpreting Section 4d(b) to reach non-FCMs is consistent with an administrative action in which the CFTC's adjudicatory arm found that a non-FCM depository was liable under Section 4d(b) for using its FCM-client's customer funds to extend credit to the FCM-client. *See In re JP Morgan Chase Bank, N.A.*, Comm. Fut. L. Rep. [Current Transfer Binder] (CCH) ¶ 32, 156 (CFTC Apr. 4, 2012).

Moreover, accepting Defendants' argument that we ruled correctly the first time would require us to construe Section 4d(b) as a shield to liability for non-FCMs who legally accept FCMs' customers' funds but then commingle or misappropriate those funds. Such a reading is contrary to the purpose of the statute: protecting investors' funds and limiting the impact of serious market disruptions. *See Financial and Segregation Interpretation No. 9, Money Market Deposit Accounts and Now Accounts* ("[I]t has always been the Division's position that customer funds deposited in a bank cannot be restricted in any way, that such funds must be held for the benefit of customers and must be available to the customer and the FCM immediately upon demand."); *Financial and Segregation Interpretation No. 10, Treatment of Funds Deposited in Safekeeping Accounts* (when there is a market disruption, any impediment or restriction on the ability to immediately withdraw funds "could magnify the impact of any market disruption and cause additional repercussions."). Because the statute favors protecting investors' liquidity over providing a safe harbor for non-FCMs that misappropriate Section 4d(a)(2) funds, the CFTC's argument is persuasive.

As is demonstrated by the language of Section 4d(b) and its underlying purpose, Sentinel was required to comply with Section 4d(b).

We hold that granting Defendants' cross-motion for summary judgment on these grounds was in error and reverse our holding to the extent it relied on that rationale. * * *

NOTES

1. To become registered as a FCM, the applicant firm must file a Form 7-R with the NFA. Like the Form BD, the Form 7-R requires basic information about the FCM including:

A. Organizational structure and ownership

B. List of all Officers and Directors

C. List of the Headquarters and all Branch Offices

D. Net capital of the FCM (the FCM must file a recent audited financial statement)

E. Answers to several questions regarding its past activities and whether any fines, sanctions or other orders have ever been issued against the FCM.

2. If the FCM is jointly registered as a BD, then the firm may file several of the documents that it had previously filed with FINRA, including its Focus Reports on its financial condition, in lieu of the forms required by the CFTC (e.g., Form 1-FR-FCM).

3. Individuals file a Form 8-R to become registered as an Associated Person (AP) of an FCM or as a Principal. This form requires information similarly required by the Form U-5 for RRs as noted above. If the person is applying to become registered as an AP, then the individual must show proof that he or she has successfully completed the Series 3 exam. This is the only examination that a salesperson must have in the futures industry. Individuals who act as a Branch Manager must have taken either the Series 9/10 exam if the FCM is jointly registered as a BD/FCM or the Series 30 exam if the FCM is solely registered as an FCM. There are some other limited examinations for persons who are registered as RRs but these limitations are not actively used.

4. If a BD or FCM is not a clearing member firm of the respective stock or futures exchange, that BD or FCM must establish a clearing arrangement with a BD or FCM that is a clearing member firm. The two most common of these clearing arrangements are omnibus clearing arrangements or fully-disclosed clearing arrangements.

5. An omnibus clearing arrangement simply means that the non-clearing member firm opens an account with the clearing member firm in the name of the non-clearing member firm. The non-clearing member firm does not disclose the names or other information of its underlying customers and, therefore, must provide all of the required reports directly to its customers. The non-clearing member firm must also be registered as either a general BD

and/or as an FCM because it must be able to hold and maintain funds of its customers.

6. In a "fully disclosed" clearing arrangement, the non-clearing member firm actually discloses the names and account information of its customers to the clearing member firm. In fact, the customers introduced by the non-clearing member firms actually become customers of the clearing member firm. Therefore, the clearing member firm must treat these customers as if the clearing member firm directly solicited that customer. However, through the Clearing Agreement that establishes the fully disclosed clearing arrangement, the clearing member firm may seek to delegate several of its responsibilities and obligations to the non-clearing member firm.

7. Only BDs and FCMs can hold and maintain customer funds or property. Therefore, firms that may act like an BD or as an FCM but which do not intend to hold customer funds or property may register instead as an Introducing Broker-Dealer with the SEC or as an Introducing Broker with the CFTC.

8. In the securities industry, the firm registers as an Introducing Broker-Dealer by filing the same Form BD as General Broker-Dealers. In the futures industry, the applicable registration categories are Non-Guaranteed Introducing Broker and Guaranteed Introducing Broker.

The difference between these two CEA registration categories involve two principal themes. Generally, a Non-Guaranteed IB must have an adjusted net capital of $45,000. In contrast a Guaranteed IB is not required to have any net capital. [17 C.F.R. § 1.17]. A Guaranteed IB must open all of its customer accounts with the one FCM that must agree to guarantee all of the obligations of the Guaranteed IB.

In contrast, a Non-Guaranteed IB may open futures customer accounts with more than one FCM and the respective FCMs do not guarantee the acts or activities of the Non-Guaranteed IB. However, depending on the particular facts, and to what extent the FCM discloses the existence of the independent contractor relationship with the Non-Guaranteed IB, the IB may be deemed an agent of the FCM. That relationship could impose liability on the FCM for the acts of even a Non-Guaranteed IB if those acts are within the scope of the agency. [See, 7 U.S.C. § 2(a)(1)(B)].

See sample of an Introducing Broker Agreement that is typically signed when a Non-Guaranteed IB desires to introduce its futures customers to an FCM on a fully-disclosed clearing basis (See, Appendix D to this Casebook).

PRESTWICK CAPITAL MANAGEMENT, LTD. V. PEREGRINE FINANCIAL GROUP, INC.

727 F.3d 646 (7th Cir. 2013)

BARKER, DISTRICT JUDGE.

Author-*cum*-rabbi Chain Pothook once observed that life presents "absolutely no guarantee that things will automatically work out to our best advantage." Given the regulatory mandate that certain financial entities guarantee other entities' performance, and acknowledging that guarantees of all sorts can turn out to be ephemeral, we grapple here with the truth of Pothook's aphorism. More specifically, the instant lawsuit requires us to clarify the scope of a futures trading "guarantee gone wrong," presenting sunk investments and semantic distractions along the way.

In 2009, Prestwick Capital Management Ltd., Prestwick Capital Management 2 Ltd., and Prestwick Capital Management 3 Ltd. (collectively, "Prestwick") sued Peregrine Financial Group, Inc. ("PFG"), Acutest Inc., Acutest Brokers, LLC, and two of Acuvest's principals (John Caiazzo and Philip Grey), alleging violations of the Commodity Exchange Act ("CEA"), 7 U.S.C. § 1 *et seq.* Prestwick asserted a commodities fraud claim against all defendants, a breach of fiduciary duty claim against the Acuvest defendants, and a guarantor liability claim against PFG. After the district court awarded summary judgment to PFG in August 2011, Prestwick moved to dismiss the remaining defendants with prejudice in order to pursue its appeal of right against PFG. The district court subsequently dismissed the Acuvest defendants from the lawsuit, rendering its grant of summary judgment a final order which Prestwick now appeals. We affirm the district court

This commodities fraud lawsuit presents a corporation's attempt to recoup investments allegedly depleted during commerce involving an underfunded trading pool. * * *

. . . [F]utures commission merchants ("FCMs") are akin to securities brokerage houses. The CEA defines FCMs as "individual[s], association[s], partnership[s], corporation[s], or trust[s] . . . that [are] engaged in soliciting or in accepting orders for . . . the purchase or sale of a commodity for future delivery." 7 U.S.C. § 1a(28)(A)(i)(I)(aa)(AA).

Prior to 1982, it was customary for FCMs to outsource various projects to independent agents. *See* S. Rep. No. 97–384, at 40 (1982). The business dealings of these agents—many of whom were individuals or small businesses—troubled the CFTC for many reasons which soon came to the attention of Congress. As the House Committee on Agriculture noted in its May 17, 1982 report on the Futures Trading Act of 1982:

Although agents may perform the same functions as branch officers of [FCMs], agents generally are separately owned and run. [FCMs] frequently disavow any responsibility for sales abuses or other violations committed by these agents. The Committee believes that the best way to protect the public is to create a new and separate registration category for "agents". . . . Activities of agents and those of commodity trading advisors or associated persons of [FCMs] may be virtually identical, yet commodity trading advisors and such associated persons are registered and regulated under the [CEA], while many agents are not.

H.R. Rep. No. 97–565(I), at 49 (1982). The CFTC originally suggested requiring "agents" to register as FCMs' "associates," but Congress rejected that proposal. On that point, the Senate Committee on Agriculture, Nutrition, and Forestry reported, "[I]t would be inappropriate to (1) require these independent business entities to become branch offices of the [FCMs] through which their trades are cleared or (2) to impose vicarious liability on a [FCM] for the actions of an independent entity." S. Rep. No. 97–384, at 41. Yet Congress could no longer avoid the demand "to guarantee accountability and responsible conduct" of entities that "deal with commodity customers and, thus, have the opportunity to engage in abusive sales practices." *Id.* at 111. This quandary incited new legislation: the Futures Trading Act of 1982, Pub. L. No. 97–444, 96 Stat. 2294 (1983).

One legislative tactic Congress employed to remedy the CEA's perceived shortcomings was to launch a new futures trading entity: the introducing broker ("IB"). Like its "agent" predecessor, the IB was intended to procure customer orders independently, relying on FCMs to retain customer funds and maintain appropriate records. S. Rep. No. 97–384, at 41. This change was discernible in amended § 1a of the CEA, which defines an IB as "any person (except an individual who elects to be and is registered as an associated person of a futures commission merchant) . . . who . . . is engaged in soliciting or in accepting orders for . . . the purchase or sale of any commodity for future delivery." 7 U.S.C. § 1a(31)(A)(i)(I)(aa). To improve IB accountability, the Futures Trading Act of 1982 also supplemented the CEA's registration requirements. The amended CEA provides: "It shall be unlawful for any person to be an [IB] unless such person shall have registered with the [CFTC] as an [IB]." *Id.* § 6d(g). Registration as an IB is contingent upon the broker's ability to "meet[ ] such minimum financial requirements as the [CFTC] may by regulation prescribe as necessary to insure his meeting his obligation as a registrant." *Id.* § 6f(b). In a House Conference Report of December 13, 1982, Congress justified these amendments as follows:

Because many introducing brokers will be small businesses or individuals, as contemplated by the definition of this class of registrant, the conferees contemplate that the [CFTC] will establish financial requirements which will enable this new class of registrant to remain economically viable, although it is intended that fitness tests comparable to those required of associated persons will also be employed. The intent of the conferees is to require commission registration of all persons dealing with the public, but to provide the registrants with substantial flexibility as to the manner and classification of registration.

H.R. Rep. No. 96–964, at 41 (1982) (Conf. Rep.). Pursuant to 7 U.S.C. § 21(*o*), the CFTC has delegated this registration function to the National Futures Association ("NFA"), a private corporation registered as a futures association under the CEA. *See* 7 U.S.C. § 21(j) (discussing requirements for registered futures associations).

In August 1983, the CFTC promulgated a final rule setting forth minimum financial benchmarks for IBs. 48 Fed. Reg. 35,248, 35,249 (Aug. 3, 1983). This, too, was a compromise; the draft version of the rule would have required IBs, *inter alia*, to maintain a minimum adjusted net capital level of $25,000 and to file monthly financial reports if capital fell to "less than 150 percent of the minimum" amount (the "early warning" requirement). *Id.* at 35,249; *see also* 48 Fed. Reg. 14,933, 14,934, 14,945 (Apr. 6, 1983) (original version of rule). After the notice and comment period, the CFTC reduced the minimum adjusted net capital requirement to $20,000 and permitted IBs to credit toward this balance 50 percent of guarantee or security deposits maintained with FCMs 48 Fed. Reg. at 35,249. The current requisite minimum adjusted net capital is $45,000 or "[t]he amount of adjusted net capital required by a registered futures association of which [an IB] is a member." 17 C.F.R. § 1.17(a)(1)(iii)(A)–(B). Each IB must annually report its net capital position on CFTC Form 1-FR-IB. *Id.* § 1.10(b)(2)(ii)(A). However, an IB "shall be deemed to meet the adjusted net capital requirement" if it is a party to a binding guarantee agreement satisfying the conditions outlined in 17 C.F.R. § 1.10(j). *Id.* § 1.17(a)(2)(ii). A guaranteed IB, in other words, is not subject to the same reporting requirements imposed on an IB that has assumed an independent status. According to the CFTC, this dispensation is appropriate because "the guarantee agreement provides that the FCM . . . will guarantee performance by the [IB] of its obligations under the Act and the rules, regulations, and order thereunder. . . . [and] is an alternative means for an [IB] to satisfy the [CFTC's] standards of financial responsibility." 48 Fed. Reg. at 35,249.

In the case before us, the plaintiff, Prestwick, is a conglomerate of Canadian investment companies operating primarily out of Chestermere,

Alberta. The defendant, PFG, is an Iowa corporation with its principal place of business in Chicago, Illinois; it also conducts business in New York as an active foreign corporation. Importantly, PFG is registered with the CFTC as an FCM that guarantees compliance with the CEA by certain registered IBs, including two of the Acuvest defendants (Acuvest Inc. and Acuvest Brokers, LLC). Acuvest Inc. is a Delaware corporation with its principal place of business in Temecula, California; Acuvest Brokers, LLC, a branch of Acuvest Inc., is a New York corporation with its principal place of business in the State of New York. Caiazzo and Grey, the remaining Acuvest defendants, are Acuvest Inc. executives who have registered with the NFA in personal capacities.

In 2004, pursuant to the CFTC regulations discussed *supra*, Acuvest and PFG executed a guarantee agreement ("the 2004 Guarantee Agreement"). *See* 17 C.F.R. § 1.3(nn). The portion of their 2004 Guarantee Agreement that is the focus of this lawsuit provided, in relevant part, as follows:

> PFG guarantees performance by [Acuvest] . . . of, and shall be jointly and severally liable for, all obligations of the IB under the Commodity Exchange Act ("CEA"), as it may be amended from time to time, and the rules, regulations, and orders which have been or may be promulgated thereunder with respect to the solicitation of and transactions involving all commodity customer, option customer, foreign futures customer, and foreign options customer accounts of the IB entered into on or after the effective date of this Agreement.

Thus, the arrangement between PFG and Acuvest contemplated (1) Acuvest's solicitation of customers and subsequent engagement with customers for business dealings, and (2) PFG's willingness to assure Acuvest's customers that Acuvest would conform its conduct to the mandates of the CEA. Further, as the district court noted, this provision made PFG responsible for any fraudulent conduct engaged in by Acuvest.

Two years later, PFG's compliance director, Susan O'Meara, sent a memorandum to the NFA to inform the NFA of a change in PFG's relationship with Acuvest. This correspondence, titled "Guaranteed IB Termination," was dated August 25, 2006 and advised, "As of August 24, 2006, [PFG] will terminate its guarantee agreement with Acuvest. . . . This termination has been done by mutual consent."

Acuvest and PFG executed an agreement of a slightly different nature the very same month—a "Clearing Agreement for Independent Introducing Broker" ("the 2006 IIB Agreement"). Section 25 of the 2006 IIB Agreement stated that this contract "supersede[d] and replace[d] any and all previous agreements between [Acuvest] and PFG." Under the new arrangement, PFG agreed to "execute[,] buy[,] and sell orders and perform settlement and accounting services for and on behalf of [c]ustomers introduced by [Acuvest]." PFG's other obligations under this Agreement pertained to customers and included preparing activity reports, mailing account statements, distributing payments, conducting "all cashiering functions," and maintaining records. Acuvest, by contrast, assumed significantly more responsibilities to PFG and its customers. Notably, Acuvest's signature on the 2006 IIB Agreement evinced its consent to:

> comply with the rules and regulations of all relevant regulatory entities, exchanges[,] and self-regulatory organizations related to the purchase and sale of [f]utures [i]nvestments. . . . [Acuvest] shall use its best efforts to assure that [a] [c]ustomer complies with all applicable position limits established by the CFTC or any contract market. [Acuvest] shall not knowingly permit any transaction to be effected in any [c]ustomer account in violation of such limits. [Acuvest] shall promptly report to PFG any [c]ustomer's [c]ustomer [sic] [a]ccount exceeding any applicable limit.

From a financial perspective, the 2006 IIB Agreement dramatically expanded Acuvest's obligations. This adjustment was consistent with the CFTC's official differentiation between guaranteed and independent IBs: "By entering into the agreement, the [guaranteed IB] is relieved from the necessity of raising its own capital to satisfy minimum financial requirements. In contrast, an independent [IB] must raise its own capital to meet minimum financial requirements." Here, Acuvest was accountable for all customer losses, charges, and deficiencies, as well as initial and maintenance margin requirements. Acuvest also accepted absolute financial responsibility for its own actions and pledged to indemnify PFG from any harm resulting therefrom. Perhaps the most salient feature of the 2006 IIB Agreement was its treatment of guarantees. As an independent IB, Acuvest was bound by a new indemnification provision: "[Acuvest] guarantees all the financial obligations of the [c]ustomer accounts of [c]ustomers serviced by [Acuvest] and/or carried on the equity run reports produced by PFG for [Acuvest]."

PFG and Acuvest altered the nature of their relationship again on July 3, 2008 by entering into yet another agreement ("the 2008 Guarantee Agreement"). As was true of the 2006 IIB Agreement, this contract superseded all previous agreements between Acuvest and PFG. However, the new arrangement restored Acuvest to its prior status as a guaranteed IB. The provision in which PFG guaranteed Acuvest's obligations involving "customer accounts of [Acuvest] entered into on or after the effective date of th[e] Agreement" was specified by regulation and, therefore, identical to the text cited *supra* from the 2004 Guarantee

Agreement. *See* 17 C.F.R. § 1.3(nn) (requiring guarantee text from CFTC Form 1-FRIB Part B).

Acuvest's role as an IB eventually intersected with Prestwick. The Acuvest-Prestwick business relationship arose when Acuvest advised Prestwick to become a limited partner in Maxie Partners L.P. ("Maxie"), a New York commodity trading pool registered with the NFA as an "Exempt Commodity Trading Advisor. For purposes of the instant litigation, Acuvest was the IB for all of Maxie's accounts. Prestwick elected to join the Maxie trading pool and invested approximately $7,000,000 in that fund between 2005 and 2006. During this time period, the Acuvest defendants assumed full responsibility for Maxie's management and investment decisions regarding the account holding Prestwick's funds and maintained open lines of communication with Prestwick.

In April 2007, Prestwick informed Grey (one of Acuvest's executive vice presidents) of its intent to redeem Prestwick's limited partnership interest in Maxie. Grey transmitted Prestwick's redemption notice to Winell (the trading pool operator), told Prestwick that an accountant would perform a valuation of its investment in the pool, and indicated that Prestwick's funds would be wired sometime between July 10 and July 15, 2007. Believing that Maxie's assets were valued at approximately $20,000,000, Prestwick was understandably alarmed to learn on August 7, 2007 that much of its $7,000,000 investment in Maxie was unavailable. Prestwick attributes this circumstance to the "losing trading" decisions of Acuvest and Winell in July 2007. Specifically, Prestwick alleges a causal relationship between the pool's significant losses and the redepositing of nearly $4,000,000 of Prestwick's funds in Maxie's PFG account to meet frequent margin call demands. Prestwick avers that Grey, as an agent of Acuvest, knew that none of Prestwick's funds should have been redeposited into the pool's PFG account— especially not for purposes of trading or covering margin calls.

Ultimately, Prestwick's notice of redemption did not generate the anticipated payout. Prestwick claims to have received only two disbursements of its original investment in the pool—one in August 2007, and the other in October 2007—totaling approximately $3,000,000. Despite Prestwick's allegation that Winell provided assurances of forthcoming payments, Prestwick's efforts to collect the remaining balance since October 2007 have been wholly unsuccessful. Prestwick contends that it is presently owed the remainder of its limited partnership interest in Maxie, which is roughly $4,000,000.

Although Prestwick initially filed suit against PFG, Acuvest, Caiazzo, and Grey in the Southern District of New York, that action was transferred to the Northern District of Illinois on the defendants' motion.

Prestwick asserted three causes of action in its complaint: (1) commodities pool fraud as to all defendants; (2) breach of fiduciary duty as to the Acuvest defendants; and (3) guarantor liability as to PFG. The district court awarded summary judgment to PFG on August 25, 2011. Invoking Federal Rule of Civil Procedure 41(a)(2), Prestwick moved to dismiss its claims with prejudice against the Acuvest defendants. On December 30, 2011, the district court granted Prestwick's motion to dismiss. The case was closed on January 3, 2012, and Prestwick filed its timely notice of appeal on January 27, 2012.

Prestwick raises two issues for our review. The first is whether termination of PFG's guarantee of Acuvest's obligations under the CEA also terminated such protection "for existing accounts opened during the term of the guarantee," a result Prestwick vehemently repudiates. The second is whether PFG may be equitably estopped from arguing that the 2004 Guarantee Agreement was effectively terminated, which Prestwick contends should be answered in the affirmative. Because Prestwick's arguments cannot be harmonized with law or logic, we reach contrary results on both questions presented and affirm the entirety of the district court's decision. * * *

Prestwick's challenge to the district court's decision regarding the temporal scope of the 2004 Guarantee Agreement is threefold. First, Prestwick contends that the district court erroneously disregarded the plain contractual language. Prestwick's suggested construction of the 2004 Guarantee Agreement would render PFG liable for Acuvest's obligations concerning any account *opened* with PFG "during the term of" that agreement—no matter when any subsequent wrongdoing related to such account occurred. Second, Prestwick accuses the district court of misinterpreting and rewriting the 2006 IIB Agreement when the court concluded that this document, not the 2004 Guarantee Agreement, governed the PFG account containing Prestwick's funds. According to Prestwick, the parties did not intend the 2006 IIB Agreement to end PFG's guarantee of Acuvest's obligations for accounts predating its execution. Third, Prestwick argues that the district court's ruling contravenes significant consumer protection policies underlying the CFTC's regulatory scheme for guaranteed IBs. We respectfully disagree with Prestwick as to all arguments it has advanced on this issue. * * *

First, we turn to the practical aspects of terminating a guarantee agreement consistent with the CEA and its attendant rules and regulations. The CFTC explicitly addressed the contours of termination in its final rule on "Registration and Other Regulatory Requirements" for IBs, dated August 3, 1983, as follows:

> If [a] guarantee agreement does not expire or is not terminated
> in accordance with the provisions of § 1.10(j). . ., it shall remain

in effect indefinitely. The [CFTC] wishes to make clear that the termination of a guarantee agreement by an FCM or by an introducing broker, or the expiration of such an agreement, does not relieve any party from any liability or obligation arising from acts or omissions which occurred during the term of the agreement.

48 Fed. Reg. 35,248, 35,265 (citation omitted). This rule corresponds to Title 17, Section 1.10(j) of the Code of Federal Regulations, which provides the protocol for ending a guaranteed IB relationship. Termination of a guarantee agreement may take place at any time during its effective term through one of three procedures:

> (i) [b]y mutual written consent of the parties, signed by an appropriate person on behalf of each party, with prompt written notice thereof, signed by an appropriate person on behalf of each party, to the Commission and to the designated self-regulatory organizations of the [FCM] or retail foreign exchange dealer and the [IB];

> (ii) [f]or good cause shown, by either party giving written notice of its intention to terminate the agreement, signed by an appropriate person, to the other party to the agreement, to the Commission, and to the designated self-regulatory organizations of the [FCM] or retail foreign exchange dealer and the [IB]; or

> (iii) [b]y either party giving written notice of its intention to terminate the agreement, signed by an appropriate person, at least 30 days prior to the proposed termination date, to the other party to the agreement, to the Commission, and to the designated self-regulatory organizations of the [FCM] or retail foreign exchange dealer and the [IB].

17 C.F.R. § 1.10(j)(6). * * *

Our view that the district court properly heeded the plain language of the 2004 Guarantee Agreement is bolstered by record evidence confirming that the contract was effectively terminated on August 24, 2006, *i.e.*, an authenticated screenshot of information from the NFA's "External Tracking" electronic database The NFA maintains data repositories like these to log start and end dates of guarantee agreements for registered IBs. This undertaking is critical because "[a]n introducing broker may not simultaneously be a party to more than one guarantee agreement." 17 C.F.R. § 1.10(j)(8). * * *

Having Denied PFG's motion to dismiss the instant appeal, we likewise reject its contention that summary judgment for PFG was improper. For the foregoing reasons, we Affirm the judgment of the district court in favor of PFG.

NOTE

1. PFG filed for bankruptcy in July 2012 after it was discovered that its principal officer, Russell Wassendorf, Sr., had fraudulently misappropriated approximately $200,000,000 in customer assets. Wassendorf pled guilty to several criminal counts filed against him.

4. RECORD-KEEPING AND REPORTING REQUIREMENTS

Every firm registered either as a BD or as an FCM must maintain all records for a minimum period of five years. The first two years must be kept on premises and the prior three years may be kept at an offsite location [17 C.F.R. § 1.31]. Today, all such firms primarily maintain the required records on a computerized system. The records that must be kept include but are not limited to:

1. All customer account opening documents

2. All statements that have been sent to a customer including the Daily Confirmations and Monthly Statements

3. All correspondence between the Firm and its customers including but not limited to all written correspondence, emails, text messages and other electronic media

4. All complaints filed by any customer against the Firm or an Employee of the Firm

5. All orders and tickets that have been prepared including all electronic records

6. All reports that have been filed with any regulatory agency or exchange

7. All litigation matters filed against the Firm or any of its Employees relating to the Firm's business.

[See e.g., 17 C.F.R. § 1.35].

MARKOWSKI V. SEC
34 F.3d 99 (2d Cir. 1994)

JACOBS, CIRCUIT JUDGE:

Petitioner Michael Markowski, pro se, petitions for judicial review pursuant to 15 U.S.C. § 78y(a)(1) of an order of the Securities and Exchange Commission ("SEC") sustaining disciplinary action taken against him by the National Association of Securities Dealers, Inc. ("NASD") [now FINRA]. These disciplinary proceedings arose from a series of confrontations in March and April 1991, between staff of the

NASD and the representatives of Global America Inc. ("Global"), a member of the NASD that had ceased brokerage operations and was then winding down its business. Markowski was at that time the Chairman of Global, its Chief Executive Officer, and the majority stockholder in Global's parent company, and was himself a member of the NASD. The NASD's staff was seeking immediate on-site access at Global's offices to the books and records Global was required to prepare and maintain, pursuant to SEC Rules 17a–3 and 17a–4, with respect to the 19 securities in which Global made a market.

Following proceedings before the Market Surveillance Committee ("MSC") of the NASD and the National Business Conduct Committee ("NBCC") of the NASD, the SEC affirmed (i) the conclusion of the NBCC that Markowski had violated the NASD's Rules of Fair Practice and (ii) the disciplinary sanctions imposed by the NBCC: a fine of $50,000, a two-year suspension from association with any member firm in any capacity, and a bar on any debt or equity interest in any firm.

In his petition, Markowski contends that he fulfilled any responsibilities he had in respect of the NASD's document demand by delegating responsibility for maintaining and producing documents to a records custodian and by reasonably relying upon advice of counsel. Markowski faults the NASD for failing to locate the proper records custodian and for denying Markowski due process in connection with the hearing before the MSC. Finally Markowski claims that he is the subject of "administrative selective persecution."

Markowski was first registered with the NASD in November 1977. Global became a member in August of 1988 and Markowski registered as General Securities Principal with Global in May 1989. During the time Global operated as a brokerage business, Markowski was Chairman and Chief Executive Officer, and was majority stockholder of its parent company. Net capital deficiencies compelled Global to cease operating as a brokerage business on January 16, 1991. At some point, Markowski took steps to resign as Chairman.

On March 5, 1991, members of the NASD staff arrived at the business premises of Global to conduct an unannounced, on-site inspection of books and records Global was required by the securities laws to prepare and maintain in respect of the 19 stocks of which it made a market. The NASD examiners were met at the door by Markowski's mother, a registered Global representative; Markowski was not present. Mrs. Markowski contacted her son's attorney, Martin H. Kaplan, Esq., who soon arrived at Global's offices and demanded that the examiners put down the books and records, and leave. After some further exchanges, one of Kaplan's law partners summoned the New York City police, who expelled the examiners from the premises. Later on March 5, Daniel M.

Sibears, Director of the NASD's Compliance Division, spoke by telephone with Markowski who at that time was working at a securities firm called Paragon Capital Corporation ("Paragon"). In conversations with Markowski on that date, as well as on subsequent days, Sibears protested that the NASD was being denied access to Global's records. Recollections diverge as to what was said in conversations between NASD staff and Markowski on March 5; but Markowski concedes this much: that he discussed access to the records on that date with Sibears and that he agreed to meet the examiners at Global's offices the following day to afford them access to the firm's records.

The NASD's examiners appeared on March 6, but no one answered the door. A short while later, the staff received a letter from Mr. Kaplan, either by hand or by fax. Mr. Kaplan characterized Sibears's telephone calls to Markowski as "an effort to end run Global's position", sought to interpose an ethical impediment to further direct contact with Markowski by identifying Leonard Bloom, Esq., as counsel representing Markowski in "this matter," and offered to make Global's records available for review by the NASD staff "subject to reasonable identification of the items sought and a reasonable methodology being agreed to for said production." Kaplan solicited a prompt response to "avoid the need for further disagreement and acrimony" (probably an allusion to the police). Later that day, the examiners went to Paragon's office and delivered a letter addressed to Markowski in which Sibears requested immediate access to records. A woman on the premises accepted the letter on Markowski's behalf. The examiners looked up Markowski's home address in the NASD's federal registration depository, and tried to deliver a copy of the letter to him there, but discovered that he had not lived there for six months or more. Markowski had failed to notify the NASD of his change of address.

Further discussions ensued on March 7 between Sibears and Kaplan's law firm. Sibears telecopied a letter to Bloom stating that the NASD was making a final demand for access to Global's records at 2 p.m. that day. Although Bloom did not respond to the letter, one of Kaplan's colleagues telephoned Sibears and informed him that (i) Global would not provide access to its records on March 7, (ii) some of Global's records would be available for review at Kaplan's law office at 10 a.m. on March 8, and (iii) Sibears would receive a letter later in the day indicating when all of the requested records would be available and describing the "methodology" Global would follow in making the records available to the NASD. Sibears faxed a letter to Kaplan's colleague "confirming our conversation of . . . this afternoon" to the effect that "certain" books and records would be available at the offices of Global's counsel the following morning, and that Global would advise as to when "all of the requested records" would be available to the NASD staff and what "methodology"

Global would follow for the document production. Sibears, however, was unable to reach the examiners who were en route to Global's offices; when the examiners arrived there at 2 p.m. on March 7, they were denied access to the records. A fax from Mr. Kaplan the following morning duly noted that the NASD examiners failed to appear at Kaplan's office at the appointed time.

Over the following days, the antagonists exchanged legalistic correspondence expressing dismay and disappointment at each other's conduct, characterizing and re-characterizing each other's offers and positions, and proceeding generally at cross purposes concerning arrangements for the production of the documents. This exchange produced an impasse in which Global undertook to produce less than all of the documents at the offices of its counsel and to comply with all reasonable requests in due course, while the NASD examiners, having been denied on-site review of all records at Global's offices, demanded that all the documents be shipped immediately to Washington.

In the end, Global did not provide the NASD access to any documents until May 17, 1991, after the NASD had instituted disciplinary proceedings and obtained an order of production. Even then, Markowski produced less than all of the requested records; the rest were produced on June 5, 1991, the second day of the disciplinary hearings.

On April 9, 1991, a month after the NASD staff first arrived at Global's premises, the Anti Fraud Department of the NASD commenced disciplinary proceedings against Global and Markowski. The complaint before the Market Surveillance Committee alleged violations of Sections 17(a) and 17(b) of the Securities and Exchange Act of 1934, 15 U.S.C. § 78q, and Rule 17a–4 promulgated thereunder, as well as various provisions of the NASD's By-Laws and Rules of Fair Practice.

The disciplinary proceedings before the MSC were instituted on May 13, 1991. On the scheduled date of the hearing, Markowski did not appear; Kaplan did appear, but stated that he was not prepared to go forward and sought a continuance. The continuance was granted. On June 5, the re-scheduled hearing date, Markowski appeared with new counsel, who was also unprepared and who also sought a continuance. The second continuance was denied, and the hearing was conducted. On September 18, 1991, the MSC found that Markowski and Global had (i) violated Section 17(a) and Section 17(b) of the Exchange Act and Rule 17a–4 promulgated thereunder; (ii) failed to comply with the NASD's record-keeping requirements in Article III, Section 21, of the NASD Rules of Fair Practice; (iii) failed to submit to the examination of their books and records, as required by Article IV, Section 5 of the NASD Rules; (iv) failed to observe "high standards of commercial honor and just and equitable principles of trade", as required by Article III, Section 1 of the

NASD Rules; and (v) failed to update their registrations to reflect their current addresses, as required by Article IV, Section 2(c) of the NASD By-Laws. The MSC ordered Global expelled from membership and, as to Markowski, ordered that he be fined $50,000, suspended from association with any member firm in any capacity for six (6) months, barred from association with any member in a principal capacity and barred from maintaining a debt or equity interest in any member firm.

Markowski appealed to the NBCC, which set aside the MSC's findings with respect to the record-keeping violations of Sections 17(a) and (b) of the Securities and Exchange Act and Article III, Section 21 of the NASD's Rules of Fair Practice. The NBCC affirmed in all other respects except that Markowski's suspension was lengthened from six months to two years. The NBCC modified certain findings of the MSC as follows:

As to the critical events of March 5, 1991, we credit the testimony of the staff that the staff did not engage in an unreasonable search or other violation of the respondent's rights, although we note that when a member firm orders the staff off its premises in response to a request for production of documents pursuant to Article IV, Section 5 of the Rules, a violation is complete and it is unnecessary to test the limits of applicable state property law. We do not consider the fact that the police were called to have been a factor in aggravation of the respondent's violation, but observe that the respondent was notified of the staff's situation at a time when compliance and cooperation could have avoided the confrontation that ensued. We believe that Markowski's decision to temporize when confronted by Sibears' calls on March 5 constituted a refusal to comply, not reliance on counsel. We further believe, as observed by the regional attorney, that Markowski did not rely on advice of counsel in refusing access to the NASD staff on March 5, 1991, since he admitted that he did not consult with Kaplan until that day was over.

As to Markowski's argument that he reasonably relied upon the advice of counsel and the steps taken by Mr. Kaplan on behalf of Global, the NBCC concluded:

> Markowski knew or should have known that he could not delegate responsibility for satisfying the investigative demands of the NASD to Kaplan, particularly after learning of the NASD's dissatisfaction with Kaplan's refusal to grant unconditional access.

The NBCC imposed sanctions against Markowski for his violations of Article IV, Section 5 and Article III, Section 1 of the Rules of Fair Practice, but not for his violation of Article IV, Section 2(c) of the By-Laws. In relevant part, Article IV, Section 5 of the Rules of Fair Practice stated as follows:

For the purpose of any investigation . . . any Local Business Conduct Committee, any District Business Conduct Committee, the Board of Governors or any duly authorized member and members of any such Committees or Board or any duly authorized agent or agents of any such Committee or Board shall have the right . . . to investigate the books, records and accounts of any [member of the Corporation] with relation to any matter involved in any such investigation. . . . No member or person associated with a member shall . . . refuse to permit any inspection of books, records and accounts as may be validly called for under this section.

(That version of Section 5 was substantially amended and reworded effective April 15, 1992.)

Markowski appealed the NBCC ruling to the SEC, which affirmed the disciplinary sanctions on June 30, 1993. On August 23, 1993, Markowski filed a timely petition for review by this Court pursuant to 15 U.S.C. § 78y(1). On September 3, 1993 the SEC granted Markowski a stay of the sanctions pending the disposition of his petition by this Court.

Administrative findings of fact are conclusive if they are supported by substantial evidence. *Higgins v. SEC*, 866 F.2d 47, 49 (2d Cir. 1989); *see* 15 U.S.C. 78y(a)(4). "We review conclusions of law for arbitrariness, capriciousness and abuse of discretion." *Higgins*, 866 F.2d at 49.

Markowski chiefly relies upon *In Re Mark James Hankoff*, 48 S.E.C. 705 (1987), for the proposition that a senior officer of a brokerage firm is responsible for compliance by the firm, but may rely upon the reasonable delegation of particular functions to others, absent knowledge or reason to know of non-compliance by the person to whom the function is delegated. That is a fair statement of the law, but it does not assist Markowski. The facts found below support the view that, as early as March 5, 1991, immediately after the police escorted the NASD examiners from Global's premises, Markowski was made aware that the NASD's demand for access to documents was not being met. Markowski's briefs to this Court repeatedly emphasize that he designated a competent employee, named Carol Zervoulei, to maintain and produce Global's documents as needed, and that the NASD would have been able to find her and review the documents if the NASD had merely consulted Markowski's designation of her in the NASD's own records. That might have avoided the encounter with the police on March 5. However, Markowski's conduct has not been faulted at any administrative level by reason of anything preceding the phone call on the afternoon of March 5 when Sibears advised Markowski personally of the NASD's unmet demands. At that point, Markowski knew (or certainly should have known) that Ms. Zervoulei was not involved in the NASD's document request. See Patrick v. SEC, 19 F.3d 66, 69 (2d Cir. 1994) (per curiam) (high-level officers of a broker-dealer responsible for supervision of appointed representatives). It is not altogether clear whether Kaplan thereafter functioned as counsel for Global only or as counsel for Markowski as well, but there is no reason to doubt that Markowski, either individually or as officer of Global, controlled Kaplan or had the power to do so. Markowski therefore cannot evade responsibility for what Kaplan did and did not do. Id.

It is clear that from the outset the NASD's examiners demanded access to Global's files at Global's premises on an immediate basis. Markowski argues here (and presumably argued below) that "such urgency was inappropriate for the review of books and records of a firm that was winding down." However, the need for urgency may be heightened when it comes to reviewing the books and records of a brokerage firm that has ceased doing business by reason of financial distress. In one of his letters, Kaplan justified his refusal to permit immediate access to Global's books and records on its premises on the ground that the documents were "haphazardly filed and not indexed". But the disarray of business records does not argue forbearance on the part of regulators. * * *

For the foregoing reasons the petition for review is denied and the order of the SEC is affirmed.

AMERICAN INTERNATIONAL TRADING CO. V. BAGLEY
536 F.2d 1196 (7th Cir. 1976)

CLARK, ASSOCIATE JUSTICE.

On March 29, 1976, the Commodity Futures Trading Commission (CFTC), in accordance with Section 6b of the Commodity Exchange Act, as amended, 7 U.S.C. § 1 (Supp. IV, 1974), authorized an investigation into the business activities of American International Trading Company (Trading Company). Previously the CFTC had examined records of the Trading Company under its inspection powers; had requested and received a list of its customers and was initiating interviews of the latter pursuant to a number of complaints that the Trading Company was victimizing its customers in commodity futures transactions through fraudulent and deceptive acts and practices. On the same day of the CFTC authorization of the investigation, the Trading Company brought this action seeking an order enjoining CFTC from contacting its customers, other than those who had initially contacted the Commission, on the ground that it would destroy its business. The CFTC moved to dismiss for lack of jurisdiction and failure to exhaust administrative remedies, etc. Then on March 31, the district court issued a temporary restraining order enjoining the CFTC from interviewing the Trading

Company's customers, which order was succeeded on April 16th by a preliminary injunction which prohibited the use of the customer list of Trading Company for interview purposes. However, the court found no basis for laying venue in the Northern District of Illinois and ordered the case transferred to the District of Columbia but continued the injunction in effect. The CFTC appealed, a stay was granted, and briefing was expedited. We reverse and direct that, on remand, the complaint be dismissed.

We need not consider the claim of insufficiency of evidence nor other defects in procedure, etc., since we find the Trading Company's claim utterly frivolous. First, the Act itself authorizes the CFTC to "make such investigations as it may deem necessary to ascertain the facts regarding operations of boards of trade and other persons subject to any of the provisions of this Act," Section 8. In addition, the Congress for "the purpose of securing effective enforcement of this Act, and for the purpose of any investigation or proceedings under this Act," made "the provisions, including penalties, of the Interstate Commerce Act . . . applicable to the power, jurisdiction and authority of the Commission [CFTC]." And, as if these provisions were not sufficient, the Congress in Section 6g(1) required futures commission merchants or floor brokers to make such reports as CFTC required, keep such books and records pertaining to all transactions as the CFTC directed, and keep them open to inspection by any representative of the Commission. There are a host of cases on the power of an agency to require production, most of which stem from *Oklahoma Press Pub. Co. v. Walling*, 327 U.S. 186, 90 L. Ed. 614, 66 S. Ct. 494 (1946), where the Court said that it was for the agency rather than the district courts to determine in the first instance the question of coverage in the course of a preliminary investigation into possible violations. Id., at 214. It will be soon enough on direct appeal from agency action to determine the question of power. See *Federal Trade Commission v. Feldman*, 532 F.2d 1092 (7th Cir. 1976), where this court enforced a subpoena *duces tecum* holding the defenses alleged were premature. This eliminates the problem of delays which is of the essence in agency administration. If there be a legitimate purpose to which the investigation is pertinent, if the agency does not have the information sought and the formal administrative steps provided in its creative Act have been followed, then courts should not intervene in the initial determinations; they are for the agency to decide at this stage of the inquiry. *United States v. Powell*, 379 U.S. 48, 57–58, 13 L. Ed. 2d 112, 85 S. Ct. 248; *FTC v. Crafts*, 355 U.S. 9, 2 L. Ed. 2d 23, 78 S. Ct. 33 (1957); *Oklahoma Press Pub. Co. v. Walling, supra; Endicott v. Johnson Corp. v. Perkins*, 317 U.S. 501, 87 L. Ed. 424, 63 S. Ct. 339 (1948); 1 Davis Admr. Law § 3.12 (1958).

Nor do we find that CFTC was conducting its investigation in an unauthorized manner. As the Second Circuit observed in *Securities & Exchange Commission v. Brigadoon Scotch Distributing Co.*, 480 F.2d 1047, 1056 (1973), cert. den., 415 U.S. 915, 94 S. Ct. 1410, 39 L. Ed. 2d 469 (1974):

> Every person doing business and every investor knows that government agencies conduct investigations for a variety of reasons, and most of them feel the duty to respond to a proper inquiry. As for those whose practices are investigated, *it is a necessary hazard of doing business to be the subject of inquiry by a government regulatory agency.* (Emphasis supplied.)

While the CFTC proposed to contact the customers of the Trading Company by telephone, we cannot say that the use of such technique was unusual or that the questions proposed were abusive or harassing. Perhaps questions (3) and (4) smacked of the "When did you stop beating your wife" technique, but then fire sometimes has to be fought with fire.

Accordingly, the judgment of the district court is reversed, the injunction is vacated, and the case is remanded to the district court with instructions to dismiss.

Reversed.

Dissent by: CAMPBELL * * *

NOTES

1. The CFTC's inspection powers under section 4g(a) of the CEA [7 U.S.C. § 6g(a)] are tied to the requirement of registration of FCMs and others. That requirement allows the CFTC to require registrants to keep specified books and records. Section 4g(a) then allows the CFTC to inspect those records without issuing a subpoena.

2. The CFTC staff has claimed that CEA inspection powers authorize it to require registrants to search their files for an unlimited amount of documents and that registrants must copy and transfer those files to the CFTC when and where the staff demands. In re Merrill Lynch, Pierce, Fenner & Smith, CFTC Doc. No. 86–14 (settled by consent).

5. DISCLOSURE REQUIREMENTS

Each BD and FCM has a duty to disclose material risks associated with any investment made by its respective customers. The amount and type of such disclosures vary depending upon the product being sold and the investment sophistication of the respective customer. If the customer is a high net worth individual, then less disclosure may be required. The decision to provide or not provide any such disclosures is based on a customer-by-customer analysis. This principle is best explained in FINRA

Rule 2111 which requires the BD and the RR to determine that the customer is suitable for any recommendation or market strategy involving a security before making any such recommendation or providing any market strategy to that customer. However, as described in Chapter 8, there is no "suitability rule" in futures. Nevertheless, both the federal securities and NFA futures regulations require the BD and FCM to "know your customer" before opening any account with that customer.

The timing as to when to provide the disclosures varies for BDs and FCMs. For example, CFTC Rule 1.55 [17 C.F.R. § 1.55] requires the FCM to provide a Uniform Risk Disclosure Statement to the futures customer before the customer's futures account is opened. In contrast, various securities disclosures, such as prospectuses and stock option disclosures are required to be sent along with the confirmation (e.g., on a post-trade basis).

The degree of the disclosure requirement also varies depending on the background, experience and investment sophistication of the respective customer. Regulatory principles are designed to provide greater information to a "retail" customer than to a more sophisticated "institutional" customer. Unlike the retail customer, the institutional investor has sufficient assets to protect itself without government oversight. FINRA Rule 2111 now defines an "institutional account" as any firm or person who has more than $50,000,000 in assets.

6. NET CAPITAL REQUIREMENTS

To be registered as a BD or as an FCM, the firm must maintain a certain minimum amount of net capital. The applicable term is "adjusted net capital," which means the amount of the Firm's liquid current assets in excess of the Firm's total liabilities. Unlike a company's shareholder value accounting, the financial requirements for a BD and an FCM are much higher as all of its fixed assets and goodwill do not apply to this calculation. See, Jerry W. Markham, The CFTC Net Capital Rule— Should a More Risk-Based Approach be Adopted, 71 Chicago-Kent L. Rev. 1091 (1996) (describing the role of the net capital requirement).

Even current assets are reduced by a percentage "haircut" based on the riskiness of the current assets. For example, the market value discounts (or haircuts) range from .5 percent for government securities with maturities between three and six months to 6.0 percent for government securities with maturities over twenty-five years to 15 percent for stocks. See, SEC Rule 15c3–1 [17 C.F.R. § 240.15c3–1].

BDs are required to have an adjusted net capital equal to the greater of (a) $250,000 or (b) an amount based on one of two formulas. These two formulas are: (a) the Aggregate Indebtedness Standard, and (b) the Alternative Standard. Under the Aggregate Indebtedness Standard, the

BD may not permit its aggregate indebtedness to all other persons to exceed 1500 percent of its net capital (800 percent during its first twelve months after commencing business as a BD). Under the Alternative Standard, the BD must maintain adjusted net capital in an amount that is the greater of (i) $250,000, or (ii) 2 percent of its aggregate debit items. See, SEC Rule 15c3–1 [240 C.F.R. § 15c3–1].

FCMs are required to have an adjusted net capital equal to the greater of (a) $1,000,000 or (b) 8 percent of the risk-based margin amounts held at the FCM. See, CFTC Rule 1.17. [17 C.F.R. § 1.17]. See also "FCM Financial Data", which can be found on the cover page of the CFTC website at: www.cftc.gov. This chart, updated monthly, provides important financial information on all FCMs, including, among other things, their adjusted net capital, the excess amount of their adjusted net capital and the amount of customer assets held by each FCM in their customer protected accounts.

Both BDs and FCM are subject to another test, commonly referred to as the "early warning" test. The early warning amount is a percentage above the minimum net capital requirements noted above. [17 C.F.R. § 1.12]. Therefore, the BD and the FCM must, as a practical matter, maintain adjusted net capital in excess of the early warning test.

To understand this better, an example is helpful: Assume that the required adjusted net capital amount is $10,000,000 under the 8 percent of the risk-based margin amounts held at the FCM. The early warning amount is 10 percent in excess of that amount, which would make the early warning level $11,000,000. [17 C.F.R. § 1.12]. If the adjusted net capital of that firm ever falls below the early warning level of $11,000,000 but is still above the minimum net capital requirement of $10,000,000, then the Firm must give immediate notice to its respective federal regulatory agency (SEC or CFTC or both for jointly registered BD/FCMs) and to its designated self-regulatory organization (DSRO). The firm then has twenty-four hours to add additional net capital to bring its adjusted net capital amount to an amount in excess of $11,000,000.

If this Firm's adjusted net capital falls below the required level of $10,000,000 in this example, then the Firm must cease to operate as a BD or FCM and must give immediate notice to its respective regulatory agency and DSRO.

7. PROTECTION OF CUSTOMER FUNDS

Customers often have excess margin funds (excess funds) in their commodity futures accounts that are not needed to margin their open commodity futures contracts. That excess arises for many reasons, such as the closing of futures trading positions, which frees up the funds that were used to margin those positions. A favorable gain from variation margin can also create excess funds.

Section 4d of the CEA [7 U.S.C. § 6d] requires all customer assets, including the excess commodity futures and commodity options customer funds, to be held in a specially segregated account until the customer authorizes the transfer of those funds to accounts that are not subject to CEA regulation (unregulated accounts).

A brokerage firm must maintain customer assets in compliance with applicable SEC and CFTC regulations. For broker-dealers, the applicable regulation is SEC Rule 15c3–3 [17 C.F.R. § 240.15c3–3]. For FCMs, the applicable CFTC regulations are CFTC Rule 1.20 et seq. [17 C.F.R. § 1.20 et seq.]; CFTC Rule 30.7 [17 C.F.R. § 30.7]; and CFTC Part 22 [17 C.F.R. Part 22]. See, Jerry W. Markham, Custodial Requirements for Customer Funds, 8 Brook. J. Corp. Fin. & Com. L. 1 (2013) (describing those requirements).

UPTON V. SEC
75 F.3d 92 (2d Cir. 1996)

LUMBARD, CIRCUIT JUDGE:

Kevin Upton petitions for judicial review, pursuant to section 25(a)(1) of the Securities Exchange Act, 15 U.S.C. § 78y(a)(1), of an order of the Securities and Exchange Commission censuring him for failing reasonably to supervise a subordinate employee who aided and abetted a violation of Rule 15c3–3(e), the Commission's Customer Protection Rule. 17 C.F.R. § 240.15c3–3(e). The Rule is designed to prevent broker-dealers from using funds or securities held on behalf of customers to finance proprietary and other non-customer transactions, by requiring that the broker-dealer keep a separate bank account for the benefit of customers, based on a weekly calculation. The Rule begins by stating that every registered broker-dealer

> shall maintain with a bank or banks at all times . . . a "Special Reserve Bank Account for the Exclusive Benefit of Customers" . . . and it shall be separate from any other bank account of the broker or dealer. Such broker or dealer shall at all times maintain in such Reserve Bank Account, through deposits made therein, cash and/or qualified securities in an amount not less than the amount computed in accordance with the formula set forth in [Rule 15c3–3a].

17 C.F.R. § 240.15c3–3(e)(1). Unless a broker-dealer falls into a very limited exception (which does not apply here), the Rule specifies that

> computations necessary to determine the amount required to be deposited as specified in paragraph (e)(1) of this section shall be

made weekly, as of the close of the last business day of the week, and the deposit so computed shall be made no later than 1 hour after the opening of banking business on the second following business day.

17 C.F.R. § 240.15c3–3(e)(3). The actual computation of the amount of the deposit is done according to a complex formula found in Rule 15c3–3a. In general though, the deposit is the excess of "customer credits" over "customer debits" as defined in the Rule.

From May 1985 to December 1989, Kevin Upton was chief financial officer of Financial Clearing and Services Corporation ("FiCS"), a now-defunct brokerage firm. Beginning in July 1988, Upton assumed responsibility for supervising FiCS's money management department, headed by John Dolcemaschio. During fifty-eight of the sixty weeks between April 8, 1988 and May 26, 1989, the money management department paid down loans collateralized by customer securities just before the weekly Rule 15c3–3(e) computation and replaced them with unsecured loans; on the next business day, FiCS reinstated the customer-secured loans. As a result of this paydown practice, FiCS reduced its weekly reserve requirement by as much as $40 million.

On October 21, 1991, the Commission issued an order instituting public proceedings against Upton and Dolcemaschio. Dolcemaschio consented to an order imposing sanctions. On May 18, 1993, after an evidentiary hearing and post-hearing briefing, an Administrative Law Judge found that FiCS's paydown practice violated Rule 15c3–3(e) and that Upton had failed reasonably to supervise Dolcemaschio with a view toward preventing a Rule 15c3–3(e) violation. Accordingly, the judge ordered that Upton be censured. On January 30, 1995, the Commission issued a final decision and order upholding the judge's findings and affirming his choice of sanctions. This petition followed. * * *

In May 1985, Upton became chief financial officer of FiCS. As chief financial officer, Upton was responsible for overseeing FiCS's internal accounting. Upton later became supervisor of the new accounts department and the margin department as well. In November 1985, Upton was given responsibility over FiCS's money management department, although the department was reassigned to another supervisor one year later.

In February 1988, FiCS's parent corporation, Security Pacific Corporation, a bank holding corporation, sold FiCS to Integrated Resources Life Insurance Company. Prior to the sale, FiCS had access to a virtually unlimited unsecured line of credit from Security Pacific National Bank ("SPNB"), another subsidiary of Security Pacific. After the sale, SPNB limited its unsecured line of credit to FiCS but provided FiCS with a loan facility collateralized by customer securities.

Confronted with this reduced ability to obtain unsecured financing, John Dolcemaschio, the head of FiCS's money management department, began using SPNB's customer-secured credit line to finance FiCS's routine business. Such loans, however, were considered "customer credits" under Rule 15c3–3a and required FiCS to increase its reserve requirement. Beginning on April 8, 1988 and continuing through May 26, 1989, Dolcemaschio implemented the following weekly routine: FiCS substantially paid down loans secured by customer securities, ranging from $4 million to $52 million, just before the weekly Rule 15c3–3(e) computation and replaced them with unsecured loans at a higher interest rate. The next business day, FiCS substantially paid down the unsecured loans and reinstated the customer-secured loans. FiCS performed this substitution fifty-eight of the sixty weeks in question, reducing its weekly reserve requirement by $20 million on average and by as much as $40 million in some weeks.

It is undisputed that FiCS complied with the literal terms of the Rule at all times. In fact, FiCS's paydown practice was standard procedure at several other brokerage firms, including two prior firms where Dolcemaschio had worked before coming to FiCS. The Commission, however, had already begun to investigate the practice, and on March 30, 1988, issued a consent order imposing sanctions on a broker-dealer engaged in such customer loan substitutions. *See In re Underwood, Neuhaus & Co.*, Exchange Act Release No. 25,531 (Mar. 30, 1988), 40 S.E.C. Docket 785.

Upton was reappointed supervisor of the money management department in July 1988, approximately three months after the paydown practice began. Although Upton had never been responsible for supervising a Rule 15c3–3(e) computation prior to working at FiCS, he had attended a discussion on the Rule at an Institute of Finance seminar. He knew about FiCS's customer-secured loan facility and was responsible for approving any adjustments to the Rule 15c3–3(e) account. As chief financial officer, he reviewed the firm's monthly Financial and Operational Combined Uniform Single (FOCUS) reports, the basic financial and operational report required of broker-dealers by the New York Stock Exchange, which included Rule 15c3–3(e) computations. He also received the firm's daily profit and loss report, which beginning in January 1989 listed the firm's customer-secured credit facility as a separate line item.

In November 1988, Colette Rex, the assistant manager of the money management department, was informally advised by an NYSE examiner, Mon Eng, that the paydown practice was questionable and should be stopped. Although Rex instructed her subordinates to discontinue the loan substitutions, her instructions were countermanded by Dolcemaschio, who remarked that "everybody on the Street does it and if they cite us, they have to cite everybody." Rex unsuccessfully attempted to inform Upton of her conversation with Eng and the problems with the paydown practice on several occasions.

In May 1989, Upton received a telephone call from the Commission staff advising him that the paydown practice violated the spirit of Rule 15c3–3(e). Upton immediately instructed the money management department to stop paying down customer loans on the Rule 15c3–3(e) computation date. Several months later, on August 23, 1989, the Exchange circulated Interpretation Memo 89–10, in which for the first time it advised its members and member organizations that the paydown practice might violate Rule 15c3–3(e). New York Stock Exchange, *Broker-Dealer Censured for Violation of SEC Rule 15c3–3 and Discussion of the Intent and Objective of the Rule*, Interpretation Memo 89–10 (Aug. 23, 1989).

Two years later, on October 21, 1991, the Commission instituted public proceedings against Upton and Dolcemaschio. *In re Upton*, Exchange Act Release No. 29,842 (Oct. 21, 1991). The Commission's order alleged that FiCS's paydown practice resulted in a reserve bank account deficiency averaging $20 million per week between April 8, 1988 and May 30, 1989, placing over 114 broker-dealers who cleared through FiCS and over 200,000 customers at substantial risk. The order also alleged that Dolcemaschio had aided and abetted FiCS's violation of the Rule by implementing the paydown practice and that Upton had failed reasonably to supervise Dolcemaschio because he did not discover and stop the loan substitutions. * * *

After an independent review of the record, on January 30, 1995, the Commission affirmed the judge's finding of liability and his choice of sanctions. *In re Upton*, Exchange Act Release No. 34–35,292 (Jan. 30, 1995), 58 S.E.C. Docket 1864 (final decision). An order censuring Upton was issued that same day. *In re Upton*, Exchange Act Release No. 34–35,292 (Jan. 30, 1995), 58 S.E.C. Docket 1871. * * *

Subparagraph (e) of Rule 15c3–3 was promulgated pursuant to section 15(c)(3) of the Securities Exchange Act of 1934, which authorized the Commission to prescribe rules and regulations "requiring the maintenance of reserves with respect to customers' deposits or credit balances." 15 U.S.C. § 78o(c)(3). The purpose of the Rule is clear:

> to insure that customers' funds held by a broker-dealer . . . and the cash which is realized through the lending, hypothecation and other permissible uses of customers' securities are deployed in safe areas of the broker-dealer's business related to servicing his customers, or to the extent that the funds are not deployed in these limited areas, that they be deposited in a reserve bank account.

Adoption of Rule 15c3–3 under the Securities Exchange Act of 1934, Exchange Act Release No. 9856 (Nov. 10, 1972). Earlier drafts of the Rule required broker-dealers to perform the reserve computation on a daily basis. *See Notice of Revision of Proposed Rule 15c3–3 Under the Securities Exchange Act of 1934*, Exchange Act Release No. 9775 (Sept. 14, 1972). The Commission revised the Rule to allow weekly, and in some cases monthly, computation of the reserve requirement based on a variety of considerations raised by the securities industry during the comment period: the prohibitive cost of performing daily computations for smaller broker-dealers; the difficulty of tracing and separating customer and non-customer transactions on a daily basis given established accounting, clearance and settlement procedures; and the increased burden on firms employing outside computer service facilities for recording transactions.

As early as 1986, the Commission began investigating the use of the paydown practice in several brokerage firms. The Commission referred several such "violations" of Rule 15c3–3(e) to the New York Stock Exchange and instructed individual broker-dealers to discontinue the practice. The Exchange, however, informed the Commission that it would not cite any of these firms for rule violations because "there had been no written interpretation with respect to this practice." Furthermore, in a letter to the Commission dated February 29, 1988, one firm subjected to the Commission's auditing process "respectfully suggested that this interpretation [of Rule 15c3–3(e)] should be communicated formally to the broker-dealer community rather than on a firm-by-firm basis through the audit process."

On December 16, 1987, the Commission ordered public administrative proceedings against the brokerage firm Underwood, Neuhaus & Co. and two of its operations managers for paying down loans secured by customer securities on its Rule 15c3–3(e) computation day and reinstating them shortly thereafter on six occasions. *In re Underwood, Neuhaus & Co.*, Exchange Act Release No. 25,200 (Dec. 16, 1987). The order also charged that Underwood, Neuhaus had pledged customer securities to obtain loans on six occasions. The Commission accepted an offer of settlement in that case and issued a consent order. *Underwood, Neuhaus*, 40 S.E.C. Docket at 785.

In light of the number of brokerage firms engaged in the paydown practice, in late 1987 the Commission and the Exchange established a Joint Industry Rule 15c3–3(e) Committee, composed of members of the Commission's staff, members of the New York Stock Exchange, and industry representatives, to discuss the impact of the *Underwood, Neuhaus* decision on securities firms as well as to clarify the Commission's interpretation of Rule 15c3–3. On August 23, 1989, after Upton had stopped the paydown practice at FiCS, the Exchange issued to its members and member organizations Interpretation Memo 89–10, entitled "Broker-Dealer Censured for Violation of SEC Rule 15c3–3 and Discussion of the Intent and Objective of the Rule." Noting the sanctions imposed on Underwood, Neuhaus, the Memo stated the Commission's position that "substitution of proprietary or non-customer bank loans for customer bank loans only for the week-end or on the day of the Reserve Formula Computation may be regarded as an intentional circumvention of the rule if the customer loans are reinstated shortly thereafter."

The Commission is entitled to interpret Rule 15c3–3(e) expansively in order to proscribe conduct that would otherwise constitute an evasion of the reserve requirement. Rule 15c3–3(e) technically requires only that broker-dealers perform a precise computation on a specific day of the week; nonetheless, as a result of FiCS's loan manipulations, FiCS's customer loans may have been exposed to substantial risk most of the week. Adopting Upton's narrow construction of the Rule "would be to exalt artifice above reality and to deprive the [rule] in question of all serious purpose." *Gregory v. Helvering*, 293 U.S. 465, 470, 79 L. Ed. 596, 55 S. Ct. 266 (1935). The Commission may therefore broadly construe its rules to prevent such conduct. Likewise, because the Commission cannot foresee every possible evasion of the Rule, it may determine specific applications of the Rule on a case-by-case basis. *Cf. Shalala v. Guernsey Mem. Hosp.*, 131 L. Ed. 2d 106, 115 S. Ct. 1232, 1237 (1995) ("The APA does not require that all the specific applications of a rule evolve by further, more precise rules rather than by adjudication.").

Upton, however, claims that he should not be held liable for evading the literal proscriptions of Rule 15c3–3(e) because the Commission knew about the paydown practice well before the underlying events in this action took place and yet did not publicly condemn it until Interpretation Memo 89–10 was released on August 23, 1989. In rejecting Upton's argument, the Commission held that "the language of the Rule, coupled with the releases preceding its adoption," clearly evinced the Commission's intent to forbid any evasion of the Rule and that "any remaining uncertainty should have been erased by [the 1988 consent order] in *Underwood, Neuhaus*." *Upton*, 58 S.E.C. Docket at 1867.

Due process requires that "laws give the person of ordinary intelligence a reasonable opportunity to know what is prohibited." *Grayned v. City of Rockford*, 408 U.S. 104, 108, 33 L. Ed. 2d 222, 92 S. Ct. 2294 (1972). Although the Commission's construction of its own regulations is entitled to "substantial deference," *Lyng v. Payne*, 476 U.S. 926, 939, 90 L. Ed. 2d 921, 106 S. Ct. 2333 (1986), we cannot defer to the Commission's interpretation of its rules if doing so would penalize an individual who has not received fair notice of a regulatory violation. *See United States v. Matthews*, 787 F.2d 38, 49 (2d Cir. 1986). This principle applies, albeit less forcefully, even if the rule in question carries only civil rather than criminal penalties. *See Village of Hoffman Estates v. Flipside,*

Hoffman Estates, Inc., 455 U.S. 489, 498–99, 71 L. Ed. 2d 362, 102 S. Ct. 1186 (1982).

Because there was substantial uncertainty in the Commission's interpretation of Rule 15c3–3(e), Upton was not on reasonable notice that FiCS's conduct might violate the Rule. The Commission was aware that brokerage firms were evading the substance of Rule 15c3–3(e) by temporarily substituting customer loans on the Rule's computation date as early as 1986, two years before the events in this case took place. Apart from issuing one consent order carrying "little, if any, precedential weight," *In re Shipley*, 45 S.E.C. 589, 591 n.6 (1974), the Commission took no steps to advise the public that it believed the practice was questionable until August 23, 1989, after Upton had already stopped the practice. The Commission may not sanction Upton pursuant to a substantial change in its enforcement policy that was not reasonably communicated to the public. *Cf. Gerstle v. Gamble-Skogmo, Inc.*, 478 F.2d 1281, 1294 n.13 (2d Cir. 1973) ("For the future the Commission should proceed by a rule or a statement of policy that would receive wider public attention. . . ."). * * *

The petition is granted, and the Commission's order is vacated.

NOTES

1. The SEC adopted rule changes in 2013 that require broker-dealers holding customer funds to file a new, quarterly Form Custody Report with the SEC that describes the broker-dealer's custodial arrangements. Those broker-dealers must also file a Compliance Report with the SEC to verify they are properly protecting customer assets. Broker-dealers holding customer assets must also employ an independent public accountant to examine the broker-dealer's Compliance Report. In addition, broker-dealers must allow the SEC's staff to examine the work papers of their accountants and to interview those accountants. Jerry W. Markham, Custodial Requirements for Customer Funds, 8 Brook. J. Corp. Fin. & Com. L. 1, 11 (2013).

2. If a BD files for bankruptcy, pursuant to the Securities Investor Protection Act (SIPA), a SIPC trustee is appointed to handle the affairs and to wind down the business of the BD. Each customer of that BD receives insurance up to a maximum of $500,000 (but no more than $250,000 in cash) with respect to securities held at the failed BD. See, Ronald H. Filler, Are Customer Segregated/Secured Amount Funds Properly Protected After Lehman? 28 Fut. & Deriv. L. Reports 1 (Nov. 2008) (excerpted below).

The following case identifies some of the difficulties of determining the availability of SIPA coverage.

IN RE BERNARD L. MADOFF INVESTMENT SECURITIES LLC

654 F.3d 229 (2d Cir. 2011)

DENNIS JACOBS, CHIEF JUDGE:

In the aftermath of a colossal Ponzi scheme conducted by Bernard over a period of years, Irving H. Picard has been appointed, pursuant to the Securities Investor Protection Act, 15 U.S.C. § 78aaa et seq. ("SIPA"), as Trustee for the liquidation of Bernard L. Madoff Investment Securities LLC, id. § 78eee(b)(3). Pursuant to SIPA, Mr. Picard has the general powers of a bankruptcy trustee, as well as additional duties, specified by the Act, related to recovering and distributing customer property. Id. § 78fff–1. Essentially, Mr. Picard has been charged with sorting out decades of fraud. The question presented by this appeal is whether the method Mr. Picard selected for carrying out his responsibilities under SIPA is legally sound under the language of the statute. We hold that it is. Accordingly, we affirm the order of the United States Bankruptcy Court for the Southern District of New York (Lifland, J.).

The facts surrounding Bernard's multibillion dollar Ponzi scheme are widely known and were recounted in detail by the bankruptcy court. In re Bernard L. Madoff Inv. Sec. LLC, 424 B.R. 122, 125–32 (Bankr. S.D.N.Y. 2010); see also, e.g., In re Beacon Assocs. Litig., 745 F. Supp. 2d 386, 393–94 (S.D.N.Y. 2010); Anwar v. Fairfield Greenwich Ltd., 728 F. Supp. 2d 372, 387, 389–90 (S.D.N.Y. 2010); In re Tremont Sec. Law, State Law & Ins. Litig., 703 F. Supp. 2d 362, 363, 367–68 (S.D.N.Y. 2010). For our purposes, a few facts suffice. When customers invested with Bernard L. Madoff Investment Securities LLC ("BLMIS"), they relinquished all investment authority to Madoff. Madoff collected funds from investors, claiming to invest those funds pursuant to what he styled as a "split-strike conversion strategy" for producing consistently high rates of return on investments.1 J.A. Vol. II at 292. The split-strike conversion strategy supposedly involved buying a basket of stocks listed on the Standard & Poor's 100 Index and hedging through the use of options. However, Madoff never invested those customer funds. Instead, Madoff generated fictitious paper account statements and trading records in order to conceal the fact that he engaged in no trading activity whatsoever. Even though a customer's monthly account statement listed securities transactions purportedly executed during the reporting period and purported individual holdings in various Standard & Poor's 100 Index stocks as of the end of the reporting period, the statement did not reflect any actual trading or holdings of securities by Madoff on behalf of the customer. "In fact, the Trustee's investigation revealed many occurrences where purported trades were outside the exchange's price range for the trade date." In re Bernard L. Madoff, 424 B.R. at 130. Other now revealed irregularities make it clear that "Madoff never executed his split-strike investment and hedging strategies, and could not possibly have done so."

Id. To point out just two examples, "an unrealistic number of option trades would have been necessary to implement the . . . [s]trategy" and "one of the money market funds in which customer resources were allegedly invested through BLMIS . . . has acknowledged that it did not even offer investment opportunities in any such money market fund from 2005 forward." Id.

As is true of all Ponzi schemes, see Cunningham v. Brown, 265 U.S. 1, 7, 44 S. Ct. 424, 68 L. Ed. 873 (1924) (describing the "remarkable criminal financial career of Charles Ponzi"), Madoff used the investments of new and existing customers to fund withdrawals of principal and supposed profit made by other customers. Madoff did not actually execute trades with investor funds, so these funds were never exposed to the uncertainties or fluctuations of the securities market. Fictional customer statements were generated based on after-the-fact stock "trades" using already-published trading data to pick advantageous historical prices. J.A. Vol. I at 365–66, 371, 512; J.A. Vol. II at 291, 293. The customer statements documented an astonishing pattern of continuously profitable trades, approximating the profits Madoff had promised his customers, but reflected trades that had never occurred. Although Madoff's scheme was engineered so that customers always appeared to earn positive annual returns, the dreamt-up rates of return Madoff assigned to different customers' accounts varied significantly and arbitrarily. In re Bernard L. Madoff, 424 B.R. at 130. Thus, the customer statements reflected unvarying investor success; but the only accurate entries reflected the customers' cash deposits and withdrawals. J.A. Vol. I at 513.

Madoff's scheme collapsed when the flow of new investments could no longer support the payments required on earlier invested funds. See Eberhard v. Marcu, 530 F.3d 122, 132 n.7 (2d Cir. 2008) (describing typical Ponzi scheme "where earlier investors are paid from the investments of more recent investors . . . until the scheme ceases to attract new investors and the pyramid collapses"). The final customer statements issued by BLMIS falsely recorded nearly $64.8 billion of net investments and related fictitious gains. J.A. Vol. I at 505. It is not contended on this appeal that any victim knew or should have known that the investments and customer statements were fictitious. It is unquestioned that the great majority of investors relied on their customer statements for purposes of financial planning and tax reporting, to their terrible detriment.

When Madoff's fraud came to light, the Securities and Exchange Commission filed a civil complaint in the United States District Court for the Southern District of New York, alleging that Madoff and BLMIS were operating a Ponzi scheme. The Securities Investor Protection Corporation ("SIPC"), a nonprofit corporation consisting of registered broker-dealers and members of national securities exchanges that supports a fund used to advance money to a SIPA trustee, then stepped in.3 15 U.S.C. § 78ccc; Sec. & Exch. Comm'n v. Packer, Wilbur & Co., 498 F.2d 978, 980 (2d Cir. 1974). SIPC filed an application in the civil action seeking a decree that the customers of BLMIS are in need of the protections afforded by SIPA. 15 U.S.C. § 78eee(a)(3)(A). The district court granted SIPC's application; the protective order appointed Mr. Picard as Trustee for the liquidation of the business of BLMIS and the SIPA liquidation proceeding was removed to the bankruptcy court. Id. § 78eee(b)(3)–(4); see also Sec. Investor Prot. Corp. v. BDO Seidman, LLP, 222 F.3d 63, 67 (2d Cir. 2000).

SIPA establishes procedures for liquidating failed broker-dealers and provides their customers with special protections. In a SIPA liquidation, a fund of "customer property," separate from the general estate of the failed broker-dealer, is established for priority distribution exclusively among customers. The customer property fund consists of cash and securities received or held by the broker-dealer on behalf of customers, except securities registered in the name of individual customers. 15 U.S.C. § 78lll(4). Each customer shares ratably in this fund of assets to the extent of the customer's "net equity." Id. § 78fff–2(c)(1)(B). Under SIPA:

> The term "net equity" means the dollar amount of the account or accounts of a customer, to be determined by—
>
>> (A) calculating the sum which would have been owed by the debtor to such customer if the debtor had liquidated, by sale or purchase on the filing date, all securities positions of such customer . . .; minus
>>
>> (B) any indebtedness of such customer to the debtor on the filing date. . . .
>
> Id. § 78lll(11).

In many liquidations, however, the assets in the customer property fund are insufficient to satisfy every customer's "net equity" claim. In such a case, SIPC advances money to the SIPA trustee to satisfy promptly each customer's valid "net equity" claim. For securities accounts, the maximum advance is $500,000 per customer. Id. § 78fff–3(a). For customers with claims for cash, the maximum advance is substantially less. Id. § 78fff–3(a)(1), (d). Under SIPA, all claims must be filed with the trustee, id. § 78fff–2(a)(2), who is charged with determining customer claims in writing. A customer's objection must be filed with the bankruptcy court.

In satisfying customer claims in this case, Mr. Picard, as the SIPA Trustee, determined that the claimants are customers with claims for securities within the meaning of SIPA. The Trustee further concluded that each customer's "net equity" should be calculated by the "Net Investment Method," crediting the amount of cash deposited by the customer into his or her BLMIS account, less any amounts withdrawn from it. J.A. at 274. The use of the Net Investment Method limits the class of customers who have allowable claims against the customer property fund to those customers who deposited more cash into their investment accounts than they withdrew, because only those customers have positive "net equity" under that method. Some customers objected to the Trustee's method of calculating "net equity" and argued that they were entitled to recover the market value of the securities reflected on their last BLMIS customer statements (the "Last Statement Method"). After the filing of a number of objections, the Trustee moved the bankruptcy court for an order affirming his use of the Net Investment Method of calculating "net equity." Both SIPC and the SEC submitted briefs supporting the Trustee's motion.

After a hearing, the bankruptcy court upheld the Trustee's use of the Net Investment Method on the ground that the last customer statements could not "be relied upon to determine [n]et [e]quity" because customers' account statements were "entirely fictitious" and did "not reflect actual securities positions that could be liquidated. . . ." In re Bernard L. Madoff, 424 B.R. at 135. The bankruptcy court reasoned that the definition of "net equity" under SIPA "must be read in tandem with SIPA section 78fff–2(b), which requires the Trustee to discharge [n]et [e]quity claims only 'insofar as such obligations are [1] ascertainable from the books and records of the debtor or [2] are otherwise established to the satisfaction of the trustee.' " Id. (quoting 15 U.S.C. § 78fff–2(b)(2)). The bankruptcy court emphasized that the "BLMIS books and records expose a Ponzi scheme where no securities were ever ordered, paid for or acquired[,]" and concluded the Trustee could not "discharge claims upon the false premise that customers' securities positions are what the account statements purport them to be." Id. The Net Investment Method, unlike the Last Statement Method, allowed Mr. Picard to (in the bankruptcy court's phrase) "unwind[ ], rather than legitimiz[e], the fraudulent scheme." Id. at 136. The bankruptcy court reserved decision on the issue of whether the Net Investment Method should be adjusted to account for inflation or interest. Id. at 125 n.8. The bankruptcy court certified an immediate appeal to this Court, over which this Court accepted jurisdiction, pursuant to 28 U.S.C. § 158(d)(2)(A). * * *

The threshold issues are whether the BLMIS claimants are "customers" within the meaning of SIPA and, if so, whether they are customers with claims for securities or customers with claims for cash. If the objecting BLMIS claimants are not "customers," 15 U.S.C. § 78lll(2)(A), they are not entitled to the protection of SIPA at all, see Sec. Inv. Prot. Corp. v. Pepperdine Univ. (In re Brentwood Sec., Inc.), 925 F.2d 325, 327 (9th Cir. 1991). Under SIPA, "[t]he term 'customer' includes . . . any person who has deposited cash with the debtor for the purpose of purchasing securities." 15 U.S.C. § 78lll(2)(B)(i); see also Tew v. Res. Mgmt. (In re ESM Gov't Sec., Inc.), 812 F.2d 1374, 1376 (11th Cir. 1987) (observing "that it is the act of entrusting the cash to the debtor for the purpose of effecting securities transactions that triggers the customer status provisions" (emphasis omitted)). It also includes:

> . . . [a person] who has a claim on account of securities received, acquired, or held by the debtor in the ordinary course of business as a broker or dealer from or for the securities accounts of such person for safekeeping, with a view to sale, to cover consummated sales, pursuant to purchases, as collateral, security, or for purposes of effecting transfer.

15 U.S.C. § 78lll(2)(A). We conclude that the BLMIS claimants are customers with claims for securities within the meaning of SIPA.

While SIPA does not—and cannot—protect an investor against all losses, it "does . . . protect claimants who attempt to invest through their brokerage firm but are defrauded by dishonest brokers." Ahammed v. Sec. Inv. Prot. Corp. (In re Primeline Sec. Corp.), 295 F.3d 1100, 1107 (10th Cir. 2002). SIPA provides this protection by ensuring that claimants who deposited cash with a broker "for the purpose of purchasing securities," 15 U.S.C. § 78lll(2)(B)(i), are treated as customers with claims for securities. This is so because the "critical aspect of the 'customer' definition is the entrustment of cash or securities to the broker-dealer *for the purposes of trading securities*." Appleton v. First Nat'l Bank of Ohio, 62 F.3d 791, 801 (6th Cir. 1995) (emphasis added). * * *

For the reasons set forth above, we affirm the order of the United States Bankruptcy Court for the Southern District of New York (Lifland, J.) and hold that use of the Net Investment Method for calculating the "net equity" of the BLMIS customers was proper.

NOTES

1. One issue in the Madoff debacle involves whether the SIPC Trustee has the right to claw back funds distributed to Madoff customers in excess of their actual investments before the bankruptcy. This claw back issue is now before the Second Circuit in another Madoff case. As described below, another claw back case, which involved funds of both commodity futures customers and customers of an investment adviser, was decided by the Seventh Circuit in 2014. Both of these cases are also discussed in Ronald H. Filler, Ask the Professor: How Will the Seventh Circuit Rule in Sentinel II? 33 Fut. & Deriv. L Rep. 21 (Nov. 2013).

2. As noted in the Madoff case, which customer is entitled to the SIPC insurance and by what amount can vary depending on the customer's respective situation. In that case, since all profits shown on customer statements were fabricated and did not reflect actual securities transactions,

the SIPC trustee took the position that not all of Madoff customers should be treated in an equitable manner.

3. The SIPC styled insurance is similar to bank account insurance provided by the Federal Insurance Deposit Corp. (FDIC), although the FIDC insurance amount is capped at $250,000. However, SIPC does not cover losses from securities investments; it only covers losses caused by a BD's insolvency. The FDIC insures funds held in a bank even if they are invested, say in a certificate of deposit. As SIPC has noted:

> When a member bank fails, the FDIC insures all depositors at that institution against loss up to a certain dollar limit. The FDIC's no-questions-asked approach makes sense because the banking world is "risk averse." Most savers put their money in FDIC-insured bank accounts because they can't afford to lose their money.

SIPC, How SIPC Protects You (2011).

4. Both the SIPC and the FIDC insurance programs are funded primarily through the U.S Treasury; although BDs and banks also contribute to the respective funds.

RONALD H. FILLER
ARE CUSTOMER SEGREGATED/SECURED AMOUNT FUNDS PROPERLY PROTECTED AFTER *LEHMAN*?
28 Fut. & Derv. L. Rep. 1 (2008)

The short answer is "yes" for the most part with respect to customer assets held in a customer segregated account in the United States but major changes to the procedures and policies now in place are needed to provide greater customer protection safeguards, especially in connection with assets held outside the United States in CFTC Regulation 30.7 secured amount accounts, regarding trading on non-U.S. futures exchanges.

Most mystery authors normally wait until the last few pages of the last chapter to provide the final clues and solve the mystery. This is, however, a different mystery story even if it's filled with suspense, exciting themes and horror. And for those who do not believe that the role that segregated and secured amount funds play in today's global futures markets is not mysterious and challenging, then they must have slept through the period of the last two weeks in September and most of October. What we all believed were the rules to be applied in the event of an FCM's bankruptcy were all interpreted differently by the various global exchanges and clearing houses. Some clearing houses, like EUREX Clearing AG, LCH Clearnet SA, the CME Clearing House, ICE Clear US and The Clearing Corporation, acted admirably and professionally while others acted in a manner that was not necessarily in the best interests of futures customers.

With the demise of Bear Stearns Securities ("Bear") in March 2008 and now the bankruptcy of LBI, many futures customers have raised serious questions and concerns regarding how and whether their funds held by a futures commission merchant ("FCM") are protected under such circumstances. Similarly, given the recent credit crisis, the government loans provided to American International Group ("AIG"), the acquisition of Merrill Lynch by Bank of America, the $700 billion bailout approved by Congress and numerous other financial-related matters, customers of broker-dealers ("BD"), insurance companies and banks have raised similar concerns. Not to underestimate the importance of insolvencies involving these other financial institutions, this article will only address the laws, regulations and policies that impact futures customers globally under such circumstances.

Substantial financial safeguards and customer protections exist within the futures industry that are designed to protect customer funds in the event of an FCM bankruptcy. Assets held in a futures account at an FCM are protected and governed specifically by applicable laws and CFTC regulations that require the segregation of cash and collateral deposited by customers in conjunction with their futures trading. Pursuant to the Commodity Exchange Act ("CEA") and applicable CFTC regulation, an FCM, must maintain its futures customer assets in at least two different types of customer fund accounts (e.g., segregated and secured amount accounts) and may use a third type (e.g., a non-regulated account), each of which have different priority rights in the event of the FCM's insolvency.

The three types of customer fund accounts used by an FCM are:

SEGREGATED FUNDS: The first such account, established pursuant to Section 4d(a) (2) of the CEA and CFTC Rule 1.20, is referred to as the "customer segregated funds account". It holds the assets of *all customers* (U.S. and non-U.S.) deposited in conjunction with transactions on all *U.S. futures markets*. All customer assets are required to be held only in accounts maintained at custodial banks and other permitted financial institutions, including other FCMs and clearing houses that are registered with the CFTC as "derivatives clearing organizations" (DCOs). All customer segregated accounts are required to be clearly identified as segregated pursuant to CFTC Rule 1.20. These segregated funds are not permitted to be commingled with the FCM's proprietary funds or used to finance its futures or broker-dealer businesses. The amounts held in the segregated funds accounts are calculated daily as required by CFTC Rule 1.32, and the FCM must take immediate action in the unlikely event that there is ever a shortfall in its segregated funds accounts. This daily calculation must be completed by each FCM by not later than noon on the next business day. However, the customer segregated required amount needs to be in a good control location the night before. Otherwise, the

FCMs deemed to be "under segregated", and, if the FCM is "under-segregated", this must be reported promptly to the CFTC and its respective DSRO. Given this same-day deposit requirement, most large FCMs will deposit a large amount of their own capital in the customer segregated account to ensure that such accounts are never "under-segregated". This capital infusion can amount to several hundred million dollars, depending on the total amount held in the segregation pool.

SECURED AMOUNT FUNDS: The second type of account, governed by CFTC Rule 30.7, is known as the "customer secured amount account" and holds the assets of *U.S. residents* deposited in conjunction with their transactions on *non-U.S. futures markets*. These funds are also required to be held in accounts at banks and other permitted financial institutions, including non-U.S. clearing houses and members of non-U.S. exchanges, provided such non-U.S. clearing houses and non-U.S. member firms are deemed to be a "good secured" location. Like segregated funds, secured amount funds are not permitted to be commingled with the FCM's proprietary assets and are calculated daily and represent 100 percent of that day's customer requirements. FCMs are permitted to secure more than the minimum requirement stated above and can elect to deposit all funds used to trade on non-U.S. markets by all of its clients, including foreign domiciled clients. Like segregated funds as noted above, the calculation for the secured amount requirements must be completed by the following morning but the secured amount requirement must be deposited in a good secured location the night before or the FCM will be deemed to be in default. As noted above with customer segregated accounts, most large FCMs will also deposit their own capital in a secured amount account to prevent any under-funding from occurring

NON-REGULATED FUNDS: The third type of account, called the "Non-Regulated Customer Credit" calculation, contains the assets (cash and open trade equity) of *non-U.S. customers* deposited in conjunction with transactions on *non-U.S. futures markets* if such amounts are not included in the secured amount account as noted above. An FCM, also registered as a broker-dealer, may use this third account type, which is governed by Securities and Exchange Commission ("SEC") Rule 15c3–3. The amounts held in this account reflect the total of the credit balances calculated for each individual account owed by the FCM to its non-U.S. customers for transactions on *non-U.S.* futures markets less any deposits of cash or securities held with a clearing organization or correspondent clearing broker. Any amounts held in a non-regulated account are not covered by the provisions of the Securities Investor Protection Act ("SIPA").

Each "bucket", noted above, contains funds used by customers to margin the relevant futures products, with the difference being whether the futures products are traded on U.S. or non-U.S. futures markets and, for non-US markets only, whether the customer is a U.S. or a non-U.S. entity.

In addition to the segregation and secured amount requirements, CFTC regulations restrict where client funds may be placed. CFTC Rule 1.20 requires the FCM to maintain customer segregated funds, whether in the form of cash or collateral, either with a clearinghouse of a U.S. futures exchange registered with the CFTC as a DCO, in a customer segregated account with a bank or with another FCM. In connection with its custodial arrangement, the FCM must obtain what is known as a "segregation acknowledgement letter," in which the respective custodial bank or FCM acknowledges and agrees that all assets deposited in this segregated account are for the sole benefit of the FCM's futures customers and are not subject to the claims of any of the FCM's creditors, including that bank or FCM, respectively.

Similar letters must also be obtained for the Rule 30.7 secured amount account and the Rule 15c3–3 non-regulated account at the respective custodial bank. All customer assets are therefore held at all times in these accounts at the respective custodial bank or FCM, in accounts at the various clearing houses or with other clearing brokers that act as clearing brokers on the various exchanges around the globe on behalf of the FCM. * * *

An FCM is also required by CFTC regulations to properly account for and calculate on a daily basis both the amount that it is required to hold in segregation and the amount that actually is in its customer segregated accounts. Any deficiencies in the amounts required must be remedied and reported immediately to the appropriate regulators.

Most large FCMs deposit a substantial amount of their own capital in the customer segregated account to provide excess funds in the event a futures customer does not timely meet its margin requirements. This capital infusion may also be used to satisfy customer claims in the event of the FCM's insolvency. * * *

In the event of the FCM's bankruptcy, futures customer assets are normally protected except as described below. First, assuming no material futures customer-related default exists or was the cause of the FCM's bankruptcy (e.g., the insolvency was the direct result of a non-futures customer or transaction), a bankruptcy filing should have no material impact on customers' assets held in the three aforementioned accounts. Under such circumstances, each account should contain 100% of the required amounts and should be transferred back to customers in an orderly fashion.

An FCM bankruptcy would be administered under Chapter 7 of the U.S. Bankruptcy Code, which contains specific provisions for the protection of customers in the event of an FCM's insolvency. Under Part

190 of the CFTC's rules, the bankruptcy trustee would have the responsibility of returning the custodies assets back to each futures customer. Creditors of the FCM's bankrupt estate would have no claim to any of the assets held in these three accounts. The assets would be held solely for the benefit of the FCM's futures customers.

If, on the other hand, the FCM's bankruptcy resulted from a futures customer's failure to deliver the required margin for its futures trading positions, and the default was greater than all of the shareholder equity of the FCM, then each of the three accounts held at the custodian bank (or an FCM) would be treated independently of each other. Customers' assets held in one of these three accounts may not be used to satisfy any shortfalls in another account (e.g., the amounts held in the segregated account at the respective custodial bank or at a DCO may not be used to cover a shortfall held in the non-regulated account). However, as noted in greater detail below, a clearing house, including a DCO, may apply a clearing member firm's customer assets that are on deposit with that respective clearing house to satisfy margin amounts owed to the clearing house by that clearing member firm (and that clearing member firm only) for its customer accounts. In other words, customer assets held by a clearing house may not be used to cover a shortfall in the FCM's "house" account nor may assets held at one clearing house be applied to cover a shortfall at another clearing house unless a cross-margining arrangement exists with respect to the two clearing houses.

The assets of an FCM's futures customers, which trade on the U.S. futures markets, are normally wired directly by those customers into the customer segregated account at the respective custodial bank. The custodian bank would typically maintain different segregated accounts to hold cash and any non-cash collateral, such as U.S. Treasury bills, respectively. This firewall between the bank and the FCM provides important protections to the FCM's futures customers. As noted above, the assets held in these accounts at the bank do not fall within the bankrupt estate and are reserved for payment to customers if the FCM files for bankruptcy. If the bank mishandles futures customers' assets held with the FCM, its full shareholder capital should stand behind the accounts.

If the FCM is required by an exchange to send cash or collateral to a DCO to meet its customers' initial or variation margin requirements, the required amounts are typically sent via wire transfer from the customer segregated account at the respective custodial bank or FCM to another customer segregated account held in the name of the DCO for the benefit of the FCM's futures customers.

Therefore, at all times, assets of the FCM's futures customers, who trade on U.S. futures markets, are held in a customer segregated account at the FCM's or the DCO's custodial bank. Similarly, assets that need to be transferred to clearing brokers or clearing houses outside the U.S. are also sent directly from the 30.7 Secured Amount Account at the bank to the required good secured location.

There are also customer protections relating to the types of permissible investments that an FCM may make with customer assets held by the FCM. Pursuant to CFTC Rule 1.25, the FCM is permitted to invest its futures customers' assets in a limited number of permissible investments. In today's marketplace, the most commonly used investment product are money market mutual funds that meet the requirements of CFTC Rule 1.25 and SEC Rule 2a–7 under the Investment Company Act of 1940 (the "1940 Act"). However, any investment loss that may be incurred as a result of such investment must be borne solely by the FCM; its futures customers assume no such investment risk. This concern has been heightened recently by The Reserve Fund which lost a substantial amount of its investment assets through its purchase of commercial paper held in the name of Lehman Brothers and AIG, causing the fund to "break the buck." Also, the FCM must receive an acknowledgement from each money market fund that the amounts invested by the FCM on behalf of its customers with the respective money market fund may not be applied to any creditor of the FCM. This is similar to the segregation acknowledgement letter received by FCMs from their custodial banks, as noted above. * * *

The Lehman Events

On September 15, 2008, Lehman Brothers Holdings Inc. ("LB Holdings"), the holding company of all Lehman Brothers entities and the publicly-traded company (NYSE symbol: LEH) filed a petition for bankruptcy under Chapter 11 of Title 11 of the U.S. Bankruptcy Code with the U.S. Bankruptcy Court for the Southern District of New York.

Its principal U.S. subsidiary, Lehman Brothers Inc. ("LBI"), a registered broker-dealer and FCM, did not file its petition (a Chapter 7 filing) until the following weekend. The principal U.K. affiliate of LB Holdings, Lehman Brothers International (Europe) ("LBIE"), also submitted its filing on September 15th. The U.K. Financial Services Authority ("FSA") appointed Price Waterhouse Coopers ("PWC") as the Administrator for LBIE. This is similar to the role of a trustee in bankruptcy had LBI made such a filing. LBI had opened a Customer Omnibus Account on the books of LBIE to permit LBI futures customers to trade on the various European exchanges. LBIE was either directly a general clearing member firm ("GCM") on the clearing houses in Europe, such as LCH Clearnet SA and EUREX Clearing AG, or had established their own customer omnibus accounts on the books of a third party clearing firm on other European exchanges. LBI was the clearing member firm on the U.S. futures exchanges and had opened a futures customer omnibus account with other Lehman Brothers affiliates or third party clearing firms in Canada and Asia. LBIE had opened a customer omnibus account on the books of LBI to allow its futures customers to trade on the U.S., Canadian and Asian markets. All futures customer accounts were opened with either LBI or LBIE.

Note that LBIE had many direct futures accounts opened on its books, including some accounts, especially hedge fund accounts, that involved a prime brokerage and cross margin netting arrangement. LBI had similar arrangements with hedge funds on its books but also had a large number of futures-only accounts that were managed by large investment advisory firms.

As noted above, the concept of segregated funds is designed to protect the cash and collateral deposited by futures customers to margin their futures positions. These regulations do not directly address the actual futures positions themselves.

Given the uncertainty of the situation and the volatility in the marketplace, senior Lehman futures officials worked closely with their futures clients and governmental and exchange officials to transfer the client futures positions to other clearing firms in order to provide these customers with a new home that was properly capitalized.

This process started immediately after LB Holdings filed its petition for bankruptcy in the U.S. but not so outside the U.S. PWC, as the newly-appointed Administrator, did not permit the transfer of the open futures positions until late in the day on Wednesday, September 17th, with the vast majority of the futures positions being transferred on Thursday, September 18th or Friday, September 19th.

Most of the futures positions held by Lehman's customers, whether they were held on the books of LBI or LBIE, were either moved to other clearing member firms per the instructions of such customers by the close of business on Friday, September19th, or they became futures customers of Barclays Capital Inc. ("BCI"), the U.S. affiliate of Barclays Bank PLC. BCI acquired all of the remaining futures customer accounts on the books of LBI after the close of business on September19th. Therefore, the system worked for the most part although, as noted above, quicker action was needed. Through the tremendous efforts of many governmental agencies, SROs, firms, exchanges, clearing houses and clients, the goal of transferring the open futures positions was effectively achieved within five days. This reflects the strong working relationships that exist within the global futures community. No other product area or industry can make a similar claim. * * *

While open futures positions were, for the most part, transferred within the first five days, the cash and collateral used to margin those positions were not timely transferred. While part of the delay resulted from some difficulty in the accounting and trade confirmation processes, some banks simply refused to transfer the amounts held in customer protected accounts in a timely manner. For example, JP Morgan Chase Bank NA, the U.S. bank that held all of the cash and collateral in the LBI Customer Segregated Account, stopped releasing customer funds on Thursday, September 18th and continued this "hold" for many more days. Eventually, it agreed to transfer the cash and collateral held in the Customer Segregated Account. * * *

NOTES

1. For a comparative analysis of U.K. and U.S. segregation requirements see Ronald H. Filler, Consumer Protection: How U.K. Client Money Rules Differ From U.S. Customer Segregation Rules When a Custodian Firm Fails to Treat Customer Property Properly, 24 J. of Tax & Reg. of Fin. Instit. 25 (2011) and Ronald H. Filler, Ask The Professor: What Is The Impact On MF Global From The Recent UK Supreme Court Decision Involving Lehman Brothers International (Europe)? 32 Fut. & Deriv. L. Rep. 16 (Apr. 2012).

2. The legislation that created the CFTC in 1975 included a provision that required the CFTC to determine whether account insurance was needed for commodity futures customers, such as that provided to securities customers under SIPA. The CFTC conducted a study on this issue and issued a report in 1976, which examined the failures of FCMs between 1938 and 1974. Report to Congress Concerning Commodity Futures Account Insurance, Comm. Fut. L. Rep. (CCH) ¶ 20,235 (Nov. 1, 1976).

The CFTC report compared losses to customers in government-sponsored insurance programs with loss ratios for commodity futures accounts. It found that loss ratios in uninsured commodity futures accounts were substantially lower than those in insured accounts. The CFTC also concluded that the loss rate for customers of FCMs was so low that government account insurance would not be cost-effective. See, Jerry W. Markham, Custodial Requirements for Customer Funds, 8 Brook. J. Corp. Fin. & Com. L. 1, 37–38 (2013) (describing the CFTC study).

3. In 2013, a study commissioned by the NFA, the Futures Industry Association, the Institute of Financial Markets and the CME Group, the largest futures exchange complex in the U.S., concluded that private insurance for customer accounts suffering losses due to the bankruptcy of an FCM was basically impracticable, but a group of insurers recently proposed such a scheme. The industry study also determined that a government sponsored fund like SIPC would also be problematic. For example, the study estimated that it would take fifty-five years to amass a $2.5 billion government controlled insurance fund that would be funded by a 0.5 percent tax on the annual gross revenue of FCMs. Matthew Leising, Insurance for Futures Seen Feasible After Mf Global's Collapse, Bloomberg, Nov. 15, 2013, available at http://www.bloomberg.com/news/2013–11–15/insurance-for-

futures-seen-feasible-after-mf-global-s-collapse.html1 (accessed on Nov. 18, 2013)). See also, Customer Asset Protection Insurance for U.S. Futures Market Customers, by Compass Lexecon (Nov. 15, 2013).

4. The CFTC requires FCMs to advise customers through a mandated risk disclosure document that there is no SIPC-like account insurance for futures customers. [17 C.F.R. § 1.55]. Instead of insurance, futures customers continue to be protected only by customer segregation requirements. However, a breach of those requirements may result in customer losses that are not insured.

5. FCMs must report the amount of customer assets held in segregated accounts to the NFA and the CFTC. If, for any reason, the amount required to be held in each account class is less than the actual amount held, then the FCM must immediately report this "shortfall" to the CFTC and its DSRO. [17 C.F.R. § 1.12(h)]. However, pursuant to recent CFTC rules, how a shortfall is now treated varies by the type of the account. When and how the shortfall occurred can affect the customers whose property is held in each of the following three account classes.

A. If the shortfall resulted from actions taken by the FCM with respect to funds under the direct control of the FCM, then each customer will be treated on a *pro rata* basis and share the shortfall equitably.

B. If the shortfall resulted from trades that were cleared at a designated clearing organization (DCO), then the DCO's rules play a role.

C. If the shortfall resulted in the Customer Segregated Account held at the DCO, the DCO may apply assets from the defaulting FCM's non-defaulting futures customers to pay any amount owed as a result of the underlying transaction.

6. The CFTC adopted a different approach in 2012 with respect to cleared swaps. If the shortfall occurred as a result of a swap cleared at a DCO, then the DCO may not apply assets of the defaulting FCM's non-defaulting customers to cover the shortfall. This CFTC rule is called the Legally Separated but Operationally Commingled rule (LSOC). [17 C.F.R. Part 20].

The LSOC model rule provides special protections to customers who cleared their swaps through an FCM. However, the U.S. Bankruptcy Code has not been amended to reflect the LSOC model rule. So, arguably, the pro rata application involving a shortfall of a failed FCM would apply to a shortfall in both the Customer Segregated Account and the Cleared Swap Account. See, Section 766(h) of the U.S. Bankruptcy Code.

IN RE SENTINEL MANAGEMENT GROUP

728 F.3d 660 (7th Cir. 2013)

TINDER, CIRCUIT JUDGE.

The collapse of investment manager Sentinel Management Group, Inc., in the summer of 2007 left its customers in a lurch. Instead of maintaining customer assets in segregated accounts as required by law, Sentinel had pledged hundreds of millions of dollars in customer assets to secure an overnight loan at the Bank of New York, now Bank of New York Mellon. This left the Bank in a secured position on Sentinel's $312 million loan but its customers out millions. Once Sentinel filed for bankruptcy, Sentinel's Liquidation Trustee, Frederick J. Grede, brought a variety of claims against the Bank—including fraudulent transfer, equitable subordination, and illegal contract—to dislodge the Bank's secured position. After extensive proceedings, including a seventeen-day bench trial, the district court rejected all of the Trustee's claims. Although we appreciate the district court's painstaking efforts, we cannot agree with its conclusion that Sentinel's failure to keep client funds properly segregated was insufficient to show an actual intent to hinder, delay, or defraud. We also find significant inconsistencies in both the factual and legal findings of the district court with respect to the equitable subordination claim. For these reasons, we reverse the judgment of the district court with respect to Grede's fraudulent transfer and equitable subordination claims. * * *

Before filing for bankruptcy in August 2007, Sentinel was an investment manager that marketed itself to its customers as providing a safe place to put their excess capital, assuring solid short-term returns, but also promising ready access to the capital. Sentinel's customers were not typical investors; most of them were futures commission merchants (FCMs), which operate in the commodity industry akin to the securities industry's broker-dealers. In Sentinel's hands, FCMs' client money could, in compliance with industry regulations governing such funds, earn a decent return while maintaining the liquidity FCMs need. "Sentinel has constructed a fail-safe system that virtually eliminates risk from short term investing," proclaimed Sentinel's website in 2004.

To accept capital from its FCM customers, Sentinel had to register as a FCM, but it did not solicit or accept orders for futures contracts. Sentinel received a no-action" letter from the Commodity Futures Trading Commission (CFTC) exempting it from certain requirements applicable to FCMs. But Sentinel represented that it would maintain customer funds in segregated accounts as required under the Commodity Exchange Act, 7 U.S.C. § 1 *et seq.* Maintaining segregation meant that at all times a customer's accounts held assets equal to the amount Sentinel owed the customer, and that Sentinel treated and dealt with the assets "as belonging to such customer." 7 U.S.C. § 6d(a)(2) ("Such money, securities, and property shall be separately accounted for and shall not be commingled with the funds of such commission merchant or be used to margin or guarantee the trades or contracts, or to secure or extend the credit, of any customer or person other than the one for whom the same are held . . .").

Maintaining segregation serves as commodity customers' primary legal protection against wrongdoing or insolvency by FCMs and their depositories, similar to depositors' Federal Deposit Insurance Corporation protection, *see* 12 U.S.C. § 1811 *et seq.*, or securities investors' Securities Investor Protection Corporation protection, *see* 15 U.S.C. § 78aaa *et seq.* Sentinel also served other investors such as hedge funds and commodity pools, and as early as 2005, began maintaining a house account for its own trading activity to benefit Sentinel insiders. In 2006, Sentinel represented that non-FCM entities made up about one-third of its customer base. By 2007, Sentinel held about $1.5 billion in customer assets but maintained only $3 million or less in net capital.

Sentinel pooled customer assets in various portfolios, depending on whether the customer assets were CFTC-regulated assets of FCMs or unregulated funds such as hedge funds or FCMs' proprietary funds. But Sentinel handled "its and its customers' assets as a single, undifferentiated pool of cash and securities." *Grede*, 441 B.R. at 874. When customers wanted their capital back, Sentinel could sell securities or borrow the money. Sentinel's borrowing practices, and in particular an overnight loan it maintained with the Bank of New York, is this appeal's focal point. This arrangement allowed Sentinel to borrow large amounts of cash while pledging customers' securities as collateral.

Sentinel's relationship with the Bank began in 1997 in the Bank's institutional-custody division but within months moved to the clearing division (technically dubbed broker-dealer services) because Sentinel actively traded securities and frequently financed transaction settlements. Under the old arrangement, for each segregated account, Sentinel had a cash account for customer deposits and withdrawals. Assets could not leave segregation without a corresponding transfer from a cash account. But the risks of overdrafts prompted a switch to an environment where securities would be bought and sold from clearing accounts lienable by the Bank. In an email, one bank official said in reference to Sentinel's original arrangement that "THIS ACCOUNT IS AN ACCIDENT WAITING TO HAPPEN. . . . **I AM NOTIFYING YOU THAT I NO LONGER FEEL COMFORTABLE CLEARING THESE TRANSACTIONS AND REQUEST AN IMMEDIATE RESPONSE FROM YOU**. THANK YOU."

Under the new arrangement, Sentinel maintained three types of accounts at the Bank. First, clearing accounts allowed Sentinel to buy or sell securities, including government, corporate, and foreign securities and securities traded with physical certificates. The Bank maintained the right to place a lien on the assets in clearing accounts. Second, Sentinel maintained an overnight loan account in conjunction with its secured line of credit. To borrow on the line of credit, Sentinel would call bank officials to confirm whether it had sufficient assets in lienable accounts to serve as collateral. A senior bank executive had to approve requests that put the line of credit above a predetermined "guidance line." Third, Sentinel maintained segregated accounts that held assets that could not be subject to any bank lien. These included accounts (corresponding with the lienable clearing accounts) for government, corporate, and foreign securities but no corresponding segregated account for physical securities. To receive FCM funds in the segregated accounts, the Bank countersigned letters acknowledging that the funds belonged to the customers and that the accounts would "not be subject to your lien or offset for, and on account of, any indebtedness now or hereafter owing us to you. . . ." The agreement between Sentinel and the Bank provided that the "Bank will not have, and will not assert, any claim or lien against Securities held in a Segregated Account nor will Bank grant any third party . . . any interest in such Securities."

Sentinel could independently transfer assets between accounts by issuing electronic desegregation instructions without significant bank knowledge or involvement. This system allowed for hundreds of thousands of trades worth trillions of dollars every day at the Bank. Sentinel maintained responsibility for keeping assets at appropriate levels of segregation. The Bank's main concern was ensuring Sentinel had sufficient collateral in the lienable accounts to keep its overnight loan secured. In fact, at no point does it appear that the Bank was under-secured. If Sentinel sought to extend the line of credit beyond the value of the assets held in the lienable accounts, the Bank made sure Sentinel moved enough collateral into the lienable accounts. Sentinel used cash from the overnight loan for customer redemptions or failed trades and provided collateral in the form of the customers' redeemed securities. When customers redeemed investments, Sentinel could provide cash, via the loan, without waiting for the securities to sell. This arrangement did not violate segregation requirements. When a customer cashed out, the amount needed in segregation dropped by the amount lent by the Bank via the line of credit. The line of credit was in turn secured by assets moved out of customers' segregated accounts and into clearing accounts.

But in 2001, and increasingly in 2004, Sentinel started using the loan to fund its own proprietary repurchase arrangements with counterparties such as FIMAT USA and Cantor Fitzgerald & Co. Sentinel would finance most of a security's purchase price by transferring ownership of the security to a counterparty, who would lend Sentinel an amount of cash equal to a percent of the asset's market value. Sentinel used the overnight loan to cover the difference (known as a "haircut") between the security's cost and the repo loan. Sentinel had to buy the security back at some point for the amount loaned plus interest. By 2007, Sentinel held more than $2 billion in securities through repo arrangements. Meanwhile, Sentinel's guidance line for the Bank loan grew from $30 million pre-May 2004, to $55 million in May 2004, to $95 million in December 2004, to $175 million in June 2005, to $300 million in September 2006. The average loan balance from June 1, 2007, to August 13, 2007, was $369 million. The line topped out at $573 million at one point, while all along customer assets served as collateral. In 2004, Sentinel faced a segregation shortfall of about $150 million, and by July 2007, that figure reached nearly $1 billion.

During the summer of 2007, the cloud of a liquidity and credit crunch settled in. Repurchase lenders became nervous. The type of securities Sentinel held became a focus of the market as counterparties stopped accepting securities previously used as collateral. They wanted cash. But the crunch prevented selling the securities. Cash was tough to obtain. As Sentinel turned increasingly to its line of credit for cash, the Bank's thirst for the highest-rated, most-liquid securities to secure the loan intensified.

On June 1, a counterparty returned $100 million in physical securities, and as a result, the Bank loan jumped from $259.7 million to $353 million over the course of a day. To meet the Bank's demands for collateral, Sentinel moved about $88 million in government securities from segregated accounts to the lienable account. There was no way to maintain segregation levels via the returned physical securities because Sentinel did not keep segregated accounts for physical securities. Sentinel's segregation deficit grew to $644 million. On June 13, the Bank became suspicious, and a managing director emailed various bank officials involved with the Sentinel account, asking how Sentinel had "so much collateral? With less than $20MM in capital I have to assume most of this collateral is for somebody else's benefit. Do we really have rights on the whole $300MM??" After speaking to several bank officers, a Bank of New York client executive responded, "We have a clearing agreement which gives us a full lien on the box position outlined below."

The client executive testified that this was a well-advised and carefully worded statement, but both the managing director and the client executive knew Sentinel had an agreement that gave the Bank a lien on any securities in clearing accounts. *Grede*, 441 B.R. at 889–90. Then on June 26, a counterparty returned $166 million in physical securities. The Bank loan balance accordingly grew to $497.5 million. For collateral, Sentinel moved $66.6 million in government securities out of segregated accounts and into the lienable account. These securities, however, were not enough for the Bank. In turn, Sentinel pledged $165 million in physical securities, and the segregation deficiency grew to $667 million. On June 27, Sentinel's loan balanced peaked at $573 million. Two days later, the Bank told Sentinel it would no longer accept physical securities as collateral. That day, Sentinel transferred $166 million in corporate securities from segregated accounts to the lienable account. Sentinel's under-segregation problem grew to $813 million.

A similar transaction occurred on July 17, with a counterparty returning about $150 million in corporate securities. Sentinel transferred $84 million in corporate securities from a segregated account to a lienable account. The Bank loan settled at $496.9 million and Sentinel's segregation shortfall grew to $935 million. At the month's end, Sentinel briefly sent capital in the other direction. On July 30, Sentinel moved $248 million in corporate securities back into segregation from a lienable account and on July 31, $263 million in government securities back into segregation from a lienable account. Yet that same day, Sentinel moved $289 million in corporate securities from a segregated account to a lienable account. Sentinel's loan settled at $356 million and its segregation deficit at $700 million.

After these transactions, Sentinel could not hang on and told customers on August 13 that it was halting redemptions because of problems in the credit markets. Once Sentinel told the Bank about this decision the next day, the Bank cut Sentinel's remote access to its systems, sent its officials to Sentinel's offices, demanded full repayment of the loan, and threatened to liquidate the collateral. Sentinel filed for bankruptcy on August 17, owing the Bank $312,247,000.

Plaintiff Frederick J. Grede was appointed Chapter 11 Trustee for Sentinel's estate and, subsequent to the Chapter 11 plan's confirmation, the Trustee of the Sentinel Liquidation Trust. The Bank filed a $312 million claim as the only secured creditor. Grede filed an adversary proceeding against the Bank alleging that Sentinel fraudulently used customer assets to finance the loan to cover its house trading activity. Grede further alleged that the Bank knew about it and, as a result, acted inequitably and unlawfully. Grede brought claims of fraudulent transfer under the Bankruptcy Code and state law, 11 U.S.C. §§ 544(b)(1), 548(a)(1)(A); 740 ILCS 160/5(a)(1), and preferential transfer, 11 U.S.C. § 547(b), all to avoid the Bank's lien, *see* 11 U.S.C. § 550(a). Grede also brought claims of equitable subordination of the Bank's claim, 11 U.S.C. § 510(c), and invalidation of the Bank's lien, 11 U.S.C. § 506(d), among others. The district court dismissed the lien invalidation count on the pleadings, *Grede v. Bank of New York*, No. 08 C 2582, 2009 U.S. Dist. LEXIS 6184, 2009 WL 188460, at *8 (N.D. Ill. Jan. 27, 2009), and the Bank moved for summary judgment on the other claims. The court reserved ruling on the Bank's motion and held a bench trial that lasted seventeen days. After hearing from more than a dozen witnesses, listening to audio recordings between bank and Sentinel officials, and reviewing hundreds of exhibits, the district court ruled in the Bank's favor on the remaining counts. The court found that Grede had "failed to prove that Sentinel made the Transfers with the actual intent to hinder, delay or defraud its creditors." *Grede*, 441 B.R. at 881. The court also rejected the preference claim because the Bank was over-collateralized on the transfer dates. *Id.* at 886. With respect to equitable subordination, the court rejected Grede's claim because it did not believe that the Bank's conduct was "egregious or conscience shocking." *Id.* at 901. Moreover, the court found that the Bank employees "had no legal obligation . . . to seek out or analyze the data" that would have revealed Sentinel's misuse of the segregated funds. *Id.* at 895.

11 U.S.C. § 548(a)(1)(A) allows the avoidance of any transfer of an interest in the debtor's property if the debtor made the transfer "with actual intent to hinder, delay, or defraud" another creditor. Grede claims that the transfers of customer assets out of segregation and into the lienable accounts (which Sentinel used as collateral for its overnight loan with the Bank of New York) in June and July 2007 constituted fraudulent transfers under 11 U.S.C. §§ 548(a)(1)(A) & 544(b), and should thus be avoided.

At the conclusion of the bench trial, the district court acknowledged that Sentinel "was already insolvent at the time of the transfers" and had "missed] creditor assets." But the district court did not believe such behavior was enough to prove that Sentinel possessed the actual intent to hinder, delay, or defraud other creditors besides the Bank (including its FCM clients), as required to avoid a lien under 11 U.S.C. § 548(a)(1)(A). In reaching this conclusion, the district court relied on Grede's expert witness, James Feldman, who had testified that "three of the transfers in question 'had to do with the closing out of repo positions[,]' and the remaining two were related to what Feldman called 'structuring of collateral, the movement of securities between accounts.' " Based on this testimony, the district judge appeared to believe that Sentinel had robbed Peter (Sentinel's FCM clients) to pay Paul (the Bank of New York) in the months before it filed for Chapter 11 bankruptcy. While the district court's opinion certainly did not condone such behavior, it concluded that this behavior was not enough to show that Sentinel had actual intent to hinder, delay, or defraud its FCM clients. Rather, the opinion characterized Sentinel's behavior as a desperate "attempt to stay in business."

This finding that Sentinel's pledge of segregated funds as collateral for loans with the Bank of New York was driven by a desire to stay in business correctly identified the motive. Nonetheless, we disagree with the district court's legal conclusion that such motivation was insufficient to constitute actual intent to hinder, delay, or defraud Sentinel's FCM clients. Such a result too narrowly construes the concept of actual intent to hinder, delay, or defraud. When Sentinel pledged the funds that were supposed to remain segregated for its FCM clients, Sentinel's primary purpose may not have been to render the funds permanently unavailable to these clients (although Sentinel falsely reported to both its FCM clients and the CFTC that the funds remained in segregation). But Sentinel certainly should have seen this result as a natural consequence of its actions. In our legal system, "every person is presumed to intend the natural consequences of his acts." *In re Danville Hotel Co.*, 38 F.2d 10, 21 (7th Cir. 1930); *see also Reno v. Bossier Parish Sch. Bd.*, 520 U.S. 471, 487, 117 S. Ct. 1491, 137 L. Ed. 2d 730 (1997); *Trzcinski v. Am. Cas. Co.*, 953 F.2d 307, 313 (7th Cir. 1992).

Consequently, we conclude that Sentinel's transfers of segregated funds into its clearing accounts demonstrate an "actual intent to hinder, delay, or defraud" under 11 U.S.C. § 548(a)(1)(A). To treat these transfers as fraudulent is consistent with our construction of actual intent to defraud in other contexts. For example, in *United States v. Segal*, 644 F.3d 364, 367 (7th Cir. 2011), Michael Segal appealed his conviction of, among other crimes, mail and wire fraud under 18 U.S.C. §§ 1341, 1343. Segal argued that his fraud convictions should be overturned because he lacked "a specific intent to cause injury." *Id.* We rejected this argument, finding that a defendant could have an actual intent to defraud without having an actual intent to cause harm. *Id.* * * *

Sentinel's pledge of the segregated funds as collateral for its own loan becomes particularly egregious when viewed in light of the legal requirements imposed on Sentinel by the Commodity Exchange Act (CEA). Again, even if we assume that Sentinel eventually intended to replace the segregated funds and earn greater returns for their FCM clients, Sentinel knew that its pledge of the segregated funds violated the CEA. The CEA exists explicitly for the purpose of "ensur[ing] the financial integrity of all transactions" involving FCMs, "avoid[ing] systemic risk," and "protect[ing] all market participants from . . . misuses of customer assets." 7 U.S.C. § 5(b). In order to further these aims, the CEA requires that the "money, securities, and property [belonging to clients] shall be separately accounted for and shall not be commingled with the funds of such commission merchant." 7 U.S.C. § 6d(a)(2). Moreover, 7 U.S.C. § 6d(b) makes it "unlawful" for an FCM "to hold, dispose of, or use any such money, securities, or property as belonging to the depositing futures commission merchant."

The language of the CEA makes clear that Sentinel did more than just expose its FCM clients to a substantial risk of loss of which they were unaware; Sentinel, *in an unlawful manner*, exposed its FCM clients to a substantial risk of loss of which they were unaware. Thus, even if Sentinel did not intend to harm its FCM clients, Sentinel's intentions were hardly innocent. For this reason, we find that Sentinel's actions, as determined by the factual findings of the district court, demonstrate an actual intent to hinder, delay, or defraud. As such, Grede should be able to avoid the Bank of New York's lien under 11 U.S.C. § 548(a)(1)(A). * * *

NOTES

1. In a separate action, the Sentinel liquidation trustee challenged Sentinel's fraudulent pre-bankruptcy petition transfer of customer funds from Sentinel's segregated account for non-CEA customer funds (which were segregated under the provisions of the Investment Advisers Act of 1940 (IAA) and SEC rules) to Sentinel's CEA segregated customer funds account. That transfer occurred shortly before Sentinel declared bankruptcy. The Trustee also challenged an emergency post-petition transfer authorized by the bankruptcy court from Sentinel's CEA segregated funds account to various FCMs for distribution to their CEA customers. Without those transfers several FCMs could have failed. The bankruptcy court later ruled that it had entered that relief without prejudice to the rights of others who might later seek to claw it back. On January 4, 2013, Federal District Court Judge James Zagel ruled that $14,479,000 that had been distributed from Sentinel to the CEA customer segregated account of an FCM in the post-petition transfer had to be returned to the bankrupt estate of Sentinel. This was a "test" case for the remainder of the approximately $300,000,000 that had been distributed in the emergency post-petition transfer. Grede v. FCStone, LLC, 48 B.R. 854 (N.D. Ill. 2013).

Judge Zagel's decision was appealed to the Seventh Circuit. See, Ronald H. Filler, Ask The Professor: How Will The Seventh Circuit Rule In Sentinel II? 33 Fut. & Derv. L. Rep. 21 (Nov. 2013) (describing the issues raised in that appeal). The Seventh Circuit reversed Judge Zagel's ruling. Grede v. FCStone, LLC, Nos. 13–1232 and 13–1278, (7th Cir. March 19, 2014). The Seventh Circuit held that both the pre-petition transfer and the post-petition transfers fell within the safeguards set forth in Sections 546(e) and 549 of the U.S. Bankruptcy Code, 11 U.S.C. §§ 546(e) & 549, respectively. This meant that those funds should not be avoided i.e., they were not subject to a claw-back. The Seventh Circuit narrowly addressed only the validity of the pre- and post-petition transfers with respect to the U.S. Bankruptcy Code. However, the Seventh Circuit agreed with Judge Zagel that (i) the separate pools of customer funds that were subject to the CEA and CFTC regulations and the IAA and SEC regulations, were both equitable statutory trusts and "that there is no legal basis for placing one trust ahead of the other",and (ii) that FCStone was either an "initial transferee" or a "beneficiary of the transfer" under the Bankruptcy Code. The Seventh Circuit also opined that, in light of the harsh result of its decision on the IAA statuory trust beneficaries injured by the transfers, a new rule may be needed in order for competing statutory trust claimants to be treated fairly in the future.

The Seventh Circuit's decision was a victory for the FCMs receiving the post-petition transfers. However, in the view of the authors, who served as expert witnesses representing the different parties, the victory left open some serious policy concerns. For example, FCMs seeking emergency post-petition transfers of futures customer assets held at a bankrupt FCM may have difficulty in obtaining such an order in the future. A bankruptcy court considering those requests may be reluctant to issue such an order, which may prejudice the rights of other statutory trust fund beneficiaries, without a lengthy hearing and time consuming briefing before disbursing funds. Such a delay could result in the failure of FCMs seeking such emergency relief. The Seventh Circuit's decision also leaves open the possibility that, in a future case, the shoe may be on the other foot i.e., a depository may fraudulently transfer funds out of CEA segregated accounts to other statutory trusts in a pre-petition transfer, leaving the CEA customers with no recourse for recovery.

2. There have been other segregation failures at FCMs over the last several years. Refco, Inc. (Refco), a large FCM, failed in 2005 after the exposure of a massive fraud by its officers. Refco failed shortly after it announced a loss from uncollectible receivables in the amount of $430 million and advised that investors could not rely upon its financial statements. The uncollectible receivables had arisen from customer losses in the late 1990s, which eventually reached some $1 billion. Refco hid those losses on its books through an elaborate "round robin" loan scheme that took the receivable off Refco's book at the end of each accounting period and restored it immediately afterwards. The customer accounts at Refco, LLC were held in segregation under the Commodity Exchange Act of 1936. Those accounts were quickly transferred in bulk to another FCM without significant loss to those customers. However, customer funds held in an unregulated affiliate of Refco were lost. See generally, In re Refco, Inc. Sec. Litig., 503 F. Supp. 2d 611 (S.D.N.Y. 2007).

RONALD H. FILLER
ASK THE PROFESSOR: OMG! WHAT DID MF GLOBAL DO?

31 Fut. & Deriv. L. Rep. 1 (Nov. 2011)

MF Global Inc. ("MFG") was registered as a broker-dealer ("BD") with the U.S. Securities and Exchange Commission ("SEC") and as a futures commission merchant ("FCM") with the U.S. Commodity Futures Trading Commission ("CFTC").

In fact, it was one of the largest U.S. FCMs with approximately $7,270,000,000 in customer segregated funds as of August 31, 2011.3 On or about Sunday, October 30, 2011, MFG reported to regulators that a material shortfall appeared to exist in the amount of customer funds required to be segregated under the Commodity Exchange Act and CFTC Regulation 1.20 promulgated thereunder. Shortly thereafter, MFG's clearing privileges at several clearing houses were suspended and MFG was put on liquidation only trading status.

James W. Giddens, the Bankruptcy Trustee appointed by the U.S. Bankruptcy Court, stated in the SIPC's Trustee Emergency Motion:

1. More than 150,000 customer accounts were frozen on October 31st;

2. Of this total, more than 50,000 accounts were trading futures contracts as of that date;

3. The Chicago Mercantile Exchange ("CME") estimated that MFG's customer segregated funds should total approximately $5.45 billion, and that the CME held approximately $4.0 billion in cash or collateral as of that date.

4. The Securities Investor Protection Corporation ("SIPC") filed an application under the Securities Investor Protection Act of 1970, as amended ("SIPA") for the entry of a protective order placing MFG in liquidation under SIPA as MFG could no longer comply with the requirements regarding financial responsibility under Section 15(c)(3) of the Securities Exchange Act of 1934 ("1934 Act") and SEC Rules 15c3–3 and 17a–3.11

5. On October 31, 2011, the Honorable Paul Engel Mayer, U.S. District Court for the Southern District of New York, entered an Order ("the MFG Liquidation Order") which commenced liquidation of MFG pursuant to SIPA in a case captioned as: *Securities Investor Protection Corp. v. MF Global Inc.*, Case No. 11–CIV–7750 (PAE). * * *

According to the SIPC Trustee's Emergency Motion, there appears to be a shortfall in the amount of customer funds required to be held in segregation pursuant to CEA Section 4d13 and CFTC Regulation 1.20. According to numerous media reports, the amount of this shortfall has ranged between $900 million on the high end to $600 million on the low end. * * *

NOTES

1. The shortfall in funds at MF Global was later attributed to the fact that CFTC Rule 30.7 [17 C.F.R. § 30.7] did not require the complete segregation of funds held in Secured Amount Accounts for customers trading on foreign exchanges (referred to as the "alternative method"). That computation method was abandoned after the MF Global failure. See, Jerry W. Markham, Custodial Requirements for Customer Funds, and 8 Brook. J. Corp. Fin. & Com. L. 1, 35 (2013) (describing that change).

2. There was some good news. The MF Global bankruptcy judge approved a plan in November 2013 that would return all of the monies lost by its customers after the firm's failure. Ben Protess, MF Global Customers Will Collect All They Lost, N.Y. Times, Nov. 6, 2013, at B1.

3. MF Global was not the last large failure of an FCM. In a CFTC press release issued in July 2012, it was announced that:

> Washington, DC—The U.S. Commodity Futures Trading Commission (CFTC) announced today that it filed a complaint in the United States District Court for the Northern District of Illinois against Peregrine Financial Group Inc. (PFG), a registered futures commission merchant, and its owner, Russell R. Wasendorf, Sr. (Wasendorf). The Complaint alleges that PFG and Wasendorf committed fraud by misappropriating customer funds, violated customer fund segregation laws, and made false statements in financial statements filed with the Commission.

> The National Futures Association (NFA) is PFG's Designated Self-Regulatory Organization and is responsible for monitoring and auditing PFG for compliance with the minimum financial and related reporting requirements. According to the Complaint, in July 2012 during an NFA audit, PFG falsely represented that it held in excess of $220 million of customer funds when in fact it held approximately $5.1 million.

> The Commission's action alleges that from at least February 2010 through the present, PFG and Wasendorf failed to maintain adequate customer funds in segregated accounts as required by the Commodity Exchange Act and CFTC Regulations. The Complaint further alleges that defendants made false statements in filings required by the Commission regarding funds held in segregation for customers trading on U.S. Exchanges.

> According to the Complaint, Wasendorf attempted to commit suicide yesterday, July 9, 2012. In the aftermath of that incident, the staff of the NFA received information that Wasendorf may have falsified certain bank records.

CFTC Press Release No. PR6300–12 (July 10, 2012).

4. As a result of these failures, the CFTC adopted changes to its segregation requirements that were intended to strengthen customer protection. Among other things, the rules as proposed would have required "moment-to-moment" segregation, which would have meant that FCMs would not be able to use customer segregated funds in their operations or to cover a margin call of a customer between daily segregation calculations. Rather, the FCM would have to post its own funds to cover margin deficiencies until the customer met a margin call. However, industry participants complained that FCMs did not have the necessary computer systems needed to make moment-to-moment calculations and margin calls are, in any event, usually issued

and collected overnight. Moreover, most FCMs do not have the capital to cover every momentary deficient in customer accounts, and they do not wish to incur the expense.

5. The adopted rules took a modified approach to the proposed moment-to-moment requirement. FCMs will now be required to maintain residual interest of their own funds in customer segregated accounts equal to the customers' aggregate under-margined amounts at the end of each trade date. This requirement will be phased in over a period of five years. CFTC, Enhancing Protections Afforded Customers and Customer Funds Held by Futures Commission Merchants and Derivatives Clearing Organizations, 78 Fed. Reg. 68506 (Nov. 14, 2013). This was a shift from the moment-to-moment proposal, but it raised concerns that FCMs would require pre-funding of margin, a requirement that could increase the cost of hedging by farmers and others.

6. The CFTC rule amendments in 2013 also required FCMs to adopt risk management programs for customer segregated funds and to make additional disclosures to customers regarding potential threats to their funds and the lack of SIPC-like account insurance. Id.

7. The CFTC rule amendments require FCMs to establish a "targeted residual amount" of excess funds of the FCM that will be available to meet any shortfall in segregation as a result of a customer failing to meet a margin call. That targeted amount must be based on an assessment by the FCM of the amount of such potential exposure. Notice must be given to the CFTC if the FCM withdraws more than twenty-five percent of that targeted residual amount in a single transaction. [17 C.F.R. § 1.23].

8. Following the enactment of the Dodd Frank Act in 2010, another category of customer accounts was established by the CFTC. This new account class is referred to as a Cleared Swap Account [See, 17 CFR Part 22]. An FCM must now establish three customer protected accounts if they trade (1) domestic futures, (2) foreign futures and (3) swaps—Customer Segregated Account, Secured Amount Account and Cleared Swap Account. Each of these accounts must be maintained separate and apart from each other.

9. See above, Ronald Filler, Are Customer Segregated/Secured Amount Accounts Protected After Lehman? 28 Fut. & Deriv. L. Rep. 1 (Nov. 2008), which raises issues regarding how futures customer funds held outside the U.S. do not necessarily receive the protections contemplated by CFTC Part 30 [17 C.F.R. Part 30]. This is because bankruptcy laws in foreign jurisdictions may trump the protections provided by Part 30.

8. FCM AND BD LIABILITY FOR CUSTOMER LOSSES

Customers sometimes blame their trading losses on their BD or FCM. As described in Chapter 8, there are certain duties owed by brokers to customers and brokers that prohibit them from misleading customers or abusing their accounts. The next case addresses whether any duties are owed to prevent customer losses in positions initiated by the customer in a "non-discretionary" account.

DE KWIATKOWSKI V. BEAR, STEARNS & CO.
306 F.3d 1293 (2d Cir. 2002)

DENNIS JACOBS, CIRCUIT JUDGE:

In a period of less than five months in 1994–95, plaintiff Henryk de Kwiatkowski ("Kwiatkowski") made and lost hundreds of millions of dollars betting on the U.S. dollar by trading in currency futures. Kwiatkowski traded on a governmental scale: At one point, his positions accounted for 30 percent of the total open interest in certain currencies on the Chicago Mercantile Exchange. After netting over $200 million in the first trading weeks, Kwiatkowski's fortunes turned; between late December 1994 and mid-January 1995, Kwiatkowski suffered single-day losses of $112 million, $98 million, and $70 million. He continued losing money through the winter. Having lost tens of millions over the preceding several days, Kwiatkowski liquidated all his positions starting on Sunday, March 5 and finishing the next day. In all, Kwiatkowski had suffered net losses of $215 million.

In June 1996, Kwiatkowski sued the brokerage firm (and related entities) that had executed his trade orders, Bear, Stearns & Co., Inc., Bear, Stearns Securities Corporation, and Bear Stearns Forex Inc. (collectively, "Bear Stearns" or "Bear"), as well as his individual broker, Albert Sabini ("Sabini"), alleging (*inter alia*) common law negligence and breach of fiduciary duty. At trial, Kwiatkowski contended that Bear and Sabini failed adequately to warn him of risks, failed to keep him apprised of certain market forecasts, and gave him negligent advice concerning the timing of his trades.

In May 2000, a jury in the United States District Court for the Southern District of New York (Marrero, *J.*) found Bear negligent and awarded Kwiatkowski $111.5 million in damages. The jury found for Bear on the breach of fiduciary duty claim. Sabini prevailed on both claims.

Bear made timely motions for judgment under Fed. R. Civ. P. 50, arguing principally that Kwiatkowski's account was a "nondiscretionary" trading account (i.e., one where all trades require the client's authorization), and that as to such accounts (as a matter of law) a broker has none of the advisory duties that Bear was found to have breached.

In an opinion dated December 29, 2000, the district court denied Bear's motion for judgment. *de Kwiatkowski v. Bear, Stearns & Co., Inc.*, 126 F. Supp. 2d 672 (S.D.N.Y. 2000). The court ruled that the unique facts and circumstances of the parties' relationship permitted the jury reasonably to find that Bear undertook to provide Kwiatkowski with services beyond those that are usual for nondiscretionary accounts, and that there was evidence sufficient to find that Bear provided those services negligently. The district court added $53 million to the jury's damages award for prejudgment interest dating back to March 6, 1995, bringing Kwiatkowski's total recovery to $164.5 million.

On appeal, Bear argues principally: [1] that as a matter of law, because Kwiatkowski was a nondiscretionary customer, Bear had no ongoing duty to provide him with information and advice; [2] that Bear did not undertake to provide ongoing advice and account-monitoring services; and [3] that Bear was not negligent in performing any of the services it did provide. We reverse. * * *

For the most part, the operative facts are undisputed. Kwiatkowski first opened an account at Bear Stearns in 1988, when his broker, Albert Sabini, relocated there from the defunct E.F. Hutton firm. The account was handled by Bear's "Private Client Services Group," which provides large private investors with enhanced services, including access if requested to the firm's executives and financial experts. As a member of this group, Sabini was in regular contact with Kwiatkowski, often communicating several times a day. Sabini provided his client with news and market reports, and sometimes sent him Bear Stearns documents containing market forecasts and investment recommendations.

At first, Kwiatkowski's account at Bear was limited to securities trading. His currency trading was conducted through Bank Leu, a bank in the Bahamas, where Kwiatkowski maintained his principal residence. In January 1991, Kwiatkowski opened a futures account at Bear by transferring from Bank Leu a position consisting of 4000 Swiss franc short contracts traded on the Chicago Mercantile Exchange ("CME"). Kwiatkowski effected the transfer because he thought Bear would be better able to service the account, Sabini having "extolled the capacity of Bear Stearns to provide him the full services and resources he needed for large-scale foreign currency trading." *Kwiatkowski*, 126 F. Supp. 2d at 679. The Private Client Services Group provided its clients with access to Bear's financial experts and executives, *id.* at 678, and advertised "a level of service and investment timing comparable to that which [Bear] offered [its] largest institutional clients." *Id.* at 702.

Kwiatkowski's futures account at Bear was at all times "nondiscretionary," meaning that Bear executed only those trades that Kwiatkowski directed. When the account was opened in January 1991, Kwiatkowski signed a number of documents and risk-disclosure statements (some of which were mandated by federal regulations). These reflect in relevant part that:

• Kwiatkowski declared his net worth to be in excess of $100 million, with liquid assets of $80 million;

• He was warned that "commodity futures trading is highly risky" and a "highly speculative activity," that futures "are purchased on small margins and . . . are subject to sharp price movements," and that he should "carefully consider whether such [futures] trading is suitable for [him]";

• He was warned that because, under some market conditions, he "may find it difficult or impossible to liquidate a position"— meaning that he "may sustain a total loss" of his posted collateral—he should "constantly review [his] exposure . . . and attempt to place at risk only an amount which [he knew he could] afford to lose";

• He was warned that if he chose to trade on margin, he could lose more than what he posted as collateral; He gave Bear a security interest in all his accounts at the firm, authorized Bear to transfer funds from his other account to his futures account if necessary to avoid margin calls, and authorized Bear to protect itself by liquidating his futures account if Kwiatkowski failed to meet margin requirements.

126 F. Supp. 2d at 679.

Kwiatkowski's trading strategy reflected his belief in the long-term strength of the U.S. dollar. As he testified at trial, he had believed "the dollar should appreciate" over time, though he conceded that he always understood that the dollar would experience "ups and downs" in the near term. Tr. 472–74.

Kwiatkowski had been an experienced currency trader before he opened his Bear Stearns futures account. As an entrepreneur and founder of Kwiatkowski Aircraft-which leases and sells airplanes internationally—he developed a background in trading to hedge the risks associated with his company's foreign currency transactions. Kwiatkowski also had experience betting on the dollar in hopes of earning speculative profit. In 1990, shortly before transferring his Bank Leu position to Bear Stearns, Kwiatkowski lost nearly $70 million in that account when the dollar declined against the German mark and Swiss franc.

Before Kwiatkowski did his first currency transaction at Bear in September 1992, he met with Bear's then-Chief Economist, Lawrence Kudlow, who expressed the view that the dollar was undervalued worldwide and therefore was a good investment opportunity. In the weeks following this meeting, Kwiatkowski executed several trades betting on the rise of the dollar, ultimately acquiring 16,000 open contracts on the

CME. He closed his position in January 1993, having made $219 million in profits in about four months. At trial, Kwiatkowski testified that he consulted Bear prior to liquidating: "We discussed it and they thought the advisement was a change of feelings about it." Tr. at 483. The record is vague as to who at Bear said what, but (construing ambiguities in Kwiatkowski's favor) a fair reading is that Kwiatkowski was encouraged by someone at Bear to liquidate his position.

Kwiatkowski's futures account was dormant between January 1993 and October 1994. Kwiatkowski testified that in an October 1994 phone call, Sabini told him that "this is the time to buy the dollar," and that "this time the dollar will do what [Kwiatkowski] always believed it would do." Tr. 490. Kwiatkowski began aggressively short-selling the Swiss franc, the British pound, the Japanese yen, and the German mark. Within a month, Kwiatkowski amassed 65,000 contracts on the franc, pound, yen, and mark in equal proportions—a position with a notional value of $6.5 billion. All of the transactions were executed on the CME. At one point, Kwiatkowski's position amounted to 30 percent of the CME's total open interest in some of the currencies. According to David Schoenthal, the head of Bear Stearns Forex, Kwiatkowski's position was more than six times larger than any other position Schoenthal had ever seen in 27 years on the CME. Tr. 1111–12.

In mid-November 1994, after Kwiatkowski had acquired the bulk of his position (approximately 58,000 contracts), Sabini sent him a copy of a report by Wayne Angell, then-Chief Economist at Bear, entitled "Dollar Investment Opportunity," expressing the view that the dollar was still undervalued. According to Kwiatkowski, the report influenced him to "roll over" his entire 65,000-contract position past the December date on which the contracts came due.

Like many speculative investors, Kwiatkowski traded on margin, meaning he put up only a fraction of the $6.5 billion notional value, as specified by the brokerage firm. As the dollar fluctuated, Kwiatkowski's position was "marked-to-market," meaning that his profits were added to his margin and his losses were deducted. As he earned profits, his margin increased, meaning he could opt (as he did) to have profits paid out to him daily; when losses reduced his margin, Kwiatkowski was compelled to meet the margin requirement by depositing more money or by liquidating contracts. Thus, while Kwiatkowski put up only a small percentage of the notional value (well under ten percent, which is apparently not unusual), his personal profits and losses reflected the full $6.5 billion position, and magnified vastly the slightest blip in the dollar's value.

As Kwiatkowski acquired his colossal position in the volatile futures market, Bear took precautions. In November 1994, the firm's Executive Committee and senior managers assumed oversight of Kwiatkowski's account. Bear also required Kwiatkowski to increase his posted margin collateral to $300 million in cash and liquid securities.

In late November or early December, Schoenthal told Bear's Executive Committee that Kwiatkowski's position was too conspicuous on the CME to allow a quick liquidation, and (with Sabini) recommended to Kwiatkowski that he move his position to the over-the-counter ("OTC") market, the unregulated international commodities market whose traders generally consist of governments and large financial institutions. Schoenthal told Kwiatkowski that he could trade with less visibility on the larger and more liquid OTC market, and more easily liquidate without impacting the market. According to Kwiatkowski, Schoenthal told him that, when and if Kwiatkowski needed to liquidate, Schoenthal could get him out of the OTC market "on a dime." Tr. 502. Kwiatkowski accepted Schoenthal's recommendation in part: when it came time to roll over his contracts in early December, Kwiatkowski moved half of them to the OTC market.

By late January 1995, Kwiatkowski's account had booked breathtaking gains and losses. As of December 21, 1994—less than two months after he resumed currency speculation at Bear—Kwiatkowski had made profits of $228 million. When the dollar fell a week later, Kwiatkowski lost $112 million in a single day (December 28). When the dollar fell again, on January 9, 1995, Kwiatkowski lost another $98 million. Ten days later, on January 19, he lost $70 million more. After absorbing these hits, Kwiatkowski was still ahead $34 million on his trades since October 28, 1994.

As the dollar fell, Kwiatkowski consulted with Bear at least three times. After the December 28 shock, Kwiatkowski told Schoenthal and Sabini he was concerned about the dollar and was thinking of closing his position. They advised him that it would be unwise to liquidate during the holiday season, when the markets experience decreased liquidity and prices often fall. The dollar rebounded on December 29, and Kwiatkowski recouped $50 million of the previous day's losses.

After the January 9 decline, Kwiatkowski spoke with Sabini and Wayne Angell, Bear's Chief Economist. According to Kwiatkowski, Angell thought that the dollar remained undervalued and would bounce back. Kwiatkowski decided to stand firm. In late January, he spoke with Schoenthal about the U.S. Government policy of strengthening the Japanese yen, and afterward Kwiatkowski liquidated half of his yen contracts.

The dollar remained volatile through the winter, due in large part (it was thought) to geopolitical currents. Two salesmen in Bear's futures department, William Byers and Charles Taylor, who wrote a monthly report called Global Futures Market Strategies, announced in their

February 1995 issue that they were downgrading the dollar's outlook to "negative," principally because of the Mexican economic crisis, certain steps taken by the Federal Reserve Board, and an anticipated increase in German interest rates. The report cited the German mark and the Swiss franc as especially likely to strengthen—two of the currencies in which Kwiatkowski held short positions. Kwiatkowski testified that he never received a copy of this report.

As of February 17, Kwiatkowski was down $37 million since October 1994. In mid-February, rather than deposit more cash, Kwiatkowski instructed Bear to meet future margin calls by liquidating his contracts. As the dollar declined, Bear gradually liquidated Kwiatkowski's position (obtaining his approval of each trade). By the close of business on Thursday, March 2, 1995, Kwiatkowski's total position had been reduced to 40,800 contracts in the Swiss franc and the German mark. He had suffered net losses of $138 million in slightly over four months.

Over the next three days, the dollar fell sharply against both the franc and the mark, and Kwiatkowski's remaining contracts were liquidated at a further loss of $116 million.

On the morning of Friday, March 3, Bear tried to reach Kwiatkowski for authorization to liquidate 18,000 of his contracts in order to meet a margin call. Kwiatkowski was unavailable, so (as the account agreement allowed) Bear effected the liquidation unilaterally and secured Kwiatkowski's approval later that day. At that time, Kwiatkowski expressed interest in liquidating his position altogether. Schoenthal and Sabini advised Kwiatkowski that because market liquidity generally lessens on Friday afternoons, it would be prudent to hold on and take the chance that the dollar would strengthen. According to Kwiatkowski, he relied on this advice in deciding to hold on to the balance of his contracts.

When the overseas markets opened on Sunday (New York time), the dollar fell. Schoenthal was in his office to monitor Kwiatkowski's account and was in touch with Kwiatkowski throughout the day, obtaining Kwiatkowski's authorization for necessary liquidating trades. By the early hours of Monday, the liquidation was complete. In order to cover his losses, Kwiatkowski was forced to liquidate his securities account and pay an additional $2.7 million in cash. 126 F. Supp. 2d at 682.

In all, Kwiatkowski suffered a net loss of $215 million in his currency trading from October 1994 through Monday, March 6, 1995. At trial, Kwiatkowski's expert witness testified that Kwiatkowski could have saved $53 million by liquidating on Friday, March 3. The same expert surmised that $116.5 million would have been saved if Kwiatkowski had liquidated on Wednesday and Thursday, March 1 and 2.

Of the various federal, state, and common law claims in the complaint, all but the claims for negligence and breach of fiduciary duty were dismissed in August 1997 by Judge Koeltl (who had initially been assigned to the case). By the consent of the parties, Kwiatkowski filed a Second Amended Complaint in October 1998, which re-pleaded the original claims on somewhat different theories. The amended pleading alleged that Bear had failed to give adequate warning about trading risks and adequate advice regarding liquidation of Kwiatkowski's position. Bear again moved for summary judgment on all claims, arguing that under New York law, the duties it owed to a nondiscretionary customer such as Kwiatkowski were limited to the faithful execution of the client's instructions, and did not entail ongoing advice. In November 1999, the district court granted the motion in part, but refused to dismiss the breach of fiduciary duty and negligence claims, citing issues of fact as to whether Bear had undertaken advisory duties notwithstanding that Kwiatkowski's account was at least nominally of the nondiscretionary kind. *de Kwiatkowski v. Bear Stearns & Co., Inc.*, 1999 U.S. Dist. LEXIS 19966, 96 Civ. 4798, 1999 WL 1277245, at *11–*16 (S.D.N.Y. Nov. 29, 1999).

The case was reassigned to Judge Marrero, who conducted a jury trial in May 2000. At trial, Kwiatkowski contended that Bear had breached its duties in three ways: [1] Bear failed adequately to advise him about unique risks inherent in his giant currency speculation; [2] Bear failed to provide him with market information and forecasts, generated by Bear personnel, that were more pessimistic about the dollar than views Kwiatkowski was hearing from others at Bear; and [3] Bear should have advised Kwiatkowski well before March 1995 to consider liquidating his position, and specifically should have advised him on Friday, March 3 to liquidate immediately rather than hold on through the weekend.

At the close of evidence, Bear moved for judgment under Fed. R. Civ. P. 50, arguing that it had owed Kwiatkowski no duty to give advice. Bear's motion was denied. As to negligence, the district court instructed the jury (*inter alia*) that the defendants owed Kwiatkowski "a duty to use the same degree of skill and care that other brokers would reasonably use under the same circumstances." Tr. 2283.

The jury found Bear liable on the negligence claim, and awarded Kwiatkowski $111.5 million in damages. It found for Bear on the breach of fiduciary duty claim, and for Sabini on both claims (verdicts from which no appeals have been taken). Bear renewed its motion for judgment as a matter of law on the negligence claim under Rule 50(b), and moved in the alternative for a new trial pursuant to Fed. R. Civ. P. 59.

The district court denied both motions, ruling (*inter alia*) that the evidence supported the finding of an "entrustment of affairs" to Bear that included "substantial advisory functions," and that the services that Bear provided "embodied the full magnitude of 'handling' Kwiatkowski's accounts, with all the considerable implications that such responsibility entailed." *Kwiatkowski*, 126 F. Supp. 2d at 701, 708.

We must decide whether the facts of this case support the legal conclusion that Bear Stearns as broker owed its nondiscretionary customer, Kwiatkowski, a duty of reasonable care that entailed the rendering of market advice and the issuance of risk warnings on an ongoing basis. If so, we must decide whether a reasonable juror could find that Bear breached that duty.

It is uncontested that a broker ordinarily has no duty to monitor a nondiscretionary account, or to give advice to such a customer on an ongoing basis. The broker's duties ordinarily end after each transaction is done, and thus do not include a duty to offer unsolicited information, advice, or warnings concerning the customer's investments. A nondiscretionary customer by definition keeps control over the account and has full responsibility for trading decisions. On a transaction-by-transaction basis, the broker owes duties of diligence and competence in executing the client's trade orders, and is obliged to give honest and complete information when recommending a purchase or sale. The client may enjoy the broker's advice and recommendations with respect to a given trade, but has no legal claim on the broker's ongoing attention. *See, e.g., Press v. Chem. Inv. Servs. Corp.*, 166 F.3d 529, 536 (2d Cir. 1999) (broker's fiduciary duty is limited to the "narrow task of consummating the transaction requested"); *Independent Order of Foresters v. Donaldson, Lufkin & Jenrette, Inc.*, 157 F.3d 933, 940–41 (2d Cir. 1998) (in a nondiscretionary account, "the broker's duties are quite limited," including the duty to obtain client's authorization before making trades and to execute requested trades); *Schenck v. Bear, Stearns & Co.*, 484 F. Supp. 937, 947 (S.D.N.Y. 1979) (noting that the "scope of affairs entrusted to a broker is generally limited to the completion of a transaction"); *Robinson v. Merrill Lynch, Pierce, Fenner & Smith, Inc.*, 337 F. Supp. 107, 111 (N.D. Ala. 1971) ("The relationship of agent and principal only existed between [broker and nondiscretionary customer] when an order to buy or sell was placed, and terminated when the transaction was complete."); *Leib v. Merrill Lynch, Pierce, Fenner & Smith, Inc.*, 461 F. Supp. 951, 952–54 (E.D. Mich. 1978) (same; drawing distinction between discretionary and nondiscretionary accounts); *accord Paine, Webber, Jackson & Curtis, Inc. v. Adams*, 718 P.2d 508, 516–17 (Colo. 1986) (observing same distinction, and holding that existence of broad fiduciary duty depends on whether broker has "practical control" of customer's account). As the district court observed, these cases generally are cast in terms of a fiduciary duty, and reflect that a broker owes no such duty to give ongoing advice to the holder of a nondiscretionary account.

The giving of advice triggers no ongoing duty to do so. *See, e.g., Caravan Mobile Home Sales, Inc. v. Lehman Bros. Kuhn Loeb, Inc.*, 769 F.2d 561, 567 (9th Cir. 1985) (securities broker had no duty to provide customer with information about stock after purchase was complete); *Leib*, 461 F. Supp. at 953 (broker has no duty to keep nondiscretionary customer abreast of "financial information which may affect his customer's portfolio or to inform his customer of developments which could influence his investments"); *Robinson*, 337 F. Supp. at 112 ("The broker has no duty to relay news of political, economic, weather or price changes to his principal, absent an express contract to furnish such information."); *Puckett v. Rufenacht, Bromagen & Hertz, Inc.*, 587 So. 2d 273, 280 (Miss. 1991) ("If a broker were under a duty to inform all of its customers of every fact which might bear upon any security held by the customer, the broker simply could not physically perform such a duty."); *Walston & Co. v. Miller*, 100 Ariz. 48, 410 P.2d 658, 661 (Ariz. 1966) ("Any continuing duty to furnish all price information and information of all facts likely to affect the market price would be so burdensome as to be unreasonable.").

From these principles, Bear argues that: it had no ongoing duty to give Kwiatkowski financial advice about his dollar speculation; its sole obligation was to "execute [Kwiatkowski's] transactions at the best prices reasonably available and . . . offer honest and complete information when recommending [a] purchase or sale"; and it had no "open-ended duty of reasonable behavior, or to provide such investment advice as a trier of fact decides would have been prudent." As Bear points out, Kwiatkowski makes no claim that any of his instructions were improperly carried out, or that he was given dishonest or incomplete information about any trade. Thus, when the district court instructed the jury to evaluate Bear's overall conduct according to whatever a "reasonable broker" would have done under the circumstances, Bear argues, it allowed the jury to enforce advisory obligations that do not exist.

This argument, addressed to the features of nondiscretionary accounts, misses the point. The theory of the case is that this was no ordinary account (an observation that is true enough as far as it goes). Kwiatkowski contends that in the course of dealing, Bear voluntarily undertook additional duties to furnish information and advice, on which he came to rely (as Bear surely knew); that his trading losses were caused or enlarged by Bear's failures to perform those duties; and that Bear's liability arises from generally applicable tort rules requiring professionals to exercise due care in performing whatever services they undertake to provide, as measured against the standard observed by reasonable and prudent members of the profession. * * *

No doubt, a duty of reasonable care applies to the broker's performance of its obligations to customers with nondiscretionary accounts. *See, e.g., Conway v. Icahn & Co., Inc.*, 16 F.3d 504, 510 (2d Cir. 1994) * * *

The claim of negligence in this case, however, presupposes an *ongoing* duty of reasonable care (i.e., that the broker has obligations between transactions). But in establishing a nondiscretionary account, the parties ordinarily agree and understand that the broker has narrowly defined duties that begin and end with each transaction. We are aware of no authority for the view that, in the ordinary case, a broker may be held to an open-ended duty of reasonable care, to a nondiscretionary client, that would encompass anything more than limited transaction-by-transaction duties. Thus, in the ordinary nondiscretionary account, the broker's failure to offer information and advice between transactions cannot constitute negligence.

All of the cases relied on by Kwiatkowski in which brokers have been found liable for their nondiscretionary customers' trading losses involve one or more of the following: unauthorized measures concerning the customer's account (i.e., the account became discretionary-in-fact because the broker effectively assumed control of it); failure to give information material to a particular transaction; violation of a federal or industry rule concerning risk disclosure upon the opening of the account; or advice that was unsound, reckless, ill-formed, or otherwise defective when given. *See, e.g., Conway*, 16 F.3d at 510 (broker liable where he liquidated part of nondiscretionary account in order to satisfy margin call without obtaining client's authorization, where client never received notification that margin requirement had changed); *Vucinich*, 803 F.2d at 459–61 (vacating directed verdict for broker where evidence showed broker may have violated Securities Exchange Act by failing to disclose material facts relating to risk to his unsophisticated client, disregarded client's clearly-stated wish to avoid speculative trades, and may effectively have exercised control over the account); *Lehman Bros. Commercial Corp. v. Minmetals Int'l Non-Ferrous Metals Trading Co.*, 179 F. Supp. 2d 118, 2000 WL 1702039, at *26–*28 (S.D.N.Y. Nov. 13, 2000) (denying summary judgment for broker on breach of fiduciary duty claim, ruling that issues of fact existed concerning the "true nature of the relationship" between the parties); *Dime Sav. Bank*, 886 F. Supp. at 1080–81 (negligence verdict upheld where broker failed to evaluate client's financial situation before opening margin account, in violation of "suitability rule" of the National Association of Securities Dealers); *Cheng*, 697 F. Supp. at 1227 (negligence claim was adequately stated where it was based on broker's alleged failure to comply with NASD suitability rule).

Kwiatkowski does not claim any unauthorized trading, any omission of information material to a particular transaction, any violation of government or industry regulations concerning risk disclosures at the time he opened his account, or (except for Schoenthal's advice that he not liquidate on Friday, March 3, 1995) any unsound or reckless advice. Indeed (with that exception, discussed *infra*), Kwiatkowski is in no position to complain about any of these things. He can hardly contend that Bear negligently induced his speculations in the dollar (Kwiatkowski made early profits in excess of $200 million); or that Schoenthal was negligent in advising him to move the position to the OTC market (he claims that Bear was negligent in failing to give him that advice in the first place); or that Schoenthal was negligent in advising him after the late-December loss that the dollar would probably bounce back (Kwiatkowski made about $50 million the following day). Kwiatkowski does not allege that any of this advice was given negligently or in bad faith; he does not even allege that it was bad advice—nor could he, given the immense profits he made when he acted on it.

In sum, aside from the March liquidation, the claimed negligence is not in the advice that Bear gave, but in advice that Bear did not give. Specifically, Kwiatkowski finds a breach of duty in: [1] Bear's failure to volunteer certain advice, namely the Byers-Taylor prediction in early 1995 that the dollar was likely to fall; [2] Bear's failure to advise him, on an ongoing basis, of risks associated with his dollar speculation; and [3] Bear's negligence in connection with the March 1995 liquidation.

Kwiatkowski does not dispute that in the ordinary case, a broker's failure to offer ongoing, unsolicited advice to a nondiscretionary customer would breach no duty. Kwiatkowski's claim is viable, therefore, only if there is evidence to support his theory that Bear, notwithstanding its limited contractual duties, *undertook* a substantial and comprehensive advisory role giving rise to a duty on Bear's part to display the "care and skill that a reasonable broker would exercise under the circumstances."

We conclude that the district court's judgment must be reversed because there was insufficient evidence to support the finding that Bear undertook any role triggering a duty to volunteer advice and warnings between transactions, or that Bear was negligent in performing those services it did provide. Liability cannot rest on Bear's failure to give ongoing market advice that it had no duty to give, on Bear's failure to issue warnings that it had no duty to give (concerning risks about which Kwiatkowski surely knew more than anyone), or on Bear's failure to foretell the short-term gyration of the dollar. * * *

Kwiatkowski's remaining argument is that Bear negligently handled the liquidation of his account in March 1995. He contends first that Bear should have advised him to liquidate no later than Wednesday, March 1, in order to avoid being forced into liquidation by margin calls over the ensuing weekend. His expert testified that Kwiatkowski's risk of loss was ten times greater in March 1995 than it had been in November 1994.

Kwiatkowski also claims that Bear should have advised him in the weeks leading up to the March liquidation that his positions were much too large given the volatility of the dollar. Finally, he charges negligence in Bear's advice that Friday afternoon, March 3, was a dangerous time to start liquidating. He cites expert testimony that it is well-known in the industry that Sunday in New York (when only the Asian markets are open) is a worse time to liquidate than Friday afternoon, when American markets are still open. On this basis, Kwiatkowski contends that it was "foreseeable" to Bear that as Kwiatkowski's position deteriorated over the weekend, he would encounter even more difficulty liquidating in a relatively illiquid market, and that as a result his effort to exit his massive position on Sunday had proportionately greater impact on the price of the dollar, driving it downward and further exacerbating Kwiatkowski's losses.

Kwiatkowski's expert testified that Kwiatkowski would have saved $116.5 million if the position had been liquidated on Wednesday, March 1; $53 million, if it had been liquidated on Friday, March 3. The jury's damages award ($111.5 million) roughly approximates the former figure.

Kwiatkowski's arguments concerning the liquidation depend on the premise that, at various times, Bear knew or should have known whether in the course of a day or two the dollar would go up or go down. Wholly aside from whether Bear was obliged to give advice at all, the idea that Bear should have advised Kwiatkowski in February to exit the market because of the dollar's "volatility" implies knowledge on Bear's part that the dollar's volatility would work to Kwiatkowski's disadvantage. If the dollar had gone up, Kwiatkowski would of course have profited from volatility, as he had richly done in the past.

The same applies to the March liquidation. Assuming that Bear did undertake to assist Kwiatkowski and guide him through the liquidation, there is no evidence of negligence in that process. The notion that Bear negligently failed to advise a Wednesday liquidation in order to avoid a forced weekend liquidation presupposes that Bear knew that liquidation would be forced over the weekend. But there is no evidence that Bear knew this; no one could. There is evidence that Sunday afternoon is a worse time to liquidate a large position than Friday afternoon, but there is no evidence that Bear knew better than Kwiatkowski whether he would be forced to liquidate at all. Kwiatkowski was well aware, as he testified at trial, that the dollar would experience "ups and downs" in the short term. There is no evidence that Bear knew better than Kwiatkowski whether the dollar would go up or down between Friday and Monday. Indeed, there can be no such evidence; it is the nature of markets to go up and down. Schoenthal's advice on Friday afternoon was not that Sunday would be a better time to liquidate than Friday; his advice (as Kwiatkowski himself testified) was that the market "may improve next week." Tr. 516. There is no suggestion that Schoenthal failed to exercise reasonable care in forming or expressing that view; Kwiatkowski had no reasonable basis for relying on it, if indeed he did; and the fact that Schoenthal turned out to be wrong does not imply negligence. *See, e.g., Hill v. Bache Halsey Stuart Shields, Inc.*, 790 F.2d 817, 824–25 (10th Cir. 1986) ("Regarding trading advice, brokers cannot be liable for honest opinions that turn out to be wrong. Otherwise brokers would refuse to take discretionary accounts and would refuse to advise on nondiscretionary accounts."); *cf. In re Bank of New York*, 35 N.Y.2d 512, 364 N.Y.S.2d 164, 169, 323 N.E.2d 700, 704 (N.Y. 1974) (prescience not required of trustee in investment decisions).

For the reasons stated, we reverse the judgment of the district court and remand for entry of judgment dismissing the complaint.

NOTES

1. As seen from the de Kwiatkowski case, to the extent a broker-dealer is handling only non-discretionary accounts, the courts see no need to impose anything other than the most basic duties on the broker, such as refraining from engaging in unauthorized trades. One court summarized the case law on broker-dealer duties for a non-discretionary account as imposing the following duties:

> (1) the duty to recommend a stock only after studying it sufficiently to become informed as to its nature, price and financial prognosis;

> (2) the duty to carry out the customer's orders promptly in a manner best suited to serve the customer's interest;

> (3) the duty to inform the customer of the risks involved in purchasing or selling a particular security;

> (4) the duty to refrain from self dealing or refusing to disclose any personal interest a broker may have in a particular recommended security;

> (5) the duty not to misrepresent any fact material to the transaction; and

> (6) the duty to transact business only after receiving prior authorization from the customer.

Leib v. Merrill Lynch, Pierce, Fenner & Smith Inc., 461 F. Supp. 951, 953 (E.D. Mich. 1978), aff'd, 647 F.2d 165 (6th Cir. 1981).

2. In contrast, where discretion is exercised over trading in a customer's account by a broker-dealer, a broad range of fiduciary duties is imposed. The same court described the broader and additional duties imposed in a discretionary account as follows:

> (1) the duty to manage the account in a manner directly comporting with the needs and objectives of the customer as stated in the

authorization papers or as apparent from the customer's investment and trading history;

(2) the duty to keep informed regarding the changes in the market which affect his customer's interest and act responsibly to protect those interests;

(3) the duty to keep his customer informed as to each completed transaction; and

(4) the duty to explain forthrightly the practical impact and potential risks of the course of dealing in which the broker is engaged.

Id.

3. Section 913 of the Dodd-Frank directed the SEC to conduct a study on the effectiveness of existing standards of care for broker-dealers, investment advisers and their associated persons in providing personalized investment advice to retail customers. Among other things, the SEC report is to determine whether there are regulatory shortcomings in those standards that should be addressed by rule or statute.

Traditionally, investment advisers have been viewed to be fiduciaries for their clients, while broker-dealers handling non-discretionary accounts have not been held to such a high standard. An earlier study commissioned by the SEC found that there was confusion on the part of the public with respect to those differing standards. Rand Corp., Investor and Industry Perspectives on Investment Advisers and Broker-Dealers (2007). It was that confusion that led to this provision in the Dodd-Frank Act.

The study conducted by the SEC saff under Section 913 of Dodd-Frank Act recommended the creation of a uniform fiduciary standard for investment advisers and broker-dealers that is consistent with the existing standard for investment advisers. SEC Staff, Study on Investment Advisers and Broker-Dealers (Jan. 2011), available at https://www.sec.gov/news/studies/2011/913 studyfinal.pdf (accesed on March 12, 2014).

CHAPTER 5

OPTIONS AND SINGLE STOCK FUTURES

■ ■ ■

1. EXCHANGE TRADED STOCK OPTIONS

JERRY W. MARKHAM & DAVID J. GILBERG
STOCK AND COMMODITY OPTIONS—TWO REGULATORY
APPROACHES AND THEIR CONFLICTS
47 Alb. L. Rev. 741 (1982–1983)

Possibly it would be in the interest of clarity if a brief historical summary of puts and calls were presented to the committee. These contracts have been developed and sanctioned by business practice over a period of two to three centuries. Undoubtedly, they had their origin in transactions involving the merchandising of commodities, and in this respect are closely akin to the futures contract system now in vogue and such an indispensable part of the marketing of all great staple commodities.

Statement made in 1933 during Hearings on the Securities Exchange Act.

Essentially, an option grants the holder the right to purchase or sell a particular item at a specified price for a specified period of time. For example, a common type of option on stock entitles the holder to buy a specified number of shares of stock from a second party (the option "writer") at an agreed upon price (the "exercise" or "striking" price). The option right then exists for a specified period of time, measured by an expiration date. The holder is entitled to receive the shares from the writer upon payment of the exercise price. The holder will also pay the writer an agreed upon consideration for the option right, which is referred to as the "premium."

The option contract just described is often referred to as a "call" option. A second type of option, a "put" option, works in much the same way, except that the writer of a put agrees to purchase the underlying security at an agreed upon exercise price, and the holder of the put has the right to sell the stock to the writer during the term of the option at that price.

Until 1973, stock option trading was generally limited to executive compensation plans and individualized transactions conducted over the counter and to members of the New York Stock Exchange and its Association of Member Firm Option Departments.' The latter were not large markets, principally because of the difficulty of bringing buyers and sellers together and having all parties agree on the terms of the options.' Moreover, there was no "secondary" market for stock options, which often precluded a party to the option agreement from liquidating the right or obligation before its expiration. These problems were eliminated, however, in 1973 with the advent of "listed" stock options on the CBOE, a concept created by a special committee of the Board of Trade of the City of Chicago (Chicago Board of Trade), a commodity futures exchange. That committee had been appointed to study the feasibility of applying commodity futures trading principles to options on securities, "to develop futures contracts in securities."

Exchange listed options standardized the terms of option contracts and created an auction market, as well as a secondary market, where option buyers and sellers could competitively bid for and offset their positions by opposite transactions, thereby granting flexibility and liquidity to option traders." Standardization was further effected by using a single buyer and seller for each transaction, the CBOE Clearing Corporation, later renamed the Options Clearing Corporation (OCC). The OCC is the ultimate writer and holder of each option, a concept that was also borrowed from commodity futures trading.' "

The following example illustrates how trading is effected on the CBOE: The customer calls his broker to purchase a call option contract. The broker sends the order to the floor of the CBOE where it is received and transmitted to a "floor broker" who executes the order on an agency basis for the customer. If the order is a "limit" order, which means it is to be executed at a specified price rather than a market price,' the order may be given instead to a "board broker" [now a computer] who maintains a "book" of such limit orders and acts solely as an agent in executing customer orders. The board broker thereby performs the agency function of a traditional exchange specialist.

There are also individuals called "market makers" on the CBOE floor who bid for customer orders and who have roles equivalent to the specialist's dealer function; they trade for their own account and are required to maintain a fair and orderly market. Unlike the specialist system, however, there is more than one CBOE market maker assigned to each class of options, and they compete with each other in their market making activities.

The customer's order is executed by announcing it in a public auction to the market makers or other floor brokers. Upon execution, the order is confirmed as being executed to the broker who in turn confirms to the customer. At the same time, the trade is confirmed with the OCC which becomes the seller of the contract to the customer. The opposite side of the transaction is also formally undertaken by the OCC in that it intercedes between the customer and the opposite party, the market maker or other customer who was the writer of the contract. Consequently, the

> obligation of the seller of a call option to deliver stock upon payment of the exercise price runs to the OCC, and the OCC is obligated to pay him the exercise price if the option is exercised. The buyer of a call option is obligated to pay the OCC the exercise price if he chooses to exercise, and the OCC is then obligated to [obtain the stock from the writer and to deliver it to the purchaser].

This system offers several advantages to investors. For example, for a low premium, a call option holder may obtain a great deal of leverage and can profit from that leverage by price changes in stock, with liability limited to the premium cost. A writer owning the stock, on the other hand, can obtain additional income from stockholdings during periods when the writer does not expect the stock to increase in value.

Following the CBOE's market creation, other security exchanges sought entry into this new field. The American Stock Exchange (Amex) was the first, later to be followed by others. The exchanges initially traded only call options, but later added put options as well.

Stock options, albeit non-exchange listed options, were at the center of the Congressional investigations that followed the stock market crash of 1929. It was found that "[t]he granting of options to pool syndicates has been . . . at the bottom of most manipulative [stock] operations, because the granting of these options permits large-scale manipulations to be conducted with a minimum of financial risk to the manipulators."

In order to eliminate such abuses, the initial drafts of the legislation that ultimately led to the enactment of the Securities Exchange Act of 1934 proposed to ban all forms of stock options contracts. The Committee of Put and Call Brokers and Dealers in the City of New York argued, however, that stock options had been traded successfully for over two hundred years and that they should not be banned because they served important functions in the securities markets. Stock options offered "assurance against loss"; they had a "stabilizing quality"; and they "afforded the operator of moderate means [an opportunity] to protect a position in the market at a minimum risk," thereby serving as "insurance" in a manner similar to "hedging" operations which guard against price changes in commodity futures trading.

As a result of this testimony, the Securities Exchange Act of 1934, as adopted, did not ban options, but rather subjected them to the rule-making authority of the SEC under Section 9 of the Securities Exchange Act of 1934. No rules were adopted by the SEC under that authority, however, until the creation of the CBOE, when Rule 9b–1 was adopted. That rule prohibited options trading on any exchange except in accordance with a plan regulating options trading approved by the SEC. The rule also permitted the SEC to require changes in approved options plans and to disapprove amendments to such plans. In adopting this rule, the SEC stressed that option trading on exchanges was on a "pilot basis" only and that the flexible regulatory control permitted by Rule 9b–1 was necessary because of the novelty of exchange option trading, and because such trading might involve complex problems and pose special risks to investors and to the integrity of the marketplace. In granting the CBOE application to trade options, the SEC emphasized that it was recognizing the CBOE as an "experimental project," a "test market," and the SEC cautioned that it would maintain close surveillance over its progress. * * *

On July 18, 1977, as a result of growing abuses and the rapid expansion of exchange listed options, the SEC announced that it had decided to conduct a comprehensive investigation of standardized options trading. Later, on October 17, 1977, the SEC announced a proposed temporary rule that deferred the expansion of the existing options trading programs and prohibited initiation of new programs pending completion of the investigation. The SEC also announced that it would initiate disapproval proceedings for all rule change proposals of exchanges that would expand options trading. As a result, the exchanges agreed to a "voluntary moratorium" on the expansion of further trading.

The SEC investigation was conducted as a "Special Study of the Options Markets" and was carried out by a group of some twenty SEC staff members for over a year. The report of this investigation, the "Options Study," found that a number of abuses had occurred in the trading of exchange listed stock options. These included "chumming," which involves the use of fictitious trades on an exchange to increase volume trading figures in an option that is also traded on another exchange. Such fictitious trading is designed to attract orders to a particular exchange because brokerage firms will direct customer orders to the exchange with the highest volume to assure greater liquidity and better order execution.

The Options Study focused on other trading problems as well, including attempts to manipulate the price of stocks underlying options in order to profit illegally from option transactions. Also examined was "front running," where options transactions were engaged in to take advantage of advance, non-public information, such as knowledge of an impending block sale, that would have an impact on the underlying stock and options price.

Sales practices were reviewed by the Options Study and a number of abuses were found. These included numerous instances where customers "had been solicited for listed options trading even though, by any reasonable standards, they had neither the sophistication to understand, nor the financial resources to bear, the risks they were undertaking."

Instances of churning (excessive trading of a customer account in order to generate commissions) were examined, as well as other abuses including: 1) exaggerated claims of rates of return and misleading calculations; 2) recommendations by brokers to customers for options trading that had no reasonable basis in fact and exaggerated profit claims; 3) "touting the expert," a number of firms claimed to have a special formula or programs that the firm's options "expert" could use for obtaining profitable option results; 4) flamboyant language, misleading "educational" seminars that were really promotions, "prepackaged sales presentations," and high pressure "team tactics."

The Options Study further considered and found deficiencies in self-regulatory oversight by the options exchanges and by broker-dealers in hiring, training and supervising their sales force. It also focused on the problems engendered by having the same options traded on more than one exchange and possible market fragmentation resulting therefrom; the problems engendered by the proposed expansion of options trading by the entry of the New York Stock Exchange and the National Association of Securities Dealers, Inc.; and the implementation of a national market system for options trading.

The Options Study made some eighty recommendations to correct the abuses and problems it had discovered. Generally, it recommended further studies, clarification of rules, and publicity as to the illegality of various practices and increased and strengthened self-regulatory efforts. It also recommended that a simplified disclosure document be prepared and disseminated to all customers before they could open an account.

NOTES

1. In Board of Trade of the City of Chicago v. SEC, 677 F.2d 1137 (7th Cir. 1982), vacated as moot sub nom., Chicago Board Options Exchange, Inc. v. Board of Trade of the City of Chicago, 459 U.S. 1026 (1982), the Seventh Circuit held that the Commodity Futures Trading Commission (CFTC) had exclusive jurisdiction over options on futures on Government National Mortgage Association mortgage-backed pass-through certificates (GNMA's), which represented interests in government underwritten mortgages. The Court in the Board of Trade case noted that that much of the regulatory division between futures and options was "fortuitous." It stated that:

Had the plan [for exchange-traded options] emerged after the 1974 amendments to the Commodity Exchange Act, when the term "commodity" was broadened to encompass securities and the CFTC was awarded exclusive regulatory jurisdiction, the Chicago Board of Trade could have retained its original objective of trading securities futures contracts on its own floor under the same statute-the Commodity Exchange Act-governing its other activities.

677 F.2d at 1140, n.2.

2. The Board of Trade decision was rendered moot by the Shad-Johnson Jurisdictional Accord, as discussed in Chapter 2. The legislation that later codified the Accord divided options jurisdiction between the futures and stock markets. The Securities and Exchange Commission (SEC) was given exclusive jurisdiction over options on single stocks, narrow-based stock indexes and certain other financial instruments. The CFTC was given exclusive jurisdiction over futures and options on futures on treasury securities and on broad-based stock indexes and other financial instruments. Pub. L. No. 97–303, 96 Stat. 1409 (1982)

3. On January 9, 2014, the SEC approved a new rule amendment to SIPC Rule 400 (Satisfaction of Customer Claims for Standardized Options) that addresses the treatment of exchange traded options in the event of a broker-dealer (BD) bankruptcy. SIPC sought greater flexibility in dealing with such positions after the failure of Lehman Brothers in 2008. The new amended Rule 400 now gives the SIPC Trustee the flexibility to liquidate Standardized Options upon the liquidation of a BD or to transfer the Standardized Options to another broker-dealer. SIPC believed that this rule amendment was necessary to "effectuate bulk transfers of customer accounts to other brokerages enabling customers to regain access to their accounts in the form in which the accounts existed pre-liquiodation . . ." The rule amendment also revised the term "Standardized Options" to include both exchange-traded options and certain OTC options. See SEC Release No. SIPA-172, Rules of the Securities Investor Protection Corporation, dated January 9, 2014.

A NOTE ON SECURITIES OPTIONS COMPETITION

The Chicago Board Options Exchange, Inc. (CBOE) opened a high tech trading floor in 1984, in order to better compete with electronic trading systems. The CBOE's floor operations then involved open out cry trading but incorporated market making obligations for floor traders. Other options exchanges employed the specialist system for market making, while NASDAQ used a competing market maker system. In 1999, however, the CBOE adopted a Designated Primary Market Maker System, which had aspects of the specialist system.

The CBOE also began an after hours electronic trading program in 2001. In 2003, the CBOE began a "hybrid" program of side-by-side trading of electronic executions and open outcry executions, again reflecting events that were also occurring on the stock and futures markets. The CBOE also demutualized, transforming itself from a member owned organization to a publicly traded company, which is the course that other security and futures exchanges had followed.

For many years, the option equity exchanges did not actively compete against one another for individual listings of equity options. If one exchange traded options on a given underlying stock, the other exchanges generally abstained from listing those options. This system created a single market for each stock option contract and insulated the exchanges from competition with each other, just as was the case in the futures industry.

Initially, the stock option exchanges used a NFL style draft to select contracts so that there would be no competition in options trading on the stocks of the companies selected in this draft. Later, a form of lottery was used to allocate trading and options on particular securities among exchanges until the SEC ordered the exchanges to stop that practice and to permit multiple listings. The stock option exchanges ignored that SEC order.

Starting in the early 1990s, the stock options exchanges agreed among themselves not to list options that were already listed on another exchange. Any exchange seeking a breach of this agreement was met with threats of retaliatory listings or adverse action against market makers. As a result of that arrangement, most equity options were traded only on one exchange for most of the 1990s, a situation mimicking the commodity futures exchanges. In 2000, the Justice Department attacked the agreement of the stock options exchanges not to compete with each other in an antitrust suit. A consent decree in that action was entered into by the stock option exchanges. It required those exchanges to stop such anti-competitive practices. United States v. American Stock Exchange, LLC, 2000 WL 33400154 (D.D.C.). See also, In the Matter of Certain Activities of Options Exchanges, 2000 WL 1277616 (SEC 2000) (parallel charges by SEC).

The Justice Department consent decree opened up the stock option exchanges to competition. The International Securities Exchange (ISE), an electronic exchange that was started in 2000, was then able to compete head-to-head with the floor trading operations of the traditional floor trading stock options exchanges. ISE's business plan was to trade equity options on a broad range of stocks already listed on other option exchanges. ISE announced that it would list options securities that were then accounting for about 90 percent of exchange trading volume. The first cross-listings were done in 1999, and by the end of 2001, nearly all options were cross-listed.

The result of ISE's market entry was to introduce broad-based competition in stock option exchange products. ISE became one of the world's largest equity options exchanges, competing with the CBOE, which had long dominated that market. ISE was acquired by Eurex, the large derivatives exchange based in Frankfurt, Germany, in 2007.

The ISE competition had some salutary effects for traders. As ISE noted with respect to the effects of its competition with the stock option exchanges:

> The new willingness of the traditional floor-based exchanges to initiate cross-listings introduced a competitive element that was unprecedented. The competitive pressure on the traditional floor-based exchanges intensified following our launch of operations in May 2000. A major consequence of this increase in competition was a dramatic tightening of average spreads between the bid and ask prices in listed options. A special study entitled Payment for Order Flow and Internalization in the Options Markets published in December 2000 by the SEC (the Special Study) found that the trade-weighted consolidated NBBO spreads, which represent the best bids and best offers for given listings across all exchanges, dropped 38% between August 1999 and October 2000.

The SEC also found that, in addition to narrowing spreads, the expansion of multiple trading led to "market structure innovations that were designed to attract more order flow by enhancing the efficiency, transparency and liquidity of their markets." 69 Fed. Reg. 6124, 6126 (Feb. 9, 1004).

An important factor in the ISE's success was its ability to clear through the Options Clearing Corp. (OCC), which jointly clears equity options contracts for all U.S. exchanges trading those instruments. The OCC allows equity options contracts traded on more than one exchange to be treated as fungible for margining and offset.

2. COMMODITY OPTIONS

JERRY W. MARKHAM & DAVID J. GILBERG
STOCK AND COMMODITY OPTIONS—TWO REGULATORY
APPROACHES AND THEIR CONFLICTS
47 Alb. L. Rev. 741 (1982–1983)

In many respects, stock options are similar to commodity futures contracts." Both constitute agreements to buy or sell a given quantity of a particular security or commodity and both are intended for use principally as hedging and speculative investments, not as contracts for actual delivery. Like stock options, commodity options and commodity futures in various forms have been traded for hundreds of years, serving a wide range of economic and speculative functions.

Under a commodity futures contract, the trader is responsible for the total change in value of the contract during the period of his ownership; if the price of the commodity moves adversely, the trader is obligated to make additional payments equal to the amount of the adverse price change. "Because options carry no such obligations for the option holder, they are often more popular among small investors. Thus, because the option can be permitted to lapse, the holder can limit losses to the initial price of the option, the premium paid. The writer of the option, however, would not be so limited and would be liable for delivery of the commodity regardless of any adverse price changes. This can cause serious loss to the writer where the writer is uncovered or "naked"; that is, where the writer does not own the commodity or an offsetting futures contract." Another type of commodity option is issued by the producer of a particular commodity. It gives the holder of the option the right to buy or sell a given quantity of the goods produced by that company at a fixed price. These became known as "dealer" options because they were backed by the actual physical inventory of the issuing company. This type of investment, also known as "Mocatta" options after the Mocatta Metals Corporation, which initiated the plan, is based on more secure backing but, as is true of naked options, the investor undertakes the risk that the issuing company will be unable to fulfill its obligations when the option is exercised.

Still another type of option is the so-called "London" option, so named because of the relationship it bears to options traded on London exchanges. These exchanges have, for many years, conducted a reputable and respected trading in options and have developed a sound system by which the options traded are backed by the credit of the International Commodity Clearing House (ICCH), which in turn has established margin requirements and imposed other safeguards successfully used by futures exchanges to assure performance. American firms marketing such options in the United States, however, often failed to effect the transaction on the London exchanges, thus "bucketing" the order and creating a "naked" option. Moreover, even if the order was effected, it was done in the name of the London broker through an omnibus account of the American dealer, who generally was not a member of the London exchange. As a consequence, the customer had no contractual relationship whatsoever with any individual on that exchange, and thus was dependent solely on the financial integrity of the American dealer, integrity which was often sorely lacking. Only the American dealer, or some other entity, such as the record owner of the option, was known to the London broker. As a result, none of the protections afforded to option traders by the ICCH were extended to the American customer.

Commodity options have been traded on exchanges in the United States for over one hundred years, but they too have encountered serious abuses. Indeed, after speculation on commodities and options in particular had been blamed in large part for the collapse of the wheat market in the Great Depression, Congress enacted the Commodity Exchange Act (CEA), which imposed a flat prohibition on the trading of any options in the agricultural commodities then regulated under the

CEA.[1] For more than thirty years, this legislative proscription operated to ban commodity options both on and off exchanges and was only later removed by Congress.

In the early 1970's, a loophole in the law was discovered, which ultimately allowed a resurgence of off-exchange options trading far beyond anything previously experienced. The mastermind of this loophole was a twenty-six-year-old trader named Harold Goldstein, who put his scheme into operation in 1971. Starting with an initial capitalization of $800, by the end of 1972, Goldstein's firm, Goldstein-Samuelson, Inc., had offices worldwide and a gross income of $45 million. Goldstein relied on high pressure, mass-marketing techniques, and the naiveté and greed of unsophisticated investors.

The loophole used by Goldstein was simple. The CEA prohibited only the trading of options on those agricultural commodities within its scope. Several commodities, including the so-called "world" commodities, such as silver, platinum and coffee, were not then subject to the option ban contained in the CEA, and it was on these commodities that Goldstein conducted his trading.

Goldstein's adventure quickly turned to disaster because he was selling naked options. As large price increases in certain commodities began to occur, Goldstein became unable to pay, and by 1973 he was out of business, leaving behind some $85 million in unpaid "options.' " These were not the only losses, however, because several other firms had followed Goldstein's lead and losses of many millions more ensued.

As a result of these and other abuses, Congress sought to create a stronger and more coherent federal regulatory structure in the commodities field. The Commodity Futures Trading Commission Act of 1974 (CFTC Act) was enacted to meet this concern. The CFTC Act, which constituted amendments and extensions of the CEA, established the CFTC as an independent federal agency and vested it with "exclusive" jurisdiction over futures contracts trading and other activities, including the trading of commodity options.

In particular, the CFTC Act attempted to fill the legislative gaps and "loopholes." The CFTC Act extended the coverage of the CEA to all previously unregulated commodities, and it maintained the ban on options trading in the previously regulated commodities.' " It did not, however, prohibit options trading in the previously unregulated commodities. Rather, it gave the CFTC plenary authority to regulate such transactions. As a result of the enactment of the CFTC Act and its grant of exclusive jurisdiction to the CFTC, the authority of the SEC and the

---

[1] [Auth. note: The Supreme Court held in *Trusler v. Crooks*, 269 U.S. 475 (1926), that a provision in the Futures Trading Act of 1921 that sought to tax trading in options on grain out of existence was unconstitutional].

states was preempted. Although initially ineffective, by 1974 the states and the SEC had taken action to prevent abuses in the sale of commodity options. With the preemption of that authority, however, the widespread sale of commodity options began once again. The result was a debacle vividly illustrated by a number of cases against brokers dealing in the so-called London options.

NOTE

1. One court stated that:

> This would not be the first time . . . that Congress has frustrated would-be options traders out of concern for its larger constituency. Prior to enactment of the CEA in 1936, Mr. James J. Coughlin, a member of the Chicago Board of Trade, presented the Senate Committee on Agriculture and Forestry a petition "signed by something in excess of 1,500 members of the contract grain markets" requesting that the prohibition against trading "indemnities" be lifted. Hearings on H.R. 6772 Before the Senate Committee on Agriculture & Forestry 137–138 (1936). Indemnities were options on commodity futures whose trading would, in the judgment of Mr. Coughlin's petitioners, "result in a substantial broadening of the capacity of the futures markets to absorb the great volume of hedges necessarily attendant upon crop movements and, to that extent, furnish an infinitely more liquid market than exists at present, thereby not only resulting in a higher price level but likewise reducing the necessary price differential between farm and terminal." Id. But there was also substantial testimony from farm organizations and others to the effect that "this character of transaction (is) the cheapest form of gambling that can be practiced." Id. at 222 (statement of Mr. Clifford Thorne). In 1936, Congress sided with those wary of options by enacting the original Section 4c. CEA of 1936, ch. 545, s 5, 49 Stat. 1491, 1494 (now codified as s 4c(a), 7 U.S.C. s 6c(a)). In 1974, to the displeasure of putative options traders, Congress again sided with the cautious by placing all commodity options trading within the authority of a single independent agency. In 1978, Congress went even further by generally banning all options trading.

Board of Trade of the City of Chicago v. SEC, 677 F.2d 1137, 1152 (7th Cir. 1982), vacated as moot sub nom., Chicago Board Options Exchange, Inc. v. Board of Trade of the City of Chicago, 459 U.S. 1026 (1982).

BRITISH AMERICAN COMMODITY OPTIONS CORP. V. BAGLEY

552 F.2d 482 (2d Cir.), *cert denied*, 434 U.S. 938 (1977)

FEINBERG, CIRCUIT JUDGE:

Nine commodity options dealers and the National Association of Commodity Option Dealers (NASCOD) in this consolidated action challenge new rules that regulate the commodity options industry. The Commodity Futures Trading Commission (Commission) promulgated the rules under authority granted in 1974 by the Commodity Futures Trading Commission Act, Pub. L. 93–463, 88 Stat. 1389, 7 U.S.C. ss 1–22 (Supp. V, 1975). Plaintiffs claim that the regulatory scheme violates various requirements of the Administrative Procedure Act, 5 U.S.C. ss 551 et seq. (1970), and the United States Constitution. Prior to the effective dates of the new rules, plaintiffs brought suit in the federal courts for declaratory relief, and moved for a preliminary injunction against implementation of the rules. With the certified record of the informal rule-making proceeding before him, Judge Whitman Knapp of the United States District Court for the Southern District of New York enjoined the regulation that required segregation of customers' funds, but otherwise denied plaintiffs' motion and granted summary judgment for the Commission. We reverse the injunction against the segregation rule, and in other respects affirm the judgment of the district court.

The commodities business operates as a marketplace of contracts. The contracts traded are for the purchase, or sale, of specific amounts of a commodity either that have already been produced, or that will be produced in the future and delivered by a specific date. This latter group of contracts are known as "commodity futures." A "commodity option" is a contractual right to buy, or sell, a commodity or commodity future by some specific date at a specified, fixed price, known as the "striking price." A contract entitling its owner to purchase the commodity is known as a "call," and a contract entitling its owner to sell is called a "put." In the plainest case, an option is created, or "written," by the owner of a commodity or commodity futures contract, who commits himself to sell his goods or contract. But an option can also be written by anyone else willing to take the chance that he will be able to cover his obligation in the futures market, if the option purchaser decides to exercise the option. Such an option is described as "naked."

The Commodity Futures Trading Commission Act, 7 U.S.C. s 2 (Supp. V, 1975), defines "commodity" as wheat, cotton, rice, corn, oats, barley, rye, flaxseed, grain sorghums, mill feeds, butter, eggs, Solanum tuberosum (Irish potatoes), wool, wool tops, fats and oils (including lard, tallow, cottonseed oil, peanut oil, soybean oil and all other fats and oils), cottonseed meal, cottonseed, peanuts, soybeans, soybean meal, livestock,

livestock products, and frozen concentrated orange juice, and all other goods and articles, except onions as provided in section 13–1 of this title, and all services, rights, and interests in which contracts for future delivery are presently or in the future dealt in. . . .

The plaintiff firms in this case deal in "London options," which are options on futures contracts for certain commodities that are traded in London, England, on either the London Metals Exchange (LME) or several other exchanges whose transactions are cleared through the International Commodity Clearing House (ICCH). The plaintiff firms sell London options in the United States and, according to plaintiffs British American Commodity Options Corp. and Lloyd, Carr & Co., operate as follows: Plaintiffs actively solicit customers through direct mail and telephone contacts, as well as by newspaper and television advertising. When a customer orders the purchase of a commodity option, the dealer furnishes him with a notice giving the details of the transaction including the nature of the underlying futures contract, the price the writer charges for the option, known as the "premium," the dealer's commission, and the market on which the trade will be executed. The customer may or may not have paid for the option when this notice is sent; only payment of the purchase price to the dealer commits the customer to buying the option. The price quoted in the notice is firm, however, for five days, which means that the dealer assumes the risk of a price increase during that period. Once the dealer receives cash payment, he executes the trade through a "clearing member" of one of the English exchanges. The dealer then immediately forwards the premium amount to the clearing member, who pays the option writer. At the same time, the dealer sends another notice to the customer giving final details of the transaction.

To profit from this purchase, the customer must exercise the option before it expires. Exercising the option means buying the underlying futures contract. Since the customer normally has no interest in actually receiving the commodity on the delivery date, the clearing member then sells a futures contract short for the customer. The difference between the price at which the option is exercised plus the cost of purchasing the option (premium and commission) and the price at which the futures contract is sold is the customer's profit. If, however, the market price for the futures contract has dropped below the striking price, the customer allows the option to expire, in which case he loses his entire investment.

Intimations of difficulties in the commodity options market came to the attention of Congress in the early 1970's; existing laws had not worked well in preventing abuses in the options industry. Options were an especially hospitable environment for abuse because a naked option could be created out of nothing, if the writer was willing to run the risk of not covering his obligation by acquiring an offsetting position in the futures market. Thus, entry into the business of options required little capital. In addition, options bear lower price tags than the futures contracts underlying them, so the options market may be peculiarly attractive to individual investors of relatively modest means and with a propensity for taking risks.

Before 1974, regulation of trading in commodity futures and options derived mainly from the Commodity Exchange Act, 7 U.S.C. ss 1–17b (1970). That Act empowered the Commodity Exchange Authority of the Department of Agriculture to administer certain limited regulations on trading in a number of agricultural commodities, and completely banned options on them. 7 U.S.C. s 6c (1970). On October 23, 1974, Congress enacted the Commodity Futures Trading Commission Act, supra, which created the Commission as an independent regulatory agency with plenary rulemaking power. The Act also substantially broadened the field of regulation, to include virtually all "goods and articles," see note 2, supra The Commission was given exclusive jurisdiction with respect to accounts, agreements (including any transaction which is of the character of, or is commonly known to the trade as, an "option", "privilege", "indemnity", "bid", "offer", "put", "call", "advance guaranty", or "decline guaranty"), and transactions involving contracts of sale of a commodity for future delivery. 7 U.S.C. s 2 (Supp. V, 1975).

The new Act perpetuated the old Act's absolute ban on option trading for the commodities listed in the old Act, 7 U.S.C. s 6c(a) (Supp. V, 1975), but permitted other options to be written and to trade in compliance with rules promulgated by the Commission. 7 U.S.C. s 6c(b) (Supp. V, 1975). The Act authorized the Commission "to make and promulgate such rules and regulations as, in the judgment of the Commission, are reasonably necessary to effectuate any of the provisions or to accomplish any of the purposes of this chapter." 7 U.S.C. s 12a(5) (Supp. V, 1975).

On April 25, 1975, soon after the Commission came into official existence, it published for public comment a proposed anti-fraud rule, 40 Fed.Reg. 18187 (1975), that broadly proscribed fraudulent and deceptive practices and the making of false statements in connection with commodity options transactions. The anti-fraud rule became effective June 24, 1975. The Commission explained that its swift action was necessary because the Act's grant of exclusive jurisdiction to the Commission had left the public without regulatory protection.

In October 1975, the Commission announced that it was considering rules to regulate or prohibit all options trading. The Commission also announced the appointment of an Advisory Committee on the Definition and Regulation of Market Instruments to study the options situation and recommend suitable regulations. The public notice solicited suggestions of temporary rules to be adopted, and offered for consideration a number of alternative approaches: prohibition of all commodity options transactions;

restricting options trading to established contract markets; allowing trading only of options written as part of a Commission-approved "business plan"; prohibition of "naked" options; or registration by the Commission of dealers who comply with certain Commission fiduciary requirements. 40 Fed.Reg. 49360–62 (1975). The Commission did receive some comments from the public, although apparently none from any plaintiff.

On February 20, 1976, the Commission published its proposed temporary rules to govern commodity options transactions. 41 Fed.Reg. 7774 (1976). The proposal called for all options dealers, among other things, to register with the Commission, to maintain at least $100,000 of working capital, to keep certain records, and to disclose to options customers that certain information about the options dealer could be obtained from the Commission. Notably absent from the proposal was any requirement that the dealer set aside, or "segregate," any portion of the customer's cash payment until the option is sold or exercised. The Commission did, however, indicate that it was "particularly interested" in comments on the wisdom of such a requirement. 41 Fed.Reg. 7776 (1976).

At an oral hearing in March 1976, the Commission received the views of various witnesses, including counsel for British American. The Commission also received written comments, some supporting segregation, and in July 1976, the Advisory Committee transmitted its report, which also supported segregation.

On October 8, 1976, the Commission published proposed interim regulations, intended to become effective on November 22. Written comments from the public were invited on or before November 8. British American submitted comments and requested oral hearings, which the Commission did not provide. The Commission adopted the regulations, substantially in the form it had proposed, on schedule and gave public notice on November 24, 41 Fed.Reg. 51808 (1976), but delayed effectiveness for 15 days, except that the segregation requirement was delayed 30 days.

The new rules forbid an option dealer to do business after January 17, 1977 unless he is registered as a "futures commission merchant" (FCM) under the Act. 17 C.F.R. s 32.3 (1976). To be registered, a dealer has to comply with a new minimum capital requirement, 17 C.F.R. s 1.17 (1976), that the dealer maintain adjusted working capital in excess of the greater of $50,000 or a formula figure, one of whose components is five percent of the dealer's aggregate indebtedness. The new disclosure rule, 17 C.F.R. s 32.5 (1976), requires the option customer to be furnished a "summary disclosure statement" prior to the commodity option transaction. The statement must contain, among other things, a brief description of the "total quantity and quality" of the commodity under the option, its duration, the elements comprising its purchase price, the method by which the striking price is established, the amount of the commission to be charged, a statement that the price rise (for a call) or price fall (for a put) must exceed the premium amount plus costs in order for the option customer to make money, and a clear explanation of the possible effects of currency fluctuations on options executed through foreign facilities. Section 32.6 of the new regulations requires an FCM to segregate 90 percent of the payment received from the customer in a United States bank account until expiration or exercise of the option. Also, the rules require an FCM to keep pertinent records of each transaction. 17 C.F.R. s 32.7 (1976).

The new rules announced on November 24 differed in several respects from the October 8 version. In addition to postponing the effective dates, as indicated above, the new rules relaxed the earlier proposed requirement that the summary disclosure statement be furnished no less than 24 hours before the transaction. The Commission changed this requirement to allow the statement to be furnished merely "prior" to the transaction, because of public comments that the proposed rule was unrealistic in light of the volatile nature of the commodities markets. In addition, the new rules change the requirement that particularized price information be disclosed before rather than after the transaction. And the amount to be segregated was reduced from 100 percent to 90 percent so that an FCM could immediately get funds for commissions, salaries, and administrative expenses. See 41 Fed.Reg. 51811–13 (1976).

As indicated above, plaintiffs' efforts in the district court to enjoin operation of the new rules were unsuccessful, except for the segregation requirement. Except for that portion of the order, plaintiffs urge us to reverse the judgment of the district court. The Commission cross-appeals and seeks reversal of the injunction against the segregation requirement.
* * *

On the basis of the Commission's justifications and the record before us, we disagree with the district court that the segregation requirement should be enjoined. The Commission's conclusion that in light of past abuses, the public now needs this minimal protection carries great weight. And in any event, the requirement is not unreasonable even if it threatens to restrict participation in the industry to soundly capitalized firms. Nor does it appear that the Commission adopted the requirement with undue haste. * * *

KELLEY V. CARR

567 F. Supp. 831 (W.D. Mich. 1983)

NOEL P. FOX, SENIOR DISTRICT JUDGE.

Presently before the court is plaintiff Commodity Futures Trading Commission's ("Commission") motion for summary judgment. The Commission seeks permanent injunctive relief, the appointment of an Equity Receiver, an accounting, and an order directing all defendants to disgorge to the Receiver all benefits derived from the violative actions discussed below.

This case originated on October 13, 1977, when Michigan Attorney General Frank J. Kelley ("Kelley") filed a complaint against defendants in the Circuit Court for Ingham County, Michigan. The complaint charged violations of the anti-fraud and other provisions of the Michigan securities and consumer protection statutes in defendants' solicitation and sale of options on futures contracts for London commodities. On October 31, 1977, defendants removed to this court, and on November 2, 1977, the State amended its complaint to include violations of the anti-fraud provisions of the Commodity Exchange Act as amended by the Commodity Futures Trading Commission Act, Pub.L. 93–463, 88 Stat. 1389, 7 U.S.C. §§ 1–22.

A temporary restraining order was granted by this court on November 7, 1977, upon the amended complaint of Kelley, and the Commission was granted leave to intervene on November 8, 1977. The Commission's complaint included three counts: fraud in connection with the sale of commodity options, under 17 C.F.R. § 32.9; failure to disclose required information, under 17 C.F.R. § 32.5; and failure to secure prompt execution of commodity option orders, under 17 C.F.R. § 32.8(c). The Commission also requested relief in the form of an injunction against further violations of the Act, the appointment of a Receiver for Lloyd Carr & Co., an accounting, disgorgement, and a protective order *pendente lite.*

On December 5, 1977, the court granted the preliminary injunction requested by the Commission, enjoining defendants from defrauding and deceiving customers with misleading information, and from destroying records. *Kelley v. Carr,* 442 F. Supp. 346 (W.D.Mich.1977), *aff'd in part and rev'd in part,* 691 F.2d 800 (6th Cir.1980). It also compelled the defendants to provide the Commission access to Lloyd Carr & Co. records and to give notice of the injunction to all employees. In addition, a Special Master was appointed.

Subsequent to this preliminary injunction, Lloyd Carr & Co. branch offices in a number of cities failed to provide the Commission access to records as mandated, and on January 9, 1978, the U.S. Attorney for the Western District of Michigan and the Commission filed an application for an order to show cause why defendants and other Lloyd Carr employees should not be held in criminal contempt. On or about January 10, 1978, defendant Carr, a/k/a Alan Abrahams ("Abrahams")[1] was taken into federal custody on the contempt citation, and upon discovery of his true identity, was also held as an escaped fugitive from New Jersey. On January 19, 1978, Lloyd Carr & Co. and Lloyd Carr Financial Co. were placed in equity receivership in a pending injunctive action filed by the Commission in Boston against the same defendants as in the instant action.

On or about February 1, 1978, the companies were placed in involuntary bankruptcy receivership, with Walter McLaughlin Sr., the Equity Receiver appointed in the injunctive case, appointed as bankruptcy receiver/trustee. An involuntary bankruptcy petition was also filed against Alan Abrahams. *In re Alan Abrahams and Lloyd, Carr & Co.,* Nos. 78–204–Z, 78–208–Z, 78–209–Z (D. Mass. filed 2/1/1978).

On January 30, 1978, on the motions of plaintiffs Kelley and the Commission, this court amended its preliminary injunction to terminate all solicitation and sales activities of the defendants, as a result of information received which indicated additional fraud, and the discovery of Abrahams' aliases and outstanding state and federal charges. At the same time the appointment of the Master was vacated, in deference to the appointment of the Receiver by the Federal District Court in Boston.

Following a hearing on the contempt question, this court found defendants in contempt for violation of the earlier order. Defendant Abrahams received a six-month prison sentence, which was added to the sentence he was then serving for crimes in New Jersey. Abrahams has since pled guilty, in the Southern District of New York, to a multi-count mail and wire fraud conspiracy based on the same activities alleged in the Commission's pleadings in this action. He received 54 months additional prison time. *United States v. Abrahams,* 79 Cr. 425 (WCC) (S.D.N.Y. 3/31/80). Abrahams was recently released from the Federal Correctional Institution at Raybrook, New York.* * *

From 1976, when Lloyd Carr Financial first began to sell options, until January 1978, when Lloyd Carr was placed in receivership and then bankruptcy, legions of inadequately trained telephone salespeople made thousands of unsolicited or "cold" calls to unsuspecting members of the public to solicit orders for London Commodity options sold through Lloyd Carr. Representing to customers Lloyd Carr's supposed commodities

---

[1] When arrested on this contempt charge in Massachusetts and fingerprinted, James Carr was found to be Alan Abrahams, an escaped fugitive from a New Jersey prison. [Auth. Note: Abrahams had been serving a sentence for aiding and abetting the obtaining of money under false pretenses in New Jersey when he escaped from prison. Under the alias "James A. Carr" he formed Lloyd, Carr & Co. and Lloyd Carr Financial Corp., which became one of the largest brokerage firms in the U.S.]

expertise, these salespeople, often reading from prepared scripts and assisted by misleading and incomplete promotional materials, provided to actual and potential customers exaggerated predictions of huge, virtually certain profits that would follow the purchase of London options through the Company.

Lloyd Carr was a classic "boiler room" operation, utilizing:

unqualified, improperly supervised salesmen; high pressure long distance telephone sales designed to induce hasty investor decisions by customers about whose financial conditions the salesmen knew very little; and heavy dealings in speculative [transactions] about whose [terms and] conditions there was little disclosure.

Securities & Exchange Commission v. Charles A. Morris & Associates, 386 F. Supp. 1327, 1336 (W.D.Tenn.1973). Here, as usual, the boiler room operation involved a high pressure sales organization selling speculative ventures to unsophisticated investors. Defendants did not require that their salespeople be experienced. Salespeople were given no substantive training in commodities trading theory. The only significant training was in *sales* techniques, with only a brief description of commodities. Salespeople labored under high pressure conditions intended to spur sales without regard to investor suitability. Their telephone calls consisted primarily of "canned" sales pitches. *See, e.g.,* 442 F. Supp. at 350–351 n. 7.

Naggingly repetitive phone calls were employed in an attempt to pressure customers into buying options. Customers were exhorted to act hastily to avoid missing out on profits. Prices were deliberately misquoted to convince customers that opportunities to profit had already been lost by the customers' inaction.

Defendants regularly solicited and made sales to individuals without regard to investor suitability. As a result, many persons invested and lost funds they could ill afford to invest in high-risk investment schemes. These sales resulted in large part from defendants' misrepresentations of risk, profitability, and the nature of the transactions involved.

In the course of their solicitations, Lloyd Carr salespeople failed to disclose, obscured, or simply misrepresented numerous material facts concerning the transactions. Examples include: the risks involved in options transactions; profit potentials; the size and nature of Lloyd Carr's fees and commissions; the size and reliability of the Lloyd Carr research department; the nature of the "break-even" point at which an option becomes profitable to the customer; the effect of foreign currency fluctuations; Lloyd Carr's registration status with the Commodity Futures Trading Commission; Lloyd Carr's reputation in the industry; and the nature of "one-half" option contracts sold to customers.

Misrepresentations took the form of statements made to customers by salespeople, misleading sales pitches, and misrepresentations contained in various sales literature given to customers. Misrepresentations were also inherent in the failure to disclose certain material information.

In some instances salespeople induced customers to purchase more than one option, by misrepresenting the additional options as "hedges" when, in fact, they were identical to the first option.

On other occasions, salespeople placed orders for customers without their knowledge or consent, or refused to return funds to customers by explaining that the funds had already been used to purchase options when the funds had, in fact, not been spent.

At least through December 1976, Lloyd Carr sold "naked" options to customers without so informing them. The sale of naked options resulted in situations where customers had to look to Lloyd Carr, rather than an exchange member, for payment of any profits. Customers were led to believe that an actual London option had been purchased by Lloyd Carr, on their behalf. Customers were not informed of the risk involved in such a situation.

Defendants' fraudulent activities were not isolated instances of misconduct. Rather, they were pervasive and intentional acts done with the intent of defrauding unsuspecting investors. The actions took place on a massive scale. The Detroit office, alone, made more than seventy thousand calls in one month, at a cost of over fifty thousand dollars. Nationwide, telephone charges approached one million dollars monthly.

The vast majority of investors lost all of their investment. Only a very small number made any profit by investing through Lloyd Carr.

Defendants consistently failed to properly disclose the essence of the transactions being offered, including the duration of the options and the quantity and quality of the underlying commodities; the elements comprising the purchase price; the services provided for those charges; and the break-even point and how it differed from the striking price.

Defendants failed to provide a clear explanation of the effect of any foreign currency fluctuations on the transactions entered into.

Defendants often failed to send prospective purchasers a bold-faced disclosure of risk statement, or any other disclosure statement. When defendants made disclosure statements, they were generally made only *after* the deal was closed; were generally insufficient to overcome the repeated high-pressure misrepresentations and recommendations; and failed to disclose various material facts including cost components, *i.e.*, commissions, fees, and other charges.

Upon receipt of orders for commodity option transactions, defendants unreasonably failed to secure prompt execution of such orders. Orders were withheld for days or weeks prior to execution in the London markets, to the detriment of the customer.

In other instances, where customers ordered, and were told they were purchasing contracts for commodity options purchased on the London exchanges, defendants failed to purchase options, instead providing customers with naked options. * * *

NOTES

1. As the result of the Lloyd Carr and other options trading scandals, the CFTC suspended trading in 1978 for non-commercial options. The Futures Trading Act of 1978 amended the CEA to include the CFTC's ban on options trading. That statute also included an exemption for trade and dealer options. It additionally permitted the CFTC to develop a new program for regulating options traded on DCMs.

2. The CFTC, thereafter, acted to allow options on registered commodity futures exchanges where that trading could be closely regulated. The trading of commodity options on exchanges is conducted in a manner similar to that of stock options and commodity futures contracts. See, Jerry W. Markham & David J. Gilberg, Stock and Commodity Options—Two Regulatory Approaches and Their Conflicts, 47 Albany L. Rev. 741 (1983) (describing this background).

3. DEFERRED DELIVERY CONTRACTS

The switch to exchange traded options did not stop widespread fraud in retail over-the-counter transactions. The options dealers simply restructured their trading operations and claimed that they were selling "deferred delivery" (forward) contracts, which were not subject to the CFTC's jurisdiction. Forward contracts, which historically involved agricultural products and, today, several types of financial products, have been exempt from regulation pursuant to the CEA. This exemption was designed to ensure that the CEA would not interfere with normal commercial transactions involving grains. However, to qualify as a forward contract, the commercial parties to the contract must contemplate that actual delivery will occur. A payment of a net price differential does not satisfy the forward contract exemption.

The CFTC brought numerous cases charging that instruments claimed to be deferred delivery contracts were actually futures or options and that a mere name change in an instrument did not remove the CFTC's jurisdiction.

CFTC v. CO PETRO MARKETING GROUP, INC.

680 F.2d 573 (9th Cir. 1982)

Opinion by: CANBY

Co Petro Marketing Group, Inc., and individual appellants, Harold Goldstein and Michael Krivacek, (Co Petro) appeal from an order of the district court, 502 F. Supp. 806, permanently enjoining them from offering, selling, or otherwise engaging in futures contracts in petroleum products, in violation of §§ 4 and 4h of the Commodity Exchange Act, as amended, (the Act), 7 U.S.C. §§ 6, 6h (1976). Co Petro contends that the contracts it sold were not subject to the Act. Co Petro also appeals from the district court's award of relief ancillary to the permanent injunction. The district court appointed a receiver, ordered Co Petro to permit the receiver access to the firm's books and records, ordered an accounting, and generally ordered the disgorgement of unlawfully obtained funds. Co Petro further assigns as error the district court's taking judicial notice of three prior proceedings against defendant Goldstein. We affirm the district court's judgment that Co Petro was offering and selling "contracts of sale of a commodity for future delivery" (futures contracts) within the meaning of section 2(a)(1) of the Act, 7 U.S.C. § 2 (1976). We also agree with the district court that Co Petro violated sections 4 and 4h of the Act, 7 U.S.C. §§ 6, 6h (1976), by trading these contracts otherwise than by or through a member of a board of trade which has been designated by the Commodity Futures Trading Commission as a contract market. Finally we affirm the award of ancillary relief and find no error in the district court's taking judicial notice of the three prior proceedings against defendant Goldstein.

Co Petro is licensed by the State of California as a gasoline broker. It operated a chain of retail gasoline outlets and also acted as a broker of petroleum products, buying and reselling in the spot market several hundred thousand gallons of gasoline and diesel fuel monthly. While part of its business operations involved the direct sale of gasoline to industrial, commercial, and retail users of gasoline, Co Petro also offered and sold contracts for the future purchase of petroleum products pursuant to an "Agency Agreement for Purchase and Sale of Motor Vehicle Fuel" (Agency Agreement).

Under the Agency Agreement, the customer (1) appointed Co Petro as his agent to purchase a specified quantity and type of fuel at a fixed price for delivery at an agreed future date, and (2) paid a deposit based upon a fixed percentage of the purchase price. Co Petro, however, did not require its customer to take delivery of the fuel. Instead, at a later specified date the customer could appoint Co Petro to sell the fuel on his behalf. If the cash price had risen in the interim Co Petro was to (1) remit the difference between the original purchase price and the subsequent sale price, and (2) refund any remaining deposit. If the cash price had decreased, Co Petro was to (1) deduct from the deposit the difference between the purchase price and the subsequent sale price, and (2) remit the balance of the deposit to the customer. A liquidated damages clause provided that in no event would the customer lose more than 95% of his initial deposit.

Co Petro marketed these contracts extensively to the general public through newspaper advertisements, private seminars, commissioned telephone solicitors, and various other commissioned sales agents. The Commodity Futures Trading Commission brought this statutory injunctive action under section 6c of the Act, 7 U.S.C. § 13a–1 (1976), seeking to enjoin Co Petro's sales of petroleum products pursuant to its Agency Agreements. The Commission's complaint generally charged and the district court held that Co Petro was in violation of the Act by offering and selling contracts of sale of commodities for future delivery outside of a licensed contract market.

Co Petro contends that the Commission lacks jurisdiction over transactions pursuant to its Agency Agreements because these agreements are "cash forward" contracts expressly excluded from regulation by section 2(a)(1) of the Act, 7 U.S.C. § 2 (1976). While section 2(a)(1) provides the Commission with regulatory jurisdiction over "contracts of sale of a commodity for future delivery," it further provides that the term future delivery "shall not include any sale of any cash commodity for deferred shipment or delivery." Cash commodity contracts for deferred shipment or delivery are commonly known as "cash forward" contracts, while contracts of sale of a commodity for future delivery are called "futures contracts". See H.R.Rep.No.93–975, 93d Cong., 2d Sess. 129–30 (1974). The Act, however, sets forth no further definitions of the term "future delivery" or of the phrase "cash commodity for deferred shipment or delivery." The statutory language, therefore, provides little guidance as to the distinctions between regulated futures contracts and excluded cash forward contracts and, to our knowledge, no other court has dealt with this question. Where the statute is, as here, ambiguous on its face, it is necessary to look to legislative history to ascertain the intent of Congress. See United States v. Turkette, 452 U.S. 576, 580, 101 S. Ct. 2524, 2527, 69 L. Ed. 2d 246 (1981). Our examination of the relevant legislative history leads us to conclude that the Co Petro's Agency Agreements are not cash forward contracts within the meaning of the Act.

The exclusion for cash forward contracts originated in the Future Trading Act, Pub.L.No.67–66, § 2, 42 Stat. 187 (1921). Congress passed the Future Trading Act as a result of excessive speculation and price manipulations occurring on the grain futures markets. S.Rep.No.212, 67th Cong., 1st Sess. 4–5 (1921). See S.Rep.No.93–1131, 93d Cong., 2d Sess. 13 (1974), reprinted in (1974) U.S. Code & Ad. News 5843, 5854–55.

To curb these abuses, the Future Trading Act imposed a prohibitive tax on all futures contracts with two exceptions. Section 4(a) of the Act exempted from the tax future delivery contracts made by owners and growers of grain, owners and renters of land on which grain was grown, and associations of such persons. 42 Stat. 187. Section 4(b) of the Act exempted from the tax future delivery contracts made by or through members of boards of trade which had been designated by the Secretary of Agriculture as contract markets. Id. During hearings on the bill that became the Future Trading Act, various witnesses expressed concern that the exemption for owners and growers of grain, owners and renters of land on which grain was grown, and associations of such persons, was too narrow. By its terms, this section might not exempt from the tax a variety of legitimate commercial transactions, such as cash grain contracts between farmers and grain elevator operators for the future delivery of grain. Hearings on H.R. 5676 Before the Senate Committee on Agriculture and Forestry, 67th Cong., 1st Sess. 8–9, 213–214, 431, 462 (1921). As a result, the Senate added language to section 2 of the bill, excluding "any sale of cash grain for deferred shipment" from the term "future delivery". S.Rep.No.212, 67th Cong., 1st Sess. 1 (1921). There is no indication that Congress drew this exclusion otherwise than to meet a particular need such as that of a farmer to sell part of next season's harvest at a set price to a grain elevator or miller. These cash forward contracts guarantee the farmer a buyer for his crop and provide the buyer with an assured price. Most important, both parties to the contracts deal in and contemplate future delivery of the actual grain.

The exclusion was carried forward without change into the Grain Futures Act, Pub.L.No.67–331, § 2, 42 Stat. 998 (1922). In 1936, Congress enacted the Commodity Exchange Act, Pub.L.No.74–675, 49 Stat. 1491 (1936). This Act expanded the scope of federal regulation to include certain specified commodities in addition to grain, id., § 3, and reworded the exclusion to except "any cash commodity for deferred shipment or delivery." Id., § 2. The Commodity Exchange Act also deleted the express exemption for owners and growers of grain, owners and renters of land, and associations of such persons. Congress considered the exemption redundant since section 2 of the Act, which excluded cash commodity contracts for deferred shipment or delivery, served to protect the same interests that had been protected by the exemption for owners and growers. H.R.Rep.No.421, 74th Cong., 1st Sess. 4–5 (1935). Although the Act has been amended numerous times since 1936, the language excluding cash commodities for deferred shipment or delivery has remained the same.

A more recent House Report on the 1974 Amendments to the Act reconfirms the narrowness of the exclusion. H.R.Rep.No.93–975, 93d Cong., 2d Sess. 129–30 (1974). The House Report describes a typical cash transaction as involving, for example, a farmer who wants to convert 5,000 bushels of wheat into cash. He seeks a buyer such as a grain elevator for whom the wheat has "inherent value." The wheat has "inherent value" for the grain elevator because the elevator "is in contact with potential buyers such as the flour miller, and has the facilities to store, condition, and load out the grain and earn additional income from these services." Id. at 129. The wheat also has "inherent value" to the flour miller, who can increase its utility and value by grinding it into flour. Id. A cash forward contract is common in these kinds of transactions because it guarantees the miller, for example, a price but allows delivery to be deferred "until such time as he could process the wheat." Id. This House Report therefore supports prior history indicating that a cash forward contract is one in which the parties contemplate physical transfer of the actual commodity.

The situation for which the exclusion for cash forward contracts was designed is not present here. Co Petro's Agency Agreement customers were, for the most part, speculators from the general public. The underlying petroleum products had no inherent value to these speculators. They had neither the intention of taking delivery nor the capacity to do so. Yet it was to the general public that Co Petro made its strongest sales pitches. For example, in an advertisement in the Los Angeles Times under the headline "Invest in Gasoline," Co Petro stated: "The Sophisticated Small Investor Can Make Money Buying Gasoline. It's a high risk-high potential yield opportunity." In addition to advertising extensively in newspapers of general circulation, Co Petro ran seminars to explain its investment vehicle to the general public. It also hired sales agents experienced in marketing commodities to investors. In an apparent attempt to protect itself, Co Petro required the investor in one version of its Agency Agreement to initial the following statement: "I realize that a motor vehicle fuel purchase is a high risk speculative venture and I fully understand that I could lose most or all of my entire deposit and by virtue of my own business experience or independent advice, I am capable of evaluating the hazards and merits of this motor vehicle fuel purchase."

There is nothing in the legislative history surrounding cash forward contracts to suggest that Congress intended the exclusion to encompass agreements for the future delivery of commodities sold merely for purposes of such speculation. Congress has recognized the vital role speculators play in the proper functioning of futures markets, H.R.Rep.No.93–975, supra, at 138, and has expressed its desire to protect speculators through expansive federal regulation. See Merrill Lynch, Pierce, Fenner & Smith, Inc. v. Curran, 456 U.S. 353, 102 S. Ct. 1825, 1845, 72 L. Ed. 2d 182 (1982). Prior to the 1974 Amendments to the Act, only certain specified commodities were regulated. In 1974, Congress not only expanded the list of commodities subject to regulation, but also extended regulation to "all other goods and articles, . . . and all services, rights, and interests in which contracts for future delivery are presently or in the future dealt with." 7 U.S.C. § 2 (1976). The House Report on these amendments stated: "There is no reason why a person trading in one of the currently unregulated futures markets should not receive the same protection afforded to those trading in the currently regulated markets." H.R.Rep.No.93–975, supra, at 76. See S.Rep.No.93–1131, supra, at 19. This recent expression of legislative intent to protect persons like Co Petro's customers, who deal in previously unregulated commodity futures, is consonant with a narrow reading of the exclusion for sales of cash commodities for deferred shipment or delivery. We hold, therefore, that this exclusion is unavailable to contracts of sale for commodities which are sold merely for speculative purposes and which are not predicated upon the expectation that delivery of the actual commodity by the seller to the original contracting buyer will occur in the future. See In re Stovall, (Current) Commodity Futures Law Reports (CCH) § 20,941 at 23, 778 (Dec. 6, 1979).

This does not end our inquiry, however. Even though Co Petro's Agency Agreements do not fall within the exclusion for cash forward contracts, there remains the question whether they are "contracts of sale of a commodity for future delivery" (futures contracts) within the meaning of section 2(a)(1) of the Act, 7 U.S.C. § 2 (1976). Co Petro contends that its Agency Agreements cannot be futures contracts because they lack most of the common distinguishing features of futures contracts as they are known in the industry. Futures contracts traded on the designated markets have certain basic characteristics. Except for price, all the futures contracts for a specified commodity are identical in quantity and other terms. The fungible nature of these contracts facilitates offsetting transactions by which purchasers or sellers can liquidate their positions by forming opposite contracts. The price differential between the opposite contracts then determines the investor's profit or loss. * * *

While contracts pursuant to Co Petro's Agency Agreements were not as rigidly standardized as futures contracts traded on licensed contract markets, neither were they individualized. Tables furnished by Co Petro to its sales agents demonstrate uniformity in the basic units of volume, multiples of which were offered for sale. Similarly, relevant dates in Co Petro's Agency Agreements were uniform. The date on which an investor had to notify Co Petro of his intent to take delivery or appoint Co Petro as his agent to resell the contract was set at approximately eight months from the purchase date. An investor could not give notice prior to the specified notice date. The delivery date was always ten months from the purchase date.

More important, however, than the degree to which Co Petro's Agency Agreements conform to the precise features of standardized futures contracts is the rationale for standardization in futures trading. Standardized form contracts facilitate the formation of offsetting or liquidating transactions. The ability to form offsetting contracts is essential, since investors rarely take delivery against the contracts. Pursuant to provisions in Co Petro's Agency Agreements, Co Petro was obliged to perform an offsetting service for its customers by reselling contracts for their accounts. Customers also could liquidate their positions in the face of adverse price movements by cancelling their contracts with Co Petro and paying only the liquidated damages provided for in the Agency Agreements. Therefore, Co Petro's customers, like customers who trade on organized futures exchanges, could deal in commodity futures without the forced burden of delivery. Disregarding form for substance, Tcherepnin v. Knight, 389 U.S. 332, 336, 88 S. Ct. 548, 553, 19 L. Ed. 2d 564 (1967), we find without merit Co Petro's argument that its Agency Agreement represents a radical departure from the classic elements of a standardized futures contract. We also reject Co Petro's final contention that, contrary to the practice in organized futures markets where price is established by public auction, it negotiated prices directly with its Agency Agreement customers. The evidence indicates that, for the most part, Co Petro unilaterally set prices for its products according to the then-prevailing market rates, with the spot market determining resale prices to subsequent purchasers. Moreover, the fact that public auction did not determine Co Petro's prices is merely a result of Co Petro's failure to seek Commission licensing for organized exchange trading in petroleum futures.

In determining whether a particular contract is a contract of sale of a commodity for future delivery over which the Commission has regulatory jurisdiction by virtue of 7 U.S.C. § 2 (1976), no bright-line definition or list of characterizing elements is determinative. The transaction must be viewed as a whole with a critical eye toward its underlying purpose. The contracts here represent speculative ventures in commodity futures which were marketed to those for whom delivery was not an expectation. Addressing these circumstances in the light of the legislative history of the Act, we conclude that Co Petro's contracts are "contracts of sale of a commodity for future delivery." 7 U.S.C. § 2 (1976).

We further decline to accept Co Petro's contention that sections 4 and 4h of the Act, 7 U.S.C. §§ 6, 6h (1976), have no application to its activities. * * * Section 4 of the Act, 7 U.S.C. § 6 (1976), makes it "unlawful for any person to deliver . . . any offer to make . . . any contract of sale of commodity for future delivery on or subject to the rules of any board of trade in the United States, or . . . to make or execute such contract of sale, . . . except . . . where such contract is made by or through a member of a

board of trade which has been designated by the Commission as a
"contract market.'" (emphasis added). Co Petro contends that even if it
were selling commodity futures contracts, the statutory language
demonstrates that section 4 only prohibits transactions in futures
contracts which currently are on or subject to the rules of a commodity
exchange, as that institution is commonly understood. The statutory
definition of "board of trade," however, is broad enough to encompass Co
Petro's activities here. Section 2(a)(1) of the Act, 7 U.S.C. § 2 (1976),
defines "board of trade" to "include or mean any exchange or association,
whether incorporated or unincorporated, of persons who shall be engaged
in the business of buying or selling commodity or receiving the same for
sale on consignment."

Where Congress has, as here, intentionally and unambiguously
drafted a particularly broad definition, it is not our function to undermine
that effort. Co Petro clearly was an association of persons engaged in the
business of selling commodities (petroleum products) within the plain
meaning of the statute defining "board of trade." * * *

The decision of the district court is affirmed.

Dissent by: SMITH * * *

NAGEL V. ADM INVESTORS SERVICES
217 F.3d 436 (7th Cir. 2000)

POSNER, CHIEF JUDGE.

This is another chapter in the continuing saga of "flexible" or
"enhanced" hedge-to-arrive contracts (we'll call these "flex HTAs"); for the
earlier chapters see *Lachmund v. ADM Investor Services, Inc.,* 191 F.3d
777 (7th Cir. 1999), and *Harter v. Iowa Grain Co.,* 211 F.3d 338, 2000 WL
426366 (7th Cir. 2000), in light of which we can be brief.

The plaintiffs in these five consolidated cases are farmers who
entered into contracts to deliver grain to grain elevators and other grain
merchants, the defendants, at a specified future date. So far, we are
describing an ordinary forward (sometimes called "cash forward")
contract, a contract that provides for delivery at some future date at the
price specified in the contract. The hedging feature that gives the HTA
contract its name comes from the fact that the contract price is a price
specified in a futures contract that the merchant buys on a commodity
exchange and that expires in the month specified for delivery under the
merchant's contract with the farmer (the HTA contract). This
arrangement hedges the merchant against price fluctuations between
signing and delivery. The merchant is "long" in his contract with the
farmer (the forward contract) in the sense that, if price rises, he's to the
good, because the price was fixed earlier, in the contract, and so he

bought the farmer's grain cheap. But if the price of grain falls, he's hurt, because he's stuck with a contract price that is higher than the current price. To offset this risk he goes "short" in the futures contract—that is, he agrees to sell an offsetting quantity of grain at the same price as fixed in the forward contract. If the price of grain falls during the interval between the signing of and delivery under the forward contract, though he loses on the forward contract, as we have seen, he makes up the loss in the futures contract, where he is the seller and therefore benefits when the market price falls below the contract price: The loss he would otherwise sustain as a result of having to resell the farmer's grain at a lower price than the price fixed in his contract with the farmer is offset by his profit on the futures contract. In sum, the price in the contract between farmer and merchant fixed by reference to the futures contract made by the merchant protects the farmer against price fluctuations between the signing of the contract and the delivery of the grain (just because it is a fixed price and so is unaffected by any change in market price during this interval), while the futures contract itself protects the merchant from the risk of loss should the price plummet during that interval.

That's a simple HTA contract; the "flex" feature of the HTA contracts involved in this case comes from the fact that they allow the farmer to defer delivery of the grain. (On the difference between simple and flex HTAs, see the lucid discussion in Charles F. Reid, Note, "Risky Business: HTAs, The Cash Forward Exclusion and *Top of Iowa Cooperative v. Schewe,"* 44 Vill. L. Rev. 125, 134–37 (1999).) Such a contract specifies a delivery date but allows the farmer, upon the payment of a fee and an appropriate adjustment in the price to reflect changed conditions, to defer delivery beyond that date. A farmer who exercises this deferral option is doing what is called "rolling the hedge." The merchant, if he wants to hedge against price fluctuations during the extended period of the contract, will close out his existing futures contract by buying an offsetting contract and will then buy a new futures contract to expire at the new delivery date. When the new delivery date arrives, the farmer can again roll the hedge. Why might a farmer want to roll the hedge? If the market price rose between the signing of the original contract with the merchant and the delivery date specified in the contract, and the farmer expected it to fall later, he could, by rolling the hedge, sell his grain at the current market price (since he wouldn't have to deliver it to the merchant), which by assumption is higher than the price fixed in the contract; and then, just before the new delivery date, he could buy at the then current price, expected to be lower, the amount of grain he was obligated to deliver and deliver it at the price fixed in the contract. The flex feature thus enables the farmer to speculate on fluctuations in the market price of his grain.

The plaintiffs did this in 1995, but unfortunately for them prices stayed up and to satisfy their contractual obligations they had to buy grain at prices above the prices fixed in their contracts with the merchants, sustaining large losses as a consequence. They seek in these suits to get out of the contracts by arguing that flex HTA contracts are futures contracts. The Commodity Exchange Act, requires that futures contracts be sold through commodity exchanges and the futures commission merchants registered on those exchanges, 7 U.S.C. sec. 6(a); the defendants fall into neither category. The section just cited declares futures contracts not sold through commodity exchanges and registered futures commission merchants unlawful, and the parties assume that futures contracts rendered unlawful by section 6(a) are indeed unenforceable. * * *

The Act defines a futures contract as a contract for future delivery, but defines future delivery to exclude "any sale of any cash commodity for deferred shipment or delivery," 7 U.S.C. sec. 1a(11), that is, any forward contract. *Lachmund v. ADM Investor Services, Inc., supra,* 191 F.3d at 787. The plaintiffs argue that since the flex feature of their contracts permits delivery to be deferred indefinitely, the contracts are not forward contracts, but instead futures contracts. The district court disagreed and dismissed the suits, believing it plain that the language of the contracts showed they were forward contracts. Some of them contain arbitration clauses, so in addition to dismissing the suits the court confirmed arbitral awards for the defendants for the plaintiffs' breaches of contract in failing to make delivery when due.

Although futures contracts specify delivery as a possible method of satisfying the short's obligations, it is much more common for such contracts to be closed out by the "buyer's" taking an offsetting position in a new contract identical but for its price. This option for getting out enables people who are not agriculturalists, and wouldn't know an ear of corn from a soybean if it slapped them in the face, to speculate in the prices of commodities. In other words, these contracts are really a type of security, like common stock, rather than a means of fixing the terms by which farmers ship their output to grain elevators and other agricultural middlemen. It is because commodity-futures contracts are a type of security that Congress has seen fit to subject them to a regulatory scheme, the Commodity Exchange Act, which parallels that administered by the SEC for trading in corporate stock. There was no intention of regulating the commerce in agricultural commodities itself. But because futures contracts do contain a provision for delivery as an optional mode of compliance with obligations created by such contracts, rare as the exercise of that option is, it isn't always easy to determine just from the language of a contract for the sale of a commodity whether it is a futures contract or a forward contract.

The flex feature in the HTA contracts moves these contracts in the direction of futures contracts by attenuating the obligation to deliver, and there is anxiety that by loading such features onto what would otherwise seem to be garden-variety forward contracts the regulatory scheme will be evaded. This led our court in the Lachmund case to look with favor upon a "totality of the circumstances" approach for determining whether a contract is a futures contract or a forward contract, 191 F.3d at 787–88, as have other courts as well. See *Grain Land Co-op v. Kar Kim Farms, Inc.,* 199 F.3d 983, 991 (8th Cir. 1999); *Andersons, Inc. v. Horton Farms, Inc.,* 166 F.3d 308, 317–21 (6th Cir. 1998); *CFTC v. Co Petro Marketing Group, Inc., supra,* 680 F.2d at 579–81. But as noted by Judge Easterbrook, also a member of this court though sitting by designation as the trial judge in this case, the "totality of the circumstances" approach invites criticism as placing a cloud over forward contracts by placing them at risk of being reclassified as futures contracts traded off-exchange and therefore illegal. Of course, if the legality of a contract cannot easily be determined in advance, that might be a factor rebutting the presumption noted earlier that illegal contracts are unenforceable; but this is not a possibility that we need consider in this case, or perhaps in any flex HTA case, since the problem of legal uncertainty under the "totality of circumstances" is less serious than it appears to be.

As is often true of multifactor legal tests, the "totality of circumstances" approach turns out in practice to give controlling significance to a handful of circumstances; and fortunately they can usually be ascertained just by reading the contract. The cases indicate that when the following circumstances are present, the contract will be deemed a forward contract:

> (1) The contract specifies idiosyncratic terms regarding place of delivery, quantity, or other terms, and so is not fungible with other contracts for the sale of the commodity, as securities are fungible. But there is an exception for the case in which the seller of the contract promises to sell another contract against which the buyer can offset the first contract, as in *In re Bybee,* 945 F.2d 309, 313 (9th Cir. 1991), and *CFTC v. Co Petro Marketing Group, Inc., supra,* 680 F.2d at 580. That promise could create a futures contract.

> (2) The contract is between industry participants, such as farmers and grain merchants, rather than arbitrageurs and other speculators who are interested in transacting in contracts rather than in the actual commodities.

> (3) Delivery cannot be deferred forever, because the contract requires the farmer to pay an additional charge every time he rolls the hedge.

As long as all three features that we have identified are present, eventual delivery is reasonably assured, unlike the case of a futures contract—and remember that the Commodity Exchange Act is explicit that a contract for delivery in the future is not a futures contract. If one or more of the features is absent, the contracts may or may not be futures contracts.

This refinement of the "totality of circumstances" approach that we adopt today, while it will not resolve every case, will protect forward contracts from the sword of Damocles that these plaintiffs wish to wave above the defendants' heads, yet at the same time will prevent evasion of the Commodity Exchange Act by mere clever draftsmanship.

The three features are present here, as can be ascertained from the contracts themselves; and while the plaintiffs allege that there are oral as well as written terms in some of the contracts with the defendants, they have not alleged any oral terms that would prevent eventual delivery or cancel the fee for rolling, which places a practical limit on how long delivery can be deferred. The district court was therefore correct to dismiss the plaintiffs' complaint * * *

4. FOREX TRANSACTIONS

Another loophole was found for fraudulent transactions in foreign currencies. The so-called "Treasury Amendment" to the CEA, which was so named because it was added at the request of the Department of the Treasury in 1974, stated that the CEA did not apply to, among other things, "transactions in foreign currency."

The CFTC was plagued by a large number of fly-by-night firms selling leveraged products for speculation in foreign currencies. Those firms claimed they were exempt from regulation by the CFTC under the Treasury Amendment. The CFTC contended that the Treasury Amendment applied only to the commercial interbank market participants and not to wealthy or other individuals trading in the over-the-counter market.

DUNN V. CFTC
519 U.S. 465 (1997)

Opinion by: STEVENS

The question presented is whether Congress has authorized the Commodity Futures Trading Commission (CFTC or Commission) to regulate "off-exchange" trading in options to buy or sell foreign currency.

The CFTC brought this action in 1994, alleging that, beginning in 1992, petitioners solicited investments in and operated a fraudulent scheme in violation of the Commodity Exchange Act (CEA), 7 U.S.C. § 1 *et seq.*, and CFTC regulations. App. 10. See 7 U.S.C. § 6c(b); 17 CFR § 32.9 (1996). The CFTC's complaint, affidavits, and declarations submitted to the District Court indicate that customers were told their funds would be invested using complex strategies involving options to purchase or sell various foreign currencies. App. 8. Petitioners apparently did in fact engage in many such transactions. *Ibid.; 58 F.3d 50, 51 (CA2 1995).* To do so, they contracted directly with international banks and others without making use of any regulated exchange or board of trade. In the parlance of the business, petitioners traded in the "off-exchange" or "over-the-counter" (OTC) market.[3] *Ibid.* No options were ever sold directly to petitioners' customers. However, their positions were tracked through internal accounts, and investors were provided weekly reports showing the putative status of their holdings. Petitioners and their customers suffered heavy losses. 58 F.3d at 51–52. Subsequently, the CFTC commenced these proceedings.

Rejecting petitioners' defense that off-exchange transactions in foreign currency options are exempt from the CEA, the District Court appointed a temporary receiver to take control of their property for the benefit of their customers. App. to Pet. for Cert. 5b–6b. Relying on Circuit precedent, and acknowledging a conflict with another Circuit, the Court of Appeals affirmed. 58 F.3d at 54. We granted certiorari to resolve the conflict. 517 U.S. 1219 (1996). For the reasons that follow, we reverse and remand for further proceedings.

The outcome of this case is dictated by the so-called "Treasury Amendment" to the CEA. 88 Stat. 1395, 7 U.S.C. § 2(ii). We have previously reviewed the history of the CEA and generally described how it authorizes the CFTC to regulate the "volatile and esoteric" market in futures contracts in fungible commodities. See *Merrill Lynch, Pierce, Fenner & Smith, Inc.* v. *Curran*, 456 U.S. 353, 356, 357–367, 72 L. Ed. 2d 182, 102 S. Ct. 1825 (1982).As a part of the 1974 amendments that created the CFTC and dramatically expanded the coverage of the statute to include nonagricultural commodities "in which contracts for future delivery are presently or in the future dealt in," see 88 Stat. 1395, 7 U.S.C. § 2 (1970 ed., Supp. IV), Congress enacted the following exemption, which has come to be known as the "Treasury Amendment":

---

[3] We are informed by *amici* that participants in the "highly evolved, sophisticated" OTC foreign currency markets include "commercial and investment banks, . . . foreign exchange dealers and brokerage companies, corporations, money managers (including pension, mutual fund and commodity pool managers), commodity trading advisors, insurance companies, governments and central banks." Brief for Foreign Exchange Committee et al. as *Amici Curiae* 8. These markets serve a variety of functions, including providing ready access to foreign currency for international transactions, and allowing businesses to hedge against the risk of exchange rate movements. *Id.*, at 8–9.

"Nothing in this chapter shall be deemed to govern or in any way be applicable to *transactions in foreign currency*, security warrants, security rights, resales of installment loan contracts, repurchase options, government securities, or mortgages and mortgage purchase commitments, unless such transactions involve the sale thereof for future delivery conducted on a board of trade." 7 U.S.C. § 2(ii) (emphasis added).

The narrow issue that we must decide is whether the italicized phrase ("transactions in foreign currency") includes transactions in options to buy or sell foreign currency. An option, as the term is understood in the trade, is a transaction in which the buyer purchases from the seller for consideration the right, but not the obligation, to buy or sell an agreed amount of a commodity at a set rate at any time prior to the option's expiration. We think it plain that foreign currency options are "transactions in foreign currency" within the meaning of the statute. We are not persuaded by any of the arguments advanced by the CFTC in support of a narrower reading that would exempt futures contracts (agreements to buy or sell a specified quantity of a commodity at a particular price for delivery at a set future date) without exempting options.

"Absent any 'indication that doing so would frustrate Congress's clear intention or yield patent absurdity, our obligation is to apply the statute as Congress wrote it.'" *Hubbard* v. *United States*, 514 U.S. 695, 703, 131 L. Ed. 2d 779, 115 S. Ct. 1754 (1995) (quoting *BFP* v. *Resolution Trust Corporation*, 511 U.S. 531, 570, 128 L. Ed. 2d 556, 114 S. Ct. 1757 (1994) (SOUTER, J., dissenting)). The CFTC argues, and the Court of Appeals held, that an option is not itself a transaction "in" foreign currency, but rather is just a contract right to engage in such a transaction at a future date. Brief for CFTC 30–31; 58 F.3d at 53. Hence, the Commission submits that the term "transactions in foreign currency" includes only the "actual exercise of an option (*i. e.*, the actual purchase or sale of foreign currency)" but not the purchase or sale of an option itself. Brief for CFTC 31. That reading of the text seems quite unnatural to us, and we decline to adopt it.

The more normal reading of the key phrase encompasses all transactions in which foreign currency is the fungible good whose fluctuating market price provides the motive for trading. The CFTC's interpretation violates the ordinary meaning of the key word "in," which is usually thought to be "synonymous with [the] expressions 'in regard to,' 'respecting,' [and] 'with respect to.'" Black's Law Dictionary 758 (6th ed. 1990); see *Babbitt* v. *Sweet Home Chapter, Communities for Great Ore.*, 515 U.S. 687, 697–698, 132 L. Ed. 2d 597, 115 S. Ct. 2407 (1995).There can be no question that the purchase or sale of a foreign currency option is a transaction "respecting" foreign currency. We think it equally plain as a matter of ordinary meaning that such an option is a transaction "in" foreign currency for purposes of the Treasury Amendment.

Indeed, adopting the Commission's reading would deprive the exemption of the principal effect Congress intended. The CFTC acknowledges that futures contracts fall squarely within the Treasury Amendment's exemption, Brief for CFTC 30, and there is no question that the exemption of off-exchange foreign currency futures from CFTC regulation was one of Congress' primary goals.[8] Yet on the CFTC's reasoning the exemption's application to futures contracts could not be sustained.

A futures contract is no more a transaction "in" foreign currency as the Commission understands the term than an option. The Commission argues that because a futures contract creates a legal obligation to purchase or sell currency on a particular date, it is somehow more clearly a transaction "in" the underlying currencies than an option, which generates only the right to engage in a transaction. *Id.*, at 30–32. This reasoning is wholly unpersuasive. No currency changes hands at the time a futures contract is made. And, the existence of a futures contract does not guarantee that currency will actually be exchanged. Indeed, the Commission concedes that, in most cases, futures contracts are "extinguished before delivery by entry into an offsetting futures contract." *Id.*, at 30 (citing 1 T. Snider, Regulation of the Commodities Futures and Options Markets § 2.05 (2d ed. 1995) (hereinafter Snider)); see also Munn & Garcia 414. Adopting the CFTC's reading would therefore place both futures and options outside the exemption, in clear contravention of Congress' intent.

Furthermore, this interpretation would leave the Treasury Amendment's exemption for "transactions in foreign currency" without any significant effect at all, because it would limit the scope of the exemption to "forward contracts" (agreements that anticipate the actual delivery of a commodity on a specified future date) and "spot transactions" (agreements for purchase and sale of commodities that anticipate near-term delivery).

---

[8] The amendment was enacted on the suggestion of the Treasury Department at the time of a dramatic expansion in the scope of federal commodities regulation. The Department expressed concerns in a letter to the relevant congressional committee that this development might lead, *inter alia*, to the unintended regulation of the off-exchange market in foreign currency futures. See S. Rep. No. 93–1131, pp. 49–50 (1974) ("The Department feels strongly that foreign currency futures trading, other than on organized exchanges, should not be regulated by the new agency") (letter of Donald Ritger, Acting General Counsel). The Treasury Amendment, which tracks almost verbatim the language proposed by the Department, cf. 58 F.3d at 51, was included in the legislation to respond to these concerns. No. 93–1131 at 23. The CFTC is therefore plainly correct to reject the suggestion of its *amici* that the Treasury Amendment's exemption be construed not to include futures contracts within its coverage. See Brief for Chicago Mercantile Exchange as *Amicus Curiae* 17–18; Brief for Board of Trade of City of Chicago as *Amicus Curiae* 10.

Both are transactions "in" a commodity as the CFTC would have us understand the term. But neither type of transaction for *any* commodity was subject to intensive regulation under the CEA at the time of the Treasury Amendment's passage. See 7 U.S.C. § 2 (1970 ed., Supp. IV) ("term 'future delivery,' as used in this chapter, shall not include any sale of any cash commodity for deferred shipment or delivery"); Snider § 9.01; J. Markham, The History of Commodity Futures Trading and Its Regulation 201–203 (1987). Our reading of the exemption is therefore also consonant with the doctrine that legislative enactments should not be construed to render their provisions mere surplusage. See *Babbitt*, 515 U.S. at 698 (noting "reluctance to treat statutory terms as surplusage"); *Mountain States Telephone & Telegraph Co.* v. *Pueblo of Santa Ana*, 472 U.S. 237, 249, 86 L. Ed. 2d 168, 105 S. Ct. 2587 (1985).

Finally, including options in the exemption is consistent with Congress' purpose in enacting the Treasury Amendment. Although at the time the Treasury Amendment was drafted a thriving off-exchange market in foreign currency futures was in place, the closely related options market at issue here had not yet developed. See City of New York Bar Association Committee on Futures Regulation, The Evolving Regulatory Framework for Foreign Currency Trading 18, 23 (1986). The CFTC therefore suggests that Congress could not have intended to exempt foreign currency options from the CEA's coverage. Brief for CFTC 41–42. The legislative history strongly suggests to the contrary that Congress' broad purpose in enacting the Treasury Amendment was to provide a general exemption from CFTC regulation for sophisticated off-exchange foreign currency trading, which had previously developed entirely free from supervision under the commodities laws.

In explaining the Treasury Amendment, the Senate Committee Report notes in broad terms that the amendment "provides that inter-bank trading of foreign currencies and specified financial instruments is not subject to Commission regulation." S. Rep. No. 93–1131, p. 6 (1974). Elsewhere, the Report again explains in general terms—without making reference to any distinction between options and futures—that the legislation

> "included an amendment to clarify that the provisions of the bill are not applicable to trading in foreign currencies and certain enumerated financial instruments unless such trading is conducted on a formally organized futures exchange. A great deal of the trading in foreign currency in the United States is carried out through an informal network of banks and tellers. The Committee believes that this market is more properly supervised by the bank regulatory agencies and that, therefore, regulation under this legislation is unnecessary." *Id.*, at 23.

Similarly, the Treasury Department submitted to the Chairman of the relevant Senate Committee a letter that was the original source of the Treasury Amendment. While focusing on the need to exempt the foreign currency futures market from CFTC regulation, the letter points out that the "participants in this market are sophisticated and informed institutions," and "the [CFTC] would clearly not have the expertise to regulate a complex banking function and would confuse an already highly regulated business sector." 58 F.3d at 50 (letter of Donald Ritger, Acting General Counsel). The Department further explained that "new regulatory limitations and restrictions could have an adverse impact on the usefulness and efficiency of foreign exchange markets for traders and investors." *Ibid.*

Although the OTC market for foreign currency options had not yet developed in 1974, the reasons underlying the Treasury Department's express desire at that time to exempt off-exchange commodity futures trading from CFTC regulation apply with equal force to options today. Foreign currency options and futures are now traded in the same off-exchange markets, by the same entities, for quite similar purposes. See Brief for Foreign Exchange Committee et al. as *Amici Curiae* 19. Contrary to the Commission's suggestion, we therefore think the purposes underlying the Treasury Amendment are most properly fulfilled by giving effect to the plain meaning of the language as Congress enacted it.

The CFTC rejoins that the Treasury Amendment should be construed in the light of Congress' history of regulating options more strictly than futures. See Snider §§ 7.03–7.04; Brief for CFTC 38–39. The Commission submits that this distinction was motivated by the view that options lend themselves more readily to fraudulent schemes than futures contracts. Hence, the CFTC argues that Congress would have acted reasonably and consistently with prior practice had it regulated commodities differently from options. While that may be true, we give only slight credence to these general historical considerations, which are unsupported by statutory language, or any evidence evocative of the particular concerns focused on by the legislators who enacted the Treasury Amendment. We think the history of the Treasury Amendment suggests—contrary to the CFTC's view—that it was intended to take all transactions relating to foreign currency not conducted on a board of trade outside of the CEA's ambit. This interpretation is consistent with the fact that, prior to the enactment of the CEA in 1974, foreign currency trading had been entirely unregulated under the commodities laws.

Our interpretation is also consonant with the history of evolving congressional regulation in this area. That history has been one of successively broadening the coverage of regulation by the addition of more and more commodities to the applicable legislation.[11] It seems quite natural in this context to read the Treasury Amendment's exemption of transactions in foreign currencies as a complete exclusion of that commodity from the regulatory scheme, except, of course, to the extent that the proviso for transactions "conducted on a board of trade" qualifies that exclusion. See 7 U.S.C. § 2(ii).

To buttress its reading of the statute, the CFTC argues that elsewhere in the CEA Congress referred to transactions "involving" a particular commodity to describe options or used other "more encompassing terminology," rather than what we are told is the narrower term transactions "in" the commodity, which was reserved for futures, spot transactions, and forward contracts. Brief for CFTC 30–33. Not only do we think it unlikely that Congress would adopt such a subtle method of drawing important distinctions, there is little to suggest that it did so.

Congress' use of these terms has been far from consistent. Most strikingly, the use of the word "involving" in the Treasury Amendment itself completely eviscerates the force of the Commission's argument. After setting forth exemptions for, *inter alia*, "transactions in foreign currency," the amendment contains a proviso sweeping back into the statute's coverage "such transactions *involv[ing]* the sale thereof for future delivery conducted on a board of trade." 7 U.S.C. § 2(ii) (emphasis added). As we have already noted, the CFTC agrees that futures contracts are a subset of "transactions in foreign currency." The Commission further submits that the proviso uses the word "involve" to make the exemption inapplicable to those futures contracts that are conducted on a board of trade. This contradicts the "in" versus "involving" distinction. We would expect on the Commission's reasoning that this provision would refer to "transactions *in* futures." The use of the term "involving" instead, within the very amendment that the CFTC claims embraces this distinction, weighs heavily against the view that any such distinction was intended by Congress.

The statute's general jurisdictional provision also fails to maintain the distinction the Commission presses. The CEA provides that the CFTC "shall have exclusive jurisdiction . . . with respect to accounts, agreements

---

[11] The Grain Futures Act, enacted by Congress in 1922 to authorize the Secretary of Agriculture to supervise trading in grain futures on "contract markets," defined the regulated commodities to include "wheat, corn, oats, barley, rye, flax, and sorghum." 42 Stat. 998. In 1936 Congress expanded the coverage of the legislation to add further agricultural commodities, including cotton, rice, butter, eggs, and Irish potatoes. Ch. 545, 49 Stat. 1491. (The contrast between the title of the 1936 Act—"Commodity Exchange Act"—and the title of its predecessor—"Grain Futures Act"—suggests that an easy way to describe the coverage of the legislation is to identify the commodities that it regulates.) In 1968 the coverage of the legislation was again expanded, this time to include livestock and livestock products. 82 Stat. 26. The 1974 amendment expanded the coverage of the statute to include nonagricultural commodities and, appropriately, replaced regulation by the Secretary of Agriculture with regulation by a new commission whose title included the word "Commodity."

(including any transaction which is of the character of, or is commonly known to the trade as, an 'option' . . .), and transactions *involving* contracts of sale of a commodity for future delivery." § 2(i) (emphasis added). The Commission submits that this language gives the CFTC regulatory authority over options on futures contracts, see Snider § 10.11, and argues that the use of the word "involving" is therefore in keeping with its interpretation of the statutory scheme. See Brief for CFTC 32. But § 2(i) provides the CFTC with exclusive jurisdiction over far more. Among other things, it explicitly grants jurisdiction over any "transaction *involving* contracts of sale of a commodity for future delivery," plainly meaning at a minimum ordinary futures contracts, which the Commission otherwise insists are transactions "in" commodities. * * *

Finally, the CFTC calls our attention to statements in the legislative history of a 1982 amendment to the CEA, indicating that the drafters of that amendment believed that the CFTC had the authority to regulate foreign currency options "when they are traded other than on a national securities exchange." See S. Rep. No. 97–384, p. 22 (1982). Those statements, at best, might be described as "legislative dicta" because the 1982 amendment itself merely resolved a conflict between the Securities Exchange Commission and the CFTC concerning their respective authority to regulate transactions on an exchange. See Snider § 10.24. The amendment made no change in the law applicable to off-exchange trading. Although these "dicta" are consistent with the position that the CFTC advocates, they shed no light on the intent of the authors of the Treasury Amendment that had been adopted eight years earlier. See, *e. g., Mackey* v. *Lanier Collection Agency & Service, Inc.,* 486 U.S. 825, 839–840, 100 L. Ed. 2d 836, 108 S. Ct. 2182 (1988).

Underlying the statutory construction question before us, we recognize that there is an important public policy dispute—with substantial arguments favoring each side. Petitioners, their *amici,* and the Treasury Department argue that if off-exchange foreign currency options are not treated as exempt from CEA regulation, the increased costs associated with unnecessary regulation of the highly sophisticated OTC foreign currency markets might well drive this business out of the United States. The Commission responds that to the extent limited exemptions from regulation are necessary, it will provide them, but argues that options are particularly susceptible to fraud and abuse if not carefully policed. Brief for CFTC 26, 49. As the Commission properly acknowledges, however, these are arguments best addressed to the Congress, not the courts. See *United States* v. *Rutherford,* 442 U.S. 544, 555, 61 L. Ed. 2d 68, 99 S. Ct. 2470 (1979). Lacking the expertise or authority to assess these important competing claims, we note only that "a literal construction of a statute" does not "yield results so manifestly unreasonable that they could not fairly be attributed to congressional design." *Ibid.*

The judgment of the Court of Appeals is reversed, and the case is remanded for further proceedings consistent with this opinion.

It is so ordered.

JUSTICE SCALIA, concurring in part and concurring in the judgment.

I agree with the Court that "the purposes underlying the Treasury Amendment are most properly fulfilled by giving effect to the plain meaning of the language as Congress enacted it," 519 U.S. at 474, which includes options to buy or sell foreign currency. This principle is contradicted, however, by the Court's extensive discussion of legislative history, see 519 U.S. at 471, n. 8, 473–474, 478–479, as though that were necessary to confirm the "plain meaning of the language," or (worse) might have power to overcome it. I join all except those portions of the opinion, which achieve nothing useful and sow confusion in the law.

NOTE

The decision in the Dunn case allowed a return of fly-by-night firms' fraudulent sales of foreign currency options or futures. The Commodity Futures Modernization Act of 2000 sought to extend the CFTC's jurisdiction over options to firms selling those contracts to retail customers. However, as the next case demonstrates, that too proved ineffective in stopping the defrauding of retail investors in selling options like or futures like contracts.

CFTC v. ZELENER
373 F.3d 861 (7th Cir. 2004)

EASTERBROOK, CIRCUIT JUDGE.

This appeal presents the question whether speculative transactions in foreign currency are "contracts of sale of a commodity for future delivery" regulated by the Commodity Futures Trading Commission. 7 U.S.C. § 2(a)(1)(A). Until recently almost all trading related to foreign currency was outside the CFTC's remit, even if an equivalent contract in wheat or oil would be covered. See *Dunn v. CFTC,* 519 U.S. 465 (1997) (describing the Treasury Amendment to the Commodity Exchange Act). But Congress modified the Treasury Amendment as part of the Commodity Futures Modernization Act of 2000, and today the agency may pursue claims that currency futures have been marketed deceitfully, unless the parties to the contract are "eligible contract participants". 7 U.S.C. § 2(c)(2)(B). "Eligible contract participants" under the Commodity Exchange Act are the equivalent of "accredited investors" in securities markets: wealthy persons who can look out for themselves directly or by hiring experts. 7 U.S.C. § 1a(12); 15 U.S.C. § 77b(a)(15). Defendants, which sold foreign currency to casual speculators rather than "eligible contract participants," are not protected by the Treasury Amendment except to the extent that it permits them to deal over-the-counter, while most other futures products are restricted to registered exchanges (called boards of trade) or "derivatives transaction execution facilities" (specialized markets limited to professionals).

The agency believes that some of the defendants deceived some of their customers about the incentive structure: salesmen said, or implied, that the dealers would make money only if the customers also made money, while in fact the defendants made money from commissions and markups whether the customers gained or lost. This allegation (whose accuracy has not been tested) makes it vital to know whether the contracts are within the CFTC's regulatory authority. The district judge concluded that the transactions are sales in a spot market rather than futures contracts. 2003 U.S. Dist. LEXIS 17660 (N.D. Ill. Oct. 3, 2003).

AlaronFX deals in foreign currency. Two corporations doing business as "British Capital Group" or BCG solicited customers' orders for foreign currency. (Michael Zelener, the first-named defendant, is the principal owner and manager of these two firms.) Each customer opened an account with BCG and another with AlaronFX; the documents made it clear that AlaronFX would be the source of all currency bought or sold through BCG in this program, and that AlaronFX would act as a principal. A customer could purchase (go long) or sell (short) any currency; for simplicity we limit our illustrations to long positions. The customer specified the desired quantity, with a minimum order size of $5,000; the contract called for settlement within 48 hours. It is agreed, however, that few of BCG's customers paid in full within that time, and that none took delivery. AlaronFX could have reversed the transactions and charged (or credited) customers with the difference in price across those two days. Instead, however, AlaronFX rolled the transactions forward two days at a time—as the AlaronFX contract permits, and as BCG told the customers would occur. Successive extensions meant that a customer had an open position in foreign currency. If the dollar appreciated relative to that currency, the customer could close the position and reap the profit in one of two ways: take delivery of the currency (AlaronFX promised to make a wire transfer on demand), or sell an equal amount of currency back to AlaronFX. If, however, the dollar fell relative to the other currency, then the client suffered a loss when the position was closed by selling currency back to AlaronFX.

The CFTC believes that three principal features make these arrangements "contracts of sale of a commodity for future delivery": first, the positions were held open indefinitely, so that the customers' gains and losses depended on price movements in the future; second, the customers were amateurs who did not need foreign currency for business endeavors;

third, none of the customers took delivery of any currency, so the sales could not be called forward contracts, which are exempt from regulation under 7 U.S.C. § 1a(19). This subsection reads: "The term 'future delivery' [in § 2(a)(1)(A)] does not include any sale of any cash commodity for deferred shipment or delivery." Delivery never made cannot be described as "deferred," the Commission submits. The district court agreed with this understanding of the exemption but held that the transactions nonetheless were spot sales rather than "contracts ... for future delivery." Customers were entitled to immediate delivery. They could have engaged in the same price speculation by taking delivery and holding the foreign currency in bank accounts; the district judge thought that permitting the customer to roll over the delivery obligation (and thus avoid the costs of wire transfers and any other bank fees) did not convert the arrangements to futures contracts.

In this court the parties debate the effect of *Nagel v. ADM Investor Services, Inc.,* 217 F.3d 436 (7th Cir. 2000), and *Lachmund v. ADM Investor Services, Inc.,* 191 F.3d 777 (7th Cir. 1999). These decisions held that hedge-to-arrive contracts in grain markets, which allow farmers to roll their delivery obligations forward indefinitely and thus to speculate on grain prices (while selling their crops on the cash market), are not futures contracts. The rollover feature offered by AlaronFX gives investors a similar option, and thus one would think requires a similar outcome. The CFTC seeks to distinguish these decisions on the ground that farmers at least *had* a cash commodity, which they nominally sold to the dealer that offered the hedge-to-arrive contract (though they did not necessarily deliver grain to that entity). AlaronFX and BCG acknowledge this difference but say that it is irrelevant; they rely heavily on *Chicago Mercantile Exchange v. SEC,* 883 F.2d 537, 542 (7th Cir. 1989), where we wrote:

A futures contract, roughly speaking, is a fungible promise to buy or sell a particular commodity at a fixed date in the future. Futures contracts are fungible because they have standard terms and each side's obligations are guaranteed by a clearing house. Contracts are entered into without prepayment, although the markets and clearing house will set margin to protect their own interests. Trading occurs in "the contract", not in the commodity. Most futures contracts may be performed by delivery of the commodity (wheat, silver, oil, etc.). Some (those based on financial instruments such as T-bills or on the value of an index of stocks) do not allow delivery. Unless the parties cancel their obligations by buying or selling offsetting positions, the long must pay the price stated in the contract (e.g., $1.00 per gallon for 1,000 gallons of orange juice) and the short must deliver; usually, however, they settle in cash, with the payment based on changes in the market. If the market price, say, rose to $1.50 per gallon, the short would pay $500 (50¢ per gallon); if the price fell, the long would pay. The extent to which the settlement price of a commodity futures contract tracks changes in the price of the cash commodity depends on the size and balance of the open positions in 'the contract' near the settlement date.

These transactions could not be futures contracts under that definition, because the customer buys foreign currency immediately rather than as of a defined future date, and because the deals lack standard terms. AlaronFX buys and sells as a principal; transactions differ in size, price, and settlement date. The contracts are not fungible and thus could not be traded on an exchange. The CFTC replies that because AlaronFX rolls forward the settlement times, the transactions are for future delivery in practice even though not in form; and the agency insists that fixed expiration dates and fungibility are irrelevant. It favors a multi-factor inquiry with heavy weight on whether the customer is financially sophisticated, able to bear risk, and intended to take or make delivery of the commodity. See *Statutory Interpretation Concerning Forward Transactions,* 55 Fed. Reg. 39188, 39191 (Sept. 25, 1990). See also *CFTC v. Co Petro Marketing Group, Inc.,* 680 F.2d 573, 577 (9th Cir. 1982).

Instead of trying to parse language in earlier decisions that do not wholly fit this situation, we start with the statute itself. Section 2(a)(1)(A) speaks of "contracts of sale of a commodity for future delivery". That language cannot sensibly refer to all contracts in which settlement lies ahead; then it would encompass most executory contracts. The Commission concedes that it has a more restricted scope, that it does not mean anything like "all executory contracts not excluded as forward contracts by § 1a(19)." What if there were no § 1a(19)? Until 1936 that exemption was limited to deferred delivery of crops. (Compare the Grain Futures Act of 1922, 42 Stat. 998 (1922), with the Commodity Exchange Act of 1936, 49 Stat. 1491 (1936).) Then until 1936 a contract to deliver heating oil in the winter would have been a "futures contract," and only a futures commission merchant could have been in the oil business! (Moreover, those contracts could have been secured only on boards of trade, because with rare exceptions, such as foreign currency under the Treasury Amendment, all futures contracts must be traded on exchanges or not at all.) Can it be that until 1936 all commercial contracts for future delivery of newspapers, magazines, coal, ice, oil, gas, milk, bread, electricity, and so on were unlawful futures contracts? Surely the answer is no, which means that "contract for future delivery" must have a technical rather than a lay meaning.

The Commission's candidate for that technical meaning is a multi-factor approach concentrating, as we have remarked, on the parties' goals and sophistication, plus the likelihood that delivery will occur. Yet such an approach ignores the statutory text. Treating *absence* of "delivery" (actual or intended) as a defining characteristic of a futures contract is implausible. Recall the statutory language: a "contract of sale of a commodity for future *delivery*." Every commodity futures contract traded on the Chicago Board of Trade calls for delivery. Every trader has the right to hold the contract through expiration and to deliver or receive the cash commodity. Financial futures, by contrast, are cash settled and do not entail "delivery" to any participant. Using "delivery" to differentiate between forward and futures contracts yields indeterminacy, because it treats as the dividing line something the two forms of contract have in common for commodities and that both forms lack for financial futures.

It may help to recall the text of § 1a(19): "The term 'future delivery' does not include any sale of any cash commodity for deferred shipment or delivery." This language departs from the definition of a futures contract by emphasizing *sale* for *deferred* delivery. A futures contract, by contrast, does not involve a sale *of the commodity* at all. It involves a sale *of the contract*. In a futures market, trade is "in the contract." See *Chicago Board of Trade v. SEC,* 187 F.3d 713, 715 (7th Cir. 1999); Robert W. Kolb, *Understanding Futures Markets* (5th ed. 1997); Jerry W. Markham, *The History of Commodity Futures Trading and its Regulation* (1986); Louis Vitale, *Interest Rate Swaps under the Commodity Exchange Act,* 51 Case W. Res. L. Rev. 539 (2001).

In organized futures markets, people buy and sell contracts, not commodities. Terms are standardized, and each party's obligation runs to an intermediary, the clearing corporation. Clearing houses eliminate counterparty credit risk. Standard terms and an absence of counterparty-specific risk make the contracts fungible, which in turn makes it possible to close a position by buying an offsetting contract. All contracts that expire in a given month are identical; each calls for delivery of the same commodity in the same place at the same time. Forward and spot contracts, by contrast, call for sale of the commodity; no one deals "in the contract"; it is not possible to close a position by buying a traded offset, because promises are not fungible; delivery is idiosyncratic rather than centralized. *Co Petro,* the case that invented the multi-factor approach, dealt with a fungible contract, see 680 F.2d at 579–81, and trading did occur "in the contract." That should have been enough to resolve the case.

It is essential to know beforehand whether a contract is a futures or a forward. The answer determines who, if anyone, may enter into such a contract, and where trading may occur. Contracts allocate price risk, and they fail in that office if it can't be known until years after the fact whether a given contract was lawful. Nothing is worse than an approach that asks what the parties "intended" or that scrutinizes the percentage of contracts that led to delivery *ex post*. What sense would it make—

either business sense, or statutory-interpretation sense—to say that the same contract is either a future or not depending on whether the person obliged to deliver keeps his promise? That would leave people adrift and make it difficult, if not impossible, for dealers (technically, futures commission merchants) to know their legal duties in advance. But reading "contract of sale of a commodity for future delivery" with an emphasis on "contract," and "sale of any cash commodity for deferred shipment or delivery" with an emphasis on "sale" nicely separates the domains of futures from other transactions. * * *

Recognition that futures markets are characterized by trading "in the contract" leads to an easy answer for most situations. Customers of foreign exchange at AlaronFX did not purchase identical contracts: each was unique in amount of currency (while normal futures contracts are for fixed quantities, such as 1,000 bushels of wheat or 100 times the price of the Standard & Poor's 500 Index) and in timing (while normal futures contracts have defined expiration or delivery dates). Thus the trade was "in the commodity" rather than "in the contract." Cf. *Marine Bank v. Weaver,* 455 U.S. 551 (1982) (a non-fungible contract that could not be traded on an exchange is not a security); *Giuffre Organization, Ltd. v. Euromotorsport Racing, Inc.,* 141 F.3d 1216 (7th Cir. 1998) (a sports franchise linked to a single owner is not a security). * * *

These transactions were, in form, spot sales for delivery within 48 hours. Rollover, and the magnification of gain or loss over a longer period, does not turn sales into futures contracts here any more than it did in *Nagel* and *Lachmund.* The judgment of the district court therefore is

AFFIRMED.

NOTES

1. The CFTC Reauthorization Act of 2008 (CRA) amended the CEA to provide the CFTC with broad regulatory powers over retail foreign currency options, futures and other leveraged retail forex transactions not conducted on a regulated exchange. After enactment of that legislation, only certain U.S. financial institutions were allowed to act as the principal with retail customers in leveraged forex transactions, including CFTC registered futures commission merchants, SEC registered broker-dealers and financial holding companies.

2. The CRA also created a new category of registrants that were allowed to engage in retail forex transactions—"retail foreign exchange dealers" (RFEDs). Among other things, RFEDs were required to have at least $20 million in net capital in order to assure that they are financially responsible. This requirement sought to screen out the fly-by-night, poorly capitalized firms that previously engaged in widespread fraud in retail forex transactions. RFEDs are subject to audits by the NFA.

3. In 2010, the Dodd-Frank Act divided jurisdiction over retail forex transactions among the SEC, CFTC and federal banking regulators [7 U.S.C. § 2(c)]. Dodd-Frank prohibits retail forex transactions unless they are conducted in accordance with the rules of one of those agencies. Those agencies have all adopted rules governing retail forex activities within their jurisdiction [See, e.g., 17 C.F.R. § 240.15b12–1 (SEC rule); 12 C.F.R. § 240.3 et al (Federal Reserve Board rules); 12 C.F.R. § 12 C.F.R. § 240.10 et al (OCC rules); 17 C.F.R. § 5.1 et al (CFTC rules)]. As the CFTC has noted:

> While the CEA permits several types of entities to act as counterparties to retail forex transactions, the question of who regulates the activity depends on the type of entity offering to be the counterparty. For example, SEC-registered brokers or dealers doing retail forex transactions are regulated by the SEC and financial institutions are regulated by banking regulators. The CEA provides that the CFTC has jurisdiction over FCMs, RFEDs, or entities that are not otherwise regulated.

CFTC, *Q & A-Final Retail Foreign Exchange Rules*, available at opus/public/@newsroom/documents/file/forexfinalrule_qa.pdf (visited on Sept. 21, 2013).

5. SINGLE STOCK FUTURES

The 1982 legislation that enacted the Shad-Johnson Jurisdictional Accord into law did not allow futures trading on a single stock, such as the stock of the Apple computer company. That ban was lifted by the Commodity Futures Modernization Act of 2000 (CFMA). The CFMA allowed single stock futures to be traded on exchanges regulated by the CFTC and on exchanges regulated by the SEC through jointly adopted rules.

NATIONAL FUTURES ASSOCIATION
RISK DISCLOSURE STATEMENT FOR SECURITY
FUTURES CONTRACTS
Available at http://www.nfa.futures.org/NFA-compliance/publication-library/security-futures-disclosure.pdf (visited on Nov. 3, 2013)

How Security Futures Differ from the Underlying Security

Shares of common stock represent a fractional ownership interest in the issuer of that security. Ownership of securities confers various rights that are not present with positions in security futures contracts. For example, persons owning a share of common stock may be entitled to vote in matters affecting corporate governance. They also may be entitled to receive dividends and corporate disclosure, such as annual and quarterly reports.

The purchaser of a security futures contract, by contrast, has only a contract for future delivery of the underlying security. The purchaser of the security futures contract is not entitled to exercise any voting rights over the underlying security and is not entitled to any dividends that may be paid by the issuer. Moreover, the purchaser of a security futures contract does not receive the corporate disclosures that are received by shareholders of the underlying security, although such corporate disclosures must be made publicly available through the SEC's EDGAR system, which can be accessed at www.sec.gov. You should review such disclosures before entering into a security futures contract. See Section 9 for further discussion of the impact of corporate events on a security futures contract.

All security futures contracts are marked-to-market at least daily, usually after the close of trading, as described in Section 3 of this document. At that time, the account of each buyer and seller is credited with the amount of any gain, or debited by the amount of any loss, on the security futures contract, based on the contract price established at the end of the day for settlement purposes (the "daily settlement price"). By contrast, the purchaser or seller of the underlying instrument does not have the profit and loss from his or her investment credited or debited until the position in that instrument is closed out.

Naturally, as with any financial product, the value of the security futures contract and of the underlying security may fluctuate. However, owning the underlying security does not require an investor to settle his or her profits and losses daily. By contrast, as a result of the mark-to-market requirements discussed above, a person who is long a security futures contract often will be required to deposit additional funds into his or her account as the price of the security futures contract decreases. Similarly, a person who is short a security futures contract often will be required to deposit additional funds into his or her account as the price of the security futures contract increases.

Another significant difference is that security futures contracts expire on a specific date. Unlike an owner of the underlying security, a person cannot hold a long position in a security futures contract for an extended period of time in the hope that the price will go up. If you do not liquidate your security futures contract, you will be required to settle the contract when it expires, either through physical delivery or cash settlement. For cash-settled contracts in particular, upon expiration, an individual will no longer have an economic interest in the securities underlying the security futures contract.

Although security futures contracts share some characteristics with options on securities (options contracts), these products are also different in a number of ways. Below are some of the important distinctions between equity options contracts and security futures contracts.

If you purchase an options contract, you have the right, but not the obligation, to buy or sell a security prior to the expiration date. If you sell an options contract, you have the obligation to buy or sell a security prior to the expiration date. By contrast, if you have a position in a security futures contract (either long or short), you have both the right and the obligation to buy or sell a security at a future date. The only way that you can avoid the obligation incurred by the security futures contract is to liquidate the position with an offsetting contract.

A person purchasing an options contract runs the risk of losing the purchase price (premium) for the option contract. Because it is a wasting asset, the purchaser of an options contract who neither liquidates the options contract in the secondary market nor exercises it at or prior to expiration will necessarily lose his or her entire investment in the options contract. However, a purchaser of an options contract cannot lose more than the amount of the premium. Conversely, the seller of an options contract receives the premium and assumes the risk that he or she will be required to buy or sell the underlying security on or prior to the expiration date, in which event his or her losses may exceed the amount of the premium received. Although the seller of an options contract is required to deposit margin to reflect the risk of its obligation, he or she may lose many times his or her initial margin deposit.

By contrast, the purchaser and seller of a security futures contract each enter into an agreement to buy or sell a specific quantity of shares in the underlying security. Based upon the movement in prices of the underlying security, a person who holds a position in a security futures contract can gain or lose many times his or her initial margin deposit. In this respect, the benefits of a security futures contract are similar to the benefits of *purchasing* an option, while the risks of entering into a security futures contract are similar to the risks of *selling* an option.

Both the purchaser and the seller of a security futures contract have daily margin obligations. At least once each day, security futures contracts are marked-to-market and the increase or decrease in the value of the contract is credited or debited to the buyer and the seller. As a result, any person who has an open position in a security futures contract may be called upon to meet additional margin requirements or may receive a credit of available funds.

Example:

Assume that Customers A and B each anticipate an increase in the market price of XYZ stock, which is currently $50 a share. Customer A purchases an XYZ 50 call (covering 100 shares of XYZ at a premium of $5 per share). The option premium is $500 ($5 per share X 100 shares).

Customer B purchases an XYZ security futures contract (covering 100 shares of XYZ). The total value of the contract is $5000 ($50 share value X 100 shares). The required margin is $1000 (or 20% of the contract value). * * *

The most that Customer A can lose is $500, the option premium. Customer A breaks even at $55 per share, and makes money at higher prices. Customer B may lose more than his initial margin deposit. Unlike the options premium, the margin on a futures contract is not a cost but a performance bond. The losses for Customer B are not limited by this performance bond. Rather, the losses or gains are determined by the settlement price of the contract, as provided in the example above. Note that if the price of XYZ falls to $35 per share, Customer A loses only $500, whereas Customer B loses $1500. * * *

Positions in security futures contracts may be held either in a securities account or in a futures account. Your brokerage firm may or may not permit you to choose the types of account in which your positions in security futures contracts will be held. The protections for funds deposited or earned by customers in connection with trading in security futures contracts differ depending on whether the positions are carried in a securities account or a futures account. If your positions are carried in a securities account, you will not receive the protections available for futures accounts. Similarly, if your positions are carried in a futures account, you will not receive the protections available for securities accounts. You should ask your broker which of these protections will apply to your funds.

You should be aware that the regulatory protections applicable to your account are not intended to insure you against losses you may incur as a result of a decline or increase in the price of a security futures contract. As with all financial products, you are solely responsible for any market losses in your account.

Your brokerage firm must tell you whether your security futures positions will be held in a securities account or a futures account. If your brokerage firm gives you a choice, it must tell you what you have to do to make the choice and which type of account will be used if you fail to do so. You should understand that certain regulatory protections for your account will depend on whether it is a securities account or a futures account.

If your positions in security futures contracts are carried in a securities account, they are covered by SEC rules governing the safeguarding of customer funds and securities. These rules prohibit a broker/dealer from using customer funds and securities to finance its business. As a result, the broker/dealer is required to set aside funds equal to the net of all its excess payables to customers over receivables from customers. The rules also require a broker/dealer to segregate all customer fully paid and excess margin securities carried by the broker/dealer for customers.

The Securities Investor Protection Corporation (SIPC) also covers positions held in securities accounts. SIPC was created in 1970 as a non-profit, non-government, membership corporation, funded by member broker/dealers. Its primary role is to return funds and securities to customers if the broker/dealer holding these assets becomes insolvent. SIPC coverage applies to customers of current (and in some cases former) SIPC members. Most broker/dealers registered with the SEC are SIPC members; those few that are not must disclose this fact to their customers. SIPC members must display an official sign showing their membership. To check whether a firm is a SIPC member, go to www.sipc.org, call the SIPC Membership Department at (202) 371–8300, or write to SIPC Membership Department, Securities Investor Protection Corporation, 805 Fifteenth Street, NW, Suite 800, Washington, DC 20005–2215.

SIPC coverage is limited to $500,000 per customer, including up to $100,000 for cash. For example, if a customer has 1,000 shares of XYZ stock valued at $200,000 and $10,000 cash in the account, both the security and the cash balance would be protected. However, if the customer has shares of stock valued at $500,000 and $100,000 in cash, only a total of $500,000 of those assets will be protected.

For purposes of SIPC coverage, customers are persons who have securities or cash on deposit with a SIPC member for the purpose of, or as a result of, securities transactions. SIPC does not protect customer funds placed with a broker/dealer just to earn interest. Insiders of the broker/dealer, such as its owners, officers, and partners, are not customers for purposes of SIPC coverage.

Protections for Futures Accounts

If your security futures positions are carried in a futures account, they must be segregated from the brokerage firm's own funds and cannot be borrowed or otherwise used for the firm's own purposes. If the funds are deposited with another entity (e.g., a bank, clearing broker, or clearing organization), that entity must acknowledge that the funds belong to customers and cannot be used to satisfy the firm's debts. Moreover, although a brokerage firm may carry funds belonging to different customers in the same bank or clearing account, it may not use the funds of one customer to margin or guarantee the transactions of another customer. As a result, the brokerage firm must add its own funds to its customers' segregated funds to cover customer debits and deficits. Brokerage firms must calculate their segregation requirements daily.

You may not be able to recover the full amount of any funds in your account if the brokerage firm becomes insolvent and has insufficient funds to cover its obligations to all of its customers. However, customers with funds in segregation receive priority in bankruptcy proceedings. Furthermore, all customers whose funds are required to be segregated have the same priority in bankruptcy, and there is no ceiling on the amount of funds that must be segregated for or can be recovered by a particular customer.

Your brokerage firm is also required to separately maintain funds invested in security futures contracts traded on a foreign exchange. However, these funds may not receive the same protections once they are transferred to a foreign entity (e.g., a foreign broker, exchange or clearing organization) to satisfy margin requirements for those products. You should ask your broker about the bankruptcy protections available in the country where the foreign exchange (or other entity holding the funds) is located.

NOTES

1. Single stock futures, or security futures as they are often called, are jointly regulated by the SEC and the CFTC under the CFMA. A customer who purchases a single stock futures contract may elect to place the trade in either a futures account at an FCM subject to CFTC regulations or in a securities account with a BD subject to SEC regulations.

2. A sample of an Amendment to the Futures Customer Agreement (Appendix B to this Casebook) that is typically used when a customer intends to trade security futures contracts is set forth in Appendix E to this Casebook.

JERRY W. MARKHAM
MERGING THE SEC AND CFTC—A CLASH OF CULTURES
78 U. Cinn. L. Rev. 537 (2009)

The derivative market has more reason to resist a merger between the SEC and CFTC since the advent of single stock futures. Chicago is the leading single stock futures exchange in the United States. It was created through a joint venture of the CBOE, CBOT, and CME. It should have been a sterling example of convergence between the two industries, but it has remained relatively minor because the SEC has insisted on its own brand of regulation for trading these new instruments. Most futures contracts have initial margins of less than five percent of the notional amount of the contract. The SEC, however, mandated a margin of twenty percent for single stock futures. This discouraged trading in single stock futures in the United States, and as a result, South Africa now hosts the largest single stock futures exchange.

Single stock futures are another example of how overbearing SEC regulation can be in practice. Not only did the SEC insist on a suitability requirement for single stock futures, it also imposed a prospectus-like requirement. As one author observed:

> The CFTC had mandated a single page risk disclosure document for futures contracts it regulates as a substitute for the 'suitability' doctrine imposed by the SEC. However, the SEC concluded that traders in single stock futures needed both the protection of a suitability requirements and additional disclosures. Perhaps, the SEC thought that traders of such products are particularly stupid people. The result was a twenty-six page disclosure statement, rather than the single page disclosure form used for all other futures contracts.

Lawrence Hunt Jr., The Paulson Report is a Non-Starter, 67 Financier WorldWide 53 (July 2008).

CHAPTER 6

REGULATION OF OTC DERIVATIVES

■ ■ ■

1. GROWTH OF HYBRID DERIVATIVE INSTRUMENTS

JERRY W. MARKHAM
REGULATION OF HYBRID INSTRUMENTS UNDER THE
COMMODITY EXCHANGE ACT: A CALL FOR ALTERNATIVES
1990 Columbia Bus. L. Rev. 1 (1990)

[F]inancial firms have developed a number of "hybrid" instruments that defy easy classification as either commodity futures or commodity options contracts, in which case they are subject to the CFTC's jurisdiction, or traditional securities or other instruments, in which case they are subject to the Securities and Exchange Commission ("SEC") or some other federal regulatory body. In reality the hybrid instruments have characteristics of both classes of instruments, and their dual nature has led various agencies to claim jurisdiction over them.

In particular, the CFTC has sought jurisdiction over those hybrid instruments whose characteristics appear to fall within the scope of its authority, but the CFTC has not developed a coherent theory, in light of general policy concerns and the legislative policies behind the CEA, to determine when regulation is appropriate. The CFTC has rendered several interpretations" and adopted various rules allowing some hybrid contracts to be traded outside contract markets, but at the same time it has prohibited other hybrid transactions.

These efforts have aroused much opposition and controversy because of industry concerns that the form of hybrid instruments that are permitted to be traded off the exchanges is too restrictive * * *

The CEA as adopted in 1936 did not, and still does not, contain a definition of a commodity futures contract that is subject to the restrictions of Section 4.14 Instead, the statute simply states that its terms do not apply to contracts for "deferred delivery." The task of defining and distinguishing a "futures contract" from a "deferred delivery" (or "forward") contract has been left to the CFTC and the courts.

[T]he CFTC, relying upon statements in the legislative history of the CEA, concluded that the deferred delivery exception was simply a reference to actual cash commodity transactions that were entered into with the expectation that delivery of the actual commodity would inevitably occur at some future date. This meant that the seller would necessarily have the ability to deliver and the buyer would have the ability to accept delivery in fulfillment of the contract.

The CFTC determined that Stovall's contracts were futures contracts, and it identified certain "classic" elements of a futures contract. These were: (1) standardized contracts providing for future, rather than immediate delivery; (2) contracts directly or indirectly offered to the general public; (3) contracts secured by earnest money or margin; and (4) contracts that are entered into primarily for the purpose of assuming or shifting the risk of change in the value of commodities rather than for transferring the ownership of the actual commodities. The CFTC also noted that most parties to commodity futures contracts extinguish their legal obligations to make or take delivery by offsetting their contracts with equal and opposite transactions prior to the date of delivery. In so doing, they accept a profit or loss for any differences in prices between the initial and offsetting transactions. * * *

One of the first truly hybrid instruments involved a bond offered to the public by the Sunshine Mining Company in 1980. These bonds were indexed to the price of silver and were redeemable at an "index principal amount," which, in one offering, was the greater of $1,000 or the market value of 50 ounces of silver. In the event the index principal amount was greater than $1,000, the company could deliver 50 ounces of silver, rather than the cash value. The effect of the bond was to allow purchasers to receive a minimum amount of principal and interest upon maturity of the bond, while at the same time allow them the opportunity to participate in increases in silver prices.

The bond had some aspects of an investment in the shares of Sunshine Mining Company, which is America's largest silver mining company. It also allowed purchasers to receive the benefits and increases in the value of the silver owned by the company, but at the same time it placed a floor value on the investment. These features had elements of contracts regulated by the CFTC in that purchasers were allowed to speculate on the price of silver and the seller had the option of delivering silver. The contracts were standardized, provided for the future delivery of a commodity, were subject to the fact of an increased value of the commodity, and were offered to the public. On the other hand, the contracts were not secured by earnest money or margin. Instead, they represented an actual investment or a loan obligation, and they did not appear to be entered into for the purpose of assuming or shifting the risk of a change in the value of commodities. Rather, the possible increase in value of silver prices was simply a "sweetener" to the bond terms. The Sunshine Mining Company made various offerings using this concept, and at least one other company made a similar offering without challenge by the CFTC.

The CFTC, however, subsequently restricted the use of commodities in securities-like transactions. Specifically, the CFTC held that "commodity certificates" were futures contracts that were required to be traded on a contract market. These certificates were in denominations of $1,000 and in duration of 60 to 180 days. At the expiration of the certificate, the holder would be entitled to receive the prevailing price of a commodity unit or $1,000, whichever was greater. A commodity unit was a specified quantity of an underlying commodity. The CFTC concluded that these were commodity futures contracts, and possibly commodity options, because the returns to the purchasers were based on prevailing prices of commodities traded on contract markets. * * *

In the 1980s, a major brokerage house developed agreements that effectively allowed the holder of variable rate interest obligations to hedge the risk of adverse changes in those rates. These agreements simply set floors or caps on the amount of fluctuation in a variable rate commitment. In the event that interest rates fluctuated beyond that range, the brokerage firm would pay the customer an amount equivalent to such increase over the ceiling or decrease under the floor. The differences were periodically computed and payments made to the customer, if any were due. These interest rate obligation agreements effectively assured that the variable rate was converted into a fixed rate mortgage, although a limited amount of variation could be permitted between the floor or cap. In exchange for this commitment, the brokerage firm was paid a fee. The brokerage firm would hedge its risk in this transaction on a futures exchange that offered interest rate futures contracts. Floor and cap contracts were generally offered only to large commercial customers and only for substantial amounts, which effectively excluded the public from participating. The terms of the agreements were to some extent standardized but the essential terms of the contracts such as price, duration and interest rate were individually negotiated. In addition, there were no margin requirements. Nevertheless, the contracts effectively allowed the shifting of the risk of change in value of the interest rates, just as does a commodity futures contract traded on a contract market. There is, however, no provision for an offsetting contract under the floor and cap agreements. Rather, the contract was for a specific duration. The CFTC has not concluded that these contracts are futures or options. * * *

On July 21, 1989, the CFTC approved the adoption of final rules to govern certain hybrid instruments. The rules exempt (i) hybrid debt instruments, (ii) preferred equity or depository instruments that have commodity option components, where the instrument is either registered under the Securities Act of 1933 or exempt from registration because it is a government security, a security issued by a federally-insured financial institution or by a U.S. licensed branch or agency of a foreign bank; (iii) securities issued by an insurance company and exempt from registration under the Securities Act, and (iv) demand deposits, bond deposits or transaction accounts offered by federally insured financial institutions. The value of the implied option premium in an instrument can be no greater than 40% of the issue price of the instrument. The issuer must meet certain alternate performance criteria and the instrument cannot be marketed as a futures contract or commodity option instrument that cannot provide for settlement in the form of delivery instruments used by a contract market.

In adopting the final rule, the CFTC included preferred equities for which an implied option premium meeting its exempted criteria could be calculated. Other types of equities were not excluded. The CFTC also allowed detachable hybrid option instruments sold in units with other instruments to be offered provided that the detachable hybrid instrument itself complies with the criteria for exemption. Finally, the CFTC made it clear that its exemptive rules were not exclusive and that issuers could seek no-action relief for other instruments that might not meet the CFTC's exemptive criteria.

2.   UNREGULATED MARKETS

TRANSNOR (BERMUDA), LTD. V. BP NORTH AMERICA PETROLEUM
738 F. Supp. 1472 (S.D.N.Y. 1990)

WILLIAM C. CONNER, UNITED STATES DISTRICT JUDGE

This action under the antitrust and commodity laws is before the Court on defendants' motion for summary judgment.

Plaintiff Transnor (Bermuda) Ltd. ("Transnor") is a corporation established under the laws of Bermuda and with its principal place of business there. Transnor's suit arises out of its purchase of two cargoes of North Sea Crude Oil in December 1985 at an average price of $24.50 per barrel for delivery in Scotland in March 1986. Transnor refused to take delivery of these cargoes because their market value had declined after Transnor entered into the contracts.

Transnor claims that remaining defendants Conoco Inc., Conoco (U.K.) Ltd. (collectively "Conoco") and Exxon Corporation "Exxon"), conspired with the settling defendants to cause a decline in crude oil prices by jointly selling cargoes of Brent blend crude oil ("Brent Oil") at below-market prices. Brent Oil is a blend of oils produced in various fields in the North Sea and delivered through pipelines for loading onto cargo ships at Sullem Voe in the Shetland Islands. By the end of March 1986, the price of a barrel of Brent Oil had dropped substantially to $13.80 per barrel, from $29.05 per barrel in November 1985. Transnor asserts claims against defendants for violations of the Sherman Act, 15 U.S.C. § 1 (1982), and sections 4(c), 6(b), and 13(b) of the Commodity Exchange Act ("CEA"), 7 U.S.C. §§ 6(c), 9(b) and 13(b) (1980 & 1989 Supp.).

Defendants have moved for summary judgment pursuant to Rule 56, Fed. R. Civ. P. on the grounds that (1) Transnor lacks standing to sue under the antitrust laws and the CEA or, alternatively, that the Court should decline to exercise jurisdiction under principles of comity and international law; (2) there is no evidence that defendants conspired to drive down the price of oil in violation of the antitrust laws; (3) Transnor's injury is not cognizable under Section 4 of the Clayton Act, 15 U.S.C. § 15 (1973 & 1990 Supp.) because there is no evidence that defendants' behavior caused oil prices to fall; and (4) defendants' conduct was neither governed by nor in violation of the CEA. For the following reasons, the motion is denied.

Defendants first move for summary judgment on the ground that Transnor lacks standing under both the Sherman Act, 15 U.S.C. §§ 1 *et seq.* and the Commodity Exchange Act, 7 U.S.C. §§ 1 *et seq.* In an opinion and order dated August 5, 1987 ("Order"), this Court denied defendants' motion to dismiss pursuant to Rule 12, Fed. R. Civ. P. *Transnor (Bermuda), Ltd. v. BP North America Petroleum*, 666 F. Supp. 581 (S.D.N.Y. 1987). One of the grounds advanced by defendants for dismissal was that Transnor lacked standing under the antitrust and commodity laws. Accepting the facts alleged by Transnor as true, as a court must on a motion to dismiss, I found that the Brent Oil Market, in which Transnor allegedly suffered its injury, is "primarily a U.S. market," or at least a "part of U.S. commerce." *Id.* at 583. The Court accordingly held that Transnor had standing under U.S. antitrust and commodity laws. * * *

Because 95% of the trades in the Brent Market are made for speculative or hedging purposes not calling for actual delivery of the oil, the appropriate inquiry involves a consideration of the location of the trading market. The location of the production area and the delivery point are manifestly much less relevant. *See Transnor (Bermuda) Ltd. v. BP North America Petroleum*, 666 F. Supp. 581, 583 (S.D.N.Y. 1987). Where the contracts at issue were made is equally unimportant if the market itself is considered a U.S. market or directly impacts U.S. commerce. *See id.* A plaintiff should not be penalized for the utilization of a foreign branch of a market instead of an equally accessible American branch. As this Court has previously stated, Transnor's choice to purchase the contracts through the London branch, rather than in New York or Houston, "does not lessen Transnor's ability to vindicate Congress's clearly expressed desire that foreigners have standing to sue under the U.S. antitrust laws if the alleged course of anti-competitive conduct has the requisite impact on U.S. commerce." *Transnor*, 666 F. Supp. at 584.

The unrefuted evidence establishes that of the 109 traders and brokers Transnor knew to be active in the Brent Market, 88 had offices located in the United States and at least 6 traded exclusively in the United States. It is further uncontested that two of the three principal trading centers of the Brent Market are located in the United States, specifically, New York and Boston.

Where the market in question has even slight direct ties to U.S. commerce, that market is not an exclusively foreign market and is therefore deemed a U.S. market. While the Brent Market may be a substantially foreign market, Transnor has presented sufficient proof that the Brent Market is not an exclusively foreign market, and thus a U.S. market.

Moreover, Brent Oil is imported into the United States and it may be delivered to fulfill Light Sweet crude oil contracts traded on the New York Mercantile Exchange. These indirect ties to U.S. commerce further support the determination that Transnor has standing to assert claims arising from trades executed on the Brent Market. Accordingly, the Court concludes that Transnor has standing under U.S. antitrust and commodity laws. * * *

Transnor claims that defendants carried out their conspiracy through "tax spinning"—the arm's-length sale by an integrated oil producer to a third party and a substantially simultaneous purchase of a similar quantity of oil at substantially the same price for use in that producer's refineries—which, depending on the relation between the average market price and the price at which the trades were made, created the possibility of substantial tax savings under U.K. tax law. The crux of Transnor's claim is that from approximately November 1985 through mid-March 1986, defendants conspired to tax spin Brent Oil at below-market prices in order to reduce the U.K. taxes paid by defendants. Transnor also claims that the artificially reduced price of the spin sales drove down the market price of Brent Oil, a benchmark crude oil, as well as that of other crude oils such as West Texas Intermediate ("WTI"), an oil traded on the New York Mercantile Exchange, with which Brent Oil is virtually interchangeable.

Under the U.K. Oil Taxation Act of 1975 ("Taxation Act"), the applicable petroleum revenue tax rate between April 2, 1985 and March 31, 1986 was 87%. Under the then-applicable provisions of the Taxation Act, the taxed price on sales of oil differed depending on whether the sale was at arm's length on the open market or the oil was transferred directly to an integrated producer's affiliated entity. Transfers to affiliated companies were taxed at an assessed market value, known as the tax reference price ("TRP"), which, beginning in 1984, was determined by the Inland Revenue's Oil Taxation Office ("OTO") based on an average of prices established retrospectively for a period of time prior to the interaffiliate transfer. Defendants argue that because of declining oil prices from other causes, primarily the excess supply in the world oil market caused by OPEC, the TRP was higher than the current market price and thus led to payment of taxes on sales to affiliated entities based on an artificially high rate. Rather than pay taxes based on such an inflated price, defendants entered into matched buy/sell transactions in the open market instead of transferring oil directly to their refineries. Defendants claim that tax spinning thus resulted in payment of taxes based on a more accurate market rate, not, as Transnor claims, at below-market rates. This would furnish a logical explanation of tax spinning if it was done only in a declining market, in which the tax-spin transactions were at an actual market price lower than the TRP—i.e. lower than the average market prices over the past month. Whether the tax spinning was done only in such circumstances is unclear from the present record.

Both parties spend considerable energy debating whether these transfers violate U.K. tax law. In brief, Transnor contends that while it was legal for an integrated oil company to sell its oil in the open market and to buy oil for its own needs, it was not legal to enter into a large number of matched buy/sell contracts at the same price in order to establish a "portfolio" of contracts for delivery months in the future. Defendants held these contracts open until the delivery month and then selected from their "portfolio" the lowest-priced sale and assigned to it oil they produced that month, known as "equity production." Producers were also able to choose among their affiliated businesses in assigning the sale, which was then reported to the tax authorities as the arms-length price at which they sold their equity production. In order to balance its portfolio for the month, other buy/sells for that month would be disposed of by "booking out" or by entering into an offsetting transaction.

Defendants offer a lengthy explanation for the legality of their behavior and note that after reviewing data concerning all of their Brent transactions during the relevant period, the OTO subsequently approved the portions of Conoco's and Exxon's tax returns that Transnor now challenges. Defendants state that Conoco informed the OTO that when multiple sales and purchases were made in a given delivery month, it reported the lowest-priced transaction as the arms-length sale. * * *

Next, defendants challenge the Court's subject matter jurisdiction over the commodities claims, contending that the Brent transactions were "cash forward contracts" specifically exempted from the scope of the CEA. While section 2(a)(1) of the CEA provides the Commission with regulatory jurisdiction over "contracts of sale of a commodity for future delivery," it further provides that the term future delivery "shall not include any sale of a cash commodity for deferred shipment or delivery." This case presents the Court with a novel type of transaction, which appears to be a hybrid of a futures contract and a forward contract. Examination of the distinctions between the two, their purposes and the case law construing them, leads the Court to conclude that Transnor's 15-day Brent transactions are futures contracts within the meaning of the Act, and are therefore subject to the Commission's regulatory powers.

Sales of cash commodities for deferred shipment or delivery generally have been recognized to be transactions in physical commodities in which delivery in fact occurs but is delayed or deferred for purposes of convenience or necessity. See *Commodity Futures Trading Comm. v. Co Petro Marketing Group, Inc.*, 680 F.2d 573 (9th Cir. 1982); *In re Stovall*, [1977–1980 Transfer Binder]Comm. Fut. L. Rep. (CCH) P20,941, 23,777 (CFTC 1979); 52 Fed. Reg. 47022 ("Regulation of Hybrid and Related Instruments: Advance Notice of Proposed Rulemaking") (CFTC, December 11, 1987). Forward contracts have thus been defined as transactions in which the commercial parties intend and can accommodate physical transfer of the actual commodity. *See Co Petro*, 680 F.2d at 578–79; *NRT Metals, Inc. v. Manhattan Metals (Non-Ferrous), Ltd.*, 576 F. Supp. 1046, 1050–51 (S.D.N.Y. 1983). By contrast, futures contracts are undertaken primarily to assume or shift price risk without transferring the underlying commodity. As a result, futures contracts providing for delivery may be satisfied either by delivery or offset. *See* 54 Fed. Reg. 30694, 30695 ("Policy Statement Concerning Swap Transactions") (CFTC, July 21, 1989). Once distinguished by unique features, futures and forward contracts have begun to share certain characteristics due to increasingly complex and dynamic commercial realities. The predominant distinction between the two remains the intention of the parties and the overall effect of the transaction.

The Commodity Futures Trading Commission ("CFTC") has recognized that commodity transactions between commercial participants in certain markets have evolved from privately negotiated contracts for deferred delivery of a physical commodity under which delivery generally occurs to transactions that have highly standardized terms and are frequently satisfied by payments based upon intervening market price changes. *See* Regulation of Hybrid and Related Instruments: Advance Notice of Proposed Rulemaking, *supra* at 47027. 15-day Brent is such a market. The 15-day Brent market involves sales or purchases of a cargo for delivery on an unspecified day of a given month. The actual delivery dates are determined at the seller's option, the buyer being entitled to clear notice of a three-day loading range. 15-day Brent sales are therefore highly specialized forward sales which start out "dry" but ultimately become "wet," subject to liquidation of the contract. *See* The Legal Aspects of the 15-day Brent Market, *supra*, at 110. Because the contracts do not provide for offset without the consent of the parties and because the sellers cannot predict in advance whether a particular buyer will insist on physical delivery, the market remains one based on physical trading. *Id.* at 116. Yet, because 15-day Brent oil can be sold without physical cover initially, participants can take long or short positions in the market for purposes of hedging and speculation, explaining the high ratio between barrels traded and barrels delivered. The three major motivations in Brent market activity, hedging, speculation and tax spinning, *id.*; R. Bacon, The Brent Market: An Analysis of Recent Developments, WPM8, Oxford Institute for Energy Studies (1986), have led at least one commentator to describe the market as an "unregulated and unguaranteed form of futures trading." The Legal Aspects of the 15-day Brent Market, *supra*, at 117 (quoting International Petroleum Exchange of London: "Brent Crude Oil, Trading of Brent Crude. Notes for Discussion," February 26, 1986). The 15-day Brent Market has thus assumed aspects of the futures market while retaining elements of the forward contract.

The legislative history of the forward contract exclusion, fully set forth by the Ninth Circuit Court in *Commodity Futures Trading Comm. v. Co Petro Marketing Group, Inc.*, 680 F.2d 573 (9th Cir. 1982), reveals its narrow purpose: to facilitate commodities transactions within the commercial supply chain. Policy Statement Concerning Swap Transactions, *supra*, at 30695. The exemption originated in the 1921 Act to meet the particular need of a farmer to sell part of next season's harvest at a set price to a grain elevator or miller. *See* S. Rep. No. 212, 67th Cong. 1st Sess. 1 (1921), H.R. Rep. No. 345, 67th Cong. 1st Sess. 7 (1921). The exemption was predicated upon the contemplation of actual, albeit future, delivery of the underlying commodity. *Co Petro*, 680 F.2d at 578; *NRT Metals, Inc. v. Manhattan Metals (Non-Ferrous), Ltd.*, 576 F. Supp. 1046 1050 (S.D.N.Y. 1983). The more recent 1974 version of the Act has left unchanged the exemption's limited scope, confirming the view that a forward contract is one in which the parties contemplate the future transfer of the commodity. *See Co Petro*, 680 F.2d at 578 (citing H.R. Rep. No. 975, 93rd Cong. 2d Sess. 129–30 (1974)); *NRT Metals*, 576 F. Supp. at 1050. "Nothing in the legislative history surrounding . . . [the exemption] suggests that Congress intended to encompass agreements for the future delivery of commodities sold . . . for . . . speculative purposes." *Co Petro*, 680 F.2d at 579. The *Co Petro* Court summed up that,

> this exclusion is unavailable to contracts for sale for commodities which are sold merely for speculative purposes and which are not predicated upon the expectation that delivery of the actual commodity by the seller to the original contracting buyer will occur in the future.

Id.; see NRT Metals, 576 F. Supp. at 1051.

In determining whether a particular transaction is exempt from the Act's jurisdiction as a forward contract, the Courts and the CFTC have required that the contract's terms and the parties' practice under the contract make certain that both parties to the contract deal in and contemplate future delivery of the commodity. *See Co Petro*, 680 F.2d at 578; 50 Fed. Reg. 39656, 39657–58 ("Characteristics Distinguishing Cash and Forward Contracts and 'Trade' Options") (CFTC, September 30, 1985).

In *Co Petro*, the relevant agency agreements in gasoline obligated Co Petro to perform an offsetting service for its customers which would satisfy their contractual duties without delivery. Co Petro customers could also liquidate their positions in the face of adverse price fluctuations through a cash settlement by cancelling their contracts and paying only the liquidated damages provided for in the agreements. The Ninth Circuit Court likened Co Petro's customers to those customers who trade on organized futures markets because they could deal in commodities futures without the forced burden of actual delivery, *Co Petro*, 680 F.2d at 570, 580, and accordingly held that "the contracts here represent speculative ventures in commodities which were marketed to those for whom delivery was not an expectation." *Id.* at 581.

In *Commodity Futures Trading Comm. v. Comercial Petrolera Internacional S.A.*, [1980–82 Transfer Binder]Comm. Fut. L. Rep. (CCH) P21,222 at 25,088 (S.D.N.Y. 1981), Judge Knapp similarly held that the relevant oil contracts were intended as "investment vehicles" in which the parties had never anticipated delivery. *Id.* at 25,098. The court's reasoning emphasized the language in the contracts that obligated the buyers to "purchase a specified amount of oil at a fixed price *or* to notify the dealer to sell the oil at the going price on or before a specified future date." *Id.* at 25,092–93.

In *Habas v. American Board of Trade*, [1986–87 Transfer Binder] Comm. Fut. L. Rep. (CCH) P23,500 at 33,320 (CFTC 1987), the Judgment Officer, viewing the transactions as a whole to be futures contracts, noted that "the company's literature implies the opportunity to offset and the company permits entering into an opposite offsetting transaction prior to the maturity of the contract, both of which are characteristic of a futures contract." The Judgment Officer further considered the transactions' standardized terms as a means of facilitating offsetting transactions. *Id.* at 33,321.

In determining whether the parties to copper contracts intended delivery of the commodity, Judge Carter in *NRT Metals, Inc. v. Manhattan Metals (Non-Ferrous), Ltd.*, 576 F. Supp. 1046, 1050 (S.D.N.Y. 1983), focused on whether the parties maintained facilities to accommodate physical delivery of the 500 metric tons of copper and whether the parties simultaneously bought and sold copper futures contracts. The district court concluded that both factors contraindicated any intention of actual delivery. *Id.* at 1051.

In the present case, defendants have acknowledged the tax advantages of trading in 15-day Brent and do not dispute that during the relevant period, 15-day Brent oil contracts were routinely settled by means other than delivery, most typically through the clearing techniques of offset and bookout. However, defendants maintain that because the contracts lack a contractual right to avoid delivery, they are predicated upon actual delivery of the oil and thus constitute forward contracts within the Act's definition. The Court disagrees. The high levels of speculation and performance without delivery, as well as the relatively standardized contracts, distinguish the 15-day Brent transactions from the forward contracts contemplated by the drafters of the Act.

The Court acknowledges that 15-day Brent contracts may represent binding commitments to buy or sell physical oil. The real question, however, is whether the transactions are more like bargains for the purchase and sale of crude oil than speculative transactions tacitly expected to end by means other than delivery. The Ninth Circuit Court's "forced burden of delivery" language in *Co Petro* does not mandate forward contract classification of those contracts imposing a forced burden which is not expected to be enforced. The Ninth Circuit Court held only that the *absence* of a forced burden of delivery is indicative of the speculative nature of futures contracts. That court did not have before it contracts imposing a forced burden of delivery, and thus did not rule on the effect of the *presence* of such a burden. Accordingly, this Court need not disagree with or deviate from *Co Petro*, but merely considers as relevant whether the contracts provide for an opportunity to avoid delivery. This is consistent with the reasoning of the *Habas* court, which speaks in terms of "opportunity to offset." This Court concludes that even where there is no "right" of offset, the "opportunity" to offset and a tacit expectation and common practice of offsetting suffices to deem the transaction a futures contract.

Defendants admit that the incentive to spin and respin was to ensure that taxes were paid on the basis of a more favorable market price. Defendants' 328 tax spin transactions reveal that the underlying purpose was not to transfer physical supplies of oil. Defendants' expert, Donald Miller, states in his Affidavit that,

> Many participants in the Brent Market have no intention of taking delivery of oil either to store or refine it and others who sell Brent do not produce it.

Miller Aff. para. 16. Indeed, "only a minority of transactions in the Brent market result in delivery." *Securities and Investments Board, Consultative Document on the Future Regulation of the Oil Markets* at 2 (February 1988). The customary use of offsetting and booking out strongly suggests that physical delivery was not contemplated by the parties.

Moreover, the high degree of standardization of terms such as quantity, grade, delivery terms, currency of payment and unit of measure, which facilitate offset, bookout and other clearing techniques available on the Brent market, further evidence the investment purpose of Brent trading. The 15-day Brent market does not remotely resemble the commercial trading originally excepted from the Act. While this Court recognizes that commercial transactions have increased in complexity since the predecessor to the CEA was enacted, the interests of Brent participants, which include investment and brokerage houses, do not parallel those of the farmer who sold grain or the elevator operator who bought it for deferred delivery, so that each could benefit from a guaranteed price.

While there is no contractual entitlement to satisfy Brent obligations by means other than delivery, the likelihood of avoiding delivery has enabled participants to develop what is essentially a "paper" market for speculative or hedging purposes rather than one for physical transfer. The Court therefore concludes that the 15-day Brent transactions do not constitute forward contracts excepted from the CEA.

After deciding that the relevant contracts were not forward contracts, the *Co Petro* court considered whether the contracts constituted futures contracts. In making that determination, the court found that,

> no bright line definition or list of characterizing elements is determinative. The transaction must be viewed as a whole with a critical eye toward its underlying purpose.

Co Petro, 680 F.2d at 581. The Ninth Circuit Court then held that, due to their speculative nature, the contracts at issue were "contracts for sale of a commodity for future delivery." In a recent policy statement, the Commodity Futures Trading Commission affirmed and amplified *Co Petro's* holding by declaring,

In determining whether a transaction constitutes a futures contract, the Commission and the courts have assessed the transaction "as a whole with a critical eye toward its underlying purpose" [citing *Co Petro*]. Such an assessment entails a review of the "overall effect" of the transaction as well as a determination as to "what the parties intended." Although there is no definitive list of the elements of futures contracts, the CFTC and the courts recognize certain elements as common to such contracts. Futures contracts are contracts for the purchase or sale of a commodity for delivery in the future at a price that is established when the contract is initiated, with both parties to the transaction obligated to fulfill the contract at the specified price. In addition, futures contracts are undertaken principally to assume or shift price risk without transferring the underlying commodity. As a result, futures contracts providing for delivery may be satisfied either by delivery or offset. The Commission has explained that this does not mean that all commodity futures contracts must have these elements [citation omitted]. To hold otherwise would permit ready evasion of the CEA. Policy Statement Concerning Swap Transactions, *supra*, at 30694–95. Therefore, there is no exhaustive check-list by which a contract can be measured. Addressing the essentials of the futures contract, the Court is convinced that the 15-day Brent transactions satisfy the criteria.

Transnor's contracts for 15-day Brent, a commodity within the CEA's meaning, were dated December 1985 and called for March 1986 delivery, indicating that sales of 15-day Brent could occur several months ahead of the specified loading month. Transnor's Brent contracts established a price for a standardized volume when the contract was initiated in December 1985, despite the +/–5% volume tolerance, and both parties to the contracts were obligated to fulfill the contract at the specified price. Most importantly, the Brent contracts were undertaken mainly to assume or shift price risk without transferring the underlying commodity. Defendants acknowledge that the volume of Brent contract trading greatly exceeded the amount of physical oil available to satisfy such contracts. The volume of contracts traded and the high standardization of the contracts demonstrate the essential investment character of the 15-day Brent market. "With an eye toward [their] underlying purpose," the Court concludes that Transnor's 15-day Brent transactions constitute futures contracts. * * *

For the reasons outlined above, defendants' motion for summary judgment is denied.

SO ORDERED.

NOTES

1. The Transnor decision had far reaching effects. It meant that U.S. firms could not participate in the important Brent oil market because it was not registered with the Commodity Futures Trading Commission (CFTC) as a contract market and could not operationally do so.

2. The CFTC issued an interpretation that excluded the Brent oil market from the contract market registration requirement. CFTC, Statutory Interpretation Concerning Forward Transactions (Comm. Fut. L. Rep. (CCH) ¶ 24,925 (1990). However, it was not clear whether the CFTC had such authority. Congress responded to those concerns with provisions in the

Futures Trading Practices Act of 1992, which allowed the CFTC to exempt over-the-counter energy derivatives from the contract market registration requirement and the CFTC proceeded to do so. CFTC, Exemption for Certain Contracts Involving Energy Products, 58 Fed. Reg. 21286 (April 20, 1993).

3. It is interesting to note that some derivative transactions, historically, were not regulated while others were. For example, before the creation of the CFTC in 1974, only futures contracts on commodities enumerated in the Commodity Exchange Act of 1936 (CEA) were regulated. The CEA was amended at various time to add additional commodities to the enumerated list, but the continual development of new contracts on other commodities outstripped the ability of Congress to keep up with that expansion through an enumerated list. Consequently, futures customers often had two accounts with their FCM, a "regulated" account for regulated futures and an "unregulated" account for unregulated futures. The 1974 amendments solved that problem by making futures contracts on any commodity (but see the Dunn case above) subject to the CFTC's regulation. However, the amendments did not address such things as over-the-counter swaps and other commercial instruments that had leverage features.

* * *

The following case involves a claim over transactions that were called "pre-paid forward contracts," but were alleged to be disguised loans that were used to dress up the financial statements of the Enron Corp. That company failed spectacularly in 2001 after those and other accounting manipulations were exposed. See, Jerry W. Markham, A Financial History of Modern U.S. Corporate Scandals: From Enron to Reform (2005) (describing the Enron scandal and its accounting machinations).

JPMORGAN CHASE BANK EX REL. MAHONIA LTD. V. LIBERTY MUT. INS. CO.
189 F. Supp. 2d 24 (S.D.N.Y. 2002)

JED S. RAKOFF, U.S.D.J.

By this lawsuit, plaintiff JPMorgan Chase Bank, for and on behalf of Mahonia Limited and Mahonia Natural Gas Limited (collectively "Mahonia"), seeks to compel the eleven defendant insurance companies (collectively the "Sureties") to pay Mahonia over $1 billion, pursuant to six surety bonds (the "Bonds") that guaranteed the obligations of Enron Natural Gas Marketing Corporation and Enron North America Corporation (collectively "Enron") on six corresponding natural gas and crude oil forward sales contracts (the "Contracts") entered into between June, 1998 and December, 2000.

According to plaintiff, the facts are simple and straightforward. Under each of the Contracts, Mahonia paid Enron a set sum in return for subsequent deliveries of natural gas or crude oil extending over many months. *See* Affidavit of Jeffrey Dellapina, sworn to on December 28, 2001 ("Dellapina Aff.") PP 3–4, Ex. G; Affidavit of Philip N. Bair, sworn to on February 7, 2002 ("Bair Aff.") Exs. A–F. To insure against the risk that Enron might default in part or whole on its promise to deliver the gas and oil, Mahonia not only obtained contractual guarantees from Enron to make monetary payments in the event of such failures but also simultaneously obtained from the Sureties the Bonds here in issue, which guaranteed payment to Mahonia upon any default by Enron.

In due course, Enron did indeed default, following which, on December 7, 2001, plaintiff, on behalf of Mahonia, sent written notices to the Sureties demanding payment in accordance with the terms of the Bonds. When the sureties demurred, plaintiff brought this lawsuit and promptly moved for summary judgment in Mahonia's favor, contending that, by the express terms of the Bonds, the Sureties' obligation to pay was immediate and unconditional.

In response to the motion, defendants allege quite different facts. They allege that, unbeknownst to the Sureties at the time they issued the Bonds, the Contracts between Mahonia and Enron were part of a fraudulent arrangement by which simple loans to Enron by plaintiff's predecessor, the Chase Manhattan Bank ("Chase"), were disguised as sales of assets. Specifically, they allege that Chase lent Mahonia the money used to pay Enron on the Contracts, and that, at the very time Enron was contracting to sell to Mahonia future deliveries of gas and oil, Enron was secretly contracting to repurchase the very same gas and oil from one or more entities commonly controlled with Mahonia, at a price equal to what was owed by Mahonia to Chase on the loan. The net effect was simply a series of loans from Chase to Enron; but by disguising them as sales of assets, Enron could book them as revenue while Chase and Mahonia could, among other things, induce the Sureties to issue Bonds that would effectively guarantee repayment of the loans—something the Sureties were otherwise forbidden to do under applicable New York law (which here governs). *See* §§ N.Y. Ins. Law 1102, 1113(16)(E); 6901(a)(1)(A) (McKinney 2000). In short, defendants allege that the Bonds were the product of fraudulent inducement and fraudulent concealment by the plaintiff.

Fraudulent inducement and fraudulent concealment are familiar defenses to contractual performance. Yet, New York law does not permit a contracting party to lightly evade its contractual obligations by simply crying "fraud." Thus, for example, under New York law, a claim for breach of contract cannot be converted into a fraud claim by simply alleging that the promisor intended not to perform its promise. *See Papa's-June Music v. McLean*, 921 F. Supp. 1154, 1160–1161 (S.D.N.Y. 1996) (collecting cases). Also, of particular relevance here, New York law will not permit a sophisticated party that, in negotiating a contract, has expressly disclaimed reliance on specific oral representations extrinsic to the contract to thereafter claim that the fraudulence of these representations is a defense to contractual performance. * * *

[D]efendants have managed to obtain some important evidence that, taken most favorably to them (as it must be for purposes of this motion), inferentially but materially supports their theory. For example, with respect to the last of the six underlying Contracts here in question, which was entered into between Enron and Mahonia on December 28, 2000, defendants have obtained evidence that, on that very same day, Enron entered into an agreement with an entity called Stoneville Aegean Limited ("Stoneville") to purchase from Stoneville the identical quantities of gas that Enron was that same day agreeing to sell to Mahonia, to be delivered to Enron on the very same future dates as Enron was supposed to deliver the same quantities of gas to Mahonia.

The fact that Enron would be simultaneously buying from Stoneville the very gas it was selling to Mahonia becomes even more suspicious when considered in light of the further evidence adduced by defendants to the effect that both Mahonia and Stoneville—offshore corporations set up by the same company, Mourant & Company—have the same director, Ian James, and the same shareholders.

What, finally, turns suspicion to reasonable inference is defendants' further evidence that, whereas Mahonia agreed in its Contract with Enron to pay Enron $330 million for the gas at the moment of contracting (December 28, 2000), Enron, in its agreement with Stoneville, agreed to pay Stoneville $394 million to buy back the same quantities of gas on the same delivery schedule—but with the $394 million to be paid at specified future dates.

Taken together, then, these arrangements now appear to be nothing but a disguised loan—or at least have sufficient indicia thereof that the Court could not possibly grant judgment to plaintiff.

The Court has also considered plaintiff's other arguments but finds them to be without merit. Accordingly, plaintiff's motion for summary judgment is hereby denied. * * *

SO ORDERED.

3. THE COMMODITY FUTURES MODERNIZATION ACT OF 2000

JERRY W. MARKHAM
MERGING THE SEC AND CFTC—A CLASH OF CULTURES
78 U. Cinn. L. Rev. 537 (2009)

Financial engineering became a phenomenon in the last three decades of the twentieth century. In addition to financial futures, a wave of new instruments appeared after the CFTC was created that contained elements of futures or options. The CFTC was faced with decisions on whether and how to regulate such instruments. If CFTC had jurisdiction over those instruments, the exchange-trading requirement would have precluded their use because over-the-counter dealers could not act as self-regulators or incur the expense of such regulation. In addition, institutional traders neither wanted nor needed the CEA's regulatory protection.

A fight over futures-type trading in the Brent oil market resulted in a district court decision that such transactions were futures contracts subject to the CEA, even though the institutions trading in the market needed no such protection. That decision threatened to shut down that market, at least in the United States, until Congress acted to allow the CFTC to exempt that market from contact market registration requirements. Another new contract, the swap, was immediately popular in the financial markets. It too was not tradable on the exchanges and would have perished if an exchange-trading requirement had been imposed. Other instruments with hybrid features included bonds that had a fixed interest rate of return with a commodity price kicker that would provide an additional return if a commodity, such as silver or oil, increased by a specified amount; the bond holder paid for the commodity price kicker by receiving a lower interest rate than would be paid on a combination instrument without such a feature.

The CFTC tried to regulate these and other instruments by ascertaining whether their options or futures elements outweighed their other features; this created much confusion and complexity. In 1989, the CFTC issued a policy statement that exempted swap transactions from its regulatory reach, but there was uncertainty over whether the CFTC had the power to do so. To provide more certainty, the Futures Trading Practices Act of 1992 authorized the CFTC to exempt swaps, which it did. The CFTC also exempted various over-the-counter energy contracts in the wake of the Brent oil market decision as well as other hybrid instruments.

Use of derivatives dealer firms that arranged transactions and guaranteed their performance grew the swaps market rapidly. In the

1990s, the growth of OTC derivatives trading by many large financial institutions regulated by the SEC aroused the agency's interest and led to another jurisdictional battle with the CFTC, which the SEC lost. The SEC then decided to enter derivatives regulation through the back door by creating a broker-dealer "Lite" registration program for broker-dealers that were also derivatives dealers in the over-the-counter market. The SEC required these OTC derivative dealers to establish risk management programs to monitor and manage the risks of their positions. The SEC allowed the OTC derivative dealers to use value at risk systems (VaRs), consistent with the Basel II Accord for banks, which allowed the banks to compute their capital based on the risks in their portfolios. The SEC rules for broker-dealer Lites imposed a capital requirement to prevent "excessive leverage" and cushion steep market declines. * * *

When adopted, the CFTC viewed the SEC's broker-dealer Lite program as an encroachment on its turf. In response, the CFTC proposed to study whether it should expand its own jurisdiction over the burgeoning OTC derivatives market; both Congress and the industry opposed the study. Additionally, Robert Rubin, the Secretary of the Treasury, Alan Greenspan, Chairman of the Federal Reserve Board, and Arthur Levitt, Chairman of the SEC, blasted the CFTC's proposal.

In the midst of that contretemps, a huge hedge fund, Long Term Capital Management (LTCM), which had been investing in derivatives, suffered massive losses in September 1998. Those losses raised concerns that LTCM might fail and touch off a market panic. The Federal Reserve Board intervened and pressured some large broker-dealers to infuse capital into LTCM to stop any panic—which they did. The CFTC used that event to support its claim that it should regulate OTC derivatives. Congress did not accept the CFTC's argument and responded in November 1998 with a legislative moratorium that prohibited the CFTC from asserting regulatory control of the OTC derivatives market.

Congress directed the Presidential Working Group on Financial Markets to study the OTC derivatives market and recommend whether Congress should regulate it. That report was issued in 1999 and was followed by the [Commodity Futures Trading Commission Act of 2000] ("CFMA"), which exempted OTC instruments from regulation where the transactions' parties were sophisticated. The exempted institutions included banks, investment bankers and other financial institutions, pension funds, large businesses, and high net worth individuals. The Treasury Department noted that:

> The primary justifications for recommending exclusion for such transactions were a determination that most OTC financial derivatives (e.g., interest rate swaps) were not susceptible to manipulation and that the counterparties in such transactions

did not need the same protections as smaller, unsophisticated market participants who relied on intermediaries to conduct their transactions.

After its leadership changed, the CFTC abandoned its traditional rules-based regulatory structure in favor of a principles-based system. The CFMA also created a multi-tiered derivatives market in which each tier was subject to differing levels of oversight based on the nature of the participants, the commodity traded, and the type of trading. The most regulated tier was the traditional contract market where retail traders participated, but even it was transitioned to a principles-based regimen, which allowed the exchanges more control over their operations. The CFMA did leave traditional "designated contract markets" (DCMs) saddled with cumbersome regulatory requirements, while upstart electronic execution facilities remained virtually unregulated.

The DCMs were required to continue as self-regulatory bodies in conjunction with the NFA. But the DCMs and the NFA did not consolidate their self-regulatory activities, as did the NYSE and NASD when they created FINRA. But the DCMs and NFA did form a Joint Audit Committee to better monitor and examine common member futures commission merchants.

The CFMA also exempted electronic trading facilities used by institutional traders from regulation; these facilities were called "exempt commercial markets" (ECMs). ECMs must restrict trading through their electronic facilities to principal-to-principal transactions between "eligible commercial entities." These eligible commercial entities were large institutional traders, and include hedge funds that trade "exempt" commodities, which included energy products, metals, chemicals, and emission allowances. ECMs became popular and even challenged traditional DCMs for market share.

NOTES

1. The exemption for commercial markets (ECMs) in the Commodity Futures Modernization Act of 2000 (CFMA) was often referred to as the "Enron loophole." This was because it was inserted into the CFMA at the last minute through the lobbying efforts of the Enron Corp., which was seeking to protect its popular electronic trading platform, EnronOnline, from regulation.

2. Criticism of the Enron loophole intensified after it was discovered that Enron and other energy trading firms had massively manipulated the California electricity market in 2000–2001, causing brownouts and other disruptions in that state. See, Jerry W. Markham & Lawrence H. Hunt Jr., The California Energy Crisis—Enron's Gaming of Governor Gray's Imperfect Market, 24 Fut. & Derv. L. Rep. 1 (April 2004) (describing these manipulations).

UNITED STATES V. RADLEY

632 F.3d 177 (5th Cir. 2011)

EDITH H. JONES, CHIEF JUDGE:

The United States appeals from the district court's order dismissing the indictment of Appellees for wire fraud and violations of the Commodities Exchange Act (CEA), 7 U.S.C. § 13(a)(2). Because Appellees' conduct fell within a statutory exemption for off-exchange commodities transactions, we affirm the dismissal of the indictment's price manipulation and cornering counts. Although the CEA exemption does not necessarily inoculate Appellees from the wire fraud statute, we affirm the district court's dismissal of the wire fraud counts.

Appellees Mark David Radley, James Warren Summers, Cody Dean Claborn, and Carrie Kienenberger worked as commodities traders for BP Products North America Inc. Among other things, they traded futures in "TET propane," which is propane stored in a salt dome near Mont Belvieu, Texas, and transported in a pipeline system belonging to the Texas Eastern Products Pipeline Company, LLC. TET propane, along with the propane stored in two other Mont Belvieu salt domes, is the primary supply of propane sold between Gulf Coast producers and Midwestern and Northeastern consumers.

TET propane futures do not trade on an exchange. Rather, buyers and sellers place bids on an electronic interface called Chalkboard, negotiate deals directly, or use brokers to negotiate deals on their behalf. Bids and offers are anonymous, though all market participants can see the price and quantity of each transaction. Each day, the Oil Price Information Service (OPIS) compiles data on the day's trades and publishes an average price.

Beginning in early February 2004, the Appellees began purchasing a large number of futures contracts for delivery at the end of that month—*i.e.*, taking a "long position" in February TET propane. They did so through the Chalkboard system, placing multiple bids at different prices and quantities. They also entered agreements to sell February TET propane at the OPIS average price. Because of Appellees' ambitious (and risky) buying campaign, the price of futures skyrocketed from 61 cents per gallon on February 9, 2004 to a high of 94 cents on February 27, 2004, the last trading day before delivery on February 29. After the February contracts came due, the price of propane futures plummeted. On March 1, the price of March TET propane fell almost 25 cents per gallon to settle at 61.75 cents.

BP made money from Appellees' activity in two ways. First, some of the people who sold futures contracts (the "shorts") did not actually have any propane to sell ("naked shorts"); in order to fulfill their obligation, they needed to repurchase TET propane at the high price prevailing after Appellees' buying campaign was underway, often from Appellees themselves. Second, Appellees' contracts to sell at future OPIS prices generated profits because the OPIS price increased with Appellees' voracious demand.

On October 25, 2007, following a two-year investigation, a grand jury in the Northern District of Illinois returned a twenty-count indictment against Appellees. The district court transferred that case to the Southern District of Texas, where a second grand jury returned a twenty-six-count superseding indictment on January 29, 2009. The superseding indictment charged price manipulation, attempted price manipulation, cornering the market, attempted cornering, wire fraud, and conspiracy to commit those crimes. According to the government, Appellees attempted to drive up the price of February TET propane by placing multiple bids on Chalkboard—"stacked bids"—in order to trick other market participants into believing that demand for the commodity was strong and came from more than one source. Moreover, Appellees placed bids at prices higher than other bidders had posted, allegedly perpetrating their deception by enticing other market participants to transact at higher prices. The indictment finally alleged that Appellees withheld information about the extent of their purchases and falsely denied attempting to corner the market. * * *

The CEA makes it a felony for "[a]ny person to manipulate or attempt to manipulate the price of any commodity in interstate commerce . . . or to corner or attempt to corner any such commodity. . . ." 7 U.S.C. § 13(a)(2). In 2000, Congress updated the CEA by passing the Commodity Futures Modernization Act (CFMA), Pub. L. No. 106–554, § 1(a)(5), 114 Stat. 2763. The CFMA aimed to dispel uncertainty over the reach of the CEA and prevent the commodity futures market from fleeing the United States. CFMA § 2(5)–(6),(8). As modified by the CFMA, the CEA exempts from its regulations certain off-exchange transactions in non-agricultural commodities: "No provision of this chapter . . . shall apply to or govern any agreement, contract, or transaction in a commodity other than an agricultural commodity," provided three conditions are met. 7 U.S.C. § 2(g). The conditions require that the contract was "(1) entered into only between persons that are eligible contract participants at the time they enter into the agreement, contract, or transaction; (2) subject to individual negotiation by the parties; and (3) not executed or traded on a trading facility." *Id.* The district court carefully explained how the subject matter of this case satisfies the statutory conditions of the exception. *Radley*, 659 F. Supp.2d at 811–12. On appeal, the government does not challenge the conditions' satisfaction. Instead, the parties dispute the reach of the exemption itself. * * *

The dispute focuses on the meaning of "transaction" in Section 2(g). The activities alleged in the indictment—placing "stacked bids," withholding supply from the market, falsely denying a scheme to corner the market, and falsely stating that BP intended to consume its propane—are not contracts, but whether they are part of a "transaction" or "agreement" is a more difficult question. Neither this Circuit nor the Supreme Court has defined "transaction" for purposes of the CEA. Other courts have struggled with the issue but failed to produce a test to identify which conduct is sufficiently disconnected from a purchase and sale to fall outside the definition of a transaction. * * *

The indictment alleges violations of the CEA based on Appellees' efforts to conceal their long position in February TET propane. These include Appellee Claborn's denial that he was running a corner, his statement to another trader that BP intended to consume its propane purchases, and Appellees' efforts to conceal their long position from supervisors at BP. The government maintains that these actions are analogous to the false reporting in *Futch*. As the district court explained, however, *Futch* involved false reports of sales that did not actually occur. *Radley*, 659 F. Supp. 2d at 810. By contrast, the statements here concerned genuine transactions—and transactions protected by § 2(g), no less. We reject the government's proffered construction of § 2(g) that shields every aspect of a transaction while requiring the people involved to disclose their strategy to even the most informal of inquiries from other parties. *See Dunn v. CFTC*, 519 U.S. 465, 476–77, 117 S. Ct. 913, 919, 137 L. Ed. 2d 93 (1997), (rejecting CFTC's narrow construction of an exemption for "transactions in foreign currency" and noting CFTC's agreement that "futures contracts are a *subset*" of those transactions (emphasis added)). * * *

NOTES

1. The Dodd-Frank Wall Street Reform and Consumer Protection Act, Pub. L. No. 111–203, 124 Stat. 1376, repealed § 2(g) of the CEA effective July 21, 2011.

2. The Enron Loophole also allowed the Intercontinental Exchange Inc. (ICE) in Atlanta, Georgia to become a major unregulated market for trading swaps. It became a competitor with the regulated markets and was a popular price setting mechanism. ICE was so successful that it was eventually able to purchase the New York Stock Exchange, further drawing the derivatives and securities markets even closer together.

3. As a result of concerns caused by spiking energy prices, which were blamed on unregulated speculators in the over-the-counter energy derivatives markets, the CFTC Reauthorization Act of 2008 expanded the CFTC's regulatory authority over the ECMs that were operating under the Enron

Loophole. The new act created a new regulatory category for ECMs that traded "significant price discovery contracts" (SPDCs).

A SPDC was defined as a contract traded on an otherwise exempt ECM that has a price linkage to contracts traded on a regulated contract market or was used as a material price reference to price transactions in the underlying commodity. That legislation regulates ECMs trading SPDCs in much the same manner as regulated contract markets. See, Jerry W. Markham, A Financial History of Modern U.S. Corporate Scandals: From Enron to Reform 210–211 (2005) (describing this development).

4. SWAP DEREGULATION

The Transnor decision in the preceding chapter was concerned with trading futures like instruments in an energy market. The Transnor decision also raised concerns over whether swaps could be deemed to be futures or options that would require contract market registration. Such a requirement would have destroyed that then developing market.

The CFTC issued a policy statement in 1989 that permitted swaps to be traded without any registration requirements where the participants were large commercial entities. CFTC Policy Statement Concerning Swap Transactions, 54 Fed. Reg. 30694 (July 21, 1989). However, as was the case for the over-the-counter energy contracts at issue in the Transnor case, it was not clear whether the CFTC had the authority to make such an exemption. See, Mark D. Young & William Stein, Swap Transactions Under the Commodity Exchange Act: Is Congressional Action Needed? 76 Geo. L. J. 1917 (1988) (describing those concerns).

Congress responded with provisions in the Futures Trading Practices Act of 1992 that allowed the CFTC to exempt swaps from regulation and the CFTC proceeded to do so. CFTC, Exemption for Certain Swap Agreements, 58 Fed. Reg. 5587 (Jan. 22, 1993).

PROCTER & GAMBLE CO. v. BANKERS TRUST CO.
925 F. Supp. 1270 (S.D. Oh. 1996)

Opinion by: JOHN FEIKENS

Plaintiff, The Procter & Gamble Company ("P & G"), is a publicly traded Ohio corporation. Defendant, Bankers Trust Company ("BT"), is a wholly-owned subsidiary of Bankers Trust New York Corporation ("BTNY"). BTNY is a state-chartered banking company. BT trades currencies, securities, commodities and derivatives. Defendant BT Securities, also a wholly-owned subsidiary of BTNY, is a registered broker-dealer. The defendants are referred to collectively as "BT" in this opinion.

P & G filed its Complaint for Declaratory Relief and Damages on October 27, 1994, alleging fraud, misrepresentation, breach of fiduciary duty, negligent misrepresentation, and negligence in connection with an interest rate swap transaction it had entered with BT on November 4, 1993. This swap, explained more fully below, was a leveraged derivatives transaction whose value was based on the yield of five-year Treasury notes and the price of thirty-year Treasury bonds ("the 5s/30s swap"). * * *

This motion involves questions of first impression whether the swap agreements fall within federal securities or commodities laws or Ohio Blue Sky laws. These are questions of law, not questions of fact. "The judiciary is the final authority on issues of statutory construction. . . ." Chevron, U.S.A., Inc. v. Natural Resources Defense Council, Inc., 467 U.S. 837, 843 n.9, 81 L. Ed. 2d 694, 104 S. Ct. 2778 (1984). Mr. Justice Powell stated, in determining Congressional intent, "the task has fallen to the Securities and Exchange Commission (SEC), the body charged with administering the Securities Acts, and ultimately to the federal courts to decide which of the myriad financial transactions in our society come within the coverage of these statutes." United Housing Foundation, Inc. v. Forman, 421 U.S. 837, 848, 44 L. Ed. 2d 621, 95 S. Ct. 2051 (1975).

I conclude that the 5s/30s and DM swap agreements are not securities as defined by the Securities Acts of 1933 and 1934 and the Ohio Blue Sky Laws; that these swap agreements are exempt from the Commodity Exchange Act; that there is no private right of action available to P & G under the antifraud provisions of that Act; and that the choice of law provision in the parties' agreement precludes claims under the Ohio Deceptive Trade Practices Act. Therefore, P & G's claims in Counts VII through XV of its Second Amended Complaint are dismissed. * * *

Financial engineering, in the last decade, began to take on new forms. A current dominant form is a structure known as a derivatives transaction. It is "a bilateral contract or payments exchange agreement whose value derives . . . from the value of an underlying asset or underlying reference rate or index." Global Derivatives Study Group of the Group of Thirty, Derivatives: Practices and Principles 28 (1993). Derivatives transactions may be based on the value of foreign currency, U.S. Treasury bonds, stock indexes, or interest rates. The values of these underlying financial instruments are determined by market forces, such as movements in interest rates. Within the broad panoply of derivatives transactions are numerous innovative financial instruments whose objectives may include a hedge against market risks, management of assets and liabilities, or lowering of funding costs; derivatives may also be used as speculation for profit. Singher, Regulating Derivatives: Does

Transnational Regulatory Cooperation Offer a Viable Alternative to Congressional Action? 18 Fordham Int'l. Law J. 1405–06 (1995).

This case involves two interest rate swap agreements. A swap is an agreement between two parties ("counterparties") to exchange cash flows over a period of time. Generally, the purpose of an interest rate swap is to protect a party from interest rate fluctuations. The simplest form of swap, a "plain vanilla" interest-rate swap, involves one counterparty paying a fixed rate of interest, while the other counterparty assumes a floating interest rate based on the amount of the principal of the underlying debt. This is called the "notional" amount of the swap, and this amount does not change hands; only the interest payments are exchanged.

In more complex interest rate swaps, such as those involved in this case, the floating rate may derive its value from any number of different securities, rates or indexes. In each instance, however, the counterparty with the floating rate obligation enters into a transaction whose precise value is unknown and is based upon activities in the market over which the counterparty has no control. How the swap plays out depends on how market factors change.

One leading commentator describes two "visions" of the "explosive growth of the derivatives market." Hu, Hedging Expectations: "Derivative Reality" and the Law and Finance of the Corporate Objective, Vol. 73 Texas L. Rev. 985 (1995). One vision, that relied upon by derivatives dealers, is that of perfect hedges found in formal gardens. This vision portrays

> the order—the respite from an otherwise chaotic universe—made possible by financial science. Corporations are subject to volatile financial and commodities markets. Derivatives, by offering hedges against almost any kind of price risk, allow corporations to operate in a more ordered world.

Id. at 994.

The other vision is that of "science run amok, a financial Jurassic Park." Id. at 989. Using this metaphor, Hu states:

> In the face of relentless competition and capital market disintermediation, banks in search of profits have hired financial scientists to develop new financial products. Often operating in an international wholesale market open only to major corporate and sovereign entities—a loosely regulated paradise hidden from public view—these scientists push the frontier, relying on powerful computers and an array of esoteric models laden with incomprehensible Greek letters. But danger lurks. As financial creatures are invented, introduced, and then evolve and mutate, exotic risks and uncertainties arise. In its most fevered

imagining, not only do the trillions of mutant creatures destroy their creators in the wholesale market, but they escape and wreak havoc in the retail market and in economies worldwide.

Id. at 989–90.

Given the potential for a "financial Jurassic Park," the size of the derivatives market and the complexity of these financial instruments, it is not surprising that there is a demand for regulation and legislation. Several bills have been introduced in Congress to regulate derivatives. BT Securities has been investigated by the Securities and Exchange Commission ("SEC") and by the Commodities Futures Trading Commission ("CFTC") regarding a swap transaction with a party other than P & G. In re BT Securities Corp., Release Nos. 33–7124, 34–35136 and CFTC Docket No. 95–3 (Dec. 22, 1994). Bankers Trust has agreed with the Federal Reserve Bank to a Consent Decree on its leveraged derivatives transactions. At present, most derivatives transactions fall in "the common-law no-man's land beyond regulations—. . . interest-rate and equity swaps, swaps with embedded options ('stations')," and other equally creative financial instruments. Cohen, The Challenge of Derivatives, Vol. 63 Fordham L. Rev. at 2013. This is where the two highly specialized swap transactions involved in this case fall.

Those swaps transactions are governed by written documents executed by BT and P & G. BT and P & G entered into an Interest Rate and Currency Exchange Agreement on January 20, 1993. This standardized form, drafted by the International Swap Dealers Association, Inc. ("ISDA"), together with a customized Schedule and written Confirmations for each swap, create the rights and duties of parties to derivative transactions. By their terms, the ISDA Master Agreement, the Schedule, and all Confirmations form a single agreement between the parties.

During the fall of 1993, the parties began discussing the terms of an interest rate swap which was to be customized for P & G. After negotiations, the parties agreed to a swap transaction on November 2, 1993, which is referred to as the 5s/30s swap; the written Confirmation is dated November 4, 1993.

In the 5s/30s swap transaction, BT agreed to pay P & G a fixed rate of interest of 5.30% for five years on a notional amount of $200 million. P & G agreed to pay BT a floating interest rate. For the first six months, that floating rate was the prevailing commercial paper ("CP") interest rate minus 75 basis points (0.75%). For the remaining four-and-a-half years, P & G was to make floating interest rate payments of CP minus 75 basis points plus a spread. The spread was to be calculated at the end of the first six months (on May 4, 1994) using the following formula:

$$\text{Spread} = \frac{(98.5 * [\underline{5 \text{ year CMT}}] - 30 \text{ T Price})}{100}$$

5.78%

In this formula, the "5 year CMT" (Constant Maturity Treasury) represents the yield on the five-year Treasury Note, and the "30 T Price" represents the price of the thirty-year Treasury Bond. The leverage factor in this formula meant that even a small movement up or down in prevailing interest rates results in an incrementally larger change in P & G's position in the swap.

The parties amended this swap transaction in January 1994; they postponed the date the spread was to be set to May 19, 1994, and P & G was to receive CP minus 88 basis points, rather than 75 basis points, up to the spread date.

In late January 1994, P & G and BT negotiated a second swap, known as the "DM swap", based on the value of the German Deutschemark. The Confirmation for this swap is dated February 14, 1994. For the first year, BT was to pay P & G a floating interest rate plus 233 basis points. P & G was to pay the same floating rate plus 133 basis points; P & G thus received a 1% premium for the first year, the effective dates being January 16, 1994 through January 16, 1995. On January 16, 1995, P & G was to add a spread to its payments to BT if the four-year DM swap rate ever traded below 4.05% or above 6.01% at any time between January 16, 1994, and January 16, 1995. If the DM swap rate stayed within that band of interest rates, the spread was zero. If the DM swap rate broke that band, the spread would be set on January 16, 1995, using the following formula:

Spread = 10 * [4-year DM swap rate − 4.50%]

The leverage factor in this swap was shown in the formula as ten.

P & G unwound both of these swaps before their spread set dates, as interest rates in both the United States and Germany took a significant turn upward, thus putting P & G in a negative position vies-a-vies its counterparty BT. BT now claims that it is owed over $200 million on the two swaps, while P & G claims the swaps were fraudulently induced and fraudulently executed, and seeks a declaratory verdict that it owes nothing. * * *

An option is the right to buy or sell, for a limited time, a particular good at a specified price. Five-year notes and thirty-year Treasury bonds are securities; therefore, P & G contends that the 5s/30s swap is an option on securities. It argues that because the 5s/30s swap spread was based on the value of these securities, it falls within the statutory definition: "any put, call, straddle, option or privilege on any security, group or index of securities (including any interest therein or based on the value thereof)." It describes the 5s/30s swap as "a single security which can be decomposed into a plain vanilla swap with an embedded put option. The option is a put on the 30-year bond price with an uncertain strike price that depends on the level of the 5-year yield at the end of six months."

BT contends that the 5s/30s swap is not an option because no one had the right to take possession of the underlying securities. BT argues that although both swaps contained terms that functioned as options, they were not options because they did not give either party the right to sell or buy anything. According to BT, the only "option-like" feature was the spread calculation that each swap contained; that any resemblance the spread calculations had to options on securities does not extend to the underlying swaps themselves, which had no option-like characteristics. I agree that the 5s/30s swap was not an option on a security; there was no right to take possession of any security.

The definition of a "security" in the 1933 and 1934 Acts includes the parenthetical phrase "(including any interest therein or based on the value thereof)," which could lead to a reading of the statute to mean that an option based on the value of a security is a security. Legislative history, however, makes it clear that that reading was not intended. The U.S. House of Representatives Report ("House Report") on the 1982 amendments that added this parenthetical phrase provides that the definition of "security" includes an option on "(i) any security, (ii) any certificate of deposit, (iii) any group or index of securities (including any interest therein or based on the value thereof), and (iv) when traded on a national securities exchange, foreign currency." H.R. Rep. No. 626, 97th Cong., 2d Sess., pt. 2, at 4 (1982), reprinted in 1982 U.S.C.C.A.N. 2780, 2795. Thus, even though the statute jumbles these definitions together, it is clear from the House Report that the parenthetical phrase "(. . . based on the value thereof)" was intended only to modify the immediately preceding clause—"group or index of securities"—and not the words "any option" or "any security."

Two Orders by the Security and Exchange Commission must be considered. These rulings involve transactions between BT and Gibson Greetings, Inc. in swaps that have some similarities to the 5s/30s swap. In re BT Securities Corp., Release Nos. 33–7124, 34–35136 (Dec. 22, 1994), and In the Matter of Mitchell A. Vazquez, Release Nos. 33–7269, 34–36909 (Feb. 29, 1996). In these cases, the SEC ruled that a "Treasury-Linked Swap" between BT and Gibson Greetings, Inc. was a security within the meaning of the federal securities laws. The SEC stated: "While called a swap, the Treasury-Linked Swap was in actuality a cash-settled put option that was written by Gibson and based initially on the 'spread' between the price of the 7.625% 30-year U.S. Treasury maturity maturing on November 15, 2022 and the arithmetic average of the bid and offered yields of the most recently auctioned obligation of a two-year Treasury note."

These SEC Orders were made pursuant to Offers of Settlement made by BT Securities and Vazquez. In both Orders, the SEC acknowledged that its findings were solely for the purpose of effectuating the respondents' Offers of Settlement and that its findings are not binding on any other person or entity named as a defendant or respondent in any other proceeding. They are not binding in this case, in part because of the differences between the transactions; nor do they have collateral estoppel effect. See also SEC v. Sloan, 436 U.S. 103, 118, 56 L. Ed. 2d 148, 98 S. Ct. 1702 (1978) (citations omitted) (The "courts are the final authorities on the issues of statutory construction and are not obliged to stand aside and rubber-stamp their affirmance of administrative decisions that they deem inconsistent with a statutory mandate or that frustrate the congressional policy underlying a statute.").

Even though both the Gibson Greetings, Inc. swap and the P & G 5s/30s swap derived their values from securities (Treasury notes), they were not options. While these swaps included option-like features, there is a missing essential element of an option. These swaps were exchanges of interest payments; they did not give either counterparty the right to exercise an option or to take possession of any security. Neither party could choose whether or not to exercise an option; the stream of interest payments under the swap was mandatory. Consequently, I conclude that the 5s/30s swap is not an option on a security or an option based on the value of a security. * * *

The Commodity Exchange Act ("CEA") includes in its definition of a commodity "all services, rights, and interests in which contracts for future delivery are presently or in the future dealt in." 7 U.S.C. § 1a(3). BT asserts that the swaps are not futures contracts; P & G claims that they are.

Under the CEA, The Commodity Futures Trading Commission has exclusive jurisdiction over "accounts, agreements . . . and transactions involving contracts of sale of a commodity for future delivery traded or executed on a contract market . . . or any other board of trade, exchange, or market, and transactions [in standardized contracts for certain commodities]." As of January 19, 1996, the CFTC had "not taken a position on whether swap agreements are futures contracts." Letter from Mary L. Schapiro, Chair of U.S. Commodity Futures Trading Commission to Congressmen Roberts and Bliley, p.4 (Jan. 19, 1996). This opinion does not decide that issue because the 5s/30s and DM swaps are within the Swaps Exemption to the CEA and because P & G has not stated a claim under § 4b, § 4o, or 17 C.F.R. § 32.9, as discussed below.

Even if the 5s/30s and DM swaps are defined as commodities, swap agreements are exempt from all but the antifraud provisions of the CEA under the CFTC Swap Exemption. Title V of the Futures Trading Practices Act of 1992 granted the CFTC the authority to exempt certain swaps transactions from CEA coverage. 7 U.S.C. § 6(c)(5).

In response to this directive, on January 22, 1993, the CFTC clarified its July 1989 safe-harbor policy regarding swap transactions in order to "promote domestic and international market stability, reduce market and liquidity risks in financial markets, including those markets (such as futures exchanges) linked to the swap market, and eliminate a potential source of systemic risk. To the extent that swap agreements are regarded as subject to the provisions of the Act, the rules provide that swap agreements which meet the terms and conditions [of the rules] are exempt from all provisions of the Act, except section 2(a)(1)(B)." Exemption for Certain Swap Agreements, 58 Fed. Reg. 5587, 5588 (Jan. 22, 1993).

To qualify for exemption, a transaction must fit within the CFTC's definition and meet four criteria. The CFTC defines a "swap agreement" as

(i) An agreement (including terms and conditions incorporated by reference therein) which is a rate swap agreement, basis swap, forward rate agreement, commodity swap, interest rate option, forward foreign exchange agreement, rate cap agreement, rate floor agreement, rate collar agreement, currency swap agreement, cross-currency rate swap agreement, currency option, any other similar agreement (including any option to enter into any of the foregoing);

(ii) Any combination of the foregoing; or

(iii) A master agreement for any of the foregoing together with all supplements thereto.

17 C.F.R. § 35.1(b) (1993). The 5s/30s and DM swaps fit within this definition.

The four criteria for exemption are: 1) The swap must be entered into solely between "eligible swap participants;" 2) the swap may not be part of a fungible class of agreements standardized as their material economic terms; 3) counterparty creditworthiness is a material consideration of the parties in entering into the swap agreement; and 4) the swap is not entered into and is not traded on or through an exchange market. 17 C.F.R. § 35.2 (1993).

The 5s/30s and DM swaps meet these criteria. First, the definition of "eligible swap participants" in 17 C.F.R. § 35.1(b)(2) includes a "bank or trust company (acting on its own behalf or on behalf of another eligible swap participant)" and corporations with total assets exceeding $10,000,000. BT and P & G are within this definition. Second, these swaps are customized and not fungible as they could not be sold to another counterparty without permission. Third, creditworthiness is a consideration of the parties. Fourth, the swaps are private agreements not traded on any exchange.

While exempting qualified swap agreements from CEA requirements such as trading only on an exchange, the CFTC specifically reserved the antifraud provisions in Sections 4b and 4o of the Act and Commission Rules 32.9, 17 C.F.R. § 32.9 (1992):

> A swap agreement is exempt from *all* provisions of the Act and any person or class of persons offering, entering into, rendering advice, or rendering other services with respect to such agreement, is exempt for such activities from all provisions of the Act (except in each case the provisions of sections 2(a)(1)(B), 4b, and 4o of the Act and § 32.9 of this chapter. . . .

Id. (emphasis added).

Thus, even if the 5s/30s and DM swaps are exempt from other provisions of the CEA, they may be subject to the antifraud provisions (§ 4b and § 4o). * * *

NOTES

1. The growth of the swaps market was aided by the development of swaps dealers, such as Bankers Trust in the preceding case, that acted as counterparties to other swap market participants.

2. Like a futures clearinghouse, swap dealers provided assurance of performance on the contract because they were highly capitalized and were often given triple A credit ratings by the credit rating agencies. However, those ratings were downgraded after the failure of a Lehman Brothers swap dealer during the financial crisis in 2008.

3. Another key factor in the development of the swaps market was the creation of standardized documentation by the International Swaps and Derivatives Association (ISDA). The ISDA form agreement acts as a master agreement governing the parties' transactions. It is accompanied by confirmations for individual trades. Swap agreements are secured by collateral transfers between parties in order to protect against default in much the way margin is used to secure futures contracts. Such collateral arrangements are usually documented by a Credit Support Annex to the ISDA Master Agreement (Credit Support Annex). The Credit Support Annex provides the terms under which the parties will exchange collateral. See, Wachovia Bank, N.A. v. VCG Special Opportunities Master Fund, Ltd., 661 F.3d 164, 167 (2d Cir 2011) (describing the Credit Support Annex).

5. INITIAL SEC AND CFTC JURISDICTION OVER SWAPS

CAIOLA V. CITIBANK, N.A.

295 F.3d 312 (2d Cir.2002)

B. D. PARKER, JR., CIRCUIT JUDGE:

Plaintiff-appellant Louis S. Caiola brought federal securities fraud and state law claims against defendant-appellee Citibank, N.A., New York arising from extensive physical and synthetic investments. The District Court (Denise L. Cote, *Judge*) granted Citibank's motion to dismiss the Complaint under Federal Rule of Civil Procedure 12(b)(6), finding that Caiola lacked standing under Rule 10b–5 to allege a violation of section 10(b) of the Securities Exchange Act of 1934 (the "1934 Act") because he was not a purchaser or seller of securities, his synthetic transactions were not "securities" as defined by the 1934 Act, and he failed to plead material misrepresentations. The District Court declined to exercise supplemental jurisdiction over Caiola's state law claims. Caiola v. Citibank, N.A., 137 F. Supp. 2d 362 (S.D.N.Y. 2001). Caiola appealed. We find that Caiola sufficiently alleged both purchases and sales of securities and material misrepresentations for purposes of Rule 10b–5 and therefore reverse and remand.

* * * The allegations in the Complaint are as follows. Caiola, an entrepreneur and sophisticated investor, was a major client of Citibank Private Bank, a division of Citibank, from the mid-1980s to September 1999. During this relationship, Citibank assisted Caiola with a wide range of business and personal financial services. As a result of these transactions, which involved hundreds of millions of dollars, Caiola became one of Citibank's largest customers.

Beginning in the mid-1980s, Caiola undertook high volume equity trading, entrusting funds to Citibank who in turn engaged various outside brokerage firms. Caiola specialized in the stock of Philip Morris Companies, Inc. ("Philip Morris") and regularly traded hundreds of thousands of shares valued at many millions of dollars. To hedge the risks associated with these trades, Caiola established option positions corresponding to his stock positions.

As Caiola's trades increased in size, he and Citibank grew increasingly concerned about the efficacy of his trading and hedging strategies. Caiola's positions required margin postings of tens of millions of dollars and were sufficiently large that the risks to him were unacceptable unless hedged. But the volume of options necessary to hedge effectively could impact prices and disclose his positions—effects known as "footprints" on the market. In early 1994, Citibank proposed synthetic trading. A synthetic transaction is typically a contractual agreement between two counterparties, usually an investor and a bank, that seeks to economically replicate the ownership and physical trading of shares and options. The counterparties establish synthetic positions in shares or options, the values of which are pegged to the market prices of the related physical shares or options. The aggregate market values of the shares or options that underlie the synthetic trades are referred to as "notional" values and are treated as interest-bearing loans to the investor. As Citibank explained to Caiola, synthetic trading offers significant advantages to investors who heavily concentrate on large positions of a single stock by reducing the risks associated with large-volume trading. Synthetic trading alleviates the necessity of posting large amounts of margin capital and ensures that positions can be established and unwound quickly. Synthetic trading also offers a solution to the "footprint" problem by permitting the purchase of large volumes of options in stocks without affecting their price.

Taking Citibank's advice, Caiola began to engage in two types of synthetic transactions focusing on Philip Morris stock and options: equity swaps and cash-settled over-the-counter options. In a typical equity swap, one party (Caiola) makes periodic interest payments on the notional value of a stock position and also payments equal to any decrease in value of the shares upon which the notional value is based. See Note, Tax-Exempt Entities, Notional Principle Contracts, and the Unrelated Business Income Tax, 105 Harv. L. Rev. 1265, 1269 (1992). The other party (Citibank) pays any increase in the value of the shares and any dividends, also based on the same notional value. See id.

For example, if Caiola synthetically purchased 1000 shares of Philip Morris at $50 per share, the notional value of that transaction would be $50,000. Because this notional value would resemble a loan from Citibank, Caiola would pay interest at a predetermined rate on the $50,000. If Philip Morris's stock price fell $10, Caiola would pay Citibank $10,000. If the stock price rose $10, Citibank would pay Caiola $10,000. Citibank also would pay Caiola the value of any dividends that Caiola would have received had he actually owned 1000 physical shares.

Caiola also acquired synthetic options, which were cash-settled over-the-counter options. Because these options were not listed and traded on physical exchanges, their existence and size did not impact market prices. Caiola and Citibank agreed to terms regarding the various attributes of the option in a particular transaction (such as the strike price, expiration date, option type, and premium). They agreed to settle these option transactions in cash when the option was exercised or expired, based on the then-current market price of the underlying security.

Caiola and Citibank documented their equity swaps and synthetic options through an International Swap Dealers Association Master Agreement ("ISDA Agreement") dated March 25, 1994. The ISDA Agreement established specific terms for the synthetic trading. After entering into the ISDA Agreement, Caiola, on Citibank's advice, began to enter into "coupled" synthetic transactions with Citibank. Specifically, Caiola's over-the-counter option positions were established in connection with a paired equity swap, ensuring that his synthetic options would always hedge his equity swaps. This strategy limited the amount he could lose and ensured that his risks would be both controllable and quantifiable.

Citibank promised Caiola that as his counterparty it would control its own risks through a strategy known as "delta hedging." Delta hedging makes a derivative position, such as an option position, immune to small changes in the price of an underlying asset, such as a stock, over a short period of time. See John C. Hull, Options Futures, and Other Derivatives 311–12 (4th ed. 2000). The "delta" measures the sensitivity of the price of the derivative to the change in the price of the underlying asset. Id. at 310. Specifically, "delta" is the ratio of the change in the price of the derivative to that of the underlying asset. Id. Thus, if an option has a delta of .5, a $1 change in the stock price would result in a $.50 change in the option price. Caiola's synthetic positions contained a number of components, such as a stock position plus one or more option positions. For each of these coupled or integrated transactions a "net delta" was calculated which helped Citibank determine the amount of securities necessary to establish its "delta core" position. By maintaining a "delta core" position in the physical market, Citibank could achieve "delta neutrality," a hedge position that would offset Citibank's obligations to Caiola.

Effective delta hedging is a sophisticated trading activity that involves the continuous realignment of the hedge's portfolio. Because the delta changes with movements in the price of the underlying asset, the size of the delta core position also constantly changes. Although a certain delta core position might sufficiently hedge Citibank's obligations at one point, a different delta core position may become necessary a short time later. See Hull, supra, at 310–11. Thus, as markets fluctuate, the net delta must be readjusted continuously to ensure an optimal exposure to risk. Id.; Adam R. Waldman, Comment, OTC Derivatives & Systemic Risk: Innovative Finance or the Dance into the Abyss?, 43 Am. U. L. Rev. 1023, 1044 (1994). Citibank told Caiola that as his counterparty it would continuously adjust its delta core positions to maintain delta neutrality. Also, Caiola routinely altered his transactions to account for their effect on Citibank's delta core positions. This arrangement was satisfactory so long as Citibank adhered to its delta hedging strategy, which involved comparably small purchases in the physical market. However, if Citibank fully replicated Caiola's stock and option positions in the physical market instead of delta hedging, the benefits of synthetic trading would disappear and he would be exposed to risks that this strategy was designed to avoid.

Each synthetic transaction was governed by an individualized confirmation containing a number of disclaimers. A confirmation for Caiola's purchase of 360,000 cash-settled over-the-counter options dated December 9, 1998 ("Confirmation"), for instance, provides that each party represents to the other that "it is not relying on any advice, statements or recommendations (whether written or oral) of the other party," that each is entering the transaction "as principal and not as an agent for [the] other party," and that "[Caiola] acknowledges and agrees that [Citibank] is not acting as a fiduciary or advisor to [him] in connection with this Transaction." (Confirmation P 9(a).) Further, the ISDA Agreement and accompanying Schedule, which governed the overall synthetic relationship, provides:

> This Agreement constitutes the entire agreement and understanding of the parties with respect to its subject matter and supersedes all oral communication and prior writings with respect thereto. (ISDA Agreement P 9(a).) [Caiola] has such knowledge and experience in financial, business and tax matters that render him capable of evaluating the merits and risks of this Agreement and the Transactions contemplated hereunder; [Caiola] is able to bear the economic risks of this Agreement and the Transaction contemplated hereunder; and, after appropriate independent investigations, [Caiola] has determined that this Agreement and the Transactions contemplated hereunder are suitable for him. . . . (ISDA Agreement, Schedule to the Master Agreement, Part 5, P 2(a)(ii).)

In October 1998, Citicorp, Citibank's parent company, merged with Travelers Group, Inc. ("Travelers"). Caiola feared that Salomon Smith Barney ("SSB"), a Travelers affiliate, might become involved in his account. At a November 18, 1998 meeting, Citibank informed Caiola that SSB would become involved in Caiola's synthetic equities trading. At this meeting, Caiola stated that he did not wish to become a client of SSB and that, unless his relationship with Citibank were to continue as it had previously existed, he would terminate it. Citibank assured Caiola then and subsequently that their relationship would continue unchanged and, specifically, that his synthetic trading relationship with Citibank would remain unaltered by SSB's involvement.

Relying on these assurances, Caiola maintained his account at Citibank and continued to establish sizeable positions with the understanding that they would be managed synthetically, with Citibank continuing to serve as the delta hedging counterparty. From January 1999 through March 1999, Caiola bought and sold more than twenty-two million options, established a swap position involving two million shares of Philip Morris stock with a notional value of eighty million dollars, and paid Citibank millions of dollars in commissions and interest.

However, after November 1998, and contrary to its representations and unknown to Caiola, Citibank had secretly stopped delta hedging and transformed Caiola's synthetic portfolio into a physical one by executing massive trades in the physical markets that mirrored Caiola's synthetic transactions. In other words, when Caiola sought to open an integrated synthetic position in shares of synthetic stock and synthetic options, Citibank, instead of delta hedging, simply executed physical trades on stock and options. These transactions, Caiola alleges, exposed him to the risks—"footprints" and a lack of liquidity—that synthetic trading was intended to avoid.

On March 12, 1999, Citibank told Caiola that it intended to early exercise certain options in his portfolio for physical settlement, a demand inconsistent with a synthetic relationship. One week later Citibank for the first time refused to establish a synthetic option position Caiola requested. Growing concerned, on March 26, 1999, Caiola inquired and was told that SSB was unwilling to assume the risks associated with synthetic trading. During this time period, although Caiola had taken a large position in Philip Morris stock that was declining in value, he wrote options expecting to recoup his losses and to profit from an anticipated rise in the value of the shares. The strategy, Caiola claims, failed because Citibank had secretly and unilaterally terminated synthetic trading. This termination cost Caiola tens of millions of dollars because the price of Philip Morris rebounded as he had expected.

At this point, Caiola investigated and discovered that Citibank had ceased treating his investments synthetically as early as November 1998. Two Citibank officers informed Caiola that "many" of his trades had been executed on the physical market, although they had been submitted and accepted by Citibank as synthetic transactions. The only explanation Caiola received was that "this is how SSB wanted it done." (Compl. P 136.)

Caiola unearthed additional evidence that Citibank had transformed his portfolio when he attempted to unwind his account in September 1999. When Caiola placed unwind transactions, Citibank refused to execute the trades without a commission—a further indication to Caiola that what he thought were synthetic positions were being handled by Citibank as physical transactions. In addition, as Citibank executed certain option transactions during this unwind period, Citibank sent

Caiola confirmations reflecting that the transactions were for physical, instead of cash, settlement. Caiola also was told by a Citibank official that it was holding hundreds of thousands of physical shares of Philip Morris stock in his account and that Citibank had executed certain unwind transactions by going to the physical market to sell millions of options and shares. Finally, when Citibank failed to completely unwind a certain swap position, it told Caiola that hundreds of thousands of physical shares—for which he had no hedge protection and was financially responsible—were being sold on his behalf.

In July 2000, Caiola sued Citibank alleging violations of section 10(b) and Rule 10b–5. He also asserted state law claims for fraud, breach of fiduciary duty, and breach of contract. Generally, the Complaint alleged that Citibank violated section 10(b) and Rule 10b–5 when it misrepresented that it would continue its pre-existing synthetic trading relationship but secretly abandoned its role as delta hedging counterparty and, instead, bought and sold exchange-traded stock and options on Caiola's behalf. Caiola further claims that Citibank's misrepresentations were material, he relied on them, and, as a result, he experienced massive losses. * * *

The District Court concluded—without distinguishing between options and swaps—that Caiola failed to allege the purchase or sale of a security because his synthetic transactions were not "securities." The District Court analyzed Caiola's options in light of the conventional understanding that "an option contract 'entitles a purchaser to buy or sell a commodity by some specific date at a fixed price known as the 'strike price'. . . ." Caiola, 137 F. Supp. 2d at 370 (quoting United States v. Bein, 728 F.2d 107, 111 (2d Cir. 1984)). The District Court believed that no court previously had considered "whether the types of transactions at issue in this case constitute securities, although in [Procter & Gamble], the court held that certain interest rate swap contracts were not 'securities.' " Id. 137 F. Supp. 2d 362, 369. The court concluded that "for many of the same reasons offered in Procter and Gamble, the transactions at issue were not 'securities.' " Id. In particular, the District Court held that Caiola's synthetic transactions did not fit the definition of "securities" in section 3(a)(10) of the 1934 Act because they were not investment contracts, notes, or evidence of indebtedness. Id. 137 F. Supp. 2d 362, 369–70. The court also held that the synthetic transactions were not "options on securities" as defined by that section because, drawing on Procter & Gamble, "'they did not give either counterparty the right to exercise an option or to take possession of any security.' " Id. at 370 (quoting Procter & Gamble, 925 F. Supp. at 1282).

Caiola's synthetic transactions, however, involved two distinct instruments: cash-settled over-the-counter options and equity swaps. The two must be analyzed separately. We conclude that Caiola's synthetic options are "securities" subject to section 10(b). Caiola does not argue on appeal that his equity swaps met the definition of a security under section 3(a)(10) at the time of his trades, but instead urges us to apply retroactively the Commodities Futures Modernization Act of 2000 ("CFMA"), Pub. L. No. 106–554, 114 Stat. 2763 (2000). Because Caiola did not adequately raise this issue before the District Court, we decline to consider it on appeal.

The anti-fraud provisions of the federal securities laws cover options on securities. Section 3(a)(10) of the 1934 Act defines "security" to include "any put, call, straddle, option, or privilege on any security, certificate of deposit, or group or index of securities (including any interest therein or based on the value thereof). . . ." 15 U.S.C. § 78c (a)(10) (2000). Citibank contends that this definition of "security" does not include all options without limitation. Citibank argues that only an option on a security would be covered, not an option based on the value of a security. In other words, according to Citibank, an option that involves the right to take possession of a security fits the statutory definition but a synthetic option that merely obligates the counterparty to make cash payments based on the value of a security does not. The District Court agreed with this analysis. Caiola, 137 F. Supp. 2d at 370–72. Caiola, on the other hand, alleges that his synthetic options were simply cash-settled over-the-counter options on Philip Morris stock and therefore are securities. We agree that these instruments are securities under section 3(a)(10) for a number of reasons.

The Confirmation, on which Citibank relies for its argument that Caiola's options are not securities, indicates that the transactions are commonly used cash-settled over-the-counter options. The Confirmation expressly states that the "particular Transaction to which this Confirmation relates is an Option" and the "Type of Transaction" is an "Equity Option" on the "common stock of Philip Morris Cos." Options have been covered under section 10(b) since the 1934 Act was amended in 1982. Securities Exchange Act of 1934 Amendments of 1982, Pub. L. No. 97–303, 96 Stat. 1409 (1982). The parties dispute whether cash-settled over-the-counter options on the value of a security are covered by section 10(b). We hold that they are. * * *

Both the District Court and Citibank rely heavily on Procter & Gamble for their conclusion that cash-settled over-the-counter options are not securities. Procter & Gamble, however, held that a very different type of transaction—swaps linked to the price of Treasury notes—were not securities. The plaintiff in Procter & Gamble argued that even though the instrument in question was technically an interest rate swap, it had option-like features and thus could be characterized as an "option on a security" under section 3(a)(10). Procter & Gamble, 925 F. Supp. at 1280–81. The court, however, rejected this argument because the swap "did not give either counterparty the right to exercise an option or to take possession of any security." Id. at 1282. The District Court imported this language from Procter & Gamble, finding it dispositive. Caiola, 137 F. Supp. 2d at 370 (quoting Procter & Gamble, 925 F. Supp. at 1282). Unlike the plaintiff's argument in Procter & Gamble that an interest rate swap with option-like features could be characterized as an option on a security, Caiola's transactions involve the much more straightforward question of whether a cash-settled over-the-counter option on Philip Morris stock—similar to options commonly traded on the market—is an option on a security. Procter & Gamble does not address this issue.

Further, Procter & Gamble concluded that a critical feature of an option was the right to exercise and to take possession of the security because the parenthetical "based on the value thereof" in section 3(a)(10) applied only to the immediately preceding phrase, "group or index of securities" and not to "any security." Procter & Gamble, 925 F. Supp. at 1281–82. We believe this conclusion is incorrect, and we decline to follow its lead. We hold that the parenthetical applies to "any security." The text of the statute itself includes cash-settled options by defining "option" to include an option on a "group or index of securities." This provision is sufficiently clear that a resort to legislative history is not necessary. See Lee v. Bankers Trust Co., 166 F.3d 540, 544 (2d Cir. 1999). A contrary reading would mean that the statute illogically both includes and excludes cash-settled options in the same sentence. In other words. there is no basis for reading into the term "option" as used in the phrase "option . . . on any security" a limitation requiring a particular method of settlement—a limitation that clearly does not apply to "option" as used in the phrase "option . . . on any . . . index of securities." The Procter & Gamble court's application of the parenthetical also produced the odd consequence that Rule 10b–5 would cover options based on the value of two securities but not options based on the value of single security. We do not agree with this interpretation and, accordingly, we hold that there is no textual basis for reading section 3(a)(10) to define "option" as including only transactions that give the holder the right to receive the underlying securities.

Thus, section 3(a)(10)'s broad definition of "security" to include an option on any "security" as well as an option on any "group or index of securities" permits no distinction between cash-settled options and those that are settled by physical delivery. Accordingly, Caiola's cash-settled over-the-counter options are securities under section 3(a)(10).

Caiola does not argue that, at the time of his trades, his equity swaps were covered by section 10(b), but urges us to apply retroactively the CFMA's amendments to section 10(b). In December 2000, Congress enacted the CFMA to, among other things, clarify the status of swap agreements under the securities laws. CFMA § 2, 114 Stat. at 2763A–366.

Sections 302 and 303 of the CMFA define "swap agreements" and then expressly exclude them from the definition of "securities," but amend section 10(b) to reach swap agreements. Id. §§ 302, 303, 114 Stat. at 2763A–452. Had Caiola entered into his synthetic stock transactions after the enactment of the CFMA, they clearly would now be covered under Rule 10b–5. To prevail on a retroactivity argument, Caiola faces a substantial burden. "Elementary considerations of fairness dictate that individuals should have an opportunity to know what the law is and to conform their conduct accordingly; settled expectations should not be lightly disrupted." * * *

We find it unnecessary to resolve whether Caiola has overcome this hurdle because he failed to raise the issue properly in the District Court and we generally do not consider arguments not raised below. * * *

NOTES

1. Synthetic swaps take many forms. For example, one court described cash-settled total-return equity swaps as follows:

> Total-return swaps are contracts in which parties agree to exchange sums equivalent to the income streams produced by specified assets. Total-return equity swaps involve an exchange of the income stream from: (1) a specified number of share in a designated company's stock, and (2) a specified interest rate on a specified principal amount. The party that receives the stock-based return is styled the "long" party. The party that receives the interest-based return is styled the "short" party. These contracts do not transfer title to the underlying assets or require that either party actually own them. Rather, in a total-return equity swap, the long party periodically pays the short party a sum calculated by applying an agreed upon interest rate to an agreed-upon notional amount of principal, as if the long party had borrowed that amount of money from the short party. Meanwhile, the short party periodically pays the long party a sum equivalent to the return to a shareholder in a specified company—the increased value of the shares, if any, plus income from the shares—as if the long party owned actual shares in that company. As a result, the financial return to a long party in a total-return equity swap is roughly equivalent to the return when borrowed capital is used to purchase shares in the referenced company. Long swap positions can, therefore, be attractive to parties that seek to increase the leverage of their holdings without actually buying the shares. The short party's financial return, in turn, is equivalent to the return to someone who sold short and then lent out the proceeds from that sale. However, because of the inherent risks in short-equity positions—share value can be more volatile than interest rates—persons holding short positions in

total-return equity swaps will usually choose to purchase equivalent numbers of shares to hedge their short exposure.

CSX Corp. v. Children's Inv. Fund Mgmt. (UK) LLP, 654 F.3d 276, 279–280 (2d Cir. 2011).

2. Dictum in Caiola infers that the equity swaps traded by Caiola were subject to SEC regulation under the CFMA. The CFMA, however, clearly exempted security-based swap agreements and other swaps from regulation under the federal securities and commodities laws. The Dodd-Frank Act gave the SEC jurisdiction over security-based swaps while the CFTC was given jurisdiction over swaps and security-based swap agreements. See the Joint SEC/CFTC Release below.

6. CREDIT DEFAULT SWAPS

NORMAN MENACHEM FEDER
DECONSTRUCTING OVER-THE-COUNTER DERIVATIVES
2002 Columbia Bus. L. Rev. 677

Credit derivatives are relatively recent OTC products that are intended to transfer credit exposure vis-a-vis specific obligors. Essentially, credit derivatives, like other derivatives, isolate specific risk—either credit risk only or credit risk together with market risk—and transfer that risk to a willing party. Transfer of the isolated credit risk protects the risk transferor from, and exposes the risk transferee to, the risk that an obligor—whom often is called a reference credit or reference entity—may experience a credit event, such as a default under a specified debt instrument or a certain decline in creditworthiness. Notably, the transfer need not disturb the original credit relationship between reference credit and creditor. The reference asset can be anything whose value reflects the credit of a certain entity, but tradable bonds are the most logical because their price is most easily discovered. Bank loans too may one day become important reference assets.

Credit risk protection provided by third parties is hardly new. For ages, guarantees and letters of credit have protected creditors from obligor defaults. What sets credit derivatives apart from predecessor techniques is separation of the protection from the reference asset. This allows the market to trade credit risk separately from the instrument that creates the risk. This also allows the market to price that risk and for various investors to mitigate or amplify for themselves the credit risk of specific entities with relative ease.

Credit derivatives usually comprise one of three forms: credit default swap, total return swap and credit spread option. Additionally, there is a fourth form, credit-linked debt, which is not a pure credit derivative, but a hybrid of a debt instrument and credit derivative. As a general matter, the maturities of credit derivatives do not exceed, and usually do not even match, the maturities of the underlying obligations of the reference credit. The exact form of credit derivative will determine how much credit risk is being transferred, but every form involves the sale of credit protection from a protection seller to a protection buyer (although other correlative phrasing is used with certain types of credit derivatives).

A credit default swap transfers potential credit loss, usually, but not necessarily, in connection with a specific reference asset. Under a typical credit default swap, the protection buyer makes a single payment or periodic payments to the protection seller as premium, and the protection seller is obligated to pay a credit event payment to the protection buyer if a credit event occurs. Because the reference asset may retain residual value after default by the reference credit, the benefit to the protection buyer from receipt of the credit event payment is usually structured to equal something less than the gross value of the reference asset.

Credit event payments can take on various forms. In a cash-settled arrangement, the protection seller will pay cash, and usually only the difference between the principal amount and recovery value of the reference asset. Specifically, the credit event payment will equal the difference between the market value of the reference asset after default, as determined by dealer quotes or market price, and its par value. Alternatively, the cash-settlement arrangement can be binary. In that case, the protection seller will pay a stipulated amount. This amount would likely equal the par value of the reference asset minus some amount that represents the parties' expectation of the reference asset's residual value following default, based on market experience. Or, the amount will equal a predetermined percentage of the par value of the reference asset; this amount is meant to reflect the parties' expectation when entering into the swap of prospective credit loss.

In a physically-settled arrangement, the credit event payment amount will equal the par value of the reference asset and, in exchange for payment by the protection seller of that amount, the protection buyer will physically deliver the reference asset to the protection seller. The protection seller will then have a right to claim on the reference asset from the obligor. The advantage of physical settlement, particularly to the protection buyer, is that it results in a precise credit risk transfer and lets the parties avoid valuing prospectively the post-default reference asset to predetermine the amount of the credit event payment.

The credit event commonly portends the insolvency of the issuer of the reference asset. The event can be instrument-specific, such as failure of the obligor to make a payment when due under the reference asset. Alternatively, it can be defined more generally to include a credit rating downgrade or a failure of the obligor to make any payment under any obligation. In any event, the credit-dependent trigger is the basis for the transfer of credit risk from the protection buyer to the protection seller.

For example: Party A holds a bond issued by Company C and would like to manage the risk that Company C will fail. Party A can enter into a credit-default swap with Bank B, under which Party A will periodically pay Bank B a floating rate (e.g., LIBOR plus fifty basis points) 43 on a notional amount and Bank B will be obligated to pay Party A the principal amount minus any residual value of the bond if B fails. In this example, Party A is the protection buyer and Bank B is the protection seller. Company C is unaffected by the transaction, at least until it defaults, whereupon its creditor may be Party A or Bank B, depending on whether the swap requires Party A to transfer the bond to Bank B after Bank B makes the credit-default payment to party A.

The reference asset in a credit default swap can be a single item or a basket of items. In the case of a basket, the contract will often include a first-to-default feature, whereby the protection seller's payment obligations are triggered upon the first default of any of the assets in the basket (and the derivatives contract thereafter may or may not automatically terminate). Sometimes, a contract referencing a basket of assets will include instead a green bottle feature, which allocates protection to all the assets in the basket according to proportions described in the contract. Additionally, some credit-default swaps will incorporate a materiality threshold, meaning that the protection seller's payment obligations will be triggered only if the protection buyer first experiences a pre-determined amount of loss.

Perhaps because the protection buyer's payment obligations can be periodic, or perhaps because credit default swaps sometimes refer to notional amounts for purpose of calculating the protection buyer's payment obligations or the protection seller's credit default payment amount, the transactions are considered swaps. Nevertheless, the protection seller's payment obligations are contingent; thus it may be more accurate to think of credit default swaps as options. Certainly, a credit default swap in which the protection buyer must deliver the reference asset to the protection seller to obtain the credit default payment resembles a physically-settled put option. * * *

With a total return swap, also known as a total rate-of return swap, the protection buyer, or total return seller, artificially sells a reference asset to the protection seller, or total return buyer. Technically, the total return seller agrees to pay the total return associated with a reference asset to the total return buyer. Total return equals interest plus fees and appreciation in market value at maturity. In exchange, the total return buyer agrees to make payments to the total return seller. These payments are formulated from either fixed or floating rates on a notional amount and cover depreciation in value at maturity. To compensate the total return buyer for the risk it undertakes, the notional amount is usually less than the principal amount of the reference asset. The transaction may or may not provide for termination and a cash settlement between the parties if a credit event occurs.

For example: Party A holds a bond issued by Company C, and Bank B would like to obtain both the credit risk and the market risk under the bond. Party A can swap with Bank B all the returns on the bond, including any increase in value of the bond, measured at maturity, in exchange for (i) periodic payments by Bank B to Party A at a floating rate (e.g., LIBOR plus fifty basis points) on a notional amount, and (ii) a payment equal to any decrease in value of the bond measured at maturity (or early termination of the bond, if applicable). In this example, Party A is the total return seller and the protection buyer, and Bank B is the total return buyer and the protection seller.

The nature of the risks protected distinguishes a total return swap from a credit-default swap. A credit default swap transfers only credit risk. A total return swap, however, transfers both credit risk and market risk. Indeed, because a total return swap synthetically transfers ownership in an asset, some market professionals do not see the transaction as a true credit derivative, even though credit risk is shifted. This may also explain why total return swap terminology prefers the terms total return buyer and total return seller to the terms protection seller and protection buyer, respectively.

Interestingly, a total return swap can engender a basis swap. This would occur if both the reference asset and the total return buyer's payment obligations were set at a floating rate. Because both sides of the swap relate to floating rates, the market risk that the total return swap transfers is basis risk.

Credit spread options are designed to capture changes in yield between (i) a reference asset and a relatively risk-free baseline, such as a U.S. Treasury Bill or market rate swap, of similar maturity; (ii) similar securities of two different issuers; or (iii) two obligations of the same issuer but with differing maturities. The spread between the two items is the quantification by the market of the credit risk in holding a certain asset. What makes credit spread options unique among credit derivatives is the disregard of credit events and sole focus on the differences between two references. The protection offered by a credit spread option usually can be invoked long before a true credit event occurs because yield differences express the market's anticipation of credit or credit-like events. In this sense, it might not be appropriate to call a credit spread option a credit derivative; ultimately, however, the moniker is fair because the product does address credit risk, just not credit-default alone.

In a credit spread option, the party buying protection, as it were, pays a premium and obtains a right to buy from or sell to the other party the reference asset at a predetermined price, should the spread reach a certain trigger point. When the option is a put, the option holder will sell the asset once the spread indicates unpalatable risk. When the option is a call, the option holder will buy the asset once the spread, hence return, appears sufficiently large to justify tolerating the risk. The protection provided by a credit spread option is wider than that provided by a credit swap or a total-return swap because a credit spread option protection trigger can occur long before a credit event arises and payment is due regardless of what causes the credit spread movement.

For example: Party A holding a rated bond issued by Company C with one-year maturity can buy a credit spread put option from Bank B for an upfront premium. The option gives Party A the right to sell the bond to Bank B at a predetermined strike value. The strike value is expressed in terms of credit spread over a one year U.S. Treasury bond. On the option's strike date, if the actual spread of the bond is less than the strike value, the option is worthless and simply will expire. If the spread is higher than the strike value on the strike date, Party A will deliver the underlying bond to Bank B and Bank B will pay an agreed-upon compensation. In this example, Party A is the spread buyer and Bank B is the spread seller. * * *

Credit-linked debt is only a credit derivative in part. Most commonly, it takes the form of a credit-linked note, which is a combination of a structured note and a funded credit-default swap. In a credit-linked note, the protection seller pays the protection buyer a principal amount, in exchange for a note issued by the protection buyer. Under the note, the protection buyer obligates itself to pay periodic interest. The principal is redeemed upon maturity or a credit event, whichever comes first. In the case of a first-occurring credit event, however, the note holder will suffer. If the arrangement is cash-settled, the note issuer will deduct a stipulated credit-default amount from the principal. If the arrangement is physically-settled, the note issuer will deliver the reference asset to the note holder, instead of redeeming with cash.

For example: Bank B issues a note to Party A, under which Party A lends a principal amount to Bank B at a predetermined interest rate. Bank B will pay periodic interest payments to Party A. However, if a certain Company C defaults on a certain bond that it has issued before the note's maturity, Party A will forfeit its rights to return of some or all of the principal and any remaining interest payments. In this example, Party A is the protection seller and Bank B is the protection buyer.

In contrast to the protection seller in a credit-default swap, the protection seller in credit-linked debt ensures its contingent payment obligation in advance by way of a forfeitable loan. In this manner, the protection seller finds or collateralizes the original credit risk with a principal amount. The protection buyer is thus also protected from the credit risk of the protection seller. It is this funding that most distinguishes credit-linked debt from a credit default swap. This funding is particularly attractive to regulated entities, as the credit risks of both the obligor and of the credit derivative counterparty are neutralized, reducing the need for regulatory capital. As in the case of a credit default swap, credit-linked debt transfers only credit risk.

NOTES

1. The growth of the credit default swaps market had been phenomenal. The notional amount of outstanding credit default swaps in 2000 was $900 billion. Nat'l Ass'n of Professional Ins. Agents, *Congress Exempted Credit Default Swaps From State Gaming Laws in 2000*, http://www.pianet.com/NewsCenter/BizPolitics/10–15–08–7.htm (accessed July 3, 2011). That figure increased to $62 trillion by 2008. *See* INTERNATIONAL SWAP AND DERIVATIVES ASSOCIATION INC., MARKET SURVEY (2009), http://www.isda.org/statistics/pdf/ISDA–Market–Survey-historical-data.pdf (accessed July 1, 2011).

2. Although it was estimated that 80 percent of the credit default swap market was speculative in nature before the Financial Crisis in 2008, credit default swaps also performed a hedging function. Among other things, they were used to protect a corporate bondholder from the bankruptcy of the company issuing the bond. Credit default swaps were used to enhance the creditworthiness of subprime mortgage securitizations that were bundled into collateralized debt obligations (CDOs).

As a result of credit enhancements such as credit default swaps, the credit rating agencies gave the upper tranches of CDOs triple AAA ratings. This was the same credit rating that was given to U.S. government debt before it lost that rating in 2011.

Because of their perceived safety, many financial institutions invested in super seniors, which were the upper and most protected levels of the CDO tranches. For the same reason, the banking regulators gave those instruments special capital treatment, encouraging banks to keep such investment on their books while selling off more risky lower-rated tranches of the CDOs.

3. Warren Buffett, the large scale trader and head of Berkshire Hathaway Inc., famously stated in his annual report to the shareholders of Berkshire Hathaway in 2002:

> The derivatives genie is now well out of the bottle, and these instruments will almost certainly multiply in variety and number until some event makes their toxicity clear. Knowledge of how dangerous they are has already permeated the electricity and gas

businesses, in which the eruption of major troubles caused the use of derivatives to diminish dramatically. Elsewhere, however, the derivatives business continues to expand unchecked. Central banks and governments have so far found no effective way to control, or even monitor, the risks posed by these contracts. . . . I believe Berkshire should be a fortress of financial strength—for the sake of our owners, creditors, policyholders and employees. We try to be alert to any sort of megacatastrophe risk, and that posture may make us unduly apprehensive about the burgeoning quantities of long-term derivatives contracts and the massive amount of uncollateralized receivables that are growing alongside. In our view, however, derivatives are financial weapons of mass destruction, carrying dangers that, while now latent, are potentially lethal.

Berkshire Hathaway Inc. 2002 Annual Report at 15. Buffett's words were much quoted during the Financial Crisis in 2008, which was blamed in large measure on credit default swaps associated with subprime mortgages.

JERRY W. MARKHAM
REGULATING CREDIT DEFAULT SWAPS IN THE
WAKE OF THE SUBPRIME CRISIS

Paper presented at the International Monetary Fund Seminar on
Current Developments in Monetary and Financial Law
Washington, D.C. (Dec. 2, 2009)

As a result of efforts by the Clinton administration, "[s]ubprime mortgage originations grew from $35 billion in 1994 to $140 billion in 2000, indicating an average annual growth rate of 26%."[3] Clinton certainly laid the groundwork for the subprime crisis, but subprime lending exploded during the years of the George W. Bush administration. As one source points out:

Some 80 percent of outstanding U.S. mortgages are prime, while 14 percent are subprime and 6 percent fall into the near-prime category. These numbers, however, mask the explosive growth of nonprime mortgages. Subprime and near-prime loans shot up from 9 percent of newly originated securitized mortgages in 2001 to 40 percent in 2006.

Danielle DiMartino & John V. Duca, *The Rise and Fall of Subprime Mortgages*, 2 ECON. LETTER—INSIGHTS FROM THE FED. RESERVE BANK OF

---

[3] A subprime loan is one that has a high likelihood of default because the borrower is not creditworthy. Although there are no uniform standards for classifying a mortgage as subprime, a loan is generally viewed to be such if the borrower falls within one of the following categories: (1) those with a poor credit history; (2) those with no credit history; and (3) borrowers who have existing credit, but who are over extended. *See* Note, *The Entrance of Banks Into Subprime Lending: First Union and the Money Store*, 3 N.C. BANKING INST. 149, 150–51 (1999). FICO credit scores are also used to identify subprime borrowers. *See* In re Countrywide Fin. Corp. Sec. Litig., 2008 U.S. Dist. LEXIS 102000 (C.D. Cal. 2008).

DALLAS 11, *available at* http://www.dallasfed.org/research/eclett/2007/
el0711.html.

The amount of securitized subprime mortgages grew from about $11
billion in 1994 to over $100 billion in 2002. Bear Stearns made its first
subprime securitization offering in 1997 for mortgages totaling $385
million, and it underwrote an additional $1.9 billion in CRA
securitizations over the next ten months. "By 2005, almost 68 percent of
home mortgage originations were securitized." The FDIC noted, in 2006,
that:

> A significant development in the mortgage securities market is
> the recent and dramatic expansion of 'private-label, [mortgage-
> backed securities] MBS . . . Total outstanding private-label MBS
> represented 29 percent of total outstanding MBS in 2005, more
> than double the share in 2003. Of total private-label MBS
> issuance, *two thirds comprised non-prime loans in 2005*, up from
> 46 percent in 2003.

The securitization process was carried out through CDOs
[collateralized debt obligations] that were distributed through
"warehouse" operations, in which mortgages were purchased from non-
bank originators by investment banks and then resold through
securitizations. These warehousing operations became a part of an
unregulated "shadow banking" system. A shareholder report by UBS AG
described its CDO facility as follows:

> In the initial stage of a CDO securitization, the [CDO] desk
> would typically enter into an agreement with a collateral
> manager. UBS sourced residential mortgage backed securities
> ('RMBS') and other securities on behalf of the manager. These
> positions were held in a CDO Warehouse in anticipation of
> securitization into CDOs. Generally, while in the Warehouse,
> these positions would be on UBS's books with exposure to
> market risk. Upon completion of the Warehouse, the securities
> were transferred to a CDO special-purpose vehicle, and
> structured into tranches. The CDO desk received structuring
> fees on the notional value of the deal, and focused on Mezzanine
> ('Mezz') CDOs, which generated fees of approximately 125 to 150
> bp (compared with high-grade CDOs, which generated fees of
> approximately 30 to 50 bp). . . .

> Under normal market conditions, there would be a rise and fall
> in positions held in the CDO Warehouse line as assets were
> accumulated ('ramped up') and then sold as CDOs. There was
> typically a lag of between 1 and 4 months between initial
> agreement with a collateral manager to buy assets, and the full
> ramping of a CDO Warehouse.

Subprime CDOs were broken up into separate tranches. The less secure tranches were required to absorb any larger than expected losses from mortgage defaults, providing a cushion from loss for the most secure tranche, called the "Super-Senior." As a result of this credit enhancement feature, the Super-Seniors were considered to be more credit-worthy than the underlying subprime mortgages themselves. * * *

The subprime crisis focused much attention on credit default swaps (CDS) and the role they played in the failure of the American International Group Inc. (AIG). The bailout of AIG by the U.S. government was unprecedented in size and scope, and the amount of the bill to the taxpayers for that and other failures is yet to be tallied. * * *

A CDS is an agreement by one party to make a series of payments to a counter party, in exchange for a payoff, if a specified credit instrument goes into default. As one court defined these instruments:

> a common type of credit derivative in which the protection buyer makes a fixed payment to the protection seller in return for a payment that is contingent upon a 'credit event'—such as a bankruptcy—occurring to the company that issued the security (the 'reference entity') or the security itself (the 'reference obligation'). The contingent payment is often made against delivery of a 'deliverable obligation'—usually the reference obligation or other security issued by the reference entity—by the protection buyer to the protection seller. This delivery is known as the 'physical settlement.'

Deutsche Bank AG v. Ambac Credit Products LLC, 2006 U.S. Dist. LEXIS 45322 (S.D.N.Y. 2006).

Although CDS were widely used as a form of insurance against a default from that credit instrument, they were also used for speculation on whether a default will occur. It was estimated that eighty percent or more of the giant CDS market was speculative. The CDS, in all events, proved to be a popular instrument. Outstanding notional value of the CDS was over $42 trillion in debt at year-end 2007.

CDS were used to enhance the creditworthiness of subprime securitizations. As an April 2008 UBS shareholder report noted, "[k]ey to the growth of the CDO structuring business was the development of the credit default swap ('CDS'). . . ." With the credit enhancement of a CDS, the credit rating agencies often gave the Super Seniors their highest triple-A rating. This was the same credit rating enjoyed by the federal government, which signaled to the world that a default on those Super Senior tranches was highly unlikely. Unfortunately, the rating agencies' risk models for awarding the triple-A rating on CDOs did not take into account the possibility of a major downturn in the real estate market. That flaw was not spotted until the subprime crisis arose.

A risk model developed by David Li did for CDOs what the Black-Scholes model did for options. Seemingly, it allowed a supposed precise mathematical computation of the risks posed by these instruments. That and other Gaussian Copula risk models failed, however, to predict the massive losses sustained by commercial banks in the United States, and Europe, from their exposures to subprime CDOs. Fail they did, but there was no cabal using a secret formula to deceive investors. Moody's actually published its CDO risk assessment model (CDOROM), which became the industry standard, on the Internet in 2004. The whole world was free to discover its flaws but, except for a few naysayers, the model went pretty much unchallenged.

The mathematical model used to rate CDOs proved to be badly flawed. Critics charged that these models were defective because they relied on historical prices generated by a rising market. That Pollyanna approach overlooked the possibility of a hundred-year, "perfect" storm, which arrived in the form of the subprime crisis. The possibility of such an unusual event was called a "fat tail" or "outlier." They were also called "black swans," as a metaphor for the widely held belief that there was no such thing as a black swan, until explorers reached Australia and found just such a bird. See, Nassim N. Taleb, The Black Swan: The Impact of the Highly Improbable (2007). The probability of an outlier was considered so small that they were ignored by the credit assessors. Lloyd Blankfein, the CEO at Goldman Sachs, also asserted that many financial institutions had erred in outsourcing their risk management to the rating agencies. He believed that the rating agencies had diluted their triple-A rating by giving that rating to over 64,000 structured finance instruments, while only twelve operating companies in the world had such a rating.

The high credit ratings given to the Super Senior tranches posed another problem. These securities were hard to market due to their lower interest rates, which was a function of their triple-A rating. That problem was solved after bank regulators in the United States allowed favorable capital treatment of Super Seniors on bank balance sheets, provided that the Super Senior had a triple-A credit rating. This regulatory blessing removed any residual concerns on the part of the banks of undue risk from Super-Seniors and created a demand for the Super Seniors by banks here and abroad. As a result, a large portion of the Super Senior tranches were held on the books of many major investment banks such as Citigroup, Merrill Lynch, UBS AG and Lehman Brothers. The twenty-five largest banks were also holding $13 trillion in CDS notionals on their books in March 2008.

A credit down grade at the American International Group, Inc. (AIG) in September 2008 raised concerns that large losses would be experienced in the financial community if AIG defaulted on its $500 billion CDS portfolio. This spurred the federal government to mount a $183 billion rescue of that firm. AIG entered the CDS market in a big way in 2005 through its division called AIGFP, which had been founded by a group of traders from Drexel Burnham Lambert, the failed junk bond broker of Michael Milken fame. AIGFP's risk model predicted that, based on historic default rates, the economy would have to fall into depression before AIG would experience losses from its CDS exposures. AIGFP assured investors in August 2007 that "it is hard for us, without being flippant, to even see a scenario within any kind of realm of reason that would see us losing $1 in any of those transactions."

AIG's share price dropped sharply after it reported a large 2007 fourth quarter loss that was accompanied by a $5.29 billion write-down of its mortgage related business, including a write-down of its credit CDS business by $4.88 billion. AIG reported a loss of $7.81 billion in the first quarter of 2008, largely due to a write down of $11 billion related to losses from Super Senior CDS written by the AIG Financial Products Corp. (AIGFP). Another $3.6 billion was written off by AIG for those instruments in the second quarter of 2008, adding to the $5.36 billion loss by AIG in that quarter. AIG reported a loss in the third quarter of $24.47 billion, including losses of $7.05 billion in AIGFP.

Fed chairman Ben Bernanke turned AIG and the CDS market into a pariah when he declared in congressional testimony that nothing had made him more angry than the AIG failure, which he attributed to AIG's exploitation of "a huge gap in the regulatory system." He asserted that AIGFP was nothing more than a hedge fund attached to large and stable insurance company that "made huge numbers of irresponsible bets, [and] took huge losses. There was no regulatory oversight because there was a gap in the system." Bernanke stated that the government was forced to expend billions of dollars to save AIG because its failure would have been "disastrous for the economy."

Actually, it appears that AIG's failure was the result of credit downgrades, prompted by AIG's write-downs of its CDS positions. Those write-downs were caused by a lack of a market that could accurately price the underlying Super Seniors. The subsequent credit downgrades caused large collateral calls that AIG did not have the liquidity to meet.

NOTE

1. Shortly after Lehman Brothers failed during the Financial Crisis in 2008 (and the AIG insurance company would have failed but for the U.S. bailout) several states, in particular the State of New York, issued interpretative letters on credit default swaps. Those letters declared that credit default swaps were insurance contracts and thus were subject to New York's insurance regulations. The letters stated that the payment of the premium by the Protection Buyer to the Protection Seller and the obligations

of the Protection Seller to pay the Protection Buyer in the event of certain types of defaults constitute an insurance contract. This letter raised significant concerns to the CDS industry because they did not want to become regulated insurance companies in order to sell CDS. Later, the New York State Insurance Department withdrew its letter.

7. DODD-FRANK SWAP REGULATION

The Treasury Department proposed legislation in June 2009 to repeal the Enron loophole for swaps. SEC chair Christopher Cox also sought authority from Congress to regulate the credit default swap market. He asserted that the market lacked transparency and was susceptible to fraud and manipulation.

These proposals floated about in Congress for about a year, but became bogged down in fights over the scope and application of such regulation, as well as concerns over other aspects of the Obama Administration's proposals for financial services regulation. That logjam was broken by a highly publicized case brought by the SEC against Goldman Sachs, which is set forth below, for misselling CDS. The filing of that case touched off a populist demand for the regulation of such instruments. President Obama joined the fray by announcing, just after the case was filed, that he would veto the pending financial services legislation if it did not regulate OTC derivatives, including CDS.

Congressional leaders behind the Dodd-Frank Act examined various methods to regulate swaps in the aftermath of the 2008 Financial Crisis and how best to regulate CDS, which was the principal product that resulted in the $185 billion bailout by the U.S. government of the American International Group (AIG) to keep it afloat in September 2008. AIG had guaranteed all of the financial obligations resulting from CDS transactions issued by AIGFP, its UK affiliate.

In adopting the Dodd-Frank Act, two main requirements emerged, namely that all swaps, not just CDS, would be required to be traded on an exchange or cleared on a central counterparty (CCP) with some exceptions. The basis for the mandatory clearing and trading requirements came from the exchange-traded derivatives markets, which require that the underlying derivative be traded on a regulated exchange and cleared through a regulated clearinghouse. None of the exchange-traded derivatives required any bailout or needed any special assistance in 2008. In fact, all such products were traded without issue during this period. Many experts have argued that not all swaps created any financial problems in 2008, yet Congress chose to regulate all swaps, not just CDS swaps that required the bailout of AIG, with the enactment of the Dodd-Frank Act.

Congress believed that swaps should be traded and cleared like futures contracts and thus gave significant jurisdiction to the CFTC to regulate swaps under Title VII of the Dodd-Frank Act. Approximately 90 percent of the regulatory jurisdiction relating to all swaps was given to the CFTC, with the difference being given to the SEC.

The Dodd-Frank Act amended the federal securities laws and repealed a residue of the Enron loophole in the Commodity Exchange Act of 1936, in order to authorize the SEC and CFTC to regulate swaps and swap dealers. Dodd-Frank gave the SEC broad and exclusive jurisdiction over "security-based swaps," while the CFTC was given exclusive jurisdiction over other swaps, and joint jurisdiction was declared for the SEC and CFTC over "mixed swaps," which have securities and futures like elements.

To delineate the regulatory roles of the SEC and CFTC over swaps, Dodd-Frank defined the term "swap" and then defined smaller subsets of that term—the "securities-based swap" (a swap on a narrow-based index of securities or on a single issuer) and the "mixed swap" (basically any other swap that has a financial component such as interest rates, currencies, quantitative measures, or the occurrence of a change associated with a potential financial, economic, or commercial event).

All swaps, subject to the mandatory clearing requirement, must be cleared on a designated clearing organization (DCO) that is registered with the CFTC or on a clearinghouse regulated by the SEC. The new swaps clearing requirement in the Commodity Exchange Act (CEA) states that:

> It shall be unlawful for any person to engage in a swap unless that person submits such swap for clearing to a derivatives clearing organization that is registered under this chapter or a derivatives clearing organization that is exempt from registration under this chapter if the swap is required to be cleared.

7 U.S.C. § 2(h).

Most swaps will now be exchange traded and cleared through a regulated exchange and cleared by a regulated clearinghouse. Many swap customers also trade futures through an FCM. To do so, they must open a futures account on the books of their FCM and execute a futures customer agreement required by that FCM. To clear swaps with their FCM, the swaps customer will be required to sign an Addendum to the futures customer agreement, which will permit that customer to clear swaps as well as futures with the FCM.

The Dodd-Frank Act trading mandate for swaps also allows swaps to be traded on a "swap execution facility" (SEF), a new trade execution entity established by the Dodd-Frank Act. A DCM may trade both futures and swaps, although the DCM will have separate rules relating to futures contracts traded on the DCM versus how swaps will be traded, whereas a SEF may only offer swaps for trading purposes.

As of December 2013, approximately eighteen firms had submitted applications to become registered as a SEF with the CFTC. SEFs, like DCMs that will offer swaps, must comply with several new regulations issued by the CFTC. Both DCMs that will offer swaps for trading and SEFs must allow the counterparty to select the DCO on which it wants to clear the swap. This is a unique difference from futures trading whereby the DCO and the DCM are affiliated so all futures contracts are cleared by the affiliated DCO. As described above, this vertical clearing model has received criticism by the U.S. Department of Justice as possibly being anti-competitive but, to date, no action has been taken by the Justice Department against any DCM or DCO.

As Congress was debating the Dodd-Frank Act in 2009 and 2010, before it became law in July 2010, several agricultural and energy firms lobbied Congress to provide an exemption from the mandatory clearing requirement for commercial end users of a product that is the subject of a swap agreement. Their main concern was that they did not have the requisite liquid assets and collateral, which are normally required by a DCO to satisfy the DCO's initial margin requirements. When the Dodd-Frank Act was signed into law in July 2010, there was an exemption from the mandatory clearing requirement for commercial end users, which used swaps in a bona fide hedging manner. At least one party to these swaps must be a person that is not a financial entity and is using swaps to hedge a commercial risk and must notify the CFTC of how it meets its financial obligations associated with its uncleared swaps. [17 C.F.R. § 50.50].

The CFTC will set margin requirements for uncleared swaps. As of December 2013, the regulations regarding how much margin may be required for uncleared swaps had not been finalized. It will be quite interesting to see if the margin amounts for uncleared swaps will be significantly higher than those required for cleared swaps. See, CFTC, "Swap Transaction Compliance and Implementation Schedule: Trading Documentation and Margining Requirements Under Section 4s of the CEA," 76 Fed. Reg. 58176 (Sept. 20, 2011) (describing the schedule for implementing this requirement).

Swap transactions are required to be reported to a swap data repository (SDR). Swap data repositories are regulated by the CFTC.

Swap dealers are also required to register and are subject to extensive regulation by the CFTC. "Securities-based" swap dealers are regulated by the SEC, while other commodity based swaps (referred to simply as "swaps") are regulated by the CFTC.

Among other things, customer funds associated with DCM traded swaps must be held in a segregated account, called a cleared swap account. The Dodd-Frank Act allows regulators to impose capital, reporting, recordkeeping, disclosure and margin requirements on swap dealers. In addition swap dealers are subject to new Internal Business Conduct Requirements and External Business Conduct Requirements.

Dodd-Frank added two further categories of registrants, i.e. "Major Swap Participants (MSPs) and Securities-based Major Swap Participants (SBMSPs). Like the other new swap registrants, a MSP is subject to the CEA and CFTC regulations whereas SBMSPs are subject to the federal securities laws and SEC regulations.

In essence, these new registrants are the primary counter-parties to swaps and securities-based swaps that do not fall within any other definition or qualify for any other exemption.

SEC AND CFTC, FURTHER DEFINITION OF "SWAP," "SECURITY-BASED SWAP," AND "SECURITY-BASED SWAP AGREEMENT"; MIXED SWAPS; SECURITY-BASED SWAP AGREEMENT RECORDKEEPING
77 Fed. Reg. 48207 (Aug. 13, 2012)

On July 21, 2010, President Obama signed the Dodd-Frank Act into law. Title VII of the Dodd-Frank Act ("Title VII") established a comprehensive new regulatory framework for swaps and security-based swaps. The legislation was enacted, among other reasons, to reduce risk, increase transparency, and promote market integrity within the financial system, including by: (i) Providing for the registration and comprehensive regulation of swap dealers, security-based swap dealers, major swap participants, and major security-based swap participants; (ii) imposing clearing and trade execution requirements on swaps and security-based swaps, subject to certain exceptions; (iii) creating rigorous recordkeeping and real-time reporting regimes; and (iv) enhancing the rulemaking and enforcement authorities of the Commissions with respect to, among others, all registered entities and intermediaries subject to the Commissions' oversight.

Section 712(d)(1) of the Dodd-Frank Act provides that the Commissions, in consultation with the Board, shall jointly further define the terms "swap," "security-based swap," and "security-based swap agreement" ("SBSA"). Section 712(a)(8) of the Dodd-Frank Act provides further that the Commissions shall jointly prescribe such regulations regarding "mixed swaps" as may be necessary to carry out the purposes of Title VII. In addition, sections 721(b) and 761(b) of the Dodd-Frank Act provide that the Commissions may adopt rules to further define terms included in subtitles A and B, respectively, of Title VII, and sections 721(c) and 761(b) of the Dodd-Frank Act provide the Commissions with authority to define the terms "swap" and "security-based swap," as well as the terms "swap dealer," "major swap participant," "security-based swap dealer," and "major security-based swap participant," to include transactions and entities that have been structured to evade the requirements of subtitles A and B, respectively, of Title VII.

Section 712(d)(2)(B) of the Dodd-Frank Act requires the Commissions, in consultation with the [Federal Reserve] Board, to jointly adopt rules governing books and records requirements for SBSAs by persons registered as swap data repositories ("SDRs") under the CEA, including uniform rules that specify the data elements that shall be collected and maintained by each SDR. Similarly, section 712(d)(2)(C) of the Dodd-Frank Act requires the Commissions, in consultation with the Board, to jointly adopt rules governing books and records for SBSAs, including daily trading records, for swap dealers, major swap participants, security-based swap dealers, and security-based swap participants.

Under the comprehensive framework for regulating swaps and security-based swaps established in Title VII, the CFTC is given regulatory authority over swaps, the SEC is given regulatory authority over security-based swaps, and the Commissions shall jointly prescribe such regulations regarding mixed swaps as may be necessary to carry out the purposes of Title VII.[10] In addition, the SEC is given antifraud authority over, and access to information from, certain CFTC-regulated entities regarding SBSAs,[11] which are a type of swap related to securities over which the CFTC is given regulatory authority. * * *

---

[10] Section 721(a) of the Dodd-Frank Act describes the category of "mixed swap" by adding new section 1a(47)(D) to the CEA, 7 U.S.C. 1a(47)(D). Section 761(a) of the Dodd-Frank Act also includes the category of "mixed swap" by adding new section 3(a)(68)(D) to the Exchange Act, 15 U.S.C. 78c(68)(D). A mixed swap is defined as a subset of security-based swaps that also are based on the value of 1 or more interest or other rates, currencies, commodities, instruments of indebtedness, indices, quantitative measures, other financial or economic interest or property of any kind (other than a single security or a narrow-based security index), or the occurrence, non-occurrence, or the extent of the occurrence of an event or contingency associated with a potential financial, economic, or commercial consequence (other than the occurrence, non-occurrence, or extent of the occurrence of an event relating to a single issuer of a security or the issuers of securities in a narrow-based security index, provided that such event directly affects the financial statements, financial condition, or financial obligations of the issuer).

[11] Section 761(a) of the Dodd-Frank Act defines the term "security-based swap agreement" by adding new section 3(a)(78) to the Exchange Act, 15 U.S.C. 78c(a)(78). The CEA includes the definition of "security-based swap agreement" in subparagraph (A)(v) of the swap definition in CEA section 1a(47), 7 U.S.C. 1a(47). The only difference between these definitions is that the definition of SBSA in the Exchange Act specifically excludes security-based swaps (See section 3(a)(78)(B) of the Exchange Act, 15 U.S.C. 78c(a)(78)(B)), whereas the definition of SBSA in the CEA does not contain a similar exclusion. Instead, under the CEA, the exclusion for security-based swaps is placed in the general exclusions from the swap definition (See CEA section 1a(47)(B)(x), 7 U.S.C. 1a(47)(B)(x)). Although the statutes are slightly different structurally, the

[T]he Commissions are adopting rules and interpretations regarding, among other things: (i) The regulatory treatment of insurance products; (ii) the exclusion of forward contracts from the swap and security-based swap definitions; (iii) the regulatory treatment of certain consumer and commercial contracts; (iv) the regulatory treatment of certain foreign-exchange related and other instruments; (v) swaps and security-based swaps involving interest rates (or other monetary rates) and yields; (vi) total return swaps ("TRS"); (vii) Title VII instruments based on futures contracts; (viii) the application of the definition of "narrow-based security index" in distinguishing between certain swaps and security-based swaps, including credit default swaps ("CDS") and index CDS; and (ix) the specification of certain swaps and security-based swaps that are, and are not, mixed swaps. In addition, the Commissions are adopting rules: (i) To clarify that there will not be additional books and records requirements applicable to SBSAs other than those required for swaps; (ii) providing a mechanism for requesting the Commissions to interpret whether a particular type of agreement, contract, or transaction (or class of agreements, contracts, or transactions) is a swap, security-based swap, or both (i.e., a mixed swap); and (iii) providing a mechanism for evaluating the applicability of certain regulatory requirements to particular mixed swaps. Finally, the CFTC is adopting rules to implement the anti-evasion authority provided in the Dodd-Frank Act. * * * *

The statutory definition of the term "swap" includes, in part, any agreement, contract or transaction "that provides for any purchase, sale, payment or delivery (other than a dividend on an equity security) that is dependent on the occurrence, nonoccurrence, or the extent of the occurrence of an event or contingency associated with a potential financial, economic, or commercial consequence." As stated in the Proposing Release, the Commissions do not interpret this clause to mean that products historically treated as insurance products should be included within the swap or security-based swap definitions. The Commissions are aware of nothing in Title VII to suggest that Congress intended for traditional insurance products to be regulated as swaps or security-based swaps. Moreover, the fact that swaps and insurance products are subject to different regulatory regimes is reflected in section 722(b) of the Dodd-Frank Act which, in new section 12(h) of the CEA, provides that a swap "shall not be considered to be insurance" and "may not be regulated as an insurance contract under the law of any State." Accordingly, the Commissions believe that state or Federally regulated insurance products that are provided by persons that are subject to state or Federal insurance supervision, that otherwise could fall within the definitions should not be considered swaps or security-based swaps so

---

Commissions interpret them to have consistent meaning that the category of security-based swap agreements excludes security-based swaps.

long as they satisfy the requirements of the Insurance Safe Harbor (as defined below). At the same time, however, the Commissions are concerned that certain agreements, contracts, or transactions that are swaps or security-based swaps might be characterized as insurance products to evade the regulatory regime under Title VII of the Dodd-Frank Act. * * * *

Insurance

The Commissions are adopting the Product Test as proposed, with certain modifications to respond to commenters' concerns. The Product Test sets forth four criteria for an agreement, contract, or transaction to be considered insurance. First, the final rules require that the beneficiary have an "insurable interest" underlying the agreement, contract, or transaction and thereby carry the risk of loss with respect to that interest continuously throughout the duration of the agreement, contract, or transaction. The requirement that the beneficiary be at risk of loss (which could be an adverse financial, economic, or commercial consequence) with respect to the interest that is the subject of the agreement, contract, or transaction continuously throughout the duration of the agreement, contract, or transaction will ensure that an insurance contract beneficiary has a stake in the interest on which the agreement, contract, or transaction is written. Similarly, the requirement that the beneficiary have the insurable interest continuously throughout the duration of the agreement, contract, or transaction is designed to ensure that payment on the insurance product is inextricably connected to both the beneficiary and the interest on which the insurance product is written. In contrast to insurance, a credit default swap ("CDS") (which may be a swap or a security-based swap) does not require the purchaser of protection to hold any underlying obligation issued by the reference entity on which the CDS is written. One commenter identified the existence of an insurable interest as a material element to the existence of an insurance contract. Because neither swaps nor security-based swaps require the presence of an insurable interest at all (although an insurable interest may sometimes be present coincidentally), the Commissions continue to believe that whether an insurable interest is present continuously throughout the duration of the agreement, contract, or transaction is a meaningful way to distinguish insurance from swaps and security-based swaps.

Second, the requirement that a loss occur and be proved similarly ensures that the beneficiary has a stake in the insurable interest that is the subject of the agreement, contract, or transaction. If the beneficiary can demonstrate loss, that loss would "trigger" performance by the insurer on the agreement, contract, or transaction such that, by making payment, the insurer is indemnifying the beneficiary for such loss. In addition, limiting any payment or indemnification to the value of the insurable interest aids in distinguishing swaps and security-based swaps (where there is no such limit) from insurance.

Third, the final rules require that the insurance product not be traded, separately from the insured interest, on an organized market or over the counter. As the Commissions observed in the Proposing Release, with limited exceptions, insurance products traditionally have not been entered into on or subject to the rules of an organized exchange nor traded in secondary market transactions (*i.e.,* they are not traded on an organized market or over the counter). While swaps and security-based swaps also generally have not been tradable at will in secondary market transactions (*i.e.,* on an organized market or over the counter) without counterparty consent, the Commissions understand that all or part of swaps and security-based swaps are novated or assigned to third parties, usually pursuant to industry standard terms and documents. In response to commenter concerns, the Commissions are clarifying when assignments of insurance contracts and trading on "insurances exchanges" do not constitute trading the contract separately from the related insurable interest, and thus would not violate the Product Test. The Commissions do not interpret the assignment of an insurance contract as described by commenters to be "trading" as that term is used in the Product Test. Nor do the Commissions find that the examples of exchanges offered by commenters, such as Federal Patient Protection and Affordable Care Act "exchanges," are exchanges as that term is used in the Product Test, *e.g.,* a national securities exchange or designated contract market. Mandated insurance exchanges are more like marketplaces for the purchase of insurance, and there is no trading of insurance policies separately from the insured interest on these insurance exchanges. Thus, the assignment of an insurance contract as permitted or required by state law, or the purchase or assignment of an insurance contract on an insurance exchange or otherwise, does not constitute trading an agreement, contract, or transaction separately from the insured interest and would not violate the trading restriction in the Product Test. For the foregoing reasons as clarified, the Commissions continue to believe that lack of trading separately from the insured interest is a feature of insurance that is useful in distinguishing insurance from swaps and security-based swaps.

Fourth, the final rules provide that in the case of financial guaranty insurance policies, also known as bond insurance or bond wraps, any acceleration of payment under the policy must be at the sole discretion of the provider of the financial guaranty insurance policy in order to satisfy the Product Test. Although such products can be economically similar to products such as CDS, they have certain key characteristics that distinguish them from swaps and security-based swaps. For example, under a financial guaranty policy, the insurer typically is required to make timely payment of any shortfalls in the payment of scheduled interest to the holders of the underlying guaranteed obligation. Also, for particular bonds that are covered by a financial guaranty policy, the indenture, related documentation, and/or the financial guaranty policy will provide that a default in payment of principal or interest on the underlying bond will not result in acceleration of the obligation of the insurer to make payment of the full amount of principal on the underlying guaranteed obligation unless the insurer, in its sole discretion, opts to make payment of principal prior to the final scheduled maturity date of the underlying guaranteed obligation. Conversely, under a CDS, a protection seller frequently is required to make payment of the relevant settlement amount to the protection buyer upon demand by the protection buyer after any credit event involving the issuer.

As noted in the Proposing Release, the Commissions do not believe that financial guaranty policies, in general, should be regulated as swaps or security-based swaps. However, because of the close economic similarity of financial guaranty insurance policies guaranteeing payment on debt securities to CDS, in addition to the criteria noted above with respect to insurance generally, the final rules require that, in order to satisfy the Product Test, financial guaranty policies also must satisfy the requirement that they not permit the beneficiary of the policy to accelerate the payment of any principal due on the debt securities. This requirement further distinguishes financial guaranty policies from CDS because, as discussed above, the latter generally requires payment of the relevant settlement amount on the CDS after demand by the protection buyer.

Finally, in response to comments, the Commissions are clarifying that reinsurance and retrocession transactions fall within the scope of the Product Test. The Commissions find that these transactions have insurable interests, as the Commissions interpret such interests in this context, if they have issued insurance policies covering the risks that they wish to insure (and reinsure). Moreover, the Commissions find that retrocession transactions are encompassed within the Product Test and the Provider Test because retrocession is reinsurance of reinsurance (provided the retrocession satisfies the other requirements of both tests). In addition, reinsurance (including retrocession) of certain types of insurance products is included in the list of Enumerated Products.

Requiring all of the criteria in the Product Test will help to limit the application of the final rules to agreements, contracts, and transactions that are appropriately regulated as insurance, and help to assure that agreements, contracts, and transactions appropriately subject to the regulatory regime under Title VII of the Dodd-Frank Act are regulated as swaps or security-based swaps. As a result, the Commissions believe that these requirements will help prevent the final rules from being used to circumvent the applicability of the swap and security-based swap regulatory regimes under Title VII. * * * *

The Forward Contract Exclusion

As the Commissions explained in the Proposing Release, the definitions of the terms "swap" and "security-based swap" do not include forward contracts. These definitions exclude "any sale of a nonfinancial commodity or security for deferred shipment or delivery, so long as the transaction is intended to be physically settled." The Commissions provided an interpretation in the Proposing Release regarding the applicability of the exclusion from the swap and security-based swap definition for forward contracts with respect to nonfinancial commodities and securities. The Commissions are restating this interpretation as set forth in the Proposing Release with certain modifications in response to commenters.

The CFTC provided an interpretation in the Proposing Release regarding the forward contract exclusion for nonfinancial commodities and is restating this interpretation with certain modifications in response to commenters. These clarifications include that the CFTC will interpret the forward contract exclusion consistent with the entire body of CFTC precedent. The CFTC is also clarifying what "commercial participant" means under the "Brent Interpretation." In addition, while the CFTC is withdrawing its 1993 "Energy Exemption" as proposed, it is clarifying that certain alternative delivery procedures will not disqualify a transaction from the forward contract exclusion. In response to comments, the CFTC is providing a new interpretation regarding book-out documentation, as well as additional factors that may be considered in its "facts and circumstances" analysis of whether a particular contract is a forward.

The wording of the forward contract exclusion from the swap definition with respect to nonfinancial commodities is similar, but not identical, to the forward exclusion from the definition of the term "future delivery" that applies to futures contracts, which excludes "any sale of any cash commodity for deferred shipment or delivery."

In the Proposing Release, the CFTC proposed an interpretation clarifying the scope of the exclusion of forward contracts for nonfinancial commodities from the swap definition and from the "future delivery" definition in a number of respects. After considering the comments received, the CFTC is restating substantially all of its interpretation regarding these forward exclusions set forth in the Proposing Release, but with several clarifications in response to commenters.

The CFTC is restating from the Proposing Release that the forward exclusion for nonfinancial commodities in the swap definition will be interpreted in a manner consistent with the CFTC's historical interpretation of the existing forward exclusion with respect to futures contracts, consistent with the Dodd-Frank Act's legislative history. In addition, in response to a commenter, the CFTC is clarifying that the entire body of CFTC precedent regarding forwards should apply to the forward exclusions from the swap and future delivery definitions.

The CFTC's historical interpretation has been that forward contracts with respect to nonfinancial commodities are "commercial merchandising transactions." The primary purpose of a forward contract is to transfer ownership of the commodity and not to transfer solely its price risk. As the CFTC has noted and reaffirms today:

The underlying postulate of the [forward] exclusion is that the [CEA's] regulatory scheme for futures trading simply should not apply to private commercial merchandising transactions which create enforceable obligations to deliver but in which delivery is deferred for reasons of commercial convenience or necessity.

As noted in the Proposing Release, because a forward contract is a commercial merchandising transaction, intent to deliver historically has been an element of the CFTC's analysis of whether a particular contract is a forward contract. In assessing the parties' expectations or intent regarding delivery, the CFTC consistently has applied a "facts and circumstances" test. Therefore, the CFTC reads the "intended to be physically settled" language in the swap definition with respect to nonfinancial commodities to reflect a directive that intent to deliver a physical commodity be a part of the analysis of whether a given contract is a forward contract or a swap, just as it is a part of the CFTC's analysis of whether a given contract is a forward contract or a futures contract.

Brent Interpretation[1]

In this interpretation, the CFTC is restating, with certain clarifications in response to commenters, its interpretation from the Proposing Release that the principles underlying the CFTC's "Brent Interpretation" regarding book-outs developed in connection with the forward exclusion from futures apply to the forward exclusion from the swap definition as well. Book-out transactions meeting the requirements specified in the Brent Interpretation that are effectuated through a subsequent, separately negotiated agreement qualify for the safe harbor under the forward exclusions.

As was noted in the Proposing Release, the issue of book-outs first arose in 1990 in the Brent Interpretation n216 because the parties to the crude oil contracts in that case could individually negotiate cancellation agreements, or "book-outs," with other parties.

---

[1]   [Auth. note: the reference to the Brent Interpretation was to the CFTC's exemption of energy products in the wake of the Transnor case set forth above. *See Transnor (Bermuda) Ltd.* v. *BP N. Am. Petroleum,* 738 F. Supp. 1472 (S.D.N.Y. 1990)].

The Brent Interpretation described these "book-outs" as follows: "In the course of entering into 15-day contracts for delivery of a cargo during a particular month, situations often arise in which two counterparties have multiple, offsetting positions with each other. These situations arise as a result of the effectuation of multiple, independent commercial transactions. In such circumstances, rather than requiring the effectuation of redundant deliveries and the assumption of the credit, delivery and related risks attendant thereto, the parties may, but are not obligated to and may elect not to, terminate their contracts and forego such deliveries and instead negotiate payment-of-differences pursuant to a separate, individually-negotiated cancellation agreement referred to as a book-out.' Similarly, situations regularly arise when participants find themselves selling and purchasing oil more than once in the delivery chain for a particular cargo. The participants comprising these circles' or loops' will frequently attempt to negotiate separate cancellation agreements among themselves for the same reasons and with the same effect described above." Brent Interpretation, *supra* note 207, at 39190.

It is noteworthy that while such [book-out] agreements may extinguish a party's delivery obligation, they are separate, individually negotiated, new agreements, there is no obligation or arrangement to enter into such agreements, they are not provided for by the terms of the contracts as initially entered into, and any party that is in a position in a distribution chain that provides for the opportunity to book-out with another party or parties in the chain is nevertheless entitled to require delivery of the commodity to be made through it, as required under the contracts.

Thus, in the scenario at issue in the Brent Interpretation, the contracts created a binding obligation to make or take delivery without providing any right to offset, cancel, or settle on a payment-of-differences basis. The "parties enter[ed] into such contracts with the recognition that they may be required to make or take delivery."

On these facts, the Brent Interpretation concluded that the contracts were forward contracts, not futures contracts:

Under these circumstances, the [CFTC] is of the view that transactions of this type which are entered into between commercial participants in connection with their business, which create specific delivery obligations that impose substantial economic risks of a commercial nature to these participants, but which may involve, in certain circumstances, string or chain deliveries of the type described

* * * are within the scope of the [forward contract] exclusion from the [CFTC's] regulatory jurisdiction.

Although the CFTC did not expressly discuss intent to deliver, the Brent Interpretation concluded that transactions retained their character as commercial merchandising transactions, notwithstanding the practice of terminating commercial parties' delivery obligations through "book-outs" as described. At any point in the chain, one of the parties could refuse to enter into a new contract to book-out the transaction and, instead, insist upon delivery pursuant to the parties' obligations under their contract.

The CFTC also is clarifying that commercial market participants that regularly make or take delivery of the referenced commodity in the ordinary course of their business meet the commercial participant standard of the Brent Interpretation. The CFTC notes that the Brent Interpretation applies to "commercial participants in connection with their business." The CFTC intends that the interpretation in this release be consistent with the Brent Interpretation, and accordingly is adding "commercial" before "market participants" in this final interpretation. Such entities qualify for the forward exclusion from both the future delivery and swap definitions for their forward transactions in nonfinancial commodities under the Brent Interpretation even if they enter into a subsequent transaction to "book out" the contract rather than make or take delivery. Intent to make or take delivery can be inferred from the binding delivery obligation for the commodity referenced in the contract and the fact that the parties to the contract do, in fact, regularly make or take delivery of the referenced commodity in the ordinary course of their business.

Further, in this final interpretation, the CFTC clarifies, in response to a comment received, that an investment vehicle taking delivery of gold as part of its investment strategy would not be engaging in a commercial activity within the meaning of the Brent Interpretation. By contrast, were the investment vehicle, for example, to own a gold mine and sell the output of the gold mine for forward delivery, or own a chain of jewelry stores that produces its own jewelry from raw materials and purchase a supply of gold from another entity's gold mine in order to provide raw materials for its jewelry stores, such contracts could qualify as forward contracts under the Brent Interpretation—provided that such contracts otherwise satisfy the terms thereof.

Because the Commission s interpretation does not explicitly refer to commercial market participants, it would seem to cover financial players as long as those entities regularly make or take delivery of the underlying commodity in connection with their business. Examples of such entities would be hedge funds or other investment vehicles that regularly make or take delivery of commodities (*e.g.* gold) in conjunction with their line of business—that is, as part of their investment strategies. [CME] asks that the [CFTC] confirm that the Brent safe harbor would be available to these types of market participants that technically are not "commercial" actors.

In sum, the CFTC is interpreting the term "commercial" in the context of the Brent Interpretation in the same way it has done since 1990: "related to the business of a producer, processor, fabricator, refiner or merchandiser." While a market participant need not be solely engaged in "commercial" activity to be a "commercial market participant" within the meaning of the Brent Interpretation under this interpretation, the business activity in which it makes or takes delivery must be commercial activity for it to be a commercial market participant. A hedge fund's investment activity is not commercial activity within the CFTC's longstanding view of the Brent Interpretation.

In addition, the CFTC is expanding the Brent Interpretation, which applied only to oil, to all nonfinancial commodities, as proposed. As a result, book-outs are permissible (where the conditions of the Brent Interpretation are satisfied) for all nonfinancial commodities with respect to the exclusions from the definition of the term "swap" and the definition of the term "future delivery" under the CEA.

Because the CFTC has expanded the Brent Interpretation to nonfinancial commodities in this final interpretation, the CFTC also has determined to withdraw the Energy Exemption as proposed. In response to comments received, the CFTC is clarifying that certain alternative delivery procedures discussed in the Energy Exemption will not disqualify a transaction from the Brent Interpretation safe harbor.

In the Proposing Release, the CFTC proposed to withdraw the Energy Exemption, which, among other things, expanded the Brent Interpretation to energy commodities other than oil, on the basis that the exemption was no longer necessary in light of the extension of the Brent Interpretation to nonfinancial commodities. The Energy Exemption, like the Brent Interpretation, requires binding delivery obligations at the outset, with no right to cash settle or offset transactions. Each requires that book-outs be undertaken pursuant to a subsequent, separately negotiated agreement.

As discussed above, the CFTC is extending the Brent Interpretation to the swap definition and applying it to all nonfinancial commodities for both the swap and future delivery definitions, but is withdrawing the Energy Exemption. With regard to netting agreements that were expressly permitted by the Energy Exemption, the CFTC clarifies that a physical netting agreement (such as, for example, the Edison Electric Institute Master Power Purchase and Sale Agreement) that contains a provision contemplating the reduction to a net delivery amount of future, unintentionally offsetting delivery obligations, is consistent with the intent of the book out provision in the Brent Interpretation—provided that the parties had a bona fide intent, when entering into the transactions, to make or take delivery (as applicable) of the commodity covered by those transactions.

The CFTC also has determined that, notwithstanding the withdrawal of the Energy Exemption, a failure to deliver as a result of the exercise by a party of a "bona fide termination right" does not render an otherwise binding delivery obligation as non-binding. In the Energy Exemption, the CFTC provided the following examples of bona fide termination rights: force majeure provisions and termination rights triggered by events of default, such as counterparty insolvency, default or other inability to perform. The CFTC confirms that market participants who otherwise qualify for the forward exclusion may continue to rely on the bona fide termination right concept as set forth in this interpretation, although, as was stated in the Energy Exemption, such right must be bona fide and not for the purpose of evasion. In this regard, the CFTC further clarifies, consistent with the Energy Exemption, that a bona fide termination right must be triggered by something not expected by the parties at the time the contract is entered into.

The Energy Exemption also discussed a number of methods by which parties to energy contracts settle their obligations, including: The seller's passage of title and the buyer's payment and acceptance of the underlying commodity; taking delivery of the commodity in some instances and in others instead passing title to another intermediate purchaser in a chain; and physically exchanging (i.e., delivering) one quality, grade or type of physical commodity for another quality, grade or type of physical commodity. The CFTC clarifies that these settlement methods generally are not inconsistent with the Brent Interpretation.

Contracts for Differences[2]

As the Proposing Release notes, the Commissions have received inquiries over the years regarding the treatment of CFDs under the CEA and the Federal securities laws. A CFD generally is an agreement to exchange the difference in value of an underlying asset between the time at which a CFD position is established and the time at which it is terminated. If the value increases, the seller pays the buyer the difference; if the value decreases, the buyer pays the seller the difference. CFDs can be traded on a number of products, including treasuries, foreign exchange rates, commodities, equities, and stock indexes. Equity CFDs closely mimic the purchase of actual shares. The buyer of an equity CFD receives cash dividends and participates in stock splits. In the case

---

[2]   [Auth. note: A description of difference trading is contained in the Justh v. Holliday case set forth in Chapter One]

of a long position, a dividend adjustment is credited to the client's account. In the case of a short position, a dividend adjustment is debited from the client's account. CFDs generally are traded over-the-counter (though they also are traded on the Australian Securities Exchange) in a number of countries outside the United States.

The Commissions provided an interpretation in the Proposing Release regarding the treatment of CFDs. The Commissions are restating the interpretation set out in the Proposing Release without modification.

CFDs, unless otherwise excluded, fall within the scope of the swap or security-based swap definition, as applicable. Whether a CFD is a swap or security-based swap will depend on the underlying product of that particular CFD transaction. Because CFDs are highly variable and a CFD can contain a variety of elements that would affect its characterization, the Commissions believe that market participants will need to analyze the features of the underlying product of any particular CFD in order to determine whether it is a swap or a security-based swap. The Commissions are not adopting rules or additional interpretations at this time regarding CFDs.

In light of provisions in the Dodd-Frank Act that specifically address certain foreign exchange products, the Commissions in the Proposing Release proposed rules to clarify the status of products such as foreign exchange forwards, foreign exchange swaps, foreign exchange options, non-deliverable forwards involving foreign exchange ("NDFs"), and cross-currency swaps. The Commissions also proposed a rule to clarify the status of forward rate agreements and provided interpretations regarding: (i) Combinations and permutations of, or options on, swaps or security-based swaps; and (ii) contracts for differences ("CFDs").

The Commissions are adopting the rules as proposed without modification and are restating the interpretations provided in the Proposing Release without modification. In addition, the Commissions are providing additional interpretations regarding foreign exchange spot transactions and retail foreign currency options.

As adopted, rule 1.3(xxx)(2) under the CEA and rule 3a69–2 under the Exchange Act explicitly define the term "swap" to include certain foreign exchange-related products and forward rate agreements unless such products are excluded by the statutory exclusions in subparagraph (B) of the swap definition. In adopting these rules, the Commissions do not mean to suggest that the list of agreements, contracts, and transactions set forth in rule 1.3(xxx)(2) under the CEA and rule 3a69–2(b) under the Exchange Act is an exclusive list. * * * *

Mixed Swaps

The category of mixed swap is described, in both the definition of the term "security-based swap" in the Exchange Act and the definition of the term "swap" in the CEA, as a security-based swap that is also based on the value of 1 or more interest or other rates, currencies, commodities, instruments of indebtedness, indices, quantitative measures, other financial or economic interest or property of any kind (other than a single security or a narrow-based security index), or the occurrence, non-occurrence, or the extent of the occurrence of an event or contingency associated with a potential financial, economic, or commercial consequence (other than an event described in subparagraph (A)(ii)(III) [of section 3(a)(68) of the Exchange Act]).

A mixed swap, therefore, is both a security-based swap and a swap. As stated in the Proposing Release, the Commissions believe that the scope of mixed swaps is, and is intended to be, narrow. Title VII establishes robust and largely parallel regulatory regimes for both swaps and security-based swaps and directs the Commissions to jointly prescribe such regulations regarding mixed swaps as may be necessary to carry out the purposes of the Dodd-Frank Act. More generally, the Commissions believe the category of mixed swap was designed so that there would be no gaps in the regulation of swaps and security-based swaps. Therefore, in light of the statutory scheme created by the Dodd-Frank Act for swaps and security-based swaps, the Commissions believe the category of mixed swap covers only a small subset of Title VII instruments.

For example, a Title VII instrument in which the underlying references are the value of an oil corporation stock and the price of oil would be a mixed swap. Similarly, a Title VII instrument in which the underlying reference is a portfolio of both securities (assuming the portfolio is not an index or, if it is an index, that the index is narrow-based) and commodities would be a mixed swap. Mixed swaps also would include certain Title VII instruments called "best of" or "out performance" swaps that require a payment based on the higher of the performance of a security and a commodity (other than a security). As discussed elsewhere in this release, the Commissions also believe that certain Title VII instruments may be mixed swaps if they meet specified conditions.

The Commissions also believe that the use of certain market standard agreements in the documentation of Title VII instruments should not in and of itself transform a Title VII instrument into a mixed swap. For example, many instruments are documented by incorporating by reference market standard agreements. Such agreements typically set out the basis of establishing a trading relationship with another party but are not, taken separately, a swap or security-based swap. These agreements also include termination and default events relating to one or both of the counterparties; such counterparties may or may not be entities that issue securities. The Commissions believe that the term "any agreement * * * based on * * * the occurrence of an event relating to a single issuer of a security," as provided in the definition of the term "security-based swap," was not intended to include such termination and default events relating to counterparties included in standard agreements that are incorporated by reference into a Title VII instrument. Therefore, an instrument would not be simultaneously a swap and a security-based swap (and thus not a mixed swap) simply by virtue of having incorporated by reference a standard agreement, including default and termination events relating to counterparties to the Title VII instrument.

The Commissions are adopting as proposed paragraph (a) of rule 1.9 under the CEA and rule 3a68–4 under the Exchange Act to define a "mixed swap" in the same manner as the term is defined in both the CEA and the Exchange Act. The Commissions also are adopting as proposed two rules to address the regulation of mixed swaps. First, paragraph (b) of rule 1.9 under the CEA and rule 3a68–4 under the Exchange Act will provide a regulatory framework with which parties to bilateral uncleared mixed swaps (*i.e.*, mixed swaps that are neither executed on or subject to the rules of a DCM, NSE, SEF, security-based SEF, or FBOT nor cleared through a DCO or clearing agency), as to which at least one of the parties is dually registered with both Commissions, will need to comply. Second, paragraph (c) of rule 1.9 under the CEA and rule 3a68–4 under the Exchange Act establishes a process for persons to request that the Commissions issue a joint order permitting such persons (and any other person or persons that subsequently lists, trades, or clears that class of mixed swap) to comply, as to parallel provisions only, with specified parallel provisions of either the CEA or the Exchange Act, and related rules and regulations (collectively "specified parallel provisions"), instead of being required to comply with parallel provisions of both the CEA and the Exchange Act.

Swap dealers and major swap participants will be comprehensively regulated by the CFTC, and security-based swap dealers and major security-based swap participants will be comprehensively regulated by the SEC. The Commissions recognize that there may be differences in the requirements applicable to swap dealers and security-based swap dealers, or major swap participants and major security-based swap participants, such that dually-registered market participants may be subject to potentially conflicting or duplicative regulatory requirements when they engage in mixed swap transactions. In order to assist market participants in addressing such potentially conflicting or duplicative requirements, the Commissions are adopting, as proposed with one modification explained below, rules that will permit dually-registered swap dealers and security-based swap dealers and dually-registered major swap participants and major security-based swap participants to comply with an alternative regulatory regime when they enter into certain mixed swaps under specified circumstances. The Commissions received no comments on the proposed rules.

Accordingly, as adopted, paragraph (b) of rule 1.9 under the CEA and rule 3a68–4 under the Exchange Act provide that a bilateral uncleared mixed swap, where at least one party is dually-registered with the CFTC as a swap dealer or major swap participant and with the SEC as a security-based swap dealer or major security-based swap participant, will be subject to all applicable provisions of the Federal securities laws (and SEC rules and regulations promulgated thereunder). The rules as adopted also provide that such mixed swaps will be subject to only the following provisions of the CEA (and CFTC rules and regulations promulgated thereunder):

Because mixed swaps are both security-based swaps and swaps, absent a joint rule or order by the Commissions permitting an alternative regulatory approach, persons who desire or intend to list, trade, or clear a mixed swap (or class thereof) will be required to comply with all the statutory provisions in the CEA and the Exchange Act (including all the rules and regulations thereunder) that were added or amended by Title VII with respect to swaps or security-based swaps. Such dual regulation may not be appropriate in every instance and may result in potentially conflicting or duplicative regulatory requirements. However, before the Commissions can determine the appropriate regulatory treatment for mixed swaps (other than the treatment discussed above), the Commissions will need to understand better the nature of the mixed swaps that parties want to trade. As a result, the Commissions proposed paragraph (c) of rule 1.9 under the CEA and rule 3a68–4 under the Exchange Act to establish a process pursuant to which any person who desires or intends to list, trade, or clear a mixed swap (or class thereof) that is not subject to the provisions of paragraph (b) of the rules (*i.e.,* bilateral uncleared mixed swaps entered into by at least one dual registrant) may request the Commissions to publicly issue a joint order permitting such person (and any other person or persons that subsequently lists, trades, or clears that class of mixed swap) to comply, as to parallel provisions only, with the specified parallel provisions, instead of being required to comply with parallel provisions of both the CEA and the Exchange Act. The Commissions received no comments on the proposed rules and are adopting the rules as proposed.

Security-Based Swap Agreements

SBSAs are swaps over which the CFTC has regulatory and enforcement authority but for which the SEC also has antifraud and certain other authority. The term "security-based swap agreement" is defined as a "swap agreement" (as defined in section 206A of the GLBA) of which "a material term is based on the price, yield, value, or volatility of any security or any group or index of securities, including any interest therein" but does not include a security-based swap.

The CEA does not contain a stand-alone definition of "security-based swap agreement," but includes the definition instead in subparagraph (A)(v) of the swap definition in CEA section 1a(47), 7 U.S.C. 1a(47). The only difference between these definitions is that the definition of SBSA in the Exchange Act specifically excludes security-based swaps (*See* section 3(a)(78)(B) of the Exchange Act, 15 U.S.C. 78c(a)(78)(B)), while the definition of SBSA in the CEA does not contain a similar exclusion. Instead, the exclusion for security-based swaps is placed in the general exclusions from the swap definition in the CEA (*See* CEA section 1a(47)(B)(x), 7 U.S.C. 1a(47)(B)(x)).

Although the Commissions believe it is not possible to provide a bright line test to define an SBSA, the Commissions believe that it is possible to clarify that certain types of swaps clearly fall within the definition of SBSA. For example, as the Commissions noted in the Proposing Release, a swap based on an index of securities that is not a narrow-based security index (*i.e.,* a broad-based security index) would fall within the definition of an SBSA under the Dodd-Frank Act. Similarly, an index CDS that is not based on a narrow-based security index or on the "issuers of securities in a narrow-based security index," as defined in rule 1.3(zzz) under the CEA and rule 3a68–1a under the Exchange Act, would be an SBSA. In addition, a swap based on a U.S. Treasury security or on certain other exempted securities other than municipal securities would fall within the definition of an SBSA under the Dodd-Frank Act.

The Commissions received no comments on the examples provided in the Proposing Release regarding SBSAs. Accordingly, the Commissions are not further defining SBSA beyond restating the examples above.

* * * *

CHAPTER 7

REGULATION OF COMMODITY POOLS AND TRADING ADVISORS

■ ■ ■

1. ADVISERS AND COMMODITY POOLS

A commodity pool is simply a collective investment trust or similar form of enterprise operated for the purpose of trading commodity interests. As one Court noted:

> Commodity pools, "the commodity-futures equivalent of a mutual fund," facilitate the participation of investors in the market. They are vehicles through which investors can aggregate their funds, allowing a commodity pool operator to invest them for a fee. The pooling of funds also allows the pool, and by extension its participants, to hold a diversified portfolio and ensures individual investors will not have to take delivery of commodities. Typically the pool is organized in the form of a business entity that limits the liability of individual investors. The amount of funds invested in commodity pools has grown immensely, from $75 million in 1976 to $600 billion in assets in 2005.

CFTC v. Equity Financial Group LLC, 572 F.2d 150, 155–156 (3d Cir. 2009), cert. denied, sub. nom. Shimer v. CFTC, 559 U.S. 991 (2010).

Any person or firm that sponsors, organizes or acts as an administrator to a commodity pool is a "commodity pool operator" (CPO). Pursuant to Section 4m of the Commodity Exchange Act (CEA) [7 U.S.C. § 6m], each person or firm that is defined to be a CPO must register as such.

Commodity pools are not themselves required to be registered pursuant to the CEA or Commodity Futures Trading Commission (CFTC) regulations. Instead of regulating the commodity pool itself, the CFTC regulates the operator of the pool, the CPO.

The CEA defines a commodity pool as "any investment trust, syndicate, or similar form of enterprise operated for the purpose of trading in commodity interests" regulated by the CEA, unless excluded by the CFTC. 7 U.S.C. § 1a(10).

The term CPO is defined in the CEA to be any person:

> engaged in a business that is of the nature of a commodity pool, investment trust, syndicate, or similar form of enterprise, and who, in connection therewith, solicits, accepts, or receives from others, funds, securities, or property, either directly or through capital contributions, the sale of stock or other forms of securities, or otherwise, for the purpose of trading in commodity interests, including any [transaction regulated by the CEA and not excluded by the CFTC]

7 U.S.C. § 1a(11).

The courts considering the issue of what type of activity requires CPO registration:

> require the following factors to be present in a commodity pool: (1) an investment organization in which the funds of various investors are solicited and combined into a single account for the purpose of investing in commodity futures contracts; (2) common funds used to execute transactions on behalf of the entire account; (3) participants share pro rata in accrued profits or losses from the commodity futures trading; and (4) the transactions are traded by a commodity pool operator in the name of the pool rather than in the name of any individual investor.

Lopez v. Dean Witter Reynolds, Inc., 805 F.2d 880 (9th Cir. 1986). See also, Nilsen v. Prudential-Bache, 761 F. Supp. 279, 292 (S.D.N.Y. 1991) (noting that essentially, a CPO is one who manages an investment fund, similar to a mutual fund, in which the assets of several investors are invested together with gains or losses shared pro rata by the participants.).

The person or firm who manages the trading of the commodity interests on behalf of a commodity pool must register as a commodity trading advisor (CTA) under the CEA. A CTA is often a person or firm who controls the trading of a customer's futures trading account and is not registered as an futures commission merchant (FCM) or introducing broker (IB).

A CTA is defined by the CEA "as any person who for compensation or profit, engages in the business of advising others, either directly or through publications, writings, or electronic media, as to the value of or the advisability of trading in" contracts regulated by the CEA. [7 U.S.C. § 1a(12)].

Excluded from the definition of a CTA are banks and trust companies and their employees, news reporters, or others involved in the print or electronic media, any lawyer, accountant, or teacher, and the publisher or producer of any print or electronic data of general and regular dissemination, including its employees, provided that such advice is "solely incidental to the conduct of their business or profession." Id. The CFTC was authorized to exempt other persons from the registration requirement and has done so in CFTC Regulation 4.14. [17 C.F.R. § 4.14].

Also exempted from registration as a CTA are firms "who, during the course of the preceding twelve months, has not furnished commodity trading advice to more than fifteen persons and who does not hold himself out generally to the public as a commodity trading advisor." [7 U.S.C. § 6m].

Any firm that meets the definitional tests of a CPO or CTA must register as such by filing a Form 7-R with the National Futures Association (NFA) and by complying with all of the other applicable regulatory requirements.

A collective investment trust or similar form of enterprise that trades in securities must register with the Securities and Exchange Commission (SEC) as an "investment company" under the Investment Company Act of 1940 (ICA). [15 U.S.C. §§ 80a–1 et seq.]. Likewise, the person or firm that manages the securities trading of an investment company, such as a mutual fund, or advises others on security investments must register as an "investment adviser" (IA) under the Investment Advisers Act of 1940 (IAA). [15 U.S.C. §§ 80a–1 et seq.]. As discussed below, certain limited exemptions apply to these registration categories.

IAs register with the SEC by filing a Form ADV. This form requires the IA to provide historical background and contact information about the advisory firm and its principals, a description of its trading strategies and other important disclosures. IAs file the Form ADV with the SEC. FINRA does not handle applications for registration by IAs.

A particular concern on the part of the SEC and CFTC has been whether hedge funds must register as CTAs or IAs. As noted elsewhere:

> The hedge fund is a relatively new entrant into the financial world, tracing its history back to A.W. Jones & Co., a firm that was founded in 1949 by Alfred Winslow Jones. That company rewarded its managers with an incentive fee of 20% of the profits gained from the collective investment of its clients' funds. By 1961, Jones's hedge fund had obtained a 21% annual rate of return, with gains of over 1,000 percent in one ten year period. Even so, Jones's fund operated in obscurity until an article published in 1966 in Fortune magazine described its operations. It then became the model for other funds. By 1969, there were about 150 hedge funds operating in the United States. Those funds held some $1 billion invested by about 3,000 investors. The funds used borrowed money to obtain leverage, engaged in exotic

derivative and other complex transactions and often sold short. By 1994, some 800 hedge funds were holding $75 billion in assets. The number of hedge funds had jumped to 6,000 as the new century began, and they were managing some $600 billion. In 2004, there were some 7,000 hedge funds managing an estimated $850 billion. Assets under management by hedge funds reached an estimated $1.2 trillion in 2006.

Hedge fund corporate governance sought to place investment decisions in the hands of its managers. Investors are not treated as shareholders in the enterprise who have a say in governance.

Another distinctive feature of hedge funds is their management structure. Unlike mutual funds, which must comply with detailed requirements for independent boards of directors, and whose shareholders must explicitly approve of certain actions, domestic hedge funds are usually structured as limited partnerships to achieve maximum separation of ownership and management. In the typical arrangement, the general partner manages the fund (or several funds) for a fixed fee and a percentage of the gross profits from the fund. The limited partners are passive investors and generally take no part in management activities.

Jerry W. Markham, Mutual Fund Scandals—A Comparative Analysis of the Role of Corporate Governance in the Regulation of Collective Investments, 3 Hastings Bus. L. J. 67, 99–101 (2006).

GOLDSTEIN V. SEC
451 F.3d 873 (D.C. Cir. 2006)

RANDOLPH, CIRCUIT JUDGE:

This is a petition for review of the Securities and Exchange Commission's regulation of "hedge funds" under the Investment Advisers Act of 1940, 15 U.S.C. § 80b–1 *et seq. See* Registration Under the Advisers Act of Certain Hedge Fund Advisers, 69 Fed. Reg. 72,054 (Dec. 10, 2004) (codified at 17 C.F.R. pts. 275, 279) ("*Hedge Fund Rule*"). Previously exempt because they had "fewer than fifteen clients," 15 U.S.C. § 80b–3(b)(3), most advisers to hedge funds must now register with the Commission if the funds they advise have fifteen or more "shareholders, limited partners, members, or beneficiaries." 17 C.F.R. § 275.203(b)(3)–2(a). * * *

"Hedge funds" are notoriously difficult to define. The term appears nowhere in the federal securities laws, and even industry participants do not agree upon a single definition. *See, e.g.*, SEC Roundtable on Hedge Funds (May 13, 2003) (comments of David A. Vaughan), *available at* http://www.sec.gov/spotlight/hedgefunds/hedge-vaughn.htm   (citing fourteen different definitions found in government and industry publications). The term is commonly used as a catch-all for "any pooled investment vehicle that is privately organized, administered by professional investment managers, and not widely available to the public." President's Working Group On Financial Markets, Hedge Funds, Leverage, And The Lessons Of Long-Term Capital Management 1 (1999) ("*Working Group Report*"); *see also* Implications Of The Growth Of Hedge Funds: Staff Report To The United States Securities And Exchange Commission 3 (2003) ("*Staff Report*") (defining "hedge fund" as "an entity that holds a pool of securities and perhaps other assets, whose interests are not sold in a registered public offering and which is not registered as an investment company under the Investment Company Act").

Hedge funds may be defined more precisely by reference to what they are *not*. The Investment Company Act of 1940, 15 U.S.C. § 80a–1 *et seq.*, directs the Commission to regulate any issuer of securities that "is or holds itself out as being engaged primarily . . . in the business of investing, reinvesting, or trading in securities." *Id.* § 80a–3(a)(1)(A). Although this definition nominally describes hedge funds, most are exempt from the Investment Company Act's coverage because they have one hundred or fewer beneficial owners and do not offer their securities to the public, *id.* § 80a–3(c)(1), or because their investors are all "qualified" high net-worth individuals or institutions, *id.* § 80a–3(c)(7). Investment vehicles that remain private and available only to highly sophisticated investors have historically been understood not to present the same dangers to public markets as more widely available investment companies, like mutual funds. *See Staff Report*, *supra*, at 11–12.

Exemption from regulation under the Investment Company Act allows hedge funds to engage in very different investing behavior than their mutual fund counterparts. While mutual funds, for example, must register with the Commission and disclose their investment positions and financial condition, *id.* §§ 80a–8, 80a–29, hedge funds typically remain secretive about their positions and strategies, even to their own investors. *See Staff Report*, *supra*, at 46–47. The Investment Company Act places significant restrictions on the types of transactions registered investment companies may undertake. Such companies are, for example, foreclosed from trading on margin or engaging in short sales, 15 U.S.C. § 80a–12(a)(1), (3), and must secure shareholder approval to take on significant debt or invest in certain types of assets, such as real estate or commodities, *id.* § 80a–13(a)(2). These transactions are all core elements of most hedge funds' trading strategies. *See Staff Report*, *supra*, at 33–43. "Hedging" transactions, from which the term "hedge fund" developed, *see* Willa E. Gibson, *Is Hedge Fund Regulation Necessary?*, 73 TEMP. L. REV. 681, 684–85 & n.18 (2000), involve taking both long and short positions on debt and equity securities to reduce risk. This is still the most frequently used hedge fund strategy, *see Staff Report, supra*, at 35, though there are many others. Hedge funds trade in all sorts of assets, from traditional stocks, bonds, and currencies to more exotic financial derivatives and even non-financial assets. *See, e.g.*, Kate Kelly, *Creative Financing: Defying the Odds, Hedge Funds Bet Billions on Movies*, WALL ST. J., Apr. 29, 2006, at A1. Hedge funds often use leverage to increase their returns.

Another distinctive feature of hedge funds is their management structure. Unlike mutual funds, which must comply with detailed requirements for independent boards of directors, 15 U.S.C. § 80a–10, and whose shareholders must explicitly approve of certain actions, *id.* § 80a–13, domestic hedge funds are usually structured as limited partnerships to achieve maximum separation of ownership and management. In the typical arrangement, the general partner manages the fund (or several funds) for a fixed fee and a percentage of the gross profits from the fund. The limited partners are passive investors and generally take no part in management activities. *See Staff Report, supra*, at 9–10, 61.

Hedge fund advisers also had been exempt from regulation under the Investment Advisers Act of 1940, 15 U.S.C. § 80b–1 *et seq.* ("Advisers Act"), a companion statute to the Investment Company Act, and the statute which primarily concerns us in this case. Enacted by Congress to "substitute a philosophy of full disclosure for the philosophy of *caveat emptor*" in the investment advisory profession, *SEC v. Capital Gains Research Bureau, Inc.*, 375 U.S. 180, 186, 84 S. Ct. 275, 11 L. Ed. 2d 237 (1963), the Advisers Act is mainly a registration and anti-fraud statute. Non-exempt "investment advisers" must register with the Commission, 15 U.S.C. § 80b–3, and all advisers are prohibited from engaging in fraudulent or deceptive practices, *id.* § 80b–6. By keeping a census of advisers, the Commission can better respond to, initiate, and take remedial action on complaints against fraudulent advisers. *See id.* § 80b–4 (authorizing the Commission to examine registered advisers' records).

Hedge fund general partners meet the definition of "investment adviser" in the Advisers Act. *See* 15 U.S.C. § 80b–2(11) (defining "investment adviser" as one who "for compensation, engages in the business of advising others, either directly or through publications or writings, as to the value of securities or as to the advisability of investing in, purchasing, or selling securities"); *Abrahamson v. Fleschner*, 568 F.2d 862, 869–71 (2d Cir. 1977) (holding that hedge fund general partners are "investment advisers"), *overruled in part on other grounds by Transamerica Mortgage Advisors, Inc. v. Lewis*, 444 U.S. 11, 100 S. Ct. 242, 62 L. Ed. 2d 146 (1979). But they usually satisfy the "private adviser exemption" from registration in § 203(b)(3) of the Act, 15 U.S.C. § 80b–3(b)(3). That section exempts "any investment adviser who during the course of the preceding twelve months has had fewer than fifteen clients and who neither holds himself out generally to the public as an investment adviser nor acts as an investment adviser to any investment company registered under [the Investment Company Act]." *Id.* As applied to limited partnerships and other entities, the Commission had interpreted this provision to refer to the partnership or entity itself as the adviser's "client." *See* 17 C.F.R. § 275.203(b)(3)–1. Even the largest hedge fund managers usually ran fewer than fifteen hedge funds and were therefore exempt.

Although the Commission has a history of interest in hedge funds, *see Staff Report*, *supra*, at app. A, the current push for regulation had its origins in the failure of Long-Term Capital Management, a Greenwich, Connecticut-based fund that had more than $125 billion in assets under management at its peak. In late 1998, the fund nearly collapsed. Almost all of the country's major financial institutions were put at risk due to their credit exposure to Long-Term, and the president of the Federal Reserve Bank of New York personally intervened to engineer a bailout of the fund in order to avoid a national financial crisis. *See generally* Roger Lowenstein, When Genius Failed: The Rise And Fall Of Long-Term Capital Management (2000).

A joint working group of the major federal financial regulators produced a report recommending regulatory changes to the regime governing hedge funds, and the Commission's staff followed with its own report about the state of hedge fund regulation. Drawing on the conclusions in the Staff Rep*ort*, the Commission—over the dissent of two of its members—issued the rule under review in December 2004 after notice and comment. The Commission cited three recent shifts in the hedge fund industry to justify the need for increased regulation. First, despite the failure of Long-Term Capital Management, hedge fund assets grew by 260 percent from 1999 to 2004. *Hedge Fund Rule*, 69 Fed. Reg. at 72,055. Second, the Commission noticed a trend toward "reutilization" of hedge funds that increased the exposure of ordinary investors to such funds. This retailization was driven by hedge funds loosening their investment requirements, the birth of "funds of hedge funds" that offered shares to the public, and increased investment in hedge funds by pension funds, universities, endowments, foundations and other charitable organizations. *See id.* at 72,057–58. Third, the Commission was concerned about an increase in the number of fraud actions brought against hedge funds. *See id.* at 72,056–57. Concluding that its "current regulatory program for hedge fund advisers [was] inadequate," *id.* at 72,059, the Commission moved to require hedge fund advisers to register under the Advisers Act so that it could gather "basic information about hedge fund advisers and the hedge fund industry," "oversee hedge fund advisers," and "deter or detect fraud by unregistered hedge fund advisers," *id.*

The *Hedge Fund Rule* first defines a "private fund" as an investment company that (a) is exempt from registration under the Investment Company Act by virtue of having fewer than one hundred investors or only qualified investors, *see* 15 U.S.C. § 80a–3(c)(1), (7); (b) permits its investors to redeem their interests within two years of investing; and (c) markets itself on the basis of the "skills, ability or expertise of the investment adviser." 17 C.F.R. § 275.203(b)(3)–1(d)(1). For these private funds, the rule then specifies that "[f]or purposes of section 203(b)(3) of the [Advisers] Act (15 U.S.C. § 80b–3(b)(3)), you must count as clients the shareholders, limited partners, members, or beneficiaries . . . of [the] fund." *Id.* § 275.203(b)(3)–2(a). The rule had the effect of requiring most hedge fund advisers to register by February 1, 2006.

The dissenting Commissioners disputed the factual predicates for the new rule and its wisdom. Goldstein makes some of the same points but the major thrust of his complaint is that the Commission's action misinterpreted § 203(b)(3) of the Advisers Act, a charge the Commission dissenters also leveled. This provision exempts from registration "any investment adviser who during the course of the preceding twelve months has had fewer than fifteen *clients*." 15 U.S.C. § 80b–3(b)(3) (emphasis added). The Act does not define "client." Relying on *Chevron, U.S.A., Inc. v. NRDC*, 467 U.S. 837, 842–43, 104 S. Ct. 2778, 81 L. Ed. 2d 694 (1984), the Commission believes this renders the statute "ambiguous as to a method for counting clients." Br. for Resp. 21. There is no such rule of law. The lack of a statutory definition of a word does not necessarily render the meaning of a word ambiguous, just as the presence of a definition does not necessarily make the meaning clear. A definition only pushes the problem back to the meaning of the defining terms. *See Alarm Indus. Commc'ns Comm. v. FCC*, 327 U.S. App. D.C. 412, 131 F.3d 1066, 1068–70 (D.C. Cir. 1997); *Doris Day Animal League v. Veneman*, 354 U.S. App. D.C. 216, 315 F.3d 297, 298–99 (D.C. Cir. 2003).

If Congress employs a term susceptible of several meanings, as many terms are, it scarcely follows that Congress has authorized an agency to choose *any* one of those meanings. As always, the "words of the statute should be read in context, the statute's place in the overall statutory scheme should be considered, and the problem Congress sought to solve should be taken into account" to determine whether Congress has foreclosed the agency's interpretation. *PDK Labs. Inc. v. DEA*, 360 U.S. App. D.C. 344, 362 F.3d 786, 796 (D.C. Cir. 2004) ("*PDK I*") (internal quotation marks omitted).

"Client" may mean different things depending on context. The client of a laundry occupies a very different position than the client of a lawyer. Even for professional representation, the specific indicia of a client relationship—contracts, fees, duties, and the like—vary with the profession and with the particulars of the situation. An attorney-client relationship, for example, can be formed without any signs of formal "employment." *See* Restatement (Third) Of The Law Governing Lawyers § 14 & cmt. c (2000) ("The client need not necessarily pay or agree to pay the lawyer; and paying a lawyer does not by itself create a client-lawyer relationship. . . ."). Matters may be very different for the client of, say, an architectural firm. * * *

. . . [T]he Advisers Act strongly suggests that Congress did not intend "shareholders, limited partners, members, or beneficiaries" of a hedge fund to be counted as "clients." Although the statute does not define "client," it does define "investment adviser" as "any person who, for compensation, engages in the business of advising others, either *directly* or through publications or writings, as to the value of securities or as to the advisability of investing in, purchasing, or selling securities." 15 U.S.C. § 80b–2(11) (emphasis added). An investor in a private fund may benefit from the adviser's advice (or he may suffer from it) but he does not receive the advice *directly*. He invests a portion of his assets in the fund. The fund manager—the adviser—controls the disposition of the pool of capital in the fund. The adviser does not tell the *investor* how to spend his money; the investor made that decision when he invested in the fund. Having bought into the fund, the investor fades into the background; his role is completely passive. If the person or entity controlling the fund is not an "investment adviser" to each individual investor, then *a fortiori* each investor cannot be a "client" of that person or entity. These are just two sides of the same coin.

This had been the Commission's view until it issued the new rule. As recently as 1997, it explained that a "client of an investment adviser typically is provided with individualized advice that is based on the client's financial situation and investment objectives. In contrast, the investment adviser of an investment company need not consider the individual needs of the company's shareholders when making investment decisions, and thus has no obligation to ensure that each security purchased for the company's portfolio is an appropriate investment for each shareholder." Status of Investment Advisory Programs Under the Investment Company Act of 1940, 62 Fed. Reg. 15,098, 15,102 (Mar. 31, 1997). The Commission said much the same in 1985 when it promulgated a rule with respect to investment companies set up as limited partnerships rather than as corporations. The "client" for purposes of the fifteen-client rule of § 203(b)(3) is the limited partnership not the individual partners. *See* 17 C.F.R. § 275.203(b)(3)–1(a)(2). As the Commission wrote in proposing the rule, when "an adviser to an investment pool manages the assets of the pool on the basis of the investment objectives of the participants as a group, it appears appropriate to view the pool—rather than each participant—as a client of the adviser." *Safe Harbor Proposed Rule*, 50 Fed. Reg. at 8741. * * *

Here, even if the Advisers Act does not foreclose the Commission's interpretation, the interpretation falls outside the bounds of reasonableness. "An agency construction of a statute cannot survive judicial review if a contested regulation reflects an action that exceeds the agency's authority. It does not matter whether the unlawful action arises because the disputed regulation defies the plain language of a statute or because the agency's construction is utterly unreasonable and thus impermissible." *Aid Ass'n for Lutherans v. United States Postal Serv.*, 355 U.S. App. D.C. 221, 321 F.3d 1166, 1174 (D.C. Cir. 2003); *see also id.* at 1177–78; *Am. Library Ass'n v. FCC*, 365 U.S. App. D.C. 353, 406 F.3d 689, 699 (D.C. Cir. 2005). * * *

The *Hedge Fund Rule* might be more understandable if, over the years, the advisory relationship between hedge fund advisers and investors had changed. The Commission cited, as justification for its rule, a rise in the amount of hedge fund assets, indications that more pension funds and other institutions were investing in hedge funds, and an increase in fraud actions involving hedge funds. All of this may be true, although the dissenting Commissioners doubted it. But without any evidence that the role of fund advisers with respect to investors had undergone a transformation, there is a disconnect between the factors the Commission cited and the rule it promulgated. That the Commission wanted a hook on which to hang more comprehensive regulation of hedge funds may be understandable. But the Commission may not accomplish its objective by a manipulation of meaning. * * *

The petition for review is granted, and the *Hedge Fund Rule* is vacated and remanded.

So ordered.

NOTES

1. After the Goldstein case was decided, hundreds of accounts held at a firm operated by Bernard Madoff, whose firm was registered as an investment adviser with the SEC, were found to have been defrauded through a giant Ponzi scheme. That scandal led Congress to amend the IAA. First, the fifteen client exemption noted in the Goldstein case was repealed. Second, IAs that manage less than $100,000,000 in assets could no longer register as an IA with the SEC but now have to register with each state in which they act as an IA. This meant that the managers of most large hedge funds would have to register with the SEC as an IA.

2. Ironically, Madoff had registered with the SEC as an IA after the adoption of the SEC's Hedge Fund Rule. However, unlike many hedge funds, Madoff did not resign its registration after the decision in the Goldstein case. Madoff was thus subject to the SEC's jurisdiction before and after the scandal broke, but his giant fraud went undetected by the SEC. Jerry W. Markham,

Merging the SEC and CFTC—A Clash of Cultures, 78 U. Cinn. L. Rev. 537, 563–54 (2009).

SEC ADOPTS DODD-FRANK ACT AMENDMENTS TO INVESTMENT ADVISERS ACT FOR IMMEDIATE RELEASE 2011–133

Washington, D.C., June 22, 2011—The Securities and Exchange Commission today adopted rules that require advisers to hedge funds and other private funds to register with the SEC, establish new exemptions from SEC registration and reporting requirements for certain advisers, and reallocate regulatory responsibility for advisers between the SEC and states.

The rules adopted by the Commission implement core provisions of the Dodd-Frank Wall Street Reform and Consumer Protection Act regarding investment advisers, including those that advise hedge funds.

"These rules will fill a key gap in the regulatory landscape," said SEC Chairman Mary L. Schapiro. "In particular, our proposal will give the Commission, and the public, insight into hedge fund and other private fund managers who previously conducted their work under the radar and outside the vision of regulators." * * *

A large number of individuals and institutions invest a significant amount of assets in private funds, such as hedge funds and private equity funds. However, until the passage of the Dodd-Frank Act, advisers managing those assets were subject to little regulatory oversight.

With the Dodd-Frank Act, Congress closed this regulatory gap by generally extending the registration requirements under the Investment Advisers Act to the advisers of these funds. The new law also provided the Commission with the ability to require the limited number of advisers to private funds that will not have to register to file reports about their business activities.

Further, in acknowledging the Commission's limited examination resources—and in light of the new responsibilities for private fund advisers—the Dodd-Frank Act reallocated regulatory responsibility for certain mid-sized investment advisers to the state securities authorities.

For many years, advisers to private funds have been able to avoid registering with the Commission because of an exemption that applies to advisers with fewer than 15 clients—an exemption that counted each fund as a client, as opposed to each investor in a fund. As a result, some advisers to hedge funds and other private funds have remained outside of the Commission's regulatory oversight even though those advisers could be managing large sums of money for the benefit of hundreds of investors.

Title IV of the Dodd-Frank Act eliminated this private adviser exemption. Consequently, many previously unregistered advisers, particularly those to hedge funds and private equity funds, will have to register with the Commission and be subject to its regulatory oversight, rules and examination.

These advisers will be subject to the same registration requirements, regulatory oversight, and other requirements that apply to other SEC-registered investment advisers. To provide these advisers with a window to meet their new obligations, the transition provisions the Commission is adopting today will require these advisers to be registered with the Commission by March 30, 2012. * * *

Since 1996, regulatory responsibility for investment advisers has been divided between the Commission and the states, primarily based on the amount of money an adviser manages for its clients. Under existing law, advisers generally may not register with the Commission unless they manage at least $25 million for their clients.

The Dodd-Frank Act raises the threshold for Commission registration to $100 million by creating a new category of advisers called "mid-sized advisers." A mid-sized adviser, which generally may not register with the Commission and will be subject to state registration, is defined as an adviser that:

Manages between $25 million and $100 million for its clients.

Is required to be registered in the state where it maintains its principal office and place of business.

Would be subject to examination by that state, if required to register.

As a result of this amendment to the Investment Advisers Act, about 3,200 of the current 11,500 registered advisers will switch from registration with the Commission to registration with the states. These advisers will continue to be subject to the Advisers Act's general anti-fraud provisions.

The Commission is adopting amendments to several of its current rules and forms to:

Reflect the higher threshold required for Commission registration.

Provide a buffer to prevent advisers from having to frequently switch between Commission and state registration.

Clarify when an adviser will be a mid-sized adviser.

Facilitate the transition of advisers between federal and state registration in accordance with the new requirements. Advisers registered with the Commission will have to declare that they are permitted to remain registered in a filing in the first quarter of 2012, and those no longer eligible for Commission registration will have until June 28, 2012 to complete the switch to state registration.* * *

As previously described, the Dodd-Frank Act eliminated the private adviser exemption and created three new exemptions for:

Advisers solely to venture capital funds.

Advisers solely to private funds with less than $150 million in assets under management in the United States.

Certain foreign advisers without a place of business in the United States.

The Commission is adopting rules that would implement these exemptions and define various terms.

The Dodd-Frank Act amended the Advisers Act to exempt from registration advisers that only manage venture capital funds, and directed the Commission to define the term "venture capital fund." The Commission is adopting a definition of "venture capital fund" that is designed to effect Congress' intent in enacting this exemption.

Under the definition, a venture capital fund is a private fund that:

Invests primarily in "qualifying investments" (generally, private, operating companies that do not distribute proceeds from debt financings in exchange for the fund's investment in the company); may invest in a "basket" of non-qualifying investments of up to 20 percent of its committed capital; and may hold certain short-term investments.

Is not leveraged except for a minimal amount on a short-term basis.

Does not offer redemption rights to its investors.

Represents itself to investors as pursuing a venture capital strategy.

Under a grandfathering provision, funds that began raising capital by the end of 2010 and represented themselves as pursuing a venture capital strategy would generally be considered venture capital funds. The Commission is adopting this approach because it could be difficult or impossible for advisers to conform these pre-existing funds, which generally have terms in excess of 10 years, to the new definition.

The Commission also is adopting a rule that would implement the new statutory exemption for private fund advisers with less than $150 million in assets under management in the United States. The rule largely tracks the provision of the statute.

The Dodd-Frank Act also amended the Advisers Act to provide for an exemption from registration for foreign advisers that do not have a place of business in the United States, and have:

Less than $25 million in aggregate assets under management from U.S. clients and private fund investors.

Fewer than 15 U.S. clients and private fund investors.

The Commission is adopting rules to define certain terms included in the statutory definition of "foreign private adviser" in order to clarify the application of the foreign private adviser exemption and reduce the potential burdens for advisers that seek to rely on it. The rule incorporates definitions set forth in other Commission rules, all of which are likely to be familiar to foreign advisers active in the U.S. capital markets.

http://www.sec.gov/news/press/2011/2011-133.htm

CFTC v. SAVAGE
611 F.2d 270 (9th Cir. 1979)

SNEED, CIRCUIT JUDGE:

This appeal raises several questions regarding the proper interpretation of the Commodity Exchange Act (Act), 7 U.S.C. ss 1–24. Defendant-appellant Savage appeals from an order and judgment of permanent injunction entered on a motion for summary judgment. Savage was one of several defendants in an action brought by the Commodity Futures Trading Commission (CFTC) in the United States District Court for the Central District of California. Each of the other defendants have consented to permanent injunctions or have not pursued appeals. The district court on May 6, 1977 permanently enjoined appellant Savage from engaging in future violations of antifraud, fictitious sale and commodity trading-advisor registration provisions of the Act. We note jurisdiction under 28 U.S.C. s 1291 and affirm in part, reverse in part, and remand for further proceedings.

On October 23, 1974, to remedy perceived abuses in commodity transactions, Congress extensively amended the Commodity Exchange Act by enacting the Commodity Futures Trading Commission Act of 1974, Pub.L.No.93–463, 88 Stat. 1389. The 1974 Act created the CFTC, an independent federal regulatory agency, to administer the Act and enforce its provisions. Congress determined that "(t)he public interest . . . requires that these markets operate under close scrutiny so that they serve their legitimate market functions." H.R.Rep.No.93–975, 93rd Cong.,

2d Sess. 34 (1974). The CFTC, as one aspect of this scrutiny, was empowered to go directly into federal court to seek injunctive relief restraining any person from violating the Act. 7 U.S.C. s 13a–1. The substantive content of the regulatory framework for commodity market professionals created in 1974 included a broad definition of the term "commodity trading advisor," registration and record-keeping requirements, and antifraud standards analogous to those in other federal securities laws.[3]

The CFTC brought this action July 1, 1976 under 7 U.S.C. s 13a–1. The complaint contained six counts, only three of which apply to the appellant. It sought preliminary and permanent injunctions against appellant, the American International Trading Company (AITC), and twelve other individual defendants, including employees of AITC and floor brokers at the MidAmerica Commodity Exchange (MACE), a contract market registered with the CFTC. Appellant Savage was a member of MACE; he traded on the floor for his own account and was not registered in any capacity with the CFTC. The complaint charged appellant and others with various fraudulent activities which operated to defraud the customers of AITC. All of the defendants except appellant and two others, all of whom resided in Chicago and worked at MACE, also in Chicago, allowed consent decrees to be entered against them.

Only three counts III, IV and V contain allegations against the appellant:

Count III. In Count III, the complaint alleged that Savage and others violated prohibitions against fraud and fictitious sales contained in sections 4b and 4c of the Act, 7 U.S.C. ss 6b & 6c. The complaint charged that Savage, by arrangement, took the opposite side of commodity contract trades from AITC customers in two contexts. First, the complaint charged that a series of prearranged transactions in soy beans and silver occurred on April 17 and 18, 1975. In these transactions, Savage bought contracts when contracts were sold for the account of customers of the

---

[3] The definition of "commodity trading advisor" is found in 7 U.S.C. s 2, which provides in pertinent part:

The term "commodity trading advisor" shall mean any person who, for compensation or profit, engages in the business of advising others, either directly or through publications or writings, as to the value of commodities or as to the advisability of trading in any commodity for future delivery on or subject to the rules of any contract market, or who for compensation or profit, and as part of a regular business, issues or promulgates analyses or reports concerning commodities; but does not include (i) any bank or trust company, (ii) any newspaper reporter, newspaper columnist, newspaper editor, lawyer, accountant, or teacher, (iii) any floor broker or futures commission merchant, (iv) the publisher of any bona fide newspaper, news magazine, or business or financial publication of general and regular circulation including their employees, (v) any contract market, and (vi) such other persons not within the intent of this definition as the Commission may specify. by rule, regulation, or order: Provided, That the furnishing of such services by the foregoing persons is solely incidental to the conduct of their business or profession.

AITC Managed Account Program, and Savage sold futures contracts simultaneously with the purchase of futures contracts for the accounts of AITC customers. Savage sustained losses with respect to AITC customers who had deficits in their accounts and enjoyed profits on transactions with AITC customers who had credit balances in their accounts. As a net effect of these transactions, Savage's losses and gains substantially offset, leaving him with only a small gain, and AITC customer funds shifted between accounts. In addition, Count III alleged that during at least the period July 9 to September 9, 1975, Savage engaged in or aided and abetted prearranged trades between himself and AITC customers. Savage allegedly profited by becoming the buyer in respect to AITC customer sell orders and the seller in respect to AITC customer buy orders.

The complaint alleged in Count IV that since April 21, 1975, Savage violated section 4m of the Act, 7 U.S.C. s 6m, by operating as a commodity trading advisor without registering with the CFTC. The CFTC takes the position that Savage operated as an advisor to the customers of AITC's Managed Account Program through Melvin Berman, who made the investment decisions for AITC accounts. The complaint also alleged that Savage prepared portions of a commodity advisory letter.

Count V. Count V charged violations of section 4o of the Act, 7 U.S.C. s 6o. That section forbade a commodity trading advisor "registered under this Act . . . to employ any device, scheme, or artifice to defraud any client . . . or . . . to engage in any transaction, practice, or course of business which operates as a fraud or deceit upon any client. . . ." The specific actions alleged to constitute the violation were those outlined in Count III of the complaint.

Prior to its 1978 amendment, it read the same except that the phrase "registered under this Act" followed after the term "any commodity trading advisor or commodity pool operator."

With its complaint, the CFTC filed eleven lengthy affidavits of its investigators, AITC customers, and a former AITC employee. Seven more affidavits were filed July 15, 1976. A preliminary injunction issued July 16, 1976, restraining appellant from violating section 4b of the Act by cheating or attempting to cheat a customer by making false reports or engaging in offsetting trades with a customer; from engaging in "wash" or accommodation trades; from holding himself out to the public as a commodity trading advisor without being registered pursuant to section 4m of the Act; from taking the offsetting position from that of customers of AITC and engaging in fictitious trades involving the accounts of AITC customers while acting as a commodity trading advisor to AITC, in violation of section 4o of the Act. (C.T. at 783.). * * *

It is undisputed that the appellant has never been registered as a commodity trading advisor. Although he previously sought registration, such registration was denied, and the denial upheld. Savage v. Commodity Futures Trading Commission, 548 F.2d 192, 197 (7th Cir. 1977). Savage now claims he need not have registered under section 4m because he is within an exception to the registration requirement in section 4m, Viz., he "has not furnished commodity trading advice to more than fifteen persons and . . . does not hold himself out generally to the public as a commodity trading advisor." We disagree. We hold that Savage does not come within the scope of this exception.

7 U.S.C. s 2 defines a "commodity trading advisor" as "any person who, for compensation or profit, engages in the business of advising others, either directly or through publications or writings. . . ." This language demonstrates some concern for indirectly, as well as directly, conveyed advice. The CFTC staff has interpreted this provision liberally.

> We do not believe that the definition of commodity trading advisor requires that the "compensation or profit" flow directly from the person or persons advised. It is sufficient that the compensation or profit is to result wholly or in part from the furnishing of services. . . .

CFTC Interpretive Letter No. 75–11 (1975–77 Transfer Binder) Comm.Fut.L.Rep. (CCH) P 20,098 (1975) at 20,763 n. 6. The exemption upon which appellant depends relieves from registration only advisors who, during the preceding twelve months, have not Furnished commodity trading advice to more than fifteen persons. Furnished implies indirect as well as direct provision. The CFTC staff in a related context has taken the position which lends support to our view, that nonpaying as well as paying clients must be joined for determining the exemption's availability. CFTC Interpretive Letter No. 76–9 (1975–77 Transfer Binder) Comm. Fut. L. Rep. (CCH) P 20,151 (1976).

The Act was enacted to remedy widespread abuses in commodity trading. We have recognized that "(r)emedial statutes should be liberally construed and should be interpreted (when that is possible) in a manner tending to discourage attempted evasions by wrongdoers." Westinghouse Electric Corp. v. Pacific Gas & Electric Co., 326 F.2d 575, 580 (9th Cir. 1964) (quoting Scarborough v. Atlantic Coast Line R. R., 178 F.2d 253, 258 (4th Cir. 1949)). In other security law contexts courts ordinarily defer to statutory purpose and narrowly construe exemptions from registration. See, e. g., Securities & Exchange Commission v. Ralston Purina Co., 346 U.S. 119, 73 S. Ct. 981, 97 L. Ed. 1494 (1953); Abrahamson v. Fleschner, 568 F.2d 862 (2d Cir. 1977), cert. denied, 436 U.S. 905, 98 S. Ct. 2236, 56 L.Ed.2d 403 (1978); Quinn & Co. v. Securities & Exchange Commission, 452 F.2d 943, 946 (10th Cir. 1971), cert. denied, 406 U.S. 957, 92 S. Ct. 2059, 32 L.Ed.2d 344 (1972). We believe our interpretation of section 4m is consistent with this emphasis.

The registration provisions of the Act serve an important purpose; registration assures a public source of information about those upon whom customers rely and protects the public from individuals unfit to act as advisors. Advisors should not be able to circumvent the congressionally-mandated registration scheme merely by the subterfuge of advising a person or entity who then operates as a conduit for trading advice to the actual advisees. If this were possible the registration requirement would serve little protective purpose at all. On the other hand, attributing the customers of an advisee to the advisor in all contexts would stretch the Act unjustifiably. Remedial intent must not become a rationalization for bending a statute to a court's will.

We interpret section 4m, 7 U.S.C. s 6m, to include within the persons to whom an advisor "furnishes" advice customers of an advisee when the advisor knows or should know that advice he gives is directly passed to those customers. The ultimate customers should be protected from the ultimate advisor in this situation. The fee the ultimate advisor receives will reflect the value of the advice to the ultimate customers. Absent the interpretation we have given the section, mere sham arrangements would shield those unqualified to be advisors from the registration and disclosure procedures.

AITC was a registered "futures commission merchant" under the Act. As such, AITC solicited and accepted orders for the purchase and sale of commodities for future delivery and promoted a "Managed Account Program" whereby customers placed money under the discretionary control of AITC. It had as many as 900 customers in that program. Melvin Berman was responsible for making the trading decisions for the managed account program. He was registered with the CFTC as a person associated with a futures commission merchant under 7 U.S.C. s 6k. The CFTC affidavits establish that Savage communicated trading advice to Melvin Berman and thereby to AITC itself. Savage did not communicate directly with AITC customers, although it is undisputed that he knew AITC managed a great number of customer accounts and that his advice was acted upon by AITC in its dealings for the benefit of managed account customers. Savage, by affidavit, merely asserted that he "at no time advised customers of AITC." Upon review of this summary judgment, we must decide whether appellant's denial that he "advised" AITC customers sufficiently creates an issue of fact as to whether he "furnished" advice to those customers within the meaning of section 4m.

The affidavits submitted by the CFTC support an inference that Savage knew that Melvin Berman and AITC acted upon his advice directly in making trading decisions for the managed account program. The advice did not, however, "flow through" to customers in the sense of given advice being actually communicated to AITC customers for those customers to then act upon. There is no indication that AITC acted as a mere conduit for physical passage of Savage's advice. Nevertheless, AITC customers entrusted funds to AITC and gave AITC discretion to enter commodity transactions on those customers' accounts. Savage, aware of this fact, gave advice to AITC knowing that AITC, on behalf of its customers, would incorporate that advice directly into actual transactions. Savage knew his advice impinged directly upon the fortunes of these ultimate customers; it was not merely a component of an independent investment model employed by AITC. These customers, well in excess of fifteen, are subject through this arrangement to the very risks Congress sought to eliminate by requiring registration. On these facts we find that Savage furnished commodity trading advice to more than fifteen individuals. His affidavits did not create a genuine issue of material fact.

In holding as we do, we are influenced by the interrelationship of the Act's registration provisions. If AITC had operated a commodity trading pool, appellant's relationship to the pool would have been disclosed in the pool's registration. 7 U.S.C. s 6n(1)(A) & (B). Or, if Savage supervised persons who solicited or accepted funds from customers of AITC, he would need to register as a person associated with a futures commission merchant. 7 U.S.C. s 6k. While these provisions do not apply here, they provide related but inapplicable protections. Instead, Savage provided trading advice to a futures commission merchant under unique circumstances. He knew that his advice became the direct basis for trades made by AITC on behalf of its managed account customers. Under these circumstances the district court did not err by finding no issue of material fact existed as to whether Savage furnished trading advice to more than fifteen persons within the meaning of the Act. We, therefore, affirm as to Count IV.

Section 4o of the Act, 7 U.S.C. s 6o (1), in its form at the time of the alleged violation, made it unlawful for "any commodity trading advisor . . . Registered under this Act . . . to employ any device, scheme or artifice to defraud any client . . . or prospective client" (emphasis added). Congress has since deleted the "registered under this Act" language, Pub.L.No.95–405, s 10, 92 Stat. 870 (1978). The amendment "makes it clear that persons engaged in activities which should require them to be registered . . . are subject to . . . Section 4o of the Act, even though those persons are not in fact registered with the Commission." H.R.Rep.No.1181, 95th Cong., 2d Sess. 20–21 (1978). Savage argues that because he was not registered at the time of this action, and because Congress had not yet changed the law, section 4o does not apply to him. The CFTC argues that section 4o applies to all those who Should have been registered under the Act, and therefore . . . appellant is subject to the section.

No prior court to our knowledge has interpreted this provision. The fact that Congress deleted "registered under this Act" might suggest that a gap in the law existed prior to amendment. We consider the amendment to be a clarification, however. The purpose of the statute supports this interpretation of congressional intent. It would be anomalous indeed if an advisor could escape the fiduciary duties of section 4o by avoiding required registration. This would frustrate a principal purpose of the Act. * * *

Savage's opposition affidavit admits that he entered into most of the alleged transactions. He contends, however, that his affidavit brings into dispute a critical element of each section of the Act that he is charged with having violated. He argues that violation of these sections requires a fraudulent intent or knowing violation the element of scienter. His affidavit denies: (1) an intent to enter into prearranged accommodation trades; (2) knowledge that he entered into trades away from the market price; and (3) an intent to serve as an intermediary to shift funds between accounts of AITC customers. If, as appellant contends, a fraudulent intent or knowing violation is necessary to run afoul of sections 4b, 4c and 4o (1) of the Act, then his intent and knowledge are material to the violation and his opposition affidavit has raised a genuine issue of material fact.

We say this because appellant's intent and knowledge are particularly within his personal comprehension. As this court has noted, "(g)enerally, when intent is at issue, a jury should be allowed to draw its own inferences from the undisputed facts unless all reasonable inferences defeat appellants' claims." Mutual Fund Investors v. Putnam Management Co., supra, 553 F.2d at 624. We cannot say that the facts put forward in the CFTC affidavits raise inferences so reasonable as to defeat Savage's claims. If resolution of the dispute would pit appellant's word against the CFTC's affiants, the decision is one for a trier of fact. * * *

We conclude, therefore, that summary judgment was improper provided Savage is correct in his view that to violate sections 4b, 4c, and 4O (1) of the Act a fraudulent intent or knowing violation is necessary. We now turn to this issue.

AFFIRMED as to judgment finding violations of sections 4m and 4O (1) (Counts IV and V), REVERSED and REMANDED as to judgment finding violations of sections 4b and 4c (Count III).

NOTES

1. As the result of the Savage decision, a person or a firm that managed a pool that had fifteen or more investors was required to register as a CTA with the CFTC. However, the CFTC changed its approach in 2003 by adopting a "sophisticated investor" exemption from CPO registration. That amendment exempted from registration hedge fund managers and others that were advising only wealthy and sophisticated clients. That exemption

was designed to conform to the then existing SEC pre-Hedge Fund Rule that did not look through entities to count clients for purposes of the fifteen person exemption from registration as an adviser. In February 2012, however, as noted in the Investment Company Institute case, infra, the CFTC again amended CFTC Regulation 4.5 [17 C.F.R. § 4.5] by repealing the changes made in 2003, thus bringing CFTC Regulation 4.5, with a small modification, back to its structure that had previously been in place.

2. With the addition of "swaps" within the definition of a "commodity interest" under the CEA as a result of the Dodd Frank Act, the number of registered CPOs that had previously either been exempt from the CPO registration requirements or were exempt from the definition of a CPO because the commodity pool only traded swaps and not futures contracts, increased dramatically in size. As of December 2013, there were over 1,800 firms registered as CPOs and another 2,600 firms registered as a CTA, both of which represented a large increase in just the past year.

3. The definition for a CTA under the CEA pretty much tracks that for the investment advisers under the Investment Advisers Act of 1940 except for the instruments on which they advise. There are, however, some nuances. For example, for reasons known only to history, the IAA spells the registrant as "adviser," while the CEA spells it as "advisor."

4. In SEC v. Lowe, 472 U.S. 181 (1985), the SEC sought to enjoin an investment advisor from publishing advice concerning securities without being registered as an IA under the IAA. The terms of that statute—as does the CEA—exempted bona fide newspapers from registration where they are of general and regular circulation. The Supreme Court concluded that Lowe's publication met the definition of a bona fide newspaper, even though it was published irregularly and contained mostly financial advice. The Supreme Court was of the view that registration was not required because the defendant was not providing personalized advice.

5. The CFTC did not embrace the decision in Lowe, arguing that the statutory language in the CEA is slightly different from that in the IAA, i.e., any advice in a newspaper must be incidental to the newspaper's business before it is exempt from CTA registration. See, CFTC v. Vartuli, 228 F.3d 94 (2d Cir. 2000) and Commodity Trend Service, Inc. v. CFTC, 233 F.3d 981 (7th Cir. 2000). However, because of legal uncertainty over whether the CFTC's approach was unconstitutional, the CFTC amended its Rule 4.14 [17 C.F.R. § 4.14] "to create an exemption from the Commodity Exchange Act's registration requirements for commodity trading advisors that provide standardized advice by means of media such as newsletters, prerecorded telephone newslines, Internet web sites, and non-customized computer software." CFTC, Exemption From Registration as a Commodity Trading Advisor, 65 Fed. Reg. 12938 (March 10, 2000).

2. DISCLOSURE REQUIREMENTS

One of the principal regulatory requirements for both CPOs and CTAs is the obligation to provide a Disclosure Document to each potential investor before he or she makes a purchase of the interest in the commodity pool or opens an account with the CTA. [See, 17 C.F.R. § 4.21.and 17 C.F.R. § 4.31]. A key part of that document is a risk disclosure statement that warns in stark terms of the high risk of derivatives trading, the effects of restrictions on the withdrawal of investor funds and the substantial fees that may attach to investments in commodity pools. [17 C.F.R. § 4.24].

Another centerpiece of the disclosure document is the track record provision, which requires that the Disclosure Document set forth the actual performance record in mandated form for the pool, other pools operated by the commodity pool operator, and commodity interest accounts directed by the pool's commodity trading advisor.

This requires disclosure of past trading performance, including the actual trading performance of the pool and its CTAs for the preceding five years. That performance must be in a form specified by CFTC regulations, which require, among other things, disclosure of the worst peak-to-valley drawdown during the most recent five calendar years. [17 C.F.R. § 4.25].

The Disclosure Document must also contain disclosures on other material aspects of the investment including, but not limited to:

1. Name and Address of the Commodity Pool and the CPO,

2. List of all officers and directors of the CPO,

3. Description of the trading strategies of the commodity pool,

4. Description of all potential risks that may result from an investment in the commodity pool,

5. Description of all management fees, commission costs and other expenses associated with an investment in the commodity pool,

6. Description of all potential conflicts of interest that may apply to the commodity pool,

7. Tax consequences associated with an investment in the commodity pool,

8. Past performance of the pool and of other pools operated by the CPO or managed by the CTA to the pool at issue, and

9. Certain prescribed disclaimers and disclosure legends.

Since the interests in the commodity pool constitute a "security," the sale of such interests must either be registered pursuant to Section 5 of the Securities Act of 1933 ("1933 Act") or qualify for an exemption from such registration. In addition, if the commodity pool also trades in securities, the pool may be required to register as an investment company under the ICA unless it qualifies for an exemption from such ICA registration.

Many investment companies that trade in commodity interests must now be registered with the CFTC following the amendments to CFTC Regulation 4.5 in February 2012. The CFTC sought to make it easier to comply with several of the disclosure requirements for commodity pools that are also investment companies regulated by the SEC. See, Harmonization of Compliance Obligations for Registered Investment Companies Required to Register as Commodity Pool Operators, 78 Fed. Reg. 52308 (Aug. 22, 2013). However, in the following case, one trade association, the Investment Company Institute, which represents mutual funds, challenged the CFTC's revision of CFTC Rule 4.5 [17 C.F.R. § 4.5].

INVESTMENT COMPANY INSTITUTE V. CFTC
720 F.3d 370 (D.C. Cir. 2013)

ESTELLE, SENIOR CIRCUIT JUDGE:

The Investment Company Institute and the Chamber of Commerce of the United States brought this action against the Commodity Futures Trading Commission (CFTC), seeking a declaratory judgment that recently adopted regulations of the Commission regarding derivatives trading were unlawfully adopted and invalid, and seeking to vacate and set aside those regulations and to enjoin their enforcement. The district court granted summary judgment in favor of the Commission. Because we agree with the district court that the Commission did not act unlawfully in promulgating the regulations at issue, we affirm.

The Commodity Exchange Act (CEA), Title 7, United States Code, Chapter 1, establishes and defines the jurisdiction of the Commodity Futures Trading Commission. Under this Act, the Commission has regulatory jurisdiction over a wide variety of markets in futures and derivatives, that is, contracts deriving their value from underlying assets. *See* 7 U.S.C. § 2(a). In addition to establishing the regulatory authority of the Commission, the CEA also directly imposes certain duties on regulated entities. As relevant here, the Act requires that Commodity Pool Operators (CPOs) register with CFTC and adhere to regulatory requirements related to such issues as investor disclosures, recordkeeping, and reporting. 7 U.S.C. §§ 6k, 6n; 17 C.F.R. §§ 4.20–4.27. The CEA defines CPOs as entities "engaged in a business that is of the nature of a commodity pool, investment trust, syndicate, or similar form of enterprise" that buy and sell securities "for the purpose of trading in commodity interests." 7 U.S.C. § 1a(11)(A)(i). The CEA, however, empowers CFTC to exclude an entity from regulation as a CPO if CFTC determines that the exclusion "will effectuate the purposes of" the statute. *Id.* § 1a(11)(B).

Since 1985, the Commission has exercised its authority to exclude "otherwise regulated" entities through § 4.5 of its regulations. *See* Commodity Pool Operators, 50 Fed. Reg. 15,868 (Apr. 23, 1985) (codified at 17 C.F.R. § 4.5). Under the version of § 4.5 that applied before amendments of 2003, otherwise regulated entities could claim exclusion by meeting certain regulatory conditions. These conditions included that the entity:

> (i)   Will use commodity futures or commodity options contracts solely for bona fide hedging purposes . . . [;] (ii) Will not enter into commodity futures and commodity options contracts for which the aggregate initial margin and premiums exceed 5 percent of the fair market value of the entity's assets . . . [;] (iii) Will not be, and has not been, marketing participations to the public as or in a commodity pool or otherwise as or in a vehicle for trading in the commodity futures or commodity options markets; [and,] (iv) Will disclose in writing to each prospective participant the purpose of and the limitations on the scope of the commodity futures and commodity options trading in which the entity intends to engage[.]

Id. at 15,883. These conditions were amended slightly in 1993, when CFTC promulgated a rule removing the bona fide hedging requirement and excluding bona fide hedging from the trading threshold. Commodity Pool Operators, 58 Fed. Reg. 6,371, 6,372 (Jan. 28, 1993). Under these conditions, there was no automatic exclusion for registered investment companies, or "RICs," regulated by the Securities and Exchange Commission pursuant to the Investment Company Act of 1940, 15 U.S.C. §§ 80a–1 to –64. Therefore, a commodity pool operator that was also a registered investment company was included within CFTC's regulatory definition of CPOs unless it met all of the § 4.5 requirements for exclusion.

In 2000, Congress enacted the Commodity Futures Modernization Act of 2000, Pub. L. No. 106–554, 114 Stat. 2763. That statute barred CFTC and SEC from regulating most "swaps," a type of derivative involving the exchange of cash flows from financial instruments. *See* 7 U.S.C. § 2(d). Responsive to the statutory change, the Commission amended its requirements for exclusion to eliminate the five percent ceiling. *See* Additional Registration and Other Regulatory Relief for

Commodity Pool Operators and Commodity Trading Advisors, 68 Fed. Reg. 47,221, 47,224 (Aug. 8, 2003). These 2003 amendments "effectively excluded RICs from the CPO definition," freeing registered investment companies from most CFTC CPO regulations. *Investment Company Institute v. CFTC*, 891 F. Supp. 2d 162, 172 (D.D.C. 2013). CFTC viewed its 2003 amendments as consistent with the deregulatory spirit of the 2000 statute. *See* 68 Fed. Reg. at 47,223.

In 2010, the Commission began shifting back to a more stringent regulatory framework. This shift came in the wake of the 2007–2008 financial crisis, which many attributed to poorly regulated derivatives markets, when Congress passed the Dodd-Frank Wall Street Reform and Consumer Protection Act, Pub. L. No. 111–203, 124 Stat. 1376 (2010) (codified as amended in scattered sections of the U.S. Code). As relevant here, Dodd-Frank repealed several statutory provisions that had excluded certain commodities transactions from CFTC oversight. *Id.* §§ 723, 734. Dodd-Frank also gave CFTC regulatory authority over swaps, and amended the statutory definition of commodity pool operators to include entities that trade swaps. *Id.* §§ 721(a), 722. Dodd-Frank, however, did not affect CFTC's authority to set exclusion requirements for CPOs.

After Congress passed Dodd-Frank, the National Futures Association (NFA), to which all CPOs must belong, filed a petition of rulemaking with CFTC requesting that CFTC amend § 4.5 to limit the scope of its exclusion for registered investment companies. *See* Petition of the National Futures Association, 75 Fed. Reg. 56,997 (Sept. 17, 2010). In NFA's view, mutual funds were using the relaxed § 4.5 standards to evade CFTC oversight of their derivative operations, reducing transparency and potentially harming the public because no other regulator had rules equivalent to CFTC's. *See Investment Company Institute*, 891 F. Supp. 2d at 175–76. Therefore, NFA asked CFTC to restore the trading threshold and public marketing prohibition requirements to § 4.5 for any registered investment company seeking exclusion from CPO status. *See* 75 Fed. Reg. at 56,998. In essence, NFA sought a return to the pre-2003 regulatory framework, but only for registered investment companies.

On February 11, 2011, CFTC proposed new regulations that would amend § 4.5 "to reinstate the pre-2003 operating criteria" for all registered investment companies. Commodity Pool Operators and Commodity Trading Advisors: Amendments to Compliance Obligations, 76 Fed. Reg. 7,976, 7,984 (Feb. 11, 2011). One notable difference from the 2003 framework is that because of Dodd-Frank's extension of CFTC authority to swaps, the regulations proposed that swaps be included in the trading thresholds. *See id.* at 7,989. The proposed regulations also required certified regular reports from CPOs, a requirement that would be contained in a new § 4.27. *See id.* at 7,978. CFTC provided four explanations for these proposed regulations: First, the regulations would align CFTC's regulatory framework "with the stated purposes of the Dodd-Frank Act." *Id.* Second, they would "encourage more congruent and consistent regulation of similarly situated entities among Federal financial regulatory agencies." *Id.* Third, they would "improve accountability and increase transparency of the activities of CPOs" and commodity pools. *Id.* Fourth, they would make it easier to collect data for the Financial Stability Oversight Council ("FSOC"), a new body created by Dodd-Frank charged with "identify[ing] risks to the financial stability of the United States." *Id.*; Dodd-Frank Act § 112 (codified at 12 U.S.C. § 5322).

After the public comment period expired, CFTC promulgated a Final Rule amending § 4.5 and adding § 4.27 largely as proposed. *See* Commodity Pool Operators and Commodity Trading Advisors: Compliance Obligations, 77 Fed. Reg. 11,252 (Feb. 24, 2012), as corrected due to Fed. Reg. errors in its original publication, 77 Fed. Reg. 17,328 (Mar. 26, 2012); *see also* 17 C.F.R. §§ 4.5, 4.27. The primary difference between the proposed rule and the Final Rule is that, to be eligible for exclusion, a RIC's non-bona fide hedging trading must be less than or equal to five percent of the liquidation value of the entity's portfolio, *or* the aggregate net notional value of such trading must be less than or equal to "100 percent of the liquidation value of the pool's portfolio." 77 Fed. Reg. at 11,283. As the appellants do not directly challenge the aggregate net notional value threshold, we decline to define it further and fill the Federal Reporter with irrelevant financial lingo.

In its Final Rule, CFTC justified its decision to return to the pre-2003 regulatory framework on the basis of "changed circumstances [that] warrant revisions to these rules." *Id.* at 11,275. According to CFTC, the 2003 "system of exemptions was appropriate because [registered investment companies] engaged in relatively little derivatives trading." *Id.* Since the 2003 amendments, however, such companies have engaged in "increased derivatives trading activities" and "now offer[ ] services substantially identical to those of registered entities [that] are not subject to the same regulatory oversight." *Id.* Given this changed circumstance, and Dodd-Frank's "more robust mandate to manage systemic risk and to ensure safe trading practices by entities involved in the derivatives markets," CFTC considered it necessary to narrow the exclusions from its derivatives regulation. *Id.* Following this rule change, RICs that do not satisfy the exclusion requirements must register with CFTC per § 4.5.

In adopting the heightened disclosure requirements, CFTC explained that "there currently is no source of reliable information regarding the general use of derivatives by registered investment companies." *Id.* Such information would be useful to CFTC and FSOC in performing their statutory mandates of regulating commodities trading and identifying systemic financial risks. *See id.* at 11,281.

Several commenters called the Commission's attention to possible inconsistencies with or redundancies to SEC compliance requirements. In response to those commenters, and concurrently with the issuance of the Final Rule, CFTC issued a notice of proposed rulemaking to harmonize CFTC and SEC's compliance requirements. *See* Harmonization of Compliance Obligations for Registered Investment Companies Required To Register as Commodity Pool Operators, 77 Fed. Reg. 11,345 (Feb. 24, 2012). In this notice, CFTC stated that it may change certain disclosure requirements to harmonize them with SEC requirements but, importantly, it does not plan to change the new reporting requirements promulgated in the Final Rule and contained in 17 C.F.R. § 4.27. *See id.; see also Investment Company Institute*, 891 F. Supp. 2d at 183. The § 4.27 reporting requirements, however, are suspended for registered investment companies until CFTC and SEC promulgate a Final Rule on harmonization. *See id.* at 183–84.

Appellants contend that CFTC violated the APA in its rulemaking by: (1) failing to address its own 2003 rationales for broadening CPO exemptions; (2) failing to comply with the Commodity Exchange Act and offering an inadequate evaluation of the rule's costs and benefits; (3) including swaps in the trading threshold, restricting its definition of bona fide hedging, and failing to justify the five percent threshold; and, (4) failing to provide an adequate opportunity for notice and comment. * * *

The appellants first contend that CFTC failed to explain why it changed from its more generous exemption requirements that had existed since 2003 to the more stringent requirements contained in the Final Rule. Though it is true that the Final Rule stated that investment companies are increasing their participation in derivatives markets, the 2003 rule was explicitly designed to promote liquidity in the commodities markets by making it easier for registered investment companies to participate in derivatives markets. CFTC, according to the appellants, completely failed to address the liquidity issue, and therefore its change in position was arbitrary and capricious.

We disagree. An agency changing course "need not demonstrate to a court's satisfaction that the reasons for the new policy are *better* than the reasons for the old one; it suffices that the new policy is permissible under the statute, that there are good reasons for it, and that the agency *believes* it to be better." *FCC v. Fox Television Stations, Inc.*, 556 U.S. 502, 515, 129 S. Ct. 1800, 173 L. Ed. 2d 738 (2009). * * *

Appellants next contend that CFTC failed to adequately consider the costs and benefits of the rule. The Commodity Exchange Act requires that CFTC "consider the costs and benefits" of its actions and "evaluate[ ]" those costs and benefits "in light of" five factors: "(A) considerations of protection of market participants and the public; (B) considerations of the efficiency, competitiveness, and financial integrity of futures markets; (C) considerations of price discovery; (D) considerations of sound risk management practices; and (E) other public interest considerations." 7 U.S.C. § 19(a)(2). As a reviewing court, "[o]ur role is to determine whether the [agency] decision was based on a consideration of the relevant factors and whether there has been a clear error of judgment." *Center for Auto Safety v. Peck*, 751 F.2d 1336, 1342, 243 U.S. App. D.C. 117 (D.C. Cir. 1985) (internal quotation marks omitted) (quoting *State Farm*, 463 U.S. at 43).

First, appellants argue that CFTC ignored existing SEC regulations that could provide the necessary information about investment companies' activities in derivatives markets. Appellants point to two recent cases in which we vacated SEC regulations because SEC had failed to address existing regulatory requirements to determine whether sufficient protections were already present. *See Business Roundtable v. SEC*, 647 F.3d 1144, 1154, 396 U.S. App. D.C. 259 (D.C. Cir. 2011); *American Equity Inv. Life Ins. Co. v. SEC*, 613 F.3d 166, 179, 392 U.S. App. D.C. 1 (D.C. Cir. 2010). According to the appellants, CFTC similarly failed to consider whether existing regulations made its proposed regulation unnecessary.

We are unconvinced. In its Final Rule, CFTC explicitly discussed SEC's oversight in the derivatives markets: "In its recent concept release regarding the use of derivatives by registered investment companies, the SEC noted that although its staff had addressed issues related to derivatives on a case-by-case basis, it had not developed a 'comprehensive and systematic approach to derivatives related issues.'" 77 Fed. Reg. at 11,255 (quoting Use of Derivatives by Investment Companies Under the Investment Company Act of 1940, 76 Fed. Reg. 55,237, 55,239 (Sept. 7, 2011)). CFTC surveyed the existing regulatory landscape and concluded that it "is in the best position to oversee entities engaged in more than a limited amount of non-hedging derivatives trading." *Id.; see also id.* at 11,278. CFTC found that its registration and reporting requirements could fill gaps in current regulations, explaining that only it has the authority "to take punitive and/or remedial action against registered entities for violations of the CEA or of the Commission's regulations." *Id.* at 11,254. It explained how the new § 4.27 forms would collect information from entities registered under § 4.5 that would not otherwise be collected by SEC. *See id.* at 11,275. Further, CFTC issued a harmonization proposal to ensure that its rules do not duplicate or contradict SEC regulations. *See* 77 Fed. Reg. 11,345. * * *

The appellants challenge three particular aspects of the Final Rule. The first is CFTC's decision to include swap transactions in the registration threshold, which has the effect of requiring more investment companies to register pursuant to § 4.5. The appellants claim that this decision was arbitrary and capricious because Dodd-Frank implemented a separate reporting framework with regard to swaps. Appellants contend that one of CFTC's responses to this claim, that participation in swaps would trigger the registration requirement even if CFTC based its threshold only on futures and options, is irrational and obviously incorrect.

Though we agree that this particular response offers "less than ideal clarity," CFTC gave sufficient other explanations for including swap trades in the § 4.5 trading threshold that we can "reasonably . . . discern[ ]" its rationale. *Bowman*, 419 U.S. at 286. The Final Rule explained that "[t]he Dodd-Frank Act amended the statutory definition of the terms 'commodity pool operator' and 'commodity pool' to include those entities that trade swaps," evidencing that swaps were a central concern of the statute. 77 Fed. Reg. at 11,258. The rule further explained that CFTC would use information obtained "from CPOs transacting in swaps" to "help to bring transparency to the swaps markets, as well as to the interaction of swaps and futures markets, protecting the participants in both markets from potentially negative behavior." *Id.* at 11,283. Given these goals, it was not arbitrary or capricious to include swaps in the § 4.5 trading threshold.

The second aspect of the rule challenged by the appellants is its definition of bona fide hedging transactions, a definition that the appellants claim is too narrow and should encompass risk management strategies in financial markets. This argument amounts to nothing more than another policy disagreement with CFTC, so we must reject it. CFTC adequately explained that it was rejecting the broader "risk management" definition because "bona fide hedging transactions are unlikely to present the same level of market risk [as risk management transactions] as they are offset by exposure in the physical markets." *Id.* at 11,256. It also found that the risk management definition would be difficult to "properly limit" and make its exclusion "onerous to enforce." *Id.* Given the deference appropriate to such expert determinations, we reject the appellants' challenge to this aspect of the rule. *See Rural Cellular Ass'n v. FCC*, 588 F.3d 1095, 1105, 388 U.S. App. D.C. 421 (D.C. Cir. 2009) ("The 'arbitrary and capricious' standard is particularly deferential in matters implicating predictive judgments. . . .").

We further reject the appellants' contention that this aspect of the rule must be vacated because the bona fide hedging definition was cross-referenced to another rule that was recently vacated. *See Int'l Swaps & Derivatives Ass'n v. CFTC*, 887 F. Supp. 2d 259 (D.D.C. 2012). The decision vacating the cross-referenced rule had nothing to do with the bona fide exception in this rule, and the fact that the definition here was cross-referenced instead of reproduced does not make it automatically invalid.

The third and final particular aspect of the rule challenged by the appellants is the five percent registration threshold for § 4.5, which the appellants argue is too low. Our cases explain the appropriate deference given to these types of agency determinations:

> It is true that an agency may not pluck a number out of thin air when it promulgates rules in which percentage terms play a critical role. When a line has to be drawn, however, [CFTC] is authorized to make a rational legislative-type judgment. If the figure selected by the agency reflects its informed discretion, and is neither patently unreasonable nor a dictate of unbridled whim, then the agency's decision adequately satisfies the standard of review.

WJG Telephone Co. v. FCC, 675 F.2d 386, 388–89, 218 U.S. App. D.C. 367 (D.C. Cir. 1982) (internal quotation marks and citations omitted). CFTC offered a reasoned explanation for its choice of five percent, finding that "trading exceeding five percent of the liquidation value of a portfolio evidences a significant exposure to the derivatives markets." 77 Fed. Reg. at 11,278. According to the Final Rule, the five percent threshold is appropriate because "it is possible for a commodity pool to have a portfolio that is sizeable enough that even if just five percent of the pool's portfolio were committed to margin for futures, the pool's portfolio could be so significant that the commodity pool would constitute a major participant in the futures market." *Id.* at 11,262 (quoting 76 Fed. Reg. at 7,985). We defer to CFTC's judgment and hold that adopting the five percent threshold was neither arbitrary nor capricious. * * *

For the foregoing reasons, the decision of the district court is *Affirmed.*

NOTES

1. The amendments to CFTC Rule 4.5 [17 C.F.R. 4.5], which were at the heart of the ICI case, merely added back regulations, with minor exceptions, that were previously in existence.

2. A more interesting issue was that the D.C. Court of Appeals held that the CFTC did not act unlawfully in promulgating the amendments to CFTC Rule 4.5. In another case, the D.C. federal district court held that the CFTC, in adopting regulations on position limits, did so unlawfully. See International Swaps and Derivatives Association, et al. v. U.S. Commodity Futures Trading Commission, No. 11–cv–2146 (RLW) (Sept. 28, 2012). That case was appealed by the CFTC to the D.C. Court of Appeals but, in November 2013, the CFTC withdrew its appeal as it chose instead to propose new regulations on position limits. It would have been interesting to see how

the D.C. Court of Appeals would have decided this case if the appeal was not withdrawn.

3. REPORTING AND RECORD-KEEPING REQUIREMENTS

CFTC Rule 4.22 [17 C.F.R. § 4.22] requires CPOs to supply their investors with monthly account statements containing a report on the pool's income and identifying changes in the pool's net asset value ("NAV"). NAV is a critical indicator to investors as to whether the pool is making a profit over its last reports. Increasing NAV is a strong attractant for new investments, while a declining NAV is an inducement for investors to exit the fund. This gives the CPO an incentive to manipulate NAV, as was the case for Bernie Madoff and others.

That rule further requires CPOs to supply those investors with an annual report containing audited financial statements certified by an independent public accountant. That accountant acts as a watchdog by reviewing and certifying that the CPO's annual financial reports are properly presented and that trading in the CPO account and NAV is correctly reported to pool participants.

There are certain exemptions available from these reporting requirements. One such exemption is found in CFTC Rule 4.13(a)(4) for commodity pools in which the participants are "qualified eligible persons" (QEPs) such as very wealthy individuals and institutional investors. [17 C.F.R. § 4.13(a)(4)]. CPOs claiming that exemption are not required to prepare and send monthly NAV statements to the investors in the exempt commodity pool. Instead, the exempt CPO is required to send those investors copies of the monthly account statements that the CPO receives from its FCM clearing firm. [17 C.F.R. § 4.13(c)(3)(i)]. CPOs claiming this exemption must give notice of that claim to the NFA. *Id.*

Like all registrants that deal with customers, there is a disclosure requirement for CTAs, namely that one must properly disclose all applicable risks and other elements of the trading activities so that the customer is fully aware of all such matters. For CTAs, this disclosure requirement is embedded in CFTC Rule 4.31. [17 C.F.R. § 4.31]. Each registered CTA must also provide their clients with a disclosure brochure that discloses the following:

1. Name, address and contact information of the CTA

2. Name and background on each officer and director of the CTA

3. Trading strategy to be employed by the CTA for the customer's account

4.   All applicable risk factors

5.   All applicable conflicts of interest

6.   Past performance record of the CTA including, but not limited to, number of accounts managed by the CTA, amount of assets under management by the CTA, performance record of its accounts in table form

7.   Management and incentive fee arrangements

8.   Methods to close an account and terminate trading by the CTA

SEC ADOPTS DODD-FRANK ACT AMENDMENTS TO INVESTMENT ADVISERS ACT FOR IMMEDIATE RELEASE 2011–133

Washington, D.C., June 22, 2011

When investment advisers register with the Commission, they provide information in their registration form that is not only used for registration purposes, but that is used by the Commission in its regulatory program to support its mission to protect investors.

To enhance its ability to oversee investment advisers to private funds, the Commission is requiring advisers to provide additional information about the private funds they manage. The information obtained as a result of these amendments will assist the Commission in fulfilling its increased responsibility for private fund advisers arising from the Dodd-Frank Act.

Under the amended adviser registration form, advisers to private funds will have to provide:

- Basic organizational and operational information about each fund they manage, such as the type of private fund that it is (e.g., hedge fund, private equity fund, or liquidity fund), general information about the size and ownership of the fund, general fund data, and the adviser's services to the fund.

- Identification of five categories of "gatekeepers" that perform critical roles for advisers and the private funds they manage (i.e., auditors, prime brokers, custodians, administrators and marketers).

These reporting requirements are designed to help identify practices that may harm investors, deter advisers' fraud, and facilitate earlier discovery of potential misconduct. And this information will provide for the first time a census of this important area of the asset management industry.

In addition, the Commission is adopting other amendments to the adviser registration form to improve its regulatory program. These amendments will require all registered advisers to provide more information about their advisory business, including information about:

- The types of clients they advise, their employees, and their advisory activities.

- Their business practices that may present significant conflicts of interest (such as the use of affiliated brokers, soft dollar arrangements and compensation for client referrals).

The rules also will require advisers to provide additional information about their non-advisory activities and their financial industry affiliations.

While many private fund advisers will be required to register, some of those advisers may not need to if they are able to rely on one of three new exemptions from registration under the Dodd-Frank Act, including exemptions for:

Advisers solely to venture capital funds.

Advisers solely to private funds with less than $150 million in assets under management in the U.S.

Certain foreign advisers without a place of business in the U.S.

The Commission can still impose certain reporting requirements upon advisers relying upon either of the first two of these exemptions ("exempt reporting advisers").

Under the new rules, exempt reporting advisers will nonetheless be required to file, and periodically update, reports with the Commission, using the same registration form as registered advisers.

Rather than completing all of the items on the form, exempt reporting advisers will fill out a limited subset of items, including:

Basic identifying information for the adviser and the identity of its owners and affiliates.

Information about the private funds the adviser manages and about other business activities that the adviser and its affiliates are engaged in that present conflicts of interest that may suggest significant risk to clients.

The disciplinary history (if any) of the adviser and its employees that may reflect on the integrity of the firm. Exempt reporting advisers will file reports on the Commission's investment adviser electronic filing system (IARD), and these reports will be publicly available on the Commission's website. These advisers will be required to file their first reports in the first quarter of 2012.

4. FRAUD STANDARDS

SEC v. CAPITAL GAINS RESEARCH BUREAU, INC.
375 U.S. 180 (1963)

MR. JUSTICE GOLDBERG delivered the opinion of the Court.

We are called upon in this case to decide whether under the Investment Advisers Act of 1940 the Securities and Exchange Commission may obtain an injunction compelling a registered investment adviser to disclose to his clients a practice of purchasing shares of a security for his own account shortly before recommending that security for long-term investment and then immediately selling the shares at a profit upon the rise in the market price following the recommendation. The answer to this question turns on whether the practice—known in the trade as "scalping"—"operates as a fraud or deceit upon any client or prospective client" within the meaning of the Act. We hold that it does and that the Commission may "enforce compliance" with the Act by obtaining an injunction requiring the adviser to make full disclosure of the practice to his clients.

The Commission brought this action against respondents in the United States District Court for the Southern District of New York. At the hearing on the application for a preliminary injunction, the following facts were established. Respondents publish two investment advisory services, one of which—"A Capital Gains Report"—is the subject of this proceeding. The Report is mailed monthly to approximately 5,000 subscribers who each pay an annual subscription price of $18. It carries the following description:

> "An Investment Service devoted exclusively to (1) The protection of investment capital. (2) The realization of a steady and attractive income therefrom. (3) The accumulation of CAPITAL GAINS thru the timely purchase of corporate equities that are proved to be undervalued."

Between March 15, 1960, and November 7, 1960, respondents, on six different occasions, purchased shares of a particular security shortly before recommending it in the Report for long-term investment. On each occasion, there was an increase in the market price and the volume of trading of the recommended security within a few days after the distribution of the Report. Immediately thereafter, respondents sold their shares of these securities at a profit. They did not disclose any aspect of these transactions to their clients or prospective clients.

On the basis of the above facts, the Commission requested a preliminary injunction as necessary to effectuate the purposes of the Investment Advisers Act of 1940. The injunction would have required respondents, in any future Report, to disclose the material facts concerning, *inter alia*, any purchase of recommended securities "within a very short period prior to the distribution of a recommendation . . .," and "the intent to sell and the sale of said securities . . . within a very short period after distribution of said recommendation. . . ."

The District Court denied the request for a preliminary injunction, holding that the words "fraud" and "deceit" are used in the Investment Advisers Act of 1940 "in their technical sense" and that the Commission had failed to show an intent to injure clients or an actual loss of money to clients. 191 F. Supp. 897. The Court of Appeals for the Second Circuit, sitting *en banc*, by a 5-to-4 vote accepted the District Court's limited construction of "fraud" and "deceit" and affirmed the denial of injunctive relief. 306 F.2d 606. The majority concluded that no violation of the Act could be found absent proof that "any misstatements or false figures were contained in any of the bulletins"; or that "the investment advice was unsound"; or that "defendants were being bribed or paid to tout a stock contrary to their own beliefs"; or that "these bulletins were a scheme to get rid of worthless stock"; or that the recommendations were made "for the purpose of endeavoring artificially to raise the market so that [respondents] might unload [their] holdings at a profit." *Id.*, at 608–609. The four dissenting judges pointed out that "the common-law doctrines of fraud and deceit grew up in a business climate very different from that involved in the sale of securities," and urged a broad remedial construction of the statute which would encompass respondents' conduct. *Id.*, at 614. We granted certiorari to consider the question of statutory construction because of its importance to the investing public and the financial community. 371 U.S. 967.

The decision in this case turns on whether Congress, in empowering the courts to enjoin any practice which operates "as a fraud or deceit upon any client or prospective client," intended to require the Commission to establish fraud and deceit "in their technical sense," including intent to injure and actual injury to clients, or whether Congress intended a broad remedial construction of the Act which would encompass nondisclosure of material facts. For resolution of this issue we consider the history and purpose of the Investment Advisers Act of 1940.

The Investment Advisers Act of 1940 was the last in a series of Acts designed to eliminate certain abuses in the securities industry, abuses which were found to have contributed to the stock market crash of 1929 and the depression of the 1930's. It was preceded by the Securities Act of 1933, the Securities Exchange Act of 1934, the Public Utility Holding Company Act of 1935, the Trust Indenture Act of 1939, and the Investment Company Act of 1940. A fundamental purpose, common to these statutes, was to substitute a philosophy of full disclosure for the philosophy of *caveat emptor* and thus to achieve a high standard of business ethics in the securities industry. As we recently said in a related context, "It requires but little appreciation . . . of what happened in this country during the 1920's and 1930's to realize how essential it is that the highest ethical standards prevail" in every facet of the securities industry. *Silver* v. *New York Stock Exchange*, 373 U.S. 341, 366.

The Public Utility Holding Company Act of 1935 "authorized and directed" the Securities and Exchange Commission "to make a study of the functions and activities of investment trusts and investment companies. . . ." Pursuant to this mandate, the Commission made an exhaustive study and report which included consideration of investment counsel and investment advisory services. This aspect of the study and report culminated in the Investment Advisers Act of 1940.

The report reflects the attitude—shared by investment advisers and the Commission—that investment advisers could not "completely perform their basic function—furnishing to clients on a personal basis competent, unbiased, and continuous advice regarding the sound management of their investments—unless all conflicts of interest between the investment counsel and the client were removed." The report stressed that affiliations by investment advisers with investment bankers, or corporations might be "an impediment to a disinterested, objective, or critical attitude toward an investment by clients. . . ."

This concern was not limited to deliberate or conscious impediments to objectivity. Both the advisers and the Commission were well aware that whenever advice to a client might result in financial benefit to the adviser—other than the fee for his advice—"that advice to a client might in some way be tinged with that pecuniary interest [whether consciously or] subconsciously motivated. . . ." The report quoted one leading investment adviser who said that he "would put the emphasis . . . on subconscious" motivation in such situations. It quoted a member of the Commission staff who suggested that a significant part of the problem was not the existence of a "deliberate intent" to obtain a financial advantage, but rather the existence "subconsciously [of] a prejudice" in favor of one's own financial interests. The report incorporated the Code of Ethics and Standards of Practice of one of the leading investment counsel associations, which contained the following canon:

> "[An investment adviser] should continuously occupy an impartial and disinterested position, as free as humanly possible

from the *subtle* influence of prejudice, *conscious or unconscious*; he should scrupulously avoid any affiliation, or any act, which subjects his position to challenge in this respect." (Emphasis added.)

Other canons appended to the report announced the following guiding principles: that compensation for investment advice "should consist exclusively of direct charges to clients for services rendered"; that the adviser should devote his time "exclusively to the performance" of his advisory function; that he should not "share in profits" of his clients; and that he should not "directly or indirectly engage in any activity which may jeopardize [his] ability to render unbiased investment advice." These canons were adopted "to the end that the quality of services to be rendered by investment counselors may measure up to the high standards which the public has a right to expect and to demand." One activity specifically mentioned and condemned by investment advisers who testified before the Commission was *"trading by investment counselors for their own account in securities in which their clients were interested. . . ."*

This study and report—authorized and directed by statute—culminated in the preparation and introduction by Senator Wagner of the bill which, with some changes, became the Investment Advisers Act of 1940. In its "declaration of policy" the original bill stated that

"Upon the basis of facts disclosed by the record and report of the Securities and Exchange Commission . . . it is hereby declared that the national public interest and the interest of investors are adversely affected—. . . (4) when the business of investment advisers is so conducted as to defraud or mislead investors, or to enable such advisers to relieve themselves of their fiduciary obligations to their clients. "It is hereby declared that the policy and purposes of this title, in accordance with which the provisions of this title shall be interpreted, are to mitigate and, so far as is presently practicable to eliminate the abuses enumerated in this section." S. 3580, 76th Cong., 3d Sess., § 202.

Hearings were then held before Committees of both Houses of Congress. In describing their profession, leading investment advisers emphasized their relationship of "trust and confidence" with their clients and the importance of "strict limitation of [their right] to buy and sell securities in the normal way if there is any chance at all that to do so might seem to operate against the interests of clients and the public." The president of the Investment Counsel Association of America, the leading investment counsel association, testified that the

"two fundamental principles upon which the pioneers in this new profession undertook to meet the growing need for unbiased investment information and guidance were, first, that they would limit their efforts and activities to the study of investment problems from the investor's standpoint, not engaging in any other activity, such as security selling or brokerage, which might directly or indirectly bias their investment judgment; and, second, that their remuneration for this work would consist solely of definite, professional fees fully disclosed in advance."

Although certain changes were made in the bill following the hearings, there is nothing to indicate an intent to alter the fundamental purposes of the legislation. The broad proscription against "any . . . practice . . . which operates . . . as a fraud or deceit upon any client or prospective client" remained in the bill from beginning to end. And the Committee Reports indicate a desire to preserve "the personalized character of the services of investment advisers," and to eliminate conflicts of interest between the investment adviser and the clients as safeguards both to "unsophisticated investors" and to "bona fide investment counsel." The Investment Advisers Act of 1940 thus reflects a congressional recognition "of the delicate fiduciary nature of an investment advisory relationship," as well as a congressional intent to eliminate, or at least to expose, all conflicts of interest which might incline an investment adviser—consciously or unconsciously—to render advice which was not disinterested. It would defeat the manifest purpose of the Investment Advisers Act of 1940 for us to hold, therefore, that Congress, in empowering the courts to enjoin any practice which operates "as a fraud or deceit," intended to require proof of intent to injure and actual injury to clients. * * *

We turn now to a consideration of whether the specific conduct here in issue was the type which Congress intended to reach in the Investment Advisers Act of 1940. It is arguable—indeed it was argued by "some investment counsel representatives" who testified before the Commission—that any "trading by investment counselors for their own account in securities in which their clients were interested . . ." creates a potential conflict of interest which must be eliminated. We need not go that far in this case, since here the Commission seeks only disclosure of a conflict of interests with significantly greater potential for abuse than in the situation described above. An adviser who, like respondents, secretly trades on the market effect of his own recommendation may be motivated—consciously or unconsciously—to recommend a given security not because of its potential for long-run price increase (which would profit the client), but because of its potential for short-run price increase in response to anticipated activity from the recommendation (which would profit the adviser). An investor seeking the advice of a registered investment adviser must, if the legislative purpose is to be served, be permitted to evaluate such overlapping motivations, through appropriate disclosure, in deciding whether an adviser is serving "two masters" or only one, "especially . . . if one of the masters happens to be economic self-interest." *United States* v. *Mississippi Valley Co.*, 364 U.S. 520, 549. Accordingly, we hold that the Investment Advisers Act of 1940 empowers the courts, upon a showing such as that made here, to require an adviser to make full and frank disclosure of his practice of trading on the effect of his recommendations. * * *

Experience has shown that disclosure in such situations, while not onerous to the adviser, is needed to preserve the climate of fair dealing which is so essential to maintain public confidence in the securities industry and to preserve the economic health of the country.

The judgment of the Court of Appeals is reversed and the case is remanded to the District Court for proceedings consistent with this opinion.

Reversed and remanded.

NOTES

1. The SEC adopted various rules under the antifraud provisions of Section 206 of the IA Act, the statute at issue in the Capital Gains case. SEC Rule 206(4)–2 [17 C.F.R. § 275.206(4)–2], for example, imposes custody requirements for customer assets held by registered investment advisers (the IA Custody Rule).

2. The IA Custody Rule requires "investment advisers who have custody or possession of funds or securities of clients to segregate the securities and to hold them in safekeeping and to set up a separate trust account in a bank for funds belonging to each client." 27 Fed. Reg. 2149 (March 16, 1962). See, Grede v. FCStone, LLC, No. 09 C 136 (N.D. Ill), in which Judge Zagel held that the IA Custody Rule was equal in scope and protection as customer segregated accounts required by the CEA and CFTC regulations. As of December 2013, this case is on appeal to the Seventh Circuit. See, Ronald H. Filler, Ask the Professor; How Will the Seventh Circuit Rule in Sentinel II?, 33 Fut. & Deriv. L. Rep. 21 (November 2013), which analyzed Judge Zagel's decision.

3. CTAs are not allowed to hold customer funds associated with CEA regulated transactions. Consequently, there is no need for a CFTC rule like the IA Custody Rule.

MESSER V. E.F. HUTTON & CO.
847 F.2d 673 (11th Cir. 1988)

PER CURIAM

Upon publication of the panel opinion [833 F.2d 909], the Commodity Futures Trading Commission (CFTC) moved this Court for leave to file a brief as amicus curiae in support of rehearing. The panel granted the motion and has since received the brief in addition to responses from appellant and appellees. * * *

The district court entered a judgment n.o.v. on Messer's Commodity Exchange Act (CEA) claim on the ground that fraud claims based upon promises of future action are not actionable under Florida law. It is clear that under certain circumstances a false promise to perform future services can support a claim under the CEA's antifraud provisions. See Apache Trading Corp. v. Toub, 816 F.2d 605, 610 (11th Cir.1987). Accordingly, we disagree with the district court's grounds for disposing of Messer's CEA claim. We, however, affirm the result reached by the district court on different grounds.

Messer's claim under the Commodity Exchange Act is brought under Section 6o(1), which states:

> (1) It shall be unlawful for any commodity trading advisor . . .
>   (A) to employ any device, scheme, or artifice to defraud any client or participant or prospective client or participant; or
>   (B) to engage in any transaction, practice, or course of business which operates as a fraud or deceit upon any client or participant or prospective client or participant.

7 U.S.C.A. § 6o(1) (West 1980).

Messer's claim under Section 6o(1) presents two possible grounds for liability: the opening of the account and the unauthorized trades. Neither the Supreme Court nor this Circuit has addressed the question of whether Section 6o(1) of the CEA contains a scienter requirement. After reviewing the language of the provision, interpretations of analogous statutes, and the sparse legislative history that accompanies Section 6o(1), we conclude that Section 6o(1)(A) contains the same scienter requirement as Section 10(b) and Rule 10b–5 of the federal securities laws, while Section 6o(1)(B) does not require proof of scienter.

The focus of our analysis is the language of Section 6o. Because the case law indicates that subsections (A) and (B) under Section 6o(1) should be analyzed differently, we will discuss each subsection separately. Section 6o(1)(A) prohibits financial advisers from "employ[ing] any device, scheme, or artifice to defraud any client." This language closely tracks two other antifraud provisions, Section 17(a)(1) of the Securities Act of 1933, 15 U.S.C.A. § 77q(a)(1), and Section 206(1) of the Investment Advisers Act (IAA), 15 U.S.C.A. § 80b–6(1). Both of these analogous provisions have been interpreted by binding precedent as requiring the same proof of [678] scienter as is required to establish a violation of Section 10(b) and Rule 10b–5 of the securities laws. Aaron v. SEC, 446 U.S. 680, 695–96, 100 S. Ct. 1945, 1954–55, 64 L. Ed. 2d 611 (1980) (interpreting Section 17(a)(1) of Securities Act of 1933); Steadman v. SEC,

603 F.2d 1126, 1134 (5th Cir.1979) (interpreting Section 206(1) of Investment Advisers Act). There is nothing in the language, purpose, or legislative history of Section 6o(1)(A) to justify giving it a different interpretation. See Bromberg & Lowenfels, Securities Fraud and Commodities Fraud § 4.6(453). Accordingly, we conclude that proof of a violation of Section 6o(1)(A) requires proof of scienter.

Based on this interpretation of Section 6o(1)(A), we find that Messer's 6o(1)(A) claim fails because the record does not provide an evidentiary basis for a reasonable juror to find that E.F. Hutton acted with the requisite scienter.

The Supreme Court has held that Section 10(b) and Rule 10b–5 are not violated in the absence of a showing of scienter—an intent to deceive, manipulate or defraud. Santa Fe Industries v. Green, 430 U.S. 462, 473–74, 97 S. Ct. 1292, 1300–01, 51 L. Ed. 2d 480 (1977); Ernst & Ernst v. Hochfelder, 425 U.S. 185, 193, 96 S. Ct. 1375, 1380, 47 L. Ed. 2d 668 (1976); see also Gochnauer v. A.G. Edwards & Sons, 810 F.2d 1042, 1046 (11th Cir.1987); cf. Aaron v. SEC, 446 U.S. 680, 695, 100 S. Ct. 1945, 1955, 64 L. Ed. 2d 611 (1980) (SEC required to prove scienter in actions to enjoin violations of Section 10(b) and Rule 10b–5). This Circuit has held that the scienter requirement in securities fraud cases can also be satisfied with a showing of knowing misconduct or severe recklessness. 4 Woods v. Barnett Bank of Fort Lauderdale, 765 F.2d 1004, 1010 (11th Cir.1985); Kennedy v. Tallant, 710 F.2d 711, 720 (11th Cir.1983). Severe recklessness and knowing misconduct are limited to "those highly unreasonable omissions or misrepresentations that involve not merely simple or inexcusable negligence, but an extreme departure from the standards of ordinary care." Woods, supra, 765 F.2d at 1010 (quoting Broad v. Rockwell International Corp., 642 F.2d 929, 961–62 (5th Cir.) (en banc), cert. denied, 454 U.S. 965, 102 S. Ct. 506, 70 L. Ed. 2d 380 (1981)). In applying this scienter requirement in the context of unauthorized trading on an account, we agree with the Ninth Circuit's opinion in Brophy v. Redivo, 725 F.2d 1218, 1221 (9th Cir.1984), that an unauthorized trade does not violate the antifraud provisions of the Securities Exchange Act unless it is accompanied by an intent to defraud or a willful and reckless disregard of the client's best interests. 725 F.2d at 1220–21; see, e.g., Shemtob v. Shearson, Hammill & Co., 448 F.2d 442, 445 [679] (2d Cir.1971); cf. Lincoln Commodity Services v. Meade, 558 F.2d 469, 474 (8th Cir.1977).

A review of the record persuades us that no reasonable juror could have concluded that E.F. Hutton made the unauthorized trades with the requisite scienter. The record shows that E.F. Hutton made the unauthorized trades because the value of Messer's T-bond holdings was dropping precipitously and it wanted to protect the account. The record also shows that the trades were made without Messer's authorization because he was out of town and could not be reached at the time the decision had to be made. While opinions might differ on whether or not the decision to straddle the account was a good business decision, the expert testimony at trial established that straddling an investment is a common and accepted industry practice to protect an account against extreme losses. Far from supporting a finding that E.F. Hutton made the unauthorized trades with intent to defraud or reckless disregard for Messer's best interest, it appears that Hutton made a reasonable decision well within the bounds of accepted industry practice designed to protect the account.

Messer argues that a reasonable jury could have found that E.F. Hutton acted in reckless disregard of his interests because there was evidence that E.F. Hutton was motivated by a desire to protect itself. There is no real dispute that Hutton did in fact act to protect its own interests; however, that does not mean that in so doing E.F. Hutton acted in reckless disregard of Messer's interests. E.F. Hutton, who would have been liable for any margin call on Messer's investment, attempted to protect itself from liability by preventing a decline in the value of Messer's portfolio. Accordingly, Hutton's interests and Messer's interests were aligned rather than being antagonistical. While Messer now claims that the actions were not in fact in his interest, that does not alter the fact that the actions were not taken in disregard of his welfare. We conclude that no reasonable jury could have found that E.F. Hutton acted with the requisite scienter and accordingly that the jury verdict in favor of Messer on his securities act claim cannot stand.

The language of Section 6o(1)(B) reads slightly differently, prohibiting advisers from "engag[ing] in any transaction, practice, or course of business which operates as a fraud or deceit upon any client." (Emphasis added.) This language tracks Section 17(a)(3) of the Securities Act of 1933 and Section 206(2) of the Investment Advisers Act, which have been interpreted as not requiring proof of scienter. Aaron, 446 U.S. at 697, 100 S. Ct. at 1956 (interpreting Section 17(a)(3) of Securities Act of 1933); SEC v. Capital Gains Research Bureau, Inc., 375 U.S. 180, 195, 84 S. Ct. 275, 284, 11 L. Ed. 2d 237 (1963) (interpreting Section 206(2) of IAA); see also Steadman, 603 F.2d at 1134 (Section 206(2) of IAA). These courts reasoned that the phrase "operates as" focused the force of the prohibition on the effect of the action rather than on the actor's state of mind, thereby indicating that Congress did not intend to require proof of scienter to establish a violation. Aaron, 446 U.S. at 697, 100 S. Ct. at 1956; Capital Gains, 375 U.S. at 195, 84 S. Ct. at 284. Again, we find no reason to distinguish the interpretations of these analogous statutory provisions from the interpretation of Section 6o(1)(B).

Even with this interpretation of Section 6o(1)(B), we conclude that no reasonable juror could have concluded that E.F. Hutton's actions in placing the straddle on Messer's account in fact "operate[d] as a fraud or deceit" upon Messer. Even given that E.F. Hutton breached its contract with Messer, as the jury found, it does not necessarily follow that the breach of contract operated as a fraud or deceit on Messer. The facts and circumstances surrounding the transactions do not establish a course of unauthorized trading taking place during normal market conditions, see, e.g., Haltmier v. Commodity Futures Trading Comm'n, 554 F.2d 556, 562 (2d Cir.1977), or a "churning" case where excessive trading is carried out in order to generate commissions, see e.g., Thompson v. Smith Barney, Harris Upham & Co., 709 F.2d 1413, 1416–17 [680] (11th Cir.1983), both situations which do involve deceit and fraud. In contrast, E.F. Hutton made two isolated trades within a short period of time in response to what it reasonably perceived to be a dangerously dropping market. While it undeniably made the trades without Messer's authorization, it did so at least in part because Messer was not available to authorize the trades or otherwise respond to the changing market situation. Messer was notified as soon as it was possible to notify him that the trades had in fact been made and was given the opportunity to restore the account to its original condition by posting the required margin. In addition, as previously noted, E.F. Hutton offered to waive its commission on the trades. No reasonable juror could conclude that these facts amount to fraud or deceit. Accordingly, we AFFIRM the district court's entry of a judgment n.o.v. on Messer's CEA claim.

NOTE

1. The Sixth Circuit in First National Monetary Corp. v. Weinberger, 819 F.2d 1334 (1987) distinguished the scienter requirement in Section 4o of the CEA for CPOs and CTAs from those in the general antifraud provision in Section 4b of the CEA [7 U.S.C. § b], which, as described in Chapter 8, requires scienter. The court held that, under certain provisions of Section 4o, all that is required to be shown is that the individual acted intentionally to make statements that were not true. It is not necessary to show that the individual acted with the intent to defraud. The court noted that Section 4o focuses on the effect of the conduct and not on the intent of the actor.

5. ORDER ALLOCATION SCHEMES

STEPHENS, INC. V. GELDERMANN, INC.
962 F.2d 808 (8th Cir. 1992)

BEAM, CIRCUIT JUDGE.

Stephens, Inc., an Arkansas corporation, brought an action in federal district court against Geldermann, Inc., a Chicago based commodity futures merchant, for losses allegedly sustained through a house account

Stephens maintained at Geldermann. Stephens raised a variety of claims based on state and federal law, seeking punitive as well as compensatory damages. The district court, through summary judgment or directed verdict, dismissed several of these claims, including one based on the Racketeering Influenced and Corrupt Organizations Act (RICO), 18 U.S.C. §§ 1961–1968. Stephens' claims alleging violations of the Commodity Exchange Act, fraud, conspiracy to defraud, and breach of contract went to a jury, which returned a verdict in favor of Stephens for $1,381,000 in compensatory damages and $1,000,000 in punitive damages. Although the jury did not specify the basis of Geldermann's liability, the verdict form required that punitive damages be premised on a finding of either fraud or conspiracy. After trial, Geldermann requested, and received, a $600,000 set-off against the verdict for funds which Stephens had voluntarily ceded to another party involved in the litigation. Geldermann appeals claiming that (1) the district court improperly admitted prejudicial hearsay; (2) Stephens failed to prove proximate cause for certain damages and, regardless, such damages were speculative; and (3) the district court erred in permitting the jury to consider punitive damages and in failing to adequately review the award. Stephens cross-appeals, arguing that the district court erred (1) in dismissing its RICO claim and (2) in granting Geldermann's motion for a set-off. We affirm on all issues.

In May 1982, Stephens opened a commodity trading account at Geldermann, number 15233, in order to trade with Stephens' own funds (Stephens Account). A senior officer of Stephens, John Markle, had discretion and control over the account. About the same time, unbeknownst to Stephens, Markle opened another account at Geldermann, number 15245, in the name of his mother, Mercedes McCambridge (McCambridge Account). McCambridge alleged that she gave Markle approximately $1,000,000 to $1,100,000 to invest in certificates of deposit and other conservative investments. According to McCambridge, Markle assured her that he was following her investment directions.

Markle traded both accounts through Geldermann. A dedicated phone line ran from Markle's office at Stephens in Little Rock, Arkansas, to Geldermann's desk at the Chicago Board of Trade. Markle simply would pick up the phone in his office and direct a Geldermann employee in Chicago to buy or sell specific commodity futures. When Markle placed his orders, he never told the Geldermann employee the number of the account being traded. Under Commodity Futures Trading Commission (CFTC) regulations, however, a broker must ask a trader for the number of the account traded and write that number on the order ticket. 17 C.F.R. § 1.35(a–1)(1). In direct violation of the CFTC regulations, Geldermann employees permitted Markle to assign his trades to either the Stephens or the McCambridge Account at the end of the day, after he knew which trades had been profitable. Internal Geldermann memoranda dated from May to July 1984, supported an inference that Geldermann suspected trading improprieties involving the McCambridge Account, but actively concealed the Account's existence from Stephens to avoid losing Markle's business.

Between 1982 and 1987, the Stephens Account suffered trading losses of $5,267,638.74 and Stephens paid Geldermann commissions and fees of $959,597.53 for a total loss of $6,227,236.27. The McCambridge Account, however, performed unusually well (92% of the account's trades were profitable) and realized a total profit of $854,444.58 with commissions and fees of $167,608.92. On October 6, 1987, Geldermann finally informed Stephens about the McCambridge Account and its unusual pattern of profitability. According to Stephens, Geldermann did so only because Stephens had learned a day earlier that Markle had been operating another account in Mercedes McCambridge's name at the Elders Commodity Firm in Chicago.

Stephens began to investigate Markle's trading activities and confronted him on October 7, 1987. According to the testimony of two Stephens officers, Markle initially denied any wrongdoing, but, at several later meetings, admitted to defrauding Stephens. Markle also indicated that he had received help and, on at least one occasion, specifically stated that "Geldermann" had helped him. During the later meetings, Markle also attempted to negotiate a settlement with Stephens. Near the end of the discussions, for example, Markle offered Stephens $600,000 to be paid after Mercedes McCambridge's death. Stephens rejected the offer on November 13, 1987, demanding at least $1,000,000 within the next few weeks. Markle responded that he would need a month to work something out. At the same meeting, Warren Stephens, the president and chief executive officer of Stephens, promised Markle that Stephens would not sue him, but instead planned to sue Geldermann. Markle appeared relieved and again stated that he had been given help with his scheme. This meeting proved to be the last one between Markle and Stephens because shortly thereafter, Markle killed himself.

At the time Markle's scheme was uncovered, the McCambridge Account contained approximately $1,200,000. Geldermann transferred the funds to an account at Stephens in McCambridge's name. When McCambridge declared an intention to withdraw the funds, Stephens brought an action in state court to recover them as the proceeds of Markle's scheme to defraud Stephens. Stephens and McCambridge eventually reached a settlement whereby each received $600,000 from the McCambridge Account. Stephens further agreed to indemnify McCambridge for any liability to Geldermann and, in return,

McCambridge assigned any claim she had against Geldermann to Stephens.

At the end of the trial, the jury was asked to determine whether Geldermann was liable to either Stephens or McCambridge for the losses they each alleged to have suffered. The jury had previously learned that both Stephens and McCambridge had received $600,000 from the McCambridge Account and the court instructed the jury in separate instructions to offset any damages awarded to either Stephens or McCambridge by any monies either had already received. The jury returned a verdict in favor of Stephens against Geldermann and awarded Stephens $1,381,000 in compensatory damages and $1,000,000 in punitive damages. As to McCambridge's claims, however, the jury found in favor of Geldermann.

After trial, Geldermann requested the district court to off-set the verdict in Stephens' favor by the $600,000 that McCambridge had received in the settlement. Geldermann argued that the jury's verdict against McCambridge demonstrated that Stephens' claim to the funds in the McCambridge Account as proceeds of Markle's fraud was superior to McCambridge's claim. The funds, therefore, always belonged to Stephens and the $600,000 McCambridge received was a voluntary transfer from Stephens. Geldermann thus asserted that a set-off was necessary to prevent double recovery by Stephens. The district court agreed, and granted Geldermann's motion.

Geldermann contends that the district court improperly admitted prejudicial hearsay statements. The court permitted the two Stephens officers who had confronted Markle, Phillip Shellabarger and Warren Stephens, to testify about the statements Markle had made to them during their various conversations with him. Although Geldermann conceded that Markle's confession to defrauding Stephens was admissible, it objected to the portions of Markle's statements indicating that he had help. Relying on our decision in Smith v. Updegraff, 744 F.2d 1354, 1366 n.7 (8th Cir. 1984), the district court admitted the disputed hearsay as statements against interest made by an unavailable declarant, see Fed. R. Evid. 804(b)(3). Although we agree with Geldermann that the district court erred in admitting the disputed portions of Markle's statements, we believe that this error was harmless. * * *

The issue here, therefore, is whether those portions of Markle's statements implicating Geldermann were truly against his interest when made. We believe they were not. Stephens had accused Markle of serious fraud and had begun negotiations with Markle to settle its claims against him. Although Markle's statements admitting to the fraud were clearly against his interest, his statements implicating Geldermann were not necessarily so. Under the circumstances, it is possible that Markle was attempting to shift Stephens' attention from himself to Geldermann and thereby improve his position with Stephens in the negotiations. As such, his statements do not contain the indicia of reliability necessary for admission under Rule 804(b)(3).

Nonetheless, we have reviewed the record and conclude that the error was harmless. Substantial evidence existed to demonstrate that Geldermann facilitated Markle's scheme. In direct violation of federal regulations, Geldermann employees failed to require Markle to declare account numbers when placing orders. Moreover, internal Geldermann memoranda indicated that Geldermann actively concealed the existence of the McCambridge Account from Stephens and implied that Geldermann suspected or knew Markle may have been acting improperly. The improper admission of Markle's statement that he had "help" from Geldermann was, therefore, harmless.

Geldermann contends that the evidence at trial was not sufficient to support the compensatory damages that the jury awarded to Stephens. * * *

The evidence, when viewed most favorably to Stephens, provides sufficient support for the jury's conclusion that Geldermann's actions proximately caused damages to Stephens exceeding the profits contained in the McCambridge Account. In particular, Stephens presented an expert witness, Edward Horwitz, who testified about Markle's trading activities. Horwitz concluded that Markle was not simply skimming-off profitable trades otherwise made in the normal course of business. Horwitz explained that because Markle defrauded Stephens by allocating certain profitable trades to the McCambridge Account, he needed to initiate trades in order to create opportunities for such allocation. Markle, therefore, had an incentive to order trades so as to maximize the opportunities for profitable transactions, irrespective of the net profitability of the trades as a whole. Markle then allocated certain profitable trades to the McCambridge Account, and the remainder, whatever the net gain or loss, to the Stephens Account. Thus, according to Horwitz, the profits that Markle allocated to the McCambridge Account did not accurately reflect the total damage to Stephens. Transcript at 664–66. Although Geldermann presented experts who disagreed with Horwitz, his testimony is sufficient to support the jury's conclusion that Stephens' damages exceeded the profits Markle allocated to the McCambridge Account. Cf. York, 458 N.E.2d at 492–93 (emphasizing testimony of plaintiff's expert witness, which was contested by defendant's experts, in refusing to reverse jury's finding of proximate cause).

Geldermann criticizes Horwitz's testimony, noting that he discussed various theories concerning Markle's trading activities and even admitted that it was impossible to determine exactly which losses in the Stephens Account were attributable to Markle's scheme. Transcript at 664–65. These objections, however, are matters for the jury as fact-finder to consider in evaluating the expert's opinion. We have reviewed the evidence at trial and do not believe that it so overwhelmingly favored Geldermann so as to require reversal.

Geldermann further contends that even if its actions did proximately cause some of the losses in the Stephen's Account, the damages awarded to Stephens were unduly speculative because the jury could not ascertain the exact amount of these losses. Illinois law, however, does not require that the jury be able to ascertain damages with absolute mathematical certainty. Rhodes v. Sigler, 44 Ill. App. 3d 375, 357 N.E.2d 846, 850, 2 Ill. Dec. 626 (Ill. App. Ct. 1976); Meyer v. Buckman, 7 Ill. App. 2d 385, 129 N.E.2d 603, 613 (Ill. App. Ct. 1955). All that is needed is a reasonable basis, established with a fair degree of probability, for the jury to assess the damages. Tower Oil & Technology Co. v. Buckley, 99 Ill. App. 3d 637, 425 N.E.2d 1060, 1068, 54 Ill. Dec. 843 (Ill. App. Ct. 1981).

We believe that the jury had a reasonable basis to compute damages here. In addition to Horwitz's testimony, for example, the jury heard testimony that Markle's trading strategy would have led him to make many of the trades regardless of his scheme to defraud Stephens and that his skill as a trader was poor. Transcript at 1911–13, 1941. The chief executive officer of Stephens admitted that he knew the Stephens Account was losing money, yet allowed Markle to continue trading it. Id. at 771–72. The jury, therefore, could have reasonably concluded that a certain degree of loss in the Stephens Account was inevitable, but that Markle's scheme increased the amount of this loss. As such, the jury had a reasonable basis to assess damages and we refuse to upset its assessment as speculative. Cf. Tower Oil, 425 N.E.2d at 1068 (although exact amount of lost profits is unascertainable, reasonable basis existed for jury to estimate damages). * * *

We do not believe the district court abused its discretion in submitting the issue of punitive damages to the jury on a theory of either fraud or conspiracy to defraud. As discussed above, there was substantial evidence that Geldermann facilitated Markle's scheme and made positive efforts to prevent Stephens from learning about the McCambridge Account. As such, we agree with the district court that the evidence was sufficient under Illinois law to submit the issue of punitive damages to the jury. Cf. Federal Deposit Ins. Corp. v. W.R. Grace & Co., 877 F.2d 614, 623 (7th Cir. 1989) concealment of fraud sufficient to support award of punitive damages under Illinois law), cert. denied, 494 U.S. 1056, 108 L. Ed. 2d 764, 110 S. Ct. 1524 (1990). * * *

For the reasons discussed above, we affirm the jury's awards of compensatory and punitive damages to Stephens as well as the district court's orders dismissing Stephens' RICO claim and granting Geldermann a set-off against Stephens' compensatory damage award.

IN THE MATTER OF HAROLD LUDWIG

Comm. Fut. L. Rep. (CCH) ¶ 29,807 (C.F.T.C. 2004)

ORDER INSTITUTING PROCEEDINGS PURSUANT TO SECTIONS 6(c), 6(d) and 8a(2) OF THE COMMODITY EXCHANGE ACT, AS AMENDED, MAKING FINDINGS AND IMPOSING REMEDIAL SANCTIONS

The Commodity Futures Trading Commission ("Commission") has reason to believe that Harold Ludwig ("Ludwig") has violated Sections 4b(a)(2)(i) and (iii) and 4o(1) of the Act, 7 U.S.C. §§ 6b(a)(2)(i) and (iii) and 6o(1). Therefore, the Commission deems it appropriate and in the public interest that a public administrative proceeding be, and hereby is, instituted to determine whether Ludwig has engaged in the violations as set forth herein and to determine whether any order should be issued imposing remedial sanctions.

In anticipation of the institution of this administrative proceeding, Respondent has submitted an Offer of Settlement ("Offer") that the Commission has determined to accept. Without admitting or denying the findings herein, Respondent acknowledges service of this Order Instituting Proceedings Pursuant to Sections 6(c), 6(d) and 8a(2) of the Commodity Exchange Act, as amended, Making Findings and Imposing Remedial Sanctions ("Order"). Respondent consents to the use of the findings herein in this proceeding and in any other proceeding brought by the Commission or to which the Commission is a party.

The Commission finds that:

Respondent engaged in an illegal trade allocation scheme, pursuant to which he allocated trades to his personal trading account to the detriment of Princeton accounts over which he also had trading authority. These Princeton accounts were set up at Republic New York Securities Corporation ("RNYSC") by Martin Armstrong who, along with his two companies, Princeton Global Management, Ltd. and Princeton Economics International Ltd and Maria Toczylowski, a vice president of RNYSC's futures division, and William Rogers, president of the futures division of RNYSC, carried out the fraudulent scheme.

Ludwig, who resides in Newtown, Pennsylvania, is, along with Martin Armstrong, a co-director of Princeton Global Management, Ltd., incorporated in the Turks and Caicos, British West Indies. During the relevant time period, Ludwig had trading authority over all of the

Princeton accounts and actively traded in the PGM K-5 and Princeton Aggressive Fund accounts. In 1997, Ludwig opened a personal trading account in the name of Blue Horizon Trading, Ltd. (the "Blue Horizon" account), which is a Turks and Caicos Island unincorporated association owned and controlled by Ludwig and his wife. With the help of Rogers and Toczylowski, Ludwig allocated winning trades to the Blue Horizon account to the detriment of the Princeton accounts. Ludwig has been registered with the Commission as a Commodity Trading Advisor ("CTA") from July 1987 to the present. He has also been registered as an Associated Person from November 1986 to the present.

Ludwig was Armstrong's co-director, and was responsible for managing a few Princeton accounts, including the Princeton International Aggressive Fund (Princeton Aggressive Fund) account, and the Princeton Global Management K-5 (PGM K-5) account. Ludwig allocated winning trades to an account owned by Ludwig and his wife, and the losing trades were allocated into Princeton accounts over which Ludwig had trading authority. In particular, Ludwig received a bonus based on a percentage of the profits he made in these accounts. In 1997, Ludwig used the bonus he earned from his apparently successful trading to open a trading account designated as the Blue Horizon account. This was Ludwig's personal trading account, established as a Turks and Caicos Island unincorporated association in the name of Blue Horizon Trading, Ltd., which was owned and controlled by Ludwig and his wife. Ludwig continued to manage the PGM K-5 and Princeton Aggressive Fund accounts while trading for the Blue Horizon account. Now, however, Ludwig began to allocate winning trades to the Blue Horizon account. Ludwig's trade allocations functioned to siphon away funds from the Japanese investors for Ludwig's own benefit.

An analysis of the trading results for day trades for the S&P 500 futures contracts in the accounts managed by Ludwig show widely disparate returns that favor his Blue Horizon account. According to account documents, between June 1997 and August 1999, the Blue Horizon account day traded S&P 500 futures contracts on 98 days. Blue Horizon traded profitably on 83 of the 98 days, which translates into an 85% profitability rate and the realization of some $4.5 million in profits. In contrast, the other two accounts that Ludwig had control over were profitable only approximately 40% of the time. The Princeton Aggressive Fund account day traded S&P 500 futures contracts on 275 days between June 1997 and August 1999, and the trades were profitable on 113 of those days, providing a 40% profitability rate. The Princeton Aggressive Fund account lost approximately $550,000 during that period. The PGM K-5 account day traded S&P 500 futures on 102 days between June 1997 and August 1999 and the trades were profitable on 41 days, providing a 39% profitability rate. While the PGM K-5 account profited overall by approximately $290,000 in trades involving the S&P 500 futures contracts, a substantial portion of this amount resulted from eight trades that were held overnight. When these eight trades are not considered in the calculation, the PGM K-5 account lost approximately $363,000.

Trading records also reveal that on 51 days during the period, the Blue Horizon account received profitable day trades while the PGM K-5 and Princeton Aggressive Fund accounts did not receive any trades. On most days when there were no profitable day trades in any of the accounts at issue, the Blue Horizon account did not trade but the PGM K-5 and Princeton Aggressive Fund accounts had losing day trades.

A review of the floor order tickets supports the trade allocation scheme. A random sample of original floor order placed for "Hal," which was Ludwig's nickname. Account numbers on these tickets were written in different colored ink and/or in different handwriting than the rest of the order, indicating that pertinent information was added at a different time and/or by a tickets shows that account numbers for the Blue Horizon, PGM K-5 and Princeton Aggressive Fund accounts were added to the order tickets for day trades of S & P 500 futures contracts after the trades were executed. Many of the tickets show that the order instructions, i.e. the quantity, contract month, commodity and price instructions were in the same handwriting and writing instrument. Most of these orders indicated that the trades were different person, most likely after the execution of the order. Other tickets with trades that were never executed have no account number at all, and only identify the customer as "Hal."

In recorded telephone conversations Ludwig and another Armstrong employee discuss (1) whether specific trades could be allocated to the Blue Horizon account after having been executed, and (2) the procedure that should be followed when Ludwig placed bulk trade orders that would allow trades to be allocated after they were executed.

Ludwig violated Sections 4b(a)(2)(i) and (iii) and 4o(1) of the Act for his conduct in fraudulently allocating trades among the Blue Horizon, PGM K-5 and Princeton Aggressive Fund accounts. Ludwig allocated profitable trades to the Blue Horizon account that he owned while allocating unprofitable trades to the PGM K-5 and Princeton Aggressive Fund accounts, which he managed but did not own. Such conduct constitutes an unlawful trade allocation scheme and violates sections 4b(a)(2)(i) and (iii) and 4o(1) of the Commodity Exchange Act (the Act) 7 U.S.C. § 6b(a)(2)(i) and (iii) and 6o(1) (2002).

Section 4b(a)(2)(i) and (iii) of the act is violated when a party allocates trades in a way that consistently disadvantages a particular customer. GNP Commodities [1990–92 Transfer Binder] Comm. Fut. L. Rep. (CCH) P25,360, 39,214 (CFTC Aug. 11, 1992) (citing In re

Lincolnwood [1982–84 Transfer Binder] Comm. Fut. L. Rep. (CCH) P21,986 (CFTC Jan. 31, 1984)). The proper question is whether the defendant acted with intent by "knowingly employing an allocation scheme that was neither predetermined nor fair to all his customers." In re Nikkhah, [Current Transfer Binder] Comm. Fut. L. Rep. P28,129, 49,887 (CFTC May 12, 2000).

The mere failure to place account numbers on order tickets is not, in and of itself, a fraudulent act. GNP Commodities, at 39,214. But the failure to place account numbers on order tickets does provide the opportunity to direct profitable fills to favored accounts. Id. Therefore, the significance of the fact that trades were placed without account numbers "cannot be overstated." Id. at n. 8.

Where specific account identification is withheld from the order ticket at the time the order is communicated to the trading floor, the Commission has found that this fact "raise[s] serious questions about the allocation process. . . ." In re Nikkhah, Comm. Fut. L. Rep. P28,129, 49,885 (CFTC May 12, 2000). This is because it is consistent with the intent to eliminate the type of audit trail information that would impede post-execution allocation. Id. Additionally, the Commission has recognized that day trades are particularly susceptible to manipulation in furtherance of the kind of allocation scheme described above because day trades also reduce the evidence of ownership of a particular trade to a bare minimum. In re Lincolnwood, [1982–84 Transfer Binder] Comm. Fut. L. Rep. (CCH) P21,986, 28,226 (CFTC Jan. 31, 1984).

The wide disparity in profits among accounts that were commonly controlled, coupled with the controlling person's ability to allocate trades, is also highly indicative of an unlawful allocation scheme. See Lincolnwood, at P 28,244–45 (comparing average profit per trade and account balances). Similarly, where account numbers on order tickets are written with different writing instruments or in different handwriting, and where a name appears in place of account numbers, such evidence indicates an unlawful allocation scheme. GNP Commodities, at 39,209.

Ludwig's allocation scheme violates Section 4b(a)(2)(i) and (iii) of the Act because he consistently disadvantaged the PGM K-5 and Princeton Aggressive Fund accounts to the benefit of the Blue Horizon account. There are wide disparities in profits achieved by the Blue Horizon account in day trades of S&P 500 futures, as opposed to the profits achieved by the PGM K-5 and Princeton Aggressive Fund accounts. Further, the original trade tickets show that the fill orders and the account numbers were written with different writing instruments from the orders themselves.

In order to establish a violation of Section 4o(1) of the Act the Division must prove that the respondent was (i) a CTA and (ii) either (a) employed any device, scheme, or artifice to defraud any client or prospective client, or (b) engaged in any transaction, practice, or course of business which operates as a fraud or deceit upon any client or prospective client. Section 4o(1) of the Act which also requires the use of the mails or any means or instrumentality of interstate commerce, prohibits both registered and unregistered CTAs from defrauding their clients.

Under Section 1a(5) of the Act, in order to establish that someone is acting as a CTA, it must be shown that the person (i) advised another about the value or advisability of trading in futures contracts, (ii) "either directly or through publications, writings or electronic media," and (iii) for compensation or profit. Section 1a(5) of the Act, 7 U.S.C. § 1a(5). Ludwig is a registered CTA and AP and gave commodity futures trading advice for compensation or profit to the corporations that owned the PGM K-5 and Princeton Aggressive Fund accounts.

By engaging in a fraudulent allocation scheme, Ludwig violated Section 4o(1) of the Act just as he violated Sections 4b(a)(i) and (iii) of the Act. In re R&W Technical Services, Comm. Fut. L. Rep. (CCH) P27,582 (CFTC March 16, 1999) ("Because we have found that [respondents] violated Section 4b(a) of the Act and that they acted as CTAs, further analysis is not needed to conclude that [respondents] also violated Section 4o(1) of the Act"), *aff'd in relevant part,* R&W Technical Services v. CFTC, 205 F.3d 165 (5th Cir. 2000). * * *

NOTES

1. A concern over order allocations arises in the use of "bunch" orders, which is a collective order for a group of customer accounts controlled by a CTA or an associated person of an FCM. Frequently, such bunch orders have "split fills," which means that the entire bunch order could not be filled at the same price. In such instances, some customers will receive better prices than others. CFTC Rule 1.35(b)(5) [17 C.F.R. § 1.35(b)(5)] permits allocations of such orders among the managed accounts at the end of the trading day, rather than at time of entry of the order. However, the allocations must be done in a fair and equitable manner. Some customers will receive more favorable treatment than others because the prices allocated will differ due to the split fill. Nevertheless, that allocation cannot be intentionally unfair. See, In the Matter of U.S. Securities & Futures Corp., Comm. Fut. L. Rep. (CCH) ¶ 31,494 (C.F.T.C. 2009) (Rule 1.35 does not permit fraudulent order allocations) and In the Matter of Prudential Securities, Comm. Fut. L. Rep. (CCH) ¶ 29,617 (C.F.T.C. 2003) (same).

2. Some exchanges allow for an average pricing mechanism that permits all customers to receive the average price of a split fill that arises from a bunch order or several orders placed by the account controller or trader (e.g.,

the CTA) during a single trading day. Using the average price system (APS) model, each customer managed by the CTA receives the same price.

3. See also Kemper Financial Services, Inc. (Investment Advisers Act of 1940 Release No. 1387, [1993 Transfer Binder] Fed. Sec. L. Rep. (CCH), 85,237 (Oct. 29, 1993)) and Kemper Financial Services, Inc., Investment Advisers Act of 1940 Release No. 21113 (June 6, 1995). Both of these matters involved allocation of bunched orders of securities by an investment adviser.

CHAPTER 8

GENERAL ANTIFRAUD PROVISIONS

■ ■ ■

1. COMMODITY EXCHANGE ACT SECTION 4B

The principal antifraud provision in the Commodity Exchange Act of 1936 (CEA) is found in Section 4b. It is a long and convoluted statute, which states that:

It shall be unlawful—

(1) for any person, in or in connection with any order to make, or the making of, any contract of sale of any commodity in interstate commerce or for future delivery that is made, or to be made, on or subject to the rules of a designated contract market, for or on behalf of any other person; or

(2) for any person, in or in connection with any order to make, or the making of, any contract of sale of any commodity for future delivery, or swap, that is made, or to be made, for or on behalf of, or with, any other person, other than on or subject to the rules of a designated contract market—

(A) to cheat or defraud or attempt to cheat or defraud the other person;

(B) willfully to make or cause to be made to the other person any false report or statement or willfully to enter or cause to be entered for the other person any false record;

(C) willfully to deceive or attempt to deceive the other person by any means whatsoever in regard to any order or contract or the disposition or execution of any order or contract, or in regard to any act of agency performed, with respect to any order or contract for or, in the case of paragraph (2), with the other person; or

(D) (i) to bucket an order if the order is either represented by the person as an order to be executed, or is required to be executed, on or subject to the rules of a designated contract market; or

(ii) to fill an order by offset against the order or orders of any other person, or willfully and knowingly and without the prior consent of the other person to become the buyer in respect to any selling order of the other person, or become the seller in respect to any buying order of the other person, if the order is either represented by the person as an order to be executed, or is required to be executed, on or subject to the rules of a designated contract market unless the order is executed in accordance with the rules of the designated contract market.

(b) Clarification

Subsection (a)(2) of this section shall not obligate any person, in or in connection with a transaction in a contract of sale of a commodity for future delivery, or swap, with another person, to disclose to the other person nonpublic information that may be material to the market price, rate, or level of the commodity or transaction, except as necessary to make any statement made to the other person in or in connection with the transaction not misleading in any material respect.

(c) Buying and selling orders for commodity

Nothing in this section or in any other section of this chapter shall be construed to prevent a futures commission merchant or floor broker who shall have in hand, simultaneously, buying and selling orders at the market for different principals for a like quantity of a commodity for future delivery in the same month executing such buying and selling orders at the market price: Provided, That any such execution shall take place on the floor of the exchange where such orders are to be executed at public outcry across the ring and shall be duly reported, recorded, and cleared in the same manner as other orders executed on such exchange: And provided further, That such transactions shall be made in accordance with such rules and regulations as the Commission may promulgate regarding the manner of the execution of such transactions.

(d) Inapplicability to transactions on foreign exchanges

Nothing in this section shall apply to any activity that occurs on a board of trade, exchange, or market, or clearinghouse for such board of trade, exchange, or market, located outside the United States, or territories or possessions of the United States, involving any contract of sale of a commodity for future delivery that is made, or to be made, on or subject to the rules of such board of trade, exchange, or market.

(e) Contracts of sale on group or index of securities

It shall be unlawful for any person, directly or indirectly, by the use of any means or instrumentality of interstate commerce, or of the mails, or of any facility of any registered entity, in or in connection with any order to make, or the making of, any contract of sale of any commodity for future delivery (or option on such a contract), or any swap, on a group or index of securities (or any interest therein or based on the value thereof)—

(1) to employ any device, scheme, or artifice to defraud;

(2) to make any untrue statement of a material fact or to omit to state a material fact necessary in order to make the statements made, in the light of the circumstances under which they were made, not misleading; or

(3) to engage in any act, practice, or course of business which operates or would operate as a fraud or deceit upon any person.

NOTES

1. The original language in clause (1) of Section 4b limited its application to members of contract markets, their correspondents, agents, or employees. It was broadened in 1968 to apply its proscriptions to "any person." This language was added at the request of the Department of Agriculture, which was then administering the CEA, so that Section 4b would "cover all persons who handle customer orders or funds" and thereby "give customers who deal in commodity futures with non-members the full protection of the Act." 113 Cong. Rec. 23,652 (1967); S. Rep. No. 947, 90th Cong., 2d Sess. 6 (1968).

2. One limitation set forth in Section 4b is that the prohibited conduct must be "in or in connection with" a commodity futures contract traded on or subject to the rules of a contract market. Such limiting language has also appeared in the federal securities laws. See, Blue Chip Stamps v. Manor Drug Stores, 421 U.S. 723 (1975).

3. Section 4b does not apply to foreign futures transactions sold in the United States, but the CEA was amended in 1982 to include a specific provision authorizing the CFTC to promulgate an antifraud rule for foreign futures transactions, which it had already done. [17 C.F.R. § 30.9]. Other transactions regulated by the CEA also do not fall within the province of Section 4b. These include commodity option transactions, which are governed by a specific antifraud rule adopted by the CFTC. [17 C.F.R. § 33.10]. As noted in Chapter 7, there is also a separate antifraud provision for commodity trading advisors and commodity pool operators. [7 U.S.C. § 6o].

4. Adding more confusion, Section 4b(e) of the CEA adds a special antifraud provision for futures contracts on a group or index of securities.

That provision tracks language from Section 10b of the Securities Exchange Act of 1934 [15 U.S.C. 78j], the antifraud provision that you studied in your Business Organizations class.

2. SCIENTER

HAMMOND V. SMITH BARNEY, HARRIS UPHAM & CO., INC.
Comm. Fut. L. Rep. (CCH) ¶ 24,617 (C.F.T.C. 1990)

By the Commission (CHAIRMAN GRAMM and COMMISSIONERS HINEMAN, DAVIS and ALBRECHT) (COMMISSIONER WEST, dissenting).

Respondents appeal from the Judgment Officer's conclusion that their solicitation of complainant Hammond was fraudulent. Respondents contend that the record does not support the Judgment Officer's finding that the risk disclosure they provided was negated by their discussion of profit potential. They also challenge the Judgment Officer's legal analysis, suggesting that a finding of fraud under Section 4b(A) of the Commodity Exchange Act ("Act") requires proof respondents acted with scienter. Complainant opposes the appeal, arguing that the Judgment Officer's findings are fully supported by the record.

Based on our review of the record, we conclude that the Judgment Officer's findings are supported by the evidence and that his legal analysis is consistent with our interpretation of Section 4b(A) of the Act in Gordon v. Shearson Hayden Stone, Inc., [1980–1982 Transfer Binder] Comm. Fut. L. Rep. (CCH) ¶ 21,016 (CFTC Apr. 10, 1980). As discussed below, however, we will no longer follow the interpretation of Section 4b(A) of the Act set forth in *Gordon*. In light of our change in the applicable legal standard, we remand to the Judgment Officer for supplementation of the record and specific findings on the issue of scienter.

The parties' dispute focuses on the interpretation of two categories of information: (1) the oral and written presentation respondent King offered at seminars on commodity futures trading offered March 6 and 7, 1985 in Bend, Oregon and (2) a chart of the results of hypothetical trading King provided to complainant Hammond in early April. We begin our review of the record with the evidence relating to King's presentations at the seminars.

According to King, between 1981 and early 1986 he had given between 20 and 30 seminars a year in order to develop new futures business. In March 1985, King explained, he offered seminars in Bend, Oregon, covering: (1) the mechanics of futures trading, (2) trading in precious metals and (3) trading in foreign currencies. King testified that the subjects covered during the seminars were consistent with the outlines respondents submitted for the record and insisted that he had discussed trading risk at every seminar and in a variety of ways.

King acknowledged that his seminar presentation included a number of documents: (a) account papers, (b) commodity charts, (c) exchange brochures on specific commodities, (d) a brochure on the managed account program he offered through his employer, Smith Barney, Harris Upham & Co. ("Smith Barney"), (e) brochures describing some commodity funds and (f) examples of profitable futures transactions. King testified that he discussed the account papers during the seminars and specifically reviewed the Rule 1.55 risk disclosure document. He acknowledged, however, that he had also assured the seminar participants that a customer could earn a profit through futures trading even if the majority of his transactions showed losses.

Hammond's recollection of King's presentations at the seminars focused on the general impression King had created and his use of three written examples to illustrate his trading program. While Hammond did not recall specific representations made by King, he testified that King's presentation led him to believe that the commodity trading system devised by King and his partner, respondent Waterman, could virtually guarantee large trading profits. According to Hammond, the written examples King distributed indicated that the trading program could produce high profits with low commissions. While he had learned about the risk of trading futures contracts prior to attending King's seminars, Hammond stated, he could not recall any discussion of risk by King.

In early April, Hammond received a follow-up letter from King along with an "updated performance chart for the $25,000 Model Technical Account." The letter drew specific attention to the successful trading of the model account in March. The performance chart attached to King's letter reviewed the trading results in the model account on a month-by-month basis for the period January 1982 through March 1985. The final column listed the annual return of the model account for each month of each year. According to profit figures disclosed in the chart, a customer who had deposited $25,000 into the model account in January 1982 would have earned a net profit of almost $70,000 by March 1985. At the bottom of the chart, King made the following disclosure:

> Model, hypothetical or simulated performance results have certain inherent limitations. Unlike an actual performance record, the results do not represent actual trading. Also, since the trades have not actually been executed, the results may have under or over compensated for the impact, if any, of certain market factors such as lack of liquidity. Model or simulated trading programs in general are also subject to the claim that they are designed with the benefit of hindsight. Although we

have attempted to present the model results in as fair a manner as possible, such results are subject to the limitation inherent in all simulated performance results. NO REPRESENTATION IS BEING MADE THAT ANY ACCOUNT WILL OR IS LIKELY TO ACHIEVE PROFITS OR LOSSES SIMILAR TO THOSE SHOWN.

After reviewing this performance chart, Hammond telephoned King and expressed an interest in opening a discretionary account. King reviewed the account application with Hammond, answering questions and explaining Smith Barney's minimum financial requirements. On April 3, 1985, Hammond executed a new account form and financial questionnaire, an account agreement, a power of attorney in favor of respondent Waterman and an acknowledgement that he had read and understood the Rule 1.55 disclosure statement. He deposited $10,000 to commence trading in his account.

Complainant maintained his futures account from April through October, 1985. Trading in April produced a small profit on completed transactions that was offset by losses accrued on positions that remained open at the end of the month. Equity in the account continued to decline due to trading in May and June. By the end of July, however, completed transactions had produced a profit of almost $550 and positions remaining open in the account had accrued a net profit of $950. In August, despite continued success on transactions completed during the month, the value of Hammond's equity plunged due to open positions that had accrued losses of $9,000 by the end of the month. After these losses were realized through limited trading in September and October, Hammond closed his account. His net loss amounted to approximately $7,000.

In the complaint he filed in March 1986, complainant raised claims of fraudulent inducement and churning. Respondents denied all of Hammond's claims in their answer. * * *

[R]espondents suggest that the Judgment Officer erred by limiting his analysis of the record to whether complainant was materially misled by King's presentation. Prior to concluding that King had violated Section 4b(A) of the Act, respondents argue, the Judgment Officer should have determined whether King intended or knew that his presentation to Hammond was materially misleading. In other words, respondents contend that they cannot be held liable under Section 4b(A) of the Act for the misleading nature of King's presentation unless he acted with scienter.

Under provisions of the federal securities law roughly analogous to Section 4b(A) of the Act, it is clearly established that neither a false statement of a material fact nor a culpable failure to disclose a material fact is actionable unless the respondent has acted either intentionally or recklessly. In *Gordon, supra,* however, the Commission concluded that it was not necessary to analyze a respondent's state of mind in cases alleging a violation of Section 4b(A) of Act. Commission presiding officers are not authorized to disregard Commission precedent merely because it has not been favored in the courts of appeals. Only the Commission may determine it is appropriate to alter its precedent in the face of contrary authority. Thus the Judgment Officer did not err in failing to anticipate the change of interpretation announced in this case.

Because the ultimate result in this case rests squarely on the issue decided in *Gordon, supra,* we must resolve the conflict between the approach mandated by our precedent and the approach consistently endorsed by the federal courts. Our conclusion in *Gordon* was based on a careful review of the language, structure and legislative history of Section 4b of the Act. In analyzing Congress' intent, the Commission noted the Supreme Court's holding that scienter was a necessary element for proof of a violation of Section 10(b) of the Securities Exchange Act of 1934. Ernst & Ernst v. Hochfelder, 425 U.S. 185 (1976). The Commission declined to follow Hochfelder's specific reasoning, however, because of distinctions between the language and structure of Section 10(b) of the Securities Exchange Act and Section 4b(A) of the Commodity Exchange Act.

At the time the Commission issued *Gordon,* at least two courts of appeals had announced more restrictive interpretations of Section 4b(A). Master Commodities, Inc. v. Texas Cattle Management, 586 F.2d 1352, 1355–56 (10th Cir. 1978); Commodity Futures Trading Commission v. Savage, 611 F.2d 270 (9th Cir. 1979). Despite the Commission's decision in *Gordon,* other circuit courts of appeals have adopted interpretations of Section 4b(A) generally reflecting a symmetrical approach to the requirements of Section 10(b) of the Securities Exchange Act and Section 4b(A) of the Commodity Exchange Act. First Commodity Corporation of Boston v. Commodity Futures Trading Commission, 676 F.2d 1, 4–5 (1st Cir. 1982); McIlroy v. Dittmer, 732 F.2d 98, 102 (8th Cir. 1984); Hill v. Bache Halsey Stuart Shields, Inc., 790 F.2d 817, 822 (10th Cir. 1986); First National Monetary Corp. v. Weinberger, 819 F.2d 1334, 1342 (6th Cir. 1987); Drexel Burnham Lambert v. Commodity Futures Trading Commission, 850 F.2d 742, 748 (D.C. Cir. 1988). Cf. Messer v. E.F. Hutton & Co., 847 F.2d 673 (11th Cir. 1988) (Scienter is a necessary element for proof of a violation of Section 4o(1)(A) of the Act).

The Commission has rejected the view that the primary focus of an interpretation of the Commodity Exchange Act should be maintenance of symmetry with preexisting interpretations of the securities laws. Moreover, under applicable Supreme Court precedent, the Commission's interpretation of the meaning of the Act is entitled to significant deference from the courts. Chevron, U.S.A., Inc. v. Natural Resources Defense Council, 467 U.S. 837, 842–843 (1984). In light of the consistent view of the circuit courts of appeals, however, it does not appear that continued adherence to the interpretation of Section 4b(A) announced in *Gordon* would serve the interests of the Commission or complainants who might be called upon to litigate the issue before these courts. For this reason, we hold that scienter is a necessary element for proof of a violation of Section 4b(A) of the Act. Accordingly, in assessing the evidence in reparation cases alleging a violation of Section 4b(A) of the Act, presiding officers shall determine whether respondents' wrongful acts were committed intentionally or with reckless disregard for their duties under the Act. Absent sufficient evidence to support such a finding, a violation of Section 4b(A) of the Act shall not be found.

On the present record, we cannot conclude that King acted with scienter when he misled complainant about the risks inherent in futures trading. Nevertheless, we reject respondents' suggestion that the scienter issue must be determined in their favor because the Judgment Officer credited King's testimony that he believed he had fully disclosed the risks of futures trading. Because complainant was not on notice of his obligation to develop the record on King's state of mind, he may have mistakenly permitted King's testimony to go unchallenged. Moreover, a good faith belief is not necessarily inconsistent with a finding of scienter. See, e.g. United States v. Boyer, 694 F.2d 58, 60 (3d Cir. 1982) (Endorsing the district court's instruction that "no amount of honest belief that the enterprise would ultimately make money can justify baseless, false or reckless misrepresentations or promises."). Thus, in light of the change in our interpretation of Section 4b(A), complainant should have a fair opportunity to develop the record on respondent King's state of mind.

Accordingly, we vacate the initial decision and remand to the Judgment Officer for further proceedings. If he deems it appropriate, the Judgment Officer may reopen discovery on issues relevant to King's scienter and conduct a telephonic hearing pursuant to 17 C.F.R. § 12.209. If the Judgment Officer concludes that complainant has not established scienter for purposes of his fraudulent inducement claim, he shall make appropriate findings and conclusions on complainant's churning allegations.

Dissent By: WEST

NOTES

1. The term "fiduciary duty" is often used in customer dispute cases. However, a breach of fiduciary duty does not require a showing of scienter, while fraud prohibitions often require some degree of specific intent. See, Jerry W. Markham, Fiduciary Duties Under the Commodity Exchange Act,

68 Notre Dame L. Rev. 199 (1992) (discussing the nature and role of fiduciary duties).

2. The Supreme Court has likened Section 4b of the CEA to Section 10(b) of the Securities Exchange Act of 1934. See Merrill Lynch, Pierce, Fenner & Smith, Inc. v. Curran, 456 U.S. 353 (1982). The Commodity Futures Trading Commission (CFTC) also stated in the Hammond case, supra, that, where concepts under the CEA are directly comparable to concepts underlying provisions of the securities laws, the CFTC will generally give significant weight to the views of the courts that have interpreted the relevant securities statutes.

Nevertheless, the CFTC noted that there might be a divergence of the two industries on particular matters. For example, as will be described later in this chapter, the securities law fraud concept of "suitability" is not recognized by the CFTC for futures and options. Similarly, as will be described in Chapter 9, the insider information antifraud standards under Section 10b of the Securities Exchange Act of 1934 [15 U.S.C. § 78j] have little applicability to transactions conducted under the CEA. In addition, as described below, securities law fraud claims, such as "churning," may require different assessments and analysis than those used for commodity futures.

3. As noted in Chapter 9, the Dodd-Frank Act added a new anti-fraud standard in the CEA by establishing a disruptive trading and manipulation element of liability, which is similar in nature to Section 10(b) of the Securities Exchange Act.

3. SECONDARY LIABILITY[1]

(A) RESPONDENT SUPERIOR LIABILITY

ROSENTHAL & CO. V. CFTC
802 F.2d 963 (7th Cir. 1986)

POSNER, CIRCUIT JUDGE.

This petition by Rosenthal & Company, a commodities broker, to review an order of the Commodity Futures Trading Commission requires us to decide questions of the interpretation and application of section 2(a)(1) of the Commodity Exchange Act, 7 U.S.C. § 4. That section provides that "the act, omission, or failure of any official, agent, or other person acting for (an entity regulated by the Commodity Futures Trading Commission) within the scope of his employment or office shall be deemed the act, omission, or failure of" the entity itself.

---

[1] For further discussion of secondary liability under the CEA see, Jerry W. Markham and Ellen R. Meltzer, Secondary Liability Under the Commodity Exchange Act—Respondeat Superior, Aiding and Abetting, Supervision and Scienter, 27 Emory L. J. 1115 (1978) and Jerry W. Markham, and Kyra Bergin, Customer Rights Under the Commodity Exchange Act, 31 Vand. L. Rev. 1299 (1984).

In 1974 and 1975 Larry Pinckney and others organized three corporations to operate, among other types of investment venture, commodity pools. A commodity pool is the commodity-futures equivalent of a mutual fund; the investor buys shares in the pool and the operator of the pool invests the proceeds in commodity futures. See 1 Johnson, Commodities Regulation § 1.15, at pp. 52–53, §§ 1.59–1.64 (1982). Pinckney, the president of two of the three corporations, marketed shares in the pools through salesmen hired by the corporations. His office was on the first floor of an office building in Kansas City.

To trade commodity futures for the pools Pinckney had to use a commodities broker registered on the major commodity exchanges, such as Rosenthal & Company—a "commission house," as this kind of broker is sometimes called, see H.R. Rep. No. 975, 93d Cong., 2d Sess. 140–43 (1974). Rosenthal was eager for Pinckney's business, and by way of inducement was willing to rebate to him part of its regular commission for trading commodity futures. But Rosenthal could not lawfully split commissions with Pinckney unless Pinckney was registered with the commodity exchanges. See 1 Johnson, *supra*, § 1.89, at 197. One way of accomplishing this was for Rosenthal to register Pinckney with the Commodity Futures Trading Commission as an "associated person" of Rosenthal, 7 U.S.C. § 6k, and then designate him a registered representative of Rosenthal with the exchanges. Rosenthal took these steps. It also designated Pinckney its Kansas City branch manager, and leased office space for him on the tenth floor of the building that contained Pinckney's office as president of the two investment corporations on the first floor. Pinckney did not, however, become an employee of Rosenthal. He was compensated not by a wage but by rebates of commissions that Rosenthal charged the pools for executing their trades. In return Pinckney agreed to give Rosenthal the pools' brokerage business.

Pinckney's relationship with Rosenthal began late in 1975 and ended in 1978. There is evidence that during this period Pinckney sometimes told the salesmen for his commodity pools not to send investors the actual subscription agreement (i.e., the contract for the purchase of shares in the pool) until the investor had mailed his check, because the agreement contained alarming language (required by the Commodity Futures Trading Commission) about how risky speculation in commodity futures is. There was not a great deal of such evidence but enough to sustain the Commission's conclusion, in the proceeding we are asked to review, that Pinckney had engaged in a form of commodities fraud, in violation of sections 4b and 4o of the Commodity Exchange Act, 7 U.S.C. §§ 6b, 6o. The difficult question is whether the Commission was entitled to impute Pinckney's conduct to Rosenthal under section 2(a)(1). Rosenthal argues that it was not, and that therefore we must set aside the Commission's order, which imposed a $15,000 fine on Rosenthal for Pinckney's violation.

Section 2(a)(1), which dates back to 1921, enacts a variant of the common law principle of respondeat superior. The common law principle makes an employer strictly liable—that is to say, regardless of the presence or absence of fault on the employer's part—for torts committed by his employees in the furtherance of his business; in legalese, it "imputes" the employee's negligence to his employer, thus making the employer's own lack of fault immaterial. See Prosser and Keeton on the Law of Torts § 70 (5th ed. 1984). Section 2(a)(1) departs from the common law in two respects. It is in effect a quasi-criminal statute as well as a tort statute, for it can make the principal liable for not only the payment of damages to the victim of the tort (the statutory tort of commodities fraud) but also the payment of a fine to the government. And it applies to torts committed by agents who are not necessarily employees. The resemblance to the tort doctrine is so close, however, and the language of the statute so clear—it expressly imputes the agent's wrongdoing to the principal—that we have no doubt that section 2(a)(1) imposes strict liability on the principal (Rosenthal), provided, of course, as the statute also states expressly, that the agent's misconduct was within the scope or (equivalently but more precisely) in furtherance of the agency.

Principals are strictly liable for their agents' acts—even if the agents are not employees—if the principals authorize or ratify the acts or even just create an appearance that the acts are authorized. This is so even though in a case of ratification or apparent authority the principal does not himself direct the act and may indeed know nothing about it when it occurs, as Rosenthal (we may assume) knew nothing of Pinckney's fraud. Ratification is not the theory of section 2(a)(1), but we mention it to show that strict liability is no stranger to the principal-agent relationship even outside the narrow domain of the employment relationship. Strict liability is no stranger to the criminal law either, and anyway, technically at least, section 2(a)(1) is not a source of criminal liability—though, functionally speaking, a fine is a fine. Although there is not pre-enactment legislative history of section 2(a)(1) and no extended judicial discussions, it has long been assumed, and for the reason stated we agree, that the statute was intended to impose strict liability, under a theory of respondeat superior, for acts within its reach. See, e.g., *CFTC v. Premex, Inc.*, 655 F.2d 779, 784 n. 10 (7th Cir. 1981); H.R. Conf. Rep. No. 964, 97th Cong., 2d Sess. 48 (1982).

Rosenthal argues, however, that later additions to the Commodity Exchange Act must be taken to have modified the strict-liability standard of section 2(a)(1). Section 13(a), 7 U.S.C. § 13c(a), imposes liability for aiding and abetting violations of the Act; section 13(c), 7 U.S.C. § 13(c), imposes liability on "controlling persons," that is, persons controlling the violator. The legislative history makes plain, however, that these additions were intended to supplement rather than displace the respondeat superior liability created by section 2(a)(1). See H.R. Conf. Rep. No. 964, *supra*, at 48; S. Rep. No. 384, 97th Cong., 2d Sess. 47 (1982). The same conclusion has been reached in interpreting the "controlling person" provisions of the federal securities laws—section 15 of the Securities Act of 1933, 15 U.S.C. § 77o, and section 20(a) of the Securities Exchange Act of 1934, 15 U.S.C. § 78t(a)—on which section 13(c) of the Commodity Exchange Act is modeled, S. Rep. No. 384, *supra*, at 47. See, e.g., *Paul F. Newton & Co. v. Texas Commerce Bank*, 630 F.2d 1111, 1114–19 (5th Cir. 1980); *Marbury Management, Inc. v. Kohn*, 629 F.2d 705, 711–16 (2d Cir. 1980). These holdings have been criticized, see Fischel, *Secondary Liability Under Section 10(b) of the Securities Act of 1934*, 69 Calif. L. Rev. 80, 86–87, 89–94 (1981); cf. *Barker v. Henderson, Franklin, Starnes & Holt*, 797 F.2d 490, 494–95 (7th Cir. 1986), but on grounds unrelated to the present case. For there is no counterpart in the securities laws to section 2(a)(1) of the Commodity Exchange Act, that is, no provision creating liability on the basis of respondeat superior. And, again unlike that Act, there is no legislative history to the securities laws clearly indicating that the "controlling persons" provisions are intended to leave respondeat superior unaffected.

Nor does an aiding or abetting provision or a controlling persons provision occupy the same ground as respondeat superior, so that the three grounds of liability cannot co-exist. Section 2(a)(1) would not, for example, reach the case of an aider or abettor who was not the violator's principal. Nor would it reach an individual officer or supervisor who controlled the violator. The words "respondeat superior" imply that the doctrine is one of superior officers' liability, but it isn't; it is a doctrine about employers and (in section 2(a)(1)) other principals. It has no application to a case where A, B's supervisor, is sued because B commits a tort. There is, in fact, no common law doctrine of superior officers' liability. *McKinnon v. City of Berwyn*, 750 F.2d 1383, 1390 (7th Cir. 1984). Although a supervisor could of course be held liable by reason of his personal fault, see *id.* at 1391; *Chapman v. Pickett*, 801 F.2d 912, slip op. at 11 (7th Cir.1986); *id.* at 26 (dissenting opinion), that would not be by virtue of respondeat superior, a doctrine of imputed liability. Section 13(c), however, creates superiors' liability in or approximating a respondeat superior sense in the commodities trading industry. More important, section 13(c) makes it more difficult for a principal to escape liability by inserting a dummy corporation between itself and its agent. See S. Rep. No. 384, *supra*, at 47; cf. *Paul F. Newton & Co. v. Texas Commerce Bank, supra*, 630 F.2d at 1115. Of course common law principles would allow the corporate veil to be pierced and the shareholder of the dummy corporation (i.e., the real principal) held liable for the agent's misconduct. But these principles are rather nebulous, see, e.g., *In re Kaiser*, 791 F.2d 73, 75 (7th Cir. 1986), federal common law tends to be ill defined, and Congress apparently wanted a more straightforward route to making principals liable for their agents' wrongdoing.

So the fact that Rosenthal was not shown to know about or be involved in or careless regarding Pinckney's fraud is irrelevant; the only question is whether the fraud was within the scope of his agency. This, however, is a difficult question, though *CFTC v. Commodities Fluctuations Systems, Inc.*, 583 F. Supp. 1382, 1384 (S.D.N.Y. 1984), aff'd without opinion, 788 F.2d 4 (2d Cir. 1986), provides a bit of support for the Commission's answer, and no case is against it. The fraud was committed by Pinckney in soliciting customers for his commodity pools, and Rosenthal contends that Pinckney was its agent not to solicit investors in commodity pools but to steer commodity brokerage business its way. Indeed, Rosenthal questions whether Pinckney was an agent in any but a technical sense. It says he really was a customer, who bought brokerage services from Rosenthal; and because he was a good customer, Rosenthal agreed to give him (in effect) a discount off the price of those services. But to do this lawfully, Rosenthal argues, it had to make him an "associated person" of Rosenthal and a registered representative of the commodities exchanges. Because the rules of those exchanges require that all exchange business be done in offices exclusively dedicated to such business, Rosenthal also had to set up Pinckney in his tenth-floor office, yet so far as appears none of the customers for the commodity pools was even aware of the office. Pinckney's status as an associated person authorized him to solicit business on Rosenthal's behalf, but there is no indication he did so. As a matter of fact it would have been unlikely for him to do so. Rosenthal appears to have had no interest in having Pinckney's customers as customers for its brokerage business. It was content to have them as indirect customers, in the sense that Pinckney's brokerage business with Rosenthal depended on his success in attracting investors to his pools.

This is a good line of argument and if the Commission had accepted it we don't suppose that we or any other court would think the Commission had taken leave of its senses. But we also think the Commission was entitled, without being deemed to have acted unreasonably or without substantial evidence, to conclude that Pinckney was acting within the scope of his agency when he instructed his salesmen to delay in sending investors the subscription agreement. Rosenthal did not have to make Pinckney a branch manager, and lease an office for him, in order to be able to compensate him, by splitting commissions, for the brokerage business that he gave it. All that was required was that Pinckney register with the commodities exchanges. See 1 Johnson, *supra*, §§ 1.44, 3.15. To do this on his own he would have had to put up some capital. By becoming an associated person he was able to use Rosenthal's capital, but nothing in the law required Rosenthal to put up the money for his registration, let alone to pay for the office that Pinckney was required to have for his exchange activities or to make Pinckney a branch manager.

Rosenthal did all this in the hope that Pinckney would generate more brokerage business for it by vigorous solicitation of investors for his commodity pools. Rosenthal knew about the pools and must have known that it was encouraging Pinckney to continue and if possible augment the solicitations that had brought the existing investors into these pools. One of Rosenthal's executives described Pinckney as a "salesperson" for Rosenthal. The subscription agreements, which were reviewed and approved by Rosenthal, described Pinckney as "a commodity solicitor with Rosenthal & Company, the futures commission merchant through which the (commodity pool) will execute most of its trades." The fact that the fraud consisted of delaying the sending of these agreements to the investors does not detract from their significance in characterizing the relationship of Pinckney and Rosenthal as Rosenthal itself viewed it. Rosenthal apparently thought of Pinckney's customers as its indirect customers and Pinckney as its solicitor of these indirect customers.

Rosenthal argues that there was no way in which it could have policed Pinckney's solicitations and thereby prevented the fraud. In so arguing it appeals to the policy behind respondeat superior. That policy is to encourage employers and other principals to monitor the conduct of their often judgment-proof (or fine-proof) employees. See *Anderson v. Marathon Petroleum Co.*, 801 F.2d 936, slip op. at 3–5 (7th Cir. 1986). But Rosenthal takes too narrow a view of monitoring. It could not practicably have assigned someone to make himself Pinckney's shadow and give a shout whenever he saw Pinckney committing a fraud, but it could have investigated Pinckney's operation before signing him on, and after signing him on could have conducted discreet spot checks of the operation from time to time. We do not say it was careless in failing to do more than it did, because there is no proof that it was. But negligence is not required for respondeat superior. Liability under the doctrine is strict, in the belief that employers and sometimes other principals can in the general run of cases prevent torts committed by their employees or agents in furtherance of the employment or agency. The belief does not have to be substantiated in every case. * * *

AFFIRMED.

(B) CONTROLLING PERSON LIABILITY

IN THE MATTER OF JAMES R. BURGESS
2006 WL 237509 (C.F.T.C.)

The Commodity Futures Trading Commission ("Commission") has reason to believe that Optioneer Inc., doing business as "Optioneer Systems" ("Optioneer"), by and through its employees and/or agents, including James R. Burgess ("Burgess"), has violated Sections 4*o*(1)(A) and (B) of the Commodity Exchange Act, as amended ("the Act"), 7 U.S.C. §§ 6*o*(1)(A) and (B) (2002), and Sections 4.41(a)(1) and (2) and 4.41(b)(1) and (2) of the Commission's Regulations promulgated thereunder, 17 C.F.R. §§ 4.41(a)(1)–(2), 4.41(b)(1)–(2) (2005) ("Regulations"). Burgess is liable as a controlling person for Optioneer's violations of the Act and Commission Regulations pursuant to Section 13(b) of the Act. Therefore, the Commission deems it appropriate and in the public interest that public administrative proceedings be, and they hereby are, instituted to determine whether Optioneer and Burgess (collectively, the "Respondents") engaged in the violations set forth herein and to determine whether any order should be issued imposing remedial sanctions.

In anticipation of the institution of an administrative proceeding, Respondents have submitted a Joint Offer of Settlement ("Joint Offer"), which the Commission has determined to accept. Respondents acknowledge service of this Order Instituting Proceedings Pursuant to Sections 6(c) and 6(d) of the Act, Making Findings and Imposing Remedial Sanctions ("Order"). Respondents, without admitting or denying the findings of fact or conclusions of law herein, consent to the use of the findings contained in this Order in this proceeding and in any other proceeding brought by the Commission or to which the Commission is a party.

The Commission finds the following:

From at least August 2002 through July 2004 (the "relevant period"), Optioneer, an unregistered commodity trading advisor ("CTA"), used misleading and false advertising to solicit members of the public to purchase its Optioneer trading system, which included hardware, software, training, technical support, monthly data and market information. On its website, www.Optioneer.com ("the Optioneer website"), the company falsely touted substantial profits that could be made using the trading system and a related commodity options trading advisory service. However, the Respondents had no documentary evidence to support such claims. Finally, Optioneer failed to tell clients and prospective clients that the performance histories of the system and advisory service were based on simulated or hypothetical trading, and failed to provide those persons with the required disclosures concerning the inherent limitations of hypothetical or simulated trading.

By making such material misrepresentations about its trading system, Optioneer, by and through its agents, including Burgess, violated Sections 4o(1)(A) and (B) of the Act and Commission Regulation 4.41(a)(1) and (2). In addition, Optioneer's failure to advise clients and prospective clients about the hypothetical or simulated nature of the performance histories and advisory service, and failure to provide the required disclosure concerning hypothetical trades, violated Commission Regulation 4.41(b)(1) and (2).

At all times during the relevant period, Burgess was the controlling person of Optioneer and he is therefore liable for Optioneer's violations of Sections 4o(1)(A) and (B) of the Act and Commission Regulations 4.41(a)(1) and (2), 4.41(b)(1) and (2), pursuant to Section 13(b) of the Act.
* * *

Section 13(b) of the Act imposes liability upon "[a]ny person who, directly or indirectly, controls any person who has violated any provision" of the Act or Regulations. "A fundamental purpose of Section 13(b) is to allow the Commission to reach behind the business entity to the controlling individual and to impose liability for violations of the Act directly on such individual as well as on the entity itself." *In re Glass,* [Current Transfer Binder] Comm. Fut. L. Rep. (CCH) ¶ 27,337 at 46,561–4 (CFTC April 27, 1998); *see also In re Apache Trading Corp.,* [1990–1992 Transfer Binder] Comm. Fut. L. Rep. (CCH) ¶ 25,251 at 38,794 (CFTC March 11, 1992).

Controlling person liability attaches if a person possesses the ability to control the activities upon which the primary liability is predicated, even if that ability was not exercised. *See Monieson v. CFTC,* 996 F.2d 852, 859 (7th Cir. 1993). In addition, Section 13(b) of the Act requires that the controlling person "did not act in good faith or knowingly induced, directly or indirectly, the act or acts constituting the violation." All that is required to constitute "knowing inducement" under Section 13(b) of the Act is that the controlling person "had actual or constructive knowledge of the core activities that constitute the violation at issue and allowed them to continue." *In re Spiegel,* [1987–1990 Transfer Binder] Comm. Fut. L. Rep. (CCH) ¶ 24,103 at 34,767 (CFTC Jan. 12, 1988).

Burgess had the requisite power and control. He exercised day-to-day authority over Optioneer and its employees and performed all important managerial functions. For example, Burgess supervised the other Optioneer employees, and controlled the content posted on Optioneer's website and set forth in other promotional materials. Thus, Burgess was a controlling person of Optioneer.

At all times during the relevant period, Burgess had actual and/or constructive knowledge of the fraudulent activities, since he knew that the claims posted on the Optioneer website were not supported by any Optioneer track record and that Optioneer's customers were not consistently achieving the claims posted on its website. In fact, Burgess knew that only one of Optioneer's clients achieved the results claimed on the Optioneer website. Burgess registered the Optioneer website, helped create the website, and had the ability to control the content of the website, but nevertheless permitted the fraudulent misrepresentations to be made on the website. Burgess either included misrepresentations on the website intentionally or failed to act in good faith by failing to prevent such representations from being posted. Thus, pursuant to Section 13(b) of the Act, Burgess is liable as a controlling person for Optioneer's violations of Section 4o(1)(A) and (B) of the Act and Commission Regulations 4.41(a)(1) and (2) and 4.41(b)(1) and (2). * * *

(C) AIDING AND ABETTING LIABILITY

IN THE MATTER OF LINCOLNWOOD COMMODITIES, INC. OF CALIFORNIA
1984 CFTC LEXIS 773 (C.F.T.C.)

[T]he Administrative Law Judge found that all of the individual respondents, other than Josephine Charleton, aided and abetted respondent Lincolnwood's maintaining books and records which contained false information concerning their fictitious accounts and commingling of proprietary funds with customer funds. Respondents Lincolnwood and Baksheeff were found to have aided and abetted respondent Almgren in his unauthorized combination of customer accounts. Finally, respondent Baksheeff was found to have aided and abetted respondent Lincolnwood in failure to comply with the Commission's minimum capital requirements for FCMs and in the filing of required reports with the Commission which contained false statements of Lincolnwood's financial condition.

On appeal, respondents argue that the evidence does not support the Administrative Law Judge's findings of willful aiding and abetting under the standards enunciated by the Commission in In the Matter of Richardson Securities, Inc., 2 COMM. FUT. L. REP. (CCH) P21,145 (January 27, 1981) ("Richardson"). Respondents' arguments on appeal raise once again the issue of when, under Section 13(a) of the Act, a person may be said to have "willfully" aided and abetted violations of the Act committed by another person and thereby be held responsible as a principal for those violations.

In Richardson, we carefully reviewed the language and legislative history of Section 13(a) and concluded that the term "willfully" was inserted in this provision to assure that persons would be held liable only where "knowing participation" in aiding the unlawful conduct of the primary wrongdoer was established; that unintentional aiding of another's improper actions would not be sufficient to establish liability; and that therefore the standard of proof of 18 U.S.C. § 2, the Federal criminal aiding and abetting provision, was meant to apply in civil administrative proceedings involving Section 13(a) of the Act. Richardson, at 24,642–43. In view of this expressed congressional intent, the Commission held that "willfully" aiding and abetting for purposes of Section 13(a) required a person knowingly to associate himself with an unlawful venture and to participate in it as something he wishes to bring about and seek by his actions to make succeed. Richardson, at 24,646. Subsequently, in In the matter of Earl K. Riley & Company, et al., CFTC Docket No. 80–15 (Commission Opinion and Order, November 24, 1981), we reaffirmed our views as set forth in Richardson, holding that mere reckless behavior was insufficient to meet the knowing participation requirement subsumed within the term "willfully" in Section 13(a).

It may appear somewhat incongruous to employ a standard derived from criminal law in proving aiding and abetting in civil proceedings enforcing a remedial statute like the Commodity Exchange Act, particularly in those cases where the underlying violation may be established without proof of any elements of scienter. Yet we believe there are sound public policy reasons for this legislative approach. In those instances where concepts of general or specific intent may be disregarded in imposing civil liability on primary wrongdoers, e.g., where a violation by a futures commission merchant of the segregation provisions of Section 4d(2) of the Act is involved, Congress has struck the balance decidedly in favor of the integrity of the market place and the protection of customers. Thus, any requirement of proof of mens rea on the part of primary wrongdoers is subordinated to these greater public interests. In such cases, it is more important to stop and deter these types of violations than it is to find that they were "willfully" committed.

Irrespective of the level of proof required to establish the primary violation, however, the evidentiary standards of aiding and abetting imposed by Section 13(a) are designed to assure that remedial sanctions will not be imposed against a secondary respondent who intentionally assists a primary wrongdoer but lacks knowledge of the unlawful conduct. Knowing participation thus becomes a critical focus of the inquiry and strikes a balance between punishment of the principal wrongdoer and protection of those who unknowingly assist unlawful conduct. As stated by a leading commentator in discussing aiding and abetting in the context of securities law fraud cases:

If all that is required in order to impose liability for aiding and abetting is that illegal activity under the securities laws exists and that a secondary defendant, such as a bank, gave aid to that illegal activity, the act of loaning funds to the market manipulator would clearly fall within that category and would expose the bank to liability for aiding and abetting. Imposition of such liability upon banks would virtually make them insurers regarding the conduct of insiders to whom they loan money. If it is assumed that an illegal scheme existed and that the bank's loan or other activity provided assistance to that scheme, some remaining distinguishing factor must be found in order to prevent such automatic liability.

Under Section 13(a) of the Act, the distinguishing factor is "willful" conduct exemplified by knowing participation in and intentional assistance of unlawful conduct.

While the standards of Section 13(a) may be high, they do not pose an impossible obstacle to vigorous law enforcement. Nothing in Richardson or Earl K. Riley suggests that knowing participation and intentional assistance require the Commission to establish that the aider and abettor knew the principal's activity was unlawful. Ignorance of the law is no more a defense for the aider and abettor that it is for the primary wrongdoer. Cf. United States v. Gregg, 612 F.2d 43, 50–51 (2d Cir. 1979); United States v. McDaniel, 545 F.2d 642, 644 (9th Cir. 1976); United States v. Schilleci, 545 F.2d 519, 526 (5th Cir. 1977); See United States v. Corbin Farm Service, 444 F. Supp. 510, 524–25 (E.D. Cal. 1978); United States v. J & J Truck Leasing, Inc., 258 F. Supp. 105, 110 (D. Kan. 1966). This is especially true when the person charged with aiding and abetting a violation is himself an industry professional who operates in a highly-regulated field which imposes duties upon him that do not attach to the public at large. Cf. del Junco v. C. T. Conover, 682 F.2d 1338, 1342 (9th Cir. 1982).

Moreover, to say that the aider and abettor must be shown to have "knowingly" participated in the illegal conduct is not to say that direct proof of knowledge is necessary in all cases. Given the difficulties in probing the minds of men, the Commission is not foreclosed from inferring knowledge from the evidence adduced. As the Eighth Circuit has stated in a case involving the receipt of stolen goods (emphasis added):

> "The requisite guilty knowledge need not be actual, direct, positive, or absolute, but may be constructive, implied, or circumstantial. It is not essential to a conviction that the requisite guilty knowledge that the goods were stolen should be actual, direct or positive and absolute, such, for instance, as knowledge acquired by having personally witnessed or observed

the theft, or by information of the theft from persons who had personal knowledge, such as eyewitnesses or the person from whom the goods were received; the requisite knowledge may be circumstantial or deductive, and constructive or implied knowledge through notice of facts and circumstances from which guilty knowledge may be fairly inferred satisfies the requirements as to knowledge.

Costello v. United States, 255 F.2d 389, 400 (8th Cir. 1958), cert. denied, 358 U.S. 830 (1958). The Commission is likewise free to inter the requisite knowing conduct from all the attendant circumstances.[106] Accordingly, it is our task in any given case to determine whether the evidence establishes that a primary violation has occurred, and that the person charged with aiding and abetting that violation may fairly be found to have knowingly participated in the violation and purposefully assisted in its commission.

On the other hand, to hold an individual officer of the corporate advisor liable as an aider and abettor of the firm's violation requires satisfaction of the standards of Section 13(a) of the Act. Richardson at 24,646, n. 14. The officer must be shown to have knowingly participated and intentionally assisted in the conduct that Section 4o makes unlawful—the dissemination of market information that is false or misleading. If the evidence shows that the officer acted based on a mistake of fact (he meant to approve document A, but approved document B or that he had a good faith belief that the information was not false) he will not be held liable as an aider and abettor. If the evidence establishes, however, that the officer knows that the information is false and purposely or intentionally assists in its preparation or dissemination he will be held liable. See also IIT, an International Investment Trust v. Cornfeld, supra, 619 F.2d at 927 (aiding and abetting liability can also result from inaction where an individual knowingly and purposefully fails to act in violation of an independent duty to act). And, as noted above, such knowledge may be inferred from attendant circumstances, e.g., by evidence establishing the officer's educational background, knowledge of the business and position in the firm, and other factors that would be probative of his knowledge of the character of the information. * * *

---

[106] These inferences take on added significance in establishing aiding and abetting where scienter is not an element of the underlying violation. For example, a corporate commodity trading advisor can violate the antifraud provisions of Section 4o(1) of the Act by disseminating false market information without any showing that the firm, through its employees or other agents, intended to defraud its clients or knew that the information was false. This is consistent with the congressional goal of discouraging the enticement of unsuspecting traders and eliminating undesirable business practices. Savage v. Commodity Futures Trading Commission, 611 F.2d 270, 285 (9th Cir. 1979). This Congressional policy encourages commodity trading advisors to take every precaution that is practicable to prevent the dissemination of false information by its employees, because it will be held liable under Section 4o even if it acted in the good faith belief that the information it disseminated was true.

(D) FAILURE TO SUPERVISE

SANCHEZ V. CROWN
2006 CFTC LEXIS 4 (C.F.T.C.)

* * * We turn to the Judgment Officer's finding that Crown failed to supervise Denn diligently. Commission Rule 166.3 states:

> Each Commission registrant, except an associated person who has no supervisory duties, must diligently supervise the handling by its partners, officers, employees and agents (or persons occupying a similar status or performing a similar function) of all commodity interest accounts carried, operated, advised or introduced by the registrant and all other activities of its partners, officers, employees and agents (or persons occupying a similar status or performing a similar function) relating to its business as a Commission registrant.

"The objective of Regulation 166.3 is to protect customers from fraudulent or manipulative activities of Commission registrants." *Modlin v. Cane,* [1996–1998 Transfer Binder] Comm. Fut. L. Rep. (CCH) P 27,392 at 46,809 (CFTC July 30, 1998) *citing In re Paragon Futures Association,* [1990–1992 Transfer Binder] Comm. Fut. L. Rep. P 25,266 at 38,850 (CFTC April 1, 1992). Failure to supervise is an independent and primary violation of the Commission's rules. *Paragon,* P 25,266 at 38,849.

When it adopted the rule, the Commission stated that its "basic purpose . . . is to protect customers by ensuring that their dealings with the employees of Commission registrants will be reviewed by other officials in the firm." Customer Protection Rules, 43 Fed. Reg. 31,886, 31,889 (July 24, 1978). Nonetheless, in proposing this rule, the Commission specifically recognized that "the performance of a wrongful act by an employee . . . does not necessarily mean that the employee was improperly supervised, although it is often a strong indication of a lack of proper supervision." Protection of Commodity Customers, 42 Fed. Reg. 44,742, 44,747 (Sept. 6, 1977). The focus of an inquiry to determine whether Rule 166.3 has been violated is on whether review occurred, and if it did, whether it was diligent. *In re First Investors Group of the Palm Beaches,* [2003–2004 Transfer Binder] Comm. Fut. L. Rep. P 29,767 at 56,210 (CFTC May 24, 2004).

In a reparations case, to establish a violation of Rule 166.3, a complainant must show more than a supervisory relationship and a violation of the Act leading to damages. *Bunch v. First Commodity Corp. of Boston,* [1990–1992 Transfer Binder] Comm. Fut. L. Rep. (CCH) P 25,352 at 39,168 (CFTC Aug. 5, 1992), *citing Callahan v. Delphi Commodities, Inc.,* [1987–1990 Transfer Binder] Comm. Fut. L. Rep.

(CCH) P 24,060, at 34,645 n.4 (CFTC Dec. 18, 1987). In assessing an alleged violation of Rule 166.3, the Commission focuses on: (1) the nature of a respondent's system of supervision; (2) the supervisor's role in that system of supervision; and (3) evidence that the supervisor did not perform his assigned role in a diligent manner. In addition, a complainant must establish that the supervisor's breach of duty played a substantial role in the wrongdoing that proximately caused the damages. *Id.* at 39,168–69. To find an individual supervisor liable, the complainant must show either that the respondent had knowledge of wrongdoing and failed to take reasonable steps to correct the problem, or that the respondent failed to discharge specific responsibilities of supervision. In addition, it must be shown that respondent's failure was the proximate cause of complainant's damages. *Id.* at 39,169.

Crown's testimony included an explanation of ITG's system of supervision and his role in it. *See generally* Tr. at 135–46. Crown testified that, at the time at issue, he was the president and manager of ITG; his duties included instructing, training, and overseeing brokers. Tr. at 135. Subject to Marshall's approval, Crown established the compensation package (which included his share in the brokers' commissions) and hired and fired brokers. Tr. at 141. He confirmed that he was responsible for implementing, monitoring, and enforcing policies and procedures to detect, deter, and prevent fraudulent sales practices and other violations and that he was required to report any material problems to Marshall. Tr. at 141–42. Crown was responsible for reviewing the trading activity in all of the brokers' accounts, including Denn's, and was aware of Sanchez's account and his situation. Tr. at 142–43. Denn's fraudulent solicitation of Sanchez standing alone, however, "does not necessarily mean that [she] was improperly supervised." Protection of Commodity Customers, 42 Fed. Reg. at 44,747.

While Crown may have been aware of the status of Sanchez's account, there is no evidence that Crown was aware of Denn's material misrepresentations to him. Neither Crown nor Denn testified about his oversight of her conversations with Sanchez. There is no evidence that he listened to the conversations between Denn and Sanchez or discussed them with her, or that there were other factors that should have put him on notice to watch her more closely. Since the evidence does not show that Crown had knowledge of Denn's wrongdoing and failed to take reasonable steps to correct the problem or that he failed to discharge specific responsibilities of supervision, we conclude that there is not enough evidence to find that Crown failed to supervise Denn diligently in relation to her fraudulent solicitation of Sanchez. Accordingly, we vacate the Judgment Officer's finding that Crown violated Rule 166.3.

Crown also testified that the compliance director, Rogers, not Crown himself, was responsible for the explanation of risk and that the compliance department reviewed account opening documents. Tr. at 147–48. Rogers confirmed Crown's testimony by acknowledging that he performed the compliance responsibilities at ITG and was "in charge of the compliance people who actually recorded the trades and the initial compliance procedures for the customers." Tr. at 230. Rogers, not Crown, had the duty to supervise Denn and her compliance with the obligation to provide the required risk disclosure statement before she began trading customer accounts. Rogers, however, is not a party to this proceeding.

Based on the foregoing, we find that ITG failed to provide Sanchez with the risk disclosure statement required by Commission Rule 33.7, and that Denn aided and abetted ITG's violation. We also find TNT derivatively liable under Section 2(a)(1)(B) of the Act for the violations of Denn and ITG. We affirm the Judgment Officer's findings that Denn fraudulently induced Sanchez to open a commodity options account by overstating the likelihood of profit and that ITG and TNT are derivatively liable for Denn's violations under Section 2(a)(1)(B) of the Act. We vacate those portions of the I.D. that find Crown liable and dismiss the complaint against him. We affirm the $24,396 award of Sanchez's out-of-pocket damages. Denn, ITG, and TNT are jointly and severally liable.
* * *

NOTE

1. The NFA also imposes supervisory requirements:

NFA Compliance Rule 2–9 places a continuing responsibility on every Member to diligently supervise its employees and agents in all aspects of their futures-related activities, while NFA Compliance Rule 2–36 (and Compliance Rule 2–39 by reference to Compliance Rule 2–36), imposes the same requirements on Members with respect to their forex-related activities. NFA recognizes that, given the differences in the size and complexity of the operations of NFA Members, there must be some degree of flexibility in determining what constitutes "diligent supervision" for each firm. It is NFA's policy to leave the exact form of supervision to the Member, thereby providing the Member with flexibility to design procedures that are tailored to the Member's own situation. However, NFA believes that all Members should regularly review the adequacy of their supervisory procedures.

In order to satisfy their continuing supervisory responsibilities under Compliance Rules 2–9, 2–36 and 2–39, NFA Members must review their operations on a yearly basis using NFA's Self-Examination Questionnaire, which includes a general questionnaire that must be completed by all Members and five supplemental questionnaires (e.g. FCM, FDM, IB, CPO and CTA) that must be completed as applicable. The questionnaires are designed to aid

Members in recognizing potential problem areas and to alert them to procedures that need to be revised or strengthened. The questionnaires focus on the Member's regulatory responsibilities and solicit information regarding whether the Member's internal procedures are adequate for meeting these responsibilities.

NFA, Self-Examination Questionnaire For FCMs, FDMs, IBs, CPOs and CTAs (May 2013).

IN THE MATTER OF JOHN H. GUTFREUND
51 S.E.C. 93 (1992)

The Commission deems it appropriate and in the public interest that public administrative proceedings be and they hereby are instituted against John H. Gutfreund, Thomas W. Strauss, and John W. Meriwether pursuant to Section 15(b) of the Securities Exchange Act of 1934 ("Exchange Act").

In anticipation of the institution of these administrative proceedings, Gutfreund, Strauss, and Meriwether have each submitted Offers of Settlement which the Commission has determined to accept. Solely for the purposes of these proceedings and any other proceedings brought by or on behalf of the Commission or to which the Commission is a party, prior to a hearing pursuant to the Commission's Rules of Practice, and without admitting or denying the facts, findings, or conclusions herein, Gutfreund, Strauss, and Meriwether each consent to entry of the findings, and the imposition of the remedial sanctions, set forth below. * * *

Salomon Brothers Inc. ("Salomon") is a Delaware corporation with its principal place of business in New York, New York. At all times relevant to this proceeding, Salomon was registered with the Commission as a broker-dealer pursuant to Section 15(b) of the Exchange Act. Salomon has been a government-designated dealer in U.S. Treasury securities since 1939 and a primary dealer since 1961.

John H. Gutfreund was the Chairman and Chief Executive Officer of Salomon from 1983 to August 18, 1991. He had worked at Salomon since 1953.

Thomas W. Strauss was the President of Salomon from 1986 to August 18, 1991. During that time period, Strauss reported to Gutfreund. He had worked at Salomon since 1963.

John W. Meriwether was a Vice Chairman of Salomon and in charge of all fixed income trading activities of the firm from 1988 to August 18, 1991. During that period, Meriwether reported to Strauss. During the same period, Paul W. Mozer, a managing director and the head of Salomon's Government Trading Desk, reported directly to Meriwether.

Donald M. Feuerstein was the chief legal officer of Salomon Inc. and the head of the Legal Department of Salomon until August 23, 1991. From 1987 until August 23, 1991, the head of Salomon's Compliance Department reported directly to Feuerstein.

In late April of 1991, three members of the senior management of Salomon—John Gutfreund, Thomas Strauss, and John Meriwether—were informed that Paul Mozer, the head of the firm's Government Trading Desk, had submitted a false bid in the amount of $3.15 billion in an auction of U.S. Treasury securities on February 21, 1991. The executives were also informed by Donald Feuerstein, the firm's chief legal officer, that the submission of the false bid appeared to be a criminal act and, although not legally required, should be reported to the government. Gutfreund and Strauss agreed to report the matter to the Federal Reserve Bank of New York. Mozer was told that his actions might threaten his future with the firm and would be reported to the government. However, for a period of months, none of the executives took action to investigate the matter or to discipline or impose limitations on Mozer. The information was also not reported to the government for a period of months. During that same period, Mozer committed additional violations of the federal securities laws in connection with two subsequent auctions of U.S. Treasury securities.

The Respondents in this proceeding are not being charged with any participation in the underlying violations. However, as set forth herein, the Commission believes that the Respondents' supervision was deficient and that this failure was compounded by the delay in reporting the matter to the government.

For a considerable period of time prior to the February 21, 1991 auction, the Treasury Department had limited the maximum bid that any one bidder could submit in an auction of U.S. Treasury securities at any one yield to 35% of the auction amount. On February 21, 1991, the Treasury Department auctioned $9 billion of five-year U.S. Treasury notes. Salomon submitted a bid in its own name in that auction at a yield of 7.51% in the amount of $3.15 billion, or 35% of the auction amount. In the same auction, Salomon submitted two additional $3.15 billion bids at the same yield in the names of two customers: Quantum Fund and Mercury Asset Management. Both accounts were those of established customers of Salomon, but the bids were submitted without the knowledge or authorization of either customer. Both bids were in fact false bids intended to secure additional securities for Salomon. Each of the three $3.15 billion bids was prorated 54% and Salomon received a total of $5.103 billion of the five-year notes from the auction, or 56.7% of the total amount of securities sold at that auction.

After the auction results were announced, Paul Mozer, then a managing director in charge of Salomon's Government Trading Desk, directed a clerk to write trade tickets "selling" the $1.701 billion auction allocations received in response to the two unauthorized bids to customer accounts in the names of Mercury Asset Management and Quantum Fund at the auction price. Mozer at the same time directed the clerk to write trade tickets "selling" the same amounts from those accounts back to Salomon at the same price. These fictitious transactions were intended to create the appearance that the customers had received the securities awarded in response to the unauthorized bids and had sold those securities to Salomon.

Under Salomon's internal procedures, the trade tickets written by the clerk resulted in the creation of customer confirmations reflecting the purported transactions. Mozer directed the clerk to prevent the confirmations from being sent to either Mercury Asset Management or Quantum Fund. As a result, the normal procedures of Salomon were overridden and confirmations for the fictitious transactions were not sent to either Mercury Asset Management or Quantum Fund.

The Submission of a bid in the February 21, 1991 Auction by S.G. Warburg and the Treasury Department's Investigation of That Bid and the Salomon False Bid

In the February 21, 1991 five-year note auction, S.G. Warburg, a primary dealer in U.S. Treasury securities, submitted a bid in its own name in the amount of $100 million at a yield of 7.51%. The 7.51% yield was the same yield used for the unauthorized $3.15 billion Mercury bid submitted by Salomon. At the time the bids were submitted, S.G. Warburg and Mercury Asset Management were subsidiaries of the same holding company, S.G. Warburg, PLC. Because the unauthorized Mercury bid was for the maximum 35% amount, the submission of the $100 million bid in the name of S.G. Warburg meant that two bids had apparently been submitted by affiliated entities in an amount in excess of 35% of the auction.

The submission of the bids was noticed by officials of the Federal Reserve Bank of New York and brought to the attention of officials of the Treasury Department in Washington, D.C. The Treasury Department officials did not know that one of the bids had been submitted by Salomon without authorization from Mercury. Because the bids were to be significantly prorated, officials of the Treasury Department decided not to reduce the amount of either bid for purposes of determining the results of the February 21, 1991 auction. The Treasury Department began to review whether the relationship between S.G. Warburg and Mercury Asset Management was such that the bids should be aggregated for determination of how the 35% limitation should be applied to those entities in future auctions.

After reviewing facts concerning the corporate relationship between Mercury Asset Management and S.G. Warburg, the Treasury Department determined to treat the two firms as a single bidder in future auctions of U.S. Treasury securities. The Treasury Department conveyed that decision in a letter dated April 17, 1991 from the Acting Assistant Commissioner for Financing to a Senior Director of Mercury Asset Management in London. The April 17 letter noted that a $3.15 billion bid had been submitted by Salomon on behalf of Mercury Asset Management in the five-year U.S. Treasury note auction on February 21, 1991, and that S.G. Warburg had also submitted a bid in the same auction, at the same yield, in the amount of $100 million. The letter noted that Mercury Asset Management and S.G. Warburg were subsidiaries of the same holding company and stated that the Treasury Department would thereafter "treat all subsidiaries of S.G. Warburg, PLC as one single entity for purposes of the 35 percent limitation rule." Copies of the letter were sent to Mozer and to a managing director of S.G. Warburg in New York.

Mozer received the April 17 letter during the week of April 21, 1991. On April 24, he spoke with the Senior Director at Mercury Asset Management who had also received the April 17 letter. Mozer told the Senior Director that the submission of the $3.15 billion bid in the name of Mercury Asset Management was the result of an "error" by a clerk who had incorrectly placed the name of Mercury on the tender form. Mozer told the Senior Director that he was embarrassed by the "error," which he said had been "corrected" internally, and he asked the Senior Director to keep the matter confidential to avoid "problems." The Senior Director indicated that such a course of action would be acceptable. The Mercury Senior Director was not aware that the submission of the bid was an intentional effort by Salomon to acquire additional securities for its own account.

Mozer then went to the office of John Meriwether, his immediate supervisor, and handed him the April 17 letter. When Meriwether was finished reading the letter, Mozer told him that the Mercury Asset Management bid referred to in the letter was in fact a bid for Salomon and had not been authorized by Mercury. After expressing shock at Mozer's conduct, Meriwether told him that his behavior was career-threatening, and he asked Mozer why he had submitted the bid. Mozer told Meriwether that the Government Trading Desk had needed a substantial amount of the notes, that there was also demand from the Government Arbitrage Desk for the notes, and that he had submitted the false bid to satisfy those demands.

Meriwether then asked Mozer if he had ever engaged in that type of conduct before or since. Mozer responded that he had not. Meriwether told Mozer that he would have to take the matter immediately to Thomas Strauss. Mozer then told Meriwether of his conversation with the Mercury Senior Director in which he had told that individual that the bid was an "error" and had asked him to keep the matter confidential. Meriwether listened to Mozer's description of the conversation, but did not respond. He then gave the letter back to Mozer and Mozer left the office.

Meriwether then called Thomas Strauss. Strauss was not in, but he returned Meriwether's call later that day. Meriwether told Strauss that Mozer had informed him that he had submitted an unauthorized customer bid in an auction of U.S. Treasury securities. Strauss indicated that they should meet to discuss the matter first thing the next morning.

Meriwether met with Strauss at 9:15 a.m. the following morning, April 25, in Strauss' office. Prior to the meeting, Strauss had arranged for Donald Feuerstein, the firm's chief legal officer, to attend, and Feuerstein was in Strauss' office when Meriwether arrived. Meriwether began the meeting by describing his conversation with Mozer the previous day. He told Strauss and Feuerstein that Mozer had come to him and had informed him that he had submitted an unauthorized customer bid in an auction of U.S. Treasury securities. He said that he had informed Mozer that his conduct was career-threatening and that Mozer had denied that he had ever before or since engaged in that type of conduct. He indicated that Mozer had received a letter from the Treasury Department inquiring about the bid and that Mozer had shown him a copy of that letter. Meriwether also reported that Mozer had said that he had submitted the bid to satisfy demand for the securities from the Government Trading Desk and from Salomon's Government Arbitrage Desk. Finally, he told Strauss and Feuerstein that Mozer had informed him that he had contacted an individual at Mercury Asset Management who had also received the letter from the Treasury Department. Meriwether indicated that Mozer had told that individual that the submission of the bid was an error, and had attempted to persuade him not to inform the government of that fact.

When Meriwether was finished, Feuerstein said that Mozer's conduct was a serious matter and should be reported to the government. Feuerstein asked to see a copy of the April 17 letter. Meriwether returned to the trading floor and retrieved the letter from Mozer. He then returned to Strauss' office and provided the letter to Feuerstein. After some discussion about the letter, Strauss said he wanted to discuss the matter with Gutfreund, who was then out of town, and the meeting ended.

A meeting was then held early the following week, on either Monday, April 29 or Tuesday, April 30, with Gutfreund. The meeting was attended by Meriwether, Feuerstein, Strauss and Gutfreund and was held in Strauss' office. Meriwether summarized his conversation with Mozer. Meriwether also indicated that he believed that the incident was an aberration and he expressed his hope that it would not end Mozer's career at Salomon.

After Meriwether's description, Feuerstein told the group that he believed that the submission of the false bid was a criminal act. He indicated that, while there probably was not a legal duty to report the false bid, he believed that they had no choice but to report the matter to the government. The group then discussed whether the bid should be reported to the Treasury Department or to the Federal Reserve Bank of New York. The hostile relationship that had developed between Mozer and the Treasury Department over the adoption of the 35% bidding limitation in the Summer of 1990 was noted, as was the role of the Federal Reserve Bank of New York as Salomon's regulator in the area of U.S. Treasury securities, and the group concluded that the preferable approach would be to report the matter to the Federal Reserve Bank of New York. The meeting then ended.

At the conclusion of the meeting, each of the four executives apparently believed that a decision had been made that Strauss or Gutfreund would report the false bid to the government, although each had a different understanding about how the report would be handled. Meriwether stated that he believed that Strauss would make an appointment to report the matter to Gerald Corrigan, the President of the Federal Reserve Bank of New York. Feuerstein stated that he believed that Gutfreund wanted to think further about how the bid should be reported. He then spoke with Gutfreund the next morning. Although the April 17 letter had been sent from the Treasury Department, Feuerstein told Gutfreund that he believed the report should be made to the Federal Reserve Bank of New York, which could then, if it wanted, pass the information on to the Treasury Department. Strauss stated that he believed that he and Gutfreund would report the matter in a personal visit with Corrigan, although he believed that Gutfreund wanted to think further about how the matter should be handled. Gutfreund stated that he believed that a decision had been made that he and Strauss, either separately or together, would speak to Corrigan about the matter.

Aside from the discussions referred to above regarding reporting the matter to the government, there was no discussion at either meeting in late April about investigating what Mozer had done, about disciplining him, or about placing limits on his activities. There was also no discussion about whether Mozer had acted alone or had been assisted by others on the Government Trading Desk, about whether false records had been created, about the involvement of the Government Arbitrage Desk, which Mozer had said had sought securities from the auction, or about what had happened with the securities obtained pursuant to the bid. Similarly, there was no discussion about whether Salomon had violated the 35% bidding limitation by also submitting a bid in its own name.

For almost three months, no action was taken to investigate Mozer's conduct in the February 21 auction. That conduct was investigated only after other events prompted an internal investigation by an outside law firm, as is discussed below. During the same period, no action was taken to discipline Mozer or to place appropriate limitations on his conduct. Mozer's employment by Salomon was terminated on August 9, 1991, after an internal investigation had discovered that he had been involved in additional improper conduct.

Each of the four executives who attended the meetings in late April placed the responsibility for investigating Mozer's conduct and placing limits on his activities on someone else. Meriwether stated that he believed that, once he had taken the matter of Mozer's conduct to Strauss and Strauss had brought Feuerstein and Gutfreund into the process, he had no further responsibility to take action with respect to the false bid unless instructed to do so by one of those individuals. Meriwether stated that he also believed that, though he had the authority to recommend that action be taken to discipline Mozer or limit his activities, he had no authority to take such action unilaterally. Strauss stated that he believed that Meriwether, who was Mozer's direct supervisor, and Feuerstein, who was responsible for the legal and compliance activities of the firm, would take whatever steps were necessary or required as a result of Mozer's disclosure. Feuerstein stated that he believed that, once a report to the government was made, the government would instruct Salomon about how to investigate the matter. Gutfreund stated that he believed that the other executives would take whatever steps were necessary to properly handle the matter. According to the executives, there was no discussion among them about any action that would be taken to investigate Mozer's conduct or to place limitations on his activities.

After Mozer's disclosure of one unauthorized bid on April 24, 1991, he submitted two subsequent unauthorized bids in auctions of U.S. Treasury securities. * * *

There was no disclosure to the government of the false bid in the February 21, 1991 auction prior to August 9, 1991, when the results of the internal investigation were first made public.

In mid-May, after it had become clear to Feuerstein that the false bid had not yet been reported, Feuerstein met with Gutfreund and Strauss and urged them to proceed with disclosure as soon as possible. He was told by both that they still intended to report the matter. Feuerstein also learned from the in-house attorney who worked with the Government Trading Desk of a proposal by Mozer that Salomon finance in excess of 100% of the amount of the two-year U.S. Treasury notes auctioned on May 22, 1991. Feuerstein expressed his disapproval of the proposal to the attorney. Feuerstein believed that Mozer's support for this proposal, his submission of the unauthorized bid in the February auction, and his conduct during the Summer of 1990 which led to the adoption of the 35% bidding limitation combined to indicate that he had an "attitudinal problem." Prior to leaving for Japan on May 23, 1991, Feuerstein spoke with Strauss and conveyed these concerns to him. He also again discussed with Strauss his belief that the bid should be reported to the government as soon as possible. Feuerstein also spoke with Gutfreund in early June and again urged him to report the matter to the government.

Strauss and Gutfreund also discussed the matter of reporting the bid on several occasions during this period. On at least one occasion, Strauss also urged Gutfreund to decide how to handle the matter and to proceed with disclosure to the government. Gutfreund indicated on these occasions that he still intended to report the false bid to the government. Gutfreund stated that he believed, however, that the false bid was a minor aberration, and that the reporting of the bid was not a matter of high priority.

. . . [I]n the auction on May 22, 1991 for two-year U.S. Treasury notes, Salomon and two customers bid for and received approximately 86% of the two-year notes. On May 23, reports appeared in the press concerning rumors of a possible "squeeze" in the May two-year issue. On May 30, press reports mentioned Salomon by name in connection with a rumored short squeeze in the two-year notes.

In early June, Strauss spoke by telephone with a senior official of the Treasury Department. Strauss told the official that the firm was aware of the Department's interest in the May 22, 1991 auction and was willing to discuss the matter with the Department. Following Strauss' call, Gutfreund arranged to meet with officials of the Treasury Department to discuss Salomon's role in the May 22, 1991 auction.

On June 10, 1991, Gutfreund met with an Under Secretary of the Treasury and other Treasury Department officials in Washington, D.C. During the meeting, Gutfreund told the Treasury Department officials that he believed that the firm had acted properly in connection with the May 22, 1991 auction, and he indicated that the firm would cooperate with any inquiries by the Department into the matter. While the focus of the discussion at the meeting was the May 22, 1991 auction, Gutfreund did not disclose to the Treasury Department officials that he knew that a false bid had been submitted in the February 21, 1991 five-year note auction by the head of the firm's Government Trading Desk, the same individual responsible for the firm's activities in connection with the May two-year note issue.

On June 19, Meriwether, Strauss and Gutfreund met to discuss the allegations concerning the May 22, 1991 two-year note auction. At that meeting, Strauss and Gutfreund decided that disclosure of the unauthorized customer bid in the February 21, 1991 auction should be delayed until more information could be obtained about Salomon's activities in the May two-year note auction. No decision was made about how much time should elapse before a report was made. While Gutfreund and Strauss were under the general impression that someone in the legal department was reviewing the May 22, 1991 auction, there was not any discussion about any specific efforts or inquiries that would have to be undertaken before a report could be made. There were also no efforts or inquiries underway at that time to investigate Mozer's conduct in the February 21, 1991 auction. Feuerstein was not informed of or present at the meeting and was not informed of the decision to delay the disclosure.

For the next several weeks, there was not any further consideration of reporting the unauthorized bid in the February 21, 1991 auction to the government. Some discussion about limiting Mozer's activities did occur in late June with respect to the auction for June two-year U.S. Treasury notes. On the day of the auction, Strauss and Gutfreund told Mozer that he should not bid in an aggressive or high-profile manner in the auction because of the attention which had been focused on Salomon's role in the May two-year auction. * * *

Following an intensive investigation, on May 20, 1992, the Commission filed a complaint in U.S. District Court for the Southern District of New York charging Salomon and its publicly-held parent, Salomon Inc., with numerous violations of the federal securities laws. Among other things, the complaint charged that Salomon had submitted or caused to be submitted ten false bids in nine separate auctions for U.S. Treasury securities between August of 1989 and May of 1991. The false bids alleged in the complaint totaled $15.5 billion and resulted in the illegal acquisition by Salomon of $9.548 billion of U.S. Treasury securities. The complaint alleged that submission of the bids allowed Salomon repeatedly to circumvent the limitations imposed by the Treasury Department on the amount of securities any one person or entity may obtain from auctions of U.S. Treasury securities.

Simultaneously with the filing of the action, Salomon and Salomon Inc. consented, without admitting or denying the allegations of the complaint, to the entry of a Final Judgment of Permanent Injunction and Other Relief. The Judgment required, among other things, that Salomon pay the amount of $290 million, representing a payment of $190 million to the United States Treasury as civil penalties and asset forfeitures and a payment of $100 million to establish a civil claims fund to be administered by a Fund Administrator appointed by the Court.

On May 20, 1992, the Commission also instituted and settled, pursuant to an Offer of Settlement submitted by Salomon, an administrative proceeding against the firm pursuant to Section 15(b) of the Exchange Act. In that proceeding, the Commission found that Salomon had failed, in connection with the facts described in this Order, reasonably to supervise a person subject to its supervision with a view to preventing violations of the federal securities laws.

Section 15(b)(4)(E) of the Exchange Act authorizes the Commission to impose sanctions against a broker-dealer if the firm has:

> failed reasonably to supervise, with a view to preventing violations [of federal securities laws], another person who commits such a violation, if such person is subject to his supervision.

Section 15(b)(6) of the Exchange incorporates Section 15(b)(4)(E) by reference and authorizes the Commission to impose sanctions for deficient supervision on individuals associated with broker-dealers.

The principles which govern this proceeding are well-established by the Commission's cases involving failure to supervise. The Commission has long emphasized that the responsibility of broker-dealers to supervise their employees is a critical component of the federal regulatory scheme. As the Commission stated in Wedbush Securities, Inc.: In large organizations it is especially imperative that those in authority exercise particular vigilance when indications of irregularity reach their attention.

The supervisory obligations imposed by the federal securities laws require a vigorous response even to indications of wrongdoing. Many of the Commission's cases involving a failure to supervise arise from situations where supervisors were aware only of "red flags" or "suggestions" of irregularity, rather than situations where, as here, supervisors were explicitly informed of an illegal act.

Even where the knowledge of supervisors is limited to "red flags" or "suggestions" of irregularity, they cannot discharge their supervisory obligations simply by relying on the unverified representations of employees. Instead, as the Commission has repeatedly emphasized, "[t]here must be adequate follow-up and review when a firm's own procedures detect irregularities or unusual trading activity. . . ." Moreover, if more than one supervisor is involved in considering the actions to be taken in response to possible misconduct, there must be a clear definition of the efforts to be taken and a clear assignment of those responsibilities to specific individuals within the firm.

As described above, in late April of 1991 three supervisors of Paul Mozer—John Meriwether, Thomas Strauss, and John Gutfreund—learned that Mozer had submitted a false bid in the amount of $3.15 billion in an auction of U.S. Treasury securities. Those supervisors learned that Mozer had said that the bid had been submitted to obtain additional securities for another trading area of the firm. They also learned that Mozer had contacted an employee of the customer whose name was used on the bid and falsely told that individual that the bid was an error. The supervisors also learned that the bid had been the subject of a letter from the Treasury Department to the customer and that Mozer had attempted to persuade the customer not to inform the Treasury Department that the bid had not been authorized. The supervisors were also informed by Salomon's chief legal officer that the submission of the false bid appeared to be a criminal act.

The information learned by the supervisors indicated that a high level employee of the firm with significant trading discretion had engaged in extremely serious misconduct. As the cases described above make clear, this information required, at a minimum, that the supervisors take action to investigate what had occurred and whether there had been other instances of unreported misconduct. While they could look to counsel for guidance, they had an affirmative obligation to undertake an appropriate inquiry. If they were unable to conduct the inquiry themselves or believed it was more appropriate that the inquiry be conducted by others, they were required to take prompt action to ensure that others in fact undertook those efforts. Such an inquiry could have been conducted by the legal or compliance departments of the firm, outside counsel, or others who had the ability to investigate the matter adequately. The supervisors were also required, pending the outcome of such an investigation, to increase supervision of Mozer and to place appropriate limitations on his activities.

The failure to recognize the need to take action to limit the activities of Mozer in light of his admitted misconduct is particularly troubling because Gutfreund and Strauss did place limitations on Mozer's conduct in connection with the June two-year U.S. Treasury note auction at a time when they thought the firm had not engaged in misconduct, but press reports had raised questions about the firm's activities. Although they had previously been informed that a serious violation had in fact been committed by Mozer, they failed for over three months to take any action to place limitations on his activities to deal with that misconduct.

The need to take prompt action was all the more critical in view of the fact that the potential unlawful conduct had taken place in the market for U.S. Treasury securities. The integrity of that market is of vital importance to the capital markets of the United States, as well as to capital markets worldwide, and Salomon occupied a privileged role as a government-designated primary dealer. The failure of the supervisors to take vigorous action to address known misconduct by the head of the firm's Government Trading Desk caused unnecessary risks to the integrity of this important market.

To discharge their obligations, the supervisors should at least have taken steps to ensure that someone within the firm questioned other employees on the Government Trading Desk, such as the desk's clerk or the other managing director on the Desk. Since the supervisors were informed that Mozer had said that he submitted the false bid to obtain additional securities for another trading desk of the firm, they should also have specifically investigated any involvement of that area of the firm in the matter. The supervisors should also have reviewed, or ensured that others reviewed, documentation concerning the February 21, 1991 auction. Such a review would have revealed, at a minimum, that a second false bid had been submitted in the auction and that false trade tickets and customer confirmations had been created in connection with both false bids. Those facts would have raised serious questions about the operations of the Government Trading Desk, and inquiries arising from those questions might well have led to discovery of the additional false bids described above. For instance, two of the other false bids, those submitted in the December 27, 1990 and February 7, 1991 auctions, involved the same pattern of fictitious sales to and from customer accounts and the suppression of customer confirmations used in connection with the February 21, 1991 auction. Inasmuch as Mozer had admitted to committing one apparently criminal act, the supervisors had reason to be skeptical of Mozer's assurances that he had not engaged in other misconduct.

Each of the three supervisors apparently believed that someone else would take the supervisory action necessary to respond to Mozer's misconduct. There was no discussion, however, among any of the supervisors about what action should be taken or about who would be responsible for taking action. Instead, each of the supervisors assumed that another would act. In situations where supervisors are aware of wrongdoing, it is imperative that they take prompt and unequivocal action to define the responsibilities of those who are to respond to the wrongdoing. The supervisors here failed to do that. As a result, although there may be varying degrees of responsibility, each of the supervisors bears some measure of responsibility for the collective failure of the group to take action.

After the disclosure of one unauthorized bid to Meriwether, Mozer committed additional violations in connection with the submission of two subsequent unauthorized customer bids. Had limits been placed on his activities after the one unauthorized bid was disclosed, these violations might have been prevented. While Mozer was told by Meriwether that his conduct was career-threatening and that it would be reported to senior management and to the government, these efforts were not a sufficient supervisory response under the circumstances. The supervisors were required to take action reasonably designed to prevent a repetition of the misconduct that had been disclosed to them. They could, for instance, have temporarily limited Mozer's activities so that he was not involved in the submission of customer bids pending an adequate review of what had occurred in the February 21, 1991 auction, or they could have instituted procedures to require verification of customer bids.

Under the circumstances of this case, the failure of the supervisors to take action to discipline Mozer or to limit his activities constituted a serious breach of their supervisory obligations. Gutfreund, Strauss and Meriwether thus each failed reasonably to supervise Mozer with a view to preventing violations of the federal securities laws.

As Chairman and Chief Executive Officer of Salomon, Gutfreund bore ultimate responsibility for ensuring that a prompt and thorough inquiry was undertaken and that Mozer was appropriately disciplined. A chief executive officer has ultimate affirmative responsibility, upon learning of serious wrongdoing within the firm as to any segment of the securities market, to ensure that steps are taken to prevent further violations of the securities laws and to determine the scope of the wrongdoing. He failed to ensure that this was done. Gutfreund also undertook the responsibility to report the matter to the government, but failed to do so, although he was urged to make the report on several occasions by other senior executives of Salomon. The disclosure was made only after an internal investigation prompted by other events. Gutfreund's failure to report the matter earlier is of particular concern because of Salomon's role in the vitally-important U.S. Treasury securities market. The reporting of the matter to the government was also the only action under consideration within the firm to respond to Mozer's actions. The failure to make the report thus meant that the firm failed to take any action to respond to Mozer's misconduct.

Once improper conduct came to the attention of Gutfreund, he bore responsibility for ensuring that the firm responded in a way that recognized the seriousness and urgency of the situation. In our view, Gutfreund did not discharge that responsibility.

Strauss, as the President of Salomon, was the official within the firm to whom Meriwether first took the matter of Mozer's misconduct for appropriate action. As its president, moreover, Strauss was responsible for the operations of Salomon as a brokerage firm. Though he arranged several meetings to discuss the matter, Strauss failed to direct that Meriwether, Feuerstein, or others within the firm take the steps necessary to respond to the matter. Even if Strauss assumed that

Meriwether or Feuerstein had taken the responsibility to address the matter, he failed to follow-up and ascertain whether action had in fact been taken. Moreover, it subsequently became clear that no meaningful action was being taken to respond to Mozer's misconduct. Under these circumstances, Strauss retained his supervisory responsibilities as the president of the brokerage firm, and he failed to discharge those responsibilities.

Meriwether was Mozer's direct supervisor and the head of all fixed-income trading activities at Salomon. Meriwether had also been designated by the firm as the person responsible for supervising the firm's fixed-income trading activities, including the activities of the Government Trading Desk.

When he first learned of Mozer's misconduct, Meriwether promptly took the matter to senior executives within the firm. In so doing, he took appropriate and responsible action. However, Meriwether's responsibilities did not end with communication of the matter to more senior executives. He continued to bear direct supervisory responsibility for Mozer after he had reported the false bid to others within the firm. As a result, until he was instructed not to carry out his responsibilities as Mozer's direct supervisor, Meriwether was required to take appropriate supervisory action. Meriwether's efforts in admonishing Mozer and telling him that his misconduct would be reported to the government were not sufficient under the circumstances to discharge his supervisory responsibilities.

Donald Feuerstein, Salomon's chief legal officer, was informed of the submission of the false bid by Paul Mozer in late April of 1991, at the same time other senior executives of Salomon learned of that act. Feuerstein was present at the meetings in late April at which the supervisors named as respondents in this proceeding discussed the matter. In his capacity as a legal adviser, Feuerstein did advise Strauss and Gutfreund that the submission of the bid was a criminal act and should be reported to the government, and he urged them on several occasions to proceed with disclosure when he learned that the report had not been made. However, Feuerstein did not direct that an inquiry be undertaken, and he did not recommend that appropriate procedures, reasonably designed to prevent and detect future misconduct, be instituted, or that other limitations be placed on Mozer's activities. Feuerstein also did not inform the Compliance Department, for which he was responsible as Salomon's chief legal officer, of the false bid.

Unlike Gutfreund, Strauss and Meriwether, however, Feuerstein was not a direct supervisor of Mozer at the time he first learned of the false bid. Because we believe this is an appropriate opportunity to amplify our views on the supervisory responsibilities of legal and compliance officers in Feuerstein's position, we have not named him as a respondent in this proceeding. Instead, we are issuing this report of investigation concerning the responsibilities imposed by Section 15(b)(4)(E) of the Exchange Act under the circumstances of this case.

Employees of brokerage firms who have legal or compliance responsibilities do not become "supervisors" for purposes of Sections 15(b)(4)(E) and 15(b)(6) solely because they occupy those positions. Rather, determining if a particular person is a "supervisor" depends on whether, under the facts and circumstances of a particular case, that person has a requisite degree of responsibility, ability or authority to affect the conduct of the employee whose behavior is at issue. Thus, persons occupying positions in the legal or compliance departments of broker-dealers have been found by the Commission to be "supervisors" for purposes of Sections 15(b)(4)(E) and 15(b)(6) under certain circumstances.

In this case, serious misconduct involving a senior official of a brokerage firm was brought to the attention of the firm's chief legal officer. That individual was informed of the misconduct by other members of senior management in order to obtain his advice and guidance, and to involve him as part of management's collective response to the problem. Moreover, in other instances of misconduct, that individual had directed the firm's response and had made recommendations concerning appropriate disciplinary action, and management had relied on him to perform those tasks.

Given the role and influence within the firm of a person in a position such as Feuerstein's and the factual circumstances of this case, such a person shares in the responsibility to take appropriate action to respond to the misconduct. Under those circumstances, we believe that such a person becomes a "supervisor" for purposes of Sections 15(b)(4)(E) and 15(b)(6). As a result, that person is responsible, along with the other supervisors, for taking reasonable and appropriate action. It is not sufficient for one in such a position to be a mere bystander to the events that occurred.

Once a person in Feuerstein's position becomes involved in formulating management's response to the problem, he or she is obligated to take affirmative steps to ensure that appropriate action is taken to address the misconduct. For example, such a person could direct or monitor an investigation of the conduct at issue, make appropriate recommendations for limiting the activities of the employee or for the institution of appropriate procedures, reasonably designed to prevent and detect future misconduct, and verify that his or her recommendations, or acceptable alternatives, are implemented. If such a person takes appropriate steps but management fails to act and that person knows or has reason to know of that failure, he or she should consider what additional steps are appropriate to address the matter. These steps may include disclosure of the matter to the entity's board of directors, resignation from the firm, or disclosure to regulatory authorities.

These responsibilities cannot be avoided simply because the person did not previously have direct supervisory responsibility for any of the activities of the employee. Once such a person has supervisory obligations by virtue of the circumstances of a particular situation, he must either discharge those responsibilities or know that others are taking appropriate action.

In view of the foregoing, the Commission deems it appropriate and in the public interest to impose the sanctions specified in the Offers of Settlement submitted by John H. Gutfreund, Thomas W. Strauss, and John W. Meriwether.

4. SUITABILITY

(A) SECURITIES

A major duty imposed on broker-dealers (BDs) regulated by the SEC is that BDs and their registered representatives (RRs) must not make unsuitable securities recommendations to customers. The suitability requirement evolved from the "know-your-customer" rule of the New York Stock Exchange. That rule required broker-dealers to conduct an inquiry to assure that customers had the ability to pay for securities purchased for their accounts. The know-your customer rule was for the protection of the broker rather than the customer.

The suitability requirement for broker-dealers also evolved from the so-called "shingle theory" or "duty of fair dealing" that was created by the SEC. The shingle theory is based on a belief that broker-dealers are professionals on whose advice the public relies. In hanging out its shingle, the broker-dealer is making an implied representation that the public may seek and will receive professional advice from the broker-dealer. When brokers hold themselves out as experts, they will be held to a higher standard of care in making recommendations.

In applying the shingle theory, a broker who makes a recommendation is viewed as making an implied representation that he or she has adequate information on the security for forming the basis of his or her opinion. This also means that investment recommendations by a broker-dealer must be based on the particular needs and investment objectives of individual customers. Recommendations should not be based on the self-interest of the broker-dealer in selling securities owned by the firm or which may provide a higher commission or markup to the firm or individual registered representative.

The SEC has stated that:

> An important aspect of a broker-dealer's duty of fair dealing is a suitability obligation, which generally requires a broker dealer to make recommendations that are consistent with the interest of its customer. Broker-dealers are also required under certain circumstances, such as when making a recommendation, to disclose material conflicts of interest to their customers, in some cases at the time of the completion of the transaction. The federal securities laws and FINRA rules restrict broker-dealers from participating in certain transactions that may present particularly acute potential conflicts of interest.

Staff of the SEC, Study on Investment Advisors and Broker-Dealers, iv (January 2011).

FINRA has described its suitability requirement as follows:

> FINRA Rule 2111 requires, in part, that a broker-dealer or associated person "have a reasonable basis to believe that a recommended transaction or investment strategy involving a security or securities is suitable for the customer, based on the information obtained through the reasonable diligence of the [firm] or associated person to ascertain the customer's investment profile." In general, a customer's investment profile would include the customer's age, other investments, financial situation and needs, tax status, investment objectives, investment experience, investment time horizon, liquidity needs and risk tolerance. The rule also explicitly covers recommended investment strategies involving securities, including recommendations to "hold" securities. The rule, moreover, identifies the three main suitability obligations: reasonable-basis, customer-specific, and quantitative suitability. Finally, the rule provides a modified institutional-customer exemption.

FINRA, Frequently Asked Questions FINRA Rule 2111 (Suitability), available at www.finra.org/web/idcplg?IdcService=GET_FILE...1 (accessed on March 12, 2013).

Before FINRA Rule 211 took effect in 2012, the applicable suitability rule was NASD Rule 2310. FINRA Rule 2111 made several changes to NASD Rule 2310. FINRA Rule 2111 added the concept of market strategy to the suitability test, i.e., it applies to all recommendations and market strategies involving a security. Further, FINRA Rule expanded the types of customer profiles that a BD must obtain. They now include the customer's age and other investments, financial situation and needs, tax status, investment objectives and experience, time horizon, liquidity needs and risk tolerance.

Enhanced suitability requirements have been imposed on particular securities products, such as variable life insurance and variable annuities. Low priced speculative "penny stocks" are subject to special suitability requirements adopted under the Penny Stock Reform Act of 1990.

There has also been much debate over whether the suitability requirement should apply to institutional investors that have the wherewithal to conduct their own investigation of their suitability for securities products. Compare, Jerry W. Markham, Protecting the Institutional Investor—Jungle Predator or Shorn Lamb?' 12 Yale J. on Reg. 345 (1995), *with*, Donald C. Langevoort, Selling Hope, Selling Risk: Some Lessons for Law from Behavioral Economics About Stockbrokers and Sophisticated Customers, 84 Calif. L. Rev. 627 (1996); Norman S. Poser, Liability *of Broker-Dealers for Unsuitable Recommendations to Institutional Investor*s, 2001 Brigham Young U.L. Rev. 1493 (2001).

Under FINRA Rule 2111, if the respective customer is classified as an institutional customer, then the BD is required to apply the customer specific suitability test. This means that the BD only needs to determine that the institutional customer is capable independently to evaluate the recommendation and has made the decision independently. An "institutional customer" is one that has assets in excess of $50,000,000.

(B) COMMODITY FUTURES

PHACELLI V. CONTICOMMODITY SERVICES, INC.
Comm. Fut. L. Rep. (CCH) ¶ 23,250 (C.F.T.C. 1986)

In each of these cases, respondents appeal from initial decisions in which Administrative Law Judges ("ALJs") awarded reparations on the theory that there was a duty implied in Section 4b of the Act not to make a trade for a customer without first ascertaining that the customer was "suitable" for futures trading, and that respondents violated that duty. * * *

Complainant is a 57-year-old carpenter in Bronx, New York, retired because of a disability. He has a hearing impairment and a nervous condition. In 1979, Gabriel Borenstein, an associated person ("AP") with Conticommodity Services, Inc. ("Conti"), a registered futures commission merchant ("FCM"), received the following letter from complainant:

Dear Mr. Borenstein;

I like your philosophy on Interest Rates and the Market in general. In dealing with a firm one has to have faith in that person. To a certain degree I do have faith in your ability. If I decide to get into commodities I would like you to handle my account. Have some experience in stock but not much experience in commodities. For this reason I have to rely mostly on your good judgment.

My objective is to trade in one of the monetary futures which has the greatest potential return for the money. Was thinking of a spread in Ginnie Maes. Perhaps a spread will give me some protection. As you very well know, timing is so important in reducing the risk. One has to have some idea when Interest Rates will peak out. I remember this past May, many taught [sic] Interest Rates peaked out. You were one of the few who did not think so. You deserve a lot of credit. Let's hope you can call the next major turn on Interest rate. If you were to take an educated guess on how high do you expect interest rates to go?

What do you think of a Ginnie Mae spread? In your opinion what is the best way to place a Ginnie Mae spread, which months and which way? It is more to our advantage for the distant months to be selling above the middle months?

It would be helpful to know what risk ratio is compared to the reward. In other words what is the worst that can happen. For a number of years I have been waiting for the stock market to complete its cycle every four to five years. This time around the stock market is in such a confused state, that I decided to stay away from it and maybe go into monetary futures instead. I am ready to get into the market when you think the timing is right. Since my hearing is not so good it is necessary for me to write to you. If you feel this can be discussed further over the telephone, I will be glad to phone you, but you have to speak real loud. Please let me hear from you on this important matter. I shall be looking forward to your reply.

Borenstein gave Phacelli requisite risk disclosure materials and other documents. On September 24, 1979 Phacelli signed a customer agreement, a "New Account Worksheet" (on which he listed his income as less than $15,000/year, net worth as $50,000 to $100,000 and available risk capital as $30,000, and stated that he had not previously traded commodities); a risk disclosure statement; and a trading authorization, giving Borenstein authority to trade his account. Conti received these papers, along with Phacelli's $30,000, on September 26, 1979. Trading began on October 2, 1979 and ended October 18th, with a loss of $6,970.60. * * *

Along with the issues raised in the complaint, the ALJ addressed a claim that complainant raised later in the proceeding, namely, that he was unsuitable to trade commodity futures because of his low fixed income, disability and limited savings. As to this theory, the Judge concluded that "suitability" is implicit in the anti-fraud provisions of the Act, and that Phacelli's low income, not worth and disability supported the claim. While noting the unexplained "discrepancy" between Phacelli's statement in his first letter to Borenstein that he had not "much experience in commodities" and his statement in the New Account Worksheet that he had none, the ALJ declined to give that matter much weight because, in his view, Phacelli's initial letter to Borenstein made it clear that he would rely on the broker's judgment. Without addressing his earlier finding that Phacelli "cannot be considered a totally reliable witness," the ALJ concluded that "respondents owed complainant a fiduciary duty, this duty was breached by placing him at risk in the futures markets, that breach constituted a violation of Section 4b(A) of the Act, and damaged him in the amount of his losses, $6,970.60."

Complainant, Patrick McDowell Hannay, was a 71-year-old engineer with the Northrop Corporation when he opened his commodity trading account with First Commodity Corporation of Boston ("FCCB"), a registered FCM, in early December 1982. Hannay stated on the customer agreement form that his annual income was greater than $25,000, his net worth in excess of $100,000. Although complainant had not previously traded commodities, he had traded securities; he testified that he had subscribed to Howard Ruff's newsletter. Hannay also testified that he became acquainted with FCCB through a magazine which he had ordered from a television advertisement. The magazine rated commodity companies, including FCCB. He sent FCCB a postcard, and, after phone calls from two FCCB offices, he selected Andrew C. Anderson, a registered associated person from the Miami office, to be his account executive.

According to complainant, he told Anderson that he wanted to double his money by the time he was 72 for retirement proposes. Anderson testified that he knew of Hannay's profit objective (although not his age) and showed complainant on paper how he might be able to achieve a certain goal in terms of dollars and profit, depending on market movements. Hannay signed a risk disclosure statement in addition to the customer application and agreement. He testified that he had understood the risks of commodity futures trading and was aware of the fees and margin requirements. Anderson testified that he orally told Hannay of the risks, i.e., that he could lose his entire investment and possibly additional funds. Hannay confirmed his understanding of both the risks and the fee structure in two conversations with an FCCB employee on Dec. 7, 1982; FCCB recorded both conversations.

Hannay opened a discretionary account with FCCB in early December 1982 with a $20,000 deposit, authorizing FCCB to purchase four contracts. Complainant knew that the maintenance fee would be $1,950 per year, which would allow him to trade in and out of a contract for a year at no additional cost. Later Hannay deposited another $14,000 for two additional contracts; after a profitable December and January, he invested another $10,000 to purchase more contracts. At the close of business on February 16, 1983, complainant had invested a total of $44,400 and the net equity in the account was $55,976.92. Hannay and Anderson spoke to each other during this period two or three times a week.

Hannay's account thereafter suffered large losses due to down limit moves in silver. On March 2, 1983, after Anderson liquidated two contracts, the net value of Hannay's account was down to $5,103.00. Thereafter Hannay revoked Anderson's power of attorney to trade. Pursuant to a later letter from complainant, FCCB closed his account on April 13, remitting his balance of $6,308.60. Hannay had sustained out-of-pocket losses (including maintenance fees) of approximately $38,000. * * *

The Commission's adjudicatory opinions have consistently declined to read into Section 4b of the Act, a requirement that commodity professionals determine a customer's suitability to trade futures contracts. Beginning in 1981, in denying an application for review of an initial decision, the Commission noted that it "wishes to disavow the judge's reference to, and discussion of suitability at pp. 16–17 of the initial decision." Jensen v. Shearson Hayden Stone, Inc., et al., [1980–1982 Transfer Binder] Comm. Fut. L. Rep. (CCH) P21,324 at 25,482, n.1 (CFTC October 9, 1981). The portion disavowed by the Commission included the ALJ's determination that the concept of suitability was implicit in the existing anti-fraud provisions of the Act and was the basis for a claim (he decided, however, that there the complainant was, in fact, suitable). Jensen, [1980–1982 Transfer Binder] Comm. Fut. L. Rep. (CCH) P21,062 at 24,284 (CFTC Initial Decision July 28, 1980).

The Commission similarly rejected a judge's recognition of a suitability requirement in Avis v. Shearson Hayden Stone, Inc., et al., [1980–1982 Transfer Binder] Comm. Fut. L. Rep. (CCH) P21,379 (CFTC April 13, 1982). In that case, the Commission affirmed the ALJ's holding that the broker had violated Section 4b(A) of the Act for failing to properly monitor complainant's account after having undertaken the duty to do so. At the same time, however, the Commission specifically rejected the ALJ's conclusion that respondents also violated the Act by failing to advise complainant that his financial condition rendered him unsuitable, stating:

> At this juncture we wish to note that the Commission has never adopted any rule of suitability governing the commodity broker-

customer relationship ... The Administrative Law Judge's determination that Mr. Avis' financial status after he was forced to retire "disqualified him as suitable customer" was unnecessary to his conclusion that respondent Schanck breached a fiduciary duty by failing to disclose a material fact to complainant, i.e., what his account equity was on November 16. Therefore, we find his discussion of suitability ... to be extraneous to his conclusion that respondents Schanck and Shearson violated Section 4b of the Commodity Exchange Act. To the extent that the judge in his decision below suggests that suitability principles are implicit in any of the provisions of the Act, the Commission does not adopt such reasoning. Id. at 25,830, n.4 (emphasis added). See also, William Weeks v. International Trading Group, Ltd. and Mark Ackerman, No. R78–852–79–466, order at n.1 (CFTC January 17, 1983) (citing Avis, supra).

While acknowledging these consistent Commission disavowals of the notion that "suitability" was inherent in Section 4b, the ALJ nevertheless reached a contrary result in Phacelli. In particular he regarded a 1977 notice of proposed rulemaking as "a carefully reasoned and explicated prior position. . . .", and did not view the disavowals as controlling because they were dicta in footnotes. We respectfully disagree with the judge's approach.

This agency, on three occasions in 1981, 1982 and 1983, disclaimed that Section 4b required commodity professionals to determine a customer's suitability to trade futures contracts. It is true that the expressions were dicta, but the fact that the Commission went beyond the narrow limits of the particular circumstances to disavow the suitability requirement was itself significant. Even a district judge cannot assume that the Court of Appeals for his circuit "writes merely for intellectual exercise," and must give "great weight" to its pronouncements "even though they appear by dictum." Highland Supply Corp. v. Reynolds Metal Co., 245 F. Supp. 510, 512 (E.D. Mo. 1965); Cole v. University of Hartford, 391 F. Supp. 888, 890, fn.3 (D. Conn. 1975); Max M. v. Thompson, 585 F. Supp. 317, 324 (N.D. Ill. 1984).See also Public Service Co. of New Mexico v. General Electric Co., 315 F.2d 306, 310, fn.6 (10th Cir. 1983),cert. denied, 374 U.S. 809:

> The contention is made that the quoted phrase is dictum to which the lower courts are not required to yield. Without exploring the intricate distinctions between dictum and language necessary to the decision, we conclude that we must recognize the clear, direct, explicit and unqualified statement of the Supreme Court. That the statements appeared in footnotes was of no significance, let alone a reason to differ with them. See

Phillips v. Osborne, 444 F.2d 778, 782 (9th Cir. 1971); United States v. Egelak, 173 F. Supp. 206, 210 (D. Alaska 1959).

Nor was the 1977 rulemaking proposal "a carefully reasoned and explicated prior position" as to Section 4b's impliedly imposing a suitability requirement upon commodity professionals. As the Supreme Court has recognized, "a proposed regulation does not represent an agency's considered interpretation of its statute . . ." CFTC v. Schor, 54 USLW 5096, 5100 (decided July 7, 1986). Moreover, this omnibus proposal, setting out nine different ideas (including a suitability rule) for customer protection, rested on some fifteen different sections of the Act (id. at 44749). Nowhere did the notice articulate, focus upon, or even address the question raised and disavowed by the Commission in Jensen, Avis and Weeks. The 1977 notice did not say, and should not have been read as saying that as a matter of law, Section 4b includes a suitability requirement.

The courts have also recognized that no suitability requirement presently governs commodity futures trading. Schofield v. First Commodity Corp. of Boston, 793 F.2d 28, 34 (1st Cir. 1986) and cases there cited; Myron, et al. v. Hauser, 673 F.2d 994, 1005 (8th Cir. 1982); Trustman v. Merrill Lynch, Pierce, Fenner & Smith, Inc., et al. [1984–1986 Transfer Binder] Comm. Fut. L. Rep. (CCH) P22,490 at 30,168 (C.D. Cal. Jan. 24, 1985); Shearson Loeb Rhoades, Inc. v. Quinard, et al. [1982–1984 Transfer Binder] Comm. Fut. L. Rep. (CCH) P21,686 at 26,622 (C.D. Cal. Mar. 11, 1983); Applegate v. Dean Witter Reynolds, et al. [1982–1984 Transfer Binder] Comm. Fut. L. Rep. (CCH) P21,881 at 27,748 (S.D. Fla. Jan. 17, 1983); J.E. Hoetger & Co. v. Asencio, 558 F. Supp. 1361, 1364 (E.D. Mich. 1983); Sherry v. Diercks, et al., [1980–1982 Transfer Binder] Comm. Fut. L. Rep. (CCH) P21,221 at 25,087 (Ct. App. Wash. 1981).

It is true, as the Judge noted, that the Commission has interpreted the concept of "fraud" to include breach of a commodity professional's duties to his customer. See Avis, supra, where we held a broker liable for failure to monitor the status of a customer's account when the broker had originally agreed to do so. We stated that ". . . when a customer makes it known that he intends to rely on the commodity professional to perform special instructions given by the customer, the commodity professional, as part of his fiduciary obligation, must, in order to disavow that duty, either disclose to the customer in unequivocal language that he cannot or will not perform the additional duties requested of him or that he will only do so conditionally or without warranty as to result. Avis [1980–1982 Transfer Binder] Comm. Fut. L. Rep. at 25,831 n.8. Cf. Aronow v. First National Monetary Corporation, [1984–1986 Transfer Binder] Comm. Fut. L. Rep. (CCH) P22,282 (CFTC July 13, 1984) (interpreting fraud under Section 4O). While our broad reading of the Act's antifraud rules is consistent with their remedial purpose, we do not believe that it justifies including, under the rubric of fraud, a suitability concept which has such a limited relationship to traditional notions of fraud and fiduciary duties. That a breach of duty amounting to fraud and the breach of a suitability requirement are not interchangeable has been recognized under the federal securities laws. See, Hecht v. Harris, Upham & Co., 430 F.2d 1202, 1209 (9th Cir. 1970) ("Unlike the fraud requirement of the Securities Exchange Act, the N.A.S.D. 'suitability' rule would . . . allow recovery against a member who did not have 'reasonable grounds' to believe his investment recommendation was suitable for the customer"); See also, Buttrey v. Merrill Lynch, Pierce, Fenner & Smith, Inc., 410 F.2d 135, 143 (7th Cir. 1969) (a violation of the New York Stock Exchange "know your customer" rule gives rise to civil liability only in cases "tantamount to fraud").

Based on Commission precedent and the great weight of authority in the courts, we hold that a commodity professional does not violate Section 4b merely because he fails to determine whether a customer is suitable for commodity trading. In other words, a customer who makes a knowing and meaningful election to undertake the risks of commodity futures trading cannot recover his losses by claiming under Section 4b that his account executive should have warned him that he was unsuitable for such a risk.

This does not mean that the Act is necessarily indifferent to the individual characteristics of the complaining customer. Under traditional fraud concepts, and wholly apart from notions of "suitability," an individual's duties under the law may vary according to the characteristics and circumstances of the particular customer being solicited. Thus several courts treat conduct amounting to "overreaching," as equivalent to fraud. In analyzing the reliance element in traditional fraud cases, it has long been recognized:

> . . . that people who are exceptionally gullible, superstitious, ignorant, stupid, dim-witted, or illiterate have been allowed to recover when the defendant knew it, and deliberately took advantage of it.

Prosser and Keeton on Torts (5th Ed. 1984), p. 751 (citations omitted).

We have similarly considered the characteristics and circumstances of complainants in evaluating assertions that they have been misled or otherwise defrauded, and nothing in this opinion should be read as departing from that approach. Moreover, the instant cases do not involve liability for an express representation as to the "suitability" of a particular trade or strategy for a particular customer. Assuming proof of reliance, an affirmative misrepresentation of suitability would—like other forms of material misrepresentation—constitute fraud. See e.g., Schofield v. First Commodity Corp. of Boston, 793 F.2d 28, 34–36 (1st Cir. 1986) (distinguishing between a "suitability cause of action" and "misrepresentation of [complainant's] suitability for commodities trading"); Anderson v. Knox, 297 F.2d 702 (9th Cir. 1961).

Even if a suitability requirement could be grounded in some other provision of the Act, a question we do not here decide, we believe that the fashioning of a workable requirement and creation of the guidelines that would determine its scope and practical impact on commodity professionals and customers would be better done on an industry-wide generic basis than through the reparations process.

For present purposes, the task of developing an industry-wide approach to the issue has been undertaken by the National Futures Association (NFA), the self-regulatory organization of the commodities industry—consistent with the treatment of "suitability" for securities trading, where the principal rules are those of self-regulatory organizations. NFA adopted Compliance Rule 2–30 in November 1985 and the Commission approved the rule in April 1986. As the NFA noted in an interpretive statement that accompanied the rule, Rule 2–30 was derived from a NFA member's duty to observe high standards of commercial honor and just and equitable principles of trade in the conduct of their futures business. As such, its principles go beyond the traditional antifraud principles. For example, the rule requires that the member seek information from the customer without regard to whether such information is "material" under the particular facts and circumstances. As explained by the Commission's Division of Trading and Markets, recommending Commission approval, under NFA's own interpretation, the rule requires, in appropriate cases, disclosure "that makes [it] clear that futures trading is too risky for that particular customer."

In our view, this NFA requirement is a promising adjunct to the policy of full and fair disclosure that underlies Section 4b. The interests of customers and the reputation of the commodity industry will both be served by discouraging participation by individuals who are not prepared to undertake the inherent risks of the market. Our holding in these cases, that the antifraud principles of Section 4b do not impose a duty on commodity professionals to determine whether a customer is suitable for commodity trading, does not indicate a lessening of our support for the principles underlying the NFA rule. We again endorse NFA's efforts in enacting Rule 2–30, and encourage it to continue its efforts to develop and implement standards in this area.

The initial decision in *Phacelli* rested solely on suitability, the Judge having explicitly found against any recovery on a fraud theory. For the reasons set out above, we reverse that decision and dismiss the complaint. As noted supra, in Hannay the Judge, while unquestionably resting in part on suitability, may also have intended to award reparations on a traditional fraud basis. For that reason we reverse the initial decision insofar as it found respondents liable for "suitability" violations, but otherwise remand the proceeding to the Administrative Law Judge for further proceedings not inconsistent with this Opinion.

Concur: WEST

NOTES

1. A suitability requirement was imposed by the NFA on the trading of security futures that are jointly regulated by the SEC and CFTC. See, 13 Jerry W. Markham, Commodities Regulation: Fraud, Manipulation & Other Claims § 10:9.50 (2013) (describing this requirement).

2. CFTC Rule 23.402(b) created a "know-your-counterparty" requirement for swap contracts [17 C.F.R. § 23.402]. This requires swap dealers to obtain essential facts concerning each counterparty and the authority of any person acting for such counterparty, including facts necessary to comply with applicable laws to evaluate the client's previous swaps experience, financial wherewithal and flexibility, trading objectives and purposes of the counterparty. Major swap participants are excluded from this requirement.

The CFTC also created an "institutional suitability" requirement for recommendations a swap dealer or major swap participant makes to a counterparty in connection with a swap or swap trading strategy. This means that those registrants must have a reasonable basis to believe that any swap or swaps trading strategy that it recommends to a counterparty is suitable for that counterparty. Such a requirement does not apply if the counterparty is determined to have the independent capability of assessing the suitability of the transaction [17 C.F.R. 23.434].

WISBEY V. MERRILL LYNCH, PIERCE, FENNER AND SMITH, INC.

Comm. Fut. L. Rep. (CCH) ¶ 24,594 (C.F.T.C. 1990)

Complainant Wisbey alleged that he had lost almost $67,000 because respondents failed to make timely disclosure under Rule 1.55 or warn him that the trading in his account was too risky and affirmatively misrepresented the risks of spread trading and respondents' ability to limit his losses to $10,000. Wisbey appeals from the Administrative Law Judge's ("ALJ") dismissal of his complaint, focusing on alleged flaws in the ALJ's analysis of the factual record. Respondents suggest that Wisbey traded his account with full knowledge of the risks he was undertaking and maintain that the initial decision is fully supported by the record. As explained below, we conclude that the ALJ erred in analyzing respondents' compliance with their Rule 1.55 disclosure duty. Nevertheless, because the record establishes that complainant's trading decisions were not affected by respondents' delayed disclosure, we affirm the result of the initial decision.

Complainant's appeal is based on several of the factual disputes raised by the parties. The ALJ resolved these disputes in respondents' favor. We begin our review with a summary of the undisputed factual background. We then turn to a description of the factual disputes central to complainant's appeal.

Complainant is a high school graduate residing in Bellingham, Washington. For most of his working life, Wisbey was an owner-manager of two cabaret restaurants in Vancouver, Canada. After retiring in the early 1980s, complainant had open-heart surgery. Following the surgery, Wisbey liquidated his interest in the restaurants. He invested $250,000 of the proceeds in a new house and deposited the remaining $100,000 in a local bank. In October 1982, after reading an article on futures trading in his local newspaper, Wisbey considered investing part of the $100,000 in the futures market. Based on advertisements he had seen, Wisbey contacted respondent Merrill Lynch, Pierce, Fenner and Smith, Inc. ("Merrill Lynch").

When complainant visited the local Merrill Lynch branch office, he discovered that the Bellingham branch did not include any account executives qualified to handle futures accounts. He was referred, however, to Merrill Lynch's Seattle branch office and provided with a toll free number to call. When Wisbey telephoned the Seattle branch office, he spoke to respondent Gomez. Following this telephone conversation, Gomez mailed a Merrill Lynch account-opening package to Wisbey. It included a brochure entitled "Understanding the Futures Market," a customer agreement form, a statement of financial condition and a Rule 1.55 risk disclosure statement. Wisbey initialed an acknowledgment that he had received and understood the Rule 1.55 risk disclosure statement. He also signed an acknowledgment of the terms of the customer agreement. He did not, however, include a date with either signature. When Wisbey executed his statement of financial condition, however, he dated it October 22, 1982. He later returned the completed documents to Merrill Lynch.

On October 19, 1982, Wisbey delivered a cashier's check for $10,000 to Merrill Lynch's Bellingham branch office. The following day, October 20, Gomez executed the initial transaction in Wisbey's account, a sale of one contract of December silver futures. Four additional contracts were sold between October 25 and 27. When these positions were liquidated on October 29, Wisbey experienced a net loss of $580.

During November, December and January, there was frequent trading in Wisbey's account. With the exception of one trade in copper futures, Wisbey's transactions were limited to silver futures. By

November 9, the equity in Wisbey's futures account had risen to almost $11,500. Wisbey deposited additional funds on November 9 and 12, raising his total investment to $34,000. By the end of November, however, Wisbey's futures trading had resulted in a net realized loss of approximately $1,400. During December, the previous pattern of trading continued but losses increased. By the end of the month, Wisbey's net realized loss from futures trading had risen to over $8,000. Although the overall trading results improved in January, Wisbey's net realized trading loss increased to almost $9,500 by the end of the month.

During January, Wisbey and Gomez met to review complainant's account. At the meeting, they discussed spread trading and foreign currency futures contracts. In early February, complainant earned a profit of over $10,500 on two silver transactions. As a result, by February 3, complainant's futures trading had earned a net realized profit of approximately $1,000. Following this trading success, Wisbey began trading spread positions in silver futures and outright positions in Swiss franc and Canadian dollar contracts. These transactions produced heavy losses and, by the end of February, Wisbey's futures trading showed a net realized loss of over $17,000.

Early in March, Wisbey met margin calls for $10,000 and $15,000. When he received an additional call for $45,000, however, Wisbey was unable to assure Merrill Lynch that additional funds would be deposited. As a result, Merrill Lynch liquidated Wisbey's account. Complainant paid the debit balance of approximately $7,500, raising his trading losses to over $68,000.

The parties' initial factual dispute involves the events preceding the initial transaction in Wisbey's account. According to Wisbey, he first contacted Gomez on October 19, 1982. In that conversation, he fully advised Gomez about both his heart condition and his limited finances. In addition, he advised Gomez that $5,000 to $10,000 was the maximum he could afford to risk. According to Wisbey, Gomez assured him that his loss could be limited to that amount by using stop loss orders.

Wisbey testified that he made his initial deposit of $10,000 on the same day as his initial conversation with Gomez. At that time, Wisbey stated, he had not received either written or oral disclosure of the risks of futures trading. Wisbey received the paperwork to open his account approximately one week after Gomez began trading the account. According to complainant, Gomez instructed him to falsify the statement of financial condition by listing his income as $50,000 a year. Gomez also instructed Wisbey to back-date his signature to October 22 and return the completed form to Merrill Lynch.

Respondents vigorously dispute Wisbey's version of these events. Accordingly to respondents, the initial contact between Wisbey and

Gomez was prior to October 19. During this initial conversation, Gomez testified, Wisbey claimed he had $30,000 in risk capital and was interested in trading silver futures contracts. Gomez denied advising Wisbey that his losses could be limited to any specific amount.

According to Gomez, account-opening documents (including the Rule 1.55 disclosure statement) were provided to Wisbey and returned by complainant prior to the initial transaction in Wisbey's account. Both Gomez and Brenda Aston, a Merrill Lynch sales assistant, testified that Merrill Lynch would not assign an account number to a customer prior to receipt of properly completed account-opening documents. On this basis, respondents suggested that Gomez's recollection was corroborated by complainant's use of an account number when he made his initial deposit of funds on October 19. In addition, Gomez's supervisor, Doyle Neuenswander, testified that he had given written approval to the opening of Wisbey's account on October 28. Prior to taking this step, he stated, he had spoken with Wisbey and reviewed his understanding of the risk disclosure statement.

The level of influence Gomez exercised over Wisbey's trading is also disputed by the parties. Wisbey admitted that he had initiated many transactions in the account. He blamed respondents, however, for losses attributable to his misunderstanding of trading risk and Merrill Lynch's confusing, error-prone account statements. According to complainant, Gomez encouraged him to trade frequently and to increase the funds invested in the account so that additional positions could be maintained. Wisbey testified that Gomez recommended shifting his silver trading from the smaller contract traded at a Chicago exchange to the larger, more active contract traded in New York. Complainant also claimed that Gomez had assured him that a portion of the additional funds necessary to margin trades in the larger contract would be reserved in his money market account and thus protected from loss. After his losses mounted, Wisbey testified, Gomez assured him that the market would turn around, eliminating Wisbey's losses.

Gomez denied Wisbey's suggestion that Gomez had been the primary influence on the level and frequency of complainant's trading. Respondents presented evidence that Wisbey had continued to trade aggressively when Gomez was out of the office and had made independent efforts to increase the trading limits Merrill Lynch had imposed on complainant to protect its financial interests. They also emphasized the system Wisbey had developed to independently monitor his transactions as an indication of the close attention Wisbey had given to his account.

The parties also offered differing views about the change of complainant's trading strategy in February. Complainant contended that Gomez had initiated the discussion of spread trading in response to

Wisbey's request that his account be closed. According to Wisbey, Gomez assured him that spread trading was more conservative and that losses could be limited to $5,000. Wisbey also testified that Gomez had suggested submitting another false statement of financial condition to Merrill Lynch, inflating his net worth and risk capital in order to justify an increased trading limit. Finally, Wisbey claimed Gomez had also initiated his transactions in foreign currencies and had induced him to pay margin calls in early March by assuring him that the market was on the verge of turning in his favor.

According to Gomez, Wisbey initiated the discussion of spread trading based on a friend's assurance that it was a more conservative method for trading in the silver market. Gomez maintained he had carefully explained the mechanics of spreads to complainant. Respondents also relied upon a letter Wisbey wrote after closing his account. Enclosing a check for the debit balance in the account, Wisbey acknowledged that the trading losses he had incurred were the result of his own decisions. He suggested Merrill Lynch shared responsibility for the losses, however, and asked rhetorically: "[d]o you watch someone jump off a bridge, just because they paid the toll?" * * *

Wisbey's appeal focuses primarily on his disagreement with the ALJ's assessment of the factual record. Several of his arguments are based on the premise that his testimony was more believable than that offered by respondents. As a general rule, however, we defer to a presiding officer's assessment of the factual record in the absence of clear error. See Secrest v. Madda Trading Co., CFTC Docket No. R–81–1073–81–827 (CFTC Sept. 14, 1989), slip op. at 15. Deference is particularly appropriate when resolution of factual disputes rests on an assessment of witness credibility. Id. at 16. The decision in this case turns largely on a choice between two irreconcilable accounts of the events at issue. After an opportunity to observe the demeanor of the witnesses, the ALJ determined that respondents' version of events was generally more credible than complainant's version. With the exception of the findings discussed below, there is no evidence of the type of clear error that justifies an exception to our policy of deferring to factual findings of presiding officers. Accordingly, we reject complainant's challenge to the ALJ's credibility determination.

Complainant claims the ALJ's analysis of respondents' risk disclosure is flawed by its failure to reflect the specific requirements of Rule 1.55. He contends that the evidence establishes that respondents (1) began trading in Wisbey's account prior to his receipt of a Rule 1.55 disclosure statement, (2) subsequently provided a disclosure statement that failed to meet the format requirements of Rule 1.55 and (3) failed to retain a signed and dated acknowledgment of Wisbey's receipt and understanding of the disclosure statement. Respondents contend that the record supports the ALJ's finding that Wisbey received a Rule 1.55 disclosure statement prior to the initial trade in his account and suggest that the statement Wisbey received met the format requirements of Rule 1.55. Even if they failed to properly fulfill some of their obligations under Rule 1.55, respondents argue, the record establishes that complainant knowingly undertook the risks of futures trading. In these circumstances, they suggest, complainant cannot recover damages for a breach of Rule 1.55.

As noted above, the ALJ found that Wisbey initially contacted Gomez on October 2, rejecting Wisbey's testimony that the telephone contact was not until October 19. While we see no basis to overturn the ALJ's assessment of complainant's credibility, none of the evidence in the record refers to October 2 as the date of the initial contact. Based on our independent review of the record, we conclude that there is insufficient reliable evidence to specify the date of the initial contact. For this reason, we vacate the ALJ's specification of the October 2 date.

We also conclude there is insufficient evidence to support the ALJ's finding that Wisbey received a Rule 1.55 disclosure statement prior to October 20, 1982. Respondents argue that this finding is consistent with Gomez's testimony that he had provided a disclosure document to Wisbey and received a signed acknowledgment from Wisbey prior to entering the first transaction for complainant's account. In light of Merrill Lynch's account opening policy, respondents continue, Gomez's testimony is corroborated by Wisbey's inclusion of an account number with his October 19 deposit. The regularity of Merrill Lynch's account-opening procedure is called into question, however, by its failure to assure that a date accompanied the acknowledgment of the Rule 1.55 statement submitted by Wisbey. Moreover, neither respondents nor the ALJ have offered an explanation for the date Wisbey included on his statement of financial condition—October 22, 1989. Absent evidence that Wisbey submitted the statement of financial condition under separate cover from the other account-opening documents, there is insufficient evidence to conclude that Wisbey received a Rule 1.55 disclosure statement prior to October 22. In these circumstances, the ALJ should have concluded that respondent Merrill Lynch breached its duty under the regulation.

Proof that a customer's account was opened without compliance with Rule 1.55 raises a presumption that the customer would not have taken such a step had he been aware of information material to an assessment of the risks of futures trading. Sher v. Dean Witter Reynolds, Inc., [1984–1986 Transfer Binder] Comm. Fut. L. Rep. (CCH) P22,266 at 29,371 (CFTC June 13, 1984). In order to rebut the presumption that complainant "relied" upon the material information that was not disclosed, respondents may show that: (1) the customer was exposed to the material information reflected in the Rule 1.55 disclosure statement,

(2) following the exposure, the customer knowingly undertook the risks of trading and (3) the record supports an inference that the customer would have acted similarly had he been exposed to the information at the time and in the manner required by Rule 1.55. See Batra v. E. F. Hutton & Co., [Current Transfer Binder] Comm. Fut. L. Rep. (CCH) P23,937 at 34,287 (CFTC Sept. 30, 1987). We agree with respondents that the evidence in this case is sufficient to rebut the presumption that Wisbey's trading decisions were affected by his delayed receipt of the Rule 1.55 disclosure statement.

Doyle Neuenswander, Gomez's supervisor, testified that he spoke to Wisbey on October 28, 1982 and reviewed the information included in the Rule 1.55 disclosure statement. On this basis, the ALJ concluded that Wisbey was "again advised of the risks involved in commodity trading." Initial Decision at 3. Following this exposure to information material to an assessment of market risk, Wisbey continued to trade his account. Moreover, despite a small realized loss due to transactions completed in October, Wisbey increased the funds available for trading by $24,000 in early November. Indeed, despite realizing significant losses in December and January, Wisbey took no action to close his account even after the losses were recovered in early February. On this record, we conclude that respondents' eight-day delay in disclosing the risks of trading to Wisbey did not affect his trading decisions. Accordingly, we affirm the ALJ's denial of a damage award on complainant's Rule 1.55 claim. * * *

NOTES

1. The CFTC has ruled that a risk disclosure statement may be vitiated by oral misrepresentations. See e.g., Kahn v. First Commodity Corp., Comm. Fut. L. Rep. (CCH) ¶ 23,306 (C.F.T.C. 1986).

2. The CFTC has separate risk disclosure requirements for options [17 C.F.R. § 33.7]; for foreign futures [17 C.F.R. § 30.6]; for commodity trading advisors [17 C.F.R. § 4.31]; and for commodity pools [17 C.F.R. § 4.24]. CFTC Rule 41.41(b) requires a risk disclosure statement for security futures [17 C.F.R. § 41.41(b)]. NFA Rule 2–30 sets forth the disclosures required for single stock futures. FINRA has the same requirement for broker-dealers trading single stock futures on securities exchanges.

3. In November 2013, the CFTC amended the risk disclosure statement that FCMs must provide to their customers. It enhanced disclosures on customer segregated fund exposures and other matters. See, Enhancing Protections Afforded Customers and Customer Funds Held by Futures Commission Merchants and Derivatives Clearing Organizations. 78 Fed. Reg. 68506 (Nov. 14, 2013).

5. CHURNING

HINCH V. COMMONWEALTH FINANCIAL GROUP, INC.
Comm. Fut. L. Rep. (CCH) ¶ 27,056 (C.F.T.C. 1997)

Richard and Carol Hinch brought this summary reparation proceeding against respondents Commonwealth Financial Group, Inc. ("Commonwealth"), a registered introducing broker ("IB"), and its associated person ("AP") Carlton A. Brown, alleging breach of fiduciary duty, churning and failure to supervise in connection with losses in the Hinches' commodity options account. The Judgment Officer issued an initial decision against respondents and awarded $13,651 in damages plus interest and costs.

Respondents timely filed and perfected this appeal. * * *

The Hinches maintained their account at Commonwealth from May 1994 through August 1994. According to Richard Hinch, a machinist with a tenth-grade education, he saw a television infomercial in April 1994 that promoted an options trading strategy based upon seasonal trends in unleaded gasoline prices. This strategy called for the purchase of call options on unleaded gasoline futures contracts in anticipation of increasing prices resulting from rising demand for unleaded gasoline during the summer travel season.

Hinch spoke by telephone with Randi Levine, a Commonwealth associated person, after he responded to the television advertisement. Hinch was unclear about the sequence of events surrounding the initial contact with Levine, although he did recall that the commercial did not mention Commonwealth by name. (Tr. at 37–38) The Hinches were provided with a "Special Report on Unleaded Gasoline" ("Special Report") which was prepared by Commonwealth for its clients. The Special Report, like the commercial, promoted the seasonal strategy for trading unleaded gasoline contracts. The Special Report advised readers to buy and hold the options "now" and to ignore temporary dips in their value. The Hinches opened a nondiscretionary commodity options account and on May 5, 1994, purchased five September unleaded gasoline call options. They paid a total of $5,000 from which Commonwealth deducted $1,000 in commissions. No other trades were executed for the account while Levine handled it. At one point, Hinch rejected her recommendation to purchase corn options.

Respondent Brown became the Hinches' AP after Levine was stricken by illness in mid-June 1994. According to Hinch, he was "a little bit shook" when Brown told him that he could not understand why Levine "got you into this gas." Hinch testified that Brown recommended that the Hinches exit their unleaded gasoline position and establish a position in heating oil contracts because of "potential war in Korea or something in Africa, something about the oil or something."

The Hinches followed Brown's recommendation. They sold the unleaded gasoline contracts for a profit and established a new position in heating oil options. Hinch said that, while he maintained his Commonwealth account, his reliance on Brown's recommendations was "total."

Once Brown took over the their account, the Hinches made a series of trades in option contracts on heating oil, coffee, and Swiss franc futures from mid-June through late August 1994. Thus, on June 15, 1994, the Hinches' position in unleaded gasoline options was liquidated for a net profit of $1,185. On June 20, 1994, the Hinches purchased October heating oil options (ten calls and three puts for a partial hedge) for $11,830, from which they paid $2,600 in commissions. On June 30, July 1, and July 7, 1994, the Hinches purchased a total of six September coffee puts for a total purchase price of $6,337 and for which they paid $1,200 in commissions.

On July 18, the Hinches sold their heating oil put options for a net profit of $511. On the same day, they purchased four September Swiss franc options for a total purchase price of $2,500 from which they paid $800 in commissions. On August 1, 1994, they sold the heating oil call options for a net profit of $35. Also, on August 1, the Hinches again purchased heating oil options for a total purchase price of $6,720 from which they paid commissions in the amount of $2,000. These positions and the Swiss franc position remained open when the Hinches closed their account at Commonwealth in August 1994 and were transferred to their new account at First Pacific Group. The Swiss franc options expired worthless, and the heating oil options were sold at a loss. Overall, the Hinches invested $16,565 with Commonwealth and incurred losses of $13,651. Hinch said his new broker at First Pacific told him that his Commonwealth account had been churned.

Brown testified that, when he took over the account from Levine, Hinch explained that he never had traded commodity options before and that he was relying on Brown to advise him of "something that looked good, [that] he would take advantage of it if he could." Brown testified that Hinch never articulated an explicit trading strategy nor stated an objective other than that he wanted to make money. Brown testified that Hinch:

> specifically pointed out to me that, you know, he was there for one purpose, and that was to make money. I mean, he told me that, you know, if—basically he was here, and he wanted to make money; that's why he was in this type of market. You know, [I] spoke to the gentleman every day.

Despite Hinch's limited trading experience, Brown testified that he was "a man of his own mind" who was never afraid to ask questions. Brown said that he did not control the trading in the Hinch account and that he was surprised when he received a telephone call from Commonwealth's compliance department informing him that the Hinches were transferring their account to another firm.

Brown denied that he ever recommended trades solely for the purpose of earning commissions. He testified that he relied on an in-house commodity trading advisor employed by Commonwealth who each day recommended trades. Brown testified that he talked to Hinch "at least once a day, sometimes twice" and that during these conversations Hinch agreed to the trades made for his and his wife's account.

The Judgment Officer issued an initial decision finding that the Hinch account had been churned. He found that the trades recommended by Brown generated a total of $6,600 in commissions and resulted in out-of-pocket losses of $13,651. * * *

The respondents assign three errors on appeal. First, they argue that the evidence is insufficient to support the Judgment Officer's findings that Brown rather than the Hinches controlled the trading in the Hinches' account and that the trading was excessive. Second, the respondents argue that, even if control and excessive trading were proven, the Hinches are entitled to recover only their commissions as damages and the Judgment Officer erred in awarding them their trading losses. * * *

Churning is a violation of Section 4c(b) of the Act and Commission Rule 33.10. See Johnson v. Don Charles & Company, [1990–1992 Transfer Binder] Comm. Fut. L. Rep. (CCH) P 24,986 (CFTC Jan. 16, 1991). To prove churning, a complainant must show that (1) the AP controlled the level and frequency of trading in the account, (2) the overall volume of the AP's trading was excessive in light of the complainant's trading objectives, and (3) the AP acted with intent to defraud or in a reckless disregard of the customer's interests. Id.

Control. Respondents first argue that the record is "completely devoid" of evidence that Brown controlled the trading in the Hinches' account. They argue that the Hinches had "previous speculative investment experience" in trading precious metals and stocks; that they understood futures and options trading; that they were aware of the risks of trading; and that they were in regular contact with Levine and respondent Brown regarding the course of trading in the Commonwealth account. They also point out that the Hinches were required by Commonwealth directly to place their trades through the firm's trading department and that this further supports their contention that the Hinches, not Commonwealth's APs, controlled the trading.

The Hinches defend the Initial Decision by arguing that the evidence shows that they knew little about commodities trading and relied on the trading advice of the Commonwealth APs.

The Commission has identified six factors tending to show the existence of a broker's de facto control over a customer's nondiscretionary account. See Lehman v. Madda Trading Company, [1984–1986 Transfer Binder] Comm. Fut. L. Rep. (CCH) P 22,417 (CFTC Nov. 13, 1984). These factors are:

> (1) lack of customer sophistication, (2) lack of prior commodity trading experience by the customer and a minimum of time devoted by the customer to the trading in the account, (3) a high degree of trust and confidence reposed in the AP by the customer, (4) a large percentage of transactions entered into by the customer based upon recommendations of the AP, (5) the absence of prior customer approval for transactions entered into on his behalf, and (6) customer approval of recommended transactions where approval is not based upon full, truthful and accurate information supplied by the AP.

It is not mandatory that each of these factors be present in order to establish control in every case, and the relative weight to be accorded to each factor will depend upon the facts of each particular case. Id.

Turning to the facts of record, there is no dispute that the Hinches were first time options traders with limited education and that Richard Hinch reposed a high degree of trust in Brown. Brown admitted at the hearing that he knew the Hinches were relying upon him for trading recommendations. While Brown contended that one trade originated with Hinch, there is little real basis to dispute that all of the other trades were recommended by Commonwealth. Under these circumstances, we conclude that the respondents have failed to show error in the Judgment Officer's determination that Brown controlled the trading in the Hinches' account.

Excessive Trading. The next issue is whether Brown traded the Hinches' account excessively "for the purpose of generating commissions, without regard for the investment or trading objectives of the customer." In the Matter of Lincolnwood Commodities, Inc. of California, [1984–1986 Transfer Binder] Comm. Fut. L. Rep. (CCH) P 21,986 at 28,246 (CFTC Jan. 31, 1984). As is true with the issue of control, excessive trading is a question of fact that cannot be determined by any precise formula or rule. Rather it must be determined on a case-by-case basis. In re Paragon Futures Association, [1990–1992 Transfer Binder] Comm. Fut. L. Rep. (CCH) P 25,266 at 38,847 (CFTC April 1, 1992); Fields v. Cayman Island Associates, Ltd., [1984–1986 Transfer Binder] Comm. Fut. L. Rep. (CCH)

P 22,688 (CFTC Jan. 2, 1985). We have identified the following as relevant, but non-exclusive, factors:

> (1) a high commission-to-equity ratio, (2) a high percentage of day trades, (3) the broker's departure from a previously agreed upon strategy, (4) trading in the account while it was undermargined, and (5) in and out trading.

Paragon Futures, P 25,266 at 38,847; Lincolnwood Commodities, P 21,986 at 28,250. We note that these cases involve futures.

Respondents argue that the Judgment Officer's analysis of the excessive trading element of churning was flawed because he focused on only one factor of excessive trading—departure from a previously agreed upon strategy—to the exclusion of all other factors. Moreover, they contend that the record fails to establish even that factor. Respondents challenge the Judgment Officer's conclusion that the complainants' strategy consisted of buying and holding unleaded gasoline contracts to exploit seasonal price shifts in that commodity, contending that the Hinches' trading objectives were far more open-ended. They suggest that the Hinches were "fundamental" traders, open to trading in a wide range of contracts, and were simply interested in "making money."

The Hinches defend by arguing that, as found by the Judgment Officer, there was no convincing justification for any of Brown's trading recommendations. Trading strategy apart, they contend that the $6,600 they paid in commissions on trades recommended by Brown indicates excessive trading in light of the amount they invested.

Owing to differences in the mechanics and trading principles underlying futures and options contracts, precedent analyzing excessive trading in the context of futures may be of limited relevance in determining whether excessive trading has occurred in the context of an options account. For instance, undermargined trading, while relevant to futures accounts, ordinarily would not be relevant in the options context where the options purchaser pays the full option premium or purchase price upon acquiring the position. Similarly, the commission-to-equity ratio is not particularly meaningful in determining whether an options account has been traded excessively. Departure from agreed on strategies and objectives, however, is equally applicable in the futures and options contexts as a measure of excessive trading.

When a customer has been solicited on the basis of one specific trading strategy and soon after the account opening the AP urges a switch to another trading strategy, an AP who controls the account bears the burden of providing a credible explanation justifying the change. We place considerable weight upon the fact that the Hinches were steered away from their original trading objective as soon as Brown gained control of this account.

While Brown argues that he was trading the account on the basis of fundamentals, we agree with the Judgment Officer that he failed to support this contention or to articulate a reasonable basis to justify any of the individual trading suggestions he made to complainants. It was not enough for Brown to say that he simply relayed to his clients the generalized recommendations of Commonwealth's in-house commodity trading advisor. Brown had to show a reasoned application of those recommendations to the particular needs and desires of his clients, something he was unable to do.

The initial switch from a position in unleaded gasoline options to heating oil appears to be based on nothing more than Brown's determination to earn his own commission from an account he had inherited from Randi Levine. In addition, we find the partial hedge of the ten heating oil calls with three puts to be particularly inexplicable. Without any showing of how the dynamics of spread trading were expected to operate on this position, we can conclude only that respondent encouraged complainants to bet against themselves.

We also have considered the amount of the complainants' out-of-pocket investment and compared that amount to the level of commissions charged. During the course of this short-lived account, the Hinches deposited $16,565 and were charged $6,600 in commissions. Thus, the level of commissions charged amounted to approximately 40% of the level of the Hinches' total investment. Given the high commissions charged, the purchase of deep-out-of-the-money coffee options for this account, which were nearing expiration, strikes us as facially excessive trading undertaken to earn commissions for Brown.

Because the Hinches made a prima facie showing of excessive trading, the Judgment Officer did not err in taking into consideration Brown's failure to provide a credible explanation for the trades he made in the Hinch account. Gilbert v. Refco, Inc., [1990–1992 Transfer Binder] Comm. Fut. L. Rep. (CCH) P 25,081 at 38,057–058 (June 27, 1991); Don Charles, P 24,986 at 37,624–625. Under the circumstances, we believe that the record is sufficient to sustain the finding of excessive trading.

Damages. The second error assigned by respondents pertains to the amount of damages awarded. The usual measure of damages for churning violations is the amount of commissions and fees charged. Trading losses are not awarded absent proof that the losses would not otherwise have occurred had the account not been churned. At a minimum, a complainant must demonstrate that churning exposed the account to risks of market loss greater than those which the customer agreed to undertake. DeAngelis v. Shearson/American Express, Inc., [1984–1986 Transfer Binder] Comm. Fut. L. Rep. (CCH) P 22,753 at 31,139 (CFTC Sept. 30, 1985). Accordingly, respondents assert that the Judgment

Officer erred in awarding trading losses rather than commissions as damages to the Hinches. They claim that direct evidence is required to show fraud.

Trading losses may be awarded on a churning claim when there exists evidence of fraudulent promises, fraudulent profit guarantees, and exposure to a greater market risk than was necessary. Here, the Hinches' losses clearly resulted from trading in contracts other than the unleaded gasoline contracts they originally intended to trade, contracts which we have found they were persuaded to trade solely for the purpose of earning commissions for Carlton Brown. Accordingly, we conclude that the Judgment Officer did not err in awarding damages in the amount of complainants' trading losses and that the Initial Decision is entirely consistent with our case law. See Davis v. Murlas Commodities, Inc., [1986–1987 Transfer Binder] Comm. Fut. L. Rep. (CCH) P 23,376 at 33,033 n.1 (CFTC Nov. 12, 1986). * * *

NOTES

1. Churning is also considered to be a fraudulent practice under the federal securities laws. See e.g., Costello v. Oppenheimer & Co., 711 F.2d 1361, 1367 (7th Cir. 1983) ("The term 'churning,' in the context of securities regulation, denotes a course of excessive trading through which a broker advances his own interests (*e.g.*, commissions based on volume) over those of his customer." (citations omitted)).

2. Excessive trading in a securities account is usually measured by the turnover ratio in the account, i.e., the ratio of the total cost of purchases incurred by an account during a specified period time to the amount invested. In a securities account, excessive trading may be found for an ordinary securities account where the annual turnover ratio exceeds six. See, 23 Jerry W. Markham & Thomas Lee Hazen, Broker Dealer Operations Under Securities and Commodities Law: Financial Responsibilities, Credit Regulation, and Customer Protection, § 10:25 (2013).

3. The formula used in the securities industry to determine whether excessive trading has occurred for purposes of churning is not readily applicable to the trading of commodity futures contracts. This is because futures traders tend to be more active traders, volatile markets require quick adjustments of positions and futures contracts have only limited lives, requiring a liquidation and renewal for continued market exposures, all of which generate commissions and increase the turnover ratio. See, In re Lincolnwood Commodities, Comm. Fut. L. Rep. (CCH) ¶ 21,986, at 28,246–50 (C.F.T.C. 1984) (discussing churning of futures accounts). See also, 13 Jerry W. Markham, Commodities Regulation: Fraud, Manipulation & Other Claims § 11:3 (2013) (same).

4. Damages for churning claims are generally limited to the commissions generated by the excessive trades, unless it can be shown that the trader

intended to cause trading losses in the account through the excessive trades. See generally, Lehman v. Madda Trading Co., Comm. Fut. L. Rep. (CCH) ¶ 22,417 (C.F.T.C. 1984).

6.　UNAUTHORIZED TRADING

SHERWOOD V. MADDA TRADING COMPANY
Comm. Fut. L. Rep. (CCH) ¶ 20,728 (C.F.T.C. 1979)

By the Commission (ACTING CHAIRMAN SEEVERS and COMMISSIONERS DUNN, MARTIN and GARTNER).

Respondent Madda Trading Company has petitioned for Commission review of an initial decision filed in a reparation proceeding on March 25, 1977 by an Administrative Law Judge. The Administrative Law Judge found that respondent Christopher Jankowski ("Jankowski"), a registered associated person, had violated Section 4b of the Commodity Exchange Act, as amended ("the Act"), 7 U.S.C. § 6b (1976), by making unauthorized trades in the account of the complainant, Omar F. Sherwood ("Sherwood"), his customer. Relying on Section 2(a)(1) of the Act, 7 U.S.C. § 2 (1976), the Judge also found that respondent Madda Trading Company ("Madda"), the registered futures commission merchant for whom Jankowski worked, was jointly and severally liable with Jankowski. The Administrative Law Judge awarded Sherwood damages of $7,124 plus interest and costs, including attorney fees of $3,000. * * *

In his initial decision the Administrative Law Judge found, as we do, that Sherwood, who resides in Bremerton, Washington, responded to a newspaper advertisement placed by Madda. As a result, Jankowski, an employee at Madda's Chicago office, called the complainant in late January 1976 and solicited Sherwood to open a commodity futures account. Two customer agreements and information concerning margin and commission rates were sent to the complainant. Sherwood signed one customer agreement shortly thereafter and returned it to Madda with a check for $10,000. Sherwood instructed Jankowski to open two accounts, each for $5,000. However, on February 5, 1976, Jankowski opened only one account for Sherwood and deposited in it the entire $10,000 sum. Sherwood and Jankowski communicated frequently prior to February 9, 1976 concerning general trading philosophy and Jankowski's Maxitron System, but no actual trading took place until that date.

On or about February 9, 1976, Sherwood and Jankowski finally discussed actual trade possibilities. In fact, Sherwood authorized Jankowski to sell one silver contract and one wheat contract on the Chicago Board of Trade. On February 10, 1976, Jankowski sold and credited to Sherwood's account three April silver and three March wheat contracts. Between February 10 and 25, 1976, approximately 53 trades were effected in Sherwood's account, generating over $2,000 in commissions. Except for the two contracts actually authorized by Sherwood on February 10 (of the six traded for his account), none of these trades were authorized by Sherwood.

On February 10, 1976, Madda mailed Sherwood the first trading confirmation. Subsequent confirmations were sent the day following each trade. However, Sherwood did not actually receive any communication from Jankowski or Madda until about Monday, February 16, 1976. On or about that date, Sherwood began to receive the trading confirmations and discovered that a large number of trades were being credited to his account. Between then and February 26, Sherwood made numerous attempts to contact Jankowski by telephone at Madda's Chicago office. On each occasion Sherwood was told that Jankowski was not in the office. According to Sherwood, Jankowski returned only one call; however, Sherwood was out of the office on that occasion.

On February 26, Jankowski's employment with Madda was terminated by Madda and on that date, Mr. Wynn, Jankowski's supervisor, contacted Sherwood. Wynn apprised Sherwood of open position in the account as of that time, and he began servicing the account on February 27, 1976. The statement sent by Madda to Sherwood on February 27 noted seventy-four open positions, seventy involving a wheat spread and four involving a silver spread. These open positions were all offset by March 3, 1976. However, subsequently several additional trades were made in silver and soybeans through Wynn and Madda and with Sherwood's consent. All of these additional positions were offset and the account was closed on March 16.

Jankowski's testimony was in sharp contrast to Sherwood's. Jankowski basically testified that each trade was discussed with Sherwood the day before the trade, and that Sherwood authorized each transaction. However, the Judge found that Sherwood's testimony was more worthy of belief than Jankowski's. The Judge based his conclusions upon subjective impressions gathered at the hearing, objective conclusions based on collateral evidence, and the lack of corroborative support for Jankowski's testimony.

Although Sherwood's credibility was enhanced by the fact that the suit was limited to trades made by Jankowski and by several admissions made by Sherwood against his interest at the hearing, the Judge's findings mostly reflected a disbelief of Jankowski's testimony. First, the Judge specifically found that the trades executed on Sherwood's behalf did not manifest the general conservative philosophy that Sherwood had exhibited in the past. The Judge found it "difficult to believe" that a person with a conservative trading history would authorize trades which generated over $2,000 in commissions in only two weeks. Second, the Judge noted that Jankowski's employment at Madda was terminated over a dispute which, in part, concerned low pay. At the time Jankowski left Madda, he had only five active accounts. Thus, Jankowski, who had been arguing with his employer over money, may have had a greater motive than other account executives for executing unauthorized trades. Finally, the Administrative Law Judge found that Jankowski's explanation for failing to respond to a discovery order of November 8, 1976, and to certain correspondence sent by the Hearing Clerk during the proceeding, severely undermined Jankowski's credibility.

All findings of fact must be supported by the weight, that is, the preponderance of the evidence. Haltmier v. Commodity Futures Trading Commission, 554 F.2d 556 (2d Cir. 1977). Here, the findings of fact are based upon substantial testimony and upon an assessment of the credibility of witnesses seen and heard by the Administrative Law Judge. Generally, such findings of fact should not be disturbed by the Commission, Universal Camera Corp. v. National Labor Relations Board, 340 U.S. 474, 494 (1951). Accordingly, we find, as did the Judge, that with the exception of the one silver and one wheat contract, all transactions entered into between February 10 and February 25 and credited to Sherwood's account were without Sherwood's prior authorization or consent, and thus were unauthorized. Jankowski's actions are imputed to Madda pursuant to Section 2(a)(1) of the Act, and thus, both are in violation of Sections 4b(A) and (C) of the Act. * * *

We first turn to the issue of damages. Madda defended and appeals on grounds of ratification, estoppel and failing to mitigate, and asks that some or all of the damages awarded be overturned. Although each of these defenses is slightly different, the essence of Madda's position is that Sherwood's failure to inform Madda of unauthorized trades credited to his account and Sherwood's continued trading deprived Madda of control over the unauthorized trades.

In aid of its analysis of the question raised here, the Commission would like to clarify its views concerning the interrelated rights and duties which arise when a customer believes that trades have been made in his account without his authorization. Principal among these is the customer's absolute right not to incur liability for any trade not authorized by him. In order words, if a transaction is executed without proper customer authorization, the position belongs to the futures commission merchant, not the customer.

As a corollary, the futures commission merchant also must either inform the customer, or be demonstrably certain that the customer otherwise understands, that the customer is under a duty to make a complaint at the first reasonable opportunity should he discover unauthorized trading in his account. Any notification should be clear and unequivocal, assuring that the customer understands the import of his action or inaction. If the futures commission merchant fails to insure that its customer is on notice of this duty, the futures commission merchant must necessarily assume absolute liability for all trades ultimately found to have been executed without authorization. This notification in turn triggers the duty of the customer to complain or to attempt to complain to his futures commission merchant immediately upon discovery of unauthorized trading. Should a customer, who has been informed that he must make a timely complaint of unauthorized trades, fail to notify or to attempt to notify the futures commission merchant of unauthorized transactions, the customer will have breached his duty to the futures commission merchant and thus must absorb himself any aggravated losses resulting from subsequent liquidation of the unauthorized positions, as we shall discuss.

Here, Madda's arguments center on Sherwood's failure to make an immediate protest to Madda concerning the unauthorized trades credited to his account. Madda places great reliance upon the customer confirmation statement which states: "Note: Please Report Any Differences Immediately." The Commission finds that, while this notification was meager at best, it was sufficient to trigger Sherwood's duty to notify or to make timely and reasonable efforts to notify either Jankowski or Madda of the errors. However, this is only the starting point of our analysis.

Madda's defense as to losses arising prior to February 26 was grounded almost entirely upon the absence of an actual complaint by Sherwood to Madda or one of its officers or agents. However, the Administrative Law Judge explicitly found that Sherwood attempted to contact Jankowski on a daily basis from the date he first received confirmation disclosing the unauthorized trades. In our view these attempts were sufficient to satisfy the duty imposed upon Sherwood and to warrant recovery of the losses in Sherwood's account prior to February 26 as the result of Jankowski's unauthorized trading.

Sherwood's initial inquiry to Madda was routed to Jankowski, and from then on Sherwood's only contact with Madda was through Jankowski. Jankowski arranged a telephone call-back system whereby Sherwood's calls were initially refused, but returned by Jankowski via his WATS line. Thus, Madda, through its agent Jankowski, prescribed the manner in which customer communication would occur. It was certainly not unreasonable for Sherwood to attempt to communicate with Jankowski via the means established by him. Moreover, Sherwood's attempts were certainly not singular or summary. Sherwood testified that he called Jankowski daily over a period of eight business days. Only one call was returned. Accordingly, so long as Sherwood made reasonable efforts to contact Madda, efforts which were foiled by Jankowski, Madda's agent, Madda cannot succeed in its claim that Sherwood breached his duty to complain and is consequently estopped from recovering for all losses sustained during this period. Thus, Sherwood is entitled to recover all losses sustained prior to February 26.

Sherwood's acquiescence during and after his conversation with Mr. Wynn on February 26 clearly dictates a different legal—and monetary—consequence for Sherwood. Madda argues that Sherwood, by his silence and subsequent trading activity, actually ratified, or intended to adopt for all time and as his own, the unauthorized trades credited to his account. The burden of proving ratification rests with the respondent. McCurnin v. Kohlmeyer & Co., 477 F.2d 113, 115 (5th Cir. 1973). Although Sherwood failed to protest the unauthorized trades credited to his account on February 26, or shortly thereafter, we conclude that the Judge was correct in finding that respondents failed to prove that Sherwood, by his silence, intended to adopt for all time the open unauthorized trades credited to his account, regardless of their ultimate fate in the marketplace.

We will apply the doctrine of ratification only where it is clear from all the circumstances presented that the intent of the customer was to adopt as his own and for all time the trades executed for his account without authorization. The *caveat* contained in Madda's confirmations, while it directed Sherwood to report discrepancies immediately, was sufficiently ambiguous that we cannot conclude that Sherwood would have known that his failure to complain in timely fashion constituted permanent adoption of all unauthorized trades. Indeed, it is difficult for us to believe, absent *compelling* evidence to the contrary, that one who truly understands his rights in such a situation would remain silent with the intention of adopting what would be, when commission fees are considered, losing trades, and we find no such evidence here. We also accept complainant's averment that his lack of true understanding of his right to repudiate the trades in question explains to a great extent his silence, at least insofar as the silence can be considered to imply an intention to ratify. As complainant points out, " '[r]atification is a matter of intention; its existence is a question of fact,....' " Thus, under the circumstances, especially in the absence of a logical motive, we hold that the Administrative Law Judge did not err in finding that Sherwood's failure to complain immediately did not constitute an affirmative ratification of the unauthorized trades credited to his account.

However, Madda's estoppel argument is persuasive as to the period after February 26, the date of Sherwood's conversation with Mr. Wynn and his first real opportunity to complain. Complaining to the responsible officer or agent of one's futures commission merchant is, in the Commission's view, the mandatory first step which a customer must take to mitigate damages upon discovery of unauthorized trading. The rationale behind this rule is simple. A substantiated complaint to a broker would immediately remove the burden of the unauthorized activity from the customer and give the person or entity with ultimate legal and financial responsibility for the trade an early opportunity to close the unauthorized position according to his own market theory or trading policy. By not complaining at the first reasonable opportunity, a customer, in effect, usurps the proper role of the persons ultimately responsible for the trade, the futures commission merchant and its officers and agents. Moreover, by failing to protest, the broker would undoubtedly presume the regularity of the unprotested transactions and knowingly forego potential opportunities to liquidate the positions. In the Commission's view, any aggravation of damages occurring as the result of a customer's undue silence should not be passed on to the futures commission merchant.

This view finds legal support in the doctrine of equitable estoppel:

> Four elements must be present to establish the defense of estoppel: (1) The party to be estopped must know the facts; (2) he must intend that his conduct shall be acted on or must so act that the party asserting the estoppel has a right to believe it is so intended; (3) the latter must to ignorant of the true facts; and (4) he must rely on the former's conduct to his injury. (citations omitted). Hampton v. Paramount Pictures Corp., 279 F.2d 100, 104 (9th Cir. 1960). See also Chemetron Corp. v. McLouth Steel Corp., 522 F.2d 469, 473 (7th Cir. 1975); Hecht v. Harris, Upham & Co., 430 F.2d 1202, 1208 (9th Cir. 1970); United States v. Georgia-Pacific Co., 421 F.2d 92 (9th Cir. 1970). And the view is also supported by the related, sometimes synonymous, doctrine of waiver. Shearson Hayden Stone, Inc. v. Leach, supra, at p. 370.

Applying this rule here, it is clear that Sherwood was aware that unauthorized trades had been credited to his account. It is also clear that Madda's trade confirmations warned Sherwood to report any discrepancies immediately and thereby put Madda on notice of his duty to complain. While this notification might not have imparted to Sherwood full knowledge of his right to repudiate unauthorized transactions and to have them removed from his account without expense, it certainly placed upon him the burden of informing Madda of discrepancies. To quote a time-tested maxim, "[h]e who keeps silent when duty commands him to speak shall not speak when duty commands him to keep silent." Bigelow, LAW OF ESTOPPEL 603 (6th Ed. Carter 1913); United States v. Georgia-Pacific Co., supra, at 96; 31 C.J.S. Estoppel § 108 at p. 548. Thus, Sherwood's failure on or after February 26 to inform Madda or its agent Wynn, both of whom were unaware that unauthorized trades had been credited to Sherwood's account, caused them to presume the regularity of the transactions and deprived Madda of the opportunity to liquidate the unauthorized positions immediately. Accordingly, losses to the equity in Sherwood's account subsequent to February 26 as the result of Jankowski's unauthorized activities are not recoverable by Sherwood.

Given the principle underlying our holding here—that trades made without customer authorization belong to the futures commission merchant, not the customer—Sherwood's silence, together with his continued trading, placed Sherwood in a position whereby he was trading against positions in his account which belonged to Madda, but without Madda either knowing of the unauthorized nature of the trades or consenting to or acquiescing in Sherwood's trading strategy. If we are to place ultimate responsibility for unauthorized trades upon futures commission merchants, we must also give assurance that they will have the opportunity to assert control over such trades and extricate themselves from the market at the first reasonable opportunity.

This will assure that customers cannot take advantage of mistakes by associated persons or other employees of futures commission merchants and use unauthorized or mistaken trades as a means to play the market with impunity, only repudiating the trades in question if they finally become losing propositions. Our approach will also assure that when such complaints are made to futures commission merchants, bona fide errors will be acknowledged (or at least corrected) at the earliest possible moment, if for no other reason than the financial interests of the futures commission merchant. Thus, if a merchant chooses to disbelieve a *bona fide* complaint, he does so at his peril. For the customer, upon establishing to our satisfaction the unauthorized nature of any transaction, may recover as damages in a reparation proceeding all subsequent, albeit aggravated, market losses sustained while the unauthorized positions are being liquidated by him in a reasonable fashion. Finally, by declining to make broad application of the doctrine of ratification here, opting rather for the more *ad hoc* and more flexible principles of equitable estoppel, we signal to all a balanced regulatory approach. We will not permit a commission merchant to assert that a customer has ratified a trade made without customer authorization, such trade being patently fraudulent and illegal, absent a clear and unequivocal adoption of such a trade by the customer. However, neither will we permit recovery of damages where unfair conduct by a customer harms the financial interests of the broker. In sum, we wish to assure that all receive fair treatment in the marketplace.

As for an actual computation of damages, the Commission will make its award based upon the losses incurred by Sherwood prior to February 27, 1976, less the losses flowing from the initial two trades authorized by Sherwood. As we noted earlier, Sherwood clearly authorized the sale of one April silver contract and one March wheat contract. On February 10, the March wheat sale was executed at 3.62 and the April silver sale at 405. Both of these transactions resulted in immediate losses. Indeed, for the entire period during which Jankowski controlled Sherwood's account, these commodities traded above the contract price. Jankowski covered the first silver position credited to Sherwood's account on February 11 at 413.00, for a loss of $400 plus a commission of $48.00. The wheat position was covered on February 24 at 3.80 1/2, for a loss of $925, plus a commission charge of $48.00.

Upon review of the record here, we find no indication that Sherwood intended to or would have liquidated these positions in any better fashion. Sherwood has not shown how he suffered actual loss as the result of the unauthorized transactions which covered Sherwood's initial authorized trades. We shall neither conjecture over what trading strategy Sherwood might have employed, nor make awards simply upon an after-the-fact review of exchange records. Simply stated, the burden of proving damages accruing as the result of the unauthorized activities of Jankowski rested with Sherwood here, and he did not carry it. Thus, although the authorized open positions were liquidated without Sherwood's authorization, we find that Sherwood has failed to prove any loss as the result and we shall award Sherwood damages in the amount of $4,673.50. * * *

DREXEL BURNHAM LAMBERT, INC. V. CFTC
850 F.2d 742 (D.C. Cir. 1988)

Opinion by: EDWARDS

Drexel Burnham Lambert Inc. ("Drexel") and one of its former brokers, David Ragan, petition for review of a decision by the Commodity Futures Trading Commission ("Commission") ordering them to pay Sansom Refining Company ("Sansom") approximately $1.3 million plus interest and costs for trading losses. The Commission found Drexel liable for the losses in Sansom's account because Richard Robinson, the Sansom employee who initiated the unprofitable trades, lacked actual and apparent authority to buy or sell commodity futures on Sansom's behalf, and because Sansom never ratified these trades. The Commission further ruled that Sansom was not estopped from claiming injury.

We affirm the Commission's decision in substantial part. We agree that Ragan's reckless response to Robinson's unauthorized trading orders violated section 4b of the Commodity Exchange Act, 7 U.S.C. § 6b, and that Drexel was liable for his actions under section 2(a)(1)(A) of the Act, 7 U.S.C. § 4. We have concluded, however, that the Commission erred in ruling that the petitioners violated section 4d(2) of the Act, 7 U.S.C. § 6d(2). Accordingly, we grant the petition for review with respect to the latter finding and reverse the Commission's decision on that point. The Commission also failed to address Drexel's argument that it should not bear the entire loss because Sansom failed to mitigate damages. We therefore remand the case to the Commission for further findings on this issue.

In 1980, Sansom was engaged in the business of buying precious metal as scrap, refining it, and reselling the purified product to larger refiners. Its two officers were Jackson Loughridge, President and Treasurer, and Albert Waterman, Vice-President and Secretary. Each owned 45% of Sansom's stock. In March 1980, Loughridge discussed various means of reducing Sansom's income tax liabilities with Drexel brokers. Throughout these discussions, Loughridge considered the advice of Richard Robinson, a Sansom employee. Robinson apparently knew more about tax law and commodity trading than did Loughridge, and Loughridge often consulted with him in such matters.

In April 1980, Loughridge and Robinson met with Ragan at Drexel's Houston office. Ragan suggested that Sansom establish an interest rate arbitrage program involving the purchase and sale of Treasury bills and Treasury bill futures, in order to convert its profits from ordinary income to long-term capital gains. Shortly thereafter, Loughridge agreed on Sansom's behalf to accept Ragan's proposal, which entailed an initial commitment of between $300,000 and $500,000. In early May 1980, Loughridge and Waterman executed Drexel's standard account-opening documents. They granted Ragan discretionary authority to trade Sansom's account. They also signed a corporate resolution form provided by Drexel, which Loughridge modified (with Waterman's permission) to authorize Loughridge alone—not Waterman as well—to trade the account. Although the corporate resolution form permitted Loughridge "to appoint any other person or persons to do any and all things which [he] is hereby empowered to do, and generally to do and take all action necessary in connection with the account," Appendix ("App.") at 812, neither Robinson nor any other person was ever authorized by Loughridge to initiate trades on Sansom's behalf.

On May 15, 1980, Ragan began buying Treasury bills for Sansom's account. Ragan telephoned Loughridge to report these initial purchases, and Drexel sent Sansom a statement, marked "Attn. Jack Loughridge," confirming the transactions. After several telephone calls, Loughridge told Ragan not to call him to report his dealings in the account; all telephonic reports, he said, should be made directly to Robinson. After reviewing the first few written account statements, Loughridge apparently ceased reading them as well. Instead, he relied on Robinson to monitor the statements and to inform him of the account's status every week or so. Between May 15 and June 10, 1980, Sansom deposited $400,000 in its account with Drexel.

On June 11, 1980, Robinson telephoned Ragan and placed an order to sell 48 pork belly futures for Sansom's account. Ragan executed the order, without asking Loughridge whether he had authorized the sale or delegated to Robinson his exclusive authority to trade. Ragan had good reasons to be suspicious of the order, both because he had never been advised that Robinson had authority to trade for Sansom, and because the order was patently at odds with the well-understood tax goals of the client's account.

On June 19, 1980, Ragan, Robinson and Loughridge met in Philadelphia. Ragan spoke very generally about Sansom's trading program and reported that all was well. Ragan did not mention the sale of pork belly futures he had made eight days before at Robinson's behest, although at that meeting he could easily have verified Robinson's authority to initiate trades. Ragan also furnished Loughridge with a list of transactions in Sansom's account through June 11. Significantly, however, the list did not include the sale of pork belly futures on June 11 that Robinson had requested, even though three other transactions involving Treasury bills were listed for that date.

On July 9, 1980, Robinson directed Ragan to offset half of the pork belly futures at a loss of more than $77,000. Ragan did so, again without telephoning Loughridge to confirm Robinson's authority to initiate trades. During the rest of July, Robinson ordered numerous other unprofitable trades in pork belly and live cattle futures. In August and September, he speculated even more heavily, accumulating huge losses.

At no time did Ragan ask Loughridge whether Robinson was authorized to trade for Sansom. When Sansom's losses began to mount, however, he did express his worries to Robinson, who stated that Sansom had hedged the unprofitable trades through orders placed at Bache Halsey Stuart Shields Inc. ("Bache"). Ragan telephoned a broker at Bache to confirm Robinson's story. He was told that Sansom's account at Bache enjoyed a surplus roughly equal to Sansom's aggregate losses at Drexel. The Bache broker refused to tell Ragan, however, what trades had been made through that account. Hence, Ragan could not corroborate Robinson's assertion, although his fears were somewhat allayed. In fact, Sansom's account at Bache was *not* used to hedge Robinson's trades at Drexel.

Throughout this period, Drexel regularly sent account statements to Sansom, marked to the attention of Loughridge. The statements requested the client to report any inaccuracies immediately. Sansom never complained about the unauthorized trades, because Loughridge trusted Robinson to read the statements and apprise him of the account's status, and Robinson never mentioned the unauthorized, speculative commodity trades that he had placed with Ragan. Sansom deposited over

$1.3 million in the account between July and September 1980 in order to cover its losses. Most of the checks were signed by Waterman. Neither Loughridge nor Waterman questioned Robinson when he presented the checks for their signatures.

In mid-September 1980, Ragan and Loughridge discussed a gold trade that Ragan had made for Sansom's account. It is unclear who initiated the call, or how Loughridge learned of the trade. However, it is clear that, as soon as Loughridge became aware of the unauthorized trade, he was explicit in instructing Ragan not to trade in gold. Even though Loughridge expressed concern about commodity trading in the company's account, Ragan never volunteered any information about the orders that had been placed by Robinson, nor did he use the occasion of their September discussion to inquire regarding the efficacy of the commodity trades.

On September 21, 1980, Robinson finally confessed to Loughridge that he had speculated in Sansom's account and had incurred colossal losses. Loughridge promptly closed out all the open commodity contracts the following day. Sansom maintained its account at Drexel, however, so as not to lose the tax benefits it expected to reap from its Treasury bill spreads.

On June 3, 1982, Sansom filed a reparations claim with the Commission against Drexel and Ragan. Sansom's complaint alleged violations of section 4b of the Commodity Exchange Act, 7 U.S.C. § 6b. The Administrative Law Judge ("ALJ") who conducted a hearing on Sansom's complaint ruled in favor of Drexel and Ragan and dismissed Sansom's action on May 27, 1986. He found that, although Robinson lacked both actual and apparent authority to initiate trades in Sansom's account, Sansom was estopped from claiming injury from the unauthorized trades because Sansom had not complained of them to Drexel despite having received reports of the transactions and having paid $1.3 million to meet its margin requirements.

Sansom appealed and the Commission reversed. The Commission agreed that Robinson lacked actual and apparent authority to trade Sansom's account. Having found that Ragan accepted orders even though Robinson had no actual or apparent authority to trade for Sansom, the Commission ruled that Sansom could not be estopped from claiming injury. The Commission concluded that "Ragan was unreasonable under the circumstances to allow Robinson to begin trading the account and remained unreasonable in allowing trading to continue, even in light of Sanson's failure to protest and payment of margin. . . ." Commission Op. at 34,108. In the Commission's view, "Ragan's conduct amount[ed] to willful disregard of whether he was acting in accordance with Sansom's instructions," and thus constituted a violation of section 4b. *Id.* at 34,108 n.10.

The Commission also found Drexel and Ragan liable under section 4d(2), 7 U.S.C. § 6d(2). According to the Commission, section 4d(2) "places the burden on the commodity professional to ascertain the authority of an individual purporting to act for a customer. If the associated person fails to take reasonable steps to learn the limits of an individual's authority, and the futures commission merchant fails to take reasonable steps to prevent, detect, and correct such employee errors, complainants will not be denied recovery merely because they could have done a better job of protecting their own interest." Commission Op. at 34,108. Without considering whether Sansom had failed to mitigate damages, the Commission ordered Drexel and Ragan to pay Sansom $1,322,074.50 with interest from September 22, 1980. Drexel and Ragan seek review of the Commission's decision.

Section 4b [of the CEA] renders it unlawful "to cheat or defraud" or "willfully to deceive" any person in regard to any commodity contract in interstate commerce. Other circuits that have construed this provision are agreed that "mere negligence, mistake, or inadvertence" fails to meet section 4b's scienter requirement; "a degree of intent beyond carelessness or negligence" is necessary to violate this provision. *Hill v. Bache Halsey Stuart Shields Inc.*, 790 F.2d 817, 822 (10th Cir. 1986); *see also Greenwood v. Dittmer*, 776 F.2d 785, 789 (8th Cir. 1985); *Haltmier v. CFTC*, 554 F.2d 556, 562 (2d Cir. 1977). The question here is whether section 4b encompasses reckless conduct.

We hold that recklessness is sufficient to satisfy section 4b's scienter requirement. A reckless action, as the First Circuit said in reaching the same result, "is one that departs so far from the standards of ordinary care that it is very difficult to believe the [actor] was not aware of what he was doing." *First Commodity Corp. v. CFTC*, 676 F.2d 1, 7 (1st Cir. 1982). The language of section 4b, together with the virtually unanimous agreement among the circuits that recklessness may serve as the predicate for liability under the analogous provisions of section 10(b) of the Securities Exchange Act of 1934 and SEC Rule 10b–5, *see, e.g., Rolf v. Blyth, Eastman Dillon & Co.*, 570 F.2d 38, 46 (2d Cir.), *cert. denied*, 439 U.S. 1039, 58 L. Ed. 2d 698, 99 S. Ct. 642 (1978); *McLean v. Alexander*, 599 F.2d 1190, 1197–98 (3d Cir. 1979), convinces us that reckless inattention to obvious dangers to a client's interests in arranging a purchase or sale for the client's account triggers liability under section 4b. As Drexel's counsel acknowledged at oral argument before this court, the Commission's finding that "Ragan's conduct amounts to willful disregard of whether he was acting in accordance with Sansom's instructions," Commission Op. at 34,108 n.10, plainly fulfills section 4b's scienter requirement if it is supported by the weight of evidence.

In our view, the Commission's determination is firmly rooted in the record before it. Loughridge was the only Sansom officer authorized to trade Sansom's account, apart from the discretionary authority vested in Ragan with respect to the purchase and sale of government securities to attain Sansom's tax objectives. Loughridge modified the corporate resolution form provided by Drexel to so provide, and Ragan was or should have been aware of this fact. At no time, moreover, did Loughridge inform Ragan or Drexel that he had delegated to Robinson his authority to trade. Nor did Ragan avail himself of numerous opportunities to ascertain Robinson's authority to initiate trades when he placed commodity futures orders, even though he had reason to be suspicious of those orders. As the Commission noted, Loughridge initiated no trades himself, and those that Robinson ordered "were unmistakably intended for speculative purposes in commodities bearing no relation to Sansom's tax goals." Commission Op. at 34,107. Ragan was also aware that Loughridge was not knowledgeable about commodity trading, and he had no reason to surmise that Loughridge was eager to speculate with the money he hired Ragan to shield from income tax. Under these circumstances, the Commission properly concluded that it was highly irresponsible for Ragan to place Robinson's orders without verifying his authority. Yet, he did not even call Loughridge—not when Robinson phoned in his first trade, and not even when Sansom's losses ran to hundreds of thousands of dollars. Ragan did not mention the first pork belly futures trade when he met with Loughridge and Robinson on June 19, 1980, and the list of trades he tendered to Loughridge that day inexplicably omitted the pork belly futures trade, despite the fact that Treasury bill transactions on the same day were included. He further failed to mention Robinson's commodity futures trades when Loughridge rebuked him for trading in gold in mid-September. Given this record, the Commission had ample support for the finding that Robinson lacked both actual and apparent authority to trade Sansom's account. *See* ALJ Op. at 32,198; Commission Op. at 34,107. Furthermore, we deem the evidence adduced by the Commission more than sufficient to sustain its conclusion that Ragan's conduct constituted "willful disregard of whether he was acting in accordance with Sansom's instructions," in clear violation of section 4b. Commission Op. at 34,108 n.10.

The ALJ "concluded that Ragan, with some justification believed that Robinson had authority to trade on behalf of Sansom." ALJ Op. at 32,201. But the Commission weighed the evidence entirely differently when it found that, "in light of the facts available to Ragan, he was unreasonable in simply assuming that Robinson was authorized to trade the account. At a minimum, Ragan should have sought clarification from Loughridge, an individual Ragan knew and to whom he had reasonable access." Commission Op. at 34,107. In short, if the ALJ thought that Ragan had "some justification" for his unauthorized dealings with Robinson, the

Commission found it to be both "unreasonable" and reflective of a "willful disregard of whether he was acting in accordance with Sansom's instructions." Because the Commission's findings are reasonably supported by the record, we are bound to accept these determinations.

The Commission also expressly noted that the ALJ's estoppel ruling, which derived from the same facts that the ALJ thought warranted Ragan's erroneous belief that Robinson had been empowered to trade Sansom's account, was "fundamentally inconsistent with the judge's prior determination that Ragan did not reasonably rely on statements or activity attributed to Sansom in allowing Robinson to trade." Commission Op. at 34,108. The Commission further rejected the claim that Sansom's failure to protest and its continued payment of margin rendered reasonable Ragan's persistent neglect to inquire into Robinson's authority to trade. *See id.* In support of this conclusion, the Commission pointed out that Ragan's awareness that Loughridge looked to Robinson to supervise the account "diminishe[d] the weight he could reasonably attribute to the failure to protest." *Id.* at 34,108 n.8. It also noted that Ragan decided not to contact Loughridge when Robinson's trades produced large losses, but instead contented himself with a hasty and unsatisfactory inquiry into the status of Sansom's account at a rival investment bank—a decision which the Commission, in its expert judgment, found unjustifiable. *See id.* Finally, the Commission reasoned that Sansom's payment of amounts in excess of $500,000 to maintain its account "are not persuasive evidence of approval of Robinson's trades in light of the complex nature of the straddle strategy at issue. It is not uncommon that margin requirements will be underestimated in the course of soliciting participation in such programs." *Id.* at 34,108 n.9.

In view of the deference we owe to an agency's factual determinations, including the reasonable inferences drawn therefrom, we conclude that the Commission's finding that Ragan acted with "willful disregard" of whether he was heeding Sansom's instructions is reasonably supported by the great weight of the evidence in the record of this case. That the Commission cast the relevant facts in a different light and drew different inferences than the ALJ is not in itself reason for us to gainsay the Commission's judgment, provided—as is here the case—that it was reasonable. The Commission's conclusion fully accords with its findings of fact, and its explication of that conclusion suffices, particularly given the inconsistency at the heart of the ALJ's opinion.

As a possible affirmative defense against a finding of liability, Drexel and Ragan contend that Sansom ratified Robinson's unauthorized trades when it continued to fund its account, without protest, after receipt of Drexel's confirmation statements. This contention is insupportable in view of the prevailing legal standard and the facts of this case. The Commission has held that a customer ratifies unauthorized trading for his account "only where it is clear from all the circumstances presented that the intent of the customer was to adopt as his own and for all time the trades executed for his account without authorization." *Sherwood v. Madda Trading Co.*, [1977–1980 Transfer Binder] Comm. Fut. L. Rep. (CCH) P20,728 at 23,020 (CFTC Jan. 5, 1979). Circuit courts that have confronted the issue have also deemed knowledge of the relevant facts and an intent to approve the unauthorized action after its occurrence to be preconditions to ratification. *See, e.g., Hill v. Bache Halsey Stuart Shields Inc.*, 790 F.2d 817, 827 (10th Cir. 1986).

We embrace the Commission's standard for the affirmative defense of ratification, and agree with the Commission that Drexel and Ragan have failed to meet it in this case. Commission Op. at 34,107. There is no evidence that either Loughridge or Waterman was aware that the checks they signed were to fund Robinson's trading losses rather than the Treasury bill arbitrage program they were pursuing. *See* ALJ Op. at 32,198–99; Commission Op. at 34,107. Indeed, Loughridge's decision to close out all commodity positions as soon as Robinson confessed his unauthorized dealings, despite the heavy losses Sansom thereby incurred, strongly supports the finding that he was ignorant of Robinson's trading and that he did not intend to approve it after the fact. *See id.* Furthermore, Loughridge's decision to maintain Sansom's account at Drexel after Robinson's trading was discovered, in order not to lose the tax advantages he sought, cannot be deemed ratification of those trades Loughridge did *not* authorize. *See* ALJ Op. at 32,198.

Drexel and Ragan also argue that Sansom is estopped from claiming injury because it failed to protest upon receipt of Drexel's account statements listing the unauthorized trades, because it repeatedly sent checks to Drexel to cover Robinson's trading losses, and because it was aware of Robinson's history of gambling and embezzlement whereas Drexel was not.

We reject this argument. Normally, four elements must be present to establish the affirmative defense of estoppel: (1) the party to be estopped must have known the facts; (2) the party against whom estoppel is asserted must have acted in a manner that caused the other party reasonably to believe that it intended whatever action it is allegedly estopped from citing as the basis of its claim; (3) the party asserting estoppel must have been justifiably ignorant of the relevant facts; and (4) the party asserting estoppel must have relied on the other party's conduct to his injury. *See Sherwood v. Madda Trading Co.*, [1977–1980 Transfer Binder] Comm. Fut. L. Rep. (CCH) P20,728 at 23,021 (CFTC Jan. 5, 1979). The Commission found, and we agree, that both the second and third elements were absent in this case.

Drexel and Ragan manifestly lacked a reasonable belief that Sansom sanctioned Robinson's trades. Both the ALJ and the Commission found that Robinson lacked actual and apparent authority to initiate trades. If Robinson had neither actual nor apparent authority to trade, then Ragan and Drexel are hard-pressed to suggest that they *reasonably* believed that Robinson's orders were authorized. Furthermore, the Commission pointed out that Ragan was aware of Loughridge's reliance on Robinson and that he knew or should have realized that Loughridge and Waterman might have signed the checks necessary to maintain Sansom's account because they were ignorant of the details of Ragan's trading program and did not know how much money was necessary to finance it. *See* Commission Op. at 34,108 & nn.8–9. Hence, Drexel and Ragan cannot plausibly contend that their asserted belief in Sansom's acquiescence in Robinson's speculative trading was justified by Sansom's failure to protest and its payment of margin requirements. Ragan had clear instructions that only Loughridge had the authority to trade for Sansom, and these instructions were never amended during the course of Robinson's unauthorized trading.

Moreover, Ragan's failure to inquire into Robinson's authority to trade precludes the petitioners from claiming that they were justifiably ignorant of Sansom's disapproval of Robinson's trades. A party urging estoppel must show that it took reasonable steps to discover relevant facts. *See Keller v. Scoular-Bishop of Missouri, Inc.*, [1986–1987 Transfer Binder] Comm. Fut. L. Rep. (CCH) P23,128 at 32,336 (CFTC June 26, 1986); *Sherwood*, para. 20,728 at 23,021. The petitioners failed to do so. Ragan could easily have ascertained, at any time, whether Robinson had been authorized to trade. *See* Commission Op. at 34,108. Moreover, he plainly had a duty to verify Robinson's authorization, both because Robinson did not possess even apparent authority to trade and because his commands were highly suspicious, given that the speculative commodity trades Robinson ordered would not advance the objectives of Sansom's Treasury bill arbitrage program. Under the circumstances, Ragan did not display reasonable diligence in determining Robinson's authority or lack thereof, and a modicum of effort—a brief telephone call, or a single question to Loughridge when they met in person on June 19, 1980—would have revealed that Robinson did not possess authority to place orders for commodity futures. The Commission was therefore correct in ruling that Drexel and Ragan were not justifiably ignorant of Sansom's disapproval of Robinson's trades, and thus that Sansom was not estopped from claiming injury.

In addition to their claims with respect to *ratification* and *estoppel*, Drexel and Ragan also assert that Sansom should bear at least part of the losses incurred because it failed to take reasonable steps to *mitigate* damages. The Commission has recognized that "each of these defenses is slightly different," *Sherwood v. Madda Trading Co.*, [1977–1980 Transfer Binder] Comm. Fut. L. Rep. (CCH) P20,728 at 23,018 (CFTC Jan. 5, 1979), yet no judgment was offered in this case on the claim of mitigation.

Although Commission precedent admits of some confusion on this point, it would appear that the doctrine of mitigation of damages, unlike that of estoppel, looks solely to the conduct of the party requesting damages. As was noted in *Sherwood*, complaining to the responsible officer or agent of one's futures commission merchant is, in the Commission's view, the mandatory first step which a customer must take to mitigate damages upon discovery of unauthorized trading. *Id.* at 23,021.

Often, as in *Sherwood*, judgments on ratification and estoppel appear to subsume the inquiry on mitigation, even though the doctrinal analyses are distinct. Nonetheless, as is also clear from *Sherwood*, there are cases in which different results may obtain with respect to different trades, depending upon whether the complainant "was aware that unauthorized trades had been credited to his account." *Id.* The Commission must reach a determination on this question in order to dispose of the claim of mitigation. Accordingly, we will remand the case for the Commission's ruling on this issue.

The final issue before us concerns the Commission's purported reliance on section 4d(2) in finding Drexel and Ragan liable under the Act. Section 4d(2) requires a futures commission merchant to "treat and deal with all money . . . received by [him] to margin, guarantee, or secure the trades or contracts of any customer . . . as belonging to such customer." 7 U.S.C. § 6d(2). The Commission ruled that Ragan's trading in accordance with Robinson's unauthorized orders violated section 4d(2). The Commission explained:

> Section 4d(2) of the Act . . . places the burden on the commodity professional to ascertain the authority of an individual purporting to act for a customer. If the associated person fails to take reasonable steps to learn the limits of an individual's authority, and the futures commission merchant fails to take reasonable steps to prevent, detect, and correct such employee errors, complainants will not be denied recovery merely because they could have done a better job of protecting their own interest.

Commission Op. at 34,108. In support of this claim, the Commission cited its decision in *Hunter v. Madda Trading Co.*, [1980–1982 Transfer Binder]Comm. Fut. L. Rep. (CCH) P21,242 at 25,204 (CFTC Sept. 2, 1981).

The Commission's reading of section 4d(2) is unpersuasive. Neither the express terms of the statute nor the legislative history of section 4d(2) buttresses the Commission's assertions. Contrary to the Commission's ill-defended claims in *Hunter*, section 4d(2) was intended for one purpose: to prevent an unscrupulous broker from commingling clients' margin funds with his own and then using those funds to speculate for the broker's own account, thereby imperiling his clients' prospects of obtaining a refund of their margin deposits should the broker's gambles fail. *See* 80 CONG. REC. 6162, 6612–13, 7910–12 (1936); *see also Craig v. Refco, Inc.*, 624 F. Supp. 944, 946–47 (N.D. Ill. 1985) (recounting legislative history), *aff'd*, 816 F.2d 347 (7th Cir. 1987); *Marchese v. Shearson Hayden Stone, Inc.*, 644 F. Supp. 1381, 1384 (C.D. Cal. 1986) (same), *aff'd*, 822 F.2d 876 (9th Cir. 1987). It does not reach every failure by a broker to act in accordance with a client's orders.

Moreover, as the petitioners and amicus point out, the Commission's construction of section 4d(2) would eviscerate section 4b, rendering nugatory its scienter requirement. For if the Commission's interpretation of this section were correct, the innocent or negligent mishandling of client funds, which the Commission recognizes is immune from liability under section 4b in virtue of its scienter requirement, *see Hunter*, para. 21,242 at 25,204 n.8, would automatically generate liability under section 4d(2). Congress cannot have intended this irrational result. Hence, we reverse the Commission's decision that Drexel and Ragan are liable under section 4d(2).

We deny Drexel and Ragan's petition for review with regard to the Commission's finding that the petitioners violated section 4b of the Commodity Exchange Act by dint of Ragan's reckless compliance with Robinson's orders without attempting to verify Robinson's authority to trade Sansom's account. The Commission was also correct in ruling that Sansom was not estopped from claiming injury. We find, however, that the Commission's construction of section 4d(2) was erroneous. We therefore grant the petition for review insofar as it concerns the petitioners' liability under that section. Finally, we remand this case to the Commission with instructions to consider whether Sansom failed to mitigate damages.

So ordered.

Concur by: STARR (In Part)

Dissent by: STARR (In Part)

EVANSTON BANK V. CONTICOMMODITY SERVICES
623 F. Supp. 1014 (N.D. Ill. 1985)

JAMES B. MORAN, JUDGE, UNITED STATES DISTRICT COURT

In late May of 1982 the board of directors of the Evanston Bank discovered that the bank had lost over $1,200,000 in about one year of trading in commodities, while paying over $270,000 in commissions. The bank now brings this action for commodities fraud against ContiCommodity Services, Inc. (Conti), the futures commission merchant through which it traded in commodity futures, and Ted Thomas, the broker who handled its account.

The bank's version of how the loss occurred appears in the six counts of its complaint. Counts I and II allege violations of the Commodity Exchange Act (CEA), 7 U.S.C. § 1 *et seq.*, specifically that Conti and Thomas used the bank's account for unauthorized trading and "churned" it (traded it excessively) to generate unnecessary commissions. The bank maintains that it intended only to hedge in commodities as a protection against rising interest rates, a conservative investment strategy. It says that it got speculative trading instead. Since Conti and Thomas used the mails and the telephone in connection with the trading, count IV alleges mail and wire fraud in violation of 18 U.S.C. § 1961 *et seq.*, the Racketeer Influenced and Corrupt Organization Act (RICO). The remaining counts are pendent claims under Illinois law. Count III, for common law fraudulent misrepresentation and concealment, and count V, for fraudulent or deceptive business practices under Ill.Rev.Stat. ch. 121–1/2 para. 262, rest on Thomas' alleged assurances that the bank's account would be traded in accordance with appropriate banking regulations and Federal Deposit Insurance Corporation (FDIC) policies, and that the bank would be charged commissions at the same rate as other banks. Since an FDIC policy statement in effect then and now allows hedging in commodities but strongly discourages banks from speculative trading, and the bank was charged $94 per "round turn" (per transaction) while other Conti customers with similar account activity were charged $30 to $35 (and apparently some banks with other firms had a rate of only $11 to $20), the bank claims fraud and deception. Finally, count VI, apparently in the alternative, alleges negligence in the handling of the bank's account.

Conti, however, presents a different version of how the loss occurred and moves for summary judgment in its favor. The board of directors of the bank fully authorized Richard Christiansen, at that time both the chairman of the bank's board of directors and the bank's chief executive officer, to handle commodities trading for the bank. Conti maintains that all of the trades followed Christiansen's instructions on the bank's objectives and the overwhelming majority of them were either specifically approved or later ratified by him. Christiansen also executed a power of attorney to Thomas to make trades on behalf of the bank. The bank may now regret its choice of Christiansen as its agent (he was fired in June 1982, after the rest of the board discovered the extent of his trading), but nevertheless it chose him and so must bear the loss from his acts. And, if any further authority is needed, Conti points out that it strictly complied with the bank's instructions to send daily written confirmation of each trade to the cashier of the bank, Hindrek Ott. Neither Ott nor any other representative of the bank disavowed any trade until May 28, 1982. Since the bank was fully informed, both through its agent Christiansen and through the notice to the cashier, Conti argues, its silence ratified the trades. Therefore, Conti is not liable for the bank's losses as a matter of law. Defendant Thomas has moved to adopt Conti's motion.

This court finds to the contrary that, at least on the evidence now before us, this case needs a trial to resolve a host of unanswered questions. The primary purpose of summary judgment is to avoid the expenditure of time and money on a trial in cases where a trial would serve no real function. *Mintz v. Mathers Fund, Inc.*, 463 F.2d 495 (7th Cir. 1972). Summary judgment should not be granted when facts or the inferences to be derived from facts are in dispute, because finding facts and drawing inferences are tasks for a trier of fact. *United States v. Diebold, Inc.*, 369 U.S. 654, 8 L. Ed. 2d 176, 82 S. Ct. 993 (1962); *Wang v. Lake Maxinhall Estates, Inc.*, 531 F.2d 832 (7th Cir. 1976). Some inquiries by their very nature are fact-intensive. Fraud, for example, involves questions of intent and knowledge, which are normally questions for a trier of fact. If a reasonable person could draw more than one inference from the known facts, summary judgment is not appropriate. *Rock Island Bank v. Aetna Casualty and Surety Co.*, 706 F.2d 219 (7th Cir. 1983). Agency questions also tend to be fact intensive. A third party dealing with an agent has a legal obligation to verify both the fact and the extent of the agent's authority. *Malcak v. Westchester Park District*, 754 F.2d 239, 245 (7th Cir. 1985). The inquiry will usually focus on whether reliance on the indications of authority which were present was reasonable under all the facts and circumstances. Such questions of reasonableness also in most cases must go to triers of fact. *See e.g., Borg-Warner Leasing v. Doyle Electric Co.*, 733 F.2d 833, 836 (11th Cir. 1984); *Moreau v. James River-Otis, Inc.*, 767 F.2d 6, 9 (1st Cir. 1985). This case involves both allegations of fraud and questions of agency. It cannot be cut off at this point.

The complexity of the case requires that the facts be set out in considerable detail. In March 1981 Conti conducted a seminar on commodities trading especially tailored for financial institutions. Thomas, then head of Conti's broker training program and soon to be an account executive in Conti's Chicago office, participated. Christiansen, accompanied by Michael McGreal, the Evanston Bank's president, attended the seminar. Neither had any previous experience in trading commodities but Christiansen, who had read an article on the subject, wanted the bank to consider trading futures contracts in order to hedge the bank's assets against interest rate fluctuations.

Thomas contacted Christiansen and McGreal soon after the seminar. There is some dispute as to the exact characterization Thomas gave of himself at that point in his effort to win the bank's business. McGreal says that Thomas held himself out as a specialist in hedging for financial institutions. Thomas maintains that he represented himself merely as "knowledgeable" and "attempting to specialize." His knowledge came from one seminar on banks and commodities trading held the year before, and Thomas now admits that he was not familiar with the language of specific regulations and FDIC policy statements. During the next year the Evanston Bank was in fact his only bank client, although he had previously handled the account of one other bank. What Thomas felt he understood at that time was that banks could not open speculative accounts but could have hedge and arbitrage accounts. An FDIC policy statement of November 20, 1979, permits banks to hedge on financial futures to protect against interest rate fluctuations, but describes other transactions "such as taking futures positions to speculate on future interest rate movements" as "inappropriate futures transactions for banks." 44 Fed. Reg. 66673; *amended at* 45 Fed. Reg. 18116 (March 20, 1980) *and at* 46 Fed. Reg. 51302 (Oct. 19, 1981). Under 12 U.S.C. § 1818, conduct contrary to FDIC policy can result eventually in a bank's losing its insured status with the FDIC, which in turn would mean loss of federal insurance protection for its depositors and loss of membership in the Federal Reserve System.

The bank opened a commodity futures hedge account with Conti on May 19, 1981. The board had endorsed a corporate authorization, a standard form furnished by Conti. By its terms, the bank authorized Christiansen and McGreal to buy and sell commodities for the bank, with written confirmations to go to the cashier, Ott, "who is hereby authorized to receive and acquiesce in the correctness of such confirmations, statements and other records and documents." Christiansen then completed a standard customer's agreement and a risk disclosure statement, a new account worksheet and a hedging account designation form. According to the latter, "Any and all positions in the above-mentioned account will be bona fide hedges as defined in Regulation 1.3(2) of the Commodity Futures Trading Commission (CFTC)." McGreal asserts, and Thomas apparently does not deny, that at the time the account was opened Thomas said that the bank's account would be traded in such a fashion that there would be no problem with any relevant regulations for banks, including FDIC policies, and that Evanston Bank would be charged the same commissions that other banks trading through Conti were charged. McGreal and Christiansen told Thomas at that time that the bank's investment objective was to hedge the bank's assets against rising interest rates—a very conservative strategy of acquiring futures contracts to sell ("shorts") corresponding to assets held by the bank—and that the bank would "rather be safe than sorry." The first activity in the account was on June 2, 1981.

From July 1981 through December 1981 all parties agree that trading in the bank's account was consistent with those objectives. It averaged 22.8 transactions per month and was profitable. Thomas left Chicago to become branch manager of Conti's Houston office at the beginning of August, but continued to handle the Evanston Bank's account. A few days before he left, on July 27, Christiansen executed a document in the bank's name which gave Thomas a power of attorney over the bank's account. The origin of this document is disputed. Thomas maintains that it came in response to a concern voiced by Christiansen and McGreal that Thomas would be unable to reach them by telephone at a crucial time. McGreal disavows such a concern, and both deposition testimony and board minutes show that the board was unaware of any such document's existence throughout the period of the bank's trading. Christiansen's deposition testimony is silent on this and all other disputed matters since he relied upon his privilege against self-incrimination to decline to answer virtually all questions. The document made the bank's account a "discretionary account," a status not encouraged by Conti's own policy manual.

According to Thomas, he used his authority for a few trades over the life of the account, but most came as a result of frequent telephone conversations with Christiansen. The pattern of trading began to shift in January of 1982. In that month the bank's activity included 150 contracts in day trades, more day trades than had been placed during the entire life of the account up to that time. Approximately that volume of trading persisted through February. Then in March activity took another quantum jump, with 326 contracts day-traded. From January until the board halted all trading at the end of May, the monthly average was 297.8 trades, over ten times the average for the previous six months. Although Thomas declines to call this trading "speculative," he agrees that it was a change in position in the futures market seeking higher yield. The bank's net "open positions" in its account with Conti shifted from an overall short position in January to $27,000,000 long at the end of April. According to Irving Hankin, an expert witness whose affidavit was submitted by the bank, this trading pattern was speculative and quite inconsistent with the bank's original objectives. Since commissions were charged per transaction, this pattern also generated substantial commissions for Conti and Thomas, for example a larger charge for commissions in the month of March alone than for all trading in the account in 1981. The account's increased activity brought no reduction in the rate which the bank paid. By Thomas' admission, large volume customers normally were charged lower commission rates. Hankin found the commissions "atypically large."

According to Thomas, the shift in trading resulted from Christiansen's instructions to change the bank's investment strategy.

Though he is not clear on the precise date, at some point in early 1982 Christiansen approached him with the question of whether it was feasible to make day trades for profit; told that it was, he authorized Thomas to make such day trades. Thomas says that Christiansen informed him that the bank needed to generate profits in order to meet a major debt which was coming due. Indeed, the bank's holding company, Evco, faced a quarterly payment on a $1,350,000 loan. It had intended to meet the payment with bank stock dividends, but, in March, the Commissioner of Banks denied permission to issue a dividend because the bank had not been sufficiently profitable. All bank personnel, however, deny that the board ever looked to commodities trading to generate the amount due, or in any other way changed its investment strategy for commodities. If Christiansen indeed ordered such a change, he seems to have concealed it from the board. He also apparently lied to the bank's asset and liability committee about the size and nature of the bank's trading. The loan to Evco was secured by bank stock and Christiansen's personal guarantee.

Another apparent effort to infuse cash into Evco came in late April and May. Christiansen also was the bank's chief loan officer. The bank loaned $50,000 to Thomas, who then used the funds to purchase Evco stock. The loan was issued to Thomas' Illinois bank account, though he had then lived in Houston for several months. The 800 shares of Evco stock were actually paid for by and issued to Thomas' wife in her maiden name, which she had not used for business for over 20 years. Thomas says that these arrangements were Christiansen's idea, "to avoid unnecessary questions from the bank examiners."

In any case, daily reports of the increased trading went to Ott, the cashier. Ott testified by deposition that his only responsibilities towards these reports on Christiansen's instructions, were to "book the entries," to post the gains and losses on the bank's general ledger, and then to put the statements into a file. The Evanston Bank did not have a regular cashier's report. The board reviewed only the monthly statements, not the daily ones. By opening and closing a position on the same day, the trading pattern eliminated the need for margin calls on the bank. Thomas admits that the motive for some trades was to avoid margin calls. The directors did not actually know the bank's true position until late May. When they did, the board first ordered Christiansen to stop trading on May 28 and then began liquidating as rapidly as it could without absorbing so much of a loss as to make it insolvent. Christiansen was terminated by June 15. Conti fired Thomas in September, by his testimony for matters not related to the Evanston Bank account. * * *

Count I seeks to impose liability on Thomas for unauthorized trading and on Conti both directly and vicariously for its employee's acts. Conti's direct liability would result from its alleged aiding and abetting of Thomas, its failure to supervise its broker with procedures which would have brought his conduct to light, and its failure to investigate the investment objectives and financial resources of its client the bank to make sure its investments were suitable, as required by trade regulations. Conti argues, however, that it cannot be directly liable since even if proved true, none of those allegations states a claim under the Commodities Exchange Act as applied to losses incurred in 1982.

The CEA provides for enforcement of its provisions largely through the administrative agency it created, the CFTC. The express private right of action under the CEA, 7 U.S.C. § 25, was enacted by Congress only in the Futures Trading Act of 1982, PL 97–444 § 235, 96 Stat. 2322 (1982). It was not in effect during the period of the bank's losses. The Supreme Court has held that the general provision against commodities fraud, 7 U.S.C. § 6b, includes an implied private right of action for both acts expressly prohibited by that provision and acts prohibited by some regulations promulgated under it. *Merrill Lynch, Pierce, Fenner & Smith, Inc. v. Curran*, 456 U.S. 353, 72 L. Ed. 2d 182, 102 S. Ct. 1825 (1982). However, courts which have dealt with the question have found significant limits on that implied right of action. In *Curran*, the court reasoned that since Congress amended the CEA in 1974 aware that courts were finding private rights under it, and did nothing to correct that impression, it must have implicitly adopted the law as it found it into the CEA. 456 U.S. at 378–382, 387. In interpreting *Curran*, then, lower courts have concluded that the implied private right delineated by that decision is limited to those actions which the law recognized in 1974. Any action based on a theory of recovery not recognized in 1974—which includes most breaches of CFTC regulations—must be independently analyzed under the familiar tests of *Touche Ross & Co. v. Redington*, 442 U.S. 560, 61 L. Ed. 2d 82, 99 S. Ct. 2479 (1979), and *Cort v. Ash*, 422 U.S. 66, 45 L. Ed. 2d 26, 95 S. Ct. 2080 (1975). *See J. E. Hoetger & Co. v. Asencio*, 558 F. Supp. 1361 (E.D. Mich. 1983). So, courts have failed to find any pre-1982 right of action based on aiding and abetting, *Johnson v. Chilcott*, 590 F. Supp. 204 (D. Colo. 1984), failure to supervise, *Bennett v. E. F. Hutton Co.*, 597 F. Supp. 1547 (N.D. Ohio 1984), or failure to find investments suitable to the customer, *Asencio*, 558 F. Supp. at 1364. *Cf. Cardoza v. CFTC*, 768 F.2d 1542 (7th Cir. 1985). This court concludes that the bank has no action against Conti for a breach of any of these.

It does not follow, however, that Conti could not be found liable. The CEA makes brokerage firms vicariously liable for the CEA violations of their agents, whether authorized or not, as long as the agent was "acting for" the firm at the time. 7 U.S.C. § 4; *Poplar Grove Planting and Refining Co. v. Bache Halsey Stuart, Inc.*, 465 F. Supp. 585 (M.D. La.), *remanded on other grounds* 600 F.2d 1189 (5th Cir. 1979). The Supreme Court in *Curran* specifically held that the implied right of action under the CEA includes actions for fraud, deceit or misrepresentation. 7 U.S.C. § 6b;

Curran, 456 U.S. at 389–390. If Thomas were found liable for commodities fraud, Conti would also be liable.

The § 6b action, however, requires intentional or reckless conduct similar to the *scienter* element of common law fraud. Since the term "willfully" occurs four times in § 6b, and since its function roughly parallels that of the antifraud provision of the Securities Exchange Act, 15 U.S.C. § 78j(b), which has already been construed to cover only intentional misrepresentation, most courts construing the CEA have found that liability for commodities fraud must be based on more than negligence. *See McIlroy v. Dittmer*, 732 F.2d 98 (8th Cir. 1984); *CFTC v. Savage*, 611 F.2d 270 (9th Cir. 1979). While the broker or house need not have had a demonstrably evil motive or an affirmative intent to injure customers—a fiduciary's breach of duty in appropriate circumstances is constructive fraud—nevertheless most courts, before finding a § 6b violation, look for at least knowing and deliberate conduct. *See Marchese v. Shearson Hayden Stone, Inc.*, 734 F.2d 414 (9th Cir. 1984); *Silverman v. CFTC*, 549 F.2d 28, 31 (7th Cir. 1977); *Haltmier v. CFTC*, 554 F.2d 556 (2d Cir. 1977). The standard for private actions in both the Ninth and the First Circuits is intentional or willful conduct, including acting with knowledge of a false statement or an omission, or acting with reckless disregard of the falsity or omission. *Yopp v. Siegel Trading Co., Inc.*, 770 F.2d 1461, 1464 (9th Cir. 1985); *First Commodity Corp. of Boston v. CFTC*, 676 F.2d 1, 6 (1st Cir. 1982). Recklessness has been defined in this context as conduct which "departs so far from the standards of ordinary care that it is very difficult to believe that the speaker was not aware of what he was doing." *First Commodity*, 676 F.2d at 7. Such a standard closely parallels the standard in the Seventh Circuit for securities fraud actions, *Sundstrand Corp. v. Sun Chemical Corp.*, 553 F.2d 1033, 1044 (7th Cir.), *cert. denied*, 434 U.S. 875, 54 L. Ed. 2d 155, 98 S. Ct. 224, 98 S. Ct. 225 (1977), and so would probably be adopted here for commodities fraud as well. *See Crook v. Shearson Loeb Rhoades, Inc.*, 591 F. Supp. 40 (N.D. Ind. 1983). *But see Gordon v. Shearson Hayden Stone, Inc.*, Comm. Fut. L. Rep. (CCH) para. 21,016 (CFTC 1980) (CFTC uses negligence standard).

A genuine issue of fact exists as to whether Thomas' conduct in trading the bank's account could be characterized as intentional or reckless. Thomas, as the bank's broker, owed it a fiduciary duty, and that is a factor in the analysis. *Marchese*, 734 F.2d at 418; *Crook*, 591 F. Supp. at 48. A breach of a broker's fiduciary duty is not in every instance also a § 6b violation, *Hagstrom v. Breutman*, 572 F. Supp. 692, 697 (N.D. Ill. 1983), but when the breach appears intentional or reckless, and seems to benefit the broker at the expense of the client, as in the case at bar, it usually is grounds for a § 6b recovery. *Crook*, 591 F. Supp. at 48. For example, ignoring a client's express trading instructions is conduct so far from the ordinary standard of care that it must be either intentional or reckless. When a broker promised his customer that he would trade a discretionary account in a particular manner, and then repeatedly failed to do so, the conduct was both a breach of fiduciary duty and a violation of the CEA. *McIlroy*, 732 F.2d at 103–104. It is undisputed that Thomas initially promised to hedge the Evanston Bank account. Despite Thomas' reluctance to characterize the 1982 trades as speculative, there can be no genuine issue that they were. For the bank, any net long position was speculative and its account was $27,000,000 long. Unless a trier of fact found that Christiansen's agency, or a ratification theory, worked to release Thomas from that promise, it could infer unauthorized trading from these facts.

Also, a conscious decision not to disclose an objectively obvious danger to a client is reckless non-disclosure, which for a fiduciary amounts to misrepresentation or deceit. *Sundstrand*, 533 F.2d at 1047–1048. A trier of fact could infer that Thomas knew that the trades he made after January 1982 presented an obvious danger to the bank, given the FDIC policy with which he was at least somewhat familiar, and consciously decided not to inform his principal of that danger. If the agency issues were resolved against Conti, then a trial could find that Thomas breached his duty through unauthorized trading and reckless nondisclosure, and Conti would be liable as well. * * *

Conti and Thomas can therefore avoid a trial only if they can show that the bank authorized Thomas' trading of the account. Their arguments here fall broadly into two legal categories. First, they assert that Thomas had express actual authority to trade the account as he did, from the power of attorney he held and the instructions he received from the bank's authorized agent for trading, Christiansen. Additionally, they argue that Thomas had implied authority for the trades, since the bank's failure to repudiate any transactions effected a ratification by estoppel.

To find that the bank authorized Thomas' acts, his authority must be legally traceable, directly or indirectly, to the bank's board of directors. The authority of an agent, whether express or implied, must stem from the words or actions of his principal. *Chase v. Consolidated Foods Corp.*, 744 F.2d 566 (7th Cir. 1984). The principal in question here is not a natural person, but a corporation—the bank. The board of directors of a corporation functions more or less as its collective legal guardian, and formal actions of the board are the actions of the corporation. Since a corporation can act only through its agents, some individual agents will have authority to act for the corporation in a variety of situations. But their authority is only effective insofar as it can be traced back to a board of directors' action (or, in a few cases not relevant here, to the action of stockholders): either through an express grant of authority from the board, or impliedly, for example through the board's having placed the individual in a corporate office or position which carries the inherent authority to act for the corporation in certain transactions. *See generally Chase*, 744 F.2d at 568–569; 2 Fletcher, *Cyclopedia of the Law of Private Corporations*, §§ 434, 444, 483.1 (1982). If the authority is based on ratification, again that ratification must be traceable ultimately to the board of directors, either because the board expressly adopted a transaction, or because it knew or should have known all the material facts and behaved in a way that implied ratification. *Harris Trust & Savings Bank v. Joanna-Western Mills Co.*, 53 Ill.App.3d 542, 368 N.E.2d 629, 11 Ill. Dec. 78 (1st Dist. 1977); 2A Fletcher, *Cyclopedia*, §§ 752, 756 (1982).

With these basic principles in mind, our analysis turns first to the evidence for express actual authority. Thomas held a power of attorney ostensibly executed on behalf of the bank, which made the account discretionary. However, that document was signed by Christiansen alone and the board denies all knowledge of it. For purposes of summary judgment, then, it can function as a binding grant of authority from the bank only if Christiansen indisputably already held authority from the board to give Thomas such power. For Christiansen to have such authority, it would have to stem either from the board's express grant of authority to him for commodities transactions, or from his inherent authority as chief executive officer of the bank.

Neither line is without dispute. If the ostensible source was Christiansen's own power to buy and sell, then the power of attorney is presumptively void as a matter of law. As a general rule an agent can delegate to someone else the ministerial tasks which his principal has assigned to him, but not those which require the exercise of judgment or discretion. 1 *Restatement of the Law of Agency 2d*, §§ 18, 78 (1958). The rule is less strictly applied when the principal is a corporation. But, nevertheless, a corporate officer normally "has no authority to delegate special powers conferred on him, and which involve the exercise of judgment or discretion, unless he is expressly authorized to do so, or unless the circumstances are such that the authority is necessarily implied." 2 Fletcher, *Cyclopedia*, § 503. *Cf. Ohio Boulevard Land Corp. v. Greggory*, 46 F.2d 263 (6th Cir. 1931); *Insurance Co. of North America v. Wisconsin Central Railway*, 134 F. 794 (7th Cir. 1905). Since buying and selling commodities involves the exercise of judgment and discretion, and the bank selected Christiansen and McGreal to do it, the law presumes that neither of them has the authority to delegate that trust to another. Conti offers no proof to the contrary.

Neither is it clear that Christiansen, as the bank's chief executive officer, had the inherent authority to execute such a power of attorney on behalf of the bank. Unquestionably, the president or chief executive officer of a corporation has very broad powers to bind the corporation by virtue of the office he holds. However, those powers extend only to transactions within the usual and ordinary business of the corporation. *Harris*, 53 Ill.App.3d at 550–551, 368 N.E.2d at 635–636, 11 Ill. Dec. at 84–85. Persons doing business with a corporation are entitled to assume that a chief executive is authorized to act for it, as long as the transaction falls within ordinary bounds. Those seeking unusual or extraordinary arrangements, however, are not entitled to simply rely on the officer's own assertions of authority.

The question of what is unusual or extraordinary is normally one for the trier of fact, since it depends on the facts and circumstances of the business, the officer's position and the specific transaction. *Corn Belt Bank v. Lincoln Savings and Loan Ass'n*, 119 Ill.App.3d 238, 456 N.E.2d 150, 74 Ill. Dec. 648 (4th Dist. 1983). For example, in *Sacks v. Helene Curtis Industries, Inc.*, 340 Ill. App. 76, 91 N.E. 2d 127 (1st Dist. 1950), a corporate president had inherent authority to hire, but not to give a percentage of profits as compensation. Similarly, in *Melish v. Vogel*, 35 Ill.App.3d 125, 343 N.E.2d 17 (1st Dist. 1975), the president had inherent authority to retain an attorney, but not for fifteen years. Both decisions found that a board would not normally allow a single officer to commit that great a proportion of corporate assets to another, without at least consulting the board. Here the power of attorney involved entrusting ultimately a far greater proportion of the bank's assets to Thomas. A trier of fact could reasonably infer that the grant was extraordinary and beyond Christiansen's inherent power. With Christiansen's authority to issue the power of attorney in dispute, it cannot serve as a basis for finding that Conti and Thomas are not liable as a matter of law.

Thomas, however, also maintains that Christiansen personally either authorized or ratified all the trades. Christiansen's silence of course does not refute the claim. Ordinarily, proof of Christiansen's approval would settle the issue. The board had expressly authorized Christiansen to buy and sell commodities. Third parties can normally rely on express grants of authority. However, if a third party knows or has reason to know that the agent with whom he is dealing is in fact exceeding his authority, the right to rely is extinguished. *Chase*, 744 F.2d at 569. For example, a third party who knows that an agent is faithless and engaged in a fraud on his principal, cannot join in the fraud and then claim innocent reliance on the agent's authority. *Fustok v. Conticommodity Services, Inc.*, 577 F. Supp. 852 (S.D.N.Y. 1984), *complaint dismissed on other grounds*, 610 F. Supp. 986 (S.D.N.Y. 1985); Restatement, § 166 and comment a.

A trier of fact could reasonably infer that Thomas knew, or should have been on notice, that Christiansen was exceeding his authority from the bank. Even an agent with an express grant of authority has no authority to act contrary to the known wishes and instructions of his principal. *Old Security Life Insurance Co. v. Continental Illinois National*

Bank, 740 F.2d 1384, 1391 (7th Cir. 1984). For example, when the agent's acts or assertions conflict with the reasonable inferences that can be drawn from a corporate resolution, a third party may be found on notice of limits to that agent's authority. *Old Security*, 740 F.2d at 1391. Here the bank had authorized Christiansen and McGreal to trade, but Christiansen alone purported to grant discretionary power over the bank's account to Thomas. The contradiction might have spurred a prudent person to make further inquiry.

Further contradiction arose when Christiansen instructed Thomas to make day trades for speculation. The last communication Thomas had from Christiansen's principal, the bank, indicated that the bank wanted only to hedge and to trade within regulations. The new trading was speculative and ran afoul of an FDIC policy statement. Defendants point out that there was nothing illegal about the bank's trading. Designation of an account for hedging does not mean that only hedges may be traded from it, *Montgomery & Associates, Inc. v. Thomson, McKinnon Securities, Inc.*, Comm. Fut. L. Rep. (CCH) P22,368 (CFTC 1984), and FDIC policy statements do not have the force of law. However, the argument misses the point. To paraphrase a recent Illinois appellate decision, the mere fact that the bank had the power to make speculative trades does not of itself clothe even the highest officer of the bank with the authority to bind the bank to such trades. *Corn Belt*, 119 Ill.App.3d at 245, 456 N.E.2d at 156, 74 Ill. Dec. at 654. In that case a creditor bank sued a savings and loan association on an agreement guarantying promissory notes executed by debtors. The chief executive officer of the savings and loan, who also had express authority from his board to borrow funds from the creditor bank, made the guaranty of the promissory notes ostensibly on behalf of the savings and loan. The savings and loan argued that it had no power to make guaranties. The court found that it did. However, savings and loans rarely issue guaranties. The extraordinary nature of the transaction was therefore a matter to be considered in determining whether the officer had authority to make it. 119 Ill.App.3d at 244, 456 N.E.2d at 155, 74 Ill. Dec. at 653. Similarly, the question here is not whether the bank could make speculative trades but rather whether Christiansen's instructions to make them, given the existence of the bank's earlier instructions and the FDIC statement, should not have seemed so extraordinary to Thomas as to make him question whether Christiansen was still acting in his principal's interest. In Illinois, whether a person has notice of limits on an agent's authority, or is put on notice by circumstances, is generally a question of fact. *Corn Belt*, 119 Ill.App.3d at 245, 456 N.E.2d at 156, 74 Ill. Dec. at 654; *Schoenberger v. Chicago Transit Authority*, 84 Ill.App.3d 1132, 1138, 405 N.E.2d 1076, 1081, 39 Ill. Dec. 941, 946 (1st Dist. 1980).

The problems are compounded by the indications from which Thomas could have inferred that Christiansen was acting for his own benefit rather than for the bank. If a person knows that an agent is acting for himself, the transaction is suspicious on its face and the principal is not bound unless the agent is in fact expressly authorized to make it. Where circumstances indicate that the agent may be acting in fraud of the principal, the person must exercise care and investigate or the principal will not be liable. Whether or not the person has reason to know of the agent's improper motive is a question of fact. *See Fustok*, 577 F. Supp. at 858; Restatement, § 165 comment c, § 166 comment c. If Thomas knew that Christiansen had personally secured the $1,350,000 loan to Evco, he would know that Christiansen had a personal motive for his actions. It would not be unreasonable for a trier of fact to infer from the very strange series of transactions where the bank, through Christiansen, loaned Thomas money and his wife then bought Evco stock in her maiden name, that at least by then Thomas knew something.

Thomas was the bank's broker, owing it a fiduciary duty. The question is whether at some point that duty, plus reasonable prudence under the circumstances, did not require him to contact McGreal or some officer other than Christiansen to see if the bank's objectives truly had changed. A trier of fact might even infer from his failure to inquire that Thomas followed Christiansen's instructions, in spite of the warning signs, because Thomas benefited from the large commissions which the speculative trading generated. *Cf. Fustok*, 577 F. Supp. at 857. The evidence supporting express actual authority from the bank for a change in trading comes in a factual context which makes it equally open to an interpretation that the trading was unauthorized. In such a situation summary judgment cannot be granted.

Defendants' second line of argument looks to implied authority. Even if an agent's act exceeds his authority, it can bind his principal if the principal later ratifies it. Ratification may be express, or it may be implied from a failure to repudiate the unauthorized transaction. Restatement, §§ 82, 94. The latter variety is often called "ratification by estoppel" because the failure to repudiate can mislead a third party into concluding that the transaction was authorized, and so the principal should be estopped to deny his agent's authority. *See Harris*, 53 Ill.App.3d at 552, 368 N.E.2d at 636, 11 Ill. Dec. at 85. A series of ratifications, express or implied, of similar transactions will give implied actual authority to an agent to make such transactions in the future, even though they are beyond his express authority. Restatement, § 43. In the case at bar Thomas and Conti had been trading in a speculative pattern for five months, with Christiansen fully informed, and with daily notices of the transaction sent to the cashier according to the bank's instructions. Neither Thomas nor Conti received any hint of repudiation during that time. They therefore argue that the bank's silence ratified the trades and at some point gave Thomas the right to assume that he was authorized to trade the same way in the future.

Illinois case law, however, indicates that determining whether ratification has occurred is a complex, fact-intensive inquiry. Ratification from silence, or "ratification by estoppel," will be found only when a principal, with full knowledge of all material facts, conducts himself in a manner inconsistent with repudiation of his agent's transaction, and a third party relies on that conduct to his detriment. Each of these elements, knowledge, conduct and reliance, is a question of fact to be answered in light of the surrounding circumstances. *Harris*, 53 Ill.App.3d at 549–553, 368 N.E.2d at 635–637, 11 Ill. Dec. at 84–86.

The inquiry is fact-intensive because of the policy considerations on which the legal principles are based. The purpose of the doctrine of ratification by estoppel is to protect innocent third parties, not parties who share responsibility for the loss. Where the conduct of the party claiming the ratification has contributed to the injury, courts are reluctant to find ratification. *Old Security*, 740 F.2d at 1392; *cf.* Restatement, § 101(a). That is especially true when, as here, the party is also himself the agent who allegedly exceeded his authority in the very transaction to which he now seeks to bind his principal through ratification. Every aspect of such a transaction must be carefully scrutinized to ensure that he is not simply trying to make his principal bear the loss for his own wrongdoing. *Cf. Corn Belt*, 119 Ill.App.3d at 251, 456 N.E.2d at 160, 74 Ill. Dec. at 658; Restatement, § 101(b).

Giving these facts such scrutiny reveals problems in each of the elements. For example, ratification may be inferred from silence only when the principal has full knowledge of all material facts. *Harris*, 53 Ill. App.3d at 549–550, 368 N.E.2d at 635, 11 Ill. Dec. at 84; Restatement, § 91. Since the principal here is a corporation, the only knowledge it had was that knowledge which is imputed to it by law from its agents. An agent's knowledge is generally imputed to his principal if it is received while he is acting within the scope of his agency and concerns a matter within the scope of his authority. *Campen v. Executive House Hotel, Inc.*, 105 Ill. App.3d 576, 434 N.E.2d 511, 61 Ill.Dec. 358 (1st Dist. 1982). The rationale for the rule is that a third party may reasonably rely on an agent's fiduciary duty to convey important information to his principal. If for any reason that duty does not exist toward a particular item of knowledge, then the rule does not apply. Restatement, § 275. For that reason, when the principal is a corporation, whether the agent's knowledge will be imputed is a question of fact which takes into account the nature of the information, the circumstances in which the agent received it, and the agent's position in the corporate hierarchy. *Continental Oil Co. v. Bonanza Corp.*, 706 F.2d 1365, 1377 n.16 (5th Cir. 1983); *cf.* 3 Fletcher, *Cyclopedia*, § 807 (1975, and 1985 cum. supp.).

Considering all of those factors, only a trier of fact can determine whether the daily statements sent to the bank's cashier legally represent knowledge which can be imputed to the bank. The party seeking to establish a ratification must show that the knowledge which he seeks to impute concerns a matter within the scope of the agent's authority. In a claim involving services rendered for a fishing trawler, the fact that agents of the vessel's owner knew that it was tied up at the fleeting company's dock did not establish knowledge chargeable to the owner without proof that they had authority from him to contract for services to the vessel. *Bull v. Mitchell*, 114 Ill.App.3d 177, 448 N.E.2d 1016, 70 Ill. Dec. 138 (3d Dist. 1983).

Further, for knowledge to be imputed, the agent must have not just a duty in relation to the subject matter, but a duty to speak to his principal about the specific item of knowledge. Restatement, § 275 comment c. So, for example, in a suit over an oil and gas lease, a corporation had employed a title examiner who had read the lease. It was not charged with knowledge of the lease's unusual provisions on drilling requirements since nothing indicated that the title examiner had any duty to determine or report about drilling requirements. *Sawyer v. Mid-Continent Petroleum Corp.*, 236 F.2d 518 (10th Cir. 1956). Similarly, in an action for loss of cargo from a lighter which sank while alongside a pier, the harbormaster's knowledge that the lighter was moored at the pier was not imputed to the connecting ocean carrier because he had no duty to report the lighter's presence. *General Motors Corp. v. Pennsylvania Railroad*, 357 F. Supp. 646, 653 (S.D.N.Y. 1973), *aff'd* 506 F.2d 1395 (2d Cir. 1974). The cashier, Ott, describes his duties toward the entries as ones of recording the data on them in corporate books. Conti and Thomas have not shown that he had a duty to analyze them and report his analysis to his superiors. Such a duty does not necessarily follow from the nature of his position.

In addition, a principal is only bound by the knowledge which would appear to be important to the agent, in view of his duties and prior knowledge. The principal is not affected by information which, when acquired, reasonably seems irrelevant or insignificant to that agent. Restatement, § 275 comment d. For example, in a suit for trademark infringement, Great Plains Bag argued that Georgia-Pacific was estopped from objecting to its GP mark. Since the mark had been in use for several years corporate employees must have seen it, and Georgia-Pacific had not objected. The court found that one issue was what type of employees had seen the mark. If a professional salesperson who could recognize the significance of the mark's relation to his company's own mark had seen it, his knowledge would be imputed to the corporation. However, "knowledge of mark usage gained by bookkeepers in receiving checks . . . should not normally be imputed to the corporation. Their duties are not of the type that would require sensitivity of the value of their employer's marks in the marketplace." *Georgia-Pacific Corp. v. Great Plains Bag Co.*, 614 F.2d 757, 763 (C.C.P.A. 1980). Confirmation notices for commodities trades, like those for securities, are not necessarily readily analyzed by the average person. *Cf. Costello*, 711 F.2d at 1364; *Hecht v. Harris, Upham & Co.*, 430 F.2d 1202, 1209 (9th Cir. 1970). In the case at bar it is not clear whether the cashier's duties were routine, like a bookkeeper's, or whether he should have recognized the significance of the information on the statements. Only a trier of fact, therefore, can decide whether his knowledge should be imputed to the bank.

Nor is there any other route by which knowledge of the speculative trading can be imputed to the bank as a matter of law. At the summary judgment stage one needs uncontroverted proof that the board of directors had or should be charged with knowledge to find ratification by silence. *Harris*, 53 Ill.App.3d at 549, 368 N.E.2d at 635, 11 Ill. Dec. at 84. Knowledge of matters in the corporate files and records is generally imputed to directors, and the cashier did enter data from the statements into the corporate books. However, the principle is an equitable one, and such knowledge is only imputed after a reasonable time. In the leading Illinois case, knowledge was imputed after it had been in the records for a year and a half, while here the earliest entries had been booked less than six months previously. *Cf. Roth v. Ahrensfeld*, 373 Ill. 550, 27 N.E.2d 445 (1940).

The information was of course within the scope of both Thomas' and Christiansen's agencies, and both had a duty to speak. However, knowledge is normally not imputed when an agent is acting adversely to the principal and for his own or another's benefit. Since the agent then has a motive for concealing the information, one can no longer assume that he will fulfill his duty to speak. *McKey & Poague, Inc. v. Stackler*, 63 Ill. App.3d 142, 152, 379 N.E.2d 1198, 1205, 20 Ill. Dec. 130, 137 (1st Dist. 1978); Restatement, § 282(1). Any allegation of fraud against the agent, for example, removes the presumption that the knowledge will be imputed and triggers a factual inquiry. *Metropolitan Sanitary District v. Anthony Pontarelli & Sons, Inc.*, 7 Ill. App.3d 829, 288 N.E.2d 905 (1st Dist. 1972).

In *Pontarelli*, a case with a number of similarities to the instant one, the Sanitary District sued a contractor and its own chief engineer for fraud. The contractor admitted that there were flaws in the sewer it had constructed, but claimed that the plaintiff had acquiesced in the work. The chief engineer had approved the work at various stages and other engineers from the Sanitary District were on the construction site. Some evidence existed which could have indicated that the contractor and the chief engineer joined together to defraud the District. On the other hand, there was evidence of poor subsoil conditions and faulty design. The court found that the circumstances raised issues of material fact and denied the contractor's motion for summary judgment. The allegations of fraud against the chief engineer meant that his knowledge could not be imputed to the District. The other engineers were under no duty to report to the District, only the chief engineer was. Therefore, their knowledge could not necessarily be imputed to the District either. The court decided that only a trial could sort out the problems. *Pontarelli*, 7 Ill.App.3d at 840–841, 288 N.E.2d at 912–913.

Such reluctance to impute relates directly to the policy concern behind ratification, namely its protection of those who have innocently relied on silence. Ratification will normally not apply where the party asserting it has knowledge of or convenient access to facts contrary to those on which he purportedly relied. *In the Matter of Pubs, Inc. of Champaign*, 618 F.2d 432, 438 (7th Cir. 1980). For example, in *Perlman v. First National Bank of Chicago*, 15 Ill.App.3d 784, 305 N.E.2d 236 (1st Dist. 1973), debtors sued their lending bank for calculating annual interest on their loans by using a year of 360 days. The bank attempted to argue that the debtors were estopped by their acquiescence to the practice. The court commented that it would be "a strange twist of the law that would permit the party with knowledge of the facts to estop the party without knowledge." 15 Ill.App.3d at 797, 305 N.E.2d at 246. As the preceding discussion of express authority shows, Thomas and Christiansen both had motives which could have conflicted with their duty to speak. A trier of fact could infer that they did engage in some concealment. There seems little doubt that Thomas' actual knowledge of the transactions far exceeded the actual knowledge of the board. Under those circumstances, finding a ratification at the summary judgment stage would be inappropriate on the knowledge issue alone.

Ratification also can only be found when the principal's conduct is inconsistent with repudiation of the transaction. Silence is not itself necessarily ratification as a matter of law. Rather, it is evidence from which a trier of fact may draw an inference that the principal intended to affirm his agent's act. *Shearson Hayden Stone, Inc. v. Leach*, 583 F.2d 367, 369 (7th Cir. 1978); Restatement, § 94 comment a. The failure to object must be considered in the context of all the facts and circumstances in which it occurred. "Ratification will not be implied . . . from acts or conduct which are as consistent with an intention not to ratify as to ratify." *Arthur Rubloff & Co. v. Drovers National Bank*, 80 Ill.App.3d 867, 872, 400 N.E.2d 614, 618, 36 Ill. Dec. 194, 198 (1st Dist. 1980). A delay of a few months is not necessarily to be interpreted as a failure to object, *Shoenberger*, 84 Ill.App.3d at 1139, 405 N.E.2d at 1082, 39 Ill. Dec. at 947, and a failure to object is not necessarily to be interpreted as indicating intent to ratify, when other reasons could explain the principal's actions. *Drovers*, 80 Ill. App.3d at 873, 400 N.E.2d at 619, 36

Ill. Dec. at 199. Here the bank could have failed to object, for example, because it did not know there was anything to object to. And if its agents were engaged in concealment, a delayed response would be reasonable. Only a trier of fact can make the appropriate inference.

Also, one who claims a ratification must show not only that the principal failed to object, but that he was actually misled by that silence into doing that which he would not have done except for the silence. *Pubs*, 618 F.2d at 438; *First National*, 15 Ill.App.3d at 795, 305 N.E.2d at 245. In *Harris*, the estate of a key employee claimed that he had refrained from selling his stock in reliance on what he thought was an agreement that the corporation would repurchase it at his death. The court found that if he knew that his agreement needed to be disclosed and approved, he could not have been misled by any corporate failure to repudiate it and so could not have relied on the corporate silence to his detriment. 53 Ill.App.3d at 553, 368 N.E.2d at 637, 11 Ill. Dec. at 86. Similarly, the owner of a registered landmark, who failed to disclose its landmark status when applying for a demolition permit but rather took advantage of confusion over addresses to get a permit, could not estop the city from collecting damages for the demolition. He had not been misled by the city's failure to object but, rather, had contributed to that failure with his own deceit. *City of Chicago v. Roppolo*, 113 Ill. App.3d 602, 447 N.E.2d 870, 69 Ill. Dec. 435 (1st Dist. 1983). A trier of fact could infer that Thomas had decided to make speculative trades in any event and merely avoided any act which would bring the trades forcefully to the bank's attention. He would then not have been misled by the silence and in fact would have contributed to it. On those facts no ratification could be found.

Also, the gist of the action here is intentional misrepresentation. . . . [O]rdinarily an action for intentional fraud cannot be defeated by an assertion that the person defrauded was negligent in failing to discover the truth. This circuit, like others, has carried that principle over into actions for securities fraud. A plaintiff's ordinary negligence, or lack of due diligence, is no bar to recovery for securities fraud, although gross negligence might be. *Angelos*, 762 F.2d at 528–529; *Sundstrand*, 553 F.2d at 1048. Given the many similarities between securities and commodities claims, this court sees no reason why the same principle should not extend to commodities fraud. In *Hecht*, an action for churning of a securities account, the plaintiff recovered in spite of having received accurate confirmation slips and monthly statements for seven years. The court found that she simply could not discern from the statements whether the trading was excessive. 430 F.2d at 1209. A trier of fact could easily conclude that the bank's failure to recognize excessive trading from the statements it received for not quite six months was no more than ordinary negligence, and still find for the bank.

The end of this long trail is therefore that the arguments on express authority and ratification, like the previous arguments about level of conduct, do not provide grounds for granting summary judgment. Conti and Thomas may or may not be liable for commodities fraud. Only a trial can tell for sure. * * *

NOTES

1. Unauthorized trading was once a principal source of fraud claims under the CEA. This was because most trades were entered by telephone. The childhood game of "telephone" demonstrates the problem with such orders. In order to resolve disputes over orally entered orders, many FCMs tape recorded the conversations of their associated persons with customers. Those tapes authenticated the trades, but also often played a role in claims that risks had been misrepresented to customers. Today, much of the trading in futures is conducted through orders entered by the customer on electronic trading platforms, obviating many claims of unauthorized trading.

2. CFTC rules require that FCMs promptly confirm trades to customers, so that the customer will have the opportunity to protest a trade that was not authorized [17 C.F.R. § 1.33(b)]. The Sherwood case addressed the effectiveness of a statement in a confirm requiring timely protest of trades claimed to be unauthorized. See also, Jerry W. Markham, 13 Commodities Regulation: Fraud, Manipulation & Other Claims, § 12:3 (2013) (discussing that requirement).

3. The CFTC adopted a requirement that prohibits FCMs and associated persons from effecting a commodity interest transaction for a customer, unless properly authorized by the customer. The customer must either specifically authorize the trade orally or in writing or give the FCM written authorization to effect trades for the customer without a prior specific authorization. The rule did not require an FCM to have a written authorization where the customer directed the FCM to trade a specified amount of a specified contract. This allowed the customer to grant the FCM discretion as to the price of the trade. The rule also allows an FCM to utilize time discretion as well. This time and price discretion allowed the FCM to judge when was the best time to obtain the best price for the order. See CFTC Rule 166.2. [17 C.F.R. § 166.2].

4. Another problematic unauthorized trading situation involves so-called "rogue" traders. These are individuals who trade for the account of a large financial institution, exceed their trading authority and cause large losses to their employer. A twenty-eight year old rogue trader, Nicholas Leeson, destroyed the centuries old Barings Bank in 1995. See, Jerry W. Markham, Guarding the Kraal—On the Trail of the Rogue Trader, 21 J. Corp. L. 131 (1995) (describing the supervisory problems associated with rogue traders).

Another spectacular case of rogue trading occurred at the Société Générale S.A. in France during the Financial Crisis in 2008. That bank discovered that one of its traders, Jerome Kerviel, had incurred some $6 billion in trading losses for the bank. The disclosure of that loss touched off a global market panic. In 2011, UBS AG, sustained losses of $2.3 billion from the rogue trading of one of its employees, Kweku Adoboli.

JPMorgan Chase suffered a loss of nearly $6.2 billion in 2012 as the result of credit default swaps entered into by one of its traders in London. That trader, Bruno Iksil, was dubbed the "London Whale" because of the size of his trades.

7. SALES ABUSES

SYNDICATE SYSTEMS, INC. v. MERRILL LYNCH, PIERCE, FENNER & SMITH INC.

Comm. Fut. L. Rep. (CCH) ¶ 23,289 (C.F.T.C. 1986)

Complainants appeal from the Administrative Law Judge's denial of reparations. Abandoning claims of unauthorized trading and violation of risk disclosure requirements, complainants focus on appeal on the theory that respondents are liable because they assertedly had no reasonable basis for the particular spread positions recommended to and accepted by complainants, and because respondents failed properly to monitor the complainants' accounts.

The following is taken primarily from the Administrative Law Judge's Initial Decision.

Complainant Syndicate Systems is an Indiana corporation in the business of selling glass display fixtures to retailers. Complainant Swisher is the President and Chairman of Syndicate's Board. He has a net worth apparently in excess of one million dollars, and had substantial investment experience in the securities markets. For personal and corporate investment advice, he relied heavily on Arthur A. Angotti, Syndicate System's Treasurer and Secretary. Mr. Angotti, who held an MBA from Indiana University, with a focus in finance, had prior experience in mergers and acquisitions as an employee of the Indiana National Bank, and had experience in municipal bonds, common stocks, and interest rates. In late 1977, Mr. Angotti had helped restructure Mr. Swisher's personal investment portfolio. In that same year, Mr. Angotti had discussed with Swisher a tax straddle involving options on IBM stock, but had not advised him on it. Ultimately, Swisher attempted that straddle and apparently lost about $11,000.

In the fall of 1978 Mr. Angotti read a *BusinessWeek* article on tax straddle trading using Treasury Bill futures. After discussions with Mr. Swisher, the two men developed a proposal to use this device to defer some of Syndicate Systems' income and some of Mr. Swisher's personal income into 1979.

On Mr. Swisher's behalf, Mr. Angotti then contacted respondent Peterson, a Merrill Lynch commodity account executive. Peterson and Angotti spoke at length the telephone in late September about the *BusinessWeek* article, the mechanics of tax trading, and costs. Angotti told Peterson that the company hoped to defer $200,000 to $300,000 in 1978 income and that Swisher sought the same result as to $100,000 of his personal 1978 income. Peterson sent Angotti literature published by Merrill Lynch and the International Monetary Market regarding T-bill futures.

At Angotti's request, he and Peterson met for three to four hours during the first week of October 1978. Angotti reiterated the tax deferral goals for the corporation and for Swisher, and raised a secondary goal, to make a profit on the transaction if possible. Peterson and Angotti discussed the futures markets; risks of trading; procedures for opening an account; account documents, including monthly statements and confirmations; types of orders; limit moves; an initial and variation margin requirements.

Angotti told Peterson that he believed interest rates would rise through June 1979 and would thereafter decline, describing this predicted decline in terms of a slight "inversion" of the yield curve. He had long been familiar with graphing of yield curves and projection of interest rates, and held firm opinions about the future movement of interest rates. While no distinction is drawn in the record, these interest rate projections by Angotti were apparently based on the cash market yields, not, for example, on the T-bill futures market.

Peterson reviewed for Angotti the concept of a tax "straddle" (used below interchangeably with "spread"), which involves assuming long and short positions in two different delivery months for the same commodity. The tactic was to liquidate the losing leg of the straddle and thus recognize a loss before the end of one tax year, and liquidate the profitable leg in the following year, recognizing the gain. (More specifically, when the losing leg of the straddle was liquidated it would be replaced with an equivalent position to hedge the gain on the profitable leg until the gain could be realized in the following year.) Such trading was used, *inter alia*, to shift or "roll over" taxable income from one year to another.

Peterson also explained various costs to Angotti, including commissions and the lost opportunity cost of the money deposited as initial margin. He cautioned Angotti that Swisher and Syndicate Systems could lose some or all of their original margin, as well as additional amounts. The BusinessWeek article itself had warned that there could be a change in spread relationships and that substantial net profit or loss could result:

Your two futures contracts expire on different dates, so you have real risk * * *

Even though T-bill rollovers are hedged investments, you can end with a substantial net loss if the spread between contracts of different maturities narrows or widens. *Business Week,* 129 (Sept. 11, 1978). Peterson also said that it was late in the year to be commencing a tax straddle, since there might not be adequate time for the market to move enough to reach the loss goal of the transaction by the end of the year.

Peterson recommended a position long September '79 and short December '79. Peterson based this recommendation on the liquidity of those months and thus the case of execution of orders; the relative historical lack of volatility between these months so that they had a pattern of moving in tandem; and the flexibility that these months gave in liquidating the losing leg and replacing it with another position to hedge the profitable leg of the spread.

Following this lengthy meeting, Swisher, Angotti and Peterson scheduled another meeting for October 9, 1978. Between the two meetings, Peterson checked with two Merrill Lynch traders who concurred in his recommendation for the straddles. At Angotti's request, Peterson also obtained approval to offer a reduced commission rate from that earlier quoted.

At the second meeting involving all three men, Peterson offered significant discounts on the commission rates. He then reemphasized what he had earlier stressed to Angotti: that there were significant risks of actual loss from the proposed transaction. Peterson explained the heightened leverage effect of the very low initial straddle margins. He told them that there could be bigger equity changes relative to the size of the margins, and thus substantial margin calls might be made. The mechanics of a tax straddle were explained, and Peterson informed them the as soon as the losing position reached the desired amount it would be "switched" to the new straddle position to carry the profitable leg into the next tax year. The last leg of the straddle would be liquidated as soon as positions were proper in the new year, i.e., when the spread relationship for the new straddle was such that the gain on the profitable leg of the original spread could be obtained on liquidation.

Peterson also discussed how to take advantage of Angotti's interest rate projections. His recommendation was that the positions be put on, oriented so that they would profit from the ultimate reversion of the yield curve, i.e., long the nearby month and short the far out. Thus Peterson counseled complainants to wait until the inversion predicted by Angotti had occurred and September was trading even with or at a discount to December.

Finally, Peterson advised Angotti and Swisher to consult with their accountant regarding tax consequences. Angotti did so and decided to accept the risk that the IRS might not recognize the hoped-for favorable tax results.

On October 26, 1978, after a reminder from Peterson about the short time remaining in the tax year, Angotti and Swisher went to Peterson's office to open accounts. Account forms were prepared and signed. At this meeting Swisher and Angotti informed Peterson that they wished to proceed with fewer contracts in order to lower the amount of initial margin. Thus, 100 spreads were to be placed in the corporate account and 50 spreads in Swisher's individual account. Peterson explained that a larger movement of the market would be needed to accomplish the same dollar loss with fewer contracts. No indication was given by Angotti and Swisher that they had reduced the amount of income to be deferred.

Over Peterson's objection, Angotti and Swisher insisted that the positions be placed immediately. Because September T-bill prices were then higher than December's (i.e., reflecting lower near term interest rates), Peterson counseled against taking the positions; he wanted to wait until the yield curve inverted as Angotti anticipated (i.e., future interest rates lower). Angotti nevertheless persisted, and phoned Peterson the next morning to repeat his insistence that the positions be placed. Peterson was still reluctant. He called Swisher to tell him of Angotti's instructions, and persuaded Swisher to enter only the fifty positions for his personal account while holding off the trades for the corporate account. On Monday, October 30, when Angotti learned of the non-execution of the trades for the corporate account, he called Peterson, demanding as an officer of the company that Peterson enter the orders. Peterson then complied.

Initial margin for T-bill futures came to $80,000 for the Syndicate Systems spreads and $40,000 for the spreads for Mr. Swisher personally.

Margin calls were issued on both accounts the same day. Angotti and Swisher were upset, but met the calls. On November 2, 1978 the situation worsened when the Federal Reserve Board increased the discount rate. The Syndicate Systems account was assessed margin calls totaling $34,473. Following the discount rate change, the yield curve inverted generally and with respect to the September-December spread. This was consistent with Angotti's hypothesis and both Angotti and Swisher demanded an explanation for the margin calls. Peterson characterized the losses as due to an aberration and advised them to continue to meet the margin calls and maintain the positions.

Communications—several per week—between Peterson and the complainants continued during November. No margin calls were issued between November 9 and November 20. Complainants continued to question the losses in the accounts.

Between November 13 and 19, Angotti analyzed the positions in both accounts and formed the opinion that Peterson had put the positions on backwards. At a meeting between Peterson, Swisher and Angotti on November 20, Angotti complained that the positions were losing money even though they had asked Peterson to position them with regard to the inversion that had in fact occurred. Angotti then ordered changes in the positions. Among other things, the short December contracts, the losing leg of the spread, were liquidated to establish the tax losses. The balance of positions were reoriented so that they were short the nearby future and long the deferred, i.e., the reverse of Peterson's selection. By January 26, 1979 Angotti had directed Peterson to liquidate all positions in both accounts. Swisher's account sustained a net loss after commissions of $78,340; the corporate account had a net loss after commissions of $43,670.

Complainants sought reparations and filed the instant complaint in October 1980 Three days of hearings were held before the ALJ. The record was supplemented by depositions of complainant Swisher and of an expert witness for respondents. Two expert witnesses testified for the complainants. The 60-page Initial Decision was issued on December 20, 1984.

The ALJ found that the advice given by respondent Peterson was "sound and reasonable," and that Peterson had properly monitored the account.

In recommending a particular transaction or offering a professional opinion, a commodity professional makes an implied representation that there is a reasonable basis for the recommendation or opinion. See, Commodity Futures Trading Commission v. U.S. Metals Depository, 468 F. Supp. 1149, 1159 n.40 (S.D.N.Y. 1979); cf. Dill v. Sutton Ross Assoc., [1984–1986 Transfer Binder] Comm. Fut. L. Rep. (CCH) P22,696 at 30.968 (CFTC Aug. 22, 1985); Hanly v. Securities and Exchange Commission, 415 F.2d 589 (2d Cir. 1969). This does not mean, however, that the Commission will question the wisdom of any recommendation of a commodity professional that proves unprofitable. Whether there was or was not a reasonable basis for a particular recommendation does not turn on its ultimate success but must be determined on the facts of each case. In our view, a recommendation has a reasonable when the commodity professional has considered those relevant factors that were reasonably ascertainable in the context of the particular recommendation and exercised rational judgment in light of them. For these purposes, it is not necessary that the recommendation at issue be unassailable or even the most preferable of available alternatives. If it is within the range of acceptable alternatives, it has a reasonable basis.

Complainant has the burden of establishing that the challenged recommendation lacked a reasonable basis. This inquiry is essentially factual, involving matters of degree and judgment that rarely land themselves to clear-cut answers. And, this Commission does not generally sit to second-guess market prognoses or strategies or to second-guess its fact finders' determinations.

In this case complainants' experts failed to persuade the administrative law judge. Respondents' expert testified that given complainants' dual objectives (the tax rollover coupled with market profit), Peterson's recommendation was within the range of reasonable alternatives. After a lengthy discussion of the case, in his decision the ALJ accepted the view of respondents' expert. Our review of the contentions of the parties an appeal and of the record shows that the ALJ's factual determination was well within his broad discretion.

Complainants' experts assumed that complainants intended to profit immediately from the initial inversion of the yield curve and built upon that theory. But complainants did not so testify, and there is nothing in the record suggesting that they so instructed Peterson. More specifically there is no proof that complainants had any specific inclination to profit from the inversion itself, as distinct from other strategies which could also follow from Angotti's prediction. In short, Angotti generally explained the hypothesis (imminent inversion, followed by ultimate reversion) and left to Peterson the details of tactics and timing. Expert testimony which assumed, contrary to the record, that complainants had filled in these details is not compelling, and certainly does not support a finding of clear error by the fact finder.

Respondents' expert recognized the historic stable relationship between the September and December contract months, a factor which Peterson had considered in order to avoid volatility with resulting large margin calls. This expert viewed the strategy as first to accomplish the tax rollover goal (establish the desired loss before the end of the year). After establishing the tax loss, the position could be reoriented to protect the profitable leg and to take advantage of the clients' market prognoses. Given these assumptions, respondents' expert concluded that Peterson's advice was sound.

Complainants' position boils down to the assertion that their goals (tax rollover plus profits) envisioned simultaneous accomplishment based on the initial inversion of the yield curve. But the record fails to show that Peterson was under such instructions, let alone such severe restrictions as to foreclose any other approach. On this record, it was "reasonable" for Peterson to select a trading strategy which in essence enabled him to do one thing at a time.

That margin calls were received when complainants' hypothesis about interest rates seemed to be coming true does not establish lack of reasonable basis. Peterson reported that the losses were the product of an "aberration," i.e., the wide reversal of the historic spread relationship between September and December; instead of September's historic supremacy, December was now trading at a substantial premium. In view of Peterson's reliance on the historically stable spread relationship between September and December to limit volatility and, consistent with this relationship, Peterson's orientation of the tax straddle to take advantage of the predicated reversion of the yield curve, this occurrence does not prove the absence of a reasonable basis for Peterson's advice.

Finally, we also note that complainants put themselves into the market when Peterson had advised otherwise. Complainants' repeated and insistent decision to go forward with the trades on October 26, 27 and 30, contrary to respondents' recommendation that they wait, raises substantial doubt that they can claim to have been injured by the respondents' recommendations. Complainants, who had some degree of financial sophistication and who chose to ignore the timing aspect of the recommendation are hardly in the best position to assert that it lacked a reasonable basis.

Wholly apart from the question of a reasonable basis for the original recommendation, complainants argue that respondents are liable on a different theory. All parties agree that Peterson undertook to monitor the account in question. They differ, however, as to the focus of that monitoring duty.

Complainants say that they reduced their tax savings goals from $200,000 to $100,000 for the corporation and from $100,000 to $50,000 for Swisher. Complainants argue that Peterson breached his duty to them to take appropriate action when the above tax losses could have been achieved. It is undisputed that Peterson took no action in the account at the end of October or in mid-November of 1978 when this reduced result presumably could have been achieved for Swisher and the corporation, respectively. Peterson denies, however, that he had received any instructions regarding reduction of the originally requested tax savings.

This issue turns on a factual dispute which was resolved by the ALJ adversely to the complainants. The judge saw and heard the witnesses, and concluded that complainants had failed to prove that Peterson had any reason to monitor the accounts for losses less than the $200,000 and $100,000 for the corporation and Swisher respectively which had originally been discussed. We see no reason to disturb this factual conclusion.

Complainants claim on appeal that Peterson admitted at trial that he was aware of the complainants' reduced expectations, although subsequently recanting this testimony. They also complain that in any event the surrounding circumstances make it unbelievable that Peterson did not understand that complainants had reduced their tax loss expectations.

Complainants contend that the ALJ had an obligation to explain (but did not do so) why he had rejected the alleged damaging admission by Peterson, citing Cotter v. Harris, 642 F.2d 700, 706–707, reh. denied, 650 F.2d 481 (3rd Cir. 1981). They urge us, accordingly, to undertake de novo review of this aspect of the record and find in their favor on this issue.

Initially, however, we note that complainants' post-hearing Proposed Findings of Fact and Conclusions of Law filed with the ALJ, make no mention of Peterson's alleged admissions. The argument is made for the first time on appeal. In these circumstances, complainants are in no position to criticize the ALJ for his asserted failure to discuss the matter. Moreover, our examination of the relevant portions of the hearing transcript leads us to conclude that the purported admission need not be read as such. We quote the colloquy relied upon by complainants in its entirety:

Q.   So how many basis points in the case of Syndicate Systems where there was a hundred contracts involved at $1,000 per contract would there have to be a movement in one of the legs of the straddle in terms of a loss to decide to lift that leg?

MR. MARSHALL: Objection, Your Honor, to the form of the question. In think it is an improper characterization of the prior testimony.

JUDGE PAINTER: I see some confusion in that, as I recall, there was a $200,000 desired loss on Syndicated [sic] $100,000 on Mr. Swisher, that was reduced by half.

MR. SPINDEL: That's right, Your Honor.

JUDGE PAINTER: So what were they seeking here? I don't know whether Mr. Peterson knows. Do you?

MR. SPINDEL: Mr. Peterson earlier testified that the movement as he advised the customers was $1,000 per contract that they would be able to defer, and in a hundred contracts, we're talking about $100,000 of deferral for the corporate customer.

What I'd like to find out from Mr. Peterson, at this point, is how he determined that that $100,000 or that $1,000 per contract loss had been obtained in connection with the movement of these straddles.

JUDGE PAINTER. Mr. Peterson, can you answer that question? When did you intend to recommend, to tell them, to call them up and say, "Now, you've reached your goal. Should I lift the leg?"

THE WITNESS: Once the losing position had an open loss of $100,000.

JUDGE PAINTER: There's your answer.

MR. SPINDEL:

Q. Okay. And you would determine that by looking at the market on any given day?

A. Yes, sir.

Q. Now, prior to November the 20th, 1978, did the market ever reach that level?

A. I don't believe it did.

Q. It did not? And you looked at the market every day?

A. That's correct.

Q. Now, also the same goes for the individual account, Mr. Swisher's account? You would also be looking every day to see whether there was sufficient movement to make his $50,000 loss on his 50 contracts, is that right?

A. Yes, sir.

Q. And prior to November 20th, there was insufficient movement to make that, is that correct?

A. I believe that's correct."

It is critical to note that although the ALJ apparently asked Mr. Peterson "what [amount of loss] were [complainants] seeking," the answer was given by complainants' counsel, not Mr. Peterson, Mr. Peterson's statement that he would have advised the complainants to lift the losing leg of the straddle "once the losing position had an open loss of $100,000," apparently refers only to complainants' counsel's question how Mr. Peterson would have determined that $1000 per contract "or $100,000 for the corporate customer" had been lost and not to the amount of the tax loss sought. Mr. Peterson's response was mathematically consistent with the question's assumptions but need not be read as acknowledging that the $100,000 assumption was actually the goal. As we read the record, this testimony does not constitute an admission and raises no issue about the ALJ's factual determinations.

Complainants' related assertion must also fail. They contend that in context it is not credible that Peterson would think that complainants had not reduced their tax loss expectations when they reduced the number of contracts to be placed. The ALJ found that complainants had not instructed Peterson regarding reduced tax expectations and on this record we do not find it incredible that Peterson should believe that the expectations remained unchanged.

Complainants cite to no evidence that they ever told Peterson of the reduced expectations. Second, they do not dispute the ALJ's findings (Init. Dec. 26) that in relevant part the conversation at the critical October 26, 1978 meeting consisted only of a) complainants advising Peterson that a reduced number of contracts was desired, in order to reduce margin expense and b) Peterson observing that a greater movement in the market would be needed to accomplish the tax objective. In dealing with clients who had sought lower commissions and had already reduced the number of contracts specifically to lower margin costs, it would not be unbelievable for Mr. Peterson to assume they were merely seeking the same tax objectives but at less cost.

Nor do the circumstances corroborate the assertion that Peterson must have known of the alleged reduced tax loss objective. Nothing in his conduct evidences such an understanding and there was no evidence that Angotti, who was monitoring the accounts, ever raised this issue with Peterson while the positions were still open. We find the ALJ's conclusion, that the tax loss objectives had not been reduced when the positions were first put on, and that Peterson had not failed in his undertaking to monitor the accounts, adequately supported in the record.

Accordingly, the decision below is affirmed.

For the Commission (CHAIRMAN PHILLIPS and COMMISSIONERS HINEMAN, WEST, SEALE, and DAVIS).

NOTES

1. CFTC Rule 1.56(b) [17 C.F.R. § 1.56(b)] states that:

(b) No futures commission merchant or introducing broker may in any way represent that it will, with respect to any commodity interest in any account carried by the futures commission merchant for or on behalf of any person:

(1) Guarantee such person against loss;

(2) Limit the loss of such person; or

(3) Not call for or attempt to collect initial and maintenance margin as established by the rules of the applicable board of trade.

2. CFTC Rule 1.56 was triggered by firms that guaranteed to their customers that no trading losses would occur. This jeopardized the financial stability of those firms and misled customers as to the risks of trading. It has also arguably been applied to FCMs, which provides margin financing

directly to its customers. Compare, CFTC Rule 1.30 [17 C.F.R. § 1.30], allowing FCMs to loan funds to customers for margin using customer securities as collateral.

CFTC v. R.J. FITZGERALD & CO., INC.
310 F.3d 1321 (11th Cir. 2002), cert. denied, 543 U.S. 1034 (2004)

COWEN, CIRCUIT JUDGE:

Presented in this appeal is the question of liability for fraud and related allegations under the Commodities (sic) Exchange Act, 7 U.S.C. §§ 1 *et seq.,* (the "CEA" or "Act") and accompanying regulations. Plaintiff/Appellant Commodities Futures Trading Commission ("CFTC") appeals from a judgment finding all Defendants not liable under the Act for various solicitation and trading activities carried out at R.J. Fitzgerald & Company, Inc. ("RJFCO"). After reviewing the record in this matter, considering the submissions of the parties, and having benefitted from oral argument, we conclude that the District Court erred in not finding liability under the Act as a matter of law for two specific solicitation devices utilized by RJFCO: (1) a television commercial that aired on the "CNBC" cable network in March 1998 (The "Commercial") and (2) a promotional seminar for potential RJFCO customers that also took place in 1998 (the "Seminar"). For the reasons expressed below, we will reverse as to Raymond Fitzgerald, Leiza Fitzgerald and RJFCO, and remand only for enforcement proceedings against those two individuals and the firm.

In 1999, CFTC commenced this CEA enforcement case by filing a Complaint against Defendants/Appellees RJFCO, Raymond Fitzgerald, Leiza Fitzgerald, Chuck Kowlaski, and Greg Burnett, alleging that they were involved in fraudulent solicitations to attract potential customers throughout the United States to invest in commodity options, in violation of the Act and related federal regulations. This Complaint was dismissed essentially for failure to plead fraud with particularity.

The District Court then required CFTC to file an Amended Complaint detailing every fact it intended to prove in establishing liability under the ACT. CFTC complied with that request, filing an extensive 138 page, 15 count Complaint which sets the framework for the instant case. The Amended Complaint alleged that Defendants, or some individual Defendants, violated the Act by: (1) committing fraud by misrepresentation or omission of material facts in connection with the solicitation, maintenance, or execution of commodity futures transactions; (2) operating an introducing brokerage firm to cheat, defraud, deceive, or attempt to cheat, defraud or deceive clients; (3) trading client accounts excessively in order to generate commissions without regard to customer interests ("churning"); (4) failing to provide risk disclosure statements prior to the opening of RJFCO customer accounts; and (5) failing to supervise firm personnel diligently. Defendant Raymond Fitzgerald was charged with "controlling person" liability under the Act. The various allegations in the Amended Complaint encompass claims grounded in 7 U.S.C. § 6c(b), 17 C.F.R. § 33.10(a) and (c), 17 C.F.R. § 166.3, and 7 U.S.C. § 13c(b).

Counts one, two, seven and nine alleged that Raymond Fitzgerald, as principal of RJFCO, RJFCO, Leiza Fitzgerald and Greg Burnett committed fraud by misrepresentation or omission of material facts in connection with the solicitation of commodity futures transactions. Counts three, ten and fifteen charged Raymond Fitzgerald, as principal of RJFCO, RJFCO, Greg Burnett and Chuck Kowalski with operating an introducing brokerage to cheat, defraud, deceive, or attempt to cheat, defraud or deceive clients. Counts four and eleven charged Raymond Fitzgerald, RJFCO, and Greg Burnett with committing fraud by trading client accounts excessively to generate commissions without regard to client interests. Count five charged Raymond Fitzgerald and RJFCO with failing to provide adequate risk disclosure statements prior to opening customer accounts. Counts six, eight, and twelve charged Raymond Fitzgerald, Leiza Fitzgerald and Greg Burnett with failing to supervise diligently the sales practices and solicitations of RJFCO brokers.

After some of the claims in the Amended Complaint were dismissed on summary judgment, the parties agreed, pursuant to 28 U.S.C. § 636(c) and Fed.R.Civ.P. 73, to conduct a bench trial before a Magistrate Judge. That trial commenced on February 26, 2001. On March 8, 2001, the Court heard oral argument and granted what it labeled a "directed verdict" against a significant part of the CFTC's case. Germaine to this appeal, and as will be explained further below, the District Court granted relief to Defendants on that part of the CFTC's claim that the Commercial violated the Act as well as on the claim that Defendants had a duty to disclose their specific trading record (i.e., their success rate) to potential customers.

The trial pressed forward to completion on the remaining claims in the Amended Complaint and concluded on March 19, 2001. Thereafter, the District Court entered extensive findings of fact and conclusions of law, ruling in favor of all Defendants on all counts in the Amended Complaint. *See CFTC v. R.J. Fitzgerald & Co., Inc.*, 173 F.Supp.2d 1295 (M.D.Fla.2001). CFTC appeals, essentially arguing that regardless of the Court's factual findings based on witness credibility, Defendants committed fraud and other CEA violations as a matter of law.

RJFCO was a full service "introducing broker" at all times relevant to this appeal. *See* 7 U.S.C. § 1a. RJFCO's obligations to those with whom it dealt were guaranteed by Iowa Grain Company ("Iowa Grain"), a registered futures commission merchant. RJFCO opened for business in 1992. It operated as a firm designed to service small customer accounts, where the customer base had little experience in commodities markets. RJFCO operated in a perhaps unique manner in the commodities industry in that it used one team of sales brokers for generating customers via telephone calls and a separate team of brokers and traders to do the actual trades and monitor accounts. Defendant Raymond Fitzgerald was the principal of RJFCO and was responsible for all decisions, actions, and trading recommendations made or entered into by the firm. Defendant Leiza Fitzgerald's responsibilities at RJFCO involved developing training materials and training sales brokers. Greg Burnett was an associated person at RJFCO and was responsible for supervising traders and brokers. Chuck Kowalski was RJFCO's chief financial analyst, responsible for studying the commodities markets and developing trades and trade strategies.

At the heart of this appeal are two solicitation devices used by RJFCO to attract customers to invest in options on futures contracts: the Commercial and the Seminar.

The Commercial stated that "the El Nino [weather phenomenon] has struck where expected, and if patterns continue, the effects could be devastating. Droughts, floods, and other adverse conditions could drastically alter the supply and demand dynamics of the corn market. . . ." The Commercial also declared that "[w]ith the giant developing nations, such as China and Russia badly in need of grains and world grain supplies put to the test, conditions may exist for profits as high as 200 to 300 percent." This was accompanied by a graphic statement on the television screen that the percentages were a mathematical example of leverage. The Commercial further asserted that "the potential of the corn market may never be greater. Tight U.S. reserves coupled with domestic and worldwide demands could be the formula for a trade you won't want to miss. Find out how as little as $5,000 could translate into profits as high as 200 to 300 percent. Call R.J. Fitzgerald today. . . ."

The Commercial was initially drafted by an advertising agency. When Raymond Fitzgerald first received the script, he edited it to add additional risk disclosures that would appear just above the firm's phone number, so that anyone watching the Commercial would see the risk disclosure. He further insisted that this disclosure appear more than half the time the Commercial was running. After his edits were done, he sent the script to Iowa Grain's chief compliance officer, Anne Farris. Iowa Grain approved the script on February 18, 1998.

The Commercial actually ran on CNBC for the first half of March, 1998, but did not generate much business. In total, it appeared about eight or nine times and was then discontinued. At some point after its discontinuation, Raymond Fitzgerald was contacted by a National Futures Association ("NFA") compliance officer, who expressed concern over the Commercial's content. More specifically, the NFA officer, David Croom, informed Raymond Fitzgerald that the Commercial was in apparent violation of NFA rules because: (1) it was misleading in that it failed to tell potential customers that the options spoken of were "out-of-the money options" that would require a dramatic move in the options premium value in order for the customer to see gains equal to that claimed in the Commercial; (2) misleadingly gave the impression that weather events were inevitable; (3) did not display the risk of loss statement prominently enough on the screen; and (4) downplayed the risk of loss. In response to this concern, Raymond Fitzgerald informed Croom that the Commercial had already been discontinued and would not be aired again.

At the close of CFTC's case, and before the defense was presented, the District Court entered a directed verdict in favor of Defendants on the part of the claim that the Commercial was fraudulent and violated the CEA. The District Court addressed the Commercial again in its opinion issued after the bench trial, stating that the Commercial was not "misleading or deceptive" and that there was no "intent to defraud." 173 F. Supp.2d at 1310.

In addition to the Commercial, CFTC alleged CEA violations occurred in a promotional seminar used by RJFCO to attract customers. The Seminar was developed by Leiza Fitzgerald and RJFCO brokers Scott Campbell and Tom West after they attended a training session on the topic conducted by the National Introducing Brokers Association

The Seminar informed customers that weather patterns, political events, and historical trends can affect the prices of certain commodities. The Seminar also told customers that technical analysis could assist them in the commodity options market, since "history often repeats itself" and "past price action can provide you with clues to future action." Customers were told they could "take advantage" of "fundamental" market moves such as weather events and political events and "technical theory" such as past market movements through either futures or options investing. The Seminar also drew a distinction between investment instruments based on the quantum of risk involved:

> Which one you choose depends on how aggressive or what degree of risk you wish to take on.
>
> If you are highly aggressive and looking for unlimited profit potential as well as unlimited risk than [sic] it would be the futures. But most would like something less aggressive,

something offering unlimited profit potential but limited risk-option trade [sic].

On the topic of risk, the Seminar additionally told potential customers: "options on futures allow investors and risk managers to define risk and limit it to the loss of a premium paid for the right to buy or sell a futures contract while still providing . . . unlimited profit potential."

The RJFCO employees who conducted the Seminar offered what the Seminar script deemed a "very exciting" illustration of how profits could be made on options. Specifically, the Seminar focused on the commodity heating oil, explaining that for the last eighteen years, there was an average increase in that commodity "of 22 cents from the low to the high in the price range" and that a $5,000 investment on a heating oil futures contract would result in $46,200 if there was a 22 cent move in the price. Customers were told that if they wanted "limited risk," they could invest in an option contract, where they would receive "approximately 50% of that profit—46,200 divided by 2 equals $23,100."

In its opinion following the bench trial, the District Court concluded that the Seminar did not violate the CEA. The District Court explained that there was nothing "patently or latently misleading or deceitful" about the profit illustrations used in the seminar. 173 F. Supp.2d at 1311.
* * *

CFTC argues that the District Court erred because the Commercial is fraudulent as a matter of law. Upon review of the full text of the Commercial, we are constrained to agree. The CEA and its accompanying regulations directly proscribe attempts to deceive and defraud in connection with futures and options trading. 17 C.F.R. § 33.10 provides:

It shall be unlawful for any person directly or indirectly:

(a) To cheat or defraud or attempt to cheat or defraud any other person; . . . .

(c) To deceive or attempt to deceive any other person by any means whatsoever

in or in connection with an offer to enter into, the entry into, the confirmation of the execution of, or the maintenance of, any commodity option transaction.

See also 7 U.S.C. § 6b(a)(i), (iii) (proscribing similar conduct in connection with a futures contract).

In order to establish liability for fraud, CFTC had the burden of proving three elements: (1) the making of a misrepresentation, misleading statement, or a deceptive omission; (2) scienter; and (3) materiality. *See Hammond v. Smith Barney Harris Upham & Co.,* [1987–

1990 Transfer Binder] Comm. Fut. L. Rep. (CCH) 24,617 (CFTC Mar. 1, 1990); *CFTC v. Trinity Finan. Group, Inc.,* Comm. Fut. L. Rep. 27,179, 1997 WL 820970 (S.D. Fla. Sept. 29, 1997), *aff'd in relevant part, CFTC v. Sidoti,* 178 F.3d 1132 (11th Cir.1999). Failure to establish any one of these elements is dispositive and would preclude CFTC's fraud/deception claims.[6]

Whether a misrepresentation has been made depends on the "overall message" and the "common understanding of the information conveyed." *Hammond,* Comm. Fut. L. Rep. at 36,657 & n. 12. For purposes of fraud or deceit in an enforcement action, scienter is established if Defendant intended to defraud, manipulate, or deceive, or if Defendant's conduct represents an extreme departure from the standards of ordinary care. *See, e.g., Messer v. E.F. Hutton & Co.,* 847 F.2d 673, 677–79 (11th Cir.1988). In the similar context of federal securities law, we have previously stated that scienter is met when Defendant's conduct involves "highly unreasonable omissions or misrepresentations . . . that present a danger of misleading [customers] which is either known to the Defendant or so obvious that Defendant must have been aware of it." *Ziemba v. Cascade Int'l, Inc.,* 256 F.3d 1194, 1202 (11th Cir.2001). A representation or omission is "material" if a reasonable investor would consider it important in deciding whether to make an investment. *See Affiliated Ute Citizens of Utah v. United States,* 406 U.S. 128, 153–54, 92 S.Ct. 1456, 1472, 31 L.Ed.2d 741 (1972); *R&W Technical Servs., Ltd. v. CFTC,* 205 F.3d 165, 169 (5th Cir.2000).

In applying these various elements to the present case, we are guided by the principle that the CEA is a remedial statute that serves the crucial purpose of protecting the innocent individual investor-who may know little about the intricacies and complexities of the commodities market-from being misled or deceived. * * *

The parties obviously do not contest the textual content of the Commercial. The actual words of the Commercial and how the Commercial physically appeared on television are undisputed matters of record and do not require us to second guess what the District Court concluded with regard to witness demeanor and credibility at the bench trial. That being said, we are persuaded that these undisputed facts demonstrate fraud and deception as a matter of law.

Read for its *overall message,* and how that message would be interpreted by an objectively reasonable television viewer, the Commercial overemphasizes profit potential and downplays risk of loss, presenting an unbalanced image of the two. The Commercial suggests to

---

[6] Unlike a cause of action for fraud under the common law of Torts, "reliance" on the representations is not a requisite element in an enforcement action. *See, e.g., CFTC v. Rosenberg,* 85 F.Supp.2d 424, 446 (D.N.J.2000).

the potential investor, that truly enormous profits (200–300%) can be made on options on futures contracts by looking at known and expected weather patterns. More specifically, the Commercial affirmatively represents to potential RJFCO customers that El Nino had struck "where *expected*" and that if the "*patterns continue*," "*huge* profits" of "*200 to 300%*" could be realized. The Commercial also improperly overstated the profit potential by suggesting to potential customers that they should not pass up such a tremendous chance to make money. Rather, viewers are told to call RJFCO "now" because there may "never" be such an opportunity in the corn market again. ("The potential of the corn market may *never* be greater [and] 'could be the formula for a trade *you won't want to miss.'* Find out how as little as $5,000 could translate into profits as high as 200 to 300 percent. Call R.J. Fitzgerald today.").

Against these highly alluring statements is only boilerplate risk disclosure language. We agree with CFTC's position that these statements directly contravene the legal principles established in prior commodities fraud cases. *See, e.g., Trinity Finan. Group,* Comm. Fut. L. Rep. 27,179, *aff'd in relevant part, Sidoti,* 178 F.3d 1132; *In re JCC, Inc.,* [1992–1994 Transfer Binder] Comm. Fut. L. Rep. (CCH) 26,080 (CFTC May 12, 1994), *aff'd, JCC, Inc. v. CFTC,* 63 F.3d 1557 (11th Cir.1995); *Bishop v. First Investors Group,* [1996–1998 Transfer Binder] Comm. Fut. L. Rep. (CCH) 27,004, 44,841 (CFTC Mar. 26, 1997); *In re Staryk,* [1996–1998 Transfer Binder] Comm. Fut. L. Rep. 27,206, 45,809, 1997 WL 840840 (CFTC Dec. 18, 1997). As we have indicated in various prior commodities cases, the fact that the Commercial had a general risk disclosure statement does not automatically preclude liability under the CEA where the overall message is clearly and objectively misleading or deceptive. *See Clayton Brokerage Co. v. CFTC,* 794 F.2d 573, 580–81 (11th Cir.1986); *JCC,* 63 F.3d at 1565 n. 23, 1569–70; *Sidoti,* 178 F.3d at 1136 ("we seriously doubt whether boilerplate risk disclosure language could ever render an earlier material misrepresentation immaterial."); *see also Bishop,* Comm. Fut. L. Rep. at 44,841.

Contrary to Defendants' argument, we see no absolute, bright-line requirement in these cases that a solicitation offer a "clear guarantee[ ]" of profits before liability is triggered. Appellees' Brief at 40. Nor should there be. Such an exacting standard would thrust the door of deception wide open, allowing clearly misleading statements to escape CFTC enforcement, thereby thwarting the underlying purpose of the Act. Brokers would have free reign to abuse their knowledge by subtly manipulating customer beliefs about the functioning of commodities markets, afforded safe haven so long as no actual "guarantee" is made.

Having determined that the Commercial contained deceptive and misleading statements, we next consider the element of scienter. This element is also met here as a matter of law. Defendant acted recklessly with regard to the statements aired on television. This recklessness is premised on the fact that this Court and the CFTC have previously condemned attempts to attract customers by: (1) linking profit expectations on commodities options to known and expected weather events, seasonal trends, and historical highs; (2) suggesting that the commodities market can be correctly timed to generate large profits; and (3) substantially inflating option profit expectations while downplaying risk of loss. We hold that Defendant, as a federally registered professional, knowledgeable in the nuances and complexities of the industry, deviated in an extreme manner from the standards of ordinary care.

The final element, materiality, is satisfied as well. It is too obvious for debate that a reasonable listener's choice-making process would be substantially affected by emphatic statements on profit potential ("200–300%") and the suggestion that known and expected weather events are the vehicle for achieving those enormous profits. A reasonable investor would also be heavily influenced by the suggestion in the Commercial that, due to weather events, the present day offers an opportunity like no other to make money in the corn market. *See In re JCC,* Comm. Fut. L. Rep. at 41,576 n. 23 ("When the language of a solicitation obscures the important distinction between the possibility of substantial profit and the probability that it will be earned, it is likely to be materially misleading to customers."). *See also CFTC v. Noble Wealth Data,* 90 F.Supp.2d 676, 686 (D.Md.2000) (representations about profit potential and risk "*go to the heart of a customer's investment decision* and are therefore material as a matter of law"), *aff'd in part and vacated in part,* 278 F.3d 319 (4th Cir.2000).

Defendants argue that scienter is lacking with regard to the Commercial because Raymond Fitzgerald edited the Commercial to include more disclosures, sought and received approval from Iowa Grain, and assured NFA official Croom that the Commercial had already been discontinued after Croom expressed concern over its misleading content. None of these arguments can overcome the CFTC's position that prior cases establish the illegality of the Commercial's content as a matter of law. Moreover, Defendants should not be able to escape liability under the Act by simply claiming that a related private business entity (Iowa Grain) issued its stamp of approval. Iowa Grain does not determine with legal finality what constitutes deceptive solicitations under the CEA and its regulations. * * *7

---

7 As part of their argument that the Commercial is not deceptive, Defendants assert that investors had, in the past, actually made profits as large as 200–300%. However, just because such profits are possible, or have happened to some degree in the past, does not mean that the Commercial's total message is not misleading. *See JCC,* 63 F.3d at 1568 n. 34. Even literally true statements can be extremely and impermissibly deceptive when viewed in their overall context. *See, e.g., In re Staryk,* Comm. Fut. L. Rep. at 45,809.

Much of the discussion above on the illegality of the Commercial applies to the Seminar as well. We hold that the Seminar is also fraudulent and deceptive as a matter of law. Like the Commercial, the Seminar, when viewed in its entirety, suggests to a reasonable listener that RJFCO has a reliable strategy in place for increasing profits and limiting losses.[8] Like the Commercial, it presents a distinctly unbalanced picture between the potential for profit and the potential for loss in options, inflating one while downplaying the other. The Seminar also impermissibly suggests that profits on options on futures contracts (the specific type of investment they were promoting) are proportionally related to the cash market. *See CFTC v. Commonwealth Finan. Group, Inc.*, 874 F. Supp. 1345, 1352 (S.D.Fla.1994), *vacated on other grounds*, 79 F.3d 1159 (11th Cir.1996); *Bishop,* Comm. Fut. L. Rep. at 44,841 (deceptive to tell customer that one could earn $420 for every penny increase in heating oil); *In re JCC,* Comm. Fut. L. Rep. 26,080 (fraud to tell customer that every time sugar moves ten cents, you make $67,000); *Trinity Finan. Group,* Comm. Fut. L. Rep. 27,179 (deceptive to use cash prices to predict proportional profits on heating oil options).

Furthermore, as with the Commercial, the Seminar, in its heating oil mathematical illustration, misleads potential customers by suggesting that historical movements and known and expected seasonal patterns can be used reliably to predict profits on options. The Seminar gave those in attendance a deceptive impression that known seasonal trends will lead to their quick success and that options provide a scenario of "limited risk." In this regard, we are especially concerned with the Seminar's suggestion toward the end of the undisputed script that "greed" is a major reason people do not make money in commodities and that a customer "will *never go broke* taking a *profit.*" Despite the Seminar's use of risk disclosure material, the overall impression is that RJFCO is going to make customers money if they invest in options. Such conduct simply cannot survive under the Act, its underlying purpose, its regulations, and the interpretive case law.

As with the Commercial, the statements in the Seminar are clearly material because an objectively reasonable investor's decision-making process would be substantially affected by the Seminar's discussion on limited risk, cyclical heating oil-weather patterns, and examples and illustrations of large profits. Such representations, as a matter of law, alter the total mix of relevant information available to the potential

---

[8] This Circuit has clearly explained previously that brokers must be extremely careful when making representations in the commodities market because the standard *pro forma* risk disclosures do not "warn the customer to disbelieve *representations that certain trading strategies can . . . overcome inherent market risks, or that certain commodities are less volatile.* Those *unfamiliar* with the workings of markets are unlikely to understand that *no broker can eliminate or diminish risk.*" *Clayton,* 794 F.2d at 580–81 (emphasis added). We note that RJFCO designed its business specifically to deal with smaller, less experienced customers. *See R.J. Fitzgerald,* 173 F.Supp.2d at 1297.

commodity option investor. Scienter is also established on this record as a matter of law for the same reasons as with the Commercial. Precedent has condemned materially similar representations in the past, including specific representations on heating oil. We hold that Defendants acted with the requisite recklessness and departed in an extreme manner from the ordinary standards of care.

As explained above, CFTC contends, and we agree, that liability is established with regard to the language used in the Commercial and the Seminar. As an additional violation of the Act, CFTC claims that these two solicitation devices were fraudulent as a matter of law because they spoke of RJFCO's strategy for enormous profit potential without simultaneously informing potential RJFCO customers that more than 95% of the firm's clientele lost money in the types of investments being advertised. We agree.

Given the extremely rosy picture for profit potential painted in the Seminar and in the Commercial, a reasonable investor *surely* would want to know-before committing money to a broker-that 95% or more of RJFCO investors lost money. Such a disclosure would have gone a long way in balancing out, for example, the affirmative representation in the Commercial that the grain market was ripe for "huge" profits of "200–300 percent" and to telephone RJFCO "now" because such a corn market opportunity may "never" exist again. It would also have done much to counteract the assertion of "limited risk" in the Seminar. It is misleading and deceptive to speak of "limited risk" and "200–300" percent profits without also telling the reasonable listener that the overwhelming bulk of firm customers lose money. *See Ziemba,* 256 F.3d at 1206 (duty to disclose arises where a "defendant's failure to speak would render the defendant's *own* prior speech misleading or deceptive") (emphasis in original); *Rudolph v. Arthur Andersen & Co.,* 800 F.2d 1040, 1043 (11th Cir.1986) (same); *see also Modlin v. Cane,* [1999–2000 Transfer Binder] Comm. Fut. L. Rep. (CCH) 28,059, 49,550, 2000 WL 33678421 (CFTC March 15, 2000) ("a reasonable investor who hires a broker . . . would clearly find it material to learn that that broker had never closed an account with a profit."); W. Page Keeton et al., Prosser and Keeton on Torts § 106 at 738 (5th ed. 1984) ("half of the truth may obviously amount to a lie, if it is understood to be the whole.").

In its determination that there was no duty to disclose, the District Court was influenced by the fact that there was no evidence that other firms in the commodities industry did any worse than RJFCO and that RJFCO did not affirmatively represent that it had an attractive success rate. Given the highly misleading nature of the Commercial and Seminar, we fail to discern the legal significance of those facts in this case. As CFTC has persuasively argued, the Act should not foster a "race to the bottom," where liability for unquestionably deceptive activity is based in part on whether your competitors are not doing any better than you are. The focus of the inquiry is not on how well or how poorly others firms have done or even, in some circumstances, whether a firm has affirmatively boasted about a particular win-loss record. Rather, the judicial cross hairs in this case fall squarely on what the investor would reasonably want to know before deciding to commit money to a broker. *See, e.g.,* 17 C.F.R. § 33.7(f); *Sidoti,* 178 F.3d at 1136 n. 3 (explaining that § 33.7(f) "bolsters" 17 C.F.R. § 33.10 by stating that standard risk disclosures do not relieve a broker from the obligation of disclosing all material facts to potential or existing options customers). This of course brings us back, as it should, to the underlying remedial purpose of the Act: protecting the individual investor from being misled or deceived in the highly risky arena of commodities investment. The omission of highly material information is pernicious because it strikes at the very core of individual autonomy. The law vigorously protects the right of private individuals to exercise free choice in the marketplace. Such freedom of choice is eviscerated, and the autonomy of the individual severely undermined, if decision-altering information is withheld. * * *

This case serves as a pungent reminder that *caveat emptor* has no place in the realm of federal commodities fraud. Congress, the CFTC, and the Judiciary have determined that customers must be zealously protected from deceptive statements by brokers who deal in these highly complex and inherently risky financial instruments. Upon review of the record and controlling law, we conclude that the District Court erred in finding that the Commercial and the Seminar did not violate the CEA and its regulations. Both were deceptive and misleading, unquestionably material to the potential customer, and promulgated with the requisite scienter. These two solicitation devices also violate the Act because they failed to disclose extremely material information that any reasonable investor would want to know before committing money. * * *

TJOFLAT, CIRCUIT JUDGE, concurring

WILSON, CIRCUIT JUDGE, dissenting

IN THE MATTER OF JAMES R. BURGESS
2006 WL 237509 (C.F.T.C. 2006)

The Commodity Futures Trading Commission ("Commission") has reason to believe that Optioneer Inc., doing business as "Optioneer Systems" ("Optioneer"), by and through its employees and/or agents, including James R. Burgess ("Burgess"), has violated Sections 4*o*(1)(A) and (B) of the Commodity Exchange Act, as amended ("the Act"), 7 U.S.C. §§ 6*o*(1)(A) and (B) (2002), and Sections 4.41(a)(1) and (2) and 4.41(b)(1) and (2) of the Commission's Regulations promulgated thereunder, 17 C.F.R. §§ 4.41(a)(1)–(2), 4.41(b)(1)–(2) (2005) ("Regulations"). Burgess is liable as a controlling person for Optioneer's violations of the Act and Commission Regulations pursuant to Section 13(b) of the Act. Therefore, the Commission deems it appropriate and in the public interest that public administrative proceedings be, and they hereby are, instituted to determine whether Optioneer and Burgess (collectively, the "Respondents") engaged in the violations set forth herein and to determine whether any order should be issued imposing remedial sanctions.

In anticipation of the institution of an administrative proceeding, Respondents have submitted a Joint Offer of Settlement ("Joint Offer"), which the Commission has determined to accept. Respondents acknowledge service of this Order Instituting Proceedings Pursuant to Sections 6(c) and 6(d) of the Act, Making Findings and Imposing Remedial Sanctions ("Order"). Respondents, without admitting or denying the findings of fact or conclusions of law herein, consent to the use of the findings contained in this Order in this proceeding and in any other proceeding brought by the Commission or to which the Commission is a party.

From at least August 2002 through July 2004 (the "relevant period"), Optioneer, an unregistered commodity trading advisor ("CTA"), used misleading and false advertising to solicit members of the public to purchase its Optioneer trading system, which included hardware, software, training, technical support, monthly data and market information. On its website, www.Optioneer.com ("the Optioneer website"), the company falsely touted substantial profits that could be made using the trading system and a related commodity options trading advisory service. However, the Respondents had no documentary evidence to support such claims. Finally, Optioneer failed to tell clients and prospective clients that the performance histories of the system and advisory service were based on simulated or hypothetical trading, and failed to provide those persons with the required disclosures concerning the inherent limitations of hypothetical or simulated trading.

By making such material misrepresentations about its trading system, Optioneer, by and through its agents, including Burgess, violated Sections 4o(1)(A) and (B) of the Act and Commission Regulation 4.41(a)(1) and (2). In addition, Optioneer's failure to advise clients and prospective clients about the hypothetical or simulated nature of the performance histories and advisory service, and failure to provide the required disclosure concerning hypothetical trades, violated Commission Regulation 4.41(b)(1) and (2).

At all times during the relevant period, Burgess was the controlling person of Optioneer and he is therefore liable for Optioneer's violations of Sections 4o(1)(A) and (B) of the Act and Commission Regulations

4.41(a)(1) and (2), 4.41(b)(1) and (2), pursuant to Section 13(b) of the Act. * * *

During the relevant period, Optioneer, by and through its employees and/or agents, including Burgess, marketed and sold its trading system through the Optioneer website. The Optioneer trading system is designed to assist users in the purchase and sale of commodity options. The Optioneer system is marketed to include a mini-computer and software, six hours of training, technical support, monthly data and market information. On its website, Optioneer markets the hardware, software, and training for $5,000; technical support for $2,000; and monthly data and market information for $250/month. During the relevant period, Optioneer sold the Optioneer System to approximately 668 clients.

Also during the relevant period, Burgess exercised day-to-day authority over Optioneer and its employees, and performed all significant managerial functions, such as supervising the other Optioneer employees. He also controlled the content posted on Optioneer's website and included in other Optioneer promotional materials.

During the relevant period, Optioneer, by and through its employees and/or agents, including Burgess, posted numerous misrepresentations directed at clients and prospective clients on the Optioneer website. The misrepresentations concerned profit potential, the limited nature of the risk of options trading, and the Optioneer system's track record. For example, the Optioneer website contained the following statements:

- "Consistently earn 60% to 70% per year using the Optioneer System"

- "Even in years of market downturn, Optioneer members realized an average return of 70% per year"

- "Proven historical data"

- "Historically, Optioneer users realize 5 to 15%, for annualized returns of 60 to over 100%"

- "Using Optioneer to trade options, you make money in falling markets-not just in rising markets"

- "With Optioneer you have the opportunity to multiply your returns over and above what the market normally offers."

Optioneer, by and through its employees and/or agents, including Burgess, made these claims knowing that its clients were not consistently making the returns advertised, and without possessing or reviewing any documentary evidence to support such claims.

During the relevant period, Optioneer, by and through its employees and/or agents, including Burgess, failed to disclose to prospective and actual clients that certain trading results posted on its website were based on simulated or hypothetical trades. In addition, Optioneer, by and through its employees and/or agents including Burgess failed to disclose, in light of the purported trading track record posted on the Optioneer website, that neither Burgess nor Optioneer ever employed the system using real trades.

During the relevant period, Optioneer, by and through its employees and/or agents including Burgess, identified the following returns based on a $10,000 investment on the Optioneer website:

- Year 1–36% $13,600
- Year 2–46% $19,856
- Year 3–30% $25,812
- Year 4–46% $37,685
- Year 5–40% $52,759
- Total–527% $52,759

Optioneer, by and through its employees and/or agents including Burgess, included these performance results on the Optioneer website, knowing that the results were based on a hypothetical investment, but failed to disclose this fact on the website.

Optioneer, by and through its employees and/or agents including Burgess, also made claims such as "5 years traded" and "6 years user traded" without disclosing the fact that neither Burgess nor Optioneer ever traded the Optioneer system using actual trades. Furthermore, Optioneer, by and through its employees and/or agents including Burgess, made these claims when they did not possess or review any documentary evidence to support such claims.

Optioneer, while acting as an unregistered CTA, violated Sections 4o(1)(A) and (B) of the Act and Commission Regulations 4.41(a)(1) and (2) by falsely representing to clients and prospective clients in written statements on the Optioneer website the performance of the Optioneer system and the risk involved.

To violate Section 4o(1) of the Act, Optioneer must have acted as a CTA. Section 1a(6) of the Act defines a CTA as "any person who, for compensation or profit, engages in the business of advising others either directly or through publications, writings or electronic media, as to the advisability of trading in any" commodity futures contract or options contract. 7 U.S.C. § 1a(6). Commodity trading advice includes the sale of a trading system that generates specific trade recommendations. *CFTC v. Avco Financial Corp.,* 28 F. Supp.2d 104, 118–19 (S.D.N.Y. 1998), *aff'd in part and remanded in part on other grounds sub nom. Vartuli v. CFTC,* 228 F.3d 94 (2d Cir. 2000) (company acted as a CTA under "the plain language of the [Act]" when it marketed computer software that generated specific recommendations to buy and sell futures contracts); *In re R&W Technical Services, Ltd.,* [1998–1999 Transfer Binder] Comm. Fut. L. Rep. (CCH) ¶ 27,582 at 47,738 (CFTC March 16, 1999), *aff'd in relevant part, R&W Technical Services, Ltd. v. Commodity Futures Trading Commission,* 205 F.3d 165, 170 (5th Cir. 2000) (trading signals generated by computerized trading system together with advertisements which convince clients that the signals will be highly profitable constitute advising others). Here, Optioneer acted as a CTA because it provided commodity options trading advice for compensation or profit through the sale of the Optioneer trading system, which provides its users with specific buy and sell recommendations for commodity options contracts.

Section 4o(1)(A) and (B) of the Act prohibit both registered and unregistered CTAs from making material misrepresentations and omissions to their clients regarding commodity options transactions. *R&W Technical Services, Ltd.,* 205 F.3d at 170 (prohibiting fraud by an unregistered CTA who sold a trading system to the public). Similarly, Commission Regulations 4.41(a)(1) and (2) prohibit a CTA, whether registered or unregistered, from advertising in a fraudulent or misleading manner. *In the Matter of Stenberg,* Comm. Fut. L. Rep. (CCH) ¶ 29, 221 (CFTC Nov. 7, 2002); *CFTC v. Wall St. Underground, Inc.,* 281 F. Supp. 2d 1260 at 1270 (D. Kan., 2003).

A statement is material if it is substantially likely that a reasonable investor would consider the matter important in making an investment decision. *TSC Industries, Inc. v. Northway, Inc.,* 426 U.S. 438, 449 (1976); *Sudol v. Shearson Loeb Rhoades, Inc.,* [1984–1986 Transfer Binder] Comm. Fut. L. Rep. (CCH) ¶ 22,748 at 31,119 (CFTC Sept. 30, 1985). Generally, omissions and misrepresentations of fact concerning the likelihood of profiting from commodity options transactions are material and violate the antifraud provisions of the Act. *See, e.g., Avco Financial Corp.,* 28 F. Supp.2d at 115–16 (S.D.N.Y. 1998).

While violations of Section 4o(1)(A) and Regulation 4.41(a)(1) require proof of scienter, a violation of Section 4o(1)(B) does not. *See In re Slusser,* [1998–1999 Transfer Binder] Comm. Fut. L. Rep. (CCH) ¶ 27,701 at 48,315 (CFTC July 19, 1999), *aff'd in relevant part, Slusser v. CFTC,* 210 F.3d 783 (7th Cir. 2000). Neither does a violation of Regulation 4.41(a)(2) require proof of scienter. *See Commodity Trend Serv. v. Commodity Futures Trading Commission,* 233 F.3d 981, 993 (7th Cir. 2000).

Optioneer, by and through its employees and/or agents including Burgess, violated Sections 4o(1)(A) and (B) of the Act and Commission Regulations 4.41(a)(1) and (2) by exaggerating the performance of the Optioneer trading system and minimizing options risk on the Optioneer website, as well as making false representations concerning Optioneer's track record. During the relevant period, Optioneer did not have any actual past performance record, nor was its trading system performing as well as was claimed in the Optioneer website. Optioneer, by and through its employees and/or agents, also failed to disclose that neither Burgess nor Optioneer had ever employed the Optioneer system using actual trades.

Actual and prospective clients of Optioneer would have viewed these facts as material information. *See CFTC v. Commonwealth Financial Group, Inc.,* 874 F. Supp. 1345, 1353–54 (S.D. Fla. 1994), *citing, inter alia, Reed v. Sage Group,* [1987–1990 Transfer Binder] Comm. Fut. L. Rep. (CCH) ¶ 23,942 at 34,299 (CFTC Oct. 14, 1987) (misrepresentations regarding a firm or broker's trading record and experience are fraudulent because past success and experience are material facts to reasonable investors); *R & W Technical Services, Ltd.,* ¶ 27,582 at 47,742 ("The use of a trading system by its developers is important to reasonable consumers because it reflects a meaningful vote of self-confidence and a sign of authenticity"). A reasonable client would think it material that the trading program at issue had never been applied through actual trading. *Levine v. Refco, Inc.,* [1987–1990 Transfer Binder] Comm. Fut. L. Rep. (CCH) ¶ 24, 488 at 36,115 (CFTC July 11, 1989); *see also CFTC ex rel. Kelley v. Skorupskas,* 605 F. Supp. 923, 933 (E.D. Mich. 1985) (misrepresenting performance tables as being actual trading results violated Section 4o of the Act).

Optioneer, by and through its employees and/or agents including Burgess, also violated Sections 4o(1)(A) and (B) of the Act and Commission Regulations 4.41(b)(1) and (2) by misrepresenting hypothetical or simulated trades as actual profitable trades made by using the Optioneer trading system. *R & W Technical Svcs., Inc. v. CFTC,* 205 F.3d at 170 ("Because simulated results inherently overstate the reliability and validity of an investment method, and because extravagant claims understate the inherent risks in commodity futures and options trading, a reasonable investor would find [such] fraudulent misrepresentations to be material."); *See also Skorupskas,* 605 F. Supp. at 933 (misrepresenting performance tables as being actual trading results violates anti-fraud provisions of the Act).

In this case, Burgess acted with scienter because he knew or recklessly disregarded the fact that the Optioneer system did not perform as well as Optioneer represented to clients and prospective clients on the Optioneer website. Burgess also knew or recklessly disregarded the fact that Optioneer did not have an established track record to support the claims on the website. Optioneer therefore violated Sections 4o(1)(A) and (B) of the Act and Commission Regulation 4.41(a)(1) and (2).

Pursuant to Commission Regulation 4.41(b)(1), no person may present the performance of any simulated or hypothetical commodity interest account, transaction in a commodity interest or a series of transactions in a commodity interest unless such performance is accompanied by:

(i) The following statement: 'Hypothetical or simulated performance results have certain inherent limitations. Unlike an actual performance record, simulated results do not represent actual trading. Also, since the trades have not actually been executed, the results may have under-or over-compensated for the impact, if any, of certain market factors, such as lack of liquidity. Simulated trading programs in general are also subject to the fact that they are designed with the benefit of hindsight. No representation is being made that any account will or is likely to achieve the profits or losses similar to those shown;' or

(ii) A statement prescribed pursuant to rules promulgated by a registered futures association. . . .

Commission Regulation 4.41(b)(2) requires that:

If the presentation of such simulated or hypothetical performance is other than oral, the prescribed statement must be prominently disclosed.

Optioneer, by and through its employees and/or agents including Burgess, failed to provide the disclosure orally or in written form on its website during the relevant period, in violation of Commission Regulation 4.41(b)(1) and (2). * * *

Solely on the basis of the consents evidenced by the Offer, and prior to any adjudication on the merits, the Commission finds that Optioneer violated Sections 4o(1)(A) and (B) of the Act, 7 U.S.C. §§ 6o(1)(A) and (B) (2002), and Sections 4.41(a)(1) and (2), 4.41(b)(1) and (2) of the Commission's Regulations, 17 C.F.R. §§ 4.41(a)(1)–(2), 4.41(b)(1)–(2) (2004). Burgess, as controlling person of Optioneer, is liable for Optioneer's violations of Sections 4o(1)(A) and (B) of the Act and Sections 4.41(a)(1) and (2), 4.41(a)(1) and (2) of the Commission's Regulations pursuant to Section 13(b) of the Act, 7 U.S.C. § 13c(b) (2002). * * *

CHAPTER 9

MANIPULATION AND TRADING ABUSES

■ ■ ■

1. BACKGROUND

JERRY W. MARKHAM
THE COMMODITY EXCHANGE MONOPOLY—
REFORM IS NEEDED
48 Wash. & Lee L. Rev. 977 (1991)

Commodity futures trading evolved from the grain marketing problems that arose in the 1800s in the midwest when farmers would bring their grain to market after the harvest. The market would then become so flooded with grain that prices would drop drastically-often to levels far below production and transportation costs. At such time, grain would be dumped in the streets and left to rot. Later, as surpluses were used up, grain shortages would occur and prices would skyrocket. Crop failures and transportation problems compounded this boom and bust cycle. To alleviate these conditions "forward" contracts were developed. These were simply contracts for the delivery of grain at a time specified in the future rather than for immediate delivery. These forward, or "to arrive," contracts helped stabilize the market because farmers could sell their grain in advance for set prices and specified delivery dates. They could then store the grain either in their own facilities, or at local elevators, until the grain was needed. This also stabilized the supply situation for processors and users of the grain.

These forward contracts evolved into futures contracts with standardized terms. That is, the quantity and grade of the commodity and the delivery date became standardized with the only negotiated feature being the price. This permitted traders to offset their contracts with each other, which facilitated negotiations and allowed contracts, in effect, to be resold. This standardization also allowed speculation in these contracts. Speculation quickly became widespread.

Abuses soon followed, including efforts to corner the grain markets by maintaining large futures positions coupled with purchases of available deliverable supplies. This required sellers of futures contracts to close their contracts at artificial prices demanded by the cornering party. There was also widespread concern that speculators in Chicago were

503

driving grain prices down to levels below production costs, which created much animosity on the part of populists and members of Congress. As a result, numerous bills were introduced in Congress to regulate grain futures trading. * * *

Legislative efforts to regulate futures trading both on and off the exchanges were unsuccessful until 1921 when the Future Trading Act of 1921 was adopted. This statute, which was based on the taxation powers of Congress, imposed a prohibitive tax on futures transactions that were not conducted on an exchange licensed by the federal government. Exchanges so licensed were also required to prevent manipulation of prices. Although the Supreme Court held that this legislation was an unconstitutional extension of the Congressional taxing power, the next year Congress enacted essentially the same statute under its authority to regulate interstate commerce. This statute, the Grain Futures Act, was upheld by the Supreme Court.

The Grain Futures Act proved to be ineffective in preventing market abuses. To cite one example, the Commodity Exchange Commission, which administered the Act, held that [abusive] trading practices did not fall within the prohibitions against manipulation in the Grain Futures Act. The Commission stated that, while such transactions might be fraudulent, they were not manipulative and, therefore, were not subject to the prohibitions of the Grain Futures Act. The Supreme Court also later held that a party manipulating the markets could not be the subject of disciplinary action by the Secretary of Agriculture unless disciplinary action was imposed before the manipulation had been completed. Legal processes, however, simply did not permit the completion of such an action before a manipulation could be effectuated. Consequently, the Act was effectively gutted.

The stock market crash of 1929 was accompanied by a drastic decline in grain prices and, with the election of Franklin Roosevelt, a presidential call went out for legislation concerning both securities and commodities. Much of the securities legislation was adopted before 1934—i.e., the Securities Act of 1933 and the Securities Exchange Act of 1934. Commodities legislation, however, was not enacted until 1936. It also took a much different route from that of the securities legislation, which was handled by the banking committees. Instead, commodity futures regulation fell within the province of the agricultural committees. The result was the Commodity Exchange Act of 1936.

The Commodity Exchange Act differed in many respects from the securities legislation that was adopted during the New Deal. For example, the Commodity Exchange Act carried forward the concept of the Futures Trading Act that all futures contracts must be traded on a licensed exchange called a "contract market." Unlike the securities industry, no over-the-counter trading is permitted in futures contracts. Another concept that was carried forward in the Commodity Exchange Act was that of a regulatory oversight body called the Commodity Exchange Commission. Rather than being an independent federal agency, such as the SEC, the Commodity Exchange Commission was composed of the Secretaries of the Departments of Agriculture and Commerce and the Attorney General of the United States. Day-to-day regulation of the statute was given to the Secretary of Agriculture who assigned this duty to an agency within the department, the Commodity Exchange Authority (CEA).

NOTES

1. The Future Trading Act of 1921 was preceded by a massive study of the grain trade and the commodity exchanges by the Federal Trade Commission (FTC Study). That study was conducted as a result of concerns over grain speculations associated with World War I.

The FTC study identified various trading abuses, including "corners" and "squeezes." A corner involves a speculation in which a trader or group of traders buys up all available supplies of a commodity and also gains control of a large portion of the long commodity futures contract for the same commodity. This allows the trader to dictate prices to the shorts when they try to cover their positions.

A squeeze is a lesser form of corner. It involves gaining control of a substantial percentage of available supplies, which causes a shortage of available deliverable supplies. The effect is to squeeze prices upward to the benefit of the manipulator's futures positions. See, Jerry W. Markham, Law Enforcement and the History of Financial Market Manipulation 3 (2014) (describing corners and squeezes).

Corners and squeezes often failed because of the problem of "burying the corpse." That is, when the corner or squeeze was completed, the manipulator would be left with the problem of how to get rid of the grain acquired to complete the manipulation. Sales of the grain would drive prices down, eroding the gains made from the manipulation. See, Jerry W. Markham, "Manipulation of Commodity Futures Prices—The Unprosecutable Crime," 8 Yale J. on Reg. 281, 293 (1991) (describing this problem and the schemes used to avoid it).

2. There are three recognized forms of manipulation:

(1) Market power manipulations in which a trader uses its control of the cash market and futures in a commodity to manipulate associated futures prices, as in the case of a corner or squeeze;

(2) Rigged trading manipulations in which fictitious trades, such as wash sales discussed later in this Chapter; are used to set artificial prices;

(3) False report manipulations involve the use of false information that is used to mislead other traders on the value of a commodity.

See, 23A Jerry W. Markham and Thomas Lee Hazen, Broker Dealer Operations Under Securities and Commodities Law: Financial Responsibilities, Credit Regulation, and Customer Protection, § 9:17.50 (discussing these manipulation forms).

2. THE CFTC'S VIEWS ON MANIPULATION

IN THE MATTER OF INDIANA FARM BUREAU COOPERATIVE ASSOCIATION, INC.
Comm. Fut. L. Rep. (CCH) ¶ 21,796 (C.F.T.C. 1982)

By the Commission (COMMISSIONERS GARTNER, PHILLIPS and HINEMAN; CHAIRMAN JOHNSON and COMMISSIONER STONE concurring in result).

This enforcement proceeding was instituted on December 11, 1974, with the issuance of a "Complaint and Notice of Hearing" ("complaint") by the United States Department of Agriculture. The complaint charges that respondents Indiana Farm Bureau Cooperative Association, Inc. ("Indiana Farm") and Louis M. Johnston ("Johnston") attempted to manipulate and did manipulate the price of the July 1973 corn future contract on the Chicago Board of Trade in violation of §§ 6(b) and 6(c) of the Commodity Exchange Act, as amended, 7 U.S.C. §§ 9 and 13b (the "Act"). Specifically, the complaint alleges that respondents manipulated the market by conducting a "squeeze" on July 20, 1973, the last day of trading on the July corn contract. After extensive discovery, evidentiary hearings were held in November 1976, February and March 1977, and April, May and June 1978. Exhaustive post hearing briefs were filed by both sides. On December 12, 1979, Administrative Law Judge Arthur L. Shipe filed a ninety-two page Initial Decision ("I.D.") wherein he ruled that the Division of Enforcement ("Division") had failed to prove that respondents had attempted to manipulate or had manipulated the July 1973 corn contract.

The Administrative Law Judge made extensive findings of fact and conducted a thorough analysis of the evidence in his discussion of the law and facts. The judge's findings of fact are not in dispute and upon review of the entire record, the Commission finds them to be fully supported by the evidence. Although the judge's legal analysis of the evidence and conclusions of law are disputed by the parties, it is unnecessary for purposes of this opinion's discussion of the law to restate the facts in full detail. The following summary, as contained in the Administrative Law

Judge's initial decision, accurately presents the operative facts and basic issues:

> The July 1973 corn futures contract expired on July 20, 1973 at about 12:00 noon. On July 19, 1973, the CBOT Board of Directors voted to remove the 10-cent maximum daily limit on price fluctuation for the final day of trading in the contract. The midpoint of the closing range in the contract was 259 1/2 [cents per bushel] on July 19th. The settlement price on July 20th was 380, though trades had occurred at 390 before the session closed. The contract did not reach 300 until approximately 11:24 a.m.

> It is contended that the sharpness of the increase resulted in artificial prices and that these prices are attributable to the trading activity of respondents. Respondents held a long position of 4,705,000 bushels in the contract at the opening of trading on July 20th, and stood for delivery of 2,010,000 bushels upon expiration of the contract. They liquidated approximately 500,000 bushels at prices of 370 to 390 in the last 20 minutes of trading.

> On July 20, 1973, reported corn stocks in deliverable position in Chicago were 12,107,000 bushels, of which 4,511,000 bushels were reported to be deliverable. The Division of Enforcement (DE) claims, however, that only 511,000 bushels were in fact available for delivery.

> During the summer of 1973, there was a heavy movement of export grain to, among other countries the Soviet Union, resulting in a shortage of transportation and elevator facilities used for shipping grain. Additionally, quality problems with the corn crop of 1972–1973 developed in some areas of production. DE [Division of Enforcement] contends that the demand of respondents for delivery in these circumstances produced the alleged artificial prices, and thus constituted manipulation within the meaning of Sections 6(b) and 6(c) of the Act (7 U.S.C. §§ 9 and 13b).

> Respondents assert that DE has failed to prove that the price of the July 1973 corn futures contract was artificial on July 20, 1973, or that the respondents caused the price rise that occurred on that day, or that the respondents intended that their actions would cause an artificial price. They further dispute DE's contention that there was an insufficient supply of corn available to satisfy delivery requirements on the futures contract. Judge Shipe concluded:

> > In final summary, as the foregoing discussion has shown, prices in the CBOT 1973 corn futures contract reached artificial levels on July 20, 1973. DE's claim that the standing for delivery by respondents was the legal cause of these artificial prices rests largely on DE's further claim that the bulk of the reportable deliverable supply was unavailable for delivery on the futures market. The evidence offered to support the latter contention

consists mainly of date on the heavy corn export movements at the time. There were, however, cash transfers of ownership of corn throughout the period and futures deliveries were, in fact, made. Indeed, there were more deliveries made at prices under 300, which DE concedes were nonartificial prices, than DE claims were available for delivery. Thus, heavy export movements of corn are not proof that corn was unavailable for delivery on the futures market. At bottom, DE's claim is that the futures market cannot work where supply and demand are unusual. This cannot be concluded even on the basis of the events in issue here.

DE argues that the entry by respondents of scaled-up spread orders during July 1973 reflects an intention to manipulate the market. However, as shown, the entry of these orders was entirely consistent with the theory of hedging now embraced by DE. DE also lays heavy emphasis on the liquidation orders entered by respondents in the last twenty minutes of trading. The circumstances in which these orders were entered belie DE's contention that they reflected an intent, formed earlier in July, to manipulate the market.

The remainder of DE's claims are clearly makeweight, and without merit. Accordingly, the following conclusions are entered.

     1.   The prices in the CBOT July 1973 corn futures contract reached artificial levels on July 20, 1973. It is not possible to state precisely at what price this occurred.

     2.   The trading of respondents was not a culpable or legal cause of the prices that were reached in that contract on July 20.

     3.   Respondents did not attempt or intend to cause the prices that were reached, and could not reasonably have foreseen that such prices would be reached because of their activity. (I.D. at 91–92.) The Division of Enforcement has appealed these conclusions, arguing both by brief and at oral argument on May 21, 1982, that respondents did, indeed, manipulate the July option of this corn contract. The Division of Enforcement contends that respondents manipulated the congested market existing in the final half-hour of trading on July 20, 1973, by standing for delivery on four times what the Division views as the deliverable supply of corn and by "squeezing" prostrate shorts, who had no recourse to the cash market, into paying artificial prices to offset their contracts.

In order to consider and resolve the arguments raised, it is important to clarify at the outset the meaning the Commission attaches to various material terms. Neither manipulation nor attempted manipulation is defined in the Commodity Exchange Act. That task has fallen to case-by-case judicial development. The federal courts and judicial decisions of the Department of Agriculture have looked to the common understanding of manipulation in determining the essential elements of the offense. For example, in Cargill, Inc. v. Hardin, 452 F.2d 1154, 1163 (8th Cir. 1971), cert. denied, 406 U.S. 932 (1972), the Eighth Circuit adopted the basic definition accepted by the Seventh Circuit in an earlier case:

> The Commodity Exchange Act itself does not define "manipulation", and definitions from other sources are of a most general nature. One of the new judicial definitions is to be found in General Foods Corporation v. Brannan, 170 F.2d 220, 231 (7th Cir. 1948), where the court said:
>
>> "We are favored with numerous definitions of the word 'manipulation.' Perhaps as good as any is one of the definitions which appears in the government's brief, wherein it is defined as 'the creation of an artificial price by planned action, whether by one man or a group of men.'" In Volkart Brothers, Inc. v. Freeman, 311 F.2d 52, 58 (5th Cir. 1962), the court adopted the often cited definition of manipulation given by Arthur R. Marsh, a former president of the New York Cotton Exchange, in a hearing before a Senate subcommittee in 1928:
>>
>>> Manipulation, Mr. Chairman, is any and every operation or transaction or practice, the purpose of which is not primarily to facilitate the movement of the commodity at prices freely responsive to the forces of supply and demand; but, on the contrary, is calculated to produce a price distortion of any kind in any market either in itself or in its relation to other markets. If a firm is engaged in manipulation it will be found using devices by which the prices of contracts for some one month in some one market may be higher than they would be if only the forces of supply and demand were operative... Any and every operation, transaction, device, employed to produce those abnormalities of price relationship in the futures markets, is manipulation. In a 1971 Department of Agriculture decision, In re David Henner, 30 A.D. 1151 (1971), the Judicial Officer approved of this definition as being "consistent with the common understanding of the term." Id. at 1224 (footnote and citations omitted).

In the only manipulation case heretofore decided by this Commission, In re Hohenberg Brothers, [1975–1977 Transfer Binder] Comm. Fut. L. Rep. (CCH) P20,271 (February 18, 1977) ("Hohenberg"), the Commission, addressed manipulation in terms that have yielded some differing interpretations, as is apparent in this case. Among other things, the

Commission explained that the intent requirement, which is the same for a manipulation and an attempted manipulation, is "the performance of an act or conduct which was intended to effect an artificial price." Id. We adhere to this general description, but recognize that some refinement is in order.

Since intent is the essence of manipulation, we turn then to analyze more specifically the level of intent, or the state of mind, which must be found in order to support a finding of manipulation under the Commodity Exchange Act. The complaint in this case charges that respondents acted "for the purpose and with the intent of causing prices in the July 1973 corn future which were arbitrary and artificial. . . ." (Complaint P14).n3 This is the classic formulation of a charge requiring proof of "specific intent" as that term is generally understood in the criminal law. While the charging terms of its complaint and its subsequent proffer indicated that it would introduce evidence of purposeful conduct, the Division of Enforcement later argued to the Administrative Law Judge that a less stringent standard of "general intent" was sufficient to meet the manipulative intent requirement. The Division argued ". . . it is sufficient, for purposes of manipulative intent, that the necessary consequence of their action was an unlawful result." The Administrative Law Judge apparently reviewed the evidence in light of general intent and a negligence type standard, and concluded that "[r]espondents did not attempt or intend to cause the prices that were reached, and could not reasonably have foreseen that such prices would be reached because of their activity."

In its brief to the Commission on appeal, the Division adopted Judge Shipe's "reasonable foreseeability" alternative formulation of intent, arguing that "intentional conduct which results in a manipulated price where that result was reasonably foreseeable, as a standard, protects the innocent while permitting the Commission to relieve more effectively 'burdens on interstate commerce caused by manipulation and market control.'" At oral argument, however, counsel for the Division abandoned the "reasonably foreseeable" argument and argued in favor of its original "general intent" standard which counsel defined as knowledge "that the likely effect of [respondents'] action would be to cause a futures price that would not accurately reflect the basic forces of supply and demand."

Respondents counter that the negligence concept of "reasonable foreseeability" cannot be the standard for manipulative intent, and regardless of whether specific intent or general intent is required, the Division's proof of intent was lacking under either standard (Brief for Respondents at 91–107). At oral argument, counsel for respondents maintained, as he had below, that specific intent is the level of intent required to prove manipulation.

Upon review of the relevant federal case law and prior administrative decisions, we conclude, consistent with this Commission's opinion in In re Hohenberg Brothers, supra, that the requisite level of mens rea required to prove manipulation or attempted manipulation under the Commodity Exchange Act is that of "specific intent, "or as that term is also commonly understood to mean today, "purposeful conduct."

In Hohenberg, supra, the Commission reviewed the law of manipulative intent in the context of an alleged attempted short-side manipulation. We defined intent in terms of purposeful conduct and applied that standard to the evidence presented:

> As recognized by the court in Great Western Food Distributors, supra, 201 F.2d at 479, the intent of the parties is a determinative element of a punishable manipulation. Intent is a subjective factor and since it is impossible to discover an attempted manipulator's state of mind, intent must of necessity be inferred from the objective facts and may, of course, be inferred by a person's actions and the totality of the circumstances.* * *

> We discern no difference in the intent required to accomplish a manipulation and that required by an attempted manipulation which is simply the performance of an act or conduct which was intended to effect an artificial price.

Id. at 21,477 (footnote omitted). In so defining manipulative intent, the Commission adhered to the long line of federal court decisions and judicial opinions of the Department of Agriculture, cited supra, which have held that specific intent to create an "artificial" or "distorted" price is a sine qua non of manipulation. For example in Volkart Brothers, Inc. v. Freeman, supra, 311 F.2d at 58 the Fifth Circuit concluded: "there must be a purpose to create prices not responsive to the forces of supply and demand; the conduct must be 'calculated to produce a price distortion.'" In Cargill, Inc. v. Hardin, supra, 452 F.2d at 1163, the Eighth Circuit quoted with approval the definition of manipulation used by the Seventh Circuit in General Foods Corporation v. Brannan, supra, "'the creation of an artificial price by planned action, whether by one man or a group of men.'"

We are unable to discern any justification for a weakening of the manipulative intent standard which does not wreak havoc with the market place. It is the intent of the parties which separates otherwise lawful business conduct from unlawful manipulative activity. This being so, a clear line between lawful and unlawful activity is required in order to ensure that innocent trading activity not be regarded with the advantage of hindsight as unlawful manipulation. Many years ago, the Seventh Circuit observed in General Foods Corp. v. Brannan, supra, 170

F.2d at 231, that "self-preservation has oftentimes been referred to as the first law of nature, and we suppose it applies to traders as well as others. We see no reason way the seller respondents as well as General Foods and Metcalf should not under the circumstances make an effort to protect their own interests." Similarly this Commission recognized in Hohenberg, *supra* at 21,478, that "[e]ven though respondents' activities may have involved a 'profit motive,' absent a finding of manipulative intent, trading with the purpose of obtaining the best price for one's [commodity] . . . does not constitute, in itself, a violation of the Commodity Exchange Act. "Thus, market participants have a right to trade in their own best interests without regard to the positions of others as long as their trading activity does not have as its purpose the creation of "artificial" or "distorted" prices. Indeed, it is this very motivation which gives lifeblood to the forces of supply and demand, and makes the price discovery function of the marketplace viable. Moreover, since the self-interest of every market participant plays a legitimate part in the price setting process, it is not enough to prove simply that the accused intended to influence price.

Accordingly, we hold that in order to prove the intent element of a manipulation or attempted manipulation of a futures contract price under §§ 6(b) and 6(c) of the Commodity Exchange Act, as amended, it must be proven that the accused acted (or failed to act) with the purpose or conscious object of causing or effecting a price or price trend in the market that did not reflect the legitimate forces of supply and demand influencing futures prices in the particular market at the time of the alleged manipulative activity. Since proof of intent will most often be circumstantial in nature, manipulative intent must normally be shown inferentially from the conduct of the accused. But once it is demonstrated that the alleged manipulator sought, by act or omission, to move the market away from the equilibrium or efficient price—the price which reflects the market forces of supply and demand—the mental element of manipulation may be inferred. Further, while knowledge of relevant market conditions is probative of intent, it is not necessary to prove that the accused knew to any particular degree of certainty that his actions would create an artificial price. It is enough to present evidence from which it may reasonably be inferred that the accused "consciously desire[d] that result, whatever the likelihood of that result happening from his conduct." See United States v. United States Gypsum Co., *supra*, 438 U.S. at 445.

The intent question here must be analyzed in the context of an alleged manipulative squeeze. The term "squeeze," like manipulation, is undefined in the Act. However, the market condition giving rise to the term in a well-known phenomenon affecting the futures markets. An oft cited definition of "squeeze" is that offered by Senator Pope during debate on enactment of the Commodity Exchange Act:

> Squeeze (congestion): These are terms used to designate a condition in maturing futures where sellers (hedgers or speculators), having waited too long to close their trades, find there are no new sellers from whom they can buy, deliverable stocks are low, and it is too late to procure the actual commodity elsewhere to settle by delivery. Under such circumstances and though the market is not cornered in the ordinary sense, traders who are long hold out for an arbitrary price.

80 Cong. Rec. 8089 (1928). Baer & Saxon, Commodity Exchanges and Futures Trading (1949) explains: "A squeeze is a relatively small corner occurring in deliveries for some one month or some one grade. Some—or, in fact, most—squeezes are inevitable on both the physical and the exchange markets and are not the result of illegal manipulation." Volkart, supra, 311 F.2d at 59. In its Report on the Grain Trade (1926) the Federal Trade Commission stated:

> A 'squeeze' suggests a much milder situation than a corner. It means that there is too large a line of short sales out and that the short sellers have been somewhat obstinate in carrying their trades into the delivery month, or possibly that the various long interests are unduly or unexpectedly obstinate in reducing their lines during the delivery month. A squeeze does not imply one long holder nor conspiracy among the long interests to enhance the price. A large long interest may exist which has not been built up for manipulative or even speculative purposes, but as a hedge, and may be a hedge on which the buyer expects to take delivery to meet cash grain commitments.

7 FTC Report, pp. 284–285.

When, then, does it become unlawful to profit from a congested futures market? Or stated another way, when has unlawful intent to "squeeze" shorts during a period of congestion been proven? A significant problem in analyzing the case law and the briefs in this case is the inconsistent use of the term "squeeze." The case law and the arguments of the parties here appear to use the term "squeeze" sometimes simply to describe the condition of "congestion" and at others to describe the unlawful act of manipulation itself. We read the first sentence of Senator Pope's definition, supra, to describe a congested futures market generally; the second sentence to define what may turn such market congestion into an unlawful manipulation, i.e., a "squeeze," if manipulative intent is present. See The Report of the Federal Trade Commission on the Grain Trade (1926), at pages 243–244. For the sake of consistency, we shall hereinafter refer to the situation or "condition" in maturing futures described by Senator Pope's first definitional sentence as "congestion." We shall refer to the profiting from such congestion—Senator Pope's second sentence—as a "squeeze." This reading is consistent with the general principle that the essence of manipulative activity is "the creation [or attempted creation] of an artificial price by planned action," Cargill, supra 452 F.2d at 1163. Holding out for high prices is normally rational and lawful market behavior. See Hohenberg, supra at p. 21,478; Volkart, supra, 311 F.2d at 58–59; General Foods, supra, 170 F.2d at 231. Such activity only becomes unlawful when it is accompanied by manipulative intent as generally manifested by conduct other than simply seeking the best price in a pit in which there may be supply shortages. The Seventh Circuit stated in Great Western Food Distributors v. Brannan, supra, n. 5, 201 F.2d at 479. " * * * the intent of the parties during their trading is a determinative element of a punishable corner. Unintentional corners can develop, 7 F.T.C. Report on the Grain Trade 243 (1926), and should not carry the pain of forfeiture of trading privileges. As the Fifth Circuit observed in Volkart, supra:

> Certainly the term "manipulate" means more than the charging of what some may consider to be unreasonably high prices. Otherwise, there would be grave doubt as to the constitutionality of the statutes.

> As Mr. Marsh's testimony indicates, there must be a purpose to create prices not responsive to the forces of supply and demand; the conduct must be "calculated to produce a price distortion." There may be a squeeze not planned or intentionally brought about by the petitioners. Such a squeeze should not result in their being punished.

311 F.2d at 58–59. (Footnote omitted.)

Because intent must generally be inferred from conduct, we emphasize, as we said in Hohenberg, that seeking the best price for one's commodity is a legitimate, indeed critical, price-creating force in the futures markets that in-and-of-itself cannot be the basis for an inference of manipulative intent. It is imperative that each said of the market seek the best price in order for price discovery to occur and that "best" price is, of necessity, at the expense of the other side. This pricing process works in delivery markets only because a person with open positions—if dissatisfied that the price bid or offered to liquidate an open position reflects the value of the underlying commodity at that point in time—can make or force delivery of the actual product. Squeezes in general and manipulative squeezes in particular are possible only when the delivery option disappears and its tempering effect is lost. Thus, the adequacy of "deliverable supply," as distinguished from supply generally, and the role of market participants in the supply scenario is of great significance in any analysis. For instance, where there is evidence that the deliverable supply was intentionally and significantly reduced by a market participant, the seeking of "unreasonably high prices," which otherwise would be lawful conduct, becomes susceptible to an inference that the true purpose of the activities of the accused is to create prices not responsive to the forces of supply and demand. For example, in Cargill, supra, and G.H. Miller & Co. v. United States, supra, the longs intentionally created the conditions which led to congestion in the delivery month by intentionally acquiring control or market dominance over the cash market (delivery) and the futures market (offset) for a particular commodity, and thereafter by virtue of their dominance were able to liquidate the long futures position at prices that would not otherwise have been reached under normal pressures of supply and demand. These manipulative squeezes were possible because, by assuring that the deliverable supply was inadequate to enable liquidation of the contracts through delivery, the longs assured that at least some shorts would either have to default or pay whatever price was dictated by the longs.

The acquisition of market dominance is the hallmark of a long manipulative squeeze. For without the ability to force shorts to deal with him either in the cash or futures market, the manipulator is not able to successfully dictate prices because a short may buy grain from other sources and deliver against his commitments. See, e.g., Cargill, supra, 452 F.2d at 1164–67; Great Western, supra, n.5, 201 F.2d at 478–479. Where a trader builds up a cornering or near cornering interest in the cash market and a large long interest in the futures market, he has "laid the base for a squeeze, "Cargill, supra, 452 F.2d at 1172, and subsequent trading activity must be scrutinized carefully. The intentional acquisition of market dominance, while it may be lawful in and of itself, is compelling evidence of manipulative intent where that dominance is subsequently used to "squeeze" shorts into offsetting contracts with the manipulator at prices considerably above the market. Thus, where the intentional acquisition of market dominance is coupled with a subsequent "squeeze" of shorts who are forced to deal with the accused, it may be inferred that the charging of high prices was done with the purpose of causing a price and reaping a profit beyond that which the legitimate forces of supply and demand would otherwise have allowed.

On the other hand, where a long does not intentionally create the conditions for a squeeze, and a congested futures market arises from other causes, often a "natural" corner or low deliverable supply, manipulative intent may not be inferred where a long does not exacerbate the congestion itself, but simply seeks the best price from the existing situation. See Volkart, supra, 311 F.2d at 58–59.

Turning to the evidence presented, we conclude, consistent with the Administrative Law Judge's determination, that there was insufficient evidence to prove that respondents acted with the conscious object or purpose of causing an artificial or distorted price. The respondents did not lay the base for a squeeze and it has not been demonstrated that they took any action with the intent to effect an artificial price. Indeed, in exercise of our expertise, we conclude that no basis for a squeeze existed nor was any illegitimate factor present in the pricing aggregate in the instant case.

Judge Shipe, who had the advantage of observing the demeanor of the witnesses, including respondent Johnston, concluded that "[r]espondents did not attempt or intend to cause the prices that were reached. . . ." He so found based upon an exhaustive review of the evidence, wherein he generally refused to accept the adverse manipulative inferences sought to be drawn by the Division and generally accepted as credible respondent Johnston's testimony as to why he took the positions he took, traded when he did, and stood for delivery as he did. We have examined the evidence and have found no reason to disturb these findings of fact or question the Administrative Law Judge's ultimate conclusion of law that there was no manipulative intent proven.

The Division does not contend, and there is no evidence from which to conclude, that respondents were responsible for the market congestion which occurred on the last day of trading or that they exacerbated it. The evidence demonstrates that any relative overall cash corn shortfall that did occur in the Chicago area was the product of a "natural" corner, due to transportation shortages, heavy export shipments and quality problems. Apparently, a number of shorts who had made no delivery preparations stayed in the market speculating on the imposition of federal export controls on corn which had been threatened in June by the Department of Commerce and which would have brought prices down. This threat was not lifted until after the close of trading on July 18, and perhaps the uniqueness of this particular market situation is attributable to the confluence of these factors.

In the absence of evidence that respondents were responsible for the market congestion, it cannot be inferred that respondents' trading activity, consistent with their hedging program and commercial commitments, was intended to produce an artificial price. Standing for delivery as they did was respondents' contractual right and was motivated by pre-existing commercial needs and the uncertainty of prices in the inactive cash market. Unlike Cargill, Indiana Farm Bureau did not deplete the local cash commodity late in the delivery month; did not establish a large long speculative position at a time it knew it held virtually all of the cash commodity; and did not increase its long position on the last day of trading. Nor did it liquidate a dominant speculative long position at prices already seven to eight cents over the market price. Indiana Farm's export contracts were entered into in January and April, 1973 and its long position was established as a hedge on which it expected to, and did, take delivery in order to meet its legitimate commercial commitments. Upon taking delivery, respondents, in fact, used virtually all corn received to fill existing contractual commitments. No manipulative intent may be inferred from such activity which, moreover, was specifically cited by the FTC Grain Report as legitimate nonmanipulative activity during a congested market.

We also note in this regard the irresponsible market behavior of the shorts here. A serious contributing factor to squeezes in general and to the congestion that occurred in the instant case is the behavior of shorts who remain in the futures market during the delivery month without having made any delivery preparations. Consistent with the views expressed in Volkart, supra, 311 F.2d at 60, the testimony of numerous trade witnesses in this case and the findings of the Administrative Law Judge (I.D. at 69–72), we find that it is irresponsible market behavior for shorts to enter the delivery month, especially where low cash supplies are evident, without making adequate delivery preparations.

The decision to deliver or offset in the trading pit is one of time, price, distance and convenience. The fact that local supply of a commodity is scarce does not relieve the shorts from their obligation to honor their contractual commitment to deliver. A short who, for whatever reason, enters the delivery month unprepared or unable to deliver runs the risk that he will have to offset at the long's price. Where a long has not intentionally created or exploited a congested situation, the long has a contractual right to stand for delivery or exact whatever price for its long position which a short is willing to pay in order to avoid having to make delivery.

We also wish to emphasize that historical price comparisons of the type relied upon by the courts in Cargill and G. H. Miller are of limited probative value here because of the unique combination of circumstances which led to the price rise in the corn pit on July 20, 1973. The tight corn supply and Indiana Farm's standing for delivery were legitimate forces of supply and demand which caused futures prices to rise. The panic bidding of shorts who were totally unprepared to deliver caused the most dramatic spurt in prices. The threat of government export controls similar to those imposed on soybeans undoubtedly led to the large open short position late in the delivery month. When that possibility was removed after the close on July 18, shorts in no position to fulfill their delivery obligations bid the price up the limit on July 19 and beyond on July 20. While the resultant $1.20 price rise was the largest one day price rise ever recorded for corn, it must be remembered that the daily price limit had been removed allowing for such an unprecedented rise. Against the backdrop of an inert cash market, comparison of the futures price and nominal cash quotations is of little value in assessing the true economic value of corn in Chicago on July 20. In Cargill, the cash market was relevant to a determination of price. In the instant case, the pricing of corn was in the trading pit due to the inert cash market. Thus, given the unique market and economic forces of supply and demand operating on the July 1973 corn futures contract, while the prices reached on July 20 were high, we do not agree with the Administrative Law Judge who found that the price was artificial. To the contrary, based upon market factors we have noted, we conclude that the price trend on July 20 was indeed reflective of the legitimate forces of supply and demand.

Finally, while there may have been, overall, relatively less corn available than usual, we agree with Judge Shipe that there was adequate deliverable supply of corn in the cash market to allow responsible shorts to obtain corn to fulfill their delivery commitments without having to deal with respondents, thereby precluding a successful squeeze of the corn market by any market participant.

Excluding corn "committed" to export sales, the Division calculated deliverable supply of corn available in Chicago on July 20, 1973, at what it describes as "non-artificial" prices, at no more than 511,000 bushels. Judge Shipe rejected the Division's calculation essentially on the basis that there was no evidence to show that respondents either knew or could have known how much corn was "committed" to export sales. Judge Shipe calculated the deliverable supply to be at a minimum, 4,616,000 bushels and concluded from the combined cash supply and respondents futures positions that respondents did not have the requisite market dominance at the time the Division alleged prices to have become artificial (11:24 a.m.) to be able to "squeeze" the shorts.

The Division argues on appeal: "Judge Shipe injects absolute uncertainty into its determination, making it a factor of a trader's subjective appraisal. Deliverable supply, on the contrary, is an objective fact to be determined by looking at the terms of the futures contract and the economics of compliance with them."

Respondents argue that the deliverable supply of corn was at all times sufficient to permit the shorts to cover their positions without purchasing futures from respondents. They dispute the Division's position that deliverable supply is "an objective fact," contending, as the Administrative Law Judge found, that deliverable supply is determined on the basis of what information is known by or reasonably available to the accused.

The complaint in this case charged that respondents *knew* that there was an insufficient supply of deliverable grade corn in deliverable position on July 20 to allow shorts to satisfy their contracts except by purchasing corn futures from respondents. Judge Shipe concluded, and we agree, that there is no evidence that respondents had knowledge of "committed" corn stocks and, further, that in fact there was an adequate supply of deliverable corn in Chicago at the time, because the corn excluded by the Division was not irrevocably committed. While we agree with the Division that the basic calculation of deliverable supply may be accomplished without regard to what is known by the accused, it is the deliverable supply known to the accused which must be looked to in determining whether respondent's purchase of contracts is susceptible to an inference of manipulative intent. Manipulative intent may be inferred, for example, "through the purchase of long contracts in excess of *known* deliverable supply. . . ." Great Western Foods v. Brannan, supra, 201 F.2d at 478–479 (emphasis added), as in Cargill, where the accused knew it had a virtual corner on the existing deliverable supply. See Cargill, supra, 452 F.2d at 1159, 1170. Conversely, no such unlawful intent may be presumed where a long purchases contracts in quantity generally consistent with published reports of available stocks. Since there is no evidence that the corn supply was in fact irrevocably committed to commercial contracts, such corn was "available" to shorts and cannot be excluded from the deliverable supply.

Accordingly IT IS HEREBY ORDERED that the decision of the Administrative Law Judge is AFFIRMED and the complaint is DISMISSED.

Concur By: JOHNSON and STONE

NOTES

1. In another carry-over case inherited by the CFTC from the Commodity Exchange Authority, In re Cox, Comm. Fut. L. Rep. (CCH) ¶ 23,786 (1987), the CFTC sought to determine whether an illegal manipulation had occurred in the May 1971 wheat futures contract. In conducting its analysis, the CFTC considered available deliverable supplies to determine if the shorts could have covered their delivery obligations. The CFTC concluded that supplies that were committed to delivery at points other than the terminal market could not be included in available supplies for determining whether a manipulation was present. Nevertheless, since the traders were unaware of these commitments, the CFTC determined that this should not be marked against them. It also stated again that the shorts had an obligation to secure supplies adequate to meet their delivery obligations. The CFTC focused on the fact that the respondents could not foreclose the delivery option and thus lacked the ability to influence prices. In other words, if the short traders could have obtained supplies from other sources to meet their delivery obligations, they had an obligation to do so. If there was such an availability, there would be no basis for charging manipulation.

2. The CFTC has stated that the elements of manipulation are:

(1) a trader or group of traders who act in concert and have the capacity to affect the price of a commodity,

(2) the exercise by that trader or group of traders of their capacity to affect the price,

(3) an artificial price, and

(4) intent to create that artificial price

Report of the Commodity Futures Trading Commission on Recent Developments in the Silver Futures Market to the Senate Committee on Agriculture, Nutrition, and Forestry, 96th Cong., 2d Sess. 15, 18–19 (1980).

The CFTC has found that it was very difficult to prove these elements. Indeed, during its thirty-nine year history, the CFTC was successful in only one adjudicated manipulation case. In the Matter of DiPlacido, Comm. Fut. L. Rep. (CCH) ¶ 30, 970 (C.F.T.C. 2008), aff'd sub nom., DiPlacido v. CFTC, No. 08–5559–ag, 2009 U.S. App. LEXIS 22692 (2d Cir. 2009), cert denied, 2010 U.S. LEXIS 2461 (2010).

3. ATTEMPTED MANIPULATION

IN THE MATTER OF ECOVAL DAIRY TRADE, INC.
2011 CFTC LEXIS 44 (C.F.T.C. 2011)

The Commodity Futures Trading Commission ("Commission") has reason to believe that, from September 21, 2007 to October 17, 2007, Ecoval Dairy Trade, Inc. ("Ecoval" or "Respondent") violated Sections 6(c), 6(d), and 9(a)(2) of the Commodity Exchange Act (the "Act"), 7 U.S.C. §§ 9, 13b, and 13(a)(2) (2006). Therefore, the Commission deems it appropriate and in the public interest that public administrative proceedings be, and hereby are, instituted to determine whether Respondent engaged in the violations set forth herein and to determine whether any order should be issued imposing remedial sanctions.

In anticipation of the institution of an administrative proceeding, the Respondent has submitted an Offer of Settlement (the "Offer"), which the Commission has determined to accept. Without admitting or denying any of the findings or conclusions herein, Respondent consents to the entry of this Order Instituting Proceedings Pursuant to Sections 6(c) and 6(d) of the Commodity Exchange Act, Making Findings and Imposing Remedial Sanctions ("Order") and acknowledges service of this Order.

The Commission finds the following:

During the period from September 21, 2007 through October 17, 2007 (the "Relevant Period"), Ecoval attempted to manipulate the daily settlement prices of each of the Chicago Mercantile Exchange ("CME")

Non Fat Dry Milk ("NFDM") monthly commodity futures contracts for December 2007 through July 2008. Ecoval executed various trading strategies on the electronic market trading platform, Globex, with the intent to "push" the prices of these NFDM futures contracts higher so Ecoval could potentially establish a large short position in these NFDM futures contracts at higher prices.

Ecoval Dairy Trade, Inc. is a Pennsylvania corporation with its principal place of business located in Wayne, Pennsylvania. During the Relevant Period, Ecoval, a company of less than twenty employees, bought and sold physical dairy commodities, domestically and internationally, and regularly traded various dairy commodity futures contracts, including NFDM. Ecoval has never been registered with the Commission in any capacity.

During the Relevant Period, the NFDM futures market was illiquid and thinly traded. It carried an average total open interest across all of its twenty-four contract months of approximately 100 to 150 contracts. During the Relevant Period, market conditions reflected a disparity between near month NFDM futures prices and cash prices. The CME began electronic trading of NFDM futures contracts through Globex beginning on September 17, 2007. From this date forward, NFDM futures trading could be performed either electronically or in the trading pit, although the overwhelming majority of NFDM futures trading occurred in the electronic market. In fact, during the Relevant Period, there was minimal bid and offer activity in the pit, with only one NFDM trade occurring in the pit, and only twelve market participants active in the electronic market. This NFDM futures contract is cash-settled.

Starting on September 21, 2007, Ecoval, by and through its employees, formulated a strategy, explained in several emails, stating its intent to try to "push" NFDM futures contracts higher than existing market forces dictated so Ecoval could potentially establish large short positions in monthly NFDM futures contracts at higher prices. For example, Ecoval stated that it was, "trying to push the market a bit higher in order to get a higher sales prices [sic];" "[in] NFDM, we're adding shorts but trying to obtain a higher price;" and "[s]till selling short NFDM but at higher prices, we're trying to push the market higher in order to obtain a better sales price for 2008."

Ecoval attempted to manipulate the NFDM market by utilizing various trading strategies, including, but not limited to, the following: 1) executing trades by "lifting" offers, and then immediately bidding a higher price than just paid in the trade; 2) placing both bids and offers above prevailing market prices across multiple contract months in order to establish higher price ranges in the market; 3) consistently placing bids above the opening price or the prevailing price across multiple contracts;

and 4) bidding, and then quickly cancelling the bids, without the intent to have the bids filled.

Ecoval engaged in the foregoing conduct with the intent to affect the daily settlement prices of December 2007 through July 2008 NFDM futures contracts so Ecoval could potentially establish a large short position in these same NFDM futures contracts at higher prices.

Section 9(a)(2) of the Act makes it unlawful for "[a]ny person to manipulate or attempt to manipulate the price of any commodity in interstate commerce, or for future delivery on or subject to the rules of any registered entity. . . ." 7 U.S.C. § 13(a)(2) (2006). Sections 6(c) and 6(d) of the Act, 7 U.S.C. §§ 9 and 13b (2006), authorize the Commission to serve a complaint and provide for the imposition of, among other things, civil monetary penalties and cease and desist orders if the Commission has reason to believe that "any person . . . has manipulated or attempted to manipulate the market price of any commodity . . . for future delivery on or subject to the rules of any registered entity . . . or otherwise is violating or has violated any of the provisions of [the] Act. . . ."

The following elements are required to prove an attempted manipulation: (1) an intent to affect the market price of a commodity; and (2) an overt act in furtherance of that intent. *See In re Hohenberg Bros. Co.*, [1975–1977 Transfer Binder] Comm. Fut. L. Rep. (CCH) P 20,271 at 21,477 (CFTC Feb. 18, 1977); *CFTC v. Bradley,* 408 F. Supp. 2d 1214, 1220 (N.D. Okla. 2005). "Intent is the essence of manipulation . . . the intent of the parties is the determinative element in a punishable manipulation. . . . It is the intent of the parties which separates otherwise lawful business conduct from unlawful manipulative activity." *In re Indiana Farm Bureau* [1982–1984 Transfer Binder] Comm. Fut. L. Rep. (CCH) P 21,796 at 27,282–27,283 (CFTC Dec. 17, 1982). Proof of manipulative intent will most often be circumstantial in nature and thus it often can be shown inferentially from the conduct of the accused. *Indiana Farm Bureau,* P 21,796 at 27,283. The type of conduct alleged can be based on a particular trading strategy. *CFTC v. Amaranth Advisors, LLC,* 554 F. Supp. 2d 523, 531 (S.D.N.Y. 2008). "Because every transaction signals that the buyer and seller have legitimate economic motives for the transaction, if either party lacks that motivation, the signal is inaccurate. Thus, a legitimate transaction combined with an improper motive is commodities manipulation." *In re Amaranth Natural Gas Commodities Litigation,* 587 F. Supp. 2d 513, 534 (S.D.N.Y. 2008).

During the Relevant Period, Ecoval, by and through its employees, used various trading strategies in an attempt to "push" the NFDM futures market higher with the intent to affect the daily settlement prices in certain NFDM futures contracts.

By this conduct, Ecoval, through the acts of its employees, violated Sections 6(c), 6(d), and 9(a)(2) of the Act.

The Commission finds that, during the Relevant Period, Ecoval violated Sections 6(c), 6(d), and 9(a)(2) of the Act, 7 U.S.C. §§ 9, 13b, and 13(a)(2) (2006), by attempting to manipulate the daily settlement prices for the December 2007 through July 2008 NFDM futures contracts.

NOTES

1. In order to ease its evidentiary burdens, the CFTC brought cases charging "attempted" manipulation. The CFTC has asserted that an attempted manipulation can be proved by simply showing manipulative intent and an overt act to carry out a manipulation. In the Matter of Hohenberg Bros., Comm. Fut. L. Rep. (CCH) ¶ 20, 271, n. 39 (C.F.T.C. 1977). This obviates the very difficult task of proving that the party caused an artificial price and had market power sufficient to carry out the manipulation, all of which may be affected by numerous market factors.

2. The CFTC also charges manipulation by false reports. The CEA thus prohibits "false or misleading or knowingly inaccurate reports concerning crop or market information or conditions that affect or tend to affect the price of any commodity in interstate commerce. . . ." [7 U.S.C. § 13(a)(2)].

3. The CFTC has brought numerous cases and reached settlements involving hundreds of million dollars in penalties over charges of attempted manipulation and false price reports designed to manipulate energy prices or to present a false appearance in the market. Still, the CFTC encountered setbacks when cases were actually adjudicated. See, Jerry W. Markham, Lawrence Hunt, Jr. & Michael Sackheim, Market Manipulation—From Star Chamber to Lone Star, 23 Fut. & Deriv. L. Rep. 7 (2003) (describing those efforts).

4. The Dodd-Frank Wall Street Reform and Consumer Protection Act of 2010 (Dodd-Frank Act) sought to expand the powers of the CFTC to attack commodity price manipulations by including a provision in the CEA that tracks the anti-fraud and anti-manipulation language in Section 10(b) of the Securities Exchange Act of 1934 [15 U.S.C. § 78j(b)]. Section 753 of the Dodd-Frank Act thus prohibits any "manipulative or deceptive device or contrivance" in violation of CFTC rules adopted within one year of the enactment of that legislation. This "fraud based" provision was intended to create "a strong bright line" as to what constitutes manipulation. 156 Cong. Rec. S3348 (May 6, 2010) (remarks of Sen. Cantwell).

The new Section 10(b) language will be interpreted in the same manner as it is under the Securities Exchange Act since it was borrowed from that provision. For a comparison of the application of Section 10(b) and the pre-existing anti-manipulation provisions in the CEA see Jerry W. Markham, Law Enforcement and the History of Financial Market Manipulation (2014).

5. Section 753 in Dodd-Frank also added a "special provision" for manipulation by "false reporting." That provision establishes a "good faith mistake" exception to this prohibition. This would include mistakenly transmitting, in good faith, false, misleading or inaccurate information to a price reporting service.

6. The Dodd-Frank Act left the CFTC's pre-existing anti-manipulation authority intact. The CFTC can now proceed under the new Dodd-Frank Act authority or under its pre-existing powers against persons believed to be engaged in manipulative activities. The CFTC has adopted rules implementing both of those approaches. See CFTC Rules 180.1 and 180.2. [17 C.F.R. § 180.1 & § 180.2].

7. Following the Enron manipulations of the California energy market, the Federal Energy Regulatory Commission (FERC) brought a number of actions under its power to regulate natural gas and electricity. Congress then passed the Energy Policy Act of 2005, which expanded the FERC's powers to attack energy price manipulations. This anti-manipulation authority was also modeled after Section 10(b) of the Securities Exchange Act of 1934. See, Jerry W. Markham, Law Enforcement and The History of Financial Market Manipulation, Ch. 6 (2013) (describing the FERC actions and this new power).

FERC has aggressively used this new power. For example, in 2013, FERC fined Barclays Bank $453 million for manipulative activity in the electricity markets. The bank was accused of losing money in physical power markets between 2006 and 2008 in order to benefit its derivatives positions. FERC News Release (July 16, 2013) available at http://www.ferc.gov/media/news-releases/2013/2013–3/07–16–13.asp#.UoNxv6Wm5GA (accessed on Nov. 13, 2013)

JPMorgan Chase thereafter paid $410 million to settle FERC manipulation charges. FERC News Release, available at http://www.ferc.gov/media/news-releases/2013/2013–3/07–30–13.asp#.UoNwzaWm5GA (July 30, 2013) (accessed on Nov. 13, 2013).

8. Concerns over a spike in energy prices after hurricanes Katrina and Rita caused Congress to enact legislation that gave the Federal Trade Commission (FTC) authority to prosecute false reporting and market manipulation in the wholesale petroleum market. [Pub. L. 110–140, 121 Stat. 1492, Title VIII, Subtitle B, *codified at* 42 U.S.C. §§ 17301–17305]. The legislation granting that authority was again modeled after Section 10(b) of the Securities Exchange Act of 1934.

9. Consequently, there are now four federal agencies with power over market price manipulations, the CFTC, SEC, FERC and FTC. See, Jerry W. Markham, Law Enforcement and The History of Financial Market Manipulation, Ch. 6 (2013) (describing the development and scope of this authority). As seen in the next case those new powers resulted in a jurisdictional conflict between FERC and the CFTC.

HUNTER V. FERC

711 F.3d 155 (D.C. Cir. 2013)

TATEL, CIRCUIT JUDGE:

Pursuant to the Energy Policy Act of 2005, the Federal Energy Regulatory Commission fined petitioner $30 million for manipulating natural gas futures contracts. According to petitioner, FERC lacks authority to fine him because the Commodity Futures Trading Commission has exclusive jurisdiction over all transactions involving commodity futures contracts. Because manipulation of natural gas futures contracts falls within the CFTC's exclusive jurisdiction and because nothing in the Energy Policy Act clearly and manifestly repeals the CFTC's exclusive jurisdiction, we grant the petition for review.

Petitioner Brian Hunter, an employee of the hedge fund Amaranth, traded natural gas futures contracts on the New York Mercantile Exchange (NYMEX), a CFTC-regulated exchange. * * *

This case arises from Hunter's alleged manipulation of the "settlement price" for natural gas futures contracts, which is determined by the volume-weighted average price of trades during the "settlement period" for natural gas futures. The settlement price may affect the price of natural gas for the following month.

According to FERC, Hunter sold a significant number of natural gas futures contracts during the February, March, and April 2006 settlement periods. During these settlement periods, Hunter's sales ranged from 14.4% to 19.4% of market volume. Given their volume and timing, Hunter's sales reduced the settlement price for natural gas. Hunter's portfolio benefited from these sales because he had positioned his assets in the natural gas market to capitalize on a price decrease—that is, he shorted the price for natural gas.

Hunter's trades caught the attention of federal regulators. On July 25, 2007, the CFTC filed a civil enforcement action against Hunter, alleging that he violated section 13(a)(2) of the Commodity Exchange Act by manipulating the price of natural gas futures contracts. 7 U.S.C. § 13(a)(2). The next day, FERC filed an administrative enforcement action against Hunter, alleging that he violated section 4A of the Natural Gas Act, which prohibits manipulation. 15 U.S.C. § 717c–1. FERC claimed that Hunter's manipulation of the settlement price affected the price of natural gas in FERC-regulated markets. Following a lengthy administrative process, FERC ruled against Hunter and imposed a $30 million fine.

Hunter now petitions for review. He argues, amongst other things, that FERC lacks jurisdiction to pursue this enforcement action. The CFTC has intervened in support of Hunter on this issue. In refereeing this jurisdictional turf war, we cannot defer to either agency's attempt to reconcile its statute with the other agency's statute. Because the "premise of *Chevron* deference is that Congress has delegated the administration of a particular statute to an executive branch agency, . . . we have never deferred where two competing governmental entities assert conflicting jurisdictional claims." *Salleh v. Christopher*, 85 F.3d 689, 691–92, 318 U.S. App. D.C. 123 (D.C. Cir. 1996). * * *

Most significantly for this case, CEA section 2(a)(1)(A) provided, at the time of Hunter's trades, that:

> The Commission shall have *exclusive jurisdiction* . . . with respect to accounts, agreements (including any transaction which is of the character of, or is commonly known to the trade as, an "option", "privilege", "indemnity", "bid", "offer", "put", "call", "advance guaranty", or "decline guaranty"), and transactions involving contracts of sale of a commodity for future delivery, traded or executed on a contract market designated or derivatives transaction execution facility registered pursuant to section 7 or 7a of this title or any other board of trade, exchange, or market, and transactions subject to regulation by the Commission. . . . *Except as hereinabove provided*, nothing contained in this section shall (I) supersede or limit the jurisdiction at any time conferred on the Securities and Exchange Commission or other regulatory authorities under the laws of the United States or of any State, or (II) restrict the Securities and Exchange Commission and such other authorities from carrying out their duties and responsibilities in accordance with such laws.

7 U.S.C. § 2(a)(1)(A) (emphases added). Stated simply, Congress crafted CEA section 2(a)(1)(A) to give the CFTC exclusive jurisdiction over transactions conducted on futures markets like the NYMEX.

In response to the California energy crisis, Congress enacted the Energy Policy Act of 2005, which significantly expanded FERC's authority to regulate manipulation in energy markets. As codified at section 4A of the Natural Gas Act, the statute makes it

> unlawful for any entity, directly or indirectly, to use or employ, in connection with the purchase or sale of natural gas or the purchase or sale of transportation services subject to the jurisdiction of the Commission, any manipulative or deceptive device or contrivance . . . in contravention of such rules and regulations as the Commission may prescribe as necessary in the public interest or for the protection of natural gas ratepayers.

15 U.S.C. § 717c–1. FERC subsequently promulgated regulations prohibiting manipulative trading in natural gas. *See Prohibition of*

Energy Market Manipulation, 71 Fed. Reg. 4244–03 (Jan. 26, 2006) (codified at 18 C.F.R. § 1c.1).

The Energy Policy Act contains only two references to the CFTC. As codified at section 23 of the Natural Gas Act, the statute states:

> (1) Within 180 days of ... enactment of this section, the Commission shall conclude a memorandum of understanding with the [CFTC] relating to information sharing, which shall include, among other things, provisions ensuring that information requests to markets within the respective jurisdiction of each agency are properly coordinated to minimize duplicative information requests, and provisions regarding the treatment of proprietary trading information.

> (2) Nothing in this section may be construed to limit or affect the exclusive jurisdiction of the [CFTC] under the Commodity Exchange Act (7 U.S.C. 1 et seq.).

15 U.S.C. § 717t–2(c). In other words, section 23 requires FERC and the CFTC to enter into a memorandum of understanding about information sharing. Section 23 further provides that it has no effect on the CFTC's exclusive jurisdiction.

As we see it, this case reduces to two questions. First, does CEA section 2(a)(1)(A) encompass manipulation of natural gas futures contracts? If yes, then we need to answer the second question: did Congress clearly and manifestly intend to impliedly repeal CEA section 2(a)(1)(A) when it enacted the Energy Policy Act of 2005?

A quick glance at the statute's text answers the first question. CEA section 2(a)(1)(A) vests the CFTC with "exclusive jurisdiction ... with respect to accounts, agreements[,] ... and transactions involving contracts of sale of a commodity for future delivery, traded or executed" on a CFTC-regulated exchange. 7 U.S.C. § 2(a)(1)(A). Here, FERC fined Hunter for trading natural gas futures contracts with the intent to manipulate the price of natural gas in another market. Hunter's scheme, therefore, involved transactions of a commodity futures contract. By CEA section 2(a)(1)(A)'s plain terms, the CFTC has exclusive jurisdiction over the manipulation of natural gas futures contracts.

Against the statute's plain text, FERC marshals two counterarguments. According to FERC, although it and the CFTC "each have exclusive jurisdiction over the day-to-day regulation of their respective physical energy and financial markets, where, as here, there is manipulation in one market that directly or indirectly affects the other market, both agencies have an enforcement role." Respondent's Br. 21 (internal quotation marks omitted). But FERC's contention that the CFTC may exclusively regulate only day-to-day trading activities—not an overarching scheme like manipulation—finds no support in CEA section 2(a)(1)(A)'s text. Moreover, as the CFTC points out, "[a]cceptance of FERC's jurisdictional test would allow any agency having authority to prosecute manipulation of the spot price of a commodity to lawfully exercise jurisdiction with respect to the trading of futures contracts in that commodity." CFTC Reply Br. 3. Such an interpretation would eviscerate the CFTC's exclusive jurisdiction over commodity futures contracts and defeat Congress's very clear goal of centralizing oversight of futures contracts. *See, e.g.*, S. Rep. No. 93–1131, at 6 (1974) (stating that CEA section 2(a)(1)(A) "make[s] clear that (a) the Commission's jurisdiction over futures contract markets or other exchanges is exclusive and includes the regulation of commodity accounts, commodity trading agreements, and commodity options; [and] (b) the Commission's jurisdiction, where applicable, supersedes States as well as Federal agencies"). To be sure, CEA section 2(a)(1)(A)'s second sentence preserves the jurisdiction of other federal agencies, but its first sentence makes clear that the CFTC's jurisdiction is exclusive with regards to accounts, agreements, and transactions involving commodity futures contracts on CFTC-regulated exchanges. Thus, if a scheme, such as manipulation, involves buying or selling commodity futures contracts, CEA section 2(a)(1)(A) vests the CFTC with jurisdiction to the exclusion of other agencies. * * *

Because any infringement of the CFTC's exclusive jurisdiction would effectively repeal CEA section 2(a)(1)(A), we must next determine whether, as FERC insists, the Energy Policy Act constitutes a repeal by implication. On this front, FERC carries a heavy burden. * * *

"[A]bsent a clearly expressed congressional intention" to repeal CEA section 2(a)(1)(A), *Morton v. Mancari*, 417 U.S. 535, 551, 94 S. Ct. 2474, 41 L. Ed. 2d 290 (1974), FERC cannot demonstrate that section 4A encroaches upon the CFTC's exclusive jurisdiction. Having failed to meet the high bar of showing an implied repeal, FERC lacks jurisdiction to charge Hunter with manipulation of natural gas futures contracts.

For the foregoing reasons, we grant the petition for review.

4. "OPEN MARKET" MANIPULATIONS

UNITED STATES V. MULHEREN

38 F.2d 364 (2d Cir. 1991)

McLAUGHLIN, CIRCUIT JUDGE:

In the late 1980's a wide prosecutorial net was cast upon Wall Street. Along with the usual flotsam and jetsam, the government's catch included some of Wall Street's biggest, brightest, and now infamous—Ivan Boesky,

Dennis Levine, Michael Milken, Robert Freeman, Martin Siegel, Boyd L. Jeffries, and Paul A. Bilzerian—each of whom either pleaded guilty to or was convicted of crimes involving illicit trading scandals. Also caught in the government's net was defendant-appellant John A. Mulheren, Jr., the chief trader at and general partner of Jamie Securities Co. ("Jamie"), a registered broker-dealer.

Mulheren was charged in a 42-count indictment handed-up on June 13, 1989. The indictment alleged that he conspired to and did manipulate the price on the New York Stock Exchange (the "NYSE") of the common stock of Gulf & Western Industries, Inc. ("G & W" or the "company") in violation of 18 U.S.C. Sec. 371, 15 U.S.C. Sec. 78j(b) & 78ff and 18 U.S.C. Sec. 2, by purchasing 75,000 shares of G & W common stock on October 17, 1985 for the purpose of raising the price thereof to $45 per share (Counts One through Four); that he engaged in "stock parking" transactions to assist the Seemala Corporation, a registered broker-dealer controlled by Boesky, in evading tax and other regulatory requirements in violation of 15 U.S.C. Secs. 78j(b) & 78ff and 18 U.S.C. Sec. 2 (Counts Five through Twenty-Four); that he committed mail fraud in connection with the stock parking transactions in violation of 18 U.S.C. Secs. 1341 & 2 (Counts Twenty-Five through Thirty-Nine); and that Mulheren caused Jamie to make and keep false books and records in violation of 15 U.S.C. Sec. 78ff & 78q(a) (Counts Forty through Forty-Two).

Count Forty-One was dismissed before trial on the government's motion. At the conclusion of the government's case, the district court dismissed Counts Twenty-Nine through Thirty-Nine pursuant to Fed.R.Crim.P. 29. Of the remaining thirty counts, the jury returned a partial verdict of guilty on Counts One through Four. A mistrial was declared by the district court when the jury could not reach a verdict on the other twenty-six counts. On Counts One through Four, Mulheren was sentenced to concurrent terms of one year and one day imprisonment, a $1,681,700 fine and a $200 special assessment.

This appeal thus focuses solely on the convictions concerning Mulheren's alleged manipulation of G & W common stock. The government sought to prove that on October 17, 1985, Mulheren purchased 75,000 shares of G & W common stock with the purpose and intent of driving the price of that stock to $45 per share. This, the government claimed, was a favor to Boesky, who wanted to sell his enormous block of G & W common stock back to the company at that price. Mulheren assails the convictions on several grounds.

First, Mulheren claims that the government failed to prove beyond a reasonable doubt that when he purchased the 75,000 shares of G & W common stock on October 17, 1985, he did it for the sole purpose of raising the price at which it traded on the NYSE, rather than for his own investment purposes. Second, Mulheren argues that even if his sole intent had been to raise the price of G & W stock, that would not have been a crime because, he claims, (1) he neither misrepresented any fact nor failed to disclose any fact that he was under a duty to disclose concerning his G & W purchases; (2) his subjective intent in purchasing G & W stock is not "material"; and (3) he did not act for the purpose of deceiving others. Finally, Mulheren cites various alleged evidentiary and sentencing errors that he believes entitle him to either a new trial or resentencing.

Although we harbor doubt about the government's theory of prosecution, we reverse on Mulheren's first stated ground because we are convinced that no rational trier of fact could have found the elements of the crimes charged here beyond a reasonable doubt.

Reviewing the evidence "in the light most favorable to the government, and construing all permissible inferences in its favor," United States v. Puzzo, 928 F.2d 1356, 1357 (2d Cir.1991) (citing United States v. Diaz, 878 F.2d 608, 610 (2d Cir.), cert. denied ___ U.S. ___, 110 S.Ct. 543, 107 L.Ed.2d 540 (1989)), the following facts were established at trial.

In 1985, at the suggestion of his long-time friend, Carl Icahn, a prominent arbitrageur and corporate raider, Ivan Boesky directed his companies to buy G & W stock, a security that both Icahn and Boesky believed to be "significantly undervalued." Between April and October 1985, Boesky's companies accumulated 3.4 million shares representing approximately 4.9 percent of the outstanding G & W shares. According to Boesky, Icahn also had a "position of magnitude."

On September 5, 1985, Boesky and Icahn met with Martin Davis, the chairman of G & W. At the meeting, Boesky expressed his interest in taking control of G & W through a leveraged buyout or, failing that, by increasing his position in G & W stock and securing seats on the G & W board of directors. Boesky told Davis that he held 4.9 percent of G & W's outstanding shares. Davis said he was not interested in Boesky's proposal, and he remained adamant in subsequent telephone calls and at a later meeting on October 1, 1985.

At the October 1, 1985 meeting, which Icahn also attended, Boesky added a new string to his bow: if Davis continued to reject Boesky's attempts at control, then G & W should buy-out his position at $45 per share. At that time, G & W was, indeed, reducing the number of its outstanding shares through a repurchase program, but, the stock was trading below $45 per share. Davis stated that, although he would consider buying Boesky's shares, he could not immediately agree to a price. Icahn, for his part, indicated that he was not yet sure whether he would sell his G & W stock.

During—and for sometime before—these negotiations, Mulheren and Boesky also maintained a relationship of confidence and trust. The two had often shared market information and given each other trading tips. At some point during the April-October period when Boesky was acquiring G & W stock, Mulheren asked Boesky what he thought of G & W and whether Icahn held a position in the stock. Boesky responded that he "thought well" of G & W stock and that he thought Icahn did indeed own G & W stock. Although Boesky told Mulheren that G & W stock was "a good purchase and worth owning," Boesky never told Mulheren about his meetings or telephone conversations with Davis because he considered the matter "very confidential." Speculation in the press, however, was abound. Reports in the August 19, 1985 issue of Business Week and the September 27, 1985 issue of the Wall Street Journal indicated that Boesky and Icahn each owned close to five percent of G & W and discussed the likelihood of a take-over of the company. Mulheren, however, testifying in his own behalf, denied reading these reports and denied knowing whether Boesky and Icahn held positions in G & W.

On October 3, 1985, two days after his meeting with Boesky and Icahn, Davis met with Mulheren. Mulheren stated that he had a group of investors interested in knowing whether G & W would join them in acquiring CBS. According to Davis, Mulheren also volunteered that he could be "very helpful in monitoring the activities of Ivan Boesky [in G & W stock;] [Mulheren] knew that [Davis] considered Mr. Boesky adversarial;" and Mulheren agreed with Davis' unflattering assessment of Boesky. In a telephone conversation sometime between this October 3 meeting and a subsequent meeting between the two on October 9, 1985, Mulheren told Davis that he believed that Boesky did not own any G & W securities. Mulheren also said that he did not own any G & W stock either. When Davis and Mulheren met again on October 9, they spoke only about Mulheren's CBS proposal.

In the meantime, Boesky continued to press Davis to accept his proposals to secure control of G & W. When Boesky called Davis after their October 1, 1985 meeting, Davis "told [Boesky] as clearly as [he] could again that [G & W] had no interest whatsoever in doing anything with [Boesky]." Boesky then decided to contact his representative at Goldman, Sachs & Co. to arrange the sale of his massive block of stock to G & W. Boesky advised Goldman, Sachs that G & W common stock was not trading at $45 per share at the time, "but that should it become 45," he wanted to sell. A Goldman, Sachs representative met with Davis shortly thereafter regarding the company's repurchase of Boesky's G & W shares.

Sometime after the close of the market on October 16, 1985, Boesky called Davis, offering to sell his block of shares back to G & W at $45 per share. NYSE trading had closed that day at $44 3/4 per share, although at one point during that day it had reached $45. Davis told Boesky that the company would buy his shares back, but only at the "last sale"—the price at which the stock traded on the NYSE at the time of the sale—and that Boesky should have his Goldman, Sachs representative contact Kidder Peabody & Co. to arrange the transaction.

After this conversation with Davis, but before 11:00 a.m. on October 17, 1985, Boesky called Mulheren. According to Boesky's testimony, the following, critical exchange took place:

BOESKY: Mr. Mulheren asked me if I liked the stock on that particular day, and I said yes, I still liked it. At the time it was trading at 44 3/4. I said I liked it; however, I would not pay more than 45 for it and it would be great if it traded at 45. The design for the comment—

DEFENSE COUNSEL MR. PUCCIO: Objection to the "design of the comment." I would ask only for the conversation.

A.U.S.A. GILBERT: What if anything did he say to you?

BOESKY: I understand.

Shortly after 11:00 a.m. on October 17, 1985, Jamie (Mulheren's company) placed an order with Oliver Ihasz, a floor broker, to purchase 50,000 shares of G & W at the market price. Trading in G & W had been sluggish that morning (only 32,200 shares had traded between 9:30 a.m. and 11:03 a.m.), and the market price was holding steady at $44 3/4, the price at which it had closed the day before. At 11:04 a.m., Ihasz purchased 16,100 shares at $44 3/4 per share. Unable to fill the entire 50,000 share order at $44 3/4, Ihasz purchased the remaining 33,900 shares between 11:05 a.m. and 11:08 a.m. at $44 7/8 per share.

At 11:09 a.m., Ihasz received another order from Jamie; this time, to purchase 25,000 shares of G & W for no more than $45 per share. After attempting to execute the trade at $44 7/8, Ihasz executed the additional 25,000 share purchase at $45 per share at 11:10 a.m. In sum, between 11:04 a.m. and 11:10 a.m., Jamie purchased a total of 75,000 shares of G & W common stock, causing the price at which it traded per share to rise from $44 3/4 to $45. At 11:17 a.m., Boesky and Icahn sold their G & W stock—6,715,700 shares between them—back to the company at $45 per share. Trading in G & W closed on the NYSE on October 17, 1985 at $43 5/8 per share. At the end of the day, Jamie's trading in G & W common stock at Mulheren's direction had caused it to lose $64,406.

A convicted defendant, of course, bears "a very heavy burden" to demonstrate that the evidence at trial was insufficient to prove his guilt beyond a reasonable doubt. * * * On this appeal, however, we are reminded that "in America we still respect the dignity of the individual, and [a defendant] . . . is not to be imprisoned except on definite proof of a specific crime." United States v. Bufalino, 285 F.2d 408, 420 (2d Cir.1960)

(Clark, J., concurring). To that end, it is "imperative that we not rend the fabric of evidence and examine each shred in isolation; rather, the reviewing court 'must use its experience with people and events in weighing the chances that the evidence correctly points to guilt against the possibility of innocent or ambiguous inference.'" United States v. Redwine, 715 F.2d 315, 319 (7th Cir.1983) (quoting United States v. Kwitek, 467 F.2d 1222, 1226 (7th Cir.), cert. denied, 409 U.S. 1079, 93 S.Ct. 702, 34 L.Ed.2d 668 (1972)), cert. denied, 467 U.S. 1216, 104 S.Ct. 2661, 81 L.Ed.2d 367 (1984).

The government's theory of prosecution in this case is straightforward. In its view, when an investor, who is neither a fiduciary nor an insider, engages in securities transactions in the open market with the sole intent to affect the price of the security, the transaction is manipulative and violates Rule 10b–5.2 Unlawful manipulation occurs, the argument goes, even though the investor has not acted for the "purpose of inducing the purchase or sale of such security by others," an element the government would have had to prove had it chosen to proceed under the manipulation statute, Sec. 9(a)(2). 15 U.S.C. Sec. 78i(a)(2). Mulheren was not charged with violating Sec. 9(a)(2). When the transaction is effected for an investment purpose, the theory continues, there is no manipulation, even if an increase or diminution in price was a foreseeable consequence of the investment.

Although we have misgivings about the government's view of the law, we will assume, without deciding on this appeal, that an investor may lawfully be convicted under Rule 10b–5 where the purpose of his transaction is solely to affect the price of a security. The issue then becomes one of Mulheren's subjective intent. The government was obligated to prove beyond a reasonable doubt that when Mulheren purchased 75,000 shares of G & W common stock on October 17, 1985, he did it with the intent to raise its price, rather than with the intent to invest. We conclude that the government failed to carry this burden. * * *

The strongest evidence supporting an inference that Mulheren harbored a manipulative intent, is the telephone conversation between Boesky and Mulheren that occurred either late in the day on October 16 or before 11:00 a.m. on October 17, 1985. In discussing the virtues of G & W stock, Boesky told Mulheren that he "would not pay more than 45 for it and it would be great if it traded at 45." To this Mulheren replied "I understand." The meaning of this cryptic conversation is, at best, ambiguous, and we reject the government's contention that this conversation "clearly conveyed Boesky's request that the price of the stock be pushed up to $45 . . . [and Mulheren's] agreement to help." Boesky never testified (again, he was not asked) what he meant by his words.

We acknowledge that, construed as an innocent tip—i.e. G & W would be a "great" buy at a price of $45 or below—the conversation appears contradictory. It seems inconsistent for Boesky to advise, on one hand, that he would not pay more than $45, yet on the other to exclaim that it would be a bargain ("great") at $45. The conversation does not make any more sense, however, if construed as a request for illicit manipulation. That Boesky put a limit on the price he would pay for the stock ("I would not pay more than 45 for it") seems inconsistent with a request to drive up the price of the stock. If a conspiracy to manipulate for his own selfish benefit had been Boesky's intent, and if Davis were poised to repurchase the shares at the "last sale," Boesky would obviously have preferred to see Mulheren drive the trading in G & W stock to a price above $45. In this regard, it is noteworthy that there was no evidence whatever that Mulheren knew of Boesky's demand to get $45 per share from G & W. Moreover, during the four to six weeks preceding this conversation, Mulheren repeatedly asked Boesky what he thought of G & W—evincing Mulheren's predisposition (and Boesky's knowledge thereof) to invest in the company. In fact, Mulheren took a position in G & W when he shorted a broker 25,000 shares of G & W after the market closed on October 16.

Clearly, this case would be much less troubling had Boesky said "I want you to bring it up to 45" or, perhaps, even, "I'd like to see it trading at 45." But to hang a conviction on the threadbare phrase "it would be great if it traded at 45," particularly when the government does not suggest that the words were some sort of sinister code, defies reason and a sense of fair play. Any doubt about this is dispelled by the remaining evidence at trial.

First, and perhaps most telling, is that Jamie lost over $64,000 on Mulheren's October 17th transactions. This is hardly the result a market manipulator seeks to achieve. One of the hallmarks of manipulation is some profit or personal gain inuring to the alleged manipulator. See, e.g., Baum v. Phillips, Appel & Walden, Inc., 648 F. Supp. 1518, 1531 (S.D.N.Y.1986), aff'd per curiam, 867 F.2d 776 (2d Cir.), cert. denied, ___ U.S. ___, 110 S.Ct. 114, 107 L.Ed.2d 75 (1989); Walck v. American Stock Exchange, Inc., 565 F.Supp. 1051, 1065–66 (E.D.Pa.1981), aff'd, 687 F.2d 778 (3rd Cir.1982), cert. denied, 461 U.S. 942, 103 S.Ct. 2118, 77 L.Ed.2d 1300 (1983); SEC v. Commonwealth Chemical Securities, Inc., 410 F.Supp. 1002, 1013 (S.D.N.Y.1976), aff'd in part, modified on other grounds, 574 F.2d 90 (2d Cir.1978).

Second, the unrebutted trial testimony of the G & W specialist demonstrated that if raising the price of G & W to $45 per share was Mulheren's sole intent, Mulheren purchased significantly more shares (and put Jamie in a position of greater risk) than necessary to achieve the result. The G & W specialist testified that at the time Jamie placed its second order, 5,000 shares would "definitely" have raised the trading price from $44 7/8 to $45 per share. Yet, Jamie bought 25,000 shares.

Although there was no evidence that Mulheren received a quid pro quo from Boesky for buying G & W stock, the government, nevertheless, claims that Mulheren had a "strong pecuniary interest" in accommodating Boesky in order to maintain the close and mutually profitable relationship they enjoyed. With this argument the government is hoist with its own petard. Precisely because of this past profitable relationship, the more reasonable conclusion is that Mulheren understood Boesky's comment as another tip—this time to buy G & W stock. Indeed, there was no evidence that Boesky had ever asked Mulheren to rig the price of a stock in the past.

None of the traditional badges of manipulation are present in this case. Mulheren conspicuously purchased the shares for Jamie's account in the open market. Compare United States v. Scop, 846 F.2d 135, 137 (matched orders through fictitious nominees), modified on other grounds, 856 F.2d 5 (2d Cir.1988); United States v. Gilbert, 668 F.2d 94, 95 (2d Cir.1981) (matched orders and wash sales) cert. denied, 456 U.S. 946, 102 S.Ct. 2014, 72 L.Ed.2d 469 (1982); United States v. Minuse, 114 F.2d 36, 38 (2d Cir.1940) (fictitious accounts, matched orders, wash sales, dissemination of false literature). The government argues that Mulheren's deceptive intent can be inferred from the fact that (1) he purchased the G & W shares through Ihasz, a floor broker whom the government claims was used only infrequently by Jamie; and (2) Ihasz never informed anyone that the purchases were made for Jamie. These arguments are factually flawed.

There was no evidence that there was anything unusual about Ihasz's execution of the trades. Oliver Ihasz testified that Jamie was a customer of his company. There was no testimony that his company was used infrequently, or that Mulheren's request was in any way out of the ordinary. Nor is there anything peculiar about the fact that Ihasz disclosed only the name of the clearing broker and not Jamie, as the purchaser, when he executed the trade. As Ihasz testified, in an open market transaction, the only information the floor broker provides to the seller is the name of the clearing broker, not the ultimate buyer. Jamie was conspicuously identified as the ultimate buyer of the G & W securities on Ihasz's order tickets, where it is supposed to appear.

The government also argues that manipulative intent can be inferred from the fact that Mulheren's purchase on October 17, 1985 comprised 70 percent of the trading in G & W common stock during the period between the opening of the market and 11:10 a.m. Such market domination, the government contends, is indicative of manipulation. While we agree, as a general proposition, that market domination is a factor that supports a manipulation charge, the extent to which an investor controls or dominates the market at any given period of time cannot be viewed in a vacuum. For example, if only ten shares of a stock are bought or sold in a given hour and only by one investor, that investor has created 100 percent of the activity in that stock in that hour. This alone, however, does not make the investor a manipulator. The percent of domination must be viewed in light of the time period involved and other indicia of manipulation. * * *

The government also urges that Mulheren's manipulative intent—as opposed to investment intent—can be inferred from certain of Mulheren's actions after his purchase of the G & W shares. For example, Mulheren sold G & W call options in the afternoon of October 17, 1985 that were designed to create a hedge in the event of a drop in the price of stock. Had Mulheren known, however, that Boesky and Icahn were going to unload 6.7 million shares of G & W stock—which had the inevitable effect of driving the price down—surely Mulheren would have had the foresight to write the options before Boesky and Icahn had a chance to sell. That Mulheren wrote the options in the afternoon suggests only that he was attempting to mitigate his losses.

Finally, the government contends that the fact that Mulheren continued to do favors for Boesky after G & W repurchased Boesky and Icahn's shares is inconsistent with his claim that he was "duped" by Boesky into purchasing the 75,000 G & W shares. We disagree. First, the evidence of "favors" rests largely on the unproven "stock parking" charges. Second, Mulheren's conduct after his G & W purchases is equally consistent with that of a sophisticated businessman who turns the other cheek after being slapped by the hand that usually feeds him.

We acknowledge that this case treads dangerously close to the line between legitimate inference and impermissible speculation. We are persuaded, however, that to come to the conclusion it did, "the jury must have engaged in false surmise and rank speculation." United States v. Wiley, 846 F.2d 150, 155 (2d Cir.1988) (citing United States v. Starr, 816 F.2d 94, 99 (2d Cir.1987)). At best, Mulheren's convictions are based on evidence that is "at least as consistent with innocence as with guilt," United States v. Mankani, 738 F.2d 538, 547 (2d Cir.1984), and "on inferences no more valid than others equally supported by reason and experience." United States v. Bufalino, 285 F.2d 408, 419 (2d Cir.1960). Accordingly, the judgments of conviction are reversed and Counts One through Four of the indictment are dismissed.

NOTES

1. The Mulheren case gave rise to a debate over whether "open market" trades could be manipulative. An open market trade is a bona fide

transaction in which the actor is intending to create an artificial price that does not have price risk. A "closed market" trade is non-bona fide trade (such as a "wash sale," which is described below) that is intended to create an artificial price, and has no price risk. The SEC believes "that open-market activities amount to market manipulation if the trader's 'sole intent' in placing an order is to move the price of a stock. In other words, the SEC considers manipulation to occur when, absent manipulative intent, the trader would not have made the bid or offer." David L. Kornblau, Allison Lurton & Jonathan M. Sperling, Market Manipulation and Algorithmic Trading: The Next Wave of Regulatory Enforcement? 44 Sec. Reg. & L. Rep. (BNA) 369, 370 (Feb. 20, 2012).

2. In Markowski v. SEC, 274 F.3d 525 (D.C. Cir. 2001), cert. denied, 537 U.S. 819 (2002), the court noted the debate among commentators over the circumstances under which liability for manipulation should be imposed where open-market trades are involved. The court concluded that it could not find the SEC's interpretation to be unreasonable in light of what appears to be the determination of Congress that manipulation can be illegal solely because of the actor's purpose.

3. In ATSI Communications Inc. v. The Shaar Fund Ltd., 493 F.3d 87, 100–101 (2d Cir. 2007), the Second Circuit reviewed the manipulation standards set by the various circuit courts and noted that existing case law requires "a showing that an alleged manipulator engaged in market activity aimed at deceiving investors as to how other market participants have valued a security." The courts look to see "whether trading activity sends a false pricing signal to the market."

4. The CFTC has also asserted that open market trades may be manipulative. See, Prohibition of Market Manipulation, 75 Fed. Reg. 67657, 67661 (Nov. 3, 2010). The following unpublished opinion by the Second Circuit also concerned open market trades.

DIPLACIDO V. CFTC

364 Fed. Appx. 657 (2d Cir. 2009), cert. denied, 559 U.S. 1025 (2010)

Anthony J. DiPlacido seeks review of the Commission's 79-page decision affirming an administrative law judge's ("ALJ") determination that he manipulated settlement prices for electricity futures contracts. DiPlacido argues that (1) the decision violates due process, because he lacked notice of the theory of manipulation under which he was found liable; (2) the applied theory of manipulation was erroneous as a matter of law; (3) the weight of the evidence does not support a finding of liability; (4) the ALJ made improper evidentiary rulings and exhibited bias; and (5) the sanctions imposed were excessive. We assume familiarity with the facts and the record of prior proceedings, which we reference only as necessary to explain our decision.

DiPlacido's due process challenge is without merit. Due process requires that "a regulation carrying penal sanctions . . . give fair warning of the conduct it prohibits or requires." *Rollins Envtl. Servs. (NJ) Inc. v. U.S. EPA,* 937 F.2d 649, 653 n.2, 290 U.S. App. D.C. 331 (D.C. Cir. 1991) (internal quotation marks omitted). Although "[a]n agency is free . . . to interpret its governing statute case by case through adjudicatory proceedings rather than by rulemaking," if it "suddenly changes its view . . . with respect to what transactions are bona fide trading transactions," it may not then "charge a knowing violation of that revised standard and thereby cause undue prejudice to a litigant who may have relied on [its] prior policy or interpretation." *Stoller v. CFTC,* 834 F.2d 262, 265–66 (2d Cir. 1987) (internal quotation marks and citations omitted).

Citing the Commission's observation that his case raised "issues of first impression," *In re DiPlacido,* Comm. Fut. L. Rep. (CCH) P 30,970, 2008 CFTC LEXIS 101, at *1, 2008 WL 4831204, at *1 (CFTC Nov. 5, 2008), DiPlacido complains that this is the first time the Commission has found manipulation "based solely on trade practices," Appellant's Br. 11. We disagree. As the Commission itself observed, the theory applied in this case was adopted in *In re Henner,* a case brought by its predecessor agency under a statute that is the substantive equivalent of the one at issue here, and concerning closely analogous facts. 30 Agric. Dec. 1151 (1971) (finding manipulation where trader "intentionally paid more than he would have had to pay . . . for the purpose of causing the closing quotation [to increase]"); *see also In re Zenith-Godley,* 6 Agric. Dec. 900 (1947) (holding that actions of trader constituted manipulation). The Commission also noted that, subsequent to *Henner,* it had pursued trade-based manipulation cases.

DiPlacido argues further that the Commission denied due process by abandoning an existing requirement for proof of defendant's control over the relevant market. The Commission's well-established precedents are plainly to the contrary, indicating that market control may be a feature of some forms of manipulation, *e.g.,* a "corner" or "squeeze," but is *not* a requirement of manipulation in all its forms. *See, e.g., In re Hohenberg Bros. Co.,* [1975–1977 Transfer Binder] No. 75–4, Comm. Fut. L. Rep. (CCH) P 20,271, 1977 CFTC LEXIS 123, at *24, 1977 WL 13562, at *7 (CFTC Feb. 18, 1977) ("A dominant or controlling position in the market is not a requisite element to either manipulation or attempted manipulation. . . .").

Thus, this is not a case like *Stoller v. CFTC,* in which the agency suddenly changed its position and banned a "commonplace" practice. 834 F.2d at 265. Rather, the Commission's reading of the broad language of 7 U.S.C. § 13(a) is consistent with prior readings and with its own practice. *See, e.g., In re Indiana Farm Bureau Coop. Ass'n, Inc.,* [1982–1984 Transfer Binder] No. 75–14, Comm. Fut. L. Rep. (CCH) P 21,796, 1982

CFTC LEXIS 25, at *8, 1982 WL 30249, at *3 (CFTC Dec. 17, 1982) (citing definition of manipulation as "any and every operation or transaction or practice, the purpose of which is not primarily to facilitate the movement of the commodity at prices freely responsive to the forces of supply and demand; but, on the contrary, is calculated to produce a price distortion"). Further, DiPlacido's own actions, not least his instruction to Livingston to use the code words "don't be shy," rather than instructing him to "buy contracts worst or sell them worst," Arb. Tr. 107, suggest actual notice that his conduct was wrongful.

Accordingly, we identify no denial of due process.

DiPlacido claims that the Commission's definition of manipulation is arbitrary and capricious. Our review of the Commission's legal judgments is plenary, *Piccolo v. CFTC*, 388 F.3d 387, 389 (2d Cir. 2004), but "where a question implicates Commission expertise, we defer to the Commission's decision if it is reasonable," *id.; see also Chevron, U.S.A., Inc. v. Natural Res. Defense Council*, 467 U.S. 837, 844, 104 S. Ct. 2778, 81 L. Ed. 2d 694 (1984).

In the absence of a statutory definition of "manipulation," the Commission has established a four-part test under which it will find manipulation where a preponderance of the evidence shows "(1) that the accused had the ability to influence market prices; (2) that [he] specifically intended to do so; (3) that artificial prices existed; and (4) that the accused caused the artificial prices." *In re Cox* [1986–1987 Transfer Binder] No. 75–16, Comm. Fut. L. Rep. (CCH) P 23,786, 1987 CFTC LEXIS 325, at *9, 1987 WL 106879, at *3 (CFTC July 15, 1987). It applied this test in DiPlacido's case.

DiPlacido argues that because "[e]veryone in the market has the ability to affect the market price," the Commission erred in not imposing a further market-control requirement. Appellant's Br. 35. Even supposing that all large traders in illiquid markets possess the ability to influence those markets, the Commission's inclusion of "the ability to influence the market price," rather than market control, as an element of manipulation is hardly arbitrary or capricious, as three other elements, including specific intent, must also be satisfied to establish liability. *Cf. Colautti v. Franklin*, 439 U.S. 379, 395, 99 S. Ct. 675, 58 L. Ed. 2d 596 (1979) (collecting cases and recognizing that "constitutionality of a vague statutory standard is closely related to whether that standard incorporates a requirement of *mens rea*"); *United States v. Curcio*, 712 F.2d 1532, 1543 (2d Cir. 1983) (Friendly, J.) (same).

DiPlacido further challenges the Commission's standard on the ground that the elements of the four-part test "collapse[ ]" into one—uneconomic trading—so that a violation exists wherever bids and offers are violated, and even lawful hedging may constitute manipulation.

Appellant's Br. 39. We are not persuaded. The Commission stated that "violating bids and offers—*in order to influence prices*" was "sufficient to show manipulative intent." *In re DiPlacido*, 2008 CFTC LEXIS 101, 2008 WL 4831204, at *26 (emphasis added). Its finding of intent thus depended not merely on DiPlacido's having violated bids and offers, but also on taped conversations signaling manipulative intent and the ALJ's finding that DiPlacido's denial of intent lacked credibility. Further, the Commission cited evidence (including expert testimony) that artificial prices were a "reasonably probable consequence" of DiPlacido's large trades made during the close in an illiquid market. *Id.* 2008 CFTC LEXIS 101, [WL] at *32. Thus the Commission carefully applied all four elements of the traditional test, and DiPlacido's challenge to the reasonableness of the Commission's "new theory," Appellant's Br. 39, misses its mark.

We reject DiPlacido's claim that the evidence does not support a finding of liability for manipulation. The Commission's findings of fact, "if supported by the weight of the evidence, shall . . . be conclusive." 7 U.S.C. § 9. Our review of such findings is "narrow." *Reddy v. CFTC*, 191 F.3d 109, 117 (2d Cir. 1999); *see also Haltmier v. CFTC*, 554 F.2d 556, 560 (2d Cir. 1977) (describing court's role as "something other than that of mechanically reweighing the evidence to ascertain in which direction it preponderates; it is rather to review the record with the purpose of determining whether the finder of the fact was justified, i.e. acted reasonably" (internal quotation marks omitted)).

The Commission acted reasonably in concluding that DiPlacido had the ability to influence prices where, on the relevant dates, his trades over two minutes at the Close accounted for an average 14% of a full day's volume. Likewise reasonable was the determination that DiPlacido's trades established artificial prices, given that several witnesses testified that he violated bids and offers. *See In re Eisler*, No. 01–14, Comm. Fut. L. Rep. (CCH) P 29,664, 2004 CFTC LEXIS 9, at *18, 2004 WL 77924, at *6 (CFTC Jan. 20, 2004) (discussing artificial prices). Finally, we detect no unreasonableness either in the Commission's intent finding, based in part on the referenced taped telephone calls, or in its reliance on expert testimony that DiPlacido's actions were a likely cause of artificial prices. * * *

We have reviewed DiPlacido's remaining arguments and find them to be without merit. Accordingly, the petition for review is GRANTED, the Commission's decision is MODIFIED to reduce the civil penalty by $320,000, and the decision of the Commission as modified is AFFIRMED.

5. AIDING AND ABETTING MANIPULATION

GRACEY V. J.P. MORGAN CHASE & CO. (IN RE AMARANTH NATURAL GAS COMMODITIES LITIG.)

2013 U.S. App. LEXIS 19444 (2d Cir.)

Opinion by: DEBRA ANN LIVINGSTON:

In the fall of 2006, Amaranth Advisors LLC ("Amaranth"), a hedge fund that had heavily invested in natural gas futures, collapsed. A Senate investigation would later conclude that Amaranth, in the months leading up to its demise, had taken positions in natural gas futures and swaps so massive that its trading directly affected domestic natural gas prices and price volatility. *See Staff Report of S. Permanent Subcomm. on Investigations, Comm. on Homeland Security and Governmental Affairs, 110th Cong., Excessive Speculation in the Natural Gas Market* 6 (2007) ("Senate Report"). Plaintiffs-Appellants, traders who had bought or sold natural gas futures during these same months, filed a complaint in the United States District Court for the Southern District of New York alleging that Amaranth had manipulated the price of natural gas futures in violation of the Commodities Exchange Act ("CEA"), 7 U.S.C. § 1 *et seq.* Plaintiffs-Appellants also alleged that Defendants-Appellees J.P. Morgan Chase & Co., J.P. Morgan Chase Bank, Inc., and J.P. Morgan Futures, Inc. ("J.P. Futures") (collectively, "J.P. Morgan") had aided and abetted Amaranth's manipulation of natural gas futures through J.P. Futures's services as Amaranth's futures commission merchant and clearing broker. The district court (Scheindlin, J.), in October 6, 2008 and April 27, 2009 orders, concluded that both Plaintiffs-Appellants' complaint and amended complaint failed to state claims against J.P. Morgan.

Plaintiffs-Appellants argue on appeal that the district court did not apply the correct standard for evaluating the sufficiency of their amended complaint and likewise failed to recognize the amended complaint's well-pleaded allegations that J.P. Futures aided and abetted Amaranth's manipulation within the meaning of Section 22 of the CEA, 7 U.S.C. § 25(a). We conclude that the district court did not err in concluding that Plaintiffs-Appellants' amended complaint failed to state a claim against J.P. Futures. Because we conclude that this is so even under the pleading standards that Plaintiffs-Appellants argue should apply, we do not decide whether the district court's application of a more stringent standard was error.

The CEA prohibits manipulation of the price of any commodity or commodity future. *See* 7 U.S.C. §§ 9(1), 13(a)(2). While the CEA itself does not define the term, a court will find manipulation where "(1) Defendants possessed an ability to influence market prices; (2) an artificial price existed; (3) Defendants caused the artificial prices; and (4) Defendants specifically intended to cause the artificial price."[1] *Hershey v. Energy Transfer Partners, L.P.*, 610 F.3d 239, 247 (5th Cir. 2010). This case is about the alleged manipulation of natural gas futures traded on the New York Mercantile Exchange ("NYMEX"). The alleged manipulative scheme, however, also involved a second standardized energy contract: natural gas swaps traded on the Intercontinental Exchange ("ICE"), an electronic exchange based in Atlanta, Georgia. A full understanding of Plaintiffs-Appellants' allegations requires background on both of these financial instruments and their respective exchanges.

NYMEX is a futures and options exchange based in New York City. *N.Y. Mercantile Exch. v. IntercontinentalExchange, Inc.*, 497 F.3d 109, 110 (2d Cir. 2007). We have previously described the basic features of commodity futures trading:

> A commodities futures contract is an executory contract for the sale of a commodity executed at a specific point in time with delivery of the commodity postponed to a future date. Every commodities futures contract has a seller and a buyer. The seller, called a "short," agrees for a price, fixed at the time of contract, to deliver a specified quantity and grade of an identified commodity at a date in the future. The buyer, or "long," agrees to accept delivery at that future date at the price fixed in the contract. It is the rare case when buyers and sellers settle their obligations under futures contracts by actually delivering the commodity. Rather, they routinely take a short or long position in order to speculate on the future price of the commodity. Then, sometime before delivery is due, they offset or liquidate their positions by entering the market again and purchasing an equal number of opposite contracts, *i.e.*, a short buys long, a long buys short. In this way their obligations under the original liquidating contracts offset each other. The difference in price between the original contract and the offsetting contract determines the amount of money made or lost.

---

[1] Since the events alleged in Plaintiffs-Appellants' amended complaint, the CEA has undergone some significant changes. Among them, Congress amended 7 U.S.C. § 9(1) to prohibit the use of "any manipulative or deceptive device or contrivance, in contravention of such rules and regulations as the [Commodity Futures Trading] Commission shall promulgate." *See* Dodd-Frank Wall Street Reform and Consumer Protection Act, Pub. L. No. 111–203, Tit. VII, § 753(a), 124 Stat. 1376, 1750 (2010); *see also* 7 U.S.C. § 25(a)(2) (providing private right of action for violation of such rules and regulations). The Commodity Futures Trading Commission ("CFTC") has since promulgated a regulation making it unlawful for any person to "intentionally or recklessly" manipulate prices through various deceitful or fraudulent conduct. *See* 17 C.F.R. § 180.1(a) (2013). This regulation does not impact the present appeal, however, given the regulation's effective date of August 15, 2011. *See* Prohibition on the Employment or Attempted Employment of Manipulative and Deceptive Devices, 76 Fed. Reg. 41398, 41398 (July 14, 2011). The CFTC also promulgated a separate regulation at the same time for cases of manipulation not involving deceitful or fraudulent devices, and explained that interpretation of that regulation "will be guided" by existing law on commodities manipulation. *See* 17 C.F.R. § 180.2 (2013); 76 Fed. Reg. at 41407.

Strobl v. N.Y. Mercantile Exch., 768 F.2d 22, 24 (2d Cir. 1985).

One type of futures contract traded on NYMEX is for the delivery of natural gas. In its standard form, this contract obligates the buyer to purchase 10,000 MMBtu2 of natural gas released during the contract's delivery month at the Henry Hub distribution facility in Erath, Louisiana. Trading on the future begins five years before the delivery month and ends three business days before the first calendar day of the delivery month. To determine the future's final price, NYMEX uses a weighted average of the trades executed during the final half hour of trading—2:00 to 2:30 P.M.—on the last trading day. This final half hour is referred to as the contract's "final settlement period," and final price as the "final settlement price."

NYMEX is a designated contract market, or "DCM." As a DCM, NYMEX may offer options and futures trading for any type of commodity, but is subject to extensive oversight from the Commodity Futures Trading Commission ("CFTC"). *See* 7 U.S.C. §§ 6(a)(1). Among other things, NYMEX must maintain an internal monitoring and compliance program that meets statutory criteria listed in the CEA. *See id.* § 7. One of these criteria is that NYMEX establish position limits and accountability levels for each type of contract that it offers for trading. *See id.* § 7(d)(5). A "position limit" is a cap on the number of contracts that a trader may hold or control for a particular option or future at a particular time, with exceptions provided for traders engaged in bona fide hedging. *See id.* § 6a(a)(2)(A), (c)(1). An "accountability level" provides that once a trader holds or controls a certain number of contracts for a particular option or future she must provide information about that position upon request by the exchange and, if the exchange so orders, stop increasing her position. At the time of the events alleged in the amended complaint, NYMEX had set a position limit of 1,000 contracts, net short or net long, for any natural gas future, applicable during the last three days of trading. NYMEX had also set corresponding accountability limits, which varied in size based on the trader's capitalization and applied at all times the future was traded.

All trades on NYMEX must go through the exchange's clearinghouse. To finalize, or "clear," a trade, traders must transact with a NYMEX clearing member—a firm approved as a member of the clearinghouse. The seller's clearing firm will sell the contract to the clearinghouse, which then sells the contract to the buyer's clearing firm. Through this act of simultaneously buying and selling the contract, the clearinghouse guarantees both sides of the trade and ensures that neither buyer nor seller is exposed to any counterparty credit risk. The clearing firms, in turn, guarantee their clients' performance to the clearinghouse.

To protect itself from risk of nonpayment, the NYMEX clearinghouse requires that its members deposit margin sufficient to cover any potential short-term losses on their clients' open positions. At the end of each trading day, the clearinghouse examines the change in value to these positions and determines whether the firm must post additional margin (generally the case if value has decreased) or receives payment on margin (generally the case if value has increased). This process is called "marking-to-market." *See N.Y. Mercantile Exch.*, 497 F.3d at 111. Clearing firms engage in the same process with their customers, requiring an initial margin payment for any newly acquired position and conducting a daily recalculation of that margin requirement as the position changes in value.

In addition to clearing members, traders on NYMEX also interact with futures commissions merchants, or "FCMs." "An FCM is the commodity market's equivalent of a securities brokerage house, soliciting and accepting orders for futures contracts and accepting funds or extending credit in connection therewith." *First Am. Discount Corp. v. CFTC*, 222 F.3d 1008, 1010, 343 U.S. App. D.C. 71 (D.C. Cir. 2000); *see also* 7 U.S.C. § 1a(28). FCMs must register with the CFTC, *see id.* § 6d(a)(1), and are subject to numerous regulatory requirements. A firm may be both a clearing member and an FCM. Such dual status would enable it to both accept orders from clients and clear any resulting trades.

ICE is an electronic commodity exchange based in Atlanta, Georgia. At the time of the events alleged in the amended complaint, ICE offered trading in natural gas swaps[3] Swaps, unlike futures contracts, do not contemplate delivery of the underlying commodity. Rather, in a typical commodity swap, the buyer agrees to pay the seller a fixed amount of money and the seller agrees to pay the buyer the price of an underlying commodity at the time the swap expires. For ICE's Natural Gas Henry Hub Swap, this "floating value" paid by the seller was the final settlement value of the NYMEX natural gas future for the corresponding month. Hence, if the final settlement value of the NYMEX natural gas future was above whatever price the buyer paid for the swap, the buyer would profit; if it was below, the seller would.

Since the settlement price of an ICE Henry Hub natural gas swap was pegged to the final settlement price of the corresponding NYMEX natural gas future, the two instruments were functionally identical for risk management purposes. Indeed, arbitrageurs ensured that their prices moved in virtual lockstep with one another. Whether a trader decided to transact in ICE swaps or in NYMEX futures often depended on factors such as which market had greater liquidity.

---

[3] ICE has since stopped offering natural gas swaps for trading, and instead offers trading in natural gas futures and options. *See* Press Release, *ICE Completes Transition of Energy Swaps to Futures* (Oct. 16, 2012), http://ir.theice.com/releasedetail.cfm?ReleaseID=713717.

An important difference between the two instruments, however, was that ICE did not face the same level of regulatory oversight as did NYMEX. At the time of the events alleged in the amended complaint, ICE qualified as an "exempt commercial market," or "ECM," under the CEA.[4] While this status limited both the type of instruments ICE could offer for trading and the parties that could trade them, it also exempted ICE from most of the regulatory obligations placed upon NYMEX. *See* 7 U.S.C. § 2(h)(3) (2006). As an ECM, ICE did not have to set position limits or accountability levels, nor did it need to monitor trading to ensure compliance with market rules and prevent manipulation.

At the time of the events alleged in the amended complaint, ICE did not have a central clearinghouse. ICE did, however, permit its traders to employ clearing firms, and many of the companies that operated as clearing firms on NYMEX also operated as clearing firms on ICE.

The following facts are taken from the amended complaint, the allegations of which we accept as true, as well as from other materials referenced in the amended complaint. *See, e.g., ONY, Inc. v. Cornerstone Therapeutics, Inc.*, 720 F.3d 490, 496 (2d Cir. 2013).

Amaranth was a multi-strategy hedge fund based in Greenwich, Connecticut. Founded in 2000, Amaranth initially pursued an investment strategy that did not particularly focus on energy trading. This changed over the next half-decade, however, and by 2005 energy trading consumed over thirty percent of Amaranth's capital. Amaranth profited from this focus on energy when, in late 2005, Hurricanes Katrina and Rita disrupted domestic natural gas distribution. The resultant spike in prices produced returns on Amaranth's investments so large that energy trading would ultimately account for 98% of the fund's 2005 performance. By the beginning of 2006, Amaranth managed over $8 billion in assets and employed over 400 people.

Amaranth continued to focus on energy trading in 2006. Among other things, it began to acquire large "spread" positions in NYMEX natural gas futures.[6] Specifically, Amaranth acquired "calendar" spreads between natural gas futures for different months. Since many homes and businesses use it for indoor heating, natural gas has a highly seasonal

---

[4] In 2008, Congress increased the CFTC's oversight of any ECM that offered trading in products the CFTC deemed to be "significant price discovery contracts." *See* Food, Conservation, and Energy Act of 2008, Pub. L. No. 110–246, Tit. XIII, Sub. B, 124 Stat. 1651, 2197–2204. Two years later, the Dodd-Frank Wall Street Reform and Consumer Protection Act repealed the statutory basis for ECMs. *See* Dodd-Frank Act § 723, 123 Stat. at 1675 (repealing 7 U.S.C. § 2(h)(3)–(5)). The effective date of this repeal was July 16, 2011. *Id.* The CFTC, however, has conditionally exempted preexisting ECMs from compliance with the new laws as it works to implement Dodd-Frank's changes. *See* CFTC Letter No. 13–28, No-Action Letter (June 17, 2013) (providing conditional no-action relief until October 2, 2013).

[6] A spread position is created when a trader takes a long position in one future and a short position in another. The trader seeks to profit from changes in the difference between the two futures' prices, rather than from any absolute changes to the futures' prices themselves.

price that rises in the colder winter months and falls in the warmer summer months. By taking large spread positions, Amaranth was betting that the difference between these winter and summer prices would increase.

Amaranth started to build up short positions for the March 2006, April 2006, and November 2006 NYMEX natural gas futures, while at the same time acquiring a long position for the January 2007 future. The sizes of these positions were exceptional. Most traders consider control of only a few hundred contracts to be a substantial position; a position of 10,000 NYMEX natural gas futures contracts, meanwhile, will produce $1,000,000 in profit or loss for every cent of price change. Amaranth, however, soon acquired positions of over 40,000 March 2006 and 27,000 April 2006 contracts. These positions also represented a substantial share of the market. By February, Amaranth controlled over half of the open interest on NYMEX November 2006 natural gas futures contracts, and held a similar percentage of January 2007 contracts.

While Amaranth was building its spread positions during the first half of 2006, it also engaged in several unusual transactions, referred to by Plaintiffs-Appellants in their amended complaint as "slamming the close" trades. These trades all followed the same pattern: in the weeks leading up to a NYMEX future's expiration, Amaranth would simultaneously acquire a long position in the future and a short position in the corresponding swap on ICE. Then, during the last half hour of trading on the final trading day—the final settlement period—Amaranth would sell most or all of its long position, thus lowering the future's final settlement price. This would then lower the final settlement price of the corresponding ICE swap, allowing Amaranth to profit from its short position in that swap.

Amaranth engaged in these "slamming the close" trades for the March 2006, April 2006, and May 2006 NYMEX natural gas futures. For example, on the March 2006 future's final trading day, Amaranth acquired a long position in the future of over 3,000 contracts. It then sold off this position during the future's final settlement period, lowering the future's final price by $0.29 and realizing a gain for its short positions of over $29 million. Amaranth engaged in similar conduct the next two months, building up a large long position, selling it off during the final settlement period, and profiting by virtue of short positions on ICE as well as in other NYMEX natural gas futures also suppressed in price by the trades. Subsequent investigations would reveal that Amaranth traders discussed "smashing" the settlement price of these NYMEX futures and directed floor brokers not to sell the contracts until the final minutes of trading.

In conducting these trades, Amaranth violated NYMEX position limits and accountability levels, which prompted investigations from both NYMEX and the CFTC. NYMEX also sought to limit Amaranth's trading for the June 2006 future, even contacting J.P. Futures, Amaranth's clearing broker, in May to remind it that Amaranth needed to remain below applicable position limits. Amaranth failed to heed these warnings, and on June 1 it appeared on a list of traders exceeding applicable accountability levels. Nevertheless, NYMEX's initial response to Amaranth's having again exceeded accountability levels was to recommend their temporary increase. Then in early August, NYMEX informed Amaranth that it should reduce its positions in the September 2006 natural gas future. Amaranth responded by shifting its positions in September and October natural gas futures to the corresponding swaps on ICE. It subsequently increased the size of those positions.

By early September 2006, Amaranth had a total open position in natural gas futures and swaps of 594,455 contracts. The fund's ever-increasing positions kept the spreads between winter and summer natural gas prices artificially high. Indeed, energy traders would subsequently describe the spread between winter and summer prices as "clearly out-of-whack" and "ridiculous." The Senate Permanent Subcommittee on Investigations would later conclude that Amaranth "dominated" the domestic natural gas market in 2006, and "had a direct effect on U.S. natural gas prices and increased price volatility in the natural gas market." This investigation would reveal that Amaranth traders discussed using the fund's large positions to, among other things, "push" and "widen" spreads.

By September 2006, however, the market for natural gas moved in ways that disrupted Amaranth's positions. As the winter months approached, it became clearer that the price of natural gas would not rise considerably; the winter/summer price spreads in which Amaranth had invested consequently began to fall. Amaranth, faced with ballooning margin requirements, struggled to find the capital or credit necessary to continue buying large positions that could prop up prices. On the brink of collapse, the fund entered into negotiations with several investment banks to sell off its natural gas positions. These negotiations fell through, and on September 20, 2006, Amaranth sold most of its natural gas portfolio to J.P. Morgan. J.P. Morgan eventually earned $725 million from the takeover. Amaranth liquidated the remainder of its assets.

On July 25, 2007, the CFTC filed a complaint against Amaranth and its head energy trader, Brian Hunter, alleging that they "intentionally and unlawfully attempted to manipulate the price of natural gas futures contracts on the New York Mercantile Exchange ('NYMEX') on February 24 and April 26, 2006 . . . and that Amaranth Advisors L.L.C. made material misrepresentations to NYMEX in violation of Section 9(a)(4) of the [CEA]." *CFTC v. Amaranth Advisors L.L.C.*, No. 07–cv–6682, 2009 U.S. Dist. LEXIS 101406, 2009 WL 3270829, at *1 (S.D.N.Y. Aug. 12, 2009). The defendants settled with the CFTC for a civil penalty of $7.5 million. 2009 U.S. Dist. LEXIS 101406, [WL] at *3. On July 26, 2007, the Federal Energy Regulatory Commission ("FERC") commenced an administrative proceeding against Amaranth for civil penalties and disgorgement of profits. *See CFTC v. Amaranth Advisors, LLC*, 523 F. Supp.2d 328, 331 (S.D.N.Y. 2007). Amaranth likewise settled for a civil penalty of $7.5 million.

Throughout the class period, J.P. Futures served as Amaranth's FCM and clearing firm. This meant, among other things, that J.P. Futures processed and settled Amaranth's trades on both NYMEX and ICE.[8] J.P. Futures profited from this role: between the beginning of 2005 and September 2006, it earned over $32 million in commissions from Amaranth's trading, as well as fees and interest on Amaranth's margin deposits.

As Amaranth's clearing broker, J.P. Futures "marked to market" Amaranth's positions on a daily basis in order to determine if Amaranth needed to deposit additional margin. This, along with J.P. Futures's other roles as a clearing broker, meant that it knew of Amaranth's positions and trading activity. As the clearing broker, J.P. Futures also knew when Amaranth violated NYMEX position limits or exceeded NYMEX accountability levels. Indeed, NYMEX contacted J.P. Futures directly in May 2006 to warn it about Amaranth's position in the June 2006 NYMEX natural gas future. Additionally, J.P. Futures knew of the positions Amaranth took in connection with its "slamming the close" trades. It similarly knew about the NYMEX and CFTC investigations into Amaranth's trading.

Throughout the class period, J.P. Futures continued to service all of Amaranth's trades, including those that put Amaranth's positions above applicable NYMEX position limits and accountability levels. On one occasion in late May 2006, J.P. Futures bypassed its own internal position limits for natural gas futures in order to clear a series of large trading transactions undertaken by Amaranth. During the summer months of 2006, J.P. Futures regularly granted Amaranth credit limit increases to support its positions on ICE. J.P. Futures facilitated Amaranth's transfer of positions from NYMEX natural gas futures to ICE natural gas swaps, which were beyond CFTC and NYMEX scrutiny. This transfer resulted in

---

[8] Though the amended complaint alleges that J.P. Futures accepted Amaranth's trade orders, other sections of the complaint suggest that Amaranth placed orders directly with floor brokers. In particular, the complaint identified other third-party floor brokers as the brokers who accepted the "slamming the close" trades in March, April, and May 2006. Plaintiffs-Appellants' counsel clarified at oral argument that J.P. Futures permitted Amaranth to contact floor brokers directly to execute trades.

higher margin requirements for Amaranth, and thus increased fees and interest for J.P. Futures. * * *

Section 22 of the CEA provides a private right of action against "[a]ny person (other than a registered entity or registered futures association) who violates this chapter or who willfully aids, abets, counsels, induces, or procures the commission of a violation of this chapter." 7 U.S.C. § 25(a)(1). This language tracks that of 7 U.S.C. § 13c(a), which establishes aiding and abetting liability generally under the CEA. Congress modeled Section 13c(a) itself, moreover, after the federal statute for criminal aiding and abetting, 18 U.S.C. § 2. *See In re Richardson Secs., Inc.*, CFTC No. 78–10, 1981 CFTC LEXIS 629, 1981 WL 26081, at *5 (Jan. 27, 1981) ("The section was modeled after the federal criminal aiding and abetting statute, 18 U.S.C. § 2."); *see also Bosco v. Serhant*, 836 F.2d 271, 279 (7th Cir. 1987) (noting "that the aiding and abetting provision was modeled on, and was intended to be interpreted consistently with, the federal statute that makes aiding and abetting a crime, 18 U.S.C. § 2").

Accordingly, both the CFTC and courts have determined that the standard for aiding and abetting liability under the CEA is the same as that for aiding and abetting under federal criminal law. The CFTC has held, drawing from Judge Learned Hand's classic formulation of criminal aiding and abetting liability in *United States v. Peoni*, 100 F.2d 401, 402 (2d Cir. 1938), that "proof of a specific unlawful intent to further the underlying violation is necessary before one can be found liable for aiding and abetting a violation of the [CEA]." *In re Richardson Secs.*, CFTC No. 78–10, 1981 CFTC LEXIS 629, 1981 WL 26081, at *5. The Seventh Circuit has likewise noted that "[t]he elements that a plaintiff must allege to state a claim for aiding and abetting under § 22 of the CEA are therefore the same elements that must be established to prove a violation of 18 U.S.C. § 2." *Damato v. Hermanson*, 153 F.3d 464, 473 (7th Cir. 1998). The Seventh Circuit articulated these elements, consistent with its own case law on criminal aiding and abetting, as: "that [defendant] (1) had knowledge of the principal's . . . intent to commit a violation of the Act; (2) had the intent to further that violation; and (3) committed some act in furtherance of the principal's objective." *Id.* The Third Circuit has endorsed the same definition. *See Nicholas v. Saul Stone & Co.*, 224 F.3d 179, 189 (3d Cir. 2000).

This Circuit has yet to articulate a precise standard for aiding and abetting liability under the CEA. We agree that Section 22 should be interpreted consistently with the criminal law, and that a complaint therefore states a claim for aiding and abetting under 7 U.S.C. § 25 when it plausibly alleges conduct that would constitute aiding and abetting under 18 U.S.C. § 2. We have not typically evaluated criminal aiding and abetting under a three-part test, however, but have instead continued to follow Judge Hand's statement in *Peoni* that aiding and abetting requires the defendant to "in some sort associate himself with the venture, that he participate in it as in something that he wishes to bring about, that he seek by his action to make it succeed." 100 F.2d at 402; *see also United States v. Frampton*, 382 F.3d 213, 222 (2d Cir. 2004) (citing *Peoni* as the "traditional understanding of the law of aiding and abetting"). We do not understand this traditional articulation of the standard to differ, in substance, from the standard employed by the Seventh and Third Circuits. Because this articulation of the test for aiding and abetting is the one with which the courts of this Circuit are most familiar, however (as well as to avoid the confusion potentially generated by using two different articulations for the same substantive legal standard), we conclude that Judge Hand's formulation, understood in light of our subsequent case law on 18 U.S.C. § 2, most properly states the standard for aiding and abetting under the CEA. * * *

Commodities manipulation requires "that (1) Defendants possessed an ability to influence market prices; (2) an artificial price existed; (3) Defendants caused the artificial prices; and (4) Defendants specifically intended to cause the artificial price." *Hershey*, 610 F.3d at 247; *see also DiPlacido v. CFTC*, 364 F. App'x 657, 661 (2d Cir. 2009). There is thus no manipulation without intent to cause artificial prices. Accordingly (and because aiding and abetting requires knowledge of the primary violation and an intent to assist it), Plaintiffs-Appellants were required to allege that J.P. Futures knew that Amaranth specifically intended to manipulate the price of NYMEX natural gas futures and that J.P. Futures intended to help. Looking at the amended complaint as a whole, we conclude that Plaintiffs-Appellants' allegations of such knowledge and intent, considered in connection with the routine services that J.P. Futures allegedly provided to Amaranth, fail to state a claim for aiding and abetting manipulation under the CEA.

As stated earlier, Plaintiffs-Appellants allege that Amaranth manipulated the price of NYMEX natural gas futures in two ways: (1) the accumulation of large open positions that artificially propped up natural gas calendar spreads; and (2) its "slamming the close" trades. Plaintiffs-Appellants allege that J.P. Futures had knowledge of these manipulative schemes because it had information on Amaranth's daily trading activity and open positions on NYMEX and ICE. This information also meant that J.P. Futures knew when Amaranth was in violation of NYMEX position limits or accountability levels. Plaintiffs-Appellants further allege that J.P. Futures performed multiple overt acts to assist Amaranth in its manipulations, including the clearing of trades, the extension of credit, and assistance in moving positions from NYMEX to ICE. According to the amended complaint, J.P. Futures assisted Amaranth because of the large commissions J.P. Futures earned from the fund's trading, as well as fees and interest it earned on the fund's margin deposits.

With respect to Plaintiffs-Appellants' first theory of manipulation—the building of large open positions—the amended complaint alleges, at most, a very weak inference that J.P. Futures actually knew of Amaranth's manipulative intent, much less that it intended to assist in carrying it out. This is for a simple reason: while J.P. Futures may have known about Amaranth's large positions in natural gas futures and swaps, such large positions do not necessarily imply manipulation. A trader may indeed acquire a large position in order to manipulate prices. But a trader may also acquire a large position in the belief that the price of the future will, for reasons other than the trader's own activity, move in a favorable direction. *Cf. In re Crude Oil Commodity Litig.*, No. 06 Civ. 6677, 2007 U.S. Dist. LEXIS 47902, 2007 WL 1946553, *8 (S.D.N.Y. June 28, 2007) (declining to impute intent to manipulate market to defendants simply due to the size of their holdings). Put differently, large positions can be indicative either of manipulation or of excessive speculation. The amended complaint contains no allegation from which we can draw the conclusion that a clearing broker like J.P. Futures would know which is the goal of any particular large position held by a client.

This remains true even if a trader's positions violate applicable position limits and accountability levels. As the CEA explains, position limits and accountability levels are intended not only to prevent manipulation, but also "to diminish, eliminate, or prevent excessive speculation," "to ensure sufficient market liquidity for bona fide hedgers," and "to ensure that the price discovery function of the underlying market is not disrupted." 7 U.S.C. § 6a(a)(3)(B).[16] This makes sense: excessive speculation, just as much as manipulation, can result in market illiquidity and artificial prices. If the violation of these restrictions does not necessarily entail manipulation, moreover, then neither should their evasion: that a trader shifts contracts from NYMEX to ICE in order to maintain a large open position, standing alone, does not reveal why the trader seeks that large position.

The amended complaint's factual allegations illustrate these principles in action. By the start of the class period, Amaranth had realized large profits from the high spread between winter and summer natural gas prices that occurred after Hurricanes Katrina and Rita wreaked havoc on the Gulf Coast in 2005. The positions Amaranth then acquired were consistent with a belief that the same price pattern would

---

[16] Though subsection 6a(a)(3)(B) is specifically about position limits set by the CFTC, its description of their purpose applies to position limits and accountability levels generally. Indeed, 7 U.S.C. § 7(d)(5), which relates to position limits and accountability levels set by the exchanges, similarly states that position limits are "[t]o reduce the potential threat of market manipulation *or congestion* (especially during trading in the delivery month)." *Id.* (emphasis added).

happen again in 2006. Thus, while these positions could have suggested manipulative intent, they equally suggested undue confidence that recent history would repeat itself. This strains any inference that J.P. Futures *actually knew*—as opposed to, for example, that J.P. Futures simply *should* have known—that Amaranth was manipulating NYMEX natural gas futures.

The allegations supporting Plaintiffs-Appellants' second theory of manipulation—the "slamming the close" trades—present a closer issue. In contrast to the acquisition of large open positions, J.P. Futures has provided no obvious legitimate economic reason why Amaranth would wait until the final minutes of trading to sell large quantities of a particular future. This type of trading activity, while not dispositive of manipulation, does strongly suggest it. Indeed, the district court found that "the timing of the sales are suspicious in themselves." *Amaranth I*, 587 F. Supp. 2d at 535.

Still, per *Peoni* and *Apuzzo*, we must consider J.P. Futures's alleged knowledge and intent regarding Amaranth's "slamming the close" trades in connection with J.P. Futures's alleged actions. The amended complaint does not allege that J.P. Futures did anything more to assist Amaranth in these trades than to provide routine clearing firm services. As previous decisions from this Circuit recognize, such allegations provide only weak evidence that J.P. Futures associated itself with Amaranth's manipulation and "participate[d] in it as in something that [it] wishe[d] to bring about." *Peoni*, 100 F.2d at 402. For example, in *Greenberg v. Bear, Stearns & Co.* we stated that the mere performance of routine clearing services cannot constitute the aiding and abetting of fraud under New York law. *See* 220 F.3d at 29 (quoting *Stander v. Fin. Clearing & Servs. Corp.*, 730 F. Supp. 1282, 1286 (S.D.N.Y. 1990)). And we have observed more recently that the performance of routine clearing services, without more, cannot trigger primary liability under § 10(b) of the Securities Exchange Act. *See Levitt v. J.P. Morgan Sec., Inc.*, 710 F.3d 454, 466 (2d Cir. 2013).

Granted, *Greenberg* and *Levitt* did not involve commodities trading or the CEA. Their holdings need not control, however, for us to decide the present case. It suffices to conclude that in the circumstances presented here, the provision of routine clearing services, when combined only with allegations that the clearing firm knew of trading activity that was highly suggestive but not dispositive of manipulation, is not enough to state a claim for aiding and abetting under Section 22 of the CEA.[18]

---

[18] We accordingly need not and do not hold that the provision of routine clearing services in commodities trading can *never* constitute aiding and abetting; again, it is necessary to consider an alleged aider and abettor's actions in conjunction with its alleged knowledge and intent. As we said in *Apuzzo*, "the three components of the aiding and abetting test 'cannot be considered in isolation from one another.' " *Apuzzo*, 689 F.3d at 214 (quoting *DiBella*, 587 F.3d at 566).

Plaintiffs-Appellants argue that the amended complaint also alleges that J.P. Futures performed "non-routine" tasks to assist Amaranth, including helping to transfer positions from NYMEX to ICE, extending credit limits, and bypassing internal position limits. But these acts, even if they are "non-routine," are alleged to have been performed only in connection with Amaranth's accumulation of large open positions. Plaintiffs-Appellants do not allege that J.P. Futures transferred positions, extended credit limits, or bypassed internal position limits in connection with Amaranth's "slamming the close" trades. Without considering the relevance of such actions in other contexts, then, or in conjunction with other evidence of purposeful association with a primary violator, we need only observe here that J.P. Futures allegedly performed these "non-routine" acts in connection with trading activity that was not as suggestive of manipulation as the "slamming the close" trades, weakening the force of such allegations in stating an aiding and abetting claim.

In sum, with respect to Plaintiffs-Appellants' first theory of manipulation, the amended complaint's allegations allow only a weak inference that J.P. Futures actually knew Amaranth was manipulating natural gas futures through the acquisition of large open positions. This, when considered in connection with the amended complaint's relatively weak allegations about J.P. Futures's assistance to Amaranth, fails to state a claim that J.P. Futures aided and abetted Amaranth's market manipulation by purposefully "seeking by its own actions to make it succeed." Similarly, while the amended complaint more plausibly alleges that J.P. Futures actually knew Amaranth's "slamming the close" trades were manipulative, its allegations concerning J.P. Futures's assistance with those trades are even weaker. This too fails to state an aiding and abetting claim under the CEA. * * *

Nor does J.P. Futures's role as Amaranth's FCM change the outcome. Plaintiffs-Appellants make generalized assertions that J.P. Futures placed *some* of Amaranth's trading orders—as did floor brokers. There are no allegations that J.P. Futures accepted the "slamming the close" trades; to the contrary, the complaint specifically identifies other brokers as the persons who handled these trades. Therefore, at most J.P. Futures's role as an FCM plausibly heightened J.P. Futures's knowledge of the large positions Amaranth held—a fact already known to J.P. Futures as the clearing firm.

Case law does not suggest a different result. Crediting the facts alleged in the complaint as true, J.P. Futures's seemingly minimal involvement as an FCM distinguishes this case from *Miller v. New York Produce Exchange*, which involved a broker described by the court as playing "a dominant and knowing role" in its client's market manipulation. 550 F.2d 762, 767 (2d Cir. 1977). Plaintiffs-Appellants also cite various CFTC decisions, but these are distinguishable from the instant case because they all involved FCMs transmitting wash orders on behalf of clients. *In re Piasio*, CFTC No. 97–9, 2000 CFTC LEXIS 216, 2000 WL 1466069, at *3 (CFTC Sept. 29, 2000) *aff'd sub nom. Piasio v. CFTC*, 54 F. App'x 702 (2d Cir. 2002); *In re LFG, L.L.C.*, CFTC No. 01–19, 2001 CFTC LEXIS 121, 2001 WL 940235, at *1 (CFTC Aug. 20, 2001); *In re Mitsubishi Corp.*, CFTC No. 97–10, 1997 CFTC LEXIS 148, 1997 WL 345634, at *2–3 (CFTC Jun. 24, 1997); *In re Three Eight Corp.*, CFTC No. 88–33, 1993 CFTC LEXIS 173, 1993 WL 212489, at *1 (CFTC June 16, 1993). Wash orders are explicitly banned by the CEA and, because they involve simultaneous or shortly spaced transactions to buy and sell the same quantity of a commodity or stock, they are much more recognizable to the broker transmitting them. *See* 7 U.S.C. § 6c(a) (prohibiting "any person to offer to enter into, enter into, or confirm the execution of" a wash sale). In sum, Plaintiffs-Appellants have cited no authority establishing that an FCM must at all times monitor its clients' trading in order to prevent manipulation. Nor is this a viable theory of aiding and abetting liability pursuant to § 25.

For the foregoing reasons, we AFFIRM the judgment of the district court.

NOTE

1. The "spreads" at issue in the Amaranth case have been further described as:

> Spread contracts represent the price difference between two commodity contracts. A "calendar spread" is the price differential between the delivery of WTI in the near month and delivery of WTI in the following month. A "long" calendar spread consists of two futures contracts: (1) the purchase of WTI for delivery in the near month and (2) the sale of the same quantity of oil in the subsequent month. A "short" calendar spread is the inverse: a sale in the near month and a purchase in the subsequent month.

> For most commodities, the price of a futures contract includes such carrying costs as storage, insurance, financing, and other expenses the producer incurs as the commodity awaits delivery. Thus, typically, the further in the future the delivery date, the greater the purchase price of the futures contract. That relationship is known as "contango." See Virginia B. Morris and Kenneth M. Morris, Standard & Poor's Dictionary of Financial Terms 41 (2007); see also Barbara J. Etzel, Webster's New World Finance and Investment Dictionary 74 (2003) ("contango[:] A pricing situation in which the prices of futures contracts are higher the further out the maturities are. This is the normal pricing pattern because carrying charges such as storage, interest expense, and insurance have to be paid in order to hold onto a commodity.").

Near-term supply of crude oil is generally inelastic, meaning, supply in the near term does not increase even if prices rise significantly. Long-term supply, on the other hand, can usually increase to meet market prices and is therefore elastic. Thus, if there is a shortage or tightness in immediate supply, traders are willing to pay a high premium for near-term supply relative to long-term supply. Such a market condition is the opposite of contango and is called "backwardation." See Jerry M. Rosenberg, Dictionary of Banking and Finance 41 (1982) ("backwardation: a basic pricing system in commodities futures trading. A price structure in which the nearer deliveries of a commodity cost more than contracts that are due to mature many months in the future. A backwardation price pattern occurs mainly because the demand for supplies in the near future is greater than demand for supplies at some distant time.").

Calendar spreads are sensitive to end-of-month balances of oil supply. In particular, a market perception that the physical supply of crude oil is low will drive near term prices higher relative to long-term prices, i.e., into a pattern of backwardation. Although somewhat counterintuitive, because the price of a long calendar spread is the difference in the price of the near month and the next month, long calendar spread contract prices rise as near term prices trend higher relative to the next month price. When there is a near-term glut of supply, the price of the near month trends lower relative to the next month price and the long calendar spread contract price declines.

CFTC v. Parnon Energy Inc., 875 F. Supp.2d 233, 237–238 (S.D.N.Y. 2012).

6. POSITION LIMITS

In order to curb "excessive speculation" the CEA allows the CFTC and the futures exchanges to set speculative limits on the amount of futures contracts that may be held by any one speculator. [7 U.S.C. § 6a]. Those limits do not apply to hedgers. [*See,* 17 C.F.R. 1.3(z) (defining what is "bona fide hedging" for purposes of the application of speculative position limits)].

CORN PRODUCTS REFINING COMPANY V. BENSON
232 F.2d 554 (2d Cir. 1956)

WATERMAN, CIRCUIT JUDGE.

This is an appeal from an order of the Secretary of Agriculture denying trading privileges on all contract markets to petitioner, Corn Products Refining Company, for a period of one day because of alleged violation of the provisions of § 4a of the Commodity Exchange Act, 7 U.S.C.A. § 6a, and a regulation promulgated thereunder, 17 CFR 150.1.

The Secretary of Agriculture, acting through the Judicial Officer, found that petitioner held a net long position in corn futures contracts in excess of the 2,000,000 bushel trading limit established pursuant to the Commodity Exchange Act.

The issue presented here is whether certain of petitioner's transactions come within the coverage of § 4a, and, if so, whether they qualify under the exemption provided in the section for "bona fide hedging transactions." This Court has jurisdiction under § 6(b) of the Commodity Exchange Act, 7 U.S.C.A. § 9, and § 10(a) and (b) of the Administrative Procedure Act, 5 U.S.C.A. § 1009 (a) and (b).

The complaint below alleged, *inter alia,* that petitioner violated the provisions of the Act and the applicable regulation in that, as the result of transactions entered into on the Chicago Board of Trade, it held on April 11, 1952 a net long position in corn futures of approximately 3,650,000 bushels, of which approximately 207,000 bushels represented bona fide hedging transactions as defined in the Act. The answer admitted that petitioner had a long position in corn futures on the Chicago Board of Trade on the date and in the quantities specified, but denied that such position violated the Act or the regulation. In support of this contention, the answer set forth various circumstances relating to the business activities of petitioner, which, it alleged, justified its total long position in corn futures on the date in question. The answer also alleged that the regulation establishing trading limits for corn futures contracts, and the Act, to the extent that it authorized the regulation, are discriminatory and violative of due process of law.

The decisive facts in this proceeding are not in dispute, and may be summarized as follows: Petitioner, a nationally known manufacturer of products made from grain corn, is the largest individual buyer of corn for wet mill processing in the United States, processing annually in excess of 50,000,000 bushels of corn. Economic operation of petitioner's plans requires that they be furnished with a continuous supply of raw corn. Over the years petitioner has found it more economical to insure a continuous supply of raw corn by the purchase of corn futures than to build storage facilities of great magnitude and stock them with sufficient corn to supply its needs for periods longer than several weeks. Futures contracts, purchased in times of low offerings, are thus used by petitioner to insure delivery of the cash commodity necessary to maintain production. Delivery is occasionally taken under the futures contract itself, but petitioner's usual practice is to trade the future for the cash commodity. The price of the future, however, represents the basic cost of corn to petitioner.

Petitioner bases its purchase of corn futures on forecasts of manufacturing requirements and expected sales of corn products and by-products. These forecasts of its business activity and raw material requirements for many months ahead are based on past experience, and have proved remarkably reliable (error less than 5%). For the period involved in this case, petitioner's forecasts indicated that it would be required, in order to meet its expected sales, to obtain delivery of over 4,000,000 bushels of raw corn a month, or an aggregate of over 25,000,000 bushels during the last six months of 1952. Petitioner purchased the corn futures involved in this case in order to insure a supply of corn during this period of the above amounts. The Judicial Officer concluded, on the basis of these facts, that petitioner's trading was not done for the purpose of speculating in price differences, but in good faith for the purpose of offsetting risks and reducing costs in its business. Nevertheless, the Judicial Officer held that these facts did not remove petitioner's transactions from the coverage of § 4a and the applicable regulation, or qualify the transactions as bona fide hedging within the meaning of the Act.

The specific situation before the Judicial Officer was:

On April 11, 1952, the petitioner held a net long position of 3,650,000 bushels in corn futures contracts calling for the delivery of corn. On the same day petitioner had outstanding contracts to sell corn products and by-products, as follows:

(a) Contracts with unaffiliated purchasers to sell dextrose, for delivery within 30 days at the market price on the day of shipment. The manufacture of the requisite amount of dextrose would require 547,000 bushels of corn. Since the marketing peculiarities of dextrose tie its sales price to that of cane sugar, which price, in turn, is fixed for periods of 30 days, the Judicial Officer concluded that the price at which dextrose was to be sold under these contracts was in effect a fixed price.

(b) Contracts with unaffiliated purchasers to sell starch, syrup, and dextrin at fixed prices, the manufacture of which would require 207,000 bushels of corn. In addition, petitioner had outstanding contracts with affiliated companies for the sale of starch, syrup, and dextrin for delivery within 30 days at the market price on the day of shipment. The manufacture of the total starch, syrup and dextrin provided for in these contracts, including the contracts with affiliated companies, would require 1,059,000 bushels of corn.

(c) Contracts with unaffiliated purchasers to sell 41,000,000 pounds of gluten feed and meal for delivery within 30 days at fixed prices, the manufacture of which would require approximately 3,090,000 bushels of corn. Since gluten feed and meal are by-products representing about ¼ of the total yield from a bushel of corn, the same 3,090,000 bushels of corn would at the same time yield 105,000,000 pounds of starch or 130,000,000 pounds of syrup.

(d) Contracts with a wholly-owned sales subsidiary, Corn Products Sales Company, for the sale of dextrose for delivery within 30 days at fixed prices, the manufacture of which would require 2,007,000 bushels of corn.

In addition to the above outstanding contracts for the future sale of its products and by-products, the petitioner expected as of April 11, 1952, to sell to customers during the latter part of 1952, 15,225,000 pounds of *cerelose,* the petitioner's brand name for dextrose. The production cost of dextrose, a by-product of corn, is based upon the price of corn. However, dextrose sells in competition with cane and beet sugars, and its market price is related to sugar at an unfavorable differential of 15 or 16%. There is no commodity futures trading in dextrose. To meet the risks of non-parallelism in corn and sugar prices petitioner purchased 510,000 bushels of December corn futures and sold 7,000 long tons of raw sugar futures and 840,000 pounds of cottonseed oil futures. These purchases and sales of corn, sugar and corn oil futures were based upon reliable forecasts of the expected sales of dextrose. The closeout of these transactions as production progressed insured petitioner against loss due solely to variations in the market differential between corn and sugar. Thus the purpose and effect of these transactions was to protect the profit margins of the petitioner on future dextrose sales.

The Judicial Officer found that the transactions set forth in paragraph (a), supra, were bona fide hedging transactions; that the transactions set forth in paragraph (b), supra, were bona fide hedging transactions to the extent of 207,000 bushels of corn; that the transactions set forth in paragraph (c), supra, were bona fide hedging transactions to the extent of 770,000 bushels; and that the remaining transactions, based on contracts with affiliated companies, on contracts not containing a fixed price, or on expected sales of dextrose, were not bona fide hedging transactions within the meaning of the Act. The Judicial Officer therefore determined that futures contracts for the purchase of 1,335,500 bushels of corn should be offset against the petitioner's net long position of 3,650,000 bushels, resulting in a long futures position of 2,314,500 bushels. He concluded that petitioner had exceeded the trading limit by 314,500 bushels.

Petitioner admits that on April 11, 1952, it held a net long position in corn futures in excess of the 2,000,000 bushel trading limit, but contends that the trading limit provisions of the Act and the regulation thereunder are inapplicable to the corn futures transactions here involved. Petitioner argues that the trading limit provisions contained in § 4a of the Act apply only to *speculative* trading, that the Commission's regulation can only do likewise, and that petitioner's corn futures trading is *not speculative* because it is done to stabilize the cost of corn to it and to assure a continuing source of supply of corn for its manufacturing and selling needs. Therefore, petitioner concludes, the trading limit of 2,000,000 bushels contained in the regulation promulgated pursuant to § 4a of the Act is not applicable to its corn futures transactions, *whether or not such transactions are exempt as hedging under the Act.* Examination of this contention requires a detailed analysis of the provisions of § 4a of the Commodity Exchange Act, 7 U.S.C.A. § 6a, which section is printed in full in the margin.

Section 4a of the Act begins with a Congressional finding that "[e]xcessive speculation in any commodity under contracts of sale of such commodity for future delivery made on or subject to the rules of contract markets causing sudden or unreasonable fluctuations or unwarranted changes in the price of such commodity, is an undue and unnecessary burden on interstate commerce in such commodity." 7 U.S.C.A. § 6a (1). It then provides that the Commodity Exchange Commission for the purpose of diminishing, eliminating or preventing such burden shall, from time to time, after notice, hearing, etc., "proclaim and fix such limits on the amount of *trading* under contracts of sale * * * for future delivery on or subject to the rules of any contract market which may be done by any person as the commission finds is necessary to diminish, eliminate, or prevent such burden." [Emphasis supplied.] It should be noted that "trading" is unmodified by any reference to "speculative," and any such reference must be derived from the surrounding context.

The discretionary powers of the Commission and the exemptions from the "trading limits" established under the Act are carefully delineated in § 4a. The Commission is given discretionary power to prescribe " * * * different trading limits for different commodities, markets, futures, or delivery months, or different trading limits for buying and selling operations, or different limits for the purposes of subparagraphs (A) [i. e., with respect to trading during one business day] and (B) [i. e., with respect to the net long or net short position held at any one time] of this section * * *." The *only* exemptions to the trading restrictions provided for by the Act which are pertinent here are (1) the discretionary authority of the Commission to exempt or treat differently "transactions commonly known to the trade as 'spreads' or 'straddles' ", 7 U.S.C.A. § 6a(1), and (2) the exemption of "bona fide hedging transactions" in § 4a(3), 7 U.S.C.A. § 6a(3). Finally, § 4a(2) makes it unlawful for any person to buy or sell any amount of a commodity for such future delivery in excess of any *trading* limit fixed by the Commission.

Although § 4a expresses an intention to curb "excessive speculation," we think that the unequivocal reference to "trading," coupled with a specific and well-defined exemption for bona fide hedging, clearly indicates that *all* trading in commodity futures was intended to be subject to trading restrictions unless within the terms of the exemptions.

We think that the internal construction of the section requires this conclusion. As we have seen, § 4a provides for fixing *trading* limits, exempts certain transactions from those limits, and makes it unlawful to exceed the day limits or position limits fixed by the Commission. There is an element of speculation in all transactions involving the holding or use of property, and were we to infer that the "trading" regulated by the Act is only "speculative trading," we would impose upon the administrative body and the courts the difficult problem of determining in each instance whether a transaction was speculative or non-speculative in character within the meaning of the Act. This, perhaps, would not be an insurmountable task, but it is one which we think cannot be reasonably inferred from the words used by Congress. Moreover, if we were to accept petitioner's argument, the specific exemption of bona fide hedging transactions contained in the Act would be rendered meaningless and superfluous. For petitioner contends that the trading limits provided for in § 4a are inapplicable to non-speculative trading of all types. If this were true, there would be no need for the specific exemption of bona fide hedging transactions. Such transactions, clearly more non-speculative in character than those of petitioner here involved, would be exempt without any specific exemption.

We think that Congress, in order to prevent the harmful effects of speculation on the commodity markets, intended to limit *all* trading of any person not coming within a specified exemption such as that for bona fide hedging beyond the daily limit or net position limit fixed by the Commission. It is obvious that transactions in such vast amounts as those involved here might cause "sudden or unreasonable fluctuations * * * in the price" of corn and hence be "an undue and unnecessary burden on interstate commerce." In its attempt to diminish or prevent any harmful method of speculation in commodity futures, Congress chose the practicable course of treating all trading not "bona fide hedging," or not within one of the other exemptions as speculative in character or effect. * * *

Petitioner contends that all its futures transactions considered by the Judicial Officer constituted "bona fide hedging" within the meaning of the Act and the regulation promulgated thereunder, and he erred in holding that only some were within this exemption. Petitioner interprets the definition of "bona fide hedging" transactions contained in § 4a(3) of the Act in a manner so as to include its purchases of corn futures to offset (1) anticipated manufacturing requirements based on forecasts of expected sales, (2) contracts to sell corn products or by-products at petitioner's market price on the day of shipment, and (3) contracts to sell dextrose at fixed prices to petitioner's wholly-owned subsidiary.

Petitioner purchases corn futures in order to assure it a continuous supply of cash corn as well as to stabilize the cost of corn to it. It forecasts with substantial accuracy its need for corn and the prices at which it will sell corn products or by-products in the future, and it regards these forecasts as commitments. Petitioner argues that "sale" in § 4a(3)(B) extends to sales of products and by-products to take place in the future even though no contracts of sale exist at the time of the purchase of futures. This phase of the case therefore presents the question whether the purchase of corn futures against expected or anticipated sales of products and byproducts are hedges under the Act.

The Judicial Officer interpreted the statutory definition as one of "traditional" or "strict" hedging, i. e., he held that the statute required a contract to sell corn products or by-products *at a definite price* in order for a transaction to fall within the hedging exemption of the Act. We think that the Judicial Officer's interpretation of the Act, supported by the words of the statute, the legislative history, and trade parlance, is the correct one. * * * *

The petition for review is therefore denied and the order of the Secretary of Agriculture in all respects affirmed.

NOTES

1. Although hedgers are exempt from position limits, the commodity exchanges may set trading limits for such traders that are based on the hedging needs of the trader and liquidity availability.

2. Historically, the CFTC set position limits only on certain legacy agricultural futures contracts. However, the CFTC required all exchanges to set speculative position limits on all contracts after the Hunt family of Dallas, Texas was able to obtain massive positions in silver futures, allowing them to manipulate the market in 1979. See, Jerry W. Markham, Law Enforcement and the History of Financial Market Manipulation 402 (2014) (describing that manipulation and the CFTC's reaction). As shown in the next case, the Hunts had earlier ignored position limits that were in place for soybean futures.

3. The exchanges may also set "accountability" limits that do not prohibit positions larger than those limits, but subjects the trader to greater scrutiny by the exchange. See e.g., One Chicago, Position Limit Explanation, http://www.onechicago.com/?page_id=2101 (accessed on Nov. 13, 2013) (describing information that must be supplied when accountability level is reached). Regulations on position limits that were proposed by the CFTC would remove the accountability limits for certain energy contracts.

COMMODITY FUTURES TRADING COMMISSION v. HUNT
591 F.2d 1211 (7th Cir. 1979)

SWYGERT, CIRCUIT JUDGE.

This case presents several issues arising out of a complaint brought by the Commodity Futures Trading Commission, pursuant to the Commodity Exchange Act, against seven members of the Hunt family and an affiliated company. The complaint was instituted by the Commission on April 28, 1977 to compel the defendants to comply with limits established by the Commission on the speculative position that any individual or group may have in soybean futures contracts. See Commodity Exchange Act, § 4a(1), 7 U.S.C. § 6a(1) (Supp.1978); Rule 150.4, 17 C.F.R. § 150.4 (1977).

The Commission's complaint alleges that from at least January 17, 1977 and continuing to the commencement of the court action, two brothers, Nelson Bunker Hunt and William Herbert Hunt, five of their children, and a corporation they control, had been exceeding collectively the limit of three million bushels that had been set for soybean futures contracts. The complaint sought preliminary and permanent injunctions against future violations of these limits, the disgorgement of any profits the Hunts had obtained as a result of their unlawful conduct, and an order requiring the Hunts to liquidate all existing positions in soybean futures in excess of the speculative limits. Contemporaneous with the filing of the complaint, the Commission, pursuant to section 8a(6) of the Commodity Exchange Act, 7 U.S.C. § 12a(6) (1978), publicly disclosed the soybean trading activity and positions of the Hunts. . . .

On September 28, 1977, the district court, after hearings on the Commission's motion for a preliminary injunction, issued a memorandum opinion accompanied by findings of fact and law, and entered a judgment order. Commodity Futures Trading Comm. v. Hunt, No. 77–C–1489 (N.D. Ill., Sept. 28, 1977). The lower court concluded that the Hunts, acting in concert, had acquired soybean futures in excess of the three million bushel limit prescribed by regulation, thereby violating Rule 150.4 and section 4a(1) of the Commodity Exchange Act. The court, however, denied the Commission's motion for an order enjoining future violations of the limits and rejected the Commission's request for disgorgement of the Hunts' illegal profits. The lower court also rejected the counterclaim and third-party claims brought by the Hunts.

The Commission appealed from the lower court's decision, arguing that both the injunction and the ancillary relief of disgorgement should have been granted. The Hunts cross-appealed, seeking to overturn the district court's declaratory judgment that the Hunts had violated the speculative limit, and challenging the validity of the regulation itself. The Hunts also challenged the dismissal of their counterclaim and third-party claims. The Commission's appeal and the Hunts' cross-appeal were consolidated in November 1977 with the Commission's earlier appeal of the lower court's injunction against publication of trading information regarding the Hunts.

Section 4a(1) of the Commodity Exchange Act, 7 U.S.C. § 6a(1), authorizes the Commodity Futures Trading Commission to set commodity trading limits. Congress concluded that excessive speculation in commodity contracts for future delivery can cause adverse fluctuations in the price of a commodity, and authorized the Commission to restrict the positions held or trading done by any individual person or by certain groups of people acting in concert. Pursuant to this statutory authority, the Commodity Exchange Authority, the predecessor of the Commodity Futures Trading Commission, established trading limits on a variety of commodities, including soybeans. In 1951 the Authority set the soybean speculative position limit at one million bushels, 16 Fed.Reg. 8107 (Aug. 13, 1951). The Authority raised the limit to two million bushels in 1953, 18 Fed.Reg. 7230–31 (Nov. 14, 1953), and to three million bushels in 1971, 36 Fed.Reg. 1263 (June 6, 1971). This three million bushel position limit, Regulation 150.4, 17 C.F.R. § 150.4 (1977), was in effect at the time of the Hunt family soybean transactions.

The Hunts present multiple challenges to the soybean trading regulation, contending that there were procedural defects in its adoption and that it is an arbitrary and capricious exercise of administrative authority. The essence of the Hunts' attack on the validity of the regulation is their substantive contention that there is no connection between large scale speculation by individual traders and fluctuations in the soybean trading market. . . .

The district court found that Nelson Bunker Hunt and William Herbert Hunt, five of their children, and a corporation they control had exceeded the speculative limit of three million bushels that had been established for soybean futures contracts by Rule 150.4, promulgated pursuant to section 4a(1) of the Commodity Exchange Act. 7 U.S.C. § 6a(1). The Hunts claim that the district court misinterpreted section 4a(1) in applying it to the Hunts' activities, and that there was no factual basis for a finding that the Hunts had violated the statute and its corollary regulation.

Section 4a(1) provides for the aggregation of commodity positions for purposes of determining whether the speculative limit has been exceeded, when one person "directly or indirectly" controls the trading of another, or when two persons are acting "pursuant to an express or implied agreement or understanding. . . ." 7 U.S.C. § 6a(1). Thus, even though two persons acting in concert might each individually have a commodity position below the limit, if their combined position exceeds the limit they have violated the statute. Further, contrary to the arguments advanced by the Hunts, there is nothing in either the statutory language or legislative history which suggests that intent either to affect market prices or specific intent to exceed the speculative limits is a necessary element of a violation of section 4a(1). In fact, the Senate Report to the 1968 amendments to the statute states that a speculative futures position exceeding the limit can constitute a statutory violation "regardless of how or when or for what purpose such position was created." 1968 U.S. Code Cong. & Admin. News 1673, 1678. A violation occurs simply when an individual or several individuals acting in concert exceed the commodity position limits set pursuant to the statute.

The Hunts contend that the evidence compiled in the district court is insufficient to prove a violation of the statute. In assessing the district court's findings, we must defer to the reasonable inferences of the trial court. Fed.R.Civ.P. 52(a). See SEC v. Parklane Hoisery Co., 558 F.2d 1083, 1086 (2d Cir. 1977); Markiewicz v. Greyhound Corp., 358 F.2d 26 (7th Cir.), cert. denied, 385 U.S. 828, 87 S.Ct. 64, 17 L.Ed.2d 65 (1966). Under this rule, the trial court's conclusion that the Hunts violated section 4a(1) by collectively exceeding the speculative limits of Rule 150.4 must be upheld.

A brief survey of the Hunt family's complicated soybean trading substantiates this conclusion. Nelson Bunker Hunt and William Herbert Hunt were the principal family figures in these transactions. They are brothers, and the chief officers of the Hunt Energy Corporation. In mid-1976 N. B. and W. H. Hunt entered the soybean market. By August 1 each brother consistently held a long position at the three million bushel limit, usually for the closest delivery month. Through a series of purchases the date, timing, and size of which were virtually identical each brother, by January 1977, held a three million bushel position in March 1977 soybeans. Over the next six weeks each of the Hunt brothers entered into eight transactions on the same days, using the same broker, involving virtually identical quantities and prices. Throughout this time an employee of the Hunt Energy Corporation, Charles Mercer, prepared commodity position statements for the brothers reflecting their combined holdings and unrealized profits and losses.

On February 25, with both N. B. and W. H. Hunt at the personal position limit, N. B. Hunt ordered a purchase, through one of his brokers, of 750,000 bushels of May soybeans in the name of his son, Houston Hunt. On March 3 he ordered the purchase of 750,000 May bushels to be allocated equally among accounts he had opened on behalf of his three daughters. And, although the bank accounts of the various children lacked the funds to cover these purchases, the transactions were made possible by a short-term transfer of interest-free funds from their father's account. N. B. Hunt's children did not participate in these initial soybean transactions made in their names: they had nothing to do with opening the accounts, placing the first order, or arranging financing for their purchases. And once these family members had entered the soybean market, their transactions were added to the composite report sent to N. B. Hunt.

A similar relationship existed between W. H. Hunt and his son, Douglas. On March 1 W. H. Hunt and his wife transferred their interests in Hunt Holdings, Inc. to their three sons. Less than a week later Douglas Hunt personally and through Hunt Holdings, whose trading he controlled, began purchasing July soybeans. These purchases were financed in part by money advanced by his father.

The overall involvement of the Hunt family in the soybean market also was increased by the spread trading purchasing old crop contracts and selling contracts in new crop markets of N. B. and W. H. Hunt. Some of N. B. Hunt's purchases in this period were financed by temporary advances from his brother. As of April 14, 1977 the Hunt family's collective position involved over twenty-three million bushels of old crop soybeans: over 10.8 million in May futures, 7.7 million in July futures, and 5.2 million in August futures. These collective figures, of course, put the Hunt family well over the speculative limits in soybeans set by Rule 150.4. And the evidence presented in the district court clearly indicates that the individual positions of the family members should be aggregated. Thus, the Hunt family soybean transactions constituted a violation of section 4a(1) of the Commodity Exchange Act, 7 U.S.C. § 6a(1). * * * *

INTERNATIONAL SWAPS AND DERIVATIVES ASSOCIATION V. CFTC

887 F. Supp. 2d 259 (D.D.C. 2012)

Opinion by: ROBERT L. WILKINS

Plaintiffs International Swaps and Derivatives Association ("ISDA") and Securities Industry and Financial Markets Association ("SIFMA") (collectively "Plaintiffs") challenge a recent rulemaking by Defendant United States Commodity Futures Trading Commission ("CFTC" or "Commission") setting position limits on derivatives tied to 28 physical commodities. See Position Limits for Futures and Swaps, 76 Fed. Reg. 71,626 (Nov. 18, 2011) ("Position Limits Rule"). The CFTC promulgated the Position Limits Rule pursuant to the Dodd-Frank Wall Street Reform and Consumer Protection Act, Pub. L. No. 111–203, 124 Stat. 1376 (2010) ("Dodd-Frank").

The heart of Plaintiffs' challenge is that the CFTC misinterpreted its statutory authority under the Commodity Exchange Act of 1936 ("CEA"), as amended by Dodd-Frank. The central question for the Court, then, is whether the CFTC promulgated the Position Limits Rule based on a correct and permissible interpretation of the statute at issue. Before the Court are the following motions: 1) Plaintiffs' Motion for Preliminary Injunction (Dkt. No. 14), Plaintiffs' Motion for Summary Judgment (Dkt. No. 31) and Defendant's Cross Motion for Summary Judgment (Dkt. No. 38). For the reasons set forth below, Plaintiffs' Motion for Summary Judgment is GRANTED, the CFTC's Cross-Motion for Summary Judgment is DENIED, and Plaintiffs' Motion for Preliminary Injunction is DENIED AS MOOT.

ISDA is a trade association with more than 825 members that "represents participants in the privately negotiated derivatives industry." SIFMA is an "association of hundreds of securities firms, banks, and asset managers" whose claimed mission is to "support a strong financial industry, investor opportunity, capital formation, job creation, and economic growth, while building trust and confidence in the financial markets." According to Plaintiffs, the commodity derivatives markets are "crucial for helping producers and purchasers of commodities manage risk, ensuring sufficient market liquidity for bona fide hedgers, and promoting price discovery of the underlying market." The CFTC, of course, is an agency of the U.S. government with regulatory authority over the commodity derivatives market.

Three types of commodity derivatives are implicated in this case: futures contracts, options contracts and swaps. A futures contract is a contract between parties to buy or sell a specific quantity of a commodity at a particular date and location in the future. An options contract is a contract between parties where the buyer has the right, but not the obligation, to buy or sell a specific quantity of a commodity at a point in the future. Futures contracts and options contracts result in either physical delivery or a cash settlement between parties. In a physical delivery contract, the buyer takes physical delivery of the commodity when the contract expires. At the conclusion of a cash-settled contract, a cash transfer occurs that is equivalent to the difference between the price set forth in the contract and the market price at the time the contract expires. Swaps involve one or more exchanges of payments based on changes in the prices of specified underlying commodities without transferring ownership of the underlying commodity.

A position limit "caps the maximum number of derivatives contracts to purchase (long) or sell (short) a commodity that an individual trader or group of traders may own during a given period." A position limit may impose a ceiling on either a "spot-month" position or a "non-spot-month" position. A "spot month" is a specific period of time (which varies by commodity under the rules) that immediately precedes the date of delivery of the commodity under the derivatives contract. As Plaintiffs explain, "[a] spot-month position limit, therefore, caps the position that a trader may hold or control in contracts approaching their expiration. A non-spot-month position limit caps the position that may be held or controlled in contracts that expire in periods further in the future or in all months combined."

The main issue in this case is whether the Dodd-Frank amendments to Section 4a of the CEA (codified at 7 U.S.C. § 6a) mandated that the CFTC impose a new position limits regime in the commodity derivatives market. It is undisputed that, prior to Dodd-Frank, the CEA vested the Commission with discretion to set position limits on futures and options contracts in commodity derivatives markets. See 7 U.S.C. § 6a (stating that CFTC has authority to proclaim and fix position limits "from time to time" "as the Commission finds are necessary to diminish, eliminate, or prevent [excessive speculation]."). Title VII of the Dodd-Frank Act amended Section 6a in several respects. The full text of Section 6a, with the Dodd-Frank amendments reflected in red-lined format, is attached to this Opinion as Appendix A.

Dodd-Frank went into effect on July 21, 2010. On January 26, 2011, the CFTC issued a Notice of Proposed Rulemaking ("NPRM"), stating that Title VII of Dodd-Frank "requires" the Commission "to establish position limits for certain physical commodity derivatives." Position Limits for Derivatives, 76 Fed. Reg. 4,752 (Jan. 26, 2011). At an open meeting on January 13, 2011 prior to the issuance of the NPRM, Commissioner Michael V. Dunn stated that, "to date CFTC staff has been unable to find any reliable economic analysis to support either the contention that excessive speculation is affecting the market we regulate or that position limits will prevent excessive speculation." Transcript of Open Meeting on the Ninth Series of Proposed Rulemakings Under the Dodd-Frank Act at 9 (Jan. 13, 2011). Dunn also shared his "fear" that "at best position limits are a cure for a disease that does not exist, or at worst it's a placebo for one that does." Id. Commissioners Jill Sommers and Scott D. O'Malia also expressed fundamental concerns with the position limits proposal before the agency.

In the NPRM, the CFTC proposed to establish position limits for futures contracts, options contracts and swaps for 28 physical commodities. In discussing its statutory authority, the CFTC stated its view that it was:

> not required to find that an undue burden on interstate commerce resulting from excessive speculation exists or is likely to occur in the future in order to impose position limits. Nor is the Commission required to make an affirmative finding that position limits are necessary to prevent sudden or unreasonable fluctuations or unwarranted changes in prices or otherwise necessary for market protection. Rather the Commission may impose position limits prophylactically, based on its reasonable

judgment that such limits are necessary for the purpose of 'diminishing, eliminating, or preventing' such burdens on interstate commerce. . . .

76 Fed. Reg. at 4754 (emphasis added). The CFTC stated that the "basic statutory mandate in section [6]a of the Act to establish position limits to prevent 'undue burdens' associated with 'excessive speculation' has remained unchanged—and has been reaffirmed by Congress several times—over the past seven decades." Id. In discussing the Dodd-Frank amendments to Section 6a, the Commission noted that:

> [P]ursuant to the Dodd-Frank Act, Congress significantly expanded the Commission's authority and mandate to establish position limits beyond futures and options contracts to include, for example, economically equivalent derivatives. Congress expressly directed the Commission to set limits in accordance with the standards set forth in sections [6]a(a)(1) and [6]a(a)(3) of the Act, thereby reaffirming the Commission's authority to establish position limits as it finds necessary in its discretion to address excessive speculation.

Id. at 4755 (emphasis added). At this stage of the rulemaking, therefore, when discussing the "standards set forth in section [6]a(a)(1)," the Commission directly referred to its authority to "establish position limits as it finds necessary in its discretion to address excessive speculation." Id.

During an open meeting on October 18, 2011, the CFTC adopted the Position Limits Rule by a vote of 3 to 2. 76 Fed. Reg. at 71,699. Chairman Gary Gensler and Commissioner Bart Chilton voted in favor of the Rule, with Commissioner Dunn providing the third vote for the majority. 76 Fed. Reg. at 71,699. Dunn stated that "no one has presented this agency any reliable economic analysis to support either the contention that excessive speculation is affecting the market we regulate or that position limits will prevent the excessive speculation." Dunn expressed his opinion that "position limits may harm the very markets we're intending to protect." Despite the fact that his opinion on position limits still "ha[d] not changed," Dunn voted in favor of the Rule because he believed Congress had required the Commission to impose position limits:

> Position limits are, in my opinion, a sideshow that has unnecessarily diverted human and fiscal resources away from actions to prevent another financial crisis. To be clear, no one has proven that the looming specter of excessive speculation in the futures market re-regulated even exist, let alone played any role whatsoever in the financial crisis of 2008. Even so, Congress has tasked the CFTC with preventing excessive speculation by imposing position limits. This is the law. The law is clear, and I will follow the law.

Commissioner Gensler supported Commissioner Dunn's view, stating that by "the Dodd-Frank Act, Congress mandated that the CFTC set aggregate position limits for certain physical commodity derivatives." 76 Fed. Reg. at 71,626, 71,699. The final rule reflected the Commission's view that it was compelled to produce a certain result: "Congress did not give the Commission a choice. Congress directed the Commission to impose position limits and to do so expeditiously." 76 Fed. Reg. at 71,628 (emphasis added).

Commissioners Sommers and O'Malia voted against the final rule and published written dissents. Sommers claimed that, while she was not philosophically opposed to position limits, she did "not believe position limits will control prices or market volatility" in this market. 76 Fed. Reg. at 71,699. Sommers claimed that the rule would inflict the greatest harm on bona fide hedgers and "ironically" may "result in increased food and energy costs for consumers." Id. Sommers claimed that, in her view, the Commission had "chosen to go way beyond what is in the statute and have created a very complicated regulation that has the potential to irreparably harm these vital markets." 76 Fed. Reg. at 71,700. By enacting the Rule, she believed that "[the CFTC] is setting itself up for an enormous failure." 76 Fed. Reg. at 71,699.

Commissioner O'Malia claimed that, although he had a number of serious concerns about the Rule, his "principal disagreement is with the Commission's restrictive interpretation of the statutory mandate under Section 4a [7 U.S.C. § 6a] of the [CEA] to establish position limits without making a determination that such limits are necessary and effective in relation to the identifiable burdens of excessive speculation on interstate commerce." Id. at 71,700 (emphasis added). As O'Malia stated, "the Commission ignores the fact that in the context of the Act, such discretion is broad enough to permit the Commission to not impose limits if they are not appropriate." Id. at 71,701. In O'Malia's view, the CFTC had "fail[ed] to comply with Congressional intent" and "misse[d] an opportunity to determine and define the type and extent of speculation that is likely to cause sudden, unreasonable and/or unwarranted commodity price movements so that it can respond with rules that are reasonable and appropriate." Id. at 71,700. O'Malia also faulted the Commission for promulgating the rule without any evidence that the position limits would actually benefit the market:

- "Historically, the Commission has taken a much more disciplined and fact-based approach in considering the question of position limits; a process that is lacking from the current proposal." Id. at 71,700.

- "The Commission voted on this multifaceted rule package without the benefit of performing an objective factual analysis based on the necessary data to determine whether these particular limits . . . will effectively prevent or deter excessive speculation." Id. at 71,702.

- "By failing to put forward data evidencing that commodity prices are threatened by the negative influence of a defined level of speculation that we can define as 'excessive speculation,' and that today's measures are appropriate (i.e. necessary and effective) in light of such findings, I believe that we have failed under the Administrative Procedure Act to provide a meaningful and informed opportunity for public comment." Id.

In the Position Limits Rule, the CFTC established spot-month and non-spot-month position limits for all "Referenced Contracts" as defined under the Rule. A Referenced Contract:

> is defined as a Core Referenced Futures Contract or a futures contract, options contract, swap or swaption directly or indirectly linked to either the price of a Core Referenced Futures Contract or to the price of the commodity underlying a Core Referenced Futures Contract for delivery at the same location as the commodity underlying the relevant Core Referenced Futures Contract.

The Rule identifies 28 Core Referenced Futures Contracts that will be subject to its provisions. Id. The Rule specifies that spot-month position limits shall be based on one-quarter of the estimated spot month deliverable supply as established by the Commission, and will apply to both physical delivery and cash-settled contracts separately. For non-spot-months, different position limit rules apply for legacy Referenced Contracts and non-legacy Referenced Contracts. Legacy Referenced Contracts are contracts that were previously subject to position limits by the CFTC. Id. These contracts will remain subject to the preexisting regulations set forth in 17 C.F.R. § 150, although the Rule raised the preexisting limits to higher levels.

Non-legacy Referenced Contracts are contracts that were not previously subject to position limits. Id. The position limits for these contracts are fixed by the Commission based on "10 percent of the first 25,000 contracts of average all-months combined aggregated open interest with a marginal increase of 2.5 percent thereafter." Id. In addition to these regulations, the Rule also established circumstances where a trader must aggregate positions held in multiple accounts. Id. at 16. Subject to some exceptions, traders must aggregate all counts in which they have at least a 10% ownership or equity interest. Id.

Plaintiffs assert the following claims against the CFTC based on the Position Limits Rule: 1) Count One: Violation of the CEA and APA—

Failure to Determine the Rule to be Necessary and Appropriate under 7 U.S.C. § 6a(a)(1), (a)(2)(A), (a)(5)(A)); 2) Count Two: Violation of the CEA—Insufficient Evaluation of Costs and Benefits under 7 U.S.C. § 19(a); 3) Count Three: Violation of the APA—Arbitrary and Capricious Agency Action in Promulgating the Position Limits Rule; 4) Count Four: Violation of the APA—Arbitrary and Capricious Agency Action in Establishing Specific Position Limits and Adopting Related Requirements and Restrictions; 5) Count Five: Violation of the APA—Failure to Provide Interested Persons A Sufficient Opportunity to Meaningfully Participate in the Rulemaking; and 6) Count Six: Claim for Injunctive Relief. * * * *

The first question for the Court is whether Section 6a(a)(1) requires the Commission to find that position limits are necessary prior to imposing them. This is important, of course, because the so-called "mandate" of Dodd-Frank in Section 6a(a)(2) expressly incorporates the "standards" of paragraph (1). The relevant portion of Section 6a(a)(1) states:

> For the purpose of diminishing, eliminating, or preventing such burden, the Commission shall, from time to time, after due notice and opportunity for hearing, by rule, regulation, or order, proclaim and fix such limits on the amounts of trading which may be done or positions which may be held by any person . . . under contracts of sale of such commodity for future delivery on or subject to the rules of any contract market or derivatives transaction execution facility, or swaps traded on or subject to the rules of a designated contract market or a swap execution facility, or swaps not traded on or subject to the rules of a designated contract market or a swap execution facility that performs a significant price discovery function with respect to a registered entity, as the Commission finds are necessary to diminish, eliminate, or prevent such burden.

§ 6a(a)(1) (emphasis added).

The Commission does not argue—nor could it—that this section standing alone strips the agency of any discretion not to set position limits if it would be unnecessary to do so. In fact, the statute expressly directs the agency to set position limits "from time to time." Id. The precise question, therefore, is whether the language of Section 6a(a)(1) clearly and unambiguously requires the Commission to make a finding of necessity prior to imposing position limits. The answer is yes.

The contested language in Section 6a(a)(1) has remained largely unchanged from the initial passage of the CEA to the Dodd-Frank amendments. Compare Pub. L. No. 74–675, ch. 545, 49 Stat. 1491, 1492 (June 15, 1936) ("For the purpose of diminishing, eliminating, or preventing such burden, the commission shall, from time to time . . .

proclaim and fix such limits on the amount of trading . . . which may be done by any person as the commission finds is necessary to diminish, eliminate or prevent such burden.") (emphasis added) with Pub. L. No. 111–203, Title VII, § 737(a) to (c), 124 Stat. 1722 (July 21, 2010) ("For the purpose of diminishing, eliminating, or preventing such burden, the Commission shall, from time to time . . . proclaim and fix such limits on the amounts of trading which may be done or positions which may be held by any person . . . as the Commission finds are necessary to diminish, eliminate, or prevent such burden.") (emphasis added).

Consistent with this longstanding requirement, the Commission made necessity findings in its rulemakings establishing position limits for 45 years after the passage of the CEA. See In the Matter of Limits on Position and Daily Trading in Wheat, Corn, Oats, Barley, Rye and Flaxseed for Future Delivery, 3 Fed. Reg. 3145, 3146 (Dec. 24, 1938) ("[T]rading in any one grain for future delivery on a contract market, by a person who holds or controls a speculative net position of more than 2,000,000 bushels, long or short in any one future or in all futures combined in such grain on such contract market, tends to cause sudden and unreasonable fluctuations and changes in the price of such grain . . . in order to diminish, eliminate, or prevent the undue burden of excessive speculation in grain futures which causes unwarranted price changes, it is necessary to establish limits on the amount of speculative trading under contracts of sale of grain for future delivery on contract markets, which may be done by any one person.") (emphasis added); . . . .

The CFTC argues that, although it made necessity findings in these prior rulemakings, the agency never stated that a finding of necessity was required. (Dkt. No. 38 at 19, n.12). This argument is without merit. The plain text of the statute requires that position limits be set "as the Commission finds are necessary to diminish, eliminate, or prevent [excessive speculation]." § 6a(a)(1). The text does not state (nor has it ever) that the CFTC may do away with or ignore the necessity requirement in its discretion. There is no ambiguity as to whether the statute requires the CFTC to make such findings, and the CFTC has never apparently treated the statute as ambiguous on this point. Accordingly, the Court concludes that § 6a(a)(1) unambiguously requires that, prior to imposing position limits, the Commission find that position limits are necessary to "diminish, eliminate, or prevent" the burden described in Section 6a(a)(1).

For 45 years after the passage of the CEA, the CFTC made necessity findings prior to imposing position limits under Section 6a(a). The CFTC has not cited to any express interpretation in which the CFTC took the position that no necessity finding was required. Nor has the CFTC cited to any prior interpretation in which the CFTC took the position that the specific language of Section 6a(a) (now Section 6a(a)(1)) was ambiguous on this point. Fully aware that Section 6a(a)(1) is problematic for its current position, the CFTC makes a number of arguments in an attempt to get out from underneath the statute's plain language requiring a necessity finding. Notwithstanding the CFTC's various—and at times inconsistent—interpretations, the necessity requirement remains in Section 6a(a)(1). * * * *

For the foregoing reasons, the Position Limits Rule is vacated and remanded to the Commission for further proceedings consistent with this Opinion. Moreover, Plaintiffs' Motion for Summary Judgment is granted and Defendant's Motion for Summary Judgment is denied. An Order accompanies this Memorandum.

NOTES

1. The CFTC dropped its appeal in the ISDA case. Instead, in November 2013, it re-proposed the rules with what it asserted were economic studies supporting its position. However, these new proposed rules were basically the same as the position limit rules that were the subject of the ISDA case. See, CFTC, Proposed Regulations on Position Limits for Derivatives, available at http://www.cftc.gov/ucm/groups/public/@newsroom/documents/file/pl_150_fact sheet.pdf (accessed on November 25, 2013). See, also, CFTC, Aggregation of Positions; Proposed Rule, 78 Fed. Reg. 68945 (Nov. 13, 2013) (discussing those proposals and other action on position limits).

2. The rule stricken in the ISDA case was a resurrection of a CFTC proposal in 1978 that was called "Charlie's rule," after CFTC staff member Charles Robinson, who propounded the idea. Charlie's rule would have required the futures exchanges to limit positions of traders in maturing futures contracts to no more than twenty-five percent of the open interest in that future unless the exchange affirmatively determined that the position was not a threat to orderly trading. The 1978 proposal was highly controversial and was not adopted because of uncertainty over the application of its provisions. See, Jerry W. Markham, "Manipulation of Commodity Futures Prices—The Unprosecutable Crime," 8 Yale J. on Reg. 281, 370 (1991) (describing Charlie's rule).

3. The Dodd-Frank Act added swaps to the definition of "commodity interests." Swaps that are highly economically correlated to futures contracts must be aggregated with the futures contracts traded by the account owner or trader in determining whether position limits are exceeded.

4. In the securities industry, margin requirements were imposed under the Securities Exchange Act of 1934 as a means to limit excessive speculation [15 U.S.C. § 78g]. As described in Chapter 4, the Federal Reserve Board's Regulation T limits the amount of funds that can be borrowed to purchase a stock to fifty percent of the purchase price. Although the Federal Reserve Board subsequently concluded that such restrictions were unnecessary, Regulation T remains in place. See, Jerry W. Markham, "Federal Regulation

of Margin in the Commodity Futures Industry—History and Theory," 64 Temple L. Rev. 59 (1991) (describing this background).

5. Using margin to restrict speculation was rejected under the Commodity Exchange Act of 1936. Congress chose instead to use position limits. Congress also rejected subsequent government efforts to use margin restrictions as a means to limit speculation in futures trading. See, Id. (describing that history).

6. Commodity futures exchanges have also traditionally used "price limits," as a part of their self-regulatory role in preventing market breakdowns. When the change in the price of a commodity futures contract reaches a specified amount in a single trading day (i.e., goes up or down a specified amount in a single trading day—the trading "limit"), no new trades can occur at prices above or below the specified amount. This "timeout" allows traders to collect margins, which will be needed to be posted as a result of the large price swing. The trading halt also allows the market to absorb information that may have a destabilizing effect.

7. As noted in Chapter 2, "circuit breakers" were adopted in the securities industry after the Stock Market Crash of 1987. Those controls stopped trading market wide when the circuit breaker was tripped. In addition:

> On May 31, 2012, the SEC approved a new "Limit Up-Limit Down" mechanism to address market volatility by preventing trades in listed equity securities when triggered by large, sudden price moves in an individual stock. Additionally, the SEC approved proposed rule changes that modify existing circuit breaker procedures related to market-wide trading halts.

SEC, "Investor Bulletin: New Measures to Address Market Volatility," available at http://www.sec.gov/investor/alerts/circuitbreakersbulletin.htm (accessed on April 13, 2013).

7. WASH TRADES AND OTHER FICTITOUS TRANSACTIONS

UNITED STATES V. WINOGRAD

656 F.2d 279 (7th Cir. 1981), cert. denied sub nom., 455 U.S. 989 (1982)

Opinion by: PELL

At the conclusion of a jury trial, the defendants were found guilty of conspiracy to defraud the United States by impairing the United States Treasury Department's collection of income taxes in violation of 18 U.S.C. § 371, aiding the preparation of fraudulent United States income tax returns in violation of 26 U.S.C. § 7206(2), and entering into fixed and uncompetitive commodity futures transactions and wash sales in violation of 7 U.S.C. § 6c(a)(A). This appeal followed the entry of judgment on the jury verdict.

In the fall of 1974, Harold Brady, repeatedly characterized by the parties as "one of the world's largest copper traders," and apparently being desirous of providing himself with a tegurium protecting himself to some extent from the inevitable result of an overabundance of otherwise taxable income, employed the Siegel Trading Company to execute various commodity futures transactions in order to defer certain tax payments otherwise due that year. Appellant Siegel was the president of the company, appellant Winograd was vice-president, and both appellants were active floor-traders in commodities futures. After negotiations between the appellants and agents for Brady, it was decided that one of the procedures that would be utilized to achieve this objective was the placement of "tax straddles" in Mexican peso futures contracts on the International Monetary Market in Chicago. "Tax straddles" or "tax spreads" were, at the time at least, legitimate means to accomplish the deferring of tax payments from one year to the next and sometimes the conversion of short-term gains into long-term gains. The basis of the procedure is that normally price changes in two different future month contracts of the same commodity move in the same direction and in the same amount. The deferral or conversion is accomplished by going "long" or being a net buyer in one future month of the commodity, and going "short" or being a net seller in another month of the same commodity. When the prices of the future contracts change (generally increasing in peso futures), one account will show a loss while the other shows the corresponding, and hopefully equal, gain. The key to the transaction is to liquidate the loss-bearing account or "leg" during the first tax year or in the short-term, and to liquidate the gain-bearing account or "leg," if possible, in the following tax year or in the long-term. The legs are usually immediately reestablished for future months, thus "rolling over" the transaction. If all goes as expected, the losses should nearly or exactly equal the gains and thus there would be no real economic impact on the investor. Beneficial tax treatment results, however, when, as here, the short term "losses" shelter other unrelated short-term gains in the first year, in effect converting the amount which would have been short-term gain in the first year into gain in the second year.

As stated previously, "tax straddles" were legitimate and legal means of deferring or converting tax consequences when properly executed on an established commodities futures exchange or market and through bona fide competitive trades. The Government's position in this case, however, is that the appellants executed Brady's peso trades not through bona fide trades and open-outcry on an established market, but through prearranged and uncompetitive trades done between various employees of the Siegel Trading Company. The Government concludes, therefore, that

Brady improperly deducted his short-term losses and that the appellants are guilty of the charged violations.

Appellants' first point of contention is jurisdictional. Winograd claims that because Mexican pesos are delivered only in Mexico at the maturity of the futures contract, peso futures, in fact, all international monetary futures, do not involve commodities "in" interstate commerce as required by 7 U.S.C. § 6c(a)(A). This contention may be easily dismissed with reference to the cited section which states in part:

> (a) It shall be unlawful for any person to offer to enter into, enter into, or confirm the execution of, any transaction involving any commodity, which is or may be used for (1) hedging any transaction in interstate commerce in such commodity . . . (2) determining the price basis of any such transaction in interstate commerce in such commodity or (3) delivering any such commodity sold, shipped or received in interstate commerce for the fulfillment thereof (A) if such transaction is . . . (a wash sale, etc.). (Emphasis supplied.)

The broad language of the statute is applicable to the facts of this case. Although delivery of the pesos underlying a futures contract may take place in Mexico, the Government presented sufficient evidence that the peso futures contract could be used to hedge an interstate transaction involving pesos, could be used to determine the price basis of an interstate transaction involving pesos, and could involve the delivery of pesos in interstate commerce. The facts that, for the purpose of convenience, bank credits are often transferred instead of the actual pesos, and that in the normal course of events actual delivery of the pesos to fulfill the futures contract does not occur because the obligations are met by offsetting trades, do not alter this result. Actual delivery of the pesos to fulfill the contract is not required. Board of Trade of Chicago v. Olsen, 262 U.S. 1, 43 S. Ct. 470, 67 L. Ed. 839 (1923). Accord, In re Siegel Trading Co., Com. Fut. T. Rep. (CCH) P 20,452 (1977); and see CFTC v. Muller, 570 F.2d 1296, 1299 (5th Cir. 1978). * * *

One of the more fundamental issues appellants present is that the Government's evidence was insufficient to convict them. In this argument, appellants contend that it was the Government's burden under the income tax counts to establish that the peso transactions were "risk-free" so that the short-term "losses" were improperly deducted, and that the Government failed to establish this fact by the requisite proof.

Appellants' characterization of the Government's case is in a sense warranted. We disagree, however, with their conclusion. The Government contends, basically, that the transactions were "risk-free" because they were prearranged and thus Brady had a guaranteed seller or buyer for his position when he had accomplished his tax objectives and liquidated one leg of his position. It is true that Brady had little or no risk of market entry or exit. However, the transactions appellants executed for Brady nevertheless incorporated substantial "risks" relevant to the income tax counts because appellants did not have control over the market price of pesos and therefore Brady stood to lose substantial amounts of money if the price moved contrary to their expectations, or if the spreads between the two months' prices changed relative to each other or, in the words of Winograd on one occasion, "the spread (price) differential" had gotten "out of whack."

Notwithstanding this "risk," however, we find that the district court correctly held that the Brady "losses" were not properly deducted. Our conclusion is not based upon weighing the risks involved in the peso transactions, but is based upon the fact that the appellants did not accomplish their tax objectives through bona fide transactions in the competitive open market. The Government presented substantial evidence that Brady's trades were not done in the usual manner of open-outcry in the peso area or "pit" of the IMM, but were prearranged "crosses" done in-house between traders in the Siegel Trading Company. The trades often were not done within the relevant day's price range, and in some cases Winograd would engage in the irregular practice of "bidding" for a contract at a price lower than he was "offering." In essence, therefore, appellants appeared to be utilizing the organized market, but were in fact creating a market for their transactions at the prices they established for ulterior purposes. Such prearranged trades are not bona fide transactions supporting loss deductions.

Siegel makes the additional argument that the Government's evidence failed to establish that he knew of the prearranged trades Winograd executed for Brady. Indeed, the district judge commented: ". . . the amount of direct evidence regarding Mr. Siegel is minor at best, it is bits and pieces." We cannot fault the judge for this characterization. The entirety of the Government's case against Siegel relied upon inferences to be drawn from his vague and oblique prior comments and from the circumstances of his senior position at the trading company. Our standard of review, however, is not whether some other jury might have decided differently, but rather whether the evidence and inferences when viewed in the light most favorable to the Government's position can reasonably be said to support the jury's determination. Glasser v. United States, 315 U.S. 60, 80, 62 S. Ct. 457, 469, 86 L. Ed. 680 (1942). We hold that it can here, notwithstanding the closeness of the case, and thus affirm the district court's denial of appellant's motion for acquittal and the jury's conclusion on guilt.

For the reasons given herein the judgments of conviction are

Affirmed.

JERRY W. MARKHAM
PROHIBITED FLOOR TRADING ACTIVITIES UNDER THE
COMMODITY EXCHANGE ACT

58 Fordham L. Rev. 1 (1989)

. . . [T]raders used the commodity futures market as a tax shelter through tax straddles. A trader wishing to defer gains or to convert short-term gains into long-term capital gains would purchase the right to buy a commodity under a futures contract in a particular delivery month. At the same time, the trader could sell the same futures contract with a different delivery month. If commodity prices thereafter dropped uniformly in both contracts, the futures customer would have a gain in one leg of the transaction and a loss in the other. To illustrate, assume that a trader entered into a futures contract to sell 5,000 ounces of silver at $10 with delivery to be in March; such a tactic is called going short. At the same time, the trader agreed to buy 5,000 ounces of silver at $10.10 with delivery to be in November. The trader, in the second transaction, was going long. Assume silver prices subsequently rose $1.00 in both contracts. The trader would then have a gain of $5,000 in the long transaction and an offsetting $5,000 loss in the short leg. In the short transaction, he was agreeing to sell something that was worth more than what he had agreed to sell it for and, in the long transaction, he had agreed to buy something that was worth more than what he had agreed to pay for it. If the taxpayer then liquidated the short leg in which there was a loss, he would realize a loss for tax purposes. If he offset the gain from the profitable leg of the transaction in the following tax year, the overall result would be a loss in the first year that could be used to offset other income or to convert income into long-term capital gain, while the overall transaction had no real economic effect. If done legitimately, the tax straddle was an acceptable means of deferring taxes. Not all traders, however, wanted to engage in legitimate tax straddles because they presented a risk that actual trading losses could be incurred that would not offset the tax benefits of a transaction.

For example, if silver prices reversed themselves after liquidating the loss transaction, the trader could have an actual economic loss that would not be offset by the liquidated leg of the transaction. To legitimately foreclose this possibility, traders would, after liquidating the loss leg, reestablish a similar leg, which would continue to offset any further changes in futures prices. In the following year, the trader could then liquidate both legs and thereby avoid the possibility of large losses. Nevertheless, there remains a small risk of loss between the liquidation of the first leg and its reestablishment. In addition, variations in silver prices between different delivery months could actually result in a loss or, if a trader was lucky, an outright gain.

Possible price fluctuations motivated so-called spread or straddle traders to profit from changes between delivery months. These changes were caused by events that might not affect all prices the same way because of differing perceptions of the long-term effects of the events. To negate such risks in tax straddles, traders sometimes engaged in illegal wash transactions by entering into buy and sell transactions in the same commodity for the same delivery month. These wash sales effectively eliminated the risk of price variations in the liquidation and reestablishment of the loss legs. Tax straddle traders also engaged in transactions that were fictitious and prearranged to ensure that no outright losses occurred.

These transactions sometimes took the form of round-robin or rollover tax spreads. In these prearranged transactions, three exchange members engaged in multiple round-robin transactions in particular futures contracts. The buy and sell orders for these transactions, entered simultaneously on the floor, were generally for large blocks of futures in illiquid delivery months. Because of their simultaneous entry, large size and the illiquidity of the contracts, the participants usually were assured that their prearranged buy and sell orders would be matched. The first round of those transactions resulted in large tax losses to participants in the current tax year. In the next tax year, however, the round-robin transactions were reversed so that the prior year's loss was, for the most part, recovered as a taxable gain. Predictably, a similar but greater series of such transactions would be conducted in subsequent tax years to create tax losses to apply against the gains from the prior rollover tax spreads and from other trading activities. Tax straddle traders also sometimes manipulated prices in illiquid commodity markets to acquire the necessary gains and losses and to protect against actual outright losses. These and other fraudulent trading practices became the subject of several CFTC enforcement actions. The CFTC was also responsible for the institution of grand jury proceedings in New York and Chicago. Numerous criminal indictments were returned in both cities. Investigators also discovered that the Commodity Exchange Inc. ("Comex") in New York had special trading rules that allowed straddles to be established in after-hours trading at any price that occurred during the trading range of the day, ensuring price fluctuations for tax purposes. The CFTC later prohibited this practice. * * *

The CFTC's concern about tax straddles resulted in the passage of the Economic Recovery Tax Act of 1981, which changed the ways in which commodities futures transactions are taxed. Under the Act, tax straddles are now taxed at year-end by being marked to their market price even if the transaction has not been liquidated. If there is an open gain in one leg of a straddle and a realized loss of the closing of the other leg, the gain is taxed as if it had been closed. This eliminates the usefulness of tax straddles as well as the need for wash sales and other trading techniques which sought to reduce trading risks. Nevertheless, much of the law concerning prohibited trading practices is based on cases against traders engaging in tax straddles brought prior to the Economic Recovery Tax Act of 1981. * * *

NOTES

1. Many wealthy individuals used tax straddles to avoid or evade taxes. Among those individuals was the singer Willie Nelson, and he was bankrupted by the tax penalties associated with that trading. See, Todd Mason, Mama Don't Let Your Babies Grow up to Work for the Tax Boys, Wall Street Journal Jan. 29, 1991, at C1.

2. Chicago Mercantile Rule 534 states that:

> No person shall place or accept buy and sell orders in the same product and expiration month, and, for a put or call option, the same strike price, where the person knows or reasonably should know that the purpose of the orders is to avoid taking a bona fide market position exposed to market risk (transactions commonly known or referred to as wash trades or wash sales). Buy and sell orders for different accounts with common beneficial ownership that are entered with the intent to negate market risk or price competition shall also be deemed to violate the prohibition on wash trades. Additionally, no person shall knowingly execute or accommodate the execution of such orders by direct or indirect means.

STOLLER V. CFTC

834 F.2d 262 (2d Cir. 1987)

PIERCE, CIRCUIT JUDGE:

Manning Stoller ("Stoller"), a registered account executive with a commodities brokerage firm, petitions for review of a decision and order entered in an administrative enforcement proceeding before the Commodity Futures Trading Commission (the "Commission"). The administrative complaint charged Stoller and others with engaging in "wash sales" in violation of section 4c(a)(A) of the Commodity Exchange Act (the "Act"), 7 U.S.C. § 6c(a)(A). The Commission found that Stoller had engaged in prohibited transactions, see In re Collins, [1986–87 Transfer Binder] Comm.Fut.L.Rep. (CCH) ¶ 22,982 (Apr. 6, 1986) (hereinafter Collins I), and subsequently clarified its opinion in response to a request by the Chicago Mercantile Exchange, see In re Collins, [1986–87 Transfer Binder] Comm.Fut.L.Rep. (CCH) ¶ 23,401a (Nov. 26, 1986) (hereinafter Collins II). For the reasons stated below, we grant Stoller's petition and reverse the Commission's order.

This case concerns trading practices on the New York Mercantile Exchange (the "NYMEX") relating to May 1976 Maine potato futures contracts (the "Contracts"). The transactions in question occurred on May 5 and 6, 1976, during the last few days of trading in the Contracts, and were entered into on Stoller's instructions on behalf of his own account and those of six of his customers.

As would later be shown, *see Merrill Lynch, Pierce, Fenner & Smith, Inc. v. Curran,* 456 U.S. 353, 102 S.Ct. 1825, 72 L.Ed.2d 182 (1982), the market price of potato futures was being artificially depressed at that time by an illegal conspiracy. The conspirators planned to reap large profits when the May potato crop proved to be less plentiful than they were leading the market to believe, thereby causing the price of the futures contracts to rise. *See id.* at 369–70, 102 S.Ct. at 1834–35. In the end, holders of many Contracts failed to deliver potatoes on the specified dates, "resulting in the largest default in the history of commodities futures trading in this country." *Id.* at 367, 102 S.Ct. at 1834 (citations omitted).

In early May 1976, however, the details of this fraudulent scheme were still unknown. It apparently is clear that Stoller sensed that artificial forces were being brought to bear upon the market and recognized that the market price of the Contracts was below the level that would otherwise be indicated by an anticipated short supply of potatoes. Further, it appears that Stoller consequently believed that the artificial depression of the market would cease, either through official intervention or by investors' realization that the potato crop would be small. Futures prices would then rise, thereby creating a profit for those holding fixed-price "long" contracts to receive delivery of potatoes in May 1976.

NYMEX regulations specified that commodity deliveries were to be made first to those who had held their futures contracts the longest, with holders of the most recently acquired contracts receiving their deliveries last. Thus, when the price of the cash crop is expected to rise during the period when deliveries are made, it likely would be profitable to acquire long contracts very shortly before the close of trading in order to "get behind [i.e. at the end of] the delivery line." Those like Stoller who already owned Contracts, and who therefore expected to have to take early delivery of potatoes, probably in mid-May, would likely prefer to sell their existing Contracts and to acquire newer ones, which would entitle them to take delivery instead in late May or early June, when the value of the commodity was expected to be higher. Stoller claims that this "rollover" or "roll forward" was a commonly-used practice in Maine potato futures.

On May 5 and 6, 1976, Stoller placed orders with floor brokers to sell existing Contracts, which carried early delivery dates because of the length of time for which they had been held, and to replace them one-for-one with other Contracts at a price as near as possible to the price for which the old ones were sold. By virtue of owning newly-acquired Contracts, Stoller and his customers would be entitled to later delivery dates under applicable NYMEX regulations. The transactions were designated "market not held", which Stoller asserts signified that the floor broker was entitled to exercise discretion in placing the orders so as to minimize the price differential, but would not be held liable for any losses resulting from an error in judgment. Stoller further claims that the brokers were instructed to liquidate the old positions before acquiring the new ones, thereby subjecting him to market risk in the intervening period.

The Commission brought a three count enforcement proceeding against Stoller in June 1977, alleging, *inter alia,* that these virtually simultaneous sale and repurchase transactions at substantially the same price constituted "wash sales" within the prohibitory language of section 4c(a)(A) of the Act, 7 U.S.C. § 6c(a)(A). The Division of Enforcement moved for summary disposition in May 1978, which Stoller opposed on the ground that there were genuine issues of material fact to be resolved. In his opposition papers, Stoller sought a factual hearing at which he might seek to substantiate his claims that "roll forward" trading was a common industry practice and that his "market not held" instructions did not demonstrate an intent not to engage in a bona fide market transaction. He also cross-moved for summary disposition, claiming that his conduct could not constitute a "wash sale", as that term had been applied in prior cases almost exclusively in the context of prearranged trading or other collusive action. Both motions were denied: the Division of Enforcement's because of the existence of factual questions, and Stoller's as premature because the Division of Enforcement was entitled to seek to produce evidence that would support its allegations. *See* [1977–80 Transfer Binder] Comm.Fut.L.Rep. (CCH) ¶ 20,909 (August 23, 1978); No. 77–15 (CFTC Sept. 15, 1978).

In May 1979, when the Division of Enforcement still had not produced significant additional evidence, Stoller again moved to have the charges against him dismissed. In August 1979, the administrative law judge ("ALJ") granted summary disposition in favor of Stoller on the ground that he had demonstrated a legitimate market purpose to the transactions, thereby excluding them from the intended scope of the "wash sales" prohibition. [1977–80 Transfer Binder] Comm.Fut.L.Rep. (CCH) ¶ 20,908 (Aug. 16, 1979). In November 1979, the ALJ denied a motion by the Division of Enforcement to reconsider his August ruling. In February 1984, following the dismissal for lack of evidence of the other two counts of the complaint against Stoller, the Division of Enforcement appealed to the Commission from the ALJ's order with respect to the wash sale allegations, and in April 1986, almost ten years after the trades in question were executed, the Commission reversed the ALJ's decision and entered judgment against Stoller. In its decision, it said, "We infer from his conduct that [Stoller] initiated transactions with the intent to create the appearance of genuine purchases and sales while avoiding any bona fide market transaction." *Collins I* at 31,903.

The Chicago Mercantile Exchange requested a clarification of this decision on the ground that *Collins I* seemed to prohibit transactions in which the parties seek to minimize market risk. *See* [1986–87 Transfer Binder] Comm.Fut.L.Rep. (CCH) ¶ 23,112 (June 18, 1986). The Commission modified its holding and explained that it only sought to prohibit transactions that did not expose the principals to *any* risk of market price fluctuation. *Collins II* at 33,078. Nevertheless, it reaffirmed its decision that Stoller had violated this prohibition. This case never progressed beyond the stage of summary disposition; and no factual hearing was ever held at which Stoller would have had the opportunity to establish his defense that he did not have the requisite intent to avoid a bona fide market transaction.

Stoller's appeal raises two primary challenges to the proceedings before the Commission. First, he asserts that summary disposition was improperly granted against him because of the existence of material factual disputes. Second, he claims that the Commission did not provide adequate prior notice to the commodities industry and the public that the conduct in question would be considered to constitute prohibited "wash sales". We agree with both of his contentions.

The Commission decided this case on appeal from cross-motions for summary disposition filed pursuant to 17 C.F.R. § 10.91(a). Because there were significant disputes as to material facts, this disposition was inappropriate. *RKO General, Inc. v. FCC,* 670 F.2d 215, 226 n. 32 (D.C.Cir.1981) ("Before an agency may use such [summary] procedures, it must be able to show that evidentiary hearings could serve no purpose."); *Katz v. Goodyear Tire & Rubber Co.,* 737 F.2d 238, 244 (2d Cir.1984) (dispute over question of intent may exist even where parties agree on facts concerning their actions).

Stoller's response to the Division of Enforcement's motion for summary disposition clearly sets forth genuine questions of fact, including whether Stoller instructed the floor brokers to sell the old Contracts before purchasing new ones; whether he intended to minimize or to negate risk; and what the industry practice was concerning sales to "get behind the delivery line". The determination of these issues is critical in order to ascertain whether Stoller had the requisite intent to avoid a bona fide market transaction. The Commission even concedes that to show a violation, the Division of Enforcement "must demonstrate that respondent knowingly participated in transactions initiated with intent to avoid a *bona fide* market position." *Collins II* at 33,077; *Collins I* at 31,899–900; *see also In re Goldwurm,* 7 Agric.Dec. 265, 274 (1948) ("The essential and identifying characteristic of a 'wash sale' seems to be the intent not to make a genuine, bona fide trading transaction. . . .").

Under normal circumstances, the improper resolution of a case on summary judgment is grounds to remand the case for further proceedings. *See Katz v. Goodyear Tire & Rubber Co.,* 737 F.2d at 244 (questions of intent should be left to factfinder); *Koppel v. Wien,* 743 F.2d 129, 135 (2d Cir.1984) (same). However, remand is not appropriate in this case because, as we discuss below, we consider the absence of adequate prior notice of the Commission's construction of the term "wash sale" to constitute an incurable defect in the proceedings.

The term "wash sale" is not defined in the Act itself, in any applicable regulations, or in any interpretive releases. The Commodity Exchange Authority (the "CEA"), the predecessor organization to the Commission, had advised commodities merchants and floor brokers by memorandum in 1948 that it considered trading to "get behind the delivery line" to constitute a "wash sale". However, this document was not published as an interpretive release but merely accompanied a copy of the *Goldwurm* decision that was circulated to commodities brokers shortly after the decision was rendered. In 1959, in another unpublished memorandum to the brokers, the CEA repeated this position. The CEA took the same position with respect to "roll forward" trading in an *internal* 1955 memorandum and in a 1971 letter to the Chicago Mercantile Exchange. However, we do not consider these documents to be sufficient to apprise the public at large of the rule interpretation, particularly when the policy apparently remained unenforced for years and the allegedly proscribed conduct apparently remained commonplace, as is asserted in this case. *See generally NLRB v. Majestic Weaving Co.,* 355 F.2d 854, 860–61 (2d Cir.1966) (Friendly, J.) (where conduct generally recognized as permissible in industry, agency adjudication of retroactive invalidity may be arbitrary).

An agency is free, of course, to interpret its governing statute case by case through adjudicatory proceedings rather than by rulemaking. *NLRB v. Bell Aerospace Co.,* 416 U.S. 267, 292–94, 94 S.Ct. 1757, 1770–71, 40 L.Ed.2d 134 (1974); *SEC v. Chenery Corp.,* 332 U.S. 194, 201–03, 67 S.Ct. 1575, 1579–80, 91 L.Ed. 1995 (1947). In so doing, it may "announc[e] and apply [ ] a new standard of conduct." *SEC v. Chenery Corp.,* 332 U.S. at 203, 67 S.Ct. at 1580. However, if the Commission suddenly changes its view, as we discuss below, with respect to what transactions are "bona fide trading transactions," it may not charge a knowing violation of that revised standard and thereby cause undue prejudice to a litigant who may have relied on the agency's prior policy or interpretation. *Cities of*

Anaheim, Riverside, Banning, Colton & Azusa, California v. FERC, 723 F.2d 656, 659 (9th Cir.1984) (citing *Ruangswang v. INS,* 591 F.2d 39 (9th Cir.1978)).

Like the ALJ, we are unaware of any prior instances in which the Commission had sought sanctions against anyone who engaged in futures trading that accomplished only a modification of the delivery date of the commodity. The 1948 and 1959 memoranda from the CEA to floor brokers and the 1955 internal CEA memorandum were not generally available to the public; nor does the Commission assert that they were well-known to the commodity futures community. The 1971 letter to the Chicago Mercantile Exchange was sent to an exchange other than the one on which Stoller's alleged trading violations occurred. None of these documents was formally promulgated as an administrative interpretation or incorporated in adjudicative decisions. Thus, even if Stoller had investigated the Commission's view of "roll forward" trading, it seems unlikely that he would have been able to tell from that inquiry alone that such action was impermissible. *See Ruangswang,* 591 F.2d at 45; *cf. McKenzie v. Bowen,* 787 F.2d 1216, 1222 (8th Cir.1986) (new interpretation upheld where interpretive guidelines were contained in agency's internal operations manual, publicly available for inspection and copying). The apparently commonplace nature of such trading, *see* 1 P. Johnson, *Commodities Regulation* § 2.29, at 261 (1982); *see also Collins II* at 33,078, combined with the absence of enforcement, would further buttress a reasonable inference that the conduct was permissible.

The various prior decisions on the subject of "wash sales" had concerned transactions that were virtually risk-free, often prearranged, and intentionally designed to mislead, *see, e.g., Sundheimer v. CFTC,* 688 F.2d 150 (2d Cir.1982); *In re Platt,* 24 Agric.Dec. 93 (1965), or to serve other illicit purposes, *see, e.g., In re Goldwurm,* 7 Agric.Dec. at 275 (offsetting transactions to create artificial tax losses); *In re Eisen,* 22 Agric.Dec. 758 (1963) ("accommodation trades"). The transactions in this case, by contrast, are claimed to have been designed only to minimize risk and to fulfill a purpose generally considered legitimate in the industry. Consequently, a broker might well believe the conduct in this case to be factually distinguishable from the Commission's prior case law; and indeed the ALJ acknowledged this distinction in propounding a "legitimate market purpose" test herein for conduct alleged to constitute "wash sales". [1977–80 Transfer Binder] Comm.Fut.L.Rep. (CCH) ¶ 20,908, at 23,688.

In *Collins I,* the Commission took the same position that it had expressed in its earlier memoranda, namely that all "roll forward" trading intended solely to alter the delivery date of the underlying commodity was prohibited because it did not result in any change in the holder's market position. When the Chicago Mercantile Exchange voiced its concern at this prohibition, the Commission began to reassess its position, claiming, for example, that its 1971 letter to the Chicago Exchange, despite clear language to the contrary, did not express a per se rule. *See* [1986–87 Transfer Binder] Comm.Fut.L.Rep. (CCH) ¶ 23,112, at 32,283 n. 2 (June 18, 1986). In *Collins II,* the Commission backed away from the sweeping language of *Collins I* and instead held that trading to "get behind the delivery line" might be permissible if the contract holder only sought to minimize but not to negate market risk by the transaction.

At oral argument before this Court, counsel for the Commission conceded that a market sale followed by instructions to repurchase the same quantity at the closest possible price would not constitute a "wash sale" because the individual would be exposed to the risk of market fluctuation between the trades. *See also Collins II* at 33,078 ("[T]ransactions structured to minimize rather than negate risk . . . do not violate Section 4c(a) merely because the transaction also serves to change the individual's position in the delivery line."). The Commission contends, however, that the preceding scenario is inapplicable to this case because Stoller's "market not held" instruction somehow operated to negate the risk entirely. *See Collins I* at 31,903.

The Commission may well have the power to construe the statute in such a subtle and refined way, but the public may not be held accountable under this construction without some appropriate notice. *See Ruangswang,* 591 F.2d at 45. The Commission first held that all "transactions which give the appearance of a bona fide purchase and sale, while avoiding any actual change in ownership" are illegal. *See Collins I* at 31,899. It then revised its interpretation, claiming that the statute only prohibits transactions that negate market risk. *See Collins II* at 33,078. The fact that the Commission abruptly changed its own interpretation in the middle of the proceedings in our judgment further demonstrates the need both for a clearer and more explicit interpretation and for appropriate notice thereof to the public as to what conduct is permissible. Because we find that the public was not adequately apprised that the Commission views "roll forward" trading to be encompassed within the "wash sale" prohibition, we conclude that Stoller may not be held liable under that interpretation for his alleged violations with respect to the Contracts at issue herein.

The petition for review is granted and the Commission's order is reversed.

NOTES

1. In Elliot v. CFTC, 202 F.3d 926 (7th Cir. 2000), cert denied, 531 U.S. 1010 (2000), the Seventh Circuit upheld CFTC charges that a trader violated the CEA by engaging in the same conduct that was at issue in the Stoller

case. The Seventh Circuit noted that "freshening" a position to defer delivery is a legitimate market practice unless it is done in a non-competitive manner.

2. For a discussion on scienter requirements for wash trading violations see Charles R.P. Pouncy, The Scienter Requirement And Wash Trading In Commodity Futures: The Knowledge Lost In Knowing, 16 Cardozo L. Rev. 1625 (1995).

IN THE MATTER OF SHELL TRADING US COMPANY, ET. AL.
Comm. Fut. L. Rep. (CCH) ¶ 30,161 (C.F.T.C. 2006)

The Commodity Futures Trading Commission ("Commission") has reason to believe that Shell Trading US Company ("STUSCO"), Shell International Trading and Shipping Co. ("STASCO"), and Nigel Catterall ("Catterall") (collectively "Respondents") have violated Section 4c(a) of the Commodity Exchange Act, as amended (the "Act"), 7 U.S.C. § 6c(a) (2002), and Commission Regulation 1.38(a), 17 C.F.R. § 1.38(a). Therefore, the Commission deems it appropriate and in the public interest that public administrative proceedings be, and hereby are, instituted to determine whether Respondents engaged in the violations set forth herein, and to determine whether any order shall be issued imposing remedial sanctions.

In anticipation of the institution of an administrative proceeding, Respondents have submitted Offers of Settlement (the "Offers"), which the Commission has determined to accept. Without admitting or denying the findings of fact herein, Respondents consent to the entry of this Order, and acknowledge service of this Order Instituting Proceedings Pursuant to Sections 6(c) and 6(d) of the Commodity Exchange Act, Making Findings and Imposing Remedial Sanctions ("Order"). Respondents consent to the use by the Commission of the Findings in this proceeding and in any other proceeding brought by the Commission or to which the Commission is a party.

On at least five occasions between November 2003 and March 2004, traders for STASCO and STUSCO prearranged and executed non-competitive futures trades in crude oil on the New York Mercantile Exchange ("NYMEX"). In each instance, the traders prearranged the trade by agreeing on the quantity and the settlement month, and agreeing to take the opposite positions of the trade. There was no prearrangement as to price. The traders then placed the trades with a NYMEX floor brokerage company, which then executed the trades.

The prearranged trades by the traders of STASCO and STUSCO, including Catterall, who was the chief trader on behalf of STUSCO, constituted fictitious sales in violation of Section 4c(a) of the Act, 7 U.S.C. § 6c(a) (2002). Furthermore, by executing prearranged orders to buy and sell futures in crude oil, STASCO's and STUSCO's traders also engaged in noncompetitive transactions in violation of Regulation 1.38(a), 17 C.F.R. § 1.38(a) (2004). Because the STASCO and STUSCO traders undertook their actions within the scope of their employment, STASCO and STUSCO are liable for their respective traders' violations of Section 4c(a) of the Act and Regulation 1.38(a), pursuant to Section 2(a)(1)(B) of the Act, 7 U.S.C. § 2 (a)(1)(B) (2002). * * *

Shell Trading US Company is a Delaware corporation with its principal place of business in Houston, Texas. STUSCO's ultimate parent company is Royal Dutch Shell plc. STUSCO has been a member of the NYMEX since November 8, 2002, but has never been registered with the Commission.

Shell International Trading and Shipping Co. is a United Kingdom corporation with its principal place of business in London, UK. STASCO's ultimate parent company is Royal Dutch Shell plc. STASCO has never been registered with the Commission.

Nigel Catterall resides in Sugar Land, Texas, and is the head of the Futures desk at STUSCO. Until September 2003 he was a trader at STASCO's futures desk. Catterall has never been registered with the Commission.

On at least five occasions between November 2003 and March 2004, traders for STUSCO and STASCO prearranged noncompetitive futures orders in crude oil that were placed and executed on the NYMEX. On each occasion, prior to the orders' being placed on the NYMEX, traders for STUSCO and traders for STASCO had telephone conversations with one another to discuss the specific quantity and delivery month of the orders. STUSCO and STASCO agreed that one would buy and the other would sell the specified quantity and delivery month. Subsequently, the traders contacted a floor brokerage company, which executed the trades.

For example, on January 19, 2004, Catterall, on behalf of STUSCO, and traders from STASCO prearranged and executed an order whereby STUSCO sold and STASCO bought crude oil futures. In pre-trade conversations between the STUSCO and STASCO traders, both traders reviewed their respective companies' positions before the NYMEX opening, and agreed on the volume of crude oil futures that STUSCO would sell and STASCO would buy. No prearrangement as to price occurred. Substantially similar conduct occurred on at least four other occasions, two of which involved Catterall.

STUSCO and STASCO entered into five prearranged trades, three of which involved Catterall, which are fictitious and non competitive trades under the Act and Regulations promulgated thereunder.

Section 4c(a) of the Act makes it unlawful for any person to offer to enter into, enter into, or confirm the execution of a transaction that is a fictitious sale. In re Gimbel, [1987–1990 Transfer Binder] Comm. Fut. L. Rep. (CCH) P 24,213 at 35,003 (CFTC Apr. 14, 1988), aff'd as to liability, 872 F.2d 196 (7th Cir. 1989). By enacting Section 4c(a), Congress sought to "ensure that all trades are focused in the centralized marketplace to participate in the competitive determination of the price of the futures contracts." S. Rep. No. 93–1131. 93d Cong., 2d Sess. 16–17 (1974), see also Merrill Lynch Futures. Inc. v. Kelly, 585 F. Supp. 1245, 1251 n.3 (S.D.N.Y. 1984) (Section 4c(a)(A) was generally intended to prevent collusive trades conducted away from the pits). As a result, Section 4c(a) broadly prohibits fictitious trades intended to avoid the risks and price competition of the open market.

Although Section 4c(a) of the Act prohibits fictitious sales, the term is not defined in the Act. In re Thomas Collins, [1996–1998 Transfer Binder] Comm. Fut. L. Rep. (CCH) P 27,194 at 45,742 (CFTC Dec. 10, 1997); In re Harold Collins, [1986–1987 Transfer Binder] Comm. Fut. L. Rep. (CCH) P 22,982 at 31,903 (CFTC Apr. 4, 1986). A fictitious sale is a general category that includes, at a minimum, the unlawful practices specifically enumerated in Section 4c(a), as well as prearranged trading. Id.; In re Gimbel, P 24,213 at 35,003. The central characteristic of the general category of fictitious sales is the use of trading techniques that give the appearance of submitting trades to the open market while negating the risk or price competition incident to such a market. In re Fisher, [Current Transfer Binder] Comm. Fut. L. Rep. (CCH) P 29,725 at 56,052 n.11 (CFTC Mar. 24, 2004); Thomas Collins, P 27,194 at 45,742; Harold Collins, P 22, 982 at 31, 902.

The Commission has long held that prearranged trading is a form of fictitious sales. Harold Collins, P 22,982 at 31,903. By determining trade information such as price and quantity outside the pit, and then using the market mechanism to shield the private nature of the bargain from public scrutiny, both price competition and market risk are eliminated. Id.

In this case, the various telephone conversations between the STASCO and STUSCO traders, including Catterall, pertaining to the specific quantity and delivery month of the contracts to be traded prior to the submission of the orders and the execution of the trades, and agreeing to take the opposite positions in the trades, establish that the resulting trades were prearranged, and thus fictitious sales. Consequently, the traders of STASCO and STUSCO, including Catterall, violated Section 4c(a), which makes it unlawful to offer to enter into, or to enter into, any commodity futures transaction that is a fictitious sale.

STUSCO and STASCO are liable for the violations of the traders they employed. Under Section 2(a)(1)(B) of the Act, 7 U.S.C. § 2(a)(1)(B) (2002), and Section 1.2 of the Commission's Regulations, 17 C.F.R. § 1.2 (2004), the act, omission, or failure of any official, agent, or other person acting for any individual, association, partnership, corporation, or trust within the scope of his employment or office shall be deemed the act, omission, or failure of such individual, association, partnership, corporation or trust, "It does not matter if the principal participated in or even knew about the agent's acts; he is strictly liable for them." Stotler and Co. v. CFTC, 855 F.2d 1288, 1292 (7th Cir. 1988) (citing Cange v. Stotler, 826 F.2d 581, 589 (7th Cir. 1987). As the traders, including Catterall, were each acting within the scope of their employment, STUSCO and STASCO are liable for their respective traders' violations of the Act.

Commission Regulation 1.38(a) requires that all purchases and sales of commodity futures be executed "openly and competitively." The purpose of this requirement is to ensure that all trades are executed at competitive prices and directed into a centralized marketplace to participate in the competitive determination of the price of futures contracts. Noncompetitive trades are generally transacted in accordance with express or implied agreements or understandings between and among the traders. Gilchrist, P 24,993 at 37,652. Noncompetitive trades are also a type of fictitious sale, because they negate the risk incidental to an open and competitive market. Fisher, P 29,725 at 56,052 n. 11. Trades can be noncompetitive even though they are executed in the pit. In re Buckwalter, [1990–1992 Transfer Binder] Comm. Fut. L. Rep. (CCH) P 24,994 at 37,683 (CFTC Jan. 25, 1991) (citing Laiken v. Dep't of Agriculture, 345 F.2d 784,785 (2d Cir. 1965)). Prearranged trading is a form of anti-competitive trading that violates Commission Regulation 1.38(a). Gimbel, P 24,213 at 35,003.

By entering into prearranged noncompetitive trades, STASCO and STUSCO traders, including Catterall, violated Commission Regulation 1.38(a). * * *

JERRY W. MARKHAM
PROHIBITED FLOOR TRADING ACTIVITIES UNDER THE
COMMODITY EXCHANGE ACT
58 Fordham L. Rev. 1 (1989)

CFTC Regulation 1.38 embodies a concept critical to the conduct of commodity futures trading: trades must be competitive Unfortunately, the CFTC has apparently equated this desirable goal with a requirement that there be no discussion or "shopping" of orders before their entry into the pit. The CFTC's narrow view of competition guarantees that the only competition allowed is that of floor brokers, many of whom are trading for their own account and enjoying the time and place advantage of a position on the floor where all trades are executed. Those advantages, coupled with dual trading and the lack of an adequate audit trail to uncover misconduct, foster abuses, reduce competition and give floor traders significant control over orders flowing into the pits.

Large block trades are an area of particular concern in this regard. Block trades are large orders entered by institutions that may have an undue effect on market prices if entered in the trading pit without being previously positioned with an opposite buyer or seller. A large block trade may drive down prices disproportionately, particularly in illiquid markets where prior placement may be the only method of execution. Realizing that block trades can have such effects, the securities exchanges have long allowed traders to arrange and negotiate large block trades off the exchange floors. The CFTC, however, has not allowed such block trading to occur because of its concern that such transactions are by their very nature prearranged.

The result is that a block trader who prearranges a trade in securities is considered to be undertaking the beneficial task of ensuring sufficient liquidity in the marketplace and the best possible price is being obtained for the block trader, as well as precluding an undue effect upon prices caused by a large block transaction. In contrast, the CFTC deems the same broker providing the same service to a customer in the commodities industry to be in violation of a federal law.

There is no basis for this distinction between securities and commodities. Indeed, as a result of the stock market crash of 1987, the SEC recommended that this disparity in regulation be examined, because large stock index futures trades could have an adverse effect on securities prices.

A recent report issued by the Committee on Futures Regulation of the Association of the Bar of the City of New York examined block trading at length. The report noted that the CFTC had considered a form of "sunshine trading" where orders would be announced prior to their entry on the floor so that traders could contact customers and seek their participation in the trade before the order is entered for execution in the pit. The Bar Committee concluded the proposed sunshine trading would not undermine the purposes of competitive execution. * * *

There are other incongruities and uncertainties in the regulation of floor trading practices. For example, another prohibition contained in the Commodity Exchange Act concerns "accommodation" trading. Historically this type of trading involved transactions between two clearing firms in which one house was net long while the other was net short. As a result, both firms had to post margin funds with the clearing house to secure their exposed net long or short positions. To avoid such payment, the firm that was net long sold sufficient futures contracts to the firm that was net short to place each firm in an even or nearly even position. This reduced or eliminated the need to put up margin with the clearing house. Later, another transaction was entered to unwind the first transaction. In the meantime, each house had the use of the margin money.

After the passage of the Commodity Exchange Act in 1936, the CEA sought to expand the definition of accommodation trading to include "wash trading entered into by one broker to assist another broker to make cross trades, wash trades, etc." The CFTC has also sought to expand accommodation trading to include instances where floor brokers assist other floor brokers in noncompetitive transactions and in transactions that allow brokers to trade indirectly against their customers.

The cross trade is another type of transaction prohibited under the Commodity Exchange Act. Certain cross trades are permitted, as where a broker has in hand an order to buy and an order to sell from different customers. The orders can be matched against each other at the market prices or at the limit prices upon open outcry pursuant to exchange rules. Some exchange rules permit this practice but require approval of an exchange official, indicating that the trade was done by open outcry. Other exchanges prohibit the practice entirely.

The CFTC prohibited a type of cross trading that involves the direct or indirect offsetting of customer orders. These transactions allow a floor broker to profit by offsetting transactions in his own or a competing floor broker's account. The legislative history of the Commodity Exchange Act notes that such cross trades are fictitious trades recorded as real trades and used by pit brokers [as devices] for becoming buyers in respect to selling orders of customers and vice versa. They take the form of a recorded double purchase and sale between two brokers. Each broker is recorded as having both bought from and sold to the other the same quantity of the same futures at the same price. * * *

8. INSIDER TRADING

LAIDLAW V. ORGAN
15 U.S. 178 (1817)

The defendant in error filed his petition, or libel, in the court below, stating, that on the 18th day of February, 1815, he purchased of the plaintiffs in error one hundred and eleven hogsheads of tobacco, as appeared by the copy of a bill of parcels annexed, and that the same were delivered to him by the said Laidlaw & Co., and that he was in the lawful and quiet possession of the said tobacco, when, on the 20th day of the said month, the said Laidlaw & Co., by force, and of their own wrong, took possession of the same, and unlawfully withheld the same from the petitioner, notwithstanding he was at all times, and still was, ready to do and perform all things on his part stipulated to be done and performed in relation to said purchase, and had actually tendered to the said Laidlaw

& Co. bills of exchange for the amount of the purchase money, agreeably to the said contract; to his damage, & c. Wherefore the petition prayed that the said Laidlaw & Co. might be cited to appear and answer to his plaint, and that judgment might be rendered against them for his damages, & c. And inasmuch as the petitioner did verily believe that the said one hundred and eleven hogsheads of tobacco would be removed, concealed, or disposed of by the said Laidlaw & Co., he prayed that a writ of sequestration might issue, and that the same might be sequestered in the hands of the marshal, to abide the judgment of the court, and that the said one hundred and eleven hogsheads of tobacco might be finally adjudged to the petitioner, together with his damages, & c., and costs of suit, and that the petitioner might have such other and farther relief as to the court should seem meet, & c.

The bill of parcels referred to in the petition was in the following words and figures, to wit:

"Mr. Organ Bo't of Peter Laidlaw & Co. 111 hhds. Tobacco, weighing 120,715 pounds n't. fr. $7,54469.

"New–Orleans, 18th February, 1815."

On the 21st of February, 1815, a citation to the said Laidlaw & Co. was issued, and a writ of sequestration, by order of the court, to the marshal, commanding him to sequester 111 hogsheads of tobacco in their possession, and the same so sequestered to take into his (the marshal's) possession, and safely keep, until the farther order of the court; which was duly executed by the marshal. And on the 2d of March, 1815, counsel having been heard in the case, it was ordered, that the petitioner enter into a bond or stipulation, with sufficient sureties in the sum of 1,000 dollars, to the said Laidlaw & Co., to indemnify them for the damages which they might sustain in consequence of prosecuting the writ of sequestration granted in the case.

On the 22d of March, 1815, the plaintiffs in error filed their answer, stating that they had no property in the said tobacco claimed by the said petitioner, or ownership whatever in the same, nor had they at any time previous to the bringing of said suit; but disclaimed all right, title, interest, and claim, to the said tobacco, the subject of the suit. And on the same day, Messrs. Boorman & Johnston filed their bill of interpleader or intervention, stating that the petitioner having brought his suit, and filed his petition, claiming of the said Laidlaw & Co. 111 hogsheads of tobacco, for which he had obtained a writ of sequestration, when, in truth, the said tobacco belonged to the said Boorman & Johnston, and was not the property of the said Laidlaw & Co., and praying that they, the said Boorman & Johnston, might be admitted to defend their right, title, and claim, to the said tobacco, against the claim and pretensions of the petitioner, the justice of whose claim, under the sale as stated in his petition, was wholly denied, and that the said tobacco might be restored to them, & c.

On the 20th of April, 1815, the cause was tried by a jury, who returned the following verdict, to wit: "The jury find for the plaintiff, for the tobacco named in the petition, without damages, payable as per contract." Whereupon the court rendered judgment "that the plaintiff recover of the said defendants the said 111 hogsheads of tobacco, mentioned in the plaintiff's petition, and sequestered in this suit, with his costs of suit to be taxed; and ordered, that the marshal deliver the said tobacco to the said plaintiff, and that he have execution for his costs aforesaid, upon the said plaintiff's depositing in this court his bills of exchange for the amount of the purchase money endorsed, & c., for the use of the defendants, agreeably to the verdict of the jury."

On the 29th of April, 1815, the plaintiffs in error filed the following bill of exceptions, to wit: "Be it remembered, that on the 20th day of April, in the year of our Lord, 1815, the above cause came on for trial before a jury duly sworn and empanelled, the said Peter Laidlaw & Co. having filed a disclaimer, and Boorman and Johnston of the city of New–York, having filed their claim. And now the said Hector M. Organ having closed his testimony, the said claimants, by their counsel, offered Francis Girault, one of the above firm of Peter Laidlaw & Co., as their witness; whereupon the counsel for the plaintiff objected to his being sworn, on the ground of his incompetency. The claimants proved that Peter Laidlaw & Co., before named, were, at the date of the transaction which gave rise to the above suit, commission merchants, and were then known in the city of New–Orleans as such, and that it is invariably the course of trade in said city for commission merchants to make purchases and sales in their own names for the use of their employers; upon which the claimants again urged the propriety of suffering the said Francis Girault to be sworn, it appearing in evidence that the contract was made by Organ, the plaintiff, with said Girault, one of the said firm of Peter I Laldlaw & Co. in their own name, and there being evidence that factors and commission merchants do business on their own account as well as for others, and there being no evidence that the plaintiff, at the time of the contract, had any knowledge of the existence of any other interest in the said tobacco, except that of the defendants, Peter Laidlaw & Co. The court sustained the objection, and rejected the said witness. To which decision of the court the counsel for the claimants aforesaid begged leave to except, and prayed that this bill of exceptions might be signed and allowed. And it appearing in evidence in the said cause, that on the night of the 18th of February, 1815, Messrs. Livingston, White, and Shepherd brought from the British fleet the news that a treaty of peace had been signed at Ghent by the American and British commissioners, contained in a letter from Lord Bathurst to the Lord Mayor of London, published in the British newspapers, and that Mr. White caused the same to be made public in a handbill on Sunday morning, 8 o'clock, the 19th of February, 1815, and that the brother of Mr. Shepherd, one of these gentlemen, and who was interested in one-third of the profits of the purchase set forth in said plaintiff's petition, had, on Sunday morning, the 19th of February, 1815, communicated said news to the plaintiff; that the said plaintiff, on receiving said news, called on Francis Girault, (with whom he had been bargaining for the tobacco mentioned in the petition, the evening previous,) said Francis Girault being one of the said house of trade of Peter Laidlaw & Co., soon after sunrise on the morning of Sunday, the 19th of February, 1815, before he had heard said news. Said Girault asked if there was any news which was calculated to enhance the price or value of the article about to be purchased; and that the said purchase was then and there made, and the bill of parcels annexed to the plaintiff's petition delivered to the plaintiff between 8 and 9 o'clock in the morning of that day; and that in consequence of said news the value of said article had risen from 30 to 50 per cent. There being no evidence that the plaintiff had asserted or suggested any thing to the said Girault, calculated to impose upon him with respect to said news, and to induce him to think or believe that it did not exist; and it appearing that the said Girault, when applied to, on the next day, Monday, the 20th of February, 1815, on behalf of the plaintiff, for an invoice of said tobacco, did not then object to the said sale, but promised to deliver the invoice to the said plaintiff in the course of the forenoon of that day; the court charged the jury to find for the plaintiff. Wherefore, that justice, by due course of law, may be done in this case, the counsel of said defendants, for them, and on their behalf, prays the court that this bill of exceptions be filed, allowed, and certified as the law directs.

DOMINICK A. HALL,

District Judge.

New–Orleans, this 3d day of May, 1815."

On the 29th of April, 1815, a writ of error was allowed to this court, and on the 3d of May, 1815, the defendant in error deposited in the court below, for the use of the plaintiffs in error, the bills of exchange mentioned in the pleadings, according to the verdict of the jury and the judgment of the court thereon, which bills were thereupon taken out of court by the plaintiffs in error.

MR. CHIEF JUSTICE MARSHALL delivered the opinion of the court.

The question in this case is, whether the intelligence of extrinsic circumstances, which might influence the price of the commodity, and which was exclusively within the knowledge of the vendee, ought to have been communicated by him to the vendor? The court is of opinion that he was not bound to communicate it. It would be difficult to circumscribe the contrary doctrine within proper limits, where the means of intelligence are equally accessible to both parties. But at the same time, each party must take care not to say or do any thing tending to impose upon the other. The court thinks that the absolute instruction of the judge was erroneous, and that the question, whether any imposition was practiced by the vendee upon the vendor ought to have been submitted to the jury. For these reasons the judgment must be reversed, and the cause remanded to the district court of Louisiana, with directions to award a venire facias de novo. Venire de novo awarded.

NOTES

1. The SEC's insider trading cases are premised on a theory that all traders should have equal access to information, a theory that the CFTC has refused to accept, as did the Supreme Court in Chiarella v. United States, 445 U.S. 222 (1980).

In a study ordered by Congress in the Futures Trading Act of 1982, the CFTC rejected application of the SEC's insider trading to the futures markets. The CFTC noted that many commodity market participants, particularly hedgers, had unequal access to market-moving information that was proprietary to their businesses. The CFTC stated that:

> Numerous futures market participants may have legitimate access to what some may perceive as superior information. For example, hedgers, who comprise a substantial portion of the markets, also participate in the production, processing, distribution and/or consumption of the cash commodity underlying the futures market. By the nature of their businesses, many hedgers are privy to nonpublic information that may prove to be material in futures markets. Alternatively, speculators have knowledge of their own futures or cash market positions and some traders may have superior resources with which to purchase or develop research information. Moreover, traders on the floor of an exchange may have advantages of time and place over others. Such access to superior or more timely information is inherent in the markets, and futures market participants voluntarily accept this situation if they choose to trade.

CFTC, A Study of the Nature, Extent and Effects of Futures Trading by Persons Possessing Material, Nonpublic Information, submitted to the Committee on Agriculture of the House of Representatives and the Committee on Agriculture, Nutrition and Forestry of the Senate pursuant to Sec. 23(b) of the Commodity Exchange Act, as amended (Sept. 1984).

The CFTC's 1984 study on insider trading also considered manipulation concerns raised by the Federal Trade Commission over trading in front of private analyst reports that could have market effects. For example, a bullish market report published by a large firm could push prices upward. This would allow the firm to profit by trading in advance of the report. One such instance arose from claims that Phibro-Salomon, a large financial services firm, profited from trading in interest rate futures. That trading occurred just before the publication of a market-moving forecast by Henry Kaufman, the firm's chief economist, in August 17, 1982, which predicted that interest rates would fall. The CFTC found no basis for action because it could find no relationship between Phibro-Salomon's trading and the timing of Kaufman's report.

2. In 2008, Congress added a proviso to Section 4b of the Commodity Exchange Act, [7 U.S.C. § 6b] which adopted the approach taken by the Supreme Court in Laidlaw. This amendment states that Section 4(b) does not require disclosure of "nonpublic information that may be material to the market price, rate, or level of the commodity or transaction, except as necessary to make any statement made to the other person in or in connection with the transaction not misleading in any material respect." Similar language was added by Section 753 of the Dodd-Frank Wall Street Reform and Consumer Protection Act of 2010 to the CFTC's new anti-manipulation authority.

3. The CEA prohibits insider trading by members of the CFTC or its staff or the staff or directors of a self-regulatory organization (SRO). [7 U.S.C. § 6c and § 13(e)]. The STOCK Act [112 P.L. 105; 126 Stat. 291] that was enacted in 2012 prohibits such insider trading by members of Congress and their staff.

4. As described below, the CFTC adopted a misappropriation theory for information stolen from an employer, an insider trading theory like that used by the SEC. A consent order of injunction was entered in CFTC v. Kelly, COMM. FUT. L. REP. (CCH) ¶ 27,465 (S.D.N.Y. 1998) in response to charges that the respondents misappropriated and traded on market-moving information from their employer.

9. FRONT-RUNNING

UNITED STATES V. DIAL

757 F.2d 163 (7th Cir. 1985), *cert. denied*, 474 U.S. 838 (1985)

POSNER, CIRCUIT JUDGE.

Donald Dial and Horace Salmon were found guilty by a jury of mail and wire fraud (18 U.S.C. §§ 1341 and 1343) in connection with the trading of silver futures on the Chicago Board of Trade. Dial was sentenced to 18 months in prison to be followed by 5 years on probation, and was fined $16,000. Salmon was sentenced to 5 years on probation with 30 days of this period to be spent in work release (meaning that he will work during the day but sleep in jail), and was fined $15,000 and ordered to do 500 hours of community service.

The main argument of the appeals is that the conduct in which the defendants engaged was not fraudulent. To understand this argument you must know something about commodity futures. For background see Carlton, *Futures Markets: Their Purpose, Their History, Their Growth, Their Successes and Failures*, 4 J. Futures Mkts. 237 (1984); Chicago Board of Trade, Commodity Trading Manual (1982); Chicago Board of Trade, Silver Futures: Another New Dimension (1969); *Leist v. Simplot*, 638 F.2d 283, 286–88 (2d Cir. 1980), aff'd under the name of *Merrill Lynch, Pierce, Fenner & Smith, Inc. v. Curran*, 456 U.S. 353, 72 L. Ed. 2d 182, 102 S. Ct. 1825 (1982). A futures contract is a contract for the sale of a commodity at a future date; but unlike a forward contract, which it otherwise resembles, a futures contract rarely results in actual delivery of the commodity. Suppose that today, a day in March, the price of silver for delivery in June is $4 an ounce, but you think the price will go up to $5 by the time June rolls around. You would then buy June silver at $4. The person on the other side of the contract, the seller, presumably thinks differently—that the price in June will be $4 or lower. You are "long" on the contract; you expect the price to rise. He is "short"; he expects it to fall. As the months go by, the price of June silver will change as more and more information becomes available on the likely demand and supply of silver in June. Suppose in May the price hits $5 and you want to take your profit. All you have to do is sell the contract for $5; you don't have to worry about ending up with a pile of silver to dispose of. Nor need the person who sold you the silver for $4, and who probably never had any silver, have to worry about getting some and delivering it in June to the person to whom you sold your contract. All he has to do in order to take his loss and get out of the market is buy (at $5) the same amount of June silver that he had agreed to sell; the two contracts cancel, and he is out of the market.

What we have described is speculation but not, as the defendants contend, gambling. Commodity futures trading serves a social function other than to gratify the taste for taking risks—two other social functions in fact. It increases the amount of information that the actual consumers of the commodity (mainly, in the case of silver, manufacturers of film, electronics, and jewelry) have about future price trends, by creating incentives for investors and their advisors to study and forecast demand and supply conditions in the commodity. And it enables the risk-averse to hedge against future uncertainties. Suppose a jewelry manufacturer knows that it will need a certain amount of silver in June and is worried that the price might be very high by then. By buying June silver futures at $4 it can place a ceiling on what the silver will cost it (sellers can hedge similarly, by selling futures). Suppose that by June the price has risen to $5. When the manufacturer buys silver then, it will have to pay $5; but by selling its futures contract (to someone who had gone short on June silver) just before delivery is due, for $5, which is to say at a profit of $1, the manufacturer ends up paying a net of only $4 for the silver. The manufacturer could have hedged by means of a forward instead of a futures contract, that is, by signing a contract with a silver company for delivery in June at $4. But then it would have to locate and negotiate with a particular seller in advance, rather than wait till June when it will actually want the silver and buy then at the current price ($5). Since futures contracts are standard contracts—for example, the Chicago Board of Trade's silver futures contract in the period relevant to this case was a contract for 5,000 troy ounces of silver of a specified grade and quality—there is no negotiation over terms; and since the transaction is guaranteed by the clearing members of the exchange, see *Bernstein v. Lind-Waldock & Co.*, 738 F.2d 179, 181 (7th Cir. 1984), the buyer does not have to worry about whom he is dealing with.

Traders on a commodity futures exchange will, however, want some assurance that there are no people in the market who have preferential access to information. If there are known to be such people, the other traders will tend to leave the exchange for other exchanges that do not have such people—and several commodity exchanges besides the Board of Trade offer trading in silver futures contracts. If trading is "rigged" on all commodity futures exchanges, there will be less commodity futures trading, period, and the social benefits of such trading, outlined above, will be reduced. The greatest danger of preferential access comes from the brokers, who often trade on their own account as well as for their customers. Brokers have more information than any of their customers because they know all their customers' orders. Suppose a customer directs his broker to buy a large number of silver futures contracts. The broker knows that when he puts this order in for execution the price will rise, and he can make it rise further if he waits to execute the order until he can combine it with other buy orders from his customers into a "block" order that will be perceived in the market as a big surge in silver demand. If, hoping to profit from this knowledge, the broker buys silver futures on his own account just before putting in the block order and then sells at the higher price that the block order generates, he will hurt his customers. His purchase (if substantial) will have caused the market price to rise just before the block order went in, and thus the price that his customers pay will be higher than otherwise; and his sale will cause the price to fall, and thus reduce the value of his customers' contracts. So if "trading ahead"—as the practice of a broker's putting in his own orders for execution ahead of his customers' orders is called—became widespread, customers would realize that the market was rigged against them. And trading ahead serves no social function at all. The broker obtains a profit from information that he has not invested in producing but that comes to him automatically in his capacity as a broker. It is like a lawyer's discovering that his client is about to make a takeover bid for another company and rushing out and buying some of that company's stock before the bid is made public.

Against this background we consider the facts as the jury could reasonably have found them in the government's favor. Dial, an experienced silver trader, was the manager of a branch office of the Clayton Brokerage Company. Salmon was the company's president. In 1978 Dial was looking for a very large investor to make a multi-million dollar purchase of silver futures through Clayton Brokerage. In preparation for the appearance of such an investor Salmon arranged for Dial to control a trading account at Clayton Brokerage in the name of Multi-Projects (Cayman), Ltd., a Cayman Islands corporation. An "equity raiser" named Kirst located on Dial's behalf the putative grand investor in the person of Nasrullah Khan, who said he represented a group of investors organized as the International Monetary Corporation (IMC). While negotiations between Khan and Dial's son were proceeding, Dial began buying silver futures for the Multi-Projects account. But he put up no cash or cash equivalent for these purchases. To understand the significance of this omission, recall that a futures contract commits each of the contracting parties to buy or sell the underlying commodity at a date in the future at whatever the market price then is. Since the brokerage house (here, Clayton Brokerage) is responsible for the undertakings in its customers' futures contracts, it wants to be sure that each customer has the financial wherewithal to make good on his obligation under his futures contract should the price move in the opposite direction from his expectations. To this end, the brokerage house requires each of its customers to put up "margin"—cash or a cash equivalent such as a Treasury bill—as a guarantee of solvency. The required margin is a (small) percentage of the contract price and fluctuates as the price fluctuates.

Brokerage houses naturally keep very close tabs on their margin accounts, insisting that as the price of the futures contracts bought on margin fluctuates the buyer increase his margin (if necessary—it will be necessary for the long if the market price of the futures contract falls, and for the short if the price rises) so that the brokerage house will always have a cushion under its guarantee of its customers' transactions. Therefore when Dial bought silver futures for the Multi-Projects account without putting up any cash or cash equivalent—bought a lot of silver futures, 200 in all, worth $5 million—Clayton Brokerage Company's computer department notified its margin department that margin calls amounting to $100,000 should be issued to Multi-Projects, and they were. But Salmon instructed the director of the computer department to delete the Multi-Projects account from its computer programs and as a result the margin calls (which were never met) stopped.

On the weekend of November 10, 1978, at a time when Dial's personal trading account was in a perilous position (he had put up $1 million in Treasury bills against margin calls and all but $6,000 had been debited to meet them), negotiations with Khan were successfully concluded and Kirst was dispatched to London to pick up IMC's check for $25 million. On the same weekend Dial engaged in intensive solicitation of his regular customers to create a block order for silver futures to put in for execution on Monday, November 13. Kirst as directed deposited IMC's check—drawn on the Oxford International Bank in the Turks and Caicos Islands, and not certified—on Monday morning in Clayton Brokerage Company's account in a Chicago bank. Between 8:43 a.m. and 12:15 p.m. Salmon transmitted to the floor of the Board of Trade an order to buy 12 February (1979) silver futures contracts, and Dial transmitted orders on behalf of Multi-Projects, himself, his son, and Kirst and other associates, including two secretaries, for a total of 262 February futures. During this period the price of February silver fluctuated between $5.83 and $5.86 an ounce. At 12:40 p.m. Dial put in the block order, which was to buy 583 February futures, at higher prices—between $5.88 and $5.90. At 12:59 (two minutes after having bought 2,000 December futures for IMC), Dial bought 1,192 February futures for IMC at $5.92. Later that afternoon Salmon sold 10 of his 12 February futures at $5.91, seven cents more than he had bought them for that morning. The price kept on rising as the afternoon wore on, until it reached its limit—a 20 cent rise from the opening price. (Exchanges impose daily limits on price fluctuations; no trading is allowed at prices outside of the limits.)

At some point during the day, Dial and Salmon learned that Khan's check had not been certified. Yet Dial, authorized by Salmon, continued in the following days to buy silver futures heavily for IMC's account, even as it became increasingly likely from communications with the Oxford Bank that the check would never clear. On November 28 Dial decided the price of silver was now too high. He placed an order to sell 200 February silver futures contracts for the Multi-Projects account at $6.13. He had again assembled a block order (also to sell) from his customers, which he placed ten minutes after the Multi-Projects order and which was executed at lower prices than all but eight of the Multi-Projects contracts. The IMC check never did clear, and eventually the account was liquidated—at a profit. However, we were told at argument that in subsequent silver trading Dial was wiped out.

The surge of buy orders on November 13 caught the attention of Board of Trade officials and the Commodity Futures Trading Commission. Only 1,587 February silver futures contracts had been traded on the most recent trading day, November 10; 4,756 were traded on November 13. The closing price for February silver futures on the Board of Trade on November 13 had been 13 cents higher than the closing price on the New York Commodity Exchange, where a similar futures contract is traded—an unusual discrepancy between such close substitutes. The Board and the Commission began an investigation of Clayton Brokerage Company's trading of the IMC account. Dial and Salmon lied (under oath) a number of times in the course of this investigation—Dial saying for example that he had not learned that IMC's check was not certified until the week of November 28 (and later admitting that he had known this on November 13), Salmon for example denying his interest in Multi-Projects.

The question for decision is whether the conduct we have described amounts to a fraud; if so, the defendants are guilty of federal wire and mail fraud, as there is no dispute that the telephone and the mails were used extensively. Although stiff federal criminal penalties for commodity dealers who defraud or attempt to defraud their customers were added to the Commodity Futures Trading Act on October 1, 1978, see 7 U.S.C. §§ 6b(A), 13(b), about six weeks before the defendants' scheme fructified in the trading on November 13, 1978, the defendants were not charged under these sections (they were, however, charged with and acquitted of filing a false report under another section), perhaps because the ambiguous wording of section 6b, on which see 1 Bromberg & Lowenfels, Securities Fraud & Commodities Fraud § 4.6(452) (1984), makes it an uncertain vehicle for a criminal prosecution.

The defendants do not argue that the Commodity Futures Trading Act supersedes the federal mail or wire fraud statutes, and are wise not to make the argument. See e.g., *United States v. Brien*, 617 F.2d 299, 309–11 (1st Cir. 1980). But they emphasize that none of the defendants' customers, or the defendants' employer, Clayton Brokerage Company, lost money as a result of their acts and that there is no statute, regulation, or Board of Trade rule that specifically forbids insider trading in commodity futures (as in securities), or block trading, or trading ahead (other than by floor brokers—the brokers who actually execute the trades on the floor of the exchange—which the defendants were not). Rule 150(b) of the Board of Trade, forbidding "trad[ing] systematically against the orders or position of his customers," may implicitly forbid trading ahead by any broker; but the only specific rule the defendants violated was the Board of Trade's Rule 210, which requires that accounts be margined. Neither the Multi-Projects account nor the IMC account was margined—the latter not only because IMC's check was no good but because margin must be in cash or a cash equivalent, such as a certified check.

But we think there was a scheme to defraud in a rather classic sense, which is obscured only because commodity futures trading is an arcane business—though not to these defendants. Fraud in the common law sense of deceit is committed by deliberately misleading another by words, by acts, or, in some instances—notably where there is a fiduciary relationship, which creates a duty to disclose all material facts—by silence. See Prosser and Keeton on the Law of Torts §§ 105–06 (5th ed. 1984). Liability is narrower for nondisclosure than for active misrepresentation, since the former sometimes serves a social purpose; for example, someone who bought land from another thinking that it had oil under it would not be required to disclose the fact to the owner, because society wants to encourage people to find out the true value of things, and it does this by allowing them to profit from their knowledge. See *Laidlaw v. Organ*, 15 U.S. (2 Wheat.) 178, 195, 4 L. Ed. 214 (1817); Kronman, *Mistake, Disclosure, Information, and the Law of Contracts*, 7 J. Legal Stud. 1 (1978). But if someone asks you to break a $10 bill, and you give him two $1 bills instead of two $5's because you know he cannot read and won't know the difference, that is fraud. Even more clearly is it fraud to fail to "level" with one to whom one owes fiduciary duties. The essence of a fiduciary relationship is that the fiduciary agrees to act as his principal's alter ego rather than to assume the standard arm's length stance of traders in a market. Hence the principal is not armed with the usual wariness that one has in dealing with strangers; he trusts the fiduciary to deal with him as frankly as he would deal with himself—he has bought candor.

As a broker, and therefore, the defendants concede (as they must, see, e.g., *Marchese v. Shearson Hayden Stone, Inc.*, 734 F.2d 414, 418 (9th Cir. 1984)), a fiduciary of his customers, Dial, when he solicited his customers to participate in block orders, implicitly represented to them that he would try to get the best possible price. He could have gotten a better price by putting their orders in ahead of the orders he placed for his own accounts and those of his friends. In trading ahead of his customers without telling them what he was doing, he was misleading them for his own profit, and conduct of this type has long been considered fraudulent. See *SEC v. Capital Gains Research Bureau, Inc.*, 375 U.S. 180, 183, 194–95, 11 L. Ed. 2d 237, 84 S. Ct. 275 (1963).

Although the defendants' expert witness testified to the effect that trading ahead does not violate the ethical standards of commodity futures trading, the jury did not have to believe this improbable testimony—by a witness who was a personal friend of Dial. (And the government presented its own expert, who gave contrary testimony.) It is true that the Board of Trade has no express rule against trading ahead of a customer (other than by a floor broker) and that there is no other specific prohibition (relevant to this case) of insider trading on commodity futures exchanges. See CFTC, A Study of the Nature, Extent and Effects of Futures Trading by Persons Possessing Material, Nonpublic Information, submitted to H.R. Comm. on Agriculture and Sen. Comm. on Agriculture, Nutrition and Forestry (Sept. 1984). But it is apparent that such a practice, when done without disclosure to the customer, is both contrary to a broker's fiduciary obligations and harmful to commodity futures trading, because it means that a person wanting to engage in such trading can trade only through an agent who has a conflict of interest. Cf. *Chasins v. Smith, Barney & Co.*, 438 F.2d 1167, 1172 (2d Cir. 1970).

The federal mail and wire fraud statutes have often been used to plug loopholes in statutes prohibiting specific frauds, see *United States v. Maze*, 414 U.S. 395, 405–08, 94 S. Ct. 645, 38 L. Ed. 2d 603 (1974) (dissenting opinion), a pertinent example being the application of the mail fraud statute to insider trading in securities before the promulgation of the SEC's Rule 10b–5. See *United States v. Groves*, 122 F.2d 87, 89 (2d Cir. 1941). Although some scholars question the appropriateness of prohibiting insider trading by corporate officers, pointing out for example that (at least if short selling by insiders is prohibited) it gives officers a greater incentive to take risks that may benefit the shareholders, see, e.g., Carlton & Fischel, *The Regulation of Insider Trading*, 35 Stan. L. Rev. 857 (1983), we would be surprised to find anyone saying a good word for insider trading by a broker; the only information he exploits is his knowledge of his customers' intentions.

The fraud was not only Dial's, but Salmon's, who was Dial's boss, knew what was going on, furthered the scheme by arranging for Dial to use the Multi-Projects account, and profited personally from the fraud along with Dial (indeed, more directly than Dial, who did not sell silver on his own account, as Salmon did, on November 13). Dial and Salmon not only defrauded their own customers; they also defrauded the people from whom they bought silver futures contracts, and their employer, the Clayton Brokerage Company, by trading, without margin, the Multi-Projects and IMC accounts. Trading without margin gives a misleading signal, because a signal not backed by any cash. If you had no assets at all, and could buy futures contracts at will (say $25 million worth), you could have a powerful influence on futures prices. Yet you might be totally irresponsible and incompetent in forecasting such prices, and might therefore reduce the accuracy of the market as a device for forecasting price; for you would lack the stimulus to sober reflection that comes from having to put one's money where one's mouth is. Trading without margin also shifts risk from the trader to the broker, in this case from Dial and Salmon to their employer, the Clayton Brokerage Company, which would have had to make good any losses on the Multi-Projects and IMC accounts. This risk was not disclosed to Clayton Brokerage any more than trading ahead was disclosed to the defendants' customers or the lack of cash backing for the enormous buying by Multi-Projects and IMC was disclosed to those who sold futures contracts to the defendants and their associates. Far from disclosing what they were doing, Dial and Salmon actively concealed it by using an account with an uninformative name (Multi-Projects) and by Salmon's ordering the deletion of the Multi-Projects account from Clayton Brokerage Company's computer records. The defendants' failure to disclose to their employer what was going on was a breach of the defendants' fiduciary duty as employees. Although they owed no similar duty to people on the other side of their silver futures transactions, their trading an unmargined account was an active misrepresentation and hence actionable even without a breach of fiduciary duty.

It is true that no one "lost money," because silver prices were rising for reasons other than the defendants' unmargined trading. If that trading had been the only thing jacking up the price, the price would have collapsed when the IMC account was liquidated—and it did not; between November 1978 and February 1980, the average monthly price of silver rose to $38.27 per ounce. But the analysis is incomplete. The defendants' customers did lose money—the additional profit they would have made if the defendants had placed their customers' orders ahead of rather than behind their own orders. And Clayton was subjected to the risk of having to make good what might have been $25 million in trading losses in the IMC account. The risk did not materialize, but just as it is embezzlement if an employee takes money from his employer and replaces it before it is missed, see, e.g., *United States v. Bailey*, 734 F.2d 296, 304 (7th Cir. 1984), so it is fraud to impose an enormous risk of loss on one's employer through deliberate misrepresentation even if the risk does not materialize. See, e.g., *United States v. Lindsey*, 736 F.2d 433, 436–37 (7th Cir. 1984); *United States v. Bush*, 522 F.2d 641, 648 (7th Cir. 1975); cf. *United States v. Feldman*, 711 F.2d 758, 763–64 (7th Cir. 1983). Finally, the defendants confused the market by signaling the presence of big buyers who had not in fact put up any money (IMC and Multi-Projects); and to undermine the confidence on which successful futures trading depends is to harm the exchanges, and the society at large. The evidence that the defendants' misrepresentations were deliberate was overwhelming, beginning with the establishment of an offshore trading operation in an uninformative name; continuing with the timing of the defendants' purchases for their own and their friends' accounts ahead of the block order and the IMC orders, all carefully orchestrated over the preceding weekend; culminating in the defendants' repeated lies to the investigating authorities; and including the violation of the margin requirements (Rule 210 of the Board of Trade) and the concealment of the defendants' interests in the Multi-Projects account. It is inessential whether the defendants also violated Rule 150(b).

Concern has been expressed with the possible abuse of the mail and wire fraud statutes to punish criminally any departure from the highest ethical standards. When the broad language of the statutes ("Whoever, having devised or intending to devise any scheme or artifice to defraud . . ."), which punishes the scheme to defraud rather than the completed fraud itself, is read by the light of the broad concept of fraud that has evolved in civil cases and the precept that the mail and wire fraud statutes are not confined to common law fraud, *Durland v. United States*, 161 U.S. 306, 312–13, 40 L. Ed. 709, 16 S. Ct. 508 (1896), concern naturally arises that the criminal law will be used to hold businessmen to the maximum, rather than minimum, standards of ethical behavior. See, e.g., Coffee, *Some Reflections on the Criminalization of Fiduciary Breaches and the Problematic Line Between Law and Ethics*, 19 Am. Crim. L. Rev. 117 (1981). It is not allayed by such popular formulations of the test for mail or wire fraud as the Fifth Circuit's in *Gregory v. United States*, 253 F.2d 104, 109 (5th Cir. 1958), which continues to be repeated with approval, see, e.g., *United States v. Bohonus*, 628 F.2d 1167, 1171 (9th Cir. 1980): fraud is whatever is not a "reflection of moral uprightness, of fundamental honesty, fair play and right dealing in the general and business life of members of society." Courts have been more concerned with making sure that no fraud escapes punishment than with drawing a bright line between fraudulent, and merely sharp, business practices, even though the universality of telephone service has brought virtually the whole commercial world within the reach of the wire-fraud statute. But we need not explore the outer bounds of mail and wire fraud in this case. The defendants' elaborate efforts at concealment provide powerful evidence of their own consciousness of wrongdoing, cf. *United States v. Bryza*, 522 F.2d 414, 422 (7th Cir. 1975), making it unnecessary for us to decide whether the same conduct, done without active efforts at concealment, would have been criminal. * * *

AFFIRMED.

NOTE

As noted above, the CFTC adopted a misappropriation theory for information stolen from an employer in CFTC v. Kelly, COMM. FUT. L. REP. (CCH) ¶ 27,465 (S.D.N.Y. 1998). The respondents in that case misappropriated market-moving information from their employer, John W. Henry & Co., a trading firm located in Boca Raton, Florida. One of the respondents, Thomas E. Kelly, was a trader at J. W. Henry. He passed the firm's trading plans on to another respondent, Andrew D. Rhee, who traded ahead (front runned) of J. W. Henry's trades. Kelly and Rhee made about $4.7 million from this scheme. The respondents were accused of violating the cheating and defrauding provisions in Section 4b of the CEA [7 U.S.C. § 6b], as opposed to the false reporting provision in that section. The traders also pleaded guilty to criminal charges under the CEA. For additional discussion of front running see Jerry W. Markham, "Front-Running": Insider Trading Under the Commodity Exchange Act, 38 Cath. U. L. Rev. 69 (1988).

10. "SPOOFING" AND "BANGING THE CLOSE"

IN THE MATTER OF PANTHER ENERGY TRADING LLC
CFTC Docket No. 13–26 (C.F.T.C. 2013)

The Commodity Futures Trading Commission ("Commission") has reason to believe that from August 8, 2011 through October 18, 2011, Panther Energy Trading LLC and Michael J. Coscia violated Section 4c(a)(5)(C) of the Commodity Exchange Act (the "Act"), 7 U.S.C. § 6c(a)(5)(C). Therefore, the Commission deems it appropriate and in the public interest that public administrative proceedings be, and hereby are, instituted to determine whether Respondents engaged in the violations set forth herein and to determine whether any order should be issued imposing remedial sanctions.

In anticipation of the institution of an administrative proceeding, Respondents have submitted an Offer of Settlement ("Offer"), which the Commission has determined to accept. Without admitting or denying any of the findings or conclusions herein, Respondents consent to the entry of this Order Instituting Proceedings Pursuant to Sections 6(c) and 6(d) of the Commodity Exchange Act, as Amended, Making Findings and Imposing Remedial Sanctions ("Order") and acknowledge service of this Order.

Beginning on August 8, 2011 through and including October 18, 2011 (the "Relevant Period"), Panther Energy Trading LLC ("Panther") and Michael J. Coscia ("Coscia") (collectively, "Respondents") engaged in the disruptive practice of "spoofing" (bidding or offering with the intent to cancel the bid or offer before execution) through algorithmic trading utilizing a program that was designed to place bids and offers and to quickly cancel those bids and offers before execution.

Because the Respondents engaged in conduct that is, or is of the character of, or is known to the trade as, spoofing, the conduct violated Section 4c(a)(5)(C) of the Act, 7 U.S.C. § 6c(a)(5)(C), which, *inter alia,* makes it unlawful for any person to engage in any trading, practice or conduct on or subject to the rules of a registered entity that is, is of the character of, or is commonly known to the trade as, spoofing.

Panther Energy Trading LLC is a trading company organized under Delaware law with its principal place of business in Red Bank, New Jersey. It is not and has never been registered with the Commission.

Michael J. Coscia is the manager and sole owner of Panther and has been registered with the Commission as a floor broker since 1988.

During the Relevant Period, Respondents placed on Globex, CME Group's electronic trading platform, algorithmic bids or offers which they intended to, and did, cancel prior to execution, and therefore engaged in a disruptive trading practice known as spoofing, in futures contracts traded on four exchanges owned by CME Group. The futures contracts in which the Respondents engaged in spoofing involved a wide spectrum of commodities including energy, metals, interest rate, agricultural, stock index, and foreign currency commodities, including for example, the widely-traded Light Sweet Crude Oil futures contract as well as the Natural Gas, Com, Soybeans, Soybean Oil, Soybean Meal, and Wheat futures contracts.

Respondents made money by employing an algorithm that was designed to rapidly place bids and offers in the market and to cancel those bids and offers prior to execution. The following example of Respondents' trading in the Light Sweet Crude Oil futures contract is illustrative of how the algorithm worked. First, the algorithm placed a relatively small order on one side of the market at or near the best price being offered to buy or sell, in this instance a sell order for 17 contracts at a price of $85.29 per barrel, which was a lower price than the contracts then being offered by other market participants. Thus, the Respondents' offer was at the lowest, *i.e.* best, offered price. Second, within a fraction of a second, the Respondents entered orders to buy a relatively larger number of Light Sweet Crude Oil futures contracts at progressively higher prices: the first bid at $85.26, the second bid at $85.27, and the third bid at $85.28. The prices of Respondents' bids were higher than the contracts then being bid by other market participants.

Thus, Respondents' placed their bids at the highest, *i.e.* best, prices. By placing the large buy orders, Respondents sought to give the market the impression that there was significant buying interest, which suggested that prices would soon rise, raising the likelihood that other market participants would buy the 17 lots the Respondents were then offering to sell. Although Respondents wanted to give the impression of buy-side interest, Respondents entered the large buy orders with the intent that these buy orders be canceled before the orders were actually executed.

In the above example, the program sought to capture an immediate profit from selling the 17 lots. Thus, if the program successfully filled the small 17-lot sell order, the large buy orders were immediately cancelled and the algorithm was designed to promptly operate in reverse. That is, the algorithm would then enter a small buy order in conjunction with relatively large sell orders at progressively lower prices, which sell orders Respondents intended to cancel prior to execution.

All trading using this algorithm was in an account that was owned and controlled exclusively by Coscia. The episodes of bidding, offering, canceling, and, if the program successfully filled the small order, liquidation activity, occurred over a very short time frame. In some instances, the Respondents utilized the spoofing algorithm hundreds of times in an individual futures contract in a single day. During the Relevant Period, Respondents accumulated net profits of approximately $1.4 million using the spoofing algorithm.

Section 4c(a)(5)(C) of the Act, 7 U.S.C. § 6c(a)(5)(C), makes it "unlawful for any person to engage in any trading, practice, or conduct on or subject to the rules of a registered entity that . . . is, is of the character of, or is commonly known to the trade as, 'spoofing' (bidding or offering with the intent to cancel the bid or offer before execution)."

In this case, Respondents intended when placing bids or offers to cancel the bids or offers prior to execution. Respondents designed the algorithmic trading program to place orders on one side of the market to give the impression of market interest on that side of the market and to increase the likelihood that their smaller orders sitting on the opposite side of the market would be filled. Respondents used an algorithm designed to cancel orders prior to execution. Consequently, Respondents, engaged in trading that was spoofing, in violation of Section 4c(a)(5)(C) of the Act, 7 U.S.C. § 6c(a)(5)(C). * * *

IN THE MATTER OF HOLD BROTHERS ON-LINE INVESTMENT SERVICES, LLC

2012 SEC LEXIS 3029 (SEC)

The Securities and Exchange Commission ("Commission") deems it appropriate and in the public interest that public administrative and cease-and-desist proceedings be, and hereby are, instituted pursuant to Sections 15(b) and 21C of the Securities Exchange Act of 1934 ("Exchange Act") and Section 9(b) of the Investment Company Act of 1940 ("Investment Company Act") against Hold Brothers On-Line Investment Services, LLC ("Hold Brothers"), Steven Hold ("Steve Hold"), Robert Vallone ("Vallone"), and William Tobias ("Tobias"); and that cease-and-desist proceedings be, and hereby are, instituted pursuant to Section 21C of the Exchange Act against Demostrate, LLC ("Demostrate") and Trade Alpha Corporate, Ltd ("Trade Alpha," and together with Hold Brothers, Steve Hold, Vallone, Tobias, and Demostrate, the "Respondents").

In anticipation of the institution of these proceedings, Respondents have submitted Offers of Settlement (the "Offers") which the Commission has determined to accept. Solely for the purpose of these proceedings and any other proceedings brought by or on behalf of the Commission, or to which the Commission is a party, and without admitting or denying the findings herein, except as to the Commission's jurisdiction over them and the subject matter of these proceedings, which are admitted, Respondents consent to the entry of this Order Instituting Administrative and Cease-and-Desist Proceedings Pursuant to Sections 15(b) and 21C of the

Securities Exchange Act of 1934 and Section 9(b) of the Investment Company Act of 1940, Making Findings, and Imposing Remedial Sanctions and Cease-and-Desist Orders ("Order"), as set forth below.

As gatekeepers to the capital markets, broker-dealers have a responsibility to establish, maintain, and enforce adequate policies and procedures and risk controls in light of the specific risks associated with the broker-dealer' s business. In particular, broker-dealers that provide access to the markets must ensure that they have policies and procedures and systems of controls in place that are reasonably designed to ensure, among other things, compliance with all regulatory requirements that are applicable in connection with the access they provide. These controls must be reasonably designed to identify and prevent, among other things, abusive trading practices. Further, if a broker-dealer identifies suspicious activity, whether through the access it provides or not, it must address such activity in an appropriate and timely manner.

From at least January 2009 through September 2010 (the "Relevant Period"), overseas traders who accessed the U.S. markets through respondent Hold Brothers, a registered broker-dealer, engaged in a manipulative trading strategy typically referred to as "layering" or "spoofing" (hereinafter, collectively, "layering"). Hold Brothers failed to adequately monitor for and investigate, in light of red flags, the manipulative trading by these overseas traders. The manipulative trading was profitable.

Certain of the overseas traders conducted their manipulative trading on the U.S. markets through two Hold Brothers "customer" accounts, which were accounts of two foreign companies—respondents Trade Alpha and Demostrate—created and partially owned by Steve Hold. Steve Hold funded Demostrate and Trade Alpha, and Demostrate and Trade Alpha provided the capital for the manipulative trading by these traders. Hold Brothers controlled the overseas traders by, among other things, determining and allocating buying power, establishing stop-loss limits, and, through Hold Brothers affiliated personnel, dictating the profit distribution between Demostrate and Trade Alpha and the traders.

Throughout the Relevant Period, the three individual respondents— Steve Hold, Vallone, and Tobias—became aware of red flags, including several emails, suggesting that the overseas traders who traded through Hold Brothers were engaging in manipulative trading. The individual respondents recklessly continued to provide traders with buying power and/or access to the U.S. markets, and failed to conduct adequate follow-up despite these warnings. In addition, Hold Brothers failed to make and keep current the requisite records related to certain brokerage orders given or received for the purchase or sale of securities and failed to furnish promptly to the staff certain order records requested by the staff.

By virtue of this conduct, (a) Trade Alpha and Demostrate violated Section 9(a)(2) of the Exchange Act; (b) Hold Brothers willfully violated Sections 9(a)(2) and 17(a) of the Exchange Act and Rules 17a–4 and 17a–8 thereunder, and failed reasonably to supervise the Demostrate traders in connection with their violations of the securities laws; (c) Steve Hold, Vallone, and Tobias willfully aided and abetted and caused Hold Brothers', Demostrate's and Trade Alpha's violations of Section 9(a)(2) of the Exchange Act; and (d) Steve Hold failed reasonably to supervise Vallone in connection with Vallone's violations of the securities laws.

Hold Brothers is a Delaware limited liability company wholly-owned by, among others, respondent Steve Hold. Hold Brothers is a FINRA member that has been registered as a broker-dealer pursuant to Section 15(b) of the Exchange Act since January 1995. Hold Brothers has branch offices in several states, including New York, New Jersey, Pennsylvania, and California.

Demostrate is a limited liability company organized under the laws of Nevis. Steve Hold is an owner of Demostrate. Overseas traders who traded for Demostrate were organized in groups by location, and the groups were assigned alpha-numeric identifiers.

Trade Alpha is a limited liability company organized under the laws of the British Virgin Islands. Steve Hold is an owner of Trade Alpha.

Steve Hold, age 41, resides in Warren, New Jersey. Steve Hold is the president and co-founder of Hold Brothers. Steve Hold holds Series 7, 24, 55, and 63 licenses.

Tobias, age 43, resides in Hoboken, New Jersey. Tobias is an associated person of Hold Brothers and is the managing member of Demostrate. Tobias holds Series 7, 27, 28, 55, and 63 licenses.

Vallone, age 62, resides in Princeton Junction, New Jersey. Until August 2012, Vallone was the Chief Compliance Officer and Chief Financial Officer of Hold Brothers. Vallone holds Series 7, 8, 23, 27, and 63 securities licenses.

During the Relevant Period, Hold Brothers was a limited liability company made up of one Class A member, Hold Brothers, Inc., which was wholly owned by Steve Hold and another individual, and a number of Class B members who conducted proprietary day trading activities. In addition to the Class B proprietary trading members, Hold Brothers executed trades on behalf of retail customer traders, all of whom engaged in some form of day trading. The firm's primary business was to provide market access to its proprietary and customer traders.

The majority of Hold Brothers' Class B proprietary traders were located in the United States, while the majority of Hold Brothers' customer traders were located in other countries. Hold Brothers' proprietary trading business consisted of approximately 40 traders. These proprietary traders traded the firm's capital, were monitored for risk and compliance purposes by Hold Brothers personnel, were licensed by the appropriate self-regulatory organization, were associated persons of the firm, and shared with Hold Brothers profits derived from their trading.

The vast majority of Hold Brothers' traders located overseas were associated with one of two "customers," either Trade Alpha in 2009 or Demostrate in 2010 (hereinafter, collectively, "Demostrate" or the "Demostrate traders"). These traders traded Demostrate's capital and were monitored for risk and compliance purposes by personnel of Hold Brothers and a Hold Brothers affiliate. As an owner, Steve Hold shared in the Demostrate trading profits. Unlike Hold Brothers' proprietary traders, however, Hold Brothers did not consider the Demostrate traders to be associated with the firm, nor did any of these traders hold licenses from any self-regulatory organization.

Demostrate maintained a brokerage account at Hold Brothers. Demostrate's managing member was Tobias. Demostrate was Hold Brothers' largest "customer," both in terms of the number of trades and revenues generated. All Demostrate trading occurred in a single account held at Hold Brothers. All of the persons who traded through Demostrate's account were located outside the United States, primarily in China. Hold Brothers assisted Demostrate and its traders in accessing the securities markets by providing these foreign traders with access to front-end trading platforms and access to the U.S. securities markets. * * *

During the Relevant Period, certain Demostrate traders repeatedly manipulated the markets of U.S. listed and over-the-counter stocks by engaging in the practice of layering.

Layering concerns the use of non-bona fide orders, or orders that the trader does not intend to have executed, to induce others to buy or sell the security at a price not representative of actual supply and demand. More specifically, a trader places a buy (or sell) order that is intended to be executed, and then immediately enters numerous non-bona fide sell (or buy) orders for the purpose of attracting interest to the bona fide order. These non-bona fide orders are not intended to be executed. The nature of these orders is to induce, or trick, other market participants to execute against the initial, bona fide order. Immediately after the execution against the bona fide order, the trader cancels the open, non-bona fide orders, and repeats this strategy on the opposite side of the market to close out the position.

Certain overseas traders trading for Demostrate engaged in extensive manipulative activity. Such traders induced algorithms to trade in a particular security by placing and then cancelling layers of orders in that security, creating fluctuations in the national best bid or offer of that security, increasing order book depth, and using the non-bona fide orders to send false signals regarding the demand for such security, which the algorithms misinterpreted as reflecting sincere demand. These overseas traders' orders were intended to deceive and did deceive certain algorithms into buying (or selling) stocks from (or to) the Demostrate traders at prices that had been artificially raised (or lowered) by the Demostrate traders.

The pattern of layering against algorithmic traders is illustrated by the activity of a Demostrate trader who traded under the identifier "PEBC" in group P69 from Nanjing, China. On June 4, 2010, the trader layered the stock of W.W. Grainger (NYSE: "GWW") on NASDAQ and the Boston Stock Exchange.

That day, at 11:08:55.152 a.m., the trader placed an order to sell 1,000 GWW shares at $101.34 per share. Prior to the trader placing the order, the inside bid was $101.27 and the inside ask was $101.37. The trader's sell order moved the inside ask to $101.34. From 11:08:55.164 a.m. to 11:08:55.323 a.m., the trader placed eleven orders offering to buy a total of 2,600 GWW shares at successively increasing prices from $101.29 to $101.33. During this time, the inside bid rose from $101.27 to $101.33, and the trader sold all 1,000 shares she offered to sell for $101.34 per share, completing the execution at 11:08:55.333. At 11:08:55.932, less than a second after the trader placed the initial buy order, the trader cancelled all open buy orders. At 11:08:55.991, once the trader had cancelled all of her open buy orders, the inside bid reverted to $101.27 and the inside ask reverted to $101.37.

Because the trader was now short 1,000 GWW shares, at 11:09:00.881, the trader placed an order to buy 1,000 GWW shares at $101.30, thereby changing the inside bid to $101.30. From 11:09:00.929 a.m. to 11:09:01.060 a.m., the trader placed eleven orders offering to sell a total of 2,600 GWW shares at successively decreasing prices from $101.35 to $101.31. During this time, the inside ask declined from $101.37 to $101.31, and the trader bought all 1,000 GWW shares she offered to buy for $101.30 per share, completing the execution at 11:09:00.977. At 11:09:01.662, less than a second after the trader placed the initial sell order, the trader cancelled all open sell orders. At 11:09:01.792, once the trader had cancelled all of her open sell orders, the inside bid reverted to $101.24 and the inside ask reverted to $101.37. This round trip transaction, which took less than seven seconds to complete, yielded the trader approximately $40. As described below, this strategy was repeated over and over again.

The manipulative trading consisted of anywhere from 67 percent to 95 percent or more of the overall trading activity in several of the groups of overseas traders trading for Demostrate—and it was profitable. During the Relevant Period, overseas traders trading for Demostrate in the several groups that engaged in layering entered into more than 325,000 layered transactions which corresponded to the entry of more than 8 million layered orders.

The two Demostrate trading groups that engaged in the most layering were also the most profitable, cumulatively making the owners of Demostrate approximately $1.8 million dollars in trading revenue.

Because the overseas traders were agents of Demostrate and traded through Demostrate's accounts, the traders' conduct can be imputed to Demostrate. In addition, because Hold Brothers controlled the Demostrate traders, the overseas traders' conduct can be imputed to Hold Brothers. * * *

As a result of the conduct described above, Demostrate and Trade Alpha violated Section 9(a)(2) of the Exchange Act, which prohibits any person from "effect[ing], alone or with one or more other persons, a series of transactions in any security . . . creating actual or apparent active trading in such security, or raising or depressing the price of such security, for the purpose of inducing the purchase or sale of such security by others."

As a result of the conduct described above, Hold Brothers willfully violated Section 9(a)(2) of the Exchange Act, which prohibits any person from "effect[ing], alone or with one or more other persons, a series of transactions in any security . . . creating actual or apparent active trading in such security, or raising or depressing the price of such security, for the purpose of inducing the purchase or sale of such security by others."

As a result of the conduct described above, Hold Brothers willfully violated Section 17(a) of the Exchange Act, which requires, in pertinent part, that registered brokers or dealers make and keep for prescribed periods records that the Commission deems necessary or appropriate in the public interest for the protection of investors, and certain rules adopted under Section 17(a), including (i) Rule 17a–4(b)(1), which requires that registered brokers and dealers preserve for a period of not less than three years, the first two years in an easily accessible place, among other things, "a memorandum of each brokerage order, and of any other instruction, given or received for the purchase or sale of securities, whether executed or unexecuted," (ii) Rule 17a–4(j), which requires that registered brokers and dealers "furnish promptly to a representative of the Commission legible, true, complete, and current copies of those records" that are required to be preserved under Section 17(a), and (iii) Rule 17a–8, which requires that brokers and dealers comply with the reporting, recordkeeping, and record retention requirements of the rules promulgated under the Currency and Financial Transactions Reporting

Act of 1970 (commonly known as the Bank Secrecy Act), 12 U.S.C. § 1829b, 12 U.S.C. §§ 1951–1959, and 31 U.S.C. §§ 5311–5330.

As a result of the conduct described above, Hold Brothers failed reasonably to supervise their associated persons, the Demostrate traders, within the meaning of Section 15(b)(4)(E) of the Exchange Act with a view to preventing and detecting their violations of Section 9(a)(2) of the Exchange Act.

As a result of the conduct described above, Steve Hold, Vallone, and Tobias willfully aided and abetted and caused Demostrate's, Trade Alpha's, and Hold Brothers' violations of Section 9(a)(2) of the Exchange Act, which prohibits any person from "effect[ing], alone or with one or more other persons, a series of transactions in any security . . . creating actual or apparent active trading in such security, or raising or depressing the price of such security, for the purpose of inducing the purchase or sale of such security by others."

As a result of the conduct described above, Steve Hold failed reasonably to supervise Vallone within the meaning of Section 15(b)(4)(E) of the Exchange Act, as incorporated by reference in Section 15(b)(6) of the Exchange Act, with a view toward preventing and detecting Vallone's violation of the federal securities laws.

In view of the foregoing, the Commission deems it appropriate to impose the sanctions agreed to in Respondents' Offers. * * *

NOTES

1. Section 747 of the Dodd-Frank Wall Street Reform and Consumer Protection Act of 2010 amended section 4c(a) of the CEA [7 U.S.C. § 6c(a)] to add a new subsection (5) entitled "Disruptive Practices" that makes it unlawful for any person to engage in any trading, practice that: (A) violates bids or offers; (B) demonstrates intentional or reckless disregard for the orderly execution of transactions during the closing period; or (C) is, is of the character of, or is commonly known to the trade as, "spoofing" (bidding or offering with the intent to cancel the bid or offer before execution).

The CFTC has published guidance interpreting the type and manner of conduct that will be subject to this prohibition. Among other things, the CFTC stated that the violation of existing bids and offers did not require a showing of manipulative intent, but that at least reckless conduct must be shown to establish a violation of closing period disruptions known as "banging the close." The CFTC further stated that a "spoofing violation will require the showing of specific intent, at a level above recklessness. 78 Fed. Reg. 31890 (May 28, 2013).

2. As described previously in this chapter, in its only successful contested manipulation case, the CFTC found that banging the close constituted a violation of the anti-manipulation provisions of the CEA. In the Matter of

DiPlacido, Comm. Fut. L. Rep. (CCH) ¶ 30, 970 (C.F.T.C. 2008), aff'd sub nom., DiPlacido v. CFTC, No. 08–5559–ag, 2009 U.S. App. LEXIS 22692 (2d Cir. 2009), cert denied, 2010 U.S. LEXIS 2461 (2010).

3. The Wall Street Journal reported in 2012 that it had found that the practice of "marking-the-close," also called "portfolio pumping," was widespread in the stock markets. It analyzed trading in some 10,000 stocks going back to 2004. The newspaper found that on the last trading day of each accounting quarter there was a steep jump in the number of stocks that beat the S & P market index by at least 5 percent and which then declined by more than 3 percent on the following trading day. The trades that boosted prices at the end of the quarter usually occurred late in the trading day in illiquid stocks. Those trades were often entered by hedge funds and other money managers seeking to improve the quarterly net asset value (NAV) of their portfolios reported quarterly to their investors. NAV is what attracts investors and determines much of the managers' fees. See, Jacob Zweig and Tom McGinty, Fund Managers Lift Results With Timely Trading Sprees, Wall St. J., Dec. 6, 2012, at A1.

4. A controversy arose over "hide-not-slide" orders. These are complex orders designed to free up "locked" markets. A locked market occurs where the bid and ask prices are the same, a once unusual occurrence because profits are made by market makers from the spread between the bid and ask prices. The SEC prohibited trading in locked markets because matching orders can be used to generate fees through manipulative trading. Market orders are displayed publicly and will slide to a lower or higher price in a locked market, but a hide-not-slide order will be given priority at the original price when the market unlocks. The hide-not-slide order achieves priority by not displaying the order at all in the locked market. See, Jerry W. Markham, Law Enforcement and the History of Financial Market Manipulation 402 (2014) (describing these orders).

5. The "PL Select" order used by high frequency traders has also been criticized. This type of order allows high frequency traders to place a small order to sell at a set price, but directing that the order not be executed against a larger order, even one at a better price. Larger buy orders, such as those from a mutual fund, would pay more than the price offered by the PL Select order. The result was that smaller orders executed against the PL Select trade receive more favorable prices than that paid by the large buy order trader. Scott Patterson and Jean Eaglesham, Exchanges Retreat on Trading Tool, Wall St. J., Oct. 24, 2012, at C1.

CHAPTER 10

LITIGATION INVOLVING DERIVATIVES

$$\blacksquare \; \blacksquare \; \blacksquare$$

1. CFTC INVESTIGATIONS

The Securities and Exchange Commission (SEC) and the Commodity Futures Trading Commission (CFTC) have investigative and enforcement powers that are similar in nature. For a description of the SEC's enforcement process see, Colleen P. Mahoney, et al., The SEC Enforcement Process: Practice and Procedure in Handling an SEC Investigation (BNA No. 77–4th) (2013). The focus of this Chapter is on the CFTC's enforcement powers under the Commodity Exchange Act of 1936 (CEA) because the CFTC deals more broadly with derivatives issues.

CFTC v. TOKHEIM
153 F.3d 474 (7th Cir. 1998), cert. denied, 525 U.S 1122 (1999)

This is an appeal by Richard W. Tokheim of an order granting enforcement of an administrative subpoena issued by the Commodity Futures Trading Commission (CFTC or "the Commission"). For the reasons stated herein, we affirm the district court's order.

The CFTC, which is charged with implementing the Commodity Exchange Act ("the Act"), 7 U.S.C. §§ 1–25—the basic purpose of which is the comprehensive regulation of the "volatile and esoteric futures trading complex," CFTC v. Schor, 478 U.S. 833, 836, 106 S.Ct. 3245, 92 L.Ed.2d 675 (1986) (quotation omitted)—is granted broad powers under the Act to investigate compliance with the Act's provisions. See, e.g., American Int'l Trading Co. v. Bagley, 536 F.2d 1196, 1197–98 (7th Cir.1976) (Clark, J.). On August 29, 1996, the Commission entered an order of investigation entitled "In the Matter of Richard W. Tokheim." The order empowered certain CFTC officials to investigate whether Tokheim or entities associated with him (including his business, the Investment Research Company ("IRC")) had violated provisions of the Act and CFTC regulations. According to the order, the investigation would focus on, inter alia, whether Tokheim had violated 7 U.S.C. § 6m(1), which requires individuals who provide advice regarding commodities to register with the CFTC as commodity trading advisors (CTA),1 and 7 U.S.C. §§ 6b & 6o(1), both of which prohibit fraudulent conduct in connection with the commodity futures markets.

According to the Commission, Tokheim, through his business, has held himself out to the public as a commodity broker for a number of years. Tokheim, who resides in Omaha, Nebraska, publishes a "report" analyzing the past price performance of various commodities. He has advertised his various commodity trading systems to the public through direct-mail solicitations, in a futures industry trade publication, in the Omaha telephone book "yellow pages," and on the internet, and he offers personal contact to his customers, who are invited by Tokheim's materials to "please call Rich" if they have any questions. The Commission believes that Tokheim's activities merit an investigation into whether he is operating as an unregistered CTA, in violation of 7 U.S.C. § 6m(1). In addition, the Commission asserts that, based upon complaints from some of Tokheim's customers, it has reason to believe that Tokheim has advertised fraudulently and provided his customers with fraudulent advice, in violation of 7 U.S.C. §§ 6b & 6o(1).

As part of its investigation into Tokheim's activities, officers in the Commission's Chicago Regional Office issued a subpoena to Tokheim on January 8, 1997, ordering him to appear at the United States Attorney's Office in Omaha on February 19, 1997. The subpoena sought Tokheim's testimony, and it also sought documents relating to his business, including IRC's client lists, advertisements, risk disclosure statements, and any statements for commodity accounts owned either by Tokheim or IRC. Tokheim sent a letter to CFTC officials on February 12, 1997, informing them that he would not comply with the subpoena because he was not under the CFTC's jurisdiction, and he did not appear at the Office of the United States Attorney on February 19. Subsequent repeated efforts by Commission investigators and attorneys to secure Tokheim's compliance with the subpoena proved unavailing.

On August 29, 1997, the Commission therefore filed its subpoena enforcement action in the district court, pursuant to 7 U.S.C. § 9. The magistrate judge to whom the proceedings were referred issued an order requiring Tokheim to appear before the court and to show cause why the subpoena issued by the Commission should not be enforced. The magistrate judge ultimately set October 23, 1997, as the date for the hearing; however, neither Tokheim nor his lead counsel appeared at the hearing. Although local counsel represented Tokheim at the hearing, he had no familiarity with the facts of the case. Accordingly, the magistrate judge, upon reviewing the documents submitted by the CFTC, in conjunction with Tokheim's failure to explain why the subpoena should not be enforced, ordered Tokheim to testify and produce the requested documents on November 13, 1997. The district court judge subsequently adopted this order.

Tokheim appeared at the Omaha Office of the United States Attorney on November 13, and he answered questions from CFTC investigators regarding his activities in the commodity futures industry. While he did provide the CFTC with some documents related to his business, he refused to relinquish a list of his subscribers, of which Tokheim claims there are approximately 45, as well as the materials that he sends to his subscribers. The Commission believes that the withheld materials would help it to determine whether Tokheim has violated the Act. It would like to use Tokheim's subscriber list to telephone the subscribers and determine whether the possible violations can be substantiated. Though the Commission filed a motion to hold Tokheim in contempt for failing to comply with the district court's enforcement order, see 7 U.S.C. § 9, the motion was deferred by the Commission pending the resolution of this appeal.

On appeal Tokheim raises two principal arguments, neither of which has any merit. First, he argues that the Commission lacks authority to enforce its investigatory subpoena against him because his activities fall under an exclusion from the Act's coverage. His second argument is that the Commission lacked probable cause to enforce the subpoena. We consider these arguments in turn.

Tokheim argues that he provides only "impersonal" trading advice to his subscribers, much as a newspaper would, and that he is not required to register as a CTA. He contends that he is exempt from the Act's coverage because he does not furnish commodity trading advice as defined by the Act.4 See 7 U.S.C. §§ 1a(5)(B) & 6m(1); see also supra note 1. Tokheim argues that the CFTC must demonstrate to the court that it has jurisdiction over him before it can enforce the subpoena against him.

The basic failing of this argument is that it conflates the issue of whether the Commission may investigate to determine whether conduct falls within its jurisdiction with the ultimate issue of whether conduct does in fact fall within its jurisdiction. While Tokheim's argument goes to the latter issue, the issue presently before us is only the scope of the Commission's investigatory powers. If, as Tokheim argues, the Commission first had to make a valid finding of coverage before it could enforce an investigatory subpoena, it would be unable to fulfill its investigatory responsibilities under the Act. The traditional understanding of an agency's investigatory powers is precisely to the contrary. See, e.g., United States v. Morton Salt Co., 338 U.S. 632, 642–43, 70 S.Ct. 357, 94 L.Ed. 401 (1950) (recognizing that, like a grand jury, an agency is empowered to "investigate merely on suspicion that the law is being violated, or even just because it wants assurance that it is not"); American Int'l Trading Co. v. Bagley, 536 F.2d 1196, 1198 (7th Cir.1976) (Clark, J.) (holding that it is the role of the CFTC, and not the courts, "to determine in the first instance the question of coverage in the course of a preliminary investigation into possible violations"). Tokheim's contention that he is exempt from the Act may prove to be true following the

Commission's investigation. This possibility, however, does not necessitate that the Commission establish that Tokheim is covered by the Act even before it begins its investigation.

Tokheim also argues that the Commission failed to establish probable cause to enforce its subpoena, particularly with respect to his customer lists and proprietary documents. This argument overlooks the fact that this threshold never has been required by the federal courts with respect to administrative subpoenas. See, e.g., United States v. Powell, 379 U.S. 48, 57, 85 S.Ct. 248, 13 L.Ed.2d 112 (1964); Morton Salt Co., 338 U.S. at 642–43, 70 S.Ct. 357. Rather, we require agencies to satisfy a lower threshold requirement, which is the inquiry to which we now turn.

In Powell, the Supreme Court discussed the threshold showing required of an agency in order to obtain judicial enforcement of an administrative subpoena. See 379 U.S. at 57–58, 85 S.Ct. 248. The Commission must establish that (1) its investigation is being conducted pursuant to a legitimate purpose, (2) the specific inquiry may be relevant to that purpose, (3) the information sought is not already in the Commission's possession, and (4) the proper administrative procedures required by the applicable statutes and regulations have been followed. See id. We have stated the standard somewhat differently. See, e.g., EEOC v. Quad/Graphics, Inc., 63 F.3d 642, 644–45 (7th Cir.1995) ("As a general proposition, courts enforce an administrative subpoena if it seeks reasonably relevant information, is not too indefinite, and relates to an investigation within the agency's authority."); see also In re Sealed Case (Administrative Subpoena), 42 F.3d 1412, 1415 (Fed.Cir.1994) (applying the same standard). In any event, both articulations of the standard have the same effect in operation, particularly in light of the fact that we have also emphasized that the court must be satisfied that the demand for information has not "been made for an illegitimate purpose," and that an "excessively burdensome" demand, compliance with which would threaten the normal operation of a respondent's business, will not be enforced. See Quad/Graphics, Inc., 63 F.3d at 645.

In the instant case, the district court did not evaluate the propriety of enforcing the subpoena against Tokheim according to the analyses set out in either Powell or Quad/Graphics. We recognize that this was largely due to the fact that Tokheim did not adequately appear in the district court at the hearing scheduled to contest the subpoena's validity, rendering the district court's order akin to a default judgment. Nonetheless, it would have been helpful if the district court had referenced the materials entered into the record by the Commission and proffered some analysis in this regard. In any event, in light of the long delay in enforcing the subpoena that has already resulted from Tokheim's contumacy, as well as the clear support for the subpoena that is contained in the record, we shall proceed to consider the propriety of enforcing the subpoena, rather than order a remand that would lead to an even longer delay.

The Commission concedes that its power to investigate is not unfettered and that its subpoenas may only be issued in good faith and to serve legitimate purposes. Cf. Quad/Graphics, 63 F.3d at 644–45. Applying Powell's inquiry to the facts of this case, see 379 U.S. at 57–58, 85 S.Ct. 248, we agree with the Commission that this is not an instance of impermissible overreaching. First, the purpose of the investigation is legitimate, as 7 U.S.C. § 12(a) authorizes the Commission to investigate potential violations of the Act. In response to evidence that Tokheim may be violating certain provisions of the Act, including documents and solicitations that the Commission has placed in the record, the Commission seeks information from Tokheim in order to determine whether he has indeed violated registration and fraud provisions of the Act, id. §§ 6m(1), 6b & 6o(1), and the requested documents and materials are manifestly relevant to this inquiry. Third, there is no dispute that the Commission does not already possess the requested information, including Tokheim's customer lists. Finally, Tokheim has pointed to no procedural irregularities in connection with the Commission's investigation. The Commission issued both its order of investigation and its subpoena as authorized under 7 U.S.C § 9, and it filed the instant enforcement proceedings when Tokheim refused to comply with the subpoena. Moreover, Tokheim has not demonstrated that the Commission is engaged in a wide-ranging fishing expedition supported by indefinite investigatory demands. Cf. Quad/Graphics, Inc., 63 F.3d at 645. Rather, the Commission has requested specific information from Tokheim after receiving evidence indicating that Tokheim may be violating certain provisions of the Act. Under these circumstances, we hold that the district court appropriately enforced the Commission's subpoena.

Tokheim also argues that the CFTC is conducting its investigation in bad faith and that his business will be destroyed if he turns over his customer lists and proprietary documents to the Commission. Quad/Graphics indicates that the courts will consider such arguments in determining whether to enforce an administrative subpoena. See 63 F.3d at 644–45. In the instant case, however, Tokheim makes these allegations without any factual support in the record. Tokheim had an opportunity to establish factual support for his claims, but he forfeited it when he failed adequately to appear at the district court's hearing on October 23. Accordingly, we reject Tokheim's remaining arguments because they are unsupported by the record.

For the foregoing reasons, we affirm the district court's order enforcing the subpoena of the CFTC.

NOTES

1. The CFTC staff may conduct "informal" or "formal" investigations. An informal investigation involves a request that a party voluntarily supply information to the CFTC staff. A formal investigation involves a formal order of investigation that authorizes the CFTC enforcement staff to subpoena documents and witnesses. The formal order of investigation may name potential targets and the possible sections of the CEA that may have been violated [See, 17 C.F.R. Part 11 for CFTC rules governing its investigations. See also, Jerry W. Markham, Investigations Under the Commodity Exchange Act, 31 Admin. L. Rev. 285 (1979) (describing the development of the CFTC investigative procedures)].

2. The targets of a CFTC investigation will usually be notified if the CFTC staff is recommending to the CFTC that civil administrative or injunctive proceedings be brought. The targets will then generally be allowed to make a "Wells submission" to the CFTC explaining why such action should not be filed. The CFTC will then examine those arguments and decide whether a proceeding is appropriate. [See Appendix A to 17 C.F.R. Part 11].

3. Frequently, parties that are given a Wells submission notice will seek to settle with the CFTC staff, a settlement that must be approved by the CFTC. If accepted, the CFTC will issue an order that describes the parties and makes findings of fact. The CFTC order will also set forth the statutory sections and rules that were violated. In order to avoid collateral estoppel claims of private litigants who may have been injured by the conduct, these settlements are usually made without admitting or denying the CFTC charges. However, the Financial Crisis of 2008 resulted in criticism of that practice. Those critics asserted that wrongdoers should not be allowed to settle without an admission of wrongdoing. The CFTC and SEC then began seeking admissions of wrongdoing in some high profile cases.

4. The CFTC may refer violations discovered in its investigations to the Justice Department, which may decide to seek a criminal prosecution.

5. The CFTC has entered into a Memorandum of Understanding (MOU) with several foreign prosecutors. Those MOUs reciprocally pledge that the CFTC and the foreign regulator will supply the other with information in their jurisdiction that will aid the investigation of the other. These arrangements provide access by the CFTC to the trading activities of foreign persons operating in a country where a MOU is in place.

2. CFTC ADMINISTRATIVE PROCEEDINGS

The CEA authorizes the CFTC to conduct disciplinary administrative proceedings before its own hearing officers. If violations are found after a hearing, the hearing officer may impose sanctions, including large civil penalties, cease and desist orders, suspension or revocation of registrations and suspension or revocation of trading privileges on contract markets.

The CFTC adopted a series of rules governing the procedures that are to be employed in these administrative proceedings. [17 C.F.R. § 10.1 et seq.].

In re Trillion Japan Co.

COMM. FUT. L. REP. (CCH) ¶ 26,082 (C.F.T.C. 1994)

In October 1993, the Division of Enforcement ("Division") filed a motion requesting the Commission to dismiss Counts One and Two of the Complaint in this proceeding. The Administrative Law Judge ("ALJ") assigned to this matter undertook sua sponte consideration of the motion, interpreted it as a request for summary disposition under Commission Rule 10.91, and issued an order dismissing Counts One and Two. For the reasons explained below, we vacate the ALJ's order as an abuse of discretion and grant the Division's request for dismissal of Counts One and Two. * * *

In October 1989, the Commission filed an eight-count Complaint charging Trillion Japan Co., Ltd. ("Trillion") and several other respondents with wash sale violations under Section 4c(a) of the Commodity Exchange Act ("Act"). The Complaint's allegations focused on respondents' participation in the filling of paired orders for matching executions submitted by customer omnibus accounts maintained at several foreign brokers, including Trillion. Because the Division's theory in this case was similar to that rejected by an ALJ in In re Three Eight Corporation, et. al., [1990–1992 Transfer Binder] COMM. FUT. L. REP. (CCH) P 24,944 (Initial Decision Oct. 18, 1990) ("Three Eight"), the ALJ initially assigned to this matter stayed this proceeding pending Commission resolution of the Division's appeal in Three Eight.

In June 1993, the Commission affirmed the result of the ALJ's analysis in Three Eight. In reaching this conclusion, the Commission declined to follow its precedent regarding paired orders for matching executions submitted by customer omnibus accounts, holding that the analysis should focus on the intent of the ultimate customers rather than the intent of the account taken as a whole. [Current Transfer Binder] COMM. FUT. L. REP. (CCH) P 25,749 at 40,445 (CFTC June 16, 1993).

Following the Commission's denial of its motion for reconsideration in Three Eight, the Division re-evaluated its wash sale theory in this case in view of the Commission's revised precedent. In light of this review, the Division concluded that it should not proceed to a hearing on Counts One and Two of the Complaint. Because the Commission's Rules of Practice do not specifically contemplate motions to dismiss a Complaint, the Division filed its request under the general authority of Commission Rule 10.26. Moreover, because Commission precedent suggested that ALJs are not authorized to consider motions to dismiss Commission complaints, the

Division filed its request with the Commission, specifically requesting a waiver of a portion of Rule 10.26. Respondents did not oppose the Division's motion.

Shortly thereafter, the second ALJ assigned to this matter undertook sua sponte consideration of the Division's motion and dismissed Counts One and Two. In an opinion explaining his action, the ALJ focused primarily on the Division's suggestion that he was not authorized to consider a request for dismissal. The judge acknowledged that the Commission has previously stated that an ALJ has no authority "either by rule or statute" to dismiss a Commission-instituted enforcement action. He criticized this statement as "musty" dicta, however, suggesting that Commission reservation of dismissal authority to itself would raise "fundamental separation of powers and due process considerations" in the enforcement context.

Turning to the source of his authority, the judge noted that the Administrative Procedure Act ("APA") grants him broad powers that cannot be taken away by the agency. In addition, he noted that the Rules of Practice give him responsibility for the "fair and orderly conduct of a proceeding" (Rule 10.8) and specifically authorize him to (1) consider motions for summary disposition (Rule 10.91), (2) regulate the course of hearings and consider and rule upon motions (Rule 10.8) and (3) waive or modify the Rules of Practice (Rule 10.3). On this basis, he concluded that he was "explicitly, undeniably and absolutely empowered to grant" the relief requested by the Division. Accordingly, he dismissed Counts One and Two of the Complaint.

Having reviewed the record, we agree with the Division that in light of the shift in our precedent made in Three Eight, continued proceedings on Counts One and Two of the Complaint would not serve the public interest. As discussed below, we also believe the Division acted properly in raising this issue with the Commission in the first instance. Accordingly, we grant both its request for a waiver of Rule 10.26's requirement that the motion be directed to the ALJ and its request to dismiss Counts One and Two of the Complaint.

We also vacate the ALJ's order of dismissal as an abuse of his discretion. In considering the Division's motion, the ALJ overlooked the fact that it was not directed to him. While Commission Rule 10.91 authorizes presiding officers to grant summary disposition, he may only act on the motion of a party. Compare Commission Rule 12.308(c) (an ALJ may dismiss a reparation complaint on his own motion). Even if the Division's motion can be fairly interpreted as a motion for summary disposition rather than a motion to dismiss, the motion was clearly not filed with the judge. If the Commission believed that the motion should have been directed to the ALJ, it could have easily entered an order referring the matter to the ALJ.

Moreover, we believe the Division made an appropriate judgment in raising this matter with the Commission in the first instance. Unlike the ALJ, we believe there are substantial questions about his authority to grant the relief sought by the Division. The age of a Commission decision is simply not an appropriate guide to its precedential value. "Musty" or not, presiding officers are bound by Commission decisions until they are reversed or otherwise refined by the Commission. Moreover, in the absence of a clear statement of contrary Commission intent, classifying a Commission statement as "dicta" is not an appropriate basis for failing to follow the guidance contained in Commission decisions.

Even in the absence of Commission precedent, however, there would be substantial doubt about a presiding officer's authority in this instance. While the APA does directly grant ALJs broad adjudicatory powers, the authority to dismiss agency complaints is not one of the enumerated powers. See 5 USC § 556(c). Moreover, we do not think the authority to "regulate the course of the hearing," 5 USC § 556(c)(5), can be reasonably interpreted as a direct grant of authority to dismiss complaints.

In any case, as we recently explained in a related context, the authority the APA grants to presiding officers is "subject to the published rules of the agency." In re Bilello, CFTC Docket No. 93–5 (CFTC March 25, 1994). Absent some fundamental incompatibility between the APA and the Commission's Rules of Practice, "an analysis of an ALJ's authority in an enforcement proceeding should primarily focus on the intent expressed in the Rules of Practice." Id., slip op. at 9. Because the APA says nothing about an ALJ's authority to dismiss agency complaints, the ALJ should have focused his analysis on the Rules of Practice.

As noted above, nothing in the Rules of Practice suggest that the Commission intended an ALJ to have the authority to either dismiss a complaint or grant summary disposition sua sponte. Nor does the ALJ's authority to waive the Rules of Practice (Rule 10.3(c)) amount to a license for presiding officers to do what they think is best in all circumstances. We expect that this authority will be used sparingly to assure fairness and expedition in unusual circumstances. It is certainly not an appropriate basis for exercising jurisdiction not conveyed by the Rules of Practice.

The ALJ abused his discretion by deciding a motion directed to the Commission. Given the unusual circumstances presented, it is appropriate for the Commission to rule on the Division's request for relief in the first instance. In light of our review of the record, the Division's motion to dismiss Counts One and Two of the Complaint is granted.

IT IS SO ORDERED.

By the Commission (ACTING CHAIRMAN HOLUM, COMMISSIONERS BAIR, DIAL and TULL).

SILVERMAN V. CFTC
549 F.2d 28 (1st Cir. 1980)

SPRECHER, CIRCUIT JUDGE.

This appeal tests the validity of a suspension of trading privileges on commodity futures markets imposed upon an account executive in the commodity brokerage business.

The Commodity Futures Trading Commission (CFTC or Commission) is an independent federal regulatory agency, which began operating on April 21, 1975, pursuant to the Commodity Futures Trading Commission Act of 1974 (CFTC Act or Act), Pub. L. No. 93–463, 88 Stat. 1389, *et seq.*, which amended the Commodity Exchange Act, 7 U.S.C. §§ 1–17a.

The CFTC's principal responsibility relates to contracts of sale of commodities for future delivery traded or executed on boards of trade, that is, commodity exchanges which have been designated by the Commission as "contract markets" for specific commodity futures contracts. 7 U.S.C. § 7. It is unlawful to affect a commodity futures transaction other than by or through a member of a "contract market." 7 U.S.C. § 6.

All futures commission merchants (7 U.S.C. § 6d), floor brokers (§ 6e), persons associated with futures commission merchants (§ 6k), commodity trading advisors, and commodity pool operators (§ 6m) must register with the CFTC.

The Commission is entrusted with enforcing the regulatory requirements and proscriptions of the Act against registrants and other persons subject to the Act. One of the statutory provisions which the Commission enforces is section 4b, 7 U.S.C. § 6b, which makes it "unlawful . . . for any member of a contract market . . . or employee of any member . . . in or in connection with any order to make, or the making of, any contract of sale of any commodity for future delivery, made, or to be made, on or subject to the rules of any contract market, for or on behalf of any other person . . . to cheat or defraud or attempt to cheat or defraud such other person."

On March 13, 1973, a complaint was brought before the Secretary of Agriculture, alleging violations by the petitioner, Jeffrey L. Silverman, of section 4b of the CFTC Act. On May 5, 1976, a final order was entered by the CFTC, prohibiting the petitioner from trading on or subject to the rules of any contract market for a period of two years. The petitioner was also ordered to permanently cease and desist from placing, or causing to be placed, in any customer's account, any contracts of sale of any commodity for future delivery, without the prior knowledge, consent or authorization of such customer.

The petitioner filed his petition for review of the final order pursuant to 7 U.S.C. § 9, contending that (1) the evidence does not support the finding of willful violation of section 4b of the Act; (2) the petitioner was denied due process by the arbitrary conduct of the CFTC; and (3) the CFTC violated its operational guidelines. * * *

The petitioner has argued that he was denied due process during the administrative proceedings in several ways, many of which relate to the pre-hearing production of documents by the CFTC.

There is no basic constitutional right to pretrial discovery in administrative proceedings. *Starr v. Commissioner of Internal Revenue*, 226 F.2d 721, 722 (7th Cir. 1955), *cert. denied*, 350 U.S. 993, 76 S. Ct. 542, 100 L. Ed. 859 (1955); *N.L.R.B. v. Interboro Contractors, Inc.*, 432 F.2d 854, 857 (2d Cir. 1970). The Administrative Procedure Act contains no provision for pretrial discovery in the administrative process (1 Davis, ADMINISTRATIVE LAW TREATISE (1958) § 8.15, p. 588) and the Federal Rules of Civil Procedure for discovery do not apply to administrative proceedings (*N.L.R.B. v. Vapor Blast Mfg. Co.*, 287 F.2d 402, 407 (7th Cir. 1961)). The regulations of the Commodity Exchange Authority of the Department of Agriculture did not provide, at the time of the administrative hearing, for pre-hearing discovery.

Nevertheless the due process clause does insure the fundamental fairness of the administrative hearing. We have said:

> True it is that administrative convenience or even necessity cannot override the constitutional requirements of due process. *Ohio Bell Telephone Co. v. Public Utilities Commission of Ohio*, 301 U.S. 292, 304, 57 S. Ct. 724, 81 L. Ed. 1093. However, in administrative hearings the hearing examiner has wide latitude as to all phases of the conduct of the hearing, including the manner in which the hearing will proceed. *Radio Corp. of America v. United States*, 341 U.S. 412, 420, 71 S. Ct. 806, 95 L. Ed. 1062; *Wallace v. N.L.R.B.*, supra, 323 U.S. at page 253, 65 S. Ct. at page 240; *N.L.R.B. v. Algoma Plywood & Veneer Co.*, 7 Cir., 121 F.2d 602, 604. Administrative agencies should be "free to fashion their own rules of procedure and to pursue methods of inquiry capable of permitting them to discharge their multitudinous duties." *Federal Communications Comm. v. Pottsville Broadcasting Co.*, 309 U.S. 134, 143, 60 S. Ct. 437, 441, 84 L. Ed. 656.

Cella v. United States, 208 F.2d 783, 789 (7th Cir. 1953); *see also, Swift & Co. v. United States*, 308 F.2d 849, 852 (7th Cir. 1962) (and at 851: "Due process in an administrative hearing, of course, includes a fair trial, conducted in accordance with fundamental principles of fair play and applicable procedural standards established by law.")

The petitioner was provided in advance of the hearing with copies of all proposed exhibits, a list of all proposed witnesses, the identity of the government employees who had investigated the case and copies of memoranda reflecting petitioner's own statements to administrative representatives.

The petitioner also sought under the Freedom of Information Act, 5 U.S.C. § 552, the agency's internal non-public guidelines relating to the conduct of investigations. The three such guidelines which were applicable to the investigation of the kind involved herein were furnished to the petitioner prior to the hearing. Upon the petitioner's filing of a proceeding in the federal district court for the Northern District of Illinois under the Freedom of Information Act, the agency voluntarily provided the petitioner with all of the remaining guidelines, but this occurred after the administrative hearing. The petitioner then moved to dismiss the complaint, merely stating that he "was unable to obtain and use for the purposes of that hearing, the requested information so as to prepare a line of defense or to properly cross-examine the investigators who participated in the preparation of the case." Prior to rendering his decision and order, the Administrative Law Judge denied the petitioner's motion to dismiss, stating in part:

> [Silverman] . . . fails to make any showing of the subject matter to be explored in the requested supplemental cross-examination opportunities, its relationship to the issues herein, the relevancy or materiality to said issues . . . and the relative merit or prejudice expected to be established by it. [Silverman] . . . fails to show that it would be anything other than merely cumulative, and that it involves anything other than speculation and hypothesis.

For all of these reasons, the denial of the petitioner's motion to dismiss, or in the alternative to reopen, the proceedings was not a denial of due process. Administrative proceedings would become a shambles if they could be reopened upon mere request and without a supportive showing of need.

The petitioner also sought copies of statements received from customers and reports the administrative investigators had prepared concerning their interviews with customers. Although the Jencks Act, 18 U.S.C. § 3500, applies by its terms only "in any criminal prosecution brought by the United States," the agency here complied with the Act's requirements that statements of witnesses be produced after the witnesses have testified on direct examination, by furnishing the petitioner during the course of the hearing with witnesses' statements and reports of interviews with them.

The petitioner also complained that he was entitled (1) to "a statement of the procedure employed by . . . [the investigators] in interrogating the five customers," (2) to take depositions of the investigators, and (3) to show that the investigators deviated from the administrative guidelines. The denial of these requests did not constitute deprivation of due process in the light of the whole record. Obviously an administrative hearing cannot be diverted into a trial of the mechanics of the preliminary investigation unless some flagrant abuses are shown, and such a showing could be made upon cross-examination of the witnesses during the hearing. Nor is it necessary for an investigator to scrupulously adhere to each detail of a "guideline." Every investigation must necessarily differ from all others and guidelines are only that. Guidelines are intended to generally facilitate the business of the agency and not as conferring important procedural benefits upon the subjects of investigation. *American Farm Lines v. Black Ball Freight Service*, 397 U.S. 532, 538–39, 25 L. Ed. 2d 547, 90 S. Ct. 1288 (1970); *United States v. Lockyer*, 448 F.2d 417, 420–21 (10th Cir. 1971). * * *

For these reasons the order of the Commodity Futures Trading Commission should be affirmed.

In the Matter of First Guaranty Metals Co.
Comm. Fut. L. Rep. (CCH) ¶ 21,074 (C.F.T.C. 1980)

* * * The complaint alleged that Monex International, Ltd., ("Monex") was involved in conducting an office or place of business for the purpose of soliciting and accepting orders for the purchase or sale of commodities for future delivery in violation of § 4h of the Commodity Exchange Act as amended, 7 U.S.C. § 6h, which provides that any purchase or sale of a contract for future delivery must be consummated through a member of a contract market.

After being granted an enlargement of time, on September 18, 1979 Monex filed its answer generally denying the allegations in the complaint and setting forth several affirmative defenses. On September 25, 1979 Administrative Law Judge Mason filed a prehearing order setting the manner in which discovery would proceed in this case. He specifically ordered, *inter alia,* that the Division "serve on counsel for respondents the materials specified in 17 C.F.R. § 10.42(b) (1979)." On October 26, 1979 the Division of Enforcement filed a statement advising the Administrative Law Judge that the Division had no statements of witnesses who would testify at the hearing. Thereafter on November 19, 1979 respondent Monex filed motions to modify the prehearing order, to compel discovery, and to compel compliance with Judge Mason's order.

Respondent submitted that it could not complete discovery because the Division of Enforcement had failed to serve upon Monex the requested § 10.42(b) investigatory material. On November 27, the Division filed responses to these motions. On January 24, Chief Administrative Law Judge Eugene E. Hunt ordered the Division to provide the following materials to respondents:

(1) Names and addresses of all persons interviewed by the Commission during its investigation leading to the filing of the Complaints in this consolidated action;

(2) Copies of all transcripts of testimony, signed statements, and substantially verbatim reports of interviews, as provided by Commission Regulation § 10.42(b), of all witnesses the Division of Enforcement intends to call to testify at the hearing in this action, and any officer or representative of respondents interviewed by the Commission;

(3) Copies of all exculpatory material, *Brady* v. *Maryland,* 373 U.S. 83, not otherwise privileged.

On February 15, the Division responded to the Judge's order as follows:

"(1) None; (2) None; and (3) None."

Contending that the Division failed to comply with paragraph two of the prehearing order, requiring it to provide investigatory material to the respondent as set forth in § 10.42(b), on February 26, 1980 respondent Monex filed a notice and application to take the deposition of the Director of the Division of Enforcement, John A. Field, III. The pleading also requested the issuance of a subpoena *duces tecum* to require Mr. Field to bring with him to the deposition all documents which he or any person subject to his supervision or acting at his direction reviewed in responding to Judge Hunt's order of January 24, 1980.

On March 25, 1980 Judge Hunt issued an order denying respondent's motion to depose the Director of the Division of Enforcement stating:

Although Monex in its motion alluded to occurrences [*sic*] which in its view potentially generated the requested materials, there is no reason to believe that exculpatory materials or other materials listed on the order would be in the possession of the Division contrary to its response.

On March 31, 1980 respondent submitted a motion requesting an extension of time within which to complete discovery. On April 7, 1980 the Administrative Law Judge denied that motion ordering discovery to be completed by May 16, 1980. On April 3, 1980 respondent Monex filed an application for interlocutory appeal pursuant to § 10.101 of the

Commission's Rules of Practice from the denial of the application to take the deposition of the Director of the Division of Enforcement. The Division filed a written response on April 14, to which Monex replied on April 30. * * *

For the reasons set forth below we direct the Administrative Law Judge to reconsider the adequacy of the Division's response to his underlying order to produce in light of the Division's admission in its pleading before the Commission that "persons at Monex have been interviewed in other circumstances by employees of this Commission," a fact about which the Administrative Law Judge may have been unaware at the time he ruled. *Cf. In the Matter of Siegel Trading Company, Inc.,* [1977–1980 Transfer Binder] Comm. Fut. L. Rep. (CCH) ¶ 20,862 at p. 23,535 (July 27, 1979).

The underlying discovery order provided, *inter alia,* that the Division provide

> (2) Copies of all transcripts of testimony, signed statements, and substantially verbatim reports of interviews, as provided by Commission Regulation § 10.42(b), of all witnesses the Division of Enforcement intends to call to testify at the hearing in this action, *and* any officer or representative of respondents interviewed by the *Commission* . . . (emphasis added).

On February 15, 1980, the Division responded "none" to this part of the order, thereby representing to the Administrative Law Judge that there existed no such material. The Division implied in a later pleading before the Administrative Law Judge that it had no duty to produce the ordered material because any such materials, if they exist were gathered "in other circumstances" than "the investigation" leading to the complaint at issue In its response to the application for interlocutory review, the Division states that it responded as it did because

> no investigation took place which lead to the institution of this proceeding. To be sure, persons at Monex have been interviewed in other circumstances by employees of this Commission. We have no objection to providing Monex those materials upon its making a proper application therefor under Section 10.68 of the Commission's Rules of Practice.

Thus, it is not clear, perhaps for the first time in these proceedings, that there exists testimonial materials and exhibits from interviews conducted by Commission employees of which the Division is aware—but which the Division does not feel compelled to produce under Section 10.42(b). Nevertheless, it is impossible for the Commission to ascertain from this record or the Division of Enforcement's cryptic pleadings whether these materials were properly withheld. This is not, in any event, a matter about which the Commission should have to speculate.

This is a matter which should have been inquired into by the Administrative Law Judge in the first instance, based upon the rather detailed and specific "declarations" filed with Monex' application to depose Mr. Field. *See, e.g., Williams* v. *United States,* 328 F.2d 178, 180 (D.C. Cir. 1963); *United States* v. *Keig,* 320 F.2d 634 (7th Cir. 1963).

Moreover, apart from the judge's role in assuring that discoverable material is produced, it is crucial that the Division of Enforcement fully appreciate its obligation to the fair and orderly administration of justice with respect to the disclosure of discoverable evidence. It was error for the Division to decide unilaterally not to produce or fully acknowledge to the Administrative Law Judge the existence of arguably discoverable material of which it was aware, based upon its apparent view that the material did not fall as a matter of law within § 10.42(b) or the scope of the judge's order to produce. The decision whether material is discoverable or producible as "Jencks" material[11] is not for the prosecutor to make, but rather is a matter for judicial decision, if the material even arguably falls close to the reach of the Commission's rule. *See, e.g., United States* v. *Conroy,* 589 F.2d 1258, 1272–1273 (5th Cir. 1979); *United States* v. *Harrison,* 524 F.2d 421, 427–428 (D.C. Cir. 1975), and cases cited therein. "Questions of production of statements are not to be solved through one party's determination that they are not to be produced to defense counsel or to the trial judge for his determination as to their coverage." *Palermo* v. *United States,* 360 U.S. 343, 360–361 (1959) (Brennan, J., concurring).

While there is no constitutional right to discovery in administrative proceedings, *Silverman* v. *Commodity Futures Trading Commission, supra,* 549 F.2d at 33, once a class of discovery is provided for, as the Commission has seen fit to do in § 10.42, the Commission must insure that its legitimate scope is not circumvented or its purpose frustrated. *See, e.g., Gardner* v. *F.C.C.,* 530 F.2d 1086 (D.C. Cir. 1976). Section 10.42(b) requires, *inter alia,* that the Division of Enforcement provide to respondents prior to the date of hearing "copies of the following documents obtained during the investigation preceding the initiation of the complaint, all transcripts of testimony, signed statements and substantially verbatim reports of interviews which were obtained during the investigation which preceded institution of the proceeding from or

---

[11] As the Division acknowledges, § 10.42(b) of the Commission's rules incorporates the rule set forth by the Supreme Court in *Jencks v. United States,* 353 U.S. 657 (1957) codified by Congress in 18 U.S.C. § 3500 ('Jencks Act'), that a criminal defendant 'is entitled to relevant and competent reports and statements in possession of the Government touching the events and activities as to which a Government witness has testified at the trial.' *Goldberg v. United States,* 425 U.S. 94, 104 (1976), quoting S.Rep.No. 981, 85th Cong., 1st Sess. 3, *reprinted in* [1957] U.S. Code Cong. & Admin. News 1861 at 1862. *See, generally,* Mezines, Stein, & Gruff, *Administrative Law,* ¶ 23.03[7] (1980). Unlike the Jencks Act, *supra,* where Congress limited the production of 'statements' in criminal trials until after the witness testified on direct examination. 18 U.S.C. § 3500(a), our rule provides for disclosure 'prior to the scheduled hearing date.'

concerning witnesses to be called at the hearing and all exhibits to those transcripts, statements and reports." We interpret the words "during the investigation preceding the initiation of the complaint" to mean that any material specified in the rule which is obtained during the course of an investigation or inquiry by any Commission entity must be provided so long as it can be viewed as having served as a basis for the initiation of a complaint by the Division of Enforcement, regardless of whether Part II of the Commission's Rules, relating to investigations, has been explicitly invoked. We do not find it significant that the material at issue might be physically located in files within the Commission other than those of the Division of Enforcement itself, or that the material may have been amassed or compiled by non-Division employees of the Commission. If other Commission entities gather evidence which is in turn used by the Division as a basis for the filing of a complaint, that evidence is subject to the production requirements of § 10.42(b). In this connection we have some difficulty in reconciling the Division of Enforcement's statement that "no investigation took place which lead [sic] to the institution of this proceeding" and its acknowledgement that Monex employees were interviewed by Commission employees "in other circumstances." We are unable to conclude, based on this record, that no one employed by the Commission "investigated" Monex prior to the Division's filing of the complaint and thus generated materials arguably within the scope of § 10.42(b) or the judge's discovery order.

Moreover, we are of the opinion that the failure to construe § 10.42(b) as providing for the production of documents discoverable thereunder, regardless of where they may physically be within the files of the Commission and regardless of who generated them, would violate due process, *i.e.,* "a fair trial, conducted in accordance with fundamental principles of fair play and applicable procedural standards established by law." *Swift & Co.* v. *United States,* 308 F.2d 849, 851 (7th Cir. 1962), quoted in *Silverman* v. *Commodity Futures Trading Commission, supra,* 549 F.2d at 33. In the words of a recent District of Columbia Circuit decision involving the producibility of a report potentially relevant to issues raised in an administrative discharge proceeding, *McClelland* v. *Andrus,* 606 F.2d 1278, 1285–1286 (D.C. Cir. 1979):

> Some agencies have of their own accord adopted regulations providing for some form of discovery in their proceedings. In addition to being bound by those rules, the agency is bound to ensure that its procedures meet due process requirements. *Withrow* v. *Larkin,* 421 U.S. 35 (1975). Therefore, discovery must be granted if in the particular situation a refusal to do so would so prejudice a party as to deny him due process. (Citations and footnote omitted.)

Accordingly, as a matter of regulatory interpretation, and as a matter of fundamental fairness, we interpret § 10.42(b) to require that material arguably specified therein that is in the possession, custody or control of the Commission, the existence of which is known, or by the exercise of due diligence may become known to the attorney for the Division of Enforcement be produced either directly to respondent or for inspection by the Administrative Law Judge. Thus, in this matter we hold that the Division should have confirmed the existence of any material even arguably discoverable of which it was aware, produced it to the respondent or proffered it to the Administrative Law Judge for consideration. In proffering material to the judge the Division would be free, of course, to argue that the material is not producible, but the ultimate decision is properly that of the impartial arbiter. In so holding, we expressly do not suggest that the Division of Enforcement must routinely cause a search to be made of the files of other Commission divisions offices for potentially discoverable or exculpatory material where the Division has no knowledge that such material might exist and is not directed to it by a focused and specific defense request. Nor do we mean to suggest that the Division must produce or proffer to the judge material which clearly bears no relation to any investigatory activity of the Commission's staff relevant to the ongoing proceeding. While we do not require "fishing expeditions," we do expect the Division of Enforcement to exercise due diligence in fulfilling its obligations in this area. Accordingly, where, as here, the request for investigatory materials is specific, the Division should seek out the materials, wherever they may exist within the Commission, and at a minimum turn them over to the Administrative Law Judge for his decision as to their producibility.

We also direct the administrative Law Judge to order the Division of Enforcement to produce, as a matter of due process and pursuant to paragraph three of Judge Hunt's order, any material of which it is aware that is arguably exculpatory as to either guilt or punishment. The request here is specific and gives the Division of Enforcement notice of exactly what the respondent desires. See *Brady* v. *Maryland,* 373 U.S. 83 (1963). The *Brady* rule is not a discovery rule rather it is a rule of fairness and minimum prosecutorial obligation. *United States* v. *Beasley,* 576 F.2d 626 (5th Cir. 1978), *cert. denied,* 99 S.Ct. 1426 (1979). Since *Brady* is premised upon due process grounds we hold that its principles are applicable to administrative enforcement actions such as this which, while strongly remedial in nature, may yield substantial sanctions. *See Collins Securities Corp.* v. *S.E.C.,* 562 F.2d 820, 825 (D.C. Cir. 1979). Disclosure under the doctrine is only required when the evidence is "material" to guilt or punishment, *Moore* v. *Illinois,* 408 U.S. 786 (1972). Because materiality is "an inevitably imprecise standard, and because the significance of an item of evidence can seldom be predicted accurately until the entire record is complete, the prudent prosecutor will resolve doubtful questions in favor of disclosure." *United States* v. *Agurs,* 427 U.S. 97, 108 (1976). As with questions of producibility under § 10.42, questions as to whether material must be provided as a matter of due process under *Brady* are judicial, not prosecutorial decisions. As the Supreme Court recently emphasized in *United States* v. *Agurs, supra,* at 106:

> Although there is, of course, no duty to provide defense counsel with unlimited discovery of everything known by the prosecutor, if the subject matter of such interest is material, or indeed if a substantial basis for claiming materiality exists, it is reasonable to require the prosecutor to respond either by furnishing the information or by submitting the problem to the trial judge. When the prosecutor receives a specific and relevant request, the failure to make any response is seldom, if ever, excusable.

Any material, therefore, known to the Division of Enforcement, or which by the exercise of due diligence may become known to the Division, that is arguably exculpatory and material to guilt or punishment within the meaning of *Brady, Moore,* and *Agurs, supra,* should be either provided to respondent directly, or provided to the Administrative Law Judge, for his determination as to whether it is producible or not.

Accordingly, IT IS ORDERED that the application of respondent Monex for interlocutory review of the Administrative Law Judge's March 25, 1980 order denying Monex' motion to depose the Director of the Division of Enforcement is DENIED. IT IS FURTHER ORDERED that the Administrative Law Judge conduct further proceedings consistent with Part IIB of this Order.

By the Commission (CHAIRMAN STONE and COMMISSIONERS DUNN, MARTIN and GARTNER).

GIMBEL V. CFTC
872 F.2d 196 (7th Cir. 1989)

Amended Opinion FLAUM, CIRCUIT JUDGE

Stuart Gimbel petitions for review of a final order of the Commodity Futures Trading Commission ("Commission"). The Commission, after determining that Gimbel had committed several violations of the Commodity Exchange Act ("Act"), imposed a civil monetary penalty of $115,000, denied petitioner's application for registration as a floor broker at the Chicago Mercantile Exchange and permanently barred him from trading on any contract market. On appeal, Gimbel challenges both the Commission's liability determinations and its imposition of sanctions without a separate hearing. For the reasons stated below, we affirm the Commission's liability determinations and imposition of non-monetary sanctions but reverse its imposition of a civil monetary penalty.

Over the past twenty years, Stuart Gimbel has been one of the largest and most successful commodities traders at the Chicago Mercantile Exchange ("Exchange"). In early 1980, Gimbel, in a series of transactions, invested heavily in lumber futures contracts. This investment, however, ultimately proved to be unsuccessful due to a precipitous drop in the lumber market in April, 1980.

The sharp reversal in the lumber market prompted an investigation by the Chicago Mercantile Exchange. Based on this investigation, the Exchange charged Gimbel and several others with various abuses in connection with the trading of lumber futures in early 1980. Gimbel eventually entered a plea of nolo contendere to these charges, accepting a fifteen month suspension of trading privileges and a $150,000 fine as a penalty.

Petitioner's problems, however, were not yet over. In 1984, the Commission's Division of Enforcement ("Division") filed a complaint against Gimbel containing additional allegations of misconduct stemming from the 1980 transactions in lumber futures. The complaint alleged *inter alia* that Gimbel engaged in a single "wash sale" in February, 1980, thereby violating section 4c(a)(A) of the Act, failed to disclose the extent of his investments in lumber futures in required reports to the Commission in violation of section 6(b) of the Act, obtained reportable futures positions without filing the required reports in violation of section 4(i) of the Act, and violated a prior cease and desist order of the Secretary of Agriculture.

The charges against Gimbel were evaluated by an administrative law judge ("ALJ") who conducted eight days of hearings over a four-month period in late 1984 and early 1985. At the hearing, the Division, over petitioner's objection, introduced evidence of Gimbel's extensive history of trading abuses in support of its request for a permanent trading ban. In contrast, Gimbel introduced no evidence in mitigation of possible sanctions.

In January, 1986, the ALJ entered an order finding Gimbel liable on all counts. As punishment, the ALJ permanently barred petitioner from trading on any contract market and denied his application for registration as a floor broker at the Exchange. The ALJ, however, did not impose any monetary penalty.

Upon receiving the ALJ's decision, petitioner's counsel filed a motion seeking a separate hearing on the issue of sanctions which was denied by the Assistant Chief of the Commission's Opinions Section. Gimbel then appealed the ALJ's decision to the Commission and the Division cross-appealed the ALJ's refusal to impose a monetary penalty. The Commission affirmed the ALJ's liability determinations and imposition of non-monetary sanctions and also assessed a $115,000 civil monetary penalty. Gimbel appeals from this decision.

Gimbel initially challenges the ALJ's liability determinations on a variety of grounds. First, Gimbel claims that the ALJ was biased. In support of this assertion, petitioner refers us to several places in the record where the ALJ exhibited impatience with Gimbel's counsel.

In order to set aside an ALJ's findings on the grounds of bias, "the ALJ's conduct must be so extreme that it deprives the hearing of that fairness and impartiality necessary to that fundamental fairness required by due process." *N.L.R.B. v. Webb Ford, Inc.*, 689 F.2d 733, 737 (7th Cir. 1982). The ALJ's conduct in this case did not even remotely approach this level. Although the ALJ exhibited impatience with petitioner's counsel at times, he also expressed displeasure with opposing counsel. Moreover, on at least two occasions, the ALJ remarked that petitioner's counsel was a good lawyer. Finally, the ALJ ruled in petitioner's favor several times during the course of the hearing. Given these facts, we cannot say that the ALJ's conduct deprived the hearing of the fairness and impartiality required by due process.

Gimbel next argues that the ALJ's credibility determinations were erroneous. In his order, the ALJ expressly credited the testimony of Mondi and Sasin, two witnesses who testified against Gimbel, finding them to be "honest, truthful and straightforward." In contrast, the ALJ refused to believe petitioner's testimony, finding that Gimbel was not "an honest witness."

Our review of the Commission's adoption of an ALJ's factual findings, which include his credibility determinations, is severely circumscribed. *Chapman v. U.S. Commodity Futures Trading Commission*, 788 F.2d 408, 410 (7th Cir. 1986). We review the record in order to determine whether the factual findings of the Commission are supported by the weight of the evidence. 7 U.S.C. § 9. Under this standard we will uphold the Commission's findings if we deem them to have been justified. *Stotler and Co. v. Commodity Futures Trading Comm'n*, 855 F.2d 1288, 1291 (7th Cir. 1988); *Silverman v. CFTC*, 549 F.2d 28, 30–31 (7th Cir. 1977).

Although a reviewing court generally gives substantial deference to the factual findings of an ALJ, this deference is even greater when credibility determinations are involved. *See Impact Industries, Inc. v. N.L.R.B.*, 847 F.2d 379, 381 (7th Cir. 1988). The present case presents a paradigm of when a reviewing court should defer to the credibility assessments of an ALJ. Mondi and Sasin, the witnesses who testified against Gimbel, were vigorously cross-examined by petitioner's counsel who raised substantial difficulties with their testimony. Gimbel's conflicting testimony, however, was also suspect. In these circumstances, the demeanor of the witnesses, is crucial. As the ALJ was the only individual who had the opportunity to observe the demeanor of the witnesses and expressly relied upon his observations in rendering his decision we cannot say that his credibility determinations were erroneous.

Petitioner also challenges the ALJ's reliance on damaging hearsay statements made by Philip Getson, a co-defendant in the case, to Thomas Utrata, an investigator for the Exchange. Utrata testified that Getson told him that Gimbel in fact controlled trades in an account that nominally belonged to Getson. Getson invoked the privilege against self-incrimination at the hearing and was thus not amenable to cross-examination about these statements.

It is well settled that hearsay may constitute substantial evidence in administrative hearings if factors assuring the underlying reliability and probative value of the evidence are present. *Richardson v. Perales*, 402 U.S. 389, 402, 28 L. Ed. 2d 842, 91 S. Ct. 1420 (1971); *Consolidation Coal Co. v. Chubb*, 741 F.2d 968, 972 (7th Cir. 1984). In the present case, Utrata's testimony was independently corroborated by another witness at the hearing. Given this fact, we cannot conclude that the ALJ's reliance on Utrata's testimony was erroneous.

Finally, Gimbel challenges the ALJ's extensive adoption of the Division's proposed findings. The ALJ adopted 88 of the Division's 93 proposed findings in toto. In contrast, the ALJ rejected all 257 of petitioner's proposed findings.

Although we recognize the time constraints under which most ALJ's operate, we strongly disapprove of the practice of adopting the findings submitted by one party and will scrutinize these findings closely. *See Machlett Laboratories, Inc. v. Techny Industries, Inc.*, 665 F.2d 795, 797 (7th Cir. 1981); *Garcia v. Rush-Presbyterian-St. Luke's Medical Center*, 660 F.2d 1217, 1220 (7th Cir. 1981). Among other things, this practice may create a negative impression about the ALJ's diligence and impartiality. The findings, themselves, however are supported by substantial evidence. Consequently, they will not be overturned on appeal. *See U.S. v. Crescent Amusement Co.*, 323 U.S. 173, 185, 89 L. Ed. 160, 65 S. Ct. 254 (1944).

In sum, we find that the ALJ was not biased and properly relied on the hearsay statements of Philip Getson. In addition, we find that the ALJ's factual findings and credibility determinations were supported by the weight of the evidence. Therefore, we affirm the ALJ's findings that Gimbel committed several violations of the Commodity Exchange Act in early 1980. * * *

AFFIRMED IN PART AND REVERSED IN PART.

Notes

1. The CFTC's Division of Enforcement must prove its case by a preponderance of the evidence. This requires more than a showing of suspicious circumstances. Rather, the evidence must be persuasive in drawing the inferences necessary to show a violation. In the Matter of Bielfeldt, Comm. Fut. L. (CCH) ¶ 29,923 (C.F.T.C. 2004).

2. The CFTC has ruled that in its administrative proceedings an adverse inference may be drawn where a respondent claims the fifth amendment right against self-incrimination. However, such an inference may not be the sole basis for finding liability. In re Citadel Trading Co. of Chicago, Ltd., Comm. Fut. L. Rep. (CCH) ¶ 23,082 (C.F.T.C. 1986).

Vercillo v. CFTC
147 F.3d 548 (7th Cir. 1998)

Bauer, Circuit Judge.

In 1991, appellant John Vercillo, a floor broker at the Chicago Board of Trade, was convicted of numerous criminal offenses arising out of four trades in which he participated in 1988. The Commodity Futures Trading Commission ("CFTC" or "Commission"), Division of Enforcement ("Division"), subsequently filed a three-count administrative complaint against Vercillo, charging him with violating various sections of the Commodity Exchange Act and seeking appropriate remedies. After a rather tangled history and several hearings before an administrative law judge ("ALJ"), the ALJ denied Vercillo's application for registration as a floor broker with leave to reapply in five years, and found that Vercillo should be banned from trading on Commission regulated markets for a period of five years. Both Vercillo and the Division appealed to the CFTC, which, after a de novo review of the record, issued a final agency decision denying Vercillo's application for registration and imposing a permanent trading ban against him. Vercillo filed a petition for review with this court, seeking reversal of the denial of his registration and the permanent ban. For the reasons set forth below, Vercillo's petition is denied and the order of the CFTC is enforced.

This case has a long and tangled procedural history which we will attempt to summarize. Vercillo became a member of the Chicago Board of Trade ("CBOT") in 1975, and was registered with the CFTC as a floor broker in 1982. As a floor broker, Vercillo was engaged in the trading of contracts for soybean futures in the "pit" of the Board of Trade. Things apparently went smoothly for Vercillo until January 1991, when he was convicted of various criminal offenses stemming from four trades in which he had participated between July 27 and September 12, 1988. In the four trades, Vercillo engaged in curb trading with James Nowak ("Nowak"), a broker in the soybean pit, buying or selling soybean lots from Nowak after the market had closed for the day.[1]

Vercillo, Nowak, and a number of other traders and brokers at the CBOT were indicted for their participation in these and other illegal schemes. The case went to trial, and in January 1991, Vercillo was convicted of 11 felony counts, including RICO conspiracy, mail fraud, wire fraud, and various violations of sections of the Commodity Exchange Act ("CEA") (specifically, §§ 4b(B) and (D), 7 U.S.C. §§ 6b(B) and (D)). On June 4, 1991, Vercillo was sentenced to 27 months in prison, placed on three years of supervised release, ordered to pay restitution in the amount of $1,800, and fined $10,000. Vercillo's conviction was upheld by this court on October 30, 1992. *United States v. Ashman,* 979 F.2d 469 (7th Cir. 1992), *cert. denied,* 510 U.S. 814, 114 S. Ct. 62, 126 L. Ed. 2d 32 (1993).

In June 1991, the Division filed a three-count administrative complaint against Vercillo. Counts I and II alleged that Vercillo had violated §§ 4b(B) and (D) of the CEA, 7 U.S.C. §§ 6b(B) and (D), and sought a cease and desist order against him, a suspension or revocation of all his registrations, a trading prohibition, and a civil monetary penalty. Count III alleged that Vercillo, by virtue of his 11 felony convictions, was subject to statutory disqualification from registration with the CFTC under §§ 8a(2)(D) and (E) of the CEA, 7 U.S.C. §§ 12a(2)(D) and (E). The complaint ordered an ALJ to hold a hearing on Count III to determine whether Vercillo was subject to the statutory disqualification and, if so, to suspend his registration and order him to show cause why it should not be revoked.

A hearing was held on June 25, 1991, before Administrative Law Judge George Painter, and shortly thereafter ALJ Painter concluded that Vercillo was statutorily disqualified from registration. Accordingly, ALJ Painter suspended Vercillo's floor broker registration for six months and ordered him to show cause why his registration should not be revoked. In October 1991, Vercillo's registration was revoked because he had failed to provide any evidence that his continued registration would be in the public interest. Vercillo was also ordered to answer Counts I and II of the complaint. After his answer was filed, the Division moved for summary disposition on the issue of liability, which ALJ Painter granted. Both parties briefed the ALJ on the issue of sanctions, the Division recommending that a cease and desist order and permanent trading ban be imposed and Vercillo arguing that the minimum sanction would suffice. Vercillo also requested a hearing on the issue of sanctions. In

---

[1] "Curb trading" refers to trades taking place after the closing bell has sounded to end official trading for the day. While against the CBOT's rules at the time surrounding Vercillo's illegal trades, "curb trading" has since been officially recognized and is allowed to a limited extent.

December 1992, ALJ Painter, without regard to Vercillo's request for a hearing, issued an order imposing a cease and desist order and a seven year trading ban on Vercillo. Both Vercillo and the Division appealed the ALJ's decision to the CFTC.

In August 1993, the Commission found that the ALJ had abused his discretion by failing to hold a hearing on the issue of sanctions. The Commission determined that the ALJ must give weight to the congressional mandate in § 9(b) of the CEA, 7 U.S.C. § 13(b), and found that the large number of felonies for which Vercillo was convicted under § 4b of the CEA raised a presumption that he should be permanently banned from trading. Accordingly, the CFTC reversed the decision of the ALJ and remanded the case for a hearing to permit Vercillo to attempt to rebut the presumption. The Commission directed ALJ Painter to impose a permanent trading prohibition on Vercillo unless he could demonstrate by the weight of the evidence that his access to Commission-regulated markets would pose no substantial threat to their integrity. *In re Vercillo,* [1992–94 Transfer Binder] Comm. Fut. L. Rep. (CCH) P 25,836 (CFTC Aug. 13, 1993) ("*Vercillo I*").

While the appeal was pending before the CFTC, Vercillo applied for registration as a floor trader and briefly returned to the CBOT under a "no action" status. The Division challenged the application by filing a second complaint against Vercillo in July 1993, giving notice of its intent to deny his registration. This second complaint ordered the ALJ to ascertain whether Vercillo was subject to a statutory disqualification from registration. In August 1993, the ALJ determined that Vercillo was subject to statutory disqualification of his registration under §§ 8a(2)(D) and (E) of the CEA, 7 U.S.C. §§ 12a(2)(D) and (E). The ALJ suspended Vercillo's no action status and directed him to show cause why his application for registration should not be denied. Subsequently, however, the ALJ vacated his order and consolidated the proceedings under the second complaint with those under the first complaint. The Division took an interlocutory appeal of the ALJ's decision, which the CFTC reversed, reinstating the suspension of Vercillo's no-action status and vacating the consolidation order. *In re Vercillo,* [1992–94 Transfer Binder] Comm. Fut. L. Rep. (CCH) P 25,837 (CFTC Sept. 13, 1993).

In January 1994, the ALJ conducted a simultaneous hearing on both the first and second complaints. In support of its case, the Division presented the testimony of FBI agent Richard Ostrom, as well as documentary evidence establishing that Vercillo had been convicted of numerous felonies. Vercillo testified on his own behalf, and also presented the testimony of three character witnesses. Vercillo's testimony, and the documents in the record, described the four transactions underlying his convictions. In each of the four instances, Vercillo had either bought contracts from, or sold contracts to, Nowak after trading on the CBOT had closed for the day and at pre-determined (i.e., other than market) prices. In May 1994, the ALJ issued a decision, concluding that Vercillo had presented sufficient evidence to establish that he was rehabilitated and that he should not be permanently barred from registering as a floor trader. The ALJ also found that Vercillo had rebutted the presumption that he should be permanently barred from trading on any CFTC regulated markets. ALJ Painter held that Vercillo could reapply for registration after five years had elapsed, and that Vercillo should be banned from trading for five years. Both Vercillo and the Division appealed.

On appeal, the CFTC overruled the decision of the ALJ. It found that Vercillo had failed to rebut either the presumption that his registration should be permanently denied or the presumption that he should be permanently banned from trading on any CFTC-regulated market. The Commission entered a final decision to this effect on May 30, 1997. *In re Vercillo*, [Current Transfer Binder] Comm. Fut. L. Rep. (CCH) P 27,071, 1997 WL 291441 (CFTC May 30, 1997) ("*Vercillo II*"). Vercillo filed a timely petition for review on June 12, 1997, and we have jurisdiction over this case pursuant to 7 U.S.C. § 9. In his petition for review, Vercillo argues that the CFTC abused its discretion by not affording proper deference to the findings of the ALJ, and that the permanent trading ban imposed on him violates the Double Jeopardy Clause of the United States Constitution. We discuss each of these arguments in turn.

We review decisions of the CFTC deferentially. The Commission's findings of fact are conclusive, and we will not disturb them, if they are supported by the weight of the evidence. 7 U.S.C. § 9; *Monieson v. CFTC*, 996 F.2d 852, 858 (7th Cir. 1993). Review of questions of law, or of the application of law to facts, is dependent upon the nature of the question and the comparative qualifications and competence of the decisionmakers. If the answer to a question implicates an agency's expertise, we defer to the agency's decision if it is reasonable; when the question is one of the sort that courts frequently encounter, we review it *de novo*. *Id.* (citations omitted). When reviewing an agency's imposition of sanctions, the choice of sanction will be overturned only if it is unwarranted in law or unjustified in fact. *Id.* (citing *Butz v. Glover Livestock Comm'n Co., Inc.*, 411 U.S. 182, 185–86, 36 L. Ed. 2d 142, 93 S. Ct. 1455 (1973)). A sanction which falls within the statutory limits "must be upheld unless it reflects an abuse of discretion." *Flaxman v. CFTC*, 697 F.2d 782, 789 (7th Cir. 1983).

First, Vercillo argues that the CFTC abused its discretion by failing to defer to the factual findings and determinations of the ALJ and by reviewing the ALJ's determinations *de novo*. He alleges that the Commission, at the time the hearings began, accorded deference to the ALJ's factual determinations, citing *In re Ferragamo*, 1991 CFTC LEXIS

13, [1990–92 Transfer Binder] Comm. Fut. L. Rep. (CCH) P24,982 at 37,576 (CFTC Jan. 14, 1991). However, in *In re Grossfeld,* 1996 CFTC LEXIS 242, [Current Transfer Binder] Comm. Fut. L. Rep. (CCH) P26,921, 1996 WL 709219 at *11 (CFTC Dec. 10, 1996), the Commission announced that it was abandoning the deferential standard and returning to its previous de novo standard of review. Beyond pointing out these historical facts, and citing several other cases that support the proposition that an ALJ's determinations must be accorded deference, Vercillo's brief does not elucidate why he believes that the Commission erred in applying a de novo standard in the present case.

To the extent Vercillo is arguing that the CFTC acted arbitrarily in applying a de novo standard in general or was without the power to use that standard at all, his claim is without merit. In a recent decision, *Ryan v. CFTC,* 145 F.3d 910, 1998 U.S. App. LEXIS 10226 (7th Cir. 1998), this court found that *de novo* review of an ALJ's determinations by the CFTC does not constitute an abuse of discretion. *Ryan,* No. 97–2120, Slip Op. at 11–12. We reaffirm the reasoning in Ryan today. The Administrative Procedure Act ("APA") states that "on appeal from or review of [an] initial decision, the agency has all the powers which it would have in making the initial decision except as it may limit the issues on notice or by rule." 5 U.S.C. § 557(b). *See also Containerfreight Transp. Co. v. ICC,* 651 F.2d 668, 670 (9th Cir. 1981) (APA authorizes agency reviewing findings of ALJ to decide all issues before it *de novo*). The CFTC has not, however, so limited its powers. The regulations set forth by the Commission regarding review of an ALJ's decision, at all times relevant to Vercillo's case, stated:

> On review, the Commission may affirm, reverse, modify, set aside or remand for further proceedings, in whole or in part, the initial decision by the Administrative Law Judge and make any findings or conclusions which in its judgment are proper based on the record in the proceeding.

17 C.F.R. § 10.104(b). *See also JCC, Inc. v. CFTC,* 63 F.3d 1557, 1566 (11th Cir. 1995) (Commission's regulations are in accord with the APA). The CFTC's own rules thus parallel, rather than limit, the standard of review contained in the APA, and the Commission is not limited in its review by those rules. The ability of the Commission to perform a de novo review is also supported by case law. *See, e.g., Drexel Burnham Lambert Inc. v. CFTC,* 271 U.S. App. D.C. 49, 850 F.2d 742, 747 (D.C. Cir. 1988) (when the CFTC and the ALJ disagree on factual inferences to be drawn from the record, courts of appeals must look to see "not whether the agency has 'erred' in 'overruling' the ALJ's findings, but whether its own findings are reasonably supported by the entire record.") (citing *FCC v. Allentown Broadcasting Corp.,* 349 U.S. 358, 364, 99 L. Ed. 1147, 75 S. Ct. 855 (1955)). It is clear that the CFTC is authorized to undertake a *de novo* review of the initial decision of an ALJ.

Furthermore, as the Commission itself noted in *In re Grossfeld,* it had, in the past, reviewed the imposition of sanctions by an ALJ *de novo.* It moved to the abuse of discretion standard, however, to "discourage appeals which simply asked [it] to second-guess the sanctions imposed by the ALJs." 1996 WL 709219 at *11. In determining that a return to the *de novo* standard was proper, the Commission noted the increasingly important role that sanctions play in deterring wrongful conduct and maintaining market integrity. The CFTC concluded that exercising its own independent review, and not being limited by the choices made by the ALJ, is "consistent with the Commission's ultimate responsibility to determine the appropriate sanction in each case that comes before it." *Id.* This explanation is well-reasoned and cannot be characterized as arbitrary.

While Vercillo emphasizes that the Commission was utilizing a deferential standard of review at the time of his hearings before the ALJ, he does not provide any reason why its *de novo* review of his appeal was arbitrary. It is true that Vercillo's appeal was pending before the Commission at the time it issued its decision in In re Grossfeld; however, it is established that "generally, a decision which changes existing law or policy is given retroactive effect unless retroactive application would cause 'manifest injustice.'" *NLRB v. Bufco Corp.,* 899 F.2d 608, 611 (7th Cir. 1990) (citations omitted). Vercillo has not attempted to, nor do we find that he could, establish any prejudice from the retroactive application of *In re Grossfeld.* The CFTC's actions in undertaking a *de novo* review of Vercillo's appeal, then, were not arbitrary or erroneous.

Vercillo next asserts that the Commission abused its discretion by discarding the order of ALJ Painter and imposing its own sanctions against him. First, Vercillo challenges the Commission's denial of his registration, which is governed by §§ 8a(2)(D) and (E) of the CEA. * * *

Once the Commission proves that an individual is statutorily disqualified under § 8a(2)(D) (and, presumably, § 8a(2)(E) as well), a presumption is raised that he is unfit to act as a Commission registrant. *In re Horn,* [1990–92 Transfer Binder] Comm. Fut. L. Rep. (CCH) P 24,836 at 36,939 (CFTC April 18, 1990). This presumption is based on the inference that an individual who has already undertaken serious wrongdoing presents a substantial risk of engaging in wrongdoing again. *Id.* (citing *In re Akbar,* [1986–87 Transfer Binder] Comm. Fut. L. Rep. (CCH) P 22,297 at 31,708 (CFTC Feb. 24, 1986)). In order to rebut the presumption, the petitioner must show by clear and convincing evidence that his continued registration would be in the public interest (that is, that his registration would not raise a substantial risk to the public). *In re Horn,* Comm. Fut. L. Rep. P 24,836 at 36,939; *see also Flaxman,* 697 F.2d at 788 (once a prima facie case of unfitness for registration is established, the burden shifts to petitioner to prove rehabilitation and mitigation). In

Vercillo I, the Commission held that the ALJ should assess the following in determining whether Vercillo's registration would pose a risk to the public or to market integrity: the nexus between the wrongdoing underlying his conviction and a threat to the market mechanism; circumstances that mitigate the wrongdoing for which Vercillo was convicted; evidence of rehabilitation or a "changed direction"; and the role Vercillo intended to play in CFTC-regulated markets. *Vercillo I,* Comm. Fut. L. Rep. P 25,836 at 40,739.

Vercillo does not question on appeal whether the Division proved that he was statutorily disqualified from being registered as a floor agent; rather, he asserts that the CFTC erred when it found, contrary to the decision of the ALJ, that he had not sufficiently rebutted the presumption against registrability. Much of Vercillo's brief is devoted to questioning the weight certain evidence was given by the Commission and arguing that the ALJ's determinations should have been accorded deference. It is true, as Vercillo alleges in his brief, that credibility determinations of an ALJ are entitled to great deference and should be overturned only in extraordinary circumstances. *See, e.g., J.C. Penney Co., Inc. v. NLRB,* 123 F.3d 988, 995 (7th Cir. 1997). In the present case, however, the Commission did not attempt to assess the credibility of any of Vercillo's witnesses, but rather determined how much weight their testimony should be given in light of Vercillo's burden of proof. This is entirely within the Commission's discretion when undertaking a de novo review of the ALJ's decision, and the Commission did not err in giving its own weight to the testimony elicited in favor of Vercillo. *See Ryan v. CFTC,* 145 F.3d 910, 1998 U.S. App. LEXIS 10226, *13. However, on appeal, we may review the ALJ's decision as part of the record to see if the Commission's decision was supported by the weight of the evidence. *Morris v. CFTC,* 980 F.2d 1289, 1293 (9th Cir. 1992). Furthermore, agency findings which run counter to those of the ALJ are given less weight than they would otherwise receive. *Id.* (citing *Saavedra v. Donovan,* 700 F.2d 496, 498 (9th Cir.), *cert. denied,* 464 U.S. 892, 78 L. Ed. 2d 227, 104 S. Ct. 236 (1983)).

Our review of the Commission's decision to deny Vercillo's registration shows that it is supported by the evidence and was not an abuse of discretion. * * *

Vercillo next asserts that the Commission erred in finding that he had not presented enough evidence of rehabilitation to overcome the presumption of non-registrability. First, we note that Vercillo, in his brief, sets forth an incorrect burden of proof. Therein, he states that "there is simply no evidence that he is not rehabilitated." This misstates the burden of proof, since it is up to Vercillo to show that he is rehabilitated and not up to the Commission to show that he is not. In any event, the record contains substantial evidence to support the CFTC's decision.

First, Vercillo argues that the CFTC abused its discretion by not giving weight to his character witnesses. At the hearing before the ALJ, Vercillo called as character witnesses Scott Early, the general counsel of the CBOT, Mark Gold, an independent trader at the CBOT, and Henry Shatkin, the CEO of a trading company which operates at the CBOT. The Commission stated that it did not accord significant weight to the testimony of any of these witnesses because it does not do so "unless such witness was qualified as an expert." *Vercillo II,* 1997 WL 291441 at *10. None of Vercillo's witnesses had been so qualified. We recently addressed the issue of the Commission's requirement of expert rehabilitation witnesses in *Ryan,* No. 97–2120, Slip Op. at 21, noting that the Commission has not set forth any criteria for determining when a person is considered an "expert in rehabilitation." This is not the first time we have brought this lack of guidance to the attention of the Commission. *See Cox v. CFTC,* 138 F.3d 268, 275 (7th Cir. 1998) (stating that "for the opportunity to present witnesses on the issues of rehabilitation to be meaningful, the Commission must establish some guidelines regarding the kind of testimony it will accept."); *LaCrosse v. CFTC,* 137 F.3d 925, 934 n. 5 (7th Cir. 1998) ("the Commission has not provided much guidance on who, other than a probation officer, qualifies as an expert in rehabilitation.").

Reflecting our increasing frustration with the lack of criteria, we set forth in Ryan that "until the Commission provides some guidance regarding the kind of testimony it will accept, we will consider it to be an abuse of discretion for the Commission to discount the testimony of character witnesses solely for not being experts." *Ryan,* No. 97–2120, Slip Op. at 21. We agree that this is the appropriate way to proceed, and we add our voice to the chorus of decisions calling for the Commission to set forth guidelines regarding "experts in rehabilitation." Accordingly, we find that the CFTC's decision to discount the testimony of Vercillo's witnesses simply because they were not "experts in rehabilitation" was an abuse of discretion.

As in *Ryan,* however, we find that notwithstanding the CFTC's abuse of discretion, reversal is not warranted in this case because the Commission offered a valid reason to accord the testimony of Vercillo's witnesses limited weight. In its decision, the Commission stated that the testimony of Vercillo's witnesses was "not persuasive" because it only showed "at best a perfunctory concern with the customers harmed by Vercillo's wrongdoing," and therefore showed that they had a limited appreciation of the interest of the public. *Vercillo II,* 1997 WL 291441 at *9. This is a legitimate reason for declining to fully credit the testimony of the witnesses, and is amply supported by the record. For example, Henry Shatkin stated that he noticed that Vercillo was a changed person, lacking his old "spunkiness and cockiness." He also stated that Vercillo was an active trader, which was good for the market, and that his formerly "wild" trading style had been subdued. *Id.* at 12–13. Outside of these general observations, however, Shatkin did not provide any detailed explanation as to why he felt that Vercillo would not be a threat to the market if he were allowed to return and resume trading. Mark Gold testified similarly, repeatedly noting that Vercillo was remorseful for his prior conduct and is a "changed individual." While he also opined that Vercillo would not pose a threat to the public or the market, Gold stated that this was because Vercillo's active trading style was beneficial to the market. Scott Early testified that he believed that Vercillo would not pose a threat to the market if he returned, but admitted that, at the time Vercillo committed the illegal acts, he only knew Vercillo by reputation. In sum, none of Vercillo's witnesses testified in any detail as to why they believed he would not pose a threat to the public if he were allowed to resume trading, and the Commission was within its discretion in finding that this testimony did not persuasively establish that Vercillo has been rehabilitated.

Second, Vercillo asserts that his expression of remorse shows that he is rehabilitated. The Commission gave this evidence little weight as well, finding that the wrongful nature of Vercillo's actions was clear at the time he committed his acts. This result is consistent with the CFTC's previous position on statements of contrition. In *In re Horn,* the Commission stated that "when the wrongful nature of the conduct at issue is clear at the time of the violation, expressions of contrition following detection of the wrongdoing do not necessarily indicate a significant change in character." *In re Horn,* Comm. Fut. L. Rep. P 24,836 at 36,940. The record supports the inference that Vercillo knew, at the time of his illegal actions, that his conduct was improper. At the time, CBOT rules prohibited noncompetitive trading like that engaged in by Vercillo, and all traders were therefore on notice that they should not participate in such activity. The CFTC did not abuse its discretion.

Finally, Vercillo argues that the fact he has committed no violations of the law since his conviction demonstrates that he is rehabilitated. He also notes that he traded at the CBOT for nine weeks in 1993 without getting into trouble, and that the Commission should have taken this into account. The CFTC acknowledged this evidence, but found that nine weeks of trading was too little to demonstrate that Vercillo had undertaken a changed direction in life. This view was in accord with Commission precedent that while such evidence may be probative of rehabilitation, it is not given substantial weight when the period in question is limited. In re Bryant, [1990–92 Transfer Binder] Comm. Fut. L. Rep. (CCH) P 24,847 at 36,999 (CFTC April 18, 1990) (citations omitted). Additionally, at the time Vercillo was allowed to engage in limited trading, he was the subject of an outstanding administrative complaint. CFTC precedent establishes that the weight to be accorded evidence of absence of wrongdoing is limited when the respondent is subject to an outstanding administrative complaint during the time at issue. *LaCrosse,* 137 F.3d at 932 (citing *In re Silverman,* No. 76–18, 1977 WL 13527 at *2 (CFTC Mar. 14, 1977)). Accordingly, the Commission did not err in not placing great weight on this evidence.

In sum, the record supports the Commission's conclusion that Vercillo did not rebut the presumption that his registration should be denied. Accordingly, we affirm the CFTC's decision to deny Vercillo's registration as a floor broker.

Vercillo also challenges the permanent trading ban placed on him by the Commission. At the evidentiary hearing, the Division submitted proof that Vercillo had been convicted of six felonies arising under § 4b of the CEA. Pursuant to § 9(b) of the CEA, 7 U.S.C. § 16(b), such felony convictions give rise to a presumption that Vercillo should be permanently banned from trading on Commission-regulated markets unless he can show by the weight of the evidence that his continued access to such markets will not pose a risk to their integrity. The relevant statute states:

> Any person convicted of a felony under this section shall be . . . barred from using, or participating in any manner in, any market regulated by the Commission for five years or such longer period as the Commission shall determine, on such terms and conditions as the Commission may prescribe, unless the Commission determines that the imposition of such . . . market bar is not required to protect the public interest.

7 U.S.C. § 13(b).

Vercillo asserts generally that the evidence he presented on rehabilitation was unrebutted, noting that the Division relied solely on the fact that he had been convicted of numerous felonies in support of levying sanctions against him. Our discussion above, finding that the Commission did nor err in finding that Vercillo's evidence did not meet his burden of proof, is equally applicable with regard to the imposition of a trading ban, and we need not repeat ourselves here.

Vercillo also argues that he established that he was not a threat to the marketplace. His sole argument on this point, however, consists of comparing the length of his permanent trading ban with trading bans imposed on others engaged in allegedly comparable conduct. For instance, Vercillo asserts that Nowak received only a six year trading ban even though his "participation in the same conduct [as Vercillo] makes him equally unfit" to trade. Appellant's Brief at 24. Part of the reason for Nowak's ban being shorter than Vercillo's, as the brief notes, is the fact that Nowak reached a settlement with the Commission. Vercillo also cites several other cases in which traders were given shorter bans or registration suspensions than he was. This comparison misses the point, however, since, as Vercillo notes in his brief, "sanctions must be fashioned on a case by case basis." Appellant's Brief at 23 (citing *In re Thomas McKinnon Futures, Inc.,* [1986–87 Transfer Binder], Comm. Fut. L. Rep. (CCH) P 23,753 at 33,970 (CFTC June 25, 1987)). What has happened in other cases, even those which may appear factually similar to Vercillo's circumstances, is irrelevant here. The record substantiates the Commission's finding that Vercillo did not rebut the presumption that he should be permanently banned from trading on CFTC-regulated markets, and we find that there was no abuse of discretion by the Commission. * * *

The record demonstrates that the Commission's choice to deny Vercillo's registration and permanently ban him from trading on CFTC-regulated markets is not unwarranted in law or without justification in fact. Accordingly, Vercillo's petition for review is DENIED and the order of the CFTC is ENFORCED.

NOTES

1. The CFTC may also issue a cease and desist order prohibiting future violations [7 U.S.C. § 13]. The CFTC has stated that:

> A cease and desist order is appropriate where there is a reasonable likelihood that a respondent will repeat his wrongful conduct in the future. In general, evidence of a knowing violation or a pattern of violative conduct is sufficient to support an inference that it is likely wrongful conduct will be repeated.

In the Matter of U.S. Securities & Futures Corp., Comm. Fut. L. Rep. (CCH) ¶ 31,494 (C.F.T.C. 2009).

2. Alternatively, the CFTC may seek an injunction in federal court against future violations. [7 U.S.C § 13a–1]. The Seventh Circuit has described the standards for granting such relief as follows:

> Actions for statutory injunctions need not meet the requirements for an injunction imposed by traditional equity jurisprudence. Once a violation is demonstrated, the moving party need show only that there is some reasonable likelihood of future violations. While past misconduct does not lead necessarily to the conclusion that there is a likelihood of future misconduct, it is "highly suggestive of the likelihood of future violations." In drawing the inference from past violations that future violations may occur, the court should look at the "totality of circumstances, and factors suggesting that the infraction might not have been an isolated occurrence are always relevant."

Other circuit decisions analyzing the problem whether or not to grant statutory injunctive relief after a violation has been proven have looked to a variety of factors to determine whether there is a reasonable likelihood of future misconduct. The fact that a violator has continued to maintain that his conduct was blameless has prompted several courts to look favorably on injunctive relief. Similarly, when a defendant persists in its illegal activities "right up to the day of the hearing in the district court . . . the likelihood of futures violations, if not restrained, is clear." More importantly, courts have analyzed the nature of the past misconduct and the violator's occupation or customary business activities to determine whether an injunction should be granted. When the violation has been founded on systematic wrongdoing, rather than an isolated occurrence, a court should be more willing to enjoin future misconduct. And when a defendant, because of his professional occupation or career interest, will be in a position in which future violations could be possible, relief is appropriate.

CFTC v. Hunt, 591 F.2d 1211, 1220 (7th Cir.), cert. denied, 442 U.S. 921 (1979) (citations omitted).

3. The CFTC may also seek ancillary relief when seeking an injunction, including an order requiring the disgorgement of illicit profits and restitution. The courts have assumed that ancillary equitable relief is available by implication in CFTC injunctive actions. See, e.g., CFTC v. Hunt, 591 F.2d 1211 (7th Cir.), cert. denied, 442 U.S. 921 (1979).

The Dodd-Frank Wall Street Reform and Consumer Protection Act of 2010 made such relief explicit by adding a new subparagraph (d)(3) to 7 U.S.C.A. § 13a–1, which states that:

(3) Equitable remedies In any action brought under this section, the Commission may seek, and the court may impose, on a proper showing, on any person found in the action to have committed any violation, equitable remedies including—

(A) restitution to persons who have sustained losses proximately caused by such violation (in the amount of such losses); and

(B) disgorgement of gains received in connection with such violation.

4. Monetary sanctions are authorized in both CFTC administrative proceedings and in its injunctive actions in federal court. The CFTC is authorized to impose a civil penalty in the amount of $500,00 for each violation or $1 million for violation of the manipulation prohibition [7 U.S.C. § 13a]. A federal district court may impose a civil penalty of the greater of $100,000 ($1 million for a manipulation violation) or triple the monetary gain to the violator for each violation [7 U.S.C.§ 13a–1].

3. SRO DISCIPLINARY PROCEEDINGS

MBH COMMODITY ADVISORS, INC. V. CFTC

250 F.3d 1052 (7th Cir. 2001)

CUDAHY, CIRCUIT JUDGE.

The National Futures Association (NFA) imposed sanctions on Jacob Bernstein and MBH Commodity Advisors, Inc. (MBH) in connection with an infomercial and web site on which both appeared. Following an unsuccessful appeal to the NFA Appeals Committee, Bernstein and MBH brought their case to the Commodity Futures Trading Commission (CFTC or Commission), which summarily affirmed the NFA Appeals Committee. Bernstein and MBH now appeal to this court, arguing that the CFTC applied a too-lenient standard of review in evaluating the NFA Appeals Committee decision; failed to make and declare required findings; and applied expansive readings of NFA rules in violation of their due process rights. We affirm.

Bernstein has been active in the commodities industry since 1972 and has developed a "seasonal trading method." This method is based on Bernstein's study of the historical behavior of futures markets—a study that allegedly revealed that trades of certain futures products will almost certainly produce a profit when executed on specified dates. The method is described in Bernstein's book, Key Date Seasonals—The Best of the Best in Seasonal Trades, as well as a series of newsletters, videotape lectures and other such materials, all of which he markets to the public.

In the spring of 1995, Ramy El-Batrawi of Genesis/Positive Response Television (Genesis) approached Bernstein at a seminar in Burbank, California about the possibility of marketing Bernstein's futures trading products through the creation of an infomercial. On October 27, 1995, Bernstein, acting for himself and on behalf of MBH,1 entered into a marketing and distribution agreement with Genesis. Bernstein testified before the NFA panel that, during the negotiations leading up to the final marketing agreement, he stressed the need for assurances that the infomercial would comply with NFA and CFTC regulations. Bernstein also stated that he insisted on the right to review the infomercial before it aired. However, the final agreement between Bernstein and Genesis granted Genesis the unrestricted and exclusive right to advertise and market Bernstein's commodity trading products. (Thus, Bernstein retained no right to pull the infomercial from the air, even if the infomercial raised regulatory concerns.) In exchange, Bernstein received four percent of Genesis' gross receipts from the sales of his products through the infomercial.

Prior to the infomercial's production, Genesis provided Bernstein with the infomercial script, which he reviewed. As part of his review, Bernstein independently verified the testimonials of three customers who were to appear in the infomercial as having successfully traded using his method. According to Bernstein, he satisfied himself that they had indeed profited from the use of his method although he did not continue to monitor their accounts to ensure that they remained profitable for the time during which the infomercial aired. For additional scrutiny, Bernstein sent an unspecified excerpt from the script to his attorney for review. Bernstein also requested that Genesis and Jeffrey Fox of Fox Investments, a broker to whom Bernstein referred customers for their trades, send the infomercial's script to their attorneys. All three attorneys suggested changes to the infomercial, which Genesis made. Following these preliminaries, Bernstein approved the script. Genesis produced the infomercial, entitled Success and You, in the spring of 1996.

The infomercial was ultimately aired by 390 television stations throughout the United States in 1996. The infomercial opens with a shot of two men who appear to represent contrasting degrees of wealth and poverty. A narrator states:

> Both of these men have had the same opportunities throughout their lives. One struggles paycheck to paycheck trapped in a dead-end job, while the other has financial independence and the freedom to enjoy it. Why are some people stuck living a dull and meager existence while others succeed and lead the good life?

One of the host figures in the infomercial then appears on-screen and exclaims, "Today we'll reveal how you can change your humdrum existence into a life of financial independence on Success and You." Following some preliminary profiles, the infomercial focuses on Bernstein, who tells the audience, "I think trading futures is one of the best possible ways to achieve wealth in America today." Bernstein then recounts his own "rags to riches" story, concluding with a description of the seasonal trading methodology he developed along the way.

Bernstein next tells the viewer that his seasonal trades are "no-brainers," which require no guesswork because the trader is instructed when to enter and exit from the futures market. Bernstein notes that he has done all of the hard work for his customers, and emphasizes that his trades have been historically correct 70 percent of the time. (In fact, Bernstein claims that he doesn't even "fool around with anything that's been correct less than 70 percent of the time.") However, Bernstein also gives examples during the course of the infomercial of his more successful trades, naming, for example, a heating oil trade that he claims has an 87 percent probability of producing a profit.

Following the spotlight on Bernstein, the infomercial turns to three traders who testify to their success using Bernstein's seasonal method. Ken Whisenhunt, a truck driver, is shown telling his wife, "We're going to get that Lincoln now." Whisenhunt also tells the audience that "[i]t's fantastic when you make a trade and come up with several thousand dollars in your favor." Next, the audience is introduced to a Texas farmer named Harold Hinkle, who tells them, "I'm trading for one reason and one reason only, to make money. I'm trading Jake's methodology, because I believe in it, and it's working for me." Lastly, a housewife named Pam Smith is introduced. Near the end of the infomercial she declares, "Jake is so easy to follow in what he teaches you. . . . So, by keeping it simple, I've doubled my account and made a lot of money, and I feel like I'm on my way to making a lot more money." Following other segments, the infomercial concludes with a casino dealer who tells the viewer that "[m]ost people lose in a casino because their odds of winning are less than 50 percent. Imagine if your odds of winning were over 80 percent. If you were able to win on this table eight out of ten times, would you walk out a winner?"

The infomercial superimposes cautionary statements on six scattered occasions throughout its run. These statements are: (1) "There is a risk of loss in futures trading. Past results are not necessarily indicative of future results;" (2) "Statistical probabilities do not assure that any particular trade will be profitable;" and (3) "Persons who wish to commit money to the futures market should understand the risks before they do so."

In addition to the infomercial, Genesis created an internet web site, entitled Amazing Discoveries, to promote Bernstein's materials. The web site's address is provided in the infomercial, and the site includes content similar to the infomercial. For example, the site states that "Jake Bernstein's Trade Your Way to Riches will give you the exact skills it takes to make money as a disciplined, successful commodities trader," and states that Bernstein's trades are "no-brainer" trades with "unbelievable accuracy rates of 70, 80, even 90%." The web site only contains one small-print statement at the bottom of the web page warning of the risk inherent in futures trading: "There is a risk of loss in futures trading." The record does not indicate how many visitors viewed the web site.

The infomercial and web site came to the attention of the NFA, which is charged with creating and implementing a comprehensive program for self-regulation of the commodity futures industry. To further this goal, the NFA is required to adopt rules governing the conduct of its membership. These rules are subject to Commission approval and must provide standards governing the sales practices of NFA members. See 7 U.S.C. sec. 21(p)(3); 17 C.F.R. sec. 170.5. In addition, these rules must be "designed to prevent fraudulent and manipulative acts and practices, to promote just and equitable principles of trade, in general, to protect the public interest, and to remove impediments to and perfect the mechanism of free and open futures trading." 7 U.S.C. sec. 21(b)(7).

Pursuant to its statutory mandate, the NFA has adopted numerous rules governing member conduct. See generally National Futures Association, NFA Manual (updated on an on-going basis). Because Bernstein and MBH were both members of the NFA at the time of the conduct relevant to this case, they were both subject to these rules, the most relevant of which is NFA Compliance Rule 2–29, entitled "Communications With the Public and Promotional Material." The following provisions of this rule are especially relevant:

(a) General Prohibition. No Member or Associate shall make any communication with the public which:

(1) operates as a fraud or deceit; * * *

(3) makes any statement that futures trading is appropriate for all persons.

(b) Content of Promotional Material. No Member or Associate shall use any promotional material which:

(1) is likely to deceive the public;

(2) contains any material misstatement of fact or which the Member or Associate knows omits a fact if the omission makes the promotional material misleading;

(3) mentions the possibility of profit unless accompanied by an equally prominent statement of the risk of loss; * * *

(c) Hypothetical Results.

(1) Any Member or Associate who uses promotional material which includes a measurement or description of or makes any reference to hypothetical performance results which could have been achieved had a particular trading system of the Member or Associate been employed in the past must include in the promotional material the following disclaimer prescribed by the NFA's Board of Directors [lengthy disclaimer omitted]

NFA Compliance Rule 2–29.

After reviewing the infomercial and web site, the NFA determined that they misled viewers and violated NFA Compliance Rule 2–29 for several reasons. The NFA believed that the infomercial and web site falsely implied that customers would profit on the trades recommended by Bern stein without adequately disclosing the risk of loss. This violated

Compliance Rule 2–29(b)(3), which prohibits the use of promotional material that mentions the possibility of profit without featuring an equally prominent warning of the risk of loss. The NFA also concluded that the infomercial falsely represented that anyone could trade futures, in violation of Compliance Rule 2–29(a)(3), which prohibits any communication with the public that contains any statement that futures trading is appropriate for all persons. In addition, the NFA charged that the infomercial and web site advertised hypothetical results without a required disclaimer, in violation of Compliance Rule 2–29(c)(1), which requires promotional materials that make use of hypothetical results to include a disclaimer stating the limitations of reliance on hypothetical results.

Following its review of the accounts of the three customers shown in the infomercial (Whisenhunt, Hinkle, and Smith), the NFA concluded that the infomercial falsely implied that these customers made money using Bernstein's recommended trades. In fact, these customers all lost money on their trades or failed to realize the returns they claimed in the infomercial during the time the infomercial aired. In addition, these customers for the most part did not even trade using Bernstein's seasonal methodology. Accordingly, the NFA believed that the infomercial's claim of the traders' successes violated Compliance Rules 2–29(a)(1) (prohibiting communications with the public that operate as a fraud or deceit), (b)(1) (prohibiting use of promotional material that is likely to deceive the public) and (b)(2) (generally prohibiting use of promotional material that contains material misstatements of fact).

Lastly, the NFA believed that the infomercial and web site falsely stated that Bernstein was a successful trader. Bernstein provided the NFA with monthly statements from November 1992 through November 1996 for MBH's proprietary account, through which he made his own trades. The NFA's analysis of this account showed that the account had lost $3,286.33 during 1992, $8,499.13 during 1993, $1,793.82 during 1994, $14,300.26 during 1995, and $8,374.34 during the first 11 months of 1996. Accordingly, the NFA believed that Bernstein's claim that he was a successful trader violated Compliance Rules 2–29(a)(1) and (b)(1).

As a result of its investigation, the NFA requested that Bernstein stop airing the infomercial. In turn, Bernstein relayed this request to El-Batrawi. (Remember, Bernstein had contracted away his ability to control airing of the infomercial, so, presumably, his only recourse was to ask that El-Batrawi honor the NFA's request.) After initial resistance, El-Batrawi agreed to stop airing the infomercial, and Genesis pulled it off the air sometime in July 1996. While the infomercial was off the air, Bernstein attempted to revise its script to address the NFA's concerns. Ultimately, the NFA did not accept the revised script because the script did not include disclaimers about hypothetical results. When Bernstein informed El-Batrawi of this, El-Batrawi lost patience and began re-airing the infomercial in October or November 1996, notwithstanding its alleged non-compliance with NFA rules.

Following its review of the infomercial and web site, the NFA filed a four-count complaint against Bernstein and MBH, alleging various violations of the NFA's Compliance Rules. Specifically, count one of the complaint charged Bernstein and MBH with violating Compliance Rules 2–29(a)(1), (b)(1) and (b)(2) by presenting misleading information in the infomercial and web site. Count two alleged that Bernstein and MBH violated Compliance Rule 2–29(b)(3) because the infomercial and web site promised profit without giving equal prominence to the risk of loss. Count three alleged that Bernstein and MBH violated Compliance Rule 2–29(a)(3) because the infomercial represented that futures trading was appropriate for all persons. Lastly, count four alleged that the infomercial and web site failed to disclose the limitations of using hypothetical performance results, as required by Compliance Rule 2–29(c)(1). Bernstein and MBH denied the allegations and requested a hearing before an NFA panel in accordance with Part Three of the NFA Compliance Rules. See also 7 U.S.C. sec. 21(b)(9); 17 C.F.R. sec. 170.9.

After briefing by both parties, the assigned NFA panel issued a decision finding Bernstein and MBH liable on all counts. As a sanction, the panel barred both Bernstein and MBH from the NFA for a period of 18 months, after which both could reapply for membership. In addition, the panel imposed a $200,000 fine on Bernstein and MBH, for which they incurred joint and several liability. The parties appealed to the NFA's three-person Appeals Committee, and the Committee affirmed the panel decision in all respects. The parties then appealed to the CFTC. The CFTC summarily affirmed the NFA decision, adopting the NFA's findings and conclusions after applying a weight of the evidence standard of review as dictated by 17 C.F.R. sec. 171.34. Bernstein and MBH now appeal to this court.

Bernstein raises three arguments on appeal: (1) that the CFTC erred by summarily affirming the NFA decision without making its own, independent findings of fact; (2) that the CFTC erred by failing to make the findings required by 7 U.S.C. sec. 21(i); and (3) that the NFA violated his due process rights by applying novel constructions of Compliance Rule 2–29 to him.

Bernstein first argues that 7 U.S.C. sec. 21(i) requires de novo fact finding, rather than the weight of the evidence review that the CFTC chose. * * *

Under the weight of the evidence standard, the Commission:

> does not mechanically reweigh the evidence to ascertain in which direction it preponderates. The Commission focuses its inquiry

on whether the fact finder acted reasonably in reaching material findings in light of the evidence . . . the reasonable inferences drawn therefrom, and other pertinent circumstances.

55 Fed. Reg. at 24,256. "Several courts have equated the 'weight of the evidence' standard with the 'preponderance of the evidence' standard used in other contexts." Monieson v. CFTC, 996 F.2d 852, 858 (7th Cir. 1993) (and cases cited therein). * * *

The SEC—which, under 15 U.S.C. sec. 78s, is subject to statutory requirements for reviewing securities association disciplinary decisions that are virtually identical to the CFTC's—apparently reviews NASD disciplinary actions de novo. See, e.g., Shultz v. Securities & Exchange Comm'n, 614 F.2d 561, 568 (7th Cir. 1980). Even though this might be Bernstein's most telling point, he has merely pointed out this interagency discrepancy without making the obvious point that two agencies should not draw conflicting conclusions from similar language. See Rapaport v. United States Dept. of the Treasury, Office of Thrift Supervision, 59 F.3d 212, 216–17 (D.C. Cir. 1995) (one agency's interpretation of a statute is not entitled to deference when several other agencies share administration of the statute). But here there appears to be a sound basis for the SEC and CFTC's conflicting interpretations of similar statutory language.

Perhaps most obviously, the statute guiding the SEC (the Securities Exchange Act, of which 15 U.S.C. sec. 78s is relevant here) and the statute guiding the CFTC (the CEA) are different statutes, which have a different history, even though they now contain similar language applicable to disciplinary proceedings More importantly, if any interpretation needs to be declared unreasonable, the SEC's use of a de novo standard of review appears the better candidate, for in amending the SEA Congress stated that "[t]he scope of the hearings [to review disciplinary sanctions] would be within the discretion of the appropriate regulatory agency, thus permitting the agency to consider the matter de novo if it deems this appropriate or simply on the record before the self-regulatory agency as would be the normal situation." S. Rep. No. 94–75, at 132 (1975) (emphasis added). Thus, sec. 78s appears at best to grant the SEC discretion to choose a standard of review, and certainly does not dictate a de novo standard of review. Likewise, sec. 21(i) grants discretion to the CFTC, even if this means that the CFTC and SEC may reach different conclusions in exercising their discretion.

Bernstein also argues that the structure of the CEA supports the inference that sec. 21(i) requires de novo fact finding. Bernstein begins his argument by noting that "[w]here Congress includes particular language in one section of a statute but omits it in another section of the same Act, it is generally presumed that Congress acts intentionally and purposely in the disparate inclusion or exclusion." Russello v. United States, 464 U.S. 16, 23 (1983) (quoting United States v. Wong Kim Bo, 472 F.2d 720, 722 (5th Cir. 1972)). Thus, because sec. 21(i) does not explicitly mandate a weight of the evidence review for disciplinary actions—whereas sec. 21(o) specifically prescribes this standard for the review of registration actions—Bernstein argues that Congress must have intended for the CFTC's review of disciplinary actions to be de novo.

However, given the similar reputational and financial consequences that attach to parties under both sec. 21(i) membership actions and sec. 21(o) registration actions, it would make little sense to apply differing standards of review to each. Further, sec. 21(i) explicitly states that the CFTC is only required to "review" final disciplinary decisions of the NFA, and that the CFTC may limit its review to the record below. In "reviewing" NFA decisions, the CFTC is acting in an appellate capacity, and appellate tribunals generally do not make de novo factual determinations. See Lawson Products, Inc. v. Avnet, Inc., 782 F.2d 1429, 1439 (7th Cir. 1986). Lastly, de novo review would require the CFTC to ignore the NFA's own "expertise in evaluating factual issues in the context of day-to-day industry practice." Commission Review of National Futures Association Decisions in Disciplinary, Membership Denial, Registration and Membership Responsibility Actions, 55 Fed. Reg. 24,254, 24,256 (June 15, 1990). For all of these reasons, we cannot conclude that the CFTC has adopted an unreasonable reading of sec. 21(i), even if sec. 21(o) explicitly mandates a weight of the evidence review while sec. 21(i) does not. * * *

Bernstein next argues that, in its summary opinion, the CFTC failed to make the findings and declarations required by 7 U.S.C. sec. 21(i)(1) & (3). The required declarations include a finding that the member engaged in the acts that the NFA found the member to have engaged in, sec. 21(i) (1)(A)(i) & (3)(A)(i); that the member's acts are in violation of NFA rules, sec. 21(i)(1)(A)(ii) & (3)(A)(ii); and that the rules have been applied in a manner that is consistent with the CEA, sec. 21(i)(1)(A)(iii) & (3)(A)(iii).

Here, the CFTC determined that the findings and conclusions of the NFA were supported by the weight of the evidence and that the NFA committed no error material to the outcome of the case. As such, the CFTC clearly met the requirements of sec. 21(i)(1)(A)(i) & (ii), as well as sec. 21(i)(3)(A) (i) & (ii). Further, on appeal to the Commission, Bernstein argued that the NFA erred by applying Rule 2–29 in a manner that was inconsistent with the purpose of the CEA. Since this argument was raised before the Commission, it was necessarily resolved by the Commission's order of summary affirmance. Accordingly, the requirements of sec. 21(i)(1) (A)(iii) & (3)(A)(iii) were satisfied as well, for the Commission implicitly found that the NFA applied its rules in a manner consistent with the CEA.

We are also (just barely) satisfied that the CFTC order of summary affirmance met sec. 21(i)'s requirement that the CFTC declare its findings. We will "uphold a decision of less than ideal clarity if the agency's path may reasonably be discerned." Bowman Transp., Inc. v. Arkansas-Best Freight Sys., Inc., 419 U.S. 281, 286 (1974). Here, the CFTC did not explicitly state its path, but the path is nonetheless easily discerned, for the CFTC adopted the NFA's findings and conclusions, finding no material error in the NFA proceedings. Bernstein argues that the CFTC's decision is not clear enough because it does not state what the non-material errors are. However, the non-material errors are, by definition, not material and need not be elaborated on. Accordingly, the CFTC has here made all of the findings and declarations required by sec. 21(i).

Because we believe that in this case the Commission's order of summary affirmance met the bare minimum of sec. 21(i)'s finding and declaration requirements, we need not address the Commission's argument that its occasional use of summary orders, codified at 17 C.F.R. sec. 171.33(b), is entitled to Chevron deference. However, we note that given sec. 21(i)'s express requirement that the CFTC make and declare findings, it is difficult to imagine that the Commission's use of summary affirmance orders—which need not set forth any reasoning or findings of fact—will never run afoul of sec. 21(i). * * *

For the foregoing reasons, the decision of the Commodity Futures Trading Commission is AFFIRMED.

MESIROW V. CHICAGO MERCANTILE EXCHANGE
Comm. Fut. L. Rep. (CCH) ¶ 30,552 (C.F.T.C. 2007)

ORDER DENYING STAY

By the Commission (CHAIRMAN JEFFERY COMMISSIONERS LUKKEN and DUNN).

On April 16, 2007, the Chicago Mercantile Exchange ("CME") notified Richard Mesirow ("Mesirow") that it found he had breached his fiduciary duty to his customers by revealing information concerning customer orders to another trader and by altering prices to his customers' disadvantage. The CME fined Mesirow $75,000, suspended his membership and trading floor access privileges for six months, and ordered him to pay $5,500 restitution. On May 14, 2007, Mesirow filed an appeal from the CME's decision and asked for a stay of the May 21, 2007 effective date pending appeal.

Mesirow argues that there is a likelihood that he will succeed on the merits of his appeal because the CME did not prove the alleged violations by a preponderance of the evidence. He claims that the CME's case is based upon circumstantial evidence that amounts to "mere speculation." Pet. at 6. Mesirow also argues that he will succeed on the merits because the proceeding was fundamentally unfair. He contends that the CME refused to make available videotape evidence of trades on other dates so that "he could demonstrate that locals routinely anticipated market on close orders he was filling and to establish the degree of difficulty of filling closing orders." Pet. at 14. Mesirow contends that denial of the stay would result in a six-month suspension, which "in and of itself constitutes irreparable harm." Pet. at 16. He argues that CME's failure to make the suspension effective immediate upon its April 16, 2007 decision shows that it would not endanger orderly trading or the public interest. The CME filed a response in opposition.

In determining whether to grant a stay, we consider whether the petitioner has established that: (1) there is a likelihood of success on the merits; (2) denial of the stay would cause the petitioner irreparable harm; (3) granting the stay would not endanger orderly trading or otherwise cause substantial harm to the market or market participants; and (4) granting the stay would not be contrary to the Commodity Exchange Act, and the rules, regulations and orders of the Commission, or otherwise be contrary to the public interest. Commission Rule 9.24(d), 17 C.F.R. § 9.24(d).

Mesirow's contention, that a six-month suspension "in and of itself constitutes irreparable harm," falls short of Rule 9.24's requirement. A party seeking a stay must demonstrate that the injury claimed is "both certain and great." *In re GNP Commodities,* [1990–1992 Transfer Binder] Comm. Fut. L. Rep. (CCH) P 25,399 at 39,363 (CFTC Sept. 25, 1992); *Global Futures Holdings. Inc. v. National Futures Association,* [1998–1999 Transfer Binder] Comm. Fut. L. Rep. (CCH) P 27,467 at 47,241 (CFTC Nov. 24, 1998) (*citing Cuomo v. U.S. Nuclear Regulatory Commission,* 772 F.2d 972, 976 (D.C. Cir. 1985)); *Grandview Holding Corp. v. NFA,* [1994–1996 Transfer Binder] Comm. Fut. L. Rep. (CCH) P 26,708 at 43,954 (CFTC May 30, 1996). A mere assertion of irreparable harm does not demonstrate certain injury. *Grandview,* P 26,708 at 43,954.

The six-month suspension imposed requires Mesirow to take a hiatus from trading; it does not amount to a termination of his business in the futures industry. *Auciello v. Commodity Exchange, Inc.,* [1994–1996 Transfer Binder] Comm. Fut. L. Rep. (CCH) P 26,799 at 44,270 (CFTC Sept. 27, 1996). Mesirow has not particularized either the amount of his potential loss or how his trading business will be destroyed by a six-month hiatus. *GNP Commodities,* P 25,399 at 39,363 ("[Petitioner has not] demonstrated that the imposition of a 24-month trading ban will cause him irreparable harm. Even if we assume that suspensions from personal trading can produce financial harm in the sense that business once lost cannot be recouped, it is not the kind of monetary loss considered irreparable."). *Citing Gilchrist,* P 25,024 at 37,805 and *Sampson v. Murray,* 415 U.S. 61, 90 (1974) (temporary loss of income does not usually constitute irreparable injury).

In rare instances a suspension may have consequences that are comparable to a termination of business. *Auciello,* P 26,799 at 44,270. There is nothing before us to establish that the six-month suspension at issue here will have such a draconian result. Mesirow has not presented any evidence to show that "his livelihood would be irretrievably lost." *Butler v. NYMEX,* [1990–1992 Transfer Binder] Comm. Fut. L. Rep. (CCH) P 25,089 at 38,080 (CFTC July 22, 1991). Consequently, Mesirow has not established that he is likely to suffer irreparable harm in the circumstances presented. Because Mesirow has not made the requisite showing of irreparable harm, we need not consider the other factors for issuing a stay.

Accordingly, Mesirow's petition for stay is denied.

NOTES

1. The CEA creates an appeal procedure to the CFTC from an NFA disciplinary action. [7 U.S.C. § 21(h)]. Such an appeal does not stay the imposition of NFA sanctions unless ordered by the CFTC. As typified by the preceding case, the CFTC has rarely granted a stay request. See also e.g., Stephen Bronte Advisors, LLC v. NFA, Comm. Fut. L. Rep. (CCH) ¶ 28,674 (C.F.T.C. 2001).

2. The CFTC is also empowered to review membership denial proceedings by the NFA and bars from association with NFA members. [7 U.S.C. § 21].

3. The NFA may also bring "Member Responsibility Actions" (MRAs) that impose restrictions on a member's business activities pending an adjudication before the NFA. Such actions are reviewable by the CFTC. See, e.g., Private Capital Futures Management, Inc. v. NFA, Comm. Fut. L. Rep. (CCH) ¶ 25,168 (C.F.T.C. 1991).

4. REPARATIONS

JERRY W. MARKHAM
THE SEVENTH AMENDMENT AND CFTC
REPARATIONS PROCEEDINGS
68 Iowa L. Rev. 87 (1982)

The CFTC Act [of 1974] created a "reparations" procedure, pursuant to which persons injured by violations of the Commodity Exchange Act can seek redress before the CFTC. * * *

The CFTC Act made the CFTC the adjudicative body for resolving both questions of law and fact in its reparations procedure. Thus, while the CFTC's factual findings and holdings in reparations awards are subject to judicial review in courts of appeals, the CFTC Act makes no provision for a jury trial. Nor is a jury trial available when reparations awards are sought to be enforced in a federal district court, because the order of the CFTC awarding reparations in those actions is by statute "final and conclusive." * * *

Section 14 of the Commodity Exchange Act states that any person may complain to the CFTC and seek reparations for violations of the Commodity Exchange Act and the rules, regulations, and orders thereunder. The complaint must be made within two years after the cause of action has accrued and may be made only against certain persons registered under specified provisions of the Act. Those registered persons include floor brokers, futures commission merchants, associated persons of futures commission merchants, commodity trading advisors, and commodity pool operators. * * *

Section 14 requires a complainant to file its complaint with the CFTC. The complaint must briefly state the facts upon which the complainant contends a violation has occurred. If the CFTC determines that a violation may be present, a copy of the complaint is forwarded by the CFTC to the respondent, who must either satisfy the complaint or answer it in writing. The CFTC may, in its discretion, conclude that a complaint will be rejected without affording the complaining party an opportunity for a hearing. The CFTC has also promulgated its own rules specifying similar procedures for reparations proceedings.

When the CFTC has investigated a complaint and served the complaint on the respondent, the respondent is afforded the opportunity for a hearing before an administrative law judge designated by the Commission. In cases in which a complaint is less than $5000, however, the statute provides that a hearing need not be held and that proof may be submitted in the form of depositions, verified statements of fact, or a complaint. After a hearing on the papers, or, if the claim involves over $5000, after a hearing before an administrative law judge, the CFTC will determine whether a violation has occurred and the amount of damages, if any, to which the complainant is entitled as a result of the violation. If damages are found, the CFTC will direct the respondent to pay the amount of the damages to the complainant.

Section 14 of the Commodity Exchange Act also provides for review of the CFTC's findings and reparations awards before a United States Court of Appeals. No provision is made for a jury trial at any point in this review process. Instead, section 14 incorporates another provision of the Commodity Exchange Act that allows judicial review of the CFTC's factual findings in administrative disciplinary proceedings in the courts of appeals. The provision states, however, that the factual findings of the CFTC, "if supported by the weight of evidence, shall . . . be conclusive." This may mean that, for the most part, the weight attributed to particular evidence and the inferences to be drawn from particular facts "are for the Commission to determine, not the courts."

Section 14 of the Commodity Exchange Act also provides that a complainant may enforce a reparations award by filing a certified copy of the CFTC order in an appropriate United States District Court. In those cases, subject to the right of appeal to the court of appeals as discussed above, the CFTC order awarding reparations shall be final and conclusive. * * *

The CFTC administrative law judge who conducts the factual hearing on the reparations complaint is crucial to the reparations procedure. The administrative law judge, a CFTC employee, is given broad authority in conducting the hearing, including the authority to issue subpoenas, rule on offers of proof, receive evidence, examine witnesses, regulate the course of the hearing, consider and rule on all motions and render an initial decision. The initial decision must state whether a violation has occurred and set the amount of damages, if any, suffered by the complainant.

In determining whether violations have occurred, the administrative law judge necessarily must make factual findings based on the evidence presented, and the CFTC is empowered to review these factual determinations. The CFTC has stated that findings of fact made by an administrative law judge in a reparations proceeding "must be supported by the preponderance of the evidence," which must be "substantial in nature." The CFTC also stated, however, that findings of fact made by an administrative law judge based on credibility determinations should not be disturbed "unless error is clearly shown." * * *

The effects of a CFTC decision may be far reaching. If the damage award is not paid, the registrant may have its registration suspended and be prohibited from trading futures contracts. The CFTC also has stated that a reparations award, even if paid, may become the basis for collateral estoppel in an administrative proceeding to revoke the registrant's license or impose other remedial sanctions.

MURRAY V. CARGILL, INC.

Comm. Fut. L. Rep. (CCH) ¶ 27,932 (C.F.T.C. 1999)

OPINION AND ORDER

By the Commission (CHAIRMAN RAINER, and COMMISSIONERS HOLUM, SPEARS, NEWSOME, and ERICKSON).

David Murray appeals the March 4, 1999 Order of the Administrative Law Judge ("ALJ") dismissing his reparation complaint against Cargill Incorporated ("Cargill"). We affirm in part the ALJ's ruling and dismiss this case without prejudice.

Murray is a farmer who produces corn and soybeans. Between March 31, 1995 and November 30, 1995, Murray entered into 11 purchase contracts known as "Hedge to Arrive" ("HTA") contracts with Cargill, a grain dealer. Murray failed to deliver under these contracts, and Cargill commenced an arbitration proceeding before the National Grain and Feed Association on June 30, 1998.

On November 23, 1998, Murray filed his reparation complaint with the Commission, along with a notice of parallel proceeding and a request for exception to allow the reparation proceeding to go forward, notwithstanding the pending arbitration. He alleged that Cargill violated the Commodity Exchange Act ("Act") with regard to the HTA contracts. Murray requested that the Commission make a determination that his HTA contracts with Cargill "are void, voidable, and unenforceable," as off-exchange and therefore illegal futures contracts. He claimed as damages the amount that Cargill is seeking to recover through the pending arbitration, and requested an order requiring Cargill to pay his attorney fees and costs.

The Director of the Office of Proceedings forwarded Murray's complaint to Cargill. Cargill filed a motion for reconsideration of the determination to forward the complaint, which was denied by the Director on January 14, 1999. On February 9, 1999, Cargill filed a motion to dismiss on the ground that the matters alleged in Murray's complaint were not within the reparation jurisdiction of the Commission. Specifically, Cargill argued that Murray sought only declaratory relief in his complaint, which is not available in reparations. Moreover, Cargill asserted that the Commission lacks jurisdiction over it as a non-registrant. * * *

On March 4, 1999, the ALJ issued an order dismissing the complaint. The ALJ ruled that the complaint was not cognizable in a reparation proceeding both because it sought declaratory relief rather than damages, and because the case was not ripe for adjudication, as Murray had not yet sustained any present injury. As a result, the ALJ did not reach the issue of whether Cargill is subject to reparations under Section 4m(1) of the Act. The appellant timely filed a notice of appeal to the Commission, which was duly perfected under the reparations rules. 17 C.F.R. § 12.401(a) and 12.401(b). * * *

We affirm the ALJ's dismissal of Murray's complaint as not cognizable in reparations because it fails to show actual damages and seeks declaratory relief which is unavailable in the reparations forum. Section 14(a) of the Act, as currently amended, provides the following:

> Any person complaining of any violation of any provision of this Act or any rule, regulation, or order issued pursuant to this Act by any person who is registered under this Act may, at any time within two years after the cause of action accrues, apply to the Commission for an order awarding—
>
> > (A) actual damages proximately caused by such violation. . . .
> >
> > (B) in the case of any action arising from a willful and intentional violation in the execution of an order on the floor of a contract market, punitive or exemplary damages . . .

7 U.S.C. § 18(a). The Act, therefore, provides only for actual damages proximately caused by a violation of the Act in a reparation proceeding, as well as punitive or exemplary damages. There is no provision in the Act for any other form of relief. The Commission's implementing regulations likewise provide only for damages as a reparation remedy. Commission Rule 12.13, 17 C.F.R. § 12.13, states that any person complaining of a violation of the Act may "apply to the Commission for a reparation award by filing a written complaint." A reparation award is defined in 17 C.F.R. § 12.2 as "the amount of monetary damages a party may be ordered to pay." The complaint must include "the amount of damages the complainant claims to have suffered and the method by which those damages have been computed. . . ." 17 C.F.R. § 12.13(b)(v).[2]

In his complaint, Murray states that Cargill is "attempting to collect damages from Murray for alleged breaches of two (2) contracts in the amount of $10,000 and additional damages on the remaining nine (9) contracts in the amount of $44,695." Compl. at P15. He then requests the Commission to determine that the HTA contracts "are void, voidable, and unenforceable." Murray is essentially seeking a declaratory order that his contracts are unenforceable. He does not allege that he has sustained actual damages and does not expressly ask the Commission for an award of damages. In his brief filed with his appeal, Murray argues that he did allege monetary damages in paragraph 15 of his Complaint in the amount of $54,695. Significantly, however, he states that the "respondent is attempting to collect [these damages] from Murray for an alleged breach of contract." Brief at 7 (emphasis supplied). He therefore admits that he has not been required to pay any award, and thus has not suffered any

---

[2] We note that there is a related arbitration proceeding in this case, which may have warranted dismissal of the complaint under the parallel proceeding rule, 17 C.F.R. § 12.24. However, because Cargill failed to raise this issue as a defense before the ALJ, we deem it to be waived, and we decline to exercise *sua sponte* review because of the alternate ground for dismissal herein demonstrated. 17 C.F.R. § 12.401(f).

present actual damage. His alleged damages are wholly contingent on the outcome of the arbitration proceeding.

There is no language in the Commodity Exchange Act providing for the declaratory relief requested by Murray. As stated by the U.S. Supreme Court, "a frequently stated principle of statutory construction is that when legislation expressly provides a particular remedy or remedies, courts should not expand the coverage of the statute to subsume other remedies." *National R.R. Passenger Corp. v. National Assoc. of R.R. Passengers*, 414 U.S. 453, 458 (1974). Following this principle of statutory construction, we will not expand the remedies allowed under Section 14 of the Act to include declaratory orders. Such a result comports with the legislative history of the Act. In 1978, Congress recognized that the 1974 legislation, which first created the reparations program, "envisioned the Commission's reparations proceedings as being analogous to the operation of a small claims court." 95th Cong., 2d Sess., 1978 U.S.C.C.A.N. 2087, 2104. Moreover, in 1992, Congress amended the Act, which formerly provided only for actual damages in reparations, to provide for punitive damages. Had Congress intended for the Commission to liberally construe the remedies available under the Act in reparations, this amendment, specifically adding punitive damages as a remedy, would have been unnecessary.

We note that the Administrative Procedure Act provides that agencies may "issue a declaratory order to terminate a controversy or remove uncertainty." 5 U.S.C. § 554(e). However, this Section only applies in "cases of adjudication required by statute to be determined on the record after opportunity for an agency hearing." 5 U.S.C. § 554 (a). Section 14 of the Commodity Exchange Act does not require a hearing in cases of reparation proceedings, but authorizes the Commission to promulgate "rules, regulations, and orders" necessary for "the efficient and expeditious administration of this section." 7 U.S.C. § 18(b). The Commission's regulations provide that an ALJ may dispose of a case without a hearing, 17 C.F.R. § 12.311, and authorize an ALJ to dismiss an entire proceeding if he finds "that none of the matters alleged in the complaint state a claim that is cognizable in reparations." 17 C.F.R. § 12.308(c)(1)(i). Therefore, the Administrative Procedure Act's provision for declaratory orders is not applicable to the Commission's reparations proceedings. Accordingly, the Administrative Procedure Act does not provide authority for the issuance of a declaratory order in the reparations context.

Murray's arguments that it would be procedurally improper to dismiss the case are without merit. His reliance on the Second Circuit's decision in *Schultz v. CFTC*, 716 F.2d 136 (2d Cir. 1983) is misplaced, because the court in *Schultz* was construing the version of Section 14 that was in effect prior to its amendment by the Futures Trading Act of 1982.

At that time, Section 14(e) of the Act provided that "if the Commission determines that the respondent has violated any provision of this chapter . . . the Commission shall . . . determine the amount of damage, if any, to which [the complainant] is entitled as a result of such violation." 7 U.S.C. § 18(e) (1976). The current version of Section 14 does not contain this procedural requirement. Rather, as has been noted, Congress delegated to the Commission the authority for promulgating procedures in Section 14(b) of the Act. 7 U.S.C. § 18(b). There is no requirement in the regulations that the Commission first find whether a violation of the Act has occurred, and then determine damages as indicated in *Schultz*. Rather, 17 C.F.R. § 12.308 specifically authorizes the ALJ, "at any time after he has been assigned the case," to dismiss the entire proceeding if he finds that the complaint does not state a claim cognizable in reparations.

Murray also cites *Schaefer v. Cargill, Inc.*, [1996–1998 Transfer Binder] Comm. Fut. L. Rep. (CCH) P26,962 (CFTC February 27, 1997) for the proposition that the issue of damages "is a question of fact that will depend on the development of the record by both sides." However, *Schaefer* is distinguishable because the complainants there alleged present, albeit difficult to measure, damages, while Murray has not alleged any present injury. In addition, Murray cites *Judd v. The Churchill Group, Inc.*, [1992–1994 Transfer Binder] Comm. Fut. L. Rep. P25,589 (CFTC September 30, 1992), in which the Commission held that the presiding officer's dismissal of the reparations complaint denied the claimant, who was acting *pro se*, the opportunity to prove his claim. However, *Judd* does not help Murray. Further development of the record would not cure Murray's defective pleading, which does not allege any actual damage as required by the Commission's rules. Murray also relies on *Hall v. Diversified Trading Systems*, [1992–1994 Transfer Binder] Comm. Fut. L. Rep. P26,131 (CFTC July 7, 1994), for the proposition that the Commission has favored "the holistic interpretation of parties' submissions over more technical interpretations." In that case, the Commission vacated the ALJ's order of dismissal in light of the complainant's *pro se* status, and because the complaint contained sufficient detail to provide notice of a claim. Unlike Murray, Hall in her complaint alleged that she had sustained actual damages due to the respondents' alleged misconduct, and, therefore, that case is distinguishable because Murray does not allege actual damages.

Because Murray fails to allege actual damages and seeks declaratory relief which is unavailable in reparations, we affirm the ALJ's dismissal of this case on that basis. Accordingly, Murray's complaint is dismissed without prejudice. We therefore do not reach the issues of whether this case should have been dismissed under the parallel proceeding rule or whether the Commission has jurisdiction over Cargill as a non-registered grain dealer. IT IS SO ORDERED.

NOTES

1. The Eighth Circuit has held that the mandatory CFTC reparations procedures for registrants do not violate the Seventh Amendment right to a jury trial. Myron v. Hauser, 673 F.2d 994 (1982).

2. Reparation proceedings are less formal than judicial proceedings before a federal court. Consequently, litigation costs in reparations proceedings are usually much lower than those in federal court. Nevertheless, the CFTC has adopted a formal set of rules governing reparations procedures. [17 C.F.R. § 12.1 et seq.].

3. The party initiating a reparations proceeding before the CFTC must be a "customer" of a CFTC registrant and must be injured by violations of the CEA or CFTC rules committed by the registrant. Congress amended the CEA reparations procedure in 1982 by removing the words "or required to be registered." This means that reparations cannot be brought against a person who should have been registered but was not. As noted in Section 5 below, the most prevalent forum used today to address civil claims against registered firms is through an arbitration proceeding.

4. The CFTC created three forms of reparations proceedings, each of which vary in degrees of formality, depending on the choice of the parties and amount at issue. For example, a complainant may seek an informal "Voluntary Decisional Proceeding" in which all evidence is submitted in writing to a CFTC Judgment Officer. [17 C.F.R. § 12.100]. These proceedings may be brought for claims involving any amount, provided that all parties agree to this procedure. There is no oral hearing in these cases, no findings of fact and no appeal is allowed. See, Louis F. Burke, ed., Alternate Dispute Resolution in the Futures Industry Ch. 3 (2013) (describing those proceedings).

5. If the party seeking reparations is a foreign resident, it must file a non-resident bond with the CFTC upon commencement of the proceeding. This bond must be double the amount of the claim, and a party specified in CFTC rules must issue that bond. However, this bond may be waived by the CFTC if it is shown that the country in which the complaint is a resident permits the filing of a complaint by a U.S. resident against a citizen of that country without furnishing a bond. [17 C.F.R. § 12.13].

5. ARBITRATION

INGBAR V. DREXEL BURNHAM LAMBERT INCORPORATED
683 F.2d 603 (1st Cir. 1982)

BREYER, CIRCUIT JUDGE.

Dr. Sidney Ingbar, the plaintiff/appellee, is a professor at Harvard Medical School. In 1979, he opened an account with the defendant/appellant, a commodities brokerage firm called Drexel

Burnham Lambert Incorporated ("Drexel"). When he opened the account, he signed Drexel's two-page form account contract. That form contained a provision stating that Ingbar and Drexel would submit "any controversy" to arbitration (before either the American Arbitration Association or the Board of Arbitration of the New York Stock Exchange). The provision also stated in large bold type:

WHILE the COMMODITY FUTURES TRADING COMMISSION (CFTC) RECOGNIZES the BENEFITS of SETTLING DISPUTES BY ARBITRATION, IT REQUIRES THAT YOUR CONSENT TO SUCH AN AGREEMENT BE VOLUNTARY. YOU NEED NOT SIGN THIS AGREEMENT TO OPEN AN ACCOUNT WITH DREXEL BURNHAM LAMBERT INCORPORATED.

Dr. Ingbar placed a separate signature beneath the arbitration clause containing this language.

Ingbar and Drexel soon found themselves in a "controversy." Ingbar invested about $40,000 through Drexel; he lost about $24,000; and he believes Drexel is legally liable for the loss. But, instead of seeking arbitration, he sued Drexel in federal district court. Drexel moved for a stay under the Federal Arbitration Act, 9 U.S.C. § 3. The district court denied the stay and Drexel appealed. Although not a "final" order, the denial of Drexel's request for a stay in Ingbar's damage action is properly appealable under 28 U.S.C. § 1292(a) (1). *See Warren Brothers Co. v. Cardi Corp.*, 471 F.2d 1304, 1306 (1st Cir. 1973); *Curran v. Merrill Lynch, Pierce, Fenner and Smith, Inc.*, 622 F.2d 216, 218 n.1 (6th Cir. 1980), *aff'd on other matters*, 456 U.S. 353, 102 S. Ct. 1825, 72 L. Ed. 2d 182, 50 U.S.L.W. 4457 (1982); 9 Moore's Federal Practice para. 110.20[4.–1] at 248 (2d ed. 1970). In considering this appeal, we understand the district court's order to comprise only claims under the Commodity Exchange Act, 7 U.S.C. §§ 1–24. So understood, we have examined the relevant statutes and regulations, and have concluded that the arbitration agreement is valid and that the stay should have issued. Accordingly, we reverse.

Section 3 of the Federal Arbitration Act, 9 U.S.C. § 3, requires a district court to "stay the trial of an action" if "the issue involved" is "referable to arbitration" under "an agreement in writing for such arbitration." Ingbar admits that there is an agreement in writing, signed before the dispute arose, for arbitration. He does not admit, however, that the agreement is *valid*. Indeed, he claims that either the Commodity Exchange Act, 7 U.S.C. §§ 1–24, or, alternatively, regulations of the CFTC, make the agreement in this case invalid and therefore unenforceable. We do not agree.

Ingbar's broadest claim is that the statute implicitly forbids all arbitration agreements, entered into before a dispute arises, between commodities brokers and their customers. This claim derives from the Supreme Court's decision in *Wilko v. Swan*, 346 U.S. 427, 98 L. Ed. 168, 74 S. Ct. 182 (1953), invalidating broker-customer agreements to arbitrate future controversies involving claims under the Securities Act of 1933, 15 U.S.C. § 77a *et seq.* The *Wilko* doctrine has been extended to claims under the Securities Exchange Act of 1934, 15 U.S.C. § 78a *et seq.*, *see, e.g.*, *Weissbuch v. Merrill Lynch, Pierce, Fenner and Smith, Inc.*, 558 F.2d 831 (7th Cir. 1977); *but cf. Scherk v. Alberto-Culver*, 417 U.S. 506, 41 L. Ed. 2d 270, 94 S. Ct. 2449 (1974), and, several years ago, by a federal district court in California, to claims involving the Commodity Exchange Act as well. *Milani v. Conticommodity Services, Inc.*, 462 F. Supp. 405 (N.D. Cal. 1976). *Cf. Bache Halsey Stuart, Inc. v. French*, 425 F. Supp. 1231, 1233–34 (D.D.C. 1977). *But see Romnes v. Bache & Co., Inc.*, 439 F. Supp. 833, 838 (W.D. Wis. 1977).

In our view, however, neither *Wilko* nor its progeny implies that the Commodity Exchange Act should now be read to forbid pre-dispute broker-customer arbitration agreements. For one thing, *Wilko* concerned the Securities Act of 1933, 15 U.S.C. § 77a *et seq.*, not the Commodity Exchange Act ("CEA"), 7 U.S.C. §§ 1–24. And, it turned on the language of specific provisions in the 1933 Act—one conferring on Securities Act plaintiffs "the right to select the judicial forum," 346 U.S. at 427, *see* 15 U.S.C. § 77v(a); the other making "void" any "condition, stipulation or provision binding any person acquiring any security to waive compliance with any provision" of the Act, 15 U.S.C. § 77n. The Court interpreted this language as showing a congressional intent to bar pre-dispute arbitration agreements. 346 U.S. at 435. The Securities Exchange Act contains at least a similar antiwaiver provision. *See* 15 U.S.C. § 78cc(a). No similar language, however, either as to the selection of forums or the waivability of statutory requirements, appears in the CEA. * * *

Moreover, the strict conditions imposed by the CFTC regulations assure that broker-customer arbitration agreements are entered into voluntarily and are fair. The regulations therefore meet the practical concerns as to relative bargaining power and broker overreaching that underlay the decision in *Wilko* (and, for that matter, *Milani*, which relied on *Wilko*). This much is clearly implicit in the two leading appellate decisions which applied the regulations "retroactively" to invalidate noncomplying broker-customer arbitration agreements. *See Curran v. Merrill Lynch, Pierce, Fenner and Smith, Inc., supra; Ames v. Merrill Lynch, Pierce, Fenner and Smith, Inc.*, 567 F.2d 1174 (2d Cir. 1977). * * *

Dr. Ingbar claims that the arbitration agreement was not "voluntary." *See* 17 C.F.R. §§ 180.3(a) and (b)(1) [renumbered hereinafter as 17 C.F.R. § 166.5 (a) and (b)]. Specifically, he claims it violates § 166.5(b)(1), which states that "signing the agreement must not be made a condition for the customer to utilize the services offered by the futures commission merchant" (*i.e.*, Drexel). Dr. Ingbar claims that Drexel's account executive told him he had to sign the contract (which, he says, he "understood" to mean the arbitration clause, as well as the account agreement), in order to open his account. The language, of course, in bold letters and signed by Dr. Ingbar, says the contrary. Dr. Ingbar says he did not read the language, or anything else in the contract. The district court held, however, that without evidence of fraud, Dr. Ingbar was barred by the terms of what he signed. *See McLaughlin v. Maduff & Son, Inc.*, Comm. Fut. L. Rep. (CCH) P 21,217 (C.D. Cal. 1981); *O'Neel v. National Ass'n of Securities Dealers, Inc.*, 667 F.2d 804 (9th Cir. 1982); *Pimpinello v. Swift & Co.*, 253 N.Y. 159, 170 N.E. 530 (1930) (New York law); *Abbasciano v. Home Lines Agency, Inc.*, 144 F. Supp. 235, 236 (D. Mass. 1956) (Massachusetts law). And, given Dr. Ingbar's education, the bold type, the language, the separate signature, and the circumstances under which he opened the account and signed the agreement (as revealed in the affidavits), the court found not even "the slightest evidence of fraud." We find no error in the district court's determination.

Finally, language in the district court's opinion suggests that it may have believed the arbitration agreement violated a condition laid down in CFTC rule 166.5. This section states that

> the customer must be advised in writing that he or she may seek reparations under section 14 of the Act by an election made within 45 days after the futures commission merchant [*i.e.* Drexel] . . . notifies the customer that arbitration will be demanded under the agreement. This notice must be given at the time when the futures commission merchant . . . notifies the customer of an intention to arbitrate.

Id. Although the arbitration clause at issue specifically mentions the right to seek reparations (and describes as well the 45-day election period), Drexel did not notify Ingbar in writing of his right to seek reparations "at the time when [it] . . . notifie[d him] of [its] intention to arbitrate." 17 C.F.R. § 166.5(b)(3).

Drexel argues that this condition is inapplicable because it (Drexel) has not "demanded" arbitration. Rather, it has simply notified Ingbar of its right to have suits settled through arbitration; it has moved for a stay of the court proceedings; and it has announced that it assumes Dr. Ingbar will demand arbitration in an effort to obtain what he believes Drexel owes him.

We need not pass on the merits of Drexel's contention, however, for, in any event, we do not believe that § 166.5(b)(3) invalidates the arbitration agreement before us. The obvious purpose of the (b)(3) "notice" requirement is to guarantee that a customer learns about his reparations right in time to invoke it. Given that Dr. Ingbar filed a law suit and made elaborate arguments based upon these regulations, he must have been aware of this right. Indeed, Ingbar does not say he was not aware of this right; he does not now seek, and never has sought, a reparations proceeding; he states in his brief that he did not ask the district court to deny arbitration for this reason; and, finally, he concedes that it would be "inappropriate" to seek affirmance of the district court decision on this ground. Even were the facts otherwise, it is doubtful that we would go beyond the remedy that the regulation would require to make a claimant whole—an extension of the 45-day time limit for electing reparation proceedings. *See Rothberg v. Loeb, Rhoades & Co.*, 445 F. Supp. 1336, 1339 (S.D.N.Y. 1978). There is no reason here, however, to impose even that remedy, let alone (for purposes of deterrence, enforcement, or the like) so serious a sanction as invalidation of the arbitration agreement.

For these reasons, the district court's decision is reversed. Its order denying the stay is vacated, and the case is remanded for proceedings consistent with this opinion.

Reversed and remanded.

NOTES

1. As noted in the Ingbar case, the Supreme Court had ruled in Wilko v. Swan, 346 U.S. 427 (1953) that pre-dispute clauses requiring mandatory arbitration of customer disputes with their broker-dealers were not permissible. The Supreme Court later abandoned that position. See, e.g., Shearson/American Express, Inc. v. McMahon, 482 U.S. 220 (1987). As a result, the only forum to resolve a dispute with a broker-dealer is the FINRA arbitration program.

Section 921 of the Dodd-Frank Act authorized the SEC to prohibit mandatory pre-dispute arbitration agreements between broker-dealers, investment advisers and their customers. Section 1028 of that legislation also directed the new Bureau of Consumer Financial Protection to prepare a report for Congress on the use of mandatory arbitration provisions and was authorized to prohibit such agreements. Those agencies had not adopted rules restricting such clauses as of the date of the publication of this casebook.

2. As noted in the Ingbar case, CFTC rules allow customers to opt out of otherwise binding pre-dispute arbitration agreements in favor of a reparation proceeding before the CFTC. Nevertheless, the signing of a pre-dispute arbitration agreement by a customer will have the effect of barring a private right of action in court. [17 C.F.R. § 166.5(c)(3)]. In addition, "eligible contract participants," *i.e.*, institutional investors, may be required by their broker to sign an agreement waiving the right to reparations, and that waiver will be upheld. [7 U.S.C. § 18(g)].

3. The CEA requires the NFA to "provide a fair, equitable, and expeditious procedure through arbitration or otherwise for the settlement of

customers' claims and grievances against any member or employee thereof. . . ." [7 U.S.C. § 21(b)(10)]. However, such procedures must be voluntary on the part of the customer.

4. Arbitration has many advantages, i.e., it is less expensive and usually results in a decision much more quickly than through the judicial process. Nevertheless, arbitration may result in an arbitrary decision and judicial review is extremely limited. As the Second Circuit has stated:

> A motion to vacate filed in a federal court is not an occasion for de novo review of an arbitral award. "It is well established that courts must grant an arbitration panel's decision great deference. A party petitioning a federal court to vacate an arbitral award bears the heavy burden of showing that the award falls within a very narrow set of circumstances delineated by statute and case law." The FAA [Federal Arbitration Act] sets forth certain grounds upon which a federal court may vacate an arbitral award, but "all of [these] involve corruption, fraud, or some other impropriety on the part of the arbitrators." Id.; see 9 U.S.C. § 10(a). * * *
>
> Our circuit has long held that "an arbitration award may be vacated if it exhibits 'a manifest disregard of the law.' " But we have also been quick to add that "manifest disregard of law" as applied to review of an arbitral award is a "severely limited" doctrine. Indeed, we have recently described it as "a doctrine of last resort—its use is limited only to those exceedingly rare instances where some egregious impropriety on the part of the arbitrators is apparent, but where none of the provisions of the FAA apply." Accordingly, we have said that the doctrine "gives extreme deference to arbitrators."
>
> An arbitral award may be vacated for manifest disregard of the law "only if 'a reviewing court . . . finds both that (1) the arbitrators knew of a governing legal principle yet refused to apply it or ignored it altogether, and (2) the law ignored by the arbitrators was well defined, explicit, and clearly applicable to the case.' " We have emphasized that an arbitral panel's refusal or neglect to apply a governing legal principle " 'clearly means more than error or misunderstanding with respect to the law.' " A federal court cannot vacate an arbitral award merely because it is convinced that the arbitration panel made the wrong call on the law. On the contrary, the award "should be enforced, despite a court's disagreement with it on the merits, if there is a barely colorable justification for the outcome reached.
>
> In sum, a court reviewing an arbitral award cannot presume that the arbitrator is capable of understanding and applying legal principles with the sophistication of a highly skilled attorney. Indeed, this is so far from being the case that an arbitrator "under the test of manifest disregard is ordinarily assumed to be a blank slate unless educated in the law by the parties." There is certainly

no requirement under the FAA that arbitrators be members of the bar and we have recognized "that arbitrators often are chosen for reasons other than their knowledge of applicable law." Further, "arbitrators are not required to provide an explanation for their decision." * * *

Our cases demonstrate that we have used the manifest disregard of law doctrine to vacate arbitral awards only in the most egregious instances of misapplication of legal principles.

Wallace v. Buttar, 378 F.3d 182, 189–190 (2d Cir. 2004).

6. PRIVATE RIGHTS OF ACTION

In 1946, a federal district court in Kardon v. National Gypsum Co., 69 F. Supp. 512 (E.D. Pa. 1946) held that there was an implied private right of action under the antifraud provisions of Section 10(b) of the Securities Exchange Act of 1934. [15 U.S.C. § 78j(b)]. That decision led to an explosion of private litigation charging violations of Section 10(b). As Justice Rehnquist remarked in reference to Rule 10b–5, " 'we deal with a judicial oak which has grown from little more than a legislative acorn.' " Morrison v. National Australian Bank Ltd., 561 U.S. 247, ___, 130 S.Ct. 2869, 2889 (2010) (cited in concurring opinion of Stevens and Ginsburg).

The Supreme Court also held in Merrill Lynch, Pierce, Fenner & Smith, Inc. v. Curran, 456 U. S. 353 (1982) that there was an implied private right of action under the CEA. The Curran decision raised concerns because the scope of the remedy was in no way limited or defined. There was, for example, no provision for any statute of limitations, and other limiting concepts, such as privity, were rejected by the Supreme Court in Curran. In response to those concerns, the CEA was amended in 1982 to provide a statutory provision for an express right of action.

This statute, Section 22 of the Commodity Exchange Act [7 U.S.C § 25], contains a two-year statute of limitations and places restrictions on the persons who can bring such an action. For example, only persons who at least indirectly dealt with a defendant can sue that defendant, i.e., persons only tangentially affected by CEA violations are not allowed to sue. Further, manipulation claims were limited to persons who actually engaged in futures trading and who were, therefore, directly affected by the manipulation. This means, for example, that consumers who paid an artificially high price for a commodity because of a manipulation have no right of recovery under the CEA unless they traded in the affected futures contracts.

DAMATO V. HERMANSON

153 F.3d 464 (7th Cir. 1998)

RIPPLE, CIRCUIT JUDGE.

The plaintiffs filed a complaint against several defendants alleging violations of various state and federal laws in connection with the plaintiffs' purchases of interests in a commodity pool operated by defendant Buff Hoffberg. This appeal involves only the district court's dismissal of Count VI of the plaintiffs' second amended complaint. In that count, the plaintiffs alleged that defendant First Commercial Financial Group, Inc. violated the Commodity Exchange Act ("CEA"), see 7 U.S.C. §§ 1–25, by aiding and abetting Hoffberg in his scheme to defraud the plaintiffs. For the reasons set forth in the following opinion, we affirm the judgment of the district court.

The plaintiffs in this case are a group of investors in the Echo One Trading Pool ("the Echo One pool"), a commodity pool operated by defendant Buff Hoffberg. The plaintiffs purchased limited partnership interests in the Echo One pool under the impression that Hoffberg would use their money to trade in the commodities markets. Hoffberg, however, operated the Echo One pool as a classic Ponzi scheme: He paid so-called "profits" to current investors with monies invested by new customers. Out of the $2.2 million invested in the Echo One pool, only $250,000 was lost due to trading in the commodities markets; the balance was either converted by Hoffberg for his own use or paid out to other investors as "profits."

In furtherance of his scheme, Hoffberg enlisted the services of defendant John Hermanson. Hermanson was the president of First Trading Group ("FTG"), a subsidiary of defendant First Commercial. FTG solicits and accepts orders for the purchase or sale of commodities for future delivery on behalf of First Commercial. In 1989, Hoffberg opened a trading account in the name of Echo Trading at First Commercial (through Hermanson and FTG). After Hoffberg opened the account, he made a loan to Hermanson from monies that the plaintiffs intended to be invested in Echo One. In return, Hermanson prepared a false confirmation statement to be sent to current and prospective investors which showed inflated balances in the Echo One pool. This confirmation statement was issued on First Commercial letterhead. These allegations concerning Hermanson's and First Commercial's roles in Hoffberg's scheme are at the heart of the issues raised in this appeal.

As we noted earlier, this appeal concerns only the plaintiffs' allegations that First Commercial violated the CEA by aiding and abetting Hoffberg in the operation of his fraudulent scheme. Specifically, in Count VI of their second amended complaint, the plaintiffs alleged that Hoffberg violated §§ 4b and 4o, 7 U.S.C. §§ 6b & 6o, of the CEA by fraudulently inducing the plaintiffs to purchase and retain their interests in the Echo One pool and further violated § 4o by failing to provide the plaintiffs with disclosure documents describing the Echo One pool investment. The plaintiffs alleged that First Commercial aided and abetted Hoffberg's fraudulent scheme by permitting him to operate the Echo One pool through his account with First Commercial despite the fact that Hoffberg was not properly registered with the CFTC. In addition, the plaintiffs alleged that First Commercial, through Hermanson, further aided and abetted Hoffberg by preparing false confirmation statements for the Echo One account thereby lulling the plaintiffs into retaining their investment in the Echo One pool. * * *

This case requires this court, for the first time, to interpret the extent to which § 22(a) of the CEA provides a private right of action against entities that aid and abet a violation of the CEA. In addressing this issue, we begin, of course, with the language of the statute. Section 22(a)(1) provides in pertinent part:

Private rights of action

(a) Actual damages; actionable transactions; exclusive remedy

(1) Any person (other than a contract market, clearing organization of a contract market, licensed board of trade, or registered futures association) who violates this chapter or who willfully aids, abets, counsels, induces, or procures the commission of a violation of this chapter shall be liable for actual damages resulting from one or more of the transactions referred to in subparagraphs (A) through (D) of this paragraph and caused by such violation to any other person—

(A) who received trading advice from such person for a fee;

(B) who made through such person any contract of sale of any commodity for future delivery (or option on such contract or any commodity); or who deposited with or paid to such person money, securities, or property (or incurred debt in lieu thereof) in connection with any order to make such contract;

(C) who purchased from or sold to such person or placed through such person an order for the purchase or sale of—

(i) an option subject to section 6c of this title (other than an option purchased or sold on a contract market or other board of trade);

(ii) a contract subject to section 23 of this title; or

(iii) an interest or participation in a commodity pool; or

(D) who purchased or sold a contract referred to in subparagraph (B) hereof if the violation constitutes a manipulation of the price of any such contract or the price of the commodity underlying such contract.

7 U.S.C. § 25(a)(1).

More precisely stated in terms of this statutory language, the issue in this case is straightforward: whether a plaintiff may bring a private cause of action under § 22(a)(1) of the CEA against persons who aid and abet a violation of the CEA, even if such aiders and abettors do not satisfy independently the requirements of subsections (A) through (D) of that statute.

Although this court has yet to address this issue, several distinct views on this issue have emerged in the decisions of the district courts and in the submission of the CFTC. We shall first summarize each of these views on the appropriate reading of the statute.

Several district courts have grappled with this question and concluded that a plaintiff may bring a private cause of action under § 22(a)(1) against persons who aid and abet a violation of the CEA only if those same persons participated in one of the transactions listed in subsections (A) through (D) of that statute. Those courts adopting this position have focused on the "such person" language in § 22(a)(1)(A)–(D). In their view, the "plain language" of § 22(a)(1) requires a plaintiff to demonstrate that a defendant is one of the "such persons" listed in subsections (A) through (D). *See In re Lake States Commodities, Inc.*, 936 F. Supp. 1461, 1467 (N.D. Ill. 1996); *Davis v. Coopers & Lybrand*, 787 F. Supp. 787, 794 (N.D. Ill. 1992). In addition, these courts have refused to imply a private right of action for aiding and abetting under § 13(a) of the CEA, which provides that "any person who commits, or who willfully aids, abets, counsels, commands, induces, or procures the commission of, a violation of the provisions of this chapter . . . may be held responsible for such violation as a principal." CEA § 13(a), 7 U.S.C. § 13c(a). Although these courts recognized that § 13(a) was amended in 1983 to remove the language that limited its applicability to administrative proceedings, they held that the alteration did not override the exclusivity proviso in § 22(a)(2). *See Lake States*, 936 F. Supp. at 1467–68; *Davis*, 787 F. Supp. at 795 n.15. Instead, they concluded that the amendment to § 13(a) "granted additional power to the CFTC [but not private litigants] to bring judicial, as well as administrative, proceedings against those who aid and abet violations" of the CEA. *Lake States*, 936 F. Supp. at 1467–68.

In this case, the district court applied this analysis and concluded that the plaintiffs could not bring a private cause of action against First Commercial because it had not sold interests in the commodity pool to the plaintiffs, see CEA § 22(a)(1)(C)(iii).

A contrary position was embraced by a district court in *In re ContiCommodity Services, Inc.*, 733 F. Supp. 1555 (N.D. Ill. 1990), *rev'd on other grounds*, 976 F.2d 1104 (7th Cir. 1992). In that case, the plaintiffs sought to bring a private cause of action against several defendants for aiding and abetting a violation of the CEA despite the fact that the defendants were not "such persons" within the meaning of § 22(a)(1)(A)–(D). In assessing whether § 22(a)(1) authorized such an action, the court stated that, looking solely to the plain language of § 22(a)(1), only defendants who qualify as "such persons" could be liable in a private cause of action. *See id.* at 1567. Nonetheless, the court reasoned that § 22(a)(1) should not be read in isolation but rather should be read in conjunction with § 13(a). Accordingly, the court held that § 13(a) "enables an injured party to bring a court suit against an aider, abetter, inducer, combiner, etc. who was not the 'such person' under § 22(a)(1)(A)–(D)." *Id.*

A third view is brought to us by the CFTC, the agency charged with the administration of the statute. The CFTC submits that § 22(a)(1) creates, without any dependence on § 13(a), a private right of action against a person who aids and abets a primary violator in undertaking one of the transactions listed in subsections (A) through (D) of that statute. In analyzing § 22(a)(1), the CFTC divides the statutes into two parts. The first part of § 22(a)(1) identifies the persons potentially liable of damages as "any person who" violates the CEA or "willfully aids, abets, counsels, induces, or procures the commission of a violation of this chapter." Then, the second part of that section limits the universe of plaintiffs who have standing to sue for damages and limits the damages recoverable under the private right of action to those resulting from certain specified transactions. See § 22(a)(1) (limiting damages recoverable under private right of action to "actual damages resulting from one or more of the transactions referred to in subparagraphs (A) through (D) of this paragraph and caused by such violation to any other person").

Accordingly, in the CFTC's view, the statutory language of § 22 supports the conclusion that an aider and abettor of the primary violator can be held liable in a private action for damages when the "violation" for which the suit is brought is both causally and transactionally connected to the actual damages suffered by the putative plaintiff. Consistent with this reading of the statute, the CFTC submits further that § 22 does not require that an aider and abettor sued under that section independently satisfy the requirements of subsections (A) through (D). Instead, the

CFTC asserts, an aider and abettor may be held liable under that section so long as the primary violator participates in one of the transactions listed in subsections (A) through (D). In reaching this conclusion, the CFTC stresses that § 22(a)(1) does not provide that the plaintiff's damages must be caused by the *person* charged under the statute, but only that they must be "caused by *such violation*" (emphasis added). Thus, if the primary violator's wrongdoing satisfies the requirements of subsections (A) through (D), then the plaintiff's damages are "caused by such violation," regardless of whether the aider and abettor independently would satisfy the requirements of those subsections.

Having set forth the various views on the appropriate interpretation of the statute, we now turn to our own analysis.

In our view, the language of § 22(a)(1) is ambiguous. On the one hand, § 22(a)(1) clearly creates a private right of action against "any person . . . who violates this chapter or who willfully aids, abets, counsels, induces, or procures the commission of a violation of this chapter." On the other hand, as the district courts in *Lake States* and *Davis* recognized, § 22(a)(1) can be read to require that the defendant qualify as one of the "such persons" listed in subsections (A) through (D).

It is our task to resolve this ambiguity. Having studied the approaches outlined in the preceding section, we believe that the CFTC's interpretation of § 22 is correct. It is the only approach that gives meaning to every word and every phrase of § 22. *See Walters v. Metropolitan Educ. Enters.*, 519 U.S. 202, 117 S. Ct. 660, 664, 136 L. Ed. 2d 644 (1997) (Statutes must be interpreted, if possible, to give each word some operative effect."). By contrast, the interpretation adopted by the courts in *Lake States* and *Davis* effectively reads out of the text Congress' specific reference to aiders and abettors in § 22. As we noted earlier, those courts interpreted § 22 as requiring plaintiffs to demonstrate that the aider and abettor is one of the "such persons" listed in subsections (A) through (D). Such an interpretation, however, does not comport with the traditional understanding of aiding and abetting liability. By definition, an aider and abettor knowingly contributes to the principal's violation, rather than committing an independent violation of its own. In light of this definition, to say that an aider and abettor can only be liable if it performs one of the actions listed in subsections (A) through (D) renders meaningless the words of the statute because the aider and abettor would then be a principal.

Accordingly, in order for the language of § 22 to make sense—and in order for our interpretation to recognize fully the intent of the Congress— "such person" in subsections (A) through (D) must refer to the principal and not the aider and abettor. Moreover, this reading of § 22(a)(1) is consistent with the text of the statute because, as the CFTC points out, that section does not require that the plaintiffs' damages be caused by the person charged under the statute, but instead requires only that the damages be "caused by such violation." We hold, therefore, that § 22(a)(1) does not require that an aider and abettor independently satisfy subsections (A) through (D), but rather creates, on its own, a private cause of action against an aider and abettor who aids and abets a principal in undertaking one of the specifically enumerated transactions in subsections (A) through (D). * * *

We emphasize that we do not hold, as the court did in *In re ContiCommodity Services, Inc.*, 733 F. Supp. 1555, 1567 (N.D. Ill. 1990), that § 13(a) creates, on its own, a private cause of action for aiding and abetting liability under the CEA. Instead, we simply view that section as supportive of our interpretation of the text of § 22. We also note that this case presents a statutory framework different from that encountered by the Supreme Court in *Central Bank of Denver v. First Interstate Bank of Denver*, 511 U.S. 164, 128 L. Ed. 2d 119, 114 S. Ct. 1439 (1994). In that case, the Supreme Court refused to imply a private cause of action for aiding and abetting violations of § 10(b) of the 1934 Securities Exchange Act ("the 1934 Act"). In reaching that holding, the Court ruled that the extent of private liability must be governed by the statutory text of § 10(b). *See id.* at 174–76; *see also Pinter v. Dahl*, 486 U.S. 622, 653, 100 L. Ed. 2d 658, 108 S. Ct. 2063 (1988) (stating that "the ascertainment of congressional intent with respect to the scope of liability created by a particular section of the Securities Act must rest primarily on the language of that section"). The Court stressed, however, that Congress had taken a statute-by-statute approach to civil aiding and abetting liability and that its holding in that case was based on the fact "that none of the express causes of action in the 1934 Act further imposes liability on one who aids and abets a violation." *Central Bank*, 511 U.S. at 179. By contrast, the statute at issue in this case—§ 22 of the Commodity Exchange Act—explicitly provides for a private civil action against "any person who" violates the CEA or "willfully aids, abets, counsels, induces, or procures the commission of a violation" of that Act. CEA § 22(a)(1), 7 U.S.C. § 25(a)(1). Indeed, in *Central Bank,* the Supreme Court explicitly pointed to that provision as an example of a statute in which Congress explicitly created a cause of action for aiding and abetting liability. *See* 511 U.S. at 179.

We also note that, in resolving this ambiguity, we have given due consideration to the views of the CFTC. Although the CFTC's interpretation of the statute is not binding on this court, the views of the agency charged with the administration of the statute carry considerable weight. *See Cvelbar v. CBI Ill. Inc.*, 106 F.3d 1368, 1376 (7th Cir.), *cert. denied*, 139 L. Ed. 2d 20, 118 S. Ct. 56 (1997); *Time Warner Cable v.*

Doyle, 66 F.3d 867, 876 (7th Cir. 1995), *cert. denied*, 516 U.S. 1141, 133 L. Ed. 2d 894, 116 S. Ct. 974 (1996).

Accordingly, we hold that the district court erroneously interpreted § 22 of the CEA as barring the plaintiffs from bringing a private cause of action against First Commercial because it did not independently satisfy the requirements of § 22(a)(1)(A)–(D). * * *

CHAPTER 11

MARKET TRANSFORMATION

. . .

1. ELECTRONIC TRADING PLATFORMS

Historically, all futures contracts were required to be traded via "open outcry," meaning that each order was transparent and made available to be filled by anyone on the floor of the exchange. [see, 17 C.F.R. § 1.38]. Before the advent of electronic trading, the trading floors of many designated contract markets (DCMs) were filled each day with hundreds of exchange members either trading for themselves (floor traders) or filling orders on behalf of customers (floor brokers). The movie "Trading Places" depicted this frenzied trading atmosphere near the end of the movie, and you may want to review it online.

Computers may have changed the ability to trade more frequently and more easily, but the rules have not changed. The requirement that each order be traded via open outcry still remains on the books. The difference now, however, is that everyone who wants to trade futures contracts, both in the U.S. and abroad, can do so right from their own computer. They do not need to be an exchange member; they only need to contract with an exchange member to provide them with the direct market access (DMA) needed to place orders electronically.

Electronic trading platforms have also changed who is responsible for the execution of exchange orders. In the past, when a broker took the order via phone from the customer, and then made an error in executing that order, the brokerage firm was liable for the error. The broker had to make the customer whole, meaning depositing sufficient funds in the customer's account to restore its balance as if the error never took place. With customers placing their own orders directly through the DMA process, they now assume the responsibility over their trade errors.

Each member firm, which gives access to a customer to place orders via its DMA, receives a signed License Agreement which, among other things, requires the end user, e.g., the customer, to indemnify the FCM for any and all orders placed via the electronic platform and does not hold the FCM liable in any way for any electronic transmission failure. (See, Appendix F to this Casebook).

Electronic trading has also increased trade liability from a risk perspective. In the past, when a customer was required to call in his order to his broker, the broker had prior knowledge of the customer's trading profile and financials and could thus restrict his trading to satisfy his risk profile. Today, as customers place their own orders via the computer, each FCM must establish trade and risk controls to attempt, to the fullest extent possible, to prevent any large trading losses from occurring.

These trade filters can include, among other things, (i) restricting new orders to be placed after a certain amount of trade losses have occurred in a given day or which exceed a certain margin level, (ii) placing limits on the number of shares or contracts that can be traded in a given day, or (iii) requiring each customer to confirm each trade order via a pop-up window before the order is actually placed. These filters, however, do slow down the trading speed of each order.

JERRY W. MARKHAM & DANIEL J. HARTY
FOR WHOM THE BELL TOLLS: THE DEMISE OF EXCHANGE TRADING FLOORS AND THE GROWTH OF ECNS
33 J. Corp. L. 865 (2008)[1]

The colorful "open outcry" trading in the "pits" of the Chicago futures exchanges and the bell-ringing opening of trading on the floor of the New York Stock Exchange (NYSE) has long dominated the public perception of how those markets operate. However, exchange trading floors are fast fading into history because the trading of stocks and derivative instruments are moving to electronic communications networks (ECNs) that simply match trades by computers through algorithms at incredibly high speeds and volumes. Competition from ECNs has already forced the NYSE and the Chicago futures and options exchanges to demutualize, consolidate, and reduce the role of their trading floors, while expanding their own electronic execution facilities. * * *

The ECNs have provided new trading opportunities for algorithmic traders, but their trading was soon causing regulatory concerns. High frequency electronic traders are now dominating market volume in both the securities and derivatives markets, raising concerns on how their trading is affecting long-term investors. Some electronic trading practices such as "naked access" and "quote stuffing" and trading in "dark pools" are also under regulatory scrutiny. High frequency electronic traders were suspected as contributors to the "flash crash" that resulted in a 1,000-point drop in the Dow Jones Industrial Average in just a few minutes on May 6, 2010.

The futures industry's approach to computerization has been schizophrenic. It early on embraced computers into its clearing and settlement processes, allowing it to match and clear all trades overnight.

---

[1] EDS. Note: This article was also reprinted in *Jeffrey Poitras*, ed., *Handbook of Research on Stock Market Globalization*, ch. 12 (2012).

In contrast, as described below, the securities markets were slow to adopt to computerization until a paperwork crisis in the 1960s caused the industry to embrace technology. The futures industry's pioneering efforts in automating clearing and settlement were not matched with equal zeal in automating trade executions. This was because it was obvious to the traders on the floors of the exchange that electronic executions posed a threat to their existence. Since the floor traders dominated the exchanges they were able to block any efforts to replace themselves with computers.

In fact, there was little or no thought given to computerizing the trading floors on futures exchanges until the creation of the CFTC by the Commodity Futures Trading Commission Act of 1974. That legislation required the CFTC to study how computers could aid trading in the industry. The CFTC held a conference on that topic in 1977. Papers presented at the conference were critical of the perceived inefficiencies of the open outcry trading system. The response by the industry to that conference was harsh. Leo Melamed, a senior official at the CME and a leading figure in the industry, published a detailed and passionate defense of open outcry trading in a widely read article published in the *Hofstra Law Review*. Melamed conceded that the open outcry trading system was not automated but argued that the exchanges were automating the order execution process outside the trading pits. However, pit executions still required the manual transmission of orders into often overcrowded trading pits by written orders or hand signals and then the orders were bid or offered to the pit orally. After execution, the orders were transmitted back out of the pit manually. Melamed argued that the psychology of the trading pit generated information for price efficiency and brought liquidity to the market from the trading by locals. This was the oft-cited defense of floor trading *i.e.*, the physiological lift from the noise and energy of the trading crowd that inspires traders to take risks.

The futures exchanges' defense of their trading floors came under increasing criticism as volume expanded. Pits trading popular products became overcrowded and execution times were delayed in high volume periods. Orders were often traded through in "fast market" conditions. The CME's computer system crashed during trading hours in 1984, causing much confusion, but capacity constraints were an even more pressing issue. John Conheeney, chairman of Merrill Lynch Futures, then noted that "[t]here isn't a person in the industry who wouldn't agree that the system is breaking down, but we don't see any concrete moves toward a solution, which is the most frightening aspect of the problem." Conheeney concluded that merely adding more space on the trading floors, as the exchanges were then planning, was not the solution, but he also asserted that "black box" computer trading "lacks the vital human element that makes a market work." He asserted that " 'pit psychology,' eye contact and the chemistry between traders, was often as important in determining prices as the market's technical factors and fundamentals of supply and demand." * * *

The futures exchanges continued their ostrich-like approach to automated executions, but demand was growing for extended trading hours. Trading floors were open only for a limited number of hours permitted by the stamina of the floor traders, but that left market participants stranded until the next trading day. Worldwide events with market effect often occurred after the close of trading, but traders were helpless until the opening of trading on the next day and, therefore, sought access to trade outside the regular trading hours. Futures exchanges and securities intermediaries sought to capture the additional revenues this interest represented by extending trading hours with three basic options: offering open outcry sessions at night, establishing exchanges in non-U.S. jurisdictions with local partners, and later developing electronic trading systems.

The demand for extended trading hours led to a linkage between the CME and the Singapore International Monetary Exchange (SIMEX) in 1984. That link allowed trades to be opened on the SIMEX in the evening and reciprocally closed on the CME on the next day or at some other time. The SIMEX link was a substitute for computerized executions, but it was limited in scope of the futures covered and still was tied to the floor trading operations of CME members.

The International Futures Exchange Ltd. (Intex) was created in 1984 by a former Merrill Lynch executive to operate as the first computerized commodity exchange. It was based in Bermuda in order to avoid the delay of seeking contract market status from the CFTC. Intex traded futures on gold and other commodities and cleared its trades through the London International Commodity Clearinghouse. Intex was not particularly successful, but it signaled the future.

The demand for after-hours trading continued to grow. In 1987, the CBOT began open outcry sessions at night, but those sessions were sparsely attended. The CME's response came in 1989 with its development of a computerized trading system called Globex (global exchange) with Reuters Holdings P.L.C. This system matched buy and sell orders on the basis of time and price after the trading pits closed. The CBOT responded to Globex with an announcement that it was developing its own computerized trading system, named Aurora, that would compete with Globex and pose no threat to floor traders during normal trading hours. Aurora never really got off the ground, and the CBOT joined Globex.

Globex's limitations caused it to struggle to obtain a profit, and the CBOT withdrew from the venture in 1994. In the meantime, the CBOT and CME's share of futures and options trading also continued to plummet, dropping from about 75% of all futures trading in 1987 to under 50% in 1992. In particular, competition from new exchanges abroad was fierce. One such upstart was the London International Financial Futures Exchange (LIFFE) that began trading in 1982. It initially modeled its trading operations after those in Chicago, utilizing open outcry pit trading for order executions, but later became an all-electronic exchange. More competition from Europe would follow. A 1992 New York Times article noted that "[t]he [American] exchanges have been losing ground to the approximately 50 exchanges outside the United States, about half of which have been founded since 1985. Off-exchange deals between banks and other institutional investors are also a rapidly growing part of the derivatives business."

The CBOT opened a new trading floor in 1997 that was supposed to employ the newest technology, but it remained devoted to open outcry trading in the pits. New innovations were added elsewhere in the industry. Floor brokers adopted "Electronic Clerk" and "Cubs" devices that allowed them to receive orders electronically in the pits, seeking to obviate the need for phone clerks and "runners" who had traditionally relayed customer orders into the pits either in writing or by "flashing" to the floor broker through hand signals. Those efforts did not succeed in meeting the competition from foreign exchanges that were becoming increasingly all electronic. The Deutsche Terminborse, now called Eurex, a joint venture of the Deutsche Borse and the Swiss Stock Exchange, opened as an all electronic exchange in 1989. It took Eurex just two years to eclipse the largest futures exchange in America, the CBOT, in trading volume. Eurex also later bought the International Securities Exchange, an electronic exchange that became the largest equity options market in the United States, taking market share from the open outcry equity options exchanges. Ironically, futures trading was not legalized in Germany until the 1980s when U.S. brokers successfully advocated a change in German law that had, theretofore, treated futures contracts as prohibited illegal gambling.

Eurex was also competing with LIFFE, which operated a large trading floor and was the largest futures exchange in Europe until Eurex arrived. LIFFE was forced to switch from open outcry trading to electronic trading in 2000. Similarity, Matif, the Paris based derivatives exchange, tried to offer both electronic and open-outcry trading in April 1998. A month later, most trading migrated to computers and the trading floor was shut down.

The Chicago exchanges only slowly awakened to this threat, but by the end of the last century, even Leo Melamed, the most ardent defender of open outcry trading, was in full retreat. He sounded the tocsin for this pull back in a May 1999 address at an industry conference in New York. Melamed faulted the regulatory structure for the erosion of U.S. market share in futures trading, but he also stated that "[i]f the futures exchanges fail to quickly embrace current technological and competitive demands, . . . then our exchanges may well be doomed."

The Chicago exchanges were still sluggish in their response to the electronic threat. They began a desperate effort to link with foreign electronic markets in order to cling to their remaining businesses. The CME announced a link with Matif in Paris, which was then combined with its SIMEX program. The CBOT initially linked with Eurex, but then abandoned that arrangement for an electronic platform operated by LIFFE, which was then a unit of the pan-European exchange Euronext, the subsequent merger partner of the NYSE. In response, Eurex announced that it was opening its own exchange in the United States to compete directly with the Chicago exchanges. The Chicago exchanges then sought unsuccessfully to block Eurex from being designated as a contract market by the CFTC, which happened in 2004, but Eurex was not successful in that effort to compete.

Domestic electronic futures exchanges were also appearing. FutureCom Ltd. submitted the first application to the CFTC to be designated as a contract market for Internet trading only. BrokerTec Futures Exchange, an electronic futures market, had tried to compete with the CBOT but failed in that effort. The New York Cotton Exchange merged with the Coffee, Sugar and Cocoa Exchange to become the Board of Trade of New York. It entered into a joint venture with Cantor Fitzgerald, a New York government securities trader, for the creation of an electronic futures exchange, the Cantor Financial Futures Exchange (CFFE), which would compete with the CBOT floor traders. The CBOT quickly announced that it was opening its own electronic market in those contracts. Neither electronic trading system did very well, but CFFE responded with a completely interactive electronic trading platform.

Several other electronic futures markets followed, including CBOE Futures Exchange, HedgeStreet, NQLX, OneChicago, and U.S. Futures Exchange. The Intercontinental Exchange (ICE), an electronic exchange based in Atlanta, Georgia, became a major global marketplace for trading futures and OTC energy derivative contracts. The Chicago exchanges were paralyzed by this competition and exchange politics became divided between those favoring electronic trading and those seeking to preserve open outcry trading. In a hotly contested election in 1998, one candidate was labeled by his opponent as the "President of the Flat Earth Society" for his defense of the pitch of trading desks on the floor, but the real criticism of his campaign was his desire to preserve pit trading and the value of exchange memberships that were then plunging in price. Opponents of electronic trading narrowly won that election, unseating the incumbent who was seeking to modernize the exchange with more electronic trading. Compromise followed in the form of side-by-side trading of contracts electronically and in the pits. However, that was only a compromise, not a winning strategy in the new world of all electronic trading.

More pressure for electronic trading arrived in 1989 after a massive FBI sting operation on the CME and CBOT exposed widespread fraud and questionable trading activities. Those practices were made possible by archaic trading practices on the floor that involved "dual" trading floor brokers and floor traders ("locals") and the lack of an adequate audit trail that shielded those activities. Former senator (and briefly vice presidential candidate) Thomas Eagleton made headlines by resigning from the CME board after charging that the exchange was driven with conflicts of interest. He recommended that the trading floor be replaced with an electronic trading system that would provide a better audit trail.

Competition appeared from another source in the form of the OTC market in derivatives that exploded in the last part of the twentieth century. The swap became a classic in finance within ten years of its introduction in 1981. A new phenomenon also appeared—the OTC derivative. Unfortunately, trading in over-the-counter foreign currency derivatives began with some boiler room operations fraudulently selling derivative products disguised in a manner to avoid CFTC regulation. The CFTC continued to wrestle with that problem, particularly in currency trading, for a number of years. Commercial firms were also exploring OTC derivatives during the CFTC's formative years. The CFTC resisted that effort and sought to regulate these then-designated "hybrid" instruments if their options or futures elements outweighed their securities elements. The CFTC was reluctant to create a commercial trader exception that would allow OTC derivatives to be traded by institutions or sophisticated traders, such as that employed by the SEC under the federal securities laws for "accredited investors." However, the swaps market expanded so quickly that Congress and the CFTC adopted such an exemption for swaps. An exemption was also granted for the Brent oil market that had been handicapped by a district court ruling that it was a futures exchange, a decision that would have required it to register as a contract market and destroy its viability in the United States. The OTC derivative market continued to expand even after a series of large losses by numerous institutions, including the destruction of the venerable Barings Bank by a rogue trader.

The open outcry trading systems on the futures exchanges' floors were clearly being overwhelmed as the new century began. Responding to those competitive threats, the CME and CBOT merged their clearing operations in 2003, and both the CME (in 2002) and the CBOT (in 2005) demutualized and became public companies. Still, the percentage of open outcry trades declined between 2000 and 2007 from 90% to 22%. Recognizing that the end was near, the CBOT and CME merged all of their operations in 2007. That merger was nearly spoiled by a competing bid from ICE for the CBOT in the amount of $11.9 billion, but in the end ICE lost out to the CME. After their merger, the CME and CBOT announced that they were consolidating their trading floors and would be shifting several contracts to their electronic trading platform (Globex), including agricultural products such as the once very popular frozen pork belly futures contract.

Resistance on the floor to electronic trading remained. That resistance was aided by no less a personage than former Federal Reserve Board Chairman Alan Greenspan. In March 2007, Greenspan asserted at a futures industry conference that the open outcry system of trading is still "the optimum model" because, while computers are useful, human beings always prefer personal interactions and that, therefore, open outcry markets will always be around. However, the growth of electronic trading is calling that claim into question in both the securities and commodity futures industries. * * *

Automation was seemingly more prevalent in the OTC [securities] market. Nasdaq was itself an electronic "quotation" system that was developed in the 1960s after a special study of the securities markets by the SEC staff suggested the desirability of such an automated system to replace the manual printing of quotes circulated to broker-dealers through the "Pink Sheets." Nasdaq employed competing market makers, rather than a specialist auction system. Nasdaq was broken down into tiers: the National Market System (NMS) for larger companies, a SmallCap Market for small and medium size companies, and a Bulletin Board for illiquid securities.

Nasdaq did not initially provide for the automated execution of orders. Rather, a broker observing a quote on a computer screen for a stock posted on Nasdaq would contact the posting broker and negotiate the trade. Nasdaq developed a Small Order Execution System (SOES) for the automatic execution of small customer orders, but large trades still were negotiated orally with the market makers. Another improvement was SelectNet, a screen-based trading system that allowed NASD members to enter and negotiate the terms of their trades utilizing that computer system. The Nasdaq market became successful. By 1992, Nasdaq volume was accounting for some 42% of total share volume on all U.S. markets. Nasdaq volume was sometimes in excess of 2.5 billion shares a day in 2000, which was sometimes a billion more shares than were traded on the NYSE. * * *

The ECNs arrived in force in the financial markets beginning in the early 1990s in the form of automated trading systems for institutional traders in the third market. In some ways they were actually a creation of the exchanges' efforts to automate. "Electronic trading" encompasses a wide range of systems that facilitate the entry and execution of orders electronically by algorithms. The exchanges had employed algorithms for their own trading activities, using different algorithms for different contracts, often based on a contract's liquidity. They include a first-in, first-out allocation system for trade matching, a pro-rata system, or a system that combines some elements of each of the above. Without the creation of trade-matching algorithms by exchanges, the development of electronic trading systems in the remainder of the financial services industry would have likely stalled. Some commentators view the development of trade-matching algorithms as the democratization of the financial markets. They suggest that the adoption of algorithms replaces the "privileged market access," conferred by open outcry trading and permits exchanges to differentiate between each order, let alone between members and non-members. The exchanges were initially unwilling to use algorithms to replace their trading floor functions. However, where established exchanges did not willingly venture, many "new kids on the block" began filling the void. Participants in these new ventures soon learned the benefits of electronic trading systems and order matching algorithms.

These benefits include the reduction in costs and trading errors, enhancement of operational efficiencies, and benefits associated with risk management. All of the major algorithms share some common characteristics. In particular, they provide for the anonymity of market users, something more difficult to disguise when traders stand face-to-face. Algorithms that survive the exchange development and consolidation phase will strike the right balance of fundamental qualities important to users: anonymity, speed, capacity, and stability. Like any software program, however, these algorithms require regular maintenance and a certain level of revision over time.

Non-exchange intermediaries, however, design their algorithms to manage risk and profit from market-making type functions in the exchanges' electronic environment. These algorithms are most profitable when they buy or sell an exchange's standardized product as quickly, efficiently, and anonymously as possible. Other algorithms developed by non-exchange intermediaries profit from long-term market movements, often requiring the intermediaries to hold large positions over long periods of time. Often, the non-exchange intermediaries experienced "excessive" costs when executing large orders. One reason intermediaries encouraged exchanges to adopt electronic trade-matching systems was to reduce these external costs through their ability to execute smaller sized orders and eliminate slippage and piggybacking.

In contrast, an exchange's trade-matching algorithm is limited to execution functions. The trade-matching system's purpose is to provide a central trading environment and predictable methodology for matching buyers and sellers. Critical attributes of these algorithms are their stability and predictability because the non-exchange intermediaries require reliable and consistent responses to their algorithms' buy and sell signals. Exchanges soon realized that they could tweak their algorithms to maximize profits by providing platforms that execute large sized orders or many orders. Unlike exchanges, intermediaries realize profits from the exchanges' trade-matching systems and their own order routing systems and trading strategy algorithms. Thus, while the exchanges developed electronic trade-matching systems, intermediaries developed or purchased order routing systems. These systems are either developed by intermediaries or third parties focused on supplying information technology services. In addition to these services, the third parties also introduced the patent process, and concomitant litigation, to the commodity futures industry.

The ECNs were screen-based and were initially regulated as broker-dealers in the securities industry. The SEC did not require them to register as a national securities exchange like the NYSE because they were not making a continuous market in securities. Registration as an exchange would have imposed self-regulatory and other requirements that those broker-dealers were unwilling to satisfy. By 1994, those proprietary systems were executing about 13% of Nasdaq volume but only about 1.4% of NYSE volume. Broker-dealers were also operating automated systems that matched customer orders internally, but NYSE Rule 390, until it was repealed, required orders for stocks subject to that rule to be executed on the NYSE. In preserving market share, the NYSE was also reporting record profits in 1993. However, the battle with the ECNs was already joined by Nasdaq where market share would be greatly eroded by their trading. Instinet was processing some 170 million shares a day at the end of the last century. It partnered with several online brokers that were permitting their customers to enter orders through the Internet. In August 1999, Instinet also joined with several large brokerage firms, including Merrill Lynch, Goldman Sachs, and Morgan Stanley, to form Primex Trading N.A., an electronic platform for institutional traders in NYSE stocks, a project Nasdaq also joined. Other ECNs included Wit Capital, OptiMark, Easdaq, POSIT, Tradepoint, the TONTO System, which became Archipelago, Bloomberg Tradebook, the Attain System, MarketXT, the BRUT System, GFINet System, Bridge Trader, the Strike System, and the Trading System.

Charles Schwab, Fidelity Investments, DLJdirect, and Spear, Leeds & Kellogg, a NYSE specialist firm, developed MarketXT, Inc. to trade the more active stocks on the NYSE and Nasdaq. Spear, Leeds & Kellogg also created the REDI System that matched mixed-lot orders. Bloomberg's TradeBook system traded Nasdaq stocks. The BRASS Utility System was an ECN that provided automatic execution, clearance and settlement of trades in Nasdaq National Market System and Small-Cap stocks. The BRUT System matched orders in Nasdaq National Market and Small-Cap securities on an anonymous basis. Some ECNs grew so big that they sought registration as an exchange in order to compete directly with the traditional markets through their electronic facilities. Archipelago Holdings LLC became a stock exchange through an arrangement with the Pacific Exchange. Island ECN was a leading ECN at one point. It applied to the SEC to become a stock exchange, and the CFTC approved the designation of Island Futures Exchange, LLP as a contract market in February of 2002. The National Stock Exchange, an electronic stock exchange that was trading Nasdaq stocks entered into a linkage agreement with Island ECN, the largest electronic communications network. Reuters PLC, the then owner of the Instinet Group, Inc., bought Island ECN. Those two firms accounted for about 22% of Nasdaq listed stocks.

More competition was added when the SEC allowed a London ECN to operate in the United States without requiring it to register as a national securities exchange under the Securities Exchange Act of 1934. This led the NYSE and Nasdaq to seek linkages to markets in London, Paris, Tokyo, Mexico, Sao Paulo, Amsterdam, and elsewhere. Globalization was ripe for exploitation by foreign ECNs because they had the ability to overcome the "home bias" that had caused American investors to favor domestic exchanges. This was because the ECNs were simply mathematical models that were pretty much unaffected by government intervention or uncertain rule interpretations. * * *

Some regional exchanges in the United States adopted electronic trading even before the ECN competitive threat arose. The transformation to electronic trading at the Cincinnati Stock Exchange began in 1976 and was led by Bernard Madoff, who was later sentenced to 150 years in prison for running a giant Ponzi scheme through his hedge funds. That exchange changed its name in 1995 to the National Stock Exchange, Inc. and moved to Chicago. The Midwest Stock Exchange began electronic trading in 1982. It changed its name to the Chicago Stock Exchange in 1993 and became an all-electronic exchange trading Nasdaq, NYSE, and AMEX stocks through the Internet. However, those efforts to compete with the larger market centers paled in relation to trading through ECNs.

The effects from electronic competition were more dramatic on the options exchanges. Initially, there was no competition in options trading on the stocks of the companies listed on those exchanges. The SEC ordered the exchanges to stop that practice and to permit multiple listings, but the option exchanges simply ignored that order until the Justice Department attacked that arrangement in 2000. The International Stock Exchange ("ISE"), a new all-electronic exchange was then able to compete head-to-head with the floor trading operations of the stock options exchanges. ISE soon became the world's largest equity options exchange, supplanting the CBOE in that role. The SEC found that this competition was beneficial, in addition to narrowing spreads, the expansion of multiple trading led to "market structure innovations that were designed to attract more order flow by enhancing the efficiency, transparency and liquidity of their markets." The Boston Options Exchange became all-electronic, and the AMEX began electronic trading in its options in 2004.The CBOE was forced to develop a new electronic exchange called "C2."

In 2000, SEC Chairman Arthur Levitt noted that ECNs "have provided investors with greater choices, and have driven execution costs down to a fraction of a penny. As a result, these networks presented serious competitive challenges to the established market centers." Nasdaq was reeling from ECN competition. In 2002, ECNs accounted for some 70% of Nasdaq volume. Nasdaq demutualized in order to gain access to a larger capital base. Nasdaq sold a portion of itself in private placements before registering for its initial public offering. Nasdaq began competing with the ECNs through its own SuperMontage electronic trading program developed over the objections of competitors and at a cost of over $100 million. Nasdaq subsequently went a step further and bought Instinet's ECN operations for about $1.9 billion in April 2005, after the NYSE announced its merger with another ECN, Archipelago Holdings Inc. Nasdaq also tried to stem its loss of market share by mergers, first with the AMEX in 1998. A merger with the Philadelphia Stock Exchange (PHLX), the nation's first stock exchange, initially fell through, but Nasdaq did later acquire it, as well as the Boston Stock Exchange.

More competition emerged from abroad. The London and Frankfurt stock exchanges merged, and they entered into a linkage with Nasdaq. The Canadian exchanges in Montreal, Vancouver, Toronto, and Alberta reorganized into a Pan-Canadian exchange. Nasdaq responded by acquiring control of OMX, a Nordic market operator, in a joint venture with Borse Dubai for almost $5 billion. However, Nasdaq failed in its efforts to gain control of the London Stock Exchange. Nasdaq sold its 28% ownership interest in that exchange to Dubai World, a sovereign investment fund in that country, as well as a 20% stake in Nasdaq itself.

The NYSE had successfully resisted competition from the ECNs until a scandal arose concerning the $187 million retirement package given to its CEO, Richard Grasso, in 2003. Under Grasso, NYSE volume had exploded, the exchange was still executing 85% of transactions in its listed stocks, the price of NYSE seats had doubled, and the exchange had total profits of over $2 billion between 1995 and 2000. Grasso kept the NYSE competitive by constantly updating its technology even as the specialists continued to enjoy their floor monopoly. The NYSE spent over

$2 billion during the 1990s on technology and was spending $350 million per year on technology as the new century began. However, Grasso was forced from office after the scandal involving his salary, and his successors gave up the franchise. Although the NYSE had resisted electronic trading competition for many years, it threw in the towel in 2005, merging with Archipelago Holdings, a Chicago based ECN that was then trading about 500 million shares a day, mostly in Nasdaq stocks. As a part of this merger, the NYSE gave up its not-for-profit status, demutualized, and became a public company, changing its name to NYSE Group, Inc.

In 2006, the NYSE merged with Euronext, an amalgamation of European exchanges that principally trade electronically. The NYSE agreed to give up American control of the merged entity, NYSE Euronext, sharing control of the board of the merged company with its European counterpart. Euronext was also given the right to withdraw from the combined operation in the event that the SEC tried to regulate its European operations. The NYSE continued its global expansion by entering into an alliance with three foreign exchanges, one of which was the Tokyo Stock Exchange.

NYSE market share plunged after these mergers. In September 2007, the NYSE "executed only 56.1 per cent of trades involving NYSE-listed stocks, down from 69.3 per cent a year earlier, and 78.6 per cent in September 2005." The NYSE-Euronext merger was followed by the dismantling of a considerable portion of the NYSE floor, and resulted in layoffs of hundreds of NYSE employees. The number of people employed by specialists on the NYSE floor was cut in half and the number of specialist firms was reduced to seven, down from 40 in the 1990s. The specialist lost its icon status. The NYSE made a name change for the specialists, calling them "liquidity providers" and allowing others to act as "supplemental liquidity providers." Those were all blows to the NYSE's historical role, but its merger program showed signs of success. The NYSE's own stock was up 355% as revenues and earnings soared in the first months after the merger.

The NYSE-Euronext merger also had some other wide-ranging effects. In 2007, NASD Regulation merged with the NYSE Regulation to become the Financial Industry Regulatory Authority, Inc. (FINRA), thereby creating a single self-regulator and eliminating much overlap and redundancy. The NYSE and NASD additionally merged their arbitration programs.

The growth of ECNs gave rise to the question of how they were to be regulated. If ECNs were viewed as securities exchanges, they would have to register with the SEC as a national securities exchange under the Securities Exchange Act of 1934. It would have been difficult for most

ECNs to operate as registered exchanges, which have self-regulatory responsibilities and, traditionally, no profit motive. Imposing such requirements would have nipped the growth of ECNs in the bud. Instead, the SEC chose to regulate most ECNs as broker-dealers under the Securities Exchange Act. Initially, the SEC staff applied this interpretation through the issuance of no-action letters. The SEC later adopted Rule 11Ac1–1 under the Securities Exchange Act to regulate ECNs that were matching customer orders with those of an exchange specialist or an over-the-counter market maker. This rule excluded from its reach ECNs that crossed multiple orders at a single price set by the ECN by an algorithm or any derivative pricing mechanism and did not allow orders to be crossed or executed against orders or participants outside of such terms.

In 1997, the SEC issued a massive "concept release" in which the agency announced that it was "reevaluating its approach to the regulation of exchanges and other markets in light of technological advances and the corresponding growth of alternative trading systems and cross-border trading opportunities." The SEC subsequently decided to throw a wider net over ECNs with Regulation ATS (the SEC liked the moniker Alternate Trading Systems (ATS), rather than ECNs) that allowed ECNs to choose to register as national securities exchanges or as broker-dealers. However, an ECN was required to register as an exchange when it exceeded certain volume levels. The SEC adopted Rule 11Ac1–1 under the Securities Exchange Act to define an ATS as any electronic system that widely disseminates to third parties orders entered by an exchange market maker or an over-the-counter market maker and permits such orders to be executed against each other in whole or in part. This rule excluded any system that crossed orders only at prices set by an algorithm or any derivative pricing mechanism.

Regulation ATS requires an ECN that has 20% or more of the average daily volume of a stock during four of the preceding six months to establish written standards for granting access to trading on its system and must not unreasonably limit access to its trading facilities. The SEC was concerned that the private nature of ECN trades provided institutional traders with an advantage, i.e., more favorable trading opportunities were often available to institutional traders through ECNs. The SEC, therefore, required market makers and specialists to make publicly available superior prices that it privately offered through ECNs. This rule required market makers and specialists who were using ECNs to change their quotes on public quotation systems to reflect orders placed in the ECNs or to be sure that any ECN to which they sent an order was itself able to reflect that order on the public quotation system. * * *

A new form of trader—index traders who passively trade an index of commodities—accompanied the runup in energy and other commodity prices. Those traders were taking long term positions in those indexes, raising fears that they were increasing prices. Traders using the Goldman Sachs Commodity Index (GSCI) and the Dow Jones-AIG Commodity Index (DJ-AIG) were estimated to have collectively held positions valued at $100 billion. The Deutsche Bank index held additional funds. As a class, the index traders' interest represents a significant minority in the markets in which they participate. Of particular interest is a comparison of the index traders' participation in wheat contracts offered by the Kansas City Board of Trade (KCBOT) and the CBOT. Comparing the index traders' activity in these two markets can lead to the conclusion that exchanges that promote their electronic trading system will attract more market users.

In particular, the index traders' participation in the KCBOT and CBOT's wheat contracts presaged other participants' preference in choosing a market. The trend in commercial traders' participation is quite clear in this respect. Commercial traders migrated to the CBOT's wheat contract in large numbers despite the fact that a competing exchange offers a more accurate hedging product. The migration suggests that hard red winter wheat commercial hedgers prefer to use a futures contract designed for another product type—the CBOT's wheat contract is designed for the soft red winter wheat—over the KCBOT's futures contract, a contract specifically designed for hard red winter wheat hedging. To create a mature, liquid market, exchanges must attract participants willing to trade volume. In an effort to allow retail customers trade so-called "managed futures funds" were created, which acted like a regular mutual fund except that they traded in commodities. Those funds tried to mimic the strategies that resulted in large profits when commodity prices were rising in 2008, but those markets were languishing in 2010 and the managed futures fund profits were unimpressive. Futures trading volumes soared as electronic trading increased and concern was raised that index traders were responsible for some of that growth and were placing pressures on prices. However, a CFTC investigation in 2008 could find no evidence that index traders were adversely affecting the market.

Intermediaries involved in electronic trading developed order routing and strategy algorithms that required information on a sub-second basis. This led to an ever-increasing demand for information from the ECNs' servers about the current market, and could be the cause of some interruptions in trading operations early in their development. To combat this unrelenting need for messages transmitted by market participants, exchange operated ECNs developed rules and policies to regulate the contact intermediaries may have with their servers. The ECNs limit the entities that may "write" to the servers and deliver messages to those who own trading rights, memberships, or satisfy their application program interface requirements. Exchange-operated ECNs then fine those permitted entities that send too many messages. Because the exchanges want to encourage trading, these fines are relatively light, do not appear on regulatory records, and have a high minimum threshold. Ultimately, intermediaries that are fined even a trivial amount will have violated the rule on a sustained and egregious level. There is also a national security element at play with the growth of ECNs.

A significant concern that has developed is the question of when an exchange may close its doors due to external factors. As a result of the tragic events on September 11, 2001, all exchanges and intermediaries store critical documents, systems, and procedures at a back-up location. In the event of a disaster, the back-up location shall become the fully functioning headquarters. The advent of electronic trading, however, brings new meaning to what is sufficient for an exchange to close. Before electronic trading became widespread, if members were unable to reach the exchange physically, the exchange staff and pit committee members would determine whether opening was unattainable. Now, with the majority of exchange trading happening through electronic matching systems, local failures will certainly not prevent a majority of participants from accessing the system. Absent a local failure in Chicago or New York, this will virtually guarantee that exchanges will remain open under most circumstances.* * * *

NOTES

1. The securities and derivatives markets continued to consolidate with the acquisition by IntercontinentalExchange (ICE) of the NYSE Euronext. That merger was approved by the Justice Department in November 2013.

2. The sample of an Electronic Licensing Agreement indicates that an FCM may require its customers to sign in order to allow the customer to place trades on the FCM's electronic trading platform. (Appendix F to this Casebook). Are there any duties you think should be included for the FCM to meet?

2. ELECTRONIC TRADING CONCERNS

JERRY W. MARKHAM
LAW ENFORCEMENT AND THE HISTORY OF FINANCIAL
MARKET MANIPULATION
320 (2014)[2]

Electronic trading also raised problems with market crashes. An algorithmic error on February 3, 2010, on NYMEX caused a sharp

---

[2]   Copyright M.E. Sharpe 2014.

increase in price and volume in crude oil futures contracts. Such minicrashes became common on electronic trading platforms. Embarrassingly, an initial public offering by BATS Global Markets Inc. had to be cancelled on March 23, 2012, as the result of a computer error that caused its share price to plunge from $16 per share to a few cents. The price of Apple shares also plunged briefly as a result of the error. BATS was one of the largest electronic securities markets and this failure in its computer raised further questions on the reliability of electronic trading. The initial public offering by Facebook in May 2012 was also marred by a computer glitch on NASDAQ, requiring the offering to be suspended for thirty minutes on the opening. Still another computer problem disrupted trading in the stock of the Kraft Foods Group Inc. on October 3, 2012, causing a phenomenal spread of $7 per share in bid and ask prices for a brief period.

SEC chair Mary Schapiro blamed a lack of uniformity in exchange rules for furthering problems with electronic trading and urged the exchanges to build a trading data center so that future events could be more easily tracked The SEC also proposed rules that would automatically stop trading through dynamically placed bands around stock prices. Such price limits were long used in the futures industry but drew criticism from the Chicago Mercantile Exchange (CME) when the SEC proposed them for stocks.

The SEC also proposed a rule in April 2010 that sought to track high-frequency traders by assigning them codes and requiring them to report their trading to the agency when requested. Not long afterward, high-frequency electronic traders were thought to have triggered a "flash crash" on May 6, 2010, that caused a 1,000-point drop in the Dow Jones Industrial Average in the course of a few minutes. The SEC mounted an intensive investigation of the flash crash and issued a report in September 2010, which found that it was triggered by a large mutual fund complex that entered an automated algorithmic order to sell 75,000 E-Mini futures contracts valued at over $4 billion in order to hedge an existing position. The algorithm dictated an execution rate of 9 percent of trading volume without regard to time or price. High-frequency traders responded and drove prices down in the E-Mini futures contract, touching off a stock-market-wide downturn.

In the wake of the flash crash and at the request of the SEC, the exchanges agreed to adopt circuit breakers to interrupt trading when such a sharp downturn begins. Trading was halted on exchanges in various products 265 times during a one-year period after such restrictions were imposed. The trading restrictions adopted in June 2012 required "limit-up" and "limit-down" trading halts for individual stocks like those used in the commodity futures markets. Market-wide circuit breakers were also broadened.

Another computer glitch disrupted U.S. stock markets on August 1, 2012. The problem was caused by computer problems at a brokerage firm, Knight Capital Group Inc., a high-frequency trader. That firm lost some $440 million as a result of that breakdown. A flash crash occurred in crude oil futures trading on September 17, 2012, with crude oil prices dropping by $3 per barrel in less than a minute near the close of trading. The CFTC began an investigation to determine whether high-frequency traders had caused that price break. That was not the first such problem on NYMEX. An algorithmic error occurred on February 3, 2010, at NYMEX, causing a sharp increase in price and volume on the close of the sweet crude futures contract. The NYSE experienced a trading glitch on November 12, 2012 that affected trading in some 200 stocks during the day and required the exchange to set the closing prices for those stocks. The number of computing problems on electronic trading platforms continued to increase, raising further concerns.

The SEC subsequently began an examination of "kill switches"—that is, algorithms used by broker-dealers engaged in high-frequency trading to cancel orders that unexpectedly run amok. The SEC also turned to Section 13(h) of the 34 Act after the flash crash to adopt a large trader reporting system like the one used by the CFTC. Large traders under the new SEC rule 13h–1 will be given identifier numbers that will require their trades to be reported to the SEC by their broker-dealers. A large trader was defined as a person whose transactions in National Market System securities equal or exceed 2 million shares or $20 million during any calendar day, or 20 million shares or $200 million during any calendar month.

The Dodd-Frank Act required the SEC to hire an independent consultant to report on the effect of high-frequency trading and other technological advances on the market. Dodd-Frank also required the SEC and the CFTC to conduct a joint study on the feasibility of requiring the derivatives industry to adopt computer-readable algorithmic descriptions for complex and standardized financial derivatives in order to better calculate net exposures to such instruments and to define regulated contracts. The Financial Industry Regulatory Authority (FINRA), the securities industry self-regulatory body, was requiring high-frequency traders to disclose their proprietary algorithms as a part of an investigation into improper trading activities.

This was an indication of the course that future regulation was likely to take: computer vs. computer. The Dodd-Frank Act further opened that door with a provision requiring the SEC and CFTC to conduct a study on the feasibility of requiring the derivatives industry to have standardized computer-readable algorithmic descriptions of derivative products. A CFTC commissioner also sought a budget shift from more staff to technology that would allow more effective surveillance and regulation.

Other electronic trading activities such as "stub quotes" and "naked access" also came under regulatory scrutiny. Stub quotes were price quotations by market makers well away from current market prices. These off-market quotes were used to fulfill exchange market maker obligations. The NYSE and NASDAQ curbed stub quotes by requiring quotes to be within current market ranges. Naked access (sometimes referred to as "sponsored access") involved a practice by some broker-dealers that allowed high-frequency traders to access an exchange's trading facilities without broker-dealer intermediation or supervision. The SEC adopted a rule in 2010 that restricted direct access arrangements. The rule prohibits broker-dealers from providing customers with "unfiltered" or "naked" access to an exchange or ATS. It also requires brokers-dealers to adopt risk management and supervisory controls to prevent order errors and assure compliance with credit restrictions and exposure to customer defaults.

"Flash trades" were another high-frequency trading concern. These are orders that are canceled immediately upon communication or withdrawn if not executed immediately after communication. Such flash orders, sometimes referred to as "quote stuffing," were specifically authorized by the SEC in Rule 602 of its Regulation NMS. SEC Rule 602 thus allowed exchanges to exclude such orders from consolidated quotation data because of their ephemeral nature. However, electronic traders began using flash orders for a variety of purposes and in large amounts. Among other things, the SEC noted that "[f]or those seeking liquidity, the flash mechanism may attract additional liquidity from market participants who are not willing to display their trading interest publicly."

The SEC also noted that some large institutional traders were reluctant to display their own quotations publicly because they do not want to disclose their trading plans to other market participants, but are willing to respond to flash orders on an order-by-order basis. Flash orders also helped reduce the transaction costs of those institutional investors.

The SEC sought public comment in September 2009 on whether its exception from quotation reports should be continued for flash orders. Among other things, the SEC was concerned with the fact that flash orders provided professional short-term traders an advantage over long-term investors. The SEC also discovered that some firms were entering ninety orders for every one executed. The SEC, however, deferred a decision on that issue. Instead, the agency issued a concept release in January 2010 that launched a broad-based review of the current equity market structure to determine whether the agency's rules had kept pace with the growth of electronic trading, including the role of flash orders and "pinging" orders that seek to flush out other traders.

Another concern was "dark pools," which are anonymous trading platforms for stock listed on public markets. Orders placed through an exchange are visible to the public and all other market participants, but an order or an indication of interest entered on a dark pool is revealed only to other dark pool participants. This gives dark pool participants access to information unavailable to the public. "As a result, dark pool participants are able to have their orders filled, while those on publicly displayed markets go unfilled, even though dark pools use the information from publicly displayed markets to price the dark pool transactions. When dark pools share information about their trading interest with other dark pools, they can function like private networks that exclude the public investor."

The SEC proposed rules to limit such exclusions by dark pools. The agency also accused an electronic dark pool operator of improperly sharing trading information with a high-frequency trading affiliate. Another SEC case, which was settled, involved claims that an electronic trading platform had misrepresented the manner in which it filled customer orders. In still another dark pool case in October 2012, the SEC accused a pool of using an affiliate to trade ahead of customer orders. The dark pool paid $1.2 million to settle those charges. The dark pools were, in any event, pulling trading volume away from the New York Stock Exchange (NYSE) as high-frequency traders sought to avoid regulatory scrutiny.

NOTE

An order entry error in stock options by Goldman Sachs on August 20, 2013, caused a sharp drop in the price of several stocks. That mishap was followed by a Nasdaq computer glitch that halted trading for three hours on August 22, 2013. The Nasdaq "flash freeze" was attributed to software problems. A similar shutdown, but lasting for only one hour, occurred on Eurex on August 26, 2013. Earlier, in 2012, the Chicago Mercantile Exchange experienced a computer crash in its electronic oil trading platform.

3. SEC MARKET CONCEPT RELEASE

SECURITIES AND EXCHANGE COMMISSION
CONCEPT RELEASE ON EQUITY MARKET STRUCTURE
75 Fed. Reg. 3594 (Jan. 21, 2010)

The secondary market for U.S.-listed equities has changed dramatically in recent years. In large part, the change reflects the culmination of a decades-long trend from a market structure with primarily manual trading to a market structure with primarily automated trading. When Congress mandated the establishment of a national market system for securities in 1975, trading in U.S.-listed equities was dominated by exchanges with manual trading floors. Trading equities today is no longer as straightforward as sending an order to the floor of a single exchange on which a stock is listed. [T]he current market structure can be described as dispersed and complex: (1) Trading volume is dispersed among many highly automated trading centers that compete for order flow in the same stocks; and (2) trading centers offer a wide range of services that are designed to attract different types of market participants with varying trading needs. A primary driver and enabler of this transformation of equity trading has been the continual evolution of technologies for generating, routing, and executing orders. These technologies have dramatically improved the speed, capacity, and sophistication of the trading functions that are available to market participants. Changes in market structure also reflect the markets' response to regulatory actions such as Regulation NMS, adopted in 2005, the Order Handling Rules, adopted in 1996, as well as enforcement actions, such as those addressing anti-competitive behavior by market makers in NASDAQ stocks. * * * *See, e.g.,* In the Matter of National Association of Securities Dealers, Inc., Administrative Proceeding File No. 3–9056, Securities Exchange Act Release No. 37538 (August 8, 1996). The transformation of equity trading has encompassed all types of U.S.-listed stocks. In recent years, however, it is perhaps most apparent in stocks listed on the New York Stock Exchange ("NYSE"), which constitute nearly 80% of the capitalization of the U.S. equity markets. In contrast to stocks listed on the NASDAQ Stock Market LLC ("NASDAQ"), which for more than a decade have been traded in a highly automated fashion at many different trading centers, NYSE-listed stocks were traded primarily on the floor of the NYSE in a manual fashion until October 2006. At that time, NYSE began to offer fully automated access to its displayed quotations. An important impetus for this change was the Commission's adoption of Regulation NMS in 2005, which eliminated the trade-through protection for manual quotations that nearly all commenters believed was seriously outdated. In November 2009, for example, NYSE-listed stocks represented approximately 78% of the market capitalization of the Wilshire 5000 Total Market Index.

NASDAQ itself offered limited automated execution functionality until the introduction of SuperMontage in 2002. Prior to 2002, however, many electronic communication networks ("ECNs") and market makers trading NASDAQ stocks provided predominantly automated executions. *See* Pierre Paulden, *Keep the Change,* Institutional Investor (December 19, 2006) ("Friday, October 6, was a momentous day for the New York Stock Exchange. That morning the Big Board broke with 214 years of tradition when it began phasing in a new hybrid market structure that can execute trades electronically, bypassing face-to-face auctions on its famed floor."). Prior to the Hybrid Market, NYSE offered limited automated executions. The changes in the nature of trading for NYSE-listed stocks have been extraordinary—NYSE executed approximately 79.1% of the consolidated share volume in its listed stocks in January 2005, compared to 25.1% in October 2009. NYSE's average speed of execution for small, immediately executable (marketable) orders was 10.1 seconds in January 2005, compared to 0.7 seconds in October 2009. Consolidated average daily share volume in NYSE-listed stocks was 2.1 billion shares in 2005, compared to 5.9 billion shares (an increase of 181%) in January through October 2009. Consolidated average daily trades in NYSE-listed stocks was 2.9 million trades in 2005, compared to 22.1 million trades (an increase of 662%) in January through October 2009. Consolidated average trade size in NYSE-listed stocks was 724 shares in 2005, compared to 268 shares in January through October 2009.

The foregoing statistics for NYSE-listed stocks are intended solely to illustrate the sweeping changes that are characteristic of trading in all U.S.-listed equities, including NASDAQ-listed stocks and other equities such as exchange-traded funds ("ETFs"). They are *not* intended to indicate whether these changes have led to a market structure that is better or worse for long-term investors. Rather, the statistics for NYSE-listed stocks provide a useful illustration simply because the changes occurred both more rapidly and more recently for NYSE-listed stocks than other types of U.S.-listed equities. To more fully understand the effects of these and other changes in equity trading, the Commission is conducting a comprehensive review of equity market structure. It is assessing whether market structure rules have kept pace with, among other things, changes in trading technology and practices.

The review already has led to several rulemaking proposals that address particular issues and that are intended primarily to preserve the integrity of longstanding market structure principles. One proposal would eliminate the exception for flash orders from the Securities Exchange Act of 1934 ("Exchange Act") quoting requirements. Another would address certain practices associated with non-public trading interest, including dark pools of liquidity. In addition, the Commission today is proposing for public comment an additional market structure initiative to address the risk management controls of broker-dealers with market access.

The Commission is continuing its review. It recognizes that market structure issues are complex and require a broad understanding of statutory requirements, economic principles, and practical trading considerations.

In Section 11A of the Exchange Act, Congress directed the Commission to facilitate the establishment of a national market system in accordance with specified findings and objectives. The initial Congressional findings were that the securities markets are an important national asset that must be preserved and strengthened, and that new data processing and communications techniques create the opportunity for more efficient and effective market operations. Congress then proceeded to mandate a national market system composed of multiple competing markets that are linked through technology. In particular, Congress found that it is in the public interest and appropriate for the protection of investors and the maintenance of fair and orderly markets to assure five objectives:15 U.S.C. 78k–1.

(1) Economically efficient execution of securities transactions;

(2) Fair competition among brokers and dealers, among exchange markets, and between exchange markets and markets other than exchange markets;

(3) The availability to brokers, dealers, and investors of information with respect to quotations and transactions in securities;

(4) The practicability of brokers executing investors' orders in the best market; and

(5) An opportunity, consistent with efficiency and best execution, for investors' orders to be executed without the participation of a dealer.

The final Congressional finding was that these five objectives would be fostered by the linking of all markets for qualified securities through communication and data processing facilities. Specifically, Congress found that such linkages would foster efficiency; enhance competition; increase the information available to brokers, dealers, and investors; facilitate the offsetting (matching) of investors' orders; and contribute to the best execution of investors' orders. Over the years, these findings and objectives have guided the Commission as it has sought to keep market structure rules up-to-date with continually changing economic conditions and technology advances. This task has presented certain challenges because, as noted previously by the Commission, the five objectives set forth in Section 11A can, at times, be difficult to reconcile. In particular, the objective of matching investor orders, or "order interaction," can be difficult to reconcile with the objective of promoting competition among markets. Order interaction promotes a system that "maximizes the opportunities for the most willing seller to meet the most willing buyer." When many trading centers compete for order flow in the same stock, however, such competition can lead to the fragmentation of order flow in that stock. Fragmentation can inhibit the interaction of investor orders and thereby impair certain efficiencies and the best execution of investors' orders. Competition among trading centers to provide specialized services for investors also can lead to practices that may detract from public price transparency. On the other hand, mandating the consolidation of order flow in a single venue would create a monopoly and thereby lose the important benefits of competition among markets. The benefits of such competition include incentives for trading centers to create new products, provide high quality trading services that meet the needs of investors, and keep trading fees low. *See, e.g.,* Securities Exchange Act Release No. 42450 (February 3, 2000), 65 FR 10577, 10580 (February 28, 2000) ("Fragmentation Concept Release") ("[A]lthough the objectives of vigorous competition on price and fair market center competition may not always be entirely congruous, they both serve to further the interests of investors and therefore must be reconciled in the structure of the national market system."). H.R. Rep. 94–123, 94th Cong., 1st Sess. 50 (1975). The Commission's task has been to facilitate an appropriately balanced market structure that promotes competition among markets, while minimizing the potentially adverse effects of fragmentation on efficiency, price transparency, best execution of investor orders, and order interaction. An appropriately balanced market structure also must provide for strong investor protection and enable businesses to raise the capital they need to grow and to benefit the overall economy. Given the complexity of this task, there clearly is room for reasonable disagreement as to whether the market structure at any particular time is, in fact, achieving an appropriate balance of these multiple objectives. Accordingly, the Commission believes it is important to monitor these issues and, periodically, give the public, including the full range of investors and other market participants, an opportunity to submit their views on the matter. This concept release is intended to provide such an opportunity. *See* S. Rep. 94–75, 94th Cong., 1st Sess. 2 (1975) ("S. 249 would lay the foundation for a new and more competitive market system, vesting in the SEC power to eliminate all unnecessary or inappropriate burdens on competition while at the same time granting to that agency complete and effective powers to pursue the goal of centralized trading of securities in the interest of both efficiency and investor protection."); Regulation NMS Release, 70 FR at 37499 ("Since Congress mandated the establishment of an NMS in 1975, the Commission frequently has resisted suggestions that it adopt an approach focusing on a single form of competition that, while perhaps easier to administer, would forfeit the distinct, but equally vital, benefits associated with both competition among markets and competition among orders.").

This section provides a brief overview of the current equity market structure. It first describes the various types of trading centers that compete for order flow in NMS stocks and among which liquidity is dispersed. It then describes the primary types of linkages between or involving these trading centers that are designed to enable market participants to trade effectively. This section attempts to highlight the features of the current equity market structure that may be most salient in presenting issues for public comment and is not intended to serve as a full description of the U.S. equity markets. Rule 600(b)(47) of Regulation NMS defines "NMS stock" to mean any NMS security other than an option. Rule 600(b)(46) defines "NMS security" to mean any security for which trade reports are made available pursuant to an effective transaction reporting plan. In general, NMS stocks are those that are listed on a national securities exchange. * * *

Registered exchanges collectively execute approximately 63.8% of share volume in NMS stocks, with no single exchange executing more than 19.4%. Registered exchanges must undertake self-regulatory responsibility for their members and file their proposed rule changes for approval with the Commission. These proposed rule changes publicly disclose, among other things, the trading services and fees of Exchanges.

The registered exchanges all have adopted highly automated trading systems that can offer extremely high-speed, or "low-latency," order responses and executions. Published average response times at some exchanges, for example, have been reduced to less than 1 millisecond. Many exchanges offer individual data feeds that deliver information concerning their orders and trades directly to customers. To further reduce latency in transmitting market data and order messages, many exchanges also offer co-location services that enable exchange customers to place their servers in close proximity to the exchange's matching engine.

Registered exchanges typically offer a wide range of order types for trading on their automated systems. Some of their order types are displayable in full if they are not executed immediately. Others are undisplayed, in full or in part. For example, a reserve order type will display part of the size of an order at a particular price, while holding the balance of the order in reserve and refreshing the displayed size as needed. In general, displayed orders are given execution priority at any given price over fully undisplayed orders and the undisplayed size of reserve orders.

In addition, many exchanges have adopted a "maker-taker" pricing model in an effort to attract liquidity providers. Under this model, non-marketable, resting orders that offer (make) liquidity at a particular price receive a liquidity rebate if they are executed, while incoming orders that execute against (take) the liquidity of resting orders are charged an access fee. Rule 610(c) of Regulation NMS caps the amount of the access fee for executions against the best displayed prices of an exchange at 0.3 cents per share. Exchanges typically charge a somewhat higher access fee than the amount of their liquidity rebates, and retain the difference as compensation. Sometimes, however, exchanges have offered "inverted" pricing and pay a liquidity rebate that exceeds the access fee. Highly automated exchange systems and liquidity rebates have helped establish a business model for a new type of professional liquidity provider that is distinct from the more traditional exchange specialist and over-the-counter ("OTC") market maker. In particular, proprietary trading firms and the proprietary trading desks of multi-service broker-dealers now take advantage of low-latency systems and liquidity rebates by submitting large numbers of non-marketable orders (often cancelling a very high percentage of them), which provide liquidity to the market electronically. [T]hese proprietary traders often are labeled high-frequency traders, though the term does not have a settled definition and may encompass a variety of strategies in addition to passive market making

The five ECNs that actively trade NMS stocks collectively execute approximately 10.8% of share volume. Almost all ECN volume is executed by two ECNs operated by Direct Edge, which has submitted applications for registration of its two trading platforms as exchanges.

ECNs are regulated as alternative trading systems ("ATSs"). Regulation of ATSs is discussed in the next section below in connection with dark pools, which also are ATSs. The key characteristic of an ECN is that it provides its best-priced orders for inclusion in the consolidated quotation data, whether voluntarily or as required by Rule 301(b)(3) of Regulation ATS. In general, ECNs offer trading services (such as displayed and undisplayed order types, maker-taker pricing, and data feeds) that are analogous to those of registered exchanges.

Dark pools are ATSs that, in contrast to ECNs, do not provide their best-priced orders for inclusion in the consolidated quotation data. In general, dark pools offer trading services to institutional investors and others that seek to execute large trading interest in a manner that will minimize the movement of prices against the trading interest and thereby reduce trading costs. There are approximately 32 dark pools that actively trade NMS stocks, and they executed approximately 7.9% of share volume in NMS stocks in the third quarter of 2009. ATSs, both dark pools and ECNs, fall within the statutory definition of an exchange, but are exempted if they comply with Regulation ATS. Regulation ATS requires ATSs to be registered as broker-dealers with the Commission, which entails becoming a member of the Financial Industry Regulatory Authority ("FINRA") and fully complying with the broker-dealer regulatory regime. Unlike a registered exchange, an ATS is not required to file proposed rule changes with the Commission or otherwise publicly disclose its trading services and fees. ATSs also do not have any self-regulatory responsibilities, such as market surveillance.

Some OTC market makers offer dark liquidity primarily in a principal capacity and do not operate as ATSs. For purposes of this release, these trading centers are not defined as dark pools because they are not ATSs. These trading centers may, however, offer electronic dark liquidity services that are analogous to those offered by dark pools. Dark pools can vary quite widely in the services they offer their customers. For example, some dark pools, such as block crossing networks, offer specialized size discovery mechanisms that attempt to bring large buyers and sellers in the same NMS stock together anonymously and to facilitate a trade between them. The average trade size of these block crossing networks can be as high as 50,000 shares. Most dark pools, though they may handle large orders, primarily execute trades with small sizes that are more comparable to the average size of trades in the public markets, which was less than 300 shares in July 2009. These dark pools that primarily match smaller orders (though the matched orders may be "child" orders of much larger "parent" orders) execute more than 90% of dark pool trading volume. The majority of this volume is executed by dark pools that are sponsored by multi-service broker-dealers. These broker-dealers also offer order routing services, trade as principal in the sponsored ATS, or both.

Broker-Dealer Internalization: The other type of undisplayed trading center is a non-ATS broker-dealer that internally executes trades, whether as agent or principal. Notably, many broker-dealers may submit orders to exchanges or ECNs, which then are included in the consolidated quotation data. The internalized executions of broker-dealers, however, primarily reflect liquidity that is not included in the consolidated quotation data. Broker-dealer internalization accordingly should be classified as undisplayed liquidity. There are a large number of broker-dealers that execute trades internally in NMS stocks—more than 200 publish execution quality statistics under Rule 605 of Regulation NMS. Broker-dealer internalization accounts for approximately 17.5% of share volume in NMS stocks.

Broker-dealers that internalize executions generally fall into two categories—OTC market makers and block positioners. An OTC market maker is defined in Rule 600(b)(52) of Regulation NMS as "any dealer that holds itself out as being willing to buy and sell to its customers, or others, in the United States, an NMS stock for its own account on a regular or continuous basis otherwise than on a national securities exchange in amounts of less than block size." "Block size" is defined in Rule 600(b)(9) as an order of at least 10,000 shares or for a quantity of stock having a market value of at least $200,000. A block positioner generally means any broker-dealer in the business of executing, as principal or agent, block size trades for its customers. To facilitate trades, block positioners often commit their own capital to trade as principal with at least some part of the customer's block order. Broker-dealers that act as OTC market makers and block positioners conduct their business primarily by directly negotiating with customers or with other broker-dealers representing customer orders. OTC market makers, for example, appear to handle a very large percentage of marketable (immediately executable) order flow of individual investors that is routed by retail brokerage firms. A review of the order routing disclosures required by Rule 606 of Regulation NMS of eight broker-dealers with significant retail customer accounts reveals that nearly 100% of their customer market orders are routed to OTC market makers. The review also indicates that most of these retail brokers either receive payment for order flow in connection with the routing of orders or are affiliated with an OTC market maker that executes the orders. The Rule 606 Reports disclose that the amount of payment for order flow generally is 0.1 cent per share or less. * * *

Given the dispersal of liquidity across a large number of trading centers of different types, an important question is whether trading centers are sufficiently linked together in a unified national market system. Thus far in this release, the term "dispersed" has been used to describe the current market structure rather than "fragmented." The term "fragmentation" connotes a negative judgment that the linkages among competing trading centers are insufficient to achieve the Exchange Act objectives of efficiency, price transparency, best execution, and order interaction. Whether fragmentation is in fact a problem in the current market structure is a critically important issue on which comment is requested in section IV below in a variety of contexts. This section will give an overview of the primary types of linkages that operate in the current market structure—consolidated market data, trade-through protection, and broker routing services.

Consolidated Market Data: When Congress mandated a national market system in 1975, it emphasized that the systems for collecting and distributing consolidated market data would "form the heart of the national market system." [C]onsolidated market data includes both: (1) Pre-trade transparency—real-time information on the best-priced quotations at which trades may be executed in the future ("consolidated quotation data"); and (2) post-trade transparency—real-time reports of trades as they are executed ("consolidated trade data"). As a result, the public has ready access to a comprehensive, accurate, and reliable source of information for the prices and volume of any NMS stock at any time during the trading day. This information serves an essential linkage function by helping assure that the public is aware of the best displayed prices for a stock, no matter where they may arise in the national market system. It also enables investors to monitor the prices at which their orders are executed and assess whether their orders received best execution. With respect to pre-trade transparency, Rule 602 of Regulation NMS requires exchange members and certain OTC market makers that exceed a 1% trading volume threshold to provide their best-priced quotations to their respective exchanges or FINRA, and these self-regulatory organizations ("SROs"), in turn, are required to make this information available to vendors. Rule 604 of Regulation NMS requires exchange specialists and OTC market makers to display certain customer limit orders in their best-priced quotations provided under Rule 602. In addition, Rule 301(b)(3) of Regulation ATS requires an ATS that displays orders to more than one person in the ATS and exceeds a 5% trading volume threshold to provide its best-priced orders for inclusion in the quotation data made available under Rule 602.

Importantly, the Commission's rules do not require the display of a customer limit order if the customer does not wish the order to be displayed. Customers have the freedom to display or not display depending on their trading objectives. On the other hand, the selective display of orders generally is prohibited in order to prevent the creation of significant private markets and two-tiered access to pricing information. Accordingly, the display of orders to some market participants generally will require that the order be included in the consolidated quotation data that is widely available to the public. Rule 604 of Regulation NMS, for example, explicitly recognizes the ability of customers to control whether their limit orders are displayed to the public. Rule 604(b)(2) provides an exception from the limit order display requirement for orders that are placed by customers who expressly request that the order not be displayed. Rule 604(b)(4) provides an exception for all block size orders unless the customer requests that the order be displayed. With respect to post-trade transparency, Rule 601 of Regulation NMS requires the equity exchanges and FINRA to file a transaction reporting plan regarding transactions in listed equity securities. The members of these SROs are required to comply with the relevant SRO rules for trade reporting. FINRA's trade reporting requirements apply to all ATSs that trade NMS stocks, both ECNs and dark pools, as well as to broker-dealers that internalize. FINRA currently requires members to report their trades as soon as practicable, but no later than 90 seconds. Finally, Rule 603(b) of Regulation NMS requires the equity exchanges and FINRA to act jointly pursuant to one or more effective national market system plans to disseminate consolidated information, including an NBBO, on quotations for and transactions in NMS stocks. It also requires that consolidated information for each NMS stock be disseminated through a single plan processor. To comply with these requirements, the equity exchanges and FINRA participate in three joint-industry plans ("Plans").

In addition to providing quotation and trade information to the three Networks for distribution in consolidated data, many exchanges and

ECNs offer individual data feeds directly to customers that include information that is provided in consolidated data. The individual data feeds of exchanges and ECNs also can include a variety of other types of information, such as "depth-of-book" quotations at prices inferior to their best-priced quotations. Rule 603(a) of Regulation NMS requires all exchanges, ATSs, and other broker-dealers that offer individual data feeds to make the data available on terms that are fair and reasonable and not unreasonably discriminatory. Exchanges, ATSs, and other broker-dealers are prohibited from providing their data directly to customers any sooner than they provide their data to the plan processors for the Networks. The fact that trading center data feeds do not need to go through the extra step of consolidation at a plan processor, however, means that such data feeds can reach end-users faster than the consolidated data feeds. The average latencies of the consolidation function at plan processors (from the time the processor receives information from the SROs to the time it distributes consolidated information to the public) are as follows: (1) Network A and Network B— less than 5 milliseconds for quotation data and less than 10 milliseconds for trade data; and (2) Network C—5.892 milliseconds for quotation data and 6.680 milliseconds for trade data. * * *

Trade-Through Protection: Another important type of linkage in the current market structure is the protection against trade-throughs provided by Rule 611 of Regulation NMS. A trade-through is the execution of a trade at a price inferior to a protected quotation for an NMS stock. A protected quotation must be displayed by an automated trading center, must be disseminated in the consolidated quotation data, and must be an automated quotation that is the best bid or best offer of an exchange or FINRA. Importantly, Rule 611 applies to all trading centers, not just those that display protected quotations. Trading center is defined broadly in Rule 600(b)(78) to include, among others, all exchanges, all ATSs (including ECNs and dark pools), all OTC market makers, and any other broker-dealer that executes orders internally, whether as agent or principal. Rule 611(a)(1) requires all trading centers to establish, maintain, and enforce written policies and procedures that are reasonably designed to prevent trade-throughs of protected quotations, subject to the exceptions set forth in Rule 611(b).

Protection against trade-throughs is an important linkage among trading centers because it provides a baseline assurance that: (1) Marketable orders will receive at least the best displayed price, regardless of the particular trading center that executes the order or where the best price is displayed in the national market system; and (2) quotations that are displayed at one trading center will not be bypassed by trades with inferior prices at any trading center in the national market system.

Rule 611 also helps promote linkages among trading centers by encouraging them, when they do not have available trading interest at the best price, to route marketable orders to a trading center that is displaying the best price. Although Rule 611 does not directly require such routing services (a trading center can, for example, cancel and return an order when it does not have the best price), competitive factors have led many trading centers to offer routing services to their customers. Prior to Rule 611, exchanges routed orders through an inflexible, partially manual system called the Intermarket Trading System ("ITS"). With Regulation NMS, however, the Commission adopted a "private linkages" approach that relies exclusively on brokers to provide routing services, both among exchanges and between customers and exchanges. These broker routing services are discussed next. *See* Regulation NMS Release, 70 FR at 37538–37539 ("Although ITS promotes access among participants that is uniform and free, it also is often slow and limited.").

Broker Routing Services: In a dispersed and complex market structure with many different trading centers offering a wide spectrum of services, brokers play a significant role in linking trading centers together into a unified national market system. Brokers compete to offer the sophisticated technology tools that are needed to monitor liquidity at many different venues and to implement order routing strategies. To perform this function, brokers may monitor the execution of orders at both displayed and undisplayed trading centers to assess the availability of undisplayed trading interest. Brokers may, for example, construct real-time "heat maps" in an effort to discern and access both displayed and undisplayed liquidity at trading centers throughout the national market system. Using their knowledge of available liquidity, many brokers offer smart order routing technology to access such liquidity. Many brokers also offer sophisticated algorithms that will take the large orders of institutional investors and others, divide a large "parent" order into many smaller "child" orders, and route the child orders over time to different trading centers in accordance with the particular trading strategy chosen by the customer. Such algorithms may be "aggressive," for example, and seek to take liquidity quickly at many different trading centers, or they may be "passive," and submit resting orders at one or more trading centers and await executions at favorable prices. To the extent they help customers cope with the dispersal of liquidity among a large number of trading centers of different types and achieve the best execution of their customers' orders, the routing services of brokers can contribute to the broader policy goal of promoting efficient markets. Under the private linkages approach adopted by

Regulation NMS, market participants obtain access to the various trading centers through broker-dealers that are members or subscribers of the particular trading center. Rule 610(a) of Regulation NMS, for example, prohibits an SRO trading facility from imposing unfairly discriminatory terms that would prevent or inhibit any person from obtaining efficient access through an SRO member to the displayed quotations of the SRO trading facility. Rule 610(c) limits the fees that a trading center can charge for access to its displayed quotations at the best prices. Rule 611(d) requires SROs to establish, maintain, and enforce rules that restrict their members from displaying quotations that lock or cross previously displayed quotations. *See* Regulation NMS Release, 70 FR at 37540 ("[M]any different private firms have entered the business of linking with a wide range of trading centers and then offering their customers access to those trading centers through the private firms' linkages. Competitive forces determine the types and costs of these private linkages.").

Section 6(a)(2) of the Exchange Act requires registered exchanges to allow any qualified and registered broker-dealer to become a member of the exchange—a key element in assuring fair access to exchange services. In contrast, the access requirements that apply to ATSs are much more limited. Regulation ATS includes two distinct types of access requirements: (1) order display and execution access in Rule 301(b)(3); and (2) fair access to ATS services in general in Rule 301(b)(5). An ATS must meet order display and execution access requirements if it displays orders to more than one person in the ATS and exceeds a 5% trading volume threshold. An ATS must meet the general fair access requirement if it exceeds a 5% trading volume threshold. If an ATS neither displays orders to more than one person in the ATS nor exceeds a 5% trading volume threshold, Regulation ATS does not impose access requirements on the ATS. The Commission has proposed reducing the threshold for order display and execution access to 0.25%. Non-Public Trading Interest Release, 74 FR at 61213. It has not proposed to change the threshold for fair access in general.

An essential type of access that should not be overlooked is the fair access to clearance and settlement systems required by Section 17A of the Exchange Act. If brokers cannot efficiently clear and settle transactions at the full range of trading centers, they will not be able to perform their linkage function properly. The linkage function of brokers also is supported by a broker's legal duty of best execution. This duty requires a broker to obtain the most favorable terms reasonably available when executing a customer order. Of course, this legal duty is not the only pressure on brokers to obtain best execution. The existence of strong competitive pressure to attract and retain customers encourages brokers to provide high quality routing services to their customers. In this regard, Rules 605 and 606 of Regulation NMS are designed to support competition by enhancing the transparency of order execution and routing practices. Rule 605 requires market centers to publish monthly reports of statistics on their order execution quality. Rule 606 requires brokers to publish quarterly reports on their routing practices, including the venues to which they route orders for execution. * * *

4. DEMUTALIZATION

JAKE KEAVENY
NOTE: IN DEFENSE OF MARKET SELF-REGULATION AN
ANALYSIS OF THE HISTORY OF FUTURES REGULATION AND
THE TREND TOWARD DEMUTUALIZATION
70 Brooklyn L. Rev. 1419 (2005)

The trend by the world's largest exchanges to demutualize has pushed the debate about self-regulation back to the forefront. Demutualization in this context refers to the conversion of non-profit, membership-owned organizations into for-profit stock corporations. Demutualization among futures and securities exchanges has been driven by forces in the business environment, including advances in technology, globalization of markets, a concentration of investment capital, competitive pricing pressure and government deregulation. By demutualizing, management at the exchanges hope to be able to raise larger pools of money, which in turn would allow them to invest more in technology and grow their businesses. Proponents also believe that demutualization will create a fairer marketplace. The members who have traditionally run the exchanges have been driven by the profits earned from their own trading. The demutualized exchanges would in theory be directed by shareholders and experienced management teams who are more focused on the bottom line, which in a competitive environment would mean there would be pressure to provide the best possible services. There are concerns that demutualization creates new conflicts of interest. One concern is that an inherent conflict exists between the interests of the shareholders and the market users. It has been suggested, for example, that a for-profit exchange would not rigorously undertake self-regulatory obligations if those obligations negatively affect profitability. The issue is whether a commercial entity that is running an exchange and seeking to protect and promote its business can also support the integrity and efficiency of the trading markets by setting and enforcing regulations that are in the public interest. One must enter this debate with the understanding that the current structure has its own conflicts. Even traditional, not for profit exchanges are run by members interested in making money and enhancing value through trading and seat value. Furthermore, the current structure of exchange disciplinary programs, where members sanction fellow members, could arguably affect the rigor of an exchange's self-regulatory program. Therefore, to some extent, questioning the efficacy of a for-profit structure in fulfilling self-regulatory obligations is also questioning the current exchange structure.

According to a CFTC report on demutualization that was published by CFTC Commissioner Thomas Erickson in 2000, even if new conflicts arise under the for-profit context, exchanges would continue to have a self-interest in preserving their reputations for providing fair and efficient markets. Exchanges like the CME, the New York Stock Exchange and the New York Mercantile Exchange aggressively market their records of regulatory enforcement to attract new business, and as more competitors enter the market place, the reputations of these exchanges will pay a heavier price when their regulatory systems fail. During a Senate hearing in 2000, Thomas Donovan, the chief executive of the CBOT, told legislators that "the CFTC strictly should be an oversight agency, one that provides the flexibility for us to use our self—the regulatory structure as a marketing tool for people to want to come and trade. . . ." At the same hearing, James McNulty, the CEO of the CME, concurred, saying that the exchange has built "a highly disciplined self-regulatory body in the CME, and we think that is one of the reasons people come to work with our exchange."

One issue that exchanges have been forced to address is the independence of boards of directors. A scandal over governance at the New York Stock Exchange led regulators to revisit issues surrounding exchanges' governance standards. In September of 2003, NYSE Chairman and CEO Richard Grasso was pressured to resign after it was made public that he was entitled to close to $140 million in compensation and deferred retirement benefits in 2003 (the NYSE as a whole made less than $28.1 million in profits in 2002). Much of the focus since has centered on the structure of the board, and claims that it did not receive enough information to gain a sufficient understanding of the pay package it was approving. A review of the NYSE's approach is relevant to the study of futures exchanges because the futures industry has historically followed the lead of the securities industry.

Grasso, a 35-year veteran at the NYSE, had been a respected figure in the debate over demutualization for both securities and futures exchanges. In a hearing before the Senate Banking Committee in September of 1999, Grasso said that the NYSE would need to demutualize, and possibly go public, in order to fend off competition from "electronic communications networks," commercially-owned electronic trading systems known as ECNs. Grasso argued that ECNs are not subject to cumbersome self-regulatory requirements, and are often owned by wealthy corporations that are willing to invest money to expand and enhance their businesses. Demutualization would cause the members' interests to align with the success of the exchange as a whole, as opposed to being skewed toward the success of only the floor trading operations.

Under a for-profit structure the NYSE would also be able to raise money by selling stock, either publicly or to private investors. Grasso also argued that greater competition in the market place would strengthen the NYSE's commitment to regulation. At the time he made that statement, the exchange had no intentions of altering the compensation of its board—then made up of 50% industry representatives and 50% public directors unaffiliated with its members—as a way to eliminate conflicts.

The public outcry surrounding Grasso's ouster has since led the 211-year old exchange to dramatically alter its course. John Reed, the former co-CEO of Citigroup Inc. who was brought in as interim NYSE chairman, orchestrated a series of reforms. NYSE members approved a plan that the board be cut down to 8 members, less than a third of its present size, and not include any representatives of the financial firms that are members of the exchange. Under the new structure, the board is responsible for such issues as compensation, independent audits, and self-regulation, while a separate advisory committee that would include member firms would be created to help oversee issues that are strategic to the exchange's business. The Securities and Exchange Commission has approved the proposal. Such corporate governance initiatives are implemented on securities markets sooner than on futures markets because of the public nature of the companies that are listed on them. The latest board proposal at the NYSE is an extension to a similar shake-up some 31 years earlier. In 1972, significant changes were made to the NYSE constitution after release of the Martin Report, a congressionally commissioned study that was critical of the exchange. The report had recommended that the NYSE reduce the number of board seats to twenty-one from thirty-three, and that the number of members representing the public be increased to ten from three. Prior to the reforms half of the NYSE's board had been composed of public directors. Traditionally, outside directors representing the public had only a token representation on futures exchanges.

In 1989, the Federal Bureau of Investigation ran an undercover sting at the CME and CBOT that resulted in the indictment of forty-eight individuals for various trading practice violations on commodity exchange floors. The controversy surrounding the arrests led Congress to amend the Commodity Futures Act in 1992, including a provision which had previously failed that required at least 20% of the regular voting members of the exchanges' boards be independent, non-member directors. Other provisions required that a diversity of interests be represented by including the principal groups of the commodities being traded, floor brokers and at least 10% from a group that included farmers, merchants, and exporters.

A major futures exchange to come under scrutiny following the NYSE scandal was the CME. In 2000 the CME was the first exchange to demutualize (preceding plans by the CBOT and the New York Mercantile

Exchange), and in 2002 it became the only major U.S. exchange to go public. In an October, 2003 article, Business Week reporter Joseph Weber questioned the independence of the CME's board, and said that the CFTC is scrutinizing its corporate governance policies. At the time only four of the 105-year old exchange's twenty directors do not have ties to the CME or its trading floor, while fifteen were long time exchange members.

In November, 2003 the CME announced that it planned to make a number of changes to its Board that would enhance the independent oversight of key corporate governance issues. As part of the plan, the CME would create a new board level committee in 2004, comprised solely of independent, non-member directors. The committee would conduct an annual review of issues that include the independence of the CME's regulatory functions from its business operations; the CME's compliance with its statutory self-regulatory responsibilities; the funding of the CME's self-regulatory responsibilities; and the compensation of exchange employees involved in regulatory activities. By making its boards more independent, the NYSE and the CME hope to preserve its regulatory roles from encroachment by the government. Critics have suggested that self-regulatory bodies should be completely separate from the exchanges' business operations.

CHAPTER 12

COMPARATIVE AND INTERNATIONAL REGULATION

∎ ∎ ∎

1. U.S. REGULATION OF FOREIGN BROKERS AND TRADING

MORRISON V. NATIONAL AUSTRALIAN BANK
561 U.S. 247, 130 S.Ct. 2869 (2010)

JUSTICE SCALIA delivered the opinion of the Court.

We decide whether § 10(b) of the Securities Exchange Act of 1934 provides a cause of action to foreign plaintiffs suing foreign and American defendants for misconduct in connection with securities traded on foreign exchanges.

Respondent National Australia Bank Limited (National) was, during the relevant time, the largest bank in Australia. Its Ordinary Shares— what in America would be called "common stock"—are traded on the Australian Stock Exchange Limited and on other foreign securities exchanges, but not on any exchange in the United States. There are listed on the New York Stock Exchange, however, National's American Depositary Receipts (ADRs), which represent the right to receive a specified number of National's Ordinary Shares. 547 F.3d 167, 168, and n. 1 (CA2 2008).

The complaint alleges the following facts, which we accept as true. In February 1998, National bought respondent HomeSide Lending, Inc., a mortgage servicing company headquartered in Florida. HomeSide's business was to receive fees for servicing mortgages (essentially the administrative tasks associated with collecting mortgage payments, see J. Rosenberg, Dictionary of Banking and Financial Services 600 (2d ed. 1985)). The rights to receive those fees, so-called mortgage-servicing rights, can provide a valuable income stream. See 2 The New Palgrave Dictionary of Money and Finance 817 (P. Newman, M. Milgate, & J. Eatwell eds. 1992). How valuable each of the rights is depends, in part, on the likelihood that the mortgage to which it applies will be fully repaid before it is due, terminating the need for servicing. HomeSide calculated the present value of its mortgage-servicing rights by using valuation models designed to take this likelihood into account. It recorded the value of its assets, and the numbers appeared in National's financial statements.

From 1998 until 2001, National's annual reports and other public documents touted the success of HomeSide's business, and respondents Frank Cicutto (National's managing director and chief executive officer), Kevin Race (HomeSide's chief operating officer), and Hugh Harris (HomeSide's chief executive officer) did the same in public statements. But on July 5, 2001, National announced that it was writing down the value of HomeSide's assets by $450 million; and then again on September 3, by another $1.75 billion. The prices of both Ordinary Shares and ADRs slumped. After downplaying the July write-down, National explained the September write-down as the result of a failure to anticipate the lowering of prevailing interest rates (lower interest rates lead to more refinancings, *i.e.*, more early repayments of mortgages), other mistaken assumptions in the financial models, and the loss of goodwill. According to the complaint, however, HomeSide, Race, Harris, and another HomeSide senior executive who is also a respondent here had manipulated HomeSide's financial models to make the rates of early repayment unrealistically low in order to cause the mortgage-servicing rights to appear more valuable than they really were. The complaint also alleges that National and Cicutto were aware of this deception by July 2000, but did nothing about it.

As relevant here, petitioners Russell Leslie Owen and Brian and Geraldine Silverlock, all Australians, purchased National's Ordinary Shares in 2000 and 2001, before the write-downs. They sued National, HomeSide, Cicutto, and the three HomeSide executives in the United States District Court for the Southern District of New York for alleged violations of § 10(b) and 20(a) of the Securities and Exchange Act of 1934, 48 Stat. 881, 15 U.S.C. §§ 78j(b) and 78t(a), and SEC Rule 10b–5, 17 CFR § 240.10b–5 (2009), promulgated pursuant to § 10(b). They sought to represent a class of foreign purchasers of National's Ordinary Shares during a specified period up to the September write-down. 547 F.3d, at 169.

Respondents moved to dismiss for lack of subject-matter jurisdiction under Federal Rule of Civil Procedure 12(b)(1) and for failure to state a claim under Rule 12(b)(6). The District Court granted the motion on the former ground, finding no jurisdiction because the acts in this country were, "at most, a link in the chain of an alleged overall securities fraud scheme that culminated abroad." *In re National Australia Bank Securities Litigation*, No. 03 Civ. 6537 (BSJ), 2006 U.S. Dist. LEXIS 94162, 2006 WL 3844465, *8 (SDNY, Oct. 25, 2006). The Court of Appeals for the Second Circuit affirmed on similar grounds. The acts performed in the United States did not "compris[e] the heart of the alleged fraud." 547

F.3d, at 175–176. We granted certiorari, 558 U.S. ___, 130 S. Ct. 783, 175 L. Ed. 2d 513 (2009).

Before addressing the question presented, we must correct a threshold error in the Second Circuit's analysis. It considered the extraterritorial reach of § 10(b) to raise a question of subject-matter jurisdiction, wherefore it affirmed the District Court's dismissal under Rule 12(b)(1). See 547 F.3d, at 177. In this regard it was following Circuit precedent, see *Schoenbaum* v. *Firstbrook*, 405 F.2d 200, 208, modified on other grounds en banc, 405 F.2d 215 (1968). The Second Circuit is hardly alone in taking this position, see, *e.g., In re CP Ships Ltd. Securities Litigation*, 578 F.3d 1306, 1313 (CA11 2009); *Continental Grain (Australia) PTY. Ltd.* v. *Pacific Oilseeds, Inc.*, 592 F.2d 409, 421 (CA8 1979).

But to ask what conduct § 10(b) reaches is to ask what conduct § 10(b) prohibits, which is a merits question. Subject-matter jurisdiction, by contrast, "refers to a tribunal's ' "power to hear a case." ' " *Union Pacific R. Co.* v. *Locomotive Engineers and Trainmen Gen. Comm. of Adjustment, Central Region*, 558 U.S. 67, ___, 130 S. Ct. 584, 175 L. Ed. 2d 428, 443 (2009) (quoting *Arbaugh* v. *Y & H Corp.*, 546 U.S. 500, 514, 126 S. Ct. 1235, 163 L. Ed. 2d 1097 (2006), in turn quoting *United States* v. *Cotton*, 535 U.S. 625, 630, 122 S. Ct. 1781, 152 L. Ed. 2d 860 (2002)). It presents an issue quite separate from the question whether the allegations the plaintiff makes entitle him to relief. See *Bell* v. *Hood*, 327 U.S. 678, 682, 66 S. Ct. 773, 90 L. Ed. 939 (1946). The District Court here had jurisdiction under 15 U.S.C. § 78aa 3 to adjudicate the question whether § 10(b) applies to National's conduct.

In view of this error, which the parties do not dispute, petitioners ask us to remand. We think that unnecessary. Since nothing in the analysis of the courts below turned on the mistake, a remand would only require a new Rule 12(b)(6) label for the same Rule 12(b)(1) conclusion. As we have done before in situations like this, see, *e.g., Romero* v. *International Terminal Operating Co.*, 358 U.S. 354, 359, 381–384, 79 S. Ct. 468, 3 L. Ed. 2d 368 (1959), we proceed to address whether petitioners' allegations state a claim.

It is a "longstanding principle of American law 'that legislation of Congress, unless a contrary intent appears, is meant to apply only within the territorial jurisdiction of the United States.' *EEOC* v. *Arabian American Oil Co.*, 499 U.S. 244, 248, 111 S. Ct. 1227, 113 L. Ed. 2d 274 (1991) *(Aramco)* (quoting *Foley Bros., Inc.* v. *Filardo*, 336 U.S. 281, 285, 69 S. Ct. 575, 93 L. Ed. 680 (1949)). This principle represents a canon of construction, or a presumption about a statute's meaning, rather than a limit upon Congress's power to legislate, see *Blackmer* v. *United States*, 284 U.S. 421, 437, 52 S. Ct. 252, 76 L. Ed. 375 (1932). It rests on the perception that Congress ordinarily legislates with respect to domestic, not foreign matters. *Smith* v. *United States*, 507 U.S. 197, 204, n. 5, 113 S. Ct. 1178, 122 L. Ed. 2d 548 (1993). Thus, "unless there is the affirmative intention of the Congress clearly expressed" to give a statute extraterritorial effect, "we must presume it is primarily concerned with domestic conditions." *Aramco, supra*, at 248, 111 S. Ct. 1227, 113 L. Ed. 2d 274 (internal quotation marks omitted). The canon or presumption applies regardless of whether there is a risk of conflict between the American statute and a foreign law, see *Sale* v. *Haitian Centers Council, Inc.*, 509 U.S. 155, 173–174, 113 S. Ct. 2549, 125 L. Ed. 2d 128 (1993). When a statute gives no clear indication of an extraterritorial application, it has none.

Despite this principle of interpretation, long and often recited in our opinions, the Second Circuit believed that, because the Exchange Act is silent as to the extraterritorial application of § 10(b), it was left to the court to "discern" whether Congress would have wanted the statute to apply. See 547 F.3d, at 170 (internal quotation marks omitted). This disregard of the presumption against extraterritoriality did not originate with the Court of Appeals panel in this case. It has been repeated over many decades by various courts of appeals in determining the application of the Exchange Act, and § 10(b) in particular, to fraudulent schemes that involve conduct and effects abroad. That has produced a collection of tests for divining what Congress would have wanted, complex in formulation and unpredictable in application.

As of 1967, district courts at least in the Southern District of New York had consistently concluded that, by reason of the presumption against extraterritoriality, § 10(b) did not apply when the stock transactions underlying the violation occurred abroad. See *Schoenbaum* v. *Firstbrook*, 268 F. Supp. 385, 392 (1967) (citing *Ferraioli* v. *Cantor*, CCH Fed. Sec. L. Rep. P91615 (SDNY 1965) and *Kook* v. *Crang*, 182 F. Supp. 388, 390 (SDNY 1960)). *Schoenbaum* involved the sale in Canada of the treasury shares of a Canadian corporation whose publicly traded shares (but not, of course, its treasury shares) were listed on both the American Stock Exchange and the Toronto Stock Exchange. Invoking the presumption against extraterritoriality, the court held that § 10(b) was inapplicable (though it incorrectly viewed the defect as jurisdictional). 268 F. Supp., at 391–392, 393–394. The decision in *Schoenbaum* was reversed, however, by a Second Circuit opinion which held that "neither the usual presumption against extraterritorial application of legislation nor the specific language of [§]30(b) show Congressional intent to preclude application of the Exchange Act to transactions regarding stocks traded in the United States which are effected outside the United States. . . ." *Schoenbaum*, 405 F.2d, at 206. It sufficed to apply § 10(b) that, although the transactions in treasury shares took place in Canada, they affected the value of the common shares publicly traded in the United States. See *id.,* at 208–209. Application of § 10(b), the Second Circuit found, was "necessary to protect American investors," *id., at 206.*

The Second Circuit took another step with *Leasco Data Processing Equip. Corp.* v. *Maxwell*, 468 F.2d 1326 (1972), which involved an American company that had been fraudulently induced to buy securities in England. There, unlike in *Schoenbaum*, some of the deceptive conduct had occurred in the United States but the corporation whose securities were traded (abroad) was not listed on any domestic exchange. *Leasco* said that the presumption against extraterritoriality apples only to matters over which the United States would not have prescriptive jurisdiction, 468 F.2d, at 1334. Congress had prescriptive jurisdiction to regulate the deceptive conduct in this country, the language of the Act could be read to cover that conduct, and the court concluded that "if Congress had thought about the point," it would have wanted § 10(b) to apply. *Id.,* at 1334–1337.

With *Schoenbaum* and *Leasco* on the books, the Second Circuit had excised the presumption against extraterritoriality from the jurisprudence of § 10(b) and replaced it with the inquiry whether it would be reasonable (and hence what Congress would have wanted) to apply the statute to a given situation. As long as there was prescriptive jurisdiction to regulate, the Second Circuit explained, whether to apply § 10(b) even to "predominantly foreign" transactions became a matter of whether a court thought Congress "wished the precious resources of United States courts and law enforcement agencies to be devoted to them rather than leave the problem to foreign countries." *Bersch* v. *Drexel Firestone, Inc.*, 519 F.2d 974, 985 (1975); see also *IIT* v. *Vencap, Ltd.*, 519 F.2d 1001, 1017–1018 (CA2 1975).

The Second Circuit had thus established that application of § 10(b) could be premised upon either some effect on American securities markets or investors *(Schoenbaum)* or significant conduct in the United States *(Leasco)*. It later formalized these two applications into (1) an "effects test," "whether the wrongful conduct had a substantial effect in the United States or upon United States citizens," and (2) a "conduct test," "whether the wrongful conduct occurred in the United States." *SEC* v. *Berger*, 322 F.3d 187, 192–193 (CA2 2003). These became the north star of the Second Circuit's § 10(b) jurisprudence, pointing the way to what Congress would have wished. Indeed, the Second Circuit declined to keep its two tests distinct on the ground that "an admixture or combination of the two often gives a better picture of whether there is sufficient United States involvement to justify the exercise of jurisdiction by an American court." *Itoba Ltd.* v. *Lep Group PLC*, 54 F.3d 118, 122 (1995). The Second Circuit never put forward a textual or even extratextual basis for these tests. As early as *Bersch*, it confessed that "if we were asked to point to language in the statutes, or even in the legislative history, that compelled these conclusions, we would be unable to respond," 519 F.2d, at 993.

As they developed, these tests were not easy to administer. The conduct test was held to apply differently depending on whether the harmed investors were Americans or foreigners: When the alleged damages consisted of losses to American investors abroad, it was enough that acts "of material importance" performed in the United States "significantly contributed" to that result; whereas those acts must have "directly caused" the result when losses to foreigners abroad were at issue. See *Bersch*, 519 F.2d, at 993. And "merely preparatory activities in the United States" did not suffice "to trigger application of the securities laws for injury to foreigners located abroad." *Id.*, at 992. This required the court to distinguish between mere preparation and using the United States as a "base" for fraudulent activities in other countries. *Vencap*, *supra*, at 1017–1018. But merely satisfying the conduct test was sometimes insufficient without " 'some additional factor tipping the scales' " in favor of the application of American law. *Interbrew* v. *Edperbrascan Corp.*, 23 F. Supp. 2d 425, 432 (SDNY 1998) (quoting *Europe & Overseas Commodity Traders, S. A.* v. *Banque Paribas London*, 147 F.3d 118, 129 (CA2 1998)). District courts have noted the difficulty of applying such vague formulations. See, *e.g., In re Alstom SA*, 406 F. Supp. 2d 346, 366–385 (SDNY 2005). There is no more damning indictment of the "conduct" and "effects" tests than the Second Circuit's own declaration that "the presence or absence of any single factor which was considered significant in other cases . . . is not necessarily dispositive in future cases." *IIT* v. *Cornfeld*, 619 F.2d 909, 918 (1980) (internal quotation marks omitted).

Other Circuits embraced the Second Circuit's approach, though not its precise application. Like the Second Circuit, they described their decisions regarding the extraterritorial application of § 10(b) as essentially resolving matters of policy. See, *e.g., SEC* v. *Kasser*, 548 F.2d 109, 116 (CA3 1977); *Continental Grain*, 592 F.2d, at 421–422; *Grunenthal GmbH* v. *Hotz*, 712 F.2d 421, 424–425 (CA9 1983); *Kauthar SDN BHD* v. *Sternberg*, 149 F.3d 659, 667 (CA7 1998). While applying the same fundamental methodology of balancing interests and arriving at what seemed the best policy, they produced a proliferation of vaguely related variations on the "conduct" and "effects" tests. As described in a leading Seventh Circuit opinion: "Although the circuits . . . seem to agree that there are some transnational situations to which the antifraud provisions of the securities laws are applicable, agreement appears to end at that point." *Id.*, at 665. See also *id.*, at 665–667 (describing the approaches of the various Circuits and adopting yet another variation).

At least one Court of Appeals has criticized this line of cases and the interpretive assumption that underlies it. In *Zoelsch* v. *Arthur Andersen & Co.*, 824 F.2d 27, 32, 262 U.S. App. D.C. 300 (1987) (Bork, J.), the District of Columbia Circuit observed that rather than courts' "divining what 'Congress would have wished' if it had addressed the problem[, a] more natural inquiry might be what jurisdiction Congress in fact thought about and conferred." Although tempted to apply the presumption against extraterritoriality and be done with it, see *id.,* at 31–32, that court deferred to the Second Circuit because of its "preeminence in the field of securities law," *id.,* at 32. See also *Robinson* v. *TCI/US West Communications Inc.*, 117 F.3d 900, 906–907 (CA5 1997) (expressing agreement with *Zoelsch*'s criticism of the emphasis on policy considerations in some of the cases).

Commentators have criticized the unpredictable and inconsistent application of § 10(b) to transnational cases. See, *e.g.,* Choi & Silberman, Transnational Litigation and Global Securities Class-Action Lawsuits, 2009 Wis. L. Rev. 465, 467–468; Chang, Multinational Enforcement of U. S. Securities Laws: The Need for the Clear and Restrained Scope of Extraterritorial Subject-Matter Jurisdiction, 9 Fordham J. Corp. & Fin. L. 89, 106–108, 115–116 (2004); Langevoort, *Schoenbaum* Revisited: Limiting the Scope of Antifraud Protection in an Internationalized Securities Marketplace, 55 Law & Contemp. Probs. 241, 244–248 (1992). Some have challenged the premise underlying the Courts of Appeals' approach, namely that Congress did not consider the extraterritorial application of § 10(b) (thereby leaving it open to the courts, supposedly, to determine what Congress would have wanted). See, *e.g.,* Sachs, The International Reach of Rule 10b–5: The Myth of Congressional Silence, 28 Colum. J. Transnat'l L. 677 (1990) (arguing that Congress considered, but rejected, applying the Exchange Act to transactions abroad). Others, more fundamentally, have noted that using congressional silence as a justification for judge-made rules violates the traditional principle that silence means no extraterritorial application. See, *e.g.,* Note, Let There Be Fraud (Abroad): A Proposal for A New U. S. Jurisprudence with Regard to the Extraterritorial Application of the Anti-Fraud Provisions of the 1933 and 1934 Securities Acts, 28 Law & Pol'y Int'l Bus. 477, 492–493 (1997).

The criticisms seem to us justified. The results of judicial-speculation-made-law—divining what Congress would have wanted if it had thought of the situation before the court—demonstrate the wisdom of the presumption against extraterritoriality. Rather than guess anew in each case, we apply the presumption in all cases, preserving a stable background against which Congress can legislate with predictable effects.

Rule 10b–5, the regulation under which petitioners have brought suit, was promulgated under § 10(b), and "does not extend beyond conduct encompassed by § 10(b)'s prohibition." *United States* v. *O'Hagan*, 521 U.S.

642, 651, 117 S. Ct. 2199, 138 L. Ed. 2d 724 (1997). Therefore, if § 10(b) is not extraterritorial, neither is Rule 10b–5. * * *

Petitioners argue that the conclusion that § 10(b) does not apply extraterritorially does not resolve this case. They contend that they seek no more than domestic application anyway, since Florida is where HomeSide and its senior executives engaged in the deceptive conduct of manipulating HomeSide's financial models; their complaint also alleged that Race and Hughes made misleading public statements there. This is less an answer to the presumption against extraterritorial application than it is an assertion—a quite valid assertion—that that presumption here (as often) is not self-evidently dispositive, but its application requires further analysis. For it is a rare case of prohibited extraterritorial application that lacks *all* contact with the territory of the United States. But the presumption against extraterritorial application would be a craven watchdog indeed if it retreated to its kennel whenever *some* domestic activity is involved in the case. The concurrence seems to imagine just such a timid sentinel, see *post*, at ___–___, 177 L. Ed. 2d, at 562–563, but our cases are to the contrary. In *Aramco*, for example, the Title VII plaintiff had been hired in Houston, and was an American citizen. See 499 U.S., at 247, 111 S. Ct. 1227, 113 L. Ed. 2d 274. The Court concluded, however, that neither that territorial event nor that relationship was the "focus" of congressional concern, *id.*, at 255, 111 S. St. 1227, 113 L. Ed. 2d 274, but rather domestic employment. See also *Foley Bros.*, 336 U.S., at 283, 285–286, 69 S. Ct. 575, 93 L. Ed. 680.

Applying the same mode of analysis here, we think that the focus of the Exchange Act is not upon the place where the deception originated, but upon purchases and sales of securities in the United States. Section 10(b) does not punish deceptive conduct, but only deceptive conduct "in connection with the purchase or sale of any security registered on a national securities exchange or any security not so registered." 15 U.S.C. § 78j(b). See *SEC* v. *Zandford*, 535 U.S. 813, 820, 122 S. Ct. 1899, 153 L. Ed. 2d 1 (2002). Those purchase-and-sale transactions are the objects of the statute's solicitude. It is those transactions that the statute seeks to "regulate," see *Superintendent of Ins. of N. Y.* v. *Bankers Life & Casualty Co.*, 404 U.S. 6, 12, 92 S. Ct. 165, 30 L. Ed. 2d 128 (1971); it is parties or prospective parties to those transactions that the statute seeks to "protec[t]," *id.*, at 10, 92 S. Ct. 165, 30 L. Ed. 2d 128. See also *Ernst & Ernst* v. *Hochfelder*, 425 U.S. 185, 195, 96 S. Ct. 1375, 47 L. Ed. 2d 668 (1976). And it is in our view only transactions in securities listed on domestic exchanges, and domestic transactions in other securities, to which § 10(b) applies.

The primacy of the domestic exchange is suggested by the very prologue of the Exchange Act, which sets forth as its object "[t]o provide for the regulation of securities exchanges . . . operating in interstate and foreign commerce and through the mails, to prevent inequitable and unfair practices on such exchanges. . . ." 48 Stat. 881. We know of no one who thought that the Act was intended to "regulat[e]" *foreign* securities exchanges—or indeed who even believed that under established principles of international law Congress had the power to do so. The Act's registration requirements apply only to securities listed on national securities exchanges. 15 U.S.C. § 78*l*(a).

With regard to securities *not* registered on domestic exchanges, the exclusive focus on *domestic* purchases and sale10 is strongly confirmed by § 30(a) and (b) [of the Securities Exchange Act of 1934]. The former extends the normal scope of the Exchange Act's prohibitions to acts effecting, in violation of rules prescribed by the Commission, a "transaction" in a United States security "on an exchange not within or subject to the jurisdiction of the United States." § 78dd(a). And the latter specifies that the Act does not apply to "any person insofar as he transacts a business in securities without the jurisdiction of the United States," unless he does so in violation of regulations promulgated by the Commission "to prevent evasion [of the Act]." § 78dd(b). Under both provisions it is the foreign location of the *transaction* that establishes (or reflects the presumption of) the Act's inapplicability, absent regulations by the Commission.

The same focus on domestic transactions is evident in the Securities Act of 1933, 48 Stat. 74, enacted by the same Congress as the Exchange Act, and forming part of the same comprehensive regulation of securities trading. See *Central Bank of Denver, N.A.* v. *First Interstate Bank of Denver, N. A.*, 511 U.S. 164, 170–171, 114 S. Ct. 1439, 128 L. Ed. 2d 119 (1994). That legislation makes it unlawful to sell a security, through a prospectus or otherwise, making use of "any means or instruments of transportation or communication in interstate commerce or of the mails," unless a registration statement is in effect. 15 U.S.C. § 77e(a)(1). The Commission has interpreted that requirement "not to include . . . sales that occur outside the United States." 17 CFR § 230.901 (2009).

Finally, we reject the notion that the Exchange Act reaches conduct in this country affecting exchanges or transactions abroad for the same reason that *Aramco* rejected overseas application of Title VII to all domestically concluded employment contracts or all employment contracts with American employers: The probability of incompatibility with the applicable laws of other countries is so obvious that if Congress intended such foreign application "it would have addressed the subject of conflicts with foreign laws and procedures." 499 U.S., at 256, 111 S. Ct. 1227, 113 L. Ed. 2d 274. Like the United States, foreign countries regulate their domestic securities exchanges and securities transactions occurring within their territorial jurisdiction. And the regulation of other countries often differs from ours as to what constitutes fraud, what disclosures must be made, what damages are recoverable, what discovery is available in litigation, what individual actions may be joined in a single suit, what attorney's fees are recoverable, and many other matters. See, *e.g.,* Brief for United Kingdom of Great Britain and Northern Ireland as *Amicus Curiae* 16–21. The Commonwealth of Australia, the United Kingdom of Great Britain and Northern Ireland, and the Republic of France have filed *amicus* briefs in this case. So have (separately or jointly) such international and foreign organizations as the International Chamber of Commerce, the Swiss Bankers Association, the Federation of German Industries, the French Business Confederation, the Institute of International Bankers, the European Banking Federation, the Australian Bankers' Association, and the Association Francaise des Entreprises Privees. They all complain of the interference with foreign securities regulation that application of § 10(b) abroad would produce, and urge the adoption of a clear test that will avoid that consequence. The transactional test we have adopted—whether the purchase or sale is made in the United States, or involves a security listed on a domestic exchange—meets that requirement. * * *

Section 10(b) reaches the use of a manipulative or deceptive device or contrivance only in connection with the purchase or sale of a security listed on an American stock exchange, and the purchase or sale of any other security in the United States. This case involves no securities listed on a domestic exchange, and all aspects of the purchases complained of by those petitioners who still have live claims occurred outside the United States. Petitioners have therefore failed to state a claim on which relief can be granted. We affirm the dismissal of petitioners' complaint on this ground.

It is so ordered.

JUSTICE SOTOMAYOR took no part in the consideration or decision of this case.

Concur by: BREYER; STEVENS

NOTES

1. The Morrison case was decided only a few days before enactment of the Dodd-Frank Wall Street Reform and Consumer Protection Act of 2010 (Dodd-Frank Act). Congress responded to that decision by including a provision in the Dodd-Frank Act that amended the Securities Act of 1933 and the Securities Exchange Act of 1934 to extend the SEC's jurisdiction to:

    (A) conduct within the United States that constitutes significant steps in furtherance of a violation, even if the securities transaction occurs outside the United States and involves only foreign investors; or

(B) conduct occurring outside the United States that has a foreseeable substantial effect within the United States."

Dodd-Frank Act § 929P (amending 15 U.S.C. § 77v(a) and 15 U.S.C. § 78aa). See also, 15 U.S.C. § 80b–14 (amending the Investment Advisers Act of 1940 by adding the same language).

2. The Dodd-Frank Act essentially sought to restore the prior "conduct" and "effects" test that had been applied by the circuit courts before Morrison, at least in enforcement cases brought by the SEC. See e.g., SEC v. Berger, 322 F.3d 187 (2d Cir. 2003) (describing those tests).

As noted by the District of Columbia Court of Appeals, however, in a pre-Morrison case, there were varying jurisdictional tests applied by different circuits:

> Several tests have been devised for determining when American courts have jurisdiction over domestic conduct that is alleged to have played some part in the perpetration of a securities fraud on investors outside this country. The Second Circuit has set the most restrictive standard. It has declined jurisdiction over alleged violations of the securities laws based on conduct in the United States when the conduct here was "merely preparatory" to the alleged fraud, that is, when the conduct here did not "directly cause" the losses elsewhere. *See, e.g., Bersch*, 519 F.2d at 992–93; *IIT v. Vencap, Ltd.*, 519 F.2d 1001, 1018 (2d Cir. 1975). In later cases, the line between domestic conduct that is "merely preparatory" and conduct that "directly causes" the losses elsewhere has been significantly clarified. The Second Circuit's rule seems to be that jurisdiction will lie in American courts where the domestic conduct comprises all the elements of a defendant's conduct necessary to establish a violation of section 10 (b) and Rule 10b–5: the fraudulent statements or misrepresentations must originate in the United States, must be made with scienter and in connection with the sale or purchase of securities, and must cause the harm to those who claim to be defrauded, even though the actual reliance and damages may occur elsewhere. *See IIT v. Cornfeld*, 619 F.2d 909, 920–21 (2d Cir. 1980); *cf. Vencap*, 519 F.2d at 1018 (finding of jurisdiction "is limited to the perpetration of fraudulent acts themselves"); *Leasco*, 468 F.2d at 1335 ("if defendants' fraudulent acts [occurred] in the United States . . . it would be immaterial . . . that the damage resulted, not from the contract . . . procured in this country, but from interrelated action which he induced in England").

The Third, Eighth, and Ninth Circuits appear to have relaxed the Second Circuit's test. They too have asserted jurisdiction only when the conduct in this country "directly causes" the losses elsewhere. *See SEC v. Kasser*, 548 F.2d 109, 115 (3d Cir.), *cert. denied*, 431 U.S. 938, 97 S. Ct. 2649, 53 L. Ed. 2d 255 (1977); *Continental Grain (Australia) Pty. Ltd. v. Pacific Oilseeds, Inc.*, 592 F.2d 409, 418–20

> (8th Cir. 1979); *Grunenthal GmbH v. Hotz*, 712 F.2d 421, 424 (9th Cir. 1983). But in *Continental Grain* the court explicitly repudiated the Second Circuit's requirement that "domestic conduct constitute the elements of a rule 10b–5 violation," 592 F.2d at 418, in favor of a test that would find jurisdiction whenever the domestic conduct "was in furtherance of a fraudulent scheme and was significant with respect to its accomplishment." *Id.* at 421. The Third Circuit's formulation seems more permissive, allowing subject matter jurisdiction "where at least some activity designed to further a fraudulent scheme occurs within this country." *Kasser*, 548 F.2d at 114. The consequence of these approaches has been a loosening of the jurisdictional requirements: any significant activity undertaken in this country—or perhaps any activity at all—that furthers a fraudulent scheme can provide the basis of American jurisdiction over the domestic actor.
>
> We believe that a more restrictive test, such as the Second Circuit's, provides the better approach to determining when American courts should assert jurisdiction in a case such as this.

Zoelsch v. Arthur Andersen & Co., 824 F.2d 27, 30–31 (D.C. Cir. 1987). See also, SDN BHD v. Sternberg, 149 F.3d 659 (7th Cir. 1998), cert. denied, 525 U.S. 1114 (1999) (describing the different approaches taken by the various circuits in applying these jurisdictional tests).

3. The Dodd-Frank Act also directed the SEC to conduct a study to determine whether private rights of action should be allowed for claims falling under the same broadened jurisdictional umbrella adopted for the SEC in Dodd-Frank. See, Richard W. Painter, The Dodd-Frank Extraterritorial Provision: Was It Effective, Needed or Sufficient? 1 Harv. Bus. L. Rev. 195 (2011) (discussing the effects of Section 929P of Dodd-Frank on Rule 10b–5 claims).

4. The SEC has taken a "territorial" approach for the application of the broker-dealer registration requirements to the international operations of broker-dealers.

> Under this approach, broker-dealers located outside the United States that induce or attempt to induce securities transactions with persons in the United States are required to register with the Commission, unless an exemption applies. Entities that conduct such activities entirely outside the United States do not have to register. Because this territorial approach applies on an entity level, not a branch level, if a foreign broker-dealer establishes a branch in the United States, broker-dealer registration requirements would extend to the entire foreign broker-dealer entity. The registration requirements do not apply, however, to a foreign broker-dealer with an affiliate, such as a subsidiary, operating in the United States. Only the U.S. affiliate must register and only the U.S. affiliate may engage in securities transactions and perform related functions on

behalf of U.S. investors. The territorial approach also requires registration of foreign broker-dealers operating outside the United States that effect, induce or attempt to induce securities transactions for any person inside the United States, other than a foreign person temporarily within the United States.

S.E.C. Exemption of Certain Foreign Brokers or Dealers, 2008 WL 2566725 (June 27, 2008). SEC Rule 15a–6, however, allows unregistered foreign brokers to deal with qualified U.S. investors provided that they are "chaperoned" by an associated person of a U.S. registered broker-dealer. [17 C.F.R. § 240.15a–6].

5. Compare the CFTC approach for futures to the SEC approach under its Rule 15a–6. Under Part 30 of the CFTC rules [17 C.F.R. Part 30], a non-U.S. foreign broker may solicit a U.S. person to trade futures on a non-U.S. futures exchange on which the "foreign broker" is a member firm. The foreign broker must merely file a Notice of Exemption with the National Futures Association (NFA) and, in such letter, consents to the CFTC's jurisdiction.

Part 30 applies to all U.S. persons desiring to trade futures outside the U.S., including retail customers. However, the CFTC ignored this flexible regulatory policy by adopting the Cross Border Guidance as noted in Section 3 below. There, the CFTC, in essence, is requiring all non-U.S. swap dealers who deal with U.S. persons in excess of a notional amount of $8 billion (an amount that is later scheduled to be substantially reduced) in any rolling 12-month period, must register as a swap dealer with the CFTC. See also Section 12 of Chapter 3 above.

6. Cross-border regulation has raised other issues. The merger of the New York Stock Exchange and Euronext in 2007 was arranged so that the merger would remain in place only so long as each institution was not subject to the regulatory jurisdiction of the other's country.

7. It is unclear what effect Morrison will have on claims under the Commodity Exchange Act of 1936 (CEA). In SDN BHD v. Sternberg, 149 F.3d 659 (7th Cir. 1998), cert. denied, 525 U.S. 1114 (1999), the Seventh Circuit equated jurisdictional issues under the CEA with those under the Securities Exchange Act of 1934. The Supreme Court in Morrison specifically cited and discussed SDN BHD v. Sternberg in its opinion, describing it as a "leading" case before rejecting its assertion that the Securities Exchange Act applied extraterritorially. 561 U.S. at ___, 130 S.Ct. 2869, 2880. Rather, "the focus of the Exchange Act is not upon the place where the deception originated, but upon purchases and sales of securities in the United States. Section 10(b) does not punish deceptive conduct, but only deceptive conduct 'in connection with the purchase or sale of any security registered on a national securities exchange or any security not so registered.' " Id.

8. The CFTC adopted an antifraud rule that prohibited fraud in the United States in connection with trading of commodity futures contracts on foreign exchanges. [17 C.F.R. § 30.9]. Congress subsequently amended

Section 4b of the CEA in 1982 to confirm that the CFTC had authority to regulate trading by U.S. customers on foreign futures exchanges. The CFTC adopted rules that further regulate such trading, including Rule 30.7 [17 C.F.R. § 30.7] discussed in Chapter 4 on the treatment of customer funds. CFTC rules allow exemptions from registration, except as a futures commission merchant (FCM), persons soliciting orders for foreign futures provided that the trades are conducted through a registered FCM. [17 C.F.R. § 30.5].

9. Title VII of the Dodd-Frank Act also added Section 2(i) of the CEA [7 U.S.C. 4(i)], which provides, in essence, that the Dodd-Frank Act should not apply to activities of non-U.S. swap dealers unless those activities had a "direct or significant" effect on the U.S. economy. See Section 3 below on the Cross Border Guidance issued by the CFTC in July 2013.

2. FUNCTIONAL REGULATION—A SECOND LOOK

As described in Chapter 1, the United States employees a "functional" regulatory model in which different regulators were created to regulate particular financial services, even if the same firm offers those services. Elsewhere in the world financial services regulation is consolidated into one or two regulators. It is unclear whether those models perform better than the functional system here, but clearly the functional system is more costly and results in much regulatory overlap. The following is a description and critique of the new super regulator created in the U.S. after the Financial Crisis in 2008.

JERRY W. MARKHAM

THE FINANCIAL STABILITY OVERSIGHT COUNCIL—RISK
MANAGER OR DEBATING SOCIETY

33 Capco Instit. J. of Fin. Trans. 35 (2011)

* * * Marking the regulatory response during the financial crisis was dysfunction and quarrelling among regulators. A popular book that was made into a HBO movie, *"Too big to fail,"* depicted SEC Chairman Christopher Cox as a cowardly and uninvolved regulator. The SEC was otherwise shown to have been impotent and incompetent regulator during the crisis over issues ranging from short sale restrictions to its refusal to suspend fair value accounting standards. The largest of the investment banks under the SEC's supervision also failed during the financial crisis and were either taken over by commercial banks or converted to bank holding companies, which placed them beyond SEC's jurisdiction. They included Bear Stearns, Merrill Lynch, Lehman Brothers, Goldman Sachs, and Morgan Stanley.

There was also much discord among the regulators. Shelia Bair, the head of the FDIC, was narrowly focused on protecting the FDIC's insurance fund. She attacked the large banks during and after the financial crisis, at a time when they did not need attacking. The FDIC also had a long history of disdain for the SEC. The SEC and CFTC had also been antagonists since the creation of the CFTC in 1975. They continued their jurisdictional fights after the financial crisis as they battled for control over swaps.

A particularly heated debate occurred over the proposal by the Obama administration that eventually led to the creation of FSOC. Tim Geithner, in his new role as Secretary of the Treasury, advocated that the Fed be given a supervisory role over other financial regulators in order to assure more effective decision-making during the next crisis. The FDIC objected because it wanted a new financial oversight regulatory council on which all the regulators would sit, presumably as equals. The Obama administration wanted only working group status for those other regulators. The OCC, SEC, and CFTC joined the FDIC in its criticism of the Geithner proposal. Geithner was reportedly reduced to cursing and threatening those regulators over their intransigence at one meeting. In the end, Congress had to resolve the issue, and FSOC was the rather imperfect result.

In response to a populist backlash from the TARP legislation,[1] FSOC was charged with promoting market discipline by eliminating any belief on the part of shareholders, creditors, and counterparties that the federal government will bail out a financial services firm that is about to fail. The Fed, in consultation with the Treasury Department, is required to adopt regulations designed to assure that any emergency lending program or facility is for the purpose of providing liquidity to the financial system, and not to aid a failing financial company; that the security for emergency loans is sufficient to protect taxpayers from losses; and that any such program is terminated in a timely and orderly fashion. * * *

Dodd-Frank tasked FSOC with identifying risks to the financial stability of the U.S. that could arise from large (U.S. $50 billion plus in consolidated assets) interconnected bank holding companies or nonbank financial companies, or that could arise outside the financial services marketplace. FSOC was also charged with responding to emerging threats to the stability of the U.S. financial system. FSOC is authorized to require regulation by the Fed of nonbank financial companies upon approval by two-thirds of the voting members and the affirmative vote of the chair (the Secretary of the Treasury). That vote is to be based on a determination that there will be negative effects on the financial system if the company fails or its activities would pose a risk to the financial stability of the U.S. FSOC may order the break up of large complex

---

[1]   [Auth. note: TARP stands for Troubled Asset Relief Program, which was the legislation that provided for a $700 billion bailout of large financial institutions during the Financial Crisis of 2008].

companies or require divestment of some of such companies' holdings, if it poses a grave threat to the financial stability of the U.S.—but only as a last resort.

Dodd-Frank also expanded the powers of the Fed over large systemically important bank and non-bank financial companies. The Fed is authorized to require reports and to conduct examinations of their activities and to recommend enforcement actions by their functional regulator, or take its own action if the functional regulator fails to respond. The Fed is further authorized to establish prudential risk standards for these nonbank financial companies and to direct divesture of assets in order to accomplish an orderly resolution in the event of failure. The Fed may require nonbank financial committees to establish risk committees and to undergo financial stress tests to determine their vulnerability to adverse economic events. The Fed may also establish leverage ratios limiting debt to equity of no more than 15 to 1.

Congress sought, through FSOC, to replace the *ad hoc* decision-making process used during the financial crisis by the Fed and Treasury and the unhelpful PWG. FSOC sought to create a more formal and broader based decision-making body for anticipating and dealing with the next financial crisis. However, the structure of FSOC does not portend well for reaching that goal. It is composed of ten voting members and five non-voting members who are likely to disagree, if history is any guide, over any policy affecting finance and large institutions. Those quarrels may very well derail effective and decisive decision-making that is needed for a crisis.

The Secretary of the Treasury was designated to chair FSOC and was given primacy among the regulators sitting on FSOC. Although FSOC will generally act by majority vote, critical FSOC actions require a two-thirds affirmative vote of its ten voting members, including the affirmative vote of the chair. The other voting members of FSOC are the Fed chair; the Comptroller of the Currency (OCC); the chairs of the FDIC, the SEC, the CFTC and the National Credit Union Administration (NCUA); the director of the Federal Housing Finance Agency (FHFA); the director of the Bureau of Consumer Financial Protection (BCFP), which was created by Dodd-Frank; and an independent member appointed by the President and confirmed by the Senate for a term of six years who is knowledgeable about insurance. FSOC also has five non-voting (advisory) members, which include the directors of the Federal Insurance Office and the Office of Financial Research (two more Dodd-Frank creations), and three delegates, each serving terms of two years, selected respectively by organizations of state insurance commissioners, banking supervisors, and securities commissioners.

NOTE

It will be interesting to see if the large body of regulators comprising FSOC will be effective in dealing with the next financial crisis. In past crises rescue efforts were mounted in the course of just a few days by a small number of regulators from Treasury and the Federal Reserve Board. Other regulators were often quarreling with the Treasury and Fed over what actions should be taken during the Financial Crisis in 2008. One of the reasons behind the creation of FSOC was the lack of communication among the various federal financial regulatory agencies.

3. CROSS-BORDER ISSUES

Section 722 of the Dodd-Frank Act added Section 2(i) to the CEA [7 U.S.C. § 2(i)], which states that the CEA provisions relating to swaps:

"shall not apply to activities outside the United States unless those activities have

(1) a direct and significant connection with activities in, or effect on, commerce of the United States, or

(2) contravene such rules or regulation as the Commission may prescribe or promulgate as are necessary or appropriate to prevent the evasion of any provision of this Chapter . . ."

The CFTC has asserted that Section 2(i)'s language requires it to find that swaps have a "direct and significant" effect on commerce, citing Gonzales v. Reich, 545 U.S. 1 (2005). The CFTC interpreted the term "direct" to mean a reasonably proximate nexus rather than requiring an effect to be foreseeable.

On July 12, 2013, the CFTC issued an Exemptive Order Regarding Compliance with Certain Swap Regulations, 78 Fed. Reg. 43,785 (July 22, 2013) (Cross Border Guidance). This order provided interpretative guidance, rather than a regulation, on certain regulatory requirements for non-U.S. swap dealers that engage in swaps with U.S. Persons.

The Cross Border Guidance addresses, among other things, (i) the definition of a "U.S. Person," (ii) the registration requirements of non-U.S. swap dealers, (iii) the application of "entity-level" and "transaction-level" requirements for swap dealers, and (iv) the concept of substituted compliance with U.S. regulations through compliance by the non-U.S. swap dealer with comparable laws or regulations in their home country. 78 Fed. Reg. 45291 (July 26, 2013).

The CFTC, through the Cross Border Guidance, has created a regulatory storm. Many foreign regulators have criticized the Guidance as having an adverse effect on firms located in their home country. These foreign regulators believe that they, and not the CFTC, should be regulating firms located within their borders, and that several of the requirements set forth in the Guidance would violate local law. Instead, those foreign regulators are advocating that, given the global nature of swaps, all countries should work together to harmonize applicable swap regulations, just as all of the major countries agreed to do at the G-20 Summit held in Pittsburgh, Pennsylvania in September 2009.

The Cross Border Guidance thus raises numerous issues, in particular:

1. Whether the CFTC should have issued a regulation rather than an interpretative guidance (as of December 2103, the SEC has proposed regulations on this issue);

2. Whether the definition of "U.S. Person" is too expansive, especially regarding non-U.S. funds, which are incorporated outside the U.S. but which have U.S. investors;

3. Why did the CFTC not apply a Part 30 regulatory concept to swaps (see Section 1 above);

4. How will the CFTC determine whether another country's laws and regulations will satisfy the "substituted compliance" test;

5. If a non-U.S. swap dealer is subject to comparable regulation in its home country, what was the need to require these non-U.S. swap dealers to register with the CFTC;

6. The SEC and the CFTC had previously determined that, if a U.S. swap dealer only engaged in less than $8 billion in notional value of swaps over a 12-month period, that such de minimis amount did not subject the U.S. swap dealer to the swap registration and regulatory requirements established by the two agencies. The CFTC applied this same de minimis test for non-U.S. swap dealers. Query, if a non-U.S. swap dealer engages in swaps with U.S. persons that total $8 billion, how can this de minimis amount constitute a "direct and significant" effect on the U.S. economy. Should the de minimis test for non-U.S. swap dealers have been set at a much larger amount, such as $500 billion or even a larger amount? It will be interesting to see how the CFTC ultimately enforces the Cross Border Guidance.

The CFTC staff issued a controversial "Advisory" letter on November 14, 2013, which advised that the CFTC staff believes that persons regularly arranging, negotiating, or executing swaps for or on behalf of a swap dealer are performing core, front-office activities for the swap dealer. This would mean that a non-U.S. swap dealer (whether an affiliate or not of a U.S. person) regularly using personnel or agents located in the U.S. to arrange, negotiate, or execute a swap with a non-U.S. person would be subject to CFTC regulation as a swap dealer. CFTC Staff Advisory No. 13–69 (Nov. 14, 2013). See, Floyd Norris, A Trading Tactic is Foiled, and Banks Cry Foul, N.Y. Times, Nov. 22, 2013, at B1 (describing objections by foreign banks to this interpretation). The CFTC's Global Markets Advisory Committee held hearings on February 14, 2014, to discuss this Advisory. See 79 FR 4454 (January 28, 2014).

As noted in Section 1 above, the CFTC did not elect to apply a Part 30 regulatory model to non-U.S. swap dealers as it did to non-U.S. brokerage firms who engage in futures trading with U.S. persons. It claimed that the Dodd-Frank Act did not give it the authority to do so.

Three industry groups, the International Swaps and Derivatives Association (ISDA), the Securities Industry Financial Markets Association (SIFMA) and the Institute of International Bankers (IIB), sued the CFTC over that interpretation. Landon Thomas Jr., Wall Street Challenges Overseas Swaps Rules, N.Y. Times, Dec. 5, 2013, at B5. See also the Complaint in Securities Industry Financial Markets Association et al. v. U.S. Commodity Futures Trading Commission (Civil Action No. 13–CV–1916) filed in the U.S. District Court for the District of Columbia on December 4, 2013. ISDA was successful in its lawsuit against the CFTC's adopted rules on position limits, as noted in Chapter 9 above. It will be interesting to see who prevails in this case and how this case might affect the application of the Cross Border Guidance from moving forward.

On December 20, 2013, the Commission approved Comparability Determinations for Australia, Canada, the European Union, Hong Kong, Japan and Switzerland, in which the CFTC determined whether the Business Conduct Rules relating to the Entity-Level Requirements for Swap Dealers and Major Swap Participants were or were not comparable to the CFTC regulations in these six jurisdictions, and thus satisfied the "substituted compliance" test noted above. The CFTC did not address whether other countries had a comparable regulatory scheme in place for these rules.

The CFTC was also seeking a further agreement in 2014 with the European Commission over cross border trading regulation. The proposed agreement would allow swaps trading to be done by U.S. firms on European Union markets under comparable regulatory structures. Andrew Ackerman and Katy Burne, CFTC is Set to Ease Rules on Trading Swaps Overseas, Wall St. J., Feb. 11, 2014, at C5.

4. THE U.K. FINANCIAL CONDUCT AUTHORITY

JERRY W. MARKHAM
MERGING THE SEC AND CFTC—A CLASH OF CULTURES
78 U. Cinn. L. Rev. 537 (2009)

Before the subprime crisis, the Financial Services Authority (FSA), Great Britain's single regulator, was a model for regulatory agencies around the world. That agency was created after earlier regulatory reform efforts in London failed. The FSA was given regulatory authority over all financial services in the U.K., and in the process, assumed the duties of nine other regulatory bodies. In so doing, Great Britain abolished self-regulatory organizations. Among other things, the FSA consolidated six separate insurance funds for compensating investors who suffer losses from failed financial institutions into one. The FSA also merged fourteen separate rulebooks governing various financial activities into one.

The single rulebook approach taken by the FSA was appealing, at least compared with the multitude of regulators in the United States. FSA regulation, at least initially, appeared successful. Despite the reduced regulation under the FSA, Great Britain was spared the Enron-era scandals that occurred under functional regulation in the United States. Critics contended that the FSA was understaffed and remained a weak regulator that deferred to the industry. Critics also argued that FSA unified regulations still imposed significant costs. Indeed, principles-based regulation under the FSA still required many rules, and the FSA handbook, which consolidated the rulebooks of earlier regulators, still totaled more than 8,000 pages.

The FSA also had controversial powers. It could veto decisions by large financial institutions to hire executives with "significant influence." The FSA also had authority to monitor the performance of such executives through regular reviews and was authorized to require an executive be fired if its appraisal was negative. Additionally, the FSA interviewed and approved hiring senior executives at "high-impact" firms. This meant, of course, that financial institutions had to kowtow to their regulators because if, for any reason, they displeased the FSA, their executives could be fired.

A favorable impression of FSA regulation was created after it adopted a unified approach to capital requirements and risk management. That program, however, proved to be an empty shell during the subprime crisis in 2007. The FSA was also strongly criticized for failing to prevent a bank run on Northern Rock PLC during the subprime crisis, the first run on a bank in England in more than 100 years. The English government nationalized that bank and put up $30 billion to rescue it and stop the panic. The British government also rescued the Royal Bank of Scotland and Lloyds at a tremendous cost. * * *

In January 2008, the House of Commons Treasury Committee issued a report criticizing the FSA for its laxness in regulating Northern Rock. The report asserted that the FSA failed to allocate sufficient resources to monitor the bank whose "business model was so clearly an outlier." The committee recommended that the Bank of England be the lead regulator when a bank faces financial difficulties. That recommendation was an apparent effort to turn back the clock on the single regulator concept, which had given the Bank of England's regulatory authority to the FSA because of perceived inadequacies in the Bank of England's regulatory abilities.

NOTES

1. After the Financial Crisis in 2008, Great Britain dropped its single regulator approach in favor of a "twin peaks" model. The government created a new Financial Conduct Authority (FCA) that began operations in 2013. It assumed the regulatory functions of the FSA. The FCA has described its role as follows:

> We regulate the financial services industry in the UK. Our aim is to protect consumers, ensure our industry remains stable and promote healthy competition between financial services providers. We have rule-making, investigative and enforcement powers that we use to protect and regulate the financial services industry. We are fair and principled in our approach to regulation.

FCA, *About Us*, available at http://www.fca.org.uk/about (accessed on April 1, 2013).

2. The second "peak" in the new English regulatory system is the Prudential Regulatory Authority (PRA), which is a part of the Bank of England. The PRA's role is defined in terms of two statutory objectives; (1) to promote the safety and soundness of financial services firms and for insurers, and (2) to contribute to the securing of an appropriate degree of protection for policyholders.

5. GERMANY

SECURITIES AND EXCHANGE COMMISSION V. TOURRE
2013 WL 2407172 (S.D.N.Y. 2013)

KATHERINE B. FORREST, DISTRICT JUDGE.

This case involves a three-year dispute between the SEC and Fabrice Tourre concerning allegations of fraud in the marketing and sale of interests in a synthetic collateralized debt obligation ("CDO").[1] The SEC alleges various misstatements and omissions concerning the role of Paulson & Co., Inc., ("Paulson") in structuring the CDO in issue: ABACUS 2007–AC1 ("AC1"). Although Paulson helped to select the assets that would determine AC1's value, it also shorted over $1 billion of those assets through credit default swaps ("CDS").[3]

Whether Tourre's statements or omissions about Paulson's interests and his role in the AC1 transaction were, in fact, fraudulent will be determined at trial, scheduled to commence in six weeks. The present motions for summary judgment focus primarily on the narrower question of whether the events that took place in the United States are sufficient to render any fraud that occurred actionable under Section 10(b) of the Securities Exchange Act of 1934 ("Exchange Act"), Rule 10b–5, 17 C.F.R. § 240.10b–5, or Section 17(a) of the Securities Act of 1933 ("Securities Act"). The reason the parties ask that question—as well as the answer to it lies in the Supreme Court's watershed decision Morrison v. National Australia Bank Ltd., 130 S. Ct. 2869 (2010), which redefined what it means for a claim of securities fraud to be "domestic" for purposes of Section 10(b) and Rule 10b–5. * * *

The transactions at the heart of this action involved AC1, a synthetic CDO. AC1 referenced a portfolio of ninety sub-prime and mid-prime residential mortgage-backed securities ("RMBS"). Through notes and CDS arrangements, AC1 offered investors a way to bet on the performance of its reference portfolio without actually owning the underlying mortgages. The value of the reference portfolio depended in large part on the likelihood of "credit events," such as a failure to pay the principal on underlying assets, or the writedown or downgrade of components of the portfolio. Investors with a net long interest in AC1 (i.e., investors who bought AC1 notes or who sold protection through CDS) were betting against the likelihood of credit events in the referenced portfolio. Investors with a net short interest in AC1 (i.e., investors who

---

[1] A CDO represents a pool of assets, which can be sliced into tranches of different payment priorities. (See Def.'s Resp. SEC's Rule 56.1 Statement Material Facts ¶ 7, ECF No. 228 ("DCSOF").) A CDO is synthetic when, rather than owning the pool of assets, it uses credit default swaps ("CDS") to reference those assets. (Id. ¶ 8.) Tranches typically range from super senior (highest priority) to equity or first loss (lowest priority).

[3] The Second Circuit has described CDS as follows:

"A credit default swap is the most common form of credit derivative, i.e., '[a] contract which transfers credit risk from a protection buyer to a credit protection seller.' . . . Simply put, a credit default swap is a bilateral financial contract in which '[a] protection buyer makes[ ] periodic payments to . . . the protection seller, in return for a contingent payment if a predefined credit event occurs in the reference credit,' i.e., the obligation on which the contract is written."

Eternity Global Master Fund Ltd. v. Morgan Guar. Trust Co. of N.Y., 375 F.3d]68, 171–72 (2d Cir. 2004) (internal citations omitted). In other words, CDS permit parties to assume or hedge against risk associated with assets without purchasing or selling the assets referenced.

bought protection through CDS) were betting that credit events would occur in the reference portfolio.

Tourre worked with Paulson and ACA Management LLC (referred to, along with ACA Capital Holdings, Inc., as "ACA") to structure AC1. He, along with other colleagues, then worked with ACA to market AC1.

The crux of the SEC's complaint is that Tourre knew Paulson was both participating in the selection of the reference portfolio and taking a short position on AC1, but, through misstatements or omissions, he: (1) gave ACA the impression that Paulson was taking a long position on AC1, and (2) gave potential investors the impression that ACA selected the reference portfolio without input from Paulson. The SEC essentially argues that Tourre handed Little Red Riding Hood an invitation to grandmother's house while concealing the fact that it was written by the Big Bad Wolf. Tourre disputes the SEC's characterization writ large and also points out that the alleged victims were not be-hooded children, but rather large financial institutions, operating in a dog-eat-dog world.

At present, however, the parties focus on the location of the alleged fraud, rather than whether the conduct in issue was fraudulent. The Court limits its recitation of the facts accordingly.

From the end of 2006 through October 2007, Tourre worked as a vice president on the structured products correlation desk at Goldman Sachs & Co. ("Goldman") in New York. While there, his responsibilities were primarily to develop, structure, trade, and market synthetic CDOs and to hedge those products. At that time, Paulson was a New York-based company "that managed the investments of certain hedge funds."

In late 2006, Paulson expressed interest to Goldman in buying protection on (i.e., shorting) a portfolio of sub-prime RMBS. ACA was invited to serve as portfolio selection agent, in part to help make potential long investors more comfortable with the transaction. On January 8, 2007, Tourre met with representatives of Paulson and ACA to discuss the possible AC1 transaction.

On January 10, 2007, Tourre sent an e-mail to Laura Schwartz (the head of ACA's portfolio management team) summarizing ACA's proposed role in AC1. The e-mail described the equity (or first loss) tranche of AC1 as "pre-committed" and stated that "the compensation structure" aligned the "incentives" of Paulson, Goldman, and ACA. At that time, however, Tourre did not anticipate that the equity tranche of AC1 would be placed, and he knew that Paulson contemplated taking a short interest in AC1.

ACA was formally engaged as the portfolio selection agent for the AC1 transaction by February 2007. In that capacity, ACA worked with Paulson to select the reference portfolio, which eventually included ninety Baa2-rated sub-prime and mid-prime RMBS

Tourre, along with colleagues at Goldman, Goldman Sachs International ("GSI"), and ACA, then worked together to market and negotiate the AC1 transaction. They made a term sheet, flip book, and offering circular, each of which described the reference portfolio as selected by ACA, without mentioning Paulson's role in the selection process or its contemplated short position. Tourre e-mailed a preliminary draft of the offering circular to Jorg Zimmermann and Thomas Schirmer of IKB [a bank based in Düsseldorf, Germany.]. He and his colleagues at Goldman and GSI also discussed the AC1 transaction with IKB over the phone and e-mailed other AC1 offering materials to IKB and to numerous other individuals. Tourre also e-mailed ABN discussing its potential role in intermediating a CDS transaction involving the super senior tranche of AC1. The e-mail indicated that the reference portfolio was "selected by ACA."

On April 26, 2007, the AC1 transaction closed. That day, three ACA-managed funds purchased $42 million in Class A2 notes. The trade confirmations for those purchases show a trade from Goldman to the three ACA-related entities with an account address for each entity listed as 140 Broadway, 48th Floor, New York, NY 10005. Two Loreley entities (advisory clients of IKB) also purchased $150 million in Class Al and A2 notes. Title and irrevocable liability passed to the Loreley entities in Europe. Also on April 26, 2007, Paulson purchased protection on $192 million of Class Al and A2 notes.

On approximately May 31, 2007, ACA LLC entered into a CDS in which it sold protection on $909 million of the super senior (50%–100%) tranche of the AC1 reference portfolio. ACA LLC entered into that transaction pursuant to a master agreement and a trade confirmation, each of which were signed by Nora Dahlman on behalf of ACA LLC in the United States. ACA LLC also issued a financial guaranty insurance policy on that same tranche of the AC1 reference portfolio. On May 31, 2007, Paulson purchased protection on approximately $1 billion of the super senior (45%–100%) tranche of the AC1 reference portfolio. * * *

[F]or conduct that predates the Dodd-Frank Wall Street Reform and Consumer Protection Act of 2010, the SEC must also prove that the fraud is domestic for purposes of Morrison. See generally Morrison, 130 S. Ct. 2869; SEC v. Goldman Sachs & Co., 790 F. Supp. 2d 147, 164 (S.D.N.Y. 2011) (applying Morrison to claims under Section 17(a) of the Securities Act); see also 15 U.S.C. § 77v(c) (delineating the extraterritorial scope of post-Dodd Frank enforcement actions). Section 10(b) of the Exchange Act and Rule 10b–5 also prohibit securities fraud. Section 10(b) and Rule 10b–5 claims share, inter alia, the domestic transaction element of Section 17(a) claims. See generally Morrison, 130 S. Ct. 2869.

The primary question of law that the parties dispute on these motions is what it means for fraud made "in the offer" of securities to be domestic for purposes of Section 17(a) and Morrison. * * *

The bulk of Tourre's motion for summary judgment is devoted to the argument that the Court must reject the SEC's claims to the extent they assert that Tourre violated Section 17(a) in connection with the "offer" of securities that were later sold in non-domestic transactions. For the reasons discussed at length above, the Court rejects that construction of Section 17(a) and Morrison.

Instead, to the extent the SEC seeks to hold Tourre liable for fraudulent conduct in the offer of securities to IKB and ABN, Morrison requires only that the SEC prove that Tourre engaged in fraudulent conduct in connection with a domestic offer of those securities. To make that showing, the SEC must prove only that the offeror was in the United States at the time he or she made the relevant offer. Because the SEC has not cross-moved for summary judgment on these claims, however, its burden on this motion is only to cite record evidence that would allow a reasonable jury to find that Tourre's allegedly fraudulent conduct occurred in connection with a domestic offer.

The SEC has satisfied that burden. It has cited to record evidence that would allow a reasonable jury to find that Tourre worked in New York at all relevant times. It has also cited to record evidence that would allow a reasonable jury to conclude that he e-mailed and called both IKB and ABN to discuss possible transactions involving AC1. A reasonable jury could conclude that such conduct amounted to an "offer."

These materials suffice to defeat summary judgment on the domestic element of the SEC's claims under Section 17(a) for fraud in connection with the offer of securities to IKB and ABN. * * *

For the reasons set forth above, Tourre's motion for partial summary judgment is denied.

NOTES

1. As described in Chapter 1, speculation in commodity futures contracts was prohibited in Germany for almost 100 years. After that ban was lifted in the 1990s, futures and other derivatives trading became an important part of German finance and Frankfort became a leading derivatives market center. See, William P. Rogers & Jerry W. Markham, The Application of West German Statutes to United States Commodity Futures Contracts: An Unnecessary Clash of Policies, 19 Geo. J. of L. & Policy in Intern. Bus. 273 (1987) (describing Germany's ban on futures speculation).

2. In Germany the largest banks, rather than broker-dealers and exchanges, dominate finance, including equities and lending. Until 2002, the German Financial Supervisory Authority was responsible for licensing banks

and other financial institutions. That Authority was divided into three separate units that separately regulated banking, insurance and securities. In 2002, those units were consolidated into a single regulator, a new German Financial Supervisory Authority, generally referred to as BaFin. That regulator is contained within the portfolio of the German Federal Ministry of Finance.

3. Several large German banks, including IKB, suffered large losses from investments in U.S. collateralized debt obligations during the Financial Crisis in 2008. The German government created a $750 billion rescue package for those financial institutions. BaFin required stress testing of trading positions at all levels, increased risk management controls and required bank directors to be given greater control over management. BaFin also sent out directive to firms engaging in high frequency trading (HFTs) and directed them to take actions to prevent manipulative trading practices, including "spoofing" and "layering."

4. Germany enacted legislation in 2013 that requires HFTs to register with BaFin and subjects those traders to special organizational requirements.

6. JAPAN

JERRY W. MARKHAM
SUPER REGULATOR: A COMPARATIVE ANALYSIS OF
SECURITIES AND DERIVATIVES REGULATION IN THE UNITED
STATES, THE UNITED KINGDOM, AND JAPAN
28 Brooklyn J. Int'l L. 319 (2003)

[T]he form of Japan's present regulatory structure is best explained by its history. After World War II, General Douglas MacArthur's Supreme Command required the adoption of provisions from U.S. laws regulating finance, including the securities laws and the Glass-Steagall Act. This new legislation established a Securities Commission for the Supervision of Securities Business based on the American SEC. Japan did not permit bank holding companies, but banks became members of the keiretsu, i.e., large companies joining in cooperative units with cross-shareholding, which became the dominant force within the Japanese economy after World War II. The Bank of Japan acted as the country's central bank, setting monetary policy, while the Ministry of Finance ("MoF") was responsible for financial policy. The MoF became a monolithic component of Japanese finance and managed the economy on both a micro and macro level, leaving only a limited central banking role to the Bank of Japan. To secure its position, the MoF abolished the Securities Commission for the Supervision of Securities Business in 1952 and replaced it with its own Securities Bureau. Other aspects of the U.S.-style regulatory system were also abandoned in later years. The MoF then assumed a dual role of regulator and business promoter. Though it was the sole governmental financial regulator, SROs, including the exchanges and the Japanese Securities Dealers Association, also provided some minimal regulatory functions. The Japanese economy prospered, experiencing growth rates of 10% a year between 1950 and 1970. The period of growth continued into the 1980s. * * *

The stock market boomed, and real estate prices more than doubled between 1986 and 1990. Scandals soon unfolded. In the "Recruit Cosmos" affair, Prime Minister Noboru Takeshita resigned after it was discovered that some 160 influential politicians had been given Recruit Cosmos stock at bargain prices in 1986, just before the company went public. In another scandal, the Hanshin Sogo Bank sold a large amount of stock it held in the Tateho Chemical Company the day before the company announced large losses. No wrongdoing was found, to the consternation of many. Nui Onoue, the "Bubble Lady," became famous for borrowing billions of dollars on her restaurants in order to invest in the stock market. The amounts she borrowed were greater than the value of those properties. She had also used forged certificates of deposit for her trading activities. Eventually, the Bubble Lady, who used seances to pick stocks, was sentenced to twelve years in prison. The bursting of the Japanese economic bubble at the beginning of the 1990s sent the economy into a deep recession that the country is still struggling with today—massive deflation was experienced; the Nikkei 225 index dropped from 39,000 to 11,000; land prices in large cities dropped eleven years in a row; government debt grew to 150% of GDP, as compared with 33% in the U.S.; and bad debt held by Japanese banks grew to some 30% of GDP. The Hokkaido Takushoku Bank failed, the first to do so in Japan since World War II. Nineteen of Japan's largest banks had capital shortages that threatened their ability to meet the Basel Committees guidelines for international banks. Yamaichi Securities, the fourth largest securities firm in Japan, also failed. Yamaichi had hid its losses in off book accounts, apparently with the knowledge of at least one MoF official. In the early 1990s there were a series of "loss compensation" scandals, in which it was discovered that the country's four largest brokerage firms were covering the trading losses of important clients and politicians.

In 1997, the nation's largest securities firm, Nomura, became mired in scandal, after it was discovered that the firm had covered the trading losses of a gangster and engaged in widespread abusive sales practices. The Japanese government took several steps to deal with this deteriorating situation. The Japanese Diet passed the Financial Reform Act of 1992, which allowed the MoF to establish capital requirements for banks and allowed banks to own securities affiliates. The act also aimed to further competition among financial institutions. Furthermore, a Securities Exchange and Surveillance Commission ("SESC") was created in 1992 to police the securities markets. This legislation ostensibly reduced the MoF's role as the director agency for the placement of financial resources. In application, however, the MoF remained firmly in control of financial services firms and the SESC.

Greater reform was attempted in 1996 by means of a "Japanese Big Bang" that sought to emulate the one in the U.K. and deregulate Japan's financial services. The Japanese Big Bang tried to ease market entry and remove noncompetitive practices. Commissions were unfixed. The plan was formulated by a Financial System Research Council to allow banks, insurance companies, and brokerage firms to compete with each other without the prior restrictions that had kept these sectors separate. The government also announced a "Total Plan" to deal with the mass of non-performing debt in the economy and to dissolve bankrupt companies. Although public funds were used to shore up shaky banks, Japan's banks still maintain some $1.3 trillion in bad debts. Another scandal arose after the Tokyo Prosecutor's Office staged a large-scale raid involving 100 investigators on the MoF offices in 1998. The Prosecutor was seeking information on bribes in the form of lavish entertainment and discount loans allegedly paid to MoF bank examiners by those being examined. Two examiners were arrested and a third committed suicide.

More legislation followed in the form of a Financial Reconstruction Law for failed financial institutions and a Financial Early Strengthening Law that allowed public funds to be used to shore up weak or failing banks. These laws were to be administered by a five-member governmental body called the Financial Reconstruction Commission. The SESC was transferred out of the MoF in 1998, along with an independent Financial Supervisory Agency, which was succeeded by the Financial Services Agency ("FSA-Japan") in 2000. The FSA-Japan was also given the power, previously held by the MoF, to set securities policy and to regulate securities and banking. The SESC continued its operations under authority from the FSA-Japan, which in turn was supervised by the Financial Reconstruction Commission. More reform legislation was adopted: the ban on holding companies was removed, and consumer protection was enhanced through the Law Concerning the Sale of Financial Products. Some have expressed concern that all of these reforms may not have accomplished very much.

The SESC lacked strong enforcement mechanisms—it is only an investigative agency. The SESC has no authority to impose sanctions, but may refer matters for sanctions. In practice, however, few referrals have been made to date. In 2001, the SESC had a relatively small staff, at least in comparison to the SEC in the U.S., and most of them had been transferred from the MoF. To be sure, the MoF does appear to retain some policy control. FSA-Japan also experienced a faltering start. When FSA-Japan did try to take aggressive action by urging vast bad debt write-offs, many small and medium sized companies went bankrupt. FSA-Japan then eased off, pressuring the banks and using public funds to save the Daiei supermarket chain and Koizumi, a construction company, both of which had massive amounts of bad debt. However, there were no bailouts for small companies. The government nationalized the Long-Term Credit Bank of Japan and the Nippon Credit Bank, after these institutions could no longer be kept afloat. Public funds were also injected into all but one major bank. FSA-Japan announced that it was undertaking inspections of large troubled banks in order to address their bad debt problems. The project was supposed to be a "Japanese sword" for dealing with the problem, but the result was largely to shore up some troubled banks. Critics claimed that FSA-Japan was "whitewashing" the bad debt problem in Japan.

After downgrading Japan's debt, a credit rating agency claimed that FSA-Japan was engaging in regulatory forbearance as a way to aid the economy "in the hope that something will turn up." The agency was waffling on reform in other areas. Japan dropped its insurance guaranty for customer funds held in time deposit accounts, limiting claims to about $83,000. This was intended to assure more market discipline, but it instead raised concerns that funds would be pulled out of already unstable institutions, weakening them further. When a similar proposal limiting deposit insurance on ordinary deposit accounts met political opposition FSA-Japan started backtracking. It then extended government insurance on some deposits, a breach of its promise to eliminate unlimited guarantees. FSA-Japan seemed to be retreating from promised reform measures in the insurance industry and was stalling on allowing commercial banks, such as the one sought by Sony, to be licensed. The Japanese government continued the old MoF role of trying to manage the economy in other ways.

Most recently, despite FSA-Japan's push for a market solution, the government suggested that more banks should merge and that it would offer a higher government guarantee to encourage such actions. In fact, several of Japan's largest banks did merge to form colossal enterprises, the largest being Mizuho Holdings, Inc., composed of Daiichi Bank, Fuji Bank, and the Industrial Bank of Japan. FSA-Japan was accused of trying to manipulate the Nikkei 225 index through short sale restrictions, which were modeled after those of the SEC in the U.S. Like the MoF, FSA-Japan has often been lenient, at least on Japanese banks. For example, FSA-Japan merely issued a warning to a Japanese bank that hid key information from inspectors. FSA-Japan has shown that it does know how to play tough, at least where foreigners are involved. FSA-Japan accused two American firms of improper short sales, in another attempt to support the market. In 1999, the Tokyo branch of Credit Suisse was excluded from engaging in the derivatives business in Japan after several abuses. FSA-Japan denied the consequent claims that it was discriminating against foreign firms.

NOTES

1. Japan enacted a new Financial Instruments and Exchange Law ("FIEL") in 2006. The FIEL consolidated four existing statutes including those regulating financial futures and mortgage-backed securities. The Japanese Financial Services Authority (JFSA) was given authority over derivatives related to securities and other financial instruments. FIEL applies to derivatives that are transacted through a Japanese or foreign exchange or over the counter.

2. In 2013, the Bank of Japan began an effort to stop the years of price deflation experienced in that country by doubling the amount of money in circulation and by seeking an annual inflation rate of 2 percent. Hiroko Tabuchi, Japan Initiates Bold Bid to End Years of Tumbling Prices, N.Y. Times, April 4, 2013 (available at http://www.nytimes.com/2013/04/05/business/global/japan-initiates-a-bold-bid-to-end-years-of-fallingprices.html?pagewanted=all&_r=0, accessed on August 28, 2013). Do such currency manipulations raise regulatory issues?

3. On March 10, 2014, the CFTC and the Financial Services Agency of Japan entered into a Memorandum of Cooperation (MOC) to exchange information regarding supervision and oversight of regulated entities that operate on a cross-border basis in the two countries. See, www.cftc.gov/PressRoom/PressRealeases/pr6876-14 (accessed on March 16, 2014).

7. THE EUROPEAN UNION

THOMAS L. HAZEN AND JERRY W. MARKHAM
BROKER-DEALER OPERATIONS UNDER SECURITIES
AND COMMODITIES LAW
Vol. 23A at § 16:5 (2012)

The European Union ("EU") is playing an increased role in financial services regulation. Under a 1993 Directive banks licensed in one member state had to be recognized in all other member states with regulation to be conducted by the bank's home state. This allowed cross-border branches and offices. Securities activities were also subject to similar requirements. The EU also adopted a Financial Services Action Plan in 1999 that sought complete integration of financial services among member states.

An EU Directive issued in 2002 required foreign financial services firms with operations in the EU to demonstrate holding company supervision that is equivalent to EU consolidated supervision. The SEC and CFTC reacted to that directive by allowing such entities to used risk based capital requirements as substitutes for the current net capital regimen.

The European Union has also issued a Markets in Financial Instruments Directive that seeks to develop a single market in member states in all financial transactions. That directive includes a best execution requirement. * * *

Several large European banks made substantial investments in U.S. subprime mortgages and were severely crippled when those investments became illiquid during the subprime crisis. UBS AG, for example, became heavily involved in the U.S. subprime mortgage market through its Dillon Read Capital Management LLC (Dillon Read), which the Swiss Bancorp had acquired for $600 million before its merger with UBS. By the end of September 2007, the losses from the Dillon Read positions ballooned to over $3 billion. UBS losses associated with the U.S. residential mortgage, mostly from CDOs, grew to $18.7 billion for all of 2007.

The European Central Bank (ECB) injected $210 billion into its financial markets on August 10 and 11, 2007 in order to provide liquidity as the subprime crisis spread to Europe. The Bank of England and the European Central Bank (ECB) also worked in tandem with the Federal Reserve Board to make unlimited funds available to their banks in order to ease the credit crunch. On December 12, 2007, the Federal Reserve Board, the ECB in the European Union, the Bank of England, the Bank of Canada and the Swiss National Bank announced that they would be coordinating their efforts to provide liquidity to their banks. The ECB announced on December 18, 2007 that it would offer unlimited amounts of funds to its member banks at bargain interest rates. The ECB stunned the financial community when it disclosed that it had already pumped over $500 billion into 390 euro-zone private banks, twice the amount expected.

Charlie McCreevy, the European Commissioner in charge of the Internal Market and Services, declared in October 2008 that an immediate goal of the Commission was to require central clearing of credit default swaps (CDS). The Commission was seeking the prompt creation of a central registry for such instruments that would record credit derivative instruments after trades have been confirmed. This would create a "golden" copy of those transactions. That goal was accomplished on July 31, 2009 when CDS on European reference entities began clearing through central counterparties regulated in the EU.

A Report of the High-Level Group on Financial Supervision in the EU, commonly referred to as "the de Larosière Report," that was published in February 2009, called for the "simplification and standardization of most OTC derivatives and the development of appropriate risk-mitigation techniques plus transparency measures." The de Larosière Report recommended strengthening the Level 3 committees on coordination of national regulators in the Lamfalussy process. It advocated the creation of a European Banking Authority, a European Insurance Authority and a European Securities Authority. These regulators would co-ordinate and arbitrate among national supervision regarding cross-border financial institutions; take steps to move towards a common European rulebook; and directly supervise the credit rating agencies.

Legislative proposals for implementing these recommendations were issued by the European Commission in September 2009. However, concerns were being raised over whether these regulators would interfere in the fiscal affairs of the individual member states. The proposed legislation would also create a European Systemic Risk Board, which would be composed of the 27 central bank governors from the EU member states. The de Larosière Report further recommended the creation of at least one well-capitalized "central counter party" (CCP), a.k.a. clearinghouse, to be supervised by the Committee of European Securities Regulators (CESR) and the European Central Bank (ECB).

The de Larosière Report called for "international level issuers of complex securities to retain on their books for the life of the instrument a meaningful amount of the underlying risk (non-hedged)." Regulators in the EU were also pressing for the immediate creation of a European based warehouse for CDS. They were seeking a central registry for such instruments that would record credit derivative instruments after trades have been confirmed. This would create a "golden" copy of those transactions. EU market participants were already acting on some of these recommendations. By July 2009, CDS dealers committed to start clearing eligible CDS on European reference entities and indices on these entities through one or more European CCP.

The European Commission has also identified four main goals for improving financial stability by regulating OTC derivatives markets:

> a) allow regulators and supervisors to have full knowledge about the transactions that take place in OTC derivatives markets[,] as well as the positions that are building in those markets; b) increase the transparency of OTC derivatives markets vis-à-vis their users; in particular more and better information about prices and volumes should be available; c) strengthen the operational efficiency of derivatives markets so as to ensure that OTC derivatives do not harm financial stability[;] and d) mitigate counterparty risks and promote centralized structures.

To achieve these goals, the EC wishes to use the following tactics: "(i) promoting further standardization, (ii) using central data repositories,

(iii) moving to CCP clearing, and (iv) moving trading to more public trading venues."

Regarding standardization, the European Commission would like to see as many CDS standardized as possible so that, ultimately, they could all be cleared through a clearinghouse. It views this as "a core building block in the Commission's endeavor to make derivatives markets efficient, safe and sound." * * *

The Leaders' Statement from the Group of 20 summit in Pittsburgh, Pa. also called for standardized OTC derivative contracts to be traded on exchanges or electronic trading platforms, where appropriate, and cleared through CCP by year-end 2012. The Group of 20 wanted other OTC derivative contracts to be reported to trade repositories and that non-centrally cleared contracts be subjected to higher capital requirements. To coordinate financial markets reform around the world, the Group of 20 also established the Financial Stability Board (FSB).The Group of 20 requested the "FSB and its relevant members to regularly assess implementation and whether it is sufficient to improve transparency in the derivatives markets, mitigate systemic risk, and protect against market abuse." * * *

The European Union announced to the Group of Twenty that it intended to create three pan-European regulatory bodies that would enforce common rules for banking, securities, and insurance. The three bodies would essentially involve beefing up three existing EU coordinating regulatory bodies for financial services. However, concerns were being raised over whether these regulators would interfere in the fiscal affairs of the individual member states. The proposed legislation would also create a European Systemic Risk Board, which would be composed of the 27 central bank governors from the EU member states. In addition, a new European System of Financial Supervisors would be created to regulate particular banks.

A renewed crisis broke out in Europe in early 2010. European markets fell in February over concerns with Greek government debt. Speculators using credit default swaps were blamed for worsening the situation, and it was claimed that Goldman Sachs & Co and others arranged swaps that concealed Greece's true financial condition (and debt) when it was seeking approval from the European Union to use the euro as its currency. Greece was offered a $40 billion support package from the European Union, but it turned out that the Greek debt problem was even worse than expected. Greece then sought to increase the bailout to $60 billion, seeking funds from the European Union and the IMF. That amount proved to be inadequate and $146.5 billion rescue package was agreed upon at the end of April. However, deadly violence broke out in Greece after the government acted to impose the harsh austerity measures demanded as a condition for the loan. The financial crisis that began in Greece spread to Spain and Portugal. The European Union announced a $1 trillion bailout for the affected countries on May 10, 2010. It had been prodded into action by the Obama administration, which reopened a swap facility with the European Union Central Bank that had been employed during the subprime crisis to assure liquidity in Europe. The crisis was driving down the euro and pushing gold to a new record $1,219.90 per ounce. The euro hit a four-year low on May 19, 2010, falling to $1.21. Germany imposed restriction on naked short sales on that day as a renewed credit crunch struck European borrowers. This unilateral and unexpected action by Germany sent stock markets reeling and irritated other European Union members.

RONALD FILLER AND ELIZABETH RITTER
ASK THE PROFESSORS: DID THE EUROPEAN COURT OF JUSTICE PROPERLY RULE BY DISMISSING THE U.K.'S ATTEMPT TO ANNUL ESMA'S REGULATION BANNING SHORT SELLING?
34 Fut. & Deriv. L. Rep (March 2014)

On January 22, 2014, the European Court of Justice ("ECJ") dismissed a case brought by the United Kingdom (U.K.), in which the U.K. sought to annul Article 28 of Regulation (EU) No. 236/2012 of the European Parliament and of the Council of the European Union regarding short selling activities. The U.K. government had brought this case on May 31,

Short selling, in general, consists of selling shares of common stock that are not owned by the Seller, who typically is betting that the price of that common stock will decline and thus be cheaper to buy back, resulting in a profit. In a "naked" short sale, the Seller does not borrow or arrange to borrow the securities in time to make delivery of the underlying stock to the Buyer within the standard three-day settlement period. Short selling can often result in sudden price volatility of a particular stock, especially if there is a large amount of short selling on a particular stock within a relatively short period of time. Many believe that short selling, in addition to reckless credit default swap (CDS) trading, created major price volatility in the months of September and October, 2008, that contributed, in part, to the 2008 financial crisis.

The Securities and Exchange Commission (SEC) has taken many different positions on short selling, ranging from permitting the activity either on a temporary or final basis, to restricting it with respect to certain types of stocks traded. In one press release, the SEC stated:

> "Short selling often can play an important role in the market for a variety of reasons, including contributing to efficient price discovery, mitigating market bubbles, increasing market liquidity, promoting capital formation, facilitating hedging and

other risk management activities, and, importantly, limiting upward market manipulations. There are, however, circumstances in which short selling can be used as a tool to manipulate the market."

As a result of "fails-to-deliver," which is a common occurrence in connection with short selling and the potential of abuse that may result from short selling, the SEC adopted Regulation SHO in 2005, which requires, among other things, firms that clear and settle trades, to purchase the shares to close out these fails-to-deliver within 13 days.

The SEC imposed a ban on short selling on financial stocks on September 19, 2008. Shortly thereafter, the SEC also adopted SEC Rule 10b–21, the "Naked Short Selling Antifraud Rule," to make it unlawful for any person:

> "to submit an order to sell a security if that person deceives a broker-dealer, participant of a registered clearing agency, or purchaser regarding his/her intention, or ability, to deliver the security by settlement date and that person fails to deliver the security by settlement date."

The SEC later established an interim temporary rule, which it made final on July 29, 2009, that resulted in the adoption of SEC Rule 204. Rule 204 was designed to make it a violation of Regulation SHO if a clearing firm does not purchase or borrow shares to close-out a fail-to-deliver that may result from a short sale within one day after the required settlement date, or T+4.

Many other countries also established bans on short selling, some of which continue to the present date. Given the importance of the financial services industry in London, the UK government has always taken a more aggressive view relating to restrictions placed on its financial services industry. This case is an example of other actions taken by the UK government to challenge other ESMA Regulations involving, among other things, restrictions on executive compensation.

This action was brought by the U.K. against the European Parliament and the Council of the European Union. The principal argument raised by the U.K. was simply that the European Securities and Market Authority ("ESMA") did not properly apply Regulation (EU) No 236/2012 (hereinafter referred to as "Regulation (EU) No 236").

ESMA was initially established by Regulation (EU) No 1095/2010 of the European Parliament ("EP") and of the Council of the European Union ("Council") on November 24, 2010 (hereinafter referred to as the "ESMA Regulation"). ESMA is part of the European System of Financial Supervision ("ESFS"), whose purpose is to supervise the EU's financial system. ESFS also comprises a Joint Committee of the various European Supervisory Authorities and those of the respective Member States.

Article 1(2) of the ESMA Regulation gives ESMA certain powers to legally bind the EU, and Articles 8 and 9 of the ESMA Regulation sets out its tasks regarding financial market participants. Specifically, ESMA Regulation 9(5) provides that ESMA may prohibit or restrict certain financial activities that may threaten the integrity or stability, in whole or in part, of the EU's financial system. Pursuant to Article 44(1), a Member State, such as the U.K., may request ESMA to reconsider any decisions that it may make. The U.K. government brought this case based on this Article.

Regulation (EU) No 236, which was adopted in March 2012, lays the foundation for regulations established by ESMA. In particular, ESMA may establish regulations relating to financial instruments, certain derivatives and certain debt instruments. Article 2(1) of Regulation (EU) No 236 defines a "short sale" to mean:

> "any sale of the share or debt instrument which the seller does not own at the time of entering into the agreement to sell, including such a sale where at the time of entering into the agreement to sell the seller has borrowed or agreed to borrow the share or debt instrument for delivery . . ."

Pursuant to Article 28 of Regulation (EU) No 236, ESMA may prohibit or impose conditions by natural or legal persons with respect to such short sales provided that such actions taken by ESMA (i) address a threat to the orderly functioning and integrity of the EU's financial markets or to its financial system, in whole or part, and (ii) no other competent authority (e.g., another EU country) has taken the necessary actions to address this threat. This is a conjunctive test. In making these determinations, ESMA must determine that its actions do not, among other things, create a risk of regulatory arbitrage or result in a detrimental effect on the efficiency of financial markets by, for example, reducing the liquidity in the market. If another EU country adopts, for example, a specific regulation that may differ from or conflict with ESMA's fundamental regulatory policies, then ESMA may notify that other EU country, after consulting with the European Systemic Risk Board ("ESRB") or with other authorities, that ESMA intends to take measures against the regulation adopted by that other EU country. The measure takes effect immediately after ESMA posts the notice on its website.

This threat to the orderly functioning and integrity of the EU financial system implies a very high standard before ESMA may act, that is: (i) any threat of serious financial, monetary or budgetary instability concerning a Member State, (ii) the possibility of a default by a Member State; (iii) any serious damage to the physical structures of important financial issuers, clearing and settlement systems and supervisors; or (iv) any serious disruption in any payment system or settlement process.

The U.K. government thus challenged the right of ESMA, pursuant to Article 28, to ban short selling, even if just for a temporary period.

The action, as noted above, was brought by the U.K. to annul Article 28 of Regulation (EU) No 236, which gave ESMA the powers noted above to ban short selling within the EU. Interestingly, Spain, France, Italy and the European Commission joined the action in support of the EP, thus opposing the U.K. action. * * *

The ECJ opinion noted that all of the parties in this case had cited the importance of the case of *Meroni & Co., Industrie Metallurgiche, S.A.S. v High Authority* of the European Coal and Steel Community, a case decided by this same court back on June 13, 1958. However, each party interpreted Meroni differently. The ECJ cited *Meroni* as holding that:

> " . . . the consequences resulting from a delegation of authority are very different depending on whether it involves clearly defined executive powers the exercise of which can, therefore be subject to strict review in the light of objective criteria determined by the delegating authority, or whether it involves a 'discretionary power implying a wide margin of discretion which may, according to the use which is made of it, make possible the execution of the actual economic policy."

The *Meroni* court ruled against the decision made by the regulatory bodies in that case. The ECJ, however, distinguished *Meroni* as that case involved entities governed by private law whereas ESMA is a EU entity, created by the EP. It then stated that, unlike the powers delegated to the bodies at issue in *Meroni*, in this case, Article 28 of Regulation (EU) No 236 is "circumscribed by various conditions and criteria which limit ESMA's discretion." The ECJ then stated:

1. ESMA clearly has the authority to adopt measures under Article 28(1) provided, however, that such measures address a threat to the orderly functioning and integrity of the EU financial system.

2. ESMA must take into account the extent to which the measure (e.g., the ban on short selling in this case) significantly addresses the so-called threat noted above. ESMA must therefore examine a significant number of the factors set forth in Articles 28(2) and (3) of Regulation (EU) No 236 before taking any such measure.

3. Pursuant to Articles 28(4) and (5), before adopting any such measure, ESMA must also consult with the ESRB and, if necessary, other relevant European bodies. Therefore,

ESMA's margin of discretion in adopting any such measure (e.g., the ban on short selling in this case) is circumscribed by both this consultation requirement and the temporary nature of the measure being taken.

4.   The ECJ then stated that ESMA's powers to temporarily ban short selling clearly complied with the requirements laid down in *Meroni*.

* * * The ECJ held that, under Article 28, ESMA may adopt rules affecting natural persons who enter into specific financial instruments and that Article 28 . . . Therefore, the U.K. failed to establish that the delegation of powers granted to ESMA under Article 28 is at odds with the condition that "only clearly defined executive powers may be delegated."

* * * The ECJ then held that, while the treaties did not contain any specific provision delegating powers to a EU body or agency, there is a presumption that such a possibility exists. The ECJ then inferred that the judicial review mechanisms that apply to EU bodies and agencies, as included in the treaties, are comparable to the decision-making powers granted to ESMA under Article 28. Therefore, Article 28 cannot be considered in isolation, and that ESMA was granted the necessary powers to intervene to deal with adverse developments that threaten the financial stability within the EU, including the power to impose temporary restrictions on short selling. * * *

The ECJ [further] held . . . that the EP may clearly delegate powers to an EU body or agency to implement harmonization among the Member States (e.g., EU countries) and those measures may be directed at certain persons, including natural persons or companies. The ECJ also held that the EP permitted rules to take a legislative form to ensure that regulations, such as on short selling, are applied in a uniform manner. The ECJ then held that Article 28, which was the basis behind ESMA's regulation to ban short selling, was clearly intended to harmonize the laws and regulations in the Member States relating to stock transactions and to improve the conditions for the establishment and functioning of the financial markets. . . .

What does this decision mean? While the heart of the decision deals with the validity of the delegation of authority by the Trilogue to European agencies, such as ESMA, the real test lies with the growth and powers granted to these agencies and whether these agencies actually improve the effectiveness and credibility of the European regulatory policies versus retaining that authority and power within the European Commission itself or by a Member State. The U.K. government clearly believed that it can and should be allowed to regulate financial firms located, and products sold, within the U.K. and should not be subject to the more harmonized EU rules established by ESMA. Some claimed that this case dealt a serious blow to the U.K.'s attempt to limit the power of the EU regulatory bodies. It will be interesting to see whether these agencies, such as ESMA, will work closely with regulatory agencies located within a EU country, such as the U.K. Financial Conduct Authority, or take on a more autonomous role.

On the specific issue of short selling, things have changed dramatically since the 2008 financial crisis. For many years, it has been a roller-coaster ride on this issue with prohibitions, followed by temporary permissibility, followed by additional regulatory approaches around the globe. In this case, the interest of a major financial center, London, lost its battle to regulate itself to the need for a more harmonized financial regulatory world within the entire EU. It will also be interesting to see whether this movement toward greater harmonization within the EU has an effect on U.S. regulations. Just witness the recent Joint Statement made by Acting CFTC Chair Mark Wetjen and European Commissioner Michel Barnier, in which they announced that the staffs at the CFTC and the EC have made significant progress toward harmonizing a regulatory framework for CFTC- regulated swap execution facilities ("SEFs") and EU-regulated multilateral trading facilities ("MTFs").

Another important policy issue is whether the increased amount of financial regulations within Europe produces the necessary results. This same debate is taking place here in the U.S. Moreover, in the U.S., we have a very large number of regulatory agencies, especially when you consider the roles played by the States in regulating banks, insurance companies and even securities firms. An interesting regulatory policy argument lies with whether more or less regulatory agencies prove to be beneficial or not.

One final point is the response by the U.K. government to the ECJ decision. On February 3, 2014, in a Written Answer issued by the U.K. government to a question raised by Lord Myners, in which the Commercial Secretary to the Treasury, Lord Deighton, stated:

> "The Government is disappointed that the Court of Justice of the European Justice has not upheld the UK's challenge to annul Article 28 of the Short Selling Regulation. We have consistently said we want tough financial regulation that works, but any powers conferred on EU agencies must be consistent with the EU treaties and ensure legal certainty. However, this ruling bears no impact on the day-to-day application of the Regulation."

NOTES

1. The European Court of Justice (ECJ) decision in the short selling case clearly favored the interest of the entire EU to provide a more harmonized

regulatory model, rather than to allow each Member State to permit trading that other Member States opposed.

2. The short selling decision by the ECJ was the culmination of a major effort to update financial regulation in the European Union (EU). In 2011, the EU created three committees that exercise "advisory powers" over financial services in member states. They are the European Securities and Markets Authority (ESMA), the European Banking Authority (EBA), and the European Insurance and Occupational Pensions Authority (EIOPA), as well as the Joint Committee of the European Supervisory Authorities (Joint Committee). In addition, a European Systemic Risk Board (ESRB) was established. Together with national supervisory authorities, these new authorities are meant to ensure improved and harmonized financial supervision in the EU. /internal% market/"nances/committees/index% en.htm (Nov. 13,2009).

3. The new European Securities and Marketing Authority (ESMA) began operations in 2012. Its mission is to create a multi-dimensional supervisory approach to financial services regulation in the EU and to develop a single rulebook for Europe. ESMA will seek to drive the convergence of national supervisory activities with EU regulations.

4. The European Commission (EC) adopted a European Market Infrastructure Regulation (EMIR) that became effective on August 16, 2012. EMIR:

> will require entities that enter into any form of derivative contract, including interest rate, foreign exchange, equity, credit and commodity derivatives, to:
>
>> report every derivative contract that they enter to a trade repository;
>>
>> implement new risk management standards, including operational processes and margining, for all bilateral over-the-counter (OTC) derivatives i.e. trades that are not cleared by a CCP [central counterparty]; and
>>
>> clear, via a CCP, those OTC derivatives subject to a mandatory clearing obligation.

FSA, *EMIR—What You Need to Know*, available at http://www.fsa.gov.uk/about/what/international/emir (accessed on August 28, 2013). ESMA will also supervise Trade Repositories under EMIR and will coordinate supervision for Central Counterparties.

5. The EC published proposals for a second Markets in Financial Instruments Directive (MiFID II) in October 2011. It also proposed a new Markets in Financial Instruments Regulation (MiFIR). Agreement on MiFID II and MiFIR was reached by the Trialogue (European Council, European Parliament and European Commission) on January 14, 2014. Among other things, they will increase regulation over derivatives trading, including, (i)

mandatory trading for cleared OTC derivatives; (ii) establishment of new trading facilities (organized trading facilities (OTFs) and multilateral trading facilities (MTFs); (iii) position limits on certain commodity derivatives; (iv) new enhanced reporting and record-keeping obligations; (v) increased investor protections; and (vi) new trading rules for equity instruments. Implementation of these rules may not be complete until 2016, and maybe even later.

6. As noted above, the EC has been one of the stronger critics of the CFTC's Cross Border Guidance. See the transcript of the Global Markets Advisory Committee hearing that was held on February 12, 2014, which can be found at www.cftc.gov.

7. In July 2013, the CFTC, ESMA and the European Council sought to work together to harmonize cross border conflicts, with each agreeing to establish "substituted compliance" concepts. One such matter involves the recognition of central counterparties (CCPs) located outside the respective jurisdiction (e.g., the CFTC recognizing non-US CCPs). This has been referred to as the "Path Forward Statement." This regulatory harmonization is still a work in progress. See also the "Statement by the CFTC and the European Commission on progress relating to the implementation of the 2013 Path Forward Statement", issued by CFTC Acting Chair Mark Wetjen and European Commissioner Michel Barnier on February 12, 2014; CFTC Press Release 6857–14, February 12, 2014), which can be found at: http:www.cftc.gov/PressRoom/PressReleases/pr6857-14. As a result, the Division of Market Oversight at the CFTC issued CFTC No-Action Letter 14–15, which provided time-limited relief for multilateral trading facilities (MTFs) overseen by competent authorities within a European Mamber State from the swap execution facility (SEF) registration requirements set out in Section 5h(a)(1) of the CEA. CFTC No-Action Letter 14–15. See also Questions and Answers, Implementation of the Regulation (EU) No 648/2012 on OTC derivatives. Central counterparties and trade repositories (EMIR), issued by ESMA on December 20, 2013, ESMA/2013/1959.

8. IOSCO

The International Organization of Securities Commissions (IOSCO) is a coordinating body for financial services regulation around the globe. IOSCO's website describes its role as follows:

> The International Organization of Securities Commissions (IOSCO), established in 1983, is the acknowledged international body that brings together the world's securities regulators and is recognized as the global standard setter for the securities sector. IOSCO develops, implements, and promotes adherence to internationally recognized standards for securities regulation, and is working intensively with the G20 and the Financial Stability Board (FSB) on the global regulatory reform agenda.

IOSCO's membership regulates more than 95% of the world's securities markets. Its members include over 120 securities regulators and 80 other securities markets participants (i.e. stock exchanges, financial regional and international organizations etc.). IOSCO is the only international financial regulatory organization which includes all the major emerging markets jurisdictions within its membership.

The member agencies currently assembled together in the International Organization of Securities Commissions have resolved, through its permanent structures:

> to cooperate in developing, implementing and promoting adherence to internationally recognized and consistent standards of regulation, oversight and enforcement in order to protect investors, maintain fair, efficient and transparent markets, and seek to address systemic risks;

> to enhance investor protection and promote investor confidence in the integrity of securities markets, through strengthened information exchange and cooperation in enforcement against misconduct and in supervision of markets and market intermediaries; and

> to exchange information at both global and regional levels on their respective experiences in order to assist the development of markets, strengthen market infrastructure and implement appropriate regulation.

http://www.iosco.org/about/ (accessed on August 29, 2013).

Among other things, IOSCO has adopted thirty-eight Objectives and Principles of Securities Regulation that are devoted to protecting investors; ensuring that markets are fair, efficient and transparent; and reducing systemic risk. http://www.iosco.org/about/?section=obj_prin (accessed on August 29, 2013).

ROBERTA S. KARMEL
IOSCO'S RESPONSE TO THE FINANCIAL CRISIS
37 J. Corp. L. 849 (2012)

The International Organization of Securities Commissions (IOSCO) was transformed in 1983 from an inter-American regional association of securities regulators into an international body. It is now an association of securities commissions and main financial regulators for more than 100 countries that regulate more than 90% of the world's securities markets. IOSCO's primary role is to promote high standards of securities regulation and to act as a forum for national regulators to cooperate with one another. Like other international financial bodies, IOSCO has responded to the financial crisis of 2008. Previously, in response to the Asian financial crisis of 1998, IOSCO developed its Objectives and Principles of Securities Regulation to establish a framework for the regulation of securities markets, intermediaries, securities issuers, and collective investment schemes. Ten years later, IOSCO determined that its objectives and principles were not designed to prevent systemic risk and were therefore insufficient. IOSCO thus revised its objectives and principles and added eight new principles, including two that specifically focused on systemic risk. IOSCO's ongoing efforts to support these new Principles are parallel to efforts by other financial regulators to deal with systemic risk. Yet, IOSCO's efforts focus on somewhat different issues in the capital markets than the issues of interest to bank regulators.

Systemic risk in the securities markets is not primarily about prudential regulation. Rather, it concerns activities by non-banking intermediaries, sometimes referred to as the shadow banking sector, transparency and soundness in the capital markets, trading practices, and risks from market innovations. The risks posed by these intermediaries are in some ways more subtle and difficult to understand and control than the risks posed by too-big-to-fail banks. Further, in a number of the areas in which IOSCO is attempting to set standards, the United States and the European Union have taken some divergent regulatory paths, and Asian markets may be engaging in competitive regulatory strategies that pose a threat to established markets in the United States and Europe. * * *

Since IOSCO has no enforcement mechanisms aside from peer pressure, and its members are so numerous and varied, it is unrealistic to expect rigorous and detailed harmonization of new standards of conduct or regulation. Nevertheless, IOSCO can play a useful role in highlighting critical emerging areas where securities regulation is in need of reform, and it has done so with regard to a number of systemic risk issues in the trading markets. II. IOSCO's Objectives and Principles. The IOSCO principles report of June 2010 sets forth three objectives of securities regulation. These objectives include: protecting investors (including customers or other consumers of financial services); ensuring that markets are fair, efficient, and transparent; and reducing systemic risk. It is worth noting at the outset that since the United States is the only country in the world that separates securities and financial futures regulation, IOSCO's references to security markets include the derivatives markets. The 38 IOSCO principles are grouped into nine categories: regulators; self-regulation; securities regulation enforcement; cooperation in regulation; issuers; auditors, credit rating agencies, and other information providers; collective investment schemes; market intermediaries; and secondary markets. The first four relate to the organization, powers, and functioning of regulatory agencies. When

IOSCO revised its principles in an attempt to provide guidance on how to address the issues highlighted by the crisis, it adopted two of its eight new principles relating to the regulator that focus on risk. Principle six addresses the securities regulator's role and conduct in identifying, assessing, and mitigating systemic risk, and Principle seven exhorts the regulator to regularly review the regulatory perimeter. IOSCO is currently developing an appropriate methodology to support these new principles and has already incorporated the identification and mitigation of systemic risk in its strategic mission and goals for the next five years. It also believes that it is well suited to lead responses to emerging regulatory issues. IOSCO's fifth category of principles relating to issuers touches on risk in that it states that there should be "full, accurate and timely disclosure of financial results, risk and other information which is material to investors' decisions."

Like the principles relating to issuers, the remaining principles relate to players in the capital markets, who are gatekeepers, members of the shadow banking system, or non-bank intermediaries. Some of these principles now focus on risk. Principle 27 relates to collective investment shares, which promotes regulation that ensures "a proper and disclosed basis for asset valuation and the pricing and redemption of units in a collective investment scheme," and Principle 28, which calls for regulation to "ensure that hedge funds and/or hedge fund managers are subject to appropriate oversight." Under the principles for market intermediaries, Principle 30 provides that there should be initial and ongoing capital and other prudential requirements for market intermediaries that reflect the risks they undertake, and Principle 32 provides that there should be procedures for dealing with the failure of a market intermediary to contain systemic risk. Finally, under the principles for secondary markets, Principle 37 provides that regulation should aim to ensure the proper management of large exposures, default risk, and market disruption, and Principle 38 provides that securities settlement systems and central counterparties should be subject to regulation to reduce risk. The IOSCO objectives and principles are very general, so it is necessary to look to more specific papers to appreciate the strictures on regulating risk by securities commissions. IOSCO published one such paper, entitled Mitigating Systemic Risk: A Role for Securities Regulators, in February 2011. IOSCO's Technical Committee prepared this paper; the committee is comprised of regulators from the major capital markets, and U.S. and European regulators often dominate it. The paper points out that securities regulation has traditionally focused on disclosure and business conduct oversight instead of systemic risk, which was relegated by monetary authorities and financial regulators. This traditional split in oversight proved insufficient in the 2008 crisis, particularly when risks arose from areas not within the traditional oversight of securities regulators. Examples of factors that threatened financial stability and were not mitigated by business conduct oversight included: the role of the shadow banking system; "the interconnectedness of the global market place"; the lack of incentives that market participants had to curb inappropriate risks; the innovation and complexity of financial products that resulted in information asymmetries and inadequate disclosure; the increasingly more difficult and costly management of conflicts; "the cyclicality of financial markets"; and the inherent risks in over-the-counter (OTC) markets' "lack of transparency and robust infrastructure." The IOSCO paper analyzed the sources and transmission of systemic risks as coming from size, interconnectedness, lack of substitutes and concentration, lack of transparency, leverage, market participant behavior, and information asymmetry and moral hazard. The Technical Committee urged regulators to be mindful of regulatory gaps and explained how these gaps can contribute to the build-up of systemic risk. Most notably, exemptions for particular market elements from regulatory oversight and the policy considerations underlying these exemptions should be considered and evaluated on an ongoing basis. Similarly, regulators should address gaps that arise from activities that are currently lightly regulated, as well as new market activities for which there are not yet regulatory responses. To address regulatory gaps arising outside of its jurisdiction, a securities regulator should conduct regular reviews of the perimeter of its regulation, coordinate with other regulators who do have the supervisory authority, and cooperate with international regulators.

This analysis might seem very general, but it pinpoints several of the causes of the financial meltdown: the failure to regulate swaps and credit derivatives; the failure to regulate mortgage brokers; the failure to regulate hedge funds or credit rating agencies; the inadequate regulation of securitized products; and U.S. Securities and Exchange Commission (SEC) exemptions for sophisticated investors. These failures were endemic to a deregulatory philosophy in the United States and elsewhere. It is difficult to blame securities regulators when, at least in the United States, Congress and the courts were also responsible for these regulatory failures. Where regulated industries have so much power and influence over lawmakers, there is a lack of political will to engage in vigorous regulation even when regulators perceive the dangers of insufficient market place standards. Nevertheless, IOSCO is now starting to build a research capacity and to adopt a strategy emphasizing the need for securities regulators to identify, monitor, and manage systemic risks. The IOSCO paper on mitigating systemic risk explains the tools available to securities regulators that can reinforce the stability of the financial system. These tools are "transparency and disclosure; business conduct oversight; organizational, prudential and governance requirements; prevention of risk transmission" through rules regarding trading infrastructure; and "emergency powers." In addition, IOSCO, as an international body of regulators, stressed "intra-jurisdictional communication and exchange of information among regulators about systemic risk . . . to help prevent the emergence of gaps in oversight and identify possible transfers of risk or cross-sectorial risks." Regulators were asked to leverage the work of other regulators and call on self-regulatory organizations to help, when applicable.

On the international level, securities regulators were encouraged to continue their collaboration "through IOSCO to improve transparency and disclosure in various international securities markets" and "be active participants in international supervisory colleges." The paper also recommended that regulators promote confidence in markets through adequate communication about risk. Since its onset, the financial crisis' causes have been widely debated, but the consensus is that the main culprits are financial innovations creating leverage, such as collateralized debt obligations, credit default swaps, and other structured investment vehicles. According to IOSCO: [A] new framework for financial innovation [should] therefore include greater consideration of the risks attached to innovations at the level of financial institutions and regulators; close collaboration between supervisors and regulators to consider the various potential impacts of innovations and transfers of risk; implication for the resources of regulators needed to maintain appropriate levels of surveillance and control; and consideration of the international dimension of financial innovation in order to prevent regulatory arbitrage. IOSCO also urges securities regulators to periodically review their regulatory coverage of financing activities to ensure that none escape appropriate regulation.

Regulators should do so by "regularly surveying activity in the financial and securities markets to understand the development in those markets and [to] identify opportunities for cooperation and changes; setting internal thresholds for intervening in new and expanding markets and activities; and setting regulatory goals for intervention" [to] evaluate the appropriateness of and need for such measures. One of the key concerns of financial regulators in the wake of the crisis is the shadow banking sector. This is of special importance to securities regulators since shadow banking enterprises are not banks subject to supervision by others. If such an enterprise is considered a systemically important financial institution in the United States by the Financial Stability Oversight Commission (FSOC), the enterprise will become subject to regulation by the Federal Reserve Board. It is unclear whether large hedge funds, for example, will fall into this category. IOSCO has recommended that, together with prudential regulators, securities regulators should consider whether any action should be taken with respect to shadow banking entities and activities, and if so, how the monitoring and regulation should be carried out.

IOSCO's role is to provide guidance and develop policies and standards on when and how to use the tools available to securities regulators. Its first commitment to this effort is to build a research capacity that will initially focus on the research of systemic risk and put forth an annual report to identify the most important systemic risks for securities regulation at a global level. IOSCO also intends to conduct risk analyses that focus on risks in specific products, market segments, or technologies. Members are encouraged to enter into a bilateral or multilateral "Memoranda of Understanding" to address cooperation and collaboration on the global level, especially with regard to sharing data and coordinating action on risks. IOSCO has also engaged member-SROs on specific risk topics since SROs are one step closer to the markets than their supervisory authorities.

The organization is also considering holding stakeholder consultation, where "IOSCO policy makers discuss their work program with representatives of major industry organizations" and "organizing an intensive dialogue with top-level industry groups to discuss important systemic risks." "On certain topics, IOSCO recognizes that it needs to work closely with other global bodies, such as the G-20, FSB, BCBS, CPSS, IAIS, ESRB, IMF and World Bank and when appropriate, [certain] domestic bodies." Finally, another "activity that could be within the realm of IOSCO's global work could be the improvement to transparency and disclosure through setting standards for the collection of data and standardizing documentation relevant to systemic risk."

NOTES

1. David Wright, the Secretary General of IOSCO, in a speech before the Securities and Futures Commission 2014 Regulatory Reform Program held in Hong Kong on January 27, 2014, expressed concern that the U.S. and Europe were imposing a global regulatory standard that was ignoring other countries. He stated:

> Today, we have two sharks in the pond. As they draw up rules, they say 'abide by our rules or you won't do business with the U.S. or EU.' Effectively, the rest of the world is a regulatory taker and that's not fair. Fast forward 10 years when there are more big markets, what's to stop China, Brazil, India or Indonesia saying 'if you want to do business with us, here's our rulebook.'

Viren Vaghela, writing for Asia Risk, available at http://www.risk.net/asia-risk/news/2324849/iosco-secretary-general-slams-us-and-europe-as-regulatory-sharks (accesed on March 14, 2013).

2. On January 29, 2014, IOSCO published recommendations regarding the protections of client assets held at intermediaries as well as a survey of the cient protection regimes in some twenty countries. See, www.iosco/org/library/pubdocs/pdf/IOSCOPD436.pdf (accessed on March 17, 2014). IOSCO

also published a report in March 2014 that compares differences and gaps in the capital adequacy standards of securities commissions around the world. See, IOSCO, A Comparison and Analysis of Prudential Standards in the Securities Sector, available at http://www.iosco.org/library/pubdocs/pdf/ IOSCOPD438.pdf (visited on March 17, 2014).

Professors Ronald H. Filler and Jerry W. Markham

PROFESSOR RONALD H. FILLER

Ronald H. Filler is a Professor of Law and Director of the Financial Services Law Institute at New York Law School, located in New York City. He is also the Program Director of its LL.M. in Financial Services Law Graduate Program. Prior to joining the faculty of NYLS in 2008, Professor Filler was a Managing Director in the Capital Markets Prime Services Division at Lehman Brothers Inc., where he was responsible for various business, legal and regulatory matters involving the global futures markets. Prior to joining Lehman Brothers in 1993, he was a Partner and Member of the Executive Committee at Vedder Price Kaufman & Kammholz, a large law firm located in Chicago, IL and worked at various other law firms and brokerage firms earlier in his career. He is a member of, or has served on, numerous industry boards and risk advisory committees, once served as the Chair of the Global Markets Advisory Committee of the U.S. Commodity Futures Trading Commission. He is currently a Public Director and Member of the Executive Committee of the National Futures Association, a Public Director and Chair of the Regulatory Oversight Committee (ROC) of Swap-EX, a swap execution facility, and a member of the Board of Directors of Global Clearing & Settlement, Inc., a firm providing insurance to the financial industry. Professor Filler has spoken at over 200 business and law programs during his 35+ year career in the global futures and derivatives industry. He is also the President of Ronald H. Filler & Associates, LLC, a firm that provides consulting, training and expert witness testimony services. He received a B.A. degree from the University of Illinois in 1970, a J.D. degree from George Washington University Law School in 1973 and an LL.M. in Taxation degree from Georgetown University Law Center in 1975.

WORK TELEPHONE:　　(212) 431-2812

CELL:　　　　　　　　(973) 495-8609

WORK EMAIL:　　　　ronald.filler@nyls.edu

PROFESSOR JERRY W. MARKHAM

Jerry W. Markham is Professor of Law at Florida International University at Miami (FIU). He came to FIU from the University of North Carolina where he was a Professor of Law for twelve years. Before that, he served for ten years as an adjunct professor at the Georgetown Law Center.

In addition to numerous law journal articles, Markham is the author of a three-volume financial history of the United States that was selected as a Choice Outstanding Academic Title. He also published a book on the Enron era scandals, and has published a two-volume work on the subprime crisis that shook the nation in 2008.

Markham has co-authored four casebooks on corporate law and banking regulation. He also has published a two-volume treatise and a history book on the law of commodity futures regulation, and was the principal author of a two-volume treatise on broker-dealer regulation.

Before his move to academia, Professor Markham served as secretary and counsel, Chicago Board Options Exchange, Inc.; chief counsel, Division of Enforcement, United States Commodity Futures Trading Commission; attorney, Securities and Exchange Commission; and a partner with the international firm of Rogers & Wells (now Clifford Chance) in Washington, D.C. In law school, he served as Editor-in-Chief of the Kentucky Law Journal and was named to the Order of the Coif.

Professor Markham is also the chairman of Markham Consulting Inc., where he serves as a consultant and expert witness on financial industry issues.

APPENDIX A

CROSS MARGINING AND NETTING AGREEMENT OF FILLER & MARKHAM INC.

■ ■ ■

Cross Margining and Netting Agreement

Cross Margining and Netting Agreement ("**CMN Agreement**") dated as of _____, 20__, by and among _____ ("**Counterparty**"), Filler & Markham Inc. ("FMI") Filler & Markham International, ("FMIE"), Filler & Markham Capital Markets, Ltd. ("FMCM"), FMI, FMIE and FMCM are hereinafter referred to collectively as the "**FMI Entities**" and each as a "**FMI Entity**".

WITNESSETH:

WHEREAS, the FMI Entities have made, and may from time to time make, extensions of credit to Counterparty pursuant to Base Contracts that the FMI Entities have entered into, or may from time to time enter into, with Counterparty;

WHEREAS, Counterparty has requested the FMI Entities to enter into this CMN Agreement in order to reduce its operational expense in respect of the Base Contracts; and

WHEREAS, the FMI Entities wish to reduce their collective risk in respect of Counterparty.

NOW, THEREFORE, in consideration of the foregoing premises and for other good and valuable consideration, the receipt and adequacy of which is hereby acknowledged, the parties hereto hereby agree as follows:

1. Definitions.

Capitalized terms used in this CMN Agreement and not otherwise defined herein shall have the meanings ascribed thereto in Exhibit I.

2. Margin Requirements; Excesses and Deficits.

2.1. *Calculation of Margin Requirement.* By the Margin Notification Deadline on each Business Day, one or more FMI Entities shall (i) determine the Basic Margin Requirement for each Base Contract, (ii) determine the Additional Margin Requirement for all of the Base Contracts, and (iii) determine the Margin Requirement for each Base Contract by allocating the Additional Margin Requirement between the Base Contracts as they shall determine in their sole discretion.

2.2. *Transfer of Margin Requirement.* Subject to Sections 2.3 and 2.4, (i) to the extent that the Margin Requirement determined in respect of any Base Contract pursuant to Section 2.1 is due to a FMI Entity from Counterparty, Counterparty shall Transfer Eligible Credit Support with a Value equal to that Margin Requirement to that FMI Entity and (ii) to the extent that the Margin Requirement so determined in respect of any Base Contract is due to Counterparty from a FMI Entity, that FMI Entity shall Transfer Eligible Credit Support with a Value equal to that Margin Requirement to Counterparty.

2.3. *Application of Excesses to Deficits.* If Eligible Credit Support is due from one or more FMI Entities to Counterparty pursuant to Section 2.2 in respect of any Base Contract (that Base Contract being "in **Excess**") at the same time that Eligible Credit Support is due from Counterparty to one or more FMI Entities in respect of any other Base Contract (that Base Contract being "in **Deficit**"), each FMI Entity that is a party to a Base Contract that is in Excess (each such FMI Entity, a "**FMI Transferor**") shall, subject to Section 4.2, Transfer on behalf of Counterparty Eligible Credit Support otherwise due to Counterparty to one or more FMI Entities party to a Base Contract in Deficit (each such FMI Entity, a "**FMI Transferee**") to reduce the amount such Base Contract is in Deficit, until such Base Contract in Excess is no longer in Excess or there are no more Base Contracts in Deficit; provided, however, that if the FMI Transferor does not Transfer Eligible Credit Support pursuant to this Section 2.3, the FMI Transferor shall not be in breach of this Section 2.3 or Section 2.2 but Counterparty shall be relieved of its obligations to Transfer Eligible Credit Support to the FMI Transferees to the extent (but only to the extent) the FMI Transferor does not Transfer such Eligible Credit Support. Eligible Credit Support to be Transferred by the FMI Transferors shall be allocated among the FMI Transferees as they agree.

2.4. *Return of Remaining Excesses.* Subject to Section 5.8 hereof, to the extent that a Base Contract remains in Excess after the Transfers set forth in Section 2.3 (a "**Remaining Excess**"), upon receipt of a written request from Counterparty, the relevant FMI Transferor shall Transfer to Counterparty Eligible Credit Support the Value of which does not exceed such Remaining Excess.

2.5. *Manner of Delivery and Holding Transferred Credit Support.* Eligible Credit Support Transferred pursuant to this Section 2 in respect of any Base Contract shall be delivered and held subject to the terms on which Eligible Credit Support is required to be Transferred and, if applicable, held under that Base Contract, whether such Eligible Credit Support is Transferred to fulfill a Basic Margin Requirement or the portion of the Additional Margin Requirement allocated to that Base Contract.

3. Timing of Transfers.

3.1. *Transfers by the FMI Entities.* Any Transfer that is required to be made pursuant to Section 2.3 or 2.4 shall be made by the Transfer Deadline on the Business Day written request is received by the relevant FMI Entity unless such request is sent after the Margin Notification Deadline, in which case such FMI Entity shall make such Transfer by the Transfer Deadline on the following Business Day.

3.2. *Transfers by Counterparty.* By the Margin Notification Deadline on each Business Day, a FMI Entity shall, by a single notice, notify Counterparty of the aggregate amount of Eligible Credit Support required to be Transferred by Counterparty in respect of the Margin Requirements (after taking account of any Transfers that will be made by the FMI Entities on Counterparty's behalf as set forth in Section 2.3). By the Transfer Deadline on each Business Day, Counterparty shall make all Transfers required to be made pursuant to such notice, unless such notice is sent after the Margin Notification Deadline, in which case Counterparty shall make all Transfers required to be made pursuant to such notice by the Transfer Deadline on the following Business Day.

4. Allocation of Credit Support; Netting of Transfers; Cash Transfers; Regulatory Requirements; U.S. Dollar Equivalent.

4.1. *Allocation of Credit Support.* To the extent that any Transfer from one FMI Entity to another takes place or is deemed to take place pursuant to Section 2.3, this Section 4.1 or Section 4.2, the Transfer shall be deemed to satisfy (in whole or, as the case may be, in part) the obligation pursuant to Section 2.2 of the FMI Transferor to Transfer the relevant Eligible Credit Support to Counterparty and Counterparty's obligation to Transfer the relevant Eligible Credit Support to the FMI Transferee. Accordingly, any such Transfer or deemed Transfer shall be deemed to constitute the Transfer of Credit Support from the FMI Transferor to Counterparty and the Transfer of

Credit Support from Counterparty to the FMI Transferee as a return of, or an addition to, Credit Support pursuant to the terms of a Base Contract, or as a repricing of a Base Contract, as determined by the FMI Transferor or the FMI Transferee, as applicable, in its sole discretion pursuant to the terms of the Base Contract in Excess or in Deficit, as applicable. Without prejudice to Section 2.2, which FMI Entity will act as FMI Transferor or FMI Transferee shall be determined by the FMI Entities in their sole discretion, except that where a Transfer is necessary for any Regulatory Requirements to be satisfied, the Transfer shall first be effected in such a way as to satisfy those Regulatory Requirements.

4.2. *Optional Netting.* If Counterparty and any FMI Entity would otherwise be required pursuant to one or more Base Contracts to Transfer on the same day Credit Support, payments or deliveries to or among one another in the same currency or in the same type of non-cash asset, one or more FMI Entities may, at their option, calculate the netting of any or all such Transfers so that fewer Transfers need be made. One or more FMI Entities shall determine whether and the extent to which any such netting results in a deemed Transfer from a FMI Entity to Counterparty and from Counterparty (acting through a FMI Entity or Entities on its behalf) to a FMI Entity, the nature of such Transfer, and the allocation of such Transfer to one or more Base Contracts pursuant to Section 4.1.

4.3. *Reallocation of Credit Support and Collateral.* One or more FMI Entities may for any purpose and at any time, including to satisfy or secure one or more Obligations of any FMI Affiliate to Counterparty or Counterparty to any FMI Affiliate, or to reallocate any Credit Support from a Base Contract with one FMI Entity to another Base Contract with another FMI Entity, elect to Transfer, cause to be Transferred, or allocate Credit Support, Collateral or payments to one or more FMI Affiliates or to itself (the "**Transferee**"). Any such Transfer shall be deemed to constitute (a) the Transfer to Counterparty of Credit Support or Collateral from the FMI Entity to which such Credit Support or Collateral had been allocated and (b) the Transfer of Credit Support or Collateral from Counterparty to the Transferee pursuant to the terms of any Base Contract or other arrangement between Counterparty and the Transferee and (where applicable) this Agreement. Any Transfer by a FMI Affiliate of a payment otherwise due from a FMI Entity to Counterparty to a FMI Entity shall be considered to be a collection by such other FMI Entity on Receivables Collateral.

4.4. *Cash Transfers.* Notwithstanding anything to the contrary in any Base Contract, if a FMI Entity has been Transferred non-cash Credit Support under a Base Contract and such FMI Entity is required pursuant to Section 2 to Transfer Eligible Credit Support in respect of such Base Contract to Counterparty, such FMI Entity may satisfy such Obligation by Transferring cash, even if such Base Contract does not provide for repricing. In such a case, such FMI Entity shall be deemed to have Transferred such cash as Eligible Credit Support to Counterparty under such Base Contract and to have retained the non-cash Eligible Credit Support as Eligible Credit Support under such Base Contract.

4.5. *Regulatory Requirements.* Notwithstanding anything to the contrary herein, all actions of each party hereto, and all calculations hereunder, are subject to all Regulatory Requirements. Without limiting the foregoing, no Transfer of Credit Support or payment (including by means of netting) shall be made or required if such Transfer would violate any Regulatory Requirement, and any FMI Entity shall have the right to require any Transfer of Credit Support from Counterparty at any time in order to satisfy any Regulatory Requirement. Notwithstanding anything to the contrary herein, no FMI Entity shall be required under any provision of this Agreement to take any action to satisfy a Regulatory Requirement applicable to Counterparty if, after taking such action, any Regulatory Requirement applicable to any FMI Entity would fail to be satisfied.

4.6. *U.S. Dollar Equivalents.* All Basic Margin Requirements and Additional Margin Requirements in currencies other than U.S. Dollars shall be converted into and expressed in their U.S. Dollar Equivalents, unless otherwise determined by one or more FMI Entities in their sole discretion.

4.7. *Interest.* (a) In the event there is no other agreement that provides for interest to be paid upon cash Credit Support Transferred by a FMI Entity to Counterparty in respect of a Base Contract, Counterparty shall pay interest upon any cash Credit Support Transferred by a FMI Entity in respect of such Base Contract at the Applicable Rate from (and including) the date such cash Credit Support is Transferred to (but excluding) the date on which such cash Credit Support is returned.

(b) In the event there is no other agreement that provides for interest to be paid upon cash Credit Support Transferred by Counterparty to a FMI Entity in respect of a Base Contract, FMI shall pay interest upon any cash Credit Support Transferred by Counterparty in respect of such Base Contract at the customary rate for such market.

5.   Remedies upon Close-out Event.

5.1. *Close-out.* Upon the occurrence of any Close-out Event, each FMI Entity shall be entitled at any time and from time to time, without notice, to cause the Close-out of any or all Base Contracts, determine related Settlement Amounts, and take such other actions as may be permitted or provided for under any of the Base Contracts (but without regard to any cure periods, notice requirements, dispute resolution provisions or other timing requirements specified in any such Base Contract) or Applicable Law. Subject to Section 5.2, upon Close-out of any Base Contract, the Settlement Amount for such Base Contract shall be due.

5.2. *Other Remedies upon Close-out Event.* Upon the occurrence of any Close-out Event, each FMI Entity shall have the right to net the U.S. Dollar Equivalents of the Settlement Amounts due from it to Counterparty and from Counterparty to such FMI Entity under all Base Contracts between Counterparty and such FMI Entity, so that a single settlement payment (the "**Net Settlement Payment**") shall be payable by or to Counterparty and such FMI Entity, which Net Settlement Payment shall be immediately due and payable (subject to the other provisions hereof, to the provisions of any Base Contract, except as modified hereby, or Applicable Law granting a FMI Entity rights relating to collateral, setoff, netting and recoupment). Each FMI Entity shall also be entitled to:

(a) exercise all rights and remedies of a secured party under the UCC in respect of the Collateral;

(b) retain, liquidate, apply, collect on and set off any or all Collateral delivered under any Contract against any Net Settlement Payment or other Obligation owed to it or any other FMI Entity under any Contract;

(c) set off and net any Net Settlement Payment or other Obligation owed by it or any other FMI Entity under any Contract against (i) any Securities and Cash Collateral delivered to Counterparty by any FMI Entity under any Contract and (ii) any Net Settlement Payment or other Obligation owed by Counterparty to it or any other FMI Entity; and

(d) exercise any other remedies provided under this CMN Agreement or Applicable Law.

5.3. *Interest.* Interest shall be payable on each Net Settlement Payment (or any other amount) owed to a FMI Entity by Counterparty, after taking into account the provisions herein in relation to collateral, setoff, netting and recoupment, at the Applicable Default Rate, as determined by the FMI Entity to which such Net Settlement Payment is owed, from (and including) the date such Net Settlement Payment (or any other amount) is due to (but excluding) the date that such Net Settlement Payment (or any other amount) is paid or otherwise satisfied.

5.4. *Priorities.* Unless otherwise agreed by the relevant FMI Entities, the exercise of remedies under this Section 5 shall be subject in all events to the priority of security interests as set forth in Section 6 hereof, the relative rights of a First Priority FMI Entity and of the Second Priority FMI Entities, and the setoff, recoupment and other rights of a FMI Entity party to a Base Contract that is Receivables Collateral being prior to the security interest of the FMI Entities in such Receivables Collateral.

5.5. *Collection and Similar Rights.* In the event any Obligation of Counterparty to a FMI Affiliate is satisfied by application of Credit Support or Collateral held by or transferred to another FMI Affiliate or by any offset or netting of an Obligation to Counterparty from another FMI Affiliate, such other FMI Affiliate shall immediately Transfer to such FMI Affiliate the amount so applied or netted. If a FMI Entity exercises its rights against Receivables Collateral by collecting on such Receivables Collateral from another FMI Entity that is the account debtor thereon, such other FMI Entity shall immediately Transfer to such FMI Entity the amount to be collected thereunder.

5.6. *No Discharge.* Counterparty's Obligations to the FMI Entities shall not be discharged by the exercise of any remedy set forth in any Contract or otherwise except to the extent the exercise of such remedies is final and complete and has not been objected to by any person or entity prior to the expiration of all applicable statutes of limitations.

5.7. *Stays.* If the exercise of any right pursuant to this Section 5 shall be avoided or set aside by a court or shall be restrained, stayed or enjoined under Applicable Law, then the Obligations in respect thereof shall be reinstated, or in the event of restraint, stay or injunction, preserved in the amounts (including any interest thereon) as of the date of restraint, stay or injunction between the applicable FMI Entities, on the one hand, and Counterparty, on the other, until such time as such restraint or injunction shall no longer prohibit exercise of such right.

5.8. *No Transfers.* No FMI Entity shall be required to Transfer any Credit Support or any other amounts hereunder to Counterparty (including for Transfer by Counterparty to any FMI Entity) if a Close-out Event, or an event that with the passage of time or the giving of notice, or both, would become a Close-out Event, has occurred with respect to Counterparty, or if such Transfer would cause a Base Contract to be in Deficit.

5.9. *Order of Remedies.* Subject to Section 6.2, in exercising any remedies under any Contract or otherwise, each FMI Entity shall be entitled to exercise such remedies, with respect to such of the Obligations, and in such order, as it determines in its sole discretion.

6.   Collateral.

6.1. *Grant of Security Interest.* Without prejudice to any prior security interest granted in favor of any FMI Entity, Counterparty hereby grants to each FMI Entity a security interest in and assigns by way of security, all Collateral, to secure all of Counterparty's Obligations to such FMI Entity.

6.2. *Priority; Waiver*

6.2.1.   All Securities and Cash Collateral pledged by Counterparty in connection with a particular Base Contract shall secure first Counterparty's Obligations under that Base Contract and second, Counterparty's Obligations under all other Base Contracts and this CMN Agreement. Each FMI Entity that does not have a first lien on any Securities and Cash Collateral (with respect to such Securities and Cash Collateral, a "**Second Priority FMI Entity**") shall take no action in respect of such Securities and Cash Collateral without the consent of the FMI Entity having a first lien on such Securities and Cash Collateral (with respect to such Securities and Cash Collateral, the "**First Priority FMI Entity**"), and the First Priority FMI Entity shall be entitled to exercise all remedies in respect thereof (without being required to consult with any Second Priority FMI Entity except to the extent required by Applicable Law, and each Second Priority FMI Entity hereby waives any right to be so consulted to the extent permitted by Applicable Law). Each Second Priority FMI Entity agrees that its security interest is subject and subordinate to any interest in such Securities and Cash Collateral in favor of any derivatives clearing organization, contract market or futures commission merchant in respect of any futures or commodity option position of Counterparty that is subject to regulation under the Commodity Exchange Act, and in no event will such Second Priority FMI Entity have any right to exercise any remedies in respect of such Securities and Cash Collateral until such time as all Obligations with respect to the First Priority FMI Entity and any related obligations to any such derivatives clearing organization, contract market or futures commission merchant have been satisfied in full. Each Second Priority FMI Entity acknowledges that Counterparty's rights in such Securities and Cash Collateral, and such FMI Entity's lien thereon, are subject to the insolvency of the First Priority FMI Entity, including the customer property allocation rules under the applicable securities and commodities laws.

6.2.2.   All Receivables Collateral (and all Securities and Cash Collateral delivered but not yet allocated to a particular Base Contract) shall secure all Obligations under all Base Contracts without preference or priority, and all FMI Entities shall be entitled to take such actions as they determine in their discretion in respect of any foreclosure or other application of, or collection on, any such Securities and Cash Collateral and Receivables Collateral, including, without limitation, the priority of each FMI Entity's rights in the proceeds of any such foreclosure, application or collection. Any conflicting claims to Securities and Cash Collateral and Receivables Collateral between the FMI Entities shall be resolved as the FMI Entities shall agree. The setoff, recoupment and other rights of each FMI Entity with respect to a Base Contract to which such FMI Entity is a party are prior to any other rights in respect of that Base Contract that constitute Receivables Collateral.

6.2.3.   Counterparty waives any right it may have of first requiring any FMI Entity to proceed against or claim payment from any other person or enforce any guarantee or security before enforcing its rights against the Collateral.

6.3. Control; Notification of Security Interest; Further Assurances.

6.3.1. Counterparty and each FMI Entity acknowledge and agree that any Securities and Cash Collateral held by a FMI Entity shall be held by such FMI Entity for itself as secured party and also as agent, representative and bailee for each other FMI Entity and, as such, each FMI Entity shall, subject to Section 6.2, comply with any entitlement orders or other instructions or directions originated by such other FMI Entity with respect to the Securities and Cash Collateral without any further consent of Counterparty. Each FMI Entity and Counterparty further agree that, subject to Section 6.2.1., with respect to any commodity contracts carried in an account maintained on the books of any FMI Entity, each such FMI Entity shall apply any value distributed on account of any commodity contract carried in any such account as directed by any other FMI Entity without further consent by Counterparty. Each FMI Entity and Counterparty agree that all Securities and Cash Collateral credited to any securities account maintained on the books of any FMI Entity shall be treated as a financial asset for purposes of the UCC. For purposes of Articles 8 and 9 of the UCC, to the extent that Counterparty has any control with respect to any Collateral, upon the occurrence of a Close-out Event, Counterparty shall no longer have any control over such Collateral. For purposes of Articles 8 and 9 of the UCC, to the extent that Counterparty has any right to originate entitlement orders or other instructions or directions with respect to any Securities and Cash Collateral or any commodity contracts, Counterparty shall no longer have any such right upon the occurrence of a Close-out Event.

6.3.2. Each FMI Entity hereby notifies each other FMI Entity of its security interest and assignment by way of security under Section 6.1, each FMI Entity acknowledges such notice from each other FMI Entity and each FMI Entity consents to the security interest and assignment by way of security. Counterparty and each FMI Entity agree that Counterparty's grant of the security interest and assignment by way of security under Section 6.1 shall not be a breach of any restriction on assignment in this CMN Agreement or any Base Contract or otherwise.

6.3.3. Counterparty agrees that at any time and from time to time, at the expense of Counterparty, it will promptly execute and deliver all further instruments and documents, and take all further action, that may be necessary or desirable, or that any FMI Entity may request, in order to perfect and protect each grant of a security interest and assignment by way of security under Section 6.1 or to enable any FMI Entity to exercise or enforce its rights and remedies hereunder with respect to the Collateral or any part thereof (including, without limitation, the filing of any UCC financing statements, whether initial filings, amendments or continuations deemed necessary or appropriate by any FMI Entity).

6.3.4.   Counterparty hereby irrevocably grants each FMI Entity a power of attorney, with full authority to act in the place and stead of Counterparty, under a power coupled with an interest, and in the name of Counterparty or otherwise, from time to time in such FMI Entity's discretion to take any action and to execute any instrument which such FMI Entity may deem necessary or advisable to accomplish the purposes of this CMN Agreement or to effectuate each grant of a security interest and assignment by way of security under Section 6.1. Each FMI Entity is authorized, without limitation, to prepare and file UCC financing statements, whether initial filings, amendments or continuations, with respect to the Collateral, at Counterparty's expense.

6.3.5.   Without at least 90 days' prior written notice to each FMI Entity, Counterparty shall not change its name, type of organization or jurisdiction of organization (or the organizational identification number, if any, issued by such jurisdiction to Counterparty), its place of business, or if it has more than one place of business, its chief place of business and chief executive office, each as set forth in Schedule III hereto, or otherwise change its form.

6.4. *Characterization.* It is the parties' intention that Title Transfer Credit Support characterized as such under the terms of a Base Contract shall continue to be characterized as such.

7.   Non-Exclusive.

Each FMI Entity's rights under this CMN Agreement (including in respect of the Basic and Additional Margin Requirements and remedies upon a Close-out Event) are in addition to, and not in limitation or exclusive of, any other rights which it may have (whether under the Base Contracts, any other agreement, by operation of law or otherwise), and nothing herein shall prevent any FMI Entity from exercising any right such party may have under any Base Contract, Applicable Law or otherwise to cause the termination, liquidation or acceleration of any Base Contract or exercising any right under any security or credit support arrangement relating to any Base Contract, any right to net or set off payments which may arise under any Base Contract, under Applicable Law or otherwise, or any other right or remedy of such party. The provisions of this CMN Agreement shall supersede any provisions contained in any of the Base Contracts that would otherwise limit the rights and remedies given to the FMI Entities herein, including without limitation any provisions relating to the valuation of Credit Support, the delivery of Credit Support, the amount and nature of Credit Support required to be Transferred, the delivery of notices, the timing of notices, Credit Support deliveries or Close-out and dispute resolution procedures relating to Credit Support or Close-out. All determinations and calculations by a FMI Entity of any amounts hereunder or under any Base Contract, including the Basic Margin Requirement for each Base Contract and the Additional Margin Requirement, shall be conclusive absent manifest error. Each Base Contract is hereby incorporated into this CMN Agreement, and this CMN Agreement is hereby incorporated into each Base Contract; and any transfer (including any pledge) hereunder or under any Base Contract shall be a transfer "under" and "in connection with" each Base Contract.

8. Representations and Warranties.

   8.1. *Representations and Warranties of each Party.* Each party hereto represents and warrants, and shall be deemed to represent and warrant as of the date hereof and as of the time it enters into any Base Contract, to each of the other parties hereto as follows:

      (a) it has full power and authority to execute and deliver this CMN Agreement, to enter into such Base Contract and to perform its obligations hereunder and thereunder and has taken all necessary action to authorize such execution, delivery and performance;

      (b) it has entered into or, as the case may be, will enter into the Contracts as principal;

      (c) the person signing this CMN Agreement on its behalf is, and any person representing it in entering into a Base Contract is, duly authorized to do so on its behalf;

      (d) it has obtained all authorizations of any governmental or regulatory body required in connection with the Contracts and such authorizations are in full force and effect;

(e) the execution, delivery and performance of this CMN Agreement, and any Base Contract either have been or will be, prior to entering into each Base Contract, duly authorized by all necessary corporate action and do not and will not violate any law, ordinance, charter, by-law, or rule applicable to it or any transactional restriction or agreement binding on or affecting such party or any of its assets; and

(f) this CMN Agreement has been, and any Base Contract has been or will be at the time it is entered into, duly and properly executed and delivered by such party and constitutes and will constitute the legal, valid and binding obligation of such party enforceable in accordance with its terms, except as the enforcement of rights and remedies may be limited by bankruptcy, insolvency, reorganization, moratorium, or other similar laws now or hereafter in effect relating to creditors' rights, and general principles of equity (regardless of whether such enforceability is considered in a proceeding in equity or at law).

8.2. *Additional Counterparty Representations.* Counterparty represents and warrants, and shall be deemed to represent and warrant as of the date hereof, as of the time it enters into any Base Contract and as of the time it pledges any Collateral or transfers any Credit Support thereunder or hereunder, to each of the FMI Entities as follows:

(a) the FMI Entities have a valid, perfected and enforceable security interest in, the Collateral pledged by Counterparty to a FMI Entity;

(b) it is the sole owner of or otherwise has the right to Transfer any Credit Support it transfers to a FMI Entity under the relevant Base Contract free and clear of any security interest, lien, encumbrance or other restriction (other than a lien routinely imposed on all securities in a relevant clearance system);

(c) each transfer made or obligation incurred pursuant to each Base Contract (i) is being made without intent to hinder, delay, or defraud any entity to which it is or will become, on or after the date that such transfer is made or such obligation is incurred, indebted, (ii) is being made in exchange for reasonably equivalent value and (iii) will not cause it to become insolvent;

(d) it is not engaged in business or a transaction, or is about to engage in business or a transaction, for which its remaining property is an unreasonably small capital;

(e) it is not insolvent or unable to pay its debts within the meaning of Applicable Law and is not unable to pay its debts as they mature and it is paying and it anticipates for the foreseeable future that it will continue to pay, its debts as they mature;

(f) except for security interests or encumbrances created by the Base Contracts or hereunder in favor of the FMI Entities, no person has or will have any right, title, claim or interest (by way of lien, mortgage, pledge, charge, security interest or other encumbrance, or otherwise) in, against, or to the Collateral or Credit Support;

(g) no pledge of Collateral or delivery of Credit Support violates any agreement by which it is bound;

(h) it has and will materially benefit from executing and delivering this CMN Agreement and from entering into the Base Contracts;

(i) it has entered into, is entering into and will enter into the Contracts in good faith and for the purpose of carrying on its business and there are reasonable grounds for believing that entering into the Contracts will benefit it;

(j) Counterparty's exact legal name, type of organization and jurisdiction of organization (together with the organizational identification number, if any issued by such jurisdiction to Counterparty), its place of business, or if it has more than one place of business, its chief place of business and chief executive office, at the date of this Agreement and for the four months immediately preceding the date of this Agreement are as set forth in Schedule III; and

(k) Counterparty is a "financial institution" as defined in and pursuant to FDICIA.

8.3. Counterparty Acknowledgements.

8.3.1. Counterparty recognizes that the FMI Entities, in allocating Credit Support, in exercising remedies upon a Close-out Event, or in taking any other action contemplated hereby, will be attempting, but will be under no obligation to Counterparty, to minimize the FMI Entities' economic risks in connection with the Base

Contracts and otherwise and the impact to the FMI Entities of any insolvency or bankruptcy of Counterparty (including, without limitation, application of any safe harbor provisions for financial contracts under the Bankruptcy Code).

8.3.2.   Each party recognizes that there are no third-party beneficiaries of this CMN Agreement other than the FMI Affiliates. Counterparty hereby acknowledges that FMI Affiliates are intended to be third party beneficiaries of this CMN Agreement.

8.3.3.   Each Party intends that (i) each transfer of Collateral and Credit Support and each payment to be made under any Contract is a "margin payment", "settlement payment", and "transfer" within the meaning of Sections 362 and 546 of Title 11 of the Bankruptcy Code; (ii) each obligation under any Contract is an obligation to make a "margin payment", "settlement payment" and "payment" within the meaning of Sections 362 and 560 of the Bankruptcy Code; (iii) this CMN Agreement constitutes a "netting contract" within the meaning of and as defined in FDICIA; (iv) each payment entitlement and payment obligation hereunder constitutes a "covered contractual payment entitlement" or "covered contractual payment obligation", respectively, as defined in FDICIA; (v) this CMN Agreement is a "master netting agreement" and the parties are "master netting agreement participants" within the meaning of and as such terms are used in any law, rule, regulation, statute, or order applicable to the parties' rights herein, whether now or hereafter enacted or made applicable; (vi) each Base Contract is a "swap agreement," "forward contract," "securities contract", "repurchase agreement" or "commodity contract" within the meaning of the Bankruptcy Code; (vii) all pledges of Collateral under the Base Contracts and hereunder are transfers under and in connection with "swap agreements", or "margin payments" or "settlement payments" within the meaning of the Bankruptcy Code; (viii) all Collateral and Credit Support is held or has been transferred to margin, guarantee, secure and settle "swap agreements", "forward contracts", "securities contracts", "repurchase agreements" and "commodities contracts" as part of a single integrated business relationship and arrangement; and (ix) the exercise of remedies under Section 6 are protected by FDICIA and Sections 362, 555, 556, 559 and 560 of the Bankruptcy Code.

8.3.4. COUNTERPARTY ACKNOWLEDGES THAT ALLOCATIONS OF CREDIT SUPPORT PURSUANT TO SECTION 4.1 TO A FMI ENTITY OTHER THAN LBI AND TRANSFERS OF CREDIT SUPPORT OR COLLATERAL FROM LBI PURSUANT TO SECTION 2 OR 5 MAY RESULT IN THE LOSS BY COUNTERPARTY OF RIGHTS AND PROTECTIONS AFFORDED BY RULES 15C3–3, 8C–1 AND 15C2–1 UNDER THE SECURITIES EXCHANGE ACT OF 1934, THE SECURITIES INVESTOR PROTECTION ACT OF 1970 AND ANY "EXCESS" SIPC COVERAGE LBI MAY MAINTAIN.

8.3.5. In connection with the negotiation of and the entering into this CMN Agreement and each Base Contract, Counterparty acknowledges and agrees that: (i) each FMI Entity is acting for its own account and is not acting as a fiduciary for, or a financial or investment advisor to Counterparty (or in any similar capacity); (ii) Counterparty is not relying upon any communications (whether written or oral) from any FMI Entity as investment advice or as a recommendation to enter into this CMN Agreement or any Base Contract, it being understood that information and explanations related to the terms and conditions of this CMN Agreement or any Base Contract shall not be considered investment advice or a recommendation to enter into this CMN Agreement or any Base Contract; (iii) Counterparty has not received from any FMI Entity any assurance or guarantee as to the expected results of this CMN Agreement or any Base Contract; and (iv) Counterparty has consulted with its own legal, regulatory, tax, business, investment, financial, and accounting advisors to the extent it has deemed necessary, and it has made its own independent investment, hedging, and trading decisions based upon its own judgment and upon any advice from such advisors as it has deemed necessary and not upon any view expressed by any FMI Entity.

9. Miscellaneous.

9.1. *Entire Agreement.* This CMN Agreement shall constitute the entire and exclusive understanding and agreement by the parties with respect to the matters addressed herein.

9.2. *Single Relationship.* Each party acknowledges and agrees that (a) each Contract has been entered into in consideration of and in reliance upon the fact that all Contracts constitute a single business relationship and have been made in consideration of each other, and (b) the performance by Counterparty of each and every Obligation under any Contract is a condition precedent to the performance by each FMI Entity of any Obligation to Counterparty, whether or not arising under such Contract or any other Contract. No failure by any FMI Entity to fulfill any obligation under this CMN Agreement shall constitute a breach or default under any Contract, nor shall it discharge or affect in any way Counterparty's obligations under any Contract.

9.3. *Assignment.* Each FMI Entity shall have the right to assign its rights and delegate its obligations in respect of any Base Contract or any transaction under any Base Contract to another FMI Entity, and, upon such delegation, the assignee FMI Entity may release the assignor FMI Entity from its obligations to Counterparty in respect of such Base Contract or transaction without further consent of Counterparty. Counterparty may not assign its rights or delegate its obligations under any Contract without the prior written consent of each FMI Entity, and any purported assignment or delegation absent such consent is null and void. To the extent the prior sentence is unenforceable under Applicable Law, and consistent with Section 9.2, Counterparty may not assign its rights or delegate its obligations under any Contract without the prior written consent of each FMI Entity unless it assigns its rights and delegates its obligations under all Contracts, and any purported assignment or delegation absent such consent is null and void. Subject to the foregoing, all Contracts shall be binding upon and shall inure to the benefit of the parties and their respective successors and assigns.

9.4. *Termination.* Any FMI Entity may terminate this CMN Agreement on five days' prior written notice to Counterparty and the other FMI Entities, or immediately with contemporaneous written notice if required by any Regulatory Requirement (in each case, the date such termination becomes effective, the "**CMN Agreement Termination Date**"), but no such termination shall affect any Base Contract, the security interest of any FMI Entity in any Collateral, or the ownership, setoff, netting and recoupment rights of any FMI Entity in any Title Transfer Credit Support. Notwithstanding the provisions of any Base Contract, on or prior to the CMN Agreement Termination Date, each FMI Entity party to a Base Contract shall in its sole discretion determine and notify Counterparty of the margin requirements under such Base Contract necessary to comply with any applicable Regulatory Requirements and to protect itself from any potential credit exposure to Counterparty in respect of such Base Contract. Such margin requirements shall be effective as of the CMN Agreement Termination Date and Counterparty's obligations in respect of such margin requirements shall survive the termination of this CMN Agreement.

9.5. *Adjustment Relating to Interest.* The obligations of the FMI Entities in respect of interest provided in Section 5.3 shall be reduced to the same extent that interest provided therein may not lawfully be included in calculating the obligations of Counterparty in respect of any Settlement Amount or Net Settlement Payment.

9.6. *Notices.* Unless otherwise specified, all notices and other communications to be given to a party hereunder orally or in writing and shall be given to the address, telex (if confirmed by the appropriate answerback), fax (confirmed if requested) or telephone number and to the individual or department specified with respect to such party on Schedule II or such other address, telex, telecopy or telephone number as such party may hereafter specify for the purpose of notice given in accordance with this paragraph. Unless otherwise specified, any notice, instruction or other communication, shall be effective upon receipt if given in accordance with this paragraph. Without limiting the provisions of Section 7, the notice provisions of this CMN Agreement supersede the notice provisions of any Base Contract in respect of determinations of margin requirements, transfers of Credit Support, the occurrence of a Close-out Event and the Close-out of such Base Contract.

9.7. *Interpretation; Headings and Subheadings.* References in this CMN Agreement to "pledge" or "pledgor" include a grant of a security interest in Collateral and to the party granting such security interest and references to Base Contract Collateral or Credit Support "held by" or "transferred to" a party include Base Contract Collateral or Credit Support held directly or indirectly by such party or over which such party has direct or indirect control, or with respect to which such party has perfected a security interest by filing or registration. The headings and subheadings of this CMN Agreement are for convenience of reference only and shall not affect the meaning or construction of any provision hereof.

9.8. *Governing Law; Severability.* THIS AGREEMENT AND EACH BASE CONTRACT THAT IS NOT EXPRESSED TO

HAVE A GOVERNING LAW PROVISION AND ALL MATTERS ARISING FROM OR RELATING TO THIS AGREEMENT AND EACH SUCH BASE CONTRACT SHALL BE CONSTRUED IN ACCORDANCE WITH AND GOVERNED BY THE LAW OF THE STATE OF NEW YORK, WITHOUT REFERENCE TO CONFLICTS OF LAW DOCTRINE. Wherever possible, each provision of this CMN Agreement shall be interpreted in such manner as to be effective and valid under applicable law, but if any provision of this CMN Agreement shall be prohibited by or invalid or unenforceable under such laws, such provision shall be ineffective to the extent of such prohibition, invalidity or unenforceability without otherwise affecting the validity or enforceability of such provision or the remaining provisions of this CMN Agreement.

9.9. *Jurisdiction; Process.*

9.9.1.   With respect to any suit, action, claim, or proceedings relating to this CMN Agreement (collectively, "**Proceedings**"), each party irrevocably and unconditionally:

(i) submits to the jurisdiction of the courts of the State of New York and United States federal courts located in New York, New York;

(ii) waives any objection which it may have at any time to the laying of venue of any Proceedings brought in any such court, waives any claim that such Proceedings have been brought in an inconvenient forum, and further waives the right to object, with respect to such Proceedings, that such court does not have jurisdiction over such party.

(iii) WAIVES ANY AND ALL RIGHTS TO TRIAL BY JURY IN ANY PROCEEDINGS.

9.9.2.   Counterparty hereby appoints the Process Agent specified in Schedule IV hereto to receive, for it and on its behalf, service of process in any suit, action or proceedings relating to this CMN Agreement and any Base Contract. If for any reason the Process Agent is unable to act as such, Counterparty will promptly notify the FMI Entities and within thirty (30) days appoint a substitute process agent acceptable to the FMI Entities. Counterparty irrevocably consents to service of process given in the manner provided for written notices in Section 9.6 hereof. Nothing in this CMN Agreement will affect the right of any party to serve process in any other manner permitted by law.

9.10.   *Costs of Enforcement.* Counterparty shall be liable for and shall, on demand, indemnify and hold harmless each FMI Entity for and against all reasonable out-of-pocket expenses, including, without limitation, legal fees and any stamp, registration, documentation or similar taxes or costs of collection, incurred by such FMI Entity by reason of the enforcement or protection of its rights under any Contract.

9.11.   *Counterparts.* This CMN Agreement may be executed in any number of counterparts, each of which when so executed and delivered shall be deemed an original, but all such counterparts together shall constitute but one and the same instrument.

9.12.   *Amendments;   Waivers.* No amendment, modification, supplement or waiver in respect of this CMN Agreement shall be effective unless in writing and signed by all of the parties hereto. No failure or delay by any party hereto in exercising any right, power, or privilege hereunder shall operate as a waiver thereof.

IN WITNESS WHEREOF, the parties have signed this CMN Agreement as of the date stated above.

[COUNTERPARTY]

By:_____

Name:_____

Title:_____

FMI

By:_____

Name:_____

Title:_____

FMIE

By:_____

Name:_____

Title:_____

FMCM

By:_____

Name:_____

Title:_____

APPENDIX B

FUTURES CUSTOMER AGREEMENT OF FILLER & MARKHAM INC.

■ ■ ■

In consideration of the acceptance of its account by Filler & Markham Inc. ("FMI") and FMI's agreement to act as its broker and/or dealer, the undersigned, _____ (the "Customer") agree to the following with respect to the Customer's account with FMI (the "Account") for the purchase and sale of commodities, exchange-traded contracts for the future delivery of commodities and options on such contracts (collectively, "Futures Contracts"), commodity option contracts and forward commodity and foreign exchange contracts (together with Futures Contracts, "Contracts"):

1. GOVERNMENTAL AND EXCHANGE RULES.

The Customer's account shall be maintained in accordance with, and all transactions therein shall be subject to, the constitution, statutes, by-laws, rules, regulations, customs, usages, rulings and interpretations, including the provisions of the Employee Retirement Income Security Act of 1974 as amended ("ERISA") and all applicable rules, regulations and interpretations issued pursuant thereto (collectively, "Applicable Law") of all applicable governmental and self-regulatory agencies, including, but not limited to, all exchanges or their clearing houses, if any, on which or subject to whose rules such transactions are executed. FMI shall not be liable to the Customer as a result of any actions taken to comply with Applicable Law or of any independent floor broker transacting the Customer's Contracts at FMI's or the Customer's request, including, without limitation, any liquidation, in whole or in part, of the Customer's positions or any other action taken in the event that any exchange declares an emergency, except to the extent that any such action constitutes the negligence or willful misconduct of FMI. The Customer appoints FMI to act as agent of, and not as counterparty or principal for, the Customer in connection with any Futures Contracts purchased and/or sold for the Customer's account. All Property (as defined in Section 4 below) held by FMI for the Customer shall be held subject to Applicable Law or as the parties mutually agree.

2. MARGIN.

The Customer agrees to maintain such margin in Customer's account as FMI in its reasonable discretion may require in addition to the amounts required by Applicable Law, and to deposit immediately on demand cash or property in any such amount as may reasonably be required by FMI or required by Applicable Law. The amount of the initial margin requirements for the Account shall be set forth in writing in the daily confirmation statement sent to the Customer. The Customer agrees to make all margin deposits in United States Dollars unless FMI in its discretion permits otherwise.

3. EVENTS OF DEFAULT.

In the event that:

(a) the Customer timely fails to deposit sufficient monies, funds or such other Property (as defined in Section 4 below) acceptable to FMI in its reasonable discretion to satisfy any demands for original and/or variation margin or such other amounts as FMI may, in its reasonable discretion, require;

(b) the Customer is dissolved or liquidated;

(c) a proceeding under any applicable bankruptcy law is filed by the Customer or a general assignment for the benefit of creditors or the Customer files an application for, or a receiver or trustee is appointed for, the Customer or

any of its affiliates or an involuntary proceeding under applicable bankruptcy law is commenced against the Customer and is not dismissed within thirty (30) calendar days thereafter;

(d) any attachment, execution or distress is levied against or sought to be levied against, or an encumbrancer takes possession of the whole, the Property, undertaking or assets of the Customer or against the assets being held at or being sent to FMI for the Customer's benefit;

(e) the Customer fails to perform or comply with any material obligation contained herein;

(f) the Customer's account incurs a deficit balance;

(g) FMI determines that any representation, statement or warranty made by the Customer to FMI in this Agreement or in any notice or other document, certificate or statement delivered by it pursuant hereto or in connection herewith is untrue, inaccurate or misleading in any material respect;

(h) anything analogous to any of the events specified above occurs under the laws of any applicable jurisdiction.

(each of such events referred to in the foregoing clauses (a) through (i) being referred to herein as an "Event of Default"), then FMI may, at the Customer's sole risk and expense, without prejudice to any other rights which FMI may have, exercise the rights set forth in Section 4 below. If the Customer knows or should know or becomes aware of any event in this Section 3, the Customer shall immediately notify FMI thereof.

4. CONSEQUENCES OF AN EVENT OF DEFAULT.

At any time following the occurrence of an Event of Default, FMI shall be entitled at its sole discretion, as soon as it has made every reasonable effort to give or has given written or oral notice thereof to the Adviser and Customer, to take one or more of the following actions to the extent necessary to satisfy all of the obligations of the Customer hereunder:

(i)   liquidate, sell or close out any or all of the Contracts and monies, funds, securities of all kinds, commodities and other property or collateral (collectively, "Property") in the Customer's Account;

(ii)   hedge and/or offset such Contracts and Property in the cash or other market, including a related but separate market;

(iii) sell any Contracts or Property held by FMI belonging to the Customer or in which the Customer it has an interest;

(iv)   cancel any open orders for the purchase and/or sale of any Contracts or Property;

(v)   borrow and/or buy any Contracts or Property required to make delivery against any sales, including a short sale, effected for the Customer;

(vi)   exercise any or all option contracts to which FMI and the Customer are the parties; or

(vii) take such action as FMI reasonably deems necessary for its protection.

If any such sale or purchase occurs, it may be public or private, and FMI itself may be the counterparty of such transaction(s). The proceeds of any such transactions shall be applied by FMI to reduce any and all indebtedness owed to FMI by the Customer. All costs, fees, expenses and liabilities reasonably incurred by FMI in the exercise of the rights detailed in this Paragraph 4 shall be borne by the Customer.

5. SECURITY.

All Contracts and other Property belonging to the Customer which FMI or any of its subsidiaries or affiliates may at any time be carrying for the Customer or holding in its or their possession or control on behalf of the Customer for any purpose, including safekeeping, shall be held by FMI as security and be subject to a general lien and right of setoff for the discharge of all liabilities and obligations of the

Customer owed to FMI, wherever or however arising, and without regard to whether or not FMI has made advances with respect to such Property, and FMI is hereby authorized to sell and/or purchase, loan, hypothecate or rehypothecate any and all such Property, provided FMI has made every reasonable effort to give or has given written or oral notice to the Customer, to satisfy such general lien and security interest, provided that it does so with respect to any Property of the Customer held by FMI, FMI may deliver to Customer securities or other Property of like or equivalent kind or amount.

6. PAYMENT OBLIGATIONS OF CUSTOMER.

The Customer shall pay FMI upon demand:

(a) all brokerage charges, give-up fees, commissions and service fees as FMI may from time to time charge;

(b) all exchange, clearinghouse, National Futures Association ("NFA"), clearing member or electronic trading system fees or charges;

(c) any tax imposed on such transactions by any competent taxing authority;

(d) the amount of any realized or unrealized losses in the Customer's account;

(e) any debit balance or deficiency in the Customer's account;

(f) interest on any debit balance or deficiency in the Customer's account, at the prevailing rate as determined by FMI unless otherwise agreed to by Customer and FMI in writing, together with costs and reasonable attorneys' and accountants' fees actually incurred in collecting any such debit balance or deficiency; and

(g) any other amounts owed by the Customer to FMI with respect to its account or any transactions therein.

7. INTEREST.

FMI shall pay interest on the Customer's cash held by FMI based on interest rates mutually agreed to by the parties. Notwithstanding the above, the Customer understands that FMI may retain for its own account any interest, increment, profit, gain or benefit, direct or indirect, resulting from or relating to the deposit or investment of funds, including Property of the Customer, held in commodity customer segregated accounts, customer secured amount accounts and non-regulated accounts.

8. CUSTOMER'S REPRESEN-TATIONS AND WARRAN-TIES.

The Customer represent and warrant at the time this Agreement is entered into and at the time each subsequent transaction is entered into under this Agreement that:

(a) the Customer has full right, power, capacity and authority to enter into this Agreement and each and every transaction entered into hereunder, and that each person executing this Agreement and giving instructions or orders on behalf of the Customer is authorized to do so;

(b) this Agreement and obligations expressed to be assumed by the Customer herein are legal, valid and binding on the Customer and enforceable against the Customer in accordance with the terms hereof;

(c) the Customer may lawfully establish and open the accounts for the purpose of effecting purchases and sales of Contracts through FMI and any financing thereof;

(d) transactions entered into pursuant to this Agreement will not violate any Applicable Law, including any law to which the Customer is subject or any agreement to which the Customer is subject or a party;

(e) the Customer will provide on request such information regarding the Customer's financial or business affairs as FMI may reasonably require or as required by Applicable Law, and that all information provided by the Customer to FMI hereunder or otherwise is true and correct, and the Customer shall promptly notify FMI of any change in such information and the Customer shall not omit or withhold any information that would render the information so supplied to be false or inaccurate in any material respect;

(f) the Customer has satisfied itself and will continue to satisfy itself as to the tax, accounting, legal and other implications, if any, of the transactions contemplated hereunder;

(g) the Customer has the full and unqualified right to transfer margin to FMI as required under the terms of this Agreement, and any such margin so transferred shall be beneficially owned by the Customer and free and clear of any mortgage, lien, claim, charge or other encumbrance whatsoever;

(h) no Event of Default described in Section 3 above has occurred with respect to it and is continuing, and no such event or circumstance would occur as a result of its entering into or performing its obligations under this Agreement; and

(i) if applicable, the Customer is not an authorized person or the employee of an authorized person under the Financial Services Act 1986 unless the Customer has specifically notified FMI to that effect in writing.

8A. FMI'S REPRESENTATIONS AND WARRANTIES.

FMI represents and warrants at the time this Agreement is entered into that:

(a) FMI has the full right, power, capacity and authority to enter into this Agreement, and that each person executing this Agreement on behalf of FMI is authorized to do so; and

(b) this Agreement and obligations expressed to be assumed by FMI herein are legal, valid and binding on FMI and enforceable against FMI in accordance with the terms hereof.

9. TRADING RECOMMENDATIONS.

The Customer acknowledges and understands that any market recommendations or information or other communication (written or oral) provided by FMI or by any of its affiliates or agents with respect to the Customer's trading activities is solely incidental to the conduct of its business, shall not serve as a primary basis for any decision by the Customer and does not constitute investment advice nor a recommendation to enter into a transaction unless there is a written agreement between FMI and the Customer to the contrary. No fiduciary or advisory relationship between FMI and the Customer is created by this Agreement or by ERISA, and FMI shall have no responsibility for compliance with any law or regulation governing the conduct of fiduciaries of Customer. All decisions of the Customer are made solely by and at the discretion of the Customer and are based upon the Customer's judgment and upon advice from such professional advisors as the Customer deems it necessary to consult (FMI is not nor can be considered a professional advisor for the purpose of this Agreement) and do not constitute the exercise of discretionary or fiduciary authority or control by FMI. Any information provided by FMI may be incomplete, may not have been verified and may be changed without notice to the Customer. The Customer understands that FMI makes no representation or warranty as to the accuracy, completeness, reliability or prudence of any such information. The Customer further understands that FMI, its affiliates, its officers and its employees may take or hold positions in or advise other customers concerning such transactions which are the subject of advice from FMI to the Customer, which positions and advice may be inconsistent with or contrary to positions which are held by the Customer. FMI is not acting as a fiduciary, foundation manager, commodity pool operator, commodity trading advisor or investment adviser in respect of any accounts opened by the Customer. FMI shall have no responsibility hereunder for compliance with Applicable Law governing the conduct of fiduciaries, foundation managers, commodity pool operators, commodity trading advisors or investment advisors. Upon entering into a transaction, the Customer acknowledges and agrees that by entering in to the transaction, that it understands the terms, conditions and risks of such transaction and is willing to assume those risks, financially or otherwise.

The Adviser and FMI acknowledge and agree that the Trustee has no duty or responsibility to make any investment decisions regarding the assets in the Account, that the Trustee has executed this Agreement at the direction of the Adviser and that the Trustee shall only act as directed by the Adviser and/or the Customer, and any representations or statements made herein have been made by Trustee for or on behalf of the Account in accordance with such directions. No liability is intended to attach to the Trustee, as trustee or in its individual capacity. The Trustee will send to FMI copies of the unaudited monthly statements it sends to the sponsor of the plans funded by the Customer.

10. POSITION LIMITS.

The Customer understands that FMI has, at its discretion, the right to limit positions in the Customer's account, to decline to accept any orders from the Customer, and to require that the Customer's account be transferred to another firm. The Customer shall file or cause to be filed all applications or reports required under Applicable Law with the relevant governmental authority or exchange, contract market or clearing house, and shall provide FMI with a copy of such applications or reports and such other information as FMI may reasonably request in connection therewith.

11. STATEMENTS AND CON-FIRMATIONS.

Final written confirmation of actual transactions and/or orders, purchase and sale notices, correction notices and statements of the Customer's account shall be conclusive if not objected to in writing within seven days of the receipt by Customer of the statement. Communications mailed or electronically transmitted to the Customer's address shown on FMI's books and records shall, until FMI has received notice in writing from the Customer of a different address, be deemed to have been personally delivered to the Customer, and the Customer agrees to waive all claims resulting from any failure to receive such communications.

Any notice or other communication in respect of this Agreement must be given to the other party in writing and delivered in person, sent by certified or registered mail or by overnight courier or by telex or facsimile at the address or number set forth opposite such party's name below or as may be subsequently specified in writing between the parties from time to time. Notices delivered by mail shall be deemed to have been received on the third business day thereafter where such notice is sent to or from the United States or another country. Notices sent by messenger shall be deemed duly given when delivered to the address of the receiving party as reflected on the messenger's records. Notices sent by overnight air courier shall be deemed fully given when delivered to the address of the receiving party as reflected on the air courier's records. If delivered by telex or facsimile, such notice shall be deemed to have been delivered on the date that the answerback is received or the date of the date stamp on the facsimile. Notices sent by electronic transmission from the mainframe used by FMI shall be deemed given when sent. All communications to FMI shall be sent to the address set forth below or such other place as FMI notifies in writing to the Customer.

12. EXCLUSION OF LIABILITY AND INDEMNITY.

FMI shall have no responsibility or liability to the Customer

(i)   in connection with the performance or non-performance by any exchange, clearinghouse, clearing firm or other third party (including floor brokers and banks) of their obligations in respect of any order, bid, offer, Contract or other Property of the Customer;

(ii) as a result of any prediction or recommendation made or information given by a representative of FMI whether or not made or given at the request of the Customer;

(iii) as a result of FMI's reliance on any instructions, notices or communications that it believes to be that of an individual authorized to act on behalf of the Customer;

(iv) as a result of any delay in the performance or non-performance of any of FMI's obligations hereunder directly or indirectly caused by the occurrences of any contingency beyond the control of FMI including, but not limited to, the unscheduled closure of an exchange, clearinghouse or delays in the transmission of bids, offers, orders or instructions due to slowdowns, breakdowns or failures of transmission or communication facilities, execution, and/or trading facilities or other systems (including, without limitation, electronic trading systems, facilities or services), it being understood that FMI shall be excused from performance of its obligations hereunder for such period of time as is reasonably necessary after such occurrence to remedy the effects therefrom;

(v)   as a result of any action reasonably taken by FMI or any clearing firm or executing firm, including floor brokers selected by FMI, to comply with Applicable Law;

(vi) for any acts or omissions of those neither employed nor supervised by FMI; or

(vii) for losses suffered by the Customer resulting directly or indirectly from government action, war, strike or national disaster.

FMI shall not be responsible for any loss, liability, damage or expense except to the extent that it is judicially determined that such loss, liability, damage or expense resulted directly from its gross negligence or willful misconduct. In no event shall FMI be liable to the Customer for consequential, incidental or special damages hereunder.

Nothing in this Agreement, express or implied, is intended to confer or does confer upon any person or entity other than the parties hereto or their respective successors and assigns any rights or remedies under or by reason of this Agreement or as a result of the services to be rendered by FMI hereunder.

13. OPTIONS TRANSACTIONS.

If a transaction involves a commodity option contract, the Customer acknowledges and agrees that it is responsible for taking or failing to take action to exercise any commodity option contract in the Customer's account and that, unless such commodity option contract is automatically exercised subject to Applicable Law, FMI shall not take any action to exercise any commodity option contract in the Customer's account without instructions from the Customer.

14. INDEPENDENT INVESTMENT ADVISOR.

If the Customer directs FMI in writing to accept trading instructions from an independent commodity trading advisor or investment adviser ("Advisor"), unless otherwise agreed in writing, Customer hereby appoints such Advisor as the Customer's agent for the purpose of receiving all communications, notices and requests for instructions related to this Agreement and the transactions effected pursuant to this Agreement, including, without limitation, trading recommendations or market information, confirmations of trades, statements of account and margin calls. Nothing in this Clause 14 shall relieve the Customer of any of its obligations under this Agreement. The Customer acknowledges that FMI is not responsible for the conduct of such Advisor, that such Advisor is independent of and not FMI's agent and that FMI's sole responsibilities relate to the execution, clearing and bookkeeping of transactions in the Customer's account with respect to any orders given to FMI by such Advisor and to those representations of FMI set forth in this Agreement. The Customer represents that it has reviewed the registration requirements of Applicable Law relating to the Advisor and itself and has determined that each is in compliance with such requirements.

15. CURRENCY RISK.

If the Customer initiates transactions in a Contract on an exchange where such transaction is effected in a currency other than U.S. dollars, any profit or loss from a fluctuation in the exchange rate of such currency shall be for the Customer's account and risk. Unless the Customer gives FMI contrary written instructions, FMI will debit and credit the Customer's account in U.S. dollars at an exchange rate determined by FMI in its reasonable discretion based on prevailing currency exchange rates. Unless the Customer instructs FMI otherwise, monies it deposits with FMI in currency other than U.S. dollars and unrealized profits in currencies other than U.S. dollars are not intended to margin, guarantee or secure transactions on United States exchanges. FMI shall be entitled, without prior notice to the Customer, to make any currency conversions FMI reasonably considers necessary or desirable for the purposes of complying with FMI's obligations or exercising any of FMI's rights hereunder. Any such conversion shall be effected by FMI in such manner and at such rates as FMI may, in its reasonable discretion, determine having regard to the prevailing rates for freely convertible currencies. If for the purposes of any claim, proof or order, a liability which the Customer owes to FMI must be converted into a currency other than that in which it would otherwise have been due, the Customer shall pay to FMI such additional amounts as may be necessary to ensure that, when received and reconverted, FMI will receive the full amount in the original currency as would have been received had no such conversion been required.

16. RECORDING.

Each of the parties hereto understands that the other, in its sole discretion, may record, on tape or otherwise, any telephone conversation between such parties. Each of the parties hereto hereby agrees and consents to such recordings and waives any right it may have to object on the basis of consent to the admissibility into evidence of such recordings in any legal or regulatory proceeding between the Customer and FMI or in any proceeding to which such party is a party or in which such party's records are subpoenaed. Neither party shall have any obligation hereunder to retain or preserve any tapes so made.

17. INFORMATION.

FMI may from time to time be required to provide information regarding the Customer or the Customer's Contracts to one or more regulatory bodies or exchanges. The Customer irrevocably authorizes FMI to provide any such information as may be required by Applicable Law. FMI agrees to provide prior written notice to Customer of any such non-routine requests.

18. TERM.

This Agreement shall remain in effect until terminated by the parties. Termination may occur immediately at any time provided the party so terminating this Agreement has given five days' written notice to the other party in accordance with the terms hereof. In the event of the Customer committing an Event of Default as outlined in Section 3 FMI may immediately terminate this Agreement effective at the time of occurrence of the Event of Default with prior written notice to the Customer. Sections 3, 4, 5, 6, 8, 9, 12, 16, 23, 24, 25 and 28 shall survive the termination of this Agreement.

19. GOVERNING LAW.

This Agreement is governed by the laws of the State of New York without reference to the choice of law or conflicts of law provisions thereof. Each party agrees that the other party may, in its reasonable discretion, initiate proceedings in the courts of any jurisdiction in which a party is resident or in which its assets are situated. In any legal action permitted by or against any party, that party agrees that the United States courts sitting in the State of New York shall have jurisdiction over it, and that the venue of any such action shall be the Southern District of New York. Each party hereby waives any objection to such jurisdiction and venue.

20. NO WAIVER.

A party's failure to insist at any time upon strict compliance with this Agreement or with any of its terms or any continued course of such conduct on the on the other party's part shall not constitute a waiver by such party of any of its rights hereunder.

21. SEVERABILITY.

If any provision of this Agreement is or becomes inapplicable or unenforceable due to a change in Applicable Law, such provision shall be deemed to be rescinded or modified in accordance with any such change. In all other respects, this Agreement shall continue and remain in full force and effect.

22. BINDING EFFECT.

This Agreement shall be binding upon and inure to the benefit of the parties hereto and their respective successors and assigns.

23. RIGHTS AND REMEDIES CUMULATIVE.

All rights and remedies and powers arising under this Agreement as amended and modified from time to time are cumulative and not exclusive of and shall not prejudice any rights, remedies or powers that may be available to FMI at law or otherwise.

24. WAIVER OF JURY TRIAL.

Each party hereby waives a trial by jury in any action arising out of or relating to this Agreement or any transaction in connection herewith.

25. ENTIRE AGREEMENT.

This Agreement represents the entire agreement between the Customer and FMI and supersedes all prior negotiations and understandings between the Customer and FMI, whether written or oral, as to the terms hereof. This agreement may not be amended or modified except in writing signed by each of the parties. No employee of FMI is authorized to make any representations contrary to the terms of this Agreement.

26. ADDITIONAL TERMS.

This Agreement is supplemental to and in addition to any other Agreement between the parties relating to other investment or services.

27. ASSIGNMENT.

Neither party may assign or transfer any rights or obligations arising under this Agreement except that FMI may assign or delegate to any affiliate of FMI and any of FMI's rights or obligations hereunder and in the event of any reorganization, reconstitution or merger, FMI may assign or transfer those rights or obligations to any successor company or any other affiliate of FMI without the Customer's prior consent.

28. AUTHORIZATION TO TRANSFER FUNDS.

FMI is hereby authorized to transfer from the Customer's commodity accounts to any of its other accounts such excess funds as may be required to avoid a margin call or for any other reason not in conflict with the rules and regulations of Applicable Law. Any such transfer shall be in compliance with Applicable Law. It is understood that, within a reasonable time after making any such transfer, FMI will confirm the same to the Customer and Adviser.

29. HEDGE LETTER.

If this account is to be designated as a bona fide hedge account, the Customer hereby represents that all orders given by the Customer for the purchase and sale of all Futures Contracts for its account at FMI shall represent bona fide hedges, as defined by the Commodity Futures Trading Commission ("CFTC"), against any spot position or commitments in accordance with Section 4a(3) of the Commodity Exchange Act ("CEA") and with any amendments or CFTC interpretations which have been made or which may be made in the future. Customer further agrees to notify FMI if any orders for the purchase or sale of Futures Contracts are not bona fide hedge transactions.

CUSTOMER HEREBY ACKNOWLEDGES THAT IT HAS RECEIVED THE SEPARATE RISK DISCLOSURE STATEMENT REQUIRED BY CFTC REGULATIONS AND THE U.S.A. PATRIOT ACT PRIOR TO THE OPENING OF THIS ACCOUNT AND UNDERSTANDS ITS TERMS AND CONTENT.

_____(CUSTOMER) Title:

Name: Address for notices to Customer:

SCHEDULE A

THIRD PARTY LIMITED TRADING AUTHORIZATION FORM

The undersigned Customer ("the Customer") hereby authorizes the advisory firm listed below as its agent and attorney-in-fact to buy, sell (including short sales) and trade in futures contracts and options on futures contracts, forwards and foreign exchange (collectively "Contracts") on margin or otherwise for the Customer's account and risk on your books. It is understood that any such Contracts may be effected with FMI as agent or broker for the Customer.

In all such purchases, sales and trades, FMI is authorized to follow the instructions of the advisory firm listed below in every respect concerning the Customer's account with FMI, and such advisory firm is authorized to act for the Customer and in the Customer's behalf in the same manner and with the same force and effect as the Customer might or could do with respect to such purchases, sales and trades. This authorization includes sales, purchases and trades in Contracts on both U.K., and non-U.K futures exchanges.

If the advisory firm is registered with the Commodity Futures Trading Commission ("CFTC") as a Commodity Trading Advisor ("CTA"), the Customer acknowledges receipt of the CTA's Disclosure Document as required by CFTC regulations.

The Customer hereby ratifies and confirms any and all transactions with FMI heretofore or hereafter made by the advisory firm for the Customer's account. The Customer hereby agrees to indemnify and hold FMI, its affiliates, subsidiaries and agents, harmless from and to pay FMI promptly on demand any and all losses and costs, including reasonable attorney's fees, arising from any actions taken by, or Contracts purchased, sold or traded by, such advisory firm for the Customer, except to the extent that such loss and cost are directly caused by the negligence or willful misconduct of FMI.

This authorization and indemnity will remain in full force and effect until terminated in writing and shall enure to the benefit of FMI, its affiliates, subsidiaries and agents, and successor corporations of them irrespective of any change or changes in the personnel thereof for any cause whatsoever, and of the assigns of FMI and these affiliated firms or any successor corporations thereof. To revoke this authorization, the Customer hereby agrees to submit a written notice addressed to the Futures Department at FMI, Two World Financial Center, New York, NY 10285, or such other address as

FMI may provide in writing, but such revocation shall not affect any liability in any way resulting from transactions in Contracts initiated prior to such revocation.

NAME OF ADVISORY FIRM: _____

NAME OF CUSTOMER: _____

BY: _____

PRINT NAME: _____

APPROVED BY BRANCH MANAGER: _____

SCHEDULE B

Commodity Hedge Letter

Specific Commodities, Products or By-Products to be Hedged

1. _____

2. _____

3. _____

4. _____

5. _____

6. _____

I hereby confirm to you that all orders which I give you for the purchase or sale of the aforementioned listed futures contracts for my account(s) will represent bona fide hedges, as defined by the Commodity Futures Trading Commission ("CFTC"), against my spot position or commitments in accordance with section 4a(3) of the Commodity Exchange Act, and with any amendments or CFTC interpretations which may be made in the futures. Should I place orders for the purchase or sale of futures contracts which are not hedge transactions, I will advise you to that effect.

I hereby request hedge margins whenever they properly apply. CFTC regulations 190.06(d)1) requires "A commodity broker must provide an opportunity for each customer to specify when undertaking its first hedging contract whether, in the event of bankruptcy, such customer prefers that open commodity contracts held in a hedging account be liquidated by the trustee without seeking customer instructions."

Please indicate by a check mark in the following box if you prefer to have positions **not** liquidated until the trustee seeks your specific instructions.

Yes, I prefer to have my positions **not** liquidated until the trustee seeks my specifics instructions.

Account Number	Name (*Please **print***)
Signature	Date

Risk Disclosure Statement for Futures and Options-on-Futures

This brief statement does not disclose all of the risks and other significant aspects of trading in futures and options. In light of the risks, you should undertake such transactions only if you understand the nature of the contracts (and contractual relationships) into which you are entering and the extent of your exposure to risk. Trading in futures and options is not suitable for many members of the public. You should carefully consider whether trading is appropriate for you in light of your experience, objectives, financial resources and other relevant circumstances.

Futures

1. Effect of "Leverage" or "Gearing"

Transactions in futures carry a high degree of risk. The amount of initial margin is small relative to the value of the futures contract so that transactions are "leveraged" or "geared". A relatively small market movement will have a proportionately larger impact on the funds you have deposited or will have to deposit: this may work against you as well as for you. You may sustain a total loss of initial margin funds and any additional funds deposited with the firm to maintain your position. If the market moves against your position or margin levels are increased, you may be called upon to pay substantial additional funds on short notice to maintain your position. If you fail to comply with a request for additional funds within the time prescribed, your position may be liquidated at a loss and you will be liable for any resulting deficit.

2. Risk-reducing orders or strategies

The placing of certain orders (e.g. "stop-loss" orders, where permitted under local law, or "stop-limit" orders) which are intended to limit losses to certain amounts may not be effective because market conditions may make it impossible to execute such orders. Strategies using combinations of positions, such as "spread" and "straddle" positions may be as risky as taking simple "long" or "short" positions.

Options

3. Variable degree of risk

Transactions in options carry a high degree of risk. Purchasers and sellers of options should familiarize themselves with the type of option (i.e. put or call) which they contemplate trading and the associated risks. You should calculate the extent to which the value of the options must increase for your position to become profitable, taking into account the premium and all transaction costs.

The purchaser of options may offset or exercise the options or allow the options to expire. The exercise of an option results either in a cash settlement or in the purchaser acquiring or delivering the underlying interest. If the option is on a future, the purchaser will acquire a futures position with associated liabilities for margin (see the section on Futures above). If the purchased options expire worthless, you will suffer a total loss of your investment which will consist of the option premium plus transaction costs. If you are contemplating purchasing deep-out-of-the-money options, you should be aware that the chance of such options becoming profitable ordinarily is remote.

Selling ("writing" or "granting") an option generally entails considerably greater risk than purchasing options. Although the premium received by the seller is fixed, the seller may sustain a loss well in excess of that amount. The seller will be liable for additional margin to maintain the position if the market moves unfavorably. The seller will also be exposed to the risk of the purchaser exercising the option and the seller will be obligated to either settle the option in cash or to acquire or deliver the underlying interest. If the option is on a future, the seller will acquire a position in a future with associated liabilities for margin (see the section on Futures above). If the option is 'covered' by the seller holding a corresponding position in the underlying interest or a future or another option, the risk may be reduced. If the option is not covered, the risk of loss can be unlimited.

Certain exchanges in some jurisdictions permit deferred

payment of the option premium, exposing the purchaser to liability for margin payments not exceeding the amount of the premium. The purchaser is still subject to the risk of losing the premium and transaction costs. When the option is exercised or expires, the purchaser is responsible for any unpaid premium outstanding at that time.

Additional risks common to futures and options

4. Terms and conditions of contracts

You should ask the firm with which you deal about the terms and conditions of the specific futures or options which you are trading and associated obligations (e.g. the circumstances under which you may become obligated to make or take delivery of the underlying interest of a futures contract and, in respect of options, expiration dates and restrictions on the time for exercise). Under certain circumstances, the specifications of outstanding contracts (including the exercise price of an option) may be modified by the exchange or clearing house to reflect changes in the underlying interest.

5. Suspension or restriction or trading and pricing relationships

Market conditions (e.g. illiquidity) and/or the operation of the rules of certain markets (e.g. the suspension of trading in any contract or contract month because of price limits or "circuit breakers") may increase the risk of loss by making it difficult or impossible to effect transactions or liquidate/offset positions. If you have sold options, this may increase the risk of loss.

Further, normal pricing relationships between the underlying interest and the future, and the underlying interest and the option may not exist. This can occur when, for example, the futures contract underlying the option is subject to price limits while the option is not. The absence of an underlying reference price may make it difficult to judge "fair" value.

6.   Deposited cash and property

You should familiarize yourself with the protections accorded money or other property you deposit for domestic and foreign transactions, particularly in the event of a firm insolvency or bankruptcy. The extent to which you may recover your money or property may be governed by specific legislation or local rules. In some jurisdictions, property which has been specifically identifiable as your own will be pro-rated in the same manner as cash for purposes of distribution in the event of a shortfall.

7.   Commission and other charges

Before you begin to trade, you should obtain a clear explanation of all commissions, fees and other charges for which you will be liable. These charges will affect your net profit (if any) or increase your loss.

8.   Transactions in other jurisdictions

Transactions on markets in other jurisdictions, including markets formally linked to a domestic market, may expose you to additional risk. Such markets may be subject to regulation which may offer different or diminished investor protection. Before you trade you should inquire about any rules relevant to your particular transactions. Your local regulatory authority will be unable to compel the enforcement of the rules of regulatory authorities or markets in other jurisdictions where your transactions have been effected. You should ask the firm with which you deal for details about the types of redress available in both your home jurisdiction and other relevant jurisdictions before you start to trade.

9.   Currency risks

The profit or loss in transactions in foreign currency-denominated contracts (whether they are traded in your own or another jurisdiction) will be affected by fluctuations in currency rates where there is a need to convert from the currency denomination of the contract to another currency.

10. Trading facilities

Most open-outcry and electronic trading facilities are supported by computer-based component systems for the order-routing, execution, matching, registration or clearing of trades. As with all facilities and systems, they are vulnerable to temporary disruption or failure. Your ability to recover certain losses may be subject to limits on liability imposed by the system provider, the market, the clearing house and/or member firms. Such limits may vary: you should ask the firm with which you deal for details in this respect.

11. Electronic trading

Trading on an electronic trading system may differ not only from trading in an open-outcry market but also from trading on other electronic trading systems. If you undertake transactions on an electronic trading system, you will be exposed to risks associated with the system including the failure of hardware and software. The result of any system failure may be that your order is either not executed according to your instructions or is not executed at all.

12. Off-exchange transactions

In some jurisdictions, and only then in restricted circumstances, firms are permitted to effect off-exchange transactions. The firm with which you deal may be acting as your counterparty to the transaction. It may be difficult or impossible to liquidate an existing position, to assess the value, to determine a fair price or to assess the exposure to risk. For these reasons, these transactions may involve increased risks. Off-exchange transactions may be less regulated or subject to a separate regulatory regime. Before you undertake such transactions, you should familiarize yourself with applicable rules and attendant risks.

ELECTRONIC TRADING AND ORDER ROUTING SYSTEMS DISCLOSURE STATEMENT*

Electronic trading and order routing systems differ from traditional open outcry pit trading and manual order routing methods. Transactions using an electronic system are subject to the rules and regulations of the exchange(s) offering the system and/or listing the contract. Before you engage in transactions using an electronic system, you should carefully review the rules and regulations of the exchange(s) offering the system and/or listing contracts you intend to trade.

DIFFERENCES AMONG ELECTRONIC TRADING SYSTEMS

Trading or routing orders through electronic systems varies widely among the different electronic systems. You should consult the rules and regulations of the exchange offering the electronic system and/or listing the contract traded or order routed to understand, among other things, in the case of trading systems, the system's order matching procedure, opening and closing procedures and prices, error trade policies, and trading limitations or requirements; and in the case of all systems, qualifications for access and grounds for termination and limitations on the types of orders that may be entered into the system. Each of these matters may present different risk factors with respect to trading on or using a particular system. Each system may also present risks related to system access, varying response times, and security. In the case of internet-based systems, there may be additional types of risks related to system access, varying response times and security, as well as risks related to service providers and the receipt and monitoring of electronic mail.

RISKS ASSOCIATED WITH SYSTEM FAILURE

Trading through an electronic trading or order routing system exposes you to risks associated with system or component failure. In the event of system or component failure, it is possible that, for a certain time period, you may not be able to enter new orders, execute existing orders, or modify or cancel orders that were previously entered. System or component failure may also result in loss of orders or order priority.

SIMULTANEOUS OPEN OUTCRY PIT AND ELECTRONIC TRADING

Some contracts offered on an electronic trading system may be traded electronically and through open outcry during the same trading hours. You should review the rules and regulations of the exchange offering the

---

* Each exchange's relevant rules are available upon request from the industry professional with whom you have an account. Some exchanges' relevant rules also are available on the exchange's internet home page.

system and/or listing the contract to determine how orders that do not designate a particular process will be executed.

LIMITATION OF LIABILITY

Exchanges offering an electronic trading or order routing system and/or listing the contract may have adopted rules to limit their liability, the liability of FCMs, and software and communication system vendors and the amount of damages you may collect for system failure and delays. These limitations of liability provisions vary among the exchanges. You should consult the rules and regulations of the relevant exchange(s) in order to understand these liability limitations.

DISCLOSURE FOR THE U.S.A. PATRIOT ACT

FMI is committed to complying with U.S. statutory and regulatory requirements designed to assist the Federal Government in combating money laundering and any activity which facilitates the funding of terrorist or criminal activities. The U.S.A. PATRIOT ACT enhances the money laundering prevention requirements imposed on securities firms and other financial institutions. As part of our customer identification procedures, FMI may ask the Customer or its respective Advisor to provide identification documents or other information as necessary to comply with these procedures. Until such information or documents is provided, FMI may not be able to open an account or effect any transactions for the Customer.

DISCLOSURE STATEMENT ON FUTURES EXCHANGE OWNERSHIP INTERESTS AND INCENTIVE PROGRAMS

U.S. Futures Exchange Rule 315(a) specifically requires us to inform you that your Futures Commission Merchant ("FCM"), or one or more of its affiliates, has a direct or indirect ownership interest in the U.S. Futures Exchange. In addition, your FCM or one or more of its affiliates has entered into an agreement to prepay quarterly commissions to the U.S. Futures Exchange and is permitted to claim a credit against those prepaid commissions for orders that you elect to have your FCM execute on that exchange. Your FCM and its affiliates are not, however, permitted to claim a credit against those prepaid commissions for orders that your FCM or its affiliate exercises the discretion to direct to that exchange.

You should also be aware that your FCM or one or more of its affiliates, also owns stock or has some other form of ownership interest in the Chicago Mercantile Exchange, the Board of Trade of the City of Chicago, The Clearing Corporation, and certain other U.S. and foreign exchanges and clearing houses that you may trade on or that may clear your trades.

As a result, you should be aware that your FCM or its affiliate might receive financial benefits related to its ownership interest when trades are executed on such an exchange or cleared at such a clearing house.

In addition, futures exchanges from time to time have in place other arrangements that call for participating members to pre-pay fees based on volume thresholds, or may provide members with volume or market making discounts or credits, or other incentive or arrangements that are intended to encourage market participants to trade on or direct trades to that exchange. Your FCM, or one or more of its affiliates, may participate in and obtain financial benefits from such an incentive program.

You should contact your FCM directly if you would like to know whether it has an ownership interest in a particular exchange or clearing house, or whether it participates in any incentive program on a particular exchange or clearing house. You may also contact any particular futures exchange directly to ask if it has any such incentive program for member firms.

* * *

APPENDIX C

INTERNATIONAL UNIFORM BROKERAGE EXECUTION SERVICES ("GIVE-UP") AGREEMENT: CUSTOMER VERSION 2008[1, 2]

■ ■ ■

CAUTION: THIS AGREEMENT IS DESIGNED AS A BASIC DOCUMENT FOR MARKET PARTICIPANTS ENGAGING IN "GIVE-UP" TRANSACTIONS. IT IS NOT INTENDED TO SERVE AS AN ALL ENCOMPASSING DOCUMENT FOR USE BY ALL PARTIES UNDER ALL CIRCUMSTANCES. PARTIES SHOULD CAREFULLY CONSIDER THE FULL SCOPE OF REGULATORY (INCLUDING EXCHANGE) AND COMMERCIAL TERMS THAT MAY BE APPLICABLE TO THEIR PARTICULAR CIRCUMSTANCES AND MAY ELECT TO ENTER INTO MORE DETAILED CUSTOMER AGREEMENTS AT THE OUTSET OR DURING THE COURSE OF THEIR RELATIONSHIP.

Agreement made this _____ day of _____, 20 _____, by and among

_____ ("Executing Broker")

_____ ("Clearing Broker")

_____ ("Customer")

1. All transactions executed orally, in writing or through an electronic order facility or cleared hereunder shall be subject to applicable laws, governmental, regulatory, self-regulatory, exchange or clearing house rules, regulations, interpretations, protocols and the customs and usages of the exchange or clearing house on which they are executed and cleared, as in force from time to time ("Applicable Law"). All disputes relating to transactions executed or cleared under this

---

[1] For instructions as to how to use this International Give-Up Agreement, go to the FIA website at: www.futuresindustry.org/giveup-agreements2.asp

[2] This Uniform Agreement was prepared in consultation with the FIA, FOA and MFA. Any changes or additions to the wording of this standard document must be clearly indicated. Failure to do so constitutes a representation that the document is the International Uniform Brokerage Execution Services ("Give-Up") Agreement: Customer Version 2008 and has not been modified in any respect.

Agreement shall be governed by and settled pursuant to Applicable Law and shall be subject to the jurisdiction of the exchange (and, if applicable, its clearing house) upon which the dispute arises. The parties to this Agreement shall perform their respective obligations and exercise their respective rights under this Agreement (including, but not limited to, rejecting a Customer order, calling a Customer for margin or providing any notice specified herein) using commercially reasonable judgement, in a commercially reasonable manner under the circumstances, and consistent with Applicable Law.

2. Customer authorizes Executing Broker to execute orders for Customer as transmitted orally, in writing or through an electronic order facility by Customer to Executing Broker, or, as permitted by Applicable Law, directly to an exchange. Executing Broker reserves the right to reject an order that Customer may transmit to Executing Broker for execution and shall promptly notify Customer of any such rejection. Clearing Broker may, upon prior notice to Executing Broker and Customer, place limits or conditions on the positions it will accept for give-up for Customer's account.

3. Unless otherwise agreed in writing, each of the parties authorizes Executing Broker and Clearing Broker to use the services of one or more other persons or entities in connection with their obligations under this Agreement; provided, however, that Executing Broker and Clearing Broker remain responsible to Customer for the performance (or failure of performance) of their respective obligations and responsibilities under this Agreement.

4. Customer, whether placing orders orally, in writing or through an electronic order facility, will be responsible for accurate and valid placement of orders. Executing Broker, and not Clearing Broker, will be responsible for determining that all orders are placed or authorized by Customer. Additionally, except as otherwise agreed in writing, Executing Broker will: (a) upon placement of orders by Customer, confirm the terms of the orders with Customer if customary and practicable; (b) be responsible for the accurate execution of all orders; (c) confirm the execution of such orders to Customer as soon as is practicable thereafter; and (d) transmit such executed orders to Clearing Broker as soon as practicable, but in no event later than the period mandated by Applicable Law. Subject to Section 2 herein, Clearing Broker shall be responsible for clearing all executed orders transmitted to Clearing Broker. Unless otherwise provided by Applicable Law, neither Executing Broker nor Clearing Broker shall be responsible or liable for losses or damages resulting from: (x) error, negligence or misconduct of Customer and/or exchange or clearing house; (y) failure of transmission,

communication or electronic order facilities; or (z) any other cause or causes beyond their control.

5. Executing Broker will, where applicable, bill commissions for executing trades, as elected in Section 12 below, on a monthly basis. Customer or Clearing Broker, as elected in Section 12 below, shall be responsible for verifying billing and making payment. Clearing Broker will, where applicable, pay floor brokerage fees, as well as any exchange or clearing house fees, incurred for all transactions executed by Executing Broker for and on behalf of Customer and subsequently accepted by Clearing Broker.

6. In the event that Customer disputes or denies knowledge of any transaction, Clearing Broker or Executing Broker shall be authorized to liquidate or otherwise offset the disputed position. Where practicable, prior notice of such liquidation or offset shall be provided to the other parties to this Agreement.

7. In the event that Clearing Broker does not, for any reason, accept a trade transmitted to it by Executing Broker, Clearing Broker shall promptly notify Customer and Executing Broker of such non-acceptance, and Executing Broker, or its designated clearing broker if applicable, shall at its option be entitled to:

   (a) close out Customer's trade by such sale, purchase, disposal or other cancellation transaction as Executing Broker may determine, whether on the market, by private contract or any other appropriate method. Executing Broker shall promptly notify Customer of such close out. Any balance resulting from such close out shall be promptly settled between Executing Broker and Customer; or

   (b) transfer Customer's trades to another clearing broker as instructed by Customer; or

   (c) clear Customer's trade in accordance with the following terms:

      i. Customer shall be fully liable for any and all obligations arising out of or related to transactions entered into or carried in Customer's account by Executing Broker, including, but not limited to: 1) debit balances, 2) exchange or clearing house fees, and 3) brokerage, commissions, and applicable fees charged by Executing Broker;

      ii. Executing Broker shall have the right to call Customer for margin in such amounts, in such form, by such time and in such manner as may be required by Executing Broker. If Customer fails to meet such margin call within such specified time, or if Executing Broker, in its discretion, otherwise deems it appropriate for Executing Broker's protection, Executing Broker may close out Customer's trade pursuant to sub-paragraph (a) above;

    iii. Customer acknowledges that Customer's trades may be subject to exercise or delivery assignments, where applicable.

8. Customer acknowledges that all notices and disclosures that are provided by Clearing Broker to Customer (or Customer's representative) pursuant to Applicable Law, will be deemed, for purposes of Section 7 of this Agreement, as if received by Customer from Executing Broker as well as from Clearing Broker. Clearing Broker represents, warrants and covenants to Executing Broker that it has provided, and will provide, all required notices and disclosures to Customer (or Customer's representative).

9. This Agreement may be terminated by any of the parties hereto upon prior written notice to the other parties. Any such termination shall have no effect upon any party's rights and obligations arising out of transactions executed prior to such termination.

10. This Agreement shall be exclusively governed by, and construed in accordance with, the laws of _____ without regard to principles of choice of law.

11. This Agreement shall not amend or vary any clearing or electronic services agreement between Clearing Broker and Customer or Executing Broker and Customer. In the event of a conflict between this Agreement and such other clearing or electronic services agreement with respect to the execution, clearing or carrying of Customer's trades, such other clearing or electronic services agreement will control with respect thereto.

12. Executing Broker, where applicable, will bill commissions per contract, per half turn, as specified on attached Addendum, rate schedule, or as separately agreed.

13. Each party consents to the electronic recording, without the use of an automatic warning tone, of all telephone conversations between or among the parties and their representatives.

14. Unless otherwise prohibited by Applicable Law, any party to this Agreement, from time to time, may add additional accounts of Customer to be governed by this Agreement by prior written notice (which may be by facsimile or other electronic transmission) to the other parties, *provided that* (i) the same fees agreed to herein apply

and (ii) valid clearing accounts for such accounts exist at the Clearing Broker.

15. This Agreement may be executed and delivered in counterparts (including by facsimile or other electronic transmission), each of which will be deemed an original

16. Any party that has manually executed this Agreement represents, covenants and agrees that the version electronically executed by the other parties and stored on EGUS is the final version and sets forth the complete terms and conditions as agreed to by all of the parties.

17. Conformed signatures were executed electronically in accordance with the FIA Electronic Give-Up Agreement System User Agreement.

IN WITNESS WHEREOF, the parties hereto have caused this Agreement to be duly executed and delivered by their respective authorized officers as of the date set forth above.

_____

[Name of Customer]

By_____

_____

[Print Name and Title]

_____

[Name of Clearing Broker]

By_____

_____

[Print Name and Title]

_____

[Name of Executing Broker]

By_____

_____

[Print Name and Title]

ADDENDUM TO INTERNATIONAL UNIFORM BROKERAGE EXECUTION SERVICES ("GIVE-UP") AGREEMENT

MADE THIS _____ DAY OF _____, 20

CONTACT PERSONS

Any notices or problems regarding these transactions should immediately be brought to the attention of the contact persons of each of the parties hereto, whose names, addresses, and numbers are set forth below. Each party may change its operational contact by notice to the others.

Executing Broker	*Clearing Broker*
For Trading	**For Trading**
Name:	Name:
Name of Person:	Name of Person:
Address:	Address:
Telephone No.:	Telephone No.:
Fax No.:	Fax No.:
Email	Email:
For Documentation	**For Documentation**
Name of Person:	Name of Person:
Address:	Address:
Telephone No.:	Telephone No.:
Fax No.:	Fax No.:
Email:	Email:

Customer

For Trading

Name:

Name of Person:

Address:

Telephone No:

Fax No.:

Email:

For Documentation:

Name of Person:

Address:

Telephone No.:

Fax No.:

Email:

CUSTOMER'S ACCOUNT

Customer's account number with Clearing Broker

BILLING ADDRESS

Invoices to be sent to the address set forth below.

Name:

Address:

APPENDIX D

INTRODUCING BROKER AGREEMENT OF FILLER & MARKHAM INC.

■ ■ ■

This Agreement is made in New York, New York on the ____ day of _____, 20__ by and among Filler & Markham Inc. ("FMI"), a Delaware corporation with its principal office located at _____, New York, New York _____, and _____ ("Introducing Broker"), a _____ corporation with its principal office located at _____.

W I T N E S S E T H:

WHEREAS, FMI is presently engaged in a general brokerage business in securities and commodities; and

WHEREAS, Introducing Broker is desirous of having FMI carry commodity accounts for the Introducing Broker's customers referred to FMI, such accounts to be carried on a fully-disclosed basis.

NOW, THEREFORE, in consideration of the mutual covenants contained herein, and other good and valuable consideration, the receipt and sufficiency of which are acknowledged, the parties agree as follows:

I. FINANCIAL ARRANGEMENTS

A. As compensation for FMI's services as a clearing firm, FMI will charge an amount for brokerage commissions as set forth in Schedule A attached hereto with respect to the accounts introduced by Introducing Broker.

B. No allocation of FMI commissions will be payable to Introducing Broker on any transaction executed by FMI which, except as otherwise provided hereinafter, must be closed out by FMI pursuant to exchange rules or internal FMI policies.

C. All amounts payable to Introducing Broker shall be paid by FMI on a monthly basis within thirty (30) days after the end of the month for transactions on which a commission is charged by FMI during said month.

II. APPLICABLE LAW

As used herein, the term "Applicable Law" shall mean, to the extent applicable to the activities of FMI and Introducing Broker, and as constituted from time to time, (i) all United States federal and state statutes and laws and all statutes and laws of foreign countries, (2) all rules and regulations of all regulatory agencies, organizations and bodies, (3) all rules and regulations of all exchanges and their clearing associations, corporations and organizations, if any, and (4) all rules and regulations of all self-regulatory agencies, organizations and bodies.

III. OPENING OF ACCOUNTS

A. In connection with the opening of each new disclosed account for Introducing Broker's customers introduced hereunder, Introducing Broker agrees that it will not request FMI to carry such an account until Introducing Broker has in its possession all of the necessary account documents and information as required below and as required by Applicable Law. Therefore, Introducing Broker agrees as follows:

1. Introducing Broker will obtain all background information required by Applicable Law or by FMI for any new customer accounts and, if requested by FMI, shall promptly provide such information to FMI. Such information shall include, at a minimum, all information required under Applicable Law, including applicable know-your-customer rules, financial and credit information and such other reasonable information as may be requested by FMI.

2. Introducing Broker will obtain a duly-executed and dated Commodity Client Agreement used by FMI or such other Customer Agreement in a form acceptable to FMI, including customer acknowledgements of the CFTC Risk Disclosure Statements, the disclosure statement for all electronic trading systems and all other disclosures required by Applicable Law, and all other required commodity account documents required by FMI. With respect to discretionary accounts, Introducing Broker will obtain a duly executed and dated FMI discretionary trading authorization document, all other documents or acknowledgements required from time to time by Applicable Law, including NFA Rule 2–8. Introducing Broker will promptly provide copies of such foregoing agreements and account documents to FMI.

3. No customer account may be opened and no brokerage commission rate may be set for each customer account by Introducing Broker without the prior approval of FMI.

C. FMI may, upon prior notification and consent of Introducing Broker, which shall not be unreasonably withheld, independently obtain any information about any account introduced by Introducing Broker, and may independently seek any documents from any account introduced by Introducing Broker.

D.   FMI, in its sole and absolute discretion, may accept or reject any account introduced by Introducing Broker and may terminate any previously-accepted account or request any previously-accepted account to be transferred to another futures commission merchant. The fact that an account introduced by Introducing Broker is rejected, terminated or requested to be transferred shall not be a bar against FMI soliciting such account and accepting it as a FMI customer.

E.   Introducing Broker is solely and exclusively responsible for compliance with Applicable Law with respect to the opening of accounts hereunder and all applicable record-keeping requirements, and no action by FMI in requesting information, agreements or documents, either from Introducing Broker or its customers, shall be construed as an acceptance of such responsibility by, or delegation thereof to, FMI.

IV. TRANSACTIONS

A.   FMI shall have the right, in all cases, to set, raise or lower original and maintenance margin requirements, as long as they are not below the minimum margin requirements of the applicable exchanges and boards of trade, and may apply any changes retroactively so long as such retroactive changes are made for the protection of FMI as FMI may determine in the exercise of its good faith judgment. Whenever FMI notifies Introducing Broker of the need for margin funds, other funds, documents or assurances, Introducing Broker will contact the appropriate customer promptly. FMI may, upon prior notice to Introducing Broker or reasonable attempt thereof, contact Introducing Broker's customers to call for margin funds, other funds, documents or assurances. Any notification hereunder may be made by telephone. When an account fails to satisfy FMI's margin and other requirements, FMI may proceed with the liquidation of such account and may take any reasonable remedial actions as it may deem necessary or desirable, all in FMI's sole and absolute discretion, with or without notice to Introducing Broker or its customers, although FMI will make reasonable attempts to contact Introducing Broker prior to taking such actions. Notwithstanding the above, Introducing Broker shall be obligated to pay FMI promptly any amount due FMI or owed by FMI to the respective Exchange, Clearing House or a third party.

B.   FMI shall have the right, in all cases, to set, raise or lower position limits and may apply any changes retroactively so long as such retroactive changes are made for the protection of FMI as FMI may determine in the exercise its good faith judgment. Introducing Broker agrees to adhere to and abide by all such position limits. FMI shall have the right, in all cases, to decline to accept for clearance or liquidate any futures or option transaction causing a violation of established position limits or margin requirements, including without limitation transactions executed directly by Introducing Broker and given up to FMI for clearance by FMI.

C.   FMI shall have the right, in all cases, to refuse to accept any order or other transaction regardless of whether it continues to carry the account for which an order or transaction is refused.

D.   FMI shall not be responsible for any funds or other property paid or delivered by or on behalf of any customer and Introducing Broker until such funds or property are (1) paid or physically delivered to FMI at FMI's offices at Three World Financial Center, 7th Floor, New York, New York 10285–0700 and the receipt of which has been acknowledged in writing by FMI, or (2) received or credited to a FMI bank account and the receipt has been acknowledged by such bank.

E.   FMI agrees to send to Introducing Broker's customers disclosed to FMI confirmations, purchases and sales statements, monthly statements and other customary statements of accounts, with copies to Introducing Broker.

V.   REPRESENTATIONS AND WARRANTIES

A.   Introducing Broker represents and warrants to FMI as follows:

1.   Introducing Broker is registered with the Commodity Futures Trading Commission ("CFTC") as an introducing broker or as a futures commission merchant, is a member in good standing with the National Futures Association ("NFA") and has all the required licenses and registrations required under Applicable Law to perform its activities set forth herein.

2.   Introducing Broker is and shall remain in full compliance with any legal and regulatory requirements applicable to its activities, including, without limitation, financial, reporting and recordkeeping requirements.

3.   All of Introducing Broker's partners, officers, principals and employees are registered with the CFTC as associated persons or indicated as principals, and all of such persons, who are required to be, are associate members of NFA.

B.   FMI represents and warrants to Introducing Broker as follows:

1.   FMI is and shall remain properly registered with the CFTC as a futures commission merchant and a member in good standing with the NFA as a futures commission merchant.

2.   FMI is and shall remain in full compliance with all legal, regulatory and customer requirements applicable to its activities, including, without limitation, all financial, reporting and recordkeeping requirements.

VI. COMPLIANCE AND SUPERVISION

A.   Introducing Broker is solely and exclusively responsible for compliance with Applicable Law and the supervision of its activities and the activities of its agents, servants, officers, employees, partners and principals, including but not limited to, compliance with all broker-client relationships, order execution and entry procedures, order ticket preparation, record-keeping requirements, and registration of all personnel required to be registered.

VII. INDEMNITIES AND RELATED MATTERS

A.   The parties agree to indemnify and hold each other harmless from and against any loss, damage, liability or expense which either may sustain as the result of (i) willful misconduct, errors or omissions made by the other or employees or agents of the other, or (ii) violations of Applicable Law by the other or employees or agents of the other.

B.   Any aforesaid indemnification and hold harmless obligation shall remain in effect without limit of time after the termination of this Agreement for any act or omission which shall have occurred during the period of this Agreement, whether discovered then or at any time subsequent to the termination of this Agreement.

C.   If FMI or Introducing Broker or both FMI and Introducing Broker are involved in any customer complaint, civil suit, reparations, arbitration or regulatory proceeding or reasonably expect to become so involved, FMI and Introducing Broker will cooperate with each other by furnishing all documents necessary to conduct an investigation and defend a claim or proceeding, unless it would be clearly prejudicial for a party to so cooperate.

D.   In the event of an action described in C above, FMI and Introducing Broker will permit appropriate persons in their respective organizations or their attorneys, insurance representatives or auditors to interview employees of the other in the presence of representatives of both firms.

E.   In the event of a customer complaint, civil suit, reparations, arbitration or regulatory proceeding joining FMI as a party thereto, FMI may contact the customer(s) who initiated such action, upon prior notification to Introducing Broker.

F.   Each of Introducing Broker and FMI shall promptly notify the other in writing of the institution against Introducing Broker or FMI of any suit, action, investigation or proceeding by any customer of Introducing Broker introduced to FMI or by any regulatory agency, exchange or board of trade with respect to a customer of Introducing Broker and of every material development in any such claim, suit, action, investigation or proceeding.

G.   Notwithstanding any of the above, Introducing Broker shall be liable for and shall pay FMI for any and all obligations, expenses, costs, debts, and liabilities or any kind or amount owed FMI from any customer account on FMI's books which was referred to by Introducing Broker pursuant to this Agreement.

H. FMI reserves the right to withhold payments due the Introducing Broker for the purposes of creating a surplus reserve amount which FMI can debit to pay any such obligations due FMI by Introducing Broker pursuant to this Agreement. FMI agrees to notify Introducing Broker of any such amounts withheld pursuant hereto.

VIII.   RELATIONSHIP

It is expressly understood and agreed that FMI is not entering into any partnership, agency arrangement, correspondent arrangement, joint account or joint venture with Introducing Broker. It is the purpose and intent of the parties that Introducing Broker shall be and remain an independent contractor and that Introducing Broker shall not represent the relationship to the contrary or use FMI's name in any manner which states, or from which a prospective or existing customer may infer, that Introducing Broker is an agent, representative or employee of FMI, or that Introducing Broker is acting in any capacity other than as an independent contractor. In addition, Introducing Broker may not prepare, distribute or use any written materials which bear FMI's name without the prior written consent of FMI.

FMI has no interest in Introducing Broker's profits or losses and shall not be liable, except as expressly provided herein, for any debts or obligations now existing or hereinafter incurred for any reason by Introducing Broker or any officer, director, agent, servant or employee of Introducing Broker.

IX. NOTICES

All notices required under the terms and provisions of this Agreement shall be in writing, given in person, by mail or by fax, promptly confirmed by letter, and that any such notice shall be effective when received at the address specified below (which may be changed with written notice as described in this paragraph).

If to FMI: _____

_____

_____

Attention: _____

If to Broker: _____

_____

_____

Attention: _____

X.   MISCELLANEOUS

A.   This Agreement shall be governed by the laws of the State of New York without reference to choice of law doctrine. Any controversy arising out of or relating to this Agreement, or the breach thereof, shall be settled by arbitration in accordance with the rules, then in effect, of the National Futures Association. Judgment upon any award rendered by the arbitrators may be entered in any court having jurisdiction. The laws of the State of New York shall govern any arbitration to the extent they are not superseded by the laws of the chosen forum.

B.   This Agreement shall become effective on the date first indicated above unless another date shall be mutually agreed upon by the parties and, except as otherwise provided herein, shall continue in effect until terminated at the option of either party upon thirty (30) days written notice delivered to and received by the other at the address specified herein.

C.   This Agreement represents the entire agreement between the parties with respect to the matters covered hereunder. This agreement may be modified only by a writing duly executed by the party to be charged with such modification.

D.   The failure on the part of FMI or Introducing Broker to require compliance with any provision of this agreement on any occasion shall not be construed as a waiver with respect to compliance upon any other occasion or with any other provision of this agreement. No course of conduct between the parties shall be or be construed as any waiver of any rights by the parties.

E.   The headings of the sections of this agreement are intended for identification and convenience only and shall not be used to effect the construction of interpretation of the text of this Agreement.

FMI

By: _____

Name: _____

Title: _____

_____
(Introducing Broker)

By: _____

Name: _____

Title: _____

SCHEDULE A

Name of Customer	Brokerage Commissions Paid to FMI	Brokerage Commissions Paid to Introducing Broker
_____	Round-turn Brokerage Commissions and Exchange Clearing and NFA Fees charged to the account, less $____ per round-turn futures contract	$____ per round-turn futures contract.

APPENDIX E

SECURITY FUTURES ADDENDUM TO THE INSTITUTIONAL FUTURES CUSTOMER AGREEMENT, CORPORATE COMMODITY CLIENT AGREEMENT OR COMMODITY ACCOUNT AGREEMENT OF FILLER & MARKHAM INC.

■ ■ ■

This Addendum, dated as of the _____ day of _____, 200_, supplements the terms and conditions of the Filler & Markham Inc. Institutional Futures Customer Agreement, Corporate Commodity Client Agreement or Commodity Account Agreement, as the case may be (each referred to as the "Futures Agreement"), with respect to security futures contracts carried in Customer's futures account, entered into by and between _____ ("Customer") and Filler & Markham Inc. ("FMI"), a broker-dealer registered with the Securities and Exchange Commission ("SEC") and a futures commission merchant registered with the Commodity Futures Trading Commission ("CFTC").

In consideration of FMI accepting and carrying one or more accounts for Customer for execution, clearance and/or carrying security futures contracts traded on or subject to the rules of various national securities exchanges, alternative trading systems, contract markets, derivatives transaction execution facilities and other exchanges or markets (domestic or foreign), the parties agree as follows:

Relationship to Agreement. Except as otherwise provided in this Addendum, the terms and conditions of the Futures Agreement shall remain in full force and effect and shall apply to all security futures contracts that FMI may execute, clear and/or carry on behalf of Customer. If there are any conflicts between the terms and conditions of this Addendum and the Futures Agreement, the terms and conditions of this Addendum will govern with respect to all transactions in security futures contracts. Customer hereby acknowledges, adopts and reaffirms, with respect to any and all transactions in security futures, any and all representations, warranties and covenants made by it in the Futures Agreement.

Definitions. All terms used but not otherwise defined in this Addendum shall have the meanings ascribed to them in the Futures Agreement. The term "futures contracts" in the Futures Agreement shall be defined to include the term security futures contracts. The term "exchange" in the Futures Agreement shall be defined to include any national securities exchange, alternative trading system, contract market, derivatives transaction execution facility or other exchange or market (domestic or foreign) on which security futures contracts are traded, and the term "clearinghouse" shall be amended to include The Options Clearing Corporation or any other applicable clearinghouse clearing security futures contracts for an exchange.

Account Designation. All security futures contracts and associated margin carried by FMI for Customer will be deemed to be carried in Customer's futures account at FMI unless otherwise specifically directed by Customer upon approval by FMI or unless FMI transfers such positions and margin upon notice to Customer to a securities account. Customer understands and agrees that any security futures contracts, whether traded on a domestic or foreign exchange, and associated margin, property and collateral carried in its futures account will be subject to the CFTC's customer segregated funds or secured amount rules, as applicable. Customer also understands that security futures contracts carried in its futures account will not be afforded protection under SEC Rules 8c–1, 15c2–1, 15c3–2 or 15c3–3 or the Securities Investor Protection Act of 1970 and will not be entitled to Securities Investor Protection Corporation ("SIPC") or excess SIPC insurance coverage, and in the unlikely event of FMI's insolvency Customer's rights shall be determined pursuant to the commodity broker liquidation provisions of the Bankruptcy Code and the CFTC's Part 190 Regulations.

Customer Information. Customer represents and warrants that: (a) Customer has the requisite capacity, power and authority to execute, deliver and perform its obligations under this Addendum and each and every transaction entered into hereunder; (b) Customer is an "eligible contract participant" as defined in Section 1a(12) of the Commodity Exchange Act, as amended; (c) all information provided for or on the Security Futures Qualification Form is complete and accurate; (d) if Customer is a collective investment vehicle, Customer is in compliance with any applicable registration requirements (or applicable exemptions therefrom) under the Commodity Exchange Act and the rules of the CFTC promulgated thereunder; and (e) if Customer's account is being managed by a third party, Customer has specifically authorized such third party to engage in security futures transactions for Customer's account. In the event of any change in such information or status, Customer agrees to promptly notify FMI of such change.

Acknowledgment of Risks. Customer acknowledges and agrees that Customer will not enter an order for security futures contracts unless and until Customer has received and fully read the current Risk Disclosure Statement for Security Futures Contracts (the "Disclosure Document") attached hereto, which advises Customer of the duties, responsibilities and risks associated with trading security futures contracts. Customer hereby acknowledges receipt of the current Disclosure Document and agrees to comply with any applicable duties and responsibilities set forth in the Disclosure Document. Customer represents that it is aware of the risks and obligations of trading security futures contracts and is fully prepared to assume such risk and obligations.

CUSTOMER UNDERSTANDS THAT TRANSACTIONS IN SECURITY FUTURES CONTRACTS INVOLVE A HIGH DEGREE OF RISK AND OFFER NO GUARANTEE OF GAIN OR ASSURANCE AGAINST LOSS. CUSTOMER ALSO UNDERSTANDS THAT PRIOR TO ENGAGING IN ANY SECURITY FUTURES TRANSACTIONS CUSTOMER SHOULD REVIEW ITS PRESENT FINANCIAL SITUATION AND OBJECTIVES AND DETERMINE IF A PARTICULAR TRANSACTION OR STRATEGY IS SUITABLE. FURTHERMORE, CUSTOMER UNDERSTANDS THAT IT SHOULD NOT BUY OR SELL UNCOVERED SECURITY FUTURES POSITIONS UNLESS IT IS PREPARED TO SUSTAIN LARGE LOSSES, WHICH ARE NOT LIMITED TO THE AMOUNT OF MARGIN DEPOSITED WITH RESPECT TO SUCH POSITION. CUSTOMER UNDERSTANDS THAT IT SHOULD NOT BUY PHYSICALLY SETTLED SECURITY FUTURES CONTRACTS UNLESS IT IS PREPARED TO TAKE DELIVERY OF, AND PAY FOR, THE UNDERLYING SECURITIES, AND THAT IT SHOULD NOT SELL PHYSICALLY SETTLED SECURITY FUTURES CONTRACTS UNLESS IT IS PREPARED TO DELIVER THE UNDERLYING

SECURITIES UPON THE EXPIRATION OF THE CONTRACT. CUSTOMER FURTHER UNDERSTANDS THAT NOT ALL SECURITY FUTURES CONTRACTS PERMIT THE DELIVERY OF UNDERLYING SHARES OF STOCK IN SETTLEMENT OF THE CONTRACT. CUSTOMER ALSO UNDERSTANDS THAT IT MAY NOT BE ABLE TO OFFSET PURCHASES AND SALES OF SECURITY FUTURES CONTRACTS THAT ARE EXECUTED ON DIFFERENT EXCHANGES, AND AS A RESULT, CUSTOMER MAY BE REQUIRED TO POST MARGIN FOR AND PERFORM ITS OBLIGATIONS UNDER LONG AND SHORT CONTRACTS EVEN THOUGH THOSE CONTRACTS ARE ECONOMICALLY OFFSETTING.

Order Execution.

Order Routing. Customer is solely responsible for its order routing decisions and for determining the exchange venue at which each order for security futures contracts entered through FMI is to be executed. Customer agrees and acknowledges that FMI may reject any security futures order submitted by Customer that does not include Customer's order routing instructions. FMI makes available order entry and order routing facilities that permit Customer to route such orders to the exchange venue of its choice. FMI does not make any recommendation as to where such orders should be executed and does not undertake to notify Customer of price improvement opportunities or more advantageous execution quality at particular exchange venues.

Cross Trades. Customer agrees that, without prior notice from FMI, when FMI executes orders on Customer's behalf, FMI, its directors, officers, employees, agents and affiliates may take the opposite side of Customer's orders or engage in pre-execution discussions with other market participants to facilitate execution of Customer's orders, subject to the limitations and conditions, if any, contained in any applicable regulations or exchange rules.

Block Trades. Exchange rules provide that eligible customers may enter into privately negotiated transactions in security futures contracts that satisfy certain minimum order size requirements whose price terms may be outside of the prevailing exchange bid-offer for smaller transaction sizes ("block trades"). Customer acknowledges that pursuant to the rules of the various exchanges, FMI has designated Customer as a "Wholesale Customer," "Block Trader," and "Eligible Contract Participant," as applicable, for purposes of executing block trades with or on behalf of Customer, and Customer hereby consents to such designation and to the execution of its orders pursuant to the block trading rules of the various exchanges. Customer further understands that on some exchanges designated Market Makers have the right, but not the obligation, to participate in responding to a block trade order, and that such Market Maker's election to participate in a block trade, may, under certain circumstances where Customer is acting as a responder to another party's block trade order, reduce Customer's participation in such block trade.

Offsetting Orders. Customer agrees and acknowledges that when Customer transmits to the Firm an order to purchase a security futures contract(s) at a time when Customer is short security futures contracts for the same underlying security or narrow-based security index, or when Customer transmits to the Firm an order to sell a security futures contract(s) at a time when Customer is long security futures contracts for the same underlying security or narrow-based security index, unless Customer expressly directs otherwise, the Firm may, but is not obligated to, treat such order as an offsetting order to close (fully or partially, as the case may be) the preexisting position at the respective exchange. Customer also agrees and acknowledges that, in the circumstances described above, should Customer carry open security-futures positions on the same underlying security or narrow-based security index on more than one exchange or marketplace, absent instruction to the contrary from the Customer, the Firm is authorized to offset or close the position on the exchange(s) of the Firm's choice.

Margin. Customer agrees at all times to maintain such margin with FMI on security futures contract positions as FMI may from time to time request in accordance with the terms of the Futures Agreement.

Delivery of Shares of Stock. Customer agrees to honor all delivery notices and to deliver the shares of stock underlying physically settled security futures contracts to FMI in a timely manner, in accordance with applicable delivery requirements. If Customer fails to timely deliver, or provide evidence satisfactory to FMI of Customer's ability to deliver, the underlying shares of stock, FMI may, but is not required to, buy-in such shares at the current market price, liquidate Customer's security futures contracts and/or roll forward Customer's security futures contracts to a later delivery month for Customer's account and risk. Customer understands and agrees that Customer is responsible, and Customer's account will be debited, for any loss, cost or expense incurred by FMI in connection with Customer's failure to timely deliver underlying shares of stock.

Payment of Shares of Stock. Customer agrees to pay for all shares of stock underlying a physically settled security futures contract delivered to its account. FMI is authorized to sell any such underlying shares at the current market price if Customer fails to timely pay for, or provide evidence satisfactory to FMI of its ability to pay for, such shares and Customer understands and agrees that Customer is responsible, and Customer's account will be debited, for any loss, cost or expense incurred by FMI in connection with Customer's failure to timely pay for underlying shares of stock.

Industry Affiliates. Customer, if an individual, represents and warrants to FMI that, except as notified by Customer to FMI in writing, it is not an employee of: (a) any corporation, firm or individual engaged in the business of dealing, either as a broker or as a principal, in securities or futures; (b) an exchange or any entity of which an exchange is a majority owner; or (c) the National Association of Securities Dealers, Inc. ("NASD"), and neither Customer nor any member of Customer's immediate family is associated with a firm that is a member of the NASD or the National Futures Association.

Securities Account. Customer agrees and acknowledges that any delivery of securities underlying physically settled security futures contracts will be effectuated by and through Customer's securities account at FMI. Customer agrees, represents and warrants that it has opened, or will open, prior to making or taking delivery of securities underlying physically settled security futures contracts, a securities account at FMI by completing and executing all documents, and taking any and all other actions, required by FMI to open such an account.

Applicable Law. All security futures contract transactions effected under this Addendum shall be subject to applicable federal and state laws, the rules of the SEC and CFTC, and the rules, interpretations, bylaws, constitutions, and customs and usages of all applicable self regulatory organizations, including but not limited to the NASD, exchanges and clearinghouses where such transactions are executed or cleared. Customer is aware of and agrees to be bound by such laws and rules applicable to the trading of security futures contracts.

Transfer of Funds. Customer authorizes FMI to transfer funds, securities or other property to, between or among any of Customer's securities or securities margin account(s), futures account(s) or non-regulated account(s) when in FMI's judgment a transfer of any excess funds in such account(s) may be necessary to satisfy margin calls, debit balances or for such other reasons as FMI deems appropriate. Promptly following such transfer, FMI will confirm the transfer in writing to Customer. All such transfers shall be made in compliance with the Commodity Exchange Act, Securities Exchange Act of 1934 and the applicable regulations promulgated thereunder.

EFP and EFS Transactions. If Customer engages in exchange for physical ("EFP") or exchange for swaps ("EFS") transactions involving security futures contracts Customer agrees to provide FMI, upon request, with documentation of the cash or swap transaction in the security(ies) underlying the security futures contract(s) associated with the EFP or EFS transaction, as applicable.

Position Limits. Customer is aware and agrees to abide by position limits applicable to security futures contracts as may be established from time to time and agrees not to violate such limits alone or acting in concert with others. If at any time Customer's account is in violation of any applicable position limit, Customer agrees that FMI may liquidate any security futures contract or other positions in any of Customer's accounts with FMI without prior notice to Customer and/or exercise any other remedy permitted under the Futures Agreement as FMI deems appropriate to protect itself.

17. <u>Customer Acknowledgements</u>.

Customer represents that it has received and understands the following disclosure statements. Please acknowledge receipt by checking or initialing the box next to the numbered items:

   ☐   Risk Disclosure Statement for Security Futures Contracts
   ☐   Authorization to Transfer Funds (Paragraph 15 hereof)
   ☐   NQLX Pre-Negotiated Transactions Disclosure Statement

WHEREAS, the parties have entered into this Addendum as of the date set forth above.

	FMI
_____	
Customer Name	
By: _____	By: _____
Name: _____	Name: _____
Title: _____	Title: _____
Date: _____	Date: _____
	By: _____
	Title: <u>Security Futures Principal</u>
	Date: _____

SECURITY FUTURES QUALIFICATION FORM

(A form must be completed for all beneficial owners, prior to Security Futures Principal approval)

I.A. Customer Information (for individuals):

Name _____

Address _____

Home Phone _____   Business Phone _____

E-Mail Address _____   Date of Birth _____

Occupation _____   Employer _____

Tax ID# _____   Annual Income from all Sources $___

Marital Status _____   Number of Dependents _____

Net Worth $_____   Liquid Net Worth $_____
(Excluding Primary Residence)   (*i.e.*, cash, securities, etc.)

I.B. Customer Information (for institutions):

Institution_____

Type of Institution   □ Corporation   □ Limited Liability Corporation
□ Partnership   □ Trust   □ Pension Fund   □ Other_____

Purpose of Institution_____ Nature of the Account_____

Authorized Agent_____ Position_____

Address_____

Business Phone_____ Facsimile_____

E-Mail Address_____ Tax ID#_____

Total Assets of Entity_____ (for funds, assets under management)

Please Attach Most Recent (Audited) Financial Statement, if available

II. <u>Does the customer currently, or has the customer in the past, maintained any of the following accounts with the Firm?</u>

    ☐   Securities Margin Account (Please specify Account Number _____)

    ☐   Futures Account (Please specify Account Number _____)

    ☐   Options Account (Please specify Account Number _____)

    ☐   Foreign Currency (Please specify Account Number _____)

III. <u>Investment Objectives</u>:

☐ Speculation
       OR
☐ Hedging

| | Please Specify | Avg. $ Size | Avg. Frequency of |

IV. <u>Other Investment Experience: Years of Experience of Transactions</u>

	Please Specify	Avg. $ Size	Avg. Frequency of Transactions
☐ Exchange Listed Stocks	___	___	___
☐ OTC Stocks	___	___	___
☐ Corporate Bonds/Debentures	___	___	___
☐ Government Securities	___	___	___
☐ Foreign Securities	___	___	___
☐ Listed Options	___	___	___
☐ OTC Options and Derivatives	___	___	___
☐ Futures	___	___	___
☐ Foreign Currency	___	___	___
☐ Real Estate	___	___	___
☐ Investment Partnerships	___	___	___
☐ Private Placements/Direct Participation Programs	___	___	___

V. <u>Third Party Discretion</u>:

Is the customer represented by a third party account manager?
☐ Yes ☐ No.

If yes, please provide the name, address and experience of the account manager. _____

_____

Copy of customer's discretionary authorization agreement received?
☐ Yes ☐ No

Does discretionary authorization agreement explicitly allow for security futures trading? ☐ Yes ☐ No

Relationship to customer: _____

Will the investment advisor have authority to trade for the account? ☐ Yes ☐ No.

VI. Is the customer employed by an exchange or an NASD or NFA member firm? ☐ Yes ☐ No. If yes, please provide written employer consent with this form.

Is the customer a director, 10% shareholder or policy making officer of any publicly trading company?

☐ Yes ☐ No. If yes, please specify name of company: _____

Amount of Initial Deposit: _____

Form (e.g., cash, securities, etc.) of Initial Deposit: _____

The form was completed by ☐ Customer ☐ Firm Registered Representative/Associated Person.

By signing below, customer understands, agrees and acknowledges: (1) that customer has received, read and executed the FMI. Security Futures Account Addendum and agrees to be bound by the terms and conditions therein (which terms and conditions are hereby incorporated by reference); and (2) that customer has supplied all of the information contained on this Security Futures Qualification Form and attests that all such information is true and accurate and further agrees to promptly notify FMI in writing of any material changes.

Customer Signature_____ Date_____
(*If completed by customer*)

For Associated Person/Registered Representative Use Only

If form was completed by a Firm Representative:

Customer Information obtained by ☐ Mail ☐ Telephone ☐ Interview ☐ E-mail ☐ Facsimile

☐ Other Documents (please specify) _____

☐ Other (please specify) _____

Date Risk Disclosure Statement for Security Futures Contracts Sent to Customer _____

Date NQLX Pre-Negotiated Transactions Disclosure Statement Sent to Customer _____

Name of Registered Representative/Associated Person

AP/RR Signature _____ Date _____

Notes (e.g., information not provided by customer) _____
_____
_____

For Security Futures Principal Use Only

This customer is (check one) ☐ **APPROVED** or ☐ **DISAPPROVED** for security futures trading because:

Provided All Required Information	☐ Yes	☐ No
Provided:	☐ Yes	☐ No
Executed Security Futures Account Addendum	☐ Yes	☐ No
Executed Securities Account Opening Documents	☐ Yes	☐ No
All Other Required Supplemental Documentation	☐ Yes	☐ No
(e.g., tax forms, joint account agreement, etc.)	☐ Yes	☐ No
Sufficient Total Net Worth (Individuals Only)	☐ Yes	☐ No
Sufficient Liquid Net Worth (Individuals Only)	☐ Yes	☐ No
Sufficient Annual Income (Individuals Only)	☐ Yes	☐ No
Sufficient Total Assets (Institutions Only)	☐ Yes	☐ No
Other: _____		

[If customer is approved for security futures, despite not meeting the Firm's standard criteria or providing all required information, state rationale for approval _____
_____]

Notes (e.g., limitations on trading authority)

If approved for security futures trading, and this form was completed by a Firm representative, indicate date on which the completed form was sent to customer_____

(*Must be sent within **fifteen (15)** days of approval by Security Futures Principal*) **[ONLY REQUIRED FOR INDIVIDUAL CUSTOMERS AND ONLY IF CUSTOMER NOT REQUIRED TO EXECUTE THE QUALIFICATION FORM]**

SPF Signature _____ Date _____

The approval of the Security Futures Principal is needed before the customer can engage in security futures trading.

RISK DISCLOSURE STATEMENT FOR SECURITY FUTURES CONTRACTS

This disclosure statement discusses the characteristics and risks of standardized security futures contracts traded on regulated U.S. exchanges. At present, regulated exchanges are authorized to list futures contracts on individual equity securities registered under the Securities Exchange Act of 1934 (including common stock and certain exchange-traded funds and American Depositary Receipts), as well as narrow-based security indices. Futures on other types of securities and options on security futures contracts may be authorized in the future. The glossary of terms appears at the end of the document.

Customers should be aware that the examples in this document are exclusive of fees and commissions that may decrease their net gains or increase their net losses. The examples also do not include tax consequences, which may differ for each customer.

Section 1—Risks of Security Futures

1.1. Risks of Security Futures Transactions

Trading security futures contracts may not be suitable for all investors. You may lose a substantial amount of money in a very short period of time. The amount you may lose is potentially unlimited and can exceed the amount you originally deposit with your broker. This is because futures trading is highly leveraged, with a relatively small amount of money used to establish a position in assets having a much greater value. If you are uncomfortable with this level of risk, you should not trade security futures contracts.

1.2. General Risks

- *Trading security futures contracts involves risk and may result in potentially unlimited losses that are greater than the amount you deposited with your broker.* As with any high risk financial product, you should not risk any funds that you cannot afford to lose, such as your retirement savings, medical and other emergency funds, funds set aside for purposes such as education or home ownership, proceeds from student loans or mortgages, or funds required to meet your living expenses.

- *Be cautious of claims that you can make large profits from trading security futures contracts.* Although the high degree of leverage in security futures contracts can result in large and immediate gains, it can also result in large and immediate losses. As with any financial product, there is no such thing as a "sure winner."

- *Because of the leverage involved and the nature of security futures contract transactions, you may feel the effects of your losses immediately.* Gains and losses in security futures contracts are credited or debited to your account, at a minimum, on a daily basis. If movements in the markets for security futures contracts or the underlying security decrease the value of your positions in security futures contracts, you may be required to have or make additional funds available to your carrying firm as margin. If your account is under the minimum margin requirements set by the exchange or the brokerage firm, your position may be liquidated at a loss, and you will be liable for the deficit, if any, in your account. Margin requirements are addressed in Section 4.

- *Under certain market conditions, it may be difficult or impossible to liquidate a position.* Generally, you must enter into an offsetting transaction in order to liquidate a position in a security futures contract. If you cannot liquidate your position in security futures contracts, you may not be able to realize a gain in the value of your position or prevent losses from mounting. This inability to liquidate could occur, for example, if trading is halted due to unusual trading activity in either the security futures contract or the underlying security; if trading is halted due to recent news events involving the issuer of the underlying security; if systems failures occur on an exchange or at the firm carrying your position; or if the position is on an illiquid market. Even if you can liquidate your position, you may be forced to do so at a price that involves a large loss.

- *Under certain market conditions, it may also be difficult or impossible to manage your risk from open security futures positions by entering into an equivalent but opposite position in another contract month, on another market, or in the underlying security.* This inability to take positions to limit your risk could occur, for example, if trading is halted across markets due to unusual trading activity in the security futures contract or the underlying security or due to recent news events involving the issuer of the underlying security.

- *Under certain market conditions, the prices of security futures contracts may not maintain their customary or anticipated relationships to the prices of the underlying security or index.* These pricing disparities could occur, for example, when the market for the security futures contract is illiquid, when the primary market for the underlying security is closed, or when the reporting of transactions in the underlying security has been delayed. For index products, it could also occur when trading is delayed or halted in some or all of the securities that make up the index.

- *You may be required to settle certain security futures contracts with physical delivery of the underlying security.* If you hold your position in a physically settled security futures contract until the end of the last trading day prior to expiration, you will be obligated to make or take delivery of the underlying securities, which could involve additional costs. The actual settlement terms may vary from contract to contract and exchange to exchange. You should carefully review the settlement and delivery conditions before entering into a security futures contract. Settlement and delivery are discussed in Section 5.

- *You may experience losses due to systems failures.* As with any financial transaction, you may experience losses if your orders for security futures contracts cannot be executed normally due to systems failures on a regulated exchange or at the brokerage firm carrying your position. Your losses may be greater if the brokerage firm carrying your position does not have adequate back-up systems or procedures.

- *All security futures contracts involve risk, and there is no trading strategy that can eliminate it.* Strategies using combinations of positions, such as spreads, may be as risky as outright long or short positions. Trading in security futures contracts requires knowledge of both the securities and the futures markets.

- *Day trading strategies involving security futures contracts and other products pose special risks.* As with any financial product, persons who seek to purchase and sell the same security future in the course of a day to profit from intra-day price movements ("day traders") face a number of special risks, including substantial commissions, exposure to leverage, and competition with professional traders. You should thoroughly understand these risks and have appropriate experience before engaging in day trading. The special risks for day traders are discussed more fully in Section 7.

- *Placing contingent orders, if permitted, such as "stop-loss" or "stop-limit" orders, will not necessarily limit your losses to the intended amount.* Some regulated exchanges may permit you to enter into stop-loss or stop-limit orders for security futures contracts, which are intended to limit your exposure to losses due to market fluctuations. However, market conditions may make it impossible to execute the order or to get the stop price.

- *You should thoroughly read and understand the customer account agreement with your brokerage firm before entering into any transactions in security futures contracts.*

- *You should thoroughly understand the regulatory protections available to your funds and positions in the event of the failure of your brokerage firm.* The regulatory protections available to your funds and positions in the event of the failure of your brokerage firm may vary depending on, among other factors, the contract you are trading and whether you are trading through a securities account or a futures account. Firms that allow customers to trade security futures in either securities accounts or futures accounts, or both, are required to disclose to customers the differences in regulatory protections between such accounts, and, where appropriate, how customers may elect to trade in either type of account.

Section 2—Description of a Security Futures Contract

2.1. What is a Security Futures Contract?

A security futures contract is a legally binding agreement between two parties to purchase or sell in the future a specific quantity of shares of a security or of the component securities of a narrow-based security index, at a certain price. A person who buys a security futures contract enters into a contract to purchase an underlying security and is said to be "long" the contract. A person who sells a security futures contract enters into a contract to sell the underlying security and is said to be "short" the contract. The price at which the contract trades (the "contract price") is determined by relative buying and selling interest on a regulated exchange.

In order to enter into a security futures contract, you must deposit funds with your brokerage firm equal to a specified percentage (usually at least 20 percent) of the current market value of the contract as a performance bond. Moreover, all security futures contracts are marked-to-market at least daily, usually after the close of trading, as described in Section 3 of this document. At that time, the account of each buyer and seller reflects the amount of any gain or loss on the security futures contract based on the contract price established at the end of the day for settlement purposes (the "daily settlement price").

An open position, either a long or short position, is closed or liquidated by entering into an offsetting transaction (i.e., an equal and opposite transaction to the one that opened the position) prior to the contract expiration. Traditionally, most futures contracts are liquidated prior to expiration through an offsetting transaction and, thus, holders do not incur a settlement obligation.

Examples:

> Investor A is long one September XYZ Corp. futures contract. To liquidate the long position in the September XYZ Corp. futures contract, Investor A would sell an identical September XYZ Corp. contract.

> Investor B is short one December XYZ Corp. futures contract. To liquidate the short position in the December

XYZ Corp. futures contract, Investor B would buy an identical December XYZ Corp. contract.

Security futures contracts that are not liquidated prior to expiration must be settled in accordance with the terms of the contract. Some security futures contracts are settled by physical delivery of the underlying security. At the expiration of a security futures contract that is settled through physical delivery, a person who is long the contract must pay the final settlement price set by the regulated exchange or the clearing organization and take delivery of the underlying shares. Conversely, a person who is short the contract must make delivery of the underlying shares in exchange for the final settlement price.

Other security futures contracts are settled through cash settlement. In this case, the underlying security is not delivered. Instead, any positions in such security futures contracts that are open at the end of the last trading day are settled through a final cash payment based on a final settlement price determined by the exchange or clearing organization. Once this payment is made, neither party has any further obligations on the contract.

Physical delivery and cash settlement are discussed more fully in Section 5.

2.2. Purposes of Security Futures

Security futures contracts can be used for speculation, hedging, and risk management. Security futures contracts do not provide capital growth or income.

Speculation

Speculators are individuals or firms who seek to profit from anticipated increases or decreases in futures prices. A speculator who expects the price of the underlying instrument to increase will buy the security futures contract. A speculator who expects the price of the underlying instrument to decrease will sell the security futures contract. Speculation involves substantial risk and can lead to large losses as well as profits.

The most common trading strategies involving security futures contracts are buying with the hope of profiting from an anticipated price increase and selling with the hope of profiting from an anticipated price decrease. For example, a person who expects the price of XYZ stock to increase by March can buy a March XYZ security futures contract, and a person who expects the price of XYZ stock to decrease by March can sell a March XYZ security futures contract. The following illustrates potential profits and losses if Customer A purchases the security futures contract at $50 a share and Customer B sells the same contract at $50 a share (assuming 100 shares per contract).

Price of XYZ at Liquidation	Customer A Profit/Loss	Customer B Profit/Loss
$50	$500	- $500
$50	0	$ 0
$45	- $500	$500

Speculators may also enter into spreads with the hope of profiting from an expected change in price relationships. Spreaders may purchase a contract expiring in one contract month and sell another contract on the same underlying security expiring in a different month (e.g., buy June and sell September XYZ single stock futures). This is commonly referred to as a "calendar spread."

Spreaders may also purchase and sell the same contract month in two different but economically correlated security futures contracts. For example, if ABC and XYZ are both pharmaceutical companies and an individual believes that ABC will have stronger growth than XYZ between now and June, he could buy June ABC futures contracts and sell June XYZ futures contracts * * * Speculators can also engage in arbitrage, which is similar to a spread except that the long and short positions occur on two different markets. An arbitrage position can be established by taking an economically opposite position in a security futures contract on another exchange, in an options contract, or in the underlying security.

Hedging

Generally speaking, hedging involves the purchase or sale of a security future to reduce or offset the risk of a position in the underlying security or group of securities (or a close economic equivalent). A hedger gives up the potential to profit from a favorable price change in the position being hedged in order to minimize the risk of loss from an adverse price change.

An investor who wants to lock in a price now for an anticipated sale of the underlying security at a later date can do so by hedging with security futures. For example, assume an investor owns 1,000 shares of ABC that have appreciated since he bought them. The investor would like to sell them at the current price of $50 per share, but there are tax or other reasons for holding them until September. The investor could sell ten 100-share ABC futures contracts and then buy back those contracts in September when he sells the stock. Assuming the stock price and the futures price change by the same amount, the gain or loss in the stock will be offset by the loss or gain in the futures contracts.

Price in September	Value of 1,000 Shares of ABC	Gain or Loss on Futures	Effective Selling Price
$40	$40,000	$10,000	$50,000
$50	$50,000	$ 0	$50,000
$60	$60,000	$10,000	$50,000

Hedging can also be used to lock in a price now for an anticipated purchase of the stock at a later date. For example, assume that in May a mutual fund expects to buy stocks in a particular industry with the proceeds of bonds that will mature in August. The mutual fund can hedge its risk that the stocks will increase in value between May and August by purchasing security futures contracts on a narrow-based index of stocks from that industry. When the mutual fund buys the stocks in August, it also will liquidate the security futures position in the index. If the relationship between the security futures contract and the stocks in the index is constant, the profit or loss from the futures contract will offset the price change in the stocks, and the mutual fund will have locked in the price that the stocks were selling at in May.

Although hedging mitigates risk, it does not eliminate all risk. For example, the relationship between the price of the security futures contract and the price of the underlying security traditionally tends to remain constant over time, but it can and does vary somewhat. Furthermore, the expiration or liquidation of the security futures contract may not coincide with the exact time the hedger buys or sells the underlying stock. Therefore, hedging may not be a perfect protection against price risk.

Risk Management

Some institutions also use futures contracts to manage portfolio risks without necessarily intending to change the composition of their portfolio by buying or selling the underlying securities. The institution does so by taking a security futures position that is opposite to some or all of its position in the underlying securities. This strategy involves more risk than a traditional hedge because it is not meant to be a substitute for an anticipated purchase or sale.

2.3. Where Security Futures Trade

By law, security futures contracts must trade on a regulated U.S. exchange. Each regulated U.S. exchange that trades security futures contracts is subject to joint regulation by the Securities and Exchange Commission (SEC) and the Commodity Futures Trading Commission (CFTC).

A person holding a position in a security futures contract who seeks to liquidate the position must do so either on the regulated exchange where the original trade took place or on another regulated exchange, if any, where a fungible security futures contract trades. (A person may also seek to manage the risk in that position by taking an opposite position in a comparable contract traded on another regulated exchange.)

Security futures contracts traded on one regulated exchange might not be fungible with security futures contracts traded on another regulated exchange for a variety of reasons. Security futures traded on different regulated exchanges may be non-fungible because they have different contract terms (e.g., size, settlement method), or because they are cleared through different clearing organizations. Moreover, a regulated exchange might not permit its security futures contracts to be offset or liquidated by an identical contract traded on another regulated exchange, even though they have the same contract terms and are cleared through the same clearing organization. You should consult your broker about the fungibility of the contract you are considering purchasing or selling, including which exchange(s), if any, on which it may be offset.

Regulated exchanges that trade security futures contracts are required by law to establish certain listing standards. Changes in the underlying security of a security futures contract may, in some cases, cause such contract to no longer meet the regulated exchange's listing standards. Each regulated exchange will have rules governing the continued trading of security futures contracts that no longer meet the exchange's listing standards. These rules may, for example, permit only liquidating trades in security futures contracts that no longer satisfy the listing standards.

2.4. How Security Futures Differ from the Underlying Security

Shares of common stock represent a fractional ownership interest in the issuer of that security. Ownership of securities confers various rights that are not present with positions in security futures contracts. For example, persons owning a share of common stock may be entitled to vote in matters affecting corporate governance. They also may be entitled to receive dividends and corporate disclosure, such as annual and quarterly reports.

The purchaser of a security futures contract, by contrast, has only a contract for future delivery of the underlying security. The purchaser of the security futures contract is not entitled to exercise any voting rights over the underlying security and is not entitled to any dividends that may be paid by the issuer. Moreover, the purchaser of a security futures contract does not receive the corporate disclosures that are received by shareholders of the underlying security, although such corporate disclosures must be made publicly available through the SEC's EDGAR system, which can be accessed at www.sec.gov. You should review such disclosures before entering into a security futures contract. See Section 9 for further discussion of the impact of corporate events on a security futures contract.

All security futures contracts are marked-to-market at least daily, usually after the close of trading, as described in Section 3 of this document. At that time, the account of each buyer and seller is credited with the amount of any gain, or debited by the amount of any loss, on the security futures contract, based on the contract price established at the end of the day for settlement purposes (the "daily settlement price"). By contrast, the purchaser or seller of the underlying instrument does not have the profit and loss from his or her investment credited or debited until the position in that instrument is closed out.

Naturally, as with any financial product, the value of the security futures contract and of the underlying security may fluctuate. However, owning the underlying security does not require an investor to settle his or her profits and losses daily. By contrast, as a result of the mark-to-market requirements discussed above, a person who is long a security futures contract often will be required to deposit additional funds into his or her account as the price of the security futures contract decreases. Similarly, a person who is short a security futures contract often will be required to deposit additional funds into his or her account as the price of the security futures contract increases.

Another significant difference is that security futures contracts expire on a specific date. Unlike an owner of the underlying security, a person cannot hold a long position in a security futures contract for an extended period of time in the hope that the price will go up. If you do not liquidate your security futures contract, you will be required to settle the contract when it expires, either through physical delivery or cash settlement. For cash-settled contracts in particular, upon expiration, an individual will no longer have an economic interest in the securities underlying the security futures contract.

2.5. Comparison to Options

Although security futures contracts share some characteristics with options on securities (options contracts), these products are also different in a number of ways. Below are some of the important distinctions between equity options contracts and security futures contracts.

If you purchase an options contract, you have the right, but not the obligation, to buy or sell a security prior to the expiration date. If you sell an options contract, you have the obligation to buy or sell a security prior to the expiration date. By contrast, if you have a position in a security futures contract (either long or short), you have both the right and the obligation to buy or sell a security at a future date. The only way that you can avoid the obligation incurred by the security futures contract is to liquidate the position with an offsetting contract.

A person purchasing an options contract runs the risk of losing the purchase price (premium) for the option contract. Because it is a wasting asset, the purchaser of an options contract who neither liquidates the options contract in the secondary market nor exercises it at or prior to expiration will necessarily lose his or her entire investment in the options contract. However, a purchaser of an options contract cannot lose more than the amount of the premium. Conversely, the seller of an options contract receives the premium and assumes the risk that he or she will be required to buy or sell the underlying security on or prior to the expiration date, in which event his or her losses may exceed the amount of the premium received. Although the seller of an options contract is required to deposit margin to reflect the risk of its obligation, he or she may lose many times his or her initial margin deposit.

By contrast, the purchaser and seller of a security futures contract each enter into an agreement to buy or sell a specific quantity of shares in the underlying security. Based upon the movement in prices of the underlying security, a person who holds a position in a security futures contract can gain or lose many times his or her initial margin deposit. In this respect, the benefits of a security futures contract are similar to the benefits of *purchasing* an option, while the risks of entering into a security futures contract are similar to the risks of *selling* an option.

Both the purchaser and the seller of a security futures contract have daily margin obligations. At least once each day, security futures contracts are marked-to-market and the increase or decrease in the value of the contract is credited or debited to the buyer and the seller. As a result, any person who has an open position in a security futures contract may be called upon to meet additional margin requirements or may receive a credit of available funds.

Example:

> Assume that Customers A and B each anticipate an increase in the market price of XYZ stock, which is currently $50 a share. Customer A purchases an XYZ 50 call (covering 100 shares of XYZ at a premium of $5 per share). The option premium is $500 ($5 per share X 100 shares). Customer B purchases an XYZ security futures contract (covering 100 shares of XYZ). The total value of the contract is $5000 ($50 share value X 100 shares). The required margin is $1000 (or 20% of the contract value).

Price of XYZ at expiration	Customer A Profit/Loss	Customer B Profit/Loss
65	1000	1500
60	500	1000
55	0	500
50	-500	0
45	-500	-500
40	-500	-1000
35	-500	-1500

The most that Customer A can lose is $500, the option premium. Customer A breaks even at $55 per share, and makes money at higher prices. Customer B may lose more than his initial margin deposit. Unlike the options premium, the margin on a futures contract is not a cost but a performance bond. The losses for Customer B are not limited by this performance bond. Rather, the losses or gains are determined by the settlement price of the contract, as provided in the example above. Note that if the price of XYZ falls to $35 per share, Customer A loses only $500, whereas Customer B loses $1500.

2.6. Components of a Security Futures Contract

Each regulated exchange can choose the terms of the security futures contracts it lists, and those terms may differ from exchange to exchange or contract to contract. Some of those contract terms are discussed below. However, you should ask your broker for a copy of the contract specifications before trading a particular contract.

2.6.1.   Each security futures contract has a set size. The size of a security futures contract is determined by the regulated exchange on which the contract trades. For example, a security futures contract for a single stock may be based on 100 shares of that stock. If prices are reported per share, the value of the contract would be the price times 100. For narrow-based security indices, the value of the contract is the price of the component securities times the multiplier set by the exchange as part of the contract terms.

2.6.2.   Security futures contracts expire at set times determined by the listing exchange. For example, a particular contract may expire on a particular day, e.g., the third Friday of the expiration month. Up until expiration, you may liquidate an open position by offsetting your contract with a fungible opposite contract that expires in the same month. If you do not liquidate an open position before it expires, you will be required to make or take delivery of the underlying security or to settle the contract in cash after expiration.

2.6.3. Although security futures contracts on a particular security or a narrow-based security index may be listed and traded on more than one regulated exchange, the contract specifications may not be the same. Also, prices for contracts on the same security or index may vary on different regulated exchanges because of different contract specifications.

2.6.4. Prices of security futures contracts are usually quoted the same way prices are quoted in the underlying instrument. For example, a contract for an individual security would be quoted in dollars and cents per share. Contracts for indices would be quoted by an index number, usually stated to two decimal places.

2.6.5. Each security futures contract has a minimum price fluctuation (called a tick), which may differ from product to product or exchange to exchange. For example, if a particular security futures contract has a tick size of 1¢, you can buy the contract at $23.21 or $23.22 but not at $23.215.

2.7. Trading Halts

The value of your positions in security futures contracts could be affected if trading is halted in either the security futures contract or the underlying security. In certain circumstances, regulated exchanges are required by law to halt trading in security futures contracts. For example, trading on a particular security futures contract must be halted if trading is halted on the listed market for the underlying security as a result of pending news, regulatory concerns, or market volatility. Similarly, trading of a security futures contract on a narrow-based security index must be halted under such circumstances if trading is halted on securities accounting for at least 50 percent of the market capitalization of the index. In addition, regulated exchanges are required to halt trading in all security futures contracts for a specified period of time when the Dow Jones Industrial Average ("DJIA") experiences one-day declines of 10-, 20- and 30-percent. The regulated exchanges may also have discretion under their rules to halt trading in other circumstances—such as when the exchange determines that the halt would be advisable in maintaining a fair and orderly market.

A trading halt, either by a regulated exchange that trades security futures or an exchange trading the underlying security or instrument, could prevent you from liquidating a position in security futures contracts in a timely manner, which could prevent you from liquidating a position in security futures contracts at that time.

2.8. Trading Hours

Each regulated exchange trading a security futures contract may open and close for trading at different times than other regulated exchanges trading security futures contracts or markets trading the underlying security or securities. Trading in security futures contracts prior to the opening or after the close of the primary market for the underlying security may be less liquid than trading during regular market hours.

Section 3—Clearing Organizations and Mark-to-Market Requirements

Every regulated U.S. exchange that trades security futures contracts is required to have a relationship with a clearing organization that serves as the guarantor of each security futures contract traded on that exchange. A clearing organization performs the following functions: matching trades; effecting settlement and payments; guaranteeing performance; and facilitating deliveries.

Throughout each trading day, the clearing organization matches trade data submitted by clearing members on behalf of their customers or for the clearing member's proprietary accounts. If an account is with a brokerage firm that is not a member of the clearing organization, then the brokerage firm will carry the security futures position with another brokerage firm that is a member of the clearing organization. Trade records that do not match, either because of a discrepancy in the details or because one side of the transaction is missing, are returned to the submitting clearing members for resolution. The members are required to resolve such "out trades" before or on the open of trading the next morning.

When the required details of a reported transaction have been verified, the clearing organization assumes the legal and financial obligations of the parties to the transaction. One way to think of the role of the clearing organization is that it is the "buyer to every seller and the seller to every buyer." The insertion or substitution of the clearing organization as the counterparty to every transaction enables a customer to liquidate a security futures position without regard to what the other party to the original security futures contract decides to do.

The clearing organization also effects the settlement of gains and losses from security futures contracts between clearing members. At least once each day, clearing member brokerage firms must either pay to, or receive from, the clearing organization the difference between the current price and the trade price earlier in the day, or for a position carried over from the previous day, the difference between the current price and the previous day's settlement price. Whether a clearing organization effects settlement of gains and losses on a daily basis or more frequently will depend on the conventions of the clearing organization and market conditions. Because the clearing organization assumes the legal and financial obligations for each security futures contract, you should expect it to ensure that payments are made promptly to protect its obligations.

Gains and losses in security futures contracts are also reflected in each customer's account on at least a daily basis. Each day's gains and losses are determined based on a daily settlement price disseminated by the regulated exchange trading the security futures contract or its clearing organization. If the daily settlement price of a particular security futures contract rises, the buyer has a gain and the seller a loss. If the daily settlement price declines, the buyer has a loss and the seller a gain. This process is known as "marking-to-market" or daily settlement. As a result, individual customers normally will be called on to settle daily.

The one-day gain or loss on a security futures contract is determined by calculating the difference between the current day's settlement price and the previous day's settlement price.

> For example, assume a security futures contract is purchased at a price of $120. If the daily settlement price is either $125 (higher) or $117 (lower), the effects would be as follows:

> (1 contract representing 100 shares)

Daily Settlement Value	Buyer's Account	Seller's Account
$125	$500 gain (credit)	$500 loss (debit)
$117	$300 loss (debit)	$300 gain (credit)

The cumulative gain or loss on a customer's open security futures positions is generally referred to as "open trade equity" and is listed as a separate component of account equity on your customer account statement.

A discussion of the role of the clearing organization in effecting delivery is discussed in Section 5.

Section 4—Margin and Leverage

When a broker-dealer lends a customer part of the funds needed to purchase a security such as common stock, the term "margin" refers to the amount of cash, or down payment, the customer is required to deposit. By contrast, a security futures contract is an obligation and not an asset. A security futures contract has no value as collateral for a loan. Because of the potential for a loss as a result of the daily marked-to-market process, however, a margin deposit is required of each party to a security futures contract. This required margin deposit also is referred to as a "performance bond."

In the first instance, margin requirements for security futures contracts are set by the exchange on which the contract is traded, subject to certain minimums set by law. The basic margin requirement is 20% of the current value of the security futures contract, although some strategies may have lower margin requirements. Requests for additional margin are known as "margin calls." Both buyer and seller must individually deposit the required margin to their respective accounts.

It is important to understand that individual brokerage firms can, and in many cases do, require margin that is higher than the exchange requirements. Additionally, margin requirements may vary from brokerage firm to brokerage firm. Furthermore, a brokerage firm can increase its "house" margin requirements at any time without providing advance notice, and such increases could result in a margin call.

For example, some firms may require margin to be deposited the business day following the day of a deficiency, or some firms may even require deposit on the same day. Some firms may require margin to be on deposit in the account before they will accept an order for a security futures contract. Additionally, brokerage firms may have special requirements as to how margin calls are to be met, such as requiring a wire transfer from a bank, or deposit of a certified or cashier's check. You should thoroughly read and understand the customer agreement with your brokerage firm before entering into any transactions in security futures contracts.

If through the daily cash settlement process, losses in the account of a security futures contract participant reduce the funds on deposit (or equity) below the maintenance margin level (or the firm's higher "house" requirement), the brokerage firm will require that additional funds be deposited.

If additional margin is not deposited in accordance with the firm's policies, the firm can liquidate your position in security futures contracts or sell assets in any of your accounts at the firm to cover the margin deficiency. You remain responsible for any shortfall in the account after such liquidations or sales. Unless provided otherwise in your customer agreement or by applicable law, you are not entitled to choose which futures contracts, other securities or other assets are liquidated or sold to meet a margin call or to obtain an extension of time to meet a margin call.

Brokerage firms generally reserve the right to liquidate a customer's security futures contract positions or sell customer assets to meet a margin call at any time without contacting the customer. Brokerage firms may also enter into equivalent but opposite positions for your account in order to manage the risk created by a margin call. Some customers mistakenly believe that a firm is required to contact them for a margin call to be valid, and that the firm is not allowed to liquidate securities or other assets in their accounts to meet a margin call unless the firm has contacted them first. This is not the case. While most firms notify their customers of margin calls and allow some time for deposit of additional margin, they are not required to do so. Even if a firm has notified a customer of a margin call and set a specific due date for a margin deposit, the firm can still take action as necessary to protect its financial interests, including the immediate liquidation of positions without advance notification to the customer.

Here is an example of the margin requirements for a long security futures position.

A customer buys 3 July EJG security futures at 71.50. Assuming each contract represents 100 shares, the nominal value of the position is $21,450 (71.50 x 3 contracts x 100 shares). If the initial margin rate is 20% of the nominal value, then the customer's initial margin requirement would be $4,290. The customer deposits the initial margin, bringing the equity in the account to $4,290.

First, assume that the next day the settlement price of EJG security futures falls to 69.25. The marked-to-market loss in the customer's equity is $675 (71.50 − 69.25 × 3 contacts × 100 shares). The customer's equity decreases to $3,615 ($4,290 − $675). The new nominal value of the contract is $20,775 (69.25 × 3 contracts × 100 shares). If the maintenance margin rate is 20% of the nominal value, then the customer's maintenance margin requirement would be $4,155. Because the customer's equity had decreased to $3,615 (see above), the customer would be required to have an additional $540 in margin ($4,155 − $3,615).

Alternatively, assume that the next day the settlement price of EJG security futures rises to 75.00. The mark-to-market gain in the customer's equity is $1,050 (75.00 − 71.50 × 3 contacts × 100 shares). The customer's equity increases to $5,340 ($4,290 + $1,050). The new nominal value of the contract is $22,500 (75.00 × 3 contracts × 100 shares). If the maintenance margin rate is 20% of the nominal value, then the customer's maintenance margin requirement would be $4,500. Because the customer's equity had increased to $5,340 (see above), the customer's excess equity would be $840.

The process is exactly the same for a short position, except that margin calls are generated as the settlement price rises rather than as it falls. This is because the customer's equity decreases as the settlement price rises and increases as the settlement price falls.

Because the margin deposit required to open a security futures position is a fraction of the nominal value of the contracts being purchased or sold, security futures contracts are said to be highly leveraged. The smaller the margin requirement in relation to the underlying value of the security futures contract, the greater the leverage. Leverage allows exposure to a given quantity of an underlying asset for a fraction of the investment needed to purchase that quantity outright. In sum, buying (or selling) a security futures contract provides the same dollar and cents profit and loss outcomes as owning (or shorting) the underlying security. However, as a percentage of the margin deposit, the potential immediate exposure to profit or loss is much higher with a security futures contract than with the underlying security.

For example, if a security futures contract is established at a price of $50, the contract has a nominal value of $5,000 (assuming the contract is for 100 shares of stock). The margin requirement may be as low as 20%. In the example just used, assume the contract price rises from $50 to $52 (a $200 increase in the nominal value). This represents a $200 profit to the buyer of the security futures contract, and a 20% return on the $1,000 deposited as margin. The reverse would be true if the contract price decreased from $50 to $48. This represents a $200 loss to the buyer, or 20% of the $1,000 deposited as margin. Thus, leverage can either benefit or harm an investor.

Note that a 4% decrease in the value of the contract resulted in a loss of 20% of the margin deposited. A 20% decrease would wipe out 100% of the margin deposited on the security futures contract.

Section 5—Settlement

If you do not liquidate your position prior to the end of trading on the last day before the expiration of the security futures contract, you are obligated to either 1) make or accept a cash payment ("cash settlement") or 2) deliver or accept delivery of the underlying securities in exchange for final payment of the final settlement price ("physical delivery"). The terms of the contract dictate whether it is settled through cash settlement or by physical delivery.

The expiration of a security futures contract is established by the exchange on which the contract is listed. On the expiration day, security futures contracts cease to exist. Typically, the last trading day of a security futures contract will be the third Friday of the expiring contract month, and the expiration day will be the following Saturday. This follows the expiration conventions for stock options and broad-based stock indexes. Please keep in mind that the expiration day is set by the listing exchange and may deviate from these norms.

5.1. Cash settlement

In the case of cash settlement, no actual securities are delivered at the expiration of the security futures contract. Instead, you must settle any open positions in security futures by making or receiving a cash payment based on the difference between the final settlement price and the previous day's settlement price. Under normal circumstances, the final settlement price for a cash-settled contract will reflect the opening price for the underlying security. Once this payment is made, neither the buyer nor the seller of the security futures contract has any further obligations on the contract.

5.2. Settlement by physical delivery

Settlement by physical delivery is carried out by clearing brokers or their agents with National Securities Clearing Corporation ("NSCC"), an SEC-regulated securities clearing agency. Such settlements are made in much the same way as they are for purchases and sales of the underlying security. Promptly after the last day of trading, the regulated exchange's clearing organization will report a purchase and sale of the underlying stock at the previous day's settlement price (also referred to as the "invoice price") to NSCC. If NSCC does not reject the transaction by a time specified in its rules, settlement is effected pursuant to the rules of NSCC within the normal clearance and settlement cycle for securities transactions, which currently is three business days.

If you hold a short position in a physically settled security futures contract to expiration, you will be required to make delivery of the underlying securities. If you already own the securities, you may tender them to your brokerage firm. If you do not own the securities, you will be obligated to purchase them. Some brokerage firms may not be able to purchase the securities for you. If your brokerage firm cannot purchase the underlying securities on your behalf to fulfill a settlement obligation, you will have to purchase the securities through a different firm.

Section 6—Customer Account Protections

Positions in security futures contracts may be held either in a securities account or in a futures account. Your brokerage firm may or may not permit you to choose the types of account in which your positions in security futures contracts will be held. The protections for funds deposited or earned by customers in connection with trading in security futures contracts differ depending on whether the positions are carried in a securities account or a futures account. If your positions are carried in a securities account, you will not receive the protections available for futures accounts. Similarly, if your positions are carried in a futures account, you will not receive the protections available for securities accounts. You should ask your broker which of these protections will apply to your funds.

You should be aware that the regulatory protections applicable to your account are not intended to insure you against losses you may incur as a result of a decline or increase in the price of a security futures contract. As with all financial products, you are solely responsible for any market losses in your account.

Your brokerage firm must tell you whether your security futures positions will be held in a securities account or a futures account. If your brokerage firm gives you a choice, it must tell you what you have to do to make the choice and which type of account will be used if you fail to do so. You should understand that certain regulatory protections for your account will depend on whether it is a securities account or a futures account.

6.1. Protections for Securities Accounts

If your positions in security futures contracts are carried in a securities account, they are covered by SEC rules governing the safeguarding of customer funds and securities. These rules prohibit a broker/dealer from using customer funds and securities to finance its business. As a result, the broker/dealer is required to set aside funds equal to the net of all its excess payables to customers over receivables from customers. The rules also require a broker/dealer to segregate all customer fully paid and excess margin securities carried by the broker/dealer for customers.

The Securities Investor Protection Corporation (SIPC) also covers positions held in securities accounts. SIPC was created in 1970 as a non-profit, non-government, membership corporation, funded by member broker/dealers. Its primary role is to return funds and securities to customers if the broker/dealer holding these assets becomes insolvent. SIPC coverage applies to customers of current (and in some cases former) SIPC members. Most broker/dealers registered with the SEC are SIPC members; those few that are not must disclose this fact to their customers. SIPC members must display an official sign showing their membership. To check whether a firm is a SIPC member, go to www.sipc.org, call the SIPC Membership Department at (202) 371–8300, or write to SIPC Membership Department, Securities Investor Protection Corporation, 805 Fifteenth Street, NW, Suite 800, Washington, DC 20005–2215.

SIPC coverage is limited to $500,000 per customer, including up to $100,000 for cash. For example, if a customer has 1,000 shares of XYZ stock valued at $200,000 and $10,000 cash in the account, both the security and the cash balance would be protected. However, if the customer has shares of stock valued at $500,000 and $100,000 in cash, only a total of $500,000 of those assets will be protected.

For purposes of SIPC coverage, customers are persons who have securities or cash on deposit with a SIPC member for the purpose of, or as a result of, securities transactions. SIPC does not protect customer funds placed with a broker/dealer just to earn interest. Insiders of the broker/dealer, such as its owners, officers, and partners, are not customers for purposes of SIPC coverage.

6.2. Protections for Futures Accounts

If your security futures positions are carried in a futures account, they must be segregated from the brokerage firm's own funds and cannot be borrowed or otherwise used for the firm's own purposes. If the funds are deposited with another entity (e.g., a bank, clearing broker, or clearing organization), that entity must acknowledge that the funds belong to customers and cannot be used to satisfy the firm's debts. Moreover, although a brokerage firm may carry funds belonging to different customers in the same bank or clearing account, it may not use the funds of one customer to margin or guarantee the transactions of another customer. As a result, the brokerage firm must add its own funds to its customers' segregated funds to cover customer debits and deficits. Brokerage firms must calculate their segregation requirements daily.

You may not be able to recover the full amount of any funds in your account if the brokerage firm becomes insolvent and has insufficient funds to cover its obligations to all of its customers. However, customers with funds in segregation receive priority in bankruptcy proceedings. Furthermore, all customers whose funds are required to be segregated have the same priority in bankruptcy, and there is no ceiling on the amount of funds that must be segregated for or can be recovered by a particular customer.

Your brokerage firm is also required to separately maintain funds invested in security futures contracts traded on a foreign exchange. However, these funds may not receive the same protections once they are transferred to a foreign entity (e.g., a foreign broker, exchange or clearing organization) to satisfy margin requirements for those products. You should ask your broker about the bankruptcy protections available in the country where the foreign exchange (or other entity holding the funds) is located.

Section 7—Special Risks for Day Traders

Certain traders who pursue a day trading strategy may seek to use security futures contracts as part of their trading activity. Whether day trading in security futures contracts or other securities, investors engaging in a day trading strategy face a number of risks.

- *Day trading in security futures contracts requires in-depth knowledge of the securities and futures markets and of trading techniques and strategies*. In attempting to profit through day trading, you will compete with professional traders who are knowledgeable and sophisticated in these markets. You should have appropriate experience before engaging in day trading.

- *Day trading in security futures contracts can result in substantial commission charges, even if the per trade cost is low*. The more trades you make, the higher your total commissions will be. The total commissions you pay will add to your losses and reduce your profits. For instance, assuming that a round-turn trade costs $16 and you execute an average of 29 round-turn transactions per day each trading day, you would need to generate an annual profit of $111,360 just to cover your commission expenses.

- *Day trading can be extremely risky*. Day trading generally is not appropriate for someone of limited resources and limited investment or trading experience and low risk tolerance. You should be prepared to lose all of the funds that you use for day trading. In particular, you should not fund day trading activities with funds that you cannot afford to lose.

Section 8—Other

8.1. Corporate Events

As noted in Section 2.4, an equity security represents a fractional ownership interest in the issuer of that security. By contrast, the purchaser of a security futures contract has only a contract for future delivery of the underlying security. Treatment of dividends and other corporate events affecting the underlying security may be reflected in the security futures contract depending on the applicable clearing organization rules. Consequently, individuals should consider how dividends and other developments affecting security futures in which they transact will be handled by the relevant exchange and clearing organization. The specific adjustments to the terms of a security futures contract are governed by the rules of the applicable clearing organization. Below is a discussion of some of the more common types of adjustments that you may need to consider.

Corporate issuers occasionally announce stock splits. As a result of these splits, owners of the issuer's common stock may own more shares of the stock, or fewer shares in the case of a reverse stock split. The treatment of stock splits for persons owning a security futures contract may vary according to the terms of the security futures contract and the rules of the clearing organization. For example, the terms of the contract may provide for an adjustment in the number of contracts held by each party with a long or short position in a security future, or for an adjustment in the number of shares or units of the instrument underlying each contract, or both.

Corporate issuers also occasionally issue special dividends. A special dividend is an announced cash dividend payment outside the normal and customary practice of a corporation. The terms of a security futures contract may be adjusted for special dividends. The adjustments, if any, will be based upon the rules of the exchange and clearing organization. In general, there will be no adjustments for ordinary dividends as they are recognized as a normal and customary practice of an issuer and are already accounted for in the pricing of security futures.

Corporate issuers occasionally may be involved in mergers and acquisitions. Such events may cause the underlying security of a security futures contact to change over the contract duration. The terms of security futures contracts may also be adjusted to reflect other corporate events affecting the underlying security.

8.2. Position Limits and Large Trader Reporting

All security futures contracts trading on regulated exchanges in the United States are subject to position limits or position accountability limits. Position limits restrict the number of security futures contracts that any one person or group of related persons may hold or control in a particular security futures contract. In contrast, position accountability limits permit the accumulation of positions in excess of the limit without a prior exemption. In general, position limits and position accountability limits are beyond the thresholds of most retail investors. Whether a security futures contract is subject to position limits, and the level for such limits, depends upon the trading activity and market capitalization of the underlying security of the security futures contract.

Position limits apply are required for security futures contracts that overlie a security that has an average daily trading volume of 20 million shares or fewer. In the case of a security futures contract overlying a security index, position limits are required if any one of the securities in the index has an average daily trading volume of 20 million shares or fewer. Position limits also apply only to an expiring security futures contract during its last five trading days. A regulated exchange must establish position limits on security futures that are no greater than 13,500 (100 share) contracts, unless the underlying security meets certain volume and shares outstanding thresholds, in which case the limit may be increased to 22,500 (100 share) contracts.

For security futures contracts overlying a security or securities with an average trading volume of more than 20 million shares, regulated exchanges may adopt position accountability rules. Under position accountability rules, a trader holding a position in a security futures contract that exceeds 22,500 contracts (or such lower limit established by an exchange) must agree to provide information regarding the position and consent to halt increasing that position if requested by the exchange.

Brokerage firms must also report large open positions held by one person (or by several persons acting together) to the CFTC as well as to the exchange on which the positions are held. The CFTC's reporting requirements are 1,000 contracts for security futures positions on individual equity securities and 200 contracts for positions on a narrow-based index. However, individual exchanges may require the reporting of large open positions at levels less than the levels required by the CFTC. In addition, brokerage firms must submit identifying information on the account holding the reportable position (on a form referred to as either an "Identification of Special Accounts Form" or a "Form 102") to the CFTC and to the exchange on which the reportable position exists within three business days of when a reportable position is first established.

8.3. Transactions on Foreign Exchanges

U.S. customers may not trade security futures on foreign exchanges until authorized by U.S. regulatory authorities. U.S. regulatory authorities do not regulate the activities of foreign exchanges and may not, on their own, compel enforcement of the rules of a foreign exchange or the laws of a foreign country. While U.S. law governs transactions in security futures contracts that are effected in the U.S., regardless of the exchange on which the contracts are listed, the laws and rules governing transactions on foreign exchanges vary depending on the country in which the exchange is located.

8.4. Tax Consequences

For most taxpayers, security futures contracts are not treated like other futures contracts. Instead, the tax consequences of a security futures transaction depend on the status of the taxpayer and the type of position (e.g., long or short, covered or uncovered). Because of the importance of tax considerations to transactions in security futures, readers should consult their tax advisors as to the tax consequences of these transactions.

Section 9—Glossary of Terms

This glossary is intended to assist customers in understanding specialized terms used in the futures and securities industries. It is not inclusive and is not intended to state or suggest the legal significance or meaning of any word or term.

Arbitrage—taking an economically opposite position in a security futures contract on another exchange, in an options contract, or in the underlying security.

Broad-based security index—a security index that does not fall within the statutory definition of a narrow-based security index (see Narrow-based security index). A future on a broad-based security index is not a security future. This risk disclosure statement applies solely to security futures and generally does not pertain to futures on a broad-based security index. Futures on a broad-based security index are under exclusive jurisdiction of the CFTC.

Cash settlement—a method of settling certain futures contracts by having the buyer (or long) pay the seller (or short) the cash value of the contract according to a procedure set by the exchange.

Clearing broker—a member of the clearing organization for the contract being traded. All trades, and the daily profits or losses from those trades, must go through a clearing broker.

Clearing organization—a regulated entity that is responsible for settling trades, collecting losses and distributing profits, and handling deliveries.

Contract—1) the unit of trading for a particular futures contract (e.g., one contract may be 100 shares of the underlying security), 2) the type of future being traded (e.g., futures on ABC stock).

Contract month—the last month in which delivery is made against the futures contract or the contract is cash-settled. Sometimes referred to as the delivery month.

Day trading strategy—an overall trading strategy characterized by the regular transmission by a customer of intra-day orders to effect both purchase and sale transactions in the same security or securities.

EDGAR—the SEC's Electronic Data Gathering, Analysis, and Retrieval system maintains electronic copies of corporate information filed with the agency. EDGAR submissions may be accessed through the SEC's Web site, www.sec.gov.

Futures contract—a futures contract is (1) an agreement to purchase or sell a commodity for delivery in the future; (2) at a price determined at initiation of the contract; (3) that obligates each party to the contract to fulfill it at the specified price; (4) that is used to assume or shift risk; and (5) that may be satisfied by delivery or offset.

Hedging—the purchase or sale of a security future to reduce or offset the risk of a position in the underlying security or group of securities (or a close economic equivalent).

Illiquid market—a market (or contract) with few buyers and/or sellers. Illiquid markets have little trading activity and those trades that do occur may be done at large price increments.

Liquidation—entering into an offsetting transaction. Selling a contract that was previously purchased liquidates a futures position in exactly the same way that selling 100 shares of a particular stock liquidates an earlier purchase of the same stock. Similarly, a futures contract that was initially sold can be liquidated by an offsetting purchase.

Liquid market—a market (or contract) with numerous buyers and sellers trading at small price increments.

Long—1) the buying side of an open futures contact, 2) a person who has bought futures contracts that are still open.

Margin—the amount of money that must be deposited by both buyers and sellers to ensure performance of the person's obligations under a futures contract. Margin on security futures contracts is a performance bond rather than a down payment for the underlying securities.

Mark-to-market—to debit or credit accounts daily to reflect that day's profits and losses.

Narrow-based security index—in general, and subject to certain exclusions, an index that has any one of the following four characteristics: (1) it has nine or fewer component securities; (2) any one of its component securities comprises more than 30% of its weighting; (3) the five highest weighted component securities together comprise more than 60% of its weighting; or (4) the lowest weighted component securities comprising, in the aggregate, 25% of the index's weighting have an aggregate dollar value of average daily trading volume of less than $50 million (or in the case of an index with 15 or more component securities, $30 million). A security index that is not narrow-based is a "broad based security index." (See Broad-based security index).

Nominal value—the face value of the futures contract, obtained by multiplying the contract price by the number of shares or units per contract. If XYZ stock index futures are trading at $50.25 and the contract is for 100 shares of XYZ stock, the nominal value of the futures contract would be $5025.00.

Offsetting—liquidating open positions by either selling fungible contracts in the same contract month as an open long position or buying fungible contracts in the same contract month as an open short position.

Open interest—the total number of open long (or short) contracts in a particular contract month.

Open position—a futures contract position that has neither been offset nor closed by cash settlement or physical delivery.

Performance bond—another way to describe margin payments for futures contracts, which are good faith deposits to ensure performance of a person's obligations under a futures contract rather than down payments for the underlying securities.

Physical delivery—the tender and receipt of the actual security underlying the security futures contract in exchange for payment of the final settlement price.

Position—a person's net long or short open contracts.

Regulated exchange—a registered national securities exchange, a national securities association registered under Section 15A(a) of the Securities Exchange Act of 1934, a designated contract market, a registered derivatives transaction execution facility, or an alternative trading system registered as a broker or dealer.

Security futures contract—a legally binding agreement between two parties to purchase or sell in the future a specific quantify of shares of a security (such as common stock, an exchange-traded fund, or ADR) or a narrow-based security index, at a specified price.

Settlement price—1) the daily price that the clearing organization uses to mark open positions to market for determining profit and loss and margin calls, 2) the price at which open cash settlement contracts are settled on the last trading day and open physical delivery contracts are invoiced for delivery.

Short—1) the selling side of an open futures contract, 2) a person who has sold futures contracts that are still open.

Speculating—buying and selling futures contracts with the hope of profiting from anticipated price movements.

Spread—1) holding a long position in one futures contract and a short position in a related futures contract or contract month in order to profit from an anticipated change in the price relationship between the two, 2) the price difference between two contracts or contract months.

Stop limit order—an order that becomes a limit order when the market trades at a specified price. The order can only be filled at the stop limit price or better.

Stop loss order—an order that becomes a market order when the market trades at a specified price. The order will be filled at whatever price the market is trading at. Also called a stop order.

Tick—the smallest price change allowed in a particular contract.

Trader—a professional speculator who trades for his or her own account.

Underlying security—the instrument on which the security futures contract is based. This instrument can be an individual equity security (including common stock and certain exchange-traded funds and American Depositary Receipts) or a narrow-based index.

Volume—the number of contracts bought or sold during a specified period of time. This figure includes liquidating transactions.

APPENDIX F

SOFTWARE LICENSE AND ROUTING SYSTEM ACCESS AGREEMENT OF FILLER & MARKHAM INC.

■ ■ ■

This Software License and Routing System Access Agreement ("**Agreement**") is executed and entered into this ___ day of _____, 20___, by and between Filler & Markham, Inc., a Delaware corporation ("**FMI**") with a place of business at _____, New York, NY _____ and _____, a _____ corporation/LLC/partnership/individual [circle one] ("**Licensee**") with its principal address at _____.

WHEREAS, FMI provides a license to Licensee to use the front-end software ("**Software**") and provides equipment, servers and other devices ("**Equipment**") in connection therewith (collectively the "**System**") that provides, among other functions, (1) electronic order entry (2) order routing connectivity to the Destinations (as defined below); and (3) a quotation module for access to and/or display of market information consisting of futures, options, securities and other financial quotes and other data (collectively "**Market Data**") that is provided by certain exchanges, news vendors and other information sources (collectively "**Data Sources**").

WHEREAS, Licensee desires to be granted a license to use the System and FMI desires to grant to Licensee such License on the terms and conditions set forth in this Agreement.

NOW, THEREFORE, and in consideration of the terms and conditions set forth below, FMI and Licensee agree as follows:

1. **LIMITED LICENSE.**

(a) Grant of License. FMI grants to Licensee a limited, non-exclusive, non-transferable license to use the System and accompanying documentation for Licensee's use and the use of its brokerage customers which maintain futures positions with Licensee ("**Authorized Users**") for the purpose of accessing the System.

(b) Ownership Rights Reserved. No title or ownership of intellectual property rights in and to the Software or the System or any copy, translation, compilation or other derivative works are transferred to

Licensee or any third party hereunder. Licensee agrees that unauthorized copies or disclosure of the Software and other intellectual property of FMI will cause great damage to FMI, which damage far exceeds the value of the copies or information involved. Licensee shall not assign, pledge, encumber, sell or otherwise transfer to any third party its license to use the Software or Equipment, or any rights of Licensee under this Agreement. Licensee shall keep its license to use the Software and to use the Software to access the System and other property of FMI and/or the Data Sources free and clear of any and all liens, levies and encumbrances.

(c) License Restrictions. Licensee agrees that Licensee and its Authorized Users shall not: (a) sell, lease, license or sublicense the Software or any part thereof; (b) modify, change, alter, translate, create derivative works from, reverse engineer, disassemble or decompile the Software or any part thereof for any reason; (c) provide, disclose, divulge or make available to, or permit use of the Software, or any part thereof, by any third party; (d) copy or reproduce the Software, or any part thereof, [except that Licensee may make one (1) copy of the Software for archival or emergency backup purposes]; (e) interfere with the Software or System in any way; (f) engage in spamming, or any other fraudulent, illegal, disruptive or unauthorized use of the Software; or (g) introduce into or transmit through the Software any virus, worm, clock, counter or other limiting routine, instruction or design.

This Agreement does not include the right to sublicense the Software or to use the Software to provide timeshare services, service bureau services, outsourcing services or consulting services, or for any unlawful purpose. Licensee shall be responsible and liable to FMI and any third party for any use, display or access of the Software or the Market Data through use of Licensee's access granted under this Agreement by any person or entity who is not a party to or covered by this Agreement, including, without limitation, any direct or indirect use or access, whether authorized or unauthorized by Licensee and its Authorized Users.

2.   ACCESS RIGHTS.

(a) Licensee Responsibilities. FMI will issue to Licensee an individual logon identifier and password for purposes of using the Software and FMI hereby grants Licensee access to the System. Licensee shall be responsible solely for distributing the logon identifier and password to its Authorized Users. Licensee and each Authorized User shall: (a) be responsible for the security and/or use of his/her/its logon identifier and password; (b) not disclose such logon identifier and password to any other person or entity; and (c) not permit any other person or entity to use such logon identifier and/or password and (d) be required to read the System User Manual provided with this Agreement prior to the first use of the System (e) abide by all regulatory organization and exchange rules and regulations applicable to Licensee (**"Applicable Law"**) and specifically those set forth in the Futures Customer Agreement or other comparable customer or execution agreement entered into between FMI and Licensee (each an **"Customer Agreement"**) and any addendum thereto, which has previously been entered into between FMI and Licensee or shall be executed in conjunction with this Agreement and (f) ensure that Licensee and all Authorized Users abide by and comply with this Agreement and all applicable provisions of federal and state laws, including securities and futures laws, rules and regulations applicable to Licensee. Licensee shall be responsible solely for: (g) advising each Authorized User of his/her/its obligations under this Agreement and of the license restrictions and indemnities set forth in this Agreement; and (h) each Authorized User's use of his/her/its logon identifier, password and/or the System. Licensee shall be bound by the content of all such orders transmitted through the System and by the terms of any transaction resulting therefrom. In particular, but without limitation, Licensee and its Authorized Users will be bound by such orders and transactions notwithstanding any typographical or keystroke errors made when such instructions are entered by Licensee or its Authorized Users.

FMI reserves the right to deny or revoke access to the System if FMI believes Licensee and/or its Authorized Users are in breach of this Agreement or are otherwise engaged in unlawful use of the System. Licensee shall include in its agreements with its Authorized Users terms that: (x) advise Authorized Users of the restrictions set forth in this Agreement; (y) disclaim any and all liability of FMI or the Data Sources with respect to any Authorized User and (z) require the Authorized User to abide by the rules and regulations set forth in any Customer Agreement entered into by Licensee and FMI.

(b) Limited Access to the System. Licensee acknowledges and agrees that the System is used for routing electronic messages to certain exchanges, exchange automated systems, market makers or electronic communication networks as designated by Licensee (collectively, **"Destinations"**). Licensee understands that these Destinations are not owned, controlled, operated, managed, monitored or overseen by FMI and FMI is not responsible for any disruption of service at the Destinations. Licensee shall be responsible for selecting the Destinations it requires within the System. In connection therewith, Licensee may be required to enter into agreements directly with the Destinations or Data Sources in order to receive access to such Destination or Market Data. Licensee agrees to enter into such agreements if so required.

Licensee agrees that neither Licensee nor any authorized User shall take an action to purposely or willfully interfere with or disrupt the System or any Destination or violate any rule of a Destination.

(c) Change in System Access. FMI, in its sole discretion or at the discretion of a third party, including but not limited to, FMI's third party communications and/or software providers and licensors or Regulatory Authorities, may from time to time make additions to, deletions from, or modifications to, the System. FMI shall make reasonable efforts to notify Licensee of changes in the System, (other than minor changes) prior to any such change(s), unless a malfunction necessitates modifications on an accelerated basis or an emergency precludes such advance notice or a shorter time period is required pursuant to an order or other action of a court, arbitrator or Regulatory Authority. Access to or use of the System after any change shall constitute acceptance of the System or Data Sources as modified. Licensee acknowledges and agrees that nothing in this Agreement constitutes an undertaking by FMI to provide access to System in the present form or under the current specification or requirements, with the current software interface or to continue to use existing communications providers.

(d) Equipment Requirements. Except for the Equipment provided by FMI, Licensee shall be responsible for providing all equipment, connection and telecommunications requirements for accessing the System, including for any frame relay access or Internet access approved by FMI.

(e) Distribution of Access to the System. In the event Licensee provides access to the System to its Authorized Users, Licensee understands that it is liable for all transactions sent to the System and all actions and omissions by its Authorized Users. Licensee agrees that it has not been granted a license to sub-license the Software or System and agrees not to charge its Authorized Users any additional fee for the licensing of the System.

(f) Market Data and Data Sources. Licensee acknowledges and agrees that (i) the Data Sources each retain exclusive property rights over the Market Data they provide; (ii) the Market Data constitutes valuable copyrighted and proprietary information of the Data Sources; (iii) but for the use of the System, Licensee would have no rights to the Market Data and Licensee shall safeguard the confidentiality of all such Market Data; (iv) Licensee will not distribute the Market Data in any format, including but not limited to the Internet to any news organization or any other person or entity which is not a party to this Agreement; (v) it will maintain reasonable security to prevent any entry to its place of business for the purpose of accessing the Market Data. and (vi) Licensee has received and read the notices attached hereto relating to Market Data. Licensee understands and agrees that any distribution of the Market Data by Licensee in violation of this Agreement may result in a fee adjustment from the Data Sources.

3. FEES. Licensee shall pay to FMI the fees as set forth in the Customer Agreement. FMI reserves the right to change the fees at any time upon mutual agreement with Licensee. All fees are payable as set forth in the Customer Agreement, upon completion of each transaction or upon receipt of the billing invoice.

4. SECURITY DEPOSIT. FMI may require Licensee to deposit with FMI, and keep in place, as and when requested by FMI, during the term of this Agreement, funds in a security deposit ("**Deposit**") to secure any Equipment provided by FMI. After termination of this Agreement, FMI shall refund to Licensee the Deposit less any outstanding amounts due and owing FMI at the time.

5. RIGHT OF SET-OFF. Without limiting any other rights or remedies available to FMI hereunder, or under applicable law, any amount payable to Licensee by FMI, at the option of FMI in its sole and reasonable discretion, may be reduced by its set-off against any amounts payable (whether at such time or in the future) by Licensee to FMI under any other agreements or arrangement between Licensee and FMI (including amounts owed pursuant to this Agreement). FMI shall have a right of set-off against all

Deposits, money, securities and other property of Licensee now or hereafter in the possession of or on deposit with FMI. No security interest or right of set-off shall be deemed to have been waived by any act or conduct of FMI or by any neglect to exercise such right of set-off or to enforce such security interest or by any delay in doing so; all such waivers by FMI hereunder must be in writing and signed by an authorized FMI officer.

6. AUDIT RIGHTS. During the term of this Agreement and for a period of six (6) months thereafter, FMI or any of the Data Sources shall have the right upon reasonable notice to Licensee to access Licensee's location and files during normal business hours, for purposes of: (a) confirming Licensee's compliance with the terms of this Agreement; and/or (b) inspecting Licensee's use of the System or Market Data, including, without limitation, computers and equipment used in connection therewith. Licensee shall cooperate fully with any such audit or inspection. FMI shall have the right to copy any item that Licensee may possess with respect to a violation or breach of this Agreement and/or terminate Licensee's access to the Software and/or System as a result of such violation or breach.

7. SUPPORT AND MAINTENANCE.

(a) Technical Support. FMI shall provide by telephone or online, either directly or through a third party, reasonable technical support during hours announced from time to time by FMI, Monday through Friday, excluding exchange trading holidays. Licensee shall designate an employee who is familiar with Licensee's computer systems, network and hardware to serve as the single point of contact for obtaining technical support from FMI. FMI shall not be obligated to provide support to any other person. Licensee may change its single support contact upon written notice to an authorized FMI officer. On-site support or other Licensee-specific support may be provided to Licensee on a time-and-materials basis pursuant to a separate written agreement between Licensee and FMI.

(b) Upgrades. Licensee shall receive normal maintenance upgrades of the Licensed Product during the term of this Agreement at no additional charge. Upgrades shall not include Market Data, Software and/or System features and/or functionality that FMI decides, in its sole discretion, to make generally available for a separate fee or charge.

(c) Limitations; Other. FMI shall not be obligated to provide network advice or to provide technical support or maintenance upgrades for any version of the Software other than the then-current release version. Licensee shall not receive support or upgrades for use of the Software with hardware or software configurations not included in FMI's then-current configuration list. FMI shall have the right to change its support and maintenance at any time upon notice to Licensee.

8.   Proprietary and Third Party Vendor Systems. If Licensee uses a proprietary system or third party vendor system (each a "**Sub-System**") to interface via the AACES interface ("**Interface**") to the System, FMI shall not be liable for losses, damages or claims arising out of any delay, malfunction or error due to Licensee's use of such Sub-System. FMI shall only be responsible for the transaction under the terms as transmitted by the Sub-System from the point the System receives the order from the Sub-System and on the terms the System receives the order up and until FMI reports the disposition of the order from the System to the Sub-System. **Licensee acknowledges that FMI has no control over the Sub-System and agrees, for itself and all other parties for which it is responsible or authorized to act, that neither FMI nor any affiliate, employee, officer or agent of FMI, shall be liable for any loss, damage, cost or expense whatsoever, direct or indirect, regardless of the cause, which may arise out of or be in any way related to the transmission or reception of an order from a Sub-System, including, but not limited to: (a) any fault or failure in the operation of the Interface or the Interface feed from any Sub-System; (b) the suspension or termination of, or the inability to use, all or part of the Sub-System, or any inaccuracies or omissions in any information or documentation provided by the Sub-System; (c) any failure or delay suffered or allegedly suffered by Licensee in concluding trades; or (d) any other cause in connection with the furnishing, performance, maintenance or use**

of, or inability to use, all or any part of the Sub-System. The foregoing shall apply regardless of whether a claim arises in contract, tort, negligence, strict liability or otherwise.

9. INDEMNITY.

(a) By Licensee. Licensee agrees to defend, indemnify and hold FMI, its affiliates, members, managers, officers, employees, representatives, agents, attorneys, successors, assigns, and the Data Sources, harmless from and against any and all claims, losses, damages, liabilities, obligations, judgments, causes of action, costs, charges, expenses and fees (including reasonable attorneys' fees and costs and such fees and/or penalties as any of the Data Sources may impose) arising out of: (a) any breach or alleged breach by Licensee or any Authorized User of its obligations, representations, warranties or covenants hereunder; (b) the use by Licensee or by others on Licensee's premises of any of the Software, Equipment and/or System, (c) errors or unauthorized or negligent transactions by Licensee or its employees or agents through the use of the Software, Equipment and/or System, (d) any and all regulatory actions, suits, arbitrations, claims, fines or judgments or the defense of any such proceedings arising from or in any way relating to the use by Licensee of the Software, Equipment and/or System, (e) any claims by any third party relating to Licensee, including, but not limited to, any customer or affiliate of Licensee for whom Licensee executes trades, arising out of the use of the Software, Equipment and/or System; (f) any delay, inaccuracies, errors, or omissions in the Market Data or by any Destination system or (g) any negligence, or willful or reckless actions or misconduct of Licensee, any Authorized User or Licensee's employees or agents with respect to the use of the Software, Equipment and/or System. FMI reserves the right to select its own attorneys at Licensee's cost. Licensee shall hold harmless FMI from and against any losses, claims, damages or liabilities arising out of any failure, halt or delay by any exchange or Destination system or connectivity thereto, including, but not limited to, those provided by Chicago Board of Trade, Chicago Mercantile Exchange, the New York Mercantile Exchange, SIAC, the New York Stock Exchange, the American Stock Exchange and the NASDAQ. This Section shall survive any termination or expiration and non-renewal of this Agreement.

(b) By FMI. FMI will indemnify, defend and hold Licensee harmless from and against any claim, suit or proceeding brought against Licensee alleging that the Software or Licensee's use of the Software constitutes a misappropriation of, or infringement upon, any United States of America patent or copyright of a third party, provided that: (i) Licensee promptly notifies FMI, in writing, of any such claim, suit or proceeding; (ii) FMI has sole control of the investigation, defense and settlement of any such claim, suit or proceeding; and (iii) Licensee provides FMI, upon FMI's request, with all reasonable assistance in investigating, defending and settling any such claim, suit or proceeding. If the Software or any part thereof is held to infringe upon any United States of America patent or copyright of a third party, and Licensee's use of the Software is enjoined or prohibited by a court of competent jurisdiction, FMI shall, at its sole option, within thirty (30) calendar days of such injunction or prohibition, either: (iv) procure for Licensee the right to continue using the Software free of any liability for infringement; (v) replace or modify the Software with a non-infringing product of equivalent functionality; or (vi) in the event FMI is unable, after exercising its best efforts to implement one of the options set forth in **subsection (iv)** or **(v)** above, accept return of the Software and Equipment and refund to Licensee a prorated amount equal to the fees actually paid by Licensee to FMI for use of the Software for that number of days of the calendar month during which Licensee's use of the Software was enjoined or prohibited by a court of competent jurisdiction. Such refund shall not include any commission costs incurred by Licensee. FMI shall have no obligation to indemnify, defend or hold Licensee harmless hereunder in the event any such claim, suit or proceeding arises from: (vii) changes or modifications to the Software not authorized, in writing, by FMI; (viii) the combination of the Software with any software, hardware or other product not authorized, in writing, by FMI; (ix) use of the Software not in accordance with the System User's Manual; or (x) use of a superseded or altered release or version of the Software if the infringement would have been avoided by use of the current unaltered release or version of the Software. This Section shall survive any termination or expiration and non-renewal of this Agreement. **THE RIGHTS AND OBLIGATIONS SET FORTH IN THIS SECTION 9(b) ARE FMI'S SOLE LIABILITY AND OBLIGATION AND LICENSEE'S SOLE AND EXCLUSIVE REMEDIES FOR ANY CLAIM, SUIT OR PROCEEDING WITH RESPECT TO INFRINGEMENT.**

10. CONFIDENTIALITY.

(a) General. Licensee acknowledges and agrees that this Agreement does not constitute a sale of the Software and that ownership of the Software remains with FMI. Licensee further acknowledges and agrees that the Software constitutes and incorporates confidential and proprietary information developed or acquired by, or licensed to, FMI or the Data Sources. Licensee shall take all reasonable precautions necessary to safeguard the confidentiality of the Software, including at a minimum, those taken by Licensee to protect Licensee's own confidential information which, in no event, shall be less than a reasonable standard of care. Licensee shall not allow the removal, eradication, or defacement of any confidentiality or proprietary notice placed on the Software. The placement of copyright notices on these items shall not constitute publication or otherwise impair their confidential nature. Upon termination of this Agreement, Licensee agrees to return to FMI all originals and any copies of the Software or shall certify, upon FMI's request, that all originals and copies have been destroyed.

(b) Disclosure. Licensee shall not disclose, in whole or in part, the Licensed Product or other information that has been designated as confidential by FMI to any individual or entity, except for use in acceptance with this Agreement or to Authorized Users for use in accordance with this Agreement or as otherwise required by any applicable law or the Regulatory Authorities. Licensee acknowledges that any unauthorized use or disclosure of the Software or any portion thereof may cause irreparable damage to FMI and/or the Data Sources. If an unauthorized use or disclosure occurs, Licensee shall immediately notify FMI and, at Licensee's expense, shall take all steps necessary to recover the Software and prevent subsequent unauthorized use or dissemination. If requested by any Regulatory Authorities or the Data Sources, FMI may provide information and data to Regulatory Authorities or Data Sources with respect to Licensee and any Authorized Users. To enable FMI to meets its obligations, Licensee agrees to inform FMI in writing whenever its usage, including number of Authorized Users or their locations, changes.

11. LIMITED WARRANTIES. Each party represents and warrants to the other that it has the right to enter into this Agreement. FMI warrants that it has the authority to grant Licensee the license to use the Software in accordance with the terms of this Agreement.

12. DISCLAIMER OF LIABILITY AND WARRANTY. THE SOFTWARE AND EQUIPMENT ARE PROVIDED "AS IS" AND WITHOUT ANY EXPRESS OR IMPLIED WARRANTIES INCLUDING, WITHOUT LIMITATION, ANY WARRANTIES AS TO ACCURACY, FUNCTIONALITY, PERFORMANCE OR MERCHANTABILITY. FMI, ITS PARENT AND AFFILIATES, EXPRESSLY DISCLAIM ALL OTHER WARRANTIES, EXPRESS, IMPLIED OR STATUTORY, INCLUDING, WITHOUT LIMITATION, THE WARRANTIES OF MERCHANTABILITY AND FITNESS FOR A PARTICULAR PURPOSE AND ANY WARRANTIES ARISING FROM TRADE USAGE, COURSE OF DEALING OR COURSE OF PERFORMANCE. FMI, ITS AFFILIATES AND THE DATA SOURCES MAKE NO REPRESENTATION, WARRANTY OR COVENANT CONCERNING THE ACCURACY, COMPLETENESS, SEQUENCE, TIMELINESS OR AVAILABILITY OF THE SOFTWARE, EQUIPMENT, SYSTEM, OR ANY OTHER INFORMATION OR THE LIKELIHOOD OF PROFITABLE TRADING USING THE SOFTWARE, EQUIPMENT AND/OR THE SYSTEM.

Licensee has independently evaluated the Software, Equipment and/or System and has concluded that the use of such Software, Equipment and/or System is useful to Licensee and understands that electronic trading contains certain risks. LICENSEE ASSUMES ALL LIABILITIES AND RISKS ASSOCIATED WITH THE USE OF THE SOFTWARE, EQUIPMENT AND/OR SYSTEM AND ACCEPTS FULL RESPONSIBILITY FOR ANY INVESTMENT DECISIONS OR TRANSACTIONS MADE BY LICENSEE AND/OR ITS AUTHORIZED USERS USING THE SOFTWARE, EQUIPMENT AND/OR SYSTEM. NO SALES PERSONNEL, EMPLOYEES, AGENTS OR REPRESENTATIVES OF FMI, ITS AFFILIATES OR ANY THIRD PARTY ARE AUTHORIZED TO MAKE ANY REPRESENTATION, WARRANTY OR COVENANT ON BEHALF OF FMI. ACCORDINGLY, ORAL STATEMENTS DO NOT CONSTITUTE WARRANTIES AND SHOULD NOT BE RELIED UPON AND ARE NOT PART OF THIS AGREEMENT. NEITHER FMI NOR ANY OF ITS AFFILIATES OR THE DATA SOURCES REPRESENT OR WARRANT THAT THE SOFTWARE, FMI DATA, EQUIPMENT AND/OR SYSTEM WILL BE UNINTERRUPTED OR ERROR-FREE. LICENSEE EXPRESSL Y AGREES THA T USE OF THE SOFTWARE, EQUIPMENT AND/OR SYSTEM IS AT LICENSEE'S SOLE RISK AND THAT FMI AND ITS PARENT AND AFFILIATES SHALL NOT BE RESPONSIBLE FOR ANY INTERRUPTION OF SERVICES, ERRORS OR DELAYS CAUSED BY ANY TRANSMISSION OR DELIVERY OF THE SOFTWARE OR SYSTEM OR CAUSED BY ANY COMMUNICATIONS SERVICE PROVIDERS.

LICENSEE AGREES THAT NEITHER FMI, NOR THE DATA SOURCES, THEIR VENDORS OR SUBVENDORS, OR THEIR MEMBERS, SHAREHOLDERS, DIRECTORS, OFFICERS, EMPLOYEES OR AGENTS, GUARANTEE THE TIMELINESS, SEQUENCE, ACCURACY OR COMPLETENESS OF THE DESIGNATED MARKET DATA, MARKET INFORMATION OR OTHER INFORMATION FURNISHED OR THAT THE DESIGNATED MARKET DATA HAVE BEEN VERIFIED. LICENSEE AGREES THAT THE DESIGNATED MARKET DATA AND OTHER INFORMATION PROVIDED HEREUNDER IS FOR INFORMATION PURPOSES ONLY AND IS NOT INTENDED AS AN OFFER OR SOLICITATION WITH RESPECT TO THE PURCHASE OR SALE OF ANY SECURITY OR COMMODITY AND THAT THE DESIGNATED MARKET DATA AND OTHER INFORMATION SHOULD NOT SERVE AS THE BASIS FOR ANY INVESTMENT DECISION. **DATA SOURCES MAY TERMINATE THE PROVISION OF ANY DATA WITH OR WITHOUT NOTICE AND NEITHER ANY SUCH DATA SOURCE NOR FMI SHALL HAVE ANY LIABILITY IN CONNECTION THEREWITH.**

13. LIMITATION OF LIABILITY. IN NO EVENT WILL FMI OR ITS AFFILIATES OR THE DATA SOURCES OR THEIR AFFILIATES OR MEMBERS BE LIABLE FOR ANY DIRECT, INCIDENTAL, INDIRECT, SPECIAL, OR CONSEQUENTIAL DAMAGES (INCLUDING, BUT NOT LIMITED TO, LOSS OF USE, LOSS OF PROFITS, TRADING LOSSES OR LOSS OF OTHER COSTS OR SAVINGS), RESULTING FROM OR IN CONNECTION WITH THIS AGREEMENT WHETHER SUCH DAMAGES OR LOSSES ARE THOSE OF LICENSEE OR ANY THIRD PARTY. Regardless of cause or form of action, whether in contract, tort, strict liability, statutory liability or otherwise, and whether or not such damages were foreseen, unforeseen or foreseeable, even if FMI has been advised of the possibility of such damages, FMI's sole liability and obligation and Licensee's sole and exclusive remedy shall be with respect to any claim, suit or proceeding brought against Licensee alleging that the software or licensee's use of the software constitutes a misappropriation of, or infringement upon, any United States of America patent or copyright of a third party, the remedies stated in section 9(b).

Notwithstanding the foregoing, in the event the terms of this section, or any part thereof, shall be held invalid and unenforceable by a court of competent jurisdiction, FMI's total liability under the terms of this agreement shall not exceed an amount equal to any licensee fee (but not commissions or brokerage fees) paid by Licensee to FMI for the one (1) calendar month in which such damages first accrued. This section shall not relieve FMI from liability for damages that result from its own gross negligence or willful misconduct. This section shall survive any termination or expiration and non-renewal of this Agreement. Notwithstanding the foregoing, in the event the terms of this section, or any part thereof, shall be held invalid and unenforceable by a court of competent jurisdiction, Data Sources total liability under this Agreement shall be only the actual amount of loss or damage or the amount of the monthly fee paid by Licensee to FMI for the Market Data, whichever is less.

14. LICENSEE REPRESENTATIONS. Licensee hereby represents and warrants to FMI as follows:

(a). Licensee is engaged in trading for its own account or is a futures commission merchant or commodity trading advisor acting on behalf of its Authorized Users. Licensee shall maintain all regulatory licenses and registrations required by Applicable Law during the term of this Agreement.

(b). Licensee will use the System only for executing trades in the ordinary course of conducting its business and will not use or permit the use of the information provided by the Data Sources and/or the System for any illegal purpose.

(c). Licensee shall use the System in compliance Applicable Law and the rules and regulations set forth in the Customer Agreement.

(d). Customer and its Authorized Users will use the System, the information provided by the Data Sources and the Equipment only in accordance with the terms of this Agreement.

15. GOVERNING LAW. This Agreement shall be governed by and construed in accordance with the laws of the State of New York without regard to conflicts of law principles.

16. ARBITRATION. Licensee and FMI agree that any disputes arising under this agreement shall be determined by arbitration before the National Futures Association or the exchange where any transaction that is the subject of the dispute hereunder took place. All such arbitration hearings shall be conducted in Chicago, Illinois.

17. RELATIONSHIP BETWEEN THE PARTIES. The relationship between Licensee and FMI is that of independent contractors and nothing contained in this Agreement shall be construed to constitute the parties as employees, partners, joint venturers, or agents of the other.

18. FORCE MAJEURE. Neither party shall have any liability for any failure or delay in performing any obligation under this Agreement (other than payments to FMI) due to circumstances beyond its reasonable control including, but not limited to, acts of God or nature, actions of the government, fires, floods, strikes, civil disturbances or terrorism, or power, communications line, satellite or network failures.

19. ASSIGNMENT. Licensee shall not assign, delegate or otherwise transfer this Agreement or any of its rights or obligations hereunder, in whole or in part, without FMI's prior written consent.

20. PAYMENT OF LEGAL COSTS AND FEES. In the event any legal action is taken by either party to enforce the terms of this Agreement, the non-prevailing party shall pay all related court costs and expenses including, without limitation, disbursements and reasonable attorneys' fees of the prevailing party.

21. TERM OF AGREEMENT, SURVIVAL. Either party may terminate this Agreement with or without cause, at any time, effective immediately if the other party has breached this Agreement in any manner. Otherwise, either party may terminated this Agreement upon 10 days written notice to the other party. The Software and Equipment shall be returned to FMI immediately upon termination of this Agreement in the same condition as when initially received by Licensee, ordinary wear and tear excepted. Licensee shall be responsible to FMI for any damage beyond normal wear and tear. Upon return of the Equipment, FMI shall inspect the Equipment and shall determine in its sole and absolute discretion if the Equipment is damaged beyond ordinary wear and tear. If the returned Equipment is damaged, or in the even that Licensee refuses or is unable to return the Equipment, FMI shall charge Licensee the cost to replace the Equipment or deduct such amounts from any Deposit. Sections **6, 9, 13, 17 and 20** shall survive the termination of this Agreement.

With respect to the data received by Licensee from Data Sources, Licensee agrees that its agreement with FMI for receipt of information from any Data Source is subject to immediate termination in the event that the Data Source terminates its agreement with FMI for any reason.

22. MISCELLANEOUS.

(a) Notices. All notices or approvals required or permitted under this Agreement must be given in writing and sent by mail to the addresses set forth in this Agreement below. Licensee shall give prompt written notice to FMI of any change of the name, nature or address of Licensee's business.

(b) Headings. The headings of the sections of this Agreement are inserted for convenience only and shall not constitute a part hereof or affect in any way the meaning or interpretation of this Agreement.

(c) Waiver and Modification. Any waiver or modification of this Agreement shall not be effective unless executed in writing and signed by an authorized representative of FMI and Licensee. The failure of either party to enforce, or the delay by either party in enforcing, any of its rights under this Agreement shall not be deemed to be a waiver or modification by the parties of any of their rights under this Agreement.

(d) Electronic Document. Licensee attests that if Licensee has downloaded this Agreement, Licensee has printed it directly from the PDF file provided and has not made any changes to the text. Further, Licensee understands that FMI has not authorized or agreed to any change herein.

(e) Recording. Each party may record on tape or otherwise, any telephone conversation between itself and the other party, although neither party assumes responsibility to do such or to retain such recordings. Each party hereby agrees and consents to such recording and waives any rights said party may have to object to the admissibility into evidence of such recording in any legal proceeding between the parties or in any other regulatory proceeding involving said party.

(f) Separability. If any provision of this Agreement is held to be unenforceable by a court of competent jurisdiction, in whole or in part, such holding shall not affect the validity of the other provisions of this

Agreement, unless FMI in good faith deems the unenforceable provision to be essential, in which case FMI may terminate this Agreement effective immediately upon notice to Licensee.

(g) Complete Agreement. The recitals appearing at the beginning of this Agreement are incorporated into its terms and conditions in full by this reference thereto. This Agreement, together with all of the Exhibits, Schedules, Attachments hereto, are incorporated into this Agreement in full by this reference, constitutes the complete and entire agreement between the parties and supersedes any prior agreements or understandings between the parties with respect to its subject matter.

(h) Authorized Signatory. Licensee represents that the signatory below is authorized to act in behalf of the named party. FMI represents that the Chairman, President, any Executive Vice President or any Senior Vice President of FMI are the only persons authorized to enter into this Agreement or other agreements with Licensee or modify any portion of the Agreement.

IN WITNESS WHEREOF the parties have entered into this Agreement as of the date first written above.

LICENSEE

_____ Signature

_____ Print Name and Title

_____ Date

FMI

_____ Print Name and Title

_____ Date

MARKET DATA NOTICES

UNIFORM   NOTIFICATION   REGARDING   ACCESS   TO EXCHANGE MARKET DATA

As a market user you may obtain access to exchange Market Data available through an electronic trading system, software or device that is provided or made available to you by a broker or an affiliate of such. Market Data may include, but is not limited to, "real time" or delayed market prices, opening and closing prices and ranges, high-low prices, settlement prices, estimated and actual volume information, bids or offers and the applicable sizes and numbers of such bids or offers.

You are hereby notified that Market Data constitutes valuable confidential information that is the exclusive proprietary property of the applicable exchange, and is not within the public domain. Such Market Data may only be used for your firm's internal use. You may not, without the authorization of the applicable exchange, redistribute, sell, license, retransmit or otherwise provide Market Data, internally or externally and in any format by electronic or other means, including, but not limited to the Internet.

You must provide upon request of the broker through which your firm has obtained access to Market Data, or the applicable exchange, information demonstrating your firm's use of the Market Data in accordance with this Notification. Each applicable exchange reserves the right to terminate a market user's access to Market Data for any reason. You also agree that you will cooperate with an exchange and permit an exchange reasonable access to your premises should an exchange wish to conduct an audit or review connected to the distribution of Market Data.

NEITHER THE EXCHANGE NOR THE BROKER, NOR THEIR RESPECTIVE MEMBERS, SHAREHOLDERS, DIRECTORS, OFFICERS, EMPLOYEES OR AGENTS, GUARANTEE THE TIMELINESS, SEQUENCE, ACCURACY OR COMPLETENESS OF THE DESIGNATED MARKET DATA, MARKET INFORMATION OR OTHER INFORMATION FURNISHED NOR THAT THE MARKET DATA HAVE BEEN VERIFIED. YOU AGREE THAT THE MARKET DATA AND OTHER INFORMATION PROVIDED IS FOR INFORMATION PURPOSES ONLY AND IS NOT INTENDED AS AN OFFER OR SOLICITATION WITH RESPECT TO THE PURCHASE OR SALE OF ANY SECURITY OR COMMODITY.

NEITHER THE EXCHANGE NOR THE BROKER NOR THEIR RESPECTIVE MEMBERS, SHAREHOLDERS, DIRECTORS, OFFICERS, EMPLOYEES OR AGENTS, SHALL BE LIABLE TO YOU OR TO ANY OTHER PERSON, FIRM OR CORPORATION WHATSOEVER FOR ANY LOSSES, DAMAGES, CLAIMS, PENALTIES, COSTS OR EXPENSES (INCLUDING LOST PROFITS) ARISING OUT OF OR RELATING TO THE MARKET DATA IN ANY WAY, INCLUDING BUT NOT LIMITED TO ANY DELAY, INACCURACIES, ERRORS OR OMISSIONS IN THE MARKET DATA OR IN THE TRANSMISSION THEREOF OR FOR NONPERFORMANCE, DISCONTINUANCE, TERMINATION OR INTERRUPTION OF SERVICE OR FOR ANY DAMAGES ARISING THEREFROM OR OCCASIONED THEREBY, DUE TO ANY CAUSE

WHATSOEVER, WHETHER OR NOT RESULTING FROM NEGLIGENCE ON THEIR PART. IF THE FOREGOING DISCLAIMER AND WAIVER OF LIABILITY SHOULD BE DEEMED INVALID OR INEFFECTIVE, NEITHER THE EXCHANGE NOR THE BROKER, NOR THEIR RESPECTIVE SHAREHOLDERS, MEMBERS, DIRECTORS, OFFICERS, EMPLOYEES OR AGENTS SHALL BE LIABLE IN ANY EVENT, INCLUDING THEIR OWN NEGLIGENCE, BEYOND THE ACTUAL AMOUNT OF LOSS OR DAMAGE, OR THE AMOUNT OF THE MONTHLY FEE PAID BY YOU TO BROKER, WHICHEVER IS LESS. YOU AGREE THAT NEITHER THE EXCHANGE NOR THE BROKER NOR THEIR RESPECTIVE SHAREHOLDERS, MEMBERS, DIRECTORS, OFFICERS, EMPLOYEES OR AGENTS, SHALL BE LIABLE TO YOU OR TO ANY OTHER PERSON, FIRM OR CORPORATION WHATSOEVER FOR ANY INDIRECT, SPECIAL OR CONSEQUENTIAL DAMAGES, INCLUDING WITHOUT LIMITATION, LOST PROFITS, COSTS OF DELAY, OR COSTS OF LOST OR DAMAGED DATA.

INDEX

References are to Pages
